Threatened Birds of Africa and Related Islands

The ICBP/IUCN Red Data Book, Part 1

Threatened Birds of Africa and Related Islands

The ICBP/IUCN Red Data Book, Part 1

THIRD EDITION

N. J. COLLAR and S. N. STUART

with 12 colour plates by
NORMAN ARLOTT

INTERNATIONAL COUNCIL FOR BIRD PRESERVATION
and
INTERNATIONAL UNION FOR CONSERVATION OF NATURE AND
NATURAL RESOURCES

CAMBRIDGE, U.K., 1985.

Published by ICBP, Cambridge, U.K., and IUCN, Gland, Switzerland, 1985.

Prepared with the financial assistance of the World Wildlife Fund, the United Nations Environment Stamp Conservation Fund and the United Nations Environment Programme. A contribution to the Global Environment Monitoring System.

ISBN No. 2-88032-604-4

Printed by Page Bros (Norwich) Ltd.
Typeset by Gee Graphics Ltd.

Cover illustration: Prince Ruspoli's Turaco *Tauraco ruspolii* by Brian Groombridge.

Book Design by James Butler.

ICBP

ICBP (International Council for Bird Preservation) was founded in 1922, the first global organisation to be set up for wildlife conservation. It is devoted entirely to the protection of wild birds and their habitats. Today ICBP is a federation of 270 member organisations in 87 countries.

Birds are important indicators of the state of the environment. Drawing on the expertise of a worldwide network of scientists and conservationists, ICBP

* monitors the status of the world's threatened birds and their habitats;
* identifies, develops and implements priority projects to achieve conservation through its annual Conservation Programme;
* provides expert advice to governments on bird conservation issues;
* promotes public awareness at all levels of the ecological importance of wild birds.

IUCN

IUCN (International Union for Conservation of Nature and Natural Resources) is a network of governments, non-governmental organisations (NGOs), scientists and other conservation experts, joined together to promote the protection and sustainable use of living resources.

Founded in 1948, IUCN has more than 450 member governments and NGOs in over 100 countries. Its six Commissions consist of more than 700 experts on threatened species, protected areas, ecology, environmental planning, environmental policy, law and administration, and environmental education. IUCN

* monitors the status of ecosystems and species throughout the world;
* plans conservation action, both at the strategic level through the World Conservation Strategy and at the programme level through its programme of conservation for sustainable development;
* promotes such action by governments, inter-governmental bodies and non-governmental organisations;
* provides assistance and advice necessary for the achievement of such action.

Contents

Appendices

Table of illustrations

between pages 348-349

Foreword

Advertising experts tell us that people prefer hearing cheerful news rather than doomsday stories. In their eyes, therefore, the Red Data Book, which deals almost exclusively with bad news, might not be the most suitable vehicle for achieving one of its most important objectives, namely to publicise the need for conservation. Moreover, some conservationists may question the concept behind this species-oriented book, maintaining that to give too much attention to the fate of individual species diverts us from the more fundamental task of conserving habitats and ecosystems.

Despite all that, I am convinced that a focus on threatened species remains crucial for achieving and promoting conservation. Preservation of an entire ecosystem frequently results from the efforts to save a particular species. Readers of this book will grasp this fact and realise that, to take just one example, the threatened Taita Thrush could be the salvation of the Taita Hills. Perhaps because almost all species listed in the Red Data Books have been put at risk by man-induced changes in their habitats, the plight of an individual species is still the best way to concentrate public attention on broader environmental problems. This is particularly true for birds. Birds, because of their immense popularity, are especially potent issue-raisers. ICBP owes its very existence to this fact.

And whether the advertising experts like it or not, there is a lot of bad news concerning conservation. However, I trust that most people who read this book will read it as a call for action – and revel in the occasional pieces of good news. Accurate information on the status of threatened birds throughout the world is an essential component of ICBP's programme priorities. Unfortunately, we are still responding to emergencies rather than working on preventive measures to ensure that no new species are added to the critical list. This holds true for most of today's conservation work: the list of threatened species is still growing so fast that it is almost impossible to keep pace with it, let alone to catch up.

For this reason a book about the threatened birds of Africa is sorely needed. Africa has the highest population growth rate of any continent. Even in so enormous a land mass, the natural resources on which the survival of both man and wildlife depend are finite. In the never-ending quest for more land to provide a livelihood for more people, wildlife is the loser. If man needs more timber to keep his exploitation-based economy going, numerous animals lose their habitat, as they do when wetlands must give way to agricultural land and industrial development. Such stories are repeated over and over again in this volume.

Its publication, once again drawing attention to these urgent problems, will not by itself change things for the better. No single event will. However, it is an important scientific contribution that ICBP and IUCN can make to the on-going task of publicising the fate of vanishing species. *Threatened Birds of Africa*, researched on a solid scientific basis and free from the political considerations which are often the ultimate cause of the demise of many species, points out the action required to avert their deadly fate.

This book is the first part of the third edition of the international Bird Red Data Book. The content and appearance of the Red Data Books have undergone substantial transformation in recent years. While the early volumes were compiled by scientists working part-time in different locations, recent Red Data Books have been written by full-time staff at the Conservation Monitoring Centre (CMC) specially set up in Cambridge by IUCN in 1979. As ICBP had traditionally been responsible for the Bird Red Data Book, it seemed advantageous to move the recently established professional ICBP secretariat from London to Cambridge and to set up joint offices with CMC. The compiler of the bird volume now has the benefit of working at ICBP headquarters, in close contact with his colleagues at CMC in charge of the other Red Data Books. This arrangement, together with the availability of new computer and word processing facilities at CMC, makes it possible to produce these more detailed regional treatments of threatened species.

New ground is broken with this particular Red Data Book. Hundreds of pages of print tend to make us forget that we are dealing here with a variety of fascinating and often amazingly beautiful birds. The twelve superb colour paintings by Norman Arlott in this volume, the first time a Red Data Book is illustrated in this manner, should remind the reader of this. Some of the depicted species have never been illustrated before; some of them have not been seen for decades; some, sadly, may never be seen again by any human being; others, it is to be hoped, may be rediscovered, perhaps resulting from stimulation given by this book.

I would like to thank the two authors and their principal assistant, Tim Dee, for this very fine and thoroughly researched volume prepared on behalf of ICBP and IUCN. The two organisations can be very proud of it, and it will surely be an invaluable source of information for those who want to join in the task of stemming the tide of species extinction.

Christoph Imboden

Director, International Council for Bird Preservation

September 1984

Introduction

This is the first thing
I have understood:
Time is the echo of an axe
Within a wood.

Background and region covered

The decision to prepare a Red Data Book on the birds of Africa and its related islands was taken at a meeting of ICBP delegates to the Fifth Pan-African Ornithological Congress held in Lilongwe, Malawi, in August 1980. The feeling in the meeting was that a "regional" book would be of greater local impact and usefulness than the "global" books that had preceded it. A candidate list of taxa for treatment in such a book was compiled and circulated in the course of 1981 by NJC, and a small collection of species and subspecies accounts (Collar 1982) was produced for the XVIII World Conference of ICBP in August the following year; in early 1983 SNS was appointed as an assistant compiler and co-author, a position he has held up to the present apart from a period of absence as leader of the ICBP Cameroon Montane Forest Survey from November 1983 to May 1984. Although responsibility for authorship of the entire text is shared, NJC compiled the material concerning the islands, North Africa and north-east Africa while SNS, with a few exceptions, took charge of the remainder of the continent. Except in the case of the last account compiled (Cape Vulture *Gyps coprotheres*) and for some minor instances, the cut-off date for textual alterations and the incorporation of material was 21 September 1984, but this does not mean that all literature (especially in the less specialist sources) published immediately prior to this date will have been covered.

Although this is a "regional" book serving a "regional" need, and although the number of species treated in it is greatly in excess of the number for the same area treated in the two previous editions of what we now term the "*ICBP/IUCN Red Data Book*" (Vincent 1966-1971, King 1978-1979; also King 1981), the criteria used in its compilation have not been consciously relaxed or altered from those laid down by IUCN as global definitions of threat; however, we have added, for four species, an entirely unofficial category, "Species of Special Concern" (this and the IUCN definitions are discussed below). Most "regional" Red Data Books (e.g. Siegfried *et al.* 1976; comprehensive list in Burton 1984) deal not only (and in some cases not even) with species or subspecies that are globally threatened with extinction, but with those that are threatened within the region concerned although perfectly safe elsewhere. The number of species in Africa and its related islands that fall into the latter category is probably very low, an example perhaps being the Magnificent Frigatebird *Fregata magnificens*, widespread in the waters of central America but with just two tiny colonies in the Cape Verde Islands (see Cramp and Simmons 1977); but in any case, this "African" book is not regional in that sense, and treats only those species that we deem to be globally at risk of extinction. While therefore it attempts to serve a specific need in African ornithology and conservation, it is also simply the first part of the third edition of the *ICBP/IUCN Red Data Book*.

The area covered in this volume is continental Africa, plus the adjacent or outlying islands in the Atlantic Ocean on or east of the Mid-Atlantic Ridge (hence the Tristan da Cunha group), and equivalent islands in the Indian Ocean west of 80°E (hence Amsterdam Island). Thus Palearctic Africa is included, as well as islands which on socio-political precedent are considered and function as part of Europe (the Canaries, Madeira, the Azores) or of the Middle East (Socotra). The next step will be a book covering the Americas, and it is at present anticipated that this will be followed and the process of global coverage completed by two further volumes, to cover Europe and Asia, and Australasia and the Pacific Ocean respectively, though not necessarily in that order. It should be noted that threatened species whose main area of distribution lies outside Africa or its related islands are not treated in this volume, but will mostly be treated in the proposed Europe and Asia volume; a candidate list of such species is given in Appendix D. Discounting non-breeding seabird movements, only one species treated in this volume has a distribution extending beyond the area defined above, this being the Northern Bald Ibis *Geronticus eremita*.

While the stepwise process proposed here of updating the *ICBP/IUCN Red Data Book* may appear unfair (or even be considered an arbitrary form of "triage") in respect of the regions that have to wait their turn for treatment, we should stress that gathering of information on known threatened species in these regions will continue and ICBP will, of course, be seeking to take action in many cases, based on King (1978-1979) and any newer evidence that emerges. Considerable effort is being made, for example, to keep abreast of the increasingly critical situation of forest birds in South-East Asia – there is now (e.g.) a computerised monitoring system for Indonesian wildlife (Ali 1984) which ICBP is to operate on behalf of IUCN/WWF – and, at the same time, ICBP has sought further insurance against species extinction with the development of a South Pacific project (Hay in prep.) and a world list of bird species confined to single islands and island groups (Bishop in prep.). Moreover, extensive taxonomic revisions are currently in preparation for ornithological publications concerning Indonesia and the Philippines (E. C. Dickinson pers. comm. 1983, M. D. Bruce pers. comm. 1983), and there is obvious sense in awaiting the development of these projects before embarking on Red Data Book analysis of the region concerned.

The problem of subspecies

In late 1982 a decision was reached to exclude subspecies from this and all subsequent volumes of the third edition of the *ICBP/IUCN Red Data Book*. It was a decision forced by considerations of time, man-power and subjectivity. It became apparent in the first eighteen months of preparatory work on the book that a very wide range of subspecies could be considered as candidates for inclusion; and while the previous compiler indicated (W. B. King pers. comm. 1981) that he had attempted to use his discretion in allowing the morphological distinctiveness of a subspecies to determine whether or not it merited treatment, reliance on this essentially subjective procedure became less and less comfortable the longer the candidate list became and the more the possibilities arose that a subspecies might not be as distinct in its external morphology as in its ecology or perhaps even voice. It was felt that, in a comprehensive review of the region in question, to allow equal weight and consideration to subspecies (which is practically inevitable in the research that must precede the preparation of an account, however much the latter may itself be abbreviated) would enormously retard the writing of the book without necessarily adding to its value (so many subspecies at risk occur in localities or habitats already harbouring threatened full species that the conservation measures needed for the latter would very often be identical to those needed for the former). The matter was clinched by the receipt at ICBP's offices of a copy of Schodde (1978) who, in an analysis of threatened Papuasian birds, listed over 500 taxa as meriting inclusion in the international Red Data Book, over 400 of which are subspecies. It hardly needs to be said that to follow such recommendations – and their veracity is not at issue – would not only cripple the scheduling of the book but also raise fundamental questions concerning its function and value. Until such time as it is accepted that forms of animals and plants can be given IUCN Red Data Book categories without having to be written up in book (or at least "data-sheet") form, an option which has considerable dangers, it seems pointless to pretend to offer global coverage at the subspecific level, for birds at least, unless the world is prepared to wait many more years while many of its species die off unnoticed and unlamented or unless the compilation of this book is entrusted to a team of researchers; but even if any of these options were affordable or acceptable, there remains the question of whether many subspecies (e.g. those with ranges identical to those of threatened species, as mentioned above) truly need such attention and, more poignantly, whether in any case they would benefit from it, given that many full species whose plight has long since been documented in Red Data Books evidently still find it hard enough to make their appeal heard.

Exclusion of subspecies from this Red Data Book might be interpreted as indicating that ICBP and IUCN are not concerned for their conservation, that the problems facing birds are fewer and smaller than is the case, that there is no need to preserve closely related forms in the wild, and that keeping subspecies pure in captivity is of little importance; moreover, our decision appears to forfeit the opportunity to foster local conservation interest and to promote site-oriented protection through endemic subspecies (all these important points are from R. Wirth *in litt.* 1984). Certainly, no-one should be in doubt that the environmental crisis of our planet is now so great that to focus merely on species is to fail to recognise the considerable loss of genetic diversity we are about to sustain (and doubtless are sustaining) at the subspecific level, nor should there be any doubt that either ICBP or IUCN remains unconcerned at this prospect. Indeed, both organisations continue to gather data on threatened subspecies and readily act, as and when appropriate, to promote their conservation. Nevertheless, both are also sensitive to the fact that resources (time, manpower, money) spent on subspecies are almost inevitably resources denied to species, and for the former to be saved at the expense of the latter is largely unacceptable, in theory at least. Our decision to exclude subspecies was primarily governed, as we have stated, by the scarcity of our resources; but if in turn it means that species are allowed a greater share of the scarce resources available for bird conservation, our regret must be somewhat moderated. At some stage it may be feasible to compile a Red Data Book for threatened bird subspecies, using abbreviated entries, but meanwhile many countries, rather than awaiting this development, could help the situation by preparing their own lists of the threatened subspecies within their borders: ICBP would strongly welcome and encourage such initiatives, so long as they did not result in the distortion of national priorities at species level.

Necessary and correct as we believe the decision to exclude subspecies to have been, we have made several attempts to provide some compensation. Subspecies that were treated in the previous edition (King 1978-1979) are briefly discussed with, where possible, updated information in Appendix F. A list of subspecies which are so distinct as to be regarded as "incipient species", and which because of their highly restricted ranges must be considered as at some risk, is given in Appendix E. Most importantly, perhaps, the principle has been adopted that, in cases where the taxonomic arguments for species or subspecies status are in balance, we come down in favour of accepting the status of species, even if this is sometimes in defiance of most current opinion; mention of the issue is then made under the section in the account headed Remarks. In this way, for example, the Gon-gon *Pterodroma feae* and the Freira *P. madeira* part company from each other (and from the "parent" Soft-plumaged Petrel *P. mollis*), the Macaronesian pigeons *Columba trocaz* and *C. bollii* also part company, as do the Somali and South African Long-clawed Larks *Heteromirafra archeri* and *H. ruddi*, and the Olive Ibis of São Tomé *Bostrychia bocagei*, Black-cheeked Lovebird *Agapornis nigrigenis*, Grand Comoro Scops Owl *Otus pauliani*, Usambara Eagle Owl *Bubo vosseleri*, Seychelles Swiftlet *Collocalia elephra*, Mauritius Black Bulbul *Hypsipetes olivaceus*, Fernando Po Swift *Apus sladeniae*, Monteiro's Bush-shrike *Malaconotus monteiri*, Taita Thrush *Turdus helleri*, Kabobo Apalis *Apalis kaboboensis*, Banded Wattle-eye *Platysteira laticincta*, Banded Green Sunbird *Anthreptes rubritorques*, Marungu Sunbird *Nectarinia prigoginei*, Yellow-throated Serin *Serinus flavigula* and Anambra Waxbill *Estrilda poliopareia* are each also upgraded to species level. There is only one instance where we have not followed this general principle, and that concerns the Ngoye Green Barbet *Stactolaema olivacea woodwardi*, which has recently been determined as a full species in a new genus *Cryptolybia woodwardi* (Clancey 1979a,b, Brooke in press), a view that has met with sufficient resistance (R. J. Dowsett *in litt.* 1982, L. L. Short *in litt.* 1984) for us to prefer caution (although the form is treated in Appendix E as an incipient species).

Taxonomy and names

Sequence and nomenclature follow Morony *et al.* (1975) including their "corrections and additions – 1 August 1978", with certain exceptions requiring mention here. To begin with, several species we treat have been described or established through taxonomic revision during or since 1978, these being

Amsterdam Albatross *Diomedea amsterdamensis*, Canarian Black Oystercatcher *Haematopus meadewaldoi*, Albertine Owlet *Glaucidium albertinum*, Yellow-footed Honeyguide *Melignomon eisentrauti*, Ash's Lark *Mirafra ashi*, Kibale Ground-thrush *Turdus kibalensis*, Rufous-winged Sunbird *Nectarinia rufipennis*, Marungu Sunbird *N. prigoginei*, Ankober Serin *Serinus ankoberensis* and Lake Lufira Weaver *Ploceus ruweti* (the appropriate references for which may be found in the relevant accounts). Other findings contemporary with or subsequent to Morony *et al.* (1975) which we follow are those concerning the systematic position of the Dappled Mountain Robin *Modulatrix orostruthus* and Madagascar Yellow-brow *Crossleyia xanthophrys*, the merging of *Bebrornis* in *Acrocephalus* (affecting the Seychelles Warbler *A. sechellensis* and the Rodrigues Warbler *A. rodericanus*), and the naming of the Mauritius Parakeet *Psittacula eques* (see relevant accounts). We further diverge from Morony *et al.* (1975) in allowing specific status to the birds listed in the previous paragraph (except in the cases of the pigeons and the thrush, which they also recognise), in recognising the River Prinia *Prinia "fluviatilis"*, and in the generic placing of the Slaty Egret *Egretta* (not *Hydranassa*) *vinaceigula*, Sakalava Rail *Amaurornis* (not *Porzana*) *olivieri*, Gough Moorhen *Gallinula* (not *Porphyriornis*) *comeri*, Pink Pigeon *Nesoenas* (not *Columba*) *mayeri*, Botha's Lark *Spizocorys* (not *Calandrella*) *fringillaris*, Raso Lark *Alauda* (not *Calandrella*) *razae*, Mount Kupe Bush-shrike *Malaconotus* (not *Telophorus*) *kupeensis*, Swynnerton's Forest Robin *Swynnertonia* (not *Pogonocichla*) *swynnertoni*, the akalats *Sheppardia* (not *Erithacus*) *gabela* and *S. gunningi*, the ground robins *Dryocichloides* (not *Alethe*) *montanus* and *D. lowei*, Benson's Rockthrush *Monticola* (not *Pseudocossyphus*) *bensoni*, and the ground-thrushes *Turdus* (not *Zoothera*) *oberlaenderi* and *T. fischeri* (not *Z. guttata*). We note that the specific name of the São Tomé Short-tail *Amaurocichla bocagii* is not *bocagei*, and are informed (D. W. Snow pers. comm. 1983) that that for the Scaly Ground-roller *Brachypteracias squamiger* should apparently be masculine, rather than the widely current *squamigera*. It will be noted that some further divergence occurs in the names of other species listed in the various appendices, but these are all readily identifiable by reference to other standard sources.

It may have been observed from the above that a certain amount of latitude has been allowed in the provision of suitable English vernacular names. In general there has been a policy – flexible, and not strictly applied – to seek or establish names that denote the significance of locality or sometimes character at the expense of those with possessive personal proper names. This is done in the belief that conservation of a species might better be promoted using a name which characterises it in terms of a particular site which itself requires conservation, and at any rate not in terms of something which may have no positive significance or association to those best placed to undertake the conservation needed. If some of the names invoked here prove controversial or unacceptable, African orni-thologists might nonetheless give consideration, in view of certain species' need for "marketability", to the provision of names most appropriate to the promotion of their security.

In the matter of vernacular names and taxonomy concerning plants and animals other than birds, we have relied largely on the sources we cite which refer to them; but it is a general principle that, where possible, we give scientific names to all species but domesticated forms, so that where the source does not provide a scientific name we have commonly done so, by reference to standard works or, in the case of certain plants, to authorities whose judgement derives from recent first-hand experience. Vernacular names of bird species have been given initial capital letters, but to avoid complications those of other animals and plants are uniformly in the lower case (except where proper names are involved). Scientific names of animals are provided only once in an account, when the species is first mentioned.

Methods and rationale

The process of identifying candidates for treatment in this book was greatly facilitated by the existence of such material as Hall and Moreau (1962,1970), Vincent (1966-1971), Greenway (1967), Snow (1978) and King (1978-1979), plus the lists of new species provided by Meise (1938a,b), Zimmer and Mayr (1943), Mayr (1957,1971), Morony *et al.* (1975), Mayr and Vuilleumier (1983) and the bibliographies of African ornithology compiled by Fry (1979-1982). Four unpublished documents provided important pointers, by Forbes-Watson and Turner (1972-1973), Brown (undated [but post-1972]), Dowsett (1981) and an untitled, uncredited and undated typescript which was brought back to the ICBP secretariat from the Malawi Pan-African Ornithological Congress in 1980. There was much consultation in the early stages of writing with C. W. Benson (see Acknowledgements).

Research and writing of this volume were carried out principally in the Balfour and Newton Libraries in the Department of Zoology, Cambridge University; in the Bird Room of the Cambridge University Museum of Zoology where C. W. Benson kept his very extensive library of African ornithological literature, now bequeathed to the Museum; in the Cambridge University Library; in the Alexander Library of the Edward Grey Institute of Field Ornithology, Department of Zoology, Oxford University; and at the Sub-department of Ornithology, British Museum (Natural History), Tring, where the libraries and also the skin collections were consulted. Libraries at the British Museum (Natural History) in London and at the Royal Society for the Protection of Birds, Sandy, Bedfordshire, were also used.

The part played by specimen-labels in museums has been of some value in this study, and apart from working extensively at the British Museum in Tring both NJC and SNS paid short visits to natural history museums in north-western Europe, notably those in Paris, Brussels, Tervuren, Leiden, Amsterdam, Bonn, Frankfurt and Stuttgart, in the pursuit of new distributional information on particular species.

Correspondence and discussion with individual ornithologists, naturalists and conservationists, both amateur and professional, have been very extensive throughout the preparation of the text, and the importance of their testimony is easily recognised in the very high proportion of information cited as received in letters (*"in litt."*) or by verbal communication ("pers. comm."). The usual procedure has been to prepare a draft account of a species by reference to the literature and then circulate it to individuals likely to be able to provide informed comment, corrections and additional data, which have then been incorporated into the text for publication. Accounts are stored and revised on a computerised word-processing facility at the IUCN Conservation Monitoring Centre (CMC) in Cambridge, U.K.

We make no apology for the detail into which we have gone. The trend towards greater attention to detail was initiated with the present series of Red Data Books emanating from CMC (in order of appearance: Thornback and Jenkins 1982, Groombridge and Wright 1982, Wells *et al.* 1983). IUCN Red Data Books previous to these have had the character of adumbration; they were, intentionally, anterior to the conservation process, and it was the fact of treatment rather than the manner of treatment that most mattered. In this study, however, by drawing on as wide a range of material as is available and giving what detail we can, our intention has not been just to indicate the species that need attention, why, where and when, but to provide an independent analysis to enable project managers (by which we mean anyone planning to intervene to help a species) to understand, decide on and carry out the work to be done with the maximum efficiency and confidence that circumstance allows. Many projects are, we believe, initiated and funded with insufficient reference to the available information; so the more carefully the facts about a species are researched, the more (in theory at any rate) the right species and the right projects on them should become apparent. Indeed, it has been our experience that only after very considerable attention to detail has it been possible to discern the true plight of certain species, and to have suppressed such detail in our account of it would therefore have been patently wasteful. Naturally where a species is well known and already evidently in safe hands, detailed treatment of it here may equally appear wasteful, but we feel that equality of treatment between species must be a clear principle, and that detailed independent review of species that are subject to much conservation attention is in fact fundamental to our responsibilities. (It is also, incidentally, fundamental to these responsibilities not to go into particular detail, in print, concerning localities for birds whose main threat is from collectors: there is one case in this volume where not only such localities, but all references that disclose them, have been suppressed.)

Textual organisation

The species accounts are divided up into seven sections, namely Summary, Distribution, Population, Ecology, Threats, Conservation Measures Taken and Conservation Measures Proposed, following which there is an optional section, Remarks, before references are listed. Some of these sections require comment here, but several general points need to be made first. Metric measurement is used throughout, except in quotations, and it should be noted that conversion to metric from miles, feet, etc., will often have been done by the authors and that we are therefore responsible for necessary approximations (if the original text indicates approximate miles or feet, we have generally adjusted the metric equivalent accordingly: "roughly 15 miles" would thus become "c. 25 km"). Direct quotation is used on occasions when it is felt likely to be helpful. It commonly occurs in the Population section when the source being cited offers some simple qualitative remark concerning abundance, e.g. "not very common", "not rare". It may also be used when we are anxious to indicate that a particular ambiguity, imprecision or ostensible error or contradiction lies in the original to which we refer rather than in our representation of it. We have taken the liberty of making direct quotation in translation. Responsibility for all translation of material, whether directly quoted or merely cited, rests entirely with us. Naturally, however, we do not take responsibility for errors in published material which we cite, although we do, where possible, indicate those errors we notice where they seem worthy of correction. While we have often sought to exercise our judgement independently of the sources we use (see below where we discuss References), in cases of conflicting evidence or viewpoint we have endeavoured to indicate to the reader that such conflict exists, so that judgement of the issue passes out of our hands.

Under Distribution we regret that no standard procedure for the spelling of place-names or the indication of position was developed in advance of producing the accounts, and that considerations of time later precluded a full exercise to impose such standardisation on the material. Where possible, however, names are spelt in accordance with *The Times Atlas of the World* (TAW 1980) and, if a locality is not treated there, and if its position is not fairly obvious from context, we usually attempt to provide some guidance on its location according to another source. Alternative spellings, where appropriate, are given in brackets after names; superseded (or sometimes superseding) names are commonly provided in brackets after an equal sign (=), although in the case of Madagascar, apart from using "Antananarivo" against "Tananarive", we have retained the colonial names of major towns, since these have invariably been used in all the literature we cite (alternatives now to be used are in TAW 1980). Although generally we follow anglicised versions of names, we deliberately retain "São Tomé e Príncipe" to distinguish the country from São Tomé and Príncipe as islands (birds that occur in the former do not necessarily do so on both of the latter).

Under Ecology we have attempted to provide a digest of biological information which might be expected to be of use in the planning or implementation of conservation measures. The section begins with what details of habitat are known, moves on to food, and thence to breeding and, if appropriate, migration (though this may be catered for partly or wholly under Distribution). A few other comments may also be added, e.g. concerning the tameness or otherwise of the bird in question.

In the first edition of the *ICBP/IUCN Red Data Book* (Vincent 1966-1971) and in the most recent editions of the IUCN Mammal and Amphibia/Reptilia Red Data Books (Thornback and Jenkins 1982, Groombridge and Wright 1982) there have been standard sections on Captive Breeding. We have not followed this precedent, very largely because there are far too few species of bird in the area under review for which captive breeding does or could play a significant role in their conservation. This fact need not, however, be used to obscure our personal view that captive breeding, being almost always a holding operation and not an end in itself, needs to be played down as an element in conservation, even where it is feasible (or believed to be). We are certainly not indifferent to the achievements of captive breeding, and this book bears witness to the great contribution of zoos in preserving, e.g., the Northern Bald Ibis *Geronticus eremita*, and even makes suggestions for action to take into captivity such Endangered birds as the Madagascar Pochard *Aythya innotata* and White-breasted Guineafowl *Agelastes meleagrides* (if either can still be found); but in general we follow the principle that conservationists should address themselves to the resolution of a species's problem or problems *in situ*, and we are concerned that any undue emphasis on captive breeding may in certain cases provide a spurious alternative to the confrontation of the root issues. Hence although captive breeding is referred to under Conservation Measures Taken where it has proved possible to propagate a species behind bars, irrespective of what action has then been taken in returning stock to the wild, in Conservation Measures Proposed we only mention captive breeding if this seems likely to be a successful stop-gap in the face of currently intractable environmental problems; and in a few cases, e.g. Shoebill *Balaeniceps rex* and Grey-necked Picathartes *Picathartes oreas*, where we are at pains to demonstrate that maintenance in zoos has done nothing to enhance a species's survival prospects, the issue is relegated to Remarks.

Remarks is, as noted above, an optional section and although we have attempted to use it consistently (and principally) as a means of cross-reference, indicating what other threatened species occur in the same localities as the one under review, etc., there has also been a certain latitude in the choice of comment to be made, almost always concerning taxonomic details. Thus in some cases superspecies relationships are referred to, in others they are not; in some cases debate on phylogenetic position is mentioned, in others it is not. While, as under Distribution, we regret this lack of standardisation, its relevance to the conservation of the species involved is relatively limited.

Initials and referencing

Museums, institutions or conventions referred to in the text by their initials are as follows: AMNH = American Museum of Natural History, New York; ANSP = Philadelphia Academy of Natural Sciences, U.S.A.; BMNH = British Museum (Natural History), Tring; CITES = The Washington Convention on International Trade in Endangered Species of Wild Fauna and Flora; ICONA = Instituto Nacional para la Conservacion de la Naturaleza, Spain; IRSNB = Institut Royal des Sciences Naturelles, Brussels; JWPT = Jersey Wildlife Preservation Trust, U.K.; MCZ = Museum of Comparative Zoology, Cambridge, U.S.A.; MNHN = Museum National d'Histoire Naturelle, Paris; MRAC = Musée Royale de l'Afrique Centrale, Tervuren (Belgium); NMK = National Museum of Kenya, Nairobi; NHMW = Naturhistorisches Museum, Vienna; NYZS = New York Zoological Society, U.S.A.; PFIAO = Percy FitzPatrick Institute of African Ornithology, Cape Town, South Africa; RMNH = Rijksmuseum van Natuurlijke Historie, Leiden; SMF = Senckenbergmuseum, Frankfurt; SMNS = Staatliches Museum für Naturkunde, Stuttgart; UMZC = University Museum of Zoology, Cambridge, U.K.; VIREO = Visual Resources for Ornithology (at ANSP); WWF = World Wildlife Fund; ZMA = Zoologisch Museum, Amsterdam; ZMK = Zoologisk Museum, Copenhagen; ZFMK = Zoologisches Forschungsinstitut und Museum Alexander Koenig, Bonn.

For the sake of brevity and textual clarity, citation of maps, atlases and some gazetteers in the species accounts has involved using initials (e.g. "TAW 1980"), although in the reference list at the end the full name is normally given

("*The Times Atlas of the World* [1980] Comprehensive [sixth] edition. London: Times Books"): it is assumed that readers will have no difficulty in matching names and initials thus presented. In citing book titles, we have often taken the liberty of inserting appropriate punctuation where for reasons of presentation it does not appear on the title page. For books, locality of publication is always given if disclosed; publisher is given (if disclosed) for books published in and after 1900. Concerning journals, where there is no author to cite the name of the journal is usually inserted into the text itself along with volume, year and pages; where there is no title of paper to cite (a common situation for original descriptions of species up to around the 1930s) one has usually been sought from the wording of the introductory sentence and is provided in square brackets. Journal titles are abbreviated generally in accordance with common practice; we use "Nat." for "Natural", "Natn." for "National". Letters and verbal communications are cited with year of receipt; those to other or former members of ICBP staff (R. D. Chancellor, A. M. Dixon, P. D. Goriup, W. B. King, R. F. Pasquier) are cited accordingly; those to correspondents or informants are indicated by use of "*per*".

A somewhat complicated problem exists concerning the sharing of information prior to publication. In certain cases we have exchanged draft material with workers who have also been engaged in writing on a particular species, and this has led to modifications of texts by both parties, and to one quoting the other as "in press". This in turn may lead to a situation where the party quoted as "in press" has actually altered the text – usually in direct response to information received in the text now quoting it – so that the quoted information will no longer be found in the source cited. Under Wattled Crane *Bugeranus carunculatus*, for example, the draft we have seen by G. W. Howard and D. R. Aspinwall, forwarded to *Ostrich* for consideration, quotes our work as "ICBP in press" to the effect that the species is "Vulnerable", a view we have had to modify very largely on the evidence they present. Again, through the great kindness of C. G. Jones on Mauritius we have been able to draw on his material scheduled for publication in the major forthcoming book *Studies in Mascarene island birds*, but since seeing some of this we understand certain revisions have been made, so that we cannot now be sure that everything attributed to "Jones (in press)" will be traceable in the published version. Users of this book should therefore beware of accepting with total confidence material we cite as in press, and should refer to that material when published for confirmation; conversely, they should not necessarily accept any publication that quotes this book as in press or in preparation without checking back here first. (Where a completed paper has been copied to us and been offered but not yet accepted for publication to a particular journal, we refer to it as "in press" with the journal in square brackets.)

Throughout this book, we have endeavoured to ensure that every statement is fully and consistently attributed to its source. It should therefore be noted that, unless the context clearly indicates otherwise, any sentence ending without accreditation either represents a summary whose sources are to follow or else carries a judgement or deduction that is attributable to ourselves. Sentences carrying our own judgement or opinion are most frequently to be found in the Conservation Measures Proposed sections, but no such sentences (there or elsewhere) should be construed as representing the official view or policy of either

ICBP or IUCN. Information (as opposed to opinion or judgement) provided by us is accompanied by our respective initials.

Red Data Book categories of threat

Categories of threat as defined by IUCN are given below and have, naturally, been followed as closely as information and judgement allow, except that we have declined to apply the term Extinct with the rigidity required, and have preferred that, for our purposes, the category Indeterminate be considered to cover also the possibility that a species is extinct. For four species, the Jackass Penguin *Spheniscus demersus*, Shoebill *Balaeniceps rex*, Congo Peacock *Afropavo congensis* and Wattled Crane *Bugeranus carunculatus*, we have invoked the term "Of Special Concern". Having researched all four in the belief that they merited full treatment as threatened species, we were persuaded by our findings that they are, at present, safe, but since there is great interest in their conservation and a widely held belief that they are at risk in the sense defined by IUCN, we chose to complete and publish data sheets on them as a matter of information.

IUCN status categories for Red Data Books are as follows. "Extinct" is used for "species not definitely located in the wild during the past 50 years" (but not in this volume, where we have used the term flexibly for just two species that are most probably but by no means certainly extinct; for species not seen in the wild for 50 years see Appendix B). "Endangered" applies to "taxa in danger of extinction and whose survival is unlikely if the causal factors continue operating" (because of this specific definition it is standard practice in this book to use the term "threatened", or also occasionally "at risk", in the general sense, to cover any or all specific status categories). "Vulnerable" is used for "taxa believed likely to move into the Endangered category in the near future if the causal factors continue operating" and "Rare" for "taxa with small world populations that are not at present Endangered or Vulnerable, but are at risk" (the risk commonly being merely a function of range restriction). "Indeterminate" applies to "taxa known to be Endangered, Vulnerable or Rare but where there is not enough information to say which of the three categories is appropriate" (as noted above, we also use this for species that may be extinct; it should also be noted that, since an Indeterminate species can be at best Rare, Indeterminate is a category of threat higher than Rare, and indeed those attempting to provide an account of the most threatened birds in this or any other region should refer not only to the Extinct and Endangered species but also to those treated as Indeterminate, since the latter caters for forms that are most likely either Extinct or Endangered, e.g. Yellow-throated Serin *Serinus flavigula*, Golden-naped Weaver *Ploceus aureonucha*). "Insufficiently Known" is used for "taxa that are suspected but not definitely known to belong to any of the above categories, because of lack of information" (whether or not technically correct, in practice species in this category have to be counted as "threatened"). "Out of Danger" is defined as for "taxa formerly included in one of the above categories [except Insufficiently Known], but which are now considered relatively secure because effective conservation measures have been taken or the previous threat to their survival has been removed": this definition does not allow for good fieldwork proving that a species is far better off than had previously been thought, which is essentially what has happened in the case of the one bird in this study that merits this category (Seychelles Kestrel *Falco araea*), although its introduction to Praslin certainly counts as a valuable conservation measure taken.

Decisions not only on appropriate category of threat but also on the designation of species as threatened or not have often been taken only after considerable hesitation. Naturally, however, there remain very grey areas where choice becomes a matter of chance and where single small facts, so easily missed, can hold enormous sway. Other compilers – and indeed we ourselves, given different measures of time – would doubtless have made somewhat different decisions. In order therefore to reduce the rather artificial distinction between "threatened" and "safe" species, and as an indication of the tentativeness that has informed many of our rationalisations, we have compiled an annotated list of "fringe" ("near-threatened") species which at least merit monitoring and which others may judge to merit more (see Appendix C). We also offer, in the interests of free debate, a complete list of species that were considered for treatment in either the main text or Appendix C (see Appendix G). Some further commentary is provided in the introductory paragraphs to these appendices.

The number and geography of threatened species

The number of species treated as threatened in this volume is 172, with a further one being "Out of Danger" and four "Of Special Concern" (there are, in addition, 93 "near-threatened" species briefly treated in Appendix C, 16 threatened or near-threatened incipient species in Appendix E, and 23[-24] species that occur or have occurred in the region and are candidates for inclusion in a subsequent part of this edition – see Appendix D). Of the 172 threatened species, two (1%) are accounted Extinct, 28 (16%) Endangered, 15 (9%) Vulnerable, 31 (18%) Indeterminate, 78 (45.5%) Rare, and 18 (10.5%) Insufficiently Known. For the same area the previous edition of this work (King 1978-1979) treated 65 species (this number includes forms there treated as subspecies but here considered full species), of which 19 (29%) were Endangered, 13 (20%) Vulnerable, four (6%) Indeterminate and 29 (45%) Rare.

The great difference in the number of species treated between this edition and that of King (1978-1979) and indeed that of Vincent (1966-1971) is explicable through at least five factors. The first two of these are very simple: one is that the introduction in 1980 of the category "Insufficiently Known" created an extra dimension to Red Data Book work, and the other is that certain new species have been described or established since the mid-1970s, almost all of which have required treatment as threatened (the birds in question are listed above under "Taxonomy and names" and along with those others in the Insufficiently Known category constitute 24 new entries). Third, a generous allocation of time coupled with dual authorship and a year's assistance from T. J. Dee has permitted a more exhaustive coverage than was previously possible: earlier omission of birds like the Dwarf Olive Ibis, White-breasted Guineafowl, São Tomé Short-tail and Golden-naped Weaver must be attributed to insufficient opportunity for their proper investigation. Fourth, our interpretation of IUCN categories of threat has been somewhat broader (though, as we state earlier, not more relaxed) than in previous editions, notably King (1978-1979). The two categories which show greatest numerical increase are "Indeterminate" and "Rare" and, in the latter case at least, a high proportion of the new entries is constituted by birds whose main threat is simply a function of their restricted range, e.g. Mount Cameroon Francolin *Francolinus camerunensis*, White-tailed Swallow *Hirundo megaensis*, Appert's Greenbul *Phyllastrephus apperti*, Swynnerton's Forest Robin *Swynnertonia swynnertoni*, Rockefeller's Sunbird *Nectarinia rockefelleri* and Ethiopian Bush-Crow *Zavattariornis stresemanni*. Moreover, we "restore" eight species treated by Vincent (1966-1971) but omitted by King: Prince Ruspoli's Turaco *Tauraco ruspolii*, African Green Broadbill *Pseudocalyptomena graueri*, Mauritius Black Bulbul *Hypsipetes (borbonicus) olivaceus*, Taita Thrush *Turdus helleri*, Seychelles Warbler *Acrocephalus (Bebrornis) sechellensis* (Out of Danger in King), Fernando Po Speirops *Speirops brunneus*, Warsangli Linnet *Acanthis (Warsanglia) johannis* and Tristan Bunting *Nesospiza acunhae*. At the same time we omit only one species treated by Vincent (Taita Falcon *Falco fasciinucha*) and four by King (Jackass Penguin *Spheniscus demersus*, Madagascar Crested Ibis *Lophotibis cristata*, Pitta-like Ground-roller *Atelornis pittoides* and Bernier's Vanga *Oriolia bernieri*), although all these are treated in Appendix C except Jackass Penguin, which becomes "Of Special Concern".

The fifth factor affecting the number of species treated here is again very simple: it is that the environmental situation in Africa and its related islands has, in general, become progressively worse over the past 20 years, so that the number of bird species coming under threat has correspondingly increased. Thus in West Africa, i.e. from Cameroon westwards, where loss of habitat is now known to have been particularly serious in recent decades, we treat some 22 species where King (1978-1979) treated only three; and in the Central Refugium (see below), where habitat destruction is becoming locally serious, we treat some 18 species where King treated none. Africa is, of course, in the grip of a terrible crisis over land-usage and development, and conservationists can hardly expect easy or happy resolution of all the ornithological issues presented here. It is not, however, entirely the case that Red Data Books are for emergencies rather than preventive measures, since the category "Rare" has allowed us to include species for early attention mainly at the preventive level. As the crisis in Africa intensifies, that attention will become all the more crucial.

An analysis of the distribution patterns of the threatened species in the area under review reveals some interesting trends. Only two species, the Northern Bald Ibis *Geronticus eremita* and the Algerian Nuthatch *Sitta ledanti*, represent a continental Palearctic influence. A high proportion of threatened species (44%) is restricted to oceanic islands. This includes 28 species from Madagascar, 11 from the Mascarene Islands, nine from the Seychelles and Aldabra, seven from São Tomé e Príncipe, six from the Comoro Islands (including Mayotte), five from the Tristan da Cunha group (including Gough), five from the Canary Islands, three from Madeira, two from the Cape Verde Islands and one each from Fernando Po, Ascension Island, St.Helena and Amsterdam Island. The high incidence of threatened species on islands is as expected. In an analysis of early material in the previous edition of the *ICBP/IUCN Red Data Book* (King 1978-1979) island forms were anticipated to account for 53% of the total taxa treated (King 1978). This figure was an underestimate since in that analysis large islands such as Madagascar, Taiwan and Borneo were considered to be continental (King 1978), and indeed no fewer than 46 (71%) of the 65 species treated in King (1978-1979) for the area here under review were island forms. Some of the most threatened birds considered in this volume are island species, such as the Pink Pigeon *Nesoenas mayeri*, Mauritius Parakeet *Psittacula eques* and Aldabra Warbler *Nesillas aldabranus*, and of course the Mascarene Islands (on which the first two of these examples survive) are well known for their extensive history of avian extinctions.

By contrast, no recent avian extinction is documented from the African mainland, though one bird, the Yellow-throated Serin *Serinus flavigula*, has not been seen for almost a century and another, the Golden-naped Weaver *Ploceus aureonucha*, not for over 50 years. Ninety-seven Afrotropical species are included in this volume of the Red Data Book. Moreau (1966) estimated the total number of Afrotropical species to be 1,481, of which some 6.5% must now be considered to be facing some sort of threat (compared with about 25% of the endemic avifauna of Madagascar). There have been several attempts to write a synopsis of the Afrotropical avifauna, the most noteworthy being those of Chapin (1923,1932), Moreau (1952,1966) and Crowe and Crowe (1982). In general it has been agreed that the forest avifauna (both lowland and montane) is very distinct from the avifauna in non-forest plant communities. Of the 97 threatened Afrotropical species, a disturbingly high number (63, i.e. 65%) are forest or forest-dependent species. Moreau (1966) estimated that there are 409 forest and 1,030 non-forest species in sub-Saharan Africa. If we accept these figures as being broadly correct, then it emerges that forest species have been about five times more susceptible to serious decline than have non-forest species (15% of forest birds are threatened as against 3% of non-forest birds).

If the distributions of the 63 threatened Afrotropical forest species are examined further, some remarkable patterns can be seen. The overwhelming majority of them (92%) have their ranges centred on just five areas. These are (i) the Upper Guinea lowland forest, from Sierra Leone to Ghana, (ii) the montane and lowland forests of western and southern Cameroon, (iii) the forests along the escarpment of western Angola, (iv) the lowland and montane forests along the Albertine Rift, in north-eastern Zaire, south-western Uganda and Rwanda, and (v) the forests of eastern Kenya and mountains of eastern Tanzania. Three of these five areas, Cameroon, the Albertine Rift and eastern Kenya and Tanzania, are well known as centres of forest bird diversity and endemism in Africa (Moreau 1966, Hamilton 1976, Diamond and Hamilton 1980). It has been suggested that these three areas form the main forest refugia in Africa, where the forest is believed to have survived throughout the driest periods of the Pleistocene (Livingstone 1975, Hamilton 1976, Diamond and Hamilton 1980). Whether or not the refugium hypothesis is accepted as an explanation of high bird species diversity and endemism, it is undeniable that these three areas are of critical conservation importance for African birds. In the so-called Western Refugium (Cameroon) perhaps the most important areas are Mounts Cameroon and Kupe, the Bamenda Highlands and the lowland forest around the Dja River. In the Central Refugium (Albertine Rift) the Itombwe Mountains and the Ituri Forest in north-eastern Zaire, the Nyungwe Forest in Rwanda and the Impenetrable Forest in south-western Uganda are of particular importance. In the Eastern Refugium (Kenya, Tanzania) the most crucial areas are the Sokoke Forest in coastal Kenya and the Usambara, Uluguru and Uzungwa Mountains in eastern Tanzania. The escarpment of western Angola has also been suggested as a minor forest refugium, at least for birds (Moreau 1966, Hamilton 1976). Although the forest avifauna of western Angola is not particularly diverse, it contains several species with very limited distributions.

By contrast, the Upper Guinea forests are less often considered to be a major forest refugium. Most of the threatened bird species from this area probably once ranged fairly widely through the forest block that formerly existed between Sierra Leone and Ghana. Their rarity today is a reflection of the devastation of forest which has taken place in this area. Some of these species are amongst the most threatened in continental Africa. For most of them their continued survival depends very largely on the adequate conservation of the Tai National Park in south-western Ivory Coast, although several other areas, e.g. Mount Nimba, are no less valuable if they could realistically be expected to survive.

Threatened non-forest Afrotropical species, relatively small in number, show no very striking trends in their distribution patterns. Most are not very adaptable to habitat change and are therefore vulnerable to the same processes that threaten many forest species, namely the deleterious modification of their habitat by man. We plan to analyse and discuss all the species in this volume, their geography, ecology and threats, in one or more review papers to be prepared during 1984 and 1985.

Acknowledgements

This book is the result of many kindnesses by many people. The pooling of knowledge has been consistently generous, and we have been sustained and encouraged by the goodwill of our many correspondents, helpers and friends. We have been given free use of a vast quantity of unpublished data, sometimes as personal records, sometimes as typescript reports, sometimes as material in preparation for publication or in press. We have been helped with guidance, opinion, correction, and criticism. It has all been welcome and useful, and we thank everyone who has been associated with the making of this volume for the time and the trouble they have taken.

Very special thanks are owed to a number of people: to the late C. W. Benson, for whom we reserve our appreciation until last in these acknowledgements; to R. J. Dowsett for his detailed and enthusiastic initiation of the work and his unflagging support throughout; and to J. S. Ash for drawing so readily and extensively on his notes on birds in north-eastern Africa; F. M. Benson for all her help and encouragement; W. R. P. Bourne for the careful scrutiny and correction of certain seabird and Tristan da Cunha texts; R. K. Brooke for a very detailed response (with J. Cooper) to our initial request for comments and for access to his *Rare and vulnerable birds of South Africa*, currently in press; A. S. Cheke for hours of consultation concerning the Mascarenes and full access to his library and to his material currently in press for *Studies in Mascarene island birds*; J. Cooper for a very detailed response (with R. K. Brooke) to our initial request for comments and for the constant supply of relevant PFIAO reprints and his comments on certain seabird texts; K. W. Emmerson for much new information concerning birds on the Canary Islands; G. D. Field for extensive help with West African bird species; A. D. Forbes-Watson for unpublished information concerning birds in West and East Africa and Madagascar; M. W. Fraser for much new information concerning birds on the Tristan da Cunha group; W. Gatter for extensive help with West African bird species; C. G. Jones for much new information concerning birds in Mauritius and Rodrigues, and for access to his material currently in press for *Studies in Mascarene island birds*; W. B. King for his early advice and encouragement in the project; R. de Naurois for his help in assessing threats to birds in the Gulf of Guinea islands, the Cape Verdes and elsewhere; A. Prigogine for his extensive and very painstaking help with Central Refugium species; D. A. Turner for equally extensive and painstaking help with birds of East Africa and Madagascar; and J. Watson for much new information concerning birds in Seychelles.

In addition, we must mention the following for their great kindness in supplying valuable information or for helping in other ways: P. A. Agland, P. Ahimaz, H. R. Akçakaya, J. Alamargot, J. S. M. Albrecht, D. G. Allan, O. Appert, G. W. Archibald, C. P.-J. Ash, D. R. Aspinwall, N. E. Baker, J. Barnes, G. M. Bathe, H. V. Bathe, A. J. Beakbane, M. A. S. Beaman, J. S. S. Beesley, L. Bennun, H.-H. Bergmann, K. D. Bishop, J. Blot, E. M. Boswell, S. J. Bousfield, Mrs S. J. Bousfield, C. G. R. Bowden, P. L. Britton, M. de L. Brooke, S. Brogger-Jensen, A. Brosset, J. Burlison, M. Carswell, C. Carter, P. A. Clancey, G. C. Clarke, D. R. Collins, N. M. Collins, P. R. Colston, J. E. Cooper, K. H. Cooper, S. Cramp (for access to material in draft for *Birds of the western Palearctic*, 4), Q. C. B. Cronk, G. R. Cunningham-van Someren, G. Davies, I. Dawson, W. R. J. Dean, J.-P. Decoux, P. Devillers, A. W. Diamond, I. H. Dillingham, the late B. G. Donnelly, F. Dowsett-Lemaire, E. Duffey, E. K. Dunn, A. R. Dupuy, M. Dyer, C. Edelstam, M. Eisentraut, J. H. Elgood, D. Elias, C. C. H. Elliott, H. F. I. Elliott, O. Elter, S. K. Eltringham, C. Erard, R. D. Etchécopar, P. G. H. Evans, A. Fayard, M. O. Fedden, C. T. Fisher (for data from the collections in the Merseyside County Museums, Liverpool), C. H. Fry, N. R. Fuggles-Couchman, R. W. Furness, I. C. J. Galbraith, A. B. Gammell, M. C. Garnett, J. S. Gartlan, M. E. Gartshore, J. P. Gee, C. W. D. Gibson, P. J. Ginn, K. Goodspeed, P. D. Goriup, A. A. Green, L. G. Grimes, H. Grossmann, A. Guillet, C. Hambler, D. B. Hanmer, C. Harbard, J. T. Hardyman, C. J. O. Harrison, J. C. den Hartog, J. Heinze, L. Hepworth, U. Hirsch, P. A. R. Hockey, M. C. Hodgson, M. W. Holdgate, M. V. Hounsome (for data from the collections in Manchester Museum), G. W. Howard, K. M. Howell, S. V. Hunter, C. R. Huxley, C. Inskipp, T. P. Inskipp, M. P. S. Irwin, P. C. James, F. P. Jensen, E. D. H. Johnson, M. J. Jones, P. J. Jones, P. Jouventin, F. Kämmer, Z. J. Karpowicz, J. Kear, G. S. Keith, M. G. Kelsey, P. Kerswill, J. Kielland, J. Kingdon, P. J. Knight, C. König, P. M. Konrad, M. Kraft, H. Kumerloeve, V. Laboudallon, L. A. Lace, F. R. Lambert, O. Langrand, M. LeCroy, J.-P. Ledant, G. Le Grand, A. D. Lewis, H. Löhrl, M. Louette, C. Luthin, K. Lynn, M. A. Macdonald, A. Machado, J. A. Mackenzie, H. L. Macleod, D. E. Manry, A. J. Manson, R. W. Markham, A. Martín, R. P.

Martins, A. N. B. Masterson, G. E. Maul, G. F. Mees, J. M. Mendelsohn, H. Mendelssohn, G. Merz, B.-U. Meyburg, W. Möller, J. F. Monk, A. Moore, G. J. Morel, D. C. Moyer, N. Muddiman, P. J. Mundy, D. Newsome, G. Nikolaus, A. Nørrevang, J. N. Novais, P. J. S. Olney, A. W. Owadally, R. H. W. Pakenham, S. Parry, R. F. Pasquier, H. A. W. Payne, D. S. Peacock, S. Peters, B. Phillips, N. J. Phillips, A. A. da R. Pinto, W. J. Plumb, W. Poduschka, J. I. Pollock, D. E. Pomeroy, P. Portas, R. F. Porter, R. Potvliege, K. L. Pruitt, O. E. Prys-Jones, R. P. Prys-Jones, M. E. Quigley, R. M. Randall, D. K. Read, J. F. Reynolds, M. E. Richardson, H. A. Robertson, W. A. Rodgers, W. Ruttledge, T. Searight, H. Schifter, H.-H. Schleich, K.-L. Schuchmann, W. Serle, R. E. Sharland, L. L. Short, K. E. L. Simmons, J. P. Skorupa, C. A. Spinage, M. Smart, D. A. Smith, P. A. Smith, D. W. Snow, R. J. Stjernstedt, D. R. Stoddart, the late B. W. H. Stronach, W. Strahm, the late C. J. Stutterheim, S. J. A. Sumba, M. K. Swales, A. R. H. Swash, W. R. Tarboton, I. R. Taylor, J. L. Tello, J.-M. Thiollay, J. Thomas, D. M. Todd, A. J. Tree, N. A. Tucker, A. Tye, H. Tye, S. J. Tyler, E. K. Urban, J.-P. Vande weghe, C. J. Vernon, J. D. R. Vernon, J. Vincent, C. G. Violani, M. Voisin, K. H. Voous, M. P. Walters, R. K. Walton, C. Warman, S. Warman, G. E. Watson, J. Wattel, G. Welch, H. Welch, D. R. Wells, O. West, A. J. Williams, J. G. Williams, T. A. van der Willigen, E. O. Willis, J. R. Wilson, M. G. Wilson, R. Wirth, V. E. Wood, W. Woulkoff, P. A. Zino.

As we mention under "Methods and rationale", the bulk of the research for this book was undertaken in five major libraries, and it is a pleasure to acknowledge the very positive assistance we have received from A. Randall and her staff in the Department of Zoology, Cambridge; the staff of the University Museum of Zoology, Cambridge; R. Fairclough and his staff in the Map Room of the University Library, Cambridge; A. S. Richford, L. Ratcliffe and L. Birch, successive keepers of the Alexander Library, Edward Grey Institute, Department of Zoology, Oxford; and A. Vale, librarian at the Sub-department of Ornithology, British Museum (Natural History), Tring. We must equally thank the director and other staff members of the Sub-department of Ornithology in Tring for their generosity and patience in allowing us full access to the collections in their care; and we extend our gratitude also to the directors and staff of the other museums and libraries (listed under "Methods and rationale") we have been privileged to work in.

Our friends the staff of the ICBP international secretariat and of the IUCN Conservation Monitoring Centre have been ever cheerful and supportive, and we must acknowledge especially the forbearance, help and encouragement of Ch. Imboden, director of ICBP. S. Vernon typed most of the material into the word-processor and L. Wright has most efficiently prepared the way for its publication; V. Greenwood and E. M. Schierbeek worked well beyond appointed hours to bring the text to completion, and their kindness, commitment and drive are recorded with the greatest appreciation. D. Mackinder and N. Phillips developed the computer programme for type-setting. T. J. Dee, our assistant and *eminence grise* for the past year, has adapted with skill, patience and energy to the many and varied demands we have made of him, and our gratitude for his dedicated work cannot be overstated.

Parts of this book have very kindly been read in proof for errors and means of improvement by T. J. Dee, J. Fenton, P. D. Goriup, V. Greenwood, R. F. Grimmett, B. Groombridge, M. D. Jenkins, E. M. Schierbeek, T. A. Urquhart, S. M. Wells and L. Wright.

We thank N. Arlott for painting the colour plates, B. Groombridge for his dust-jacket illustration, J. Butler for the overall book-design, and J. A. F. Humphrey of Gee Graphics Ltd. for his skilful, painstaking and speedy type-setting. We also thank Faber and Faber for permission to quote (at the head of the Introduction) Poem XXVI from P. Larkin's collection, *The North Ship*.

NJC has received enormous support from his wife, Alison, and must record here the debt he owes her and their family for the many weekends and evenings together they have lost in the cause of this project over the past three years. SNS thanks Celia Deane-Drummond for her support and encouragement.

To all these people, and to the many others who have helped us whom we have not mentioned, we offer again our warmest thanks and appreciation.

Finally in this section we must pay tribute to C. W. Benson. It was he who, in the 1970s, kindled and promoted SNS's interest in the montane avifaunas of Tanzania, which led in due course to a doctorate and thence to appointment as co-author of this book; and it was he who, in 1981 and 1982, despite his own pressing studies and deadlines, gave freely of his precious time and vast knowledge to help shape and order this book at its inception. He kept his books with the UMZC bird collection he so meticulously curated (for the last decade of his life unpaid), and visit after visit to him, often when the intention was only to consult his library, would be greeted by a cheerful smile, the offer of a cup of tea, and, most typically, "I'm awfully glad you've come in, I've got something for you...": the something would invariably be a new snippet of information he had found or thought of, often retrieved from obscurity with considerable expense of time and effort. One felt singled out by such kindness, yet he was no less obliging to everyone he dealt with: one only has to skim the acknowledgements section of a bird journal commonly treating African material over the past 30 years to see how innumerable were the kindnesses he performed and the people he helped. This generosity of his, to which this book and its authors owe so much, was ultimately a matter of caring: and two of his main cares were for the birds of Africa and for truth, things he never – as it is so easy to do – regarded as somehow his personal domain or exclusive heritage. The Abbé de Naurois put it very simply and aptly when, on learning of his death, he wrote in a letter to us: "he was a charming colleague, a true friend, an excellent zoologist – and a *gentleman*!!!" It was a privilege to have known him, and we offer this book in his honour and to his memory.

31 October 1984   N. J. Collar, S. N. Stuart

References

Ali, R. (1984) Establishment of a monitoring system for habitats, species and conservation areas in Indonesia. IUCN/WWF Project no. 3132, final report.

Bishop, K. D. (in prep.) *The ICBP list of single island endemic birds*. Cambridge: ICBP Techn. Publ. no. 7.

Brooke, R. K. (in press) *Rare and vulnerable birds of South Africa*.

Brown, L. H. (undated) A report on threatened bird species in East Africa. East Africa Wildlife Society, unpublished.

Burton, J. A. (1984) Bibliography of Red Data Books (Part 1, animal species). *Oryx* 18: 61-64.

Chapin, J. P. (1923) Ecological aspects of bird distribution in tropical Africa. *Amer. Nat.* 57: 106-125.

Chapin, J. P. (1932) The birds of the Belgian Congo. Part 1. *Bull. Amer. Mus. Nat. Hist.* 65.

Clancey, P. A. (1979a) Miscellaneous taxonomic notes on African birds 53. *Durban Mus. Novit.* 12: 1-17.

Clancey, P. A. (1979b) Miscellaneous taxonomic notes on African birds 55. *Durban Mus. Novit.* 12: 47-61.

Collar, N. J. (1982) Extracts from the red data book for the birds of Africa and associated islands. Cambridge: ICBP, unpublished.

Cramp, S. and Simmons, K. E. L. eds. (1977) *The birds of the western Palearctic*, 1. Oxford: Oxford University Press.

Crowe, T. M. and Crowe, A. A. (1982) Patterns of distribution and diversity and endemism in Afrotropical birds. *J. Zool., Lond.* 198: 417-442.

Diamond, A. W. and Hamilton, A. C. (1980) The distribution of forest passerine birds and Quaternary climatic change in Africa. *J. Zool., Lond.* 191: 379-402.

Dowsett, R. J. (1981) Memorandum: an African "Red Data Book" for birds, 14 February. Unpublished.

Forbes-Watson, A. D. and Turner, D. A. (1972-1973) Report on bird preservation in Madagascar. Report to ICBP, unpublished.

Fry, C. H. (1979-1982) Coded bibliography of African ornithology, 1975-1981. *Malimbus* supplements.

Greenway, J. C. (1967) *Extinct and vanishing birds of the world*. 2nd revised edition. New York: Dover Publications.

Groombridge, B. and Wright, L. (1982) *The IUCN Amphibia – Reptilia red data book*. Part 1. Gland, Switzerland: IUCN.

Hall, B. P. and Moreau, R. E. (1962) A study of the rare birds of Africa. *Bull. Brit. Mus. (Nat. Hist.) Zool.* 8: 313-378.

Hall, B. P. and Moreau, R. E. (1970) *An atlas of speciation in African passerine birds*. London: Trustees of the British Museum (Natural History).

Hamilton, A. C. (1976) The significance of patterns of distribution shown by forest plants and animals in tropical Africa for the re-construction of Upper-pleistocene palaeoenvironments: a review. *Paleoecol. Afr.* 9: 63-97.

Hay, R. (in prep.) Report on bird conservation in the South Pacific. ICBP/Royal Forest and Bird Protection Society/South Pacific Regional Environment Programme.

King, W. B. (1978) Endangered birds of the world and current efforts towards managing them. Pp. 9-17 in S. A. Temple, ed. *Endangered birds: management techniques for preserving threatened species*. Madison, Wisconsin: University of Wisconsin, and London: Croom Helm.

King, W. B. (1978-1979) *Red data book, 2. Aves.* 2nd edition. Morges, Switzerland: IUCN.

King, W. B. (1981) *Endangered birds of the world: the ICBP bird red data book*. Washington, D.C.: Smithsonian Institution Press/ICBP [bound re-issue of King 1978-1979].

Livingstone, D. A. (1975) Late Quaternary climatic change in Africa. *Ann. Rev. Ecol. Syst.* 6: 249-280.

Mayr, E. (1957) New species of birds described from 1941 to 1955. *J. Orn.* 98: 22-35.

Mayr, E. (1971) New species of birds described from 1956 to 1965. *J. Orn.* 112: 302-316.

Mayr, E. and Vuilleumier, F. (1983) New species of birds described from 1966 to 1975. *J. Orn.* 124: 217-232.

Meise, W. (1938a) Fortschritte der ornithologischen Systematik seit 1920. *Proc. VIII Internat. Orn. Congr. (1934)*: 49-189.

Meise, W. (1938b) Exposition de types d'oiseaux nouvellement décrits au Muséum de Paris. *Proc. IX Internat. Orn. Congr. (1938)*: 46-51.

Moreau, R. E. (1952) Africa since the Mesozoic: with particular reference to certain biological problems. *Proc Zool. Soc. Lond.* 121: 869-913.

Moreau, R.E.(1966) *The bird faunas of Africa and its islands*. London: Academic Press.

Morony, J. J., Bock, W. J. and Farrand, J. (1975) *Reference list of the birds of the world*. New York: American Museum of Natural History (Department of Ornithology).

Schodde, R. (1978) The status of endangered Papuasian birds, and Appendix. Pp. 133-145 and 185-206 respectively in M. J. Tyler, ed. *The status of endangered Australasian wildlife*. [Adelaide:] Royal Zoological Society of South Australia.

Siegfried, W. R., Frost, P. G. H., Cooper, J. and Kemp, A. C. (1976) South African red data book – Aves. Pretoria: South African National Scientific Programmes Report no. 7.

Snow, D. W. ed. (1978) *An atlas of speciation in African non-passerine birds*. London: Trustees of the British Museum (Natural History).

Thornback, J. and Jenkins, M. (1982) *The IUCN mammal red data book*. Part 1. Gland, Switzerland: IUCN.

The Times Atlas of the World (1982) Comprehensive (sixth) edition. London: Times Books.

Vincent, J. (1966-1971) *Red data book, 2: Aves*. Morges, Switzerland: IUCN.

Wells, S. M., Pyle, R. M. and Collins, N. M. (1983) *The IUCN invertebrate red data book*. Gland, Switzerland: IUCN.

Zimmer, J. T. and Mayr, E. (1943) New species of birds described from 1938 to 1941. *Auk* 60: 249-262.

Threatened species accounts

JACKASS PENGUIN   OF SPECIAL CONCERN
Spheniscus demersus (Linnaeus, 1758)

Order SPHENISCIFORMES   Family SPHENISCIDAE

Summary Although still plentiful, this penguin, which breeds only in Namibia and South Africa, suffered a drastic population decline in the nineteenth century and earlier this century from egg-harvesting and guano-scraping. It is now subject to further declines from competition for food with the pelagic fishing industry, from harbour developments near breeding islands and from oil pollution.

Distribution The Jackass Penguin is restricted as a breeding species to 25 islands off the coasts of Namibia and South Africa and a few sites on the mainland (Frost *et al.* 1976b, Brooke in press, Shelton *et al.* in press). Sixteen of these islands are in the cold, nutrient-rich Benguela Current zone along the coast of Namibia and western Cape Province (Frost *et al.* 1976b). In Namibia the species breeds on the following islands (from north to south): Hollamsbird (although there has been no confirmed evidence of breeding at this site in the last 30 years: Shelton *et al.* in press), Mercury, Ichaboe, Halifax, North Reef, Possession, Pomona, Plumpudding and Sinclair (Rand 1963b, Frost *et al.* 1976b, Shelton *et al.* in press). Along the western coast of Cape Province there are colonies on the following islands: Bird (in Lambert's Bay), Malgas, Marcus, Jutten, Vondeling, Dassen and Robben (Rand 1963a, Frost *et al.* 1976b, Shelton *et al.* in press). On the southern Cape coast (away from the Benguela Current) the species breeds on Seal Island (in False Bay), Dyer and Geyser islands and the following islands in Algoa Bay: St.Croix, Jahleel, Brenton Rock, Bird, Seal and Stag (Courtenay-Latimer and Gibson-Hill 1946, Rand 1963a, Frost *et al.* 1976b, Randall *et al.* 1981b, Shelton *et al.* in press). In 1981 a pair was found nesting on the mainland at Cape Recife on the southern end of Algoa Bay (Every 1983). Another mainland nest was located in the following year at Stony Point between the colonies at Seal Island (in False Bay) and Dyer Island (Broni 1982) and breeding was recorded again at this site in 1983-1984 (Shelton *et al.* in press). A third and much larger mainland breeding colony has recently been discovered at Sylvia Hill on the Namibian coast (Cooper *et al.* in press, Shelton *et al.* in press). Despite these records it is clear that mainland breeding is the exception rather than the rule. Four colonies are known to have died out in historical times. These were at Seal Island (near Lüderitz) and Penguin Island (also off the Namibian coast), both of which were extinct before 1900 (Shelton *et al.* in press), Quoin Rock (just east of Quoin Point) where birds nested until about 1902 (Rand 1963a) and Seal Island (in Mosselbaai) where the species bred until about 1930 (Shaughnessy and Shaughnessy 1978, Brooke in press). Other possible breeding colonies, now almost certainly extinct, may have occurred along the Namibian coast on an island in Hottentot Bay, on North Long Island and Albatross Rock, and on the coast of Cape Province on Jacob's Reef (Shelton *et al.* in press). Rumours that the species used to breed at the mouth of the Kei River (Shortridge and Sclater 1904) are almost certainly unfounded. Juveniles, and to a lesser extent sub-adults (Cooper and Randall 1981), wander considerable distances from their breeding grounds: there are many records from along the Namibian coast (Maclean

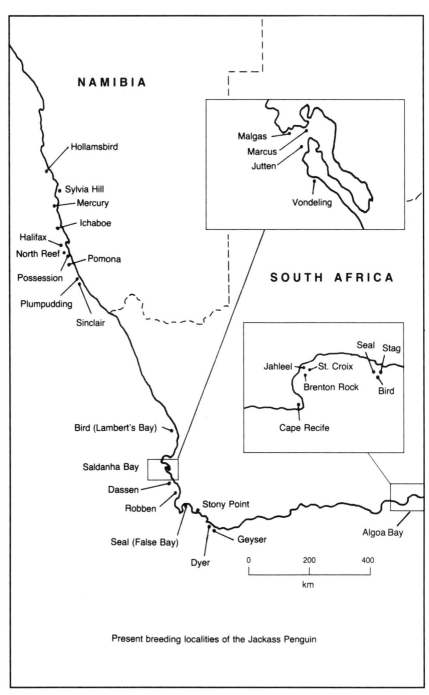

Present breeding localities of the Jackass Penguin

1960, Niethammer 1961, Brooke and Sinclair 1978, Shelton *et al.* in press) and at least six records from Angola, where it is probably a regular visitor to coastal waters in the south of the country, at Punta de São José, Moçâmedes, Baia dos Tigres (Great Fish Bay), Porto Alexandre and Lobito (Traylor 1963, da Franca 1967, Brooke 1981 and in press, Shelton *et al.* in press). There are also two remarkable records of birds seen at Pointe Noire in Congo in March 1954 and at Setté Cama (3°S) in southern Gabon in late December 1956 (Malbrant and Maclatchy 1958,1959). Along the south-east coast of Africa the species is less frequent, there being occasional records from Transkei (Shortridge and Sclater 1904, Winterbottom and Hare 1947, Siegfried 1979, Shelton *et al.* in press), Natal (Cyrus and Robson 1980, Shelton *et al.* in press) and southern Mozambique at Inhaca Island and Delagoa Bay (Pinto 1958, Clancey 1971), mainly in the winter months (McLachlan and Liversidge 1978). Most records of the species from localities far removed from the breeding grounds are of dead or exhausted birds washed ashore (Shortridge and Sclater 1904, Maclean 1960, Niethammer 1961, Siegfried 1979, Cyrus and Robson 1980). The Jackass Penguin is mainly an inshore species, most commonly recorded near the coast (Stanford 1953, Liversidge and Thomas 1970, Summerhayes *et al.* 1974, Siegfried *et al.* 1975, Shelton *et al.* in press) and it has even been recorded in Cape Town docks (Stanford 1953, van Oordt and Kruijt 1954). There are, however, several records of the species occurring over 80 km from land (Stanford 1953, Liversidge and Thomas 1970), and in one case at 190 km from the coast (Siegfried *et al.* 1975). Records of this species from Tristan da Cunha (Elliott 1953) were later considered to refer to the Magellanic Penguin *Spheniscus magellanicus* (Elliott 1957), although Shelton *et al.* (in press) consider the identification of these penguins off Tristan da Cunha to be still uncertain.

Population Although a wealth of population data exists for the Jackass Penguin, many different census methods have been used and the results are, therefore, confusing and difficult to interpret, or to use for comparative purposes (Frost *et al.* 1976b). In this section the different census methods are briefly reviewed to aid in the understanding of the population estimates that have been obtained. The various estimates of the breeding population for each island are then given and the section is concluded with estimates of the world population. Jackass Penguins are very difficult to count at their breeding colonies because some birds nest in burrows and because during the daytime those adults which are not incubating are out at sea or resting on the beach (Frost *et al.* 1976b). The species also has a very protracted breeding season and not all the adult birds are likely to be present at any one time of year (Frost *et al.* 1976b, Randall and Randall 1981). In 1956 counts were made of nearly all known Jackass Penguin colonies based on aerial photographs (Rand 1963a,b). Obviously birds nesting in burrows and birds out at sea cannot be counted by this method (Frost *et al.* 1976b). Because of these problems Rand (1963a,b) calculated estimates of the real population from the actual counts of birds on the aerial photographs (for details of this method see Rand 1963a). The extent to which this method corrects for absenteeism from the colonies is, however, completely unclear and there are problems with some of Rand's (1963a,b) computations, which are not always adequately explained (Shelton *et al.* in press). In 1978 further aerial photographs were taken of most

3

penguin colonies (Shelton *et al.* in press) (some were also taken in 1967 and 1969) and comparisons have been made between the numbers of birds present on the photographs in 1956 and 1978 (Crawford and Shelton 1981). Shelton *et al.* (in press) have calculated minimum estimates of the real populations on nearly all of the islands from the actual counts of birds on the 1978 aerial photographs. These calculations correct for absenteeism from these colonies, using information obtained by studies of absenteeism on Mercury and Possession islands (Shelton *et al.* in press). Shelton *et al.* (in press) have also re-calculated the population estimates from the 1956 aerial photographs, thus making comparisons between the 1956 and 1978 results possible (Shelton *et al.* 1982). Although the actual numbers of birds counted on the photographs are doubtless very different from the real populations, comparison between the 1956 and 1978 counts probably give a reasonable indication of population trends (Shelton *et al.* 1982, in press). Also in 1978-1979 ground counts were carried out in nearly all of the colonies (Shelton *et al.* 1982) and estimates of the absolute population, corrected for absenteeism, have been calculated (Shelton *et al.* in press). For details of this census technique and correction calculation see Shelton *et al.* (1982 and in press). The mean ratio between the number of birds counted on aerial photographs and the number of nests counted on ground surveys is 2.89 (Shelton *et. al.* in press). This suggests that a number of non-breeders are counted in the aerial censuses (Shelton *et al.* in press). The most frequently quoted population estimates of the Jackass Penguin in recent years are those provided by Frost *et al.* (1976b): these figures are based on census data taken in 1970-1972 for Halifax, Possession, Marcus, Dassen, Dyer and St.Croix Islands and on unpublished rough estimates by the Division of Government Guano Islands for all other sites (Shelton *et al.* in press) and are not, strictly speaking, comparable with the results from the aerial photographs, and are not necessarily even comparable among themselves. Another method that has proved useful in estimating minimum populations for colonies in the early years of this century is based on egg-crop data (Cott 1953, Frost *et al.* 1976b). Fortunately the South African government has kept detailed figures on the number of eggs cropped from each island, making it possible to estimate the minimum number of birds that must have been present (Frost *et al.* 1976b, Shelton *et al.* in press). Because the Jackass Penguin has a staggered breeding season, any census based on counts made only once a year can be very misleading (Frost *et al.* 1976b, Shelton *et al.* in press). This criticism can be applied to most of the census methods that have been used. One exception is the method used by Cooper (1979) and Furness and Cooper (1982) on Marcus, Malgas and Jutten Islands: this method involves counting the number of moulting birds on each island every 18 days over a 350-day period. Moulting penguins spend all their time on their breeding islands (Cooper 1979). The mean moulting period is 18 days and studies of ringed birds show the moulting interval to be c. 350 days (Cooper 1979). Although laborious, this method is probably the most accurate yet devised for estimating the total number of adults (not necessarily breeding birds) using each island and, interestingly enough, it has resulted in much higher population estimates than those obtained by any other method (Cooper 1979, Shelton *et al.* in press, R. M. Randall *in litt.* 1984). This suggests that all previous surveys have grossly underestimated the Jackass Penguin population (Shelton *et al.* in press), although more work will be needed to test this possibility. The results of the many censuses that have been carried out at the breeding sites are given below (north to south to east, the first ten being in Namibia).

Hollamsbird (Hollam's Bird) In the last century there might have been a few hundred Jackass Penguins on this island but by 1951 only two or three pairs could be found (Rand 1952b). In the early 1970s the population was assumed to be in the order of ten adult birds (Frost *et al.* 1976b) and in 1977 five birds were seen within 8 km of the island (Shaughnessy 1977). Clearly this colony is very small and no penguins could be detected on the aerial photographs taken in 1956 and 1978 (Rand 1963b, Crawford and Shelton 1981). There has been no confirmed record of breeding on Hollamsbird Island in the last 30 years (Shelton *et al.* in press).

Sylvia Hill This is the largest and best established mainland site, the highest count being 254 birds in 1984 (Shelton *et al.* in press). Earlier counts of 30 in 1981 and 60 in 1983 suggest that this colony is increasing in size (Shelton *et al.* in press).

Mercury On the 1956 aerial photographs 3,264 birds can be counted and the real population for this time was estimated at 9,500 birds (Rand 1963b) though this has since been corrected to 4,896 birds (Shelton *et al.* in press). On aerial photographs taken in 1967, 1969 and 1978, 2,964, 4,078 and 10,820 birds respectively can be counted (Shelton *et al.* in press). An analysis of the 1978 aerial photographs indicates a three-fold increase since 1956, all this increase taking place since 1967 (Crawford and Shelton 1981). When the counts on the 1978 aerial photographs are corrected for absenteeism the real population is estimated at 12,655 birds (Shelton *et al.* in press). Ground censuses, also carried out in 1978, resulted in a count of 3,218 nests and a population estimate of 6,436 breeding birds (Shelton *et al.* in press). In the light of these figures it seems that a rough estimate of 3,000 birds in the early 1970s (Frost *et al.* 1976b) is much too low, as is a head count of 2,906 adults in 1980 (Shelton *et al.* in press). In 1977 several thousand birds were found nesting on the island (Shaughnessy 1977).

Ichaboe On the 1956 aerial photographs 4,179 birds can be counted and the real population was estimated at 8,400 birds (Rand 1963b, Shelton *et al.* in press). On aerial photographs taken in 1967, 1969 and 1978, 2,882, 3,226 and 10,437 birds respectively can be counted (Shelton *et al.* in press). An analysis of the 1978 aerial photographs indicates an increase by a factor of 2.5 since 1956 (Crawford and Shelton 1981). When the counts on the 1978 aerial photographs are corrected for absenteeism the real population is estimated at 12,207 birds (Shelton *et al.* in press). Ground censuses, also carried out in 1978, resulted in a count of 3,598 nests and a population estimate of 7,196 breeding birds (Shelton *et al.* in press). In the light of these figures it seems that a rough estimate of 2,000 birds in the early 1970s (Frost *et al.* 1976b) is much too low, as is a head count of 4,200 adults in 1980 (Shelton *et al.* in press). In 1977 several thousand birds were found nesting on the island (Shaughnessy 1977).

Halifax On the 1956 aerial photographs 8,639 birds can be counted and the real population was estimated at 10,000 birds (Rand 1963b, Shelton *et al.* in press). On aerial photographs taken in 1969, 1978 and 1979, 5,412, 2,755 and 1,802 birds respectively can be counted (Shelton *et al.* in press). An analysis of the 1978 aerial photographs indicates a decline with only 32% of the 1956 population surviving, most of this decrease taking place since about 1970 (Crawford and Shelton 1981). When the counts on the 1978 aerial photographs are corrected for absenteeism the real population is estimated at 3,222 birds (Shelton *et al.* in press). Ground censuses carried out in 1978 and 1981 resulted in counts of 1,750 and 1,007 nests respectively and a population estimate of 3,500 breeding birds in 1978 (Shelton *et al.* in press). A series of head-count censuses in 1971 and 1972 produced a maximum count of 5,269 birds (Berry *et al.* 1974) and the rough estimate by Frost *et al.* (1976b) of 5,400 birds is presumably based on this work. Further head-counts in 1977, 1980 and 1981 resulted in totals of 2,129, 1,850 and 2,162 adult birds respectively (Shelton *et al.* in press). A count of 1,200 birds in 1949 (Meinertzhagen 1950) is clearly much too low.

North Reef On the 1956 aerial photographs 1,360 birds can be counted and the real population was estimated at 3,500 birds (Rand 1963b) though this has since been corrected to 2,040 birds (Shelton *et al.* in press). On aerial photographs taken in 1967 and 1978, 389 and 256 birds respectively can be counted (Shelton *et al.* in press). An analysis of the 1978 aerial photographs indicates a drastic decline with only about 20% of the 1956 population surviving (Crawford and Shelton 1981). When the counts on the 1978 aerial photographs are corrected for absenteeism the real population is estimated at 289 birds (Shelton *et al.* in press). Ground censuses carried out in 1978 and 1980 resulted in counts of 151 and 58 nests respectively and a population estimate of 302 breeding birds in 1978 (Shelton *et al.* in press). Also in 1978 and 1980 there were head-count censuses of 200 and 181 adult birds respectively (Shaughnessy and Meyer 1979, Shelton *et al.* in press).

Possession On the 1956 aerial photographs 37,192 birds can be counted and the real population was estimated at 46,000 birds (Rand 1963b) though this has since been corrected to 55,788 birds (Shelton *et al.* in press). On aerial photographs taken in 1967, 1978 and 1979, 14,528, 3,757 and 1,833 birds respectively can be counted (Shelton *et al.* in press). An analysis of the 1978 aerial photographs indicates a drastic decline with only 10% of the 1956 population surviving (Crawford and Shelton 1981). This decrease has apparently been taking place at a fairly constant rate since 1956 (Crawford and Shelton 1981). When the counts on the 1978 aerial photographs are corrected for absenteeism the real population is estimated at 4,393 birds (Shelton *et al.* in press). A ground census in 1978 resulted in a count of 2,568 nests and a population estimate of 5,136 breeding adults (Shelton *et al.* in press). In the early 1970s the population, including that on nearby North Reef, was estimated at 25,000 birds (Frost *et al.* 1976b) but head-count censuses in 1977 and 1978 produced a maximum of only 5,020 birds, again including birds on North Reef (Shaughnessy and Meyer 1979). Another head-count of 2,250 birds on Possession Island was made in 1980 (Shelton *et al.* in press).

Pomona On the 1956 aerial photographs 9,676 birds can be counted and the real population was estimated at 12,000 birds (Rand 1963b) though this has since been corrected to 14,511 birds (Shelton *et al.* in press). On aerial photographs taken in 1967, 1969, 1978 and 1979, 6,357, 8,974, 149 and 310 birds respectively can be counted (Shelton *et al.* in press). An analysis of the 1978 aerial photographs indicates a catastrophic decline to only 1.5% of the 1956 level, most of this decrease taking place since 1970 (Crawford and Shelton 1981). Other censuses confirm this trend: a rough estimate of 7,000 birds in the early 1970s and head-counts of 740 in 1977, 339 in 1979 and 116 in 1980 (Frost *et al.* 1976b, Shaughnessy 1977,1980, Shelton *et al.* in press). The 1977 count is likely to have under-recorded birds since it was carried out at midday when many are at sea (Shaughnessy 1977). When the counts on the 1978 aerial photographs are corrected for absenteeism the real population is estimated at 174 birds (Shelton *et al.* in press). Ground censuses carried out in 1978 and 1980 resulted in counts of 123 and 20 nests respectively and a population estimate of 246 breeding adults in 1978 (Shelton *et al.* in press). From the figures quoted above, there can be no doubt that a serious decrease has taken place on Pomona Island.

Plumpudding On the 1956 aerial photographs 4,801 birds can be counted and the real population was estimated at 6,000 birds (Rand 1963b) though this has since been corrected to 7,201 birds (Shelton *et al.* in press). On aerial photographs taken in 1967, 1969, 1978 and 1979, 5,515, 4,547, 803 and 96 birds respectively can be counted (Shelton *et al.* in press). An analysis of the 1978 aerial photographs indicates a drastic decline to about 17% of the 1956 level, most of this decrease taking place since 1970 (Crawford and Shelton 1981). Other censuses confirm this trend: a rough estimate of 3,000 in the early 1970s and head counts 881 in 1978, 1,068 also in 1978 and 592 in 1980 (Frost *et al.* 1976b, Shaughnessy 1980, Shelton *et al.* in press). When the counts on the 1978 aerial photographs are corrected for absenteeism the real population is estimated at 939 birds (Shelton *et al.* in press). Ground censuses carried out in 1978 and 1980 resulted in counts of 438 and 100 nests respectively and a population estimate of 876 breeding birds in 1978 (Shelton *et al.* in press).

Sinclair On the 1956 aerial photographs 2,370 birds can be counted and the real population was estimated at 3,000 birds (Rand 1963b) though this was later corrected to 3,555 birds (Shelton *et al.* in press). In 1948 the population was estimated to be 3,000 pairs (Rand 1949). If correct this indicates a severe decrease in the late 1940s and early 1950s. On aerial photographs taken 1967, 1971, 1976, 1977, 1978 and twice in 1979, 632, 373, 314, 283, 343, 158 and 321 birds respectively can be counted (Shaughnessy 1980, Shelton *et al.* in press). An analysis of the 1978 aerial photographs indicates a drastic decline to only 14% of 1956 level, most of this decrease taking place before 1970 (Crawford and Shelton 1981). By the late 1970s it seemed that the decline had levelled off following conservation measures (Shaughnessy 1980; see also under Conservation Measures Taken). When the counts on the 1978 aerial photographs are corrected for absenteeism the real population is estimated at 401 birds (Shelton *et al.* in press). Ground censuses carried out in 1978 and 1980 resulted in counts of 246 and 124 nests respectively and

7

a population estimate of 492 breeding birds in 1978 (Shelton *et al.* in press). A rough estimate of 200 birds in the early 1970s (Frost *et al.* 1976b) is probably too low. There were head-counts of 358 adults in 1978, 398 in 1979 and 308 in 1980 (Shelton *et al.* in press).

Bird Island, Lambert's Bay Between 1900 and 1909 the minimum population must have been 2,700 birds, calculated from egg-crop data (Frost *et al.* 1976b). This island was not included in any aerial surveys but the population was estimated to be 500 birds in 1956, apparently increasing (Rand 1963a). However, in the early 1970s Frost *et al.* (1976b) estimated the population to be only 150 birds. Between 1977 and 1980 20 ground censuses and 13 head counts were carried out on Bird Island, giving maximum counts of 50 nests and 309 adult birds respectively (Shelton *et al.* in press).

Malgas In 1903 the minimum population must have been 13,100 birds, calculated from egg-crop data (Shelton *et al.* in press). On the 1956 aerial photographs 1,063 birds can be counted, but because so many birds were concealed by boulders the real population was estimated to be about 5,000 birds (Rand 1963a, Shelton *et al.* in press). On the aerial photographs taken in 1978, 4,448 birds can be counted (Shelton *et al.* in press). When the counts on the 1978 aerial photographs are corrected for absenteeism the real population is estimated at 5,202 birds (Shelton *et al.* in press). Ground censuses carried out in 1978-1979 resulted in a maximum count of 1,022 nests in 1979 and a population estimate of 2,044 breeding birds in 1978 (Shelton *et al.* in press). Rough estimates of 2,000-3,000 birds in the mid-1950s (Stewart and Currey 1957) and of 1,000 birds in the early 1970s (Frost *et al.* 1976b) are probably too low, especially in the light of an estimate of 12,700 birds in 1977-1978 (Cooper 1979). This high figure was obtained by counting the number of moulting birds throughout the year (Cooper 1979) and is probably the most accurate estimate so far obtained, although it includes non-breeding adult birds (J. Cooper *in litt.* 1984) (see introductory remarks in this section).

Marcus Between 1900 and 1909 the minimum population must have been 19,500 birds, calculated from egg-crop data (Frost *et al.* 1976b). On the 1956 aerial photographs 5,834 birds can be counted and the real population was estimated at 9,500 birds (Rand 1963a) though this was later corrected to 8,751 birds (Shelton *et al.* in press). On aerial photographs taken in 1967 and 1978, 2,915 and 2,941 birds can be counted (Shelton *et al.* in press). An analysis of the 1978 aerial photographs indicates a decline to 50% of the 1956 level, most of this decrease taking place prior to 1967 (Crawford and Shelton 1981). When the counts on the 1978 aerial photographs are corrected for absenteeism the real population is estimated at 3,440 birds (Shelton *et al.* in press). Ground censuses carried out in the late 1970s resulted in counts of 374 nests in 1978 and 1,243 nests in 1979, and a population estimate of 2,486 breeding birds in 1978 (Shelton *et al.* in press). However, most estimates during the 1970s put the population at 9,000-10,000 (Frost *et al.* 1976b; also *Afr. Wildl.* 27 [1973]: 162-164; 32 [1978]: 24-26), and Cooper (1979), by counting the number of moulting birds throughout the year, estimated the population in 1977-1978 to be 14,200 adult birds.

Jutten Between 1900 and 1909 the minimum population must have been 78,000 birds, calculated from egg-crop data (Frost *et al.* 1976b). On the 1956 aerial photographs 9,444 birds can be counted and the real population was estimated at 15,000 birds (Rand 1963a) though this was later corrected to 14,166 birds (Shelton *et al.* in press). On aerial photographs taken in 1978, 3,861 birds can be counted (Shelton *et al.* in press). An analysis of the 1978 aerial photographs indicates a decline to 40% of the 1956 level (Crawford and Shelton 1981). When the counts on the 1978 aerial photographs are corrected for absenteeism the real population is estimated at 4,516 birds (Shelton *et al.* in press). Ground censuses carried out in the late 1970s resulted in counts of 712 nests in 1978 and 2,878 nests in 1979, and a population estimate of 5,756 breeding birds in 1978 (Shelton *et al.* in press). In the early 1970s a rough estimate put the population at 7,000 birds (Frost *et al.* 1976b). However Cooper (1979), by counting the number of moulting birds throughout the year, estimated the population in 1977-1978 to be 25,500 adult birds.

Vondeling Between 1900 and 1909 the minimum population must have been 44,400 birds, calculated from egg-crop data (Frost *et al.* 1976b). On the 1956 aerial photographs only 375 birds can be counted and the real population was estimated at 600 birds (Rand 1963a) though this was later corrected to 562 birds (Shelton *et al.* in press). On aerial photographs taken in 1978, 304 birds can be counted, and when this is corrected for absenteeism the real population is estimated at 356 birds (Shelton *et al.* in press). In the early 1970s Frost *et al.* (1976b) estimated the population to be 400 birds. Clearly, this colony was decimated during the first half of this century.

Dassen (Dasseneiland) Early estimates of 9,000,000 pairs (Nicoll 1906) and 5,000,000 birds (Kearton 1930) are much too high for so small an island and it is doubtful if the population has ever been greater than 1,500,000 birds (Westphal and Rowan 1969). Nevertheless it is certain that a drastic decline has taken place at this colony (Frost *et al.* 1976b). Evidence for this comes from photographs in Kearton (1930) and from egg-crop data (Frost *et al.* 1976b). Between 1900 and 1930 an average of 450,000 eggs was collected annually on Dassen (Cott 1953, Frost *et al.* 1976b). Assuming that each pair laid two eggs and that half the pairs re-nested and were exploited again, then at least 300,000 birds would have had to be present to sustain such a rate of exploitation (Frost *et al.* 1976b). In practice only part of the island was worked in any one year so the real number of penguins present must have been much higher (Frost *et al.* 1976b). Since 1930 the egg-crop yields have declined enormously (Cott 1953, Frost *et al.* 1976b) and the guano yields have also declined in a very similar fashion (Siegfried and Crawford 1978). These decreases provide strong evidence for a real decrease in the numbers of Jackass Penguins since 1930 (Siegfried and Crawford 1978). On the 1956 aerial photographs 80,652 birds can be counted (Rand 1963a). Because coverage of the island was not complete the real population was estimated to be much higher, at 145,000 birds (Rand 1963a, Shelton *et al.* in press). On aerial photographs taken in 1978 only 16,049 birds can be counted (Shelton *et al.* in press). An analysis of the 1978 aerial photographs indicates a drastic decline to only 20% of the 1956 level (Crawford and Shelton 1981). When the counts on the 1978 aerial photographs are corrected for

9

absenteeism the real population is estimated at 18,771 birds (Shelton *et al.* in press). Ground censuses carried out in 1978 resulted in a count of 11,220 nests and a population estimate of 25,292 birds (Shelton *et al.* in press). A population estimate of 70,000 birds in the early 1970s (Frost *et al.* 1976b) is probably too high. There can be no doubt that a very serious decrease has taken place at the Dassen Island colony, and it is no longer the largest in the world. The suggestion that the colony accounts for 40% of the total population (see Siegfried and Crawford 1978) must be mistaken.

Robben Island The large colony on Robben Island was extinct before 1700 (Frost *et al.* 1976b, Brooke in press). In 1983 breeding was noted again on the island and in the following year 45 adult birds and 24 nests were found (Shelton *et al.* in press).

Seal Island, False Bay In 1874 the minimum population must have been 5,000 birds, calculated from egg-crop data (Shelton *et al.* in press). No penguins can be seen on the 1956 aerial photographs (Rand 1963a) or on photographs taken of this island during the 1978 aerial survey (Crawford and Shelton 1981). However, in about 1950 200 nests and 502 adults were counted on the island (Rand 1951). In the early 1970s the population was estimated at only 50 birds (Frost *et al.* 1976b) but this is probably too low since annual censuses from 1977 to 1979 obtained counts of 111, 102 and 118 adult birds and 24, 23 and 43 occupied nests in respective years (Cooper and Shaughnessy 1977,1978, Shaughnessy *et al.* 1979). Later in 1979 (June) 82 nests were counted (Shelton *et al.* in press).

Stony Point One nest was found at this site in 1982 (Broni 1982) and 1983 (Shelton *et al.* in press). In 1984 four nests were found (Shelton *et al.* in press).

Dyer In 1905 the minimum population must have been 41,400 birds, calculated from egg-crop data (Shelton *et al.* in press). On the 1956 aerial photographs 4,982 birds can be counted and the real population was estimated at 8,000 birds (Rand 1963a). It has been suggested that this estimate is quite accurate since penguins do not burrow on Dyer Island (Cooper 1977a). On aerial photographs taken in 1967 and 1978, 17,926 and 26,599 birds respectively can be counted (Shelton *et al.* in press). An analysis of the 1978 aerial photographs indicates a greater than five-fold increase since 1956, this increase having taken place steadily over 20 years (Crawford and Shelton 1981). When the counts on the 1978 aerial photographs are corrected for absenteeism the real population is estimated at 31,110 birds (Shelton *et al.* in press). Other censuses point to an overall increase at Dyer Island: in 1972 38,000 birds were reported though this estimate was later revised down to 15,000 birds (Frost *et al.* 1976b, Cooper 1977a); in 1976 11,243 birds were counted on the beach of the island but a full census was not carried out (Cooper 1977a); and more recently an estimate of 37,000 birds has been made (Morant *et al.* 1981). Ground censuses carried out in 1978 and 1979 resulted in counts of 18,712 and 22,655 nests respectively, and a population estimate of 45,310 breeding birds in 1978 (Shelton *et al.* in press). The Dyer Island colony has increased in size very markedly and is now probably the largest in the world (Shelton *et al.* in press). A report that the entire population of Jackass Penguins on Dyer Island was wiped out in 1968 by an oil spillage (Westphal and Rowan 1969) is without foundation.

Geyser Island Ground censuses carried out in 1978 and 1979 resulted in counts of 151 and 318 nests respectively and a population estimate of 636 breeding birds in 1978 (Shelton *et al.* in press).

Quoin Rock It seems that breeding on Quoin Rock ceased around 1902 (Rand 1963a) although one adult was seen there in 1978 (Shelton *et al.* in press).

Seal Island, Mosselbaai In the early years of this century 130 birds were reported from this island and some birds were still present in 1923 but in 1978 only one moulting bird was seen (Shaughnessy and Shaughnessy 1978).

Cape Recife Three adults and one nest were found at this mainland site in 1981 (Every 1983).

Jahleel Island Censuses were carried out between 1973 and 1981, the maximum count being one of 2,200 birds (Randall *et al.* 1981b).

Brenton Rock Censuses were carried out between 1973 and 1981, the maximum count being one of 92 birds (Randall *et al.* 1981b).

St.Croix Island On the 1956 aerial photographs 7,470 birds can be counted and the real population was estimated at 12,000 birds (Rand 1963a) though this was later corrected to 11,205 birds (Shelton *et al.* in press). On aerial photographs taken in 1969 and 1978, 17,696 and 11,053 birds respectively can be counted (Shelton *et al.* in press). An analysis of the 1978 aerial photographs indicates an increase to about 1.5 times the 1956 level (Crawford and Shelton 1981). It seems that the colony increased until about 1970 when it numbered more than twice the 1956 level, since when it has decreased (Crawford and Shelton 1981). In 1971 a census on St.Croix revealed a population of 21,043 birds (Ross 1971a,b) and Frost *et al.* (1976b) made a rough estimate of 23,000 birds in the early 1970s. When the counts on the 1978 aerial photographs are corrected for absenteeism the real population is estimated at 12,927 birds (Shelton *et al.* in press). In 1978 there was a head-count of 11,591 adult birds and the breeding population was estimated at 21,000 birds (Shelton *et al.* in press). The estimate by Frost *et al.* (1976b) of 23,000 birds in the early 1970s is presumably for St.Croix, Jahleel and Brenton Rock. Randall (1983), using Cooper's (1979) moult count method, estimated the population in 1979-1980 to be 46,500 birds (including birds on Jahleel and Brenton Rock).

Seal Island, Algoa Bay In 1945 100 pairs were counted on Seal Island (Courtenay-Latimer and Gibson-Hill 1946). On the 1956 aerial photographs no birds can be seen on Seal Island (Rand 1963a). However, in 1958 300 birds (perhaps 100 pairs) were found (Rand 1963a). On aerial photographs taken in 1978, 639 birds can be counted (Shelton *et al.* in press). An analysis of the 1978 aerial photographs indicates a five-fold increase since the 1950s, all of this increase taking place since 1970 (Crawford and Shelton 1981). When the counts on the 1978 aerial photographs are corrected for absenteeism the real population is estimated at 747 birds (Shelton *et al.* in press). The maximum count of 2,200 birds between 1973 and 1981 confirms that a considerable increase has taken place (Randall *et al.* 1981b). A population estimate for all three islands of only 500 birds in the early 1970s (Frost *et al.* 1976b) is probably much too low.

Stag Island In 1945 60 pairs were counted on Stag Island (Courtenay-Latimer and Gibson-Hill 1946). On the 1956 aerial photographs 42 birds can be counted (Rand 1963a) and the real population was estimated at 63 birds (Shelton *et al.* in press). In 1958 80 birds were found (Rand 1963a). No aerial photographs were taken in 1978 but the maximum count between 1973 and 1981 is one of 118 birds (Randall *et al.* 1981b). It seems that the population on Stag Island has not showed a very marked increase, as has been the case on the nearby Seal and Bird Islands.

Bird Island, Algoa Bay In 1945 80 pairs were counted on Bird Island (Courtenay-Latimer and Gibson-Hill 1946), and in 1954 50 pairs were counted (Taylor 1954). On the 1956 aerial photographs no birds can be seen but in 1958 60 pairs were found (Rand 1963a). No aerial photographs were taken in 1978 but the maximum count between 1973 and 1981 is one of 2,100 birds (Randall *et al.* 1981b) suggesting that a considerable increase has taken place. A rough estimate of 500 birds in the early 1970s (Frost *et al.* 1976b) is probably too low.

Estimates of the total population of Jackass Penguins give very conflicting results. On the basis of the 1956 aerial photographs Rand (1963a,b) counted 81,967 birds in Namibia and 109,772 in South Africa, giving a total of 191,739 birds. After correcting for absenteeism from the colonies and other possible errors, Rand (1963a,b) estimated the real populations to be 99,000 birds in Namibia and 196,000 birds in South Africa, giving a total of 295,000 birds. Corrections of Rand's (1963a,b) population estimates give very similar results: 106,391 birds in Namibia and 190,314 in South Africa, giving a total of 296,705 birds in 1956 (Shelton *et al.* in press) . Using the 1978 aerial photographs Shelton *et al.* (in press) counted 29,320 birds in Namibia and 68,063 birds in South Africa, giving a total of 97,383 birds. After these counts have been adjusted for absenteeism, population estimates are obtained of 34,291 birds in Namibia and 79,538 in South Africa, giving a total of 113,829 birds (Shelton *et al.* in press). A comparison of the 1956 and 1978 results therefore suggests that the world population was more than halved in just 22 years. Crawford's (1982) estimate of the world population at only 50,000 pairs is presumably based on the 1978 aerial survey. Although the overall decrease in the population is very pronounced, there are some interesting local trends. The colonies on the Namibian coast north of Lüderitz (Mercury and Ichaboe Islands) and along the southern Cape coast (Dyer Island and the islands in Algoa Bay) are showing marked increases (Crawford and Shelton 1981). It has been shown that the population increases north of Lüderitz and on the southern Cape coast are so rapid that some immigration, presumably from rapidly declining colonies, must be taking place (Shelton *et al.* in press). The establishment of new colonies at Sylvia Hill, Geyser Island, Stony Point and Cape Recife, all near large and rapidly expanding colonies, may be the result of lack of space for breeding birds on islands such as Mercury and Dyer (Shelton *et al.* in press). All other colonies are tending to decrease in population size, the rate being particularly rapid in the Namibian colonies south of Lüderitz and on Dassen Island (Crawford and Shelton 1981). The aerial surveys are probably most useful in revealing the population trends discussed above but the actual numbers of birds counted by such methods are unlikely to be anything more than an index of abundance (Frost *et al.* 1976b). Ground censuses carried out in 1978-1979 resulted in counts of 12,092 nests in Namibia and 39,519 in South Africa, giving a total of 51,611 nests (Shelton *et al.* in press). When these counts are corrected for absenteeism and other errors, population estimates of 24,184 breeding birds in Namibia, 109,430 in South Africa and 133,614 in the world are obtained (Shelton *et al.* in press). This last figure is considered by Shelton *et al.* (in press) to be the best estimate of the minimum breeding population in 1978. The most frequently quoted population estimate is one of 171,710 birds (comprising 45,610 in Namibia and 126,100 in South Africa), obtained in the early 1970s by a variety of field census techniques (Frost *et al.* 1976b): thus population estimates of 170,000-172,000 (Cooper 1980, Siegfried 1982, Brooke in press, Cooper *et al.* in press) are based on this figure. More recently another population estimate has been made, of 183,500 birds (35,500 in Namibia, 87,500 on the western Cape islands, 37,000 on Dyer Island and 23,500 in Algoa Bay) (Morant *et al.* 1981), but it is not clear how these figures were obtained. The fact remains that almost all the censuses so far carried out are likely to be gross under-estimates (see introductory remarks in this section). If Cooper's (1979) method of estimating populations from the number of moulting birds is a more reliable way to count Jackass Penguins, then the world population is likely to be two or three times greater than the most recent studies have indicated. Even so, there can be little doubt that a drastic decline has taken place and that this is still continuing (Crawford and Shelton 1981). Evidence from egg-crop data and aerial photographs shows that these declines have been very severe (Frost *et al.* 1976b, Crawford and Shelton 1981), and although it is impossible to estimate what the original total number might have been, it seems likely that the species has lost 75%, possibly more, of its population in the course of this century (Brooke in press). One suggestion that the Jackass Penguin increased by 100,000 birds following the banning of egg-collecting in 1969 (see Ripley 1974) is based on no data at all (Frost *et al.* 1976b).

Ecology Jackass Penguins nest on low-lying islands, often close to cold currents and receiving very low rainfall (Frost *et al.* 1976b). Apart from the "fattening up" periods before and after the annual moult (see below), adult Jackass Penguins are resident on or in the vicinity of their breeding islands (Randall and Randall 1981, Randall *et al.* 1981b). Breeding birds usually forage at sea within a few kilometres of their breeding islands (Brooke in press, Cooper in press). Research has been carried out on digestion rates of Jackass Penguins as part of an attempt to calculate the theoretical foraging range of adults around their breeding islands (details in Furness and Laugksch 1983). They forage in flocks of up to 200 birds, though the mean group size is only eight (Siegfried *et al.* 1975), juveniles being probably more solitary at sea than adults (Cooper and Randall 1981). Within a flock all the birds tend to perform the same behaviour at the same time, such as synchronised diving, which is presumably adaptive in prey location and capture, birds not submerging for long or diving deeply (Siegfried *et al.* 1975). Studies carried out in the 1950s showed that three species of fish, the pilchard *Sardinops ocellata*, anchovy *Engraulis capensis* and maasbanker or horse-mackerel *Trachurus trachurus* were the most important components of the Jackass Penguin's diet (Davies 1955,1956, Rand 1960). Other important food items include at least 22 species of fish, amongst them the mackerel *Scomber japonicus*, mullet *Mugil*, *Scomberesox*, *Ammodytes* and *Etrumeus*, as well as three species of cephalopods (squids), 18 species of crustaceans and one species of polychaete (Davies 1955,1956, Rand 1960, Frost *et al.* 1976b). In the late 1950s pilchards were the dominant component of the diet by weight with anchovies and maasbanker filling lesser roles; on the basis of frequency of occurrence in the stomach contents, however, squids were the most important item in the diet, pilchards, anchovies and maasbankers all being taken less frequently (Rand 1960). Following the collapse of the South African and Namibian pilchard (and also maasbanker) stocks during the 1960s as a result of over-fishing by man (see Crawford and Shelton 1981), the Jackass Penguin has had to adjust its diet: anchovies are now the main component and very few pilchards are taken, though the fish *Etrumeus* and the squid *Loligo* may be seasonally important (Cooper 1979, in press). These studies (Rand 1960, Cooper 1979, in press) were in the same area, thus showing that a major change in diet has taken place in just 20 years. It seems that Jackass Penguins prefer fish to squid, turning to the latter mainly during lean times: they generally take smaller squid than those harvested by trawlers, especially *Loligo reynaudi*, but also *Heterotuthus* and *Argonauto argo* (Randall *et al.* 1981c). The penguin colonies on Mercury and Ichaboe Islands north of Lüderitz on the Namibian coast have increased in recent years, probably due to the abundance, since the early 1970s, of the bearded goby *Sufflogobius bibarbatus*: in 1980 this fish was found to comprise 92 and 71% by mass of the penguin's diet at Mercury and Ichaboe Islands respectively, compared with only 53 and 17% at Halifax and Possession Islands, south of Lüderitz, where the fish is less common (Crawford and Shelton 1981). It is significant that the colonies north of Lüderitz are increasing, presumably due to the recent superabundance of the bearded goby, whereas most colonies south of Lüderitz are declining, probably due to the collapse in the pilchard stock (Crawford and Shelton 1981; see also under Threats). Along the southern Cape coast there seems to have been a shift in the centre of the pilchard population, resulting in increases in the Jackass Penguin colonies at Dyer Island and probably also in Algoa Bay (Crawford and Shelton 1981). It has been estimated that Jackass Penguins take 47,600 tons of pelagic fish each year, a small figure compared with the 1,320,000 tons taken annually in the region by man (Cooper 1981). The birds feed mainly during the daytime and details of the feeding behaviour are given in Rand (1960). The chicks are fed mainly in the afternoon on regurgitated fish (Kearton 1930, Cooper 1977b, Brown *et al.* 1982). Jackass Penguins have a number of behavioural adaptations to prevent over-heating on land: they are mainly crepuscular and nocturnal at their colonies, numbers on land being generally highest at night and lowest during the day (birds that are not moulting, incubating or guarding chicks leaving the colony for the sea just after dawn and returning in late afternoon), while those that remain on land try to nest in burrows, if possible, these being much cooler during the daytime than outside, or seek shelter under rocks (Frost *et al.* 1976a,b, Siegfried 1982). Moreover, breeding colonies might be positioned in places exposed to cool sea-breezes (Siegfried 1977). Being susceptible to hypothermia if they enter the sea during their brief (c. 18-day) moulting period (Erasmus *et al.* 1981) the birds then also remain on land throughout the day, losing 50% of their weight and using up an even higher proportion of their fat reserves (Cooper 1978b); for this reason the birds leave the island 3-6 weeks before the onset of moult to feed and build up their fat and return to the sea after moulting for 2-6 weeks, this time to build up the necessary reserves for breeding (Rand 1960,1963a, Randall and Randall 1981, Randall *et al.* 1981b). The timing of moult varies between different islands, though much of it occurs in the October/November period (details in Rand 1951, Cooper 1978b,1979, Randall and Randall 1981, Randall *et al.* 1981b). Jackass Penguins have a very staggered breeding season and at most colonies some birds may be found breeding at any time of the year (Sclater 1904, Courtenay-Latimer and Gibson-Hill 1946, Rand 1949, Moreau 1950, McGill 1970, Cooper 1979,1980). On St.Croix Island egg-laying spans nine months, with peaks in January, March/April, May/June and sometimes September (Randall and Randall 1981, Randall *et al.* 1981b). The January peak is the initial post-moult laying, and subsequent peaks are unsuccessful birds re-laying or successful breeders laying second clutches (Randall and Randall 1981). It is possible for birds to breed twice a year and still moult at the normal time (Randall and Randall 1981). Birds have also been recorded breeding twice a year on Sinclair Island, especially in March and November, though incubation has been noted in all months (Rand 1949). On the Saldanha Bay islands (Malgas, Marcus and Jutten) breeding also takes place throughout the year (Cooper 1979). The breeding peak on Marcus Island is from December to May, but from April to July on the nearby Malgas and Jutten islands (Cooper 1979). The difference might be caused by guano-scraping which no longer takes place on Marcus Island (Cooper 1979). On Possession Island there is one breeding peak, in November (Cooper 1980). On Bird Island, Lambert's Bay, there are two laying peaks, in January and April, in one undisturbed nesting area, but a nearby nesting group which is frequently visited by tourists has only one breeding peak in May (Cooper 1980). The situation on Dassen Island is particularly confusing: research carried out in the 1950s suggested that the birds bred twice a year, in September and February/March (Rand 1960,1963a); a more recent study has shown, however, that there are egg-laying peaks in June and in November/December, and it has also been shown that the mean interval between breeding for birds which have nested successfully is 10.5 months, and four months if the breeding attempt was a failure, these figures suggesting that there is no consistent annual cycle on Dassen Island and that the timing of breeding peaks may vary from year to year (Cooper 1980). Burrows are probably the most favoured nest-sites (Betham 1929, Courtenay-Latimer and Gibson-Hill 1946, Newman 1966, Siegfried 1977, McLachlan and Liversidge 1978), which the birds dig out with their feet in sand or guano (Nicoll 1906, Brooke in press). Where birds are unable to burrow they nest among rocks and boulders (Rand 1951, Stewart and Currey 1957, Cooper and Shaughnessy 1977, Shaughnessy *et al.* 1979), in abandoned buildings and plastic pipes (J. Cooper *in litt.* 1984), in crevices (Courtenay-Latimer and Gibson-Hill 1946), under rock overhangs (Betham 1929, McGill 1970), under plants (Nicoll 1906, Betham 1929), in simple depressions in rocks (Rand 1949,1951), under sea-wall foundations (Newman 1966), among driftwood and debris (Courtenay-Latimer and Gibson-Hill 1946, Rand 1952) or in the open (Courtenay-Latimer and Gibson-Hill 1946, Rand 1949, Siegfried 1977, Brooke in press). There are also records of pairs nesting in the old nest of a cormorant (Phalacrocoracidae) and an abandoned pig-sty (Courtenay-Latimer and Gibson-Hill 1946). On some islands penguins have to nest under some sort of cover to prevent their nests being destroyed by movements of Cape fur seals *Arctocephalus pusillus* (Rand 1951,1952, Cooper and Shaughnessy 1977, Shaughnessy *et al.* 1979). Jackass Penguins are generally colonial breeders and one study on Marcus Island showed that only 6% of the birds nest outside the main colonies (Siegfried 1977). The birds use the same nest-sites in consecutive seasons (Siegfried 1977). The Marcus Island study also showed that colonially surface-breeding birds are spatially distributed in a remarkably regular pattern, their nest-sites almost forming a pattern of hexagons with sides of 4-6 m, this efficient packing of nests possibly being a response to predation pressures (Siegfried 1977). The clutch-size is usually two, occasionally one (Betham 1929, Kearton 1930, Meinertzhagen 1950, Newman 1966, McGill 1970, Ross 1971a, McLachlan and Liversidge 1978, Williams 1983, Brooke in press, Williams and Cooper in press). Each parent bird normally incubates for 24 hours at a time and is relieved by its partner during the night; if food-supply is limited this change-over period can become extended, having a deleterious effect on nesting success (Cooper 1980). In general, birds nesting in burrows have a greater reproductive output than birds nesting in other sites (Siegfried 1977, Cooper 1980). Studies on Dassen Island have shown that in burrows 75% of eggs hatch and 35% of young fledge, equivalent figures for birds nesting under rocks being 73% and 30% and for birds nesting in the open 67% and 20% (Cooper 1980). On St.Croix Island it has been shown that birds fledging successfully from the first peak breeding season in January have a higher survival rate than birds fledged from subsequent breeding peaks (Randall and Randall 1981). First-year mortality at St.Croix is very high, 80-96% (mean 89%) (Brown *et al.* 1982). There is very little movement of adults between islands (Cooper and Randall 1981) but after fledging the chicks leave the breeding island (Brown *et al.* 1982) and young birds disperse much further along coasts (Brooke in press) possibly to avoid competition with adults on their foraging grounds (Cooper and Randall 1981). Juveniles ringed on Dassen Island have been recovered as far afield as Walvis Bay and Port Elizabeth (Cooper 1974b). Some juveniles undergo a partial head-moult at sea, thereby becoming "mock adults" and so evoking less aggression from foraging groups of adults when they enter the latter's feeding areas (Cooper and Randall 1981). Birds are able to cover considerable distances in a relatively short time, e.g. one rehabilitated oiled bird released at Robben Island on 6 August 1971 was recovered dead at Port Elizabeth on 11 September 1971, having travelled 800 km (Ross 1972). Over long distances they average speeds of 81 km per day (Randall *et al.* 1981a). There is also strong evidence that Jackass Penguins are good navigators: in July 1979 many were oiled at St.Croix Island in Algoa Bay, some of these being sent to the oiled bird rehabilitation centre, and of the rehabilitated birds released from Robben Island, at least 87% had returned to St.Croix by Feburary 1980 (Randall *et al.* 1980). The Jackass Penguin is one of the species wrecked in largest numbers on the coast of the mainland (Cooper 1978a, Avery 1979, 1980, 1981, 1982) and this is presumably one reason why the recovery rate of ringed birds is so high. Of 14,104 birds ringed between 1948 and 1978, 414 (2.9%) have been recovered or controlled (Morant 1979). The mean longevity is 7.23 years (Morant 1979) and on St.Croix some birds are known to be at least 15 years old (R. M. Randall *in litt.* 1984). Females probably first breed at two years of age (Brooke in press). Adult penguins are occasionally taken as food by Cape fur seals (Bourne and Dixon 1973, Cooper 1974a, Shaughnessy 1978) and sharks (Brooke and Wallet 1976). There is also one record of 15 Jackass Penguins being found in the gut of a Bryde's whale *Balaenoptera edeni* (Cooper 1974a). Another possible predator is the killer whale *Orcinus orca* (Cooper 1974a). Experiments have shown that penguins react to avoid the source of killer whale vocalisations, "porpoising" away in a tight group (Frost *et al.* 1975). Other potentially serious predators are mongooses *Herpestes* and genets *Genetta*, should these ever become established on breeding islands (see under Threats). The only known egg-predator is the Kelp Gull *Larus dominicanus* which is also known to take chicks up to one week old (Betham 1929, McGill 1970, Cooper 1974a, Siegfried 1977). The Sacred Ibis *Threskiornis aethiopicus* occasionally takes sick chicks, and feral domestic cats might also be a threat (Cooper 1974a). There is one record of a Southern Giant Petrel *Macronectes giganteus* feeding on chicks (Sinclair and Nicholls 1978).

Threats There seems to be little doubt that the initial decline of this species was caused by prolonged over-exploitation of eggs at many colonies (Westphal and Rowan 1969, Frost *et al.* 1976b, Brooke in press, Cooper *et al.* in press) and of adults on Robben Island (J. Cooper *in litt.* 1984). Most early reports refer to the enormous scale of the egg-cropping (Sclater 1896,1904,1907, Nicoll 1906). This exploitation started soon after the Cape was settled but initially no records were kept (Frost *et al.* 1976b). Official records commenced in 1871 and some details from these have been compiled (Cott 1953, Frost *et al.* 1976b, Shelton *et al.* in press). Between 1900 and 1930 almost 14,000,000 eggs were taken from Dassen Island alone (Frost *et al.* 1976b). This figure does not include partially incubated eggs which were discarded, nor well incubated eggs which were destroyed to induce re-laying, nor eggs which were broken during collection, and so the total number of eggs collected and destroyed was obviously much higher (Frost *et al.* 1976b). During egg-collecting operations Kelp Gulls took advantage of the disturbance to prey on eggs and young chicks (Berry *et al.* 1974, Frost *et al.* 1976b). Egg-collecting was restricted to certain months of the year and there was a yearly rotation of areas over which eggs were cropped, but despite these measures the Jackass Penguin continued to decline (Frost *et al.* 1976b). Between 1890 and 1950 the Government Guano Islands Administration noted a decline on several occasions and on Dassen Island, at least, excessive egg-collecting must have been responsible (Frost *et al.* 1976b). Some illegal collecting continues, despite the ban imposed in 1969 (Frost *et al.* 1976b). The effects of the cessation of large-scale egg-cropping on the penguin population are unknown (Frost *et al.* 1976b), mainly because there are now several other factors operating which are causing further declines (see below). Colonies have also been severely disturbed by guano-scraping (Jarvis and Cram 1971, Berry *et al.* 1974, Cooper 1979,1980, Shaughnessy 1980, Brooke in press), which was particularly extensive and uncontrolled on the Namibian islands before British annexation of them in 1861 (Frost *et al.* 1976b). Although guano-scraping has been stopped on some islands, e.g. on St.Croix in 1956 (Ross 1971a), on Sinclair in 1955, Plumpudding in 1962 and Pomona in 1972 (Shaughnessy 1980), it still continues on others, such as Malgas (Cooper 1979), Bird Island in Lambert's Bay (Jarvis and Cram 1971) and Possession (Cooper 1980). Guano-scraping causes severe disturbance to colonies and leads to increased predation by Kelp Gulls (Berry *et al.* 1974). There is also evidence that guano-scraping has disrupted the timing of the breeding seasons on Malgas, Jutten, Possession, and Bird Island in Lambert's Bay (Cooper 1979,1980). Penguins are less able to burrow if guano is removed and this can have a deleterious effect on reproductive output since nesting success is higher in burrows than in the open (Berry *et al.* 1974, Frost *et al.* 1976b, Brooke in press; see Ecology). On Bird Island, Lambert's Bay, nests have been destroyed by guano-scrapers (Jarvis and Cram 1971) and breeding habitat was lost when the central area of the island was paved to facilitate guano-scraping (Frost *et al.* 1976b). Recent evidence suggests that guano removal allows seals to spread on to parts of islands formerly occupied by penguins (Shelton *et al.* in press). Even low levels of human disturbance can reduce reproductive success (Jarvis and Cram 1971, Cooper 1980, Brooke in press). Human passage through a colony leads to egg loss through increased Kelp Gull predation; moreover, nest-prospecting birds are frightened away from a potential breeding site after only three or four human intrusions, some birds retreating from a colony if an observer comes closer than 30 m (Hockey and Hallinan 1981). It is possible that the decline of the colony on Possession Island was started by disturbance from sealers who use the island as a base (Crawford and Shelton 1981). The Cape fur seal, which has increased on a number of islands, has caused severe disturbance to some penguin colonies, notably on Sinclair Island and Seal Island in False Bay (Cooper and Shaughnessy 1977, Shaughnessy 1980). The increase in seal numbers can result in a lack of space for penguins (Cooper and Shaughnessy 1977, Brooke in press). Seals sometimes disturb nesting penguins, thus facilitating increased egg-predation by Kelp Gulls, and on rare occasions seals have been known to kill penguins (Shaughnessy 1978,1980). Further disturbance to penguins can result from seal-culling during peak breeding periods (Shaughnessy *et al.* 1979). Attempts have been made to protect birds from seals by building walls (see under Conservation Measures Taken) but on some islands walls have excluded penguins from suitable nesting habitat (Frost *et al.* 1976b). The Jackass Penguin is the only African seabird to be seriously affected by oil pollution, at least 7,088 birds being known to have been oiled between 1970 and 1980 (Cooper *et al.* in press) and eight serious oil slicks affecting a minimum of 6,600 birds between 1968 and 1974 (Frost *et al.* 1976b). Although first reported in the late 1940s and early 1950s (Rand 1952a, Frost *et al.* 1976b, Morant *et al.* 1981), oil pollution became much more serious after 1967 when the Suez Canal was closed, resulting in greatly increased tanker traffic around the Cape (Westphal and Rowan 1969, Frost *et al.* 1976b, Randall and Randall 1980). One of the most widely reported incidents is that caused by the tanker Esso Essen which ran aground off Cape Point in 1968 and resulted in the oiling of at least 1,700 penguins (Rowan 1969, Westphal and Rowan 1969, McGill 1973). If 8-11 birds died at sea for each oiled bird landed on the shore, as is known to be the case for some species of seabird, then 14,000-19,000 penguins would have been killed in the Esso Essen incident (Westphal and Rowan 1969, Ross 1971a). There is, however, considerable evidence that a much higher proportion of oiled Jackass Penguins are recovered than is the case for most other species and so the situation might not have been as bad as was once feared (Frost *et al.* 1976b). Between 1968 and 1974 a minimum of 4% of the total Jackass Penguin population is known to have been oiled: the incidence of oiling was higher in Cape Province than Namibia with 5.4% of the Cape population being affected over this time, these figures representing a minimum annual oiling rate of 0.7-0.9%, well below the probable adult mortality of 8.5% per year (Frost *et al.* 1976b). Studies on St.Croix have shown that at least 1,379 penguins were oiled in four years, most of these resulting from minor incidents, not major disasters (Randall and Randall 1980). Oil pollution is the commonest single mortality factor of penguins found dead on St.Croix, accounting for 39% of deaths (Randall and Randall 1980, Randall *et al.* 1980). The effects of oil pollution have, however, been exaggerated, most notably in the claim that the entire Dyer Island population was wiped out in an oiling incident in 1968 (Westphal and Rowan 1969, Ross 1971a): it is worth noting that this incident seems to have done nothing to slow down or prevent the five-fold increase in the Dyer Island population since 1956 (see Crawford and Shelton 1981). Experiments have shown that oiled penguins at sea are liable to hypothermia and can be killed by exposure, whereas those that come ashore are more likely to be killed by long-term toxic effects (Erasmus *et al.* 1981). On Bird Island in Lambert's Bay at least 108 penguins were killed when anchovy oil, illegally released from a nearby fish factory, was beaten into a thick froth by heavy seas and surrounded the island: this incident resulted from a failure in the oil recovery system of the factory and subsequent repairs and improvements were made (PFIAO 1974, Frost *et al.* 1976b). As yet there is no evidence of lethal effects to Jackass Penguins from persistent chemical biocides or heavy metal pollutants (Frost *et al.* 1976b). Probably the most severe threat currently facing this species is food shortage resulting from competition from the pelagic shoal fishing industry (Frost *et al.* 1976b, Crawford and Shelton 1978,1981, Cooper *et al.* in press). As a consequence of severe over-fishing the pilchard stock collapsed in the waters around the Cape in 1964 and in Namibian waters in 1968 (Frost *et al.* 1976b, Crawford and Shelton 1978,1981). Between the mid-1950s and mid-1970s the maasbanker declined a hundredfold (Frost *et al.* 1976b). Serious decreases in the penguin populations on the Namibian islands south of Lüderitz and on the Cape islands west of Cape Point correlate very well with the collapse of the pilchard stock (Crawford and Shelton 1981). A subsequent increase in the anchovy biomass in Cape waters during the 1970s has not helped the Jackass Penguin, probably because the penguin, being flightless, has a restricted foraging area and needs a highly predictable food-supply (Frost *et al.* 1976b, Crawford and Shelton 1981). The seasonal distribution of anchovy is much less regular than that of pilchard (Crawford and Shelton 1981). There is some evidence that this food shortage has reduced the penguins' reproductive success (Cooper 1980, Brooke in press). In a normal situation it appears that the members of a pair at a nest, either incubating or guarding young, change over their duties every 24 hours (see Ecology): the bird not at the nest is usually fishing at sea and it seems that when the food supply becomes limited it takes the bird at sea much longer to catch sufficient fish, as a consequence of which the nest change-over period can become extended, exceptionally up to 14 days, and this often results in nest failure and starvation of the chicks (Cooper 1980). There is also some evidence that the 1982-1983 warm water event in South African waters had a deleterious effect on food supply and breeding success in Jackass Penguins (Duffy *et al.* 1984). Jackass Penguins are sometimes caught in fish-nets and traps but this is probably not a serious cause of mortality (Cooper *et al.* in press). In Saldanha Bay a causeway has been built from the mainland to Marcus Island as part of the construction of a deepwater harbour and an ore-offloading berth (Frost *et al.* 1976b, Hockey 1976, *Afr. Wildl.* 27 [1973]: 162-164; 32 [1978]: 24-26). Unfortunately the Sea Fisheries Research Institute failed to act on the advice of a recommendation to build a predator-proof wall on this island before the completion of the causeway, as a result of which several potential predators got onto the island, including the Cape grey mongoose *Herpestes pulverulentus*, the lesser spotted genet *Genetta genetta*, the Cape fox *Vulpes chama*, the bat-eared fox *Otocyon megalotis* and feral cats, some penguins apparently being killed by these predators (*Afr. Wildl.* 32 [1978]: 24-26, Hockey 1983, J. Cooper *in litt.* 1984). There were also plans to build a causeway from the mainland to St.Croix Island, again for an ore-offloading berth (McGill 1973, Frost *et al.* 1976b) but this project has now been cancelled (J. Cooper *in litt.* 1984). Feral cats occur on Dassen Island where they eat mainly rabbits *Oryctolagus cuniculus*, but also penguins (Cooper 1977c, Apps 1983). Cats and rats *Rattus* occur on Bird Island, Lambert's Bay, and possibly on other islands, but their effects are unknown (Frost *et al.* 1976b). The construction of the deep water harbour in Saldanha Bay has necessitated the use of underwater explosions (*Afr. Wildl.* 27 [1973]: 162-164; 32 [1978]: 24-26, Hockey 1976, Cooper 1979): these explosions have killed large numbers of penguins (Hockey 1976, Brooke in press) and 91 blasts between March and August 1977 resulted in the deaths of at least 454 birds (*Afr. Wildl.* 32 [1978]: 24-26, Cooper 1982).

Conservation Measures Taken The Jackass Penguin is fully protected by law in Namibia and South Africa and a temporary ban on egg-collecting has been in effect since 1969 (Frost *et al.* 1976b, Brooke in press). There were also bans on egg-collecting in the years 1932-1934, 1936-1937, 1942 and 1945 (Cott 1953). These bans were enforced to allow the species to recover its numbers but they seem to have had little effect (Cott 1953). Guano-collecting has also been stopped on many islands (Brooke in press; see also under Threats) and is no longer permitted within penguin colonies (Shelton *et al.* in press). The islands of St.Croix, Jahleel and Brenton Rock form part of a Cape Provincial Marine Reserve (Brooke in press). Other colonies are strictly controlled by the Sea Fisheries Research Institute which has all but prohibited access except to *bona fide* research workers (Brooke in press). Officers of the Sea Fisheries Research Institute live on seven of the islands (Frost *et al.* 1976b). On Bird Island, Lambert's Bay, where visitor access is still quite easy, a small fence has been built to protect the penguins from disturbance (Jarvis and Cram 1971) and on Marcus Island the predator-proof wall has now been completed

(Hockey 1983, J. Cooper *in litt.* 1984). In 1940 a wall was built on Sinclair Island to protect the penguin colony from Cape fur seals (Rand 1949, Frost *et al.* 1976b): this wall has small gaps in it which allow penguins but not seals to pass through, although in 1979 it had to be repaired after seals had got through in several places (Shaughnessy 1980). In 1968 SANCCOB (the South African National Foundation for the Conservation of Coastal Birds) was founded, and as a result of its work considerable advances have been made in the rehabilitation of oiled Jackass Penguins (Cooper 1971, Frost *et al.* 1976b, Randall and Randall 1980, Morant *et al.* 1981). In the early days of this operation the mortality of treated birds was probably much higher than it is now (see Westphal and Rowan 1969). In the years 1970-1980 5,565 oiled penguins were sent to SANCCOB's cleaning station, 4,812 of these being from 14 individual incidents (Morant *et al.* 1981). Of the 4,639 birds from the seven worst oiling incidents, 2,656 (57%) were released, 788 of these have been seen alive subsequently, 158 of them breeding (Morant *et al.* 1981, Brooke in press). One of the most successful rescue operations took place on St.Croix Island in 1979: of the 150 birds sent to SANCCOB, 32% died during treatment, but it seems that about 87% of the remainder returned to St.Croix and at least 21 were incubating eggs the following year (Randall and Randall 1980, Randall *et al.* 1980). There has been a suggestion that the mortality rate of rehabilitated birds is higher than normal (Frost *et al.* 1976b) but nevertheless it seems that the success rate for treating oiled Jackass Penguins is higher than for any other species of seabird in the world (Randall and Randall 1980; details of the cleaning method in Morant *et al.* 1981). In 1971 there was a major oil pollution incident at Dyer Island and 8,000 birds were temporarily penned on the island to prevent oiling (Cooper 1971, Frost *et al.* 1976b). The Department of Transport now maintains a fleet of boats able to deal with oil spills in coastal waters before they cause disasters (Brooke in press). There have been experiments using underwater playback recordings of killer whale vocalisations to drive penguins away from the vicinity of oil-slicks (Frost *et al.* 1976b). This method has also been used together with firing guns over the water to frighten birds away from places where underwater explosions are about to take place, and there is some evidence that this did lead to a reduction in penguin mortality (*Afr. Wildl.* 32 [1978]: 24-26, Cooper 1979,1982). A restriction of the underwater blasts to one a day, at midday when fewest penguins were around, also resulted in a reduction in mortality (Cooper 1982). The Jackass Penguin is the subject of a long-term research programme at the PFIAO, and at the University of Port Elizabeth (Brooke in press). Long-term population monitoring is taking place, as well as studies on nestling growth rates, feeding ecology, population dynamics, movement patterns and pollutant effects (Brooke in press). The species is listed on Appendix II of CITES, to which South Africa is a party.

Conservation Measures Proposed A number of conservation measures should be introduced immediately. The most important and urgent action needed is a complete ban on all pelagic shoal fishing within 25 km of all Jackass Penguin breeding colonies: this should result in improved breeding success and post-fledging survival (Brooke in press, Cooper *et al.* in press). Guano-scraping should be phased out with the expiry of existing contracts: this should also lead to improved breeding success in the long-term, as a thick deposit eventually builds up and thus facilitates burrowing (Brooke in press, Cooper *et al.* in press). Efforts should be made to stamp out any remaining illegal egg trading (Brooke in press). Walls should be built on islands to protect penguins where they co-exist with seals (Brooke in press), something already recommended for Seal Island in False Bay (Shaughnessy *et al.* 1979) and for Geyser Island (Shelton *et al.* in press). Walls on islands where there are no seals should be partially dismantled to allow penguins to pass through, but they should not be completely destroyed since they are used by Crowned Cormorants *Phalacrocorax coronatus* (see Appendix C) for nesting (Brooke in press). Rehabilitated oiled birds should be completely healthy before being released; this is necessary to protect the population from epidemics and disease (Frost *et al.* 1976b). A conservation plan for Marcus, Jutten and Malgas Islands has been prepared and includes a recommendation that the islands be included within the proposed Langebaan Nature Reserve (Cooper 1979). Apart from the measures listed above, which should be introduced immediately, a number of recommendations have been outlined which should result in more effective long-term conservation of the Jackass Penguin. First, action is needed at the political level, since at present most environmental legislation tends to ignore economically unimportant species such as the Jackass Penguin: in particular, legislation is needed to establish more viable nature reserves for this species, and political pressure is also required to regulate the pelagic shoal fishing industry more strictly and to restrict the amount of fishing to a sustained yield basis (Cooper *et al.* in press). Second, action is needed at the research level to evaluate the real impact of the threats and how they can be minimised, six possible research directions having been outlined (in Frost *et al.* 1976b).

(a) Methods are needed to census the entire penguin population more accurately and to determine whether it is still declining (some progress is being made in devising improved census techniques: Shelton *et al.* 1982, Cooper *et al.* in press).

(b) Studies are needed on mortality, recruitment and the factors which influence these (a simulation model of population dynamics has been devised for use in identifying the ecological and demographic factors which have caused the species's decline: Jackson *et al.* 1976).

(c) Much more work is needed on penguin/prey interactions and the effects of the pelagic shoal fishing industry, and research on this topic is being carried out at the PFIAO (J. Cooper *in litt.* 1984).

(d) An evaluation is needed of the degree of disturbance tolerated by breeding birds so as to assess tourist impact and potential (some progress has already been made in this direction: see Hockey and Hallinan 1981).

(e) Research is required on the effects of oil pollution on the population, with the development of methods which keep birds away from oil-slicks.

(f) More work should be done on the efficacy of SANCCOB's rehabilitation programme in relation to overall Jackass Penguin conservation, along the lines of that carried out by Morant *et al.* (1981). It is possible that too much emphasis has been placed on the problems of oil pollution and too little on other threats. This is because it is easier to raise public money for the rehabilitation of oiled birds than for less popular projects which might be more relevant for the long-term conservation of the species. There has been a lack of appreciation that certain research is essential for the formulation of appropriate conservation policies.

Remarks The Jackass Penguin is closely related to the Magellanic Penguin, though they are not considered conspecific (Ross 1971c). It is the only species of penguin breeding in Africa, but it seems that there has been a much richer penguin fauna in southern Africa over the last 130,000 years (Brooke in press). There are over 300 Jackass Penguins in captivity and their breeding potential is good (Brooke in press): for details of captive breeding see Wackernagel (1952), Michelmore (1967), Gailey-Phipps (1978a,b), Lensink and Dekker (1978), van Bocxstaele (1978) and Leung and Cooper (1979).

References

Apps, P. J. (1983) Aspects of the ecology of feral cats on Dassen Island, South Africa. *S. Afr. J. Zool.* 18: 393-399.

Avery, G. (1979) Results of beach patrols conducted in southern Africa in 1978. *Cormorant* 6: 4-12.

Avery, G. (1980) Results of beach patrols conducted in southern Africa in 1979. *Cormorant* 8: 65-72.

Avery, G. (1981) Results of beach patrols conducted in southern Africa in 1980. *Cormorant* 9: 113-122.

Avery, G. (1982) Results of beach patrols conducted in southern Africa in 1981. *Cormorant* 10: 87-96.

Berry, H. H., Seely, M. K. and Fryer, R. E. (1974) The status of the Jackass Penguin *Spheniscus demersus* on Halifax Island off South West Africa. *Madoqua* (2)3: 69-73.

Betham, R. M. (1929) Observations on the nesting of birds in the vicinity of Cape Town, South Africa. *Ibis* (12)5: 71-104.

van Bocxstaele, R. (1978) Breeding and hand-rearing the Black-footed Penguin *Spheniscus demersus* at Antwerp Zoo. *Internat. Zoo Yearbook* 18: 42-46.

Bourne, W. R. P. and Dixon, T. J. (1973) Observations of seabirds 1967-1969. *Sea Swallow* 22: 29-60.

Broni, S. C. (1982) First recorded mainland breeding by the Jackass Penguin *Spheniscus demersus*. *Cormorant* 10: 120.

Brooke, R. K. (1981) The seabirds of the Moçâmedes Province, Angola. *Gerfaut* 71: 209-225.

Brooke, R. K. (in press) *The rare and vulnerable birds of South Africa*.

Brooke, R. K. and Sinclair, J. C. (1978) Preliminary list of southern African seabirds. *Cormorant* 4: 10-17.

Brooke, R. K. and Wallett, T. S. (1976) Shark predators in Natal waters. *Ostrich* 47: 126.

Brown, L. H., Urban, E. K. and Newman, K. (1982) *The birds of Africa*, 1. London: Academic Press.

Clancey, P. A. (1971) *A handlist of the birds of southern Moçambique*. Lourenço Marques: Instituto de Investigação Científica de Moçambique.

Cooper, J. (1971) The South African National Foundation for the Conservation of Coastal Birds. *Bokmakierie* 23: 52-56.

Cooper, J. (1974a) The predators of the Jackass Penguin *Spheniscus demersus*.

Bull. Brit. Orn. Club 94: 21-24.

Cooper, J. (1974b) Bird ringing on Dassen Island. *Safring News* 3(1): 19-21.

Cooper, J. (1977a) Census of the Jackass Penguin on Dyer Island. *Cormorant* 2: 15-17.

Cooper, J. (1977b) Energetic requirements for growth of the Jackass Penguin. *Zool. Afr.* 12: 201-213.

Cooper, J. (1977c) Food, breeding and coat colour of feral cats on Dassen Island. *Zool. Afr.* 12: 250-252.

Cooper, J. (1978a) Results of beach patrols conducted in 1977. *Cormorant* 4: 4-9.

Cooper, J. (1978b) Moult of the Black-footed Penguin *Spheniscus demersus*. *Internat. Zoo Yearbook* 18: 22-27.

Cooper, J. (1979) The status of seabirds at the islands in Saldanha Bay, and recommendations for their management. Report of the Percy FitzPatrick Institute of African Ornithology, University of Cape Town, to the Advisory Committee for Ecological Studies in the Langebaan-Saldanha Area.

Cooper, J. (1980) Breeding biology of the Jackass Penguin with special reference to its conservation. *Proc. IV Pan-Afr. orn. Congr.*: 227-231.

Cooper, J. (1981) Pelagic birds and mammals of the southern Benguela region. *Trans. Roy. Soc. S. Afr.* 44: 373-378.

Cooper, J. (1982) Methods of reducing mortality of seabirds caused by underwater blasting. *Cormorant* 10: 109-113.

Cooper, J. (in press) Changes in resource division among four breeding seabirds in the Benguela upwelling system, 1953-1978. *Proc. V Pan-Afr. orn. Congr.*

Cooper, J. and Randall, R. M. (1981) Range and movements of the Jackass Penguin *Spheniscus demersus* with special reference to juvenile dispersal. P. 214 in J. Cooper, ed. *Proceedings of the Symposium on Birds of the Sea and Shore, 1979*. Cape Town: African Seabird Group.

Cooper, J. and Shaughnessy, P. D. (1977) Census of the Jackass Penguin at Seal Island, False Bay. *Cormorant* 2: 20.

Cooper, J. and Shaughnessy, P. D. (1979) Second census of the Jackass Penguin on Seal Island, False Bay: January 1978. *Cormorant* 5: 23.

Cooper, J., Williams, A. J. and Britton, P. L. (in press) Distribution, population sizes and conservation of breeding seabirds in the Afrotropical Region. In J. P. Croxall, P. G. H. Evans and R. W. Schreiber, eds. *Status and conservation of the world's seabirds*. Cambridge: ICBP Techn. Publ. no. 2.

Cott, H. B. (1953) The exploitation of wild birds for their eggs. *Ibis* 95: 409-449.

Courtenay-Latimer, M. and Gibson-Hill, C. A. (1946) A preliminary note on the Bird Island group in Algoa Bay. *Ostrich* 27: 75-86.

Crawford, R. (1982) Where have all the penguins gone? *Custos* 11(4): 31-32.

Crawford, R. J. M. and Shelton, P. A. (1978) Pelagic fish and seabird interrelationships off the coast of South West and South Africa. *Biol. Conserv.* 14: 85-109.

Crawford, R. J. M. and Shelton, P. A. (1981) Population trends for some southern African seabirds related to fish availability. Pp. 15-41 in J. Cooper, ed. *Proceedings of the Symposium on Birds of the Sea and Shore, 1979*. Cape Town: African Seabird Group.

Cyrus, D. and Robson, N. (1980) *Bird atlas of Natal*. Pietermaritzburg: University of Natal Press.

Davies, D. H. (1955) The South African pilchard (*Sardinops ocellata*): bird predators, 1953-1954. *Investgl. Rep. Div. Fish. Un. S. Afr.* 18: 1-32.

Davies, D. H. (1956) The South African pilchard (*Sardinops ocellata)* and maasbanker (*Trachurus trachurus*): bird predators, 1954-1955. *Investgl. Rep.*

Div. Fish. Un. S. Afr. 23: 1-40.

Duffy, D. C., Berruti, A., Randall, R. M. and Cooper, J. (1984) Effects of the 1982-3 warm water event on the breeding of South African seabirds. *S. Afr. J. Sci.* 80: 65-69.

Elliott, H. F. I. (1953) The fauna of Tristan da Cunha. *Oryx* 2: 41-53.

Elliott, H. F. I. (1957) A contribution to the ornithology of the Tristan da Cunha group. *Ibis* 99: 545-586.

Erasmus, T., Randall, R. M. and Randall, B. M. (1981) Oil pollution, insulation and body temperatures in the Jackass Penguin *Spheniscus demersus*. *Comp. Biochem. Physiol.* 69A: 169-171.

Every, B. (1983) Second record of mainland breeding by the Jackass Penguin *Spheniscus demersus*. *Cormorant* 11: 62.

da Franca, P. (1967) Sur la présence d'*Arctocephalus pusillus* (Schreber) (Otariidae) et de *Mirounga leonina* (Linné) (Phocidae) au sud de l'Angola. *Mammalia* 31: 50-54.

Frost, P. G. H., Shaughnessy, P. D., Semmelink, A., Sketch, M. and Siegfried, W. R. (1975) The response of Jackass Penguins to killer whale vocalisations. *S. Afr. J. Sci.* 71: 157-158.

Frost, P. G. H., Siegfried, W. R. and Burger, A. E. (1976a) Behavioural adaptations of the Jackass Penguin *Spheniscus demersus* to a hot, arid environment. *J. Zool., Lond.* 179: 165-187.

Frost, P. G. H., Siegfried, W. R. and Cooper, J. (1976b) Conservation of the Jackass Penguin *Spheniscus demersus* (L.). *Biol. Conserv.* 9: 79-99.

Furness, B. L. and Laugksch, R. C. (1983) An attempt to use barium meals and X-ray photography to determine gastric evacuation rate and gut retention time in Jackass Penguins *Spheniscus demersus*. *Cormorant* 11: 3-5.

Furness, R. W. and Cooper, J. (1982) Interactions between breeding seabird and pelagic fish populations in the southern Benguela region. *Mar. Ecol. Prog. Ser.* 8: 243-250.

Gailey-Phipps, J. (1978a) A world survey of penguins in captivity. *Internat. Zoo Yearbook* 18: 7-13.

Gailey-Phipps, J. (1978b) Breeding Black-footed Penguins *Spheniscus demersus* at the Baltimore Zoo. *Internat. Zoo Yearbook* 18: 28-35.

Healy, M. I. (1978) Breeding in a newly established exhibit of Black-footed Penguins *Spheniscus demersus* at Columbia Zoo. *Internat. Zoo Yearbook* 18: 40-42.

Hockey, P. A. R. (1976) Reactions of seabirds to an underwater explosion in Saldanha Bay. *Cormorant* 1: 6.

Hockey, P. A. R. (1983) Marcus Island – the road to recovery. *Afr. Wildl.* 37: 178-179.

Hockey, P. A. R. and Hallinan, J. (1981) Effect of human disturbance on the breeding behaviour of Jackass Penguins *Spheniscus demersus*. *S. Afr. J. Wildl. Res.* 11: 59-62.

Jackson, F., Siegfried, W. R. and Cooper, J. (1976) A simulation model for the population dynamics of the Jackass Penguin. *Trans. Roy. Soc. S. Afr.* 42: 11-21.

Jarvis, M. F. J. and Cram, D. L. (1971) Bird Island, Lambert's Bay, South Africa: an attempt at conservation. *Biol. Conserv.* 3: 269-272.

Kearton, C. (1930) *The island of penguins*. London: Longmans.

Lensink, B. M. and Dekker, D. (1978) Management of Black-footed Penguins *Spheniscus demersus* at Artiszoo, Amsterdam. *Internat. Zoo Yearbook* 18: 35-40.

Leung, H. K. W. and Cooper, J. (1979) Jackass Penguins breeding in captivity at Hong Kong. *Cormorant* 7: 4-6.

Liversidge, R. and Thomas, A. (1970) Seabirds off the south-western Cape of South Africa. *Proc. XV Internat. Orn. Congr.*: 605-606.

Maclean, G. L. (1960) Records from southern South West Africa. *Ostrich* 31: 49-63.

Malbrant, R. and Maclatchy, A. (1958) A propos de l'occurrence de deux oiseaux d'Afrique australe au Gabon: le manchot du Cap *Spheniscus demersus* Linné et la grue couronnée *Balearica regulorum* Bennett. *Oiseau et R.F.O.* 28: 84-86.

Malbrant, R. and Maclatchy, A. (1959) Occurrence inattendue de deux oiseaux d'Afrique australe au Gabon: le manchot du Cap *Spheniscus demersus* Linné et la grue couronnée *Balearica regulorum* Bennett. *Proc. I Pan-Afr. orn. Congr. Ostrich* Suppl. 3: 96-97.

McGill, E. A. (1970) St.Croix birds. *Bokmakierie* 22: 54-56.

McGill, W. J. (1973) The need to preserve the Jackass Penguins of St.Croix. *Bokmakierie* 25: 89-90.

McLachlan, G. R. and Liversidge, R. (1978) *Roberts birds of South Africa*. 4th edition. Johannesburg: Trustees of the John Voelcker Bird Book Fund.

Meinertzhagen, R. (1950) The Namib of South West Africa. *Ibis* 92: 567-573.

Michelmore, A. P. G. (1967) Breeding Black-footed Penguins *Spheniscus demersus*. *Internat. Zoo Yearbook* 7: 37.

Morant, P. D. (1979) Seabird ringing in southern Africa, 1948-1978. *Cormorant* 6: 25-32.

Morant, P. D., Cooper, J. and Randall, R. M. (1981) The rehabilitation of oiled Jackass Penguins *Spheniscus demersus*, 1970-1980. Pp. 267-301 in J. Cooper, ed. *Proceedings of the Symposium on Birds of the Sea and Shore, 1979*. Cape Town: African Seabird Group.

Moreau, R. E. (1950) The breeding seasons of African birds – 2. Sea birds. *Ibis* 92: 419-433.

Newman, K. B. (1966) Lambert's Bay Island. *Bokmakierie* 18: 12-14.

Nicoll, M. J. (1906) On the birds collected and observed during the voyage of the "Valhalla", R.V.S., from November 1905 to May 1906. *Ibis* (8)6: 666-712.

Niethammer, G. (1961) Vögel der südwestafrikanischen Küste. *Vogelwarte* 21: 147-152.

van Oordt, G. J. and Kruijt, J. P. (1954) Birds observed on a voyage in the South Atlantic and Southern Oceans in 1951/1952. *Ardea* 42: 245-280.

Percy FitzPatrick Institute of African Ornithology (1974) Fish oil kills seabirds. *Afr. Wildl.* 28: 24-25.

Pinto, A. A. da R. (1958) A contribution towards the study of the avifauna of the Island of Inhaca. *Bol. Soc. Estud. Prov. Moçambique* 112: 29-62.

Rand, R. W. (1949) Notes on birds observed on Sinclairs Island (South West Africa). *Ostrich* 20: 130-136.

Rand, R. W. (1951) Birds breeding on Seal Island (False Bay, Cape Province). *Ostrich* 22: 94-103.

Rand, R. W. (1952a) Oil contamination – a sea bird menace. *Bokmakierie* 4: 63.

Rand, R. W. (1952b) The birds of Hollamsbird Island, South West Africa. *Ibis* 94: 452-457.

Rand, R. W. (1960) The biology of guano-producing sea-birds. The distribution, abundance and feeding habits of the Cape Penguin, *Spheniscus demersus*, off the south-western coast of the Cape Province. *Investgl. Rep. Div. Fish. Un. S. Afr.* 41: 1-28.

Rand, R. W. (1963a) The biology of guano-producing sea-birds. 4. Composition of colonies on the Cape islands. *Investgl. Rep. Div. Fish. Rep. S. Afr.* 43: 1-32.

Rand, R. W. (1963b) The biology of guano-producing sea-birds. 5. Composition of colonies on the South West African islands. *Investgl. Rep. Div. Fish. Rep. S. Afr.* 46: 1-26.

Randall, R. M. (1983) Biology of the Jackass Penguin *Spheniscus demersus* (L.) at St.Croix Island, South Africa. Ph.D. thesis, University of Port Elizabeth.

Randall, R. M. and Randall, B. M. (1980) Black death for penguins. *Environment R.S.A.* 7(9): 1-2.

Randall, R. M., Randall, B. M. and Bevan, J. (1980) Oil pollution and penguins – is cleaning justified? *Mar. Poll. Bull.* 11: 234-237.

Randall, R. M. and Randall, B. M. (1981) The annual cycle of the Jackass Penguin *Spheniscus demersus* at St.Croix Island, South Africa. Pp. 427-450 in J. Cooper, ed. *Proceedings of the Symposium on the Birds of the Sea and Shore, 1979*. Cape Town: African Seabird Group.

Randall, R. M., Randall, B. M. and Baird, D. (1981a) Speed of movement of Jackass Penguins over long distances and their possible use of ocean currents. *S. Afr. J. Sci.* 77: 420-421.

Randall, R. M., Randall, B. M., Batchelor, A. L. and Ross, G. J. B. (1981b) The status of seabirds associated with islands in Algoa Bay, South Africa, 1973-1981. *Cormorant* 9: 85-104.

Randall, R. M., Randall, B. M. and Klingelhoeffer, E. W. (1981c) Species diversity and size ranges of cephalopods in the diet of Jackass Penguins from Algoa Bay, South Africa. *S. Afr. J. Zool.* 16: 163-166.

Ripley, S. D. (1974) Successful protection of the Jackass Penguin. *ICBP President's Letter* 33.

Ross, G. (1971a) Our Jackass Penguins ... are they in danger? *Afr. Wildl.* 25: 130-134.

Ross, G. J. B. (1971b) The Jackass Penguin on St.Croix: a census. *East Cape Naturalist* 44: 22-44.

Ross, G. J. B. (1971c) The specific status of the Jackass Penguin. *Ostrich* 42: 150-151.

Ross, G. J. B. (1972) Recovery of a banded Jackass Penguin. *Ostrich* 43: 230.

Rowan, M. K. (1969) Oiling of marine birds in South Africa. Pp. 121-124 in P. Barclay-Smith, ed. *Proceedings of the International Conference on Oil Pollution of the Sea, 7-9 October 1968 at Rome: report of proceedings*. [London:] International Conference on Oil Pollution of the Sea.

Sclater, W. L. (1896) A visit to Dassen Island, the home of the Jackass Penguin. *Ibis* (7)6: 519-525.

Sclater, W. L. (1904) Saldanha Bay and its bird-islands. *Ibis* (8)4: 79-88.

Sclater, W. L. (1907) The birds islands of South Africa. *Condor* 9: 71-76.

Shaughnessy, P. D. (1977) Jackass Penguins on the northern guano islands. *Cormorant* 2: 18-19.

Shaughnessy, P. D. (1978) Cape fur seals preying on seabirds. *Cormorant* 5: 31.

Shaughnessy, P. D. (1980) Influence of Cape fur seals on Jackass Penguin numbers at Sinclair Island. *S. Afr. J. Wildl. Res.* 10: 18-21.

Shaughnessy, P. D., Cooper, J. and Morant, P. D. (1979) Third census of the Jackass Penguin on Seal Island, False Bay: January 1979. *Cormorant* 6: 33-34.

Shaughnessy, P. D. and Meyer, M. A. (1979) An estimate of the Jackass Penguin population on Possession Island, 1977 and 1978. *Cormorant* 6: 21-24.

Shaughnessy, P. D. and Shaughnessy, G. L. (1978) The Jackass Penguin colony at Seal Island in Mosselbaai. *Cormorant* 5: 27-28.

Shelton, P. A., Crawford, R. J. M., Cooper, J. and Brooke, R. K. (in press) Distribution, population size and conservation of the Jackass Penguin *Spheniscus demersus*. *S. Afr. J. Mar. Sci.*

Shelton, P. A., Crawford, R. J. M., Kriel, F. and Cooper, J. (1982) Methods used to census three species of South African seabirds, 1978-1981. *Fish. Bull. S. Afr.* 16: 115-120.

Shortridge, G. C. and Sclater, W. L. (1904) On a collection of birds from the neighbourhood of Port St.Johns, in Pondoland. *Ibis* (8)4: 173-208.

Siegfried, W. R. (1977) Packing of Jackass Penguin nests. *S. Afr. J. Sci.* 73: 186-187.

Siegfried, W. R. (1979) Group size of Cape Gannets at Dwesa Nature Reserve, Transkei. *Cormorant* 7: 32.

Siegfried, W. R. (1982) Ecology of the Jackass Penguin (*Spheniscus demersus*) with special reference to conservation of the species. *Natn. Geog. Soc. Res. Reports* 14: 597-600.

Siegfried, W. R. and Crawford, R. J. M. (1978) Jackass Penguins, eggs and guano: diminishing resources at Dassen Island. *S. Afr. J. Sci.* 74: 389-390.

Siegfried, W. R., Frost, P. G. H., Kinahan, J. B. and Cooper, J. (1975) Social behaviour of Jackass Penguins at sea. *Zool. Afr.* 10: 87-100.

Sinclair, J. C. and Nicholls, G. H. (1978) Southern Giant Petrel *Macronectes giganteus* foraging ashore in South Africa. *Ardea* 66: 166.

Stanford, W. P. (1953) Some sea birds in winter off the S. W. Cape. *Ostrich* 24: 17-26.

Stewart, W. S. and Currey, A. C. (1957) Malagas – Saldanha Bay – South Africa. *Sea Swallow* 10: 15-17.

Summerhayes, C. P., Hofmeyr, P. K. and Rioux, R. H. (1974) Seabirds off the southwestern coast of Africa. *Ostrich* 45: 83-109.

Taylor, J. S. (1954) Bird Island expedition, 1954. *Bee-eater* 5: 2-3.

Traylor, M. A. (1963) Check list of Angolan birds. *Publ. cult. Co. Diam. Angola, Lisboa* no. 61.

Wackernagel, H. (1952) Künstliche Aufzucht von zwei Brillenpinguinen. *Orn. Beob.* 49: 69-79.

Westphal, A. and Rowan, M. K. (1969) Some observations of the effects of oil pollution on the Jackass Penguin. *Proc. III Pan-Afr. orn. Congr. Ostrich* suppl. 8: 521-526.

Williams, A. J. (1981) Why do penguins have long laying intervals? *Ibis* 123: 202-204.

Williams, A. J. and Cooper J. (in press) Aspects of the breeding biology of the Jackass Penguin *Spheniscus demersus. Proc. V Pan-Afr. orn. Congr.*

Winterbottom, J. M. and Hare, H. L. (1947) On the birds of Port St.Johns, Pondoland. *Ostrich* 18: 86-102.

MADAGASCAR LITTLE GREBE INSUFFICIENTLY KNOWN
Tachybaptus pelzelnii (Hartlaub, 1861)

Order PODICIPEDIFORMES Family PODICIPEDIDAE

Summary This endemic Madagascar waterbird, common and widespread in the recent past, is known to have suffered a considerable decline in certain areas and, in view of the variety of threats it faces, it is treated here as a case requiring precautionary or preventive measures.

Distribution The Madagascar Little Grebe is endemic to Madagascar where it is widespread from sea-level to 1800 m, and absent only from the subdesert region in the south, including Lake Tsimanampetsotsa (Delacour 1932, Rand 1936, Milon *et al.* 1973), although there is a specimen in NHMW from the south-west coast (H. Schifter *per* Z. J. Karpowicz *in litt.* 1983).

Population The species was considered common, 1929-1931 (Delacour 1933, Rand 1936), and locally common, 1942-1944 (van Someren 1947). In 1973 it was still described as common except for at least 15 km around Antananarivo, where it was rare (Milon *et al.* 1973), but other evidence suggests that it was probably no longer common anywhere at that stage and is likely to be less so now. Thus it was found to be abundant at Lake Ihotry in the south-west in December 1929 (Rand 1936) but was extremely rare there, 1960-1966 (Appert 1971), though 100-150 were present on it in August 1983 (O. Langrand *in litt.* 1984); and, although birds were common at Lake Alaotra, 1929-1931 (Delacour 1932), in a three-month study of grebes in north-central Madagascar ranging from south and west of Antananarivo to north of Lake Alaotra, 1960, only 10 of this species were seen (at Lake Alaotra and around Andilamena 30 km to the north) and it was "definitely the rarest" of the three species seen and had "considerably decreased in numbers" (Voous and Payne 1965). Despite a report that at least 100 were present at Lake Itasy and on nearby crater-lakes around 1970, this species along with the Madagascar Pond-heron *Ardeola idae* (see Appendix C) was then regarded as in complete collapse around Antananarivo (Salvan 1972a). The factors apparently causing the decline at Lakes Ihotry and Alaotra and around Antananarivo are reportedly widespread in Madagascar (e.g. Salvan 1970,1972b, Appert 1971), and it seems likely that the species will have declined everywhere and may well now be threatened. That it has generally declined has been confirmed by occasional observations spanning the past 15 or so years (D. A. Turner *in litt.* 1983).

Ecology It inhabits lakes, pools and slow stretches of rivers (Rand 1936), preferably those most richly vegetated with aquatic plants and notably the water-lily *Nymphaea stellata*, occurring much less often on vegetation-free water (Appert 1971). The species is considered to be less exclusively piscivorous than either of its congeners in Madagascar, the Little Grebe *Tachybaptus ruficollis* (with which it is often seen: O. Langrand *in litt.* 1984) and the Alaotra Grebe *T. rufolavatus* (Voous and Payne 1965, Appert 1971) (see relevant account); of eight stomachs of birds collected, 1929-1931, all held aquatic insects, four also feathers (Rand 1936); of five stomachs, 1960, feathers were in four, fish in two, insects in two, a crustacean in one (Voous and Payne 1965). Breeding appears to occur chiefly at the end of the rainy season (February to April), when water-levels are highest and aquatic plants most developed; in favourable conditions it evidently also occurs in the austral spring (August to October) (Appert 1971; also Rand 1936). In BMNH there is a downy chick from Namoroka (north-west) in March and a female ready to lay from Iampasika (south-east) in August (NJC). Clutch-size is three to four (Milon *et al.* 1973); nests may be close to each other (see Appert 1971). The species is forced to move around because many waterbodies annually dry out while others shrink greatly in size (Appert 1971).

Threats Apart from the pollution of waters around Antananarivo (Salvan 1970, 1972b), two major and two less immediately certain threats can be identified, the first three of which are interrelated.

Introduced exotic fish The introduction of herbivorous tilapia into many waterbodies throughout Madagascar has apparently resulted in a massive reduction in their vegetation (Appert 1971), e.g. Lake Ihotry had been rich in water-lilies in 1929, but very few were seen in 1960-1966 (Appert 1971) although it was only in October 1960 that the lake was successfully stocked with tilapia (Griveaud 1960). These fish are able to colonise sites away from the release area during the rainy season; only very isolated pools or ones which dry out every year escape (Appert 1971). All waters found to hold grebes in north-central Madagascar, 1960, had abundant small fish, mainly tilapia (Voous and Payne 1965). The black bass *Micropterus salmoides* is regarded as both a food-competitor and a predator on downy young of this and other waterbird species (Salvan 1972a).

Competition with the Little Grebe The spread through Madagascar of *T. ruficollis* is outlined in Threats under Alaotra Grebe. Its post-1945 increase in abundance appears to be related to the conditions created by the introduction of exotic fish, since *ruficollis* is more piscivorous than *pelzelnii* and occurs widely on vegetation-free waters (Voous and Payne 1965, Appert 1971). "As the structural characters of the invading *ruficollis* more closely resemble *pelzelnii* than *rufolavatus*, it is not unlikely [see Remarks] that the decline of *pelzelnii* is caused by the recent colonisation of *ruficollis*. The structure and ecology of these species make it not improbable that the decline will continue" (Voous and Payne 1965).

Hybridisation with the Little Grebe A possible hybrid *ruficollis* x *pelzelnii* has been described (Benson 1971) and an apparent pair-bond between birds of these species has been observed in the wild (Benson *et al.* 1976). This evidence, though at present slight, suggests that as *ruficollis* spreads and multiplies while *pelzelnii* contracts and declines, further interbreeding could lead to genetic swamping by the former of the latter.

Reduction of wetlands Various factors over the past 50 years have resulted, in the Mangoky region at least, in less water in rivers and lakes and a lowering of the water-table, so that overall there is less grebe habitat (Appert 1971). Marshes throughout the island have been transformed into rice-fields and fish-farms (Salvan 1970,1972b).

Conservation Measures Taken None is known.

Conservation Measures Proposed A modern evaluation of the plight of the Madagascar Little Grebe is required before appropriate measures can be proposed; nevertheless it seems clear that such measures should include the safeguarding of a network of vegetation-rich lakes and pools from the introduction of exotic fish.

Remarks In the passage (from Voous and Payne 1965) quoted under Threats, the original has "likely" for the obviously correct "unlikely": this misprint has been confirmed (K. H. Voous *in litt.* 1983).

References

Appert, O. (1971) Die Taucher (Podicipidae [*sic*]) der Mangokygegend in Südwest-Madagaskar. *J. Orn.* 112: 61-69.

Benson, C. W. (1971) Quelques spécimens anciens de *Podiceps ruficollis* (Pallas) provenant de Madagascar et des Comores. *Oiseau et R.F.O.* 41: 89-93.

Benson, C. W., Colebrook-Robjent, J. F. R. and Williams, A. (1976) Contribution à l'ornithologie de Madagascar. *Oiseau et R.F.O.* 46: 103-134.

Delacour, J. (1932) Les oiseaux de la Mission Franco-Anglo-Américaine à Madagascar. *Oiseau et R.F.O.* 2: 1-96.

Delacour, J. (1933) Les grèbes de Madagascar. *Oiseau et R.F.O.* 3: 4-7.

Griveaud, P. (1960) Une mission de recherche de l'I.R.S.M. au Lac Ihotry (S. E. Morombe, Province de Tuléar). *Naturaliste Malgache* 12: 33-41.

Milon, P., Petter, J.-J. and Randrianasolo, G. (1973) *Faune de Madagascar, 35. Oiseaux.* Tananarive and Paris: ORSTOM and CNRS.

Rand, A. L. (1936) The distribution and habits of Madagascar birds. *Bull. Amer. Mus. Nat. Hist.* 72: 143-499.

Salvan, J. (1970) Remarques sur l'évolution de l'avifaune malgache depuis 1945. *Alauda* 38: 191-203.

Salvan, J. (1972a) Statut, recensement, reproduction des oiseaux dulçaquicoles aux environs de Tananarive. *Oiseau et R.F.O.* 42: 35-51.

Salvan, J. (1972b) Remarques sur l'avifaune malagasy et la protection d'espèces aviennes mal connues ou menacées. (Communication 26, pp. 179-182, in:) *C. R. Conférence Internationale sur la Conservation de la Nature et de ses Ressources à Madagascar.* Morges: IUCN (NS) Doc. suppl. no. 36.

van Someren, V. D. (1947) Field notes on some Madagascar birds. *Ibis* 89: 235-267.

Voous, K. H. and Payne, H. A. W. (1965) The grebes of Madagascar. *Ardea* 53: 9-31.

ALAOTRA GREBE

ENDANGERED

Tachybaptus rufolavatus (Delacour, 1932)

Order PODICIPEDIFORMES

Family PODICIPEDIDAE

Summary This endemic Madagascar waterbird, known chiefly from Lake Alaotra, is in the irreversible process of disappearing through hybridisation with the Little Grebe *Tachybaptus ruficollis*.

Distribution The Alaotra Grebe is known primarily from Lake Alaotra (40 km by 3-5 km) and adjacent marshes, at c. 700 m in north-eastern Madagascar (Delacour 1932, Lavauden 1937, Voous and Payne 1965). A prediction that it would be reported from Lake Itasy and other marshes in central Madagascar (Lavauden 1937) has been partially fulfilled, with records from Ankazobe (80 km north of Antananarivo) in December 1947 (Salvan 1971), a crater-lake north of Analavory (80 km west of Antananarivo) on an unknown date (but apparently around 1970) (Salvan 1972a), "Mianinarivo" (correctly, Miarinarivo: J. T. Hardyman *in litt.* 1984) (one town of this name is near Analavory and just north of Lake Itasy, another is 100 km north of Lake Alaotra) on an unknown date (Voous and Payne 1965), and Lake Kazanga (just south of Lake Itasy) in July 1971 (when at least 10 were seen) (Salvan 1972a). Moreover, the species has been collected as far south as the Isalo massif, in January 1963, and as far west as Majunga in November 1969 (see map in Salvan 1971), and it was seen between the Antsingy massif and Antsalova (near the coast due west of Antananarivo) in July 1970 (Salvan 1971) and in the Antsingy reserve (R.N.I. no. 9 du Tsingy de Bemaraha) itself on an unknown date (but apparently around 1970) (Salvan 1972b) (this and the previous record may perhaps be the same). However, it is to be observed that, since hybridisation with the longer-winged, dispersive Little Grebe *Tachybaptus ruficollis* has been taking place from at least 1929, and had seemingly intensified by 1960 (see under Threats), and since many hybrids can be extremely difficult to distinguish as such (see Voous and Payne 1965), the validity of many – if not all – of these records away from Lake Alaotra (which remains the only known breeding site) must be doubtful.

Population Numbers are unknown, but certainly very small. At Lake Alaotra in May 1929, when 15 specimens were first collected, it was found breeding in fair numbers (Delacour 1932); in May/July 1960, when 13 more specimens were collected, the estimated total number of birds seen at the lake was 50 (Voous and Payne 1965) (this presumably includes the 13 collected). More recently it has been stated that this species "seems in expansion" (Salvan 1972a), presumably as much in terms of numbers as of range; however, the records that are evidently the basis of this view, apart from the doubt cast on them under Distribution above, can be interpreted in much less encouraging ways, e.g. that they only represent the true but hitherto unrecognised distribution of the species, or even that they reflect an unprecedented dispersal from Lake Alaotra in the face of deteriorating conditions there. However, 12 birds were seen on Lake Alaotra in December 1982 (O. Langrand *in litt.* 1984).

Ecology Lake Alaotra is a large but shallow water-body, in 1929 fringed with dense vegetation (dominated by papyrus and reeds) and dotted with water-lilies (Rand 1936). The Alaotra Grebe is almost exclusively piscivorous (Voous and Payne 1965), breeding April to June in 1929 (Rand 1936), January to March in 1960 (Voous and Payne 1965). Its short wing is considered an indication of highly sedentary behaviour (Voous and Payne 1965), but subsequent records away from Lake Alaotra have been seen to call this assumption in question (Salvan 1972a).

Threats The species is threatened by hybridisation with the far more widespread and numerous Little Grebe, and by alteration of habitat in its only known breeding area. Although only first noted in any numbers in Madagascar in 1945 (Milon 1946), the Little Grebe was evidently fairly widespread in the island in the nineteenth century (up to 17 skins in museum collections), with the earliest record in 1837 and a breeding record from 1895 (Schlegel and Pollen 1868, Hartlaub 1877, Oberholser 1900, Delacour 1933, Milon 1951, Benson 1971). Despite reports that *ruficollis* disappeared from near Antananarivo around 1955 (Salvan 1972a, Milon *et al.* 1973), it was "by far the commonest species" of grebe at and around Antananarivo and Lake Alaotra in 1960 (Voous and Payne 1965) and had also become widespread in the Mangoky river region by this time (Appert 1971). Its post-1945 increase in abundance appears to be related to the conditions created by the introduction of exotic fish, especially tilapia, into many lakes and pools throughout Madagascar (Appert 1971). Hybridisation by the Little Grebe with the Alaotra Grebe, though first recognised in the 1960s (Voous and Payne 1965), has been recorded at least as far back as the 1920s (the type-specimen and up to four others of the original series of 15 appear hybrid) (Voous and Payne 1965), and even a specimen from 1862 seems suspect (Benson 1971). Of 39 grebes collected in north-central Madagascar in 1960, 13 were *rufolavatus*, 13 *ruficollis*, and 13 hybrids or suspected hybrids of the two; although there was a bias towards collecting birds that proved to fall into this last category, it seemed likely on this evidence that the pure *rufolavatus* strain was "doomed to vanish" (Voous and Payne 1965). Observations at Lake Alaotra in April 1971 confirmed that hybridisation with *ruficollis* was on a large scale (D. A. Turner *in litt.* 1983). Tilapia were already in Lake Alaotra in 1960 (Voous and Payne 1965), and while this may not have been directly injurious to the population of the piscivorous *rufolavatus* (indeed, if *rufolavatus* is truly "in expansion" this may well be due to tilapia) it may have provided greater attraction to the more mobile *ruficollis* and thus accelerated the rate of genetic swamping, and may equally have reduced cover needed by *rufolavatus* for breeding. By 1972 Lake Alaotra was said to be of limited interest only, owing to developments there for rice-growing and fish-farming (Salvan 1972b), a view confirmed by recent observations (O. Langrand *in litt.* 1984).

Conservation Measures Taken None is known.

Conservation Measures Proposed Nothing can be done to prevent the extermination of the Alaotra Grebe in the wild; however, a survey to assess its present condition would be most valuable for, if sufficient numbers of "pure" birds survive, it might be feasible to devise a programme of captive propagation for them.

References

Appert, O. (1971) Die Taucher (Podicipidae [*sic*]) der Mangokygegend in Südwest-Madagaskar. *J. Orn.* 112: 61-69.

Benson, C. W. (1971) Quelques spécimens anciens de *Podiceps ruficollis* (Pallas) provenant de Madagascar et des Comores. *Oiseau et R.F.O.* 41: 89-93.

Delacour, J. (1932) Les oiseaux de la Mission Franco-Anglo-Américaine à Madagascar. *Oiseau et R.F.O.* 2: 1-96.

Delacour, J. (1933) Les grèbes de Madagascar. *Oiseau et R.F.O.* 3: 4-7.

Hartlaub, G. (1877) *Die Vögel Madagascars und der benachbarten Inselgruppen.* Halle.

Lavauden, L. (1937) Supplément. A. Milne Edwards and A. Grandidier, *Histoire physique, naturelle et politique de Madagascar, 12. Oiseaux.* Paris: Société d'Editions Géographiques, Maritimes et Coloniales.

Milon, P. (1946) Observations sur quelques oiseaux de Madagascar. *Oiseau et R.F.O.* 16: 82-86.

Milon, P. (1951) Notes sur l'avifaune actuelle de l'île de la Réunion. *Terre et Vie* 98: 129-178.

Milon, P., Petter, J.-J. and Randrianasolo, G. (1973) *Faune de Madagascar, 35. Oiseaux.* Tananarive and Paris: ORSTOM and CNRS.

Oberholser, H. C. (1900) Catalogue of a collection of birds from Madagascar. *Proc. U. S. Natn. Mus.* 22: 235-248.

Rand, A. L. (1936) The distribution and habits of Madagascar birds. *Bull. Amer. Mus. Nat. Hist.* 72: 143-499.

Salvan, J. (1971) Observations nouvelles à Madagascar. *Alauda* 39: 37-42.

Salvan, J. (1972a) Statut, recensement, reproduction des oiseaux dulçaquicoles aux environs de Tananarive. *Oiseau et R.F.O.* 42: 35-51.

Salvan, J. (1972b) Remarques sur l'avifaune malagasy et la protection d'espèces aviennes mal connues ou menacées. (Communication 26, pp. 179-182, in:) *C. R. Conférence Internationale sur la Conservation de la Nature et de ses Ressources à Madagascar.* Morges: IUCN (NS) Doc. suppl. no. 36.

Schlegel, H. and Pollen, F. P. L. (1868) *Recherches sur la faune de Madagascar et de ses dépendances, d'après les découvertes de François P. L. Pollen et D. C. van Dam.* 2me partie. Mammifères et oiseaux. Leyde.

Voous, K. H. and Payne, H. A. W. (1965) The grebes of Madagascar. *Ardea* 53: 9-31.

AMSTERDAM ALBATROSS   **ENDANGERED**

Diomedea amsterdamensis Roux, Jouventin, Mougin, Stahl and Weimerskirch, 1983

Order PROCELLARIIFORMES   Family DIOMEDEIDAE

Summary This very recently described albatross is confined as a breeding bird to Amsterdam Island, southern Indian Ocean, where an average of merely five pairs breed per year.

Distribution The only known breeding population (the possible existence of others is discounted) occurs on Amsterdam Island (37°50'S 77°35'E) (part of the Terres Australes et Antarctiques Françaises), southern Indian Ocean: all nests recorded have been on the main plateau of the island, the Plateau de Tourbières, between 500 and 600 m (Roux *et al.* 1983). Distribution at sea is unknown (Roux *et al.* 1983).

Population On the basis of three chicks being reared in 1978, five in 1979, eight in 1981 and one in 1982 (earlier in the same text it is stated that five chicks were found in 1978, three in 1979), it is estimated that on average five eggs are laid (i.e. five pairs breed) each year, and that if pairs breed every two years as in other *Diomedea* and age of first breeding and rates of adult and first-year mortality are as in the Wandering Albatross *D. exulans* and Royal Albatross *D. epimophora*, the total population of this species is 30-50 birds (Roux *et al.* 1983). In 1983 probably four young were reared (Jouventin and Roux 1983a,1984).

Ecology Nests are in areas exposed to west winds, in low, very wet, moss-rich vegetation (Roux *et al.* 1983). Breeding occurs in the austral autumn and winter: adults arrive at Amsterdam in February, eggs are laid in early March and hatch (very synchronously) in mid-May, chicks completing moult in December and first flying at the start of January after a fledging period of c. 235 days (Roux *et al.* 1983). As in other large albatrosses, birds breed every second year (Jouventin and Roux 1983a,1984).

Threats The original population of this species was presumably much larger, but fires and the introduction of rats, cats and bovines on Amsterdam since its discovery in 1522, along with other factors, have presumably been responsible for reducing numbers to their present very precarious level (Roux *et al.* 1983, Jouventin and Roux 1984). These dangers persist (Roux *et al.* 1983): some 1,200 cattle now cover the island, which is nowhere wider than 9 km, impeding all regeneration (Jouventin and Roux 1983a,1984).

Conservation Measures Taken Owing to the tiny numbers of this species the collection of a specimen for the original description was laudably resisted; the retrievable remains of a bird found dead in 1982 form the type-material (Roux *et al.* 1983).

Conservation Measures Proposed Complete protection of this species and its 400 ha nesting area is imperative (Roux *et al.* 1983, Jouventin and Roux 1983a,1983b). Cattle should be reduced in number and fenced in (Jouventin and Roux 1984). It is clear (from Roux *et al.* 1983) that research on the bird is continuing; it is important that this work identifies all actual and potential threats to the breeding population and develops proposals for their elimination.

References

Jouventin, P. and Roux, J.-P. (1983a) The Amsterdam Albatross: a new species which is near extinction. *RAOU Newsletter* 58: 1-2.

Jouventin, P. and Roux, J.-P. (1983b) Discovery of a new albatross. *Nature* 305: 181.

Jouventin, P. and Roux, J.-P. (1984) L'Albatross d'Amsterdam va-t-il disparaître à peine découvert? *La Recherche* 15: 250-252.

Roux, J.-P., Jouventin, P., Mougin, J.-L., Stahl, J.-C. and Weimerskirch, H. (1983) Un nouvel albatros *Diomedea amsterdamensis* n. sp. découvert sur l'île Amsterdam (37°50'S, 77°35'E). *Oiseau et R.F.O.* 53: 1-11.

MASCARENE BLACK PETREL   ENDANGERED
Pterodroma aterrima (Bonaparte, 1857)

Order PROCELLARIIFORMES   Family PROCELLARIIDAE

Summary This gadfly-petrel, only known from Réunion and Rodrigues in the Indian Ocean, has been recorded so rarely that it must be considered at best endangered on Réunion and extinct on Rodrigues.

Distribution The only acceptable records (see Jouanin 1970) of the Mascarene Black Petrel are from the Mascarene islands of Réunion (France) and Rodrigues (Mauritius) in the Indian Ocean. On Réunion, the species is known from four extant nineteenth century specimens (several others were collected but are now lost) (Jouanin 1970) and two others found in March 1970 at Entre-Deux in the south-west of the island and December 1973 at Bois Rouge on the north coast (Barau 1972, Jouanin in press). Nesting is assumed to occur near Entre-Deux and, from interviews with local people, near Grand Bassin (Barau 1972). An upper jaw found amongst subfossil material gathered on Rodrigues in the nineteenth century has been identified as of this species, which is consequently considered likely to have been the "fouquet" (= shearwater) recorded breeding in the hills of the island around 1730 (Bourne 1968); but it is presumably now extinct on Rodrigues. At sea, two birds believed to have been this species were seen in 1964 (by F. B. Gill) at 27°S 55°E (Barau 1972).

Population Numbers are unknown, but in view of the extreme rarity of records any extant population must be extremely small.

Ecology The species is expected, by virtue of its affinities (see Remarks), to breed in isolated pairs under forest in mountainous regions (Jouanin 1970, in press), either in winter (Bourne 1968) or else over a protracted period (Jouanin in press), both factors being viewed as explanations for its remarkable elusiveness on so well populated an island as Réunion (Bourne 1968, Jouanin 1970, in press).

Threats It is speculated that cats, dogs and rats *Rattus* on Réunion may prey on the species when breeding (King 1978-1979), that people may take birds at nests for food, other Réunion seabirds being much exploited (King 1978-1979), and that birds may be absorbing pesticide residues harmful to their reproduction (King 1978-1979), since this is known to be happening to the Herald Petrel *Pterodroma arminjoniana* on Round Island, off neighbouring Mauritius (see Temple 1976).

Conservation Measures Taken Searches for the breeding grounds of this species have been made on a systematic basis including interviews with (and showing pictures to) islanders in every rural community on Réunion, though as yet without success (Barau 1972, Jouanin in press).

Conservation Measures Proposed Further searches for the breeding grounds are the only practical activities to be pursued at present.

Remarks No records of this species at sea have been acceptable following the discovery of Jouanin's Petrel *Bulweria fallax* (see Jouanin 1970). The closest relatives of the Mascarene Black Petrel are considered to be the Tahiti Petrel *Pterodroma rostrata* and the almost wholly unknown Beck's Petrel *P. (rostrata) becki* (Jouanin 1970; for the last-named see King 1978-1979).

References

Barau, A. (1972) A la recherche du pétrel noir de la Réunion. *Info-Nature* no. 5: 5-10 [also dated 1971].

Bourne, W. R. P. (1968) The birds of Rodriguez, Indian Ocean. *Ibis* 110: 338-344.

Jouanin, C. (1970) Le pétrel noir de Bourbon, *Pterodroma aterrima* Bonaparte. *Oiseau et R.F.O.* 40: 48-67.

Jouanin, C. (in press) Notes on the nesting of Procellariiformes in Réunion. In A. W. Diamond, ed. *Studies of Mascarene island birds*. Cambridge: Cambridge University Press.

King, W. B. (1978-1979) *Red data book, 2: Aves*. 2nd edition. Morges, Switzerland: IUCN.

Temple, S. A. (1976) Observations of seabirds and shorebirds on Mauritius. *Ostrich* 47: 117-125.

GON-GON   RARE
Pterodroma feae (Salvadori, 1900)

Order PROCELLARIIFORMES   Family PROCELLARIIDAE

Summary This gadfly-petrel breeds on four islands in the Cape Verde archipelago and on Bugio in the Desertas off Madeira, but the most recent reports suggest the total population may now only stand at several hundred pairs; the species suffers considerable exploitation by people for food.

Distribution The Gon-gon breeds on the islands of São Nicolau, Fogo, Santo Antão and São Tiago in the Cape Verde archipelago (Republic of Cape Verde), and on the island of Bugio in the Desertas group south of Madeira (Portugal), Atlantic Ocean. On São Nicolau (type-locality), it was found at the end of the last century to nest above 500 m (Salvadori 1899) and subsequently to nest among the highest peaks above Ribeira Brava (Bourne 1955), including at Canto (Bourne 1966). On Fogo, it was reported at the end of the last century to breed (Salvadori 1899), and this has subsequently been confirmed (Bourne 1966, de Naurois 1969), eggs and young being found at 600 m and also at 2,200 m in the crater of the still active volcano (de Naurois 1969). On Santo Antão, around which birds were seen in flocks in September 1912 (Murphy 1924) and which has been considered best suited for this species of all the Cape Verde islands (Bannerman and Bannerman 1968), breeding has been reported from above Ribeira Grande (Bourne 1955) and in the high valleys of Alto Mira and of Paúl (de Naurois 1969). On São Tiago in 1951, breeding was reported by locals along the central range (Serra do Pico da Antónia) above (i.e. west of) São Domingos, Orgãos and Picos, and in the northern range "above Malagueta" i.e. on the east side of Malagueta peak, notably at Pilão Cão (see also Remarks), and a bird was heard above São Domingos, and others seen and heard on the opposite side of the range some 5 km north-west of Santa Anna (Santa Ana) on the east side of the upper reaches of the Ribeira de Santa Clara (Bourne 1955, W. R. P. Bourne *in litt.* 1984), nesting occurring between 400 and 800 m, possibly up to 1,200 m (de Naurois 1969). The expectation that the species breeds on Brava (Bannerman and Bannerman 1968) is considered mistaken (W. R. P. Bourne *in litt.* 1984), while fruitless searches have been made of Maio and parts of Sal and Boavista (de Naurois 1969, R. de Naurois *in litt.* 1984; hence Bannerman and Bannerman 1968), but such small, low islands would not be expected to hold colonies (W. R. P. Bourne *in litt.* 1984). In the Madeira group, the only certain breeding site for the species now is Bugio, the most southerly of the Desertas, where eggs were first taken on 14 October 1894 (Schmitz 1894,1905), and where birds (including nestlings) have subsequently been collected at various times this century (see list of specimens in Bannerman and Bannerman 1965): birds breed on the saddle of the island, and on the steeper, inaccessible adjacent slopes (Jouanin *et al.* 1969). A single bird was collected on Deserta Grande "in the spring of 1890", i.e. 28 June 1890 (Dalgleish 1891, Schmitz 1905), four were taken there in July 1891 (Hartwig 1891) and one on 27 (specimen dated 28th) September 1895 (Schmitz 1905, Bannerman and Bannerman 1965), but, although the island remains incompletely explored, the massive destruction of seabirds by fishermen (Jouanin *et al.* 1969) coupled with the presence of cats (Cook and Yalden 1980; but see Threats) probably explains why there have been no records there this century (that the species ever bred on the island, despite the records above, is doubted: P. A. Zino *in litt.* 1984). A single bird was collected on Baixo (Cal), in the Porto Santo group north of Madeira, in July 1889 (Dalgleish 1890,1891), and another was killed on Porto Santo itself in January 1890 (Hartwig 1891; see Remarks). The species is confidently stated to be absent now from Baixo (Jouanin *et al.* 1969), while a report of its presence on Cima, also in the Porto Santo group (Bannerman and Bannerman 1965; see Remarks) remains unconfirmed: that it ever bred on either island is doubted (P. A. Zino *in litt.* 1984). On Selvagem Grande (Great Salvage Island) (Portugal), north of the Canary Islands, calls of birds very similar to tape-recorded Soft-plumaged Petrels *Pterodroma mollis* (to which the Gon-gon is closely allied: e.g. Bourne 1957,1983a) were heard on successive nights in June 1983 (James and Robertson in press), and seem likely to have been made by Gon-gons. Breeding has been speculated on the Canaries (Salvadori 1899) and the Azores (Bourne 1966,1983a), but sea conditions are not considered favourable for gadfly-petrels *Pterodroma* around the latter (G. Le Grand *in litt.* 1984). The Gon-gon may once have bred on St.Helena in the southern Atlantic (Bourne 1956). On a visit to the waters round the Cape Verdes, April 1976, birds were observed in two main areas, near the coasts of Santo Antão and São Vicente east to Santa Luzia, and in the area south from Boavista north and east of Maio to south-west of São Tiago, with a third much less frequented area around Fogo, Brava and Rombo, with singles seen off the west coast of Sal and at 20°30'N 19°00'W; in October 1976 birds were seen only south of São Vicente (one bird) and south and south-east of Boavista (five or six) (Lambert 1980). Other records at sea (some of which may refer to the apparently far rarer Freira *Pterodroma madeira*: see relevant account) include (north to south): between Madeira and Porto Santo, December 1900 (de Noronha 1902), July 1967 (Jouanin *et al.* 1969) and August 1981 (Swash in press), between Madeira and the Desertas, July 1967 and October 1968 (Jouanin *et al.* 1969), August 1981 (Swash in press) and September 1983 (P. A. Zino *in litt.* 1984), north of the Canaries at 32°30'N 17°10'W, February 1972 (P. K. Kinnear *per* W. R. P. Bourne *in litt.* 1984), south-west of the Canaries at 25°N 19°W, September 1951 (Bourne 1955), from 500 km north-west of the Cape Verdes at 23°17'N 28°19'W south to the Cape Verdes and thence to 9°N, September 1912 (Murphy 1924), off Mauritania at 19°N 17°W, September 1966 (Bourne and Dixon 1973), south of the Cape Verdes at 13°30'N 24°W, December 1970 (Bourne and Dixon 1975), off Guinea at 12°N 17°30'W, April 1963 (Bourne 1965), off Guinea approaching Sierra Leone at 11°10'N, May 1897 (Bannerman 1914, though this record is questioned: W. R. P. Bourne *in litt.* 1984), and in the central Atlantic at 6°50'N 23°46'W (specimen collected), October 1768 (Bourne 1957), and at 2°45'N 15°45'W, November 1969 (Bourne and Dixon 1975). This last and several other records in the tropical South Atlantic, e.g. at 5°30'S 6°30'W, 11°30'S 1°30'W, 15°30'S 2°E, all June 1969, 13°30'S 1°E, July 1970, 13°45'S 3°45'E, 10°S 3°W, 6°15'S 6°30'W, all November 1969 (Bourne and Dixon 1975), conceivably refer to northward-wandering Soft-plumaged Petrels rather than southward-wandering Gon-gons (or Freiras). A gadfly-petrel found dead on the west shore of the Dead Sea, Israel, February 1963, is probably referable to this species and would therefore have reached Israel via the Mediterranean (Bourne 1983b).

Population On the most recent information, stemming from the 1960s, the total population of this species only numbers a few hundred (see below), but there is rather contrary evidence stemming from the turn of the century and the 1950s. Thus although the species appeared "rare everywhere" on the Cape Verdes when first discovered there in 1898 (Salvadori 1899), "great numbers" (assuming the identification was correct) were seen off Guinea in May 1897 (Bannerman 1914) and "considerable numbers" in the north-west approaches to the Cape Verdes, with "good-sized flocks" off Santo Antão, in September 1912 (Murphy 1924). In 1951, birds were reported by locals to be abundant on Fogo (see Remarks) and Santo Antão and were found by both report and observation to be common and widespread on São Tiago, and although no estimate of abundance could be made for São Nicolau it was concluded that there was then "still a very large population in the islands" (Bourne 1955). Nevertheless, while studies in the 1960s confirmed the bird's presence on three of the above islands – a mere day's search for it on São Nicolau was unsuccessful – it was then concluded that the total population "apparently hardly reaches several hundred pairs" (de Naurois 1969). In April 1976 in the waters around the Cape Verdes the species was uncommon, one to three usually being seen, the maximum together being eight north-west of Santo Antão; in the first half of October 1976 only six or seven birds in total were seen (Lambert 1980). On Bugio (Desertas, Madeira), about 50 pairs were known to be present, 1967-1968, with an unascertainable quantity on the steeper parts of the island (Jouanin *et al.* 1969); in 1976 the situation on Bugio was considered not to have changed (P. A. Zino *in litt.* to W. B. King 1976), but by July/August 1981 a comprehensive survey of the island yielded an estimated 30(-40) pairs (G. Le Grand *in litt.* 1984; also Swash in press).

Ecology In the Cape Verdes, the Gon-gon breeds in dispersed colonies (away from other seabirds) in burrows in rubble and earth screes or in cracks in rocky outcrops, up to 2,200 m (de Naurois 1969); it is assumed formerly to have nested in burrows in the floor of mountain woods, but all woodland is now gone (Bourne 1955). The main period for egg-laying (clutch-size one) is December/ January, fledging therefore occurring around May (Bourne 1955, de Naurois 1969, W. R. P. Bourne *in litt.* 1984). On Bugio (Desertas, Madeira), the species breeds in burrows in the turfy saddle of the island and in holes in steeper adjacent slopes (Jouanin *et al.* 1969), and is even reported mainly to breed in the island's vertical cliffs (Schmitz 1899). Egg-laying there apparently mostly occurs in July/August; fledging of a bird from an egg laid in late July would probably occur in late December, though there are records well before this (Jouanin *et al.* 1969). An observation of a bird standing and feeding on what appeared to be the carcass of a squid (Murphy 1924) seems to be still the only report concerning food in this species. Observations in April 1976 showed that birds were often in company with Cory's Shearwaters *Calonectris diomedea*, but did not come near ships (Lambert 1980). Between the Desertas and Madeira, birds have been seen more commonly during windy weather than in calm conditions (P. A. Zino *in litt.* 1984).

Threats The first and main decrease in numbers on Cape Verde can be expected to have occurred as a result of deforestation, possibly by fire, and the introduction of cats, rats *Rattus* and other mammals, confining the species to inaccessible nest-sites (W. R. P. Bourne *in litt.* 1984). Human depredation of seabirds in both the Cape Verdes and the Desertas is likely to have resulted in a further reduction in numbers of this species (Bannerman and Bannerman 1968, Jouanin *et al.* 1969) and is still extremely heavy (and considered the most serious threat) on the Desertas (P. A. Zino *in litt.* 1984). Moreover, on Fogo and perhaps elsewhere in Cape Verde the species was being exploited for "pseudo-medical" purposes some 20 years ago (de Naurois 1964). Apart from human depredation, the main threats on Bugio are vegetation destruction and soil erosion by goats and rabbits *Oryctolagus cuniculus*, and possibly competition for holes from rabbits: in July 1981 a rabbit was seen to roll a Gon-gon egg out of a burrow, and when it was replaced by the observer it was again rolled out, and so on, five times in all (G. Le Grand *in litt.* 1984). The presence of cats on Deserta Grande is assumed to be a reason why it does not now breed there (Cook and Yalden 1980), although it is questioned whether the species ever did so (see Distribution) and why (if it did) three other more accessible small seabirds should have survived such predation (P. A. Zino and G. E. Maul *in litt.* 1984).

Conservation Measures Taken None is known.

Conservation Measures Proposed A fresh survey of this species in Cape Verde is now required, together with an exhaustive evaluation of the factors that might be influencing its status adversely. Abolition of the "pseudo-medical" exploitation referred to under Threats has been called for (de Naurois 1964). Regular monitoring of the population on Bugio in the Desertas is also desirable, along with a sustained campaign of education amongst the fishermen responsible for seabird exploitation there. The need for and potential benefits of clarifying the status of Madeira in relation to European legislation are stated in Conservation Measures Proposed under Madeira Laurel Pigeon *Columba trocaz*.

Remarks The birds breeding on Bugio have been named *P. (mollis) "deserta"* but they were considered almost identical to the Cape Verde birds at the time the latter were named *P. m. feae* (Salvadori 1899,1900), and this has been confirmed by measurements (Jouanin *et al.* 1969). Taxonomic caution as to the bird's specific status (Bourne 1957) is now abandoned (Bourne 1983a). Concerning the species's occurrence in São Tiago, there is a small settlement just north of Malagueta peak named "Gon Gon" (in Ministério das Colónias 1948). Concerning the two records of single birds collected on Baixo and Porto Santo, these have been judged as referring to the same incident (Hartwig 1891) but the dates are in fact published and show that they do not. Concerning the report of the species on Cima (Porto Santo group, Madeira), it is to be noted that this has mistakenly been thought to refer to Baixo and therefore dismissed as no longer relevant (Jouanin *et al.* 1969). Concerning abundance on Fogo, the statement that the original collector, L. Fea, found them common (Bourne 1955) is in error, his only comment on numbers in Cape Verde in 1898 being quoted at the start of the entry under Population.

References

Bannerman, D. A. (1914) The distribution and nidification of the tubinares in the North Atlantic islands. *Ibis* (10)2: 438-494.

Bannerman, D. A. and Bannerman, W. M. (1965) *Birds of the Atlantic islands*, 2. Edinburgh and London: Oliver and Boyd.

Bannerman, D. A. and Bannerman, W. M. (1968) *Birds of the Atlantic islands*, 4. Edinburgh: Oliver and Boyd.

Bourne, W. R. P. (1955) The birds of the Cape Verde Islands. *Ibis* 97: 508-556.

Bourne, W. R. P. (1956) Notes on a skull of the genus *Bulweria* from St.Helena. *Bull. Brit. Orn. Club* 76: 126-129.

Bourne, W. R. P. (1957) Additional notes on the birds of the Cape Verde Islands, with particular reference to *Bulweria mollis* and *Fregata magnificens*. *Ibis* 99: 182-190.

Bourne, W. R. P. (1965) Observations of seabirds. *Sea Swallow* 17: 10-39.

Bourne, W. R. P. (1966) Further notes on the birds of the Cape Verde Islands. *Ibis* 108: 425-429.

Bourne, W. R. P. (1983a) The Soft-plumaged Petrel, the Gon-gon and the Freira, *Pterodroma mollis*, *P. feae* and *P. madeira*. *Bull. Brit. Orn. Club* 103: 52-58.

Bourne, W. R. P. (1983b) A Gon-gon *Pterodroma (mollis) feae* in Israel. *Bull. Brit. Orn. Club* 103: 110.

Bourne, W. R. P. and Dixon, T. J. (1973) Observations of seabirds 1967-1969. *Sea Swallow* 22: 29-60.

Bourne, W. R. P. and Dixon, T. J. (1975) Observations of seabirds 1970-1972. *Sea Swallow* 24: 65-88.

Cook, L. M. and Yalden, D. W. (1980) A note on the diet of feral cats on Deserta Grande. *Bocagiana* no. 52.

Dalgleish, J. J. (1890) [Letter.] *Ibis* (6)2: 386.

Dalgleish, J. J. (1891) Notes on the petrels of Madeira and adjoining seas. *Proc. Roy. Phys. Soc. Edinburgh* 11: 27-30.

Hartwig, W. (1891) Die Vögel der Madeira-Inselgruppe. *Ornis* 7: 151-188.

James, P. C. and Robertson, H. A. (in press) Soft-plumaged Petrels *Pterodroma mollis* at Great Salvage Island. *Bull. Brit. Orn. Club*.

Jouanin, C., Roux, F. and Zino, A. (1969) Visites aux lieux de nidification de *Pterodroma mollis "deserta"*. *Oiseau et R.F.O.* 39: 161-175.

Lambert, K. (1980) Beiträge zur Vogelwelt der Kapverdischen Inseln. *Beitr. Vogelkd.* 26: 1-18.

Ministério das Colónias (1948) *Atlas de Portugal Ultramarino e das grandes viagens portuguesas de descobrimento e expansão*. Lisboa: Junta das Missões Geográficas e de Investigações Coloniais.

Murphy, R. C. (1924) The marine ornithology of the Cape Verde Islands, with a list of all the birds of the archipelago. *Bull. Amer. Mus. Nat. Hist.* 50: 211-278.

de Naurois, R. (1964) Les oiseaux des îles du Cap-Vert. Suggestions en vue de leur sauvegarde. *Garcia de Orta* 12(4): 609-620.

de Naurois, R. (1969) Notes brèves sur l'avifaune de l'archipel du Cap-Vert. Faunistique, endémisme, écologie. *Bull. Inst. Fond. Afrique Noire* 31, Ser. A(1): 143-218.

de Noronha, A. (1902) Aus dem Vogelleben der Insel Porto Santo. *Orn. Jahrb.* 13: 130-135.

Salvadori, T. (1899) Collezioni ornitologiche fatte nelle Isole del Capo Verde da Leonardo Fea. *Ann. Mus. Civ. Genova* (2)20: 283-312.

Salvadori, T. (1900) On *Oestrelata mollis* (Gould) and the allied species living at Madeira and the Cape Verde Islands. *Ibis* (7)6: 298-303.

Schmitz, E. (1894) [Notiz.] *Orn. Monatsber.* 2: 195.

Schmitz, E. (1899) Die Vögel Madeira's. *Orn. Jahrb.* 10: 1-34, 41-66.

Schmitz, E. (1905) Tagebuch-Notizen aus Madeira. *Orn. Jahrb.* 16: 219-226.

Swash, A. R. H. (in press) Observations of birds in the Madeiran archipelago, summer 1981. *Bol. Mus. Mun. Funchal.*

FREIRA   ENDANGERED
Pterodroma madeira Mathews, 1934

Order PROCELLARIIFORMES   Family PROCELLARIIDAE

Summary This gadfly-petrel is known only from a few localities in the mountains of Madeira; the most encouraging of reports on its population indicates perhaps only 50 pairs.

Distribution The Freira is restricted as a breeding bird to the island of Madeira (Portugal) in the subtropical north-east Atlantic Ocean, and there known only from certain localities in the mountainous region in various directions around Pico do Cedro, and from two other localities (G. Le Grand *in litt.* 1984). It is conceivable that birds of this species or the Gon-gon *Pterodroma feae*, or perhaps birds intermediate between the two, will eventually be found in the Azores or the Canaries (Bourne 1965,1966, W. R. P. Bourne *in litt.* to W. B. King), but sea conditions are not considered favourable for gadfly-petrels *Pterodroma* around the former (G. Le Grand *in litt.* 1984). The distribution of this species at sea is wholly unknown, and the statement that it ranges along the West African coast as far south as 9°N (Jouanin and Mougin 1979) is a generalisation from observations made in September 1912 of what were probably Gon-gons (see Murphy 1924; also relevant account). Two small pale gadfly-petrels, resembling *madeira*, have been found dead on beaches in South Africa (eastern Cape Province, October 1973, and south-western Cape Province, June 1979) (Clancey *et al.* 1981), but seem likely to be immature examples of the Soft-plumaged Petrel *Pterodroma mollis* (Bourne 1983, W. R. P. Bourne *in litt.* 1984).

Population That perhaps 50 pairs were present at two small colonies visited in 1969 (Cramp and Simmons 1977) was no more than a guess, a maximum of 11 occupied burrows being found (R. de Naurois *in litt.* 1984). In 1981 these two sites held 20 pairs (G. Le Grand *in litt.* 1984).

Ecology There are no data concerning this species when at sea, either outside or inside the breeding season, nor have stomach-contents of specimens been noted. The species breeds in burrows by inland cliffs at 1,500 m (Cramp and Simmons 1977). Egg-laying (clutch-size one) occurs in May, fledging during October (W. R. P. Bourne *in litt.* 1984).

Threats It is argued that ancestors of this species colonised Madeira when it was cooler and wetter during the Pleistocene, so that its restriction now to the cool, moist upper slopes of the island is a natural consequence of climatic alteration (Bourne 1983). Nevertheless, it seems likely that other factors have influenced or continue to influence its status; rats *Rattus* are reported to be widespread in Madeira (Zino 1969), and doubtless cats and shepherd dogs (as well as shepherds) will have taken their toll (P. A. Zino and G. E. Maul *in litt.* 1984). For whatever reason, it is certainly likely that the species is indeed now "in grave danger" (Bourne 1983), and the greatest threat it now faces is believed to be from bird- and egg-collectors (P. A. Zino and G. E. Maul *in litt.* 1984).

Conservation Measures Taken None is known. "The Freira .... has been well-nigh ignored" (Bourne 1983).

Conservation Measures Proposed An intensive survey of the steeper upper slopes of the mountains of central Madeira, including interviews with local people and listening at night for calls of birds, is urgently needed to establish with greater certainty the distribution and numbers of this species. Exceedingly harsh (and well advertised) penalties for the taking of eggs would also seem appropriate. The need for and potential benefits of clarifying the status of Madeira in relation to European legislation are stated in Conservation Measures Proposed under Madeira Laurel Pigeon *Columba trocaz.*

Remarks The status of the Freira as a good species has only recently been proposed (Bourne 1983), but this step has been applauded (P. A. Zino and G. E. Maul *in litt.* 1984) and had been independently considered appropriate (R. de Naurois pers. comm. 1982).

References

Bannerman, D. A. and Bannerman, W. M. (1965) *Birds of the Atlantic islands*, 2. Edinburgh and London: Oliver and Boyd.

Bourne, W. R. P. (1965) The missing petrels. *Bull. Brit. Orn. Club* 85: 97-105.

Bourne, W. R. P. (1966) Further notes on the birds of the Cape Verde Islands. *Ibis* 108: 425-429.

Bourne, W. R. P. (1983) The Soft-plumaged Petrel, the Gon-gon and the Freira, *Pterodroma mollis, P. feae* and *P. madeira. Bull. Brit. Orn. Club* 103: 52-58.

Clancey, P. A., Brooke, R. K. and Sinclair, J. C. (1981) Variation in the current nominate subspecies of *Pterodroma mollis* (Gould) (Aves: Procellariidae). *Durban Mus. Novit.* 12(18): 203-213.

Cramp, S. and Simmons, K. E. L. eds. (1977) *The birds of the western Palearctic*, 1. Oxford: Oxford University Press.

Jouanin, C. and Mougin, J.-L. (1979) Order Procellariiformes. Pp. 48-121 in E. Mayr and G. W. Cottrell, eds. *Check-list of the birds of the world*, 1. 2nd edition, revision of the work of James L. Peters. Cambridge, Massachusetts: Museum of Comparative Zoology.

Murphy, R. C. (1924) The marine ornithology of the Cape Verde Islands, with a list of all the birds of the archipelago. *Bull. Amer. Mus. Nat. Hist.* 50: 211-278.

Zino, P. A. (1969) Observations sur *Columba trocaz. Oiseau et R.F.O.* 39: 261-264.

ASCENSION FRIGATEBIRD

RARE

Fregata aquila (Linnaeus, 1758)

Order PELICANIFORMES

Family FREGATIDAE

Summary The entire breeding population of this large seabird is confined to one tiny islet in the Atlantic Ocean, and since 1982 has been at considerably increased risk of serious disturbance.

Distribution The Ascension Frigatebird formerly bred on the lowland plains of Ascension Island (a dependency of the British Crown Colony of St.Helena), 7°57'S 14°22'W, in the tropical South Atlantic Ocean, but breeding birds are now entirely confined to the top of Boatswainbird Islet, a steep-sided flat-capped rock rising to 100 m, some 250 m off the north-east coast of Ascension (Stonehouse 1962). The top of Boatswainbird Islet measures less than 3 ha (calculated from map in Stonehouse 1962): in this area, four diffuse "colonies" were present, 1957-1959, with a roost on the leeward slopes of the islet (Stonehouse 1962). On Ascension itself, birds are known to roost on the cliffs at Crater Cliff (Simmons 1972a, Olson 1977), the cliffs at the adjacent Devil's Inkpot (Olson 1977) and the cliffs north of the Letterbox (Q. C. B. Cronk *in litt.* 1983), all these localities being near Boatswainbird Islet but at the extreme eastern point of Ascension (see map in Olson 1977). Both stacks in Pillar Bay on the south coast of Ascension held loafing (and therefore probably roosting) birds, 31 December 1976 (K. E. L. Simmons *in litt.* 1984). The species is not known to have bred elsewhere in the Atlantic and appears confined to the neighbouring waters of Ascension (Stonehouse and Stonehouse 1963); its distribution at sea may be constrained by the rather narrow tongue of nutrient-rich surface-water in which Ascension lies (see map in Stonehouse 1962). There is a record from 280 km north-east of the island in February 1963 (Simmons 1967) and from 10°S 12°W in October 1971 (Bourne and Dixon 1975), while the species has wandered to the western African coast from the Gulf of Guinea to the mouth of the Congo River (Brown *et al.* 1982).

Population In the eighteenth century the species is reported to have bred in "huge numbers" on Ascension (see Remarks), but evidently rapidly died out there following human settlement and the advent of cats in 1815 (Stonehouse 1962). Some 9,000-12,000 (8,000-10,000 breeding birds and 1,000-2,000 juveniles) were estimated to live on Boatswainbird Islet in the late 1950s (Stonehouse and Stonehouse 1963). An estimated 5,000 birds (2,500 on the top, 2,500 on the slopes and ledges) were visible on Boatswainbird from Ascension, 19 December 1976, with clearly many others out of sight (K. E. L. Simmons *in litt.* 1984). In April or May 1984 the number of immature birds at Ascension suggested that recent breeding success had been adequate and the population was probably still healthy (W. R. P. Bourne *in litt.* 1984).

Ecology All the evidence suggests this bird obtains most of its food well out in the ocean, even when pelagic fish come ashore or when Sooty Terns *Sterna fuscata* have chicks (K. E. L. Simmons *in litt.* 1984); and in April or May 1984 birds

47

were noted to be finding fish-shoals before other seabirds (W. R. P. Bourne *in litt.* 1984). The species, like all frigatebirds, is exclusively a flight-feeder whose methods comprise aerial-pursuit (both of flying-fish and of other seabirds which it harries to obtain their catch) and dipping-to-surface to snatch food-items in its bill from the water itself or from the bill of a surfacing plunge-diver, notably Brown Boobies *Sula leucogaster*; birds often hover while seeking food but typically form a soaring canopy above active congregations of other seabirds, periodically sky-dropping to feed in one of the above methods (Simmons 1967,1972b, K. E. L. Simmons *in litt.* 1984; terminology from Introduction to Cramp and Simmons 1983). The mostly immature birds present over congregations of Brown Boobies and Masked Boobies *S. dactylatra* in the Georgetown area took fish for themselves, mainly from the surf and off beaches, but also from the boobies (Simmons 1967, K. E. L. Simmons *in litt.* 1984). Food piracy from other seabirds seems to be performed by adult females and immatures (probably females) only (K. E. L. Simmons *in litt.* 1984). Food has been recorded as *Cypsilurus* and *Hirundichthyes* fish and the flying-fish *Exocoetus volitans* (Stonehouse 1962); apparently also newly hatched Green Turtles *Chelonia mydas* (Murphy 1936, Rose 1974). Small numbers of birds also attend Sooty Tern colonies (fairs), eating chicks (Ashmole 1962, Olson 1973, K. E. L. Simmons *in litt.* 1984). On Boatswainbird Islet, 1957-1959, most Frigatebirds bred among the stones and guano deposits of the rough basalt cap, but also on ledges and paths in steeper areas; on the top of the islet, birds preferred slightly sloping ground with hollows and boulders (Stonehouse and Stonehouse 1963). Birds bred throughout the year, but with an identifiable breeding season of eight or nine months (April to November or December) and a peak of activity in October, although it is possible this cycle was eleven-monthly rather than annual (Stonehouse and Stonehouse 1963). Clutch-size was one (Stonehouse and Stonehouse 1963). Chicks suffered high mortality before 20 days old, through aggression of other birds, but thereafter had a low mortality; young fledged when six or seven months old, but remained at least partly dependent on parents for a further three or four months (Stonehouse and Stonehouse 1963). Nest success was low, probably c. 15-20%, affected by breeding density and seasonal factors: it was highest among early breeders, out-of-season breeders and those in low density groups (Stonehouse and Stonehouse 1963).

Threats The extinction of the Ascension Frigatebird on Ascension itself is directly attributable to predation by feral cats (Stonehouse 1962). Cats are still present there and are responsible for continuing heavy predation of roosting birds at the eastern end of the island (Simmons 1972a,1977, Olson 1977, Q. C. B. Cronk *in litt.* 1983), and are clearly therefore preventing any recolonisation of it there or elsewhere. The general conservation prospects on Ascension deteriorated in the period 1966-1972, when not only were measures to control feral cats spasmodic and largely ineffective but the human population and the concomitant number of domestic animals greatly increased (following the establishing of the BBC Atlantic Relay Station), and Boatswainbird Islet became subject to increased disturbance with three or more sightseeing visits (by parties of up to 30 people) per year (Simmons 1972a; K. E. L. Simmons *in litt.* 1984): such visits may have continued until 1977 (see Conservation Measures Taken). It was felt that the main problem since 1966 had been the lack of effective education concerning the island's wildlife for a community with a rapid population turnover (Simmons 1972a). In 1982, political considerations dictated an enormous expansion of installations and activity on Ascension, the impact of which on the island's seabirds is unknown: concerns are that Boatswainbird Islet will be disturbed by increased visits (despite Conservation Measures Taken) and low-flying aircraft, and that control measures may be instituted against the Ascension Frigatebird (and other seabirds) because of the hazard of air-strikes following the increase in air traffic (K. E. L. Simmons *in litt.* 1984).

Conservation Measures Taken The purely personal initiatives of one biologist on short visits in 1972-1973 and 1976-1977 resulted in some local education in conservation (lectures) and in the decision, in early 1977, to prohibit pleasure-trips to Boatswainbird Islet and to place visits there for scientific and conservation purposes under control of the island administrator (Simmons 1972a, 1974, 1977, K. E. L. Simmons *in litt.* 1984).

Conservation Measures Proposed To maintain the stability of seabird populations on Ascension and Boatswainbird Islet, particularly now that the human presence is vastly increased and more disruptive (potentially if not actually), a sustainable programme of education and conservation is urgently required, with concomitant research on and monitoring of the wildlife involved, with particular emphasis on the Frigatebird. Boatswainbird Islet, described (surely correctly) as "the premier breeding station for seabirds in the tropical South Atlantic" (Simmons 1972a), merits protected area status. Strict control of the numbers and behaviour of domestic cats and dogs on Ascension is necessary (Simmons 1972a). A renewal of measures to control feral cat numbers, aiming at complete extirpation, is highly desirable and, because there is a three-month starvation period for cats while Ascension's Sooty Terns are absent from the island, apparently feasible (Stonehouse 1962, Simmons 1972a): this would almost certainly result in the recolonisation of Ascension by many seabird species, including the Frigatebird, that formerly bred there. A study of factors (other than disturbance and predation) possibly detrimental to wildlife, e.g. marine pollution, is important (Simmons 1972a). For the implementation of all these measures, a full-time professional conservation officer is required (Simmons 1976) and a resident staff of biologists desirable (Simmons 1972a).

Remarks That the species was ever present in very large numbers at Ascension has been doubted, Boatswainbird Islet itself not holding birds at carrying capacity (W. R. P. Bourne *in litt.* 1984).

References

Ashmole, N. P. (1962) The biology of the Wideawake or Sooty Tern *Sterna fuscata* on Ascension Island. *Ibis* 103b: 297-364.

Bourne, W. R. P. and Dixon, T. J. (1975) Observations of seabirds 1970-1972. *Sea-Swallow* 24: 65-88.

Brown, L. H., Urban, E. K. and Newman, K. (1982) *The birds of Africa*, 1. London: Academic Press.

Cramp, S. and Simmons, K. E. L. eds. (1983) *The birds of the western Palearctic*, 3. Oxford: Oxford University Press.

Murphy, R. C. (1936) *Oceanic birds of South America*. New York: American Museum of Natural History.

Olson, S. L. (1973) Evolution of the rails of the South Atlantic Islands. *Smithsonian Contrib. Zool.* 152.

Olson, S. L. (1977) Additional notes on subfossil bird remains from Ascension Island. *Ibis* 119: 37-43.

Rose, P. J. (1974) Some visits to Ascension Island. *Sea-Swallow* 23: 25-28.

Simmons, K. E. L. (1967) The role of food-supply in the biology of the Brown Booby *Sula leucogaster* at Ascension Island. M.Sc. thesis, University of Bristol.

Simmons, K. E. L. (1972a) Ascension Island: the need for effective conservation. A draft memorandum to the B.O.U. Council.

Simmons, K. E. L. (1972b) Some adaptive features of seabird plumage types. *Brit. Birds* 65: 465-479, 510-521.

Simmons, K. E. L. (1974) Biology of the Brown Booby and conservation at Ascension Island. Report to the Royal Society.

Simmons, K. E. L. (1976) Statement: visit to Ascension Island, December 1976. Unpublished.

Simmons, K. E. L. (1977) Biology of the Brown Booby and seabird conservation at Ascension Island – a report to the Royal Society.

Stonehouse, B. (1962) Ascension Island and the British Ornithologists' Union Centenary Expedition 1957-59. *Ibis* 103b: 107-123.

Stonehouse, B. and Stonehouse, S. (1963) The frigate bird *Fregata aquila* of Ascension Island. *Ibis* 103b: 409-422.

SLATY EGRET   INDETERMINATE
Egretta vinaceigula (Sharpe, 1895)

Order CICONIIFORMES   Family ARDEIDAE
                                          Subfamily ARDEINAE

Summary Confirmation of this egret as a distinct species came only in 1971 and nothing is known of its past status. Its centres of distribution are the Okavango Delta in northern Botswana (whence come the only breeding records), the Caprivi Strip in Namibia, and the Kafue Flats, Liuwa Plain and Bangweulu Swamp in Zambia, but it is nowhere common: flood regulation has caused it to disappear from one part of Kafue Flats and there are plans that may seriously affect the ecology of the Okavango Delta.

Distribution The Slaty Egret, which for many years was considered a variant of the Black Egret *Egretta ardesiaca* (see Benson *et al.* 1971, Irwin 1975), chiefly occurs in the floodplains of Zambia and northern Botswana, and in the Caprivi Strip, Namibia. In Zambia, birds are most often reported from the floodplains of the Kafue Flats (Blue Lagoon and Lochinvar National Parks) and of the Liuwa Plain National Park, with records from several other localities from the Zambezi River north to Bangweulu Swamp and the Nchelenge District near Lake Mweru on the Zaire border (Dowsett 1981; also 1979). In Botswana, the species occurs widely throughout the Okavango Delta and Chobe National Park (Benson *et al.* 1971, Vernon 1971, Irwin 1975, Milewski 1976, Dowsett 1981, Mathews and McQuaid 1983). In the Caprivi Strip, records are from Kabuta, Schuckmannsburg, the Chobe River opposite Kasane in Botswana, and the Kwando River in the south-western bulge of the Strip (Dowsett 1981, A. J. Tree *in litt.* 1983, A. J. Williams *in litt.* 1983). The only breeding localities known are two in northern Botswana, one c. 25 km up the Chobe River from Kasane (Benson *et al.* 1971), the other in a mixed heronry at Xakanaxa lagoon in the Moremi Wildlife Reserve (Dowsett 1981), although it is likely to breed in Zambia too (Dowsett 1981). The species is expected to occur in south-eastern Angola (Benson *et al.* 1971), and may perhaps also do so in the Upemba basin in southern Zaire. There are now (at least) five acceptable sightings (of wanderers) in eastern Zimbabwe (Tree 1979, 1982, 1983, Pollard 1981), but two sight-records from Malawi (Day and Hanmer 1978) are not fully substantiated (Dowsett 1981). Although the first three specimens known were collected in the last century at Potchefstroom in Transvaal, South Africa (see Hancock and Elliott 1978), there have been no further records from that area and they may merely have been wanderers (Benson *et al.* 1971; for discussion of movements, see Ecology).

Population There are no estimates of numbers and birds are difficult to census (see Ecology), but the species is generally considered sparse and uncommon (Benson *et al.* 1971, Brown *et al.* 1982, A. J. Tree *in litt.* 1983). Assuming that its major localities are already known (which is by no means certain), then the population is unlikely to total many thousands (R. J. Dowsett *in litt.* 1982). However, in August/September 1981 it was found to be "far from rare" in the

Okavango, with sightings almost daily and increasing towards the centre of the delta as sightings of Black Egrets grew fewer; "a group of over forty" was seen (Fothergill 1983), and "particularly large numbers" were encountered (with one group of 15) in the Jau (Jao) flats region (Dryden 1982, Fothergill 1982). On the Liuwa Plain and the Kafue Flats in Zambia it occurs in parties of up to 30 (Dowsett 1981), but the tens of birds that formerly occurred in Blue Lagoon National Park up to the mid-1970s are now gone (D. R. Aspinwall *in litt.* 1984). "Large flocks" were put up from the edge of Bangweulu Swamp during an aerial survey, June 1981 (D. R. Aspinwall *in litt.* 1981), though no birds were seen there for certain during another aerial survey, October 1983 (D. R. Aspinwall *in litt.* 1984).

Ecology The chief needs of this species is shallow expanses of receding water (i.e. seasonally inundated flood-plains, swamps), with a good growth of stranded aquatic vegetation (Vernon 1971, Irwin 1981, Mathews and McQuaid 1983, R. J. Dowsett *in litt.* 1982, A. J. Tree *in litt.* 1983). In contrast to both Black Egret and Little Egret *Egretta garzetta*, it feeds in shallower, more peripheral water (Vernon 1971, Milewski 1976, Dowsett 1981); birds in varying parts of the Okavango were feeding on open grassy plains in c. 5 cm water (Milewski 1976, Dryden 1982), the herbaceous cover often being tall and dense enough to conceal birds except when they stretch or fly up or emerge at the edge, this making numbers difficult to estimate (Milewski 1976, D. R. Aspinwall *in litt.* 1984). In contrast to the Black Egret, the Slaty Egret is not known to form its wings in an "umbrella" or "canopy" when feeding (Benson *et al.* 1971, Vernon 1971, Milewski 1976, Dowsett 1981), and its wings are not structurally adapted for this (Irwin 1975). Although commonly found to be a solitary feeder (Benson *et al.* 1971, Milewski 1976, A. J. Tree *in litt.* 1983), birds may also feed in groups together and in company (even direct association) with other bird species, e.g. Greenshank *Tringa nebularia* (Mathews and McQuaid 1983; also Vernon 1971, Milewski 1976), and this variation can occur in a diurnal pattern: thus in the early morning and evening (the species being one of the earliest to arrive to feed and often the last to leave), when fish were probably mostly near the surface, birds were more solitary and used a wait-and-strike tactic, but in the early afternoon, when fish were probably mostly low in the vegetation, birds moved about much more actively and in various associations (up to eight together), using foot movements successfully to flush out prey (Mathews and McQuaid 1983; see also Milewski 1976). In the Caprivi Strip birds have been noted feeding along channels, even at the edge of relatively deep water where fish surfaced in the evening (A. J. Tree *in litt.* 1983). Food is predominantly fish (Dowsett 1981, Mathews and McQuaid 1983, A. J. Tree *in litt.* 1983), though occasionally snails are gleaned from vegetation and dragonflies snapped up as they fly past a standing bird (Mathews and McQuaid 1983); frogs and aquatic insects are probably also taken (A. J. Tree *in litt.* 1983). Nesting has been observed in May in a reed-bed (Benson *et al.* 1971) and in June in a thicket of wild fig *Ficus verruculosa*, the one nest examined containing three nestlings (Dowsett 1981). The few observations suggest breeding colonies are small (Dowsett 1981). Movements in this species certainly occur, as is expected in a bird that depends on shallowly flooded grassland (e.g. Vernon 1971, Milewski 1976), but the evidence is somewhat conflicting and no clear-cut seasonal migration is apparent: despite being recorded from Zambia in every month and with extensive observations at Lochinvar (Kafue Flats) indicating no substantial movement of birds, there are rainy season (December to April) records from areas otherwise totally dry and, conversely, increased numbers, possibly representing a post-breeding dispersal, on Liuwa Plains and Kafue Flats in the dry season (Dowsett 1981). The species disappears from the Chobe National Park, Botswana, during the rains (Vernon 1971), and there is a midsummer influx at this time into western Okavango and apparently a summer arrival at Moremi from October (Milewski 1976, Mathews and McQuaid 1983); the sight-records from Malawi (see Distribution) were from November and December and are speculated to have resulted from an eastward summer movement to the extensive areas of marsh and flooded grassland around Lake Malawi and the Shire and Zambezi Rivers, Malawi and north-western Mozambique (Day and Hanmer 1978) – this, incidentally, following a time when birds appear to be absent from Bangweulu Swamp (see Population).

Threats Habitat needs have been suggested as the cause of the Slaty Egret's limited distribution (Vernon 1971), but this is considered improbable (the necessary conditions appear widespread, year-round): it may be a relict species, declining naturally towards extinction through some unknown factor (Irwin 1975; also Hancock and Elliott 1978), e.g. unsuccessful competition with the Black Egret (Benson *et al.* 1971). Even so, land-use alterations are likely to affect its numbers seriously (Dowsett 1981): the Kafue Flats are already subject to regulation by damming (resulting in the species's complete disappearance from the Blue Lagoon National Park in the mid-1970s: D. R. Aspinwall *in litt.* 1984), Bangweulu Swamp is the subject of a hydro-electric scheme proposal, and there are plans to clear the Okavango Delta of tsetse fly *Glossina morsitans*, which may result in substantial damage either from chemicals or a subsequent invasion of cattle (see Threats under Wattled Crane *Bugeranus carunculatus*). Other Ciconiiformes breeding in southern Zambia are subjected to persecution, nestlings being reported in 1974 to be taken from the colonies for food (T. O. Osborne *per* R. J. Dowsett *in litt.* 1982).

Conservation Measures Taken All egrets are totally protected by law in Zambia (Dowsett 1971), but this is difficult to enforce (Dowsett 1981). The main areas of concentration in Zambia occur or occurred within national parks (Lochinvar, Blue Lagoon and Liuwa Plain), although the reported desertion of Blue Lagoon (see Threats above) may mean Lochinvar is also now deserted, being likewise on the Kafue Flats. A small part of the Okavango Delta in Botswana (including the two known breeding localities of Slaty Egret) is within the Moremi Wildlife Reserve and Chobe National Park (R. J. Dowsett *in litt.* 1982).

Conservation Measures Proposed Reinforcement of the integrity of Lochinvar National Park and permanent protection for a larger part of the Okavango Delta are needed (R. J. Dowsett *in litt.* 1982). Ecological studies of the species are clearly important to determine the factors affecting its numbers and distribution.

References

Benson, C. W., Brooke, R. K. and Irwin, M. P. S. (1971) The Slatey Egret *Egretta vinaceigula* is a good species. *Bull. Brit. Orn. Club* 91: 131-133.

Brown, L. H., Urban, E. K. and Newman, K. (1982) *The birds of Africa*, 1. London: Academic Press.

Day, D. H. and Hanmer, D. B. (1978) [Letter.] *Bokmakierie* 30: 108.

Dowsett, R. J. (1971) Bird conservation in Zambia. *ICBP Bull.* 11: 229-233.

Dowsett, R. J. (1979) Recent additions to the Zambian list. *Bull. Brit. Orn. Club* 99: 94-98.

Dowsett, R. J. (1981) Breeding and other observations on the Slaty Egret *Egretta vinaceigula*. *Bull. Brit. Orn. Club* 101: 323-327.

Dryden, M. (1982) Bird list, in: The Okavango Swamps Expedition 1981: a report. Privately printed.

Fothergill, A. (1982) British undergraduate expedition to the Okavango Delta – interesting observations. *Babbler* no. 4: 7-8.

Fothergill, A. (1983) Okavango: land of restless waters. *Wildlife* 25: 131-134.

Hancock, J. and Elliott, H. (1978) *The herons of the world*. London: London Editions.

Irwin, M. P. S. (1975) Adaptive morphology in the Black and Slatey Egrets *Egretta ardesiaca* and *Egretta vinaceigula*, and relationships within the genus *Egretta*. *Bonn. zool. Beitr.* 26: 155-163.

Irwin, M. P. S. (1981) *The birds of Zimbabwe*. Salisbury, Zimbabwe: Quest Publishing.

Mathews, N. and McQuaid, C. D. (1983) The feeding ecology of the slatey egret (*Egretta vinaceigula*). *Afr. J. Ecol.* 21: 235-240.

Milewski, A. V. (1976) Feeding ecology of the Slaty Egret *Egretta vinaceigula*. *Ostrich* 47: 132-134.

Pollard, C. J. W. (1981) Sighting of the Slatey Egret *Egretta vinaceigula* at Kazungula. *Honeyguide* no. 106: 38.

Tree, A. J. (1979) Recent interesting observations in Mashonaland. *Honeyguide* no. 97: 18-24.

Tree, A. J. (1982) Recent reports. *Honeyguide* no. 109: 22-28.

Tree, A. J. (1983) Recent reports. *Honeyguide* nos. 111-112 [1982]: 45-50.

Vernon, C. J. (1971) Observations on *Egretta vinaceigula*. *Bull. Brit. Orn. Club* 91: 157-159.

MADAGASCAR HERON   INSUFFICIENTLY KNOWN
Ardea humbloti Milne Edwards and Grandidier, 1885

Order CICONIIFORMES   Family ARDEIDAE
                                                        Subfamily ARDEINAE

Summary Mostly at best uncommon, this large but very little known Malagasy waterbird was reported in 1973 to have declined alarmingly and to face extinction unless completely protected, although it appears still to be safe in parts of the west coast of Madagascar.

Distribution The Madagascar Heron occurs thinly throughout western Madagascar, chiefly in coastal and adjacent areas, but apparently rarely in the east. Records of this species are relatively few and many appear to involve wandering individuals. Only three breeding sites appear to have been found, in the extreme north (locality not specified), in the extreme south-west (locality not specified), and on Nosy Manitra off the south-west coast, west of Pointe Fenambosy (Pointe Barrow) (Milon *et al.* 1973), although a specimen in BMNH from Lake Ihotry, collected on 8 December 1929, is labelled "breeding" and another in MNHN from Tuléar, 18 May 1948, had well developed testes (NJC). Other localities from which birds have been reported are chiefly in the north-west around Majunga, including Majunga itself (Muddiman 1983), Ampijoroa in the Ankarafantsika area (Milon *et al.* 1973), Ambato-Boeni (Salvan 1970), along the Betsiboka River between Ambato-Boeni and Majunga (O. Langrand *in litt.* 1984), and Lake Kinkony (Rand 1936); birds have also been found further north on the coast opposite Nosy Bé (Rand 1936), and well to the south at Berevo on the Tsiribihina River (Bangs 1918), at Lakes Masama and Bemamba near Antsalova (O. Langrand *in litt.* 1984), at Lake Ihotry (Rand 1936) and on a marsh between Lake Ihotry and Morombe (Muddiman 1983). In the central part of Madagascar there have been three records from Antananarivo (Milon 1949, Milon *et al.* 1973), two from Lake Itasy (Salvan 1970,1972, H. A. W. Payne *per* K. H. Voous *in litt.* 1983), one at the lake near Antsimangana, north of Lake Alaotra towards Andimalena, 20 June 1960 (H. A. W. Payne *per* K. H. Voous *in litt.* 1983), and an unspecified number (but more than three) from Lake Alaotra itself (Milon *et al.* 1973, H. A. W. Payne *per* K. H. Voous *in litt.* 1983). Although the type-specimen was from the "east coast" (Milne Edwards and Grandidier 1885), the only other record from the east is of an immature that stayed near Maroantsetra from December 1982 to April 1983 (O. Langrand *in litt.* 1984). Individuals have thrice been recorded from the Comoro Islands: Moheli in September 1958 (Benson 1960), Mayotte in October 1965 (Forbes-Watson 1969), and again on Mayotte in July and August 1974 (D. A. Turner *in litt.* 1983, A. D. Forbes-Watson pers. comm. 1984).

Population Numbers are evidently rather small, and perhaps localised. The colony on Nosy Manitra consisted of five to eight nests, July 1948 (Milon 1948); the other colony in the south-west consists (or consisted) of "several nests each year" (Milon *et al.* 1973); at the site in the far north it is not clear if more than one nest was found (see Milon *et al.* 1973). Thirteen birds were collected by the

Mission Franco-Anglo-Américaine, 1929-1931 (Delacour 1932), which appears to be all or almost all of the birds seen during that period of study (reported as three to four opposite Nosy Bé, "a few" at Lake Kinkony, four at Lake Ihotry: see Rand 1936). All other records appear to concern single individuals only. In 1973 it was reported that recent observations had indicated an alarming decline (Milon *et al.* 1973), but further details were not and have not subsequently been given. Despite all this, two independent observers in the 1970s and 1980s provide more encouraging information, the species being thought "not uncommon" in some areas of the west coast between Majunga and Morondava, though rare elsewhere (D. A. Turner *in litt.* 1983, O. Langrand *in litt.* 1984); it has also been found "very common" in two areas, along the Betsiboka River, where 40 were counted between Ambato-Boeni and Majunga, April 1982, and at Lakes Masama and Bemamba, date unspecified (O. Langrand *in litt.* 1984).

Ecology The ecology of this species is probably much as other large herons *Ardea*, although the large bill, sombre colouring and observed adroitness in mandibulating prey are considered evidence of specialisation for feeding on large mobile fish rather than on a wider range of aquatic prey (Hancock and Elliott 1978). Both small and large fish (including a 48 cm eel) are recorded as food (Rand 1936, Benson 1960, Forbes-Watson 1969); it feeds in shallow water in lakes and along river banks and on the seashore (e.g. on reefs, at fish-weirs and in estuaries), and is recorded also from rice-fields (Rand 1936, Benson 1960, Forbes-Watson 1969, O. Langrand *in litt.* 1984). Although apparently solitary, it nests in mixed heronries; at one site (in the far north of Madagascar) it has been found nesting at ground level in a vegetation-swathed coral hollow (Milon *et al.* 1973). Breeding (clutch-size three) has been reported in July (Milon *et al.* 1973) and is considered likely (from gonad condition) in December (Rand 1936). Natural predators may include the Madagascar Fish Eagle *Haliaeetus vociferoides*, since a bird has been seen to be attacked by one of these raptors, escaping by diving under water (Langrand and Meyburg in press).

Threats The species is perhaps naturally uncommon and localised, and very possibly in competition with the more numerous Grey Heron *Ardea cinerea* and Purple Heron *A. purpurea*. The species's large size and relative tameness were considered in 1973 to expose it to risk, presumably from native hunters, and it was asserted that, having recently suffered an alarming decline, it would soon become extinct unless completely and carefully protected (Milon *et al.* 1973). In 1961, however, under Decree no. 61-096, both Grey and Purple Herons – although represented by endemic Malagasy subspecies – were classified as harmful animals, a situation which still obtained in 1973 (Forbes-Watson and Turner 1973): to the untrained eye the Madagascar Heron is so like these species that it cannot have escaped any persecution of them that may have been – and perhaps still is – officially encouraged. Ardeid colonies commonly suffer exploitation by locals for eggs (O. Langrand *in litt.* 1984). Rice-growing is reportedly beginning to alter Lake Bemamba (O. Langrand *in litt.* 1984).

Conservation Measures Taken None is known; however, in 1948 the wood which held the colony on Nosy Manitra was protected through a local taboo (Milon 1948, Milon *et al.* 1973).

Conservation Measures Proposed Studies are needed to determine the number and distribution of colonies of this species, its ecological requirements and long-term trends: such work might be linked with similar work on the Madagascar Pond-heron *Ardeola idae* (see Appendix C), and on the endangered Madagascar Fish Eagle. Complete and active protection for it (including the banning of further collection of specimens) and for its breeding sites is essential (Milon *et al.* 1973, Hancock and Elliott 1978). The prohibition of the taking by locals of colonial waterbirds' and seabirds' eggs would be a great step forward for conservation in Madagascar (O. Langrand *in litt.* 1984). For the need for a general ornithological survey of both west and east coast wetlands in Madagascar, and for the possible importance of wetlands around Cap St.André and of a proposed faunal reserve in the Antsalova region, see Conservation Measures Proposed under Madagascar Teal *Anas bernieri*.

Remarks "This and perhaps Swinhoe's Egret [*Egretta eulophotes*, treated in King 1978-1979] may claim to be the two heron species which are most in need of every care and protection if they are to survive" (Hancock and Elliott 1978).

References

Bangs, O. (1918) [Vertebrata from Madagascar.] Aves. *Bull. Mus. Comp. Zool.* 61: 489-511.

Benson, C. W. (1960) The birds of the Comoro Islands: results of the British Ornithologists' Union Centenary Expedition 1958. *Ibis* 103b: 5-106.

Delacour, J. (1932) Les oiseaux de la Mission Franco-Anglo-Américaine à Madagascar. *Oiseau et R.F.O.* 2: 1-96.

Forbes-Watson, A. D. (1969) Notes on birds observed in the Comoros on behalf of the Smithsonian Institution. *Atoll Res. Bull.* no. 128.

Forbes-Watson, A. D. and Turner, D. A. (1973) Report on bird preservation in Madagascar, part 2. Report to ICBP, unpublished.

Hancock, J. and Elliott, H. (1978) *The herons of the world*. London: London Editions.

King, W. B. (1978-1979) *Red data book, 2: Aves.* 2nd edition. Morges, Switzerland: IUCN.

Langrand, O. and Meyburg, B.-U. (in press) Birds of prey and owls in Madagascar: their distribution, status and conservation. Second symposium on African predatory birds, 22-26 August 1983.

Milne Edwards, A. and Grandidier, A. (1885) *Histoire physique, naturelle et politique de Madagascar, 12. Histoire naturelle des oiseaux*. Tome I. Paris.

Milon, P. (1948) Notes d'observation à Madagascar. *Alauda* 16: 55-74.

Milon, P. (1949) Tableaux d'identification des échassiers blancs et des échassiers noirs observés aux abords de Tananarive. *Naturaliste Malgache* 1(2): 93-100.

Milon, P., Petter, J.-J. and Randrianasolo, G. (1973) *Faune de Madagascar, 35. Oiseaux*. Tananarive and Paris: ORSTOM and CNRS.

Muddiman, N. (1983) List of birds seen in Madagascar, 12 May – 3 December 1982. Unpublished manuscript.

Rand, A. L. (1936) The distribution and habits of Madagascar birds. *Bull. Amer. Mus. Nat. Hist.* 72: 143-499.

Salvan, J. (1970) Remarques sur l'évolution de l'avifaune malgache depuis 1945. *Alauda* 38: 191-203.

Salvan, J. (1972) Statut, recensement, reproduction des oiseaux dulçaquicoles aux environs de Tananarive. *Oiseau et R.F.O.* 42: 35-51.

SHOEBILL   OF SPECIAL CONCERN
Balaeniceps rex Gould, 1850

Order CICONIIFORMES   Family BALAENICIPITIDAE

Summary This huge, extraordinary species, which represents a monotypic family, is widely but very locally distributed through the swamps of eastern and central Africa, where it subsists on fish and other aquatic vertebrates. In most of its range it is threatened in the medium or long term by the development and disturbance of its habitat but it is apparently not yet in any serious danger of extinction.

Distribution The Shoebill is widely distributed through the swamplands of Sudan, Uganda, and parts of Zaire and Zambia; it is also present in Central African Republic, Ethiopia, Rwanda and Tanzania, and there have been reports, mostly not accepted, from Angola, Botswana, Cameroon, Kenya and Malawi. Such reports of the species outside its known main range must mostly refer to wandering individuals. It has been speculated that the species might also occur in the Lake Chad basin (Fischer 1970) but there are no records. Evidence from sculptures suggests that Shoebills occurred in ancient Egypt (von Rosen 1961), but similar evidence from a rock painting above the Maleme Dam in the Matopo (now Matobo) Hills in Zimbabwe, suggesting that the species was present in the Maleme Valley during wetter conditions 3,000 years ago (Cooke 1964), has recenty been found wanting (Brooke *et al.* 1982).

Angola A record from the upper Cunene River in southern Angola in 1882 (Johnston 1883) is of doubtful validity (Benson *et al.* 1970).

Botswana Two birds were seen near South Gate, Moremi Wildlife Reserve, in the Okavango Swamps in the late 1970s (Matthews 1979).

Cameroon One bird was reported in dry savanna at a roadside at Guetale, near Koza, in 1953 (de Lisle 1956): this record has not, however, found universal acceptance (Louette 1981).

Central African Republic A pair was seen at Lake Gata in 1939 (Blancou 1939) and another bird was seen in the same year on the Ouandjia River, upstream of the junction with the Vakaga River (Blancou 1961). Other reports are from the upper Aouk River and Lake Mamoun, and possibly also further east in the Mangueigne area (Malbrant 1952; also C. A. Spinage *in litt.* 1984). Suggestions that the species is only a migratory visitor to this part of central Africa (Dragesco 1960) have been strongly contested (Blancou 1961).

Ethiopia The Shoebill was first noted in Ethiopia in 1961 or 1962 along the Baro River (Urban 1967). In 1973 one bird was seen at Ubela Waterhole and two pairs were recorded just north of Tedo (Duckworth 1974). All these records are from the Gambela District of south-western Ethiopia (Urban 1967, Duckworth 1974).

Kenya There is an unconfirmed report of this species being occasionally seen on the "north-eastern shores" of Lake Victoria at the beginning of this century (Johnston 1902). Otherwise the Shoebill has been chiefly known in Kenya from the nearby Yala Swamp (Britton 1978,1980), but the single record for this site is now known to have been a hoax (G. R. Cunningham-van Someren *in litt.* 1983, D. A. Turner *in litt.* 1983). There are also reports of the species from Fourteen Falls, Thika, in 1971 and the Engare N'giro Swamp north of Shombole in 1976 (Preston 1976) which are now known to have involved distant views of Marabou Storks *Leptoptilus crumeniferus* (D. A. Turner *in litt.* 1983).

Malawi Reports of the Shoebill from swamps at the northern end of Lake Malawi (Fischer 1970) are very doubtful since there is no mention of the species in the latest review of the avifauna of that country (Benson and Benson 1977), and there is now no habitat suitable (R. J. Dowsett and F. Dowsett-Lemaire *in litt.* 1983).

Rwanda There are several records of this species from the Kagera River and the Akagera National Park, including at Kadjumbura, Kitobela, Lake Mihindi and Lake Ihema (Burton and Benson 1961, Curry-Lindahl 1961, Verschuren 1965, Schouteden 1966, Vande weghe 1981). Birds have also been seen between June and September in the Nyabwongo and Akanyaru Swamps in southern Rwanda, these birds presumably being non-breeding visitors (Vande weghe 1981).

Sudan The type-specimen was collected on the upper part of the White Nile (Bahr-al-Jebel) (Gould 1851). By the beginning of this century the species was known to be widespread in the Sudd region of southern Sudan, inhabiting the swamps of the Bahr-al-Ghazal from Lake No to Meshra-el-Rek, the Jur River and the swamps of the Bahr-al-Jebel near Shambe (Butler 1905). By 1955 it had been found as far north as Kodok and as far south as Malek on the White Nile, and also west along the River Lol to Aweil (Cave and Macdonald 1955, Owen 1958). A more recent survey, carried out in 1976 and 1977, shows that the Shoebill's distribution in southern Sudan has contracted considerably (Guillet 1977,1978). In the west of its Sudanese range around Aweil only three nesting populations survive at Adiang, Adorit and War Dit (Guillet 1977,1978). Further to the east the birds also nest where the Alal and Anam Rivers join the Lol River, this population also extending south to Apuk (Guillet 1977,1978). On the Pongo River a population survives where the river divides to form the Kyom and the Lol Akweir (Guillet 1977,1978). On the Jur River the species is now restricted to the lower reaches, mainly around Majak Juer, though there is also an isolated population 15 km east of Gogrial, between Fanriar and Machoir-Akaltum (Guillet 1977,1978). There are some important sites for the species along the Bahr-al-Ghazal, especially around Makwoich, Lake Ambadi and Bentiu (Guillet 1977,1978). Along the Tonj River Shoebills are now restricted to the northern part around Lol Akweir, Wunshwai, Manabuk and Akaltum (Guillet 1977,1978). They also occur at the northern end of the Bar Gel, and what is probably a different population occurs on the Bar Naam, birds going to feed but no longer breeding south of Lol Akow (Guillet 1977,1978). On the Lau River a permanent population exists around Lake Nyubor, but otherwise birds only visit in order to exploit seasonal changes in prey availability (Guillet 1977,1978). Suitable nesting sites survive on the (South Sudan) Bahr-al-Jebel (White Nile) system, though probably few birds remain in the southern part between Juba and Bor (Guillet 1977,1978). Other sightings of birds to the east of the main Sudd region, to the north of Kapoeta, may represent a further hitherto undiscovered breeding population (Guillet 1977,1978), and there is predicted to be a relict community of birds near the junction of the Sobat River and Khor Fulus, representing the last north-eastern outlier of the Sudanese population (Guillet 1977). It is clear that the Shoebill now has a very patchy distribution in southern Sudan, the reasons for this being discussed more fully under Population, Ecology and Threats.

Tanzania There have been several records of this species from western Tanzania, especially from the area west of Lake Victoria (Burton and Benson 1961). Sites from which the species is known west of Lake Victoria are Lake Mujungu, Lake Mujungwizi, Lake Burigi, the Kyerwa Tin Mine and the Kagera Swamp (Burton and Benson 1961, Britton 1980). Further south the species has been recorded at Nkilandagoga (probably the same as Nzilindagaza) near Kibondo, and in the Malagarasi Swamp east of Kigoma (Burton and Benson 1961, Britton 1980); the likelihood that the Shoebill is widely distributed in the large, but poorly explored, swamps of western Tanzania (Vande weghe 1981) is strongly increased by the frequent observations of birds in August/September 1971 during an aerial survey of Moyowosi Swamp, 4°50'S 31°24'E, the species being concentrated in the south-east side (Parker 1984). Reports of birds from Lake Rukwa in south-western Tanzania in 1955, 1957 and 1962 probably refer to wanderers, since there is no suitable breeding habitat in this area (Burton and Benson 1961, Dean 1962,1963). Most records of this species in Tanzania are from the 1950s and there is no recent information except from Moyowosi Swamp.

Uganda The Shoebill appears to be widespread in Uganda, though with a fragmented distribution due to swamp availability (Britton 1980). Records of the species are (north-west to south-east, then south-west): the Albert Nile at Dufile near Nimule and at Lake Rubi; the Kabalega Falls National Park at the Victoria Nile delta into Lake Mobutu (Lake Albert); the Tochi Swamp; Lango District; Lake Kwania; Lake Kyogo, notably at Teso near Soroti; Lake Bisina (Lake Salisbury) and adjacent Lakes Opeta, Ajama, Kasago and Kochobo; Mpologoma and Kibimba, both near Tororo; also the Buruli District (i.e. roughly around Ngoma) and near Luwero, north-west and north of Kampala respectively; Entebbe (N'tebi) and adjacent Busi; Lake Wamala, west of Kampala; Katonga Swamp, south-west of Entebbe on Lake Victoria; along the Kagera River (not clear if at the delta or further inland); Lake Edward north of Rwenshama village; Lake George west of Hamakungo village; and the Semliki River delta at Lake Mobutu (Johnston 1902, Sharpe 1902, van Someren 1922, Gyldenstolpe 1924, Jackson 1938, Owen 1958, Burton and Benson 1961, J. S. Ash *in litt.* 1983, M. Carswell *in litt.* 1983, W. Möller *in litt.* 1983, D. E. Pomeroy *in litt.* 1984). In the 1940s 40 localities were known to C. R. S. Pitman (M. Carswell *in litt.* 1983).

Zaire Early records from Pool Malebo (=Stanley Pool) (*J. Orn.* 33 [1885]: 218) and the "upper Congo" (Stanley 1878) are presumably in error (Chapin 1932). In north-eastern Zaire it apparently occurs around Lake Mobutu (Gyldenstolpe 1924) and in 1959 three were seen at Rukanbura, south of Lake Edward and the River Ishasha, near the border with Rwanda (Curry-Lindahl 1961). The main population of Shoebills in Zaire occurs in the south-east of the country where the first specimens were collected at Lake Kisale in 1909 (Hellmayr 1911) and near Bukama at about the same time (Schouteden 1912). They are now known to be widespread along the upper Lualaba between Ankoro in the north and Bukama in the south (Burton and Benson 1961). Localities from which the species is known on the upper Lualaba are Ankoro, Mulongo, Lake Kisale, Lake Upemba, Lake Kagiba-Kikondja, Kamulondo, Bukama, Lake Kazibaziba and Lake Kabwe (Chapin 1932, Schouteden 1949,1971, Burton and Benson 1961). There is also a record of a specimen collected on the Zaire side of Lake Mweru, probably near the mouth of the Luapula River (Burton and Benson 1961). In 1960 one was seen south of Lake Lufira at Mushikatala (Ruwet 1963) and in the same year a bird seen near the Choma River in Mweru Marsh was possibly just inside Zaire (Burton and Benson 1961), though there is some confusion about the status of the Zaire/Zambia border at this locality (D. R. Aspinwall *in litt.* 1984).

Zambia The distribution of the Shoebill in Zambia has been exhaustively documented (Burton and Benson 1961) though there have been a few more recent published records (Keith and Vernon 1969, Critchley and Grimsdell 1970, Buxton 1978, Buxton *et al.* 1978). The species was first noted in Zambia at Lake Bangweulu, in 1946, or possibly earlier (White and Winterbottom 1949, Burton and Benson 1961). It is probably most widespread in the Bangweulu Swamp area, where it is mainly resident (Benson 1961, Burton and Benson 1961, Critchley and Grimsdell 1970, Buxton *et al.* 1978, R. J. Dowsett and F. Dowsett-Lemaire *in litt.* 1983). Birds have also been seen around the nearby Lake Chali in 1954 and 1958 (Burton and Benson 1961). In the Kasanka National Park, south-east of Bangweulu, single birds were seen on two occasions in 1955 (Burton and Benson 1961). In the Mweru Wantipa area in the north-east of the country the species has been recorded in many localities, notably the Fungwa Swamp in 1954, near Lake Chishi in 1960, the area around the Choma and Mwawe deltas and the Chishera Swamp in 1960 and 1964, the Musombwe area in 1957 and Bulanga in 1958, and there are also reports from the Kasenga River, Mofwe and Lusangwe (Burton and Benson 1961, Keith and Vernon 1969). In 1954 and 1956 birds were also seen in Lake Kako in the north-west of Sumbu National Park, near the southern end of Lake Tanganyika (Burton and Benson 1961). In 1950 a bird was shot on the lower Luapula River at Kampemba between the estuary and Johnston Falls. A bird with a broken wing was found at Itawa Swamp near Ndola in 1943 (Burton and Benson 1961) and one was seen there in 1971 (Madge 1971), but one observer has failed to find it there despite many hours of watching (C. Carter *in litt.* 1984). The species was seen in the Lukanga Swamp near Kabwe in 1958 and 1972 (Burton and Benson 1961, van Lavieren 1973). A probable observation was made in 1960 on a plain in Balovale (now Zambezi) District in western Zambia (Burton and Benson 1961). Other localities considered likely for the Shoebill in Zambia are Lake Lusiwashi near Serenje, the swamps along the Chambeshi River in Chinsali District and the swamps along the Manyinga River in Kabompo District (Burton and Benson 1961); of these Lake Lusiwashi is now considered unsuitable, and the Manyinga River swamps are thought perhaps to have been suggested to explain the Zambezi District record, with no evidence in recent years and the likelihood of birds there slim; however a further possible site is Insangano National Park (D. R. Aspinwall *in litt.* 1983,1984). A record of a pair seen in the Kafue National Park in 1958 near the confluence of the Kafue and Lufupa Rivers (Burton and Benson 1961), formerly rejected (Benson *et al.* 1970), is now considered probably valid (R. J. Dowsett and F. Dowsett-Lemaire *in litt.* 1983).

Population No detailed census has been carried out and a world population of 1,490-1,500 birds (Guillet 1977, Brown *et al.* 1982) is now known to have been a gross underestimate (A. Guillet *in litt.* 1983).

Central African Republic Although only a few records exist of this species in the Central African Republic, reports from local people suggest that it is common in places (Blancou 1939).

Ethiopia There is no information on numbers.

Rwanda The species is known to be fairly common (also "especially common") in the Akagera National Park (Verschuren 1965,1975) where the population in the main marshy area has been estimated at about 25 birds (Vande weghe 1981).

Sudan One estimate put the Sudanese population at 960 birds (Guillet 1977) but this is certainly much too low (A. Guillet *in litt.* 1983). In 1979 over 3,000 birds were counted along the Bahr-al-Jebel in the region of the proposed Jonglei Canal, during a series of aerial survey transects (A. Guillet *in litt.* 1983), and extrapolation from these transects gives a first estimate of 10,000 birds, probably to be revised downwards once corrected for habitat preferences (J. Kingdon pers. comm. 1983). The particularly high population here might be due to the area experiencing longer duration floods since 1962, in contrast to most other places, hydrologists expecting high flood levels to be maintained for another 10 years if the Jonglei Canal does not become operative in the interim (A. Guillet *in litt.* 1983, J. Kingdon *in litt.* 1984). It was generally considered common in the Sudd region of Sudan during the earlier years of this century (Cave and Macdonald 1955), and in the early 1900s up to 20 could be counted in one day along the Jur River (Butler 1905). Today it appears to be much more patchily distributed than formerly in southern Sudan (Guillet 1977,1978; see under Distribution) but important populations appear to survive along the Lol and Jur Rivers, and the Bahr-al-Ghazal and the Bahr-al-Jebel (Guillet 1977,1978).

Tanzania More than 300 birds are estimated to have been present in Moyowosi Swamp, 1971, based on a crude estimate of 0.64 birds per km^2 and an area of suitable habitat of "200" (presumably a misprint for 500) km^2 (Parker 1984).

Uganda The population in the 1940s was considered to be in the region of 100-200 pairs (the late C. R. S. Pitman *per* M. Carswell *in litt.* 1983). In 1977 it was judged that "roughly 50% of the 7,000 km^2 of swamps and wetlands in Uganda" were "more or less" suitable for the species and the number of birds was very roughly estimated at 400-600 (W. Möller *in litt.* 1983) It is fairly common around the Entebbe peninsula (M. Carswell *in litt.* 1983).

Zaire There is no information available for the population in north-eastern Zaire. In south-eastern Zaire it is generally considered to be uncommon (Burton and Benson 1961) though one report describes it as fairly common around Lake Upemba (Chapin 1932), and another as "observed frequently in the Virunga and Upemba parks" (Verschuren 1975).

Zambia The Shoebill is apparently uncommon throughout its Zambian range (Burton and Benson 1961), only Bangweulu Swamp being sufficiently large for a substantial number of birds (R. J. Dowsett and F. Dowsett-Lemaire *in litt.* 1983): in 1970, 20 were counted there along Lulimala River between Chiunda-ponde and the Lulimala Game Camp (Critchley and Grimsdell 1970), and in October 1983 during an aerial survey 33 birds were seen and 232 estimated present in the habitat surveyed, though other unsurveyed habitats in Bangweulu may have held more (Howard and Aspinwall in press).

Ecology The Shoebill is restricted to marshes, swamps and in particular sudd (areas of floating vegetation) (e.g. Schouteden 1912, Chapin 1932, Burton and Benson 1961, Fischer 1970, Guillet 1977,1978,1979, Vande weghe 1981, Brown *et al.* 1982): in the Akagera National Park in Rwanda it has been recorded on between 25% and 75% of visits to habitats with floating vegetation, compared with less than 25% of visits to all other marshy habitats in the park (Vande weghe 1981). The floating vegetation which it frequents consists of ferns and grasses with clumps of *Cladium*, *Typha* and papyrus *Cyperus papyrus* (Vande weghe 1981). Although not a true papyrus endemic (Vande weghe 1981), it is often found in such swamps (Hellmayr 1911, Schouteden 1912, Chapin 1932, Owen 1958, Benson 1961, Curry-Lindahl 1961, Urban 1967, Critchley and Grimsdell 1970, Guillet 1977,1978, Buxton *et al.* 1978, Vande weghe 1981). In the Akagera National Park, and probably elsewhere, it avoids pure papyrus swamps, preferring mixed papyrus and *Miscanthidium* swamps and floating vegetation mosaic (Vande weghe 1981). The species has also been recorded in marshes dominated by *Pistia striolates*, *Typha*, *Miscanthidium*, *Vossia*, *Cyperus latifolius* and *Echinochloa pyramidalis* (Curry-Lindahl 1961, Buxton *et al.* 1978, Britton 1980, Vande weghe 1981). Outside the breeding season birds have been seen on flooded grassland (Butler 1905, Dean 1963, Vande weghe 1981). In general Shoebills prefer more open parts of the swamps (Owen 1958, Keith and Vernon 1969, Vande weghe 1981), avoiding places where the vegetation is higher than the birds' backs, doubtless because of the impossibility in taking flight in dense tall growth, as e.g. formed by papyrus (Vande weghe 1981, A. Guillet *in litt.* 1984). There are also few fish in dense papyrus, making it an unsuitable habitat in which to feed (Vande weghe 1981). In Sudan, the areas in which the species occurs are very remote and restricted in type (the swamps being remarkably heterogeneous): these areas are known (in hydrological terms) as "transmission zones", being overspill areas (waterways, lagoons, channels) carrying deep, slow-moving water to lower lakeland levels and thus concentrating fish that are moving through (J. Kingdon pers. comm. 1983). The Shoebill has been reported from very small swamps of only 0.8 km^2 in Zambia (Burton and Benson 1961, Fischer 1970) though successful breeding in such places is doubtful (R. J. Dowsett and F. Dowsett-Lemaire *in litt.* 1983). Birds apparently do not walk in deep water (Burton and Benson 1961) but will perch in trees (Butler 1905, Schouteden 1912, Burton and Benson 1961), regularly when available (Möller 1980, A. Guillet *in litt.* 1984). The species is solitary, unpaired birds generally not foraging closer than 200 m, and even paired birds foraging alone, usually at opposite ends of their territory (Möller 1980); occasionally two or three can be seen together, usually keeping some distance apart (Owen 1958, Schouteden 1912, Burton and Benson 1961, Curry-Lindahl 1961). Birds usually hunt by remaining motionless in ambush, waiting for prey to come near, or occasionally by stalking their food very slowly (Butler 1905, Berg 1929, Burton and Benson 1961, Curry-Lindahl 1961, Guillet 1977,1978,1979, Buxton 1978, Buxton *et al.* 1978, Möller 1979a,1980,1982). In Sudan, birds feed mainly by ambush, using banks or floating vegetation over deep water channels, but will also feed in channels widened or even created by large mammals such as hippopotamuses *Hippopotamus amphibius* and elephants *Loxodonta africana* (J. Kingdon pers. comm. 1983). In swamps in Uganda, birds may initially detect prey by slight movements of the aquatic vegetation (Möller 1979a, 1980, 1982). They catch their prey by "collapsing" on it in an apparently unique manner for a large fish-eating bird (Guillet 1977, 1978, 1979): this is an extremely rapid event (generally less than 1 s), performed with immense power, the bird flapping forward and plunging down, bill and feet breaking the water's surface together (Möller 1979a, 1980, 1982, J. Kingdon pers. comm. 1983). The diet consists of both large and small fish, including the African lungfish *Protopterus aethiopicus*, and also bichirs *Polypterus senegalus* and tilapia, as well as frogs, water-snakes, monitors *Varanus* and young turtles and crocodiles *Crocodilus niloticus*; occasionally also warm-blooded vertebrates such as rats, young waterfowl and even young lechwe *Kobus leche* (Butler 1905, Schouteden 1912, Chapin 1932, Malbrant 1952, Burton and Benson 1961, Fischer 1970, J. Kingdon pers. comm. 1983). In 50 observations when food was caught, Uganda, 24 (45%) were African lungfish, with three catfish or lungfish (identity uncertain), one catfish, two small fish (e.g. tilapia), two frogs, four turtles, one snake, and 13 not identified (Möller 1980; expanded list including items brought to nest in Möller 1982). A large snail was also recorded as food (Möller 1980). The composition of the diet varies with habitat or area: the taking of mainly larger fish in certain areas (e.g. Rwenzori National Park, Uganda) may be related to water-clouding by hippopotamuses, since in areas with clear water (and no hippopotamuses) smaller prey are taken, perhaps because more easily visible (Möller 1980). Bichirs are reported to be the main food in Sudan (Möller 1982). Birds in the wild can manage without food for several days, e.g. a female continuously incubated eggs for four days and four hours while her mate was away (Möller 1980). The chicks are fed on chewed catfish (e.g. young *Clarias mossambicus*) and snakes (Benson 1961, Buxton 1978, Buxton *et al.* 1978). The report that birds feed during both day and night

(Burton and Benson 1961) is apparently in error: birds usually change feeding site after a successful capture, e.g. by walking some metres or by flying (generally 5-200 m), but those seen at last light one day are commonly in the same place at dawn next morning (Möller 1979a,1980,1982). Feeding activity, Uganda, had two main peaks, 11.00-12.00 hrs and 15.00-16.00 hrs, the vast majority of feeding being done after 11.00 hrs (Möller 1979a, 1980). In general, Shoebills are very sluggish in their movements (Schouteden 1912, Owen 1958, Burton and Benson 1961) and inactive for much of the time (Berg 1929, Möller 1980). Soaring occurs on hot afternoons at heights up to 500 m; it occurs frequently in periods of seasonal movement, Sudan (A. Guillet *in litt.* 1984), but is considered to have a self-advertising and territorial function, at least at times (Möller 1980). The breeding season varies greatly over different parts of Africa but it generally coincides with the beginning of the dry season and flood subsidence (Butler 1905, Chapin 1932, Jackson 1938, Owen 1958, Benson 1961, Blancou 1961, Critchley and Grimsdell 1970, Guillet 1977, 1978, Buxton 1978, Buxton *et al.* 1978, Möller 1980); in Uganda it occurs apparently at any time of year (Möller 1979b, 1980), while in Sudan least activity is in April/June (J. Kingdon pers. comm. 1983). Pairs hold all-purpose territories, with the nest generally fairly central, feeding not occurring within 200 m of it (in one case the nest was in a small marsh and all feeding took place in a separate marsh); of seven territories, two were estimated to be 2.5, one each 2.8, 3.4, 3.6, 3.7 and 3.8 km^2, shape variable with topography, e.g. one on a lake shore being 7 km long and a few hundred metres wide (Möller 1980). Clutch-size varies between one and three (Chapin 1932, Schönwetter 1942, Burton and Benson 1961, Critchley and Grimsdell 1970, Buxton 1978, Buxton *et al.* 1978), two being normal (Möller 1980). There can be strong inter-sibling rivalry, and generally only one bird fledges (Möller 1978, 1979b, 1980). One nestling (4.5 kg) disappeared at nine weeks, probably eaten by a crocodile (Möller 1978, 1980). The young first leave the nest at about 95 days and can fly at 105 days (Buxton 1978, Buxton *et al.* 1978), but are still led and fed by the parents for a period thereafter (Möller 1979b). In captivity, birds assume adult plumage at 3-4 years (Möller 1978). Optimum fishing (and also nesting) sites being limited, in southern Sudan birds move seasonally between feeding and nesting sites according to the flood regime (Guillet 1977,1978,1979). The birds are generally very shy and vulnerable to disturbance (Curry-Lindahl 1961, Duckworth 1974, Guillet 1977, 1978), although there is one record of a bird in the Kabalega Falls National Park in Uganda walking 50 m out of a swamp to inspect an empty car (Gordon 1959), and one two-year-old under study (also in Uganda) lost all fear within a few weeks and would approach to within 1 m of the observer (Möller 1980).

Threats The Shoebill is presumably declining in some areas due to swamp drainage, though this is poorly documented. The conservation situation of the species has been best studied in southern Sudan (Guillet 1977,1978, A. Guillet *in litt.* 1983). The main threats to the Shoebill in this area appear to be disturbance of birds during the breeding season by people, cattle and fire (Guillet 1977, 1978, A. Guillet *in litt.* 1983). Shoebills breed during the dry season and at this time of year their nests are often easily accessible (Guillet 1977, 1978). There has been a rapid increase in both the human and cattle populations in southern Sudan in the last 10-

20 years, and a consequent degradation of the habitat, especially in the smaller swamps (Guillet 1977, 1978, A. Guillet *in litt.* 1983; J. Kingdon pers. comm. 1983). Both fires and cattle destroy permanent swamp vegetation during the dry season which cannot regenerate during the wet season (when the cattle are removed) due to flooding (Guillet 1977, 1978). Shoebills are extremely vulnerable to disturbance at their nesting and feeding sites, by people (especially fishermen), cattle and wild animals which occur locally at relatively high densities in southern Sudan (Guillet 1977, 1978). The Shoebill populations along the Lol River have been suffering from diminished breeding success for the last 10 years because the river has been seasonally very dry for unknown reasons: as a result, people taking advantage of easy fishing disturb nesting birds (Guillet 1977, 1978). Also the populations near Aweil may be at some risk from the establishment of a new rice scheme (Guillet 1977, 1978). In some areas the birds are probably threatened by large water projects which often lead to a reduction in the water flow, upsetting the ecological balance (Guillet 1977, 1978, A. Guillet *in litt.* 1983). The construction of the Jonglei Canal along the Bahr-al-Jebel will have widespread and ecologically damaging effects (Guillet 1977, 1978), with 25% of the water in the Sudd region draining down it and transmission zones shrinking (J. Kingdon pers. comm. 1983); Phase Two of the development would take 50% of the water, and Phase Three envisages re-routing the White Nile (J. Kingdon pers. comm. 1983). In Uganda, swamp drainage for rice and sugar-cane plantations threatens the species, and the increasing human population there will bring development and disturbance (cattle, fire, hunting) elsewhere (Möller 1980, W. Möller *in litt.* 1983). In the north-eastern parts of Lake Kyoga birds are commonly hunted with spears or fish-hooks and trapped on nests, while nestlings are taken for rearing and sale as food (fetching the price of a large hen): local authorities do not know the species is protected (Möller 1980, W. Möller *in litt.* 1983). In Teso (by Lake Kyoga), the skull and bill have been seen used in a tribal ceremony (M. Carswell *in litt.* 1984). In Zambia, Bangweulu Swamp is currently at risk from increased disturbance or alteration (see Threats under Wattled Crane *Bugeranus carunculatus*). In various parts of the species's range birds are caught to stock zoos in Europe and North America (see under Remarks). The recent view that the species is "severely threatened" (Brown *et al.* 1982) is evidently based on an underestimation of total numbers (see Population) and, despite the catalogue of threats above, is probably unduly pessimistic.

Conservation Measures Taken The Shoebill is protected by law in Sudan, the Central African Republic, Uganda, Rwanda, Zaire and Zambia (Johnston 1902, Butler 1905, Malbrant 1952, Burton and Benson 1961, Fischer 1970, A. Prigogine *in litt.* 1981). The species also occurs in the following protected areas: Bahr al Zaraf and Shambe National Parks in Sudan (Guillet 1977, 1978); Saint-Floris National Park (Dragesco 1960) and Ouandja-Vakaga Reserve (Blancou 1961) in the Central African Republic; Kabalega Falls and Rwenzori National Parks in Uganda (Burton and Benson 1961, W. Möller *in litt.* 1983); Akagera National Park in Rwanda (Curry-Lindahl 1961, Verschuren 1965, Vande weghe 1981); Virunga National Park (Curry-Lindahl 1961) and Upemba National Park (Chapin 1932) in Zaire; and Kasanka National Park, Mweru Wantipa

National Park and Sumbu National Park in Zambia (Burton and Benson 1961).

The number of Shoebills in zoological collections between 1966 and 1981

Zoo	1966	1967	1968	1969	1970	1971	1972	1973
1	1	1					1	
2							2	2
3	1	1	1	1	1	1	5	6
4	2	2	2	2	2	2	2	2
5			1					
6								
7							2	2
8	3	2	2	2	2	3	4	4
9	1		1	1	1		1	1
10								
11								
12								
13	2	2	2	2	2	2	2	2
14	2	3			1	1		
15	4	4	5	5	5	4	3	3
16					1	8		
17							3	
18	1	1	1	1			3	
19	3	3	2	1	1	1	1	1
20							2	1
21			2	1	3	3	3	3
22	3	3	3	1	3		2	1
23					1	1	1	1
24								
25					1	5	5	
26	1	1						
27	2	2	2	2	2	2	4	4
28	1	1	1	1	1	1	1	1
TOTAL	27	26	25	20	27	34	47	34

Conservation Measures Proposed In general the Shoebill will be effectively conserved if large areas of swamp are strictly protected. Detailed recommendations have been made to the Sudan Wildlife Administration concerning the conservation of the Shoebill in southern Sudan (Guillet 1977) but it is not known if there has been any progress in implementing them (A. Guillet *in litt.* 1983). It has been suggested that new reserves be created at War Ajak, Meshra and Nyubor (Guillet 1977, 1978). War Ajak on the Lol River is a particularly important site since this is the only place in the west of the Sudd region which contains permanent water for the mammal fauna in the plains to the north (Guillet 1977, 1978). Meshra is also on an important migration route for large mammals (Guillet 1977, 1978). There may turn out to be important nesting sites of the Shoebill

Zoo	1974	1975	1976	1977	1978	1979	1980	1981
1								
2	2	2	2	2	2	2	1	1
3	2	1						
4	2	2						
5								
6			1	1				
7	2	2	2	2	2		2	2
8	4					1	1	
9	1	1	1	1	1			
10			1	1	1	1	1	1
11			2			2		
12			2	2	2	2	1	1
13	2	2	2	3	3	3	3	2
14	1	1	1	2	2	2	2	2
15	5	4	3	3	3	3	3	3
16								
17	3		2	2	2		2	
18			2	2				
19	1							
20								
21	3	2	2	2	2		3	3
22	1	1	3	2	2	2	1	2
23	1	1	1	1				
24							1	1
25	5	5		4	5	4	3	
26								
27	3	2	2	2	2	2	2	2
28	1	1	1	1	1	1	1	1
TOTAL	39	27	30	33	30	25	27	21

Key to table: The code for the zoos is as follows:

1. Alexandria, Egypt
2. Amsterdam, Netherlands
3. Antwerp, Belgium
4. Basle, Switzerland
5. Bristol, U.K.
6. Brownsville, U.S.A.
7. Budapest, Hungary
8. Cairo, Egypt
9. Chicago Brookfield, U.S.A.
10. Copenhagen, Denmark
11. Dubai, United Arab Emirates
12. Duisburg, West Germany
13. East Berlin, East Germany
14. Entebbe, Uganda
15. Frankfurt, West Germany
16. Khartoum, Sudan
17. Kuwait
18. Lubumbashi, Zaire
19. Philadelphia, U.S.A.
20. Rotterdam, Netherlands
21. San Antonio, U.S.A.
22. Stuttgart, West Germany
23. Tampa, U.S.A.
24. Vienna, Austria
25. Walsrode, West Germany
26. Washington NZP, U.S.A.
27. West Berlin, West Germany
28. Zurich, Switzerland

further east, to the north of Kapoeta; if so it is recommended that these be incorporated into an extension of the Gebel Boma Game Reserve (Guillet 1977, 1978). Despite these specific recommendations for certain parts of the Sudd region it has been judged that the Shoebill would be best conserved by the regulation of the spatial and temporal distribution of fires, fishermen and cattle as part of an overall ecological management plan (Guillet 1977, 1978, A. Guillet *in litt.* 1983), though this is considered an impractical requirement (J. Kingdon *in litt.* 1984). Protected area status for a part (e.g. the south-east) of the Bangweulu Swamp in Zambia would be a valuable contribution to this species's conservation (D. R. Aspinwall *in litt.* 1983). In Uganda, new reserves are needed to ensure the survival of a healthy population of birds there, coupled with a campaign of education and public awareness (Möller 1980, W. Möller *in litt.* 1983). It is also most desirable that much stricter curbs (e.g. through listing in CITES) are placed upon the importation of Shoebills into North America and Europe, where they are in constant demand by zoological collections (see under Remarks).

Remarks The relationships of the Shoebill have long been a matter of dispute and there are three main lines of thought as to its affinities. One is that it is allied to the pelicans (Pelicanidae) (Gould 1851, Cottam 1957, Saiff 1978, Sibley and Ahlquist 1984). Several authorities consider it to be closest to the herons (Ardeidae) (Jardine 1852, Parker 1860, Bartlett 1861, Beddard 1888, Shufeldt 1901) and others believe it to be nearest the storks (Ciconiidae) (Reinhardt 1860,1862, Mitchell 1913, Bohm 1930, Feduccia 1977; see Olson 1982).

Birds in captivity Two Shoebills were brought to London Zoo in 1860 (*Ibis* [8]2 [1902]: 527-528). They are also known to have been kept in captivity in Khartoum, at least since 1900 (*Ibis* [8]2 [1902]: 527-528, Butler 1905, Owen 1958, Burton and Benson 1961) and two were kept in Cairo Zoo for 22 years (Berg 1929); they have long been popular zoo birds in Europe (Steinbacher 1937, Poulsen 1950). There seems to be no evidence that the species has ever bred in captivity, which is disturbing since it appears that 90-100 birds have been captured for zoos in the last 20 years: details of the captive population between 1966 and 1981 are given in the table below (data compiled from *Internat. Zoo Yearbook* 7-22 [1967-1982]; for Entebbe Zoo also from W. Möller *in litt.* 1983, M. Carswell *in litt.* 1984).

References

Bartlett, A. D. (1861) On the affinities of *Balaeniceps. Proc. Zool. Soc. Lond.*: 131-134.

Beddard, F. E. (1888) On certain points in the visceral anatomy of *Balaeniceps rex* bearing on its affinities. *Proc. Zool. Soc. Lond.*: 284-290.

Benson, C. W. (1961) The breeding of the Whale-headed Stork or Shoebill in Northern Rhodesia. *N. Rhod. J.* 4: 557-560.

Benson, C. W. and Benson, F. M. (1977) *The birds of Malawi*. Limbe, Malawi: Montfort Press.

Benson, C. W., Brooke, R. K., Dowsett, R. J. and Irwin, M. P. S. (1970) Notes on the birds of Zambia: Part V. *Arnoldia Rhod.* 4(40).

Berg, B. (1929) *Abu Markub*. Berlin: Dietrich Reimer/Ernst Vohsen.

Blancou, L. (1939) Le *Balaeniceps rex* en Afrique Equatorial Française. *Oiseau et R.F.O.* 9: 480-485.

Blancou, L. (1961) Notes sur des oiseaux de l'Afrique Centrale. *Oiseau et R.F.O.* 31: 334-336.

Bohm, M. (1930) Ueber den Bau des jugendlichen Schadels von *Balaeniceps rex* nebst Bemerkungen über dessen systematische Stellung und über das Gaumenskelett der Vögel. *Z. Morph. Okol. Tiere, Berlin* 17: 677-718.

Britton, P. L. (1978) Seasonality, density and diversity of birds of a papyrus swamp in western Kenya. *Ibis* 120: 450-466.

Britton, P. L. ed. (1980) *Birds of East Africa: their habitat, status and distribution.* Nairobi: EANHS.

Brooke, R. K., Donnelly, B. G. and Irwin, M. P. S. (1982) Comments on cave paintings supposedly depicting Whale-headed Stork in the Matopos, Zimbabwe. *Honeyguide* no. 110: 4-7.

Brown, L. H., Urban, E. K. and Newman, K. (1982) *The birds of Africa*, 1. London: Academic Press.

Burton, M. and Benson, C. W. (1961) The Whale-headed Stork or Shoe-bill: legend and fact. *N. Rhod. J.* 4: 411-426.

Butler, A. L. (1905) A contribution to the ornithology of the Egyptian Soudan. *Ibis* (8)5: 301-401.

Buxton, C. (1978) The Shoebill story. *Black Lechwe* 12: 6-17.

Buxton, L., Slater, J. and Brown, L. H. (1978) The breeding behaviour of the Shoebill or Whale-headed Stork *Balaeniceps rex* in the Bangweulu Swamps. *E. Afr. Wildl. J.* 16: 201-220.

Cave, F. O. and Macdonald, J. D. (1955) *The birds of Sudan, their identification and distribution*. London: Oliver and Boyd.

Chapin, J. P. (1932) The birds of the Belgian Congo. Part 1. *Bull. Amer. Mus. Nat. Hist.* 65.

Cooke, C. K. (1964) Animals in Southern Rhodesian rock art. *Arnoldia Rhod.* 1(13): 1-22.

Cottam, P. A. (1957) The pelecaniform characters of the skeleton of the Shoe-bill Stork *Balaeniceps rex*. *Bull. Brit. Mus. (Nat. Hist.) Zool.* 5: 49-72.

Critchley, R. A. and Grimsdell, J. J. R. (1970) Nesting of the Shoebill *Balaeniceps rex* Gould in the Bangweulu swamps. *Bull. Brit. Orn. Club* 90: 119.

Curry-Lindahl, K. (1961) Contribution à l'étude des vertébrés terrestres en Afrique tropicale. *Exploration du Parc National Albert et du Parc National de la Kagera II. Mission K. Curry-Lindahl (1951-1952, 1958-1959)* 1: 1-331.

Dean, G. J. (1962) The Whale-headed Stork. *N. Rhod. J.* 5: 86-87.

Dean, G. J. W. (1963) Whale-headed Stork *Balaeniceps rex*, Gould. *J. E. Afr. Nat. Hist. Soc. and Coryndon Mus.* 24(2): 77-78.

Dragesco, J. (1960) Le Lac Gata, paradis des ornithologistes. *Oiseau et R.F.O.* 30: 286-288.

Duckworth, F. (1974) The Whale-headed Stork in Ethiopia. *Bull. Brit. Orn. Club* 94: 3-4.

Feduccia, A. (1977) The whalebill is a stork. *Nature* 266: 719-720.

Fischer, W. (1970) *Der Schuhschnabel.* (Die Neue Brehm Bucherei – Heft 425). Wittenburg Lutherstadt: A. Ziemsen.

Gordon, H. M. (1959) The Whale-headed (Shoebill) Stork at close range. *Afr. Wildl.* 13: 83.

Gould, J. (1851) On a new and most remarkable form in ornithology. *Proc. Zool. Soc. Lond.*: 1-2.

Guillet, A. (1977) Status of the Shoe-bill Stork (*Balaeniceps rex* Gould) in southern Sudan. Report to Sudan Wildlife Administration.

Guillet, A. (1978) Distribution and conservation of the Shoebill (*Balaeniceps rex*) in southern Sudan. *Biol. Conserv.* 13: 39-49.

Guillet, A. (1979) Aspects of the foraging behaviour of the Shoebill. *Ostrich* 50: 252-255.

Gyldenstolpe, N. (1924) Zoological results of the Swedish Expedition to Central Africa 1921. Vertebrata I. Birds. *Kungl. Svensk. Vet. Akad. Handl.* (3)1(3): 1-326.

Hellmayr, C. E. (1911) [Letter.] *Ibis* (9)5: 574-575.

Howard, G. W. and Aspinwall, D. R. (in press) Recent counts of Shoebill, Saddlebill and Wattled Crane in Zambia. [*Ostrich*.]

Jackson, F. J. (1938) *The birds of Kenya Colony and Uganda Protectorate*, 1. London: Gurney and Jackson.

Jardine, W. (1852) Ornithology in 1850; *Balaeniceps rex*. *Contrib. Orn.* 1851: 11-14.

Johnston, H. H. (1883) [Letter.] *Ibis* (5)1: 578.

Johnston, H. H. (1902) On the occurrence of *Balaeniceps rex* on Lake Victoria. *Ibis* (8)2: 334-336.

Keith, G. S. and Vernon, C. J. (1969) Bird notes from eastern and north-eastern Zambia. *Puku* 5: 131-139.

van Lavieren, L. P. (1973) Shoebill Stork (*Balaeniceps rex*) in Lukanga Swamp. *Bull. Zambian Orn. Soc.* 5: 79.

de Lisle, M. (1956) Sur une observation de *Balaeniceps rex* au Cameroun. *Oiseau et R.F.O.* 26: 1-3.

Louette, M. (1981) *The birds of Cameroon. An annotated check-list.* Brussels: Verhandeling Wetenschappen, Jaargang 43, no. 163.

Madge, S. G. (1971) Shoebill Stork at Ndola. *Bull. Zambian Orn. Soc.* 3: 21-22.

Malbrant, R. (1952) *Faune du Centre Africain Français (Mammifères et oiseaux).* 2me edition. Paris: Encyclopédie biologique.

Matthews, N. J. C. (1979) Observation of the Shoebill in the Okavango Swamps. *Ostrich* 50: 185.

Mitchell, P. C. (1913) Observations on the anatomy of the Shoe-bill (*Balaeniceps rex*) and allied birds. *Proc. Zool. Soc. Lond.*: 644-703.

Möller, W. (1978) Auf den Spuren von König Walkopf. *Sielmanns Tierwelt* no. 8: 36-44.

Möller, W. (1979a) *Balaeniceps rex* (Balaenicipitidae) – Nahrungserwerb. *Publ. Wissenschaftl. Filmen*, Biol. Ser. 12, no. 9 – Film E 2516 [ISSN 0073-8417].

Möller, W. (1979b) *Balaeniceps rex* (Balaenicipitidae) – Verhalten am Nistplatz. *Publ. Wissenschaftl. Filmen*, Biol. Ser. 12, no. 10 – Film E 2517 [ISSN 0073-8417].

Möller, W. (1980) Freilandbeobachtungen am Schuhschnabel *Balaeniceps rex*. Diplomarbeit, Zool. Inst. Techn. Univ. Braunschweig.

Möller, W. (1982) Beobachtungen zum Nahrungserwerb des Schuhschnabels (*Balaeniceps rex*). *J. Orn.* 123: 19-28.

Olson, S. L. (1982) A critique of Cracraft's classification of birds. *Auk* 99: 733-739.

Owen, T. R. H. (1958) The Shoebill Stork. *Afr. Wildl.* 12: 191-194.

Parker, I. S. C. (1984) Shoebill *Balaeniceps rex* and Wattled Crane *Grus carunculatus* in the Moyowosi Swamp, Tanzania. *Scopus* 8: 24-25.

Parker, W. K. (1860) Abstract of notes on the osteology of *Balaeniceps rex*. *Proc. Zool. Soc. Lond.*: 324-330.

Poulsen, H. (1950) Beobachtungen an einem Schuhschnabel (*Balaeniceps rex* J. Gould) in der Gefangenschaft. *Z. Tierpsychol.* 7: 134-137.

Preston, I. (1976) Whale-headed Stork. *E. Afr. Nat. Hist. Soc. Bull.* (November/ December): 131-132.

Reinhardt, J. (1860) On the affinities of *Balaeniceps*. *Proc. Zool. Soc. Lond.*: 377-380.

Reinhardt, J. (1862) Some remarks on the genus *Balaeniceps*. *Ibis* 4: 158-175.

von Rosen, B. (1961) Traskostork i fornegypten. *Fauna och Flora* 56: 174-178.

Ruwet, J.-C. (1963) Notes écologiques et éthologiques sur les oiseaux des plaines de la Lufira supérieure (Katanga). I. Podicipèdes, Steganopodes, Gressores, Anseres. *Rev. Zool. Bot. Afr.* 68: 1-60.

Saiff, E. I. (1978) The middle ear of the skull of birds: the Pelicaniformes and Ciconiiformes. *Zool. J. Linn. Soc.* 63: 315-370.

Schönwetter, M. (1942) Das Ei des *Balaeniceps rex* Gould. *Beitr. Fortpfl. Biol. Vögel* 18: 41-45.

Schouteden, H. (1912) Le *Balaeniceps* roi. *Rev. Zool. Afr.* 1: 347-352.

Schouteden, H. (1949) Contribution à l'étude de la faune ornithologique du Katanga (Congo Belge). *Rev. Zool. Bot. Afr.* 42: 322-342.

Schouteden, H. (1966) La faune ornithologique du Rwanda. *Doc. Zool. Mus. Roy. Afr. Centr.* 10.

Schouteden, H. (1971) La faune ornithologique de la Province du Katanga. *Doc. Zool. Mus. Roy. Afr. Centr.* 17.

Sharpe, R. B. (1902) On the collections of birds made by Sir Harry Johnston, K.C.B., in Equatorial Africa. *Ibis* (8)2: 96-121.

Shufeldt, R. W. (1901) Notes on the osteology of *Scopus umbretta* and *Balaeniceps rex*. *J. Anat. Physiol.* 2: 405-412.

Sibley, C. G. and Ahlquist, J. E. (1984) The phylogeny of the non-passerine waterbird assemblage. Abstracts, posters and lectures presented at the 102nd stated meeting of the American Ornithologists' Union, Lawrence, Kansas, 6-9 August 1984.

van Someren, V. G. L. (1922) Notes on the birds of East Africa. *Novit. Zool.* 24: 1-246.

Stanley, H. M. (1878) *Through the dark continent*, 2. London.

Steinbacher, G. (1937) Zur Haltung und Pflege des Schuhschnabels (*Balaeniceps rex* J. Gould). *Zool. Garten* (NF) 9: 101-106.

Urban, E. K. (1967) Possible occurrence of the Whale-headed Stork in Ethiopia. *J. E. Afr. Nat. Hist. Soc. and Natn. Mus.* 114: 87-88.

Vande weghe, J.-P. (1981) L'avifaune des papyraies au Rwanda et au Burundi. *Gerfaut* 71: 489-536.

Verschuren, J. (1965) Notes ornithologiques. *Exploration du Parc National de la Kagera.* 2me Sér. 1(4): 119-126.

Verschuren, J. (1975) Wildlife in Zaire. *Oryx* 13: 149-163.

White, C. M. N. and Winterbottom, J. M. (1949) *A check list of the birds of Northern Rhodesia*. Lusaka: Department of Game and Tsetse Control.

NORTHERN BALD IBIS   ENDANGERED
Geronticus eremita (Linnaeus, 1758)

Order CICONIIFORMES   Family THRESKIORNITHIDAE
                                        Subfamily THRESKIORNITHINAE

Summary Formerly distributed in central Europe and almost certainly across North Africa and into the Middle East, this colonial cliff-nesting species now occurs in two relict, disjunct populations, one, largely resident, breeding in Morocco and Algeria, the other breeding at a single site in southern Turkey and migrating to the Red Sea coast and Ethiopia. Despite efforts using captive breeding and release, the eastern population, which consisted of thousands of birds at the start of the century when it extended into Syria, now numbers only a few pairs and appears doomed to extinction, pesticides being the principal cause. Algeria possesses one small colony and the number of colonies in Morocco has declined from at least 38 (known this century) to about 12, and the numbers of pairs from roughly a thousand in the 1930s to 93 in 1982, persecution, disturbance and agricultural change being largely to blame. As a largely insectivorous bird of semi-arid but regularly rained-on plains, progressive climatic drying-out of habitat in North Africa and the Middle East appears to be chiefly responsible for its present distribution. Only on one consistently moist stretch of the Atlantic coast around Oued Massa in southern Morocco, where a national park has recently been scheduled, does there appear to be serious hope for the survival of the species in the wild. However, it breeds well in captivity.

Distribution The Northern Bald Ibis (Waldrapp, Hermit Ibis, Bare- or Red-faced Ibis) occurs in two disjunct populations ("a classic example of a relict species": Moreau 1972), one in north-west Africa, where it breeds in Morocco and Algeria and disperses for winter largely within these countries but with some birds (at least formerly) wandering to countries to the south (Western Sahara, Mauritania, Mali), and one in a single colony (a few pairs elsewhere) in the town of Birecik on the upper Euphrates River in southern Turkey, the birds migrating almost certainly to the Red Sea coast and especially Ethiopia for the winter: birds breeding in Turkey and formerly also in Syria are thus the most likely source for all records from Egypt, Ethiopia, Saudi Arabia, Sudan, Yemen and indeed other countries away from the Red Sea (immature birds remain away from breeding colonies and would seem to be responsible for records from around the Red Sea during the Turkish breeding season). If this is not so, the winter quarters of the Turkish and former Syrian birds remain unknown (perhaps they disperse into the Syrian desert) and the origins of the birds at the Red Sea coastlands also remain unknown (perhaps Yemen) (Smith 1970a); but even if the Turkish birds are those that appear around the Red Sea, their whereabouts between August and December is almost wholly unknown (Smith 1970a). The possibility that Turkey and adjacent countries may harbour undiscovered colonies (Smith 1970a, Moreau 1972, Hirsch 1979a) seems increasingly remote. At a time several thousand years ago when the birds were evidently not rare in Egypt it seems likely that the two populations may have been joined up across North Africa (Hirsch 1981b, Kumerloeve 1983).

Between the twelfth (probably much earlier) and seventeenth centuries the species also occurred in Europe, with confirmed records from Austria, West Germany, Switzerland and Yugoslavia, and strong evidence of its presence in Hungary: reconstruction of this former range suggests Europe was colonised from the Near East, a view supported by the migratory behaviour of the European birds (Schenker 1977). Single birds obviously from Morocco have wandered to Sao Miguel in the Azores, Atlantic Ocean, in February of a year before 1905 (Hartert and Ogilvie-Grant 1905), Boavista in the Cape Verde Islands, January 1898 (Salvadori 1899), and the Seville region of Andalucia, Spain, July 1958 (Valverde 1959).

Algeria A small colony, discovered in 1974, exists in the Djebel Amour near El Bayadh, in the central Saharan Atlas (Ledant *et al.* 1981). The only previously known colony, at Ain Sba south of Ksar El Boukhari (= Boghari) in central northern Algeria, has this century been occupied only irregularly and is now abandoned (see Population: Algeria). A nineteenth century record of birds breeding "beyond Bou Guizoun, on the road to El Aghouat" (Tristram 1860) evidently refers to modern-day Boughzoul and Laghouat, and would therefore have been very close to Ksar El Boukhari; birds were again seen at Boughzoul in May 1968 (Ledant *et al.* 1981). Records from Rocher du Lion in the Chélif valley near Ksar El Boukhari and around Laghouat in November 1924 (Mathey-Dupraz 1925) and from the Chott ech Chergui desert in November 1952 (specimen in BMNH: NJC) indicate that birds may remain in the country in winter, not wandering particularly far from where they breed (see, e.g., Heim de Balsac 1925,1931). There is a record from the dayat (marshy depression) at "Djenane Khater" (correctly, Khrater) in April 1959 (Heim de Balsac and Mayaud 1962), this now being just inside the Moroccan frontier and the record presumably referring to birds from Morocco (E. D. H. Johnson *in litt.* 1984), and it has been suggested that an extension of the eastern Moroccan population may occur (or at least have occurred) into the Monts de Tlemcen in western Algeria (Rencurel 1974). A record from Bône province in eastern Algeria (Malherbe 1855) appears to be both the easternmost and the oldest confirmed record for north-west Africa (but see below under Tunisia).

Egypt Extensive evidence from Ancient Egyptian hieroglyphics, illustrations and artefacts indicates that the species must have been widely distributed (and revered) in Egypt several thousand years ago (Kumerloeve 1983) when climatic conditions were much more favourable (Moreau 1966), but the only record in more recent times is of eight birds near Giza in May 1921 (Meinertzhagen 1930, Moreau 1966): there is a possibility that these birds came from an undiscovered colony in Sinai or in the Galala mountains west of Suez (Moreau 1966, Smith 1970a), but on current evidence (see under Ecology) these were likely to have been wandering immatures. The view that the species perhaps breeds in the Red Sea hills of Egypt (Vaurie 1965) has not been espoused elsewhere (but see below under Sudan); regular migration to the Nile valley (Vaurie 1965) does not occur.

Ethiopia The explanation of the long-known occurrence of this species in

Ethiopia (and throughout the Red Sea coastlands) is almost certainly that the birds involved are wintering adults and wintering and oversummering immatures from Turkey and formerly Syria (Smith 1970a, Siegfried 1972, Cramp and Simmons 1977, Hirsch 1980a): most dates support this interpretation – e.g. abundant, Shoa province, December; none seen, April and May (Salvadori 1884; see also below) – and indeed the almost complete break in records from Ethiopia since 1954 coincides well with the massive losses from the Birecik colony (see Population: Turkey) since then. Evidence that the Northern Bald Ibis breeds in Ethiopia – mentioned as possible (Elliott 1877, Guichard 1950, Géroudet 1965, Hirsch 1977a,b), probable (Vaurie 1965) and certain (Meinertzhagen 1951, 1954, Bannerman and Bannerman 1968) – is in fact wholly lacking (Smith 1970a). That it is only a rainy season ("February") migrant to the coastal valleys was first and most emphatically claimed almost 150 year ago (Rüppell 1835-1840,1845). Records are, however, from two major areas of Ethiopia, the Red Sea coastlands around Mits'iwa (Massawa) and the central highlands around Addis Ababa. In the former area, localities mentioned are Mits'iwa (Smith 1955,1970a), Archico (Smith 1970a), Ailet (Hirsch 1980a), Asmera (Smith 1970a, Hirsch 1980a) and the valleys – including that of the "Modat" (Motad, at Ailet, in IGM 1887) – west of Mits'iwa (Rüppell 1835-1840,1845), these all being close together and almost all from the period December to February, as are records from Karora on the Sudan border 300 km to the north-west (Smith 1955). An untraced locality, Hamedo (von Heuglin 1869-1874), is believed to lie in the Mareb valley, i.e. south-west of Mits'iwa (J. S. Ash *in litt.* 1984). In the central highlands, localities mentioned (dates given where known) are: "Arussi country, about 8°N, just south of Addis [Ababa]" (Archer and Godman 1937, Smith 1970a); 35 km south of Addis Ababa, December (Urban and Brown 1971); Lake Cialalaka (Salvadori 1884), this being a small seasonal lake at 08°46'N 38°58'E (J. S. Ash *in litt.* 1984); near Addis Ababa, December (Smith 1970a); Antotto (Moltoni and Gnecchi Ruscone 1942); Sululta, November (Guichard 1950); Dabra Berhan, February (Guichard 1950); 80 km north-east of Addis Ababa, December (Smith 1970a); and Chacha, January (Ash and Howell 1977), these last three being very close together in eastern Shoa province – indeed "eastern Shoa" was identified on early but evidently good evidence as the winter quarters of this species (see Archer and Godman 1937). Other records include two from Senafe (Eritrea province), one of them in January (Blanford 1870, Hirsch 1980a), one from the high plateau of "Wogara", February (von Heuglin 1869-1874), this being Wogoro (Uogoro) at 13°48'N 39°36'E (J. S. Ash *in litt.* 1984), and one from Antalo (Tigre province) (Blanford 1870), all these localities lying on the great north/south mountain range that extends roughly from south of Mits'iwa to Addis Ababa, and this may perhaps indicate that birds use it as a corridor from the coast to the central highlands; however, the record from Antalo was of a "large flock" (Blanford 1870), traceable to 11 May (Hirsch 1980a), and is therefore presumably referable to a wandering group of immatures (see Ecology). That the species has been found in almost all provinces (Hirsch 1980a) is not the case.

Iraq It has been speculated (Vaurie 1965) and even asserted (Bannerman and Bannerman 1968) that this species breeds in Iraq, but it appears to be no more than a straggler there: records are from Tekrit on the Tigris River in February and on a second occasion when no date was given, and from Kirkuk in January (Ticehurst *et al.* 1922,1926). The basis for the assertion that it occurs on the "upper Tigris" – Iraq or Turkey not specified – (Hartert 1912-1921) is not known. Speculation that birds might breed in the higher rocky hills of the Jabal Hamrin or in the "Fatah Gorge" (i.e. at Al Fathah, on the Tigris at the north-west tip of the Jabal Hamrin) was not substantiated by fieldwork in the region (Ticehurst *et al.* 1922). Regular dispersal to Iraq after breeding (Vaurie 1965) does not occur; indeed there appear to have been no records since the early 1920s (Allouse 1953, Cramp and Simmons 1977).

Israel The only records since 1935 are of four birds seen in early April and 15-16 in mid-April 1970, Elat (Hirsch 1980a, Krabbe 1983), and one seen in early April 1980 near the Dead Sea south of Jericho (Lambert and Grimmett 1983). Although these seem certain to have been non-breeding birds, those seen in early April were noted to depart to the north, observations which complicate the issue of what immature birds do before first breeding at six years old (see Ecology) and raise a question about the regularity with which the Rift Valley north of the Gulf of Aqaba may have been (or still be) used as a corridor by migrating Northern Bald Ibises (see also Syria below).

Jordan Ibises with red legs have once been reported from Azraq oasis, suggesting that the species is a transdesert migrant (Bourne 1959).

Mali At the time before it was realised Moroccan birds mostly winter in Morocco itself, a likely wintering area was considered to be the northern edge of the Niger Inundation Zone in Mali (Smith 1970a,b), and indeed single birds were seen in December 1971 in this region at Tadjaki marsh (not Lake Oro as also reported) and Lake Faguibine (Lamarche 1980; also Snow 1978, Curry and Sayer 1979, Brown *et al.* 1982). These birds must have been two- or three-year-olds (U. Hirsch *in litt.* 1982); the species is almost certainly no more than a vagrant to Mali.

Mauritania A flock of c. 50 was seen in February 1951 at Bir Moghreim (= Fort Trinquet) in the Zemmour, in north-west Mauritania (Dekeyser 1954, Valverde 1957, Heim de Balsac and Mayaud 1962), and a flock of c. 20 was seen in February 1960 perched in acacia near Aratane wells (18°24'N 8°31'W in Office of Geography 1966) in the Djouf, southern Mauritania (Smith 1970a; also Heim de Balsac and Mayaud 1962, Lamarche 1980). Cap Blanc in north-west coastal Mauritania is also named as the locality of a record (Hirsch and Schenker 1977). See comments under Western Sahara.

Morocco In 1982, a total of 12 colonies was known, five in eastern Morocco or the High Atlas and adjacent plains, and seven along the Atlantic coast, five of the latter being inside and two outside the proposed Massa National Park (Hirsch 1982b,c). The species was formerly widely distributed across central parts of Morocco from the eastern border with Algeria to the Atlantic coast, and breeding localities published between 1900 and 1970 include: *eastern Morocco*: the

Moscarda rocks by Triffa plain on the Morocco/Algeria border, colony extinct around 1940 (Brosset 1956,1957,1961); the Wadi Lefranne (= Oued el Frane) where it meets the lower Moulouya River (Brosset 1956,1961), extinct early 1960s (Brosset and Petter 1966); another colony on the same stretch of the Moulouya (Brosset 1961); three colonies in the Zekkara massif south-west of Oujda (Brosset 1956,1957), all virtually extinct early 1960s (Brosset and Petter 1966); Gaada de Debdou (Brosset 1956,1961); north of Saka (north of Guercif) (Marçais 1935); east of Taza (Hartert and Jourdain 1923), i.e. presumably the colony anticipated to the south of Msoun (Marçais 1935); *Atlantic coast*: Dar-ben-Arousi north of Rabat (Hartert and Jourdain 1923), extinct (Bédé 1926); Salé ("Sallee") cliffs, north of Rabat (Meade-Waldo 1903,1905), extinct before 1920 (Jourdain 1922, Hartert 1925, Bédé 1926) (these two localities adjacent); Cap Blanc near El Jadida (= Mazagan) (Hartert and Jourdain 1923; also Hartert 1902, Heim de Balsac and Mayaud 1962); Cap Cantin north of Safi, reputedly (Bannerman and Bannerman 1953) but not proved (*contra* Bierman 1959); Haha cliffs near Essaouira (= Mogador) (Meade-Waldo 1903), i.e. Cape Tafetneh (Tafelney) south of Essaouira (Hartert and Jourdain 1923, Marçais 1935), extinct by 1972 (H. Kumerloeve *in litt.* 1984); Talmeste on the Atlantic coast between Safi and Essaouira (Smith 1962-1963,1965); several colonies at Oued Massa (Heim de Balsac 1964; for varying numbers of colonies see Thévenot 1981); two unspecified localities (Smith 1970a), traceable to east of Tamri, near Agadir, and to between Safi and the Oued Tensift (Smith 1962-1963); *Middle Atlas region*: Oued Oum Er Rbia ("Wad Moorbey") at the "Oolad Lasara" (Meade-Waldo 1903), a village named Lassara or El Assara being at 32°20'N 6°43'W (Geographic Names Division 1970); up to four colonies at El Hajeb (Bédé 1926, Hartert 1928, Jourdain 1929); cliffs near Azrou (Hartert 1925,1926; also a specimen from 24 May [1919], in Lynes [1920], in BMNH: NJC); Causse d'Ito west of Azrou (Hüe 1953, Heim de Balsac and Mayaud 1962); Ain Leuh (Hartert 1925, Marçais 1935), apparently extinct (Snow 1952) but see below; Foum-el-Kheneg gorge south of Timhadite (Hüe 1953, Bierman 1959, Heim de Balsac and Mayaud 1962, Géroudet 1965, Sage and Meadows 1965, Smith 1965); crater cliff at "Jebel Hebbri", evidently near Timhadite, on the plateau (Lynes 1920, Hartert 1926; "Jbel Habri" is at 33°23'N 5°10'W in Geographic Names Division 1970); unspecified locality at 2,300 m, extinct (Ruthke 1966); Recifa gorge near Boulemane (Deetjen 1968); Timdighas (colony anticipated) (Carpentier 1933), this being near El Qbab at 32°40'N 5°30'W (M. Thévenot *in litt.* 1984). *High and Anti-Atlas region*: Aoulouz in Oued Sous (Lynes 1925, Géroudet 1965, Sage and Meadows 1965, Smith 1965, Meitz 1979a); Ksar de Tasdrem east of Aoulouz (Robin 1958; apparently the same as "Anmed" in Vernon 1973); Ouarzazate (Deetjen 1964). A report of birds breeding in cliffs in the Sidi Ifni region (Valverde 1957) appears not to have been confirmed, while a major piece of evidence to support this possibility ("the flock of several hundred seen by Bannerman 20 km north of Tiznit, 17 April 1952") refers to an unconfirmed record only, on 17 March not April (see Bannerman and Bannerman 1953), which is, perhaps, better attributable to the colonies then yet to be discovered at Oued Massa. Valverde (1957) also mentions birds from "Tuisguerrentz" in August 1952 and spring 1953, the species being reported as frequently seen there: this locality (Tuinzguerremtz, Tizgui Remt, Tuisgui Remz), at 28°25'N

9°13'W (Geographic Names Division 1970), is in the strip of land between 27°40'N and the Oued Draa ceded by Spain to Morocco in April 1958 (Steinberg and Paxton 1969). Increasingly intensive researches through the 1970s have continued to find new localities, as predicted (e.g. in Géroudet 1965, Smith 1970a, Rencurel 1974, Hamel 1975, Hirsch 1976a), but differences in the use of names, deliberate suppression or vagueness apropos localities, and the problem of colony desertion or establishment all combine to render a comprehensive enumeration of colonies inappropriate. However, at least 38 sites were known from the literature or other sources as of 1966, 19 of which were deserted by that date; from 1967 to at least 1978 there was no further information concerning six others; of the remaining 13, three were deserted in the early 1970s (Ain Leuh, El Hajeb and Foum-el-Kheneg) and three new ones discovered (Le Mischliffen near Azrou, Le Jorf Arbalou and Le Jorf Ait M'Hand, both in the Timhadite region) (Rencurel 1974, Hirsch 1979b), while by 1975 of 13 colonies – evidently misprinted as "18" in Hirsch and Schenker (1977), although the existence of two further colonies (i.e. 15 estimated in total) was guessed at by Hirsch (1976a) – five seemed previously unknown (Hirsch 1979a). By 1980 five colonies that were still occupied 1975-1977 had been abandoned (with no reliable information about two others) reducing the total number to eight (Hirsch 1981a), but in 1982 a more comprehensive survey confirmed 12 extant colonies (see first sentence in this section). In winter some 70% of the Moroccan population remains in the country, utilising probably only three main areas (Hirsch 1979b), two of which are evidently the Sous and Massa estuaries (Thévenot *et al.* 1982); fog on the coast between Agadir and Tiznit may be responsible for birds' presence all year at Massa, since it prevents dessication of the coastal steppe after June (Hirsch 1981f). Autumn records from around Tiznit (Meinertzhagen 1940) and observations of oversummering immatures around Goulimine, Oued Noun and Oued Draa (Heim de Balsac and Heim de Balsac 1951, Ruthke 1977) confirm the local nature of birds' movements in Morocco. In the Middle Atlas, near Ifrane, the species was even reported to remain all winter (Snow 1952), this tending to be confirmed by a subsequent sighting of birds near Ifrane in February and the capture of an exhausted specimen in snow at Timhadite (Rencurel 1974).

Saudi Arabia Birds have been recorded from the Red Sea coast in Saudi Arabia on three occasions, February/March: two between Al Qunfuda (Al Qunfidhah) and Souk Maschkal (Suq Mashkal, at 19°09'N 41°12'E in DMATC 1978) in February 1825 (Hirsch 1980a), five or six (very probably this species) near Birq (Al Birk) in February or March 1948 (Smith 1970a), and 24 just north of Jedda in March 1950 (Meinertzhagen 1954). A bird was also seen at Turaif (31°41'N 38°39'E in DMATC 1978) near the Jordan border in April 1976 (Hirsch 1980a). Given the coastal records and those from Eritrea (see under Ethiopia above) on the opposite side of the Red Sea, it seems very likely that birds have consistently used western Saudi Arabia as either a wintering or a staging area; indeed, the tradition in Birecik (Turkey) that the species leads the Islamic faithful on their pilgrimage to Mecca (Hirsch and Schenker 1977, Hirsch 1978) may perhaps have grown from repeated sightings of it around Mecca by pilgrims who knew it from around Birecik.

Somalia Two birds were seen in September 1920 (one of the exceptionally few records – perhaps the only – of this species outside Morocco and Turkey in this month) on the Ethiopian border at the Tug Wujaleh, feeding at the edge of a pool after rains (Archer and Godman 1937). There is a specimen in Genoa of a young bird collected around 1910/1911 in "Somalia" (Hirsch 1980a), which would presumably therefore indicate former Italian Somaliland; but this might be the specimen listed as coming from Ethiopia (in Salvadori 1912) and therefore presumably the one collected in "Arussi country" (Archer and Godman 1937: see Ethiopia above), since the same collector (C. Citerni) is referred to in all three cases.

Sudan The species has been recorded from Suakin on the Red Sea and at least twice (not regularly, as implied in Vaurie 1965) from the Blue Nile, on the latter occasion just south of Singa (Sclater and Mackworth-Praed 1920, Flower 1922, Nikolaus 1984). The possibility that it breeds in the Red Sea hills of Sudan has been consistently maintained (Bowen 1926, Vaurie 1965, Smith 1970a, Hirsch 1977a,b), although the idea seems to have developed to help explain the occurrence of birds further south along the Red Sea coast and in Ethiopia before the migratory connexion between the latter phenomenon and the Turkish population became so likely (see under Ethiopia above). Gebel Elba, singled out as the one locality in the extreme south-east of the Egyptian deserts which might not yet be too dry for the species to breed in (Moreau 1966), is in fact in extreme north-east Sudan. Records of birds in winter from Karora just inside Ethiopia (see above) suggest that it may be (or have been) regular in winter along the southern half of Sudan's Red Sea coastlands; a wildlife official even reports the species to be resident on the coast, travelling inland occasionally to rivers, and migrating to Khor Hanroyet (Hanoyet, Hamoyet), Port Sudan, during the period March/April (Hirsch 1980a), but this is almost certainly all derived from statements made in Bowen (1926) (G. Nikolaus *in litt.* 1984; see Population: Sudan).

Syria This species appears to have been fairly well distributed as a breeding bird throughout northern Syria, dying out (presumably) at an unknown date after 1928. What were evidently Northern Bald Ibises were found breeding in the walls of Raqqa on the Euphrates in north-central Syria in May 1836 (Danford 1880, Kumerloeve 1962), and a colony was discovered in 1904 in the "great white cliff" (600 m above sea level) near the springs at "Jebar", some "five hours" (presumably on horseback) from El Qaryatein (Kuryatein) (Sclater 1906, Kumerloeve 1960): this locality has been identified as Ain Jebbat, c. 20 km north of El Qaryatein (Hirsch 1980a) or possibly (unless the same) Gebel el Geba, 25 km north-east of El Qaryatein (Safriel 1980). This and other localities were soon afterwards searched for by the collector J. Aharoni, whose somewhat imprecise accounts (Aharoni 1911,1929) recently became the subject of simultaneous independent investigations (Hirsch 1980a, Safriel 1980) that offered slightly differing but equally authoritative interpretations: under one of these (Safriel 1980) six breeding colonies were found, five near El Qaryatein, one near Palmyra, under the other (Hirsch 1980a) only five colonies were found, four within 50 km of El Qaryatein and one near Palmyra (that only five colonies existed in total is made explicit in Aharoni 1928). This last was also the largest (Aharoni 1911) and most difficult to reach (Aharoni 1928), and evidently persisted the longest, since the single remaining colony in 1928 bore the name "Rheme" or "Rkheme" (Safriel 1980; also thus in Fischer-Sigwart 1914; "Rehme" in Hirsch 1980a) which, though speculated to be Ein ir Rhebe 20 km north-west of El Qaryatein (Safriel 1980), was reported to be near Palmyra (Kumerloeve 1978) and is now identified with the mountains 40 km to the north of Palmyra called Jebel Abou Rejmeine (Hirsch 1980a). It is not clear if Aharoni rediscovered "Jebar" but there are specimens from 1910 labelled "Dschebe" which might be Oum el Djebab, 60 km north-west of El Qaryatein, or possibly "Geba" or "Jebar" (Safriel 1980). Another colony active in 1910 (and still so in 1918) was El Khoudriat or Hudriat ("Chudrigat" in Hirsch 1980a), a rocky promontory 27 km north-east of El Qaryatein (Safriel 1980). Certain Aharoni specimens are labelled "Wukr-ez-zbede" (Hirsch 1980a; there are two nestlings in BMNH from this locality in May 1914: NJC); Aharoni also received specimens in 1908 from "Gebel Antamai", possibly a rocky outcrop near El Qaryatein (Safriel 1980). There is a report of a colony near Es Sukhne, north-east of Palmyra, in 1911 (Kumerloeve 1978) and of another 50 km west of Abu Kemal, i.e. near the Iraq border (Moore and Boswell 1956). A sixteenth century text is taken to indicate that birds were present at Zelebiye (Selebi) near Zenobia (these two considered the same locality, "Zalabiyah", and at 35°39'N 39°51'E in Office of Geography 1967), 80 km south of Birecik (Turkey) on the Euphrates (Kumerloeve 1962,1967b), but this interpretation has been doubted (Hirsch 1980a). Nevertheless, the species does regularly penetrate into Syria from Birecik to forage, e.g. near Bumbudj (Bambeudj), c. 50 km south of Birecik, and around Djerablus, with a roost on a rock just inside Syria during the pre-nesting period (Weigold 1912-1913, Kumerloeve 1965,1967b, Hirsch 1979a). Birds have also been seen south-east of Et Tell el Abyad, i.e. near the Belikh River on the Turkish border east of the Euphrates, in May 1946 (Kumerloeve 1967b). The whole Turkish population must pass over a part of Syria each spring and autumn; the September record of birds at Amik Gölü in Turkey (see below) raises the possibility that some birds at least may use the Rift Valley as a corridor between Turkey and the Red Sea (see also Israel above).

Tunisia An immature specimen from Tunisia preserved in BMNH was thought the only record of the species there (Whitaker 1905), but was subsequently found to have come from Algeria (Hartert 1912-1913). There seem therefore to be no records whatever from the country (Heim de Balsac and Mayaud 1962, *contra* Brosset 1956, Etchécopar and Hüe 1964). Regular dispersal to Tunisia after breeding (Vaurie 1965, Brown *et al.* 1982) certainly does not occur.

Turkey The most celebrated breeding locality of the Northern Bald Ibis and perhaps of any threatened bird species is the Turkish town of Birecik (in older literature "Beredjik", "Birajik", "Biledjik", etc.) on the upper Euphrates River c. 20 km from the Syrian border, discovered in 1879 (Dresser 1871-1881, Danford 1880). The original distribution of breeding birds at Birecik is unclear: they certainly chiefly occupied the cliffs below the town's Saracenic castle, but evidently also other rock-faces in a number of groupings or sub-colonies, some immediately to the north of the town (Danford 1880, Tristram 1882, Weigold 1912-1913). In 1953 birds still chiefly occupied the cliffs below the castle, but a small group was on a cliff in the middle of the town (H. Kumerloeve *in litt.* 1984). The cliffs below the castle were abandoned around 1956-1957, birds thereafter being restricted to some cliffs south of the castle within the town itself, very close to houses (Kumerloeve 1962,1965), though in 1970 a few pairs were also on cliffs overhanging a cement works at the edge of the river (Porter 1973) and since 1979 a few pairs have bred on a cliff a few kilometres upriver (see tabulation under Population: Turkey). In 1983 and 1984 birds have bred only at a cliff near the captive breeding aviaries north of Birecik, the town now being finally deserted by the species (H. R. Akçakaya *in litt.* 1984). Birds breeding at Birecik sometimes forage and roost in Syria (see above) and north of the town (see Ecology). Some 25-40 years prior to 1965, i.e. 1925-1940, certain other localities to the north and south of Birecik were occupied, notably near Tibobür, Savi, Telmusa and Belkis, and the breeding of a few pairs at Belkis (12 km north of Birecik) was reported in 1965, although none was present in 1967 (Kumerloeve 1967a), and two or three pairs were present most years in the 1970s in the area of these localities (Hirsch 1980a). Exploration in May 1973 of 150 km of the Euphrates upstream from Birecik yielded no birds, but in June of that year two pairs were considered to have bred at Halfeti north of Birecik on the Euphrates at cliffs where 40-50 years previously many birds were said to have nested (Hirsch 1980a). The only other locality where the species has occurred in Turkey appears to be Amik Gölü (Lake Antioch), where eight birds were captured in September 1928 (Kumerloeve 1967a). The basis for the assertion that it occurs on the "upper Tigris" – Turkey or Iraq not specified – (Hartert 1912-1921) is not known.

Western Sahara (former Spanish Sahara) Birds have been recorded from Smara (Semara), August 1954, and from Tuisguerrentz, August 1952 and spring 1953, and were reported frequently seen in the latter area (now in Morocco: see above); a bird answering this species's description was seen at Dakhla (= Villa Cisneros) in October 1954 (Valverde 1957). These and the records from Mauritania (see above) indicate that at least young birds disperse (or used to disperse) through the regions to the south of Morocco with some regularity (Valverde 1957).

North Yemen and South Yemen Although long suspected of breeding in "Yemen" (Meinertzhagen 1951,1954, Vaurie 1965, Hirsch 1977a,b), this species has provided no firm evidence that its status there is anything more than accidental (Smith 1970a): one of a pair was shot at Lawdar (Lodar) in western South Yemen in December 1948 (Meinertzhagen 1948-1949, Hirsch 1980a; incorrect date – "January 1949" – in Meinertzhagen 1954). There are no other records from either country, but secondhand reports from local people refer to its presence at various times of year (Hirsch 1980a) and to its being actively persecuted for the damage it does to black pepper crops (Kumerloeve 1965). The species is included on a list of birds recorded from North Yemen (Jennings 1981).

Population About 400 birds but only about 100 pairs were known to survive in the wild in 1982, when 367, including 93 pairs, were censused in

Morocco, approximately 10 pairs were present in Algeria, and 12 birds, forming five pairs, returned to Birecik in Turkey (see below); given that there must have been an absolute minimum 2,500 birds around 1910 in Syria and Turkey – and even a claimed 3,000 pairs at Birecik (Turkey) in the 1890s – and that there were an estimated 1,000 pairs (i.e. some 3,000 birds) in Morocco in the 1930s despite the extinction of at least two major colonies earlier in the century, it seems possible that the world population of the Northern Bald Ibis around 1900 would have been very approximately 10,000 birds, on which basis 96% of the population has disappeared in about 80 years.

Algeria The number of pairs in the Djebel Amour colony is 8-12 every year (Hirsch 1981d, U. Hirsch *in litt.* 1982) and certainly not more than 14: the maximum number of individuals seen at any one time in the past three years was 16, and the maximum number of fledged young produced was 10 in 1982 (E. D. H. Johnson *in litt.* 1984); however, in both June 1983 and May 1984 only seven birds were seen (J. Farnsworth *per* E. D. H. Johnson *in litt.* 1984). The colony at Ksar El Boukhari was never known to be bigger than this, with c. 12 pairs present in 1924 (Heim de Balsac 1924), and breeding there appears to have been sporadic and dependent on sufficient rainfall, occurring in 1923, 1924, 1926 and 1929, birds being absent in 1925, 1927 and 1928 (Heim de Balsac 1931; also Hartert 1928, Jourdain 1929,1934); apart from the vague assertion of nesting occurring in "years following" 1930 (Heim de Balsac and Mayaud 1962) and the discovery of recently used nests there in October 1953 (Kumerloeve 1958), this locality is not known to have been occupied again, was certainly vacant in 1972 (Kumerloeve 1974, Cramp and Simmons 1977) and is now considered permanently abandoned (Ledant *et al.* 1981). The nineteenth century colony south of Boughzoul was presumably very small since the observer remarked on the species's apparent lack of gregariousness (Tristram 1860).

Ethiopia Evidence of several writers indicates that this species could once have been locally abundant in Ethiopia: large flocks breaking down into small "family" groups have been reported from the Red Sea coastlands (Eritrea), December to February, many hundreds of birds being involved (Rüppell 1845, Smith 1955,1970a), and birds were "abundant" in Shoa province especially at Lake Cialalaka, December (Salvadori 1884). However, most birds were evidently present for only a small part of the year (November to February – see Distribution: Ethiopia), which would explain why one observer over a two-year period found it "by no means common" (Blanford 1870), and indeed in years when conditions were favourable in Eritrea it may perhaps not have penetrated into the highlands, which would explain why another observer considered it probably of irregular occurrence (von Heuglin 1869-1874). Observations of good numbers in Eritrea in the early 1950s (Smith 1955,1970a) correspond well with the last observations of good numbers at Birecik in Turkey (Kumerloeve 1958), and in the past 30 years the only record from Ethiopia is of six birds in December 1977, Shoa province (Ash and Howell 1977), whilst observations at Lake Cialalaka in the 1970s always drew blank (J. S. Ash *in litt.* 1984).

Morocco The Northern Bald Ibis has evidently been in constant decline in Morocco throughout this century: fifty years ago it was considered a "disappearing species" (Jourdain 1934), in 1965 it was in "alarming decline" (Géroudet 1965), and in the decade since 1965 this decline became so serious that its extinction was considered a certainty (Hamel 1975). The number of colonies being so high (though never individually so large as those formerly reported from Turkey and Syria) and the accounts of them so various, a synthesised documentation of the population decrease in Morocco is not feasible, but certain examples indicate the severity of its nature. The earliest account of the species there dealt with the northernmost Atlantic coast colony known, on the cliffs at Salé: here in May 1901 it was found to breed "abundantly ... , each bay being occupied by many pairs, and most available sites being taken up; the nests were often very close together, some ledges being quite covered with them, so that they touched each other" (Meade-Waldo 1903). These birds fed and were very numerous on the downs at the edge of the Forest of Marmora, inland (Meade-Waldo 1903,1905), but the whole colony (from its description very large by Moroccan standards) and that at nearby Dar-ben-Arousi had been completely exterminated by or before 1920 (Jourdain 1922, Bédé 1926). In the 1920s there were "quantities" of birds at Aoulouz in Oued Sous, the largest individual colony holding 40 pairs (Lynes 1925), but since the 1960s the number of pairs for the whole area has never exceeded 20 (Géroudet 1965, Hirsch and Thévenot 1980). Also in the 1920s the species was "common" both on the plateau and in the foothills of the Middle Atlas (Lynes 1925), where by the start of the 1980s it had completely vanished (see below). In the late 1950s the three Zekkara colonies in eastern Morocco held 60-70(-75) pairs (Brosset 1957,1961), but only a single pair could be found during a search in the early 1960s (Brosset and Petter 1966). In 1975 a first attempt at a comprehensive analysis of records and survey of known sites (then totalled at 33) produced the following figures: where in eastern Morocco in seven colonies there had been some 200 pairs in the 1950s, there remained an estimated 30 pairs in perhaps two sites (area not visited); where in the Middle and High Atlas there had been some 100 pairs in nine colonies, there remained some 50 pairs in four; where on the Atlantic coast and the plains around Marrakech there had been over 220 pairs in 13 colonies (see also Robin 1973), there remained 100 pairs in seven; and south of the Atlas where an unknown number had bred in four colonies, 10 pairs survived at two sites (one new) (Hirsch 1976a). It was estimated that about 1,000 pairs might have been present in Morocco, 1930-1940 (Hirsch 1976b), or at least 500 pairs in 1940 (in a healthy population the breeder to non-breeder ratio is 2:1, therefore at least 1,500 birds), while in 1975 only some 200 pairs were known with perhaps 50 pairs to be found in the Middle Atlas (in unhealthy populations such as existed in all but two colonies in 1975 the breeder to non-breeder ratio is between 4:1 and 6:1, therefore 600-650 birds in all) (Hirsch 1976a; also Hirsch and Schenker 1977). In this 1975 survey 198 breeding pairs were counted in 13 colonies, but in 1977 only 119 pairs could be found in a limited survey (Hirsch 1979a,c), hence an estimated total of 210 pairs present in that year was revised downwards to 180 in a total population of 400-500 birds (Kumerloeve 1978). By 1979 only about 100 (certainly less than 125) pairs were believed to be present, in 15 colonies (Hirsch 1980a, Brown *et al.* 1982; see also Meitz 1979b). In the course of the 1970s the importance of the populations in coastal southern Morocco became increasingly apparent, these birds and those in the High Atlas being unaffected by drought (Robin 1973) and the former, unlike the latter, showing signs of being able to maintain their numbers (see, e.g., Heinze *et al.* 1978): in 1980 a study of south-west Moroccan colonies was made, with the following results (Hirsch and Thévenot 1980).

Colony	Province	Number of pairs
a	Ouarzazate	6
b	Marrakech	(4, later shot)
c	"	–
d	"	–
e	"	–
f	Essaouira	3
g	"	8
h	Agadir	8
i	"	3
j	"	32
k	"	19
TOTAL		79 (74 in Hirsch 1980c,1981a,c)

Sixty birds did not breed for lack of space at two colonies, but an encouraging total of 168 young fledged (Hirsch 1980c,1981a,c); in an independent survey of Morocco in 1980, seven colonies (only one of which was thought not threatened) with 62 breeding pairs were found, 43 pairs being in four colonies at the coast, with 15 pairs on the south side of the High Atlas and four pairs around Marrakech (Meitz 1980). In 1981, of 34 colonies visited throughout Morocco, only 10 were occupied and breeding occurred in only seven (Hirsch 1981e,1982a; slightly different data in Thévenot *et al.* 1982), with the following details (Hirsch and Thévenot 1981).

Area	Colonies with birds	Colonies breeding	Number of pairs	Total birds	Sites visited
Atlantic coast	4	3	44 (35 at Massa)	200 (111 at Massa)	5
High Atlas, etc.	3	3	20	110	7
Middle Atlas	0	0	0	0	9
Eastern Morocco	2	0	0	9	11
Haouz	1	1	(5, later shot)	(14, later shot)	2
TOTAL	10	7	64	319	34

In 1982, when good rainfall yielded optimal breeding results, what was considered probably the most comprehensive survey of former and current breeding sites gave the following figures (Hirsch 1982b,c).

Area	Colonies	Number of pairs	Total birds
High Atlas and adjacent plains/ eastern Morocco	5	26	108
Atlantic coast outside proposed Massa N.P.	2	10	76
Atlantic coast inside proposed Massa N.P.	5	57	183
TOTAL	12	93	367

Despite good climatic conditions a further decline in inland colonies took place, but along the Atlantic coast and especially within the proposed Massa National Park the number of birds increased; however, no explanation could be found for the very high number of non-breeding birds present (Hirsch 1982c). In April 1984 the five colonies around Massa held about 220 birds (Hirsch 1984).

Sudan Notwithstanding the record of a (clearly wintering) flock of several hundred, perhaps over a thousand, in February 1922 (Flower 1922), this species probably no longer occurs except perhaps occasionally along the southern Red Sea coastlands in winter, the only record since 1955 being of one on presumed spring passage at Suakin, 18 March 1983 (Nikolaus 1984). However, the official who reported it resident (see Distribution: Sudan) also called it common (Hirsch 1980a), but this is probably as a result of referring to the now outdated Bowen (1926), where the species is called "common on the coast – resident" (see Nikolaus 1984). That the species was, indeed, common on the coast, at least seasonally, in the 1920s is supported by a record of a flock of 20-30 birds, probably feeding on locust-hoppers, at Khor Hanroyet, in February/March 1926 (W. Ruttledge *in litt.* 1984).

Syria In 1836 the species nested "by thousands" at Raqqa (Danford 1880). In 1910 the colony near Palmyra may have held a thousand breeding birds (Aharoni 1911), a colony at a undisclosed locality held 50 pairs but deserted (see Remarks) on the day of observation (Aharoni 1911), and another near El Qaryatein held 300 birds (Safriel 1980).

Turkey Although reputed to have existed for hundreds of years (indeed, the legend of the species's association with Birecik goes back to Noah), the Birecik colony may in fact have been founded only a few decades before its discovery in 1879 (see Kumerloeve 1962). According to a town official, roughly 3,000 pairs were present in 1890 (Kumerloeve 1962). Total numbers in 1912 were guessed at about

1,000 (Weigold 1912-1913), a figure which has subsequently been cited and discussed as if it represented a census. In June 1953 some 1,300 birds, including young, were estimated to be present, and in the following year another observer estimated 600-800 pairs, and it was therefore reasoned that the colony had actually grown in size since 1912, perhaps as a result of the veneration the birds enjoyed (Kumerloeve 1958) or of the above-average rainfall then being experienced (Safriel 1980). The 1954 figures have been heavily revised downward in the belief that the observer failed to allow for a high proportion (up to a third) of non-breeding birds amongst those counted (Hirsch 1980a; also Kumerloeve 1978). In any case, events in the late 1950s (see Threats: Turkey) completely transformed the situation in Birecik, and the fate of the population since 1960 is charted in the following tabulation (in which a dash indicates quantity unknown and for which there are no data from 1966).

Year	Total adults	Breeding pairs	Young fledged	Source
1961	–	c. 200	–	Kumerloeve 1962
1962	c. 250	120-130	–	Kumerloeve 1962,1965
1963		[70][1]		Bezzel 1964
1964	125-130	65[2]	65	Kumerloeve 1965
1965	155	70-75	70	Kumerloeve 1967a
1966	–	–	–	
1967	114-117	45-48	–	Kumerloeve 1967a,1969
1968	96	45-46	–	Kumerloeve 1969
1969	78	37-39	–	Kumerloeve 1969
1970	–	36[3]	–	OST 1975
1971	71	35	11	Groh 1971, Warncke 1972, OST 1975, Hirsch 1978
1972	56	23-26	6-8	Hirsch 1973,1976a, OST 1975
1973	72	22[4]	21	Hirsch 1976a,1978
1974	60[5]	25	–[6]	Hirsch 1975,1978
1975	54	25	–[7]	Hirsch 1978
1976	39	13	17	Hirsch 1978
1977	34	13	[16-17][8]	Hirsch 1978
1978	30	13	[16][9]	Hirsch 1980a
1979	27	12 (9+3)	21 (16+5)[10]	Hirsch 1980a
1980	22	8 (6+2)	13 (11+2)	Hirsch 1980a
1981	17	7 (5+2)	8-12	Hirsch 1981e
1982	12	5 (3+2)[11]	5	Hirsch 1982c
1983	–	8[12]	[17][13]	Hirsch 1984
1984	–	5[14]	–	H. R. Akçakaya *in litt.* 1984, U. Hirsch *in litt.* 1984

Notes

1. This number was estimated from a count of vacated nests on 31 July.
2. A hundred pairs had been thought present by another (briefer and earlier) visitor (Warncke 1965).
3. On 5 May 1970 there were 28 occupied nests on a cliff in Birecik, eight occupied nests and five apparently unoccupied nests on cliffs below the town; of 11 nests examined in detail, three had one young, four had two young, and four had three young (R. F. Porter *in litt.* 1984).
4. Several sources give 26 pairs for 1973 (Hirsch 1974,1976a; OST 1975) but four of these did not breed (Hirsch 1978); OST (1975) gives 22 young fledged.
5. Hirsch (1975) gives 68.
6. Hirsch (1975) gives 36 young reared, Hirsch (1978) 64 young reared; however, subsequent reports indicated that only 64 birds in total left Birecik (Hirsch 1980a). The implication is that while 36 young may have hatched, (almost) no young were fledged in 1974.
7. Hirsch (1978,1980a) says 36 young were reared, but OST (1978) says only 61 birds in total left Birecik: again, the implication is that (almost) no young were reared in 1975.
8. It is evident (from Kumerloeve 1978) that the nine young birds taken for the local captive breeding project this year (see Conservation Measures Taken: Turkey) were taken from amongst birds listed here as having fledged.
9. Ten of the 16 birds fledged and three adults were captured (Hirsch 1980a).
10. Figures in brackets refer to numbers in Birecik plus numbers at a site north of Birecik; two adults were captured before the breeding season and five young before migration south (Hirsch 1980a).
11. Hüni (1982) gives six pairs in Birecik and five birds upriver.
12. Several birds released from captivity formed pairs with wild birds, hence the increased number of pairs in 1983 (Hirsch 1984).
13. This figure, based on local report, probably refers to the total number of birds that migrated away from Birecik (U. Hirsch *per* M. E. Quigley *in litt.* 1984).
14. Eight birds returned in March from the winter quarters, nine birds were released from captivity, four of these disappearing; thus there were only 13 birds in Birecik in 1984, five pairs breeding (H. R. Akçakaya *in litt.* 1984, U. Hirsch *in litt.* 1984).

Ecology A gregarious bird throughout the year, the Northern Bald Ibis inhabits arid or semi-arid plains and plateaus, breeding in colonies in traditionally used cliffs often adjacent to watercourses (Vaurie 1965, Smith 1970a). Habitats and food are basically the same in Morocco and Turkey (Hirsch 1979a,1981b). From the account by K. Gessner in the mid-sixteenth century, remarkable for its accuracy where this can be checked, the food and feeding techniques of the species in central Europe were similar to those of present-day populations, but the habitat was evidently much lusher and must have been very different (Smith 1970a, Moreau 1972), which poses problems about the bird's avoidance of such habitat in more recent time (for Gessner's text in original German, see Kumerloeve 1958; in French, Géroudet 1965; in English, Rothschild *et al.* 1897). Extinction in Europe may primarily have been due to climatic cooling (see Threats): the species's present tolerance of degrees of aridity and temperature are not clear, though its Moroccan distribution does not go below the 200 mm isohyet (Robin 1973; see below for effect of drought on breeding), while colonies at higher altitudes endure considerable cold at night, with occasional snowfalls as late as April (Géroudet

1965). The primary requirement for the species is suitable feeding terrain, sufficient food only being found in certain habitats, e.g. sandy coastal strips, river beds, sandbanks and damp soft ground in the lower areas of high plateaus: in such places a low, species-rich but often sparse vegetation provides a species-rich invertebrate fauna (Hirsch 1981b,f; also 1979a); only rarely will birds forage on tilled fields or pastures with plants higher than 20-30 cm (Hirsch and Schenker 1977, Hirsch 1979a), although they have been seen foraging on stubble-fields in autumn (Meinertzhagen 1940). In eastern Morocco its relatively strong representation was attributed to the particularly favourable habitat produced by the conjunction of continental plain and Mediterranean climate: semi-arid steppe intersected with permanently flowing watercourses, and notably areas where flower-covered (*Asphodelus*-dominated) calcareous soils produced a rich invertebrate food-supply (Brosset 1956,1957,1961). In Syria the species was considered a steppe- and desert-dweller, even apparently avoiding water (Peters 1928). However, birds in both Morocco and Turkey also forage in marshes and their environs, even wading in very shallow water (Robin 1958, Brosset 1961, Géroudet 1965, Rencurel 1974, Hirsch 1978), but there has been no precise definition of the type of marsh used, although it seems that flooded fields and grasslands (i.e. marshes with very low vegetation) are often intended. Birds from two particular nest-ledges in Birecik, Turkey, were noted to obtain food north of the town from river banks, scantly vegetated islands in the Euphrates, and other uncultivated areas (e.g. stony fields); birds from two other ledges consistently flew south of the town to feed in marshland and cultivated areas (Hirsch and Schenker 1977, Hirsch 1978). Birds will feed up to 70 km from this colony, although only travelling some 5 km away when with eggs or young (Cramp and Simmons 1977, Hirsch 1979a). The restriction of activity to within a radius of 5 km of the colony during the nesting period has also been noted in Morocco (Géroudet 1965, Rencurel 1974); the Salé cliffs birds north of Rabat foraged on the edges of and in openings made by burning in the nearby Forest of Marmora (Meade-Waldo 1903,1905). Although cliffs are not considered important as a habitat feature (Hirsch 1981b), the presence of suitable nesting sites at reasonable distances from good feeding habitat is clearly an important requisite for a stable population of birds and hence a major factor in determining distribution (Safriel 1980; also Brosset 1961). Such sites may be steep gorges, quite small rock-faces, sheer sea-cliffs (Hartert 1912-1921, Smith 1970a); in Syria the species used sheer cliffs extending over long distances through flat open desert (Aharoni 1911); one observer in Morocco considered it to prefer overhanging cliffs (Harrison 1933), and doubtless the degree of sheerness matches the degree of protection a particular site gives against mammalian nest-predators; nevertheless the location of the major Turkish colony on cliffs within the town of Birecik (see Distribution) and of one Moroccan colony on a casbah (Kumerloeve 1974) indicates that in certain contexts the species may show a curious lack of concern over the proximity of human beings. In Morocco, birds were found to nest only in localities which received no more than 4.5 hours of sunshine per day (Hirsch 1976a,1978,1979a), and nests were of three types: on open ledges, on overhung ledges, and in holes (Hirsch 1976a: for different breeding success in these, see below). Cliffs are also used for roosting, inside and outside the breeding season (Brosset 1961, Rencurel 1974), although non-breeding birds, Morocco, have been recorded using a dam (Ruthke 1977) and wintering birds, Eritrea, coastal mangroves and garden trees (Smith 1955,1970a). In a winter of good rainfall, Eritrea, birds avoided areas of high grass and kept to open, sandy, coastal plains and flats covered by short seasonal grass *Cenchrus*, *Indigofera*, and dense stands of *Heliotropium*, where they spread out in flocks, often feeding round cattle, two even being seen walking about amongst occupied huts in a village; in a drier winter, they moved more inland to areas of open acacia (Smith 1955,1970a). In the Ethiopian highlands, birds have been found on high moors, wet meadows, grassland with patches of cultivation, by mountain torrents and on the margins of a particular lake, up to 3,350 m (von Heuglin 1862,1869-1874, Salvadori 1884, Ash and Howell 1977). The Northern Bald Ibis forages almost all day long, in loose groups though sometimes solitarily, moving about over stony terrain scouring cracks and fissures with its bill and probing under stones and in tufts of vegetation or, in sandy areas or on soft earth, probing deep into the ground, sensing and tracking subterranean prey (Rencurel 1974, Hirsch 1981b). Movements while feeding are generally unhurried, but in pursuit of insects birds can run quickly, neck outstretched, and may suddenly pounce on prey (Hartert 1925, Meinertzhagen 1940, Ruthke 1977). The species's diet is mixed, like its ecology, composition reflecting both steppe and marsh (Brosset 1961), although from the following itemisations it is evident that the principal adaptation is for foraging in semi-arid steppe: Coleoptera, Orthoptera, and small reptiles appear to be the most important types of food (first-hand accounts to this overall effect in Rüppell 1845, Tristram 1860, von Heuglin 1869-1874, Dresser 1871-1881, Hartert 1902,1925, Mathey-Dupraz 1925, Aharoni 1928, Ruthke 1977, Meitz 1979a, Hirsch 1981f). Beetles that live by day in sand, also their larvae, are a typical prey (Hirsch 1981b,f); reptiles include lizards of all species, even hard-armoured ones, and snakes, even young horned vipers *Cerastes cerastes*, decapitated with vigorous shakes of the bill (Aharoni 1928) (it seems very possible that these observations refer to birds fed in captivity, since rather similar observations by this author concerning Houbara Bustard *Chlamydotis undulata* are explicitly derived from captive birds – see Aharoni 1912). Other animal prey includes caterpillars, ants and their eggs, earwigs, spiders, scorpions, centipedes, woodlice, snails, earthworms, fish, amphibians (tadpoles, frogs, young toads), rodents ("small desert mice") and birds (e.g. nestlings of larks Alaudidae) (Rencurel 1974; also Hartert 1928, Aharoni 1929, Brosset 1961, Smith 1970a, Parslow 1973); rodents and birds are doubtless only rarely taken. Vegetable matter includes rhizomes of aquatic plants, duckweed *Lemna*, young shoots, and berries taken in pastures (Rencurel 1974), but is evidently little exploited (plants in stomach analyses have apparently only been found once: see below). The differences between prey taken in Morocco and Turkey are negligible, and the same species are involved (Hirsch 1981b). One Moroccan bird held many locusts, dung- and other beetles, centipedes and two amphisbaenians *Trogonophis wiegmanni* (Hartert 1902); another was full of scorpions (Pallary 1922); others from near Rabat, May, held locusts, scorpions and large centipedes (Meade-Waldo 1903); others from elsewhere all had large quantities of beetles (Hartert 1928); those of birds that foraged close to or in a wadi consistently held frogs, fish, insects and aquatic plants (Robin 1958). Stomachs of Algerian birds showed food of adults and young to be the same: high numbers of grasshoppers, plus large spiders, small snails and a myriapod (Heim de Balsac

1924). The majority of food of the birds at Birecik, Turkey, consists of mole-crickets *Gryllotalpa gryllotalpa* and various beetles and their larvae; more rarely, birds take the lizards *Lacerta cappadocica* and *Acanthodactylus boscianus* and, in the marshes to the south, amphibians (Hirsch and Schenker 1977). Nevertheless, an adult from this locality, June, held 95% locusts, 5% bush-crickets, and one large spider; while a two-week-old chick, May, contained a mole-cricket, ants, various beetles and crustacea (Parslow 1973). Young are fed on anything animal, from large insects to dismemberable lizards (Aharoni 1929); insects and frogs have been seen brought to young, Birecik (Hirsch 1973). Although birds have been noted flying to drink and to bring water back to their young (Kumerloeve 1965), they rarely do so, obtaining water requirements from food, those breeding far from fresh water exploiting local abundances of snails (Hirsch and Schenker 1977, Hirsch 1979a; also Etchécopar and Hüe 1964). Birds in autumn, Morocco, contained small lizards, grubs, grasshoppers and masses of beetles (Meinertzhagen 1940) and one in winter, South Yemen, held nothing but black beetles (Meinertzhagen 1954); wintering birds in Eritrea appeared to be taking grasshoppers and young locusts (Smith 1970a); oversummering immatures on stony desert, southern Morocco, fed chiefly on a species of tenebrionid beetle but were also seen at a rubbish-tip (Ruthke 1977). Birds return to their breeding colonies in February, at Birecik very punctually between 11th and 15th (Hirsch 1979a). As breeding occurs at traditional sites, single pairs (as reported in Cramp and Simmons 1977) are probaby usually the last members of a dying colony (see, e.g., Brosset and Petter 1966, Rencurel 1974). The size of colonies in north-west Africa is and seems always to have been small relative to those in the Middle East at the start of the century (see under Population); colonies are often in close proximity to other cliff-nesting bird species (Sclater 1906, Aharoni 1911, Heim de Balsac 1924, Brosset 1957, Géroudet 1965), this bearing on the problem of human disturbance (see Threats). Birds are monogamous, the pair-bond being of seasonal duration only (Cramp and Simmons 1977, Schenker 1977, Sahin 1982). Clutch-size is usually three or four, but often only two (Aharoni 1911,1929; also Hirsch 1979a); extremes of one and six are attributable to accident and old females respectively (Aharoni 1929; see Remarks), though in years of drought most nests held only one egg (Robin 1973). Eggs are generally laid in late March, Birecik (Kumerloeve 1965,1967a, Hirsch 1979a), and in March or April, north-west Africa (Brosset 1961, Heim de Balsac and Mayaud 1962, Hirsch 1979a), though in the latter area the onset of breeding varies between years, e.g. at Salé in 1901 and 1902 (Meade-Waldo 1903,1905), at Aoulouz in 1924 and 1965 (Lynes 1925, Géroudet 1965), and between areas, e.g. in relation (presumably) to rainfall – pairs at the coast in 1979 having large young at a time when those in the upper Sous were still incubating (Meitz 1979b) – or to altitude (Géroudet 1965): birds at 2,300 m appeared to be starting to incubate as late as May (Ruthke 1966). Records of nestlings from March, Syria, may be in error (see Remarks). Synchronisation of activity within a colony may be promoted by certain behavioural interactions (Thaler *et al.* 1981), so it may be that colonies with offspring at very different stages of development (see, e.g., Brosset 1957, Meitz 1979a) have suffered some major disruption. Incubation usually begins with the second egg (Rencurel 1974), though at least sometimes evidently with the first (Heim de Balsac 1924, Brosset 1957, Thaler *et al.* 1981); last-hatched chicks are likely (from behaviour of siblings) to be least fed and therefore to die (Hirsch 1979a). Breeding success increases with age of birds, which as the years pass come to occupy more central positions within the colony (Hirsch and Schenker 1977). A breeding rate of 2.5 young per nest has been claimed as normal (Hirsch and Schenker 1977), and in 1968 and 1972 three Moroccan colonies, each with 13 nests holding 3-4 eggs, each produced 39 fledged young, this claimed to represent at least 90% success rate for eggs laid (Brown *et al*. 1982). Other data are considerably less encouraging, e.g. in wet years, Morocco, 20% of nests with clutches of 2-4 eggs fledge none, 60% one, 15% two and 5% three young, while in dry years 50% fledge none and almost 50% fledge one (Cramp and Simmons 1977); and in eastern Morocco, despite clutches of 3-4 eggs, often only one young would fledge, while in some cases the majority of eggs were infertile or the young died by falling or from disease (Brosset 1961). Pairs nesting on open ledges have been found to have a smaller clutch-size than those in holes (two or three as against four), and to fledge 1-1.5 less young, this being attributed to the holes' greater protection against predators and bad weather (Rencurel 1974; also Hirsch 1979a). In very dry years no breeding may take place at all in some colonies, notably those in lowland areas away from the coast (Hartert 1928, Brosset 1956, Robin 1973); members of the colony tend to remain in the region without breeding rather than moving to a colony where breeding is less hampered by conditions (Robin 1973; also Kumerloeve 1974). Breeding success and development of colonies may be related to periods of above- and below-average rainfall: expansions and contractions of breeding range, and establishment and desertion of colonies, may occur in response to nest-site availability in more stable colonies (Safriel 1980). Soon after fledging, young birds leave the colonies with their parents, often by the end of June (Rencurel 1974, Hirsch 1979a), though in some localities (including Birecik) birds may return to roost on the ledges until August (Brosset 1956, Kumerloeve 1958), in the south of Morocco even reportedly up to November (Robin 1958). In Morocco birds move south to new feeding areas (Hirsch 1981f); the statement that young birds disperse in almost every direction (Brown *et al*. 1982) appears unfounded, and the possibility that post-breeding dispersal of birds, if related to food supply (which it is: Hirsch 1981f), might be reduced in a declining species (recruitment of young being insufficient to burden resources) (Siegfried 1966) appears not to have been fulfilled by observations. Young birds evidently soon separate into their own flocks: a winter gathering of 112 birds in southern Morocco contained only four one-year-olds, all the others appearing to be eight years or older (Hirsch 1980a), while an oversummering flock entirely composed of very young birds has been observed in a completely separate area (Ruthke 1977). Birds take six years before beginning to breed in the wild (maximum age around 25), although captive birds may be stimulated by older companions to breed at three or even two years of age (Hirsch 1978,1979a,1980a, Sahin 1980). What happens to immature birds in the intervening period is not clear: those from the eastern population may chiefly remain in the Ethiopian highlands, although the older birds amongst them may undertake increasingly extended northward movements at the appropriate season (which might explain the records under Distribution for Israel and Egypt); those in Morocco may behave similarly, the very young birds remaining in the far south (hence Ruthke 1977), those approaching maturity returning to the natal area but still remaining separate (such flocks observed by Rencurel 1974).

Threats The total collapse since the 1950s of the eastern population breeding at Birecik, Turkey, is directly attributable to the massive use of toxic chemical pesticides in the late 1950s in southern Turkey, and to their continuing application on farmland in the Birecik region ever since; disturbance and disruption at the breeding site, considered to be a major factor in the decline at one stage, is now judged to have been important but secondary (see below). In Morocco the influence of pesticides has been negligible to date, but there is no question that this species's exceptional susceptibility to them – demonstrated very clearly in a study of captive birds fed partly on Mediterranean fish at Tel Aviv (see Hirsch 1980a; also below under Turkey) – means that chemical spraying must remain the single most serious potential threat to the birds wherever they occur: a single application at Oued Massa (such as was averted in 1982: see Conservation Measures Taken: Morocco) would probably now be sufficient to seal the species's fate in the wild. The main factors causing the very serious decline in Morocco are hunting and poaching, disturbance while breeding and, perhaps most critical but least documented or understood, the development of land for agriculture (see below). The reasons for the species's extinction in central Europe are not clear: the taking of young for food, albeit with prudent leaving of one nestling per nest, was documented by Gessner (see Rothschild *et al.* 1897, Kumerloeve 1958, Géroudet 1965) and is considered to have been a likely factor along with the climatic cooling after the mid-sixteenth century (Schenker 1977; also Hirsch and Schenker 1977, Hirsch 1979a). The varying intensity of agricultural use at that period is unlikely to have affected distribution; and there were no marked changes in central European agriculture during the period the birds were known to have been present (the twelfth to the seventeenth century) which might have radically altered habitat (Schenker 1977, *contra* Hirsch 1976a). The more recent extinction of the species in Syria has similarly been traced to persecution and climatic change: in 1928 it was found that local Arabs slaughtered them for their flesh (Aharoni 1928,1929), this being accepted as the likely explanation for the loss of so many birds in so short a period (Kumerloeve 1967b, Hirsch 1978), along with collection for museums and zoos of several hundred specimens (Kumerloeve 1967b; also Aharoni 1932); however the fragmentary evidence concerning the Syrian colonies has been construed as indicating that they may only have come into existence as a result of climatic amelioration in the first decade of this century, resulting in overspill from Birecik in Turkey, and that their extinction was likewise chiefly the result of considerable drought in the 1920s (Safriel 1980). Natural dessication is certainly implied as responsible for the loss of the species from Egypt (Moreau 1966). It is to be observed here that the rather steady rate of this species's decline, its seemingly inexorable nature, and the similarity and simultaneity of the process in the eastern and western populations, combined with the fact of its extinction in Europe and the likelihood that it once ranged across North Africa, all suggest that the bird is and has for centuries been naturally declining and therefore that, despite the array of threats identified here (above, below), there remain certain unidentified natural factors whose effects are merely being amplified and accelerated by human pressures and whose power is well beyond human capacity to counteract. As noted under Ecology the Northern Bald Ibis shares its cliff-face colonies with other bird species, amongst which the Raven *Corvus corax* commonly figures as its most serious nest-predator (Aharoni 1911, Heim de Balsac 1924, Jourdain 1929, Ruthke 1966): disturbance by people at colonies has been noted to provide Ravens with the opportunity to despoil nests (Ruthke 1966). Other natural enemies include the Black Kite *Milvus migrans*, noted once to displace breeding birds to make a nest of its own (Heim de Balsac 1924) and Lanner Falcon *Falco biarmicus*, seen to attack a nesting bird (Jourdain 1929,1934).

Algeria The harsher (drier) climate relative to Morocco has been considered the main reason for the few birds and breeding localities in Algeria (Heim de Balsac 1931). Disturbances at Ain Sba may have been a factor, since a new road and railway as well as shooting were feared to have affected birds there (Hartert 1912-1921, Heim de Balsac 1924). The species's decline in or (as was at one stage thought) disappearance from Algeria has been variously attributed to the draining of marshes (Dupuy 1967), hunting by local people (Hirsch 1978), unspecified actions consequent upon the Algerian War of Liberation, 1954-1962 (Kumerloeve 1978), and the use of pesticides (Kumerloeve 1978). The threats of tourist disturbance and egg- or specimen-collection at the single surviving colony are taken seriously enough for its precise location to be suppressed.

Morocco The major factors in the decline of Morocco's birds, as noted above, have been human persecution, disturbance of colonies while breeding, and agricultural development (Brosset 1961, Kumerloeve 1974, Hirsch 1976a,b, 1977a,b,1979a,b,1981d). These and other factors may come into play in combination or sequence, e.g. the colony at Aoulouz has been affected by both poachers (Rencurel 1974) and zoo-collectors (Hirsch 1976a) and threatened by a damming project (Porter 1973, Kumerloeve 1974), while the Foum-el-Kheneg colony was affected by zoo-collectors (Hirsch 1976a) and snuffed out by poachers (Rencurel 1974) or the disturbance brought by a heavy increase in passing traffic (Hamel 1975). Human persecution of the species in Morocco has been judged the most serious threat, without which it could probably maintain its numbers (Rencurel 1974), though this is perhaps now doubtful. However, the history of the problem is certainly long and by no means over, and involves shooting for either pleasure or food or both, and the capture of adults and young for food: important colonies at Salé and Zekkara were exterminated in a matter of years by hunters (Jourdain 1922, Brosset and Petter 1966), a colony at El Hajeb dropped from 50 pairs in 1927 (Hartert 1928) to under 20 pairs in 1929 owing evidently to the ambushes of local hunters (Jourdain 1929), an unnamed colony with 30 pairs was similarly persecuted in 1974, 30 birds being shot, only 16 pairs being present the following year (Hirsch 1976a), the colony at Chichaoua was completely shot out in 1980, and that at Sour was then under constant pressure from one particular hunter (Hirsch and Thévenot 1980,1981). Disturbance of colonies during the breeding period takes many forms, including, of course, hunting (in terms of the effect on those not shot: see Remarks) and results in either rapid desertion or a slow dying out owing to inadequate recruitment: although there appear to be no fully documented examples of rapid desertion, this appears to have been the case at a site where an artillery range was installed nearby (Harrison 1933), at another where a road was built beneath the cliff (Ruthke 1966), at Lalla Takerkoust when quarrying began there (Hirsch and Thévenot 1980), at Kasbah de Tikirt and Ait ben Addou following arc-light illumination of breeding birds for the making of a film (Hirsch and Thévenot 1980), and at Moscarda cliffs partially in response to the advent of bathing as a pastime there (Brosset 1956, 1961). Where disturbance does not cause rapid desertion, it causes poor breeding success (in one colony where birds were daily flushed by tourists and fishermen seven breeding pairs raised only five young between them); chronic disturbance thus results in colonies of almost exclusively old birds, dwindling in number year by year until extinct (Hirsch 1976a,b, 1977a,b, 1980a, Hirsch and Schenker 1977). In 1980 one colony remained at serious risk from tourism (Hirsch and Thévenot 1980). Disturbance also increases the risk of nest-predation (see above); for the significance of shyness of breeding birds, see Remarks. The impact of agricultural development on the species in Morocco has not been documented, but has evidently been recognised recently as very considerable: 24 colonies are now believed to have been abandoned because of drastic changes to the feeding areas (U. Hirsch *in litt.* 1982 to P. D. Goriup), and the total desertion of the previously healthy and numerous Middle Atlas colonies is attributed to agriculture and mining – the latter presumably being either a disturbance or a cause of loss of site (Hirsch 1981e,1982a, Hirsch and Thévenot 1981). Drainage of Triffa marshes for agriculture was partly blamed for the loss of the Moscarda rocks colony (Brosset 1956, 1961). In 1980 two sites faced the risk of habitat modification by agriculture (Hirsch and Thévenot 1980). Toxic chemical pesticides in agriculture are apparently not yet a problem: of two birds shot by a hunter near Marrakech, 1979 or 1980, one held no residues whatsoever, the other a mere trace (0.001 ppm DDE) (Hirsch 1981b). Nevertheless, the poor fecundity noted in eastern Moroccan birds (Brosset 1961) may perhaps have been the result of pesticides; and the threat of their eventual use is most serious (Mayaud 1982; also Meitz 1979a). Other threats in Morocco are collecting (eggs, and adults for zoos), which has affected colonies at Aoulouz, Foum-el-Kheneg and Tifnit (Hirsch 1976a, 1979b, Hirsch and Thévenot 1980; also Meitz 1979b), dam-construction, such as has been planned at Oued El Frane and Aoulouz (Brosset 1956,1961, Porter 1973, Kumerloeve 1974), rockface collapse, such as destroyed the colony at Oued El Frane (before damming could affect it) and one at Massa (Brosset and Petter 1966, Hirsch 1980b), and drought, which becomes an ever more serious problem the more the populations dwindle from other causes: no breeding occurred at all in two colonies in 1981 (Hirsch 1981e,1982a, Hirsch and Thévenot 1981).

Turkey From the reports that colonies of the Northern Bald Ibis existed at various localities north of Birecik 45-60 years ago (see Distribution: Turkey) it is possible that the species has been in decline there for the better part of this century (reinforcing the view expressed above that ineluctable natural pressures are working against it): nevertheless, the immediate causes of the Birecik population's decline can be traced to a sequence of events in the late 1950s. A road bridge was built across the Euphrates at Birecik in this period: it destroyed the old ferry system, and it was the ferrymen who particularly kept alive the tradition of the species as holy or semi-sacred (see Distribution: Saudi Arabia, and Conservation Measures Taken: Turkey), so that the annual festival to celebrate its return to Birecik, which sustained local commitment to the birds' welfare, died out after 1958 and by the 1960s children were observed throwing stones at nesting birds and the whole problem of disturbance of the colony developed, particularly as the bridge also led to the economic growth of the town, a heavy influx of people unaware of the birds' significance, and much new building (Kumerloeve 1962,1965,1967a, Hirsch 1973, Hirsch and Schenker 1977). In the period 1956-1959 insecticide spraying against malaria was undertaken throughout the Euphrates basin, and in late 1959 a malaria epidemic was countered by extensive aerial applications of DDT (Hirsch and Schenker 1977, Hirsch 1980a). At the same time, certain marshy lower regions of the Euphrates were reclaimed for agriculture and sprayed with pesticides and, moreover, a locust swarm threatening south-eastern Turkey was countered by extensive "prophylactic" chemicals (Hirsch 1980a). In this period, people fell ill, sheep died, animal life was generally eradicated ("not a snake or scorpion survived") and in total – despite earlier reports of only one or two hundred (e.g. Kumerloeve 1962, Parslow 1973) – no fewer than 600-700 Northern Bald Ibises were found dead, i.e. about 70% of the colony's total population (Hirsch 1979a,1980a). When WWF project-work began on the species in 1973 the extent of neither the contemporaneous impact nor the subsequent effects of the pesticide spraying in the late 1950s was fully appreciated: from later research and examination of photographs, however, it was determined that of the 72 birds present in 1973 four were aged 12-14 years, four were 16-20 years, and all the rest were 20 years or older, this revealing the total failure of the birds that survived the spraying of the late 1950s to produce any surviving offspring since 1960 (Hirsch 1978,1980a), and hence giving context to an observation in 1964 of poor hatching performance in the colony (Warncke 1965). Continuing pesticide usage in the Birecik region in the early 1970s was suspected of perpetuating the problem (Hirsch 1973), although levels of DDT/DDE and aldrin/dieldrin in an egg and chick from 1972 were not considered high enough to have serious sublethal effects (Parslow 1973); yet in 1973 around Birecik alone an estimated 80,000 kg of pesticides were sprayed, the birds that fed on cultivated land to the south of the town suffered 100% nest failure, and some 30 eggs and chicks taken that year for analysis (which took about four years) were found to have an average contamination of 10.5 ppm DDT/DDE, chicks having 1.2 ppm at one day rising to 181 ppm at 20 days (Hirsch 1978,1981b, Brown *et al.* 1982; details in Hirsch 1980a). Seventeen unhatched eggs at the colony in 1978 indicated that pesticides were still the major problem, and that the situation was by then probably irreversible (Hirsch 1980a). The other major problem at the colony has been increased disturbance: the single nesting-cliff in Birecik became ever more crowded by houses and in the late 1960s, despite a prohibition on disruption of the colony, a house was built directly above the cliff, and even as late as 1974 upper storeys were added to two houses, screening a previously (but never thereafter) used nest-ledge (Kumerloeve 1969, Hirsch 1974,1975). Birds in the early 1970s had to breed only a few metres away from drying laundry and working people, with rubbish often being tipped down the cliff from above; the main nest-ledge had also partially collapsed some time since 1964, leaving it dangerously narrow (Hirsch 1973,1978). In 1972 many chicks died by falling from nests when their parents panicked, others fell off ledges simply while being fed, and still others were found dead in their nests, trampled underfoot by parents and elder siblings (this was considered a pesticide-induced behaviour): of 64 birds hatched, only nine survived (Hirsch 1973,1978). In 1973 the two main causes of loss observed were again human disturbance causing birds to panic, dislodging eggs and chicks, and the resulting prolonged exposure of eggs to the sun (Hirsch 1978). Although there has been progress in remedying the disturbance problem (see Conservation Measures Taken: Turkey), the pesticide problem remains and is compounded by the Keban dam project which, on completion, will bring existing feeding grounds under cultivation: a final solution to the species's difficulties in Turkey is thus discounted, as it would conflict with social and economic objectives of a higher governmental priority (Hirsch 1978).

Conservation Measures Taken In the early 1960s, various areas of Syria were searched for colonies without success: from Deir-es-Zoor up the Euphrates to the latitude of Aleppo, through El Haseke on the Khabur and Deir-es-Zoor across to Aleppo, and in the Palmyra region (Kumerloeve 1962,1967b,1978). In Algeria, the location of the only colony is a closely guarded secret.

Morocco The species has been protected in Morocco since 1923, the laws against hunting being "exemplary and well applied"; one colony in the mid-1970s already enjoyed sufficient guarding (Hirsch 1976a,b). The species is listed on Appendix I of CITES, to which Morocco and Algeria are parties (but Turkey not). In the mid-1970s WWF project 1288 sought to determine the bird's present distribution and status in Morocco (Hirsch 1976b). Since 1979 a joint project involving Moroccan authorities, the University Mohammed V and WWF (project 1631) has built on the earlier project, resulting in the protection of most of the species's breeding and feeding areas (U. Hirsch *in litt.* 1982). Where colonies have increased in size and where rock-faces holding them have collapsed, new nesting-places have been prepared with the help of local people (Hirsch 1980c,1981a,b,c), and these have already been used (U. Hirsch *in litt.* 1982). Following the elaboration of a conservation plan for the species (Hirsch 1980b), the proposal for a national park – holding the majority of the world's breeding pairs as well as being a major wintering area – at Oued Massa in a strip of land between Agadir and Tiznit, c. 65 km long and 10-15 km wide, has involved the stabilisation and regeneration of 80,000 ha of dunes and has helped prevent the heavy use of strong pesticides against mosquitoes in the region; the park awaits designation but the core zone is already a biological reserve (Hirsch 1981d,1982b, *IUCN Bull.* 14: 39). The park is hoped to be formally declared at the end of 1984 (Hirsch 1984).

Turkey The inhabitants of Birecik and its environs have traditionally held the Northern Bald Ibis to be holy or semi-sacred and killing it to be a crime (see Tristram 1882, Weigold 1912,1913, Hirsch and Schenker 1977, Hirsch 1978), and a successful component of the WWF project (no. 945) there in the early 1970s was to revive this belief and the lapsed annual festival to celebrate its return: the bird was made the symbol of the town, and various other measures were taken to heighten local awareness of and respect for the species (Hirsch 1973,1974,1975). In 1973 a high wall was built above the colony to prevent rubbish-tipping, the existing nest-ledge was enlarged, and an experimental 13 m long platform erected as an artificial ledge (Hirsch 1974), this last proving highly successful, holding 12 of the 13 breeding pairs by 1977, because (a) it provided much improved protection from outside disturbance, (b) its total depth (60 cm) prevented double rows of nests and hence reduced territorial conflict, and (c) it received only five hours of sunlight per day as against the natural ledges' 7-9 hours (Hirsch 1978; also Hirsch and Schenker 1977). Despite these measures, in 1977 a start was made (WWF project 1062) on attempting to establish a new colony outside Birecik using captive birds in cages on cliffs to attract the wild population away from the town (*WWF Yearbook* 1977-1978: 134), and in 1978 this captive colony was established 3 km upstream using wild birds (see Terrataz 1979, Sahin 1980; more details and slightly different figures in Hirsch 1980a). In 1979 four captive pairs bred, but the 10 young hatched from 12 eggs laid all soon died, and at August the cages held eight adults and 23 immatures; the wild birds showed much interest in the captive colony but were frightened away by a successful but misguided attempt to capture some of them at the nearby site they had each day been gathering at (Hirsch 1980a). In 1980 seven captive pairs bred and 11 young fledged, but all appeared to be suffering from rickets and none was fit for either captive breeding or release into the wild, and the high number of birds captured, the method of their capture, and the condition of their keeping were a source of concern (Hirsch 1980a,1981c). In April 1981 the cages held 39 birds (Goriup and Parr 1983; in that year 10 young fledged from c. 30 eggs laid, an attempt to reinforce the wild population using six young failed (the birds being released too late to join the migratory flock), and by December 43 birds were in the aviary (Hirsch 1981d). In 1982 11 pairs raised 14 young, and 17 birds reared in 1980 and 1981 were released, again too late to join the migratory flock: 10 did not migrate, five were found dead, and two disappeared six weeks after the wild birds had left (Hirsch 1982c). Although in 1976 the Turkish Directorate of National Parks and Wildlife decided to buy the birds' feeding areas, exclude agricultural usage on them, and restrict pesticide spraying on surrounding farmland, by 1980 a solution to the pesticide problem still had not been found (Hirsch 1980a) nor even by the end of 1984 (U. Hirsch *in litt.* 1984).

Captive breeding Hope to save the species from extinction by artificial propagation was apparently first expressed in the 1920s when a consignment of Syrian birds arrived in Berlin (Peters 1928). Although these birds evidently did not prosper, the Northern Bald Ibis breeds well in captivity, current stock being derived from Moroccan birds originally established at Basle Zoo: in 1975 there were 215 birds in 29 zoos (Hirsch and Schenker 1977), and in 1981 there were 408 in 33 (U. Hirsch *in litt.* 1982), as listed below (where f = females, m = males, u = unknown sex, k = kept, b = breeding).

	Zoos	f	m	u	Total		Zoos	f	m	u	Total
k	Altreu	1	1	10	12	k	Norfolk (USA)			9	9
b	Antwerp			3	3	b	Nurenberg	4	3	25	32
b	Basle	9	7	6	22	k	Paris			1	1
k	Berlin BRD			1	1	k	Philadelphia	3	2	7	12
k	Berlin DDR			12	12	b	Rabat			52	52
b	Bern			17	17	b	Rheine			19	19
k	Casablanca			5	5	k	Rotterdam	2	2		4
k	Cologne	1	1	4	6	k	Stuttgart	1	4	4	9
k	Dortmund			3	3	b	Tel Aviv Univ.	3	4	20	27
b	Duisburg			15	15	k	Tel Aviv Zoo	1		8	9
k	Grünau			6	6	k	Tokyo	1			1
k	Hamburg		1	5	6	k	Vienna			3	3
k	Heidelberg			13	13	k	Villars			3	3
k	Helsinki	3	2	1	6	b	Walsrode			9	9
b	Innsbruck	6	6	11	23	b	Wuppertal	2	1	11	14
b	Jersey	11	10		21	b	Zurich	7	12		19
k	Munich	5	9		14		TOTAL	60	66	282	408

To this it may be added that at July 1984 Tel Aviv University possessed 100 birds, 78 adults and 22 juveniles (hatched in 1983), and thus apparently has the largest collection of captive birds of this species in the world (H. Mendelssohn *in litt.* 1984). Detailed studies of the species in captivity have been made (e.g. Wackernagel 1964, Hirsch and Schenker 1977, Mallet 1977, Oliver *et al.* 1979, Schenker 1979, Archibald *et al.* 1980, Schenker *et al.* 1980, Thaler *et al.* 1981, Michelmore and Oliver 1982). The propagation of stocks of Northern Bald Ibis is one of the major contributions zoos have made to bird preservation, and it is not inconceivable that in another century birds will only survive in collections.

Conservation Measures Proposed The conservation of the Northern Bald Ibis in both Morocco and Turkey has largely gone beyond the proposal stage. The plans for the captive breeding programme in Birecik once (as seems quite inevitable) the last wild bird has gone are not known, but it is to be hoped that some birds will be given to zoos so that the genetic composition of the eastern population can more securely be maintained (the two populations differ very slightly: see Siegfried 1972). Hope should not be entirely abandoned that small undiscovered colonies may yet linger in little explored parts of southern Turkey; and in Syria the reputed colony west of Abu Kemal still deserves to be searched for, and an exploration of the region from Raqqa to Et Tell el Abyad is needed (Kumerloeve 1967b). In 1983 and 1984 the Wildlife Research Center of Tel Aviv University, Israel, in cooperation with Frankfurt Zoo, released a quantity of birds from an aviary following breeding, in the hope they would initially stay in the vicinity, gradually learn their surroundings, and thus adapt to semi-natural and finally natural life: if these experiments were to prove successful (and as yet they have not been), additional releases in suitable habitats such as Mount Carmel have been planned (H. Mendelssohn *in litt.* 1984, U. Hirsch *in litt.* 1984 to A. M. Dixon). In

Morocco, there is a proposal to utilise surplus birds from captive stock to reinforce dwindling populations or to re-establish populations in areas from which the species has disappeared (Hirsch 1980b,c,1981a,c); the utilisation of stock held on Jersey for such purposes in north-west Africa is a policy of JWPT (Mallet 1977) and opportunities are actively being sought (D. Waugh *in litt.* 1984 to P. D. Goriup). Consideration has been given to reintroducing the species into central Europe but this is judged impractical, chiefly owing to the problem that the original wild population migrated to escape the winters, something captive-bred stock (derived from only partially migratory birds) would be wholly unlikely to do (Schenker 1981). However, it is conceivable that climatic conditions in certain undisturbed areas of Spain might prove similar enough to those where the species survives in Morocco to warrant the experiment of attempting to introduce birds there (something which should, however, be done only after exhaustive evaluation and consultation, and only in the most carefully controlled manner).

Remarks The proposed national park at Oued Massa is a major wetland site and important for other bird species, and also offers the possibility of reintroducing Dorcas and Cuvier's Gazelles *Gazella dorcas* and *G. cuvieri* (Hirsch 1981a,1982a). Concerning clutch-size in the Northern Bald Ibis (see Ecology), the maximum has been reported as seven on the authority of Aharoni (Heim de Balsac 1931, Heim de Balsac and Mayaud 1962; hence Brown *et al.* 1982) but this appears to be a misreading of a passage describing how only seven eggs could be collected from a colony because of the steepness of the cliffs (Aharoni 1911); at any rate, six was the maximum found in Syria (Aharoni 1911,1928,1929; also Hartert 1912-1921, Peters 1928). It is curious that six-egg clutches should only have been found at the (then) sporadically occupied site of Ain Sba (see Population: Algeria) and in what are argued to have been pioneer colonies in Syria (Safriel 1980), apparently never in the more stable or less tangential colonies. Concerning the problem of early nesting in Syria (mentioned under Ecology), there are three instances of young reported as collected at colonies there in March, without any apparent recognition of the problem such records creates: Safriel (1980) refers to a juvenile collected 28 March 1904 by Carruthers, and to a nestling collected in March 1918, while Kumerloeve (1978) refers to a nestling collected in March 1928. If these records are correct, several speculations may be made to explain them – e.g. that birds sometimes arrived back at their colonies much earlier than mid-February, or that they sometimes arrived back ready to lay, or even that they may not have migrated away – but the possibility exists that all are errors: what appears to be the same Carruthers record is given as 28 May 1904 in Kumerloeve (1960,1967a), suggesting that the month May is represented on the specimen label by the number "5" and that this can be misread for "3", something which may also have happened in the other two cases. Concerning the indirect effect of hunting at a colony (mentioned under Threats), there is a report of a whole colony of 50 pairs completely deserting the locality following the shooting of two pairs (Aharoni 1911), an extreme example if genuine (it is not entirely clear from context that the birds were breeding) of rapid desertion. Concerning shyness in breeding birds (mentioned under Threats), part of the case for viewing the former Syrian colonies as pioneer settlements of young birds (spilling over from more stable colonies whose rock-faces had reached saturation point) is that they were much more susceptible to disturbance, the birds much shyer (e.g. than in Birecik): and birds in semi-arid (i.e. less suitable) habitat are shyer (i.e. less experienced, younger) than those in less arid habitat (Safriel 1980). However, other examples seem to invalidate this equation: birds at Salé cliffs near Rabat, patently one of the least arid sites in Morocco, were very wild at the nest, neglecting their young (Meade-Waldo 1903), while birds at the sporadically used Ain Sba, one of the most arid of localities in North Africa, were very wild except at the nest (Heim de Balsac 1924). Tameness at one site was considered to be a sign of adjustment to disturbance (Géroudet 1965), but another observer considers tameness to reflect the absence of disturbance, disturbed colonies being shy but composed chiefly of old birds (Hirsch 1976a). It seems prudent, in the circumstances, not to make assumptions about the status of a colony from the shyness or otherwise of its birds. The genus *Geronticus* is a threatened taxon (see Remarks under Southern Bald Ibis *G. calvus*).

References

Aharoni, J. (1911) An den Brutplätzen von *Comatibis comata*, Ehrbg. *Z. Oologie* (Stuttgart) 1(2): 9-11.

Aharoni, J. (1912) *Houbara macqueeni* Gray. *Orn. Jahrb.* 23: 1-15.

Aharoni, J. (1928) Der Waldrapp – *Comatibis eremita* (L.). *Orn. Beob.* 26: 58-60.

Aharoni, J. (1929) Zur Brutbiologie von *Comatibis comata* Bp. (*Geronticus eremita* L.). *Beitr. Fortpfl.Biol. Vögel* 5: 17-19.

Aharoni, J. (1932) Bemerkungen und Ergänzungen zu R. Meinertzhagens Werk "Nicoll's Birds of Egypt". *J. Orn.* 80: 416-424.

Allouse, B. E. (1953) The avifauna of Iraq. *Iraq Nat. Hist. Mus. Publ.* 3.

Archer, G. and Godman E. M. (1937) *The birds of British Somaliland and the Gulf of Aden*, 1. London and Edinburgh: Gurney and Jackson.

Archibald, G. W., Lantis, S. D. H., Lantis, L. R. and Munetchika, I. (1980) Endangered ibises Threskiornithidae: their future in the wild and in captivity. *Internat. Zoo Yearbook* 20: 6-23.

Ash, J. S. and Howell, T. R. (1977) The Bald Ibis or Waldrapp *Geronticus eremita* in Ethiopia. *Bull. Brit. Orn. Club* 97: 104.

Bannerman, D. and Bannerman, J. (1953) A second journey to the Moroccan Sahara (in 1952) and over the Great Atlas. *Ibis* 95: 128-139.

Bannerman, D. A. and Bannerman, W. M. (1968) *Birds of the Atlantic islands*, 4. Edinburgh: Oliver and Boyd.

Bédé, P. (1926) Notes sur l'ornithologie du Maroc. *Mém. Soc. Sci. Nat. Maroc* 16: 25-150.

Bezzel, E. (1974) Ornithologische Sommerbeobachtungen aus Kleinasien. *Anz. orn. Ges. Bayern* 7: 106-120.

Bierman, W. H. (1959) Observations ornithologiques au Maroc. *Oiseau et R.F.O.* 29: 4-39, 99-128, 221-244.

Blanford, W. T. (1870) *Observations on the geology and zoology of Abyssinia*. London.

Bourne, W. R. P. (1959) Notes on autumn migration in the Middle East. *Ibis* 101: 170-176.

Bowen, W. W. (1926) *Catalogue of Sudan birds. Part 1 – Struthionidae to Picidae*. Khartoum: Sudan Government Museum.

Brosset, A. (1956) Evolution actuelle de l'avifaune au Maroc oriental. *Bull. Soc. Sci. Nat. Phys. Maroc* 36: 299-306.

Brosset, A. (1957) Etude de quelques associations en Afrique du Nord. *Alauda* 25: 122-132.

Brosset, A. (1961) Ecologie des oiseaux du Maroc oriental. *Trav. Inst. Sci. Chérifien* Sér. Zool. no. 22.

Brosset, A. and Pettter, J.-J. (1966) Dynamiques des populations d'oiseaux au Maroc oriental. *Bull. Soc. Sci. Maroc* 46: 399-406.

Brown, L. H., Urban, E. K. and Newman, K. (1982) *The birds of Africa*, 1. London: Academic Press.

Carpentier, C.-J. (1933) Contribution à l'étude de l'ornithologie marocaine: les oiseaux du Pays Zaian. *Bull. Soc. Sci. Nat. Maroc* 13: 23-68.

Cramp, S. and Simmons, K. E. L. eds. (1977) *The birds of the western Palearctic*, 1. Oxford: Oxford University Press.

Curry, P. J. and Sayer, J. A. (1979) The Inundation Zone of the Niger as an environment for Palearctic migrants. *Ibis* 121: 20-40.

Danford, C. G. (1880) A further contribution to the ornithology of Asia Minor. *Ibis* (4)4: 81-99.

Deetjen, H. (1964) Nidification de *Geronticus* auprès de Ouarzazate. *Alauda* 32: 306-307.

Deetjen, H. (1968) Notes du Moyen Atlas. *Alauda* 36: 287.

Dekeyser, L. (1954) Contribution à l'étude du peuplement de la Mauritanie: oiseaux. *Bull. Inst. Fr. Afrique Noire* 16(4) [Ser. A]: 1248-1292.

DMATC (1978) *Saudi Arabia: official standard names gazetteer*. Washington, D. C.: United States Board on Geographic Names.

Dresser, H. E. (1871-1881) *A history of the birds of Europe*, 6. London.

Dupuy, A. (1967) La faune menacée de l'Algérie et sa protection. *Bull. Soc. Sci. Nat. Phys. Maroc* 47: 329-354.

Elliott, D. G. (1877) Review of the Ibidinae, or subfamily of the Ibises. *Proc. Zool. Soc. Lond*: 477-510.

Etchécopar, R. D. and Hüe, F. (1964) *Les oiseaux du Nord de l'Afrique*. Paris: N. Boubée.

Fischer-Sigwart, H. (1914) *Comatibis eremita* Linné oder *Geronticus eremita* L. Der Waldrapp. *Orn. Beob.* 11: 73-77.

Flower, S. S. (1922) The hermit ibis in the Sudan. *Ibis* (11)4: 598-599.

Geographic Names Division (1970) *Gazetteer no. 112. Morocco*. Washington, D. C.: U. S. Army Topographic Command.

Géroudet, P. (1965) Du "Waldrapp" de Gessner aux Ibis chauves du Maroc. *Nos Oiseaux* 28: 129-143.

Goriup, P. D. and Parr, D. (1983) Report on a survey of bustards in Turkey March 22 to May 10, 1981. *International Council for Bird Preservation Study Report* no. 1.

Groh, G. (1971) Jungfernkranich und Fahlsperling Brutvögel in der Türkei mit Bemerkungen zu anderen Vogelarten. *Mitt. Pollichia* (3)18: 178-183.

Guichard, K. M. (1950) A summary of the birds of the Addis Abeba region, Ethiopia. *J. E. Afr. Nat. Hist. Soc.* 19(5) [no. 89]: 154-181.

Hamel, H. D. (1975) Ein Beitrag zur Populationsdynamik des Waldrapps *Geronticus eremita* (L., 1758). *Vogelwelt* 96: 213-221.

Harrison, B. G. (1933) The Bald Ibis (*Comatibis eremita* (L.)). *Oologists' Record* 13: 74.

Hartert, E. (1902) Aus den Wanderjahren eines Naturforschers. *Novit. Zool.* 9: 193-339.

Hartert, E. (1912-1921) *Die Vögel der paläarktischen Fauna*, 2. Berlin: R. Friedländer und Sohn.

Hartert, E. (1925) An ornithological journey in Marocco in 1924. *Bull. Soc. Sci. Nat. Maroc* 5(6): 271-304.

Hartert, E. (1926) On another ornithological journey to Marocco in 1925. *Mém. Soc. Sci. Nat. Maroc* 16: 3-24.

Hartert, E. (1928) A rush through Tunisia, Algeria, and Marocco, and collecting in the Maroccan Atlas, in 1927. *Novit. Zool.* 34: 337-371.

Hartert, E. and Jourdain, F. C. R. (1923) The hitherto known birds of Morocco. *Novit. Zool.* 30: 91-146.

Hartert, E. and Ogilvie-Grant, W. R. (1905) On the birds of the Azores. *Novit. Zool.* 12: 80-128.

Heim de Balsac[, H.] (1924) L'Ibis chauve, *Comatibis eremita* (L.), en Algérie. *Rev. fr. Orn.* 8: 469-474.

Heim de Balsac, H. (1925) Quelques oiseaux particulièrement intéressants de l'Algérie et du Sahara. *Rev. fr. Orn.* 9: 189-193.

Heim de Balsac, H. (1931) La persistance de l'Ibis chauve en Algérie. *Alauda* 3: 71-73.

Heim de Balsac, H. (1964) Les récentes acquisitions faunistiques effectuées par R. de Naurois sur la côte Atlantique, du Maroc au Golfe de Guinée. *Alauda* 32: 245-249.

Heim de Balsac, H. and Heim de Balsac, T. (1951) Les migrations des oiseaux dans l'ouest du continent africain. *Alauda* 19: 157-171.

Heim de Balsac, H. and Mayaud, N. (1962) *Les oiseaux du nord ouest de l'Afrique*. Paris: Lechevalier.

Heinze, J., Krott, N. and Mittendorf, H. (1978) Zur Vogelwelt Marokkos. *Vogelwelt* 99: 132-137.

von Heuglin, T. (1862) Beiträge zur Ornithologie Nord-Ost-Afrika's. *J. Orn.* 10: 285-307.

von Heuglin, M. T. (1869-1874) *Ornithologie Nordost-Afrikas*, 1 and 2. Cassel.

Hirsch, U. (1973) Project 945. Conservation of the Bald Ibis. *WWF Yearbook* 1972-1973: 151-152.

Hirsch, U. (1974) Project 945. Bald ibis conservation. *WWF Yearbook* 1973-1974: 198.

Hirsch, U. (1975) Project 945. Bald ibis conservation. *WWF Yearbook* 1974-1975: 196.

Hirsch, U. (1976a) Beobachtungen am Waldrapp *Geronticus eremita* in Marokko und Versuch zur Bestimmung der Alterszusammensetzung von Brutkolonien. *Orn. Beob.* 73: 225-235.

Hirsch, U. (1976b) Project 1288. Bald Ibis, Morocco – Survey. *WWF f14Yearbook* 1975-1976: 77-78.

Hirsch, U. (1977a) Co-operation invited on the protection of the Bald Ibis *Geronticus eremita*. *Bull. Brit. Orn. Club* 97: 72.

Hirsch, U. (1977b) Aufruf zur Zusammenarbeit "Zum Schutz des Waldrapps *Geronticus eremita*". *Vogelwelt* 98: 40.

Hirsch, U. (1978) Artificial nest ledges for Bald Ibises. Pp. 61-69 in S. A. Temple, ed. *Endangered birds: management techniques for preserving threatened species*. Madison, Wisconsin: University of Wisconsin Press, and London: Croom Helm.

Hirsch, U. (1979a) Studies of west Palearctic birds. 183 Bald Ibis. *Brit. Birds* 72: 313-325.

Hirsch, U. (1979b) Protection of *Geronticus eremita*. *Bull. Brit. Orn. Club* 99: 39.

Hirsch, U. (1979c) Hilfe für den Waldrapp. *Wir und die Vögel* 11(2): 12-15.

Hirsch, U. (1980a) Der Waldrapp *Geronticus eremita*, ein Beitrag zur Situation in seinem östlichen Verbreitungsgebiet. *Vogelwelt* 101: 219-236.

Hirsch, U. (1980b) Project 1631. Waldrapp or Bald Ibis. *WWF Yearbook* 1979-1980: 130.

Hirsch, U. (1980c) Waldrapp ibis *Geronticus eremita* (Morocco Project 1631 – Waldrapp ibis). Unpublished.

Hirsch, U. (1981a) Project 1631. Waldrapp Ibis. *WWF Yearbook* 1980-1981: 213.

Hirsch, U. (1981b) Morocco plans reserve for Waldrapp ibis [interview by P. Jackson]. *WWF Monthly Report* January: 21-23.

Hirsch, U. (1981c) Captive breeding for Waldrapp ibis. *WWF Monthly Report* January: 17-19.

Hirsch, U. (1981d) Morocco declares reserve for Waldrapp ibis. *WWF Monthly Report* July: 191-193.

Hirsch, U. (1981e) Waldrapp ibis *Geronticus eremita* 1981. Unpublished.

Hirsch, U. (1981f) L'importance de la région du Massa pour l'ibis chauve. Pp. 25-26 in Avant-project de creation du Parc National de Massa, Royaume du Maroc. Unpublished.

Hirsch, U. (1982a) Morocco Project 1631. Waldrapp ibis. *WWF Yearbook* 1982: 211-212.

Hirsch, U. (1982b) Mission report re: Project 1631 – Morocco, conservation of the Waldrapp ibis (Spring 1982) and advice on the establishment of the Massa National Park (project 3063). Unpublished.

Hirsch, U. (1982c) Waldrapp ibis *Geronticus eremita* 1982. Unpublished.

Hirsch, U. (1984) National Park für Waldrappen. Unpublished.

Hirsch, U. and Schenker, A. (1977) Der Waldrapp (*Geronticus eremita*). Freilandbeobachtungen und Hinweise für eine artgemässe Haltung. *Z. Kölner Zoo* 20: 3-11.

Hirsch, U. and Thévenot, M. (1980) Rapport préliminaire du project UICN no. 1631. Programme de protection de l'ibis chauve. 2° mission du 15 mars au 20 juin. Unpublished.

Hirsch, U. and Thévenot, M. (1981) Programme de protection de l'ibis chauve au Maroc. Project UICN/WWF no. 1631, rapport préliminaire (Juin 1981). Unpublished.

Hüe, F. (1953) Note sur l'Ibis noir *Geronticus eremita* (L.) au Maroc. *Alauda* 11: 194.

Hüni, M. (1982) Exkursion der Ala in die Südosttürkei, 3-17 April 1982. *Orn. Beob.* 79: 221-223.

IGM (1887) Carta dimostrativa della regione compresa fra Massaua, Keren, Aksum e Adigrat [Ethiopia]. 1: 400,000. Istituto Geografico Militare [Italy].

Jennings, M. C. (1981) A list of North Yemen birds. Ornithological Society of the Middle East. Unpublished.

Jourdain, F. C. R. (1922) Les oiseaux de la forêt de Marmara et des environs de Rabat. *Rev. fr. Orn.* 7: 149-153.

Jourdain, F. C. R. (1929) Notes ornithologiques sur le Maroc et l'Algérie, en 1928. *Alauda* 1: 173-181.

Jourdain, F. C. R. (1934) The Bald Ibis (*Comatibis eremita*). *Oologists' Record* 14: 2-5.

Krabbe, N. (1983) Bald Ibis (*Geronticus eremita*) seen on migration in Israel. *OSME Bull.* 10: 13.

Kumerloeve, H. (1958) Von der Kolonie des Waldrapps, *Geronticus eremita* (L.), bei Birecik am Euphrat. *Beitr. Vogelk.* 6: 189-202.

Kumerloeve, H. (1960) On some birds collected by Mr Douglas Carruthers in the Syrian Desert. *Alauda* 28: 284-286.

Kumerloeve, H. (1962) Zur Geschichte der Waldrapp-Kolonie in Birecik am oberen Euphrat. *J. Orn.* 103: 389-398.

Kumerloeve, H. (1965) Zur Situation der Waldrappkolonie *Geronticus eremita* (L. 1758) in Birecik am Euphrat. *Vogelwelt* 86: 42-48.

Kumerloeve, H. (1967a) Nouvelles données sur la situation de la colonie d'Ibis chevelus *Geronticus eremita* (L.) 1758 à Birecik sur l'Euphrate (Turquie). *Alauda* 35: 194-202.

Kumerloeve, H. (1967b) Recherches sur l'avifaune de la République Arabe Syrienne essai d'un aperçu. *Alauda* 35: 243-266.

Kumerloeve, H. (1969) Situation de la colonie d'Ibis chevelus *Geronticus eremita* à Birecik en 1968 et 1969. *Alauda* 37: 260-261.

Kumerloeve, H. (1974) Bemerkungen zur Situation von Waldrapp und Kahlkopfibis. *Angew. Orn.* 4: 114-116.

Kumerloeve, H. (1978) Waldrapp, *Geronticus eremita* (Linnaeus, 1758), und Glattnackenrapp, *Geronticus calvus* (Boddaert, 1783): zur Geschichte ihrer Erforschung und zur gegenwärtigen Bestandssituation. *Ann. Naturhist. Mus. Wien* 81: 319-349.

Kumerloeve, H. (1983) Zur Kenntnis altägyptischer Ibis-Darstellungen, unter besonderer Berücksichtigung des Waldrapps, *Geronticus eremita* (Linnaeus, 1758). *Bonn. zool. Beitr.* 34: 197-234.

Lamarche, B. (1980) Liste commentée des oiseaux du Mali. 1ère partie: Non-passereaux. *Malimbus* 2: 121-158.

Lambert, F. R. and Grimmett, R. F. (1983) Bald Ibis (*Geronticus eremita*) in Israel. *OSME Bull.* 10: 12.

Ledant, J.-P., Jacob, J.-P., Jacobs, P., Malher, F., Ochando, B. and Roché, J. (1981) Mise à jour de l'avifaune algérienne. *Gerfaut* 71: 295-398.

Lynes, Captain (1920) Ornithology of the Maroccan "Middle-Atlas". *Ibis* (11)2: 260-301.

Lynes, H. (1925) L'ornithologie des territoires du Sous (Maroc du Sud). *Mém. Soc. Sci. Nat. Maroc* 13(1): 1-82.

Malherbe, A. (1855) Faune ornithologique de l'Algérie. *Bull. Soc. Hist. Nat. Moselle* 7: 5-44.

Mallet, M. (1977) Breeding the Waldrapp Ibis *Geronticus eremita* at Jersey Zoo. *Internat. Zoo Yearbook* 17: 143-145.

Marçais, J. (1935) Une colonie d'Ibis chauves *Comatibis eremita* (L.) au Maroc oriental. *Alauda* 7: 254-255.

Mathey-Dupraz, A. (1925) Excursion en Algérie. *Orn. Beob.* 22: 87-89, 107-109, 123-125.

Mayaud, N. (1982) Les oiseaux du Nord-Ouest de l'Afrique: notes complémentaires. *Alauda* 50: 114-145.

Meade-Waldo, E. G. B. (1903) Bird-notes from Morocco and the Great Atlas. *Ibis* (8)3: 196-214.

Meade-Waldo, E. G. B. (1905) A trip to the forest of Marmora, Morocco. *Ibis* (8)5: 161-164.

Meinertzhagen, R. (1930) *Nicoll's birds of Egypt*. London: Hugh Rees.

Meinertzhagen, R. (1940) Autumn in central Morocco. *Ibis* (14)4: 106-136, 187-234.

Meinertzhagen, R. (1948-1949) Diary, volume 58 (76 volumes held in Rhodes House Library, Oxford).

Meinertzhagen, R. (1951) Some relationships between African, Oriental, and Palearctic genera and species, with a review of the genus *Monticola*. *Ibis* 93: 443-459.

Meinertzhagen, R. (1954) *Birds of Arabia*. Edinburgh and London: Oliver and Boyd.

Meitz, P. (1979a) Marokko, Heimat des Waldrapp. *Gefied. Welt* 103: 78-80, 94-97.

Meitz, P. (1979b) Noch einmal in Marokko – des Waldrapps wegen! *Gefied. Welt* 103: 193-194.

Meitz, P. (1980) Nochmals: vom Waldrapp in Marokko. *Gefied. Welt* 104: 119.

Michelmore, F. and Oliver, W. L. R. (1982) Hand-rearing and development of Bare-faced Ibis chicks *Geronticus eremita* at the Jersey Wildlife Preservation Trust; with comparative observations of parent-rearing behaviour. *Dodo* 19: 51-69.

Moltoni, E. and Gnecchi Ruscone, G. (1942) *Gli uccelli dell' Africa Orientale Italiana*, 2. Milan.

Moore, H. J. and Boswell, C. (1956) Field observations on the birds of Iraq. *Iraq Nat. Hist. Mus. Publ.* 9: 1-109; 10: 110-213; 12: 214-299.

Moreau, R. F. (1966) *The bird faunas of Africa and its islands*. New York and London: Academic Press.

Moreau, R. E. (1972) *The Palearctic-African bird migration systems*. London and New York: Academic Press.

Nikolaus, G. (1984) Distinct status changes of certain Palearctic migrants in the Sudan. *Scopus* 8: 36-38.

Office of Geography (1966) *Gazetteer no. 100. Mauritania*. Washington, D. C.: Department of the Interior.

Office of Geography (1967) *Gazetteer no. 104. Syria*. Washington, D. C.: Department of the Interior.

Oliver, W. L. R., Mallet, M. M., Singleton, D. R. and Ellett, J. S. (1979) Observations on the reproductive behaviour of a captive colony of Bare-faced Ibis *Geronticus eremita*. *Dodo* 16: 11-35.

Ornithological Society of Turkey (1975) *Bird Report* no. 3 1970-1973.

Ornithological Society of Turkey (1978) *Bird Report* no. 4 1974-1975.

Pallary, P. (1922) Note sur le régime alimentaire de l'ibis à tête chauve (*Gerontiacus [sic] eremita* L.), un oiseau marocain à protéger. *Bull. Soc. Sci. Nat. Maroc* 2(1-2): 48.

Parslow, J. L. F. (1973) Organochlorine insecticide residues and food remains in a Bald Ibis *Geronticus eremita* chick from Birecik, Turkey. *Bull. Brit. Orn. Club* 93: 163-166.

Peters, H. B. (1928) Aus der Biologie des Waldrapps. *Naturforscher* 5: 380-383.

Porter, R. (1973) The disappearing ibis. *Birds* 4: 227-228.

Rencurel, P. (1974) L'Ibis chauve *Geronticus eremita* dans le Moyen-Atlas. *Alauda* 42: 143-158.

Robin, Dr. (1958) Ibis à tête chauve, *Comatibis eremita*, centre de nidification de Tasdrem. *C. R. Soc. Sci. Nat. Phys. Maroc* 24: 33-34.

Robin, P. (1973) Comportement des colonies de *Geronticus eremita* dans le sud marocain, lors des périodes de sécheresse. *Bonn. zool. Beitr.* 24: 317-322.

Rothschild, W., Hartert, E. and Kleinschmidt, O. (1897) *Comatibis eremita* (Linn.), a European bird. *Novit. Zool.* 4: 371-377.

Rüppell, E. (1835-1840) *Neue Wirbelthiere zu der Fauna von Abyssinien gehörig*. Frankfurt am Main.

Rüppell, E. (1845) *Systematische Uebersicht der Vögel Nord-Ost-Afrika's*.

Frankfurt am Main.

Ruthke, P. (1966) Beitrag zur Vogelfauna Marokkos. *Bonn. zool. Beitr.* 17: 186-201.

Ruthke, P. (1977) Beobachtungen an Jugendtrupps des Waldrapps (*Geronticus eremita*). *Vogelwelt* 98: 231-233.

Safriel, U. N. (1980) Notes on the extinct population of the Bald Ibis *Geronticus eremita* in the Syrian desert. *Ibis* 122: 82-88.

Sage, B. L. and Meadows, B. S. (1965) Some recent ornithological observations in Marocco. *Bull. Soc. Sci. Nat. Phys. Maroc* 45: 191-233.

Sahin, R. (1980) Erfolgreiche Volierenbrut der Waldrappen in der Türkei. *Orn. Mitt.* 32: 72-74.

Sahin, R. (1982) Zur Form der Ehe freilebender Waldrappen (*Geronticus eremita*) in Birecik (Türkei). *Orn. Mitt.* 34: 162-163.

Salvadori, T. (1884) [Spedizione italiana nell'Africa equatoriale. Risultati zoologici.] Uccelli dello Scioa e della regione fra Zeila e lo Scioa. *Ann. Mus. Civ. Genova* (2)1, 21: 7-276.

Salvadori, T. (1899) Collezioni ornitologiche fatte nelle Isole del Capo Verde da Leonardo Fea. *Ann. Mus. Civ. Genova* (2)20: 283-312.

Salvadori, T. (1912) Missione per la frontiera Italo-Etiopica sotto il comando del Capitano Carlo Citerni. Risultati zoologici. *Ann. Mus. Civ. Genova* (3)5: 304-327.

Schenker, A. (1977) Das ehemalige Verbreitungsgebiet des Waldrapps *Geronticus eremita* in Europa. *Orn. Beob.* 74: 13-30.

Schenker, A. (1979) Beobachtungen zur Brutbiologie des Waldrapps (*Geronticus eremita*) im Zoo Basel. *Zool. Garten* 49: 104-116.

Schenker, A. (1981) Der Waldrapp – ein historiches Wildbret. *Jagd und Hege, Naturschutz* (4)7.

Schenker, A., Hirsch, U., Mallet, M., Pechlanger, H., Thaler, E. and Wackernagel, H. (1980) Keeping and breeding the waldrapp ibis. *Internat. Zoo News* 27(165): 9-15.

Sclater, P. L. (1906) On some birds collected by Mr Douglas Carruthers in the Syrian Desert. *Ibis* (8)6: 307-317.

Sclater, W. L. and Mackworth-Praed, C. (1920) A list of the birds of the Anglo-Egyptian Sudan, based on the collections of Mr. A. L. Butler, Mr. A. Chapman and Capt. H. Lynes, R.N., and Major Cuthbert Christy, R.A.M.C. (T.F). Part IV. (Concluded). Pelecanidae – Struthionidae. *Ibis* (11)2: 781-855.

Siegfried, W. R. (1966) The Bald Ibis. *Bokmakierie* 18: 54-57.

Siegfried, W. R. (1972) Discrete breeding and wintering areas of the Waldrapp *Geronticus eremita* (L.). *Bull. Brit. Orn. Club* 92: 102-103.

Smith, K. D. (1955) Recent records from Eritrea. *Ibis* 97: 65-80.

Smith, K. D. (1962-1963) Diary, Morocco. Held in the Alexander Library, Edward Grey Institute of Field Ornithology, Oxford.

Smith, K. D. (1965) On the birds of Morocco. *Ibis* 107: 493-526.

Smith, K. D. (1970a) The Waldrapp *Geronticus eremita* (L.). *Bull. Brit. Orn. Club* 90: 18-24.

Smith, K. D. (1970b) Some African enigmas. *Bristol Ornithology* 3: 118-124.

Snow, D. W. (1952) A contribution to the ornithology of north-west Africa. *Ibis* 94: 473-498.

Snow, D. W. ed. (1978) *An atlas of speciation in African non-passerine birds*. London: Trustees of the British Museum (Natural History).

Steinberg, S. H. and Paxton, J. (1969) *The statesman's year-book, 1969-1970*. London: Macmillan.

Terretaz, M. (1979) Turkey Project 1062. Bald ibis. *WWF Yearbook* 1978-1979: 122.

Thaler, E., Ettel, E. and Job, S. (1981) Zur Sozialstruktur des Waldrapps *Geronticus eremita* – Beobachtungen an der Brutkolonie des Alpenzoos Innsbruck. *J. Orn.* 122: 109-128.

Thévenot, M. (1981) Liste provisoire des oiseaux de l'oued Massa. Pp. 27-49 in Avant-project de creation du Parc National de Massa. Unpublished.

Thévenot, M., Beaubrun, P., Baouab, R. E. and Bergier, P. (1982) Compte rendu d'ornithologie Marocaine, année 1981. Documents de l'Institut Scientifique no. 7. Rabat: Institut Scientifique.

Ticehurst, C. B., Buxton, P. A. and Cheesman, R. E. (1922) The birds of Mesopotamia. *J. Bombay Nat. Hist. Soc.* 28: 650-674.

Ticehurst, C. B., Cox, P. and Cheesman, R. E. (1926) Additional notes on the avifauna of Iraq. *J. Bombay Nat. Hist. Soc.* 31: 91-119.

Tristram, H. B. (1860) On the ornithology of northern Africa. Part 3. The Sahara. *Ibis* 2: 68-83.

Tristram, H. B. (1882) Ornithological notes of a journey through Syria, Mesopotamia, and southern Armenia in 1881. *Ibis* (4)6: 402-419.

Urban, E. K. and Brown, L. H. (1971) *A checklist of the birds of Ethiopia*. Addis Ababa: Haile Sellassie I University Press.

Valverde, J. A. (1957) *Aves del Sahara Español*. Madrid: Instituto de Estúdios Africanos.

Valverde, J. A. (1959) Cuatro interesantes especies en Andalucia. *Ardeola* 5: 143-148.

Vaurie, C. (1965) *The birds of the Palearctic fauna*. Non-passeriformes. London: H. F. and G. Witherby.

Vernon, J. D. R. (1973) Observations sur quelques oiseaux nicheurs du Maroc. *Alauda* 41: 101-109.

Wackernagel, H. (1964) Brutbiologische Beobachtungen am Waldrapp, *Geronticus eremita* (L.), im Zoologischen Garten Basel. *Orn. Beob.* 61: 49-56.

Warncke, K. (1965) Beitrag zur Vogelwelt der Turkei. *Vogelwelt* 86: 1-19.

Warncke, K. (1972) Beitrag zur Vogelwelt der Turkei im Bereich der Südgrenze. *Vogelwelt* 93: 23-26.

Weigold, H. (1912-1913) Ein Monat Ornithologie in den Wüsten und Kulturoasen Nordwestmesopotamiens und Innersyriens. *J. Orn.* 60: 249-297, 365-410; 61: 1-40.

Whitaker, J. I. S. (1905) *The birds of Tunisia*, 2. London: R. H. Porter.

SOUTHERN BALD IBIS

RARE

Geronticus calvus (Boddaert, 1783)

Order CICONIIFORMES

Family THRESKIORNITHIDAE
Subfamily THRESKIORNITHINAE

Summary This species is confined to the highlands of southern Africa in Natal, Transvaal, Orange Free State (South Africa), Lesotho and probably Swaziland. During this century it has disappeared from Cape Province (South Africa) but there is no evidence of an overall decline since 1970. The population is currently estimated at 5,000-8,000 birds. Two major requirements are safe, undisturbed nesting cliffs and areas of short-grazed and recently burnt grassland.

Distribution The Southern Bald Ibis is restricted to South Africa, Lesotho and Swaziland where it is found at high elevations above 900 m (Siegfried 1966a, Brown *et al.* 1982) though perhaps down to 600 m in Natal (Cooper and Edwards 1969). Its range is centred on the Drakensberg massif (excluding the south-western slopes) and surrounding highland areas (Siegfried 1971, Brooke in press) ranging from Mount Currie in southern Natal, formerly part of Cape Province (Shephard 1962, Cochlan 1966, Siegfried 1966b, Skead 1967, Brooke in press) north to just north of Pietersburg in Transvaal (Milstein 1973). The distribution of the species is now well known in South Africa, following surveys in Natal (Cooper and Edwards 1969, Siegfried 1971, D. E. Manry *per* C. Luthin *in litt.* 1982), Orange Free State (Pocock and Uys 1967, Siegfried 1971, D. E. Manry *per* C. Luthin *in litt.* 1982) and Transvaal (Milstein and Siegfried 1970, Siegfried 1971, Grafton 1972, Milstein and Wolff 1973, van Jaarsveld 1979,1980, Aflan 1982,1983, D. E. Manry *per* C. Luthin *in litt.* 1982). Its status and distribution in Lesotho is much less well understood (D. E. Manry *per* C. Luthin *in litt.* 1982): it has been recorded from Leribe, Pinekloof, 'Ntsekele's, Roma, Malefiloane, Old Maputsoe Road, Morija Dam, Mokhotlong and the junction of the Mokhotlong and Orange Rivers (Jacot-Guillarmod 1963, Cooper and Edwards 1969, Bonde 1981). The species also survives in western Swaziland, though its distribution there is not accurately known (D. E. Manry *per* C. Luthin *in litt.* 1982). The Southern Bald Ibis used to occur in Cape Province where it appears to have been fairly widespread during the last century (Siegfried 1966b) with most records coming from the eastern part of the province (see, e.g., Shortridge 1905, Haagner and Ivy 1907, Pym 1909, Siegfried 1966b). It has, however, been recorded as far west as Cape Town, where one was collected at Milnerton in 1906 (Taylor 1909). Other old outlying records are from Tigerhoek near Caledon (Taylor 1909) and Little Namaqualand near the mouth of the Orange River (Siegfried 1966a,1971, Brooke in press). It seems likely that breeding was confined to the eastern part of Cape Province and that these outlying records to the west refer to wanderers (Siegfried 1966a,b, Brooke in press). The species's decline in Cape Province apparently started at the beginning of this century: in Transkei it was still widespread in 1900 but had probably disappeared by the 1940s (Siegfried 1966b). There is, however, no evidence of a further contraction in range since 1970 (Brooke in press). Although surveys are still locating new colonies of this species, its overall distribution is probably now reasonably well known, at least in South Africa (Siegfried 1971, D. E. Manry *per* C. Luthin *in litt.* 1982). Its distribution has been mapped in southern Africa as a whole (Siegfried 1971), in Transvaal (Milstein and Wolff 1973, Allan 1982) and in Natal (Cyrus and Robson 1980).

Population The most recent population estimate of this species throughout its range in southern Africa is 5,000-8,000 birds (D. E. Manry *per* C. Luthin *in litt.* 1982). Since the mid-1960s there have been regular surveys carried out in South Africa aimed at assessing the population of this species (see Pocock and Uys 1967, Cooper and Edwards 1969, Siegfried 1966b,1971, Milstein and Siegfried 1970, Grafton 1972, Milstein and Wolff 1973, van Jaarsveld 1979,1980). The results of all such surveys must be treated with a certain amount of caution since staggered breeding times at the colonies makes counting difficult (Siegfried 1971). Breeding can also be sporadic in both time and place, especially during years of low rainfall (Siegfried 1971). In addition, some pairs nest solitarily and these are very difficult to locate (Siegfried 1971). Although there can be no doubt that the species declined seriously in the earlier years of this century, especially in Cape Province and Transkei (Siegfried 1966a,b,1971) there is little evidence of any recent change in status (Brooke in press): thus one survey in Natal noted a big decline at one colony but increases at two others (Cooper and Edwards 1969). Earlier population estimates now appear to have been much too low: e.g. one in 1966 (when only six colonies were known) reported only 500-1,000 birds (Siegfried 1966a). By 1971, 70 colonies were known, 40 of these being in Orange Free State though colonies average larger in size in Natal and Transvaal (Siegfried 1971). The population was estimated at about 2,000 breeding birds in 1971 (Siegfried 1971), including the birds in Lesotho where no adequate survey has been carried out. This figure includes breeding population estimates of 450 birds in Transvaal, 1,000 birds in Orange Free State and 320 birds in Natal (Siegfried 1971). In addition to these breeding populations there are considerable numbers of non-breeding birds; in 1971 these non-breeders were thought to number 400 in Orange Free State and 500 in Natal (Siegfried 1971). However, even this 1971 population survey is now known to be an underestimate: for instance in Transvaal, where 15 colonies and 226 breeding pairs were counted in 1969 (Milstein and Siegfried 1970), these estimates rose to 23 colonies and 293 pairs in 1972 (Milstein and Wolff 1973) while in 1978 and 1982, 37 and 46 colonies were found respectively (van Jaarsveld 1980, Allan 1982); however, the increase in Transvaal from 1969 to the 1980s is regarded as real (Allan 1982). The largest single number of birds counted in a single breeding season in Transvaal has been reported as 1,244 birds in 1975 (D. E. Manry *per* C. Luthin *in litt.* 1982) though it is not known what percentage of these were breeders; however, in 1977 526 pairs were counted at 33 colonies, while in 1982 496 pairs were counted at 44 (the other two colonies were not censused), in addition to which counts of non-breeding birds at roosts suggested a further 1,294 birds present, i.e. a total for Transvaal of well over 2,000 (Allan 1982). In 1983 the number of breeding pairs lay between 392 and 482 (Allan 1983). In Orange Free State 64 colonies were known by 1980 and 2,400 birds (including non-breeders) have been counted in one season (D. E. Manry *per* C. Luthin *in litt.* 1982). In Natal, where a thorough survey is still needed, 50 colonies with a total breeding population of about 400 pairs were known by 1982 (D. E. Manry *per* C. Luthin *in litt.* 1982). In Lesotho the situation is even less clear. The species was reported to be declining in the lowland parts of the country in the early 1960s (Jacot-Guillarmod 1963), but there is evidence that it is still common in the mountainous districts, where there could be a large population (Bonde 1981, D. E. Manry *per* C. Luthin *in litt.* 1982). In Swaziland there are probably a few breeding sites in the western mountainous area, but the population is unlikely to be large (D. E. Manry *per* C. Luthin *in litt.* 1982).

Ecology The two main environmental requirements of the Southern Bald Ibis appear to be short-grazed or recently burnt grassland for foraging and safe, disturbance-free cliff-sites for nesting (Allan 1982). The species is largely restricted to high altitude, high rainfall grasslands (grassveld) where it forages, usually between 1,200 and 1,850 m (Sclater 1912, Vincent and Symons 1948, Cooper and Edwards 1969, Allan 1982, Brown *et al.* 1982, Manry 1982,1983,1984a, Brooke in press). During the austral winter and spring (the breeding season) the birds feed in burnt grassland and post-burn re-growth; for the rest of the year they use short-grazed grasslands and cultivated pastures (Cooper and Edwards 1969, Manry 1982). In general they prefer to forage where the level of the grass is lower than their bellies and so they usually occur where grassland is either burnt, grazed or ploughed (Manry 1983). The grassland on which this species depends is sub-climax and can only be maintained by burning and, to a lesser extent, cattle-grazing (Manry 1983). It has been speculated that the high altitude grasslands were originally formed as a result of fires started by lightning strikes: if this is the case the grasslands might be of ancient origin, perhaps dating back into the Pleistocene, suggesting that the Southern Bald Ibis has a long history of dependence on this habitat (Manry 1983). In Transvaal, 74% of observations of birds away from colonies were in short grass (including re-growth), 15% in recently burnt grass, 9% in fields, 2% in grassy pans, and 0.4% (one observation) in vlei (Allan 1982). In Natal the species has been found in dry *Acacia* sandveld, but only where it is adjacent to grassveld (Cooper and Edwards 1969). Overgrazing in the grassland can lead to a loss of grass and surface moisture followed by the establishment of dry karoo vegetation, in which the species cannot normally survive (Siegfried 1966a, Brooke in press), though the northernmost colony in Transvaal near Pietersburg is in karoo (Milstein 1973). The practice of irrigating pastures in the Natal midlands might increase available feeding habitats during the austral winter (Brooke in press). In general the current land use and management practices within the species's range normally ensure a succession of suitable feeding areas (Brooke in press). In the initial week after a fire the birds move onto the burnt ground to feed on the large numbers of fire-killed arthropods, returning again to forage in the same areas 46-82 days after burning, as the number of live insects increases (Manry 1983,1984a). The diet consists of insects, mainly caterpillars, beetles and grasshoppers, as well as snails, earthworms, frogs and small dead mammals and birds (Sclater 1912, Vincent and Symons 1948, Milstein 1973, Brown *et al.* 1982, Manry 1983,1984a). In one area the birds have been found to eat buttons which they probably mistake for beetles (Milstein 1973,1974). An earlier report that they feed on carrion (Vincent and Symons 1948) appears not to have been confirmed. The birds feed either by probing the ground or by turning over cattle dung and leaves, usually keeping in flocks of varying sizes (Davies 1911, Vincent and Symons 1948, Cooper and Edwards 1969, Brown *et al.* 1982). During the breeding season the adults may travel up to 32 km in search of food (Cooper and Edwards 1969, Brown *et al.* 1982). The birds return to their breeding colonies in June (Brown *et al.* 1982). At one colony studied in Natal breeding is timed with the prescribed annual burning periods (Manry 1983), though in general egg-laying is not very synchronised at most colonies, laying taking place between late July and October (Vincent and Symons 1948, Siegfried 1966a, Milstein and Siegfried 1970, Brown *et al.* 1982, Manry 1983, Brooke in press); in Transvaal in 1982, all egg-laying took place between 10 July and 30 November, 86% of it between 10 August and 20 September (Allan 1982). There is one breeding record from Natal in March (Brown *et al.* 1982). This species thus nests during the winter, an unusual time of year (Manry 1983), but this permits chick development during the season of grass burning when maximum foraging ground is available (Brown *et al.* 1982). The birds nest singly or in colonies of 2-72 pairs on cliffs 3-150 m in height (Vincent and Symons 1948, Cooper and Edwards 1969, Milstein and Siegfried 1970, van Jaarsveld 1980, Allan 1982, Brown *et al.* 1982, Brooke in press); in Transvaal, nest-sites are usually near water and 71% of cliffs used in 1982 faced south or east (Allan 1982). Colony size fluctuates greatly from year to year (Milstein and Wolff 1973). Nests are placed on ledges, potholes and crevices, often near waterfalls, sometimes even behind waterfalls and often supported by shrubs projecting from the rocks (Vincent and Symons 1948, Cooper and Edwards 1969, Milstein and Siegfried 1970, van Jaarsveld 1980, Brown *et al.* 1982, Brooke in press). The birds are single-brooded (Brooke in press), although re-nesting after early failure occurs (Allan 1983), and the clutch-size varies from one to five (usually two) (Vincent and Symons 1948, Milstein and Siegfried 1970, Allan 1982, Brown *et al.* 1982, Brooke in press). Colonies are probably of long duration, in one case over 40 years (Vincent and Symons 1948) and pairs probably use the same nest-sites for life (Brown *et al.* 1982), the pair-bond apparently being maintained from year to year (Manry 1984b). In general nesting success is high (Milstein and Siegfried 1970, Brown *et al.* 1982), with birds in Transvaal, 1982-1983, producing 0.6-0.8 young per pair per year, nesting attempts begun in early or mid-season being twice as likely to succeed as those begun later (Allan 1982,1983). Success is often reduced by human disturbance (van Jaarsveld 1980, Brown *et al.* 1982). Breeding success can also be lower during drought years, probably because there are fewer available arthropods (Manry 1983) and sometimes birds fail to breed at all during droughts (Milstein and Wolff 1973, Brown *et al.* 1982). The increase in numbers in Transvaal since 1969 coincided with a decade of above-average rainfall (Allan 1982), although the influence of drought in 1981-1983 appeared to have been insignificant (Allan 1983). Chicks can be killed by unfavourable weather conditions and nests, eggs and young can be blown or merely fall off the cliffs (van Jaarsveld 1980); some chicks also starve to death shortly after hatching (Brown *et al.* 1982). However, mortality in the first year of life is low, and birds have been found to live at least up to 11 years (Allan 1983). The birds can breed before three years of age (but not before two) and colour-ringing has shown that young birds may move to other colonies to breed, in one case up to 70 km away (van Jaarsveld 1980; also Allan 1982). The birds are surprisingly inconspicuous at their colonies (Vincent and Symons 1948) and are shy and leave their nests if people approach the colony (Vincent and Symons 1948, Milstein and Siegfried 1970, Brown *et al.* 1982), but although they are generally vulnerable to disturbance there is one example from Leribe in Lesotho where birds which received protection from a local chief became tame and fed among the huts in villages (Siegfried 1966a). At all colonies there appears to be a surplus of non-breeding birds, probably juveniles (Milstein and Siegfried 1970, Milstein and Wolff 1973). Birds can be adversely affected by bad weather conditions and on one occasion a flock of about 12 ibises was found in a cave sheltering from cold, misty weather which was shortly afterwards followed by snow (Hewlett 1960). They roost at colony sites, or with Cattle Egrets *Bubulcus ibis*, Sacred Ibises *Threskiornis aethiopicus* and cormorants *Phalacrocorax* in trees or on cliffs (Pocock and Uys 1967, Hecht 1981, Brown *et al.* 1982). One such roost is known to have been occupied for nearly 100 years (Brown *et al.* 1982). After the end of the breeding season in December and January the adults and juveniles disperse over relatively short distances, up to about 18 km (Brown *et al.* 1982). The feeding flocks stay in one area for up to a week (Brown *et al.* 1982) but in general they make only small-scale movements outside the breeding season (Siegfried 1966a, Milstein and Siegfried 1970, Brooke in press). In the past it is likely that more extensive wanderings took place up to 1,000 km west of the present range (Siegfried 1966a,b; see under Distribution).

Threats It seems likely that the main reason for this species's decline (and extinction in Cape Province) during the earlier years of this century was the spread of karoo vegetation following severe overgrazing of the grasslands (Siegfried 1966a,b,1971, Brooke in press). In Transkei the drainage of marshes might also have been a problem (Siegfried 1966b). The possibility of long-term habitat degradation remains a problem for the future (Milstein and Siegfried 1970) and the planting of trees can destroy suitable foraging areas (van Jaarsveld 1980, Allan 1982). The species appears to have been hunted for food by early settlers, especially during the Boer War, 1899-1902 (Siegfried 1966a,b, Pocock and Uys 1967, Brooke in press). It seems that the species was also persecuted for its feathers (Siegfried 1966a). In the 1940s the birds were hunted by the Zulu people who believed that they had medicinal powers (Vincent and Symons 1948). In Orange Free State the birds are sometimes shot by fishermen (Milstein and Siegfried 1970) and in Transvaal there is considerable human predation on (and wanton destruction of) eggs, chicks and adults, despite legal protection (Grafton 1972, Milstein and Wolff 1973, van Jaarsveld 1979,1980, Allan 1982). In one Transvaal colony 50% of the eggs had been taken (van Jaarsveld 1980) and breeding colonies are in any case vulnerable to disturbance (Siegfried 1971). There is also a roost under threat from tourist development at the Turfloop Dam near Pietersburg (Hecht 1981). A potential future problem could come from the use of pesticides (Siegfried 1966a, Milstein and Wolff 1973) which have had a disastrous effect on the related Northern Bald Ibis *Geronticus eremita* (see relevant account). Natural predators of the species include Jackal Buzzards *Buteo rufofuscus* on nestlings, Cape Eagle Owls *Bubo capensis* on adults and nestlings and, probably, Pied Crows *Corvus albus* on eggs and Gymnogenes *Polyboroides typus* on nestlings; an attack on adults by a Black Eagle *Aquila verreauxi* has been witnessed, and a colony was abandoned (birds resettling elsewhere) when a pair of Black Eagles occupied the same cliffs (Allan 1982).

Conservation Measures Taken This species has full legal protection within South Africa and is a specially protected bird in Natal (Brooke in press). In Natal it breeds in the Highmoor Forest Reserve, the Hluhluwe-Umfolozi Game Reserve complex and the Itala Game Reserve (Macdonald and Birkenstock 1980, Brooke in press). In Transvaal in 1983, one heavily disturbed colony had a successful year after cash incentives and warnings of prosecution were given to local people (Allan 1983). In Orange Free State it breeds in the Vaalbank training area of the Department of Defence, a conserved area (Brooke in press). In Swaziland there are resident colonies in the Hlane Game Reserve, and in Lesotho the species is recorded from the Setlabathebe National Park (IUCN in press). Twenty birds are at present being kept in Pretoria Zoo (Brooke in press), presumably with the aim of starting a captive breeding population. The species is listed on Appendix II of CITES, to which South Africa is a party.

Conservation Measures Proposed It has been recommended that conservation status be given to as many of the larger colonies and feeding areas as possible, since disturbance and destruction of these sites poses a major hazard to the species (Siegfried 1971, Brooke in press). Surveys are needed to assess the status of this species in Natal, Lesotho and Swaziland and to recommend appropriate conservation action.

Remarks The Southern Bald Ibis forms a superspecies with the even more threatened Northern Bald Ibis (Snow 1978; see relevant account); this being the only other member of the genus, *Geronticus* itself is a threatened taxon.

References

Allan, D. (1982) The status of the Bald Ibis in the Transvaal. 1982 progress report, Project TN/6/44/44/5. Transvaal Provincial Administration, Nature Conservation Division.

Allan, D. (1983) The status of the Bald Ibis in the Transvaal. 1983 progress report, Project TN/6/44/44/5. Transvaal Provincial Administration, Nature Conservation Division.

Bonde, K. (1981) An annotated checklist of the birds of Lesotho. Maseru: unpublished report.

Brooke, R. K. (in press) *The rare and vulnerable birds of South Africa.*

Brown, L. H., Urban, E. K. and Newman, K. (1982) *The birds of Africa*, 1. London: Academic Press.

Cochlan, A. (1966) A day in the Drakensberg in search of the Bald Ibis. *Bokmakierie* 18: 43.

Cooper, K. H. and Edwards, K. Z. (1969) A survey of the Bald Ibis in Natal. *Bokmakierie* 21: 4-9.

Cyrus, D. and Robson, N. (1980) *Bird atlas of Natal*. Pietermaritzburg: University of Natal Press.

Davies, G. C. (1911) Notes on the birds of the district of Matatiele, East Griqualand. *J. S. Afr. Orn. Union* 7: 23-48.

Grafton, R. N. (1972) Surveying the Bald Ibis. *Fauna and Flora* 23: 16-19.

Haagner, A. and Ivy, R. H. (1907) The birds of Albany Division, Cape Colony. *J. S. Afr. Orn. Union* 3: 76-116.

Hecht, T. (1981) A bird paradise in jeopardy. *Bokmakierie* 33: 12-15.

Hewlett, J. (1960) Bald Ibises sheltering in a cave from inclement weather. *Ostrich* 31: 29.

IUCN (in press) *The IUCN directory of Afrotropical protected areas*. Cambridge (U.K.) and Gland (Switzerland): IUCN Conservation Monitoring Centre and Commission on National Parks and Protected Areas.

van Jaarsveld, J. (1979) The Bald Ibis. *Fauna and Flora* 35: 12-13.

van Jaarsveld, J. (1980) Bald Ibis – a master of the air. *Afr. Wildl.* 34(6): 20-23.

Jacot-Guillarmod, C. (1963) Catalogue of the birds of Basutoland. *S. Afr. Avifauna Ser.* no. 8.

Macdonald, I. A. W. and Birkenstock, P. J. (1980) Birds of Hluhluwe-Umfolozi Game Reserve complex. *Lammergeyer* 29: 1-56.

Manry, D. E. (1982) Habitat use by foraging Bald Ibis *Geronticus calvus* in western Natal. *S. Afr. J. Wildl. Res.* 12: 85-93.

Manry, D. E. (1983) Ecology of the Bald Ibis *Geronticus calvus* and fire in the South African grassland biome. M.Sc. thesis, University of Cape Town.

Manry, D. E. (1984a) Factors influencing the use of winter-burnt grassland by foraging Bald Ibises *Geronticus calvus*. *S. Afr. J. Zool.* 19: 12-15.

Manry, D. E. (1984b) Pair bonding and promiscuity in the Bald Ibis (*Geronticus calvus*). Abstracts, posters and lectures at the 102nd stated meeting of the American Ornithologists' Union, Lawrence, Kansas, 6-9 August 1984.

Milstein, P. le S. (1973) Buttons and Bald Ibises. *Bokmakierie* 25: 57-60.

Milstein, P. le S. (1974) More Bald Ibis buttons. *Bokmakierie* 26: 88.

Milstein, P. le S. and Siegfried, W. R. (1970) Transvaal status of the Bald Ibis. *Bokmakierie* 22: 36-39.

Milstein, P. le S. and Wolff, S. W. (1973) Status and conservation of the Bald Ibis in the Transvaal. *J. S. Afr. Wildl. Mgmt. Assoc.* 3: 79-83.

Pocock, T. N. and Uys, C. J. (1967) The Bald Ibis in the north-eastern Orange Free State. *Bokmakierie* 19: 28-31.

Pym, F. A. O. (1909) A list of the birds of the Kaffrarian frontier. *J. S. Afr. Orn. Union* 5: 91-113.

Sclater, W. L. (1912) On the birds collected by Mr Claude H. B. Grant at various localities in South Africa – Part IV. *Ibis* (9)6: 1-63.

Shephard, J. B. (1962) Check list of birds of Swartberg District. *S. Afr. Avifauna Ser.* no. 6.

Shortridge, G. C. (1905) Birds collected around Hanover, Cape Colony, from July 20th to the end of September 1903. *J. S. Afr. Orn. Union* 2: 55-83.

Siegfried, W. R. (1966a) The Bald Ibis. *Bokmakierie* 18: 54-57.

Siegfried, W. R. (1966b) The present and past distribution of the Bald Ibis in the province of the Cape of Good Hope. *Ostrich* 37: 216-218.

Siegfried, W. R. (1971) The status of the Bald Ibis of southern Africa. *Biol. Conserv.* 3: 88-91.

Skead, C. J. (1967) Ecology of birds in the eastern Cape Province. *Ostrich* suppl. 7.

Snow, D. W. ed. (1978) *An atlas of speciation in African non-passerine birds*. London: Trustees of the British Museum (Natural History).

Taylor, L. E. (1909) Notes from Cape Colony. *J. S. Afr. Orn. Union* 5: 81-87.

Vincent, J. and Symons, G. (1948) Some notes on the Bald Ibis. *Ostrich* 19: 58-62.

DWARF OLIVE IBIS

INDETERMINATE

Bostrychia bocagei (Chapin, 1923)

Order CICONIIFORMES

Family THRESKIORNITHIDAE
Subfamily THRESKIORNITHINAE

Summary A small forest ibis, this enigmatic species is confined to the island of São Tomé and has not been seen for over 50 years.

Distribution The Dwarf Olive Ibis is endemic to São Tomé (São Tomé e Príncipe) in the Gulf of Guinea. Specimens were obtained before the turn of the century from "Rio de São Thomé" (Chapin 1923), "Angolares, Morro Gentio, Budo-tap'ana, São Miguel, Florestas and Triumpho" (Bocage 1903) and a single bird (the only record this century) was collected on 9 November 1928 at Roça Jou (0°07'N 6°30'E) near Rio Quija in the south-west of the island, at 1,075 m (Correia 1928-1929). This last would (according to Amadon 1953) have brought the total known specimens to six, but seven localities had already been listed (in Bocage 1903, Chapin 1923) and, moreover, two of those localities were reported to have produced more than one specimen: two from São Miguel (Bocage 1889a,b), three from Angolares (Bocage 1891). "Florestas" (= "forests") is an untraceable locality (in Office of Geography 1962, Centro de Geográfia do Ultramar 1968) but as several specimens of São Tomé birds in BMNH are labelled "São Miguel Florestas" (NJC) it is likely that "Florestas" indicates the forested area near São Miguel on the south-west coast (0°08'N 6°30'E), while Morro Gentio (0°10'N 6°38'E) is close to Angolares (São João dos Angolares, 0°08'N 6°39'E) on the south-east coast (Centro de Geográfia do Ultramar 1968): both birds from São Miguel and two of the three from Angolares may thus be accounted for. "Rio de São Thomé" (Chapin 1923) or "Ribeira de S.Tomé" (de Naurois 1973) is in the north-east of the island with its estuary in the town of São Tomé itself (R. de Naurois *in litt.* 1984), though this watercourse is marked "Agua Grande" in Ministério das Colónias (1948) and de Carvalho Rodrigues (1974); the latter, however, marks an "Agua Tomé" just south of the Roça Uba Budo and thus evidently near Budo-tap'ana. Budo-tap'ana is near Roça Uba Budo at 585 m (de Naurois 1973), this being on the east side of the island behind Santana (i.e. roughly 0°16'N 6°42'E). Triumpho (Triunfo) lies in the far north at 0°24'N 6°41'E (d'Oliveira 1885, Office of Geography 1962, Centro de Geográfia do Ultramar 1968). From this it seems possible that as many as nine specimens are or were known (the Bocage Museum in Lisbon to which all but the last of the specimens originally came has twice suffered severe fires, in 1910 and 1975: R. de Naurois *in litt.* 1983). In 1928 two old locals each reported having once seen the species: two together at Io Grande in the south-east 20 years before, and three together at Roça Jou 10 years before (Correia 1928-1929). The distribution of records, the most striking of which is that from Triumpho in the savanna belt across the north of the island (but see Ecology), suggests it is or was a widespread species outside the higher western and central parts of the island. Intermittent searches, 1963-1973, around São Miguel and Porto Alegre in the south and at Lake Amélia and Calvário (both roughly 0°16'N 6°36'E) in the centre, proved fruitless (de Naurois 1973).

Population Numbers are unknown. The species was probably always rare and was certainly considered so in 1928 (Correia 1928-1929); it is now considered very probably extinct (de Naurois 1983). Forest ibises in the genus *Bostrychia* are, however, notoriously retiring and inconspicuous (see Brown *et al.* 1982) and São Tomé remains so little studied by ornithologists that it may still survive (R. de Naurois *in litt.* 1983).

Ecology On the basis of one personal encounter and two old reports, Correia (1928-1929) noted the species as occuring "only in virgin forests". Though the record from Triumpho might appear to contradict this, it is noted that the lower watercourses in the northern savanna belt have (or had) a sort of gallery forest, which makes the record from there and perhaps also that from the Rio de São Tomé less anomalous than they seem (R. de Naurois *in litt.* 1984). The species's ecology is presumably close to that of the Olive Ibis *Bostrychia olivacea* (for which see Brown *et al.* 1982). The bird (female) collected in November 1928 had large gonads (M. LeCroy *in litt.* 1984).

Threats In 1928 an old local reported that the birds had become very rare because wild dogs destroyed their eggs and possibly ate their young (Correia 1928-1929); but since this man had only once seen the species himself (Correia 1928-1929) and since *Bostrychia* ibises nest in trees (see Brown *et al.* 1982), this information is suspect. Nevertheless other introduced mammalian predators or disease may have played a part in this species's evident decline since the nineteenth century. Forest damage (selective felling) and destruction are known to have occurred in lowland areas of the island, notably from around 1890 to 1915 (Bannerman 1915, Correia 1928-1929, Snow 1950, de Naurois 1975, R. de Naurois *in litt.* 1984), and may have affected the bird.

Conservation Measures Taken None is known.

Conservation Measures Proposed An ICBP project was developed in 1981 to investigate the status, ecology and conservation of the endemic birds of São Tomé e Príncipe, but was unable to proceed in 1982 and 1983. A search for this bird is a component of the project and conservation proposals will follow if the work goes ahead and the species is relocated.

Remarks The Dwarf Olive Ibis of São Tomé is a very small form of the Olive Ibis of West and Central Africa (see, e.g., Brown *et al.* 1982) but there is good precedent for allowing it specific status (i.e. Chapin 1923, Amadon 1953, de Naurois 1973). Not having been seen in the wild for over 50 years, by CITES criteria this species would now be considered extinct.

References

Amadon, D. (1953) Avian systematics and evolution in the Gulf of Guinea. The J. G. Correia collection. *Bull. Amer. Mus. Nat. Hist.* 100: 393-451.
Bannerman, D. A. (1915) Report on the birds collected by the late Mr Boyd

Alexander (Rifle Brigade) during his last expedition to Africa. Part II. The birds of St.Thomas' Island. *Ibis* (10)3: 89-121.

Bocage, J. V. B. (1889a) Sur deux espèces à ajouter à la faune ornithologique de St.Thomé. *Jorn. Acad. Sci. Lisboa* (2)1: 142-144.

Bocage, J. V. B. (1889b) Aves da Ilha de S.Tomé. *Jorn. Acad. Sci. Lisboa* (2)1: 209-210.

Bocage, J. V. B. (1891) Oiseaux de l'Ile St.Thomé. *Jorn. Acad. Sci. Lisboa* (2)2: 77-87.

Bocage, J. V. B. (1903) Contribution à la faune des quatre îles du Golfe de Guinée. IV. Ile de St.Thomé. *Jorn. Acad. Sci. Lisboa* (2)7: 65-96.

Brown, L. H., Urban, E. K. and Newman, K. (1982) *The birds of Africa*, 1. London: Academic Press.

de Carvalho Rodrigues, F. M. (1974) *S.Tomé e Príncipe sob o ponto de vista agrícola*. Estudos, Ensaios e Documentos 130A. Lisboa: Junta de Investigações Científicas do Ultramar (Cartas Agrícolas).

Centro de Geográfia do Ultramar (1968) *Relação dos nomes geográficos de S.Tomé e Príncipe*. Lisboa: Junta de Investigações do Ultramar.

Chapin, J. P. (1923) The Olive Ibis of Dubus and its representative on São Thomé. *Amer. Mus. Novit.* 84.

Correia, J. G. (1928-1929) Unpublished typescript concerning his São Tomé expedition, held in AMNH.

de Naurois, R. (1973) Les ibis des îles de S.Tomé et du Prince: leur place dans le groupe des *Bostrychia* (= *Lampribis*). *Arq. Mus. Bocage* (2)4: 157-173.

de Naurois, R. (1975) Le "Scops" de l'Ile de São Tomé *Otus hartlaubi* (Giebel). *Bonn. zool. Beitr.* 26: 319-355.

de Naurois, R. (1983) Les oiseaux reproducteurs des îles de São Tomé et Príncipe: liste systématique commentée et indications zoogéographiques. *Bonn. zool. Beitr.* 34: 129-148.

Office of Geography (1962) *Gazetteer no. 63. Rio Muni, Fernando Po, and São Tomé e Príncipe*. Washington, D.C.: Department of the Interior.

d'Oliveira, A. A. (1885) Carta da Ilha de S.Thomé. [Lisboa:] Commissão de Cartográphia.

Snow, D. W. (1950) The birds of São Tomé and Príncipe in the Gulf of Guinea. *Ibis* 92: 579-595.

MADAGASCAR TEAL   VULNERABLE

Anas bernieri (Hartlaub, 1860)

Order ANSERIFORMES   Family ANATIDAE
                                                   Subfamily ANATINAE

Summary This little known and evidently much persecuted duck, endemic to Madagascar, has been recorded from a few sites along the west coast and its total numbers must be very low.

Distribution Apart from an apparently unsubstantiated assertion that it occurs on the east coast (Milne Edwards and Grandidier 1885) and a specimen in Grenoble collected by L. Lavauden at Lake Alaotra on 5 September 1932 (O. Langrand *in litt.* 1984), the Madagascar Teal is known only from localities close to the western coast of Madagascar, from the far north as far south as Lake Ihotry. There are four specimens, dated 1934, from Montagne d'Ambre (far north) in MNHN, Paris (SNS). The species was collected in June 1969 at Ambilobe (far north-west) (Salvan 1970) and in the last century from the "north-western coast" (Schlegel 1866), this presumably referring to the undated specimen in RMNH from "Bonbetak Baai", i.e. the Baie de Bombetoka at Majunga (NJC). A pair was seen in September 1983 on Lake Kinkony (O. Langrand *in litt.* 1984). Two birds were collected in July/August 1930 in the western savannas near Maintirano (Delacour 1932a, Rand 1936); one was seen at Bekopaka around this time (Delacour 1956), and a possible sight-record of a pair in July 1929 at Ankavandra (Rand 1936) would constitute the most inland record for the species (up the Manambolo River east of Antsalova), although subsequently the Antsalova region (especially Lake Bemamba) was shown to be a major area for it in the 1970s (Salvan 1970,1972, Scott and Lubbock 1974): Lake Bemamba is a shallow saline lake drying up in September/October, when the species is thought to disperse either to the Soahanina estuary or to the remaining small freshwater pools and lakes in the forests and rice-fields (Scott and Lubbock 1974). The species has also been recorded in the last century from around Morondava (Grandidier 1868; two specimens in RMNH: NJC) and in 1957 (but apparently not subsequently: see Threats) from Lake Ihotry (south-east of Morombe) (Griveaud 1960). These data confirm (but slightly extend) the species's range, anticipated and mapped as from Ambilobe to north of Morombe on the basis of apparent habitat requirements within the 500 to 1,500 mm isohyets (see Salvan 1970 and under Ecology).

Population Although not considered rare on the west coast in the last century (Milne Edwards and Grandidier 1885) it was described as very rare and localised by around 1930 (Delacour 1932a,b); and although it has more recently been judged probably less rare than records suggest (Milon *et al.* 1973) the only evidence of this is from the Lake Bemamba region, where 13 birds were shot in 1970 (Salvan 1970,1972) and, on Lake Bemamba itself, 81 birds were seen (10 pairs on the eastern shore, 61 individuals maximum on the western) and no more than 120 estimated for the whole lake, August 1973 (Scott and Lubbock 1974); this concentration was considered probably "the largest for hundreds of miles" (Scott and Lubbock 1974).

Ecology In the nineteenth century the Madagascar Teal was reported as occurring in small flocks on estuaries, marshes or pools (Milne Edwards and Grandidier 1885), but at least in July and August the species appears to occur in rather isolated pairs (Salvan 1970, Scott and Lubbock 1974; see also records from 1929 and 1930 above). It appears to occur on marshes where recent alluvia and pliocene soils mingle, in herbaceous savanna (with *Hyparrhenia* and *Heteropogon*), mangrove, and dense deciduous forest (Salvan 1970). Birds feed in shallow water or on mud at the water's edge, but have not been observed to drink or fly to fresh water (Scott and Lubbock 1974). From courtship activities seen in August, birds were expected to breed from mid-September; natives reported breeding in November and April, with clutch-size variously claimed as 2-4 and 8-10 (Scott and Lubbock 1974).

Threats The hunting of waterfowl in Madagascar was, at least until recently, very widespread and very intense (Salvan 1970,1972, Forbes-Watson and Turner 1973). Although hunting pressure at Lake Bemamba did not appear to be great in August 1973, there was some poaching (Scott and Lubbock 1974) and the area had been recently opened up for hunting by the building of an airport at Ambereny (Salvan 1972), such that by the early 1980s many hunters were coming there by private airplane from (e.g.) Majunga and Antananarivo (O. Langrand *in litt.* 1984); moreover, locals have reported that they hunt the Madagascar Teal with dogs and plunder nests for eggs (Scott and Lubbock 1974). The impact of such depredations elsewhere in Madagascar is not known. The importance to the species of habitat free of the influence of tilapia and black bass *Micropterus salmoides* is also unknown, but the absence of records from Lake Ihotry after 1957 may indicate that introduced fish pose a threat to the species (for details see Threats under Madagascar Little Grebe *Tachybaptus pelzelnii*). At least in the southern part of the Teal's range (in the Mangoky region), various factors over the past 50 years have resulted in less water in rivers and lakes and a lowering of the water-table, so that overall there is less habitat for aquatic birds (see Appert 1971). Marshes throughout the island have been transformed into rice-fields and fish-farms (Salvan 1970,1972), and rice-growing is now reportedly beginning to alter Lake Bemamba (O. Langrand *in litt.* 1984).

Conservation Measures Taken Hunting is supposed to be banned on Lakes Bemamba and Masama in the Antsalova region, also on parts of Lakes Kinkony and Ihotry (Andriamampianina 1976). The species is listed on Appendix II of CITES, to which Madagascar is a party.

Conservation Measures Proposed The area west of the north-south line between Antsalova and Bekopaka is so rich ornithologically – but particularly because of its population of Madagascar Teal – that a faunal reserve there has been urged, if only at least for Lake Bemamba (Salvan 1972; also Salvan 1970), formally recommended (IUCN 1972) and supported (Milon *et al.* 1973, Scott and Lubbock

1974), but no action appears to have been taken; such a reserve would form a valuable westwards extension of the existing reserve at Antsingy (R.N.I. no. 9 du Tsingy de Bemaraha), and would be likely to provide a major sanctuary for several other threatened bird species, notably the Madagascar Fish Eagle *Haliaeetus vociferoides*, Madagascar Heron *Ardea humbloti* and Sakalava Rail *Amaurornis olivieri* (see relevant accounts), and also perhaps the Madagascar Pond-heron *Ardeola idae* (see Appendix C). Reassessment of the Lake Bemamba situation is now urgent, especially given that there were 70% more waterfowl in the 1940s than in 1973 (Scott and Lubbock 1974). In general, this species deserves a detailed study at one site to determine its annual requirements and a survey throughout western Madagascar to determine its remaining populations and strongholds. Some of this work could be coupled with attempts to locate populations of the Sakalava Rail, and with survey work on the Madagascar Fish Eagle, Heron, and Pond-heron. In this respect it is to be noted that the extensive wetlands (as shown in IGNT 1964) that lie between Ankasakasa/Cap St.André and Tambohorano appear to have been wholly unstudied by ornithologists and merit inclusion in any future survey. Moreover, the wetlands and associated shorelines along the east coast, from Sambava northwards and Tamatave southwards, have been similarly neglected at least in this century, and in view of nineteenth century records from the east for no fewer than four threatened "west coast" birds (Madagascar Heron, Teal, Fish Eagle and Plover *Charadrius thoracicus*) and of the likely importance of these wetlands for many other bird species, a general ornithological survey is clearly needed along the coastlines indicated above.

Remarks Only one specimen of this duck appears ever to have been kept in captivity; it proved hardy (Delacour 1956).

References

Andriamampianina, J. (1976) Madagascar. Pp. 125-126 in M. Smart, ed. *Proceedings, International Conference on the Conservation of Wetlands and Waterfowl, Heiligenhafen, Federal Republic of Germany, 2-6 December 1974*. Slimbridge (Glos.), England: International Waterfowl Research Bureau.

Appert, O. (1971) Die Taucher (Podicipidae [*sic*]) der Mangokygegend in Südwest-Madagaskar. *J. Orn.* 112: 61-69.

Delacour, J. (1932a) Les oiseaux de la Mission Franco-Anglo-Américaine à Madagascar. *Oiseau et R.F.O.* 2: 1-96.

Delacour, J. (1932b) On the birds collected in Madagascar by the Franco-Anglo-American Expedition, 1929-1931. *Ibis* (13)2: 284-304.

Delacour, J. (1956) *The waterfowl of the world*, 2. London: Country Life.

Forbes-Watson, A. D. and Turner, D. A. (1973) Report on bird preservation in Madagascar. Part 2. Report to ICBP, unpublished.

Grandidier, A. (1868) Notes sur les mammifères et les oiseaux observés à Madagascar, de 1865 à 1867. *Rev. Mag. Zool.* (2)20: 3-7.

Griveaud, P. (1960) Une mission de recherche de l'I.R.S.M. au lac Ihotry (S. E. Morombe, Province de Tuléar). *Naturaliste Malgache* 12: 33-41.

IUCN (1972) Recommandations: résolutions adoptées par la Conférence. Pp. 12-15 in: *C. R. Conférence internationale sur la Conservation de la Nature et de ses Ressources à Madagascar*. Morges: IUCN (NS) Doc. Suppl. no. 36.

Institut Géographique National à Tananarive (1964) Carte de Madagascar, 1: 500,000, Type 1963. Tananarive.

Milne Edwards, A. and Grandidier, A. (1885) *Histoire physique, naturelle et politique de Madagascar, 12. Histoire naturelle des oiseaux.* Tome I. Paris.

Milon, P., Petter, J.-J. and Randrianasolo, G. (1973) *Faune de Madagascar, 35. Oiseaux.* Tananarive and Paris: ORSTOM and CNRS.

Rand, A. L. (1936) The distribution and habits of Madagascar birds. *Bull. Amer. Mus. Nat. Hist.* 72: 143-499.

Salvan, J. (1970) Remarques sur l'évolution de l'avifauna malgache depuis 1945. *Alauda* 38: 191-203.

Salvan, J. (1972) Remarques sur l'avifaune malagasy et la protection d'espèces aviennes mal connues ou menacées. (Communication 26, pp. 179-182, in:) *C. R. Conférence Internationale sur la Conservation de la Nature et de ses Ressources à Madagascar.* Morges: IUCN (NS) Doc. suppl. no. 36.

Schlegel, H. (1866) [List of the most remarkable species of mammals and birds collected by Messrs. Fr. Pollen and D. C. van Dam in Madagascar.] *Proc. Zool. Soc. Lond.*: 419-426.

Scott, D. and Lubbock, J. (1974) Preliminary observations on waterfowl in western Madagascar. *Wildfowl* 25: 117-120.

MADAGASCAR POCHARD

ENDANGERED

Aythya innotata (Salvadori, 1894)

Order ANSERIFORMES

Family ANATIDAE
Subfamily ANATINAE

Summary This freshwater diving duck, endemic to Madagascar, is extremely poorly known and since 1930 it has become increasingly rare, but nothing appears to have been done to help it.

Distribution The Madagascar Pochard is apparently confined to lakes and pools in the northern central plateau of Madagascar. The main site for the species is Lake Alaotra (Delacour 1932a,b, Rand 1936, Lavauden 1937, Milon *et al.* 1973), although there have been no published records from there since the 1930s. However, two flocks (of five and three birds) were seen in the south-east part of the lake between Andreba and Ambatosoratra, 26 May 1960, a flock of 20 (one shot, now in ZMA) was seen at Ambatosoratra, 9 June 1960, and a flock of five was seen on the north-east side near Imerimandroso, 5 July 1960 (H. A. W. Payne *per* K. H. Voous *in litt.* 1983); but a recent two-week search of Lake Alaotra failed to locate the species (O. Langrand *in litt.* 1984). In the 1930s Lake Itasy (west of Antananarivo) was identified as another locality (Lavauden 1937) but there are no subsequent records despite visits in 1969-1971, when the single record for the Antananarivo area was of a pair on Lake Ambohibao, 18 March 1970 (Salvan 1970,1972a). Around 1930 the species was seen on a small pond near Antsirabe (Rand 1936; see Remarks) and it was recently noted that three were collected in 1915 at Ambatomainty, near Maevatanana (Benson *et al.* 1976). On the 15 June 1960 two were seen at a barrage near Ambadivato, in the Andilamena region 70 km north of Lake Alaotra (H. A. W. Payne *per* K. H. Voous *in litt.* 1983). The type-specimen is from Betsileo country (Warren 1966), i.e. the southernmost named area for the species (Betsileo people mapped in Deschamps 1960, also Locamus 1900).

Population Numbers are probably at best extremely small. Around 1930 the species was common and bred at Lake Alaotra, and 27 were collected (Delacour 1932a,b, Rand 1936). The lake was revisited several times in the 1930s and live birds were captured (Webb 1936,1954). Since then it has become increasingly rare (Milon *et al.* 1973). Indeed, since this time the only published record is of the pair seen in 1970 (see Distribution). Two independent observers in Madagascar during the 1970s and 1980s are united in the belief that this bird is on the brink of extinction (D. A. Turner *in litt.* 1983, O. Langrand *in litt.* 1984).

Ecology The Madagascar Pochard is (or was) found on lakes, pools and freshwater marshes with open water, where it feeds by diving; it is rather solitary, otherwise in pairs, and not easy to observe; it nests in a large tuft of reeds or aquatic vegetation, March/April, clutch-size being two (Milon *et al.* 1973).

Threats Large-scale duck-shooting has been blamed for the evidently disastrous decline of this species (Forbes-Watson and Turner 1973). The introduction of black bass *Micropterus salmoides* and other exotic fish (e.g. tilapia) into the lakes and pools of the high central plateaus has certainly had a serious impact on native wildlife (see Salvan 1970) and may be responsible for the loss of food and/or destruction of young of this species. Gill-net fishing of exotic fish may also take a heavy toll of adults (A. D. Forbes-Watson pers. comm. 1984). By 1972 Lake Alaotra was said to be of limited interest only, owing to developments there for rice-growing and fish-farming (Salvan 1972b), a view confirmed by recent observations (O. Langrand *in litt.* 1984).

Conservation Measures Taken None is known.

Conservation Measures Proposed Legal protection for this species (and many others endemic to Madagascar) was urged in a letter to the Director, Service des Eaux et Forêts, Chasse et Pêche, over 10 years ago (see King 1978-1979). It is not known if any measures were adopted. A survey is now urgently needed to determine its distribution and numbers, and to provide information from which its conservation can be planned and implemented. This is one species that ought to be savable through captive breeding (see below).

Remarks The species was frequently bred in captivity prior to World War II, but it is not known to be currently represented in captive collections (Delacour 1959). The locality Antsirabe is assumed (and almost certain) to be that at 19°51'S 47°01'E, not that at either 17°11'S 45°01'E or 13°59'S 49°59'E (in TAW 1980).

References

Benson, C. W., Colebrook-Robjent, J. F. R. and Williams, A. (1976) Contribution à l'ornithologie de Madagascar. *Oiseau et R.F.O.* 46: 103-134.

Delacour, J. (1932a) Les oiseaux de la Mission Franco-Anglo-Américaine à Madagascar. *Oiseau et R.F.O.* 2: 1-96.

Delacour, J. (1932b) On the birds collected in Madagascar by the Franco-Anglo-American Expedition, 1929-1931. *Ibis* (13)2: 284-304.

Delacour, J. (1959) *The waterfowl of the world*, 3. London: Country Life.

Deschamps, H. (1960) *Histoire de Madagascar*. Paris: Berger-Levrault.

Forbes-Watson, A. D. and Turner, D. A. (1973) Report on bird preservation in Madagascar, part 3. Report to ICBP, unpublished.

King, W. B. (1978-1979) *Red data book, 2: Aves*. 2nd edition. Morges, Switzerland: IUCN.

Lavauden, L. (1937) Supplément. A. Milne Edwards and A. Grandidier, *Histoire physique, naturelle et politique de Madagascar, 12. Oiseaux*. Paris: Société d'Editions Géographiques, Maritimes et Coloniales.

Locamus, P. (1900) Carte de Madagascar, 1: 500,000. Paris.

Milon, P., Petter, J.-J. and Randrianasolo, G. (1973) *Faune de Madagascar, 35. Oiseaux*. Tananarive and Paris: ORSTOM and CNRS.

Rand, A. L. (1936) The distribution and habits of Madagascar birds. *Bull. Amer. Mus. Nat. Hist.* 72: 143-499.

Salvan, J. (1970) Remarques sur l'évolution de l'avifaune malgache depuis 1945. *Alauda* 38: 191-203.

Salvan, J. (1972a) Statut, recensement, reproduction des oiseaux dulçaquicoles aux environs de Tananarive. *Oiseau et R.F.O.* 42: 35-51.

Salvan, J. (1972b) Remarques sur l'avifaune malagasy et la protection d'espèces aviennes mal connues ou menacées. (Communication 26, pp. 179-182, in:) *C. R. Conférence Internationale sur la Conservation de la Nature et de ses Ressources à Madagascar*. Morges: IUCN (NS) Doc. suppl. no. 36.

The Times Atlas of the World (1980) Comprehensive (sixth) edition. London: Times Books.

Warren, R. L. M. (1966) *Type-specimens of birds in the British Museum (Natural History), 1. Non-passerines*. London: Trustees of the British Museum (Natural History).

Webb, C. S. (1936) Collecting waterfowl in Madagascar. *Avicult. Mag.* (5)1: 36-39.

Webb, C. S. (1954) *A wanderer in the wind*. London: Hutchinson.

MADAGASCAR FISH EAGLE

ENDANGERED

Haliaeetus vociferoides Desmurs, 1845

Order FALCONIFORMES

Family ACCIPITRIDAE

Summary This little known Madagascar raptor, now confined to rivers and shorelines of the west coast north of Morondava, has declined to a point where it may be close to extinction, yet a project first proposed in early 1979 to survey the species and determine its needs has consistently failed to receive funding.

Distribution The Madagascar Fish (or Sea) Eagle is confined to the west coast of central to northern Madagascar, from Morondava north to Diego Suarez. It was formerly reported from the east coast (Grandidier 1867, Hartlaub 1877, Milne Edwards and Grandidier 1879), but these records all appear to be repetitions of each other and based on a single somewhat insubstantial reference to its occurrence near Tamatave in 1862 (Vinson 1865). However, a male was collected on 25 December 1879 at Ampahana (specimen in RMNH: NJC), the only locality of this name (in Office of Geography 1955) being at 14°45'S 50°13'E, with an adjacent coastal lake of the same name, i.e on the north-east coast between Antalaha and Sambava; moreover, five days later the same collector (J. Audebert) obtained another male at "Andrimpona" (specimen in RMNH: NJC), this presumably being the "Andempona" that is marked as the next village (a few kilometres) north of Ampahana, rather than the "Andempona" marked as just north of Sambava (in Locamus 1900). In 1891 it was reported as "all along the western coast and on the numerous small islands off the north-west of the mainland" (Sibree 1891) and this is probably close to the true situation at that time, although evidence of its occurrence in the southern half of the west coast is extremely feeble. Four main general regions have been identified (although these may merely reflect ornithological activity): Nosy Bé and the coastline opposite, the Lake Kinkony region, the Antsalova region, and the coastline between the Mangoky and Fiherenana Rivers, the species apparently being extinct now in this last region. In the first of these regions, eight specimens were collected in two weeks around 1930 on the mainland opposite Nosy Bé (Rand 1936) and there are recent reports of the species from Nosy Bé itself (Thiollay and Meyburg 1981, D. A. Turner *in litt.* 1983). In the second region, there are records from Majunga (Kaudern 1922), Lake Kinkony itself, Ambararatabe and Soalala (Rand 1936); in August 1969 the area in the Soalala – Namakia – Lake Kinkony triangle was identified as a major stronghold, at least 11 birds being seen in three days between Majunga and Lake Kinkony (D. A. Turner *in litt.* 1983), and a pair was seen there in 1980, east of Mitsinjo along the Mahavavy River (Thiollay and Meyburg 1981). In the third region, eight birds were seen over Lake Masama and the Manambolo River in July 1970 (Salvan 1971, Milon *et al.* 1973, Langrand and Meyburg in press) and there have been more recent records (Thiollay and Meyburg 1981), including four adults and two juveniles over Lake Masama in June 1982 (Langrand and Meyburg in press), so that the rectangle of the lakes and marshes between Antsalova, Bekopaka and the sea is now regarded as the last likely area offering hope for the species's survival (Meyburg 1979, Langrand and Meyburg in press). In the fourth region, the species was reported from near Morombe around 1930 (Rand 1936) and as frequent in one area around 1960, but not to be found a decade later (Milon *et al.* 1973); there were in fact seven sightings of single birds in the Morombe region, 1959-1975 (Langrand and Meyburg in press). It is probable that the species was recorded at several unnamed sites along the north-west coast around 1930, given that 27 specimens were collected there "from west of Montagne d'Ambre" (specimen in BMNH: NJC) "to Lake Kinkony" (Delacour 1932); it was reported near Antsohihy in the 1940s (van Someren 1947), and there are specimens in BMNH and MNHN from Anorontsangana, north of Maromandia (NJC,SNS). Breeding was reported in the early 1970s from Lake Ampijoroa (Ankarafantsika), well inland from Majunga (Salvan 1971, Milon *et al.* 1973), but the pair involved was reported not to have produced young for several years prior to 1978 (Meyburg 1979, B.-U. Meyburg pers. comm. 1983; see Remarks under Van Dam's Vanga *Xenopirostris damii*). Nesting has also recently been recorded on a small island c. 30 km west of Diego Suarez, and there is a recent record from north of Maintirano, five birds being reported shot in this region (Langrand and Meyburg in press). There appear to be two or three old records from Mauritius (Benson 1970).

Population In the last century the species was not rare and was often seen in the north-west (Schlegel and Pollen 1868), was still fairly common there around 1930 (Delacour 1932, Rand 1936) but was considered scarce in the 1940s (van Someren 1947). Despite the fairly recent records from Lakes Kinkony and Masama (see above), at the end of the 1970s it was estimated that only 10 pairs survived (Meyburg 1979, Thiollay and Meyburg 1981). More recently, this estimate has been raised to 30 pairs (O. Langrand *in litt.* 1984). Nevertheless, the species is still to be considered one of the rarest birds of prey in the world (Langrand and Meyburg in press).

Ecology It is largely a coastal species, inhabiting estuaries and mangrove-bordered bays where shallow waters facilitate fishing, but also lakes and rivers (Grandidier 1867, Schlegel and Pollen 1868, Rand 1936). It takes fish from water in a plunge-dive (Grandidier 1867, Milne Edwards and Grandidier 1879, Rand 1936), though attacks on large waterbirds (Spoonbill *Platalea alba* and Madagascar Heron *Ardea humbloti*) have been witnessed (Langrand and Meyburg in press). It is commonly found in pairs at traditional sites (Grandidier 1867, Rand 1936), and builds a large nest in the highest tree of forest along the coast or up a river (Schlegel and Pollen 1868), though the nest near Diego Suarez (see Distribution) was on a cliff 6-8 m high (Langrand and Meyburg in press). It breeds in the dry season (Milon *et al.* 1973), towards the start of the rains (Milne Edwards and Grandidier 1879), but not in November/December (Rand 1936). Only one young is raised (Milne Edwards and Grandidier 1879, Milon *et al.* 1973) though two eggs are laid (Milon *et al.* 1973, Langrand and Meyburg in press). Age of first breeding is put at four or five years (Milon *et al.* 1973). The records from Mauritius (and also perhaps from the east coast) suggest a powerful dispersive ability.

Threats The reasons for the decline of this species are unclear (Langrand and Meyburg in press). Shooting by amateur hunters was suspected to have caused its disappearance between the Mangoky and Fiherenana Rivers (Milon *et al.* 1973), and five birds have been reported shot in recent years in the Maintirano area (Langrand and Meyburg in press); deliberate destruction of nests is also stated to occur (Thiollay and Meyburg 1981). Rice-growing is reportedly beginning to alter Lake Bemamba (O. Langrand *in litt.* 1984).

Conservation Measures Taken A leaflet has been produced to increase public awareness of the species's plight (*Fonds d'Intervention pour les Rapaces* no. 9 [1983]: 44, Langrand and Meyburg in press). Along with all Falconiformes, it is included on Appendix II of CITES, to which Madagascar is a party.

Conservation Measures Proposed Full protection for this bird is merited (Milon *et al.* 1973). A faunal reserve has been urged for the Antsalova region, identified above (under Distribution) as perhaps this species's last stronghold (see Conservation Measures Proposed under Madagascar Teal *Anas bernieri*). Since early 1979, a proposal to survey and census it from the air, as a first step to determining further conservation action, has languished for lack of financial support, despite repeated inclusion in the annual ICBP programme. It is to be noted that a similar problem exists for the Madagascar Serpent Eagle *Eutriorchis astur* and that these two raptors, among the world's rarest and yet without any conservation action on their behalf, remain the highest priorities for such action at present (Langrand and Meyburg in press). For the need for a general ornithological survey of east coast wetlands in Madagascar, and for the possible importance of wetlands around Cap St.André, see Conservation Measures Proposed under Madagascar Teal.

Remarks It is to be hoped that in the course of the proposed survey and resulting research and action for this species it will be possible to accommodate the study and conservation of three other birds of considerable importance, the Madagascar Teal, the Madagascar Heron *Ardea humbloti* (see relevant accounts) and the Madagascar Pond-heron *Ardeola idae* (see Appendix C).

References

Benson, C. W. (1970) The Cambridge collection from the Malagasy Region. Part I. *Bull. Brit. Orn. Club* 90: 168-172.

Delacour, J. (1932) Les oiseaux de la Mission Franco-Anglo-Américaine à Madagascar. *Oiseau et R.F.O.* 2: 1-96.

Delacour, J. (1932) On the birds collected in Madagascar by the Franco-Anglo-American Expedition, 1929-1931. *Ibis* (13)2: 284-304.

Grandidier, A. (1867) Notes sur les mammifères et les oiseaux observées à Madagascar, de 1865 à 1867. *Rev. Mag. Zool.* (2)19: 313-321.

Hartlaub, G. (1877) *Die Vögel Madagascars und der benachbarten Inselgruppen.* Halle.

Kaudern, W. (1922) Sauropsiden aus Madagaskar. *Zool. Jahrb.* 45: 395-457.

Langrand, O. and Meyburg, B.-U. (in press) Birds of prey and owls in Madagascar: their distribution, status and conservation. Second symposium on African predatory birds, 22-26 August 1983.

Locamus, P. (1900) Carte de Madagascar, 1: 500,000. Paris.

Meyburg, B.-U. (1979) Survey of the Madagascar Sea Eagle *Haliaeetus vociferoides*. Proposal submitted to IUCN/WWF/ICBP, 16 March.

Milne Edwards, A. and Grandidier, A. (1879) *Histoire physique, naturelle et politique de Madagascar, 12. Histoire naturelle des oiseaux*. Tome I. Paris.

Milon, P., Petter, J.-J. and Randrianasolo, G. (1973) *Faune de Madagascar, 35. Oiseaux*. Tananarive and Paris: ORSTOM and CNRS.

Office of Geography (1955) *Gazetteer no. 2. Madagascar, Réunion and the Comoro Islands*. Washington, D.C.: Department of the Interior.

Rand, A. L. (1936) The distribution and habits of Madagascar birds. *Bull. Amer. Mus. Nat. Hist.* 72: 143-499.

Salvan, J. (1971) Observations nouvelles à Madagascar. *Alauda* 39: 37-42.

Schlegel, H. and Pollen, F. P. L. (1868) *Recherches sur la faune de Madagascar et de ses dépendances, d'après les découvertes de François P. L. Pollen et D. C. van Dam*. 2me partie. Mammifères et oiseaux. Leyde.

Sibree, J. (1891) On the birds of Madagascar, and their connection with native folk-lore, proverbs and superstitions. Part I. *Ibis* (6)3: 194-228.

van Someren, V. D. (1947) Field notes on some Madagascar birds. *Ibis* 89: 235-267.

Thiollay, J.-M. and Meyburg, B.-U. (1981) Remarques sur l'organisation d'un peuplement insulaire de rapaces: Madagascar. *Alauda* 49: 216-226.

Vinson, A. (1865) *Voyage à Madagascar au couronnement de Radama II*. Paris.

CAPE VULTURE   RARE
Gyps coprotheres (Forster, 1798)

Order FALCONIFORMES   Family ACCIPITRIDAE

Summary This species, restricted to southern Africa, has declined markedly in certain parts of its range and faces a variety of threats, chiefly from the direct action of man and technology. The species's reproductive rate is good but survival, particularly of the young birds, is poor. The present population is believed to be in the order of 10,000 birds.

Distribution The Cape Vulture is restricted to southern Africa, occurring in South Africa, Lesotho, Swaziland, Botswana, Namibia, Zimbabwe and Mozambique, with occasional birds wandering north to Zambia and Zaire (Mundy 1973,1982). There are two main centres of breeding distribution, the larger in Transvaal and eastern Botswana (Mundy 1982,1984, Brooke in press, P. J. Mundy *in litt.* 1984) and the smaller centred on Transkei, Lesotho and the Natal Drakensberg (Mundy 1984, P. J. Mundy *in litt.* 1984). Because immature birds habitually live and forage away from the breeding colonies, the geographical range of the species is much wider than the breeding range and birds can be seen in almost any part of southern Africa (Mundy 1973, Brooke in press).

Botswana The colony at Mannyelanong near the border with Transvaal has been known for at least 30 years (Butchart and Mundy 1981). Another colony started nearby at Manyana in 1968, probably as a result of severe disturbance at Mannyelanong (Butchart and Mundy 1981, Mundy 1983a). Two other nearby colonies, at Otse Hill and Baratani (Ledger and Mundy 1973, von Richter and Passineau 1976), probably started during the 1960s and were also composed of birds displaced from Mannyelanong. Following protection measures at Mannyelanong and severe disturbance at Manyana these three colonies died out: Baratani in 1975, Otse Hill in 1976 and Manyana in 1978, the birds presumably returning to Mannyelanong (Butchart and Mundy 1981, Mundy 1983a). In 1976 a large colony was discovered near Lerala in the Tswapong Hills (Beesley 1976, von Richter and Passineau 1976, Mundy 1983a, P. J. Mundy *in litt.* 1984).

Lesotho The Cape Vulture is widespread in Lesotho and is known from at least 20 sites, mainly in the mountainous areas, especially the Maluti, Drakensberg and Central ranges (Jilbert 1979,1982,1983). Of these 20 sites, only ten had been researched by 1982 (Jilbert 1982) and it seems that many further sites remain to be discovered, especially in the central highland part of the country (Jilbert 1979). Three breeding colonies are known at Semonkong, the Upper Quthing Valley and Sehlabathebe, and breeding colonies are suspected at Moteng Pass, Nahamali Pass, Pitseng and Thaba Tseka (Jilbert 1979,1982,1983). The Sehlabathebe site is at 2,900 m (Jilbert 1979), the highest altitude known for a Cape Vulture breeding colony. Roosting sites have been found at Mechachaneng, Mafeteng, Ntjepeleng, Thaba Putsoa, Jonathan's Village, Matlakeng, Maboloka Mountain and Tenane (Jilbert 1979,1982,1983). A site once occupied in the Langberg (mountains) near the western border of Lesotho appears now to be deserted (Jilbert 1979). Birds have also been seen near Maseru, near Lundean's Peak and along the Sekake's-Qachas road (Jilbert 1979).

Mozambique The Cape Vulture is usually considered to be a non-breeding visitor to southern Mozambique (Clancey 1971) but a large breeding colony has recently been noted in the south of the country at 26°20'S 32°10'E (P. J. Mundy *in litt.* 1984).

Namibia The distribution of the Cape Vulture in Namibia is very poorly documented. A breeding colony at Waterberg has declined greatly since the 1960s (Mundy 1983a, P. J. Mundy *in litt.* 1984) and one report states that there has been no breeding anywhere in Namibia since the mid-1970s (Brooke in press). However, recent information indicates that the species is not yet extinct as a breeding bird in Namibia and that a small population still survives (P. J. Mundy *in litt.* 1984). One roost which was known in the Namib Desert Park in the 1960s (Sauer 1973) appears now to be deserted (Underhill 1979).

South Africa: Cape Province Before 1900 the Cape Vulture seems to have been fairly widespread in Cape Province and a breeding colony was recorded from Nelspoort near Beaufort West, in the central Karoo area and well outside the present-day breeding range (Boshoff and Vernon 1980). It once occurred on the Table Mountain and Cape Peninsula (Jarvis *et al.* 1974, Steyn 1982). Many place names throughout Cape Province embrace the words "vulture", "aasvogel", "aasvoel" or "xalanga", providing evidence for the species having been widespread in former times (Jarvis *et al.* 1974, Boshoff and Vernon 1980). There appears to have been a serious decline around the turn of the century, perhaps related to the 1898 rinderpest epidemic (Boshoff and Vernon 1980) and Masterson (1916) documents its disappearance from the Humansdorp area around this time. Since 1905 there have been two isolated populations in Cape Province, the main one centred in the east and a smaller one in the south-west (Boshoff and Vernon 1980, Boshoff *et al.* 1983). The eastern population gradually increased after 1905, spreading south and west back into the Karoo area (Boshoff and Vernon 1980). This increase continued until about 1960, since when the range has contracted again and it is now probably similar to that of about 1930 (Boshoff and Vernon 1980). The largest and best known colony in the eastern Cape Province is at Karnmelkspruit, Lady Grey District (Boshoff and Vernon 1980,1981, Vernon and Boshoff 1980, Mundy 1983a). It has been suggested that Karnmelkspruit is an ancestral colony from which the species spreads out when the population is high (Boshoff and Vernon 1980). Breeding also takes place (at least as recently as 1979) at Balloch and Forest Range Farm in Cathcart District (Jarvis *et al.* 1974, Boshoff and Vernon 1980,1981). In 1972 breeding was recorded at Stadbroke Farm in Middelburg District (Jarvis *et al.* 1974). Roosting sites (some of which might represent either former or undiscovered breeding colonies) are known in eastern Cape Province at Andriesberg, Avondale, Buffelshoek, Christiana, Clifford, Clifton, Dagbreek, De Rust, Elandsberg, Goerdwacht, Hillside, Inverket, Kleinfontein, Martha Mountain, Mlengana, Nonesi Mountain, Nosi Nek,

Rooiberg, Rooipoort, Stonehenge, Tafelberg, Teebus, The Plains and Wit-kransnek (Jarvis *et al.* 1974, Boshoff and Vernon 1980,1981). The population in south-western Cape Province, which is probably completely isolated from all other populations (Robertson 1982), has been declining throughout this century (Boshoff and Vernon 1980). Colonies have become extinct near Swellendam by 1930, at Aasvoelberg in Albertinia District in about 1946 and at Gamka Mountain in Oudtshoorn District in the 1970s (Jarvis *et al.* 1974, Currie 1978, Boshoff and Vernon 1980). According to reports in the early 1970s vultures were still present at Gamka Mountain and apparently breeding (Stuart 1972, Jarvis 1974a) but the colony was extinct by 1977 (Currie 1978). The main surviving colony in south-western Cape Province is at Potberg near Bredasdorp, which has been known since 1951 (Boshoff 1981, Boshoff and Currie 1981, Robertson 1982,1984). A smaller colony, believed to be a satellite of Potberg, is found in the Langeberg range in the Herbertsdale/Van Wyksdorp area where breeding took place in 1976, 1978 and 1979 (Boshoff and Vernon 1980, Boshoff 1981, Boshoff and Currie 1981). Before the onset of the 1981 breeding season the Langeberg colony moved its location 9 km to the north-east to Aasvogelvlei (Boshoff and Robertson 1983). There is apparently some movement of birds between Potberg and Aasvogelvlei, a distance of 120 km (Robertson 1982). Breeding took place at another site in south-western Cape Province, Langkloof, in 1976 but apparently not in 1978 (Boshoff and Vernon 1980). Birds ringed as nestlings at Potberg have been recovered 547 km to the north at Calvinia and also along the Langeberg range from Swellendam, Herbertsdale and Mossel Bay (Currie 1978, Boshoff and Currie 1981). It seems that birds ringed in south-western Cape Province wander less far than those ringed in Transvaal (Jarvis 1974a). First year birds and immatures ringed as nestlings in Transvaal, especially those from the Magaliesberg colonies, tend to gather in considerable numbers in the Kimberley area in north-eastern Cape Province (Mundy 1982, Steyn 1982). The ranches near Kimberley apparently act as nurseries for young Cape Vultures, most of which seem to come from Transvaal (Mundy 1982, Steyn 1982), though this movement of birds from Transvaal to Cape Province now probably happens on a smaller scale than formerly (Vernon 1978).

South Africa: Natal Very little has been published on the distribution of this species in Natal, though it is widespread along the Drakensberg escarpment (Cyrus and Robson 1980, P. J. Mundy *in litt.* 1984) and several breeding colonies exist (Brooke in press). One roost is known 8 km outside the Hluhluwe-Umfolozi Game Reserve complex (Macdonald and Birkenstock 1980). The colony in the Umtamvuna Gorge was just inside Transkei (Mundy 1983a), but has recently moved to the Natal side of the border (Brooke in press, P. J. Mundy *in litt.* 1984).

South Africa: Orange Free State The Cape Vulture has decreased seriously in Orange Free State, where it is in danger of extinction as a breeding bird (Mundy 1984). Mundy (1983a) states that there are five breeding sites but Brooke (in press) notes only one regular breeding colony. In the mid-1970s O'Connor (1980) noted breeding at only two sites, Zastron, which has been known since 1896, and Witsieshoek, which has been known since 1955. Breeding colonies at Stillewoning, Verlange Deel, Thaba Nchu, Thaba Phatswa and the Orange River gorge in Philippolis District are now extinct (O'Connor 1980). There is also good circumstantial evidence that two breeding colonies in Bethlehem District and in Frankfurt District were deserted earlier this century (O'Connor 1980). In the mid-1970s active roosts were known at Stillewoning, Aasvoelkrans, Verlange Deel, Merriemetsie, Thaba Nchu and Bethulie (van Heerden 1980, O'Connor 1980). There was also a winter roost at Tussen die Riviere and small irregular roosts at Non Pareil and Mount Paul (O'Connor 1980).

South Africa: Transkei The Cape Vulture occurs widely in Transkei (Boshoff *et al.* 1983) and there are several breeding colonies (Brooke in press). By far the most important breeding site is at Colleywobbles on the Bashee River (Vernon *et al.* 1980,1982a,1983b). It has been suggested that this is an ancestral colony from which the species spreads during periods of high population (Boshoff and Vernon 1980). Other colonies have been reported from the Bawa Falls on the Gcuwa River, known since the 1930s (Vernon 1982), from the Umtamvuna Gorge along the border with Natal (Mundy 1983a) and from Execution Rock, between Umtata and Port St.Johns (Ross 1970, Williams 1972). Further exploration in Transkei will, no doubt, lead to the discovery of several more colonies.

South Africa: Transvaal Transvaal is the centre of the Cape Vulture's distribution and over 50% of the breeding population occurs here (Mundy 1983a, P. J. Mundy *in litt.* 1984; see Population). There are five large breeding colonies: Blouberg, Kransberg (the same as Groothoek: P. J. Mundy *in litt.* 1984), Manoutsa and two colonies at Roberts' Farm and Skeerpoort on the Magaliesberg escarpment (Tarboton 1978, Mundy 1983a, Tarboton and Allan 1984). In the 1977-1978 survey another four small colonies at Mara (discovered in 1910), Rooipoort, Penge and Loskop were located (Tarboton 1978). Nine colonies were located altogether in the 1977-1978 survey (Tarboton 1978) but it is recently reported that 11 breeding sites are now known in the province (Brooke in press), suggesting that two small colonies have been discovered in recent years. A colony survived at Nooitgedacht on the Magaliesberg escarpment until at least 1974 (Ledger and Mundy 1975), but is apparently now extinct (Tarboton 1978). In addition to these breeding colonies there are roosts in many parts of the province and wandering birds can be seen almost anywhere (Tarboton 1978, Mundy 1982), though rarely in the central and south-eastern highveld areas (Tarboton 1978). The colonies at Roberts' Farm and Skeerpoort on the Magaliesberg escarpment are the best studied, and colour-ringing has been useful in determining the movement of juvenile birds away from the colonies: the average juvenile recovery distance increases from 5.7 km in December to 14.6 km in January, 228.7 km in February, 275.2 km in March and 390.6 km in April, the maximum distance a first-year bird is known to have moved away from the Magaliesberg escarpment being 1,192 km (Mundy 1982). Immature birds (up to six years old) average 450 km (maximum 1,226 km) from the colonies (Mundy 1982). Many of these young birds move in a south-south-westerly direction through south-western Transvaal and western Orange Free State to central and eastern Cape Province, especially the Kimberley area (Mundy 1982, P. J. Mundy *in litt.* 1984). However, the proportion of the birds ringed in Transvaal that are recovered in Cape Province has been declining for many years, from 42% in the

1950s, to 25% in the 1960s and only 11% in the 1970s (Vernon 1978). A few young birds have been recorded moving north from the Magaliesberg colonies (Mundy 1982) and it may be that the proportion of birds now moving north in their first year is increasing.

Swaziland Almost nothing is on record as to the status of the Cape Vulture in Swaziland, although it apparently breeds (Mundy 1983a, Brooke in press, P. J. Mundy *in litt.* 1984). A probable breeding colony has been observed on Umkhobolondo Mountain and further small colonies are likely to exist in the Lebombo Mountains (Williams 1972).

Zaire There is one record of this species from the Upemba National Park in south-eastern Zaire in the late 1940s (Verheyen 1953), this being the most northerly record ever of the Cape Vulture (Mundy 1973).

Zambia There have been a few sight records of this species from Lochinvar National Park during the 1970s (Dowsett 1979, Conant 1980).

Zimbabwe The Cape Vulture no longer breeds in Zimbabwe but the only known former colony at Wabai Hill south of Shangani is still used as a roost (Mundy 1982, Steyn 1982). Breeding was first reported at Wabai Hill in 1965 (Fotheringham 1966) and again in 1969 and 1971 (Mundy and Steyn 1977) but not subsequently (Mundy and Scott 1979, Mundy 1982, Brooke in press). No other roosts are known in Zimbabwe but birds are regularly recorded in the south and west of the country north to the Hwange (Wankie) and Chizarira National Parks (Mundy 1982). There are also records from the midlands between Gweru and Kwekwe, near Harare and near Mutare (Mundy 1982, P. J. Mundy *in litt.* 1984). Apart from an unconfirmed sighting from Starvation Island in Lake Kariba all Zimbabwe records of this species are from south of 17.5°S (Mundy 1982).

Population There seems little doubt that the Cape Vulture was common through much of southern Africa during the last century but most reports now indicate a serious decline in numbers (Mundy 1982, Steyn 1982). Population estimates for each province and country are given below, followed by estimates of the world population. The results of censuses should be treated as minimum estimates only, because Cape Vultures are usually very difficult to count on their breeding cliffs; apparent increases at colonies usually reflect improved census techniques rather than real increases in the population.

Botswana The best known Cape Vulture colony in Botswana is at Mannyelanong near the border with Transvaal. Counts at this colony revealed 87 pairs in 1963, 74 in 1969, seven in 1973 (see Remarks), 38 in 1974, 78 in 1975, 88 in 1976, 82 in 1977, 71 in 1978, and only 80 adult birds in 1980 (Ledger and Mundy 1973,1975,1976,1977, Mundy *et al.* 1980, Butchart and Mundy 1981, Mundy 1983a). In the years 1974-1976 correction factors were calculated to take account of nests blown away during the breeding season (Mundy 1983a), from which the true population at Mannyelanong can be estimated at 51 pairs in 1974, 104 in 1975 and

104 in 1976 (Ledger and Mundy 1975,1976,1977). The trend at Mannyelanong has been one of a severe decline until 1973, followed by a rapid recovery (as a result of protection given to the colony) and then some subsequent decline in the late 1970s (Mundy 1983a). The initial decline was probably caused by disturbance at Mannyelanong and it seems that during this time many birds moved to the nearby colonies of Manyana, Otse Hill and Baratani (Mundy 1983a). With the recovery of the Mannyelanong population these three colonies all declined to extinction (Mundy 1983, see Distribution). The Manyana colony started in 1968 and censuses revealed 49 pairs in 1973 (70 pairs estimated according to Ledger and Mundy 1975, also 1973: see Remarks), 26 in 1974, 23 in 1975, nine in 1976, eight in 1977 and none thereafter (Ledger and Mundy 1975,1976,1977, Mundy *et al.* 1980, Butchart and Mundy 1981, Mundy 1983a). After applying correction factors for nests blown away the estimates of the true population for 1974-1976 are 35 pairs in 1974, 31 in 1975 and 11 in 1976 (Ledger and Mundy 1975,1976,1977). The Otse Hill colony numbered 3-4 in 1974, 2-3 in 1975 but none thereafter (Ledger and Mundy 1973,1975,1976, Mundy 1983a; see Remarks). There were 11-15 pairs at Baratani in 1974 but no records of any breeding subsequently (Ledger and Mundy 1975, Mundy 1983a). Much the largest breeding colony in Botswana is in the Tswapong Hills where 68 birds were seen when the site was first discovered (Beesley 1976) but work in 1980 showed there to be at least 166 breeding pairs (Butchart and Mundy 1981). There may be other colonies to be discovered in remote parts of Botswana (Beesley 1976) and the breeding population for the whole country is estimated to be about 300 pairs (P. J. Mundy *in litt.* 1984).

Lesotho There have been no detailed censuses of this species in Lesotho but brief counts have been carried out at a number of colonies and roosts (Jilbert 1979,1982,1983). At the Semonkong colony 67 flying birds and 31 chicks were counted in 1977 and 58 birds were counted in 1982 (Jilbert 1979,1982). In the Upper Quthing Valley colony 87 birds were counted in 1977-1978 and 128 in 1982 (Jilbert 1979,1982). No proper count has been carried out at the Sehlabathebe colony but at least 12-15 birds were seen there in 1978 (Jilbert 1979). In the suspected breeding colonies about ten birds were seen at Moteng Pass in 1978, 15 at Nahamali Pass in 1978, 105 at Pitseng in 1982 and 52 at Thaba Tseka in 1982 (Jilbert 1979,1982). Counts at roosting sites revealed about 30 birds at Mafeteng in 1978, ten at Ntjepeleng in 1978, 30 at Maboloka Mountain in 1978 and six there in 1982, and 22 at Tenane in 1982 (Jilbert 1979,1982). The Maboloka Mountain roost is probably only intermittently used (Jilbert 1982). The total breeding population in Lesotho is estimated to be about 250 pairs (P. J. Mundy *in litt.* 1984).

Mozambique The recently reported colony in southern Mozambique is thought to number about 200 pairs (P. J. Mundy *in litt.* 1984).

Namibia The well known colony at Waterberg has declined markedly, and a recent count by C. J. Brown was of about 10 pairs (Mundy 1983a, P. J. Mundy *in litt.* 1984). In 1969 there were 300 birds at this site but by 1974 only 50 survived (Mundy 1983a). The current Namibian breeding population is estimated to be in the order of 50 pairs (P. J. Mundy *in litt.* 1984) but with no indication as to where these birds might be.

    South Africa: Cape Province The Cape Vulture's main population in Cape Province is in the eastern Cape grasslands where its most important colony is at Karnmelkspruit (Boshoff and Vernon 1980). It seems that, following a population crash at the turn of the century, the eastern Cape birds slowly recovered in numbers up to 1960, then rapidly declined (Boshoff and Vernon 1980). In 1978 the Karnmelkspruit colony was estimated to number 40 pairs and 250 birds (Boshoff and Vernon 1980, Vernon and Boshoff 1980). In 1979 40 nestlings and 240 birds were counted (Boshoff and Vernon 1981). In 1980 76 nests were counted (presumably reflecting improved census techniques since the colony was said to be declining) but only 120 birds were seen (Vernon and Boshoff 1980). In 1981 there were only 66 occupied nests (Vernon *et al.* 1983a). Elsewhere in the eastern Cape Province 65 birds were counted at a breeding colony at Stadbroke Farm, Middelburg District, in 1972 (Jarvis *et al.* 1974), 11 pairs and 50 birds at Balloch in 1978 (Boshoff and Vernon 1980) with 14 nestlings at the same site in 1979 (Boshoff and Vernon 1981) and nine pairs and 36 birds at Forest Range Farm in 1978 (Boshoff and Vernon 1980). Censuses at roosting sites in eastern ·Cape Province revealed 13 birds at Andriesberg in 1979, 25 at Avondale in 1979, 160 at Buffelshoek in 1972, one at Christiana in 1972, 14 at Clifford in 1979, 80 at Clifton in 1979, 60 at Dagbreek in 1972, 30 at De Rust in 1972, 41 at Hillside in 1979, 100 at Kleinfontein in 1972, 25 at Martha in 1972 and 40 in 1979, eight at Nonesi Mountain in 1972, 32 at Rooiberg in 1979, 119 at Stonehenge in 1979, 36 at Tafelberg in 1979 and 15 at The Plains in 1972 (Jarvis *et al.* 1974, Boshoff and Vernon 1981). The isolated population in the south-western Cape has been declining all this century (Boshoff and Vernon 1980) and now probably numbers only about 80 birds (Robertson 1984). The main colony at Potberg had 26 nests in 1974, 30 in 1975 (37 according to Boshoff 1981), 19 in 1976, 18 in 1977, 12 in 1978, 13 in 1978 (10 according to Boshoff and Vernon 1981), 14 in 1980, 16 in 1981 and 17 in 1982 (Boshoff and Robertson 1983, *Afr. Wildl.* 37 [1984]: 39). These figures suggest that the decline might now have levelled off (*Afr. Wildl.* 37 [1984]: 39). Maximum counts of flying birds at Potberg show a similar trend: 111 birds in 1972, 79 in 1973, 84 in 1974, 45 in 1978 and 1979, 51 in 1980, 59 in 1981 (Boshoff and Vernon 1980,1981, Boshoff 1981, Boshoff and Currie 1981, Boshoff and Robertson 1983). At the Langeberg colony only one pair bred in 1978 and 1979, and three in 1980, maximum counts of flying birds being 28 in 1978 and 40 in 1979 (Boshoff and Vernon 1980,1981, Boshoff 1981, Boshoff and Robertson 1983). In 1981, after this colony had moved to Aasvogelvlei, there were ten nests and 20 flying birds (Boshoff and Robertson 1983). At Langkloof, where a pair bred in 1976, only ten unoccupied nests could be found in 1978 (Boshoff and Vernon 1980). In the early 1970s 80-100 Cape Vultures were seen at the Gamka Mountain colony in Oudtshoorn District but of the 50 nests counted, most were probably old (Stuart 1972). A few years later this colony was extinct (Currie 1978). In 1978 a total of 63 nests was counted at three Cape Vulture colonies in Cape Province (Mundy 1983a) and this figure could be the basis for a population estimate of 65 pairs for the whole province in 1979 (Boshoff *et al.* 1983, Brooke in press). This is likely to be an underestimate and a more likely figure is probably 100 breeding pairs in Cape Province (P. J. Mundy *in litt.* 1984). A count of 250 pairs and 889 birds in 1978, leading to an estimate of the real population of 1,200-1,600 birds in Cape Province, is misleading since this includes part of the much larger population in Transkei (see Boshoff and Vernon 1980).

South Africa: Natal Little is known of the numerical status of the Cape Vulture in Natal. Many small colonies are situated along the Drakensberg and a recent count by C. J. Brown revealed about 650 birds scattered the length of the Natal side (P. J. Mundy *in litt.* 1984). The colony on the Natal side of the Umtamvuna Gorge numbered at least 37 pairs in 1982 (Brooke in press). The Natal population is estimated to be in the order of 200 pairs (P. J. Mundy *in litt.* 1984).

South Africa: Orange Free State The Cape Vulture has seriously declined in Orange Free State and several breeding colonies are now only roosts or have died out altogether (O'Connor 1980; see Distribution). The best known colony is at Zastron which has decreased steadily over many years from 142 nests in 1948, to 102 in 1950, 72 in 1955, 52 in 1960, 41 in 1965, 34 in 1970 and 27 in 1975 (van Ee 1981). Other censuses carried out in the mid-1970s revealed 205 birds in 1974, 19 nests counted (though the real number was probably about 31) and 60 birds seen in 1975, and 18 pairs and 215 birds in 1976 (Ledger and Mundy 1976, O'Connor 1980). The breeding colony at Witsieshoek numbered 11 pairs and 150 birds in 1976 (O'Connor 1980). In 1976 censuses of roosts in Orange Free State revealed 49 birds at Stillewoning, 9 at Aasvoelkrans, 16 at Verlange Deel, 71 at Merriemetsie, 19 at Thaba Nchu, 16 at Bethulie, 131 at Tussen die Riviere, 5 at Non Pareil and 3 at Mount Paul (O'Connor 1980). Also in 1976 nine birds were counted at the roost at Merrimetsie in Excelsior District (van Heerden 1980), when 71 birds were counted in the same year (O'Connor 1980): this discrepancy illustrates the fluctuations that can occur from week to week (and even day to day) at roosts, although after 1976 conservation measures were introduced and the roost then increased to (generally at least) 42 birds (van Heerden 1980, P. J. Mundy *in litt.* 1984).

South Africa: Transkei The colony at Colleywobbles on the Bashee River is one of the largest and most important in existence (P. J. Mundy *in litt.* 1984). Incomplete censuses at Colleywobbles revealed 46 pairs in 1976, 20 in 1977 and 83 in 1978 (Ledger and Mundy 1977, Mundy *et al.* 1980). However, more detailed work has shown that the real population at Colleywobbles is much higher: 175 pairs were counted in 1977, 201 in 1978 (180 according to Boshoff and Vernon 1980), 200 in 1979, 247 in 1980, 314 in 1981 and 303 in 1982 (Vernon *et al.* 1980,1982a,1983b). This apparent increase in population is probably a reflection of improved census techniques and so population trends are difficult to assess (Vernon *et al.* 1980,1982a). The counts in 1982 were the most detailed so far and the results probably represent a real population decline of about 23% (Vernon *et al.* 1983b). In 1981 there were probably 800 flying birds present at Colleywobbles (Vernon *et al.* 1982a). In 1981 49 nests were counted at the Bawa Falls colony on the Gcuwa River and there is one report of 300 birds having been seen there (Vernon 1982). The colony on the Transkei side of the Umtamvuna Gorge is thought to number about ten pairs (Mundy 1983a). The Transkei population is estimated to be about 500 pairs (P. J. Mundy *in litt.* 1984).

South Africa: Transvaal Transvaal is very much the core of the Cape Vulture's breeding distribution and 95% of the province's birds breed in five large colonies, Blouberg, Kransberg (or Groothoek), Manoutsa and the two Magaliesberg colonies, Roberts' Farm and Skeerpoort (Tarboton 1978, Mundy 1983a, P. J. Mundy *in litt.* 1984). The Blouberg colony numbered 315-370 pairs and 825 birds in 1978 (Tarboton 1978). The Kransberg colony was estimated at 200-250 pairs and 633 birds in 1978 (Tarboton 1978) but more recent counts by P. C. Benson have shown it to number at least 700 and perhaps up to 1,000 pairs (P. J. Mundy *in litt.* 1984), making it by far the largest of any Cape Vulture colony. There have been several incomplete censuses of the Manoutsa colony giving very low population estimates of 14 pairs in 1975 (Ledger and Mundy 1976), 44 in 1976 (Ledger and Mundy 1977), 25 in 1977 and 36 in 1978 (Mundy *et al.* 1980). A count of 100 pairs and 366 birds in 1978 (Tarboton 1978) is probably a more realistic estimate. Censuses at the Roberts' Farm colony have revealed an alarming decline in recent years (Mundy *et al.* 1980). In 1974 188 pairs were counted and the real population was estimated to be 255 pairs (Ledger and Mundy 1975). In 1975 198 pairs were counted and the real population was estimated to be 249 pairs (Ledger and Mundy 1976). In 1976 the decline started with 167 pairs counted and 201 pairs estimated (Ledger and Mundy 1977). In 1977 and 1978 no estimates were made of the true population but 135 and 92 pairs were counted in the respective years (Mundy *et al.* 1980). Between 1976 and 1979 the Roberts' Farm colony decreased by 45% (*S. A. Digest*, 10 April 1981: 17). By contrast the nearby Skeerpoort colony has remained relatively stable (Mundy *et al.* 1980). In 1974 186 pairs were counted and the real population was estimated to be 271 pairs (Ledger and Mundy 1975). This compares with 188 pairs counted (282 pairs estimated) in 1975 (Ledger and Mundy 1976), 177 pairs counted (216 estimated) in 1976 (Ledger and Mundy 1977), 195 pairs counted in 1977 and 150 pairs counted in 1978 (Mundy *et al.* 1980). No estimates were made of the true population in 1977 and 1978 and the censuses were, in any case, incomplete in these two years and so the number of birds present was doubtless higher than the counts themselves suggest (Mundy *et al.* 1980). Of the smaller colonies in Transvaal, a survey in 1978 counted 50-60 pairs and 174 birds at Mara, 7-13 pairs at Rooipoort (this colony was once much bigger), 6-8 pairs at Penge and fewer than 20 pairs at Loskop (Tarboton 1978). The colony at Nooitgedacht on the Magaliesberg escarpment numbered 50 pairs in 1962, 24 pairs in 1963, 8-11 pairs in 1974 (Ledger and Mundy 1975) but is now extinct (Tarboton 1978). Cape Vultures can be seen widely over many parts of Transvaal (Tarboton 1978; see Distribution). In the Kruger National Park it is fairly common (Kemp 1969), accounting for 12.9% of the vultures at carcasses (Mundy 1982). Most of the birds feeding in the Kruger National Park probably come from the colony at Manoutsa (Kemp 1980). The breeding population in Transvaal has been estimated at 1,900 pairs (Brooke in press) and 2,000 pairs (P. J. Mundy *in litt.* 1984).

Swaziland Almost nothing is known of the numerical status of the Cape Vulture in Swaziland. In the early 1970s 8-10 birds were reported to be roosting on

Umkhobolondo Mountain (Williams 1972). The Swaziland population is estimated to be in the order of 50 pairs (P. J. Mundy *in litt.* 1984).

Zimbabwe This species has not bred in Zimbabwe since 1971 but the former breeding colony at Wabai Hill is still used as a roost (Mundy 1982, Steyn 1982). In 1965 18 birds and five nests were counted during a brief visit to the colony (Fotheringham 1966) and in 1969 four active nests were found (Mundy and Steyn 1977). Between 1969 and 1977 the number of birds using the roost halved (Mundy and Steyn 1977), probably from about 100 birds (Mundy 1973) to about 40 birds (Mundy 1982). However, about 240 birds were counted at Wabai in March 1983, illustrating the large fluctuations that can occur at roosts (P. J. Mundy *in litt.* 1984). Cape Vultures account for only 0.7% of vultures present at carcasses in Zimbabwe (Mundy 1982). In 1940 nearly 100 birds were seen at a carcass near Harare (Smith 1952) and it is clear that the species has declined greatly in Zimbabwe since then.

The world breeding population of the Cape Vulture was estimated in 1983 to be 3,700 pairs, of which 2,850 pairs (77%) were in South Africa (including Transkei) (Mundy 1984, P. J. Mundy *in litt.* 1984). Eighty-eight percent of the breeding population is centred on two main areas: the larger of these is in Transvaal and Botswana and numbers 2,300 pairs (62%); the smaller, centred on Lesotho, Transkei and Natal, numbers 950 pairs (26%) (P. J. Mundy *in litt.* 1984). A large proportion of these nesting birds occurs in eight major breeding colonies (P. J. Mundy *in litt.* 1984). Five of these colonies are in Transvaal at Blouberg, Kransberg, Manoutsa, Roberts' Farm and Skeerpoort, one is in the Tswapong Hills in Botswana, one is at Colleywobbles in Transkei and one is recently reported in southern Mozambique (Tarboton 1978, Mundy 1982, Steyn 1982, P. J. Mundy *in litt.* 1984). Probably about 25% of the total Cape Vulture population is composed of immature birds and so the world population in 1983 was in the order of 10,000 individuals (Mundy 1984, P. J. Mundy *in litt.* 1984). The 1977 population was also estimated to be 10,000 birds (King 1978-1979), but this estimate was based on the incorrect assumption that only half the birds breed in any one year: the population estimate for 1983 is the result of more accurate surveys and does not infer a stable population (P. J. Mundy *in litt.* 1984).

Ecology The Cape Vulture forages over open country, especially grassland, but also thornbush, macchia, karoo and desert (Mundy and Scott 1979, Steyn 1982, Boshoff *et al.* 1983, Mundy 1983a, Brooke in press). It avoids large tracts of woodland and forest (Steyn 1982). In Transvaal the birds forage much more frequently in the lowveld rather than in highveld and bushveld (Tarboton 1978). Cape Vultures roost colonially, usually on cliffs, but they can also use trees and pylons (Sauer 1973, Steyn 1982, Mundy 1982,1983a). The birds leave their roosts and colonies early in the morning and use air currents around the cliffs, rather than thermals, to become airborne (Mundy and Steyn 1977, Brown *et al.* 1982, Jilbert 1982, Steyn 1982). They return to the roosts in the mid-afternoon in groups of four to seven birds (Mundy and Steyn 1977, Brown *et al.* 1982, Jilbert 1982). Late arrivals have to flap strenuously in order to reach the roosting cliffs (Jilbert 1982). In the Namib Desert Cape Vultures have been seen in mixed soaring flocks with Lappet-faced Vultures *Torgos tracheliotus* (Sauer 1973). Cape Vultures were formerly dependent on large migratory mammals for food, but most populations now feed on the carcasses of open-range domestic stock (Mundy 1982, Brooke in press). The birds probably find carcasses by observing other scavengers (Steyn 1982). At carcasses they are dominant over White-backed Vultures *Gyps africanus* while they rarely confront Lappet-faced Vultures, White-headed Vultures *Trigonoceps occipitalis* and Hooded Vultures *Necrosyrtes monachus* which have different feeding habits (Steyn 1982). In the Namib Desert, however, they were observed to be subordinate to Lappet-faced Vultures at carcasses (Sauer 1973). Immature birds are poor competitors at carcasses and all birds are frequently chased away from food by jackals *Canis* (Brown *et al.* 1982). Cape Vultures are "inside" feeders, with long, bare necks and a specially adapted tongue (Steyn 1982). They can eat 1 kg of meat in 2-3 minutes, taking muscle meat and intestines and, later, small bones, if available (Steyn 1982). The colony at Potberg feeds mainly on sheep, those on the Magaliesberg escarpment take cattle, and birds at Colleywobbles feed on pigs, goats and horses (Boshoff and Currie 1981, Mundy 1983a, Robertson 1984). Cape Vultures in Lesotho probably have an abundance of food, both cattle and sheep, which die by slipping on the rugged terrain and scree slopes or are killed during the harsh winters (Jilbert 1979,1982). One study in Cape Province showed that 66% of the carcasses taken were sheep and lambs, 12% were cattle, 9% horses and donkeys, 3% springbok *Antidorcas marsupialis*, 3% dogs, 3% goats and 1% Cape Vultures (Jarvis *et al.* 1974). There is also one record of a bird taking a small mammal road casualty (Jarvis *et al.* 1974). Experiments on captive birds have shown that underfed vultures require 500-600 g of food per day in order to regain weight, but that 500 g per day is sufficient for a healthy bird; however, wild birds probably use up much more energy flying and so might require as much as 1 kg of food a day, which means that a colony of 100 birds needs 6-7 sheep per day to sustain it (Jarvis *et al.* 1974). Because the birds hunt mainly on thermals, they can cover 180-225 km a day during the 8-9 hours flying time available to them, without expending too much energy (Jarvis *et al.* 1974). Each colony, therefore, has a theoretical feeding range of 200,000 km^2, which for a colony of 100 birds would have to provide 2,000-2,500 dead sheep (or their equivalent) per year, or one carcass per year for each 80-96 km^2 (Jarvis *et al.* 1974). Around the Potberg colony there are apparently 56-67 carcasses per year for every 80-96 km^2, which indicates a food availability 50-60 times greater than the minimum required, which means that birds would not need to range more than 35 km from the colony (Jarvis *et al.* 1974) and the Potberg birds have indeed been noted to have a very small feeding range (Robertson 1984). Some areas might not be as good as this, but even so there is likely to be at least 25-30 times more food available around each colony than the minimum required (Jarvis *et al.* 1974). However, although food supply is usually plentiful, mortality amongst domestic stock is likely to be lowest during the summer months at the crucial time when young vultures become independent so that they may be at risk from food shortages at this time (Robertson 1984). Cape Vultures are efficient feeders and they clear the grassland of carcasses, thereby greatly reducing the population of blowflies *Chrysomya* and *Lucilia* (Jarvis 1974a, Steyn 1982, Mundy 1983a): blowflies are serious agricultural pests and are responsible for the spread of "sheep crutch disease" which is costly to eradicate and prevent (Mundy 1983a). After eating, Cape Vultures bathe and drink, sometimes in cattle troughs, and so have been blamed for the spreading of anthrax (see de Vos 1973, Mundy 1983a); however, it now seems that the birds curtail rather than facilitate the spread of the disease (Mundy and Brand 1978, Mundy 1983a). Cape Vultures have often been accused of killing sheep and a few instances of this have been documented (see Roberts 1931, Bradfield 1932); they might on rare occasions take weakened animals at times of drought (Jarvis 1974a) but these would probably have died anyway (Jarvis *et al.* 1974), and being very cautious when they approach carrion they are unlikely to take live animals often (Mundy and Scott 1979). The vultures themselves are vulnerable to attacks from Kelp Gulls *Larus dominicanus* and two such incidents have been reported, one at the Heuningnes Estuary and one at Mossel Bay, one bird apparently dying as a result of an attack (Boshoff 1980). It has been suggested that Cape Vultures cannot breed until they become proficient at finding food, either through practice or through enhanced social status (Vernon and Robertson 1982). They usually nest colonially on cliffs facing south, with suitable ledges and potholes (Tarboton 1978, Jilbert 1979, Mundy 1982, Steyn 1982, Brooke in press); for details of colony sizes see under Population. Vernon and Robertson (1982) have suggested that colony size is determined by food availability, though this seems to contradict the evidence given by Jarvis *et al.* (1974) that the species faces no serious food shortage problem. The nests are composed mainly of grass with sticks and feathers around the rims (Mundy 1982, Steyn 1982) and sometimes used for several years in succession (Boshoff 1980, Steyn 1982). In one colony 13 nests were built on the same ledge (Mundy 1982). Nest building starts in early March (Mundy 1982). Eggs are laid between April and July with a peak in late April and May (Mundy 1982, Steyn 1982, Vernon *et al.* 1982a,1983b). Within a colony egg-laying is apparently fairly synchronous (Steyn 1982) though this is not the case at Potberg (Boshoff and Currie 1981). Eggs are laid a little later in Botswana than on the Magaliesberg escarpment (Ledger and Mundy 1973, Mundy 1982). Clutch-size is usually one (Masterson 1916, Mundy 1982, Steyn 1982, Brooke in press) and the occasional records of two eggs in a clutch could be the result of two females using the same nest (Mundy and Ledger 1975a). Eggs laid very late in the year are probably replacement clutches (Mundy 1982). The young are fed mainly on muscle meat (Mundy 1982) but also on bones when these are available (Mundy and Ledger 1976). In recent times the absence in the environment of large mammalian carnivores which crunch up bones in carcasses has reduced the availability of this important calcium source for chicks (Mundy and Ledger 1976; see Threats). Cape Vultures collect artefacts, such as china and glass, at their colonies, probably mistaking them for bones (Mundy 1982). The chicks and eggs face several natural hazards including chilling by clouds which settle on south-facing cliffs (Brooke in press) and predation by Black Eagles *Aquila verreauxii* and White-necked Ravens *Corvus albicollis* (Bowen 1970, Boshoff 1980, Brooke in press). Relatively high rates of nest failure occur in nests situated near places where non-breeding birds congregate (Vernon *et al.* 1982a). This is probably because the adult birds spend too much time in nest defence and so the eggs and chicks are taken by predators or are inadequately incubated or fed (Vernon *et al.* 1982a). In 1976 some nestlings at Potberg were in a very poor condition owing to heavy infestations of blood-sucking simuliid flies which are often vectors of vertebrate protozoan parasites, though it is not clear if this infestation caused any chick deaths (Currie 1978, Boshoff and Currie 1981). In 1977 the infestation was reduced and in 1978-1979 it was absent altogether (Currie 1978, Boshoff and Currie 1981). Also at Potberg in 1981 breeding success was very low owing to exceptionally poor weather (Robertson 1984). Potberg is the only colony of Cape Vultures in the South African winter rainfall region and during poor weather the adults fly less and, therefore, provide less food for their chicks (Robertson 1984). Attempts have been made to assess the breeding success at several colonies. This is usually measured as the percentage of nests occupied in July with nestlings in September or October. For instance, breeding success at Colleywobbles was 68% in September 1980, 65% in October 1980, 69% in October 1981 and 67% in September 1982 (Vernon *et al.* 1980,1982a,1983b). It is possible that early layers occupy premium nest sites since birds at Colleywobbles that lay before 20 May have a higher nesting success (79%) by 12 September than those which lay afterwards (49%) (Vernon *et al.* 1982a,1983b). Most nest losses at Colleywobbles occur in the incubation rather than the nestling period (Vernon *et al.* 1982a). At the Bawa Falls colony on the Gcuwa River breeding success was 51% in September 1981 (Vernon 1982), at Karnmelkspruit nesting success was 63-72% in October 1980 and 45-54% in December 1981 (Vernon and Boshoff 1980, Vernon *et al.* 1983a) and at Aasvogelvlei in the Langeberg Range the success was 60% in October 1981 (Boshoff and Robertson 1983). The average September breeding success at Potberg is 63%, ranging from 57% in 1980 to 68% in 1977 (Boshoff 1980). Some parts of the Potberg colony have much higher nesting success than others, ranging from 33% to 93% (Boshoff 1980). Nests used for each of the six years 1975-1980 had a 75% success rate whereas those used only once had an 8% success rate (Boshoff 1980). In practice few nests are used for more than 4-5 years in succession and it may be that not all pairs attempt to breed every season (Boshoff 1980). If this is the case then censuses at colonies are likely to underestimate the true population (Boshoff 1980). In Botswana and on the Magaliesberg escarpment the number of chicks reared per nest is 0.40-0.52 with an average of 0.44 (Mundy 1982). At these colonies the most vulnerable stage appears to be when the chicks are aged 40-100 days and are growing so rapidly that sufficient food is sometimes difficult to obtain (Mundy 1982). As a result of an extensive ringing scheme a considerable amount is known about the dispersal, movements and survival of Cape Vultures (Houston 1974, Piper *et al.* 1981, Mundy 1982; details of the scheme in Paterson 1952, Ledger and Mundy 1973,1978, Jarvis 1974, Ledger 1974 and Mundy 1982). The fledglings have a 16-week post-fledging period of dependence on their parents (Vernon and Robertson 1980, Brooke in press), with whom they stay until the start of the next breeding season (Brooke in press). After this time the juvenile birds disperse (Vernon and Robertson 1980, Brooke in press) and those from the Magaliesberg escarpment tend to move south-south-west to the Kimberley area (Mundy 1982, Steyn 1982: see Distribution). Outside the breeding season adult birds might wander to good food sources (Steyn 1982) but they usually stay within 100 km of their colonies (Brooke in press). Immature birds wander much farther and live outside the normal foraging range of birds at breeding colonies (Houston 1974, Brooke in press). Female birds cannot breed until they are at least four years old

(Vernon and Robertson 1982) but most probably do not breed until they are six (Mundy 1982, Brooke in press). A breeding pair observed at Potberg consisted of a nearly seven-year-old male and a nearly five-year-old female (Robertson 1983, 1984). Most birds return to the colony at which they hatched (Mundy and Ledger 1975a, Robertson 1983) but there are a few exceptions: one bird ringed at Skeerpoort as a chick moved along the Magaliesberg escarpment to breed at Roberts' Farm (Mundy and Ledger 1975a), another ringed at Colleywobbles was subsequently seen at Karnmelkspruit (Vernon and Boshoff 1980), and another ringed at Potberg moved to Langeberg (Boshoff 1981). Annual survival rates for first-year fledged birds from the Magaliesberg colonies is only 17% (Piper *et al.* 1981). This high mortality drops off rapidly with increasing age (Houston 1974) and the survival-rate for third-year birds and older is 74% (Piper *et al.* 1981). The survival rates for adults must be even higher but information is still lacking because many of the original rings used on vultures in southern Africa are of very poor quality and have fallen off (Piper *et al.* 1981). The average life expectancy as an adult bird is given as six years (in King 1978-1979). It has been calculated that a pair of vultures needs to breed annually for at least eight years in order to replace itself (Mundy 1976). The probability of a fledgling reaching its third year is only 10.6% (Piper *et al.* 1981) and it is probably this high mortality in the early years of life which is causing the population decline (Mundy and Ledger 1977). Houston (1974) has suggested that recruitment at the Magaliesberg colonies is now insufficient to balance adult mortality. Some of this high juvenile mortality is no doubt natural (Mundy 1982), such as clumsy landing by newly fledged birds on their breeding cliffs (Brooke in press). There are, however, a number of serious man-induced mortality factors which are probably responsible for the decline (see Threats). Of juvenile deaths, 50% occur within a few weeks of fledging and a further 25% while they are still partially dependent on their parents (Mundy 1982).

Threats Because immature Cape Vultures travel so widely, individual birds must come across a wide variety of threats during their life-times (Mundy 1984). It has been suggested that changes in the availability of food have been a major factor in the population fluctuations of the Cape Vulture (Boshoff and Vernon 1980). The species's initial decline coincides with the 1898-1903 rinderpest epidemic in which two million to five million cattle were lost (Boshoff and Vernon 1980). Suggestions that Cape Vultures die if they eat rinderpest-infected meat are, however, untrue (Boshoff and Vernon 1980). The recent decline of the species in Cape Province has been considered related to a threefold decline in stock-losses between 1950 and 1971 (Boshoff and Vernon 1980), but there is very little evidence that food supply presents a serious problem to the species today (Mundy 1983a) and the food supply is generally good (see Ecology). It is, however, likely that recently fledged young birds with low social status at carcasses are particularly susceptible to food shortages (Robertson 1984). More serious food shortages are likely in the future as a result of more intensive farming practices in which carcasses are found and quickly disposed of by the farmer (Jarvis *et al.* 1974). Ultimately farming efficiency might be so improved that mortality in livestock is restricted to the abattoir; such a development would obviously be catastrophic for the Cape Vulture (Mundy 1983a). A more serious immediate threat results from a decline in food quality rather than quantity: the disappearance of large mammalian carnivores which crunch up bones in carcasses means that vultures are no longer able to feed bone flakes to their chicks (Mundy and Ledger 1976, Steyn 1982, Brooke in press), and as a consequence chicks suffer a severe calcium shortage resulting in osteodystrophy whereby the bones are deformed and very easily broken (Mundy 1982, Brooke in press). Some chicks have disastrous first flights from the nest (Steyn 1982) and others, which fledge successfully, subsequently break their bones at cliffs or carcasses (Mundy 1976). The incidence of osteodystrophy is highest in cattle-ranching areas such as Magaliesberg and Botswana (Mundy 1983a). The problem is most serious on the Magaliesberg escarpment where up to 24% of the chicks have been affected, and has led to a decline in breeding success at both Roberts' Farm and Skeerpoort and an actual population decline at Roberts' Farm (Mundy 1976, Mundy *et al.* 1980, *S. A. Digest*, 10 April 1981: 17). The incidence of osteodystrophy is lower in sheep-farming areas, perhaps because sheep bones are smaller and can be more easily swallowed, but affected birds have nevertheless been recorded from Potberg, Karnmelkspruit and Forest Range Farm (Boshoff and Vernon 1980, Boshoff and Currie 1981, Mundy 1983a). There appear to be virtually no cases of osteodystrophy from Colleywobbles or Manoutsa (Mundy *et al.* 1980, Mundy 1983a). Jarvis *et al.* (1974) have suggested that the initial decline of the Cape Vulture was caused by widespread shooting and baiting of birds with poisoned carcasses. Farmers have tended to be antagonistic towards vultures because they are believed to kill sheep (Jarvis *et al.* 1974, Boshoff and Vernon 1980, van Heerden 1980, Mundy 1982, Steyn 1982) and to spread anthrax (Mundy and Brand 1978, Mundy 1983a), and are known to foul the water in drinking troughs, preventing cattle from drinking (Mundy 1976,1982,1983a). It seems that some reports of vulture attacks on sheep are genuine (Mundy 1976) but most farmers now agree that these are rare events, probably involving livestock that would have died anyway through injury or drought (Jarvis *et al.* 1974, Boshoff and Vernon 1980). There is also evidence that Cape Vultures curtail, rather than facilitate, the spread of anthrax (Mundy and Brand 1978, Mundy 1983a). Because the vultures are still perceived to be a threat they are often shot (Mundy 1976, Ledger and Mundy 1977, Mundy and Steyn 1977, King 1978-1979, Boshoff and Vernon 1980, van Heerden 1980, Mundy 1982, Steyn 1982). A very high level of shooting probably caused the extinction of the Manyana colony and resulted in the birds moving to Mannyelanong (Ledger and Mundy 1977, King 1978-1979). A more serious threat is posed by poisoned carcasses, which are often aimed at jackals, caracals *Felis caracal* and other predatory mammals as well as vultures and White-necked Ravens (Robertson 1984, Mundy 1984, Brooke in press). Such poisoning is still quite extensive (van Heerden 1980, Boshoff and Currie 1981, Robertson 1984) and a few contaminated carcasses can exterminate all the vultures in a district (Steyn 1982, Brooke in press). Near Herbertsdale about 100 birds were killed by one farmer attempting to poison one caracal, and 28 birds were accidentally poisoned near Dordrecht in 1975 (Boshoff and Currie 1980). The recent decline at the Karnmelkspruit colony is probably at least partly caused by poisoning (Vernon *et al.* 1983a). In 1984 42 vultures, almost certainly this species, were poisoned or killed on a farm near Barkly East (Cape Department of Nature and Environmental Conservation press release, 7 May 1984). Disturbance is also a serious threat and none of the large breeding colonies is satisfactorily conserved in this regard (Mundy 1983b). There is evidence that some disturbance at colonies is deliberate (van Heerden 1980) but most is probably unintentional. Disturbance by mountaineers can lead to desertion and egg and nestling chilling and can facilitate predation by Black Eagles and White-necked Ravens (Vernon *et al.* 1982a,1983b, Brooke in press). The colony at Colleywobbles is threatened by disturbance resulting from the construction of a new hydro-electricity scheme nearby on the Bashee River (Vernon *et al.* 1983b). The Potberg colony suffers from severe disturbance by military helicopters, which frighten both adults and chicks and as a consequence the chicks are not properly fed and suffer poor growth rates (*Afr. Wildl.* 37 [1984]: 39). A colony in Bethlehem District, Orange Free State, was deserted earlier this century, apparently following the construction of a phosphate mine beneath the colony (O'Connor 1980). Part of the Semonkong colony in Lesotho has been abandoned owing to the establishment of a cattle post on the cliff-top (Jilbert 1982). Disturbance can also be caused by fire. In 1975 a fire in the cliff vegetation at Skeerpoort resulted in a 5% increase in chick mortality (Mundy and Ledger 1975b). This mortality was probably caused by predators taking advantage of the adult vultures having temporarily left their nests and by chicks panicking and falling off the cliff ledges (Mundy and Ledger 1975b). There were three major fires at the Potberg colony during the 1970s, which might have had some effect on nesting success (Boshoff and Currie 1981). Some Cape Vultures have been caught and eaten by dogs (Piper *et al.* 1981) but this is probably not a serious threat. Cape Vultures are also killed by witch-doctors who use their brains and hearts for tribal medicines (Ledger and Mundy 1975, Steyn 1982). A serious problem is the electrocution of birds, especially juveniles and a few immatures, on pylons in western Transvaal and in the Kimberley area (Markus 1972, Jarvis 1974b, Ledger 1980, Ledger and Annegarn 1981, Mundy 1983a). At least 300 birds are known to have been killed in this way between 1970 and 1977, though the real number is obviously much higher and probably 500 are killed in western Transvaal alone every five years (Ledger 1980, Ledger and Annegarn 1981). Although inexperienced juveniles may collide with wires (Steyn 1982), most birds are killed by electrocution on pylons (Ledger and Annegarn 1981, Mundy 1982) when they sit on the towers and wipe their bills on the wires (Jarvis 1974b). Most deaths occur on 88 kV suspension towers (Markus 1972, Ledger and Annegarn 1981) owing to the geometry of the tower design (Ledger and Annegarn 1981). Because the pylons that are being built now are of a safe design, further expansion of the electricity network should reduce, not increase, Cape Vulture mortality (Ledger and Annegarn 1981). A few deaths have been recorded from 11 kV power lines in Cape Province (Boshoff and Vernon 1980). Deaths have also occurred when birds have collided with communication masts in cloudy weather (Brooke in press). The notion that the corona discharge and electric field around overhead cables affect the birds' fertility is probably untrue (Brooke in press). There are occasional records of mass drownings in circular reservoirs and water tanks, but the reasons for this are not known (Mundy and Scott 1979, Brooke in press). It seems that pesticides are not presenting a serious threat to the species (Mundy *et al.* 1982, Brooke in press). Egg-shells have become thinner since 1947 when DDT was introduced into South Africa, but only by 3.5% and there are no records of broken eggs (Mundy *et al.* 1982).

Conservation Measures Taken The Cape Vulture is fully protected throughout its range (Mundy 1983a, Brooke in press) and, along with all Falconiformes, is included on Appendix II of CITES, to which Botswana, Mozambique, South Africa and Zimbabwe are parties. In Transvaal the penalty for disturbing or hunting the birds or robbing the nests is a fine of R 1,200 or 18 months' imprisonment or both (Mundy 1983a). In Botswana the penalties are P 800 or 2 years' imprisonment (Mundy 1983a). An investigation is currently under way into the illegal poisoning of vultures near Barkly East in 1984, and a prosecution is likely (Cape Department of Nature and Environmental Conservation press release, 7 May 1984). In 1978 the Potberg colony was incorporated into the De Hoop Nature Reserve, thus restricting access and reducing disturbance (Boshoff and Currie 1981, Mundy 1983a, Robertson 1984, Brooke in press). The Cape Provincial Administration is now renting the Karnmelkspruit colony from its owner (Mundy 1983a) and there is a colony in the Umtamvuna Nature Reserve in Natal (Abbot 1982, Brooke in press). A game scout has been stationed at the Mannyelanong colony in Botswana and this has helped the colony to recover following severe disturbance (Mundy 1976). In 1976 it was reported that the colony was shortly to be gazetted as a sanctuary (von Richter and Passineau 1976) but this has apparently not yet happened (Mundy 1983a). The Magaliesberg escarpment was declared a Natural Area in 1977 and it is hoped that the area will be developed as a nature reserve (Mundy 1983a). In 1973 the Vulture Study Group was started and many of the recent successes in Cape Vulture conservation are a direct consequence of the group's work (Ledger 1982, Mundy 1984). The group has a "vigilante" task force protecting the Skeerpoort colony from disturbance (Mundy 1984). A great deal of publicity about the Cape Vulture has been organised and has succeeded in arousing considerable sympathy in the public and amongst landowners (Mundy 1984). There has been a media campaign against the practice of poisoning carcasses, though it is difficult to stop government projects to control rabies in jackals (Ledger 1982). The Vulture Study Group, in conjunction with the appropriate national or provincial nature conservation bodies, is approaching the owners of breeding and roosting sites to try to effect local conservation measures (Brooke in press). As a result of the Vulture Study Group's activities, the attitudes of farmers are becoming less antagonistic (Mundy 1983a,1984) and at Dullstroom in eastern Transvaal some farmers have asked the Group to help bring vultures back (Mundy 1983a). The Vulture Study Group has instigated the establishment of vulture "restaurants" where carcasses whose bones have been smashed are put out for the birds (Tarboton 1978, Mundy *et al.* 1980, Hancock 1981, Ledger 1982, Steyn 1982, Friedman and Mundy 1983). It is intended that the birds should take the bone fragments available, thus increasing calcium intake and reducing the incidence of osteodystrophy (Ledger 1982, Steyn 1982). "Restaurants" have been set up by the group at De Wildt, Kommandonek Nature Reserve (servicing the Skeerpoort colony), Roberts' Farm, Krugersdorp Game Reserve, Impala Platinum Mine and Pilanesberg Game Reserve (Hancock 1981, *S. A. Digest*, 10 April 1981: 17, Ledger 1982, Friedman and Mundy 1983) while others have been established independently at Potberg (Boshoff 1981, Boshoff and Currie 1981) and the Umtamvuna Nature Reserve (Abbot 1982). Some farmers have started their own vulture "restaurants" (Ledger 1982, Mundy 1982), one doing so after seeing a programme about Cape Vultures on television (Mundy 1984). Contact with local farmers near Merrimetsi in Orange Free State led to reduced persecution and the establishment of "restaurants", and as a result the number of birds attending the local roost increased from nine to 42 (van Heerden 1980). The "restaurant" in the Pilanesberg Game Reserve uses donkeys killed on the roads and seems to have good tourist potential (Hancock 1981). It seems that "restaurants" have already reduced the incidence of osteodystrophy at the Skeerpoort colony (Mundy *et al.* 1980) but further research is being carried out to see whether the "restaurants" are achieving their aim (*S. A. Digest*, 10 April 1981: 17). The Vulture Study Group has been working in conjunction with the Electricity Supply Commission of South Africa (ESCOM) to find a solution to the problem of vulture electrocution (Steyn 1982). This is also in ESCOM's interest since bird electrocutions cause power inter-ruptions (Ledger 1980). The incidence of electrocution is reduced if perches are fitted to the tops of the towers (Ledger 1980,1982). More fundamental design changes have now been made to the pylons and ESCOM is now slowly replacing or modifying the existing 88 kV towers and is no longer erecting new towers on which Cape Vultures are likely to be electrocuted (Brooke in press). Conservation oriented research, some of it under the auspices of the Vulture Study Group, is being carried out on calcium requirements, feeding ecology, breeding biology and population monitoring (Robertson 1984, Mundy 1984, Brooke in press).

Conservation Measures Proposed Much stricter protection is needed for the breeding colonies which are highly vulnerable to disturbance (Mundy 1983a), e.g. it has been suggested that access to the Magaliesberg cliff-tops be controlled (Ledger and Mundy 1975) and that the Zastron colony in Orange Free State should be purchased (O'Connor 1980). In particular, more research and conservation work should be concentrated in the core areas of the population (Mundy 1984; see Population). It is most desirable to increase the amount of extension work with farmers (Mundy 1984, Brooke in press), who, in return for their increased co-operation, should be compensated for any sheep killed by Cape Vultures (Mundy 1983a). Farmers will also be helped if cattle-drinking troughs can be protected from vulture use and if separate pools can be set aside for the vultures (Mundy 1983a). Changes in the design of water tanks are needed to prevent mass drowning incidents (Brooke in press). Considerable conservation effort should be directed towards increasing juvenile survival (Piper *et al.* 1981). Special care should be given to malnourished juvenile birds that are found at the beginning of each year, to enhance their chances of survival (Mundy 1983a). More research is needed on the relationship between the Cape Vulture and the spread of anthrax, and also on the efficacy of vulture "restaurants" (Brooke in press). If the "restaurants" can be shown to be effective then they should be organised and funded on a long-term basis (Brooke in press). It may be that most colonies will eventually need a "restaurant" from late June until December (Mundy 1983a). A new "restaurant" has been recommended for the Mannyelanong colony (Butchart and Mundy 1981). The South African Defence Force should be careful to avoid using the Potberg area where military developments, especially the use of helicopters, are disturbing the colony (*Afr. Wildl.* 37 [1983]: 39). In Botswana searches should be carried out for undiscovered colonies in suitable, isolated areas (Butchart and Mundy 1981).

Remarks The Cape Vulture forms a species-group with Rüppell's Vulture *Gyps rueppellii*, the Griffon Vulture *G. fulvus*, the Indian Vulture *G. indicus* and the Himalayan Vulture *G. himalayensis* (Snow 1978). At least 50 birds are in captivity (P. J. Mundy *in litt.* 1984) but although they often lay eggs (Stuart 1970, Mundy and Marais 1981) there are very few instances of successful breeding. Successful breeding took place on several occasions in the Bloemfontein Zoo in the 1950s and 1960s (van Ee 1981) but the only recent success is of a chick hand-reared in the Pretoria Zoo in 1982 (P. J. Mundy *in litt.* 1984). Concerning reports on numbers in Botswana, Ledger and Mundy (1973) mistakenly called Manyana as Mannyelanong and Mannyelanong as Ootsi (Otse) (P. J. Mundy *in litt.* 1984).

References

Abbot, A. A. (1982) Cape Vultures at Umtamvuna Nature Reserve. *Vulture News* 7: 22-23.

Beesley, J. (1976) A new Cape Vulture colony in Botswana. *Bokmakierie* 28: 75.

Boshoff, A. F. (1980) Mobbing by Kelp Gulls *Larus dominicanus* as a possible cause of Cape Vulture *Gyps coprotheres* mortality. *Cormorant* 8: 15-16.

Boshoff, A. (1981) Notes on two Cape Vulture colonies in the south-western Cape Province, South Africa. *Vulture News* 5: 3-10.

Boshoff, A. F. and Currie, M. H. (1981) Notes on the Cape Vulture colony at Potberg, Bredasdorp. *Ostrich* 52: 1-8.

Boshoff, A. and Robertson, A. (1983). Two Cape Vulture colonies in the S.W. Cape Province: 1981 data. *Vulture News* 9/10: 37-39.

Boshoff, A. F. and Vernon, C. J. (1980) The past and present distribution and status of the Cape Vulture in the Cape Province. *Ostrich* 51: 230-250.

Boshoff, A. F. and Vernon, C. J. (1981) Active Cape Vulture breeding and roost sites in the Cape Province in 1979. *Vulture News* 6: 19.

Boshoff, A. F., Vernon, C. J. and Brooke, R. K. (1983) Historical atlas of the diurnal raptors of the Cape Province (Aves: Falconiformes). *Ann. Cape Prov. Mus. (Nat. Hist.)* 14: 173-297.

Bowen, P. (1970) Some observations of the Cape Vulture. *Afr. Wildl.* 24: 125-128.

Bradfield, R. D. (1932) Unusual experiences with birds. *Ostrich* 3: 13-16.

Brooke, R. K. (in press) *The rare and vulnerable birds of South Africa.*

Brown, L. H., Urban, E. K. and Newman, K. (1982) *The birds of Africa*, 1. London: Academic Press.

Butchart, D. and Mundy, P. (1981) Cape Vultures in Botswana. *Babbler* no. 1: 6-7.

Clancey, P. A. (1971) *A handlist of the birds of southern Moçambique.* Lourenço Marques: Instituto de Investigação Científica de Moçambique.

Conant, R. A. (1980) A further sight record of Cape Vulture *Gyps coprotheres* from Lochinvar National Park. *Bull. Zambian Orn. Soc.* 12: 38-39.

Currie, M. H. (1978) Ringing at Potberg, Bredasdorp District. *Safring News* 7(1): 16-17.

Cyrus, D. and Robson, R. (1980) *Bird atlas of Natal.* Pietermaritzburg: University of Natal Press.

Dowsett, R. J. (1979) Recent additions to the Zambian list. *Bull. Brit. Orn. Club* 99: 94-98.

van Ee, C. A. (1981) Captive breeding of the Cape Vulture at the Bloemfontein Zoo. *Vulture News* 5: 14-15.

Fotheringham, H. J. (1966) Cape Vulture (*Gyps coprotheres*) on De Beers Ranch. *Honeyguide* no. 48: 13-14.

Friedman, R. and Mundy, P. J. (1983) The use of "restaurants" for the survival of vultures in South Africa. Pp. 345-355 in S. R. Wilbur and J. A. Jackson, eds. *Vulture biology and management*. Berkeley: University of California Press.

Hancock, P. (1981) Vulture restaurant at Pilanesberg Game Reserve. *Vulture News* 6: 23.

van Heerden, J. (1980) Report on the Cape Vulture at Merrimetsi in the Excelsior District, Orange Free State. *Vulture News* 4: 13-14.

Houston, D. C. (1974) Mortality of the Cape Vulture. *Ostrich* 45: 57-62.

Jarvis, M. J. F. (1974a) Ringing Cape Vultures. *Afr. Wildl.* 28(3): 24-25.

Jarvis, M. J. F. (1974b) High tension power-lines as a hazard to larger birds. *Ostrich* 45: 262.

Jarvis, M. J. F., Siegfried, W. R. and Currie, M. H. (1974) Conservation of the Cape Vulture in the Cape Province. *J. S. Afr. Wildl. Mgmt. Assoc.* 4: 29-34.

Jilbert, J. (1979) Cape Vulture sites in Lesotho: a summary of current knowledge. *Vulture News* 2: 3-14.

Jilbert, J. (1982) Lesotho Cape Vulture project: preliminary report. *Vulture News* 8: 19-25.

Jilbert, J. (1983) Cape Vulture sites in Lesotho: a continuing investigation. *Bokmakierie* 35: 85-88.

Kemp, A. C. (1969) Vultures of the Kruger National Park. *Bokmakierie* 21: 59-60.

Kemp, A. C. (1980) The importance of the Kruger National Park for bird conservation in the Republic of South Africa. *Koedoe* 23: 99-122.

King, W. B. (1978-1979) *Red data book, 2: Aves.* 2nd edition. Morges, Switzerland: IUCN.

Ledger, J. A. (1974) Colour-rings for vultures. *Safring News* 3(2): 23-28.

Ledger, J. A. (1980) Plea to save Africa's birds from electrocution. *Megawatt* 63: 11-13.

Ledger, J. (1982) The Vulture Study Group. *Quagga* 1: 5-9.

Ledger, J. A. and Annegarn, H. J. (1981) Electrocution hazards to the Cape Vulture *Gyps coprotheres* in South Africa. *Biol. Conserv.* 20: 15-24.

Ledger, J. A. and Mundy, P. J. (1973) Cape Vulture ringing in southern Africa. *Safring News* 2(3): 5-11.

Ledger, J. and Mundy, P. (1975) Research on the Cape Vulture 1974 progress report. *Bokmakierie* 27: 2-7.

Ledger, J. and Mundy, P. (1976) Cape Vulture research in 1975. *Bokmakierie* 28: 4-8.

Ledger, J. and Mundy, P. (1977) Cape Vulture research report for 1976. *Bokmakierie* 29: 72-75.

Ledger, J. and Mundy, P. (1978) Cape Vulture recovery data. *Safring News* 7(2): 21-31.

Macdonald, I. A. W. and Birkenstock, P. J. (1980) Birds of the Hluhluwe-Umfolozi Game Reserve complex. *Lammergeyer* 29: 1-56.

Markus, M. B. (1972) Mortality of Cape Vultures caused by electrocution. *Nature* 238: 228.

Masterson, B. A. (1916) Observations on the birds of the district of Humansdorp, Cape Province. *J. S. Afr. Orn. Union* 11: 119-142.

Mundy, P. J. (1973) On the Cape and White-backed Vultures. *Honeyguide* no. 76: 10-17.

Mundy, P. J. (1976) The Cape Vulture. Pp. 116-118 in J. D. Skinner, ed. *Proceedings of a symposium on endangered wildlife in southern Africa.* Johannesburg: Endangered Wildlife Trust.

Mundy, P. J. (1982) *The comparative biology of southern African vultures.* Johannesburg: Vulture Study Group.

Mundy, P. J. (1983a) The conservation of the Cape Griffon Vulture of southern Africa. Pp. 57-74 in S. R. Wilbur and J. A. Jackson, eds. *Vulture biology and management.* Berkeley: University of California Press.

Mundy, P. J. (1983b) Cape Vulture "safe" but insecure. *Afr. Wildl.* 36: 240.

Mundy, P. J. (1984) How to conserve the Cape Vulture. *Quagga* 6: 16-18.

Mundy, P. J. and Brand, F. E. (1978) An investigation of vultures and anthrax in southern Africa. *Rhod. Vet. J.* 9: 36-39.

Mundy, P.J., Grant, K. I., Tannock, J. and Wessels, C. L. (1982) Pesticide residues and eggshell thickness of Griffon Vulture eggs in southern Africa. *J. Wildl. Mgmt.* 46: 769-773.

Mundy, P. and Ledger, J. (1975a) Notes on the Cape Vulture. *Honeyguide* no. 83: 22-28.

Mundy, P. J. and Ledger, J. A. (1975b) The effects of fire on a Cape Vulture colony. *S. Afr. J. Sci.* 71: 217.

Mundy, P. J. and Ledger, J. A. (1976) Griffon vultures, carnivores and bones. *S. Afr. J. Sci.* 72: 106-110.

Mundy, P. and Ledger, J. (1977) The plight of the Cape Vulture. *Endangered Wildlife* 1(4).

Mundy, P., Ledger, J. and Friedman, R. (1980) The Cape Vulture project in 1977 and 1978. *Bokmakierie* 32: 2-8.

Mundy, P. J. and Marais, E. (1981) Vultures in captivity in southern Africa. *Avicult. Mag.* 87: 215-222.

Mundy, P. J. and Scott, H. (1979) Research towards the conservation of the Cape Vulture. *Rhod. Sci. News* 13: 89-90.

Mundy, P. and Steyn, P. (1977) To breed or not to breed. *Bokmakierie* 29: 5-7.

O'Connor, T. (1980) The status of the Cape Vulture in the Orange Free State Province of South Africa. *Vulture News* 3: 3-6.

Paterson, J. M. (1952) Banding Cape Vultures in Magaliesberg. *Bokmakierie* 4: 58-59.

Piper, S. E., Mundy, P. J. and Ledger, J. A. (1981) Estimates of survival in the Cape Vulture *Gyps coprotheres. J. Anim. Ecol.* 50: 815-825.

von Richter, W. and Passineau, J. (1976) Endangered wildlife species in Botswana. *Botswana Notes and Records* 11: 121-126.

Roberts, A. (1931) Vultures attacking sheep. *Ostrich* 2: 68.

Robertson, A. S. (1982) Vulnerable vultures: a case study of the Potberg colony. *Vulture News* 7: 3-4.

Robertson, A. (1983) Known-age Cape Vultures breeding in the wild. *Ostrich* 54: 179.

Robertson, A. (1984) Parental problems at the Potberg vulture colony in the De Hoop Nature Reserve. *Afr. Wildl.* 37: 40-43.

Ross, G. (1970) Umlengana – vulture's retreat. *East Cape Naturalist* 40: 4-5.

Sauer, E. G. F. (1973) Notes on the behavior of Lappet-faced Vultures and Cape Vultures in the Namib Desert of South West Africa. *Madoqua* 2(2): 43-62.

Smith, K. D. (1952) Notes on some birds of Mashonaland, Southern Rhodesia. *Ostrich* 13: 40-42.

Snow, D. W. ed. (1978) *An atlas of speciation in African non-passerine birds*. London: Trustees of the British Museum (Natural History).

Steyn, P. (1982) *Birds of prey of southern Africa*. Cape Town and Johannesburg: David Philip.

Stuart, C. T. (1970) Breeding behaviour of a pair of Cape Vultures in captivity. *Bokmakierie* 22: 67.

Stuart, C. T. (1972) Notes on a Cape Vulture colony in the Gamka Mountains, Oudtshoorn District. *Ostrich* 43: 140-141.

Tarboton, W. (1978) A survey of the birds of prey in the Transvaal. Pretoria: Transvaal Nature Conservation Division.

Tarboton, W. R. and Allan, D. G. (1984) The status and conservation of birds of prey in the Transvaal. *Transvaal Mus. Mem.* no. 3.

Underhill, L. G. (1979) Waders and vultures, Walvis and Windhoek. *Bokmakierie* 31: 86-89.

Verheyen, R. (1953) Oiseaux. *Exploration du Parc National de l'Upemba. Mission G. F. de Witte (1946-1949)* 19: 1-687.

Vernon, C. J. (1978) Change in the reporting locality of the Cape Vultures ringed in the Transvaal in the period 1953-1975. *Safring News* 7(2): 17-19.

Vernon, C. J. (1982) Bawa Falls revisited – the Cape Vulture colony of the Gcuwa River, Transkei. *Vulture News* 8: 33.

Vernon, C. J. and Boshoff, A. F. (1980) The Cape Vulture colony at Karnmelkspruit, Lady Grey District, Cape Province. *Vulture News* 4: 11-12.

Vernon, C. J., Boshoff, A. F. and Robertson, A. S. (1983a) The Cape Vulture colony at Karnmelkspruit, Cape Province in 1981. *Vulture News* 9/10: 42-43.

Vernon, C. J., Piper, S. E. and Schultz, D. M. (1980) The breeding success of the Cape Vultures at Collywobbles, Transkei, in 1980. *Vulture News* 4: 21-22.

Vernon, C. J., Piper, S. E. and Schultz, D. M. (1982a) The breeding success of Cape Vultures at Collywobbles, Transkei in 1981. *Vulture News* 8: 26-29.

Vernon, C. J., Piper, S. E. and Schultz, D. M. (1982b) Tandem flying by Cape Vultures. *Vulture News* 7: 17.

Vernon, C. J., Piper, S. E. and Schultz, D. M. (1983b) The Cape Vulture at Colleywobbles, Transkei in 1982. *Vulture News* 9/10: 11-13.

Vernon, C. J. and Robertson, A. S. (1982) A discussion of the factors regulating breeding in the Cape Vulture *Gyps coprotheres*. *Vulture News* 7: 10-13.

de Vos, V. (1973) Vulture ringing in the Kruger National Park. *Safring News* 2(3): 11-13.

Williams, A. M. (1972) [Letter.] *Bokmakierie* 24: 66.

Winterbottom, J. M. (1968) A checklist of the land and fresh water birds of the western Cape Province. *Ann. S. Afr. Mus.* 53: 1-276.

MADAGASCAR SERPENT EAGLE   ENDANGERED
Eutriorchis astur Sharpe, 1875

Order FALCONIFORMES   Family ACCIPITRIDAE

Summary This very poorly known Madagascar rainforest raptor was last seen by an ornithologist over 50 years ago, and hopes for its survival are largely pinned on the conservation of adequate areas of primary forest in the central-east and north-east of the island.

Distribution The Madagascar Serpent Eagle is confined to the eastern rainforests of Madagascar, and known from only eight specimens, all collected more than 50 years ago (four in MNHN, two in AMNH, one in BMNH and one in Grenoble) (A. Fayaud *in litt.* 1983, G. S. Keith *in litt.* 1983, NJC); a further specimen reportedly in Berlin (Lavauden 1937) cannot be traced (B.-U. Meyburg *in litt.* 1984). The species was first described from a single specimen collected (presumably around 1874) "in the southern portion of Madagascar" (Sharpe 1875) though the locality was later identified as "Ampasimanavy", a hamlet in the forest a day's march from Andakana village, in the Mangoro valley between Antananarivo and Mahanoro (Milne Edwards and Grandidier 1879; see Remarks). A second bird, dated 1883 and labelled simply "Madagascar", was collected by L. Humblot (specimen in MNHN: NJC). In April 1924 a male was obtained in forest at Fito, i.e. Sihanaka forest (specimen in AMNH: G. S. Keith *in litt.* 1983). The Expédition Citroën Afrique obtained a bird at an unknown date and from an unknown locality (specimen in MNHN: NJC), although it is known that the Citroën team arrived in Antananarivo in June 1925 (R. D. Etchécopar *in litt.* 1984). Four specimens were collected in the period 1928-1930, one from Rogez at 900 m in eastern central Madagascar (18°50'S 48°35'E), December 1928 (Lavauden 1932, Benson *et al.* 1976), one from Analamazaotra near Périnet (i.e. also near Rogez), 11 June 1930 (specimen in Grenoble: A. Fayaud *in litt.* 1983), and two from around Maroantsetra (one at sea level at Bevato, 40 km north-west of Maroantsetra up the Vohémar River, 8 May 1930, the other at 600 m at "Ambohimarahavary" [see Remarks under Short-legged Ground-roller *Brachypteracias leptosomus*], two days' march north-east of Maroantsetra, 6 July 1930) in the north-east of the island (Rand 1932,1936). The species has been reported to occur as far south as Farafangana (Lavauden 1937), although there appears to be no evidence for this other than that a bird, either this species or Henst's Goshawk *Accipiter henstii* (see Remarks), was seen at Vondrozo (inland from Farafangana), June or July 1929 (Rand 1932). A forestry official reported making four or five sightings of a raptor closely answering this species's description over the period 1964-1977 in the Marojejy Reserve, north-west of Andapa in north-eastern Madagascar (Meyburg and Meyburg 1978, Meyburg 1979, Thiollay and Meyburg 1981). There have been no other reports since 1930 though it is hoped the species may also survive on the Masoala peninsula in the north-east (Meyburg and Meyburg 1978, Meyburg 1979).

Population Numbers are unknown, but the species was repeatedly described as very rare fifty years ago (Delacour 1932, Lavauden 1932, Rand 1936),

152

so presumably it is very much more so at present: indeed it is authoritatively considered one of the six rarest birds of prey in the world (Langrand and Meyburg in press). However, since it has also been said to be very shy (Lavauden 1932) it has conceivably avoided detection in several areas, although the forestry official who claimed to have seen it in the Marojejy Reserve (see above) considered it relatively fearless (B.-U. Meyburg *in litt.* 1983). At any rate, to treat the species as extinct (Day 1981) is on present information irresponsibly pessimistic.

Ecology This bird inhabits primary rainforest, although it has also been recorded in secondary growth at the edge of dense forest (Lavauden 1932, Rand 1936). Its short wings and long tail are considered adaptations for flight below the canopy (Lavauden 1932,1937), although it is also considered a bird of the tree-tops (Lavauden 1937). One of the birds collected near Maroantsetra contained part of a very large chameleon (Rand 1936), but the species is also reported to attack lemurs and even poultry belonging to forest guards (Lavauden 1932) and to feed chiefly on mammals (Lavauden 1937). There appears to be no direct evidence that it eats snakes (see Remarks). There are no breeding data (Lavauden 1937).

Threats Destruction and disturbance of primary rainforest is the single most serious threat to this and all other rainforest-dependent species in Madagascar "The present wholesale destruction of the forest" (i.e. rainforest) was being lamented almost 100 years ago (Baron 1890) but has continued unabated throughout the present century (Humbert 1927, Heim 1935, Rand 1936, Swingle 1937, Louvel 1950, Chauvet 1972, McNulty 1975, Guillaumet 1981) and is now proceeding so "incredibly fast" that "good places four or five years ago are already destroyed" and "within the next five years ... all the good [i.e. rich, lowland] forests will vanish" (B.-U. Meyburg *in litt.* 1983). It is estimated that in the years 1981-1985 loss of primary forest in Madagascar will be 35,000 ha per year, most of this in the eastern rainforests and most of it as a result of slash-and-burn ("tavy") cultivation (Jenkins in prep.). The de-gazetting of the Masoala Forest Nature Reserve (R.N.I. no. 2) is highly regrettable (see Conservation Measures Proposed).

Conservation Measures Taken The species's reported presence in the Marojejy Reserve (R.N.I. no. 12), which covers 60,150 ha (Andriamampianina 1981), reinforces the importance of this protected area; however, it has been pointed out that only the lower parts of the reserve provide suitable habitat, the higher-lying areas lacking sufficient vegetation (Meyburg 1979). A "Special Reserve" also exists at Périnet-Analamazaotra, where the Madagascar Serpent Eagle was once recorded (see Distribution), but only covers 810 ha (Andriamampianina 1981) and the species evidently does not now occur there. Along with all Falconiformes it is included on Appendix II of CITES, to which Madagascar is a party.

Conservation Measures Proposed Immediate and effective protection of as much remaining rainforest as possible would almost certainly guarantee the survival of this and all other rainforest-dependent species in Madagascar: this was formally recommended in 1970 (IUCN 1972). Complete protection of the intact parts of "Sihanaka forest" is of extreme importance, being the single most important tract of unprotected bird habitat at present known in Madagascar: with the reasonable exception of the Snail-eating Coua *Coua delalandei* and the Red-tailed Newtonia *Newtonia fanovanae* (see relevant accounts), all Madagascar rainforest birds here treated as threatened have been recorded there, namely the Brown Mesite *Mesitornis unicolor*, Madagascar Red Owl *Tyto soumagnei*, Short-legged Ground-roller, Scaly Ground-roller *Brachypteracias squamiger*, Rufous-headed Ground-roller *Atelornis crossleyi*, Yellow-bellied Sunbird-asity *Neodrepanis hypoxantha*, Dusky Greenbul *Phyllastrephus tenebrosus*, Grey-crowned Greenbul *P. cinereiceps*, Pollen's Vanga *Xenopirostris polleni* and Madagascar Yellowbrow *Crossleyia xanthophrys* (see relevant accounts), as well as several species treated in Appendix C. "Sihanaka forest" is technically a misnomer, since the Sihanaka people are to the west of the central rainforest belt, which is inhabited by the Betsimisaraka people (J. T. Hardyman *in litt.* 1984); the name appears to have been imposed by explorers to stand crudely for the broad belt of humid forest from the coast to the Mangoro valley, east and south of Lake Alaotra and in particular in the Tamatave hinterland, notably between the towns of Didy and Fito (see, e.g., the map in Delacour 1932). Proposals for a comprehensive ornithological survey of Madagascar's rainforests, to feature studies of the Sihanaka forest, the adjacent Zahamena Nature Reserve (R.N.I. no. 3), and other protected areas of rainforest, with particular emphasis on the Serpent Eagle, are to be drawn up as part of an overall plan for bird conservation and research on the island. A proposal in 1979 to search for this species in the Marojejy Nature Reserve and later on the Masoala peninsula (Meyburg 1979) was adopted as WWF Project 1368, and the required sums were raised; however these sums were not released and the project did not proceed (Langrand and Meyburg in press). It is to be noted that a similar problem has existed for the Madagascar Fish Eagle *Haliaeetus vociferoides* and that these two raptors, among the world's six rarest and yet without any conservation action on their behalf, remain the highest priorities for such action at present (Langrand and Meyburg in press). The re-gazetting of the Masoala Forest Nature Reserve (R.N.I. no. 2) was formally recommended in 1970 (IUCN 1972).

Remarks This species is the only one in its genus (see Sharpe 1875). Concerning the type-locality, Andakana is at 19°22'S 48°05'E on the Mangoro River (Office of Geography 1955, IGNT 1964); neither "Ampasimanavy" nor "Ampasmonhavo" (the name given apropos other species in Sharpe 1875) can be traced (Office of Geography 1955, IGNT 1964), but there is an "Ampasimaneva" a few kilometres to the south of Andakana (see IGNT 1964) which must surely be the site (19°24'S 48°04'E). This is also the type-locality of the Rufous-headed Ground-roller (Sharpe 1875) and it is therefore of considerable importance to establish whether good forest still stands in that part of the Mangoro valley. Concerning the name "serpent eagle", confusion may arise in field studies since one French name for the Madagascar Harrier-hawk *Polyboroides radiatus* is "serpentaire" (A. D. Forbes-Watson pers. comm. 1984): possibly "crested eagle" or "forest eagle" would be a more appropriate name for *E. astur*. It has been remarked that there is great similarity between specimens of the Madagascar Serpent Eagle and those of Henst's Goshawk (A. Fayard *in litt.* 1983), and the AMNH specimen from Fito was originally labelled as the latter species (G. S. Keith *in litt.* 1983): given the importance of museum material in clarifying the range of the former, a check needs to be made of skins of Henst's Goshawk to confirm their identity, and details of any Serpent Eagles thus (or otherwise) discovered are requested to be forwarded to ICBP. Not having been seen with certainty in the wild for over 50 years, by CITES criteria this species would now be considered extinct.

References

Andriamampianina, J. (1981) Les réserves naturelles et la protection de la nature à Madagascar. Pp. 105-111 in P. Oberlé, ed. *Madagascar, un sanctuaire de la nature*. Paris: Lechevalier.

Baron, R. (1890) A Malagasy forest. *Antananarivo Annual* 4 (no. 13): 196-211.

Benson, C. W., Colebrook-Robjent, J. F. R. and Williams, A. (1976) Contribution à l'ornithologie de Madagascar. *Oiseau et R.F.O.* 46: 103-134.

Chauvet, B. (1972) The forests of Madagascar. In R. Battistini and G. Richard-Vindard, eds. Biogeography and ecology in Madagascar. *Monog. Biol.* 21: 191-199.

Day, D. (1981) *The doomsday book of animals*. London: Ebury Press.

Delacour, J. (1932) Les oiseaux de la Mission Franco-Anglo-Américaine à Madagascar. *Oiseau et R.F.O.* 2: 1-96.

Griveaud, P. and Albignac, R. (1972) The problems of nature conservation in Madagascar. In R. Battistini and G. Richard-Vindard, eds. Biogeography and ecology in Madagascar. *Monog. Biol.* 21: 727-739.

Guillaumet, J.-L. (1981) Le monde végétal: une variété exceptionnelle. Pp. 29-46 in P. Oberlé, ed. *Madagascar, un sanctuaire de la nature*. Paris: Lechevalier.

Heim, R. (1935) L'état actuel des dévastations forestières à Madagascar. *Rev. Bot. appl. et Agr. trop.* 15 (no. 166): 418-426.

Humbert, H. (1927) La destruction d'une flore insulaire par le feu. Principaux aspects de la végétation à Madagascar. *Mém. Acad. Malgache* V: 1-80.

IUCN (1972) Recommandations: résolutions adoptées par la Conférence. Pp. 12-15 in *C. R. Conférence internationale sur la Conservation de la Nature et de ses Ressources à Madagascar*. Morges: IUCN (NS) Doc. Suppl. no. 36.

Institut Géographique National à Tananarive (1964) Carte de Madagascar, 1: 500,000, Type 1963. Tananarive.

Jenkins, M. D. (in prep.) An environmental profile of Madagascar. IUCN/CMC.

Langrand, O. and Meyburg, B.-U. (in press) Birds of prey and owls in Madagascar: their distribution, status and conservation. Second symposium on African predatory birds, 22-26 August 1983.

Lavauden, L. (1932) Etude d'une petite collection d'oiseaux de Madagascar. *Bull. Mus. Natn. Hist. Nat.* (2)4: 629-640.

Lavauden, L. (1937) Supplément. A. Milne Edwards and A. Grandidier, *Histoire physique, naturelle et politique de Madagascar, 12. Oiseaux*. Paris: Société d'Editions Géographiques, Maritimes et Coloniales.

Louvel, M. (1950) Notes sur les forêts malgaches de l'est. *Rev. internat. Bot. appl. et Agr. trop.* 30 (nos. 333-334): 370-378.

McNulty, F. (1975) Madagascar's endangered wildlife. *Defenders of Wildlife* 50: 93-134.

Meyburg, B.-U. (1979) Survey of the Madagascar Serpent Eagle *Eutriorchis astur*. Proposal submitted to IUCN/WWF/ICBP, 6 March.

Meyburg, B.-U. and Meyburg, C. (1978) Both Madagascan eagle species acutely endangered. Memorandum to ICBP.

Milne Edwards, A. and Grandidier, A. (1879) *Histoire physique, naturelle et politique de Madagascar, 12. Histoire naturelle des oiseaux.* Tome I. Paris.

Office of Geography (1955) *Gazetteer no. 2. Madagascar, Réunion and the Comoro Islands.* Washington, D.C.: Department of the Interior.

Rand, A. L. (1932) Mission Franco-Anglo-Américaine à Madagascar. Notes de voyage. *Oiseau et R.F.O.* 2: 227-282.

Rand, A. L. (1936) The distribution and habits of Madagascar birds. *Bull. Amer. Mus. Nat. Hist.* 72: 143-499.

Sharpe, R. B. (1875) Contributions to the ornithology of Madagascar – Part IV. *Proc. Zool. Soc. Lond.*: 70-78.

Swingle, C. F. (1937) Forest destruction and soil erosion in Madagascar. *Soil Conservation* 3: 102-105.

Thiollay, J.-M. and Meyburg, B.-U. (1981) Remarques sur l'organisation d'un peuplement insulaire de rapaces: Madagascar. *Alauda* 49: 216-226.

MAURITIUS KESTREL   ENDANGERED
Falco punctatus Temminck, 1823

Order FALCONIFORMES   Family FALCONIDAE

Summary The known population of this forest-dwelling species, endemic to Mauritius, was reduced to single figures in the early 1970s for uncertain reasons. Although there has apparently been a slight recovery since then, the immediate and long-term problems it faces are daunting.

Distribution The Mauritius Kestrel is confined to the remoter parts of south-west Mauritius, Indian Ocean, its range having contracted with the reduction of its forest habitat; before Mauritius was discovered, the species probably occurred throughout the island (Temple 1978b, Jones 1981a, in press, Jones *et al.* 1981). In the period 1829-1840 it was found chiefly in the extensive forests of the centre of the island (Oustalet 1897), reference to a contemporary map indicating that such forests then ranged in a broad unbroken belt from the Nicolière mountains east of Port Louis south and west to the coastal areas from Baie du Tamarin in the west to Rivière Tabac in the south (Mackenzie Fraser 1835). The species was also then found in these south-western coastal areas, e.g. Baie du Tamarin, Baie du Cap (Newton 1861, Oustalet 1897; specimens in UMZC: NJC). After the turn of the century, it was still fairly widespread in the central and south-western forests (Carié 1904, Meinertzhagen 1912), and up until the 1940s it was still to be found in the Moka range in the north-west of the island and in the Montagnes Bambous in the east (Jones in press). By the 1950s, however, it was confined to the remote forests of the south-western plateau (Rountree *et al.* 1952, Newton 1958) and all subsequent reports are from within the steep forested area of the Black River Gorges and northwards along the Magenta escarpment as far as Tamarin Gorge (Jones 1980,1981a). Reports from Réunion (Schlegel and Pollen 1868, Oustalet 1897, Meinertzhagen 1912, Berlioz 1946) probably all refer to migrant falcons, e.g. Eleonora's Falcon *Falco eleonorae* (A. S. Cheke pers. comm. 1984).

Population There is almost no historical evidence of the Mauritius Kestrel's abundance; however, in the 1850s it was "plentiful wherever the indigenous woods exist" (Clark 1859). In the twenty years between the crystallisation of concern for Mauritius's endemic birds in the early 1950s and the start of the ICBP/WWF project on them (see Conservation Measures Taken) in the early 1970s, this species was considered so rare that extinction appeared inevitable (Rountree 1951, Vinson 1956, Newton 1958, Greenway 1967, Fabian 1970). However, in the course of fieldwork, 1979-1984, it has become clear that some pairs are so extremely difficult to locate that the consideration arises of whether population reports over the past decade or so have not consistently understated the true position, and it is recommended that all "total" figures quoted below for each year, 1973-1981, be regarded with caution; it is even considered possible that numbers could have been stable throughout the 1970s at 15-20 birds (C. G. Jones *in litt.* 1984). At the start of the 1960s there were thought to be probably fewer than 10 pairs left (Vinson 1963); at the start of the 1970s one pair and two solitary birds

157

were all that could be found by one observer during frequent visits to (parts of) the bird's habitat (Staub 1971). In 1972 at least one young was reported to have fledged (during November) (Temple 1973a). In the course of 1973 it was established that eight or nine – originally reported as six or seven (Temple 1974c) – birds survived, one pair disappearing at the start of the hunting season in July, another pair being trapped for captive breeding in December, and no birds breeding successfully that season, leaving four or five birds known in the wild and two in captivity by the end of the year (Temple 1976b; also Temple 1974c,1977). In March 1974 the captive female died and in May another female was caught from the wild to replace her, so that by mid-year there were just six known birds left, only two of which were then thought to constitute a mated pair (Temple 1974a,b, Temple *et al.* 1974). However in the subsequent breeding season all these birds paired, one rearing three young, the other failing to rear any, and the captive pair hatching a single chick that died, leaving seven birds known in the wild and two in captivity by the end of 1974 (Temple 1975,1976b,1977). All seven wild birds survived Cyclone Gervaise in February 1975 and were still present in September (Temple 1976a,b), though in October only two of the three young birds were to be found in their parents' territory (Newlands 1975b), these presumably the two that were reported to have paired at around this time (Temple 1976a). Both mature wild pairs and the captive pair failed to breed in 1975 (Temple 1976a,b; see Remarks), so that there were six (or seven) birds known in the wild and two in captivity by the end of the year (Temple 1976a). Three pairs were present in 1976 (McKelvey 1977), two of these nesting in cliffs and raising three and two young respectively, the third nesting in a tree (see Remarks) and failing, while the captive pair also failed, so that there were 11 birds known in the wild and two in captivity by the end of the year (S. D. McKelvey *in litt.* 1977 to R. D. Chancellor, McKelvey 1978a,b). In 1977 four pairs were present and three nested, all in cliffs, and produced seven young between them, of which three (one from a nest of two and two from a nest of two) were brought into captivity, while the captive pair did not breed, so that there were a known 12 birds in the wild and five in captivity at the end of the year (Boosey 1978, King 1978, Staub 1979, Jones *et al.* 1981, Jones and Owadally in press). In the course of 1978 the captive adult pair died, so in July two birds (one of the three wild pairs that bred in 1977) were trapped as a replacement and fledged one young in November; in the wild, one pair fledged three young at New Year 1979 and another pair was suspected but not proved to have bred (Jones 1979, in press, King 1979, Staub 1979, Steele 1979, Jones *et al.* 1981), but as other birds were very little in evidence at other known sites during 1978 (though apparently barely if ever searched for after July) (Steele 1979), the total number of birds in the wild at the start of 1979 was unknown, while there were six (believed at the time to be three males, three females, but later found to be four and two respectively) in captivity (Jones 1979, Steele 1979, C. G. Jones *in litt.* 1984). By the start of 1980 all six captive birds had died (Jones 1980, Cooper *et al.* 1981, Jones *et al.* 1981) and the population in the wild was estimated at 15 birds, only one pair having been found to breed, fledging two young (despite Cyclone Claudette) in January 1980 (Jones 1980, in press). Exhaustive fieldwork over the 1980 breeding season extending into 1981 established that certainly "no more than ... 15 birds" survived (C. G. Jones *in litt.* 1981 to R. F. Pasquier 1981); only two breeding pairs were located, one fledging three young (of which one quickly disappeared) while the other failed to rear any (Jones 1981c, in press, Owadally 1981, C. G. Jones *in litt.* 1981 to R. F. Pasquier). In 1981 the number of wild birds remained "low" and again only two breeding pairs were located, both their clutches being taken for captive breeding (three young reared), one pair re-laying but failing to rear young (Jones 1982a,b); other pairs were, however, seen at three further sites over the 1981-1982 breeding season (Jones in press). In 1982 five or six pairs were located holding territories, three of them breeding: one laid infertile eggs, the second reared two young which disappeared soon after fledging, and the third lost their first clutch while their second was taken for captive breeding and three young were reared, bringing the total captive population to six (five males, one female) (Jones 1983). In 1983 three wild pairs nested, two pairs producing three fledglings, of which two were taken for captive breeding, the third pair being given supplementary food and producing three clutches, two of which were taken for captive breeding, two young being raised, the third clutch probably being infertile, so that by the end of the year 10 birds were in captivity with an estimated six pairs, three certainly capable and the other three probably capable of breeding, in the wild (C. G. Jones *in litt.* 1984, *ICBP Newsletter* 6,1 [1984]).

Ecology The Mauritius Kestrel inhabits mature native evergreen forest (now confined to uplands) (Procter and Salm 1974, Temple 1974a), though birds are now found mainly in sub-climax growth where trees rise to c. 15 m, dominant species belonging to the Sapotaceae and including *Sideroxylon grandiflorum*, *S. puberculum* and *Labourdonnaisia glauca* (Jones and Owadally in press); one pair has also recently been found in a lowland mature mixed plantation (see Distribution). Food has been very variously reported, and presumably is at least partly variable according to interrelated factors such as particulars of habitat, availability of prey and season, as well as ability, experience, preference, age and sex of bird. Early accounts, conceding that the species only rarely lived up to its creole name "mangeur des poules", list young rats, mice, birds, lizards and chiefly grasshoppers (Clark 1859, Newton 1883, Oustalet 1897, Carié 1904), and birds were witnessed taking a shrew (presumably *Suncus murinus*) (Meinertzhagen 1912) and chasing a Mauritius Cuckoo-shrike *Coracina typica* (Newton 1958), although this latter event is judged to have been mobbing, not hunting (C. G. Jones *in litt.* 1984). With more intensive studies in the 1970s prey has been identified as lizards (mainly *Phelsuma* geckos), birds (mainly Grey White-eyes *Zosterops borbonicus* and introduced Common Waxbills *Estrilda astrild*), and insects (mainly dragonflies and cicadas, also cockroaches and crickets) (McKelvey 1978a,b, Jones 1981a; also Temple 1974c,1977, Pasquier 1980b). Grey White-eyes have been considered the single most important prey (Jones 1981a, Temple 1981), but geckos were also thought to form 50% of the diet (McKelvey 1978a,b) and formed 94% of 218 identified prey items brought to a nest in October/November 1981 (Jones 1982a,b). The short, rounded, accipitrine wing-structure in the Mauritius Kestrel is an adaptation to hunting below the canopy (McKelvey 1978a, Jones 1981a): prey is usually caught in a rapid dash or pounce from a cliff or tree perch or following a quiet flight through or above the canopy (Staub 1971, Jones *et al.* 1981), geckos being snatched from trunks and branches or chased along branches with rapid hops (a pair sometimes cooperating to force them into exposed positions) (Staub 1976, McKelvey 1978a,b), birds surprised in tree-tops, chased across ravines or occasionally stooped at (McKelvey 1978a,b, Jones *et al.* 1981), dragonflies hunted down wooded roads and cicadas picked from the canopy (McKelvey 1978b; also Staub 1976). Insects probably form a greater proportion of prey in the non-breeding period (Jones in press). The influence of food availability on breeding density and survival is treated under Threats; the species has been stated to shift into lower areas in winter months (May to August) possibly in response to a seasonal drop in geckos and insects in the highlands (Temple 1978b). Colour-marked birds from established pairs have been seen in winter up to 1 km from the nest-site, suggesting a home-range of some 300 ha (Jones in press). Each pair has been stated to require one square mile (i.e. 250-300 ha) to survive (Temple 1974a) or even "a generous average" of 5-10 km^2 (500-1,000 ha) (Cade 1982), yet pairs have been calculated to hold territories of 600 m in diameter, i.e. about 30 ha (Temple 1978b); however, observations 1979-1984 have shown that during the breeding season the male may forage up to about 700 m from the nest, suggesting a territory size of up to about 150 ha (Jones in press). Courtship activity usually starts in September/October, eggs (usually three) being laid in any month from October to January, with most first clutches in late October; the nest-site is in a cliff or, by (still unsubstantiated) report, a hole in a tree (Jones 1981a, C. G. Jones *in litt.* 1984). Young birds are tolerated by their parents until the next breeding season, when they are harried away (McKelvey 1978a,b, Jones 1980,1981a); however, birds from adjacent territories may soar together, and "visiting" birds near nests are tolerated (Jones 1980, 1981a). The species is notably tame, but birds are often very elusive (Jones 1980; also McKelvey 1978a).

Threats The factors causing declines in all forest-dependent birds in Mauritius are deeply interrelated and largely irreversible (for popular accounts, see Jolly 1982, Pasquier and Jones 1982). The fundamental problem has been and remains chronic loss of native forest habitat: virgin forest originally covered almost all the island, but had diminished to a mere 2,800 ha in 1936, 1,600 in 1970 and 1,400 in 1980, although somewhat larger areas of degraded forest, used by some native birds, survived (see Temple 1974b, Cheke in press b, Jones and Owadally in press). This relict forest is, moreover, subject to steady degeneration, caused by the invasion of vigorous exotic plants (notably guava *Psidium cattleianum*, privet *Ligustrum robustum* var. *walkeri* and bramble *Rubus mollucensis*), the seeds of which are themselves spread by introduced (as well as native) frugivorous birds and mammals, the process being compounded by browsing by introduced deer *Cervus timorensis*, grubbing by feral pigs, seed destruction by introduced crab-eating macaques *Macaca fascicularis* and black rats *Rattus rattus*, and the effect of cyclones (A. S. Cheke pers. comm. 1984, C. G. Jones *in litt.* 1984, Cheke in press a,b). Endemic birds in these forests all suffer, in varying degrees and combinations, competition for food and nest-sites from and food-source destruction and nest-predation by introduced animals, notably monkeys, rats and Indian Mynahs *Acridotheres tristis* (Temple 1974b, Cheke in press a, Jones and Owadally in press). Introduced diseases may have affected endemic birds (Peirce *et al.* 1977) and hunting was formerly a major cause of decline and even extinction (Meinertzhagen

1912, Cheke in press b). Considerable disturbance is brought to the remaining native forest, seasonally by hunters, who still occasionally (but potentially critically) persecute endemic birds, and daily by woodcutters, who do not restrict themselves to taking exotic weeds (Cheke in press a). The threat to endemic birds from major cyclones, such as struck Mauritius in 1892, 1931, 1945, 1960, 1975, 1979 and 1983 (Niven 1965, Newlands 1975a, Cheke 1975b, Jones 1980, Pasquier 1980b, C. G. Jones *in litt.* 1984), is greatly amplified by the reduction in forest and bird population sizes to their present levels, frugivorous birds particularly suffering from loss of food supply (Cheke in press a). Critically low populations face the additional but as yet unclarified problem of inbreeding (King 1979, Cooper *et al.* 1981). Some genetic factor was proposed to explain the Mauritius Kestrel's decline over the 50 years to around 1960 (Vinson 1963), but in the early 1970s the main threats to the remaining birds were considered to be continuing habitat loss, direct human persecution (three or four birds believed shot, 1971-1973), and nest-predation by monkeys (Temple 1973a,b,1974a,b,c, McKelvey 1978a). The significance of this last factor, and of its avoidance by the development of an exclusively cliff-nesting habit (e.g. Temple 1977,1978a,b), has been doubted (Jones 1980,1981a, in press, Jones *et al.* 1981, Jones and Owadally in press), but feral cats were suspected of killing the only birds fledged in 1982 (Jones 1983). Interspecific competition for nest-sites was noted (McKelvey 1978a,b), and lack of suitable nest-sites was considered a possible restriction on the population (Jones 1979), but this view has been rejected as unproven (Jones in press, Jones and Owadally in press). The progressive spread of exotic vegetation through native forest understorey was recognised as an impediment to hunting and "no doubt significantly reduces the prey resources available" (Temple 1973b) and, despite reports of prey being abundant in the species's forest habitat (McKelvey 1978b, Pasquier 1980b), it is indeed habitat quality and food abundance that are now accounted responsible for controlling the population, such that breeding distribution within the remaining habitat is "patchy" and expectations for the species's survival in the wild "must be very poor" (Jones 1981c, in press, C. G. Jones *in litt.* 1981 to R. F. Pasquier, Jones *et al.* 1981, Jones and Owadally 1982, in press). The possibility exists that the upturn (if real) in Mauritius Kestrel numbers in the mid-1970s was related to the cessation of organochlorine pesticide usage ten years earlier (Jones 1980,1981a, Pasquier 1980b).

Conservation Measures Taken In 1973 a WWF project (managed by ICBP and with financial support from NYZS) was initiated to study and save this species, and soon afterwards it was expanded to cover other threatened forms of wildlife on Mauritius (annual reports in Temple 1974c,1975,1976a, McKelvey 1977, King 1978,1979, Pasquier 1980a,1982, Jones 1981b; see also Temple 1974b,1977, Jones *et al.* 1981, Jones 1982b). Since 1976 this project has operated in conjunction with JWPT and with the active participation of the Government of Mauritius; since 1982 it has been the concern of ICBP and JWPT and in 1984 it became part of the Mauritius Wildlife Research and Conservation Programme (MWRCP) (*ICBP Newsletter* 6,1 [1984]), which will address the conservation of all Mauritian bird species (and those from Rodrigues) treated in this volume. The bare details of the birds taken for captive breeding on Mauritius (project now located at government aviaries at Black River), and their performance to date, are given under Population above (see also Cooper *et al.* 1981, Jones *et al.* 1981). Recent manipulation of the wild population has included supplementary feeding of a pair to maximise egg-production (C. G. Jones *in litt.* 1984). Other measures that have presumably benefited the species include legal protection, first called for in 1878 (Newton 1883) and enacted before 1911 (Meinertzhagen 1912), which, combined with a campaign of public education and awareness since the early 1970s (Temple 1977,1978b), currently renders persecution of the species rare or non-existent (Jones and Owadally in press); and habitat preservation, in the form of the Macabé/Bel Ombre Nature Reserve, which was created in 1974 through the linking of existing nature reserves at Petrin, Macabé and Bel Ombre by the addition of Les Mares and Plaine Champagne, forming a large block covering 3,594 ha (Owadally 1976; see map in Procter and Salm 1974). The species is listed on Appendix I of CITES, to which Mauritius is a party.

Conservation Measures Proposed A radio-telemetry study of this species to determine the extent of individual birds' movements and their habitat utilisation has been considered essential (Jones 1980,1981a, Pasquier 1980b), and in October 1984 such a project, lasting four months, is scheduled to begin, financed by Peregrine Fund Inc. (P. D. Goriup pers. comm. 1984); study of its ecology and life history, with particular reference to its dependence on geckos, has been envisaged (Jones and Owadally 1982). The provision of nest-boxes has been considered as a means of increasing reproductive output (Jones 1981a) but it has been decided that nest-site availability is not a factor limiting the population (Jones in press, Jones and Owadally in press). Proposals in the early and mid-1970s to restrict the threat of nest-predation by controlling monkeys (Temple 1974a) and fencing trees and wardening nests (Temple 1976b) were not implemented, and the current view is that such predation is unlikely to be serious (see Threats). The long-term strategy of creating commercially viable conservation-oriented plantations (see Conservation Measures Proposed under Mauritius Cuckoo-shrike) would probably also benefit this species (Jones and Owadally 1982, in press). Re-introduction of the species into parts of its former range on Mauritius has been under consideration (Temple 1978b, C. G. Jones *in litt.* 1984), although this presupposes that the factors that caused its extinction in them no longer operate or that they can be overcome. Introduction of birds to the neighbouring French island of Réunion (Cheke 1975a, Temple 1976b) has been argued as biogeographically valid (Temple 1981), and has been supported, following successful captive breeding on Mauritius, provided that the risk of predation by the Réunion Harrier *Circus maillardi* is recognised (Cheke 1978), but is rejected on the basis that hunting pressure there is too high (Jones and Owadally 1982, in press); nevertheless, such an experiment, fully monitored at a suitably undisturbed site and with a well managed publicity campaign, appears a logical outcome of the present attempts to propagate the species in good numbers in captivity, and it is to be noted that the Réunion Harrier itself has recovered from low numbers following its legal protection in the mid-1960s (see Appendix C), indicating that hunting pressure on raptors in Réunion is under control.

Remarks Concerning the failure of wild birds to breed in 1975 (as reported under Population), the statement that successful breeding occurred in 1975 and 1976 (Temple 1978a) is evidently in error for 1976 and 1977 respectively. Concerning the attempt of a pair to nest in a tree in 1976 (also reported under Population), this is disputed (in Jones in press, Jones and Owadally in press).

References

Berlioz, J. (1946) *Oiseaux de la Réunion*. Faune de l'Empire Français, IV. Paris: Librairie Larose.

Boosey, G. (1978) A recent report from Mauritius. *Hawk Trust Ann. Rep.* (1977) 8: 22-23.

Cade, T. J. (1982) *The falcons of the world*. London: Collins.

Carié, P. (1904) Observations sur quelques oiseaux de l'île Maurice. *Ornis* 12: 121-128.

Cheke, A. S. (1975a) Proposition pour introduire à la Réunion des oiseaux rares de l'île Maurice. *Info-Nature* no. 12: 25-29.

Cheke, A. (1975b) Cyclone Gervaise – an eye-witness comments. *Birds International* 1(1): 13-14.

Cheke, A. S. (1978) Recommendations for the conservation of Mascarene vertebrates. Conservation memorandum no. 3 (arising out of the B.O.U. Mascarene Islands Expedition). Unpublished.

Cheke, A. S. (in press a) The surviving native land-birds of Mauritius. In A. W. Diamond, ed. *Studies of Mascarene island birds*. Cambridge: Cambridge University Press.

Cheke, A. S. (in press b) An ecological history of the Mascarene islands. In A. W. Diamond, ed. *Studies of Mascarene island birds*. Cambridge: Cambridge University Press.

Clark, G. (1859) A ramble round Mauritius with some excursions in the interior of that island; to which is added a familiar description of its fauna and some subjects of its flora. Pp I-CXXXII in *The Mauritius register: historical, official and commercial, corrected to the 30th June 1859*. Port Louis: L. Channell.

Cooper, J. E., Jones, C. G. and Owadally, A. W. (1981) Morbidity and mortality in the Mauritius Kestrel (*Falco punctatus*). Pp. 31-35 in J. E. Cooper and A. G. Greenwood, eds. *Recent advances in the study of raptor diseases*. Keighley: Chiron Publications.

Fabian, D. T. (1970) The birds of Mauritius. *Bokmakierie* 22: 16-17, 21.

Greenway, J. C. (1967) *Extinct and vanishing birds of the world*. 2nd revised edition. New York: Dover Publications.

Jolly, A. (1982) Island of the Dodo is down to its last few native species. *Smithsonian* 13(3): 94-102.

Jones, C. G. (1979) Mauritius/Rodrigues conservation project report for January 22nd – June 20th 1979. Unpublished.

Jones, C. G. (1980) The conservation of the endemic birds and bats of Mauritius and Rodriguez (a progress report and proposal for further activities). Unpublished.

Jones, C. G. (1981a) The Mauritius Kestrel. Its biology and conservation. *Hawk Trust Ann. Rep.* (1980) 10: 18-29.

Jones, C. G. (1981b) Mauritius Project 1082. Promotion of conservation. *WWF Yearbook* 1980-1981: 206-212.

Jones, C. G. (1981c) Mauritius: an important lesson in island biology. (A summary of activities and proposals for 1981.) Unpublished.

Jones, C. G. (1982a) The conservation of the endemic birds and bats of Mauritius and Rodrigues. (Annual report 1981, WWF Project 1082.) Unpublished.

Jones, C. G. (1982b) Struggle for survival on tropical islands. *WWF Monthly Report* February: 37-42.

Jones, C. G. (1983) The conservation of the endemic birds and bats of Mauritius and Rodrigues. Annual Report, 1982. Unpublished.

Jones, C. G. (in press) The larger land-birds of Mauritius. In A. W. Diamond, ed. *Studies of Mascarene island birds*. Cambridge: Cambridge University Press.

Jones, C. G. and Owadally, A. W. (1982) Conservation priorities for Mauritius and Rodrigues. Report submitted to ICBP, July. Unpublished.

Jones, C. G. and Owadally, A. W. (in press) The status, ecology and conservation of the Mauritius Kestrel.

Jones, C. G., Steele, F. N. and Owadally, A. W. (1981) An account of the Mauritius Kestrel captive breeding project. *Avicult. Mag.* 87: 191-207.

King, W. B. (1978) Mauritius Project 1082. Promotion of conservation. *WWF Yearbook* 1977-1978: 150-151.

King, W. B. (1979) Mauritius Project 1082. Promotion of conservation. *WWF Yearbook* 1978-1979: 137-138.

Mackenzie Fraser, F. A. (1835) [Map of] Mauritius. London.

McKelvey, S. D. (1977) Mauritius Project 1082. Promotion of conservation. *WWF Yearbook* 1976-1977: 181-182.

McKelvey, S. D. (1978a) The Mauritian Kestrel. Some notes on its breeding biology, behaviour and survival potential. *Hawk Trust Ann. Rep.* (1977) 8: 19-21.

McKelvey, S. D. (1978b) The Mauritius Kestrel. *Wildlife* 20: 47-51.

Meinertzhagen, R. (1912) On the birds of Mauritius. *Ibis* (9)6: 82-108.

Newlands, W. A. (1975a) Mauritius Conservation Project monthly reports, February – August 1975. Unpublished.

Newlands, W. A. (1975b) Letter, 4 October [duplicated to interested parties]. Unpublished.

Newton, E. (1861) Ornithological notes from Mauritius. No. II. A ten days' sojourn at Savanne. *Ibis* 3: 270-277.

Newton, E. (1883) Annexe C [Letter to V. Naz, 26 February 1878]. *Trans. Soc. Roy. Arts Sci. Maurice* (NS) 12: 70-73.

Newton, R. (1958) Ornithological notes on Mauritius and the Cargados Carajos Archipelago. *Proc. Roy. Soc. Arts Sci. Mauritius* 2(1): 39-71.

Niven, C. (1965) Birds of Mauritius. *Ostrich* 36: 84-86.

Oustalet, E. (1897) Notice sur la faune ornithologique ancienne et moderne des îles Mascareignes et en particular de l'île Maurice d'après des documents inédits. *Ann. Sci. Nat. Zool.* (8)3: 1-128.

Owadally, A. W. (1976) *Annual report of the Forestry Service for the year 1974.* Port Louis, Mauritius: L. Carl Achille, Government Printer.

Pasquier, R. F. (1980a) Mauritius Project 1082. Endangered bird species. *WWF Yearbook* 1979-1980: 128-129.

Pasquier, R. F. (1980b) Report and management plan on ICBP's project for the conservation of forest birds of Mauritius. Unpublished.

Pasquier, R. F. (1982) Mauritius Project 1082. Conservation of birds of Mauritius. *WWF Yearbook* 1982: 210-211.

Pasquier, R. and Jones, C. (1982) The lost and lonely birds of Mauritius. *Natural History* 91(3): 39-43.

Peirce, M. A., Cheke, A. S. and Cheke, R. A. (1977) A survey of blood parasites of birds in the Mascarene Islands, Indian Ocean. *Ibis* 119: 451-461.

Procter, J. and Salm, R. (1974) Conservation in Mauritius 1974. IUCN/WWF consultancy report for Government of Mauritius. Unpublished.

Rountree, F. G. R. (1951) Some aspects of bird-life in Mauritius. *Proc. Roy. Soc. Arts Sci. Mauritius* 1(2): 83-96.

Rountree, F. G. R., Guérin, R., Pelte, S. and Vinson, J. (1952) Catalogue of the birds of Mauritius. *Mauritius Inst. Bull.* 3(3): 155-217.

Schlegel, H. and Pollen, F. P. L. (1868) *Recherches sur la faune de Madagascar et de ses dépendances, d'après les découvertes de François P. L. Pollen et D. C. van Dam.* 2me partie. Mammifères et oiseaux. Leyde.

Staub, F. (1971) Actual situation of the Mauritius endemic birds. *ICBP Bull.* 11: 226-227.

Staub, F. (1976) *Birds of the Mascarenes and Saint Brandon.* Port Louis, Mauritius: Organisation Normale des Enterprises.

Staub, F. (1979) Mauritius National Section, report 1977-1978. *ICBP Bull.* 13: 188-190.

Steele, F. N. (1979) Conservation of birds on Mauritius, final report for 1978. Unpublished.

Temple, S. A. (1973a) The ecology and conservation of island raptors in the Indian Ocean: an early progress report. Unpublished.

Temple, S. A. (1973b) The survival of the Mauritius Kestrel: a report on current status and an appeal for policy endorsement. Unpublished.

Temple, S.A. (1974a) Appendix 6. The native fauna of Mauritius: 1, the land birds. In J. Procter and R. Salm, Conservation in Mauritius 1974. IUCN/WWF consultancy report for Government of Mauritius. Unpublished.

Temple, S. A. (1974b) Wildlife in Mauritius today. *Oryx* 12: 584-590.

Temple, S. A. (1974c) Project 986: Western Indian Ocean island raptores [*sic*] – conservation. *WWF Yearbook* 1973-1974: 201-204.

Temple, S. A. (1975) Project 986: Western Indian Ocean raptores [*sic*]- ecology and conservation. *WWF Yearbook* 1974-1975: 210-212.

Temple, S. A. (1976a) Project 1082: Mauritius – promotion of conservation. *WWF Yearbook* 1975-1976: 165-166.

Temple, S. A. (1976b) Conservation of endemic birds and other wildlife on Mauritius. A progress report and proposal for future activities. Unpublished.

Temple, S. A. (1977) The status and conservation of endemic kestrels on Indian Ocean Islands. Pp. 74-82 in R. D. Chancellor, ed. *Report of Proceedings, World Conference on Birds of Prey*, Vienna, 1-3 October 1975. [London:] International Council for Bird Preservation.

Temple, S. A. (1978a) Manipulating behavioral patterns of endangered birds. A potential management technique. Pp. 435-443 in S. A. Temple, ed. *Endangered birds: management techniques for preserving threatened species*. Madison, Wisconsin: University of Wisconsin Press, and London: Croom Helm.

Temple, S. A. (1978b) The life histories and ecology of the indigenous landbirds of Mauritius. Unpublished.

Temple, S. A. (1981) Applied island biogeography and the conservation of endangered island birds in the Indian Ocean. *Biol. Conserv.* 20: 147-161.

Temple, S. A., Staub, J. J. F. and Antoine, R. (1974) Some background information and recommendations on the preservation of the native flora and fauna of Mauritius. Unpublished report to the Government of Mauritius.

Vinson, J. (1956) The problem of bird protection in the island of Mauritius. *Proc. Roy. Soc. Arts Sci. Mauritius* 1(4): 387-392.

Vinson, J. (1963) The extinction of endemic birds in the island of Mauritius, with a possible way of saving some of the remaining species. *ICBP Bull.* 9: 99-101.

Summary Results of a recent study indicate that this forest-dwelling Seychelles endemic raptor is far more numerous and widespread than was previously thought; populations on Mahé and Silhouette are probably at carrying capacity, and a reintroduction attempt on Praslin appears to have been successful.

Distribution The Seychelles Kestrel is confined to the islands of Mahé (and its satellite islets), Silhouette and Praslin in the Seychelles archipelago. A century ago it probably occurred throughout granitic Seychelles, with the exception of those islands (Cousin, Cousine, Aride and Frégate) with seabird colonies (Watson 1981); there is no published evidence of occurrence on these latter (*contra* Temple 1977). It was definitely recorded in the last century from Mahé (including St.Anne), Silhouette, Praslin, Curieuse, Marianne (Newton 1867, Oustalet 1878) and Félicité (Diamond and Feare 1980, Fisher 1981), and birds were reported as frequently seen on nearly all islands, 1940 (Vesey-Fitzgerald 1940), but thereafter a contraction in range evidently occurred, with fragmentary documentation emerging in the 1960s: hence this species was seen nowhere else but two localities on Mahé, 1959 (Crook 1960), reported as widely distributed on Mahé and its satellites, with no mention of other islands, 1962 (Loustau-Lalanne 1962), seen on Mahé and Praslin but not Silhouette, and reported extinct on La Digue (the first mention of this island), 1964-1965 (Penny 1968), but then claimed confined to Mahé (Gaymer *et al.* 1969). Searches of islands including La Digue, Félicité and Curieuse, 1970-1973, were fruitless and birds were found only on Mahé, Silhouette and (marginally) Praslin (Feare *et al.* 1974, Temple 1977). Intensive searches on Praslin, in June/July 1976, drew blanks and the species was suspected of being absent for some years (Evans 1977, Watson 1981). In 1975-1977, birds were found breeding on Mahé and its satellites (including St.Anne, Cerf and Longue) and Silhouette, were seen and considered probably to breed on North Island and Thérèse, and were expected to breed on Conception (Watson 1981). Occasional records from Praslin and La Digue were considered probably to refer to young birds dispersing from Mahé (Watson 1981). The species has been reported in recent years also from Félicité (Diamond and Feare 1980), and is now reintroduced to Praslin (Watson 1981).

Population Birds are evidently somewhat elusive (possibly because of their perch-and-pounce hunting strategy: see Feare *et al.* 1974, Watson 1981) and may have been under-recorded in the past, especially by short-term visitors making more casual observations: thus in 1906 and 1960 the species was considered rare (Nicoll 1906, Meade-Waldo 1907, Crook 1960), and in August 1979 only three birds were seen in a week on Mahé (Julliard 1980), though in 1867 it was "tolerably common" on Mahé (Newton 1867) and in 1962 placed with the commoner endemic Seychelles birds whose survival was not threatened (Loustau-Lalanne 1962). Following studies in the mid-1960s, however, it was maintained that birds were actually being over-recorded through frequent sightings of what were then claimed to be only single pairs ranging through very large territories (Penny 1968), and that the population on Mahé was possibly under 30 birds (Gaymer *et al.* 1969). More intensive investigations, 1972-1974, found a minimum of 49 pairs on Mahé (including one each on St.Anne and Cerf), 10 pairs on Silhouette and one or two individuals on Praslin; while average home-range was determined as 83 ha which, by extrapolation, suggested a capacity of more than 100 pairs, with at least 150 and possibly 300 individuals (Feare *et al.* 1974, Temple 1977). Still more intensive studies, 1975-1977, yielded different results again: mean territory size was found to be only 40 ha, with limited variation, apparently the smallest known for any raptor (Watson 1981). During 1976, one study area (1,270 ha) held 33 pairs and another (825 ha) 21 pairs; observations confirmed that kestrels occurred over the whole island, and by extrapolation Mahé (14,480 ha) would be expected to hold c. 370 pairs; the satellite islands might hold 13 pairs (Watson 1981). A survey of Silhouette in October 1975 yielded five pairs in 210 ha and nine in 420 ha; habitat is homogeneous throughout, permitting a minimum estimate for the island (1,600 ha) of 36 pairs (Watson 1981). North Island might hold five pairs, and in 1980 reintroduced birds on Praslin numbered 10 pairs (Watson 1981). Altogether c. 430 pairs are thus estimated to be present on Seychelles (Watson 1981). It is not clear whether this steady rise in estimated numbers reflects an actual increase in population size, increasingly efficient observer coverage, or a combination of these two, but the second of these possibilities seems most likely.

Ecology Mahé broadly possesses four main habitat-types: mixed forest and open scrub woodland in the hills, mixed coconut plantation (with lowland forest) and open lowland country around the coasts; kestrels utilise all four, within which they establish year-round territories (not distinct from home-ranges) (Watson 1981). Nesting is not year-round, however (*contra* Temple 1977), but occurs between August and October, apparently in response to increased food supply: geckos *Phelsuma longinsulae* and *P. astriata* and the ground skink *Mabuya sechellensis* comprise the bulk of the diet (50% by number of items, 65% by biomass), though insects, rats, birds, frogs and chameleons are also taken, while almost all food brought to nestlings was vertebrates, particularly (91% by number) lizards (Watson 1981). Clutch-size is two to three, hatching success high; there is one brood per year, with a post-fledging dependence period of 9-24 (mean 14) weeks (Watson 1981). Fledging success is greater at nests in cliffs and natural tree cavities (mostly in hill areas) than at those in crowns of palms and on buildings (mostly in coastal areas): those in palms at least are highly susceptible to predation by Indian Mynahs *Acridotheres tristis*, Green-backed Herons *Butorides striatus*, Barn Owls *Tyto alba*, black rats *Rattus rattus* and feral cats (Watson 1981). Average fledged brood-size in hill areas, 1975-1976, was 1.62, in coastal areas 0.81: assuming 370 pairs present, with 50% in hill areas and 50% around coasts, suffering equally 50% first-year mortality, 225 young become available to enter the breeding population each year, while (on the basis of disappearance-rate of marked birds, 1975-1976) 167 adults die each year (Watson 1981). Stability in the population must thus result from surplus production in the hill areas (150 one-year-olds from 185 pairs), since coastal pairs fail to rear enough (75 from 185 pairs) to maintain their numbers; in a removal experiment when 13 birds were transferred from Mahé to Praslin, 100% replacement occurred within 10 weeks, 11 of the new 13 being one-year-olds (Watson 1981).

Threats Extinctions on Praslin and the other northern (all low-lying) islands is considered attributable to high adult mortality (including killing by people) plus poor reproductive success in coastal (i.e. most) areas (Watson 1981). Human persecution has elsewhere been regarded as the single most critical factor in local extinctions, especially given the bird's exceptional tameness (Newton 1867, Honneger 1966, Penny 1968, Temple 1977), though extinction on La Digue was reportedly the result of displacement at nests by (introduced) Barn Owls (Penny 1968, Gaymer *et al.* 1969).

Conservation Measures Taken This species is listed on Appendix I of CITES, to which Seychelles is a party. In the 1960s, public education programmes and increased enforcement of bird protection laws virtually eliminated widespread indiscriminate shooting of birds (Temple 1977). The ban on private ownership of firearms since 1977 has further inhibited illegal shooting (Watson 1981). The species was the subject of intensive field studies, 1975-1977 (with follow-up work and analysis through to 1981), partly designed to assess its conservation needs (see Watson 1981). The recently declared Morne Seychellois National Park, embracing 30% of land above 200 m on Mahé, holds good numbers of reproductively successful pairs (Watson 1981). The reintroduction of 13 birds to Praslin in July/August 1977 (six males and seven females, amongst which were three established pairs) resulted in at least two successful nests in 1978, and by October 1980 at least 10 pairs were present, mostly in the southern, more wooded half of the island (Watson 1981). This last measure partially fulfils a major 1975 recommendation to reintroduce the species to several northern islands (see Temple 1977).

Conservation Measures Proposed The ordnance giving full legal protection to all Seychelles endemic birds should be publicised to counter possible resurgence of prejudice against the Seychelles Kestrel (whose Creole name, "mangeur des poules", is wholly unjustified) (Watson 1981; also Penny 1968). The ban on importation of any exotic bird (other than poultry) should be maintained and enforced, to prevent the establishment of any predator or competitor (Watson 1981). Persistent agricultural chemicals should continue to be restricted and where possible replaced (Watson 1981). Regular surveys are needed to determine the results of the Praslin reintroduction; if this succeeds, further reintroductions (particularly to La Digue, Félicité, Les Soeurs and Marianne) should be considered (Watson 1981).

References

Crook, J. H. (1960) The present status of certain rare land birds of the Seychelles Islands. Seychelles Government Bulletin.

Diamond, A. W. and Feare, C. J. (1980) Past and present biogeography of central Seychelles birds. *Proc. IV Pan-Afr. orn. Congr.*: 89-98.

Evans, P. G. H. (1977) Aberdeen University Expedition to Praslin, Seychelles, 1976: preliminary report. Unpublished.

Feare, C. J., Temple, S. A. and Procter, J. (1974) The status, distribution and diet of the Seychelles Kestrel *Falco araea. Ibis* 116: 548-551.

Fisher, C. T. (1981) Specimens of extinct, endangered or rare birds in the Merseyside County Museums, Liverpool. *Bull. Brit. Orn. Club* 101: 276-285.

Gaymer, R., Blackman, R. A. A., Dawson, P. G., Penny, M. and Penny, C. M. (1969) The endemic birds of Seychelles. *Ibis* 111: 157-176.

Honneger, R. E. (1966) Ornithologische Beobachtungen von den Seychelles. *Natur u. Mus.* 96: 481-488.

Julliard, J. P. (1980) Notes sur quelques oiseaux des Seychelles. *Alauda* 48: 56-57.

Loustau-Lalanne, P. (1962) Land birds of the granitic islands of the Seychelles. *Seychelles Soc. Occ. Publ.* 1.

Meade-Waldo, E. G. B. (1907) Some remarks on birds seen during the cruise of the "Valhalla", R.Y.S. *Avicult. Mag.* N.S. 5: 144-148.

Newton, E. (1867) On the land-birds of the Seychelles archipelago. *Ibis* (2)3: 335-360.

Nicoll, M. J. (1906) On the birds collected and observed during the voyage of the "Valhalla", R.Y.S., from November 1905 to May 1906. *Ibis* (8)6: 666-712.

Oustalet, M. E. (1878) Etude sur la faune ornithologique des Iles Seychelles. *Bull. Soc. Philomath. Paris* (7)2: 161-206.

Penny, M. (1968) Endemic birds of the Seychelles. *Oryx* 9: 267-275.

Temple, S. A. (1977) The status and conservation of endemic kestrels on Indian Ocean islands. Pp. 74-82 in R. D. Chancellor, ed. *Report of Proceedings, World Conference on Birds of Prey*, Vienna, 1-3 October 1975. [London:] International Council for Bird Preservation.

Vesey-Fitzgerald, D. (1940) The birds of the Seychelles. I. The endemic birds. *Ibis* (14)4: 480-489.

Watson, J. (1981) Population ecology, food and conservation of the Seychelles Kestrel (*Falco araea*) on Mahé. Ph.D. thesis, University of Aberdeen.

DJIBOUTI FRANCOLIN   ENDANGERED

Francolinus ochropectus Dorst and Jouanin, 1952

Order GALLIFORMES   Family PHASIANIDAE
                                                  Subfamily PHASIANINAE

Summary This ground-dwelling, seed- and fruit-eating species is endemic to the Forêt du Day in Djibouti. Although some 5,000 birds exist at present, primary forest at Day has been halved in the past seven years (now covering only 1,400 ha) and, without the rapid prohibition of the human activities responsible, will disappear completely before the end of the century; whether the species would be able to survive in secondary habitat is unclear.

Distribution The Djibouti Francolin is confined to the small relict Forêt du Day (Plateau du Day) at c. 1,500 m in the south of the Goda massif and c. 25 km west of Tadjoura, Djibouti (Dorst and Jouanin 1952,1954), although unidentified francolins seen in relict secondary forest at Mabla at the eastern end of the Goda massif (60 km east of the Forêt du Day) are possibly also of this species (Welch and Welch 1984a). In March/April 1984 in the Forêt du Day the species was found to be present at six sites: Garrab, Adonta, Afambo, Wadriba, Goh and Bankoualé (Welch and Welch in press).

Population Although it was initially considered improbable that total numbers exceeded several hundred (Dorst and Jouanin 1954), recent studies by J. Blot indicate a population of around 5,000 birds (Welch and Welch 1984a). This revelation does not, however, alter the seriousness of the species's plight (see Threats).

Ecology It inhabits both primary and secondary forest: primary forest consists chiefly of juniper *Juniperus procera*, with *Buxus hildebrandtii*, *Clutia abyssinica*, *Olea chrysophylla* and *Ficus* (Dorst and Jouanin 1954, Welch and Welch 1984a,b), while in secondary forest the dominant trees are *Buxus* and *Acacia etbaica*, with juniper absent or much reduced (Welch and Welch 1984a,b). The species's main requirements are reported to be areas of dense cover for roosting and (probably) breeding (such as generally occur in wadis), and areas with graminaceous plants for feeding (such as occur on plateaus) (Welch and Welch 1984a). It also feeds on various fruits (e.g. *Buxus*, *Ficus*) and is commonly found on the edges of ravines where *Ficus* trees grow, especially in the dry season (Dorst and Jouanin 1954). The greatest density (geographically) was originally noted in the Hamboka ravine near the well at Ourano (Dorst and Jouanin 1954), and (ecologically) is related to areas of greatest plant growth, which are those least accessible to people and livestock (Welch and Welch 1984a, in press). Birds are known to breed from December to February; a presumed family party consisting of nine birds was seen, March (Welch and Welch 1984a, in press). The species is sedentary, but descends below 1,000-1,200 m (*contra* Dorst and Jouanin 1954), having been seen in 1984 at 700 m (Welch and Welch in press). Activity is greatest from 06.00 to 08.00 hrs, much of the remainder of the day being spent resting in dense cover at heights up to 4 m (Welch and Welch in press).

Threats This species conceivably faces extinction before the end of this century as a result of loss of habitat: a slow, natural dessication of the region is being compounded by extensive human interference (Welch and Welch 1984a). Two thousand years ago the primary forest on the Goda massif covered 400,000 ha; in 1977 the relict area on the Plateau du Day covered only 3,000 ha, but in just seven years to 1984 this had been more than halved to 1,400 ha and on present trends all primary forest will have disappeared by 1995 (Welch and Welch 1984a). Chief causes of habitat loss are overgrazing and trampling by livestock (mainly cattle, but also on the fringes sheep and goats, and small numbers of donkeys and camels) and cutting of trees to create pasture and for firewood (apart from local use, seven tons of firewood are transported daily to Djibouti); in addition to these factors, fires are sporadically (but deliberately) started to create pasture, trees are destroyed to obtain honey, and the army is present in the summer and causes erosion around its camps; there are also government proposals to clear parts of the forest (including on mountains) for agriculture, to extract water from major wadis to supply nearby villages, and to construct roads and dwellings inside the forest (Welch and Welch 1984a,b). The fact that the Djibouti Francolin is now known to occur in secondary forest of considerably larger extent than the remaining primary forest (see Ecology) is no guarantee of its survival there in the absence of any primary forest (for an example of breeding success in primary habitat being responsible for sustaining numbers in secondary habitat, see Ecology under Seychelles Kestrel *Falco araea*). The chief natural enemy of the species would be genets *Genetta* (Dorst and Jouanin 1954).

Conservation Measures Taken The Forêt du Day falls within the boundaries of the Day National Park. The Djibouti Francolin is listed on Appendix II of CITES, to which however Djibouti is not a party. The species is a major component of a study of the whole Forêt du Day currently being conducted by J. Blot (Welch and Welch 1984a,b).

Conservation Measures Proposed All the human factors responsible for accelerating habitat loss in the Forêt du Day need to be stopped in the next 3-5 years if the primary forest is not to disappear by around 1995 (Welch and Welch 1984a,b): interventions and proposals are now being developed by ICBP. Removal of birds for captive breeding and/or translocation to other potential forests (not yet identified) deserves urgent consideration but, even if ultimately successful, should not be allowed to diminish or disguise the fundamental need for the conservation of habitat in the Forêt du Day itself (see Remarks). The identity of the birds seen at Mabla requires confirmation.

Remarks The Forêt du Day is of exceptional botanical interest (Dorst and Jouanin 1954). Its loss would mean the loss of Djibouti's only forested area and with it most of the associated wildlife, much of which is unstudied and probably contains – particularly in the insect groups – species new to science (Welch and Welch 1984a). Owing to the presence of related francolins in the nearest highland areas in Ethiopia and Somalia, the chances of the Djibouti Francolin being found at any new locality away from the Goda massif are negligible (see Hall and Moreau 1962).

References

Dorst, J. and Jouanin, C. (1952) Description d'une espèce nouvelle de francolin d'Afrique Orientale. *Oiseau et R.F.O.* 22: 71-74.

Dorst, J. and Jouanin, C. (1954) Précisions sur la position systématique et l'habitat de *Francolinus ochropectus*. *Oiseau et R.F.O.* 24: 161-170.

Hall, B. P. and Moreau, R. E. (1962) A study of the rare birds of Africa. *Bull. Brit. Mus. (Nat. Hist.) Zool.* 8: 313-378.

Welch, H. and Welch, G. (1984a) Brief summary of findings of the Djibouti Expedition – March 1984. Unpublished.

Welch, H. and Welch, G. (1984b) Djibouti Expedition – March 1984. Outline report 1. Unpublished.

Welch, G. and Welch, H. (in press) The Djibouti Francolin. [*World Pheasant Association Journal*.]

MOUNT CAMEROON FRANCOLIN   RARE
Francolinus camerunensis Alexander, 1909

Order GALLIFORMES   Family PHASIANIDAE
                                                  Subfamily PHASIANINAE

Summary This shy francolin is only known from montane forest on Mount Cameroon, where a recent ICBP survey has shown it to be still common, despite hunting pressure.

Distribution This francolin, endemic to Cameroon, is known only from the slopes of Mount Cameroon between 850 and 2,100 m (Serle 1965, SNS). It was discovered in 1909 at 2,100 m above Musake (Alexander 1909, Bannerman 1915) and further specimens were taken in the same year above Buea (Bannerman 1930), both localities being on the south-eastern slopes of the mountain. Subsequent field observations were made or specimens collected above Buea in 1934 (Boulton and Rand 1952), 1954 (Eisentraut 1956) and 1956 (Serle 1965). Birds were also heard on the south-western slopes of the mountain above Isongo in 1938 (Eisentraut 1963). Several birds, almost certainly this species, were heard on the mountain slopes above Buea in 1971 (Grimes 1971) and two birds were seen at the same locality in 1976 and 1979 (D. A. Turner *in litt.* 1983, A. D. Forbes-Watson pers. comm. 1984). In 1983 during an ICBP survey of the mountain the species was heard on several occasions over 2,000 m in the forest above Buea (SNS) and one bird was seen (M. E. Gartshore pers. comm. 1984); survey of the forest on the southern slopes of the mountain in early 1984 showed that the species ranges widely down to an elevation of 850 m (SNS), and birds were also then heard on the north-eastern slopes of the mountain (M. O. Fedden and H. L. Macleod pers. comm. 1984).

Population In 1984 the ICBP Cameroon Montane Forest Survey showed that this species is common, especially on the southern slopes of Mount Cameroon (SNS).

Ecology This species inhabits dense undergrowth in both primary and secondary montane forest, apparently avoiding montane grassland (Serle 1965). It also occurs in forest clearings (SNS). Birds usually occur in pairs or small parties and have sand baths in the sun (Serle 1962,1965). The diet includes berries, grass seeds, insects and grit and there is evidence of breeding activity in November after the rains (Serle 1981): in January 1984 good views were had of ten birds, including four chicks, on the southern slopes of the mountain (M. E. Gartshore pers. comm. 1984). The birds are very shy and difficult to observe in the forest undergrowth (Eisentraut 1956, Serle 1962,1965) but when flushed by hunters' dogs they often perch in trees, allowing a good view (Serle 1962,1965). Also, the species can readily be detected in the evenings by its loud call (SNS). It has a slight distributional overlap with the Scaly Francolin *Francolinus squamatus*, which is a lower altitude bird on Mount Cameroon (Serle 1965).

Threats The main threat to this species is probably from hunting (SNS).

Hunters apparently catch the birds on the ground in gin-traps (Eisentraut 1956, Serle 1965) as well as with shotguns and hunting dogs (W. Serle *in litt.* 1983). There is little evidence, however, of a population decline and it is likely that the species can withstand the existing hunting pressure (SNS). It might be more at risk from the periodic eruptions of Mount Cameroon's volcano, and in 1982 a large area of suitable habitat was destroyed by a lava flow (SNS).

Conservation Measures Taken None is known.

Conservation Measures Proposed A stricter conservation policy is needed for Mount Cameroon, especially for the forests of the southern slopes where several rare species occur. The ICBP Cameroon Montane Forest Survey is preparing a preliminary conservation plan for Mount Cameroon for the consideration of the Cameroon government.

Remarks The Mount Cameroon Francolin forms a superspecies with six other montane francolins, including two other threatened species, the Djibouti Francolin *Francolinus ochropectus* and Swierstra's Francolin *F. swierstrai* (see relevant accounts). The forests of Mount Cameroon are important for the survival of many bird species, including the threatened Green-breasted Bush-shrike *Malaconotus gladiator* and the Grey-necked Picarthartes *Picathartes oreas* (see relevant accounts). It is also likely that Bates's Weaver *Ploceus batesi* occurs in the lowland forest at the southern foot of the mountain and there is even an anomalous record of Monteiro's Bush-shrike *Malaconotus monteiri* from Buea (see relevant accounts). Four species in Appendix C, the Cameroon Mountain Roughwing *Psalidoprocne fuliginosa*, the Cameroon Mountain Greenbul *Andropadus montanus*, the Grey-headed Greenbul *Phyllastrephus poliocephalus*, and Ursula's Mouse-coloured Sunbird *Nectarinia ursulae*, occur on Mount Cameroon.

References

Alexander, B. (1909) [New species ... discovered on the Peak of Cameroon.] *Bull. Brit. Orn. Club* 25: 12-13.

Bannerman, D. A. (1915) A report on the birds collected by the late Mr Boyd Alexander (Rifle Brigade) during his last expedition to Africa. Part IV: the birds of Cameroon Mountain. *Ibis* (10)3: 473-526.

Bannerman, D. A. (1930) *The birds of tropical West Africa*, 1. London: Crown Agents for the Colonies.

Boulton, R. and Rand, A. L. (1952) A collection of birds from Mount Cameroun. *Fieldiana Zool.* 34: 35-64.

Eisentraut, M. (1956) Notizen über einige Vögel des Kamerungebirges. *J. Orn.* 97: 291-300.

Eisentraut, M. (1963) *Die Wirbeltiere des Kamerungebirges.* Hamburg and Berlin: Paul Parey.

Grimes, L. G. (1971) Notes on some birds seen at Buea and on Mount Cameroun, 30 Dec. 1970 – Jan. 1971. *Bull. Nigerian Orn. Soc.* 8: 35-41.

Serle, W. (1962) The Cameroon Mountain Francolin *Francolinus camerunensis* Alex. *Nigerian Field* 27: 34-36.

Serle, W. (1965) A third contribution to the ornithology of the British Cameroons. Part I. *Ibis* 107: 60-94.

Serle, W. (1981) The breeding season of birds in the lowland rainforest and in the montane forest of West Cameroon. *Ibis* 123: 62-74.

SWIERSTRA'S FRANCOLIN   INDETERMINATE
Francolinus swierstrai (Roberts, 1929)

Order GALLIFORMES   Family PHASIANIDAE
                                             Subfamily PHASIANINAE

Summary This francolin is restricted to the mountains of western Angola where it might be threatened by forest destruction, though it has been found outside forest in various habitats.

Distribution Swierstra's Francolin is restricted to the mountains of western Angola. The type-specimen was collected on the Mombolo Plateau in 1927 (Roberts 1929, Hall and Moreau 1962) and another bird was taken at Hanha on the Angolan escarpment in 1935 (Themido 1937, Hall and Moreau 1962). In 1954 seven specimens were collected in the Bailundu (Bailundo) Highlands, three of these being from Mount Moco and four from Mount Soque (Heinrich 1958, Traylor 1960). In 1956 the species was discovered in a patch of relict forest on the Chela escarpment in Huila District 320 km to the south (Hall and Moreau 1962). Two more specimens were taken on Mount Moco in 1957 (Hall 1960) and four were collected at Tundavala in Huila District in 1962 and subsequent years (Pinto in press). In 1971 two birds were collected at Cariango in Cuanza Sul District, 200 km to the north of the known range (Pinto in press).

Population Numbers are not known, though it is apparently rare (Pinto 1970, in press).

Ecology All records of this species are from montane areas, mainly from forest and forest edge (Heinrich 1958, Hall 1960, Hall and Moreau 1962, Pinto 1970, in press). There are, however, records from rocky and grassy mountainsides (Traylor 1963), tall grass savannas on mountain tops (Heinrich 1958) and gullies (Heinrich 1958). It is not clear, therefore, to what extent this is a forest-dependent species: one observer has the impression it is "intimately linked to stony areas" (A. A. da Rosa Pinto *in litt.* 1983). When found in forest it keeps to areas of dense undergrowth, consisting of bushes, shrubs, grasses and large ferns (Heinrich 1958, Traylor 1963, Pinto 1970, in press). When disturbed, birds either run for dense cover or take flight and alight in trees (Pinto in press). They feed on insects and seeds from legumes and grasses which are obtained by searching among fallen leaves on the forest floor (Pinto in press). Information on breeding is scanty (Pinto in press): one male collected in September was observed displaying and had enlarged testes (Heinrich 1958); a female taken in March had ovaries beginning to enlarge and evidence from specimens collected in August suggests a breeding season in May or June (Pinto in press).

Threats If this species depends at all on forest it is likely to be seriously threatened by forest destruction. Much of the montane forest in Angola has been destroyed and it was suggested in 1962 that suitable habitat might be limited to "a few square miles" on the highest peaks in the Bailundu Highlands and to even smaller areas on the escarpment (Hall and Moreau 1962). The species was subsequently discovered further north at Cariango (Pinto in press; see Distribution) but it remains likely that the total area occupied is dangerously small. It is not known if the species is under threat from hunting, but the likelihood should be taken very seriously (A. A. da Rosa Pinto *in litt.* 1983).

Conservation Measures Taken Swierstra's Francolin is listed on Appendix II of CITES, to which, however, Angola is not a party nor was ever even a signatory (*contra* King 1978-1979).

Conservation Measures Proposed A survey is urgently needed to determine the distribution, population and habitat requirements of this species. If it is found to depend on montane forest, suitable nature reserves should be established. It would also be desirable to establish captive breeding populations of this species.

Remarks Swierstra's Francolin is the most distinct member of a large superspecies of montane francolins (Hall 1963) including two other threatened species, the Mount Cameroon Francolin *Francolinus camerunensis* and the Djibouti Francolin *F. ochropectus* (see relevant accounts). *Francolinus cruzi*, described in 1937 (Themido 1937), has been shown to be a synonym of Swierstra's Francolin (White 1945).

References

Hall, B. P. (1960) The ecology and taxonomy of some Angolan birds (based on a collection made in 1957). *Bull. Brit. Mus. (Nat. Hist.) Zool.* 6: 367-453.

Hall, B. P. (1963) The francolins, a study in speciation. *Bull. Brit. Mus. (Nat. Hist.) Zool.* 10: 105-204.

Hall, B. P. and Moreau, R. E. (1962) A study of the rare birds of Africa. *Bull. Brit. Mus. (Nat. Hist.) Zool.* 8: 313-378.

Heinrich, G. H. (1958) Zur Verbreitung und Lebensweise der Vögel von Angola. Part 2. *J. Orn.* 99: 322-362.

King, W. B. (1978-1979) *Red data book, 2: Aves.* 2nd edition. Morges, Switzerland: IUCN.

Pinto, A. A. da R. (1970) Um catálago das aves do distrito da Huila (Angola). *Mem. Trab. Inst. Cient. Angola* no. 6.

Pinto, A. A. da R. (in press) *Ornitologia de Angola*, 1. Lisbon.

Roberts, A. (1929) New forms of African birds. *Ann. Transvaal Mus.* 13: 71-81.

Themido, A. (1937) Un nouveau *Francolinus* de l'Angola. *C. R. 12th Congr. Int. Zool., Lisboa 1935*: 1833-1834.

Traylor, M. A. (1960) Notes on the birds of Angola, non-passeres. *Publ. cult. Co. Diam. Angola, Lisboa* no. 51: 129-186.

Traylor, M. A. (1963) Check-list of the birds of Angola. *Publ. cult. Co. Diam. Angola, Lisboa* no. 61.

White, C. M. N. (1945) Three recently described game birds from Angola. *Ibis* 87: 466-467.

NAHAN'S FRANCOLIN   RARE
Francolinus nahani Dubois, 1905

Order GALLIFORMES   Family PHASIANIDAE
                                                 Subfamily PHASIANINAE

Summary This rare francolin is known only from a few localities in lowland forest in eastern Zaire and central and western Uganda. There is little recent information on its status.

Distribution Nahan's Francolin is only known from the Ituri Forest and the Semliki Valley in eastern Zaire and a few localities in western Uganda. The type-specimen, described in 1905, was collected at Popoie, in the western Ituri Forest, on the south side of the Aruwimi River between Panga and Banalia (Dubois 1905, Chapin 1932). Another early specimen was collected at Lesse in the Semliki Valley (Schouteden 1918,1968). In 1910 a bird was taken at Gamangui, 140 km east of Popoie (Chapin 1932). More recent Zaire specimens have been collected as follows: two from the Semliki Valley in 1952, one of these being from Nailube and the other from Kisayi (specimens in IRSNB: SNS); one from Yangambi in 1954 (specimen in IRSNB: SNS); one from Irumu in 1956 (specimen in MNHN: SNS); two from Alima (0°57'N 29°18'E: A. Prigogine *in litt.* 1983) in 1960 (specimens in MRAC: SNS); four from the Mambasa area, three of these being collected around "Lima" (= Alima) in 1961 (specimens in MRAC: SNS) and the fourth, without date, from Butsha (Schouteden 1963). In Uganda the species was discovered in the Mabira Forest, east of Kampala, in 1913 (van Someren 1916). At least five specimens were collected at this locality in 1913 and another one in 1914 (van Someren 1916; specimens in BMNH: SNS). In western Uganda the species was found around this time in the Bugoma Forest, where at least eight birds were collected (Jackson 1938), and in the Budongo Forest (van Someren 1922, Chapin 1932, Jackson 1938). The only subsequent Uganda records are two specimens from Budongo Forest, one collected in 1963 (Friedmann 1966) and one in 1970 (Friedmann and Williams 1973). Its altitudinal range in Uganda is from 1,000 to 1,400 m (Britton 1980).

Population Numbers are not known. The small number of collected specimens is an indication that it is rare.

Ecology All records of this species have been from lowland rainforest (van Someren 1916, Chapin 1932, Jackson 1938, Friedmann 1966, Friedmann and Williams 1973). They are usually found in pairs, often in the company of guineafowl (Numididae) (van Someren 1916,1918). The food consists of seeds, insects, small molluscs, green shoots and bulbs which they obtain by scraping through dead leaves on the forest floor (van Someren 1918,1926, Friedmann 1966). In Bugoma Forest eight specimens were obtained by sprinkling grain on a forest track (Jackson 1938, Britton 1980).

Threats This species is presumably declining due to forest destruction but also hunting (A. Prigogine *in litt.* 1981).

Conservation Measures Taken The population in the Semliki Valley, eastern Zaire, is within the Virunga National Park (Prigogine in press), but none of the other sites from which the species has been recorded is protected.

Conservation Measures Proposed This species would be best protected if the northern section of the Virunga National Park were extended westwards to include the eastern part of the Ituri Forest (Prigogine in press). Stricter forest conservation measures are also required in Uganda and there should be a survey to ascertain whether this species occurs more widely in the western Ugandan forests.

Remarks This very distinct species is sometimes included in its own monotypic genus *Acentrortyx* (Chapin 1926). The Ituri Forest is important for three other threatened bird species, the Forest Ground Thrush *Turdus oberlaenderi*, the Golden-naped Weaver *Ploceus aureonucha* and the Yellow-legged Weaver *P. flavipes* (see relevant accounts). It is also important for several species treated in Appendix C.

References

Britton, P. L. ed. (1980) *Birds of East Africa: their habitat, status and distribution.* Nairobi: EANHS.

Chapin, J. P. (1926) A new genus, *Acentrortyx*, proposed for *Francolinus nahani* Dubois. *Auk* 43: 235.

Chapin, J. P. (1932) The birds of the Belgian Congo. Part 1. *Bull. Amer. Mus. Nat. Hist.* 65.

Dubois, A. (1905) Remarques sur l'ornithologie de l'état independant du Congo, suivies d'une liste des espèces recueillies jusqu'ici dans cet état. *Ann. Mus. Congo, Zool.* (4)1: 1-36.

Friedmann, H. (1966) A contribution to the ornithology of Uganda. *Bull. Los Angeles County Mus. Nat. Hist., Sciences* 3: 1-55.

Friedmann, H. and Williams, J. G. (1973) The birds of Budongo Forest, Bunyoro Province, Uganda. *J. E. Afr. Nat. Hist. Soc. and Natn. Mus.* 141: 1-18.

Jackson, F. J. (1938) *The birds of Kenya Colony and Uganda Protectorate*, 1. London: Gurney and Jackson.

Prigogine, A. (in press) The conservation of the avifauna of the forests of the Albertine Rift. *Proceedings of the ICBP Tropical Forest Bird Symposium, 1982.*

Schouteden, H. (1918) Contribution à la faune ornithologique de la région des lacs de l'Afrique Centrale. *Rev. Zool. Afr.* 5: 209-297.

Schouteden, H. (1963) La faune ornithologique du District de l'Ituri. *Doc. Zool. Mus. Afr. Centr.* 5.

Schouteden, H. (1968) La faune ornithologique du Kivu 1. Non passereaux. *Doc. Zool. Mus. Roy. Afr. Centr.* 12.

van Someren, V. G. L. (1916) A list of birds collected in Uganda and British East Africa, with notes on their nesting and other habits. Part 1. *Ibis* (10)4: 193-252.

van Someren, V. G. L. (1918) Another rare forest francolin *Francolinus nahani* Dubois (Type locality – Ituri Forest, Congo). *J. E. Afr. Uganda Nat. Hist. Soc.* 6(18): 199-200.

van Someren, V. G. L. (1922) Notes on the birds of East Africa. *Novit. Zool.* 29: 1-246.

van Someren, V. G. L. (1926) The birds of Kenya and Uganda. Part III. *J. E. Afr. Uganda Nat. Hist. Soc.* 7(25): 29-60.

CONGO PEACOCK

Afropavo congensis Chapin, 1936

Order GALLIFORMES

OF SPECIAL CONCERN

Family PHASIANIDAE
Subfamily PHASIANINAE

Summary This shy, ground-haunting pheasant is known from a wide area of equatorial rainforest in eastern Zaire. It appears to be in no immediate danger but it is uncommon, has disappeared from the vicinity of human settlements and faces the potential threat of forest clearance.

Distribution The Congo Peacock is endemic to Zaire. A feather from Avakubi in the Ituri Forest was the first record and, following the description of the type-material, which probably derived from the southern edge of the equatorial forest (see Remarks), other records of the bird soon came to light: one had been eaten at Angumu, 170 km south of Avakubi, in 1930 (Chapin 1936,1937, 1938,1948), in 1931 one was shot 50 km south of Stanleyville, and many years earlier one was skinned at Inkongo near Lusambo, at the southern edge of the rainforest (Schouteden 1937, Chapin 1948). Within a few years of its discovery it was clear that the species occurred widely through the south-eastern corner of the equatorial rainforest belt, in central and eastern Zaire (Chapin 1948,1954, Hostie 1955a). Three detailed reviews of its distribution have been published (Prigogine 1956, Verheyen 1963c,1965a), the last of which listed it from at least 45 localities (Verheyen 1965a). The southern limit of its distribution is set by the southern boundary of the equatorial rainforest belt (Prigogine 1956, Cordier 1959, Verheyen 1963c,1965a) and in the east it ranges up to the foothills of the Albertine Rift mountains where it occurs at middle altitudes up to 1,200 m (Prigogine 1953,1956,1971, Verheyen 1963c,1965a). In the west it has not been found beyond a line between Monkoto, Lofima and Yahuma (Prigogine 1956, Verheyen 1963c,1965a) and its northern boundary appears to be set by the lower Aruwimi River (Chapin 1954, Prigogine 1956, Cordier 1959, Verheyen 1963c). It has only been found in the southernmost part of the Ituri Forest (Chapin 1954, Prigogine 1956, Verheyen 1963c,1965a). The species is absent from the northern and western parts of the rainforest belt and it has been suggested that this is due to excessive hunting pressure (Chapin 1948,1954). This idea has not, however, found wide acceptance (Cordier 1959, Verheyen 1963c) and a more likely explanation is competition with the Black Guineafowl *Agelastes niger* (Snow 1978). This latter species occurs widely in the northern and western parts of the rainforest belt and, although the two species overlap in the southern Ituri Forest, they are largely allopatric (Snow 1978). While the Congo Peacock is quite widely distributed, it appears to be of patchy occurrence and absent from large areas of seemingly suitable habitat, even within its geographical range (Verheyen 1965a). It has certainly disappeared from areas around villages, presumably due to hunting (Prigogine 1953,1956,1971, Cordier 1959, Verheyen 1965a). During the last 20 years there has been little ornithological fieldwork within the range of this species and there is no recent assessment of its status.

Population Numbers are not known. It must be an uncommon bird to have eluded detection for so long and most reports of the species refer to it as being rare (see Verheyen 1965a). It is, however, a very secretive bird and its abundance may be underestimated.

Ecology All reports are from lowland and intermediate altitude rainforests, where it lives on the forest floor (Chapin 1948,1954, Cordier 1949a,b,1959, Hostie 1955a,b, Prigogine 1956,1971, Verheyen 1963c,1965a). It prefers forest with a light understorey, although it does not avoid patches of high secondary growth within primary forest, and also seems to prefer flat terrain but avoids the lowest areas, especially places liable to flooding (Cordier 1959; also Verheyen 1965a). It is apparently more numerous in the south of its range in Kasai Province, where the forests grow on sandy soils and have a lighter physiognomy, than in the east of its range in Kivu Province, where the forests are much denser and wetter, growing on clay (Cordier 1959, Verheyen 1965a). The birds are generally quiet, and very shy, occurring in groups of 2-3, possibly larger during the breeding season (Chapin 1948, Cordier 1959, Prigogine 1971). They roost in trees at night (Chapin 1948, Cordier 1959, Verheyen 1965a) and if chased by dogs they also fly up into the trees (Prigogine 1971). They apparently feed on the ground (Prigogine 1971), spending much time under fruiting trees (Cordier 1959). The diet is very varied, including fruits of "gringi" trees and *Strombosia grandiflora*, and grains of *Sapium ellopticum*, *Xymales monospora* and *Caesalpina sepiara* (Cordier 1959, Verheyen 1965a, Prigogine 1971). The birds also eat insects, including termites (adults and larvae), the ant *Pallothyreus tarsatus*, and even an aquatic whirligig beetle *Orectopyrus* (Hostie 1955b, Prigogine 1956,1971, Verheyen 1965a). The birds might breed at any time of year although there are apparently variations due to local differences in the rainfall regime (Verheyen 1965a). In some areas breeding takes place between mid-January and May, while in others it has been recorded in September and October (Verheyen 1965a); 300 km south of the equator young birds were found only in January/February (Cordier 1959). Nests are reported by locals to be placed on the ground, e.g. between a large tree's buttress roots or close against a fallen trunk (Cordier 1959). The clutch-size is thought to be 3-6, with 2-3 young normally surviving per brood (Verheyen 1965a), but clutches of 5-9 are also claimed, with a sighting of a female with five chicks (Cordier 1959). Birds usually call in moonlight, between 19.00 and 20.00 hrs (Verheyen 1965a, Prigogine 1971): male and female sometimes duet (Cordier 1959; also Chapin 1948), and calling is often responded to by other birds or pairs throughout the forest, although never from the same place or in the same direction on successive nights, calling generally occurring on only 2-3 nights per week (Cordier 1959). Birds appear to be great wanderers through the forest (Cordier 1959).

Threats The main threat to this species appears to be hunting (Prigogine 1953,1971, Cordier 1959, Verheyen 1965a). In many areas it has disappeared over distances of up to 25 km from each village, road and track (Cordier 1959, Verheyen 1965a). It has declined in parts of the western foothills of the mountains west of Lake Edward (Prigogine 1953) and is now completely absent from the foothills of the Itombwe Mountains, except in a small area near Kilemue (Prigogine 1971). The species is held in high regard in certain tribal cultures (Cordier 1959, Verheyen 1965a) but birds are nevertheless caught in nets and snares set up primarily for catching duikers (Cephalophinae) and guineafowl (Phasianidae: Numidinae) (Prigogine 1953,1971, Cordier 1959, Verheyen 1965a). Consumption of birds caught incidentally appeared to be fairly common at one site in eastern Zaire in 1978 (A. D. Forbes-Watson pers. comm. 1984). The cost in terms of birds lost while attempting to obtain specimens for zoological collections has been high (see Cordier 1959). Forest clearance is not yet very severe within the range of the Congo Peacock (Prigogine in press), but this is certainly a likely threat in the future.

Conservation Measures Taken This species was given full protection by Zairean law in 1938, only two years after its discovery, special permits being required to collect specimens for zoos or museums (Chapin 1953, Cordier 1959, Verheyen 1965a). It is included in the latest list of protected species (law no. 82-002 of 28 May 1982), as a result of which it can only be collected by the holder of a scientific permit (A. Prigogine *in litt.* 1983). The species is known to occur in the Maiko National Park in eastern Zaire (Verschuren 1975, Prigogine in press), has been reported from near Ikali in the south of the huge Salonga National Park (Verschuren 1978), and might also be found in the western part of the Kahuzi-Biega National Park. The Congo Peacock was first held in captivity in about 1940 when up to six birds were kept at Ikela on the Tshuapa River in central Zaire (Chapin 1942,1954). The first specimens to be exhibited outside Africa were taken to NYZS in 1949 (Cordier 1949a,1949b,1959, Crandall 1949). Most of the birds at present in captivity are descendants of birds originally brought to the Antwerp Zoo between 1957 and 1962 (Cordier 1959, Verheyen 1963a,b). Breeding success of the Congo Peacock in captivity was initially very poor (Verheyen 1963a,1965a,b) but after extensive research much better results have now been achieved at Antwerp Zoo (van der Bergh 1975). Several breeding loans have been made from Antwerp to various other zoos (van der Bergh 1975). Details of the captive population between 1962 and 1981 are given in the table below (data compiled from *Internat. Zoo Yearbooks* 4-22 [1963-1982]. It is to be hoped that viable populations of this species will be established in zoos other than Antwerp, thus rendering the captive population less vulnerable to epidemics (van der Bergh 1975).

Conservation Measures Proposed A survey is needed to make a detailed up-to-date assessment of the status of this species. If the Maiko, Salonga and Kahuzi-Biega National Parks are adequately protected, and hunting pressures are kept to a minimum, it is possible that viable populations of this species will be preserved.

Remarks This and the Ethiopian Bush-crow *Zavattariornis stresemanni* (see relevant account) may be judged to represent the two most remarkable ornithological discoveries made in Africa this century. It is a mystery how the Congo Peacock remained undiscovered for so long. The first hint that there might be a large gallinaceous bird in the Zaire rainforests came in 1913 when J. P. Chapin collected a feather from the hat of a local African at Avakubi in the Ituri Forest, but it was not until 1936 that he found two specimens of the species, mounted in a

The number of Congo Peacocks in zoological collections between 1962 and 1981 (no data for 1963)

Zoo	1962	1964	1965	1966	1967	1968	1969	1970	1971	1972
1	7	8(3)	5	14(9)	24(19)	30(28)	34(33)	43(42)	35(35)	29(28)
2					1					
3	1		2							4(4)
4	1	1	1	1	1	1	1	1	1	1
5					1(1)	1(1)	1(1)	1	1	1
6	1									
7										4(4)
8									1(1)	2(2)
9		2	2	1	1	1				
10										
11									2(2)	1(1)
12	1	1	1	1	1	1	1	1(1)	1	1
TOTAL	11	12(3)	11	17(9)	29(20)	34(29)	37(34)	46(43)	41(38)	43(39)

Zoo	1973	1974	1975	1976	1977	1978	1979	1980	1981
1	31(30)	34(32)	36(34)	31(29)	27(25)	30(28)	36(35)	38(37)	26(25)
2									
3	2(2)								
4			1(1)	1(1)	1(1)	2(2)	5(5)	6(6)	7(7)
5	2	2	2	1	1	1	1	1(1)	1(1)
6									
7	4(4)	4(4)	4(4)	3(3)	4(4)	4(4)	3(3)	6(6)	6(6)
8	3(3)	2(2)	2(2)						
9									2(2)
10								2(2)	2(2)
11	?	1(1)	1(1)	?	1(1)	1(1)	2(2)	1(1)	?
12									
TOTAL	42(39)	43(39)	46(42)	36(33)	34(31)	38(35)	47(45)	54(53)	44(43)

Key to table: Figures not in brackets are the total number of Congo Peacocks in a given zoo in a given year. Figures in brackets refer to birds bred and reared in captivity. The code for zoos is as follows.

1. Antwerp, Belgium
2. Basle, Switzerland
3. Clères, France
4. Copenhagen, Denmark
5. Dallas, U.S.A.
6. Frankfurt, West Germany
7. JWPT, U.K.
8. London, U.K.
9. NYZS (Bronx Zoo), U.S.A.
10. Rotterdam, Netherlands
11. Walsrode, West Germany
12. West Berlin, West Germany

185

cabinet in MRAC (Chapin 1936,1937,1938,1948). These two specimens, one of which was designated as the type, had been donated to MRAC in 1914, and were probably collected near the southern edge of the equatorial rainforest; they had been wrongly identified as the Blue Peacock *Pavo cristatus* from India and were assumed to be birds escaped from captivity (Chapin 1936,1937,1938,1948). The Congo Peacock is in fact the only true pheasant that occurs in Africa (Chapin 1936, Verheyen 1965a, Snow 1978), taxonomic studies having shown that it is not particularly close to the guineafowl (Numidinae) but rather to the pheasants (Phasianinae), especially to the peacocks *Pavo* of Asia (Chapin 1936,1954, Lowe 1938, Gysels and Rabaey 1962, Durrer and Villiger 1975).

References

van der Bergh, W. (1975) Breeding the Congo Peacock at the Royal Zoological Society of Antwerp. Pp. 75-86 in R. D. Martin, ed. *Breeding endangered species in captivity*, London: Academic Press.

Chapin, J. P. (1936) A new peacock-like bird from the Belgian Congo. *Rev. Zool. Bot. Afr.* 29: 1-6.

Chapin, J. P. (1937) The discovery of *Afropavo congensis*. *Bull. Brit. Orn. Club* 57: 84-86.

Chapin, J. P. (1938) The Congo Peacock. *Proc. IX Internat. Orn. Congr.*: 101-109.

Chapin, J. P. (1942) The Congo Peacock in captivity. *Avicult. Mag.* (5)7: 123-124.

Chapin, J. P. (1948) How the Congo Peacock was discovered. *Animal Kingdom* 51: 67-73.

Chapin, J. P. (1953) Protection of birds in the Congo. *Troisième Conférence Internationale pour la Protection de la Faune et de la Flore, Bukavu, Congo Belge*: 366-371.

Chapin, J. P. (1954) The birds of the Belgian Congo. Part 4. *Bull. Amer. Mus. Nat. Hist.* 75B.

Cordier, C. (1949a) Further adventures of Charles Cordier. *Animal Kingdom* 52: 2-9, 28-29.

Cordier, C. (1949b) Our Belgian Congo expedition comes home. *Animal Kingdom* 52: 99-114, 134-136.

Cordier, C. (1959) Betrachtungen über den Kongo-Pfau (*Afropavo congensis*). *Gefied. Welt* 10: 181-186.

Crandall, L. S. (1949) The Congo Peacock in captivity. *Avicult. Mag.* 55: 208.

Durrer, H. and Villiger, W. (1975) Schillerstruktur des Kongopfaus (*Afropavo congensis* Chapin 1936) im Elektronenmikroskop. *J. Orn.* 116: 94-102.

Gysels, H. and Rabaey, M. (1962) Taxonomic relationships of *Afropavo congensis* Chapin 1936 by means of biochemical techniques. *Bull. Soc. Roy. Zool. Anvers* 26: 71-79.

Hostie, P. (1955a) Note sur le Paon Congolais *Afropavo congensis* Chapin 1936. *Bull. Corps. Lieut. Hon. Chasse Congo Belge* IV (16): 164-166.

Hostie, P. (1955b) *Afropavo congensis* Chapin. *Gerfaut* 45: 82-84.

Lowe, P. R. (1938) Some preliminary notes on the anatomy and systematic position of *Afropavo congensis* Chapin. *Proc. IX Internat. Orn. Congr.*: 219-230.

Prigogine, A. (1953) Contribution à l'étude de la faune ornithologique de la région à l'ouest du lac Edouard. *Ann. Mus. Roy. Congo Belge* 8°, Sci. Zool. 24: 1-117.

Prigogine, A. (1956) Distribution de l'*Afropavo congensis* Chapin. *Bull. Corps. Lieut. Hon. Chasse Congo Belge* V (18): 249-252.

Prigogine, A. (1971) Les oiseaux de l'Itombwe et de son hinterland. Volume I. *Ann. Mus. Roy. Afr. Centr.* 8°, Sci. Zool. 185: 1-298.

Prigogine, A. (in press) The conservation of the avifauna of the forests of the Albertine Rift. *Proceedings of the ICBP Tropical Forest Bird Symposium, 1982.*

Schouteden, H. (1937) A propos du Paon Congolais. *Bull. Séances Inst. Roy. Colonial Belge* 8: 578-583.

Snow, D. W. ed. (1978) *An atlas of speciation in African non-passerine birds.* London: Trustees of the British Museum (Natural History).

Verheyen, W. (1963a) The Congo Peacock *Afropavo congensis* Chapin 1936 at Antwerp Zoo. *Internat. Zoo Yearbook* 4: 87-91.

Verheyen, W. N. (1963b) Monographie du Paon Congolais *Afropavo congensis* Chapin 1936. 1. Introduction. *Bull. Soc. Roy. Zool. Anvers* 26: 3-6.

Verheyen, W. N. (1963c) Quelques données concernant le dimorphisme sexuel, la distribution géographique d'*Afropavo congensis* Chapin, ainsi qu'un essai de bibliographie générale. *Bull. Soc. Roy. Zool. Anvers* 26: 7-15.

Verheyen, W. N. (1965a) *Der Kongopfau (Afropavo congensis Chapin, 1936).* (Die Neue Brehm Bucherei – Heft 351.) Wittenburg Lutherstadt: A. Ziemsen.

Verheyen, W. N. (1965b) Breeding the Congo Peacock at Antwerp Zoo. *Internat. Zoo Yearbook* 5: 127-128.

Verschuren, J. (1975) Wildlife in Zaire. *Oryx* 13: 25-33, 149-163.

Verschuren, J. (1978) Observations ornithologiques dans les parcs nationaux du Zaire, 1968 – 1974. *Gerfaut* 68: 3-24.

WHITE-BREASTED GUINEAFOWL   ENDANGERED
Agelastes meleagrides Bonaparte, 1850

Order GALLIFORMES   Family PHASIANIDAE
                                              Subfamily NUMIDINAE

Summary This is one of the most threatened birds in continental Africa, now extinct through most of its former range as a result of hunting and alteration to its primary rainforest habitat. It possibly now survives only in Liberia and Ivory Coast and a captive breeding programme may be necessary to ensure its long-term survival.

Distribution The White-breasted Guineafowl may now survive in viable numbers only in one or two adjacent areas of Liberia and Ivory Coast, having once occurred throughout the rainforest zone of the Upper Guinea region between Sierra Leone and Ghana. The species might occur, or at least might have occurred, in the rainforest zone of southern Guinea bordering Sierra Leone, Liberia and Ivory Coast, but there are no known records. However, an early record from Gabon (Du Chaillu 1861) is apparently in error (Bannerman 1930).

Ghana The type-specimen was collected at Dabocrom in Ghana (specimen in RMNH: NJC) and there are subsequent nineteenth century records from Dabocrom, Denkera and Elmina (Hartlaub 1855, Bannerman 1930, Bouet 1955). In the early 1950s, however, it was considered to be probably extinct in these areas (Bannerman 1953). A group of 4-5 birds was seen two miles west of the Tano River, near Bopa, in Sefine District in 1930 (Bannerman 1951,1953) and a bird was collected in 1930 in the Enchi Forest (specimen in BMNH: SNS). In 1940 a group was seen near Axim and in 1953 another group was observed in the Bia National Park (M. Horwood *per* L. G. Grimes *in litt.* 1983). Two birds were captured at an unspecified locality in Ghana, probably in 1962 or 1963, and sent to the West Berlin Zoo (Raethel 1965) but there appear to be no subsequent Ghanaian records of the species, despite thorough searches by several ornithologists (M. A. Macdonald *in litt.* 1983, I. R. Taylor pers. comm. 1983).

Ivory Coast The presence of this species in Ivory Coast has been very poorly documented. The earliest record appears to be of a specimen collected in 1929 (Bouet 1955). One was also collected from a flock of a dozen birds at Kpapekou in North Gagnoa District in 1960 (Pfeffer 1961). In 1963 two birds were collected from a group of about 30 at Guoyo (specimens in ZMA: NJC). Other localities from which the species has been collected, mainly between 1965 and 1969, are Guiglo, Sinfra, Dalao, Lamto and at Kandje near Lake Potou (Bouet 1955, Brunel and Thiollay 1969, J.-M. Thiollay *in litt.* 1983). Several observations were made at unspecified localities in 1962 and 1963 (Bechinger 1964) and between 1968 and 1973 the species was seen or heard daily in the Tai National Park (J.-M. Thiollay *in litt.* 1983) but there is little subsequent information on its status in Ivory Coast.

Liberia The species probably once occurred throughout Liberia (Johnston 1906). In the 1880s one specimen was collected at Sofore (Büttikofer 1885), a few more at Schieffelin (Büttikofer 1888), eight at Mount Gallilee, probably all from one flock (Büttikofer 1889), and 20 (possibly including the eight from Mount Gallilee) from the Farmington River (Büttikofer 1890). One specimen was taken along the St.Paul River in 1904 or 1905 (Johnston 1905). It is, however, probably extinct in all these areas (Forbes-Watson undated). In the 1960s the species was collected at Suehn in Maserrado County and Geatown in Grand Gedeh County (Schouteden 1970) and in 1978 along the Cavally River bordering Ivory Coast (specimen in BMNH: SNS). The species used to occur at Mount Nimba but rapidly became extinct when the area was opened up for mining in the late 1950s and early 1960s (Forbes-Watson undated, Colston and Curry Lindahl in press). Observations made in recent years show that the species still survives in the south-east of Liberia (W. Gatter *in litt.* 1983). Birds have been seen in Sapo National Park in Sinoe County, in the north of Maryland County, and in Grebo National Forest in the south of Grand Gedeh County (W. Gatter *in litt.* 1983). In this last locality birds, including chicks, have been seen on several occasions and two specimens were bought from local hunters (W. Gatter *in litt.* 1983).

Sierra Leone A family party was caught in the Gola Forest in the late 1960s for live export but it is not known what became of these birds (G. D. Field pers comm. 1983). Two birds were seen in December 1984 on Tiwai Island in the Moa River (c. 5 km from Gola Forest) (G. Davies *in litt.* 1984). There appear to be no other records.

Population Numbers are not known, though the contraction of the species's geographical range suggests a dramatic population crash. The species might now be extinct in Ghana and Sierra Leone. It has apparently always been a very rare bird, generally occurring at low densities (Büttikofer 1885,1888,1889, Bannerman 1930,1953, Bouet 1955, Raethel 1965, J.-M. Thiollay *in litt.* 1982, Forbes-Watson undated). One observer, who travelled over 24,000 km in Ghana and hunted a great deal in the forest, saw only one flock of 4-5 birds, in 1930 (Bannerman 1951). Another observer spent 19 years in the forest zone of Ghana but saw the species on only two occasions (M. Horwood *per* L. G. Grimes *in litt.* 1983). During the 1970s several ornithologists searched for this species in Ghana (I. R. Taylor pers. comm. 1983) and another observer looked for it for 16 years in Sierra Leone in the 1960s and 1970s (G. D. Field pers comm. 1983) but all were unsuccessful. In contrast to most localities it appears that it was once quite common in the Tai National Park although even here there has apparently been a decrease (J.-M. Thiollay *in litt.* 1983). Available evidence suggests that the species is now making its last stand in south-eastern Liberia and south-western Ivory Coast (W. Gatter *in litt.* 1983, J.-M. Thiollay *in litt.* 1983).

Ecology This species is only found in the thin undergrowth of primary lowland rainforest where it is sympatric with the Crested Guineafowl *Guttera edouardi* (Bechinger 1964). Unlike this latter species, however, the White-breasted Guineafowl cannot survive in the denser understorey of secondary forest (J.-M.

189

Thiollay *in litt.* 1982) – although this was the habitat on Tiwai Island, Sierra Leone, in 1984 (G. Davies *in litt.* 1984) – and only very rarely leaves the protection of forest cover (Bechinger 1964). The two species mix only on very rare occasions (Bechinger 1964). White-breasted Guineafowls occupy large territories in which groups of 15-20 birds, or more, constantly move about in search of food (Bechinger 1964), though some earlier workers have reported groups of only 4-5 birds (Bannerman 1951) or even pairs (Johnston 1906). The diet consists of anything obtainable in the undergrowth, both animal and vegetable matter (Bechinger 1964). The ground below a fruiting tree can be a particularly favoured feeding place (Bechinger 1964). When a bird finds some food others move in quickly in an attempt to displace it (Bechinger 1964). Such feeding skirmishes are common but serious fighting does not take place (Bechinger 1964). The nest has not been found but is thought to be made on the ground, protected by thick undergrowth, and the eggs probably number about a dozen (Bechinger 1964). Several reports indicate that the species is very shy (Johnston 1906, Allen 1930, Bannerman 1930). The red heads and white breast-feathers are easily visible in the dark understorey of the forest and are thought to facilitate group cohesion (Bechinger 1964). If a predator appears the group scatters in all directions but a "cheeping" call is used to re-establish contact between the individual birds (Bechinger 1964).

Threats This species has declined as a result of habitat destruction and hunting pressure (J.-M. Thiollay *in litt.* 1982,1983). It appears to be unable to survive in the dense understorey of secondary forest (Bechinger 1964, J.-M. Thiollay *in litt.* 1982) and areas of primary forest are now restricted to a very few places in West Africa (Dufresne and Cloutier 1982, Roth 1982, Verschuren 1982,1983, Halle 1983). The Gola Forest in Sierra Leone is seriously threatened by timber exploitation (A. Tye *in litt.* 1983, G. D. Field pers. comm. 1983), and the Tai Forest National Park in Ivory Coast is also suffering from illegal encroachment (Roth 1982, Halle 1983, J.-M. Thiollay *in litt.* 1983). The rate of forest destruction in Africa west of the Dahomey Gap is so severe that any bird species endemic to primary forest in this region must now be considered gravely at risk (see Remarks under Rufous Fishing Owl *Scotopelia ussheri* for the species in question). Severe hunting pressure has, moreover, probably eliminated this guineafowl from several areas of suitable habitat, especially in Liberia where the trapping and shooting of wildlife is particularly severe (Verschuren 1982,1983). Many of the museum specimens were bought from local people who trapped the birds on forest paths (Büttikofer 1885,1889,1890, Allen 1930, Bannerman 1930). These traps consist of nooses set at openings in a long barrier made of sticks and palm fronds in the forest (Allen 1930) though birds are no doubt shot as well. In Ivory Coast hunters mimic the call of the birds, which approach to within a few metres and are killed by a stone from a sling (Bechinger 1964). The species probably survives only in areas of primary forest at a considerable distance from human settlements and disturbance. Recent reports indicate that hunting pressure is severe, even within the Tai National Park (Roth 1982, J.-M. Thiollay *in litt.* 1983). The rapid extinction of the species around Mount Nimba following the exploitation of the area's timber (Forbes-Watson undated, Colston and Curry-Lindahl in press) is an ominous sign for its survival in West Africa as a whole.

Conservation Measures Taken None is known, other than that its occurrence in the Tai National Park in Ivory Coast and Sapo National Park and Grebo National Forest in Liberia provides some hope for its survival (see also Remarks). The species is listed on Appendix III of CITES for Ghana.

Conservation Measures Proposed This species will only survive in the wild if large areas of primary forest are protected and a hunting ban is rigorously enforced. The future of the species depends mainly on the conservation of the Tai National Park in south-western Ivory Coast and the adjoining areas of forest at Tchien and the Cavally River in eastern Liberia, including Sapo National Park and Grebo National Forest, where the species apparently survives (Forbes-Watson undated, W. Gatter *in litt.* 1983; see Distribution). This is by far the largest area of primary rainforest surviving west of the Dahomey Gap (Roth 1982, Halle 1983): a survey is needed to assess the status of the White-breasted Guineafowl there and to make comprehensive proposals for its conservation. Hunting pressure being severe throughout the Tai National Park (see Threats), it may be impossible to save the species even in this area. If sufficient protection for the species cannot be given, a captive breeding programme must be a matter of urgent consideration. A few birds were in captivity in West Berlin Zoo in the early 1960s (Raethel 1965) and at Frankfurt Zoo between 1966 and 1973 (*Internat. Zoo Yearbook* 7-14 [1967-1974]). One bird was also in Mayaguez Zoo in Puerto Rico in 1972 (*Internat. Zoo Yearbook* 13-14 [1973-1974]). However, there is no evidence that the species has ever bred in captivity and no captive population is now known to survive.

Remarks The genus *Agelastes* is thought to represent the most primitive surviving guineafowl, probably the result of an early radiation of the group into the rainforest environment (Crowe 1978). The only other member of the genus is the Black Guineafowl *A. niger* (Hall 1961), known from forests from southern Cameroon to eastern Zaire: the two birds might form a superspecies (Snow 1978). There are several rainforest areas west of the Dahomey Gap which are under varying degrees of protection (for details of these and of the ornithological importance of Tai and Gola Forests see Remarks under the Rufous Fishing Owl). The White-breasted Guineafowl survives in some of these areas but hunting pressure and logging (both legal and illegal) are serious problems in nearly all of them (IUCN 1977).

References

Allen, G. M. (1930) The birds of Liberia. Pp. 636-748 in R. P. Strong, ed. The African Republic of Liberia and the Belgian Congo, based on the observations made and material collected during the Harvard African expedition 1926-1927, 2. *Contrib. Dept. Trop. Med. and Inst. Trop. Biol. and Med.* 5.

Bannerman, D. A. (1930) *The birds of tropical West Africa*, 1. London: Crown Agents for the Colonies.

Bannerman, D. A. (1951) *The birds of tropical West Africa*, 8. London: Crown Agents for the Colonies.

Bannerman, D. A. (1953) *The birds of West and equatorial Africa*, 1. London: Oliver and Boyd.

Bechinger, F. (1964) Beobachtungen am Weissbrust-Waldhuhn (*Agelastes meleagrides*) im Freileben und in der Gefangenschaft. *Gefied. Welt.* 88: 61-62.

Bouet, G. (1955) *Oiseaux de l'Afrique tropicale.* 1ère partie. Paris: Faune de l'Union Française XVI.

Brunel, J. and Thiollay, J.-M. (1969) Liste préliminaire des oiseaux de Côte d'Ivoire. *Alauda* 37: 230-254.

Büttikofer, J. (1885) Zoological researches in Liberia. A list of birds collected by J. Büttikofer and C. F. Sala in western Liberia, with biological observations. *Notes Leyden Mus.* 7: 129-255.

Büttikofer, J. (1888) Zoological researches in Liberia. A list of birds collected by the author and Mr F. X. Stampfli during their last sojourn in Liberia. *Notes Leyden Mus.* 10: 59-106.

Büttikofer, J. (1889) Zoological researches in Liberia. Fourth list of birds. *Notes Leyden Mus.* 11: 113-138.

Büttikofer, J. (1890) *Reisebilder aus Liberia*, 2. Leyden: E. J. Brill.

Colston, P.R. and Curry-Lindahl, K. (in press) The birds of the Mount Nimba region in Liberia. *Bull. Brit. Mus. (Nat. Hist.) Zool.*

Crowe, T. M. (1978) The evolution of guinea-fowl (Galliformes, Phasianidae, Numidinae): taxonomy, phylogeny, speciation and biogeography. *Ann. S. Afr. Mus.* 76: 43-136.

Du Chaillu, P. B. (1861) *Explorations and adventures in equatorial Africa.* London.

Dufresne, A. and Cloutier, A. (1982) Conserving tropical rainforests in West Africa. *WWF Monthly Report* September: 257-262.

Forbes-Watson, A. D. (undated) Checklist of the birds of Liberia. Non-passeriformes. Unpublished.

Hall, B. P. (1961) The relationship of the guinea-fowls *Agelastes meleagrides* Bonaparte and *Phasidus niger* Cassin. *Bull. Brit. Orn. Club* 81: 132.

Halle, M. (1983) Timber pressure on last Ivory Coast forest. *WWF News* 22: 2.

Hartlaub, G. (1855) Beschreibung einiger neuen von Herrn H. S. Pel, hollandischem Residentem an der Goldküste, daselbst gesammelten Vogelarten. *J. Orn.* 3: 353-361.

IUCN (1977) *World directory of national parks and other protected areas.* Morges, Switzerland: IUCN.

Johnston, H. H. (1905) Notes on the birds and mammals of Liberia. *Proc. Zool. Soc. Lond.*: 197-210.

Johnston, H. H. (1906) *Liberia*, 2. London: Hutchinson and Co.

Pfeffer, P. (1961) Etude d'une collection d'oiseaux de Côte d'Ivoire. *Bull. Mus. Natn. Hist. Nat.* (2)33: 357-368.

Raethel, H. S. (1965) White-breasted Guinea-fowl *Agelastes meleagrides* Bp. at West Berlin Zoo. *Internat. Zoo Yearbook* 5: 165-166.

Roth, H. H. (1982) We all want trees – case history of the Tai National Park. 3rd World National Parks Congress, Bali, Indonesia. Unpublished.

Schouteden, H. (1970) Quelques oiseaux du Liberia. *Rev. Zool. Bot. Afr.* 82: 187-192.

Snow, D. W. ed. (1978) *An atlas of speciation in African non-passerine birds.* London: Trustees of the British Museum (Natural History).

Verschuren, J. (1982) Hope for Liberia. *Oryx* 16: 421-427.

Verschuren, J. (1983) Conservation of tropical rain forest in Liberia. Recommendations for wildlife conservation and national parks. Gland, Switzerland: IUCN/WWF.

WHITE-BREASTED MESITE   RARE

Mesitornis variegata (I. Geoffroy Sainte-Hilaire, 1838)

Order GRUIFORMES   Family MESITORNITHIDAE

Summary This rail-like terrestrial forest bird is currently known from only a single site (Ankarafantsika) in Madagascar, which is, however, a protected area.

Distribution Although the White-breasted Mesite was first found in 1834 at an unspecified locality in Madagascar, almost a century passed (during which all records of this species are attributable to the Brown Mesite *Mesitornis unicolor*: see Lavauden 1931) before it was rediscovered: an adult female was collected on 12 July 1929 in Ankarafantsika forest (110 km south-east of Majunga), north-west Madagascar, and a nest with two eggs was found there in October that year (Lavauden 1931,1932). A year later, on 10-11 November 1930, two males and a gravid female were collected at Ankarana cliffs, 25 km south-west of Tsarakibany, in the far north of the island (Rand 1936). A few were seen in 1971 at Ankarafantsika (Forbes-Watson *et al.* 1973) and further visits there through the 1970s consistently resulted in sightings (D. A. Turner pers. comm. 1983), but there appear to be no other records for this species. Nevertheless it has been speculated that birds may occur in the region between the two known localities, "notably in the Analalava and in the Haut-Sombirano [*sic*]" (Lavauden 1932), and that the Betsiboka River may mark the southern boundary of its distribution (Lavauden 1937). The statement that it occurs "in all western Madagascar" (Milon *et al.* 1973) is patently unsubstantiated.

Population Observations through the 1970s suggest that the species is common at Ankarafantsika (D. A. Turner pers. comm. 1983).

Ecology At Ankarafantsika the species is a ground-dweller in dry forest (Lavauden 1932), likewise at Ankarana cliffs, where a pair was found "running about together in rather low dry forest, somewhat clear of under-brush" (Rand 1936). Food probably consists of insects and fruit (Rand 1951); birds live in pairs on the ground, walking or running with frequent stops and changes of direction, but flying poorly (only if threatened by a predator) (Lavauden 1931, Rand 1936); the nest is placed low in a bush (60-80 cm above ground), evidently October/November (Lavauden 1932, Rand 1936). An association appears to exist between this species and the Rufous Vanga *Schetba rufa*, exactly as for the Subdesert Mesite *Monias benschi* (see relevant account) and Lafres-naye's Vanga *Xenopirostris xenopirostris* (A. D. Forbes-Watson pers. comm. 1984).

Threats The highly restricted range of this species must be a source of permanent concern and vigilance for its welfare. Deforestation is likely to have affected many areas where it might have been searched for in north-west Madagascar. Introduced rats, widespread in the eastern forests in the 1930s and presumably therefore present in the west, may affect the bird adversely (see under Brown Mesite).

Conservation Measures Taken The only area where it is currently known to occur falls within the Ankarafantsika Nature Reserve (R.N.I. no. 7) (see Andriamampianina 1981).

Conservation Measures Proposed A study of the status and ecology of this bird at Ankarafantsika would help determine where else it might be searched for and what management it might require. Ankarana cliffs merit revisiting and careful survey. All such work should be undertaken in conjunction with studies recommended under Conservation Measures Proposed for Van Dam's Vanga *Xenopirostris damii*.

Remarks The importance of the Ankarafantsika Nature Reserve as the only locality currently known for this species and Van Dam's Vanga cannot be overstated.

References

Andriamampianina, J. (1981) Les réserves naturelles et la protection de la nature à Madagascar. Pp. 105-111 in P. Oberlé, ed. *Madagascar, un sanctuaire de la nature*. Paris: Lechevalier.

Forbes-Watson, A. D., Turner, D. A. and Keith, G. S. (1973) Report on bird preservation in Madagascar. Part 3, Appendix. Report to ICBP, unpublished.

Lavauden, L. (1931) Note préliminaire sur les oiseaux appartenant aux genres *Mesoenas* et *Monias*. *Alauda* 3: 395-400.

Lavauden, L. (1932) Etude d'une petite collection d'oiseaux de Madagascar. *Bull. Mus. Natn. Hist. Nat.* (2)4: 629-640.

Lavauden, L. (1937) Supplément. A. Milne Edwards and A. Grandidier, *Histoire physique, naturelle et politique de Madagascar, 12. Oiseaux*. Paris. Société d'Editions Géographiques, Maritimes et Coloniales.

Milon, P., Petter, J.-J. and Randrianasolo, G. (1973) *Faune de Madagascar, 35. Oiseaux*. Tananarive and Paris: ORSTOM and CNRS.

Rand, A. L. (1936) The distribution and habits of Madagascar birds. *Bull. Amer. Mus. Nat. Hist.* 72: 143-499.

Rand, A. L. (1951) The nests and eggs of *Mesoenas unicolor* of Madagascar. *Auk* 68: 23-26.

Mesitornis unicolor (Desmurs, 1845)

Order GRUIFORMES   Family MESITORNITHIDAE

Summary This cryptic and retiring terrestrial rail-like bird of Madagascar rainforest apparently possesses a much wider distribution than has previously been appreciated, but may be at risk from both forest destruction and introduced mammalian predators.

Distribution The Brown Mesite evidently occurs throughout much of eastern Madagascar, although most records are from the circle whose diameter lies between Antananarivo and Tamatave. One usually reliable authority gave its range as from Vohémar (high north-east) to Farafangana (south-east) (Lavauden 1932) but there appear to be no records to support the choice of these extremes and indeed the same authority later speculated whether the species reached even as far south as Mananjary (Lavauden 1937). Reports of the bird from the "north-east" (Humblot 1882), the Masoala peninsula (Lavauden 1937) and south of Maroantsetra (Lavauden 1932,1937), though in themselves too vague to be regarded with confidence, are supported by specimens collected by J. Audebert at Mananara (Antongil Bay), 17 August 1876, "Savary" in February and April 1878 and "Maintinbato" in May 1878 (specimens in RMNH: NJC; also Fisher 1981): "Savary" cannot be traced (e.g. in Office of Geography 1955, IGNT 1964) but a letter from the collector to H. Schlegel, dated 4 March 1878 is headed "Savary, Antongil Bay, west of Mananara, Ancay border, seven days' journey into the interior" (G. F. Mees *in litt.* 1983), which clearly suggests that the "Maintinbato" (i.e. Maintimbato) in question is that just south of Rantabe on the shore of Antongil Bay. The type-specimen was described as from the "north-east" (Delacour 1932) but this was later refined to "around Tamatave" (Lavauden 1937). There is a specimen in MRAC labelled as from "Brickaville district", February 1928 (NJC). The species occurs in the Sihanaka forest, where four birds were taken in 1925, three in April, one in November (specimens in SMF: NJC), where an adult female was collected in May 1930 (Lavauden 1932) and whence six further specimens were obtained by purchase around this time (Delacour 1932, Rand 1936). The species is known from the forest between Rogez and Fito (Lavauden 1937), was seen at Périnet in 1939 or 1940 (Webb 1954), and collected in "Lakato forest" in 1924 (two specimens in MRAC: NJC). Four further specimens (in MRAC, SMF and RMNH) are from "Vohibazaha forest, Anivorana district", October 1923 (two) and "Marovato", November 1922 and March 1923 (NJC): Vohibazaha, at 18°48'S 48°33'E, is close to Périnet and Rogez, while of at least 34 localities named "Marovato" in Madagascar (see Office of Geography 1955) three, at 18°57'S 48°49'E, 18°41'S 48°36'E, and 18°27'S 48°41'E, all lie within the general area of forest between Antananarivo and Tamatave. The species was collected on the "south-east coast" around 1876 (Bartlett 1877,1879), and this otherwise anomalous record was vindicated when nesting birds were found at "Bemangidy" north of Fort Dauphin (Rand 1951; see Remarks). It is to be observed that the taboo on this species (see Conservation Measures Taken) extended even to speaking its name (Lavauden 1931), so that its existence may often have remained unreported to explorers in certain areas; elsewhere, where no taboo applied, its existence had gone undetected even by natives (Rand 1951). For these reasons, the assertion that the species did not occur at Fanovana (Rand 1936), which may have compounded the judgement that it is highly localised in distribution (e.g. Rand 1951, King 1978-1979), is open to doubt (although the forest at Fanovana is now all cleared – see under Red-tailed Newtonia *Newtonia fanovanae*); and on present evidence it would seem very possible that the bird may be found at many other localities to the north of Tamatave or to the south of Lakato.

Population The species was not considered rare in the last century (Milne Edwards and Grandidier 1885) and in Sihanaka forest it is apparently not very rare (Lavauden 1932). Its wariness and keen senses have been likened to those of pittas (Pittidae) so that it "may be common without being seen" (Webb 1954); nevertheless, it is recently reported as very scarce throughout its range (D. A. Turner pers. comm. 1983).

Ecology The Brown Mesite inhabits the floor of the thickest and remotest parts of rainforest, slipping swiftly on foot through thick vegetation (Lavauden 1931,1932). A bird observed by a seated observer "alternately ran rapidly and then remained motionless, its colours so harmonizing with the background that it was exceedingly difficult to see when stationary" (Webb 1954). Food is probably insects and fruit (Rand 1951); in another account "insects, ants" are mentioned (Milne Edwards and Grandidier 1885). The species flies poorly (only if threatened by a predator) (Lavauden 1931). Both nests found in the south-east in 1948 (on 24 November and 25 December) were in rainforest where a thin cover of shrubs and a few herbs grew below the trees; both were low (1 and 2 m above ground) in the fork of a sloping tree which had lower branches possibly used by the bird to hop up from below; both held one egg, and in both cases the incubating female was caught by hand (Rand 1951).

Threats Destruction and disturbance of primary rainforest is the single most serious threat to this and all other rainforest-dependent species in Madagascar (see Threats under Madagascar Serpent Eagle *Eutriorchis astur*). The hilly country in the south-east where nesting was proven in 1948 was evidently in the process of being cleared of forest (see Rand 1951). The brown rat *Rattus norvegicus* and black rat *R. rattus* may affect mesites adversely (Forbes-Watson and Turner 1973), and attention has been drawn to the observation, dating from around 1940, that "the eastern forests are now swarming with them, even in the most isolated regions where the precipitous nature of the country is unfavourable to human habitation" (Webb 1954). It is also speculated whether competition from the Madagascar Wood-rail *Canirallus kioloides* affects the species (D. A. Turner pers. comm. 1983).

Conservation Measures Taken The species has been recorded from the area now established as the Périnet-Analamazaotra Special Reserve, which covers 810 ha (Andriamampianina 1981). The strong taboo amongst the Malagasy people in the central part of the eastern forests was based on the fact or belief that when the young are captured the adult follows the hunter right back into the village, exhibiting parental concern so like that of a human being as to render the species sacred (Milne Edwards and Grandidier 1885); it is considered that such a taboo must have helped conserve the bird, at least in the past (Forbes-Watson and Turner 1973), and indeed at Périnet the taboo still persists (O. Langrand *per* A. D. Forbes-Watson pers. comm. 1984).

Conservation Measures Proposed Immediate and effective protection of as much remaining rainforest as possible would almost certainly guarantee the survival of this and all other rainforest-dependent species in Madagascar; and at least, on current knowledge, complete protection of the intact parts of Sihanaka forest is of extreme importance (see Conservation Measures Proposed under Madagascar Serpent Eagle). Any ornithological work in the other areas from which the species is known, or where it might be expected, should where possible be extended to include searches to locate it.

Remarks The locality of the two nests found to date was given as "Bemangidy, Poste Mananteina, Fort Dauphin district" with the addition that "Bemangidy is 72 kilometres north of Fort Dauphin and is about five miles west of the Indian Ocean" (Rand 1951). However, the correct names appear to be "Bemangily" and "Manantenina" and the correct distances 55 km and 5 km respectively (see IGNT 1964). It should also be noted that the view, first aired in the original description (Desmurs 1845), that the Brown Mesite might be or was only the female of the White-breasted Mesite *Mesitornis variegata* has resulted in considerable confusion; virtually everything written about the latter in Milne Edwards and Grandidier (1885) does in fact refer to the Brown Mesite; the view that two species were involved was accepted by Hartlaub (1877) and entertained by Lowe (1924) before being confirmed by Lavauden (1931,1932,1937).

References

Andriamampianina, J. (1981) Les réserves naturelles et la protection de la nature à Madagascar. Pp. 105-111 in P. Oberlé, ed. *Madagascar, un sanctuaire de la nature*. Paris: Lechevalier.

Bartlett, E. (1877) Remarks on the affinities of *Mesites*. *Proc. Zool. Soc. Lond.*: 292-293.

Bartlett, E. (1879) Second list of mammals and birds collected by Mr. Thomas Waters in Madagascar. *Proc. Zool. Soc. Lond.*: 767-773.

Delacour, J. (1932) Les oiseaux de la Mission Franco-Anglo-Américaine à Madagascar. *Oiseau et R.F.O.* 2: 1-96.

Desmurs, O. (1845) Description de quelques espèces nouvelles d'oiseaux. *Rev. Zool.* 8: 175-179.

Fisher, C. T. (1981) Specimens of extinct, endangered or rare birds in the Merseyside County Museums, Liverpool. *Bull. Brit. Orn. Club* 101: 276-285.

Forbes-Watson, A. D. and Turner, D. A. (1973) Report on bird preservation in Madagascar. Part 3. Report to ICBP, unpublished.

Hartlaub, G. (1877) *Die Vögel Madagascars und der benachbarten Inselgruppen*. Halle.

Humblot, L. (1882) Rapport sur une mission à Madagascar. *Arch. Miss. Sci. Litt.* (3)8: 153-157.

Institut Géographique National à Tananarive (1964) Carte de Madagascar, 1:500,000, Type 1963. Tananarive.

King, W. B. (1978-1979) *Red data book, 2: Aves.* 2nd edition. Morges, Switzerland: IUCN.

Lavauden, L. (1931) Note préliminaire sur les oiseaux appartenant aux genres *Mesoenas* et *Monias*. *Alauda* 3: 395-400.

Lavauden, L. (1932) Etude d'une petite collection d'oiseaux de Madagascar. *Bull. Mus. Natn. Hist. Nat.* (2)4: 629-640.

Lavauden, L. (1937) Supplément. A. Milne Edwards and A. Grandidier, *Histoire physique, naturelle et politique de Madagascar, 12. Oiseaux.* Paris: Société d'Editions Géographiques, Maritimes et Coloniales.

Lowe, P. R. (1924) On the anatomy and systematic position of the Madagascan bird *Mesites* (*Mesoenas*), with a preliminary note on the osteology of *Monias*. *Proc. Zool. Soc. Lond.*: 1131-1152.

Milne Edwards, A. and Grandidier, A. (1885) *Histoire physique, naturelle et politique de Madagascar, 12. Histoire naturelle des oiseaux.* Tome I. Paris.

Office of Geography (1955) *Gazetteer no. 2. Madagascar, Réunion and the Comoro Islands.* Washington, D.C.: Department of the Interior.

Rand, A. L. (1936) The distribution and habits of Madagascar birds. *Bull. Amer. Mus. Nat. Hist.* 72: 143-499.

Rand, A. L. (1951) The nests and eggs of *Mesoenas unicolor* of Madagascar. *Auk* 68: 23-26.

Webb, C. S. (1954) *A wanderer in the wind.* London: Hutchinson.

SUBDESERT MESITE   RARE

Monias benschi Oustalet and G. Grandidier, 1903

Order GRUIFORMES   Family MESITORNITHIDAE

Summary This rail-like terrestrial bird of restricted range within the subdesert region of south-west Madagascar, although numerically safe at present, appears to enjoy no protection whatever. It is of exceptional biological interest.

Distribution The Subdesert Mesite is restricted to a coastal strip roughly 70 km wide between the Mangoky and Fierenana Rivers, south-west Madagascar, ranging from sea-level to 130 m (Lavauden 1937, Appert 1968, Milon *et al.* 1973). Within this area its distribution was thought "extremely local" (Rand 1936) but other evidence suggests it is widespread (Appert 1968, Turner 1981). Nevertheless it has not been found north of the Mangoky, despite apparently suitable habitat (Appert 1968), and there is no evidence of its occurrence south of the Fierenana, despite records at and near Tuléar (Hartert 1912, Bangs 1918): the type-specimen is from Vorondreo, "25 km east of Tuléar" (Oustalet and Grandidier 1903), but this locality proves to be on the north bank of the Fierenana (i.e. north-east of Tuléar) at 23°17'S 43°51'E (Office of Geography 1955). The limit of its range inland up the Fierenana has been given as Fativolo (Lavauden and Poisson 1929), at 23°02'S 44°10'E (in Office of Geography 1955).

Population The species has been reported as common and at times abundant over much of its range (Turner 1981), but the experience of a very recent observer was much less encouraging, though birds were "rather common" at Ihotry village in September 1983 (O. Langrand *in litt.* 1984).

Ecology The Subdesert Mesite is a ground-dwelling bird, reasonably catholic in choice of habitat, primarily requiring areas with dense leaf-litter, at least in patches: thus it is found in both sparse and dense brush woodland with or without *Didierea*, and in open sandy scrub with isolated trees and bushes, etc., but it avoids shadeless areas and those where vegetation is so close to the ground that passage is obstructed (Rand 1936, Appert 1968). It feeds with occasional pecks as it walks along, but mainly by digging in leaf-covered soil (Appert 1968). Stomachs have been found to contain caterpillars, beetles, millipedes, cockroaches, grasshoppers, seeds, and pieces of shell and sand (Lavauden and Poisson 1929, Rand 1936, Appert 1968; also specimen-labels in MNHN: NJC). Parts of certain orchids are reported by natives to be favoured, and damage to orchids has been noted (Appert 1968). Birds are gregarious, generally in groups of four to six, occasionally up to ten, rarely alone; two together always represents a pair, at whatever season (Appert 1968). A report of groups up to 30-40 (Lavauden 1931) has apparently not been corroborated. "Territorial fighting" has been witnessed (Steinbacher 1977), but it is unclear if birds are group-territorial. Females are bolder than males (Rand 1936, Appert 1968). Although in one set of observations males were found to predominate numerically, and this was cited in support of the species possibly being polyandrous (Rand 1936), lengthier field study established no rule in the sexual

199

composition of groups (Appert 1968). On the basis of a male and two females with a nest with two eggs, an instance of polygyny was assumed (Appert 1968), but this conclusion – though perhaps correct – does not take consideration of other possibilities. Nests (one or two eggs) are placed 1-2 m up in trees or on broken-off tree-trunks, accessible without need of flight (Lavauden 1931, Rand 1936, Appert 1968). Males were reported by natives to incubate and care for the young (Rand 1936) and observations have partially supported this (Rand 1936, Appert 1968), but a female has been found incubating and a pair seen feeding young, though with the female playing more the role of lookout (Appert 1968). Nesting seems mainly to occur within the period of spring rains, October to December, but it may occur earlier or later and two young were even obtained in June, in the middle of the extended dry period (Lavauden 1932, Rand 1936, Appert 1968). The species has been stated not to fly (Delacour 1932) but it was reported to do so at the sound of a dog barking (Lavauden 1931) and there are two recent and very similar eye-witness accounts (Appert 1968, Turner 1981); moreover, in structure this bird is more adapted for flight and life in trees than the other two mesites (Lowe 1924) An association appears to exist between this species and Lafresnaye's Vanga *Xenopirostris xenopirostris*, since birds of the latter species are often found above parties of the former: the Mesites possibly flush insect prey for the Vangas and benefit in turn from the Vangas' greater vigilance (A. D. Forbes-Watson pers. comm. 1984); for a similar association between a vanga and a mesite, see Ecology under White-breasted Mesite *Mesitornis variegata*.

Threats The restricted range of this species must be a source of permanent concern and vigilance for its welfare. The Subdesert Mesite shares an identical range with the Long-tailed Ground-roller *Uratelornis chimaera* and occupies the latter's more restricted habitat (Appert 1968); this habitat has been reported as being destroyed (see Threats under Long-tailed Ground-roller). The birds are eaten by dogs and trapped by local villagers (O. Langrand *in litt.* 1984).

Conservation Measures Taken None is known.

Conservation Measures Proposed A study to determine the extent and type of habitat destruction reported in this species's range (see under Threats) is urgently needed. A detailed biological study of the bird would appear likely to yield important new information in the realm of behavioural ecology, given its existence in groups and at least partial sex-role reversal. Both this and the equally remarkable Long-tailed Ground-roller, whose ranges are exactly coincident, merit conservation by means of a protected area.

Remarks This extraordinary bird occupies a monotypic genus in an endemic Madagascar family of little obvious affinity, both of whose other members are under threat (see relevant accounts).

References

Appert, O. (1968) Beobachtungen an *Monias benschi* in Südwest-Madagaskar. *J.*

Orn. 109: 402-417.

Bangs, O. (1918) [Vertebrata from Madagascar.] Aves. *Bull. Mus. Comp. Zool.* 61: 489-511.

Delacour, J. (1932) Les oiseaux de la Mission Franco-Anglo-Américaine à Madagascar. *Oiseau et R.F.O.* 2: 1-96.

Hartert, E. (1912) On some unfigured birds. *Novit. Zool.* 19: 373-374.

Lavauden, L. (1931) Note préliminaire sur les oiseaux appartenant aux genres *Mesoenas* et *Monias. Alauda* 3: 395-400.

Lavauden, L. (1932) Etude d'une petite collection d'oiseaux de Madagascar. *Bull. Mus. Natn. Hist. Nat.* (2)4: 629-640.

Lavauden, L. (1937) Supplément. A. Milne Edwards and A. Grandidier, *Histoire physique, naturelle et politique de Madagascar, 12. Oiseaux.* Paris: Société d'Editions Géographiques, Maritimes et Coloniales.

Lavauden, L. and Poisson, H. (1929) Contribution à l'étude de l'anatomie du *Monias benschi. Oiseau* 10: 665-670.

Lowe, P. R. (1924) On the anatomy and systematic position of the Madagascan bird *Mesites* (*Mesoenas*), with a preliminary note on the osteology of *Monias. Proc. Zool. Soc. Lond.*: 1131-1152.

Milon, P., Petter, J.-J. and Randrianasolo, G. (1973) *Faune de Madagascar, 35. Oiseaux.* Tananarive and Paris: ORSTOM and CNRS.

Office of Geography (1955) *Gazetteer no. 2. Madagascar, Réunion and the Comoro Islands.* Washington, D.C.: Department of the Interior.

Oustalet, E. and Grandidier, G. (1903) Description d'une nouvelle espèce d'oiseau, type d'un genre nouveau, provenant de Madagascar. *Bull. Mus. Natn. Hist. Nat.* 9: 10-12.

Rand, A. L. (1936) The distribution and habits of Madagascar birds. *Bull. Amer. Mus. Nat. Hist.* 72: 143-499.

Steinbacher, J. (1977) Vogelleben auf Inseln im Indischen Ozean 3. Madagaskar. *Gefied. Welt* 101: 193-197.

Turner, D. A. (1981) A note on Bensch's Rail *Monias benschi* from Madagascar. *Bull. Brit. Orn. Club* 101: 240-241.

WATTLED CRANE   OF SPECIAL CONCERN
Bugeranus carunculatus (Gmelin, 1789)

Order GRUIFORMES   Family GRUIDAE
                                                     Subfamily GRUINAE

Summary This large, shy, mainly vegetarian crane occurs in marshes and floodplains in Ethiopia and central to southern Africa, but has declined in certain parts of its range and faces a variety of threats, chiefly to its habitats through damming, drainage and disturbance. Pairs require exceptionally large areas of remote open habitat (from which they exclude other pairs) for nesting, and have an exceptionally low productivity. Total numbers appear unlikely much to exceed 7,500.

Distribution The Wattled Crane is found in Ethiopia and Africa south of 5°S, with the main populations concentrated on six major wetlands – Kafue Flats, Bangweulu Swamp, Busanga Flats and Liuwa Plain in Zambia and Okavango Delta and Makgadikgadi Pans in northern Botswana – with smaller and more scattered populations in south Zaire, south-western Tanzania, Mozambique, Malawi, Zimbabwe, eastern South Africa (Transvaal and Natal), northern Namibia, and southern Angola (early data and details in Walkinshaw 1965,1973; map in Snow 1978). It is recorded as a migrant or vagrant only (uncommon in south-east, rare elsewhere) in Lesotho (West 1976,1977, Day 1979), and the few pairs resident in high areas of western Swaziland (West 1976,1977) are now extinct (Konrad 1980,1981). A specimen, considered immature, was collected in 1948 at Lake Cufada, Fulacunda, in Guinea-Bissau: this record, supported without comment by a poor photograph which indicates that two or three birds were then present, is given alongside an incomplete reference that suggests the species had previously been recorded at this locality (Frade and Bacelar 1955), but it seems certain that the birds involved were either escapes or vagrants (Snow 1978). Reports of the species in Somalia (e.g. Traylor 1973, McLachlan and Liversidge 1978) appear unfounded. The Wattled Crane, like the Ethiopian endemic Wattled Ibis *Bostrychia carunculata*, is depicted in Ancient Egyptian illustrations, and this is taken to indicate their former occurrence in lowland areas north-west of the Ethiopian highlands, perhaps in Egypt itself (Kumerloeve 1983).

Angola The species is widespread in the southern provinces of Cunene, Cuando-Cubango, and Huila (one record also from Moçâmedes), less common north to the central provinces of Cuanza Sul, Bié, Moxico and Lunda, with evidence that it was frequent in Benguela in the last century (Blaauw 1897, Ménégaux and Berlioz 1923, Monard 1934, Traylor 1963, Pinto 1965,1966,1970, in press). Breeding has been proved at Chitau (Bié) (Traylor 1963) and Chimporo (Cunene), and intimated (female with developed ovary) at Humpata (Huila) (Pinto in press). Birds are recorded from Luando Nature Reserve (Malanje/Bié provinces) and Kameia National Park (Moxico) in central Angola, and Bikuar (Huila) and Mupa (Cunene) National Parks and Mavinga and Luiana Partial Reserves(Cuando-Cubango)inthesouth(G. Asplund*inlitt.*1983;alsoHorsten 1982).

Botswana Birds are found in suitable open grasslands with vleis through-out the north-west, north and north-east (Ginn 1979, P. J. Jones *in litt.* 1983), the only known breeding site being the Okavango Delta, a 14,000 km^2 area of permanent wetland, seasonally flooded lowlands, woodland/grassland islands and adjoining savannas in Ngamiland: birds occur throughout the seasonal swamp areas (i.e. grassy floodplains up to 50 cm deep), never in small perennial swamps (P. A. Smith *in litt.* 1983). The entire length of the Botletle River (i.e. from Maun to Lake Xau) is considered an area of perhaps no less importance for the species, with a substantial number of records, 1970-1972 (P. J. Jones *in litt.* 1983), and breeding may occur there and perhaps also further east in good years (P. J. Ginn *in litt.* 1984). There is a major non-breeding site at Makgadikgadi Pans, a similarly large area of alkaline salt flats (seasonally flooded but dry for long periods in most years), in northern Central District (Konrad 1980,1981); favourite adjacent haunts are Mumpswe Pan and Goudse (Mrs S. J. Bousfield *in litt.* 1984). Lake Ngami (adjacent to Okavango), Lake Xau (adjacent to Makgadikgadi) and the Chobe/Linyanti River are also specifically named in records (Smithers 1964; for more details see Balden 1982). The majority of records in Botswana are from April to August, but the species evidently occurs in all months (see Balden 1982); the majority of birds recorded are, however, presumed to be non-breeding visitors from Zambia (Konrad 1980,1981).

Ethiopia The species is resident (though evidently a short-distance migrant) in West Highlands, South-East Highlands, and the Rift Valley (Urban and Walkinshaw 1967, Urban and Brown 1971). It is now known from ten provinces, listed here from north to south. Eritrea: between Massawa and Asmera (Moltoni and Gnecchi Ruscone 1944), though no subsequent records (Urban and Walkinshaw 1967, S. J. Tyler *in litt.* 1983). Begemdir: Fogera near Gonder (S. J. Tyler *in litt.* 1983). Gwejam (Gojjam): Dangila (breeding recorded) (Cheesman and Sclater 1935, Moltoni and Gnecchi Ruscone 1944); Wuhasa Abo (Cheesman and Sclater 1935, Moltoni and Gnecchi Ruscone 1944); between Debre Marcos and Dangila (Urban and Walkinshaw 1967); south of Debre Marcos (J. S. Ash *in litt.* 1983); north of Cima (Urban and Walkinshaw 1967); north of Dejem (Urban and Walkinshaw 1967). Shoa: Tefki area (cotton soil marshes) (Guichard 1950, Urban and Walkinshaw 1967, Alamargot 1980,1982, J. S. Ash *in litt.* 1983, S. J. Tyler *in litt.* 1983); Lake Abyata (Moltoni and Gnecchi Ruscone 1944); Lake Dila at c. 3,300 m (J. S. Ash *in litt.* 1983); Debre Zeit (J. S. Ash *in litt.* 1983); between Muketure and Weberi (J. S. Ash *in litt.* 1983). Welega: Lemkempt (Nak'amet) (breeding recorded) (J. S. Ash *in litt.* 1983). Kefa: at and near Jima (J. S. Ash *in litt.* 1983); 45 km west of Deneba (J. S. Ash *in litt.* 1983). Arusi: Tiggio (Urban and Walkinshaw 1967). Bale: Adoba at 3,500 m (Urban and Walkinshaw 1967); Saneti Plateau at 4,140 m (breeding evident) (J. S. Ash *in litt.* 1983, S. J. Tyler *in litt.* 1983); near Goba at 4,000 m (breeding recorded) (J. Alamargot *in litt.* 1983). Sidamo: between Wendo and Adola at c. 3,000 m (Urban and Walkinshaw 1967; also J. S. Ash *in litt.* 1983); 24 km west of Kibre Mengist (J. S. Ash *in litt.* 1983, S. J. Tyler *in litt.* 1983); 60 km east of Bore (J. S. Ash *in litt.* 1983). Gemu Gwefa (Gemu Gofa): Lake Chamo (Moltoni and Gnecchi Ruscone 1944).

Malawi Although birds have been recorded throughout the country at levels above 900 m (Benson and Benson 1977), the Malawi Bird Atlas project (1980-1984) had (at 14 March 1983) produced records from 10 quarter-degree squares, with historical reports for a further eight squares (total 18/180, i.e. 10%), and to most areas the species has probably always been only a wanderer (R. J. Dowsett *in litt.* 1983). It very probably bred on the Zomba Plateau (Belcher 1927) but was last recorded there in 1944 (R. J. Dowsett *in litt.* 1983); it certainly did so on the Viphya Plateau, e.g. in 1926 (Belcher 1927), but there are no recent records, both plateaus having been heavily afforested (R. J. Dowsett *in litt.* 1983). Breeding has also been recorded on the South Rukuru River, but there is no recent information and the area is now heavily populated (R. J. Dowsett *in litt.* 1983). Otherwise the species is only known to breed in the Kasungu and Nyika National Parks, and these are probably the only localities in Malawi where breeding (at least regularly) now occurs (Benson and Benson 1977, R. J. Dowsett *in litt.* 1983).

Mozambique The species is known chiefly from central Mozambique north of the Save River as far as the border with easternmost Malawi (Haagner 1948, Clancey 1970, Snow 1978). The main localities are Gorongosa – i.e. the "Rift Valley grasslands in the Urema Trough" – and Marromeu – i.e. the "Zambezi delta grasslands" – (West 1976, J. Burlison *in litt.* 1983, J. L. Tello *in litt.* 1983) and, since the species's occurrence at one never coincided with high numbers at the other, a single population may be involved (J. Burlison *in litt.* 1983; also O. West *in litt.* 1983). Presence of birds in Gorongosa (within the national park) coincided with wet season flooding of Lake Urema (J. Burlison *in litt.* 1983). Breeding was suspected in Marromeu, a large expanse of swamp south of the Zambezi estuary (J. Burlison *in litt.* 1983) and a pair at a nest, apparently with eggs, was observed there from an aircraft on 13 June 1981 (C. C. H. Elliott *in litt.* 1983). Otherwise the only reported breeding locality was the Save estuary (Haagner 1948), although observations there 1969-1974 failed to confirm this (J. L. Tello *in litt.* 1983). Birds were found in the 1930s on the Angoni highlands west of Malawi (West 1976, O. West *in litt.* 1983), and in the north three pairs are reported from the Niassa Game Reserve near the Rovuma River (J. L. Tello *in litt.* 1983). The species has now also been recorded from south of the Save River on the Govuru grasslands (inland from Vilanculos), the coastal grasslands on the São Sebastião peninsula (south-east of Vilanculos), at Inhambane, the valley plains inland from Inharrime, the lower Limpopo floodplains, the lower Incomati floodplains and the Banhime floodplains east of Malvérnia (Chicualacuala) (West 1976). All these localities south of the Save River are in lowland areas and the birds there behave nomadically: there may be a movement to highland areas adjacent to the known area of distribution around Nyanga, Zimbabwe, and a comparable population on the Mozambique side of the border in this region may exist (West 1976); it is also possible that birds occur on both sides of the Mozambique/Zimbabwe border in the Binga/Chimanimani mountain region (A. N. B. Masterson *in litt.* 1983).

Namibia Records are from the north only and chiefly the north-east (Caprivi Strip, Kavangoland, Bushmanland). In the Caprivi, earlier this century, birds were recorded "only during summer in savanna not far from water" (Leppan

1944), but despite the paucity of records for 1970-1980 in one account (Day 1980), two pairs with half-grown young were seen there (on the Chobe floodplain near Impalila Island), November 1978, along with at least 12 other birds (A. J. Williams *in litt.* 1983), and a pair was seen near Schuckmannsburg in September 1983 (A. J. Williams *in litt.* 1983). If large migrations occur between Zambia and Botswana, it seems likely that the birds involved would cross the Caprivi Strip. In north-east Kavangoland, on the west bank of the Okavango River in a proposed new reserve (Mahongo) between Andara and the Botswana border, two pairs are known to be present (and probably breed) in the wet season (A. J. Williams *in litt.* 1983). In eastern Bushmanland, 30 or more birds are reported to use flooded pans and waterholes near Tsumkwe, presumably having bred elsewhere, but breeding may occur there in wet cycles (A. J. Williams *in litt.* 1983). The species has also bred in Ovamboland, May, and is otherwise recorded from Grootfontein, Andoni (near Namutoni) and Etosha Pan, though there are only two records of single birds from the last locality in the past 11 years (Winterbottom 1971, A. J. Williams *in litt.* 1983). In the last century birds were reported as sparse in Damaraland (Blaauw 1897).

South Africa The species is reported extinct in Cape Province where it was formerly thinly but widely distributed, the last records being in the 1960s (Skead 1967, West 1976,1977, Day 1978,1979, Brooke in press a); however, one long-established breeding pair in the north-east was recently reported (O. West *in litt.* 1983). There were six records from Orange Free State, 1970-1980, but none previously, despite the former existence of much suitable habitat (West 1976,1977, Day 1979); two breeding pairs were recently reported (Konrad 1980,1981) but the species is now extinct there (Geldenhuys 1984). Prior to a new assessment of the situation in South Africa (see below), the species was reported to occur widely but locally in Natal at altitudes greater than 1,300 m and to be commonest at those above 1,650 m, the area concerned mostly being the eastern foothills of the Drakensberg escarpment, with records from Umvoti Vlei, Greytown, Howick, Balgowan, Nottingham Road, Mooi River, Underberg, Himeville, and the Giant's Castle Game Reserve (Clancey 1964, West 1977), while in the Transvaal it was reported to be restricted to two small areas (Belfast and Lake Chrissie) in the south-eastern highveld region (Tarboton in press). This information was recently updated and refined, the species being recorded from 58 quarter-degree squares in South Africa, 1978-1982 (Natal 34, Transvaal 21, Orange Free State 2, Transkei 1), ranging southwards from Dullstroom (Transvaal) over c. 800 km to Butterworth (Transkei), although the breeding range is restricted to between Dullstroom (roughly 25°25'S) and Kokstad (roughly 30°30'S) and divided into two discrete populations, one in Natal along the eastern foothills of the Drakensberg with concentrations in the catchments of the Umzimkulu River (13 pairs), Mooi River (11 pairs) and Umgeni River (17 pairs), the other in Transvaal in the high-lying south-eastern highveld with concentrations in the Steenkampsberg mountains around Belfast and Dullstroom (20 pairs) and in the catchments of the Usutu River (6 pairs) and Vaal River (3 pairs) (Tarboton *et al.* in press). The absence of breeding birds between the populations in Natal and Transvaal is partly attributable to unfavourable geomorphology; the existence of records outside these two main areas is attributable to the nomadic behaviour of non-breeding birds ("floaters"), which may range hundreds of kilometres away from the breeding areas (Tarboton *et al.* in press).

Tanzania Birds are resident in the south-west between (and including) the Ufipa Plateau (south-west of Lake Rukwa) and the Iringa Highlands (east of the Usangu Plain). Records (west to east) are from Lake Sundu, near Tatanda (90 km south of Sumbawanga, south-west of Lake Rukwa), near Tatanda (breeding reported in 1980) (D. Moyer *per* D. A. Turner *in litt.* 1983), Sumbawanga (Ufipa Plateau) and Rukwa Valley (Pitman 1935, Vesey-Fitzgerald and Beesley 1960, Britton 1980, J. S. S. Beesley *in litt.* 1983), Mwaya and Maliwungu (Britton 1980), Luchinde (Shelley 1899: see Remarks), the Njombe highland grasslands (Haldane 1956), the Usangu Plain (Procter 1968, Britton 1980, C. C. H. Elliott *in litt.* 1983,1984), the Great Ruaha River near Kimande (Britton 1980), and the Iringa Highlands at Mufindi (G. R. Cunningham-van Someren *in litt.* 1983), Sao Hill (J. S. S. Beesley *in litt.* 1983) and 80 km south-west of Iringa where breeding was finally proved for Tanzania, 9 May 1978 (Elliott 1983, C. C. H. Elliott *in litt.* 1983,1984). Outside this area there is an old record of small flocks on the Wualaba (= Ugalla) River (Blaauw 1897), a modern record from Kalo (5°49'S 31°28'E in Office of Geography 1965) on the Ugalla River in western Tanzania (B. W. H. Stronach *in litt.* 1983), and sightings of pairs and groups of up to six birds apparently resident in the huge swamp area of the Moyowosi, Nikonga and Kigosi Rivers north of Lake Sagara, approximately 5°S 31°30'E, also in western Tanzania (Parker 1984): this area may conceivably hold a large population of Wattled Cranes, but is unexplored ornithologically.

Zaire Records are almost exclusively from south of 5°S, with the majority concentrated in the south-east (Chapin 1939, Schouteden 1949,1965b,1971, Ruwet 1964, Lippens and Wille 1976, Snow 1978). The species occurs in the Kundelungus and Upemba National Parks in fair numbers, breeding being confirmed in the latter (Verheyen 1953, Lippens and Wille 1976, Verschuren 1978). Birds also breed in south-central Zaire in the region of the Kwilu River (Schouteden 1965a, Lippens and Wille 1976), and there are records of birds in the far west and at the coast (see Blaauw 1897, Snow 1978), although those from Pool Malebo (= Stanley Pool) and the Zaire (= Congo) River were at one stage rejected, presumably because improbable (Chapin 1939). Specimens from Kindu (Chapin 1939) in MRAC include a chick, but this species is now considered long exterminated from this northerly locality (A. Prigogine *in litt.* 1983).

Zambia The main breeding sites are (in order of apparent importance) the Kafue Flats, a large floodplain (6,000 km^2) along 235 km of the Kafue River west of Lusaka, this site also being of special seasonal importance for non-breeding birds and certainly the single most valuable area for the species anywhere; Liuwa Plain, a 3,500 km^2 floodplain formed in the upper Zambezi basin in westernmost Zambia at the Angola border; Busanga Flats, a permanent wetland covering 400 km^2 in the upper Kafue basin, north of Kafue Flats; and Bangweulu Swamp, an area of some 20,000 km^2 largely in Northern Province (Macartney 1968, Douthwaite 1974, Osborne 1978, Konrad 1980,1981). Overall, the Zambian Bird Atlas project (1976-1982) has records from 90 of the 296 half-degree squares (30%), with breeding records from 17, though breeding is doubtless under-recorded (R. J. Dowsett *in litt.* 1983). Individual pairs may be (semi-)resident in scattered small wetlands, perhaps more extensively than presently known (Konrad 1980,1981), and the species is probably absent as a breeding bird only from the low-lying Luangwa and middle Zambezi valleys (R. J. Dowsett *in litt.* 1983), though present on the Eastern Province plateau, east of the Luangwa valley, only as a non-breeder on the Nyika Plateau (Benson and White 1957, Benson *et al.* 1971, R. J. Dowsett *in litt.* 1983). Its reported scarcity in North-Western Province (Benson *et al.* 1971) and absence from the Lukanga Swamp (Benson and White 1957, Benson *et al.* 1971) are both now considered mistaken, the bird being widespread in the former (R. J. Dowsett *in litt.* 1983) and present in perhaps all but the most thickly vegetated parts of the latter (R. J. Dowsett *in litt.* 1983; see also Benson and Irwin 1967). Away from the four main areas, there are some extensive stretches of narrow floodplain or dambo, which hold a small but significant proportion of the breeding population (R. J. Dowsett *in litt.* 1983). It is evident that some movements, sometimes substantial, must occur between the large floodplains and those adjacent in Botswana (Konrad 1980,1981), and there may also be movement direct to Zimbabwe (Boulton *et al.* 1982).

Zimbabwe The resident population mainly occurs on the high ground (breeding probably only above 1,500 m) of the Mashonaland Plateau in the east (a large, well known flock forming on Gwebi Flats just north of Harare during the main breeding period), with scattered movements to the west and river valley systems (Irwin 1981, Boulton *et al.* 1982). The Charter Estate (presumably in the Charter District) is expected to be a major breeding area in wet years (P. J. Ginn *in litt.* 1984). Birds are also present up to 2,400 m in the Inyanga Highlands National Park (Mees 1970) and adjacent areas (Boulton *et al.* 1982, Snell 1983), and it is possible that some birds exist in the Chimanimani Mountains on the border with Mozambique south of Mutare near Chimanimani (Melsetter) (A. N. B. Masterson *in litt.* 1983). The species is very sparse in the Midlands (central) and Matabeleland (south-west), with records from Hwange (Wankie) National Park and Ngamo Pans (Irwin 1981; also Smithers *et al.* 1957, Masterson 1974), and breeding reported from the Dandanda Communal Area (Boulton *et al.* 1982). Presumably non-breeding birds visiting Makgadikgadi Pans in Botswana may sometimes penetrate into adjacent areas in south-west Zimbabwe. There may also be some movement direct from Zambia (Boulton *et al.* 1982).

Population Numbers are very difficult to judge, but on the data and guesswork below it is possible to conjecture a total world population of little more than 7,500, and conceivably as low as 6,000.

Angola The few breeding records (see Traylor 1963, Snow 1978) probably belie the size of the breeding population. The species is considered "relatively common" in the south (Pinto in press) and several other remarks (Traylor 1963, Pinto 1966,1970), and an observation of numerous small groups of

2-5 birds seen on the dambos and floodplains of south-eastern Cuando-Cubango in October 1973 (Dean and Huntley in press), suggest a reasonably sound population, but war may now be adversely affecting the birds (see Threats) and total numbers seem unlikely to exceed 500.

Botswana From a survey in February 1977 it is thought that several hundred birds were then present in the Okavango Delta, but another survey in February 1979 yielded only 21, possibly because birds had moved to Makgadikgadi (Konrad 1980,1981). However, records submitted 1979-1980 were few and suggest that only a small number of birds are usually present (Day 1980; see also Traylor 1965); a total of 74 was seen, "Santawani/Moremi/Okawango" in July and August 1981 (Balden 1982), while an expedition through the delta in August and September 1981 made no more than "several sightings", usually of pairs, and found one nest in the Jao region (Dryden 1982, Fothergill 1982). In the period from February 1970 to September 1972, the species was unquestionably uncommon throughout the Okavango, and flocks were rare (P. J. Jones *in litt.* 1983). In the same period, flocks of up to 40 were observed on the Botletle River and it is possible that a fairly large population of birds occurs along it (P. J. Jones *in litt.* 1983). At Makgadikgadi, migrant Wattled Cranes are present, January to May, and number from several hundred up to 2,000 in a given year (2,000 birds have been estimated present from counts made from a vehicle during a single day, and 300 were captured there for zoos over a 15-year period: Mrs S. J. Bousfield *in litt.* 1984); it is thought these birds may come from Kafue Flats, Zambia, with some from the Okavango Delta (Konrad 1980,1981). The species is commonly recorded at Linyanti Camp near Kasane in the far north (Balden 1982, J. Barnes *in litt.* 1983). It was recorded occasionally throughout an eighteen-month study, Lake Ngami, 1970-1972 (Balden 1982).

Ethiopia There are no data on numbers, but from recent records of flocks and counts, e.g. 20 east of Wendo (J. S. Ash *in litt.* 1983), 100 reported on the Dinsho Plain (Bale Mountains) in the south (Dorst and Roux 1972), 63 and 44 at Tefki Swamp south-west of Addis Ababa (Urban and Walkinshaw 1967, Alamargot 1980,1982) and at least 33 between Muketure and Weberi (J. S. Ash *in litt.* 1983), it is clear that at least several hundred birds exist.

Malawi Numbers are confidently assumed to have decreased (Benson and Benson 1977; also West 1976), though not necessarily by much, as the breeding population was probably never large (R. J. Dowsett *in litt.* 1983). The Nyika Plateau population is probably in the region of 25-30 pairs, with no more than 40 pairs in the whole country, overall numbers possibly therefore slightly over 100 (R. J. Dowsett and F. Dowsett-Lemaire *in litt.* 1983).

Mozambique From the Save River estuary, where the species was known to breed, 2-5 specimens were obtained annually prior to 1945, suggesting that several pairs (at least) were involved (see Haagner 1948), though none apparently now breeds (J. L. Tello *in litt.* 1983). Maximum daily counts at Gorongosa reached 15, at Marromeu 17 (in both cases birds were usually in pairs or threes) (J. Burlison *in litt.* 1983). During a flight over Marromeu, 13 June 1981, nine pairs and three single birds were seen, with only a small fraction of the area covered (C. C. H. Elliott 1983). In southern Mozambique the species is "apparently local and somewhat sparse" (Clancey 1970). The total number of birds seems unlikely to exceed 250.

Namibia The species is believed to be decreasing, but there are no numerical data (West 1976,1977); numbers in any case must be very small.

South Africa In the late 1970s, Natal, there were known to be 39 pairs on 37 farms, though probably with more in East Griqualand than the one pair reported (Day 1980), and the total was considered possibly 100 birds in all (Archibald 1981), while in Transvaal there were at least 21 pairs (18 in the Belfast area, three round Lake Chrissie) but probably less than 30 pairs (Tarboton in press) and possibly 50 birds in all (Archibald 1981), giving c. 60 pairs in South Africa (Day 1980). However, more recent work, 1978-1982, shows that the best estimate of breeding population in South Africa, in the first six months of 1982, was 110 pairs (81 Natal, 29 Transvaal), with 52 additional non-breeding birds ("floaters"), Natal, and 5-45 in the rest of the country, i.e. 277-317 or roughly 300 birds in all (Tarboton *et al.* in press). Although numbers were considered stable in Natal (West 1976,1977), "floaters" form up to 24% of total numbers, and this may indicate that suitable habitat is being lost (Tarboton *et al.* in press). There has certainly been a decrease in Transvaal (West 1976,1977) and without immediate conservation action the species is considered doomed to extinction in South Africa by the year 2000 (Brooke in press a,b). The investigators in the 1978-1982 study, despite the higher numbers found, regard this pessimism as justified (Tarboton *et al.* in press; see Threats).

Tanzania In the 1950s the species was considered "fairly common" in the Rukwa Valley (Vesey-Fitzgerald and Beesley 1960, J. S. S. Beesley *in litt.* 1983) and on high grasslands in the Njombe District (Haldane 1956), and up to 15 birds were seen at a time at Lake Sundu, 1978-1980 (D. A. Turner *in litt.* 1983). The population around Lake Sundu and Tatanda is still probably fairly healthy (D. A. Turner *in litt.* 1983), but total numbers seem unlikely to exceed a few hundred.

Zaire Some fifty years ago birds were reported to be fairly common around Lubumbashi (= Elisabethville) and 65 km to the north-east (Chapin 1939), and recent observations in the south and south-east confirm that birds continue to occur in fair numbers in this general area of the country (e.g. Lippens and Wille 1976), and are common on the bare plateaus (above 1,500 m) in Upemba and Kundelungus National Parks, particularly so in the latter (Verschuren 1978). It seems likely that several hundred birds inhabit Zaire.

Zambia Prior to the installation of a hydroelectric scheme during the 1970s, the Kafue Flats supported the world's largest population of Wattled Cranes, with at least 300 breeding pairs and up to 3,000 individuals present in favourable seasons (i.e. following widespread flooding), though at other times far fewer birds (in a normal year c. 1,000 are present at high flood) occur and, if rains are poor, little breeding may take place (Douthwaite 1974). At an unspecified time, 1978-1979, 552 birds (comprising 180 pairs, 20 young and 172 non-breeders) were counted and productivity was calculated as 3.6% (Konrad 1980,1981). It was considered possible that regulation of flooding would be causing declines in breeding numbers and success (Douthwaite 1974, Konrad 1980, 1981, D. R. Aspinwall *in litt.* 1981), but in May 1982 aerial transects of Kafue Flats resulted in a count of 762 birds (most in flocks, from eight to 200), giving an estimate of 3,282 birds for the area covered, indicating no change at least in numbers since a decade earlier (Howard and Aspinwall in press; but see Threats). On Liuwa Plain the population may number over 500 (Konrad 1980,1981): 148 were counted in a limited survey, November 1978 (Konrad 1980,1981), 80 in another in April 1980 (Morris 1981), and the birds evidently range commonly beyond the plain itself (see Traylor 1965). The Busanga Flats were estimated to hold 145-328 birds, 1971-1972 (Douthwaite 1974), but movements probably occur (Konrad 1980,1981). In Bangweulu Swamp, 1942-1944, the species was fairly common on the drier islands throughout the area, concentrations of nearly 200 forming south of Chafye Island and on Itili Plain in May when water-levels were too high in the rest of the swamp (Brelsford 1946,1947); however, on aerial transects over part of Bangweulu in October 1983 277 birds were counted and no less than 1,718 estimated to be present in the area of swamp with similar habitat to that sampled (Howard and Aspinwall in press). Although some migration in this population was considered probable (Konrad 1980,1981) there is no evidence for this and the birds may be largely sedentary in this area (R. J. Dowsett *in litt.* 1983). Although the species is sparse away from these major wetlands (D. R. Aspinwall *in litt.* 1981), it remains possible that the rest of the country holds almost as many pairs as they do (R. J. Dowsett *in litt.* 1983). However, assuming the figures above to represent discrete maximum populations it appears unlikely that there are many more than 5,500 Wattled Cranes throughout Zambia, and possibly many less.

Zimbabwe The total population is possibly no more than 250 (Irwin 1981). The traditional flock near Harare sometimes comprises half the estimated total population and is presumed to consist of immatures (Irwin 1981): if this is so, there can only be some 60 breeding pairs. A decrease in eastern Zimbabwe has probably occurred (West 1976). However, "large flocks" are reported still to gather in the extensive marshlands of the Charter Estate (P. J. Ginn *in litt.* 1984).

Ecology Wattled Cranes require very large open areas, both as territory and as security against predators: human approach to 400-500 m may be sufficient to put them to flight (Monard 1934, *Bokmakierie* 31 [1979]: 45), though habituation to human activity nearby is sometimes apparently possible (see Sievi and Manson 1974; also Snell 1983). Birds are most commonly found in pairs or threes (the latter almost invariably signifying a pair plus one offspring less than a year old) (Vincent 1945, Verschuren 1978, Pinto in press). In South Africa, pairs are sedentary and any flocks are formed by non-breeding birds ("floaters"), which are highly nomadic and utilise habitat (such as intensively farmed land) unsuitable for breeding, often in company with Grey Crowned Cranes *Balearica regulorum* and Blue Cranes

Anthropoides paradisea (Tarboton *et al.* in press). Whether flocks in other parts of the species's range are exclusively composed of "floaters" is not known, but north of Zimbabwe (and excluding Ethiopia) birds are very largely associated with areas undergoing seasonal inundation (Pitman 1935, Konrad 1980,1981, O. West *in litt.* 1983) and therefore subject to more movements, sometimes apparently extensive, and substantial flocks and aggregations then occur (see Population above). Birds inhabit wet grasslands, marshy edges of watercourses, extensive dambos and valleys, shallow pans, sponges, grassy vleis and marshes, usually in cool country and often on elevated plateaus (Chapin 1939, Vincent 1945, West 1963,1977, Smithers 1964, Pinto in press; see also Urban and Brown 1971). Some grasses and sedges present in such habitat have been identified (see Walkinshaw 1965,1973). Commonest food is sedge tubers and rhizomes (e.g. *Cyperus usitatus*: Smithers 1964), obtained by digging with the bill, but also invertebrates – including grasshoppers and crickets when abundant in meadows (Walkinshaw 1965) – and seeds, etc. (review in Konrad 1980,1981); in Angola food is given as chiefly reptiles, batrachians, fish, worms and insects (Pinto in press); elsewhere, small mammals are also mentioned (West 1982). Birds possibly feed also at night (see Cheesman and Sclater 1935, Masterson 1974). Moult (February/March in Zambia and Botswana) may temporarily render birds flightless (Benson *et al.* 1971, Konrad 1980,1981): the importance of large undisturbed expanses of wetland may then be paramount. Pronounced territorialism by breeding birds often means that only one pair can occupy a particular site (West 1977). To breed successfully, Transvaal, pairs appear to require a permanent marsh of at least 18 and preferably 40 ha, an area of surrounding grassland of at least 150 ha, and freedom from human disturbance at least during incubation (Tarboton in press). In the Belfast area, Transvaal, the population is sedentary, pairs occupying territories year-round and breeding on average on an unsynchronised 14-month cycle (Tarboton in press, Tarboton *et al.* in press); through-year breeding and sedentariness have also been noted, Natal (Dean 1971), although in the period 1980-1982 a clear midwinter peak in breeding activity (May/July) occurred, this being considered related to lower general rainfall during these years (Tarboton *et al.* in press). Elsewhere, limited available data both north and south of the equator suggest breeding activity is concentrated in the period from May to August (Benson *et al.* 1964, Urban and Brown 1971; also Traylor 1963, Benson and Pitman 1964, Cooper 1969, Douthwaite 1974). The nest is commonly in shallow water (birds deserting if the level drops too low: West 1982); very exceptionally in a tree (Irwin 1981) or in dry grassland (Ginn 1979). Clutch-size is one or two, one being commoner, South Africa (Tarboton *et al.* in press), two commoner, Zambia (Benson and Pitman 1964). Two-egg clutches have never been found to produce more than one chick, the second egg being abandoned as soon as the first young is strong enough to leave the nest (Tarboton *et al.* in press; also West 1963,1982). Nevertheless, some indications exist that two young at least hatch e.g. broods of two chicks seen on two separate occasions, Nyika Plateau (D. Elias *in litt.* 1984), though the siblings are then reportedly unstintingly hostile to each other (Bauer 1982); even so, there are sightings that suggest both may very occasionally survive (Bauer 1982). Incubation is 31-40 days, the young bird being incapable of flight up to 15-18 weeks, and first flying strongly at c. 21 weeks (West 1963,1977; also Macartney 1968, Bauer 1982).

The species has the lowest reproductive rate of all cranes (Konrad 1980,1981): 0.61 young per pair per year in Belfast, Transvaal (Tarboton in press; see also Benson and Pitman 1964), this figure reducing to 0.41 by the end of 1982 (i.e. for the period 1978-1982) presumably as a consequence of drought conditions (Tarboton *et al.* in press). Rearing success of clutches, Steenkampsberg (main Transvaal population), 1978-1982, was 0.49 (39 young reared from 80 clutches); hatching success, Natal, 0.55 (27 out of 49 clutches), while of 22 clutches that failed 15 disappeared without trace (Tarboton *et al.* in press). Of 32 broods, Natal, 15 survived to flying age (0.47 young per clutch hatched), nine disappearing without trace, five destroyed in grass fires and two in hailstorms: clutch success rate, Natal, was thus 0.26, considerably lower than in Steenkampsberg (Tarboton *et al.* in press). Nest-predation may sometimes be attributable to monitor lizards *Varanus* (Cooper 1969, Urban in press). Re-laying may occur only 3-4 weeks after loss of young (Bauer 1982, West 1982). Sexual maturity may be reached at four years (see Macartney 1968) or five or more (Brooke in press a), birds living and remaining reproductive for (at least) several decades (see Conway and Hamer 1977).

Threats The main factors adversely affecting Wattled Cranes are loss and disturbance of habitat, and disturbance and destruction of nests and young. The Itezhitezhi Dam at the west end of the Kafue Flats became operational in the mid-1970s, regulating the floodwaters on which the birds depend for the inundation of their breeding habitat, and their numbers and breeding success were consequently predicted to decline steeply (Douthwaite 1974; also Konrad 1980,1981, D. R. Aspinwall *in litt.* 1981). In fact, the reduction of inundated area in the seven years prior to 1983 has apparently only led to birds shifting to areas of the central floodplain, between Lochinvar and Blue Lagoon, which were previously perhaps too deep to occupy (G. W. Howard *in litt.* 1983). However, while numbers may not (yet) have suffered (see Population: Zambia), birds being long-lived, breeding success may be seriously affected resulting in a steady lowering of numbers in the next few decades (Konrad in press; also Howard and Aspinwall in press). A 50-60% decline on the Flats of the Kafue lechwe *Kobus leche kafuensis* (Konrad in press), an antelope vital for the maintenance of good bird habitat there (Douthwaite 1982) and a species with which the Wattled Crane has been noted to associate (White 1945), may also affect breeding success. Moreover, the areas now surrounding the central floodplain will become increasingly disturbed and exploited (by fishing and grazing) by an increasing human population (G. W. Howard *in litt.* 1983). On Liuwa Plain, despite its national nark status, fishermen rob nests, capture young birds, or cause pairs to desert nests (Konrad 1980,1981). In Bangweulu Swamp, a recently constructed road linking Serenje and Samfya with a large bridge at Mukuku, now renders the area much more accessible to hunters, poachers and fishermen, and may result in at least limited disturbance (D. R. Aspinwall *in litt.* 1983, G. W. Howard *in litt.* 1983). Moreover, a hydroelectric scheme has been proposed for Bangweulu, which would have disastrous effects on the wildlife there (Konrad 1980,1981), with at least half the area flooded as a storage reservoir (G. W. Howard *in litt.* 1983)· however this scheme could not avoid inundating the new road bridge at Mukuku and, with greater power surplusage expected from a new proposed dam on the Zambezi, it seems unlikely to proceed (D. R. Aspinwall *in litt.* 1983). The Okavango Delta (which has ten major concerns working on schemes to develop it) is subject to continued experimentation with pesticides in endeavours to control and possibly eventually eradicate tsetse fly *Glossina morsitans*; it is feared that the wildlife and ecology of the swamps are at risk through either the effects of certain chemicals or, if eradication is achieved, an invasion of domestic cattle (e.g. Konrad 1980,1981, Douthwaite *et al.* 1981, Soutter 1981, Yanchinski 1981, Fothergill 1983, J. Carter *in litt.* 1983). Birds have also been exported from Botswana (Konrad 1980,1981; see Population: Botswana), but this is not considered a problem (D. S. Peacock *in litt.* 1983): however, 30% of the 300 birds handled by one dealer over 15 years showed clinical signs of aspergillosis at the time of capture, and two-thirds of these (i.e. about 60) died within a few days (Mrs S. J. Bousfield *in litt.* 1984). Afforestation in South Africa, eastern Zimbabwe and Malawi is reducing habitat (West 1976,1977, W. R. Tarboton *in litt.* 1983). In Mozambique, the effects of the Kariba and Cabora Bassa Dams on the Zambezi delta and floodplain are still incomplete, but will eventually involve a reduction of habitat (J. Burlison *in litt.* 1983). In South Africa, the destruction of many seasonally flooded depressions by overgrazing, siltation, drainage and drop in water-table has been considered instrumental in the Wattled Crane's decline (Zaloumis and Milstein 1975), and grasslands generally have been degraded to karoo (succulent semidesert vegetation) by overgrazing by and mismanagement of domestic stock (Brooke in press b). Burning of breeding sites is also now a concern (Tarboton and Day 1980, Day 1981). Active persecution for food occurs in South Africa (possibly also Zambia: D. R. Aspinwall *in litt.* 1981), the birds being easily seen, nests easily found, and young easily caught: this is regarded as the major cause of decline in the Transvaal (West 1976,1977). Even accidental disturbance seems to be important: Lake Chrissie (crop farmland) holds far fewer pairs than around Belfast (sheep farmland) (Day 1980). Virtually all (105 out of 110) breeding pairs left in South Africa are on farmland under private ownership, with most sites on sponges in catchment areas that are especially vulnerable to damming projects (Tarboton *et al.* in press; also Mundy 1984). There is no doubt that loss of breeding habitat (directly through drainage or damming, and indirectly through adjacent development like afforestation, recreation and settlement) is the principal cause of decline in South Africa (Tarboton *et al.* in press, W. R. Tarboton *in litt.* 1983). Growing conversion of vleiland in Mashonaland, Zimbabwe, to agriculture is reducing habitat (West 1977); birds may suffer from poisons sprayed on crops to control small mammals, though no evidence yet exists (Day 1979); there is a recent case of displacement by damming (Snell 1983). The decrease in Namibia is attributed simply to "human population pressure" (West 1976), and this is true of parts of Malawi (R. J. Dowsett *in litt.* 1983). In Zambia, however, human population growth is associated (in places) with desertion of rural areas so that disturbance at certain sites may be decreasing (D. R. Aspinwall *in litt.* 1983). The war currently being fought between South Africa and forces in Angola over the future of Namibia is reported to have resulted in a seriously diminished avifauna in northern Namibia (A. J. Williams *in litt.* 1983) and this seems likely to be true of southern Angola also: Wattled Cranes would be vulnerable to both active persecution and incidental disturbance.

Conservation Measures Taken Wattled Cranes occur in a number of protected areas, e.g. Upemba and Kundelungus National Parks (Zaire), the Lochinvar, Kafue, Liuwa Plain, Nyika and Blue Lagoon National Parks (Zambia), Kasungu and Nyika National Parks (Malawi) (see relevant sections under Distribution), Gorongosa National Park and Marromeu Wildlife Utilisation Area (Mozambique) (J. Burlison *in litt.* 1983), Inyanga Highlands National Park (Zimbabwe) (Mees 1970), the Himeville and Kamberg Nature Reserves and Highmoor State Forest (Natal) and Belfast State Forest (Transvaal), South Africa (Brooke in press a), and six in Angola (see Distribution). In South Africa, a Wattled Crane Steering Group has been recently formed, representing appropriate conservation bodies, and has prepared a plan which aims to maintain the species at its present level with the active participation of the farming community (Tarboton *et al.* in press; see Conservation Measures Proposed); at Dullstroom, 7,000 ha of habitat supporting 12 pairs of birds are being acquired by the Transvaal Division of Nature Conservation to prevent development of the area for farming (Mundy 1983). In Zimbabwe, a personal campaign to persuade farmers to make islands in reservoirs during their construction has resulted in the successful adaptation of pairs to this artificial environment (P. J. Ginn *in litt.* 1984). Birds are held in several establishments including the International Crane Foundation (Baraboo, Wisconsin), and although extremely difficult to propagate in captivity pairs have bred at Pretoria Zoo (South Africa), Tama Zoo (Japan), Vogelpark Walsrode and Frankfurt Zoo (West Germany), and Baltimore Zoo and NYZS (U.S.A.) (G. W. Archibald *in litt.* 1981, *Gefied. Welt* 107 [1983]: 250, Brooke in press a). NYZS has a concerted programme with five pairs, involving removal of eggs and handrearing of young, so that numerous birds should be produced in the next few years (D. Bruning *in litt.* 1983).

Conservation Measures Proposed Concerning Kafue Flats, it is recommended that the Itezhitezhi hydroelectric regime be altered so as to restore the previous ecological conditions of the area, that Blue Lagoon National Park be reopened for public use, and that fishermen and herdsmen be kept out of Lochinvar National Park (Konrad 1980,1981). It is to be noted that the conservation of good numbers of lechwe on Kafue Flats is of considerable importance to the conservation of the birds of the area (Douthwaite 1982). More recent proposals, paying particular regard to the lechwe but also to the economic importance of the Flats for fisheries and cattle, are for Blue Lagoon and Lochinvar National Parks to be merged as a single refuge and for at least partial restoration of the flooding pattern (Marchand *et al.* 1983). Concerning Bangweulu Swamp, it is recommended that any damming proposals be dropped, since Zambia is already self-sufficient in power (Konrad 1980,1981). Concerning Liuwa Plain National Park, relocation of villages presently within park boundaries or of park boundaries away from present villages, followed by strict enforcement of park regulations and the mounting of an education campaign, is called for (Konrad 1980,1981). Negotiations are in progress to make the area used by birds near Tsumkwe, Namibia, into a nature reserve (A. J. Williams *in litt.* 1983). A reserve is also proposed at Mahongo, Namibia (see Distribution), but a proposed weir 30 km upstream on the Okavango River may affect the area's flooding regime (A. J.

Williams *in litt.* 1983). An inventory of small wetlands holding Wattled Cranes should be drawn up, and measures taken to protect them (Konrad 1980,1981). The management plan for this species in South Africa (see Conservation Measures Taken) proposes to monitor all breeding sites, to liaise with site owners, to promote greater public awareness and concern, to study habitat quality and preference, and to investigate the species's biology, especially flock structure, movements, daily routine, and food (Mundy 1984). Reintroduction of the species to certain suitable, previously inhabited areas is projected, as is a comprehensive international cooperative programme involving aerial censusing, colour-marking and radio-tracking (Konrad 1980,1981). The species merits listing in CITES. Further studies on distribution, population status, wetland usage, social structure, migrations and movements, and nesting success and productivity are needed (Urban in press). The implications of the apparently high incidence of aspergillosis in non-breeding birds at Makgadikgadi Pans (see Threats) are currently under study (J. E. Cooper *in litt.* 1984, G. W. Archibald *in litt.* 1984).

Remarks The locality Luchinde (see Distribution: Tanzania) is described as half-way between (the no longer extant) Fife (9°25'S 32°40'E, i.e. near Tunduma), and Lake Malawi (Lake Nyasa), but cannot be traced; however there is a Luchinde River whose source is a few kilometres inside Tanzania at 9°06'S 32°17'E (in FDTTS 1960).

References

Alamargot, J. (1980) Notes on the Tefki Wattled Cranes. *Ethiopian Wildl. Nat. Hist. Soc. Newsletter* 153 (October): 2.

Alamargot, J. (1982) Tefki Wattled Cranes. *Ethiopian Wildl. Nat. Hist. Soc. Newsletter* 174 (December): 2.

Archibald, G. (1981) Aerial censusing as a valuable technique in crane conservation. *Bokmakierie* 33: 60-61.

Balden, J. (1982) Records of crane species in Botswana. *Babbler* no. 3: 23-25.

Bauer, D. (1982) Notes on caring for cranes. *Honeyguide* no. 109: 14-17.

Belcher, C. F. (1927) Some African rarities. *Oologists' Record* 7: 73-76.

Benson, C. W. and Benson, F. M. (1977) *The birds of Malawi*. Limbe, Malawi: Montfort Press.

Benson, C. W. and White, C. M. N. (1957) *Check list of the birds of Northern Rhodesia*. Lusaka: Government Printer.

Benson, C. W. and Pitman, C. R. S. (1964) Further breeding records from Northern Rhodesia (No. 4). *Bull. Brit. Orn. Club* 84: 54-60.

Benson, C. W. and Irwin, M. P. S. (1967) A contribution to the ornithology of Zambia. *Zambia Mus. Pap.* 1.

Benson, C. W., Brooke, R. K. and Vernon, C. J. (1964) Bird breeding data for the Rhodesias and Nyasaland. *Occ. Pap. Natn. Mus. S. Rhodesia* 27B: 30-105.

Benson, C. W., Brooke, R. K., Dowsett, R. J. and Irwin, M. P. S. (1971) *The birds of Zambia*. London: Collins.

Blaauw, F. E. (1897) *A monograph of the cranes*. Leiden and London.

Boulton, R., Brown, D. and Morris, A. (1982) The species survey – Crowned and Wattled Cranes. *Honeyguide* no. 109: 10-13.

Brelsford, W. V. (1946) Ecological aspects of the bird life in the Bangweulu area. *Ostrich* 17: 165-171.

Brelsford, V. (1947) Notes on the birds of Lake Bangweulu area in Northern Rhodesia. *Ibis* 89: 57-77.

Britton, P. L. ed. (1980) *Birds of East Africa: their habitat, status and distribution.* Nairobi: EANHS.

Brooke, R. K. (in press a) *The rare and vulnerable birds of South Africa.*

Brooke, R. K. (in press b) An assessment of rare, vulnerable and endangered South African breeding birds. *Proc. V Pan-Afr. orn. Congr.*

Chapin, J. P. (1939) The birds of the Belgian Congo, part 2. *Bull. Amer. Mus. Nat. Hist.* 75.

Cheesman, R. E. and Sclater, W. L. (1935) On a collection of birds from north-western Abyssinia. *Ibis* (13)5: 151-191.

Clancey, P. A. (1964) *The birds of Natal and Zululand.* Edinburgh and London: Oliver and Boyd.

Clancey, P. A. (1970) *A handlist of the birds of southern Moçambique.* Lourençc Marques: Instituto de Investigação Científica de Moçambique.

Conway, W. and Hamer, A. (1977) A 36-year laying record of a Wattled Crane at the New York Zoological Park. *Auk* 94: 786-787.

Cooper, J. (1969) Observations at a nest of the Wattled Crane. *Honeyguide* no. 60: 17-20.

Day, D. (1978) S.A.O.S. Crane Study Group launched. *Bokmakierie* 30: 67.

Day, D. H. (1979) Report on the Crane Study Group for 1978/79. *Bokmakierie* 31: 61-62.

Day, D. H. (1980) The Crane Study Group, 1980. *Bokmakierie* 32: 90-92.

Day, D. (1981) Some thoughts on our cranes. *Bokmakierie* 33: 58-60.

Dean, W. R. J. (1971) Breeding data for the birds of Natal and Zululand. *Durban Mus. Novit.* 9(6): 59-91.

Dean, W. R. J. and Huntley, M. A. (in press) An updated list of the birds of Angola.

Dorst, J. and Roux, F. (1972) Esquisse écologique sur l'avifaune des Monts du Balé, Ethiopie. *Oiseau et R.F.O.* 42: 203-240.

Douthwaite, R. J. (1974) An endangered population of Wattled Cranes. *Biol. Conserv.* 6: 134-142.

Douthwaite, R. J. (1982) Waterbirds: their ecology and future on the Kafue Flats. Pp. 137-140 in G. W. Howard and G. J. Williams, eds. Proceedings of the national seminar on environment and change: the consequences of hydroelectric power development on the utilization of the Kafue Flats, Lusaka, April 1978. Lusaka: Kafue Basin Research Committee of the University of Zambia.

Douthwaite, R. J., Fox, P. J., Mathiessen, P. and Russell-Smith, A. (1981) The environmental impact of aerosols of endosulfan applied for tsetse fly control in the Okavango Delta, Botswana. Final report of the Endosulfan Monitoring Project. London: Overseas Developme..t Administration.

Dryden, M. (1982) Bird list, in: *The Okavango Swamps Expedition 1981: a report.* Privately printed.

Elliott, C. C. H. (1983) Unusual breeding records made from a helicopter in Tanzania. *Scopus* 7: 33-36.

FDTTS (1960) Northern Rhodesia. Sheet S.C.-36-6. Tunduma Edition 1. Salisbury, Rhodesia and Nyasaland: Director, Federal Department of Trigonometrical and Topographical Surveys.

Fothergill, A. (1982) British undergraduate expedition to the Okavango Delta – interesting observations. *Babbler* no. 4: 7-8.

Fothergill, A. (1983) Okavango: land of restless waters. *Wildlife* 25: 131-134.

Frade, F. and Bacelar, A. (1955) Catálogo das aves da Guiné Portuguesa. *Anais da Junta de Investigações do Ultramar* (Estudos de Zoologia) 10(4) fasc. 2.

Geldenhuys, J. N. (1984) The status of cranes (Aves: Gruidae) in the Orange Free State. *S. Afr. J. Wildl. Res.* 14: 15-18.

Ginn, P. (1979) *Birds of Botswana*. Johannesburg: C. van Rensburg.

Guichard, K. M. (1950) A summary of the birds of the Addis Abeba region, Ethiopia. *J. E. Afr. Nat. Hist. Soc.* 19: 154-181.

Haagner, A. K. (1948) A list of the birds observed in Beira and neighbourhood, with some notes on habits, etc. Part II. *Ostrich* 19: 211-217.

Haldane, L. A. (1956) Birds of the Njombe District. *Tanganyika Notes and Records* no. 44: 1-27.

Horsten, F. (1982) Os parques nacionais e as outras zonas de protecção da natureza de Angola. Material de estudo para os técnicos e agentes de conservação da natureza no. 2. Luanda: Direcção Nacional da Conservação da Natureza, Ministério de Agricultura.

Howard, G. W. and Aspinwall, D. R. (in press) Recent counts of Shoebill, Saddlebill and Wattled Crane in Zambia. [*Ostrich.*]

Irwin, M. P. S. (1981) *The birds of Zimbabwe*. Salisbury (Zimbabwe): Quest Publishing.

Konrad, P. M. (1980) The present status of the Wattled Crane in Africa. International Crane Foundation, unpublished.

Konrad, P. M. (1981) Status and ecology of Wattled Cranes in Africa. Pp. 220-237 in J. C. Lewis and Hiroyuki Masatomi, eds. *Crane research around the world*. Fort Collins, Colorado: Robinson Press.

Konrad, P. M. (in press) Wattled Cranes in peril – Kafue Flats, Zambia. Proc. 3rd Internat. Crane Symp., Bharatpur, India, 5-11 February 1983.

Kumerloeve, H. (1983) Zur Kenntnis altägyptischer Ibis-Darstellungen unter besonderer Berücksichtigung des Waldrapps, *Geronticus eremita* (Linnaeus, 1758). *Bonn. zool. Beitr.* 34: 197-234.

Leppan, A. W. (1944) Birds of the Eastern Caprivi Zipfel. *Ostrich* 15: 20-30.

Lippens, L. and Wille, H. (1976) *Les oiseaux du Zaire*. Tielt, Belgium: Lannoo.

Macartney, P. (1968) Wattled Cranes in Zambia. *Bokmakierie* 20: 38-41.

Marchand, M., Wisse, E. and Drijver, C. A. (1983) Land use possibilities on the Kafue Flats, Zambia. Centre for Environmental Studies, State University of Leiden, Report no. 10.

Masterson, A. (1974) Grassland birds around Salisbury. *Bokmakierie* 26: 69-73.

McLachlan, G. R. and Liversidge, R. (1978) *Roberts birds of South Africa*. Cape Town: Trustees of the John Voelcker Bird Book Fund.

Mees, G. F. (1970) Birds of the Inyanga National Park, Rhodesia. *Zool. Verh.* no. 109.

Ménégaux, A. and Berlioz, J. (1923) Oiseaux. Pp. 107-154 in *La Mission Rohan-Chabot Angola et Rhodesia, 1912-1914*. Paris.

Moltoni, E. and Gnecchi Ruscone, G. (1944) *Gli uccelli dell'Africa Orientale Italiana*, 3. Milan.

Monard, A. (1934) Ornithologie de l'Angola. *Arq. Mus. Bocage* 5: 1-110.

Morris, A. (1981) Africa survey. *Honeyguide* no. 105: 33-34.

Mundy, P. J. (1983) Times are changing for the Wattled Crane. *Quagga* no. 4: 19-20.

Mundy, P. J. (1984) What's up with the Wattled Crane? *Quagga* no. 5: 12-13.

Office of Geography (1965) *Gazetteer no. 92. Tanzania*. Washington, D.C.: Department of the Interior.

Osborne, T. O. (1978) Notes on the birds of Liuwa National Park and preliminary

217

checklist. *Bull. Zambian Orn. Soc.* 10: 8-24.

Parker, I. S. C. (1984) Shoebill *Balaeniceps rex* and Wattled Crane *Grus carunculatus* in the Moyowosi Swamp, Tanzania. *Scopus* 8: 24-25.

Pinto, A. A. da R. (1965) Contribuição para o conhecimento da avifauna da região nordeste do distrito do Moxico, Angola. *Bol. Inst. Invest. cient. Angola* (Luanda) 1(2): 153-249.

Pinto, A. A. da R. (1966) Notas sobre as colecções ornitológicas recolhidas em Angola nas expedições efectuadas pelo Instituto de Investigação Científica de Angola de 1959 a 1961. *Bol. Inst. Invest. cient. Angola* (Luanda) 3(2): 149-236.

Pinto, A. A. da R. (1970) Um catálogo das aves do distrito da Huila (Angola). *Mem. Trab. Inst. Invest. cient. Angola* 6.

Pinto, A. A. da R. (in press) *Ornitologia de Angola*, 1. Lisbon.

Pitman, C. R. S. (1935) The eggs of *Bugeranus carunculatus* (Gmelin) – Wattled Crane. *Oologists' Record* 15: 49-53.

Procter, J. (1968) The birds of the Usangu Plains. *Tanzania Notes and Records* no. 69: 1-14.

Ruwet, J.-C. (1964) Notes écologiques et éthologiques sur les oiseaux des plaines de la Lufira supérieure (Katanga), II. *Rev. Zool. Bot. Afr.* 69(1-2): 1-63.

Schouteden, H. (1949) De vogels van Belgisch Congo en van Ruanda-Urundi, II. *Ann. Mus. Congo Belge*, C. Zool. Ser. IV, 2, fasc. 2: 201-416.

Schouteden, H. (1965a) La faune ornithologique de la province du Kwango. (Contributions à l'ornithologie de la République du Congo, VII.) *Doc. Zool. Mus. Roy. Afr. Centr.* 8.

Schouteden, H. (1965b) La faune ornithologique des territoires de Dilolo et Kolwezi de la province du Katanga. (Contributions à l'ornithologie de la République du Congo, VIII.) *Doc. Zool. Mus. Roy. Afr. Centr.* 9.

Schouteden, H. (1971) La faune ornithologique de la province du Katanga. (Contributions à l'ornithologie de la République Démocratique du Congo, XI.) *Doc. Zool. Mus. Roy. Afr. Centr.* 17.

Shelley, G. E. (1899) On a collection of birds from the Tanganyika Plateau, in British Central Africa. *Ibis* (7)5: 364-380.

Sievi, J. and Manson, A. (1974) [Letter.] *Honeyguide* no. 77: 48.

Skead, C. J. (1967) Ecology of birds in the eastern Cape Province. *Ostrich* suppl. 7.

Smithers, R. H. N. (1964) *A check list of the birds of the Bechuanaland Protectorate and the Caprivi Strip with data on ecology and breeding.* Trustees of the National Museums of S. Rhodesia.

Smithers, R. H. N., Irwin, M. P. S. and Paterson, M. L. (1957) *A check list of the birds of Southern Rhodesia.* Rhodesian Ornithological Society.

Snell, M. L. (1983) Wattled Cranes at Inyanga. *Honeyguide* no. 113: 33.

Snow, D. W. ed. (1978) *An atlas of speciation in African non-passerine birds.* London: Trustees of the British Museum (Natural History).

Soutter, R. (1981) Chemical threat to swamps. *Johannesburg Star*, Friday 5 June.

Tarboton, W. R. (in press) The status and conservation of the Wattled Crane in the Transvaal. *Proc. V Pan-Afr. orn. Congr.*

Tarboton, W. and Day, D. (1980) The Wattled Crane. *Fauna and Flora* 36: 4-5.

Tarboton, W. R., Barnes, P. R. and Johnson, D. N. (in press) The Wattled Crane in South Africa during 1978-1982. Proc. 3rd Internat. Crane Symp., Bharatapur, India, 5-11 February 1983.

Traylor, M. A. (1963) Check list of Angolan birds. *Publ. cult. Co. Diam. Angola, Lisboa* no. 61.

Traylor, M. A. (1965) A collection of birds from Barotseland and Bechuanaland. *Ibis* 107: 137-172.

Urban, E. K. (in press) The cranes of Africa – an overview. Proc. 3rd. Internat. Crane Symp., Bharatpur, India, 5-11 February 1983.

Urban, E. K. and Brown, L. H. (1971) *A checklist of the birds of Ethiopia.* Addis Ababa: Haile Sellassie I University Press.

Urban, E. K. and Walkinshaw, L. H. (1967) The Wattled Crane in Ethiopia. *Auk* 84: 263-264.

Verheyen, R. (1953) *Oiseaux. Exploration du Parc National de l'Upemba*, fasc. 19. Bruxelles: Inst. Parcs Natn. du Congo Belge.

Verschuren, J. (1978) Observations ornithologiques dans les parcs nationaux du Zaire, 1968-1974. *Gerfaut* 68: 3-24.

Vesey-FitzGerald, D. and Beesley, J. S. S. (1960) An annotated list of the birds of the Rukwa Valley. *Tanganyika Notes and Records* no. 54: 91-110.

Vincent, A. W. (1945) On the breeding habits of some African birds. *Ibis* 87: 345-365.

Walkinshaw, L. H. (1965) The Wattled Crane *Bugeranus carunculatus. Ostrich* 36: 73-87.

Walkinshaw, L. (1973) *Cranes of the world.* New York: Winchester Press.

West, O. (1963) Notes on the Wattled Crane. *Ostrich* 34: 63-77.

West, O. (1976) Notes on the distribution and status of the southern population of Wattled Crane in Africa. Pp. 347-349 in J. C. Lewis, ed. *Proc. Internat. Crane Workshop*, 3-6 September 1975, Baraboo, Wisconsin. Oklahoma State University.

West, O. (1977) The Wattled Crane *Bugeranus carunculatus* (Gmelin), an endangered species. *Endangered Wildlife* 1(4).

West, O. (1982) The Wattled Crane *Grus carunculatus* (Gmelin), an endangered species. *Naturalist* 27(1): 2-9.

White, C. M. N. (1945) The ornithology of the Kaonde-Lunda Province, Northern Rhodesia. – Part III. *Ibis* 87: 309-345.

Winterbottom, J. M. (1971) *A preliminary check list of the birds of South West Africa.* Windhoek: S.W.A. Scientific Society.

Yanchinski, S. (1981) Must Botswana's wildlife give way to cattle? *New Scientist* 89, 5 March: 598-600.

Zaloumis, E. A. and Milstein, P. le S. (1975) The conservation of wetland habitats for waterfowl in southern Africa. *Afr. Wild Life* 29(1) Suppl.: 1-12.

INACCESSIBLE RAIL   RARE
Atlantisia rogersi Lowe, 1923

Order GRUIFORMES   Family RALLIDAE
                                                          Subfamily RALLINAE

Summary This, the smallest flightless bird in the world, is confined to uninhabited Inaccessible Island in the Tristan da Cunha group, where it is numerous but at permanent risk from the introduction of rats, cats and alien plants.

Distribution The Inaccessible Rail is endemic to Inaccessible Island (16 km^2) in the Tristan da Cunha group (a dependency of the British Crown Colony of St.Helena), South Atlantic Ocean (see Hagen 1952, Wace and Holdgate 1976). It occurs throughout the island, from sea-level to the highest point and even on the steepest slopes (Broekhuysen and Macnae 1949, Hagen 1952, Elliott 1953,1957).

Population Numbers of this tiny, retiring and partially subterranean species have proved difficult to estimate and various figures have been proposed; the most recent analysis apparently is the most comprehensive and reliable. Observations in 1938 suggested (conservatively) one family (3-5 birds) per 4 ha, thus 25 families (at least 75 birds) per km^2 and, Inaccessible being 16 km^2, 400 families totalling 1,200 to 2,000 birds (Hagen 1952); however, observations in 1950-1952 suggested 30 birds per 4 ha, and thus 5,000 to 10,000 birds for the whole island (Elliott 1957), although this observer had originally guessed as many as 10,000 to 20,000 (Elliott 1953). Density was considered highest in coastal strips (Elliott 1953), i.e. in tussock-grass *Spartina arundinacea* (Hagen 1952). However, density within tussock-grass areas was found to be variable, increasing where low ferns formed luxuriant meadows of undergrowth in more open tussock, and also where these ferns independently formed mats of vegetation (Hagen 1952). The species was numerous in tussock-grass above Blenden Hall (west coast) in March 1961 and above Waterfall and Tom's Beach (east coast) in February and March 1968, but no population estimates were then possible (Wace and Holdgate 1976). In 1974 at Salt Beach the population density varied between four pairs per ha in the mixed luxuriant vegetation of the old potato garden to c. 1 pair per ha in neighbouring tussock-grass; and in a sample of roughly 100 birds seen in January, c. 40% (excluding chicks) were adult breeding birds, suggesting 1.5 pairs per ha or 1,000-2,000 breeding pairs for the island (Richardson in press). However, in 1982-1983 more intensive studies of the species resulted in an estimate of a minimum of 10,000 adults, based on the following break-down of calculated densities in four habitat-types: 1 km^2 of mixed tussock, fern, grass and *Empetrum* held 15 birds per ha and thus 1,500 in all; 4 km^2 of virtually pure tussock held 10 birds per ha and thus 4,000; 7 km^2 of mixed short upland tussock, grass, fern, etc., held five birds per ha and thus 3,500; and 5 km^2 of fern-bush *Blechnum palmiforme*, mostly with island-tree *Phylica arborea* canopy, held two birds per ha and thus 1,000 (the extra 1 km^2 here is an attempt to allow for the steepest coastal slopes) (M. W. Fraser *in litt.* 1984). The total may be much higher as it was not possible to survey uniform tussock on the steepest slopes, and the appearance of the young obviously increases overall numbers substantially, with (e.g.) 12 chicks recorded in 1 ha of tussock-grass (M. W. Fraser *in litt.* 1984).

Ecology This flightless species occurs in all native vegetation-types on Inaccessible (characterised as four "habitat-types" in Population, elsewhere as three): the coastal tussock-grass, the fern-bush and island-tree thickets that occur on the peaty plateau, and the *Empetrum* and *Scirpus* heath at the highest altitudes (Wace and Holdgate 1976). It was, however, absent from one area of short dry tussock on cinder cones at Dune Hills in the south-west (M. W. Fraser *in litt.* 1984). It runs very rapidly among tussock-grass in almost mouse-like fashion (Lowe 1928, Broekhuysen and Macnae 1949, Wace and Holdgate 1976), occurring most commonly where low small ferns provide rodent-type tunnels of shelter up to 1 m long (Hagen 1952, M. W. Fraser *in litt.* 1984). Evidence of its early reported use of holes (Lowe 1928) is growing, birds in parts of the island (at least) apparently spending large periods of time underneath mats of vegetation, maintaining contact with others in their group by calling (Hagen 1952); moreover, one captured specimen dug a hole 0.3 m deep in the course of a night (or less), and one nest was placed at the end of a tunnel of vegetation c. 0.3 m long (Elliott 1957), while in 1982-1983 birds often entered (sometimes occupied) seabird burrows and were frequently seen to disappear under loose boulders on the beach and emerge from beneath others several metres away (M. W. Fraser *in litt.* 1984, M. K. Swales *in litt.* 1984). The species has thus been characterised as occupying the ecological niche of a mouse (*Bull. Brit. Orn. Club* 104 [1984]: 3). It is active by day, but also to a lesser extent at night (Hagen 1952, M. W. Fraser *in litt.* 1984). Early reports based on second-hand information indicated its food as insects, worms and seeds (Lowe 1928); three stomachs contained seeds of berries (*Empetrum*, *Nertera*) and dock *Rumex*, plus flies, caterpillars, weevils, beetles and a mite (Hagen 1952). A species of centipede was found to be an important component of the diet in 1982-1983, and full details on food then recorded are being prepared for publication (M. W. Fraser *in litt.* 1984, M. K. Swales *in litt.* 1984). Indications from these recent studies (prior to full data analysis) are that birds have a flexible system of territories, generally keeping to a discrete area but occasionally going outside it (M. W. Fraser *in litt.* 1984). The breeding season is presumably extended, with evidence from October to February, clutch-size two or three (Rothschild 1928, Broekhuysen and Macnae 1949, Hagen 1952, Elliott 1953). More recent evidence suggests clutch-size is mostly two, with two broods of two found, January 1974 (Richardson in press), and four nests each with two eggs in 1982-1983 (M. W. Fraser *in litt.* 1984). Two of the latter nests were in uniform beds of sedge on the plateau, the other two in the tussock/fern interface on the coastal strip at Blenden Hall; and of the eight eggs, three were infertile (M. W. Fraser *in litt.* 1984). Nests have been reported as having "ingeniously woven" roofs (Voous 1962). As chicks grow older they become more adventurous, climbing a metre or more up into sloping tussock (M. W. Fraser *in litt.* 1984). The species lives in (presumably family) parties of 3-5 birds (Hagen 1952); in 1982-1983 family groups varied from one parent with one chick to two adults, one subadult and two chicks (M. W. Fraser *in litt.* 1984). Although birds have been reported to have no natural enemies other than the Tristan Great Skua

Catharacta skua hamiltoni (Hagen 1952, Elliott 1957), the Tristan Thrush *Nesocichla eremita* was found in 1982-1983 to prey fairly heavily on chicks, taking (e.g.) four of the 12 chicks found in 1 ha of tussock at Blenden Hall (M. W. Fraser *in litt.* 1984; also Fraser 1983). Wet weather is also suspected of controlling chick numbers (M. W. Fraser *in litt.* 1984).

Threats The single most important threat to this flightless species is the risk of mammalian predators, especially rats and cats, becoming established on Inaccessible. Rails on islands are notoriously vulnerable: of 18 forms listed as extinct since 1600 in King (1978-1979) (to which should be added *Atlantisia podarces* and *Porzana astrictocarpus* from St.Helena: see Olson 1973) all were from islands, and of 16 forms currently treated as threatened in King (1978-1979) eleven are from islands. Two other *Atlantisia* rails, *elpenor* from Ascension Island and *podarces* from St.Helena, have become extinct since the advent of man to the islands (Olson 1973). Black rats *Rattus rattus* abound on Tristan da Cunha (Elliott 1953) and with every visit made by the Tristan islanders to Inaccessible there is a small but distinct risk of accidental introduction of this species. The islanders were reputed formerly to deposit unwanted cats or dogs on both Inaccessible and Nightingale Islands in preference to destroying them (Holdgate 1957). In the last century goats and pigs were loose on Inaccessible and did much damage to the vegetation (Holdgate and Wace 1961), but had been totally eradicated by 1950, to be replaced by a few cattle and a small flock of sheep, all removed before 1960 without having caused any damage (H. F. I. Elliott *in litt.* 1984); moreover, concern that the invasive exotic New Zealand flax *Phormium tenax* might overrun the island's natural vegetation have been allayed by recent observations (Wace and Holdgate 1976, M. K. Swales *in litt.* 1983). The tussock-grass on Inaccessible was deliberately set fire to in January 1909, reaching sufficient intensity to be visible from Tristan (40 km away) and to be still burning a month later (Barrow 1910): presumably this may very nearly have wiped out the (then still undescribed) rail. Around 1950, the species was much sought after by museums, though control of scientific collecting was then carefully exercised (Elliott 1953).

Conservation Measures Taken Much has been done since 1950 to establish principles for the management of Inaccessible and its wildlife and to foster understanding of these principles by the Tristan islanders, resulting in a new conservation ordinance in 1976 (see Elliott 1953, Wace and Holdgate 1976).

Conservation Measures Proposed Protected area status for Inaccessible Island has at least twice been urged (Broekhuysen 1957, Flint 1967) and, although the articles of the 1976 ordinance provide important protection for the island (see Wace and Holdgate 1976), more formal and concrete recognition of its importance to wildlife and science is still desirable (a view fully endorsed by the Denstone Expedition to Inaccessible: M. K. Swales *in litt.* 1984). The possibility of establishing a second population by introducing birds to adjacent Nightingale Island (also uninhabited and rat- and cat-free) appears not to have been considered but deserves examination: one drawback is that the island is much more regularly visited by Tristan islanders, with the concomitant risks of rats and mice escaping by accident (M. K. Swales *in litt.* 1984) or of birds becoming traded in (H. F. I. Elliott *in litt.* 1984), and one serious objection is that Nightingale may possess an endemic invertebrate fauna which could suffer extinctions as a consequence (W. R. P. Bourne *in litt.* 1984). Introduction to Gough Island (also in the Tristan da Cunha group) has also been suggested (H. F. I. Elliott *in litt.* 1984) as has the establishment of the species in captivity, as a conservation precaution, to facilitate continuing scientific research, and to improve public awareness of Inaccessible's wildlife and importance (M. W. Fraser *in litt.* 1984). Scientific collection of this species requires the strictest control (Wace and Holdgate 1976).

Remarks The Inaccessible Rail is "the smallest flightless bird known to exist, or to have existed", and moreover has been judged "probably ... in view of its remarkable anatomical and other features ... the most interesting rail now living" (Lowe 1928). Whether this opinion is shared or not, the species is unquestionably a most exceptional island form. Inaccessible Island is also important for one of two small populations of the Grosbeak Bunting *Nesospiza wilkinsi* (see relevant account), for a remarkable population of the Tristan Bunting *N. acunhae* (see relevant account) and for seabird colonies of exceptional importance (Broekhuysen and Macnae 1949, Hagen 1952, Elliott 1953,1957, Flint 1967, Wace and Holdgate 1976); it also holds an important population of the Tristan Thrush (see Appendix C). All these factors reinforce the case for protected area status for the island.

References

Barrow, K. M. (1910) *Three years in Tristan da Cunha*. London: Skeffington and Son.

Broekhuysen, G. J. (1957) [Note.] *Oryx* 4: 175-176.

Broekhuysen, G. J. and Macnae, W. (1949) Observations on the birds of Tristan da Cunha Islands and Gough Island in February and early March, 1948. *Ardea* 37: 97-113.

Elliott, H. F. I. (1953) The fauna of Tristan da Cunha. *Oryx* 2: 41-53.

Elliott, H. F. I. (1957) A contribution to the ornithology of the Tristan da Cunha group. *Ibis* 99: 545-586.

Flint, J. H. (1967) Conservation problems on Tristan da Cunha. *Oryx* 9: 28-32.

Fraser, M. W. (1983) The Denstone Expedition to Inaccessible Island. *Cormorant* 11: 69-73.

Hagen, Y. (1952) *Birds of Tristan da Cunha*. Results of the Norwegian Scientific Expedition to Tristan da Cunha 1937-1938, no. 20. Oslo: Norske Videnskaps-Akademi.

Holdgate, M. W. (1957) Gough Island – a possible sanctuary. *Oryx* 4: 168-175.

Holdgate, M. W. and Wace, N. M. (1961) The influence of man on the floras of southern islands. *Polar Record* 10: 475-493.

King, W. B. (1978-1979) *Red data book, 2: Aves*. 2nd edition. Morges, Switzerland: IUCN.

Lowe, P. R. (1928) A description of *Atlantisia rogersi*, the diminutive and flightless rail of Inaccessible Island (Southern Atlantic), with some notes on flightless rails. *Ibis* (12)4: 99-131.

Olson, S. L. (1973) Evolution of the rails of the South Atlantic islands. *Smithsonian Contrib. Zool.* 152.

Richardson, M. E. (in press) Aspects of the ornithology of the Tristan da Cunha group. *Cormorant*.

Rothschild, Lord (1928) [The hitherto unknown egg of the Flightless Rail (*Atlantisia rogersi* Lowe) of Inaccessible Island, Tristan d'Acunha group.] *Bull. Brit. Orn. Club* 48: 121-122.

Voous, K. H. (1962) Notes on a collection of birds from Tristan da Cunha and Gough Island. *Beaufortia* 9 (no. 99): 105-114.

Wace, N. M. and Holdgate, M. W. (1976) *Man and nature in Tristan da Cunha*. Morges, Switzerland: IUCN (Monograph no. 6).

WHITE-WINGED FLUFFTAIL   INDETERMINATE
Sarothrura ayresi (Gurney, 1877)

Order GRUIFORMES   Family RALLIDAE
                                                          Subfamily RALLINAE

___

Summary This is a tiny enigmatic rail, probably nomadic in pursuit of suitably "dry" marshland, rare at best: it is known from the Ethiopian highlands (but there are no records since the 1950s despite often intensive searches), South Africa (where it was first found in the last century and rediscovered in 1982), Zambia (two records) and Zimbabwe (three records).

Distribution The White-winged Flufftail is known from southern (chiefly South) Africa and Ethiopia, with records for the former area from 1877 to 1901 and 1955 to the present, and for the latter from 1905 to 1957. There has been no long-term occurrence at any known locality. A specimen was collected at King William's Town, eastern Cape Province, in August 1876 (Keith *et al.* 1970) but the species was first described from two birds shot at Potchefstroom, Transvaal, on 4 October and 24 November that year, when one or two others were seen (Ayres 1877; also Keith *et al.* 1970). A male was collected at the latter locality in August 1894 (Benson and Irwin 1971,1974), and a female at Bloemfontein, Orange Free State, on 9 October 1901 (Keith *et al.* 1970).·It was also reported (no dates) from vleis around Durban (Stark and Sclater 1906; also Keith *et al.* 1970). A specimen collected at Charada, Kaffa, south-western Ethiopia, 28 May 1905, was described as a new species, *Ortygops macmillani* (Bannerman 1911), but subsequent material showed this to be identical with South African specimens of *Sarothrura ayresi* (Graant and Mackworth-Praed 1941,1946); at least five specimens were collected at Antotto (Entotto), Sululta (these two probably the same: Ash 1978) and Akaki (a reservoir near Addis Ababa: S. J. Tyler *in litt.* 1983), 1939-1942 (Keith *et al.* 1970, Collar and Violani in press); all subsequent Ethiopian records, including a total of 22 collected specimens, are from Gefersa and Sululta, respectively 18 km west and 20 km north of Addis Abada, all (except for two undated) in the period 11 July to 22 September, and in the years 1947-1951 (Keith *et al.* 1970), except one from 1957 (see Remarks). Single birds were found in the Rustenburg district of south central Transvaal on 8 May 1955 (Wolff and Milstein 1976; same record, wrongly dated, in Tarboton 1968), and in the Gonubi Bird Sanctuary near East London, eastern Cape Province, on 15 September 1955 and 5 October 1956; one was caught unharmed by a dog at Cambridge, near East London, on 17 September 1956, kept for six months, and later released (Keith *et al.* 1970). A bird flushed from a marsh 28 km west of Chingdon on the Solwezi road, Zambia, on 5 November 1962, was the first record for the species between South Africa and Ethiopia (Brooke 1964). A specimen was found dead under a powerline in Suikerbosrand Nature Reserve adjoining Heidelberg, Transvaal, on 8 August 1975 (Wolff and Milstein 1976). Three sightings of single birds – conceivably the same individual – near Harare on 14 January, 12 February and 2 March 1977 (Hopkinson and Masterson 1977) remain the only records for Zimbabwe, though breeding there is not ruled out (Irwin 1981). A bird was found at Greystone Park Farm, near Kitwe, Zambia, on

13 February 1981 (*Zambia Orn. Soc. Newsletter*, February 1981: 26). Thirty-five birds (one collected) were found during searches of a very small proportion of Franklin Marsh, East Griqualand, south-western Natal, between 25 October 1982 and 7 January 1983, and 7-10 birds near Belfast, Transvaal, between 9 December 1982 and 9 January 1983 (Mendelsohn *et al.* 1983, J. M. Mendelsohn pers. comm. 1983). No birds were found during careful searches of (the then much drier) Franklin Marsh, March and April 1983 (J. M. Mendelsohn pers. comm. 1983). There is also a modern record from Ganspan, Jan Kempdorp, northern Cape Province (Brooke in press). The distribution of records by month of the year (based on references above and examination of specimens in MRAC: NJC) is as follows.

	J	F	M	A	M	J	J	A	S	O	N	D
South Africa	19	2	1		1			3	2	18	2	2
Ethiopia					1	1	13	5	6			
TOTAL	19	2	1		2	1	13	8	8	18	2	2

Further consideration of this evidence and its distributional implications is given under Ecology below.

Population There is no information on numbers, but they are likely to be extremely small.

Ecology Habitat of this species is difficult to characterise from the various records. Patches of Franklin Marsh, Natal, were noted to hold the bird, while other patches held Red-chested Flufftails *S. rufa*, with little mixing although the areas appeared the same; no particular type of vegetation was preferred, but most *ayresi* were flushed from areas without standing water, and the species was apparently absent when the water-level was higher (Mendelsohn *et al.* 1983). Other records would seem to support this preference for less flooded patches, but they commonly note a proximity to water, e.g. birds were found near a drainage line in dry *Carex* marsh (Mendelsohn *et al.* 1983), one was flushed from long grass bordering a small dam (Wolff and Milstein 1976), one from knee-high grass by a shallow ditch, and another from the same at the edge of a swamp (Hopkinson and Masterson 1977). However, records from Zambia (*Zambia Orn. Soc. Newsletter*, February 1981: 26) and Gefersa, Ethiopia, refer to marsh with ankle-deep water, the latter with rushes and marsh orchids; at Sululta, Ethiopia, the habitat was "close dry grass clumps partly submerged during the rains" (Guichard 1948). Both these Ethiopian sites dried out each year and could not have been used year-round by the species (Guichard 1948). However, the view that because the birds could be caught by hand at these sites (Guichard 1948, Gajdacs and Keve 1968) they are poor fliers and therefore only capable of short-distance migration (Guichard 1948) is, in the light of some post-1960 localities and observations of strong flight (Hopkinson and Masterson 1977, J. M. Mendelsohn pers. comm. 1983), no longer acceptable (catching by hand may, e.g., simply reflect a reluctance to fly during the breeding season, birds being noted to be extremely difficult to flush in July and August in Ethiopia: Moltoni and Gnecchi Ruscone 1944). Food is known only from the stomach-contents of the syntype, which were "water-insects" (Ayres 1877), and of the most recent (Franklin Marsh) specimen, which were grain-seeds and vegetable mush (J. M. Mendelsohn pers. comm. 1983). The lack of subspeciation between specimens from Ethiopia and South Africa provided the consideration that birds migrated between the two; however, the lack of records (at least until 1962) from the intervening area and the overlap of records in the August/September period militated against this possibility (Guichard 1948, Benson *et al.* 1970, Wolff and Milstein 1976). Breeding was confirmed in Ethiopia by the capture of a female with developed eggs on 18 July 1948 (Gajdacs and Keve 1968) and of a still flightless young on 22 September 1948 (Guichard 1950), and has recently been indicated in South Africa by the discovery of an empty nest "associated with" birds of this species in December 1982 (Brooke in press) and the sighting of two apparently newly fledged birds on 6 January 1983 (Mendelsohn *et al.* 1983). The alternative view, that the two populations are relict and unconnected, perhaps having been forced apart by competition from a congener such as the Streaky-breasted Flufftail *Sarothrura boehmi* (Keith *et al.* 1970), now has wide currency (Benson *et al.* 1970, Benson and Irwin 1971, Clancey 1972, Wolff and Milstein 1976, Ripley 1977, Brooke in press). On evidence gathered 1947-1948 it was thought likely that the species's migration to breed on the Ethiopian high plateau was purely local, probably from the western swamps (males arriving first); the Kaffa record in May was cited in support of this (Guichard 1948). In South Africa the Rustenburg record in May was similarly noted as within easy reach of the highveld pans with whose filling the other records seemed correlated (Wolff and Milstein 1976). To explain the monotypic status of the species and its occurrence in Zimbabwe it has been postulated that, as assumed for many swamp birds, it has no definite seasonal movement but erupts and disperses – over long distances if populations are high – in relation to rainfall: gene-exchange may therefore occur irregularly between northern and southern populations (Hopkinson and Masterson 1977). It is certainly to be noted that, owing to higher water-levels, the species was apparently absent from Franklin Marsh, Natal, throughout November 1982 and for the 10 years prior to October 1982 (Mendelsohn *et al.* 1983), suggesting a nomadic opportunist whose distribution never stabilises. It is also to be noted that often intensive searches (sometimes with dogs and up to 30 beaters) at Gefersa, Sululta, and many other marshes in Ethiopa, 1968-1976, failed to produce any evidence for the survival of the species in the country (Erard 1974, Ash 1978).

Threats The rarity of this species is possibly the result of competitive exclusion by a congener, e.g. the Streaky-breasted Flufftail (Keith *et al.* 1970, Benson and Irwin 1971). The view that economic development accompanied by destruction of habitat could also have affected it adversely in South Africa (Keith *et al.* 1970, Benson and Irwin 1971) has been discounted (Wolff and Milstein 1976), but the temporary or permanent loss of marshland there – as a result of drainage, damming, pumping, burning and grazing – has been noted with alarm (Mendelsohn *et al.* 1983). In Ethiopia, the marsh at Gefersa has been reduced by damming (Ash 1978).

Conservation Measures Taken None is known, other than that the species is fully protected by provincial and homeland conservation ordinances, South Africa (Brooke in press).

Conservation Measures Proposed Given the evidently nomadic behaviour of this species no specific measures can be invoked with confidence. However, the preservation of as much remaining South African marshland as possible, e.g. for the sake of other bird species such as the Wattled Crane *Bugeranus carunculatus* (see relevant account) and Bittern *Botaurus stellaris* (Mendelsohn *et al.* 1983, Brooke in press) would offer the best hope for the species long-term. Where possible, regulation of marsh water-levels to maintain or create suitable conditions (as understood in Mendelsohn *et al.* 1983) might prove valuable; and a programme to catch, mark and even radio-tag birds could yield important data on the species's biology and ecology.

Remarks The major study of the genus *Sarothrura* repeated but did not accept sight records of *ayresi* (Keith *et al.* 1970), a position subsequently considered over-cautious in view of the bird's unmistakability in flight (see Hopkinson and Masterson 1977, Brooke in press; also Wolff and Milstein 1976, Irwin 1981); this present analysis has accepted all sight records. It is thought that the species tends to flush once and may not do so again for several days, so that the Franklin Marsh record of 35, which strictly refers to sightings, probably involved little if any double counting (J. M. Mendelsohn pers. comm. 1983; also Stark and Sclater 1906). The record of a bird from Ethiopia in 1957 concerns a specimen in MRAC listed by Keith *et al.* (1970) as collected on 10 September 1951; examination of the manuscript on the specimen-label (NJC) shows that the year is 1957, not 1951, an opinion confirmed by A. Prigogine (pers. comm. 1983) and M. Louette (*in litt.* 1984).

References

Ash, J. S. (1978) *Sarothrura* crakes in Ethiopia. *Bull. Brit. Orn. Club* 98: 26-29.

Ayres, T. (1877) Additional notes on the ornithology of the Republic of Transvaal. Communicated by J. H. Gurney. *Ibis* (4)1: 339-354.

Bannerman, D. A. (1911) [Three new birds from south-western Abyssinia.] *Bull. Brit. Orn. Club* 29: 37-39.

Benson, C. W. and Irwin, M. P. S. (1971) A South African male of *Sarothrura ayresi*, and other specimens of the genus in the Leiden Museum. *Ostrich* 42: 227-228.

Benson, C. W., and Irwin, M. P. S. (1974) On a specimen of *Sarothrura ayresi* from the Transvaal in the Leiden Museum. *Ostrich* 45: 193-194.

Benson, C. W., Brooke, R. K., Dowsett, R. J. and Irwin, M. P. S. (1970) Notes on the birds of Zambia: Part 5. *Arnoldia (Rhod.)* 4(40).

Brooke, R. K. (1964) Avian observations on a journey across Central Africa and additional information on some of the species seen. *Ostrich* 35: 277-292.

Brooke, R. K. (in press) *The rare and vulnerable birds of South Africa.*

Clancey, P. A. (1972) A catalogue of birds of the South African Sub-region, suppl. 2. *Durban Mus. Novit.* 9(12): 163-200.

Collar, N. J. and Violani, C. G. (in press) Specimens of *Calandrella obbiensis* and

Sarothrura ayresi in Milan Museum. *Bull. Brit. Orn. Club.*

Erard, C. (1974) Notes faunistiques et systématiques sur quelques oiseaux d'Ethiopie. *Bonn. zool. Beitr.* 25: 76-86.

Gajdacs, M. and Keve, A. (1968) Beiträge zur Vogelfauna des mittleren Athiopien. *Stuttgarter Beitr. Naturk.* no. 182.

Grant, C. H. B. and Mackworth-Praed, C. W. (1941) Notes on eastern African birds. *Bull. Brit. Orn. Club* 62: 31-35.

Grant, C. H. B. and Mackworth-Praed, C. W. (1946) Notes on eastern African birds. *Bull. Brit. Orn. Club* 66: 37-39.

Guichard, K. M. (1948) Notes on *Sarothura [sic] ayresi* and three birds new to Abyssinia. *Bull. Brit. Orn. Club* 68: 102-104.

Guichard, K. M. (1950) A summary of the birds of the Addis Abeba region, Ethiopia. *J. E. Afr. Nat. Hist. Soc.* 19: 154-178.

Hopkinson, G. and Masterson, A. N. B. (1977) On the occurrence near Salisbury of the White-winged Flufftail. *Honeyguide* no. 91: 25-28.

Irwin, M. P. S. (1981) *The birds of Zimbabwe*. Salisbury, Zimbabwe: Quest Publishing.

Keith, S., Benson, C. W. and Irwin, M. P. S. (1970) The genus *Sarothrura* (Aves, Rallidae). *Bull. Amer. Mus. Nat. Hist.* 143(1).

Mendelsohn, J. M., Sinclair, J. C. and Tarboton, W. R. (1983) Flushing flufftails out of vleis. *Bokmakierie* 35: 9-11.

Moltoni, E. and Gnecchi Ruscone, G. (1944) *Gli uccelli dell'Africa Orientale Italiana*, 3. Milan.

Ripley, S. D. (1977) *Rails of the world*. Toronto: M. F. Feheley.

Stark, A. and Sclater, W. L. (1906) *The birds of South Africa*, 4. London: R. H. Porter.

Tarboton, W. R. (1968) *Check list of birds of the south central Transvaal*. Johannesburg: Witwatersrand Bird Club.

Wolff, S. W. and Milstein, P. le S. (1976) Rediscovery of the White-winged Flufftail in South Africa. *Bokmakierie* 28: 33-36.

SLENDER-BILLED FLUFFTAIL   INDETERMINATE

Sarothrura watersi (Bartlett, 1879)

Order GRUIFORMES   Family RALLIDAE
                                                  Subfamily RALLINAE

Summary This small marsh rail is known only from four well separated areas in central and east Madagascar, but is likely to be more widespread, and possibly more at risk from natural causes than from man.

Distribution The Slender-billed Flufftail was first described from "south-east Betsileo", i.e. south-central Madagascar, from which four specimens (one undated, three in December 1875) are known (Keith *et al.* 1970). One of these specimens, in BMNH, is labelled "Fangalathova" (NJC) but this is not a locality but evidently a local name for the bird (since such a name is also given for the Madagascar Flufftail *Sarothrura insularis* in Milne Edwards and Grandidier 1885; see Remarks). An early map marks the south-east of "Betsileo province" as the region north-east and south-west of Ikongo (Locamus 1900; see also map in Deschamps 1960). In April 1928 an immature male was collected by L. Lavauden at Analamazaotra near Périnet in eastern Madagascar (specimen in Grenoble: O. Langrand *in litt.* 1984). The species was subsequently found at 1,800 m near Andapa, north-east Madagascar, where 10 specimens were brought in by native hunters between 23 August and 7 September 1930 (Delacour 1932, Rand 1936, Keith *et al.* 1970). Another two specimens are known, labelled simply "Madagascar" without date or name of collector (Keith *et al.* 1970). In 1970-1971 it was found in the 1,200 km^2 area around the capital, Antananarivo, central Madagascar, at three sites at least, and was suspected of breeding in all *Cyperus* marshes in this area, which is all above 1,250 m (Salvan 1972); however, a search around Antananarivo in the mid-1970s by three ornithologists (A. D. Forbes-Watson, G. S. Keith and D. A. Turner) wholly failed to rediscover this species, raising doubts about the validity of the records from this area (D. A. Turner *in litt.* 1983). It has been speculated that this species may replace the common Madagascar Flufftail at higher altitudes and that it could occur on the Itremo massif (Benson *et al.* 1976); also that temperature may control its montane distribution (Rand 1936). However, Ikongo and its surrounding area appears to be or have been on the upper edge of the eastern rainforest belt and if the species was indeed collected there, and if the records from Antananarivo are in fact mistaken, there is a strong possibility that its distribution is determined by the distribution of rainforest in Madagascar.

Population Numbers are unknown. On the basis of uncorroborated observations (see above), density has been estimated at one pair per 2 ha of marsh, and the species perhaps breeds in small numbers around Antananarivo (Salvan 1972). If these records are invalid, however, it is to be noted that the species has not been seen in the wild for over 50 years.

Ecology This rail inhabits small swamps (an association with *Cyperus* is indicated) and adjacent grassy areas, keeping to dense vegetation though occasionally flying short distances (Delacour 1932, Rand 1936, Salvan 1972). Food is unrecorded (Keith *et al.* 1970). A male and female in breeding condition, Andapa, September, suggest the species may be a rainy season breeder at that locality (Rand 1936, Keith *et al.* 1970). An adult with a juvenile was reported near Antananarivo, May (Salvan 1972). There is no evidence of migration (Keith *et al.* 1970).

Threats Prior to its (uncorroborated) discovery around Antananarivo, this species was considered rare (Delacour 1932) and possibly "a relict on its way to early extinction" (Keith *et al.* 1970). Antananarivo being in the most densely populated and disturbed part of Madagascar (Salvan 1972), the bird may prove to be more resilient than suspected. The Laniera marshes, where the species has apparently bred (record of adult with juvenile, above), have been turned into rice-fields, and this is implied to be an ornithological disaster (Salvan 1972); but it is not clear if the breeding record was made before or after this development.

Conservation Measures Taken The species has been recorded from the area now established as the Périnet-Analamazaotra Special Reserve, which covers 810 ha (Andriamampianina 1981); birds might occur in the 60,150 ha Marojejy Reserve (R.N.I. no. 12) (see Andriamampianina 1981), since it lies immediately north of Andapa.

Conservation Measures Proposed A detailed survey of marshes near Antananarivo is needed to establish whether this species is present, and at what densities; protection of selected sites might then be given. Searches also need to be made in the three other areas where birds have been found.

Remarks This is the least typical member of the genus *Sarothrura*, evidently owing to long isolation in Madagascar, and a genus of its own, *Lemurolimnas*, has been proposed, though regarded as unnecessary (Keith *et al.* 1970). Failure to confirm its presence around Antananarivo need not totally invalidate records from this area, since the species possibly shows a volatility of site-usage akin to that shown by the White-winged Flufftail *S. ayresi* (see relevant account). Although given as quoted under Distribution, the native name of this species is correctly "fangalatrovy" (= "stealer of yams") (J. T. Hardyman *in litt.* 1984).

References

Andriamampianina, J. (1981) Les réserves naturelles et la protection de la nature à Madagascar. Pp. 105-111 in P. Oberlé, ed. *Madagascar, un sanctuaire de la nature*. Paris: Lechevalier.

Benson, C. W., Colebrook-Robjent, J. F. R. and Williams, A. (1976) Contribution à l'ornithologie de Madagascar. *Oiseau et R.F.O.* 46: 103-134.

Delacour, J. (1932) Les oiseaux de la Mission Franco-Anglo-Américaine à Madagascar. *Oiseau et R.F.O.* 2: 1-96.

Deschamps, H. (1960) *Histoire de Madagascar*. Paris: Berger-Levrault.

Keith, S., Benson, C. W. and Irwin, M. P. S. (1970) The genus *Sarothrura* (Aves, Rallidae). *Bull. Amer. Mus. Nat. Hist.* 143(1).

Locamus, P. (1900) Carte de Madagascar, 1: 500,000. Paris.

Milne-Edwards, A. and Grandidier, A. (1885) *Histoire physique, naturelle et politique de Madagascar, 12. Histoire naturelle des oiseaux.* Tome I. Paris.

Rand, A. L. (1936) The distribution and habits of Madagascar birds. *Bull. Amer. Mus. Nat. Hist.* 72: 143-499.

Salvan, J. (1972) Statut, recensement, reproduction des oiseaux dulçaquicoles aux environs de Tananarive. *Oiseau et R.F.O.* 42: 35-51.

SAKALAVA RAIL INSUFFICIENTLY KNOWN

Amaurornis olivieri (G. Grandidier and Berlioz, 1929)

Order GRUIFORMES Family RALLIDAE
Subfamily RALLINAE

Summary This marsh-dwelling rail is known from only three widely separated areas in the Sakalava country of western Madagascar, and is generally regarded as rare and localised.

Distribution The Sakalava Rail was first described from a single specimen (apparently undated) from Antsalova, west Madagascar (Grandidier and Berlioz 1929), i.e. at about 18°40'S 44°37'E, (*contra* "18°28'S 44°45'E" in Benson and Wagstaffe 1972). In recent years the species has been seen again in the region of Lakes Masama and Bemamba by G. Randrianasolo but a later search of these lakes was unsuccessful (O. Langrand *in litt.* 1984). Soon after its first discovery in this region the species was found c. 300 km to the north-east at Ambararatabe near Soalala, roughly 16°19'S 46°04'E, where seven specimens were collected in March 1931, six of them along the Tsiribahina (Tsiribehino) River (Rand 1936, Benson and Wagstaffe 1972). The only subsequent record is of a female taken from a nest at Nosy-Ambositra on the Mangoky River, 21°55'S 44°00'E, some 360 km to the south of the type-locality, on 9 March 1962 (Benson and Wagstaffe 1972). This record has done nothing to modify the description of the species, over 50 years ago, as strictly localised (Delacour 1932), which clearly implied that it had been looked for in other areas and found absent. From its behaviour (see Ecology below), it would seem less easy to overlook than, e.g., the Slender-billed Flufftail *Sarothrura watersi* (see relevant account), and new localities for it may prove to be few. However, large areas of apparently suitable but inaccessible habitat do exist (D. A. Turner pers. comm. 1983).

Population Numbers are unknown.

Ecology Birds along the Tsiribahina River at Ambararatabe were found standing on or running over floating vegetation on a narrow, deep stream bordered with tall coarse grass locally called "bararata" (apparently the reed *Phragmites communis*: see Benson and Wagstaffe 1972); though not very shy or active, the birds kept close to the "bararata" and retreated there for shelter (Rand 1936). A bird was also seen on a floating log in a flooded valley clearing; on 26 March a male and female were seen with two well-grown young (Rand 1936). The nest at Nosy-Ambositra was some 50 cm above ground level in bulrushes *Typha angustifolia* near water, in a marshy area with stretches of open water, with bulrushes, water-lilies *Nymphaea stellata* and *Phragmites communis* dominant (Benson and Wagstaffe 1972). The nest held two eggs, probably a complete clutch (Benson and Wagstaffe 1972).

Threats The species's very restricted distribution, as currently known, exposes it to a variety of potential threats. The eggs of the only recorded nest were eaten by local people (Benson and Wagstaffe 1972) and it is possible that populations could suffer locally from systematic exploitation for food. Rice-growing is reportedly beginning to alter Lake Bemamba (O. Langrand *in litt.* 1984).

Conservation Measures Taken None is known.

Conservation Measures Proposed A faunal reserve has been urged for the Antsalova region, this species's type-locality; for information on this proposal and on the possible importance of wetlands around Cap St.André, see Conservation Measures Proposed under Madagascar Teal *Anas bernieri*. Research on the Teal's distribution could incorporate fieldwork to locate populations of this rail and to determine the threats it may face.

Remarks Although commonly placed in the genus *Porzana*, the Sakalava Rail has been found to show close affinity to the African Black Crake *Amaurornis (Limnocorax) flavirostris* (Benson and Wagstaffe 1972).

References

Benson, C. W. and Wagstaffe, R. (1972) *Porzana olivieri* and *Limnocorax flavirostris*; a likely affinity. *Bull. Brit. Orn. Club* 92: 160-164.

Delacour, J. (1932) Les oiseaux de la Mission Franco-Anglo-Américaine à Madagascar. *Oiseau et R.F.O.* 2: 1-96.

Grandidier, G. and Berlioz, J. (1929) Description d'une espèce nouvelle d'oiseau de Madagascar de la famille des Rallidés. *Bull. Acad. Malgache* N.S. 10 [1927]: 83-84.

Rand, A. L. (1936) The distribution and habits of Madagascar birds. *Bull. Amer. Mus. Nat. Hist.* 72: 143-499.

GOUGH MOORHEN   RARE
Gallinula comeri (Allen, 1892)

Order GRUIFORMES   Family RALLIDAE
                                                       Subfamily RALLINAE

Summary This flightless rail is endemic to Gough Island and introduced to Tristan da Cunha, South Atlantic Ocean; it must be considered potentially (but permanently) at risk from the introduction of mammalian predators.

Distribution The Gough Moorhen is endemic to Gough Island in the Tristan da Cunha group (a dependency of the British Crown Colony of St.Helena), South Atlantic Ocean, occurring throughout the island up to 450 m, where the open mountain begins (Verrill 1895, Wilkins 1923, Holdgate 1958, Elliott 1969, Voisin 1979). The closely related Tristan Moorhen *Gallinula nesiotis* was considered extinct on Tristan da Cunha by the turn of the century, having been abundant over the whole island up to 1852 but rare by 1873 (Elliott 1953, Stresemann 1953, Beintema 1972, Olson 1973, Bourne and David 1981). On 15 May 1956 seven Gough Moorhens were released at a site east of the settlement on Tristan, near where the centre of the new volcano now lies (M. K. Swales *in litt.* 1984). In 1972-1973 birds were found in the north-eastern part of Tristan at Longwood, with evidence of their occurrence east to Big Gulch (Richardson in press), these being proved by examination of skins and skeletal material to be Gough Moorhens (H. F. I. Elliott *in litt.* 1984). In 1982-1983 birds were found still to be confined to the north-eastern sector of Tristan, mainly on the "Base" between the Ponds and Sandy Point (M. K. Swales *in litt.* 1984; see map in Wace and Holdgate 1976).

Population Numbers of this retiring, cover-haunting species have proved difficult to estimate and various figures have been proposed; the most recent analysis is apparently the most comprehensive and reliable. Early observers were united in considering it, in general, a common bird, though much more often heard than seen (Verrill 1895, Eagle Clarke 1905, Wilkins 1923, Broekhuysen and Macnae 1949, Elliott 1953), and commonest in the valley bottoms covered with bushes and dense undergrowth (= "dense forest") (Voisin 1979; also Holdgate 1957). However, in October/November 1974 birds were less common than anticipated, and an estimated 12-20 pairs per km^2 on the (lower) half of the island available to the species gave a total population of 300-500 pairs (Richardson in press). Nevertheless, including the birds on Tristan (see below) and whatever numbers were in captivity (see Conservation Measures Taken), the species in the mid-1970s was considered probably to number "a few thousand birds" (see Wace and Holdgate 1976). Subsequently in September/October 1983 16 territories were found in an area of just 7 ha, suggesting a nesting density of 230 pairs per km^2, though on the basis of further study territories were considered to be about 0.5 ha in extent: as some 10-12 km^2 of Gough consists of similar low-lying, heavily vegetated ground, the population there may thus be c. 2,000-3,000 pairs, though there are no data to indicate the observed density was typical of suitable habitat elsewhere (Watkins and Furness in press). On Tristan, 1972-1973, the population density was 20-30 pairs per km^2 in the Longwood area and the total area where birds were present was put at 8.5 km^2, giving an estimated breeding population of 170-255 pairs (Richardson in press). In 1982-1983 numbers on Tristan were considered to be "clearly increasing", six birds being heard calling from cover within a 100 m radius (M. K. Swales *in litt.* 1984).

Ecology On Gough, there are three vegetation-types occurring below 450 m, namely tussock-grass (*Spartina* and *Poa*) on cliffs and penguin rookeries, fern-bush where thickets of the island-tree *Phylica arborea* grow amongst dwarf tree-ferns *Blechnum* to form a dense tangle of vegetation up to c. 300 m and, above this, a zone of wet heath vegetation with low creeping plants, tufted grasses, sedges and moss up to c. 600 m (Wace and Holdgate 1976): of these, it is evidently the second which is chiefly used by the Moorhen, though it clearly also occurs in the flatter areas of tussock (Eagle Clarke 1905, Broekhuysen and Macnae 1949, Holdgate 1958, Wace and Holdgate 1976, Voisin 1979). Its secretive and shy behaviour (Wilkins 1923, Broekhuysen and Macnae 1949, Clancey 1981) and its absence from open mountain have been considered a defence against predation by the Tristan Great Skua *Catharacta skua hamiltoni* (Holdgate 1958, Elliott 1969, Enticott 1982). The recently discovered population on Tristan inhabits rugged, luxuriant, relatively inaccessible and little visited fern-bush *Blechnum*, with dense *Phylica*, between steep cliffs at 300 m and the tree/fern line at 900 m (Wace and Holdgate 1976, Richardson in press). Although flightless, the species on Gough readily climbs in *Phylica* (Watkins and Furness in press). Food appears to be as much vegetable matter and carrion as invertebrates (Watkins and Furness in press). Stomachs of three specimens held grass (Clancey 1981), and birds have been seen feeding on grassheads with a scythe-like motion of the bill (Elliott 1957). Birds also regularly feed on carcasses of seabirds killed by Great Skuas, e.g. Soft-plumaged Petrel *Pterodroma mollis* and Broad-billed Prion *Pachyptila vittata*, even offering strips of flesh to their offspring (Clancey 1981, Watkins and Furness in press, J. Cooper *in litt.* 1984). They take invertebrates (Elliott 1969), enter petrel burrows presumably in search of food (Watkins and Furness in press), pull vegetation out of abandoned nests of the Yellow-nosed Albatross *Diomedea chlororhynchos*, presumably looking for invertebrates (J. Cooper *in litt.* 1984), and feed on fish-paste bait and discarded fruit round the weather station (Clancey 1981). On Tristan, stomachs of four birds from the early 1970s held numerous grass-like seeds, many larger dark brown seeds, amorphous vegetable matter, egg shell and gravel; also a cephalopod beak, indicating that birds scavenge around albatross nests (Richardson in press). The breeding season is evidently extended, from mid- to late September (Wilson and Swales 1958, Clancey 1981, Watkins and Furness in press; see also Voisin 1979) to late February (Elliott 1970) or March (Richardson in press), presumably with the bulk of activity from October to December (Elliott 1953, Holdgate 1957), though a pair breeding in November produced a second brood later in the season (Holdgate 1958), and a young chick seen in late March was being fed by an immature bird (Richardson in press). Copulation has been witnessed in June and August (Richardson in press). On Tristan, juveniles have been seen in February and April, and a male in December had developed testes, suggesting an extended laying period, December to March, and that birds are perhaps double-brooded (Richardson in press). Although a clutch-size of two has been considered normal (Wilson and Swales 1958), three nests in 1983 held two, four and five eggs respectively (Watkins and Furness in press). Of six nests found, all were in *Poa flabellata* tussock (Watkins and Furness in press).

Threats The risk of mammalian predators becoming established on Gough must be considered a major threat to the species, and one which has substantially increased since the establishment of a permanently manned weather station on the island in 1955 (Holdgate 1957, Bourne 1981): a dead rat was found in a packing-case in 1967 (Elliott 1969) and another on the Gough supply ship in 1974 (Richardson in press), and rats were thought to have been seen alive and wild on the island in 1983 (R. W. Furness *in litt.* 1984). Since seabirds are present on Gough all year round and there is no harsh winter weather, rats would very probably flourish on the island (Watkins and Furness in press). Rails on islands are notoriously vulnerable, especially flightless ones (as is the Gough Moorhen): of 18 forms listed as extinct since 1600 in King (1978-1979) (to which should be added *Atlantisia podarces* and *Porzana astrictocarpus* from St.Helena: see Olson 1973) all were from islands, and of 16 forms currently treated as threatened in King (1978-1979) 11 are from islands. In the mid-1950s there was some concern over the numbers of Gough Moorhens (up to 30 recorded) being taken for zoos, although this was offset by recognition of the value of establishing self-sustaining stock in captivity (Holdgate 1957). The extinction of the closely related species on Tristan was considered probably attributable to rats (Elliott 1953) or to rats and feral pigs (Greenway 1967), although, since feral cats were preying on Moorhens in 1868, five years before they were first indicated to have declined on the island (Broekhuysen and Macnae 1949, Beintema 1972) and, moreover, the species was much hunted by islanders with dogs ("some hundreds" caught in 1810 with one dog) throughout the first half of the nineteenth century (see Beintema 1972), it seems probable that a combination of predators, and probably much habitat destruction too (e.g. by fire: Greenway 1967), was responsible. The fact that the Gough Moorhen has been able to colonise an area of Tristan that is no less rat-infested than any other on the island (Richardson in press) is taken to indicate that the cause of the Tristan Moorhen's extinction was hunting (W. R. P. Bourne *in litt.* 1984) and is a welcome signal that the species might not suffer if rats became established on Gough (though this is by no means certain).

Conservation Measures Taken The introduction of the Gough Moorhen to Tristan has resulted in a valuable reserve population on that island (see Distribution, Population). For human health reasons, domestic cats on Tristan were destroyed in 1974, and a bounty for the destruction of feral cats, then estimated at no more than 40 individuals, was simultaneously introduced (Richardson in press). In 1976 Gough Island was declared a wildlife reserve and the unauthorised collecting of birds or importation of exotic live animals prohibited (see Wace and Holdgate 1976). Captive breeding has occurred (Wilson and Swales 1958, Wace and Holdgate 1976). In England, specimens have probably interbred with the Common Moorhen *Gallinula chloropus* "and run wild there" (Wace and

Holdgate 1976). Amsterdam (Artis) Zoo in the Netherlands has maintained a captive population of these birds since acquiring five in 1956 and two more a few years later: between 1964 and 1983 at least 54 young were produced, 17 surviving more than a year (the longevity record being 13 years and a few months), and there were seven adults and three chicks in the zoo at June 1984; their importance is now fully realised, they have their own aviary, and no hybridisation is believed to have occurred (J. Wattel *in litt.* 1984; see also Voous 1961). Birds have also been held in Basel and Stuttgart Zoos (J. Wattel *in litt.* 1984). Some birds are also thought to be in a zoo in the U.S.A. (M. K. Swales *in litt.* 1984).

Conservation Measures Proposed Following the discovery of the dead rat in 1967 (see Threats) stronger measures were considered necessary at the Gough weather station's packing warehouse in Cape Town (Elliott 1969), and such vigilance must always be exercised while the station remains on the island. Indeed, whether the very recent record of rats on the island (see Threats) is confirmed or not, the interests of wildlife require that permission to man this weather station be rescinded at the earliest moment. Meanwhile, a survey is now needed to establish which zoos hold Gough Moorhens and to determine whether action is needed to create a major captive breeding nucleus. The population of birds on Tristan requires further study particularly in respect of its apparent ability to withstand predation.

Remarks Gough "is now a strong contender for the title of the most important seabird colony in the world" as well as being haven for over 100,000 Amsterdam fur seals *Arctocephalus tropicalis* (Bourne 1981); it also possesses an endemic emberizid in its own genus, the Gough Bunting *Rowettia goughensis* (see relevant account). The value of the island as a sanctuary for wildlife cannot be overstated.

References

Beintema, A. J. (1972) The history of the Island Hen (*Gallinula nesiotis*), the extinct flightless gallinule of Tristan da Cunha. *Bull. Brit. Orn. Club* 92: 106-113.

Bourne, W. R. P. (1981) Fur seals return to Gough Island. *Oryx* 16: 46-47.

Bourne, W. R P. and David, A. C. F. (1981) Nineteenth century bird records from Tristan da Cunha. *Bull. Brit. Orn. Club* 101: 247-256.

Broekhuysen, G. J. and Macnae, W. (1949) Observations on the birds of Tristan da Cunha Islands and Gough Island in February and early March, 1948. *Ardea* 37: 97-113.

Clancey, P. A. (1981) On birds from Gough Island, central South Atlantic. *Durban Mus. Novit.* 12(17): 187-200.

Eagle Clarke, W. (1905) Ornithological results of the Scottish National Antarctic Expedition. – 1. On the birds of Gough Island, South Atlantic Ocean. *Ibis* (8)5: 247-268.

Elliott, C. C. H. (1969) Gough Island. *Bokmakierie* 21: 17-19.

Elliott, C. C. H. (1970) Additional notes on the sea-birds of Gough Island. *Ibis* 112: 112-114.

Elliott, H. F. I. (1953) The fauna of Tristan da Cunha. *Oryx* 2: 41-53.

Elliott, H. F. I. (1957) A contribution to the ornithology of the Tristan da Cunha group. *Ibis* 99: 545-586.

Enticott, J. W. (1982) Subantarctic Skua *Catharacta antarctica* regurgitates an egg of the Gough Island Moorhen *Gallinula comeri*. *Cormorant* 10: 121-122.

Greenway, J. C. (1967) *Extinct and vanishing birds of the world*. 2nd revised edition. New York: Dover Publications.

Holdgate, M. W. (1957) Gough Island – a possible sanctuary. *Oryx* 4: 168-175.

Holdgate, M. W. (1958) *Mountains in the sea*. London: Macmillan.

King, W. B. (1978-1979) *Red data book, 2: Aves*. 2nd edition. Morges, Switzerland: IUCN.

Olson, S. L. (1973) Evolution of the rails of the South Atlantic islands (Aves: Rallidae). *Smithsonian Contrib. Zool.* 152.

Richardson, M. E. (in press) Aspects of the ornithology of the Tristan da Cunha group. *Cormorant*.

Stresemann, E. (1953) Birds collected by Capt. Dugald Carmichael on Tristan da Cunha 1816-1817. *Ibis* 95: 146-147.

Verrill, G. E. (1895) On some birds and eggs collected by Mr Geo. Comer at Gough Island, Kerguelen Island, and the Island of South Georgia. *Trans. Connecticut Acad. Arts Sci.* 9: 430-478.

Voisin, J.-F. (1979) Observations ornithologiques aux îles Tristan da Cunha et Gough. *Alauda* 47: 73-82.

Voous, K. H. (1961) The generic distinction of the Gough Island Flightless Gallinule. *Bijd. Dierk.* 31: 75-79.

Wace, N. M. and Holdgate, M. W. (1976) *Man and nature in Tristan da Cunha*. Morges, Switzerland: IUCN (Monograph no. 6).

Watkins, B. P. and Furness, R. W. (in press) Population status and nesting of the Gough Moorhen *Gallinula nesiotis comeri*. [*Ibis*.]

Wilkins, G. H. (1923) Report on the birds collected during the voyage of the "Quest" (Shackleton-Rowett Expedition) to the southern Atlantic. *Ibis* (11)5: 474-511.

Wilson, A. E. and Swales, M. K. (1958) Flightless Moorhens (*Porphyriornis c. comeri*) from Gough Island breed in captivity. *Avicult. Mag.* 64: 43-45.

CANARIAN BLACK OYSTERCATCHER　　　　　　　　　　　EXTINCT

Haematopus meadewaldoi (Bannerman, 1913)

Order CHARADRIIFORMES　　　　　　　　Family HAEMATOPODIDAE

Summary The evidence generally points to this shorebird being extinct, having always been uncommon and known only from the Canary Islands. Until 1968 there had been only one certain record and two sightings by naturalists this century and, despite several intensive searches in recent years, the established haunts of this species have proved vacant. However, four apparently genuine records of "black oystercatchers" (two on the coast of West Africa) since 1968 offer the slenderest hope of its survival.

Distribution The Canarian Black Oystercatcher is known with certainty only from the eastern Canary Islands (Spain), i.e. Fuerteventura, Lanzarote and the "Islas Menores" (Lobos at the north of Fuerteventura, and Graciosa, Montaña Clara, Alegranza and Roque del Oueste or Roque Infierno to the north of Lanzarote). All these islands and even the almost inaccessible Roque del Este, north-east of Lanzarote, have been listed as sites for the species (Bannerman 1919-1920,1922), and doubtless all but perhaps the last held it, yet Montaña Clara and Roque del Este have never been specified in reports and specimens are recorded only from southernmost Fuerteventura and Graciosa. On Fuerteventura, the species was reported from the remote coasts (Webb *et al.* 1842): several were seen and one collected in April 1852 near an islet (thus either Roque del Moro or El Islote, both on Playa de Cofete) on the Jandía peninsula in the south of the island (Bolle 1854-1855); the type-specimen, a female soon to lay, was collected somewhere near the lighthouse at the far point of Jandía on 7 April 1888 (Meade-Waldo 1889a, Bannerman 1913); and another female was collected on Jandía on 6 May 1889 (Dresser 1896), this latter perhaps one of the five specimens, reportedly breeding, that were shot by a boy that year (Meade-Waldo 1889b); birds were then also reported by locals to occur on the north coast (the Bocayna Straits), specifically at Corralejo, and were considered to breed there (Bolle 1854-1855, Meade-Waldo 1889a), although a search at Toston in 1913 and inquiries of the local lighthouse-keeper of six years' service drew a blank (Bannerman 1914,1922,1963), as did a general search of the island in 1905 (von Thanner 1908). On Lobos it was seen occasionally by this same lighthouse-keeper some time prior to around 1907 (Bannerman 1922,1963). On Lanzarote, it was reported from the remote coasts (Webb *et al.* 1842) and by implication from the southern coasts (the Bocayna Straits) (Bolle 1854-1855): it was reported by locals to breed on the island (Meade-Waldo 1889a) and a local name for it was obtained (Meade-Waldo 1890), but there is no more substantial evidence. From the first, Graciosa was identified as the main locality for the species (Webb *et al.* 1842), and following a local report of its breeding there (Meade-Waldo 1889a) a pair in breeding condition was collected on 6-7 April 1890 (Meade-Waldo 1890, Fisher 1981; specimen in BMNH: NJC); a search in mid-May 1913 failed to find any birds but local fishermen dentified La Baja de Ganado, Montaña Amarilla and El Hueso as favoured localities (von Thanner 1913) and three weeks later, on 3 June, a specimen was collected "on the reefs of the west coast of the island ... opposite Montaña Clara" (Bannerman 1922,1963; also Bannerman 1914). On Alegranza it was evidently regular at the turn of the century, being reported from the southern shores, especially in the evening (Polatzek 1908-1909), often seen there by a lighthouse-keeper some time prior to around 1907 (Bannerman 1922,1963), and even remembered as once regular there by locals interviewed in 1970 (Lovegrove 1971): favoured localities were Rrapatura (*sic*), El Drillo and Moribundo, but failure to find it there in 1913 led to the assumption that it was then very sparse on the island (von Thanner 1913). On Roque del Oueste (Roque Infierno) a pair was seen at close range in May 1913 (von Thanner 1913). The species is otherwise only known by an unreliable and secondhand report as occasionally seen on Tenerife (Godman 1872), and by a wholly unexpected and seemingly anomalous (therefore "probable") sight record of one flying over Puerto de la Cruz, Tenerife, in July 1968 (Bannerman 1969), and another of a bird observed near El Medano on the south-east coast of Tenerife, around midday on 19 February 1981 (M. Kraft *in litt.* 1984). The possibility that birds might be migratory and occur also on the coast of Africa opposite the eastern Canaries has been rejected (Bannerman 1919-1920,1963, Hockey 1982), but a "black oystercatcher" was well seen on the coast just south of Dakar, Senegal, on 22 February 1970 (G. Jarry *per* P. A. R. Hockey *in litt.* 1984) and two were seen on the coast of Senegal (Cap Roxo) near the border with Guinea-Bissau on 30 December 1975 (de Ridder 1977); see also Remarks.

Population Numbers of this species were evidently always small: only one naturalist is on record as ever seeing more than two together, and even in the 1850s he thought the bird "not frequent" (Bolle 1854-1855), a judgement commonly echoed by subsequent observers (Meade-Waldo 1893, Bannerman 1913, von Thanner 1913), one of whom was told that sites for the isolated pairs on Fuerteventura were hours of travel apart (von Thanner 1908). The possibility of its likely impending extinction was first raised in 1919 (Bannerman 1919-1920), at a time when ornithological studies in the Canary Islands, so active since the 1880s, were entering a period of dormancy: careful searches for the species were not made again until 1956, when Lanzarote, Graciosa and Montaña Clara were visited for the purpose (Etchécopar and Hüe 1957, Hüe and Etchécopar 1958), and 1970, when Graciosa, Montaña Clara, Alegranza and Roque del Este were repeatedly scoured (Lovegrove 1971). Much less systematic searches were conducted on Fuerteventura (including Lobos) in 1957 (Hooker 1958) and on Lanzarote in 1979 (Shirt 1983), but a fairly comprehensive investigation took place on Fuerteventura (including Lobos) in 1979 (Shirt 1983), while searches of southern and northern Fuerteventura were made in July 1978 (R. P. Martins *in litt.* 1984) and of northern Fuerteventura in April 1977, February and September 1978, January 1980 (K. W. Emmerson *in litt.* 1984) and, comprehensively, in April 1984 (*ICBP Newsletter* 6,2 [1984]). None of these studies yielded results but in 1970 local fishermen and lighthouse-keepers generally agreed that their last sightings of the species were around 1940 (Lovegrove 1971). The 1968 and 1981 sight records from Tenerife naturally offer a certain hope for its survival, although scarcely in relation to the eastern Canaries (see Remarks).

Ecology The species was found on both rocky and sandy shorelines: several pairs on Jandía were observed running busily along the sandy margin, rushing forward eagerly behind retreating waves to forage for small molluscs (Bolle 1854-1855); the bird on Graciosa in 1913 ran nimbly over rocks, head turning constantly from side to side as it evidently searched pools for molluscs (Bannerman 1963). This bird was both solitary and wary (Bannerman 1963) but other reports refer to birds being consistently in pairs (Bolle 1854-1855, Meade-Waldo 1893, von Thanner 1908,1913) and very tame (Meade-Waldo 1893, von Thanner 1913); after breeding three might be seen together, suggesting a clutch-size of only one (von Thanner 1908). No nest has ever been reported, but one observer recollected that eggs were received from the eastern islands by a taxidermist and dealer based in Tenerife (Bannerman 1963). Absence of proof of nesting, coupled with a local report (manifestly wrong) that birds first appeared each year in June (von Thanner 1908), fuelled speculation about the true status of this species in the eastern Canaries, but there seems little doubt that it was resident and bred there: it was considered sedentary when first discovered (Webb *et al.* 1842) and all eight specimens collected in three successive springs, 1888-1890, were in breeding condition (Meade-Waldo 1889a,b,1890). The report that it bred "very late" (Meade-Waldo 1893), while seemingly contradicted by published evidence (Volsøe 1951), ought not to be dismissed or ignored. Birds apparently moved around between islands habitually, but used traditional sites on each (von Thanner 1908,1913), hence presumably its reported recurrence in the evening on the southern shores of Alegranza (Polatzek 1908-1909); but see Remarks.

Threats The causes of the disappearance of this species are wholly unknown, but it is possible that introduced mammalian predators such as cats and rats *Rattus* may have been the cause, feral cats and other terrestrial mammals being known to prey upon the African Black Oystercatcher *H. moquini* (Hockey 1982; see Appendix C); this hypothesis is consistent with its apparent retreat to the Islas Menores by the turn of the century. Collecting can have played no real part in this species's decline, but by the start of the twentieth century may have posed a considerable final threat (see Conservation Measures Taken); it is not inconceivable, for example, that the male shot on Graciosa in June 1913 was the off-duty mate of the pair seen three weeks earlier on Roque del Oueste.

Conservation Measures Taken It is notable that the man who collected the last known specimen nowhere in his immediately subsequent publications (Bannerman 1913,1914,1919-1920) made it obvious that he had done so, or where; indeed, having given its range as "the eastern Canary group", he stated "it is unnecessary to be more explicit as to its particular haunts" and discouraged anyone intending to venture there for specimens (Bannerman 1919-1920), evidently for fear of over-collecting by others.

Conservation Measures Proposed Attempts to rediscover this bird cannot be a high priority on an international scale of concern. Nevertheless, there is perhaps justification (see Remarks) for incorporating systematic if occasional searches of stretches of coastline in both western and eastern Canaries in the course of other ornithological fieldwork, and birdwatching tourists are encouraged to liaise with ICONA and the Grupo Ornitológico Canario, to take the trouble to examine and work remoter coastlines assiduously, and to report back to the above organisations with the details of the areas covered. The cooperation of museums is also sought in supplying information to ICBP about any specimens of this bird which they may possess. The need for and potential benefits of clarifying the status of the Canaries in relation to European legislation are stated in Conservation Measures Proposed under White-tailed Laurel Pigeon *Columba junoniae*.

Remarks The reasons for elevating the Canarian Black Oystercatcher to the status of full species have recently been presented (Hockey 1982). The possible records of the species in 1968 and 1981 from Tenerife, coupled with a report of it being seen there a century earlier, prompts the consideration that, just possibly, it survives on one or more western Canary Islands. Since all reports of the bird from the outset were from the eastern islands, its confinement to them appears to be conclusively determined, but it is not at all clear that any systematic ornithological surveys of the somewhat inaccessible coastlines of the western islands have ever been undertaken. "This bird frequents the black water-worn lava of which the coasts ... are largely composed; the black plumage ... renders the bird extremely difficult to see" (Bannerman 1922): it is therefore at least conceivable that the species has been overlooked on the black rocky coastlines of the western islands down to the present, just as the occurrence of the White-tailed Laurel Pigeon on Tenerife was not recognised until the 1970s, although reported there in the 1870s (see relevant account) by the same man who reported the Black Oystercatcher on that island.

References

Bannerman, D. A. (1913) [A new subspecies of Oystercatcher found in the eastern islands of the Canary group.] *Bull. Brit. Orn. Club* 31: 33-34.

Bannerman, D. A. (1914) An ornithological expedition to the eastern Canary Islands. *Ibis* (10)2: 38-90, 228-293.

Bannerman, D. A. (1919-1920) List of the birds of the Canary Islands, with detailed reference to the migratory species and the accidental visitors. *Ibis* (11)1: 84-131, 291-321, 457-495, 708-764; (11)2: 97-132, 323-360, 519-569.

Bannerman, D. A. (1922) *The Canary Islands: their history, natural history and scenery*. London and Edinburgh: Gurney and Jackson.

Bannerman, D. A. (1963) *Birds of the Atlantic islands*, 1. Edinburgh and London: Oliver and Boyd.

Bannerman, D. A. (1969) A probable sight record of a Canarian Black Oystercatcher. *Ibis* 111: 257.

Bolle, C. (1854-1855) Bemerkungen über die Vögel der canarischen Inseln. *J. Orn.* 2: 447-462; 3: 171-181.

Dresser, H. E. (1896) *A history of the birds of Europe*, 9 (Supplement). London.

Etchécopar, R. D. and Hüe, F. (1957) Nouvelles données sur l'avifaune des îles Canaries recueillies au printemps 1956. *Oiseau et R.F.O.* 27: 309-334.

Fisher, C. T. (1981) Specimens of extinct, endangered or rare birds in the Merseyside County Museums, Liverpool. *Bull. Brit. Orn. Club* 101: 276-285.

Godman, F. C. (1872) Notes on the resident and migratory birds of Madeira and the Canaries. *Ibis* (3)2: 209-224.

Hockey, P. A. R. (1982) The taxonomic status of the Canary Islands Oystercatcher *Haematopus (niger) meadewaldoi. Bull. Brit. Orn. Club* 102: 77-83.

Hooker, T. (1958) Birds seen on the eastern Canary Island of Fuerteventura. *Ibis* 100: 446-449.

Hüe, F. and Etchécopar, R. D. (1958) Un mois de recherches ornithologiques aux îles Canaries. *Terre et Vie* 105: 186-219.

Lovegrove, R. (1971) B.O.U. supported expedition to northeast Canary Islands, July – August 1970. *Ibis* 113: 269-272.

Meade-Waldo, E. G. (1889a) Notes on some birds of the Canary Islands. *Ibis* (6)1: 1-13.

Meade-Waldo, E. G. (1889b) Further notes on the birds of the Canary Islands. *Ibis* (6)1: 503-520.

Meade-Waldo, E. G. (1890) Further notes on the birds of the Canary Islands. *Ibis* (6)2: 429-438.

Meade-Waldo, E. G. (1893) List of birds observed in the Canary Islands. *Ibis* (6)5: 185-207.

Polatzek, J. (1908-1909) Die Vögel der Canaren. *Orn. Jahrb.* 19: 81-119, 161-197; 20: 1-24, 117-134, 202-210.

de Ridder, M. (1977) Observation d'oiseaux en Basse-Casamance. *Biol. Jaarb. Dodonaea* 45: 84-103.

Shirt, D. B. (1983) The avifauna of Fuerteventura and Lanzarote. *Bustard Studies* 1: 57-68.

von Thanner, R. (1908) Ein Sammelausflug nach La Palma, Hierro und Fuerteventura. *Orn. Jahrb.* 19: 198-215.

von Thanner, R. (1913) Auf der Suche nach dem Austernfischer (*Haematopus niger* Meade-Waldo [*sic*]). *Orn. Jahrb.* 24: 189-193.

Volsøe, H. (1951) The breeding birds of the Canary Islands, 1. Introduction and synopsis of the species. *Vidensk. Medd. fra Dansk naturh. Foren.* 113: 1-153.

Webb, P. B., Berthelot, S. and Moquin-Tandon, A. (1842) Ornithologie Canarienne. In P. B. Webb and S. Berthelot, *Histoire naturelle des Iles Canaries*, 2, pt. II. Zoologie (Ornithologie) – 1. Paris.

MADAGASCAR PLOVER   RARE
Charadrius thoracicus (Richmond, 1896)

Order CHARADRIIFORMES   Family CHARADRIIDAE

Summary This shorebird is apparently restricted to coastal grassy areas of south-west Madagascar where it is greatly outnumbered (and possibly out-competed) by Kittlitz's Plover *Charadrius pecuarius*.

Distribution The Madagascar Plover is now (largely or exclusively) confined to coastal south-west Madagascar. It was, however, first described from Loholoka (21°44'S 48°12'E) and the Fanantara estuary (20°51'S 48°28'E) on the east coast of Madagascar (i.e. between Mahanoro and Manakara), when other specimens from the south-east coast were also mentioned (Richmond 1896,1897; coordinates in Office of Geography 1955); there is also a specimen collected by A. Lantz and received by MNHN in 1882 labelled as from the south-east coast (NJC). In the present century it has only been reported with certainty – other than an anomalous inland record of four 60 km from Antananarivo in January 1971 (Salvan 1971) – from the south-west coast between Morondava and Androka. The species has recently been reported without comment from Morondava (O. Langrand *in litt.* 1984), though this is much the most northerly coastal record, birds not otherwise being known to extend beyond the Maintapaka estuary (north of the Mangoky River) (Appert 1971). Thirteen sites were mapped for the species in the Morombe/Mangoky delta area in the 1960s (Appert 1971) and several more were found between Morombe and Lake Tsimanampetsotsa, July/August 1972 (Dhondt 1975). Previous records are from Tuléar airstrip (Milon 1950), Lake Tsimanampetsotsa (Bangs 1918, Milon 1950), "Nosy Asatra to Beheloka" (Bangs 1918; see Remarks), Androka (Ilinta estuary) (Delacour 1932, Rand 1936) and Nosy Mborono (Nosimborona), off Androka (Milon 1948). The species is not found at Lake Ihotry or near Antsalova (Dhondt 1975).

Population There are no estimates, but on published evidence the total number must be low, possibly under a thousand. The largest flocks reported are of 33 (Appert 1971) and 16 (Dhondt 1975); the relatively few other records are all in (usually low) single figures, e.g. only three were found by the Mission Franco-Anglo-Américaine, 1929-1931, after which the species was judged very rare (Delacour 1932). A two-day survey of the area between Morombe and Befandefa, July 1972, recorded a total of seven birds at four sites; 76 Kittlitz's Plover *Charadrius pecuarius* were found in the same places (Dhondt 1975). A two-day survey at Lake Tsimanampetsotsa, August 1972, recorded a total of 39 Madagascar Plovers at eight sites; at one of these, where several hundred plovers were probably present, 37 were *pecuarius* and only seven *thoracicus* (Dhondt 1975). The species is, however, reported to be "rather common" in the Morombe region (O. Langrand *in litt.* 1984).

Ecology It inhabits short-grass areas near the coast, also flat margins of saltwater expanses and pools, occurring less often on sand- or mudflats (Appert

1971). At least in July and August, it appears to prefer drier areas than Kittlitz's Plover and even to avoid flooded grassland (Dhondt 1975). The stomach of a specimen in MNHN held large and small insects ("not grasshoppers") (NJC). Eggs have been recorded in November (Appert 1971) and January (Milon 1950), young in December (Appert 1971) and August (Bangs 1918, Milon 1950). Breeding and general biology is evidently close to Kittlitz's Plover (see Appert 1971, Keith 1980; for Kittlitz's, see Cramp and Simmons 1983).

Threats The reasons for this species's rarity are unclear. What is certain is that Kittlitz's Plover is more recent in Madagascar (Keith 1980), and its relative numerical superiority and much wider distribution suggest that it may compete successfully with *thoracicus*. Hybridisation has not been recorded.

Conservation Measures Taken The species occurs in the Lake Tsimanampetsotsa Nature Reserve (R.N.I. no. 10) (Andriamampianina 1981).

Conservation Measures Proposed A study of the status, distribution and year-round ecological requirements of this species is clearly essential in order to determine the measures needed for its survival. Any such study should include a survey of the east coast of Madagascar from Tamatave southwards. For the need for a general ornithological survey of this coast and its wetlands, see under Conservation Measures Proposed for Madagascar Teal *Anas bernieri*.

Remarks Birds with black breast-bands were not recognised as a species distinct from Kittlitz's Plover until 1896 (see Richmond 1896), and it is possible that museum collections hold specimens of *thoracicus* from before that date whose locality data would be of value in determining the extent of its (at least former) distribution. Neither "Nosy Asatra" nor "Beheloka" are gazetteered (in Office of Geography 1955), but it is clear (from Agassiz 1918 and Bangs 1918) that they must lie between Tuléar and Lake Tsimanampetsotsa, along the coast, and indeed a Nosy Satrana and Pointe de Beheloka are marked in this stretch of coastline (in IGNT 1964), at 23°43'S 43°38'E and 23°55'S 43°40'E respectively.

References

Agassiz, G. R. (1918) [Vertebrata from Madagascar.] Introduction. *Bull. Mus. Comp. Zool.* 61: 475-479.

Andriamampianina, J. (1981) Les réserves naturelles et la protection de la nature à Madagascar. Pp. 105-111 in P. Oberlé, ed. *Madagascar, un sanctuaire de la nature*. Paris: Lechevalier.

Appert, O. (1971) Die Limikolen des Mangokygebietes in Südwest-Madagaskar. *Orn. Beob.* 68: 53-77.

Bangs, O. (1918) [Vertebrata from Madagascar.] Aves. *Bull. Mus. Comp. Zool.* 61: 489-511.

Cramp, S. and Simmons, K. E. L. eds. (1983) *The birds of the western Palearctic*, 3. Oxford: Oxford University Press.

Delacour, J. (1932) Les oiseaux de la Mission Franco-Anglo-Américaine à Madagascar. *Oiseau et R.F.O.* 2: 1-96.

Dhondt, A. A. (1975) Note sur les échassiers (Charadrii) de Madagascar. *Oiseau et R.F.O.* 45: 73-82.

Institut Géographique National à Tananarive (1964) Carte de Madagascar, 1: 500,000, Type 1963. Tananarive.

Keith, G. S. (1980) Origins of the avifauna of the Malagasy Region. *Proc. IV Pan-Afr. orn. Congr.*: 99-108.

Milon, P. (1948) Notes d'observation à Madagascar. *Alauda* 16: 55-74.

Milon, P. (1950) Deux jours au lac Tsimanampetsoa [*sic*]. Observations ornithologiques. *Naturaliste Malgache* 2(1): 61-67.

Office of Geography (1955) *Gazetteer no. 2. Madagascar, Réunion and the Comoro Islands*. Washington, D.C.: Department of the Interior.

Rand, A. L. (1936) The distribution and habits of Madagascar birds. *Bull. Amer. Mus. Nat. Hist.* 72: 143-499.

Richmond, C. W. (1896) Description of a new species of plover from the east coast of Madagascar. *Proc. Biol. Soc. Washington* 10: 53-54.

Richmond, C. W. (1897) Catalogue of a collection of birds made by Doctor W. L. Abbott, with descriptions of three new species. *Proc. U. S. Natn. Mus.* 19: 677-694.

Salvan, J. (1971) Observations nouvelles à Madagascar. *Alauda* 39: 37-42.

ST.HELENA PLOVER   RARE

Charadrius sanctaehelenae (Harting, 1868)

Order CHARADRIIFORMES   Family CHARADRIIDAE

Summary Restricted to the interior of St.Helena, in the southern Atlantic Ocean, this small plover is in no immediate danger but some of its habitat may be at risk and its numbers are probably very low.

Distribution The St.Helena Plover or Wirebird is found only on the island of St.Helena (British Crown Colony), southern Atlantic Ocean, where it is widespread in flatter, more open upland habitats at medium elevation, though concentrating in certain areas during the breeding season (Pitman 1965, J. C. den Hartog *in litt.* 1984). The distribution of breeding areas, October/December 1952, was mapped as 11 discrete localities in the northern half of the island, the most important being Deadwood Plain and Longwood Plain in the north-east (Haydock 1954, Basilewsky 1970). Although the description of it as a bird of the island's "outskirts" (Melliss 1870) was considered misleading (Benson 1950), it is at least partly confirmed by subsequent observations around the "edge" of the island (see Ecology below). Its distribution is thought to be shifting eastwards as urban areas spread (L. Hepworth *in litt.* 1984).

Population The species has been variously reported as "not very numerous" (Baker 1868), "scarce without being rare" (Huckle 1924), "in considerable numbers" (Simmons 1927), having "not more than 100 pairs" (Haydock 1954), having "something just under a thousand" birds (Pitman 1965), "now relatively frequent" (Basilewsky 1970) and, most recently, "quite common" although with a very small total population, owing to the size of the island (Q. C. B. Cronk *in litt.* and pers. comm. 1983). St.Helena is only 120 km^2 (Haydock 1954), not all of which is suitable terrain for the species (see Ecology). Although the estimate of nearly 1,000 was by a distinguished naturalist (A. Loveridge), it was offered as a suggestion on the basis of apparently casual observations (see Pitman 1965); the only deliberate attempt to assess numbers (in 1952) resulted in the conclusion of less than 100 pairs, with some 30 pairs on Deadwood Plain, eight pairs on Longwood Plain, four pairs on Francis Plain, and one to three pairs on Prosperous Bay Plain (Haydock 1954). Nevertheless, the species was considered commoner than this in the late 1960s and A. Loveridge estimated the population at Flagstaff to comprise some 50 pairs (Basilewsky 1970). Recent independent assessments have arrived at broadly similar conclusions: a short-term visitor (4-18 June 1983) saw some 80-100 birds and considered at least several hundred must be present (J. C. den Hartog *in litt.* 1984), and a long-term resident considers there to be 200-300 pairs at maximum (L. Hepworth *in litt.* 1984). The species is still most abundant on Deadwood Plain (Q. C. B. Cronk *in litt.* and pers. comm. 1983, J. C. den Hartog *in litt.* 1984), but it is not as numerous there as it was 10 years ago (L. Hepworth *in litt.* 1984).

Ecology The St.Helena Plover has been reported to live and breed in the

248

driest and sunniest part of the island (Huckle 1924). It inhabits upland pastures (especially where cattle have recently grazed) (Benson 1950), particularly hot stony plains with wire-grass *Cynodon dactylon* (Melliss 1870) and eroded kaffir fig *Carpobrotus edulis* areas which occur around the edge of the island between c. 350 and 500 m (Q. C. B. Cronk *in litt.* and pers. comm. 1983; also J. C. den Hartog *in litt.* 1984: see Remarks), also ploughed fields and large vegetable gardens, sometimes coming into gardens close to isolated hill cottages (Pitman 1965, L. Hepworth *in litt.* 1984); it is never seen on the shore (Benson 1950, Haydock 1954). On Deadwood and Longwood Plains it is often seen on freshly worked ground, in search of the insects and molluscs that constitute its food (Basilewsky 1970). It usually occurs in pairs, occasionally in groups of up to six (Melliss 1870, Pitman 1965, Q. C. B. Cronk *in litt.* and pers. comm. 1983), and breeds in the drier part of the year (late September to January, mainly December/January, with records from April and May); clutch-size is one or two (rarely three), birds possibly being double-brooded since copulation has been observed in a pair with a month-old chick, and fresh eggs and young birds have not uncommonly been found together (Pitman 1965, Basilewsky 1970, L. Hepworth *in litt.* 1984). Despite the evidence of breeding at times given above (confirmed in Melliss 1870), five specimens taken in December of one year were not in breeding condition (Layard 1867) and there is, presumably, considerable variation in the timing of breeding from year to year, depending on conditions. A. Loveridge considered that it breeds in all but the three winter months (July, August and September) (Basilewsky 1970). The species shows a marked disinclination to fly (Q. C. B. Cronk *in litt.* and pers. comm. 1983).

Threats Feral cats and Indian Mynahs *Acridotheres tristis* have been identified as occasional predators on eggs and young (Pitman 1965, Basilewsky 1970). The island is subject to periodic plagues of rats *Rattus*, which might also despoil nests (Pitman 1965); a large rubbish-dump near the main breeding area abounds in rats (L. Hepworth *in litt.* 1984). The species's habitat, particularly in the Bottomwoods and Longwood areas, is gradually being encroached by new dwellings (L. Hepworth *in litt.* 1984).

Conservation Measures Taken All species of bird on St.Helena have been protected by law since 1894 (Pitman 1965). Moreover, the islanders have particular affection for the Wirebird (Basilewsky 1970, Q. C. B. Cronk *in litt.* and pers. comm. 1983), which gives its name to a sports team and formerly to a magazine (Q. C. B. Cronk *in litt.* and pers. comm. 1983), has featured on a stamp (Pitman 1965) and currently features on tee-shirts (Q. C. B. Cronk *in litt.* and pers. comm. 1983).

Conservation Measures Proposed This species appears reasonably safe unless some major development of St.Helena takes place; however, research on its population dynamics and ecology is needed to clarify the importance of particular areas, e.g. fairly level grassland areas appear (in DOS 1974) to be restricted to the north-east of the island and to cover only a few square kilometres, and if these prove to be optimal habitat then they will require specific protection.

Remarks There is an exact correlation between the present distribution of the Wirebird and the past distribution of the endemic gumwood *Commidendrum robustum*, which was cleared some time after the first record of the bird on St.Helena (Q. C. B. Cronk *in litt.* and pers. comm. 1983; see also Benson 1950). Gumwood woodland had a shaded, bare soil and it is quite possible that the Wirebird evolved on St.Helena as a woodland floor species (Q. C. B. Cronk *in litt.* and pers. comm. 1983), although another opinion is that historical deforestation has favoured the bird to the extent that it is this century more numerous than it has ever been (J. C. den Hartog *in litt.* 1984). The Wirebird is often considered a very distinct race of Kittlitz's Plover *Charadrius pecuarius* and the two are obviously extremely closely related (see Pitman 1965), but the status of *sanctaehelenae* as a full species has recently been reaffirmed (Johnsgard 1981, Cramp and Simmons 1983).

References

Baker, E. (1868) The birds of St.Helena. *Zoologist* 26: 1472-1476.

Basilewsky, P. (1970) La faune terrestre de l'île de Sainte-Hélène. 1. – Vertébrés. *Ann. Mus. Roy. Afr. Centr.*, 8°, Sci. Zool. 181: 77-130.

Benson, C. W. (1950) A contribution to the ornithology of St.Helena, and other notes from a sea-voyage. *Ibis* 92: 75-83.

Cramp, S. and Simmons, K. E. L. eds. (1983) *The birds of the western Palearctic*, 3. Oxford: Oxford University Press.

DOS (1974) St.Helena, 1: 10,000, Series DOS 260. Surbiton: Overseas Development Administration (Directorate of Overseas Surveys).

Haydock, E. L. (1954) A survey of the birds of St.Helena. *Ostrich* 25: 62-75.

Huckle, C. H. (1924) Birds of Ascension and St.Helena. *Ibis* (11)6: 818-821.

Johnsgard, P. A. (1981) *The plovers, sandpipers and snipes of the world*. Lincoln and London: University of Nebraska Press.

Layard, E. L. (1867) [Letter.] *Ibis* (2)3: 248-252.

Melliss, J. C. (1870) Notes on the birds of the island of St.Helena. *Ibis* (NS)6: 97-107.

Pitman, C. R. S. (1965) The eggs and nesting habits of the St.Helena Sand-plover or Wirebird, *Charadrius pecuarius sanctae-helenae* (Harting). *Bull. Brit. Orn. Club* 85: 121-129.

Simmons, G. F. (1927) Sinbads of science. *Natn. Geog. Mag.* 52: 1-75.

DAMARA TERN   RARE
Sterna balaenarum (Strickland, 1852)

Order CHARADRIIFORMES   Family LARIDAE
                                                  Subfamily STERNINAE

Summary This scarce seabird breeds on the coast of Namibia and to a lesser extent in South Africa and probably also Angola. Birds are present throughout the year in Namibia and southern Angola but in South Africa the species is mainly a breeding visitor in the austral summer. Some birds, probably many of them young ones, move north in the non-breeding season as far as Nigeria and Ghana. Breeding birds are at risk from disturbance by tourists and man-induced vegetation changes on sand dunes.

Distribution The Damara Tern is restricted to the coasts of western and south-western Africa. Despite reports to the contrary (see for instance Alexander 1928, Bannerman 1931, Harrison 1983) the species is only known to breed in Namibia and South Africa (Clinning 1978, Brooke in press) though breeding probably also takes place in Angola (Brooke 1981).

Angola The status of the species in Angola is very poorly known and there are no breeding records (Brooke 1981). There are records of birds from the extreme south-west of the country at the Cunene River mouth, Baia dos Tigres and Porto Alexandre during November (Brinck 1955, Pinto 1973, Brooke 1977,1981). This is the beginning of the breeding season but of nine birds collected in early and mid-November none was in breeding condition (Pinto 1973, Brooke 1981). Nevertheless, suitable areas of breeding habitat exist along the Angolan coast south of Moçâmedes and so breeding populations might occur there (Brooke 1981). Further north in Angola the species is probably a non-breeding visitor and it has been recorded from Luanda and Cacuaco (Traylor 1963, Erard and Etchécopar 1970); birds seen at these localities in October 1969 were mainly in non-breeding plumage (Erard and Etchécopar 1970). The species has also been recorded in the winter months off the coast of Cabinda (Traylor 1963), especially at the mouth of the Chiluango River (Dean 1978), and on the Zaire coast at Banana at the mouth of the Zaire river (Chapin 1939).

Namibia Most records of the species come from this country, especially between Walvis Bay and Möwe Bay (Andersson 1872, Bannerman 1912, Niethammer 1961, Frost and Shaughnessy 1976, Clinning 1978, Johnson and Frost 1978, Whitelaw *et al.* 1978, Brooke in press) where it is known to breed in 14 localities (Clinning 1978). To the south, between Oranjemund (Orange Mouth) and Walvis Bay, only three nesting localities have been found, in the Meob/Conception area (Clinning 1978), at Hottentot Bay (Siegfried and Johnson 1977, Johnson and Frost 1978) and at Elizabeth Bay (Frost and Johnson 1977, Siegfried and Johnson 1977, Johnson and Frost 1978, Johnson 1979). Birds have also been seen at Sandwich Harbour (Port d'Ilheo Bay) (Prozesky 1963, Berry and Berry 1975, Whitelaw *et al.* 1978) but breeding has not been proved at this site (Berry and

Berry 1975). Observations of the species have been made at Grossebucht south of Lüderitz and it is likely that birds breed here (Clinning 1978, Cooper *et al.* 1980), though none could be found here in 1981 (Hockey 1982). They have also been seen nearby at Lüderitzbucht (Cooper *et al.* 1980). Birds seen fishing near the Marshall Rocks had probably come from the Hottentot Bay colony, only 7 km away (Cooper *et al.* 1980). A survey of other apparently suitable sites in southern Namibia, such as Baker's Bay, Jammer Bay, Prinzen Bay and the coast from Diaz Point to Wolf and Atlas Bay, found no birds, but it is possible that birds were overlooked in these areas, which were searched by helicopter (Frost and Johnson 1977). The species has also been recorded and found breeding along the northern Namibian coast in the Skeleton Coast Park as far north as the mouth of the Cunene River (Clinning 1978, Ryan *et al.* in press); the species has also been seen on the Angolan side of the Cunene estuary (Pinto 1973, Brooke 1981). It is likely that undiscovered populations occur along the northern Namibian coast (Clinning 1978). The species is normally seen along or near the coast, though in 1977 a flock of 24 birds was seen a few kilometres inland at Swakopmund salt works (Whitelaw *et al.* 1978). Damara Terns are present throughout the year on the Namibian coast (Bourne and Radford 1962, Winterbottom 1971, Berry and Berry 1975, Clinning 1978, Cooper *et al.* 1980), whereas in South Africa the species is a breeding visitor, chiefly between November and March (Robinson *et al.* 1957, Liversidge *et al.* 1958, Burger *et al.* 1980, Brooke in press; also *Afr. Wildl.* 37 [1983]: 33-34).

South Africa It occurs patchily along the coast between the Orange River mouth and Algoa Bay (Burger *et al.* 1980, Brooke in press) though there is also a record of the species as far east as East London (Bourne and Radford 1962) which has been overlooked by subsequent authors. Exact localities from which it is known are the Orange River mouth, Port Nolloth, Oubeep Pan, Dryer's Pan, Langebaan Lagoon, Robben Island, the Cape Town area, Cape Peninsula, Soetendalsvlei, Cape Agulhas, the Struisbaai/De Mond area including the Heuningnes estuary, De Hoop Nature Reserve, the Gourits River mouth, Mosselbaai, Groenvlei, Goukamma Nature Reserve, Noetzie, the Sondags River mouth (Algoa Bay) and East London (Robinson *et al.* 1957, Liversidge *et al.* 1958, Grindley 1959, Winterbottom 1960, Bourne and Radford 1962, Pitman 1977, Burger *et al.* 1980, Cape Bird Club 1981, Randall and McLachlan 1982, *Afr. Wildl.* 37 [1983]: 33-34, Ryan and Cooper in press). Birds have also been seen out at sea west of Cape Town (van Oordt and Kruijt 1954). In recent years breeding has been either proved or strongly suspected at the Orange River mouth, Port Nolloth, De Mond Nature Reserve, the Gourits River mouth and Algoa Bay east of the Sondags River mouth (Burger *et al.* 1980, Randall and McLachlan 1982). Breeding east of Cape Town is a discovery of the last few years (Brooke in press). In the earlier years of this century there was a small breeding colony north of Cape Town (Vincent 1946), now apparently abandoned (Cape Bird Club 1981).

Non-breeding areas Some birds migrate much farther north during the austral winter, as far as Gabon, Cameroon, Nigeria and Ghana. Probably many of these birds are young (Clinning 1978) though the great majority seen at Lagos, Nigeria, were adults (Wallace 1973). In Gabon the species has been recorded along the coast between April and November at Cape Lopez, Port Gentil, Port Denis, Pointe Noire and the Corisco Islands (Rougeot 1945,1946,1948,1952, Louette 1981). There are many fewer observations from Cameroon (see Germain *et al.* 1973), though it probably occurs regularly (Louette 1981): two were seen at the Sanaga River estuary in February 1978 (P. A. Agland pers. comm. 1984), a surprising month. In Nigeria there are many records from Lagos Lighthouse Beach and harbour entrance (Bourdillon 1944, Sander 1956, Elgood *et al.* 1973, Wallace 1973). There are records from this locality for every month of the year except February and March and numbers peak between July and October (Wallace 1973). The species has also been reported from Burutu near the Niger delta (Elgood 1982). In August 1967 the species was seen on the coast of Ghana at Kedezi and Cape St.Paul (Sutton 1970). There are published records of the Damara Tern from the western Indian Ocean, from Aldabra and from African Island(s) (Amirantes), Bird Island and Cousin Island in the Seychelles (Benson 1967, Mountfort 1971, Penny 1974): however, a more rigorous investigation of these records has shown that they are probably misidentified immature Little Terns *Sterna albifrons*, most likely Saunder's Little Terns *S. a. saundersi* (Benson 1967, Feare and Bourne 1977).

Population The world breeding population of the Damara Tern has been estimated at 1,000-2,000 pairs (Cooper *et al.* in press) and at 3,500-4,000 birds, one half to two-thirds of them being in Namibia (Clinning 1978). Recent work suggests, however, that this estimate is too low (J. Cooper *in litt.* 1984). Although there is no clear evidence of a decline in this species, its generally low numbers and the wide range of threats that it faces or is enduring (see below) are regarded here as sufficient grounds for treating it as Rare.

Angola In the south-west where the species probably breeds (J. Cooper *in litt.* 1984), it has been described as being abundant between the Cunene River estuary and Baia dos Tigres, though some of these birds might have been Little Terns (Brooke 1981).

Namibia The bulk of the Damara Tern population breeds along the Namibian coast (Clinning 1978, Brooke in press). There are population estimates of over 2,000 pairs in Namibia (*Afr. Wildl.* 37 [1983]: 33-34) and fewer than 3,000 birds south of the Cunene River including birds in South Africa (Johnson and Frost 1978). One of the most frequently quoted estimates of the Namibian population is one of only 2,000 birds (Clinning 1978). This estimate is based on counts of 1,200 birds between Swakopmund and Möwe Bay (Clinning 1978), 50 birds between Oranjemund and Lüderitz (Frost and Johnson 1977, Siegfried and Johnson 1977, Clinning 1978; also Johnson 1979), 100 birds in the Meob/Conception area (Clinning 1978) and 50 birds between Sandwich Harbour and Walvis Bay (Clinning 1978). At the time of this estimate no accurate survey had been undertaken between Lüderitz and Meob Bay (Clinning 1978) where a colony of nine pairs has since been discovered at Hottentot Bay (Siegfried and Johnson 1977); also c. 35 birds, probably representing an undiscovered breeding colony, have been seen at Grossebucht, south of Lüderitz (Cooper *et al.* 1980) and there were certainly several other undiscovered populations along the Namibian coast, especially in the northern area between Möwe Bay and the Cunene River (Clinning 1978). The figure of 2,000 birds in Namibia was, therefore, an underestimate which failed to take into proper account the probability of there being large populations to be discovered especially in the north of the country. In 1981 645 birds were counted in this northern area along the Skeleton Coast, including 375 north of Möwe Bay, 135 of which were at the Cunene River mouth: these counts took place before the breeding season and undoubtedly many groups were overlooked, so the real population must be much larger (Ryan *et al.* in press). Nevertheless it seems likely that a large proportion of the world population breeds along a relatively short stretch of the Namibian coast between Sandwich Harbour (Port d'Ilheo Bay) and Möwe Bay, especially between Swakopmund and Cape Cross (Frost and Shaughnessy 1976, Clinning 1978). One old report describes the species as being common within this area at Walvis Bay (Andersson 1872) where three colonies are now known (J. Cooper *in litt.* 1984) and recently it has been noted as common at Sandvis (Berry and Berry 1975) and north of Swakopmund (Frost and Shaughnessy 1976, Clinning 1978) where one flock of up to 200 birds has been seen (Niethammer 1961). Results of a detailed count of 240 birds between Sandvis and Durissa Bay have been published (see Whitelaw *et al.* 1978). Further south along the Namibian coast the species appears to be much less common (Clinning 1978).

South Africa The breeding population is estimated at only 200 pairs, one quarter of these (c. 48 pairs) being in the north-west of Cape Province at the Orange River mouth, Port Nolloth, Oubeep Pan and Dyer's Pan (Ryan and Cooper in press). Most counts of this species are very low. At Langebaan Lagoon the highest count is of eight birds in January (Liversidge *et al.* 1958) although it is likely that these birds were in fact Little Terns (J. Cooper *in litt.* 1984). In the De Mond Nature Reserve three pairs bred in 1978 and six pairs in 1979 (Burger *et al.* 1980). Eighty birds were counted between Cape Agulhas and Cape Infanta and 38 birds east of Cape Infanta in the 1982/1983 breeding season (*Afr. Wildl.* 37 [1983]: 33-34). In 1980 a colony of 29 adults was found at Algoa Bay, east of the Sondags River (Randall and McLachlan 1982). There are no clear population trends in South Africa. One small colony north of Cape Town (Vincent 1946) is long extinct (Cape Bird Club 1981, Brooke in press) but all the populations east of Cape Town have been discovered in recent years (Brooke in press). These populations were almost certainly overlooked previously and do not necessarily represent an extension of the breeding range. There is much suitable breeding habitat in eastern Cape Province which is not utilised (Brooke in press). The reasons for this are unknown but there is no evidence to suggest that the species was more common in the past (Brooke in press).

Non-breeding areas Flocks of up to 100 birds have been seen outside the breeding season at Luanda and Cacuaco in Angola (Erard and Etchécopar 1970) and the species is said to winter commonly on the Cabinda coast (Traylor 1963). At Cape Lopez in Gabon large numbers have been seen migrating south in September (Rougeot 1946). Further north at Lagos Lighthouse Beach and harbour mouth over 100 birds have been seen between July and October, peaking at 250 birds in August

(Wallace 1973). It has been suggested that the numbers of birds wintering at Lagos has increased (Wallace 1973) since the maximum number counted in August 1942 was only 150 birds (Bourdillon 1944) compared with 250 in the late 1960s and early 1970s (Wallace 1973): it is possible, however, that this discrepancy can be explained by observer variability or counting over a wider area. In Ghana flocks of 30 birds have been seen at Kedezi and 40 birds at Cape St.Paul (Sutton 1970).

Ecology The Damara Tern is a marine species and forages mainly in sheltered bays, estuaries and lagoons (Bannerman 1931, Rougeot 1948, Frost and Shaughnessy 1976, Clinning 1978, Johnson and Frost 1978, McLachlan and Liversidge 1978, Burger *et al.* 1980). Birds have been seen fishing in the surf zone along the open coast (Clinning 1978, J. Cooper *in litt.* 1984) and in the open sea behind the breaker zone (Burger *et al.* 1980, Brooke in press), even being found out to sea west of Cape Town, sitting on kelp and other drifting material (Vincent 1946); they have also been reported fishing around Cape Town docks (Pitman 1977), and there are a few records of birds foraging inland, but near the coast, in salt pans and salt works (Clinning 1978, Whitelaw *et al.* 1978). Nevertheless, it appears that the species is dependent on sheltered inshore areas in which to feed and the shortage of these throughout much of its range is probably one reason for its rarity (Johnson and Frost 1978). Although it sometimes roosts with other species of tern, it generally hunts separately from them, usually in pairs or small flocks, though occasionally singly (Bannerman 1931, Berry and Berry 1975, McLachlan and Liversidge 1978); larger flocks of up to 250 birds have been reported from the wintering grounds (Wallace 1973), though a flock of 200 birds has been seen north of Swakopmund on the Namibian coast in March, at the end of the breeding season (Niethammer 1961). The birds feed on small fish and crustacea (Bannerman 1931, Frost and Shaughnessy 1976, Johnson and Frost 1978). The chicks are fed mainly on fish (Burger *et al.* 1970) though small squid have also been recorded (Clinning 1978). At one colony north of Swakopmund the chicks were fed chiefly on an unidentified larval blenny but also a small mullet *Mugil richardsonii* and anchovies *Engraulis capensis*; there is one record of a 30 g anchovy being fed to a 40 g chick (Clinning 1978). Damara Terns are very faithful to their breeding sites (Clinning 1978), the location of which is probably at least partly determined by the availability of suitable feeding areas (Frost and Shaughnessy 1976, Clinning 1978, Johnson and Frost 1978). The availability of suitable breeding habitat almost certainly limits distribution to certain areas (R. M. Randall *in litt.* 1984). The birds nest on firm, stony ground rather than a sandy substrate (Clinning 1978). Typical sites are to be found on gravel plains (Frost and Shaughnessy 1976, Johnson and Frost 1978), the hardened surface of dried salt pans (Clinning 1978, Johnson and Frost 1978, Johnson 1979), bare rocky areas (Clinning 1978), gravel humps (Johnson 1979) and unvegetated slacks, composed either of gravel, pebbles or sun-bleached *Donax serra* shells, between sand dunes (Johnson and Frost 1978, Burger *et al.* 1980, Randall and McLachlan 1982, *Afr. Wildl.* 37 [1983]: 33-34, Brooke in press). These slacks form the typical nesting sites in southern Namibia and South Africa (Burger *et al.* 1980, Randall and McLachlan 1982, Brooke in press) and can vary in size from 500 to 15,000 m². There is usually only one pair of nesting birds per slack (Randall and McLachlan 1982) although two pairs have been recorded

(Burger *et al.* 1980). The sand dunes provide a protective "sea" around "islands" of gravel slacks, free from predators such as jackals and mongooses, the birds nesting only on slacks surrounded by bare sand and never on slacks among vegetated sand dunes in which predators can hide (Burger *et al.* 1980, *Afr. Wildl.* 37 [1983]: 33-34, Brooke in press). One colony has had to move several kilometres from its foraging grounds owing to man-induced vegetating of sand dunes (Brooke in press; see Threats). In Namibia, especially north of Swakopmund, gravel plains and dried salt pans are more characteristic breeding sites (Frost and Shaughnessy 1976, Clinning 1978, Johnson and Frost 1978). With the exception of the lichens *Parmelia* and *Telochistes* and the halophytic bush *Arthraerura*, the gravel plains are unvegetated (Frost and Shaughnessy 1976). In South Africa one colony has been found nesting on gravel spoil once mined for diamonds (*Afr. Wildl.* 37 [1983]: 33-34, Brooke in press). There is a record of birds once nesting on the beach north of Cape Town, a little above the high-tide level (Vincent 1946). In general it is thought that the birds do not nest on the shore because of unstable sand and the presence of scavenging mammals such as the black-backed jackal *Canis mesomelas* and brown hyena *Hyaena brunnea* (Frost and Shaughnessy 1976, Johnson and Frost 1978). In Namibia most colonies are found between 500 m and 3 km from the sea (Frost and Shaughnessy 1976, Johnson and Frost 1977,1978, Clinning 1978) whereas in South Africa most nests have been located 100-200 m from the sea, though some are less than 100 m from the spring high-tide level (Vincent 1946, Burger *et al.* 1980, Randall and McLachlan 1982). Some sites appear to be unsuitable breeding areas for Damara Terns because they are exposed to winds and blowing sand (Johnson and Frost 1978): there is one record of a nest and egg being covered by 100 mm of wind-blown sand (Johnson 1979). Many colonies are, therefore, situated in sheltered sites among the sand dunes (Vincent 1946, Frost and Johnson 1977, Johnson and Frost 1978, Randall and McLachlan 1982). In Algoa Bay the birds nest on the north-east side of each gravel stack, avoiding wind-blown sand from the west and south-west (Randall and McLachlan 1982). While Damara Terns seem to tolerate a limited range of environmental conditions on their breeding grounds, there are several apparently suitable sites in eastern Cape Province in which no colonies exist for reasons unknown (Randall and McLachlan 1982, Brooke in press) although it may be related to the species's foraging requirements (J. Cooper *in litt.* 1984). Damara Terns are loosely gregarious on their breeding grounds, nesting in dispersed aggregations of 2-9 pairs (Vincent 1946, Berry and Berry 1975, Frost and Shaughnessy 1976, Johnson 1979, Burger *et al.* 1980, Randall and McLachlan 1982, R. M. Randall *in litt.* 1984), though occasionally larger colonies occur, e.g. up to 18 pairs (Vincent 1946) or even 60 pairs (Clinning 1978). The average nearest-neighbour distance between nests at the Algoa Bay colony is 185 m (Randall and McLachlan 1982). North of Swakopmund at one colony the mean nearest-neighbour distance was 57.1 m (range 32-96 m) (Clinning 1978) whereas at another colony north of Swakopmund the distance between nests was 100-150 m (Frost and Shaughnessy 1976). Six pairs breeding on the beach north of Cape Town had their nests along a 100 m stretch of coastline (Vincent 1946). The nests are usually shallow scrapes in the ground never close to bushes or large stones but may be associated with small surface features such as wheel tracks, stones, discoloured gravel or tufts of lichen, this possibly rendering incubating birds less conspicuous and aiding them in nest location (Clinning 1978). There is no territorial behaviour beween adult birds but chicks which stray into neighbouring territories (which probably only occurs during man-induced disturbance: R. M. Randall *in litt.* 1984) are severely attacked (Clinning 1978, Randall and McLachlan 1982). Eggs are laid between November and February, extreme laying dates being 1 November and 25 February (Vincent 1946, Berry and Berry 1975, Frost and Shaughnessy 1976, Frost and Johnson 1977, Clinning 1978, Johnson 1979, Randall and McLachlan 1982). Re-laying almost certainly takes place if a clutch is lost and later clutches in January and February are probably replacements following nest failure (Frost and Shaughnessy 1976, Clinning 1978, Randall and McLachlan 1982). Maximum breeding activity coincides with maximum day-length in mid-December in middle Namibia (Clinning 1978). The species is single-brooded and the clutch-size is invariably one (Vincent 1946, Frost and Shaughnessy 1976, Frost and Johnson 1977, Clinning 1978, Johnson 1979, Randall and McLachlan 1982, Brooke in press): observations of two chicks being fed by two adults probably refer to two separate pairs (Clinning 1978). The young first fly at 20 days, though it seems they remain dependent upon their parents for at least 10 weeks (Clinning 1978, Brooke in press). In the area north of Swakopmund the chief natural predator at the breeding colonies is the black-backed jackal; in one study at least ten out of 54 eggs were lost to jackals, while three eggs were lost or deserted as a result of human disturbance, other possible predators in this area being crows (Corvidae), gulls (Laridae) and brown hyenas (Clinning 1978). At Algoa Bay it was found that, contrary to the situation with the Roseate Tern *Sterna dougallii*, gulls did not take Damara Tern eggs (Randall and McLachlan 1982), possibly because they are very difficult to see on the gravel slacks (Clinning 1978). North of Swakopmund the nesting success proved difficult to calculate but it seems that 33-72% of the eggs hatched and 16-35% of nesting attempts resulted in young reaching flying age (Clinning 1978). At the De Mond Nature Reserve, of six eggs laid in 1979 only one young reached flying age and even this bird may not have survived: the cause of low nesting success at the colony is not known, nor is it known whether re-laying took place, but there is evidence that nesting success might be higher in some years (Burger *et al.* 1980). The Damara Tern is unusual among small terns in having a clutch-size of only one (Frost and Shaughnessy 1976, Clinning 1978, Johnson and Frost 1978). Because the parents often have to fly long distances to find food (Johnson and Frost 1978) it might be advantageous to have only one chick in order to ensure maximum growth-rate (Frost and Shaughnessy 1976). Certainly an increase in the brood-size would limit the rate of feeding and the amount of protection individual young would obtain (Clinning 1978). Females are thought to start breeding at three years of age (Brooke in press).

Threats The Damara Tern has a low world population, a slow breeding rate in widely dispersed colonies and is at risk from disturbance (Frost and Shaughnessy 1976). The birds are particularly vulnerable throughout their range to disturbance by tourists at their breeding colonies, including people on foot, cars driven off roads, dune buggies and trail bikes (Earle 1976, Frost and Shaughnessy 1976, Clinning 1978, Johnson and Frost 1978, Burger *et al.* 1980, Randall and McLachlan 1982, *Afr. Wildl.* 37 [1983]: 33-34, Brooke in press). Unfortunately, a large proportion of the Damara Tern population breeds between Walvis Bay and the Ugab River, which comprises the National West Coast Tourist Recreation Area (Clinning 1978). This is the area most frequented by tourists along the Namibian coast and at least 15,000 people, probably many more, visited this region during the 1975-1976 tourist season (Clinning 1978). It is also most unfortunate that the peak tourist season is from mid-December to mid-January when Damara Terns are breeding, as a result of which clutches are sometimes unwittingly destroyed (Earle 1976, Frost and Shaughnessy 1976, Clinning 1978, Johnson and Frost 1978, Burger *et al.* 1980, Randall and McLachlan 1982, *Afr. Wildl.* 37 [1983]: 33-34, Brooke in press). In the Swakopmund area people drive through colonies to go angling (Clinning 1978). Dune buggies now enable the public to reach previously inaccessible places where Damara Terns breed (Earle 1976). Gravel extraction in the area between Walvis Bay and the Ugab River is causing disturbance to two major breeding sites and a proposed new road in this area crosses some tern colonies (Clinning 1978). It has been suggested that disturbance to breeding birds might cause them to move their colonies to sub-optimal areas (Johnson and Frost 1978). Opencast mining can destroy some breeding sites for a while, though the security measures associated with mining operations are likely to help the species (Brooke in press). The colony at Meob Bay is under potential threat from uranium prospecting (Clinning 1978). The area between the Ugab River and Möwe Bay receives some protection from disturbance, being part of the Skeleton Coast Park (Ryan *et al.* in press), but it is possible that mineral deposits could be mined here in the future (Clinning 1978). The colony at Port Nolloth in northern Cape Province is not protected at present and is vulnerable to disturbance (Ryan and Cooper in press). In southern Cape Province the population has probably been reduced as a result of the dune stablisation policy of the Directorate of Forestry: this policy involves the vegetating of the sand dunes, Damara Terns being unable to nest in the new habitats formed (Burger *et al.* 1980, Randall and McLachlan 1982, *Afr. Wildl.* 37 [1983]: 33-34, Brooke in press; see under Ecology). It is possible that the colony north of Cape Town (Vincent 1946), now abandoned, died out for this reason (Brooke in press). Military developments along the coast might also be a threat to this species: in an area planned as a missile testing range by Armscor and the Ministry of Defence, 38 Damara Terns were recently counted (*Afr. Wildl.* 37 [1983]: 33-34). The species is almost certainly persecuted on its West African wintering grounds, as are European terns (Brooke in press). Another possible threat in the future is industrial pollution (Frost and Shaughnessy 1976).

Conservation Measures Taken The Damara Tern is fully protected by law in both Namibia and South Africa (Frost and Shaughnessy 1976, Johnson and Frost 1978, Burger *et al.* 1980, Brooke in press). In South Africa colonies at Heuningnesmond (De Mond) and near the Sondags River are in State Forest Reserves (Burger *et al.* 1980, Brooke in press) and the Brandfontein colony is in a private nature reserve (Brooke in press). In 1979 the Directorate of Forestry was persuaded not to vegetate the sand dunes around the tern colony in the De Mond Nature Reserve (Burger *et al.* 1980). In Namibia the area from the Orange River mouth to Sandwich Harbour near Walvis Bay, with the exception of the Lüderitz area, is a restricted zone controlled by Consolidated Diamond Mines of South West

Africa: this area is closed to the public and so the terns which breed there are free from disturbance by tourists during the breeding season, though it appears that the tern population in this area is rather small (Clinning 1978, Johnson and Frost 1978; see Population). Public access is also restricted to the Skeleton Coast Park between the Ugab River mouth and Möwe Bay and north to the Cunene River where the breeding tern population is much higher (Clinning 1978, J. Cooper *in litt.* 1984). Of the 645 terns counted along this stretch of coast in 1981, 97.8% were within the Skeleton Coast Park and only 3.5% of these were in the tourist angling areas (Ryan *et al.* in press). In South Africa surveys are continuing to locate breeding colonies and to establish the size of the breeding population (Brooke in press).

Conservation Measures Proposed The Damara Tern has been listed as one of the 20 bird species requiring highest conservation action in South Africa (Siegfried *et al.* 1976). As many breeding sites as possible should be included in conserved areas to which access should be strictly controlled between November and February: in particular dune buggies and other vehicles should be excluded from the vicinity of breeding colonies during the breeding season (Frost and Shaughnessy 1976, Johnson and Frost 1978, Burger *et al.* 1980, Randall and McLachlan 1982, *Afr. Wildl.* 37 [1983]: 33-34, Brooke in press, Ryan *et al.* in press). Similar restrictions should apply to industrial technicians and military personnel, should they be stationed in breeding areas (*Afr. Wildl.* 37 [1983]: 33-34). In some cases it might be worth fencing around colonies to keep vehicles and other intruders out (Randall and McLachlan 1982, Brooke in press, Ryan *et al.* in press). The practice of vegetating sand dunes should also be discontinued in the vicinity of colonies (Burger *et al.* 1980, Brooke in press). The colony at Port Nolloth should be protected during the breeding season (Ryan and Cooper in press). A detailed conservation plan for the Damara Tern in the De Mond Nature Reserve has been devised (Burger *et al.* 1980) but it is not yet clear to what extent these proposals have been adopted. Proposals have also been made to the Executive Committee for South West Africa concerning the protection of Damara Tern breeding sites in the National West Coast Tourists Recreation Area (Clinning 1978). These have been accepted in principle and hopefully appropriate steps will be taken to protect certain sites (Clinning 1978). More research is needed on this species, in particular a more detailed assessment of the human impact on breeding colonies and more rigorous censuses to enable an understanding of population trends (Frost and Shaughnessy 1976). In northern Namibia a survey is needed to determine the population and status of the species more accurately (Ryan *et al.* in press).

References

Alexander, W. B. (1928) *Birds of the ocean.* New York and London: G. P. Putnam and Sons.

Andersson, C. J. (1872) *Birds of Damaraland.* London.

Bannerman, D. A. (1912) On a collection of birds made by Mr Willoughby P. Lowe on the west coast of Africa and outlying islands; with notes by the collector. *Ibis* (9)6: 219-268.

Bannerman, D. A. (1931) *The birds of tropical West Africa,* 2. London: Crown Agents for the Colonies.

Benson, C. W. (1967) The birds of Aldabra and their status. *Atoll Res. Bull.* no. 118: 63-111.

Berry, H. H. and Berry, C. V. (1975) A checklist and notes on the birds of Sandvis, South West Africa. *Madoqua* 9(2): 5-18.

Bourdillon, B. H. (1944) Terns on Lagos Beach, Nigeria. *Ibis* 86: 405-407.

Bourne, W. R. P. and Radford, M. C. (1962) Observations of sea birds. *Sea Swallow* 15: 7-27.

Brinck, P. (1955) Mallophaga. *S. Afr. Anim. Life* 2: 402-425.

Brooke, R. K. (1977) Sea and coastal birds collected in Angola by H. Skoog in 1912. *Bull. Brit. Orn. Club* 98: 31-32.

Brooke, R. K. (1981) The seabirds of the Moçâmedes Province, Angola. *Gerfaut* 71: 209-225.

Brooke, R. K. (in press) *The rare and vulnerable birds of South Africa.*

Burger, A. E., Cooper, J. and Furness, R. W. (1980) Conservation of the Damara Tern *Sterna balaenarum* at the De Mond Nature Reserve. Report of the Percy FitzPatrick Institute of African Ornithology, University of Cape Town, to the Department of Forestry and Environmental Conservation, Pretoria.

Cape Bird Club (1981) *A guide to the birds of the S. W. Cape.* 2nd edition. Cape Town: Cape Bird Club.

Chapin, J. P. (1939) The birds of the Belgian Congo. Part 2. *Bull. Amer. Mus. Nat. Hist.* 75.

Clinning, C. F. (1978) The biology and conservation of the Damara Tern in South West Africa. *Madoqua* 11: 31-39.

Cooper, J., Robertson, H. G. and Shaughnessy, P. D. (1980) Waders (Charadrii) and other coastal birds of the Diamond Coast and the islands off South West Africa. *Madoqua* 12: 51-57.

Cooper, J., Williams, A. J. and Britton, P. L. (in press) Distribution, population sizes and conservation of breeding seabirds in the Afrotropical Region. In J. P. Croxall, P. G. H. Evans and R. W. Schreiber, eds. *Status and conservation of the world's seabirds.* Cambridge: ICBP Techn. Publ. no. 2.

Dean, W. R. J. (1978) Cabinda. *Bokmakierie* 30: 68-71.

Earle, R. (1976) Pasop vir daardie fietse en besies! *Afr. Wildl.* 30(3): 14-15.

Elgood, J. H. (1982) *The birds of Nigeria.* London: B.O.U. Check-list No. 4.

Elgood, J. H., Fry, C. H. and Dowsett, R. J. (1973) African migrants in Nigeria. *Ibis* 115: 1-45.

Erard, C. and Etchécopar, R. D. (1970) Some notes on the birds of Angola. *Bull. Brit. Orn. Club* 90: 158-161.

Feare, C. J. and Bourne, W. R. P. (1977) The occurrence of "Portlandica" Little Terns and absence of Damara Terns and British Storm Petrels in the Indian Ocean. *Ostrich* 49: 64-66.

Frost, P. and Johnson, P. (1977) Seabirds on the Diamond Coast, South West Africa, December 1976. *Cormorant* 2: 3-4.

Frost, P. G. H. and Shaughnessy, G. (1976) Breeding adaptations of the Damara Tern *Sterna balaenarum.* *Madoqua* 9(3): 33-39.

Germain, M., Dragesco, J., Roux, F. and Garcin, H. (1973) Contribution à l'ornithologie du Sud-Cameroun. 1. Non-passeriformes. *Oiseau et R.F.O.* 43: 119-182.

Grindley, J. R. (1959) Birds of the Orange River estuary. *Ostrich* 30: 127-129.

Harrison, P. (1983) *Seabirds: an identification guide.* Beckenham: Croom Helm.

Hockey, P. A. R. (1982) Waders (Charadrii) and other coastal birds in the Lüderitz region of South West Africa. *Madoqua* 13: 27-33.

Johnson, P. (1979) Third census of the Damara Tern at Elizabeth Bay, South West Africa, December 1978. *Cormorant* 7: 32.

Johnson, P. and Frost, P. (1978) Conserving the Damara Tern. *Optima* 27: 106-107.

Liversidge, R., Broekhuysen, G. J. and Thesen, A. R. (1958) The birds of Langebaan Lagoon. *Ostrich* 29: 95-106.

Louette, M. (1981) *The birds of Cameroon. An annotated checklist.* Brussels: Verhandeling Wetenschappen, Jaargang 43, no. 163.

McLachlan, G. R. and Liversidge, R. (1978) *Roberts birds of South Africa.* 4th edition. Johannesburg: Trustees of the John Voelcker Bird Book Fund.

Mountfort, G. (1971) Wildlife treasures in the Indian Ocean. *Animals* 13: 619-623.

Niethammer, G. (1961) Vögel der südwestafrikanischen Küster. *Vogelwarte* 21: 147-152.

van Oordt, G. J. and Kruijt, J. P. (1954) Birds observed on a voyage in the South Atlantic and Southern Oceans in 1951/1952. *Ardea* 42: 245-280.

Penny, M. (1974) *The birds of Seychelles and the outlying islands.* London: Collins.

Pinto, A. A. da R. (1973) Aditamento à avifauna do Distrito de Moçâmedes, Angola. Pp. 383-419 in *Livro de homanegem ao Professor Fernando Frade Viegas da Costa 70° Aniversário – 27 de Abril de 1968.* Lisbon.

Pitman, C. R. S. (1977) Seafowl observed on a voyage, Capetown to London, 23rd January to 8th February 1967. *Bull. Brit. Orn. Club* 87: 117-120.

Prozesky, O. P. M. (1963) Ornithological results of the Transvaal Museum Namib expedition May 1959, and the subsequent trip to Sandwich Harbour during January, 1960. *Ostrich* 34: 78-91.

Randall, R. M. and McLachlan, A. (1982) Damara Terns breeding in the eastern Cape, South Africa. *Ostrich* 53: 50-51.

Robinson, J., Robinson, C. St.C., and Winterbottom, J. M. (1957) Notes on the birds of the Cape l'Agulhas region. *Ostrich* 28: 147-163.

Rougeot, P.-C. (1945) Notes sur quelques oiseaux de mer du Gabon. *Oiseau et R.F.O.* 15: 111-117.

Rougeot, P. (1946) Notes sur les laridés du Gabon. *Oiseau et R.F.O.* 16: 129-132.

Rougeot, P.-C. (1948) Nouvelles notes sur les palmipèdes du Gabon. *Oiseau et R.F.O.* 18: 94-97.

Rougeot, P.-C. (1952) Observations ornithologiques dans l'ocean Atlantique. *Oiseau et R.F.O.* 22: 14-19.

Ryan, P. G. and Cooper, J. (in press) Waders (Charadrii) and other coastal birds of the northern Cape Province. *Bontebok.*

Ryan, P. G., Cooper, J. and Stutterheim, C. J. (in press) Waders (Charadrii) and other coastal birds of the Skeleton Coast, South West Africa. *Madoqua.*

Sander, F. (1956) A list of birds of Lagos and its environs, with brief notes on their status. *Nigerian Field* 21: 147-162.

Siegfried, W. R., Frost, P. G. H., Cooper, J. and Kemp, A. C. (1976) Rare and vulnerable birds in South Africa. *Biol. Conserv.* 10: 83-93.

Siegfried, W. R. and Johnson, P. (1977) The Damara Tern and other seabirds on the Diamond Coast, South West Africa, December 1977. *Cormorant* 3: 13.

Sutton, R. W. W. (1970) Bird records from Ghana in 1967 and 1968/69. Part 1. Southern Ghana. *Bull. Nigerian Orn. Soc.* 7: 53-56.

Traylor, M. A. (1963) Checklist of Angolan birds. *Publ. cult. Co. Diam. Angola, Lisboa* no. 61.

Vincent, A. W. (1946) On the breeding habits of some African birds. *Ibis* 88: 48-67.

Wallace, D. I. M. (1973) Seabirds at Lagos and in the Gulf of Guinea. *Ibis* 115: 559-571.

Whitelaw, D. A., Underhill, L. G., Cooper, J. and Clinning, C. F. (1978) Waders (Charadrii) and other birds on the Namib Coast: counts and conservation priorities. *Madoqua* 11: 137-150.

Winterbottom, J. M. (1960) Report on the Cape Bird Club vlei counts, 1952-58. *Ostrich* 3: 135-168.

Winterbottom, J. M. (1971) *A preliminary checklist of the birds of South West Africa*. Windhoek: S.W.A. Scientific Society.

SOMALI PIGEON   RARE
Columba oliviae Clarke, 1918

Order COLUMBIFORMES   Family COLUMBIDAE

Summary An extremely poorly known ground-feeding, rock-dwelling species, endemic to the arid coastal regions of north-east Somalia, this pigeon is not known to be threatened other than by its restricted range; a survey is needed to confirm this range is not contracting.

Distribution The Somali Pigeon is known only from Somalia, where it has been found on the north coast of the country in the hills behind Berbera and, several hundred kilometres to the east, from behind Las Khoreh eastwards to Cape Guardafui, and on the east coast at several places from Cape Guardafui as far south as Eil. Speculation that the species occurs throughout the north coast of Somalia to Cape Guardafui (Archer and Godman 1937) was reinforced by records of it in the 1940s in the "Ahl Maskat [Ahl Mescat] range of mountains" (North 1964), although recent confirmation appears lacking (see Ash and Miskell 1983). However, the map (in Goodwin 1970) is technically inaccurate in indicating (first) a known continuity between Berbera and Las Khoreh, (second) an inland distribution, and (third) occurrence west of Berbera (this last specifically denied in Archer and Godman 1937; also Ash and Miskell 1983). Behind Berbera, the species has been recorded from at least four named localities, the first three immediately adjacent although all four evidently constituting a single area: Dubar (Dubar Fort, Dubbar), 11-13 km inland from Berbera on the Sheikh road, at 200 m, this originally being designated the type-locality (see Archer 1918, Clarke 1918); "Bosti (Faradera)", 20 km inland (evidently the hills marked Busta and Feradero in War Office 1946), this subsequently being named (in contradistinction to Dubar) as the type-locality (see Archer and Godman 1937); Gotareri pass at 300 m (specimen in BMNH: NJC), the watercourse bearing this name (Gudharera) extending from Dubar Fort to the north-east slopes of Busta (in War Office 1946); and Bihendula, 40 km inland on the road to Sheikh, at 600 m (Archer 1918, Archer and Godman 1937). Behind Las Khoreh in the Warsangli foothills the species was considered "strongly represented" earlier this century, but the only named locality was Damali (Damaleh in War Office 1946), 15 km inland from Las Khoreh (Archer and Godman 1937); in May 1942 birds were found breeding at 750 m at Galgalo, the mountain at 10°59'N 49°02'E behind Bender Cassim (= Bosaso) several tens of kilometres east of Damali (North 1964; also War Office 1946, SDGHME 1947; see Remarks), and in the period 1942-1944 birds were seen "at many places along the Ahl Maskat range" from around this area eastwards to Cape Guardafui, and "at several places" from Cape Guardafui south as far as Eil, almost exactly 8°N 50°E, where in August 1944 evidence of breeding was established, at 120 m (Pitman 1960, North 1964; specimen in BMNH labelled 180 m: NJC). In recent years birds have evidently been found on the Dante (Hafun) peninsula, north of Eil on the east-facing coast (see Ash and Miskell 1983).

Population The total numbers of this species are unknown, but on existing evidence are likely to be small. When first discovered behind Berbera, it was noted generally in twos and threes, sometimes in small flocks of five or six (Archer 1918), at one locality coming to feed at a large camp for camels (Archer 1918, Archer and Godman 1937): that "large numbers" were then seen there (Goodwin 1970) is apparently a mistaken interpretation of the sources. The species has been described as "scattered and local, rather than rare" (Archer and Godman 1937) and again as an "uncommon local endemic resident" (Ash and Miskell 1983), but there can be no doubt that, in global terms, it is numerically and geographically a rare bird (the term "rare" being readily invoked for it: J. S. Ash *in litt.* 1984).

Ecology Birds inhabit the barren, rocky limestone and sandstone hills and escarpments in maritime desert or semi-desert regions, never being found more than 30 km from the sea and apparently – even when visiting the camel camp (see above and below) – never more than a few hundred metres from crevices and rocky ravines (Archer 1918, Archer and Godman 1937, North 1964, Goodwin 1970, Ash and Miskell 1983); one observer found the species usually below 300 m (North 1964; also Goodwin 1970) but also recorded it from up to 750 m (see Distribution), and altitudinal distribution at least on the north coast conceivably varies with season. Water exists at the base of the hills but the surrounding vegetation is "scanty", consisting of "*khansa*" ("dense impenetrable bush" of *Acacia orphota*) 1 m high, salsolaceous plants, "*arman*" (stunted "thick creeper" *Cissus rotundifolia*; see Remarks), acacia and other thorn bushes, the country thus wholly devoid of grains (Archer and Godman 1937). Birds came to grain being used to feed camels at a large camp, but otherwise were assumed to feed on grass seeds and various molluscs (Archer and Godman 1937; also Archer 1918); the species was subsequently found to feed chiefly and probably entirely on the ground and to take seeds and berries (North 1964, Goodwin 1970; crop of August specimen in BMNH held berries: NJC). Nests have been found in near darkness in recesses in the roofs of caves situated on open hillsides, not in main gorges (North 1964; also Goodwin 1970), but the breeding season is unclear: an egg is known from May (addled) at Galgalo (North 1964; also Goodwin 1970) and another from August at Eil; in one account of the latter it was in the nest (North 1964; also Goodwin 1970), in another it was fresh but "dropped", 0.6 m from an unoccupied nest (Pitman 1960), and inasmuch as a male collected the previous day was not in breeding condition (specimen in BMNH referred to above) it seems possible that August is not a usual month for nesting. It was originally believed that the species bred in the winter months on the north coast (Archer 1918) but the same observer later assumed that it laid around May (Archer and Godman 1937); the latter speculation is confirmed by the Galgalo record (above), but the former is also reinforced by a report from local Somalis at Galgalo of a nest with an egg there in December and one with young in February (North 1964; also Goodwin 1970). The species's presence on the northern "maritime plain" solely in winter months led to the assumption that to escape the intense heat of the period from April to September it must migrate to places unknown (Archer 1918, Archer and Godman 1937), the speculation that birds would move uphill and breed (Archer and Godman 1937) being borne out by the Galgalo record (above); conceivably climatic conditions in the east at Eil are different. Birds are stated to be shy and wary, and difficult to approach in the open

(Archer 1918), but also to be not shy – this from context presumably when perching on rocky ledges (Archer and Godman 1937).

Threats None is known, except that its range is somewhat restricted. Habitat is presumably changing due to erosion, overgrazing and other factors, but the species is highly unlikely to be hunted (J. S. Ash *in litt.* 1984). Its relatively small range within a very arid area may be due to its inability to compete with the Speckled Pigeon *Columba guinea* under less extreme conditions, and its failure to secure a footing in Arabia may be due to the presence there of the Rock Pigeon *C. livia* (Snow 1978).

Conservation Measures Taken None is known.

Conservation Measures Proposed A survey is needed to confirm this species's continuing presence at the sites from which it is known and to make some preliminary assessment of its ecological requirements (by use of maps and satellite imagery further localities might be identified). If it cannot be found in certain areas or if environmental conditions appear unpropitious, a more detailed study would be appropriate to determine more exactly its conservation needs.

Remarks Several small errors, apart from those noted in the account above, have occurred in writings on this species. Most curiously, the specific name *oliviae* (from the name of the discoverer's wife) is consistently reproduced by the discoverer as *olivae* (in Archer and Godman 1937; hence also in Pitman 1960, Ash and Miskell 1983). Galgalo has been given incorrect coordinates ("8°00'N 49°00'E", in Goodwin 1970) and the existence of this second breeding locality has been missed (in Ash and Miskell 1983). Under Ecology, a component of habitat at the foot of hills is given as "thick creeper" on the assumption that "*arman*" is a misprint for "*armah*" (see text and glossary in Archer and Godman 1937).

References

Archer, G. and Godman, E. M. (1937) *The birds of British Somaliland and the Gulf of Aden*, 1 and 2. London: Gurney and Jackson.

Archer, G. F. (1918) [Observations on *C. oliviae*.] *Bull. Brit. Orn. Club* 38: 62-63.

Ash, J. S. and Miskell, J. E. (1983) *Birds of Somalia: their habitat, status and distribution. Scopus* Spec. Suppl. 1. Nairobi: Ornithological Sub-Committee, EANHS.

Clarke, S. (1918) [A new pigeon from Somaliland.] *Bull. Brit. Orn. Club* 38: 61-62.

Goodwin, D. (1970) *Pigeons and doves of the world*. Second edition. London: Trustees of the British Museum (Natural History).

North, M. E. W. (1964) *in litt.* to D. Goodwin (letter held in BMNH).

Pitman, C. R. S. (1960) The egg of the Somaliland Pigeon, *Columba olivae* [*sic*] Clarke. *Bull. Brit. Orn. Club* 80: 88.

Snow, D. W. ed. (1978) *An atlas of speciation in African non-passerine birds*. London: Trustees of the British Museum (Natural History).

Survey Directorate, General Headquarters Middle East (1947) *East Africa Index Gazetteer, 2 and 2A: Abyssinia, Eritrea, British, French and Italian Somaliland*

and part of the Sudan. Cairo (1946): Directorate of Military Survey, The War
Office.
War Office (1946) East Africa, 1: 500,000, GSGS 4355, 4th edition.

MADEIRA LAUREL PIGEON   RARE
Columba trocaz Heineken, 1829

Order COLUMBIFORMES   Family COLUMBIDAE

Summary This pigeon is confined to dense forest in the northern part of the island of Madeira, where it numbers something over 500 but is subject to continuing hunting pressure.

Distribution The Madeira Laurel Pigeon is known only from Madeira (Portugal), in the subtropical north-east Atlantic Ocean, and for at least the last 100 years it has been largely confined, like its laurel forest habitat, which now covers no more than 16% of the land surface (Jones *et al.* in press), to the northern interior slopes and valleys of the island (Harcourt 1851,1855, Meinertzhagen 1925, Zino 1969, van den Berg and de Wijs 1980). Localities from which the species is recorded extend across the whole of the north from west to east (as traced in da Silva 1934, Office of Geography 1961, IGCP 1971, with the assistance of P. A. Zino *in litt.* 1984) in the following sequence: the Lombo Alto mountains, breeding recorded (Schmitz 1897), Ribeira da Janela, breeding recorded specifically at Sitio do Cedro, Banda d'Alem and Passada da Figueira (Schmitz 1894a,1895,1905b, 1907a,b, Schindler 1965, Sturhan 1969, Zino 1969), Fanal de Baixo (Schindler 1965), Fanal at c. 1,000 m (specimen in BMNH: NJC), between Ribeira da Janela and Seixal in the caldeira high in the mountains, breeding recorded (Schmitz 1894a; see Remarks), "Ribeiro Fundo" (Ribeira Funda) (Zino 1969; see Remarks), Seixal, breeding recorded specifically at a cliff named Lombo dos Pastos (Schmitz 1893a,b,1894a,1899), São Vicente (Schmitz 1905a), the best locality in the west being between (Boca da) Encumeada and (Rocha do) Folhadal inland from São Vicente (van den Berg and de Wijs 1980; also Schindler 1965), Serra d'Agua between Ribeira Brava and Encumeada (Schmitz 1905b), Boaventura (Schmitz 1905a), Ribeiro Bonito (Zino 1969), the levada east from Caldeirão Verde to Queimadas (i.e. on the north slopes of the main peak, Pico Ruivo de Santana), this considered the best area for the species (Buxton 1960, Bannerman and Bannerman 1965, van den Berg and de Wijs 1980), several other localities in this general area and north of Pico do Arieiro, e.g. Faja da Nogueira, Achada do Teixeira (Jones *et al.* in press, Swash in press), the mountain slopes above both Santana and Faial, described as "main areas" for the species (Hartwig 1891), the Ribeiro Frio/Balcões area, breeding recorded (Zino 1969, Bradley 1976, van den Berg and de Wijs 1980), Casa de Agua dos Lamaceiros on the watercourse connecting Ribeiro Frio to Camacha (Zino 1969), Porto da Cruz, breeding recorded (Hartwig 1891), the crater lake at Santo (António) da Serra (Hartwig 1886), the Serra de Agua near Machico, breeding recorded (Schmitz 1894b,1899), and Camacha (Hartwig 1891), this last being the only published locality not truly in the northern half of the island. However, the species does exist in the southern half of Madeira, notably at Ribeira da Ponta do Sol at its source and at the base of Paúl da Serra (G. Le Grand *in litt.* 1984, P. A. Zino and G. E. Maul *in litt.* 1984). One was seen in August 1981 in the Ribeira da Santa Luzia (Swash in press), which meets the sea in the capital Funchal on the south coast; there is also a specimen in BMNH labelled as taken at São

Martinho on 23 November 1903 (NJC), the only locality of this name being just west of Funchal (da Silva 1934). The species is reported to move into valleys on the south side of the mountains when north winds blow and the cold intensifies (Sarmento 1948).

Population At the time of first settlement of Madeira this species was exceptionally plentiful (Bolle 1854-1855), and towards the end of the last century was accounted still fairly frequent on the north side of the island (Koenig 1890, Ogilvie Grant 1890, Hartwig 1891), though by report it was rare and local in 1925 (Meinertzhagen 1925). Nevertheless, c. 30 were seen in a day west of Queimadas around New Year 1959 (Buxton 1960) and 33 were apparently shot in one day in January 1969, this latter information being offered as evidence that the species was not yet rare (Zino 1969). In transects of 15 km and 37 km, July 1981, 27 and 37 birds respectively were counted, and the species was found in every part of the island where laurel exists and was therefore considered relatively abundant (G. Le Grand *in litt.* 1984). A flock of over 40 was seen at Balcões, 25 January 1984 (R. P. Martins *in litt.* 1984). That total numbers exceed 500, considered probable (Cramp in press), seems certain (G. Le Grand *in litt.* 1984).

Ecology This pigeon, originally very tame (Bolle 1854-1855) but now very shy (Godman 1862, Schindler 1965, van den Berg and de Wijs 1980), inhabits high laurel forest, occasionally feeding in cultivated land (Godman 1872, Meinertzhagen 1925, Bannerman and Bannerman 1965, Zino 1969). Distribution of birds between and within laurel forests may be patchy, some areas perhaps providing more resources than others, such as nesting sites, denser laurel, a larger surface-area of cover (Jones *et al.* in press). The species feeds on fruit of characteristic laurel forest plants, laurel *Laurus azorica*, vinhático *Persea indica*, faia *Myrica faya* and til *Ocotea foetens* (Harcourt 1855, Godman 1872, Koenig 1890, Zino 1969), this last identified as particularly favoured (Schmitz 1905b); also "watercresses, grasses" (Harcourt 1855), and all sorts of cultivated vegetables (Zino 1969). Breeding occurs throughout the year (Schmitz 1897; also 1893a,b,1905b,1907a,b), although main activity appears to be from February to June (Schmitz 1899). Clutch-size is one (Schmitz 1897; also 1894a), reportedly occasionally two (Hartwig 1893, Zino 1969); re-laying occurred twice within 14 days after the first and then the replacement egg of a clutch was taken (Hartwig 1893). A local report that various pairs utilise the same nest was taken to indicate that a second brood is reared (Hartwig 1893). On the basis of the first ten eggs ever found for science, the species was considered to nest regularly in trees and only rarely in cliffs (Schmitz 1897), but this finding has been misquoted to the effect that birds prefer cliffs (Zino 1969; hence Cramp in press), although of five further nests whose positions were described three were in trees and two in cliffs (Zino 1969). Trees used include faia and til, nests being recorded up to 15 m from the ground (Hartwig 1893, Schmitz 1894a,1895,1897, 1905b,1907a), once exceptionally almost at ground level in a bush (Schmitz 1907a). Birds may have different habitat requirements in winter, or at least prefer lower altitudes (Jones *et al.* in press). Those at Balcões in January 1984 seemed to be gathering to feed in isolated deciduous trees within the laurel forest (R. P. Martins *in litt.* 1984).

Threats In the early years of the settlement of Madeira (mid-fifteenth century), pigeons presumably of this species were so common and tame that they were snared off branches with ease, and without giving alarm to others on nearby branches (Bolle 1854-1855). This persecution and, more importantly, the irreversible destruction of laurel forest over much of Madeira had reduced its numbers and range very considerably by the last century, although it was then still widely hunted for food and served up ("excellent eating") by hoteliers (Harcourt 1851, Koenig 1890). Despite its reduced numbers it is still claimed to do damage to crops, which is why hunting is still permitted (Zino 1969); conversely, the species is still hunted on the assumption that it otherwise becomes a pest (van den Berg and de Wijs 1980). The season for hunting this pigeon is normally from around 15 September to 15 December, but in 1984, in response to complaints by local farmers, shooting of the species was permitted on the last two Sundays of February and the first two Sundays of March, the first time in 50 years such an additional concession is believed to have been made at this time of year (P. A. Zino and G. E. Maul *in litt.* 1984). Probably the worst threat to the species is poaching in areas too remote to control (P. A. Zino and G. E. Maul *in litt.* 1984). A nest at Ribeiro Frio was destroyed by rats *Rattus*; rats are numerous in Madeira forests and destroy many birds' nests (Zino 1969). A certain amount of laurel forest destruction continues (Bramwell *et al.* 1982).

Conservation Measures Taken None is known.

Conservation Measures Proposed Special protection from hunting has been advocated (Zino 1969). Proposals for the conservation of the native laurel forest have been formulated (Bramwell *et al.* 1982). A study of the ecology of this species is needed, with particular emphasis on determining the extent of the damage it is claimed to do to crops and the impact of present hunting, and with the aim of identifying key areas where its conservation would be most effective and feasible. That an island endemic species reduced to something over 500 individuals should still be legally hunted is worrying, and the circumstances require investigation. There is an urgent need to clarify the status of Madeira in relation to European legislation: this species, along with the Gon-gon *Pterodroma feae* and Freira *P. madeira* (see relevant accounts), should be added to Annex II of the Berne Convention on the Conservation of European Wildlife and Natural Habitats, thereby both confirming that this convention applies to the Madeiran archipelago (including the Ilhas Selvagens) and affording important protection to these species and their habitats; moreover, Madeira must be defined as part of the European territory of Portugal prior to the latter's joining the European Community, so that these species can immediately be added to Annex I of the Directive on the Conservation of Wild Birds (EEC/79/409) and thereby further gain from the measures this requires for the protection of their habitats (A. B. Gammell *in litt.* 1984).

Remarks Although this species has sometimes been treated as conspecific with the Dark-tailed Laurel Pigeon *Columba bollii* of the Canaries (see relevant account), recent opinion is against this (K. W. Emmerson and G. Le Grand *per*

A. Machado *in litt.* 1983, Cramp in press). Concerning the distributional records of this species, the locality "Ribeira" (as referred to in Schmitz 1894a) is here assumed to be Ribeira da Janela; also, it is to be noted that there are two localities named "Ribeira Funda" in northern Madeira, one between Ribeira da Janela and Seixal, the other west of São Jorge and north of Ribeiro Bonito.

References

Bannerman, D. A. and Bannerman, W. M. (1965) *Birds of the Atlantic islands*, 2. Edinburgh and London: Oliver and Boyd.

van den Berg, A. B. and de Wijs, W. J. R. (1980) Birding in the Madeiran islands. *Dutch Birding* 2: 22-24.

Bolle, C. (1854-1855) Bemerkungen über die Vögel der Canarischen Inseln. *J. Orn.* 2: 447-462; 3: 171-181.

Bradley, D. (1976) More winter notes from Madeira. *Bocagiana* no. 42.

Bramwell, D., Montelongo, V., Navarro, B. and Ortega, J. (1982) Informe sobre la conservación de los bosques y la flora de la isla de Madeira. Elaborada por el Jardín Botánico Canário "Viera y Clavijo" para la Sociedad Internacional de Dendrólogos y la Unión Internacional de la Conservación de la Naturaleza y los Recursos Naturales (IUCN). Unpublished.

Buxton, E. J. M. (1960) Winter notes from Madeira. *Ibis* 102: 127-129.

Cramp, S. ed. (in press) *The birds of the western Palearctic*, 4. Oxford: Oxford University Press.

Godman, F. C. (1872) Notes on the resident and migratory birds of Madeira and the Canaries. *Ibis* (3)2: 209-224.

Harcourt, E. V. (1851) Notice of the birds of Madeira. *Proc. Zool. Soc. Lond.*: 141-146.

Harcourt, E. V. (1855) Notes on the ornithology of Madeira. *Ann. Mag. Nat. Hist.* (2)15: 430-438.

Hartwig, W. (1886) Die Vögel Madeiras. *J. Orn.* 34: 452-486.

Hartwig, W. (1891) Die Vögel der Madeira-Inselgruppe. *Ornis* 7: 151-188.

Hartwig, W. (1893) Nachtrag zu meinen beiden Arbeiten über die Vögel Madeiras. *J. Orn.* 41: 1-12.

IGCP (1971) Arquipélago da Madeira. 1: 50,000. Series P 722, 2nd edition. Instituto Geográfico e Cadastral.

Jones, M. J., Lace, L. A. and Hunter, S. V. (in press) Habitat preferences and conservation of Madeiran land birds. *Bol. Mus. Mun. Funchal.*

Koenig, A. (1890) Ornithologische Forschungsergebnisse einer Reise nach Madeira und den Canarischen Inseln. *J. Orn.* 38: 257-488.

Meinertzhagen, R. (1925) May in Madeira. *Ibis* (12)1: 600-621.

Office of Geography (1961) *Gazetteer no. 50. Portugal and the Cape Verde Islands.* Washington, D.C.: Department of the Interior.

Ogilvie Grant, W. R. (1890) Notes on some birds obtained at Madeira, Deserta Grande, and Porto Santo. *Ibis* (6)2: 438-445.

Sarmento, A. A. (1948) *Vertebrados da Madeira*, 1. Funchal: Junta Geral do Distrito Autónomo.

Schindler, E. (1965) Ornithologische Beobachtungen auf Madeira. *Bol. Mus. Mun. Funchal* 19(86): 111-124.

Schmitz, E. (1893a) Tagebuchnotizen aus Madeira. *Orn. Monatsber.* 1: 136-138.

Schmitz, E. (1893b) Tagebuchnotizen von Madeira. *Orn. Jahrb.* 4: 30-32.

Schmitz, E. (1894a) Neues über die Madeirataube (*Columba trocaz* Hein.). *Orn. Monatsber.* 2: 190-191.

Schmitz, E. (1894b) Tagebuchnotizen aus Madeira. *Orn. Monatsber.* 2: 35-39.

Schmitz, E. (1895) [Notiz.] *Orn. Monatsber.* 3: 115.

Schmitz, E. (1897) Die Vögel Madeira's. Nachtrag. *Orn. Monatsber.* 5: 121-122.

Schmitz, E. (1899) Die Vögel Madeira's. *Orn. Jahrb.* 10: 1-34, 41-66.

Schmitz, E. (1905a) Tagebuch-Notizen aus Madeira. *Orn. Jahrb.* 16: 219-226.

Schmitz, E. (1905b) Oologische Tagebuchnotizen aus Madeira. *Z. Ool. Orn.* 15: 65-69.

Schmitz, E. (1907a) Oologische Tagebuchnotizen aus Madeira. *Z. Ool. Orn.* 17: 54-58, 70-72.

Schmitz, E. (1907b) Oologische Tagebuchnotizen aus Madeira. *Z. Ool. Orn.* 18: 181-182, 188-189.

da Silva, F. A. (1934) *Dicionário corográfico do Arquipélago da Madeira.* Funchal: edição do autor.

Sturhan, D. (1969) Beitrag zur Avifauna des Madeira-Archipels. *Bol. Mus. Mun. Funchal* 23(105): 36-45.

Swash, A. R. H. (in press) Observations of birds in the Madeiran archipelago, summer 1981. *Bol. Mus. Mun. Funchal.*

Zino, P. A. (1969) Observations sur *Columba trocaz. Oiseau et R.F.O.* 39: 261-264.

DARK-TAILED LAUREL PIGEON   RARE
Columba bollii Godman, 1872

Order COLUMBIFORMES   Family COLUMBIDAE

Summary Known from laurel forest on Tenerife, La Palma and Gomera in the Canary Islands, this pigeon is moderately common wherever stands of laurel remain on these three islands, and well conserved by recent measures.

Distribution The Dark-tailed Laurel Pigeon is confined to areas of (mostly closed-canopy) laurel forest on Tenerife, La Palma and Gomera in the Canary Islands (Spain), north-east Atlantic Ocean, its range having contracted with the steady reduction of its habitat (for distribution of remaining laurel forest, see Machado 1976). On Tenerife it formerly occurred in all suitable areas (Meade-Waldo 1893), i.e. throughout the laurel forest, but that its distribution was "general ... in both north and south" (Koenig 1890) is misleading, since laurel forest has always been very largely confined to northern slopes (Machado 1976); the species is now known to exist in only four areas in the north-east, east-central north, central north, and north-west (K. W. Emmerson *in litt.* 1983,1984). In the north-east, it occurs in the laurel forest on the northern slopes of the Anaga massif from Las Mercedes through Taborno to Taganana (Godman 1872, Reid 1887, Volsøe 1951, Hemmingsen 1958, Hald-Mortensen 1970, Conrad 1979, Löhrl 1981, K. W. Emmerson *in litt.* 1983), although a bird was collected in August 1889 as far west as Tegueste (specimen in BMNH: NJC). In the east-central north, the species was formerly numerous and widespread in the forests that existed on the north-facing slopes between Aguamansa (Agua Mansa) and Tacoronte (Santa Ursula, La Victória, Agua Garcia) (Godman 1872, Reid 1887, Koenig 1890, Meade-Waldo 1893, Bannerman 1963), and is still to be found above La Victória and Santa Ursula (K. W. Emmerson *in litt.* 1984; also Pérez Padrón 1983). In the central north, it occurs in the Orotava valley (K. W. Emmerson *in litt.* 1983; also Meade-Waldo 1893), having been recorded specifically from the ravine at Aguamansa (Godman 1872, Reid 1887). In the north-west, it was relatively recently (early 1970s) discovered in a fairly large area of laurel forest in the Teno massif west of Erjos (K. W. Emmerson *in litt.* 1983, H.-H. Bergmann *in litt.* 1984). There is a report of birds from northern slopes of the Cumbre above Higueste (Igueste) (Bolle 1857), this being mistakenly repeated as Tegueste (Bannerman 1963); there is laurel forest in this area (see map in Machado 1976; also F. Kämmer *in litt.* 1984) but it remains to be investigated (K. W. Emmerson *in litt.* 1984). On La Palma, when first successfully investigated there (April 1889) the species was present in the higher mountains in large stretches of laurel in the north-east (Meade-Waldo 1889b) and this situation still obtains (K. W. Emmerson *in litt.* 1984) but, remarkably, publication of specific sites – those mentioned (in Bannerman 1963) could equally well refer to the White-tailed Laurel Pigeon *Columba junoniae* – has only been very recent: a north-east slope near Los Sauces at 500 m (Conrad 1979), a north slope west of Barlovento at 900 m (Conrad 1979), a northern barranco (Lensch 1981), La Galga (Fisher 1981) and Los Tilos (Pérez Padrón 1983, unless this is based on Bannerman 1963). On Gomera, the species has been recorded from the centre and north (Bolle 1857, Meade-Waldo 1889a) and is to be found throughout the extensive area of laurel forest in the central north of the island within the confines of the Garajonay National Park (Cullen *et al.* 1952, van den Berg and Bosman 1979, K. W. Emmerson *in litt.* 1983, M. A. S. Beaman *in litt.* 1984). When the first account of this species (at that time not distinguished from the White-tailed Laurel Pigeon) was published, it was stated to occur in "forests of the western group of islands" (Webb *et al.* 1842) and indeed there is good evidence that it also occurred on both Gran Canaria and Hierro. On Gran Canaria a few pairs were expected to survive in the 1850s (Bolle 1857) and three pigeons, neither White-tailed Laurel Pigeons nor Rock Doves *Columba livia*, were seen in 1888 in the last fragments of the island's laurel forest at Doramas, between Barranco de la Virgen and Valleseco on the northern slopes (Tristram 1889). On Hierro, interviews with hunters in 1960 suggested that this species was present until at least 1948 (Hemmingsen 1963), but though hearsay indicated that it might still survive there, searches of the island in July 1983, April 1984 and June 1984 drew blanks (K. W. Emmerson *in litt.* 1984).

Population The elusiveness of this species and the failure of many ornithologists to search in the right places or for long enough have combined to fuel pessimism over its status, particularly in Tenerife: reports of its reasonable abundance on the island in the nineteenth century (Bolle 1857, Godman 1872, Reid 1887, Meade-Waldo 1889a) dissolved into a common supposition of extinction in the twentieth (Gurney 1927, Lack and Southern 1949, Mountfort 1960, Ash 1969), despite fragmentary evidence that at least a few birds survived (Volsøe 1951, Hald-Mortensen 1970, Etchécopar and Hüe 1957, Hüe and Etchécopar 1958). However, 15-20 pairs were considered present in forests visited, March 1977, with the total population estimated in dozens, not hundreds (Löhrl 1981), but the most recent and complete study of the species on Tenerife indicates that it is still fairly common and widespread in the only two large tracts of laurel forest remaining (north-east and north-west), with small populations in the Orotava valley and above La Victória and Santa Ursula, so that the total number of birds is at least 200-300 (K. W. Emmerson *in litt.* 1984; also Cramp in press). On La Palma plenty were seen and the species suspected of being commoner than was apparent, April 1889 (Meade-Waldo 1889b), but owing to the complete failure of anyone to find it after 1905 it was considered on the verge of extinction (Bannerman 1963); however, observations in recent years reaffirm that its status is evidently now much as it was a hundred years ago, i.e. fairly common in the good patches of laurel forest that remain on the island (K. W. Emmerson *in litt.* 1983; also Conrad 1979). On Gomera, where in the last century the species was considered commoner than on the other two islands (Bolle 1857) and certainly "common enough" (Meade-Waldo 1889a), and despite a report of its increasing rarity in 1949 (Cullen *et al.* 1952), it is now known to be common and widespread within the habitat available (K. W. Emmerson *in litt.* 1983). One observer reports that the number of sightings of the species on Tenerife was about the same as for those of White-tailed Laurel Pigeons, whereas the number of sightings on Gomera was about twice as many as for the White-tailed Laurel Pigeon, and on both islands sightings of the former would usually involve flocks or pairs, of the latter usually pairs or single birds (M. A. S. Beaman *in litt.* 1984). On Gran Canaria, the Dark-tailed Laurel Pigeon was reported to have been common when the laurel forest was extensive (Tristram 1889).

Ecology This is a bird of laurel forest, particularly favouring areas of climax forest where the canopy is well developed or closed such as occur in shallow valleys, on gentle slopes or along watercourses (K. W. Emmerson *in litt.* 1983); for ecological separation from the White-tailed Laurel Pigeon – with which there is little (but occasional) mixing (Meade-Waldo 1889a, von Thanner 1913, Conrad 1979) – see under that species. Birds will also sometimes utilise (and even nest in) degraded areas of laurel (K. W. Emmerson *in litt.* 1983; also Conrad 1979), and if necessary even resort to pines (von Thanner 1908). Shy, retiring and rather silent (Godman 1872, Reid 1887, Löhrl 1981), birds keep much to the shadows of trees, resting quietly, especially over the middle of the day (Godman 1872, Koenig 1890, Löhrl 1981), but will occasionally visit lower corn patches in the early morning (Godman 1872) and formerly were considered to cause much damage in late summer and autumn in rye fields and orchards (Bolle 1857). Their habit of flying to water along traditional routes above the trees between 14.00 and 17.00 hrs was much exploited by hunters (Polatzek 1908-1909, von Thanner 1913). Apart from occasional use of crops, food is chiefly the fruit of various trees that compose laurel forest, those identified in the last century as taken being viñátigo *Persea indica*, til *Ocotea foetens*, laurel *Laurus azorica* and haya *Myrica faya*; also shoots of mocán *Visnea mocanera* and leaves of a shrub (Bolle 1857, Godman 1872, Reid 1887, Koenig 1890, Cabrera y Diaz 1893). Recent studies on the Anaga peninsula, Tenerife, show the summer diet to consist mainly of viñátigo, sanguino *Rhamnus glandulosa*, palo blanco *Picconia excelsa*, barbusano *Apollonias barbusana*, laurel and haya; in autumn and early winter, laurel and haya predominate, while holly *Ilex canariensis* and sanguino are taken in winter and, together with viñátigo, in spring (K. W. Emmerson *in litt.* 1983; also Cramp in press). Breeding has been reported to occur all year round, but chiefly in winter and early spring, the only period of inactivity being October to December (Reid 1887, Koenig 1890, Meade-Waldo 1893); however, recent research indicates that birds on all three islands breed in November and December (K. W. Emmerson *in litt.* 1984); a report that the breeding season extends from January to September on Gomera but only January to May on Tenerife (Cramp in press) is thus superseded, breeding on both islands lasting almost the whole year (K. W. Emmerson *in litt.* 1984). Clutch-size is one (Reid 1887, Koenig 1890, Meade-Waldo 1889a,1893); second broods have been reported (Koenig 1890). Nests are constructed in trees: on the basis of (obviously considerable) experience haya was identified as the preferred tree for nesting (Meade-Waldo 1890), but in several other accounts tree-heath *Erica arborea* (brezo) has been noted as favoured (Godman 1872, Reid 1887, Koenig 1890, Cabrera y Diaz 1893), birds sometimes using high trees (Bolle 1857, von Thanner 1913), e.g. viñátigo and barbusano (Cabrera y Diaz 1893) but frequently low bushes and shrubbery, e.g. snowball-tree *Viburnum rigidum* (Bolle 1857, Koenig 1890); the tree-heath *E. scoparia* (tejo) is also frequently used (K. W. Emmerson *in litt.* 1983; also Cramp in press).

Threats Destruction of the endemic Canarian laurel forests was considered to have been a serious factor in the depletion of this species on all the islands where it is known to occur (Gurney 1927, Lack and Southern 1949, Volsøe 1951, Cullen *et al.* 1952) and in its extinction on Gran Canaria (Bannerman 1919-1920,1963). Hunting was blamed for its extinction on Hierro (Hemmingsen 1963) and several accounts indicate considerable hunting pressure elsewhere (Reid 1887, Polatzek 1908-1909, von Thanner 1913, Cullen *et al.* 1952), birds often being served up as food in Tenerife (Bolle 1857) and nestlings often being taken to be reared (presumably to eat) by islanders (Bolle 1857, Koenig 1890, von Thanner 1913). None of these factors is now a serious cause for concern (K. W. Emmerson *in litt.* 1983).

Conservation Measures Taken These are as for the White-tailed Laurel Pigeon.

Conservation Measures Proposed These are as for the White-tailed Laurel Pigeon.

Remarks Although this species has sometimes been treated as conspecific with the Madeira Laurel Pigeon *C. trocaz* (see relevant account), recent opinion is against this (K. W. Emmerson and G. Le Grand *per* A. Machado *in litt.* 1983, Cramp in press).

References

Ash, J. S. (1969) Midwinter notes from Tenerife. *Ibis* 111: 618-619.

Bannerman, D. A. (1919-1920) List of the birds of the Canary Islands, with detailed reference to the migratory species and the accidental visitors. *Ibis* (11)1: 84-131, 291-321, 457-495, 708-764; (11)2: 97-132, 323-360, 519-569.

Bannerman, D. A. (1963) *Birds of the Atlantic islands*, 1. Edinburgh and London: Oliver and Boyd.

van den Berg, A. B. and Bosman, C. A. W. (1979) Birding in the Canary Islands. *Dutch Birding* 1: 66-68.

Bolle, C. (1857) Mein zweiter Beitrag zur Vogelkunde der canarischen Inseln. *J. Orn.* 5: 258-292, 305-351.

Cabrera y Diaz, A. (1893) Catálogo de las aves del archipiélago canario. *Ann. Soc. Esp. Hist. Nat.* 22: 151-220.

Conrad, R. (1979) Beobachtungen zum Vorkommen der Lorbeertauben auf Teneriffa und La Palma (Kanarische Inseln). *Vogelwelt* 100: 155-156.

Cramp, S. ed. (in press) *The birds of the western Palearctic*, 4. Oxford: Oxford University Press.

Cullen, J. M., Guiton, P. E., Horridge, G. A. and Peirson, J. (1952) Birds on La Palma and Gomera (Canary Islands). *Ibis* 94: 68-84.

Etchécopar, R.-D. and Hüe, F. (1957) Nouvelles données sur l'avifaune des îles Canaries recueillies au printemps 1956. *Oiseau et R.F.O.* 27: 309-334.

Fisher, C. T. (1981) Specimens of extinct, endangered or rare birds in the Merseyside County Museums, Liverpool. *Bull. Brit. Orn. Club* 101: 276-285.

Godman, F. C. (1872) Notes on the resident and migratory birds of Madeira and the Canaries. *Ibis* (3)2: 209-224.

Gurney, G. H. (1927) Notes on birds observed at Orotava, Tenerife. *Ibis* (12)3: 634-644.

Hald-Mortensen, P. (1970). Some preliminary notes from Tenerife. *Ibis* 112: 265-266.

Hemmingsen, A. M. (1958) Field observations of birds in the Canary Islands. *Vidensk. Medd. fra Dansk naturh. Foren.* 120: 189-206.

Hemmingsen, A. M. (1963) Birds on Hierro and the relation of number of species, and of specific abundances and body weights, to island area. *Vidensk. Medd. fra Dansk naturh. Foren.* 125: 207-236.

Hüe, F. and Etchécopar, R.-D. (1958) Un mois de recherches ornithologiques aux îles Canaries. *Terre et Vie* 105: 186-219.

Koenig, A. (1890) Ornithologische Forschungsergebnisse einer Reise nach Madeira und den Canarischen Inseln. *J. Orn.* 38: 257-488.

Lack, D. and Southern, H. N. (1949) Birds on Tenerife. *Ibis* 91: 607-626.

Lensch, A. (1981) Zum Vorkommen einiger Vogelarten auf der Insel La Palma (Kanaren). *Orn. Mitt.* 33: 229-232.

Löhrl, H. (1981) Zwei extrem gefährdete Tauben des Lorbeerwaldes, *Columba (trocaz) bollii* und *C. junoniae*, auf Teneriffa. *J. Orn.* 122: 173-180.

Machado, A. (1976) Introduction to a faunal study of the Canary Islands' laurisilva, with special reference to the ground-beetles (Coleoptera, Caraboidea). In G. Kunkel, ed. Biogeography and ecology in the Canary Islands. *Monog. Biol.* 30: 347-411.

Meade-Waldo, E. G. (1889a) Notes on some birds of the Canary Islands. *Ibis* (6)1: 1-13.

Meade-Waldo, E. G. (1889b) Further notes on the birds of the Canary Islands. *Ibis* (6)1: 503-520.

Meade-Waldo, E. G. (1890) Further notes on the birds of the Canary Islands. *Ibis* (6)2: 429-438.

Meade-Waldo, E. G. (1893) List of birds observed in the Canary Islands. *Ibis* (6)5: 185-207.

Mountfort, G. (1960) Notes on the birds of Tenerife. *Ibis* 102: 618-619.

Pérez Padrón, F. (1983) *Las aves de Canarias*. 3rd edition. (Enciclopedia Canaria). Tenerife: ACT.

Polatzek, J. (1908-1909) Die Vögel der Canaren. *Orn. Jahrb.* 19: 81-119, 161-197; 20: 1-24, 117-134, 202-210.

Reid, S. G. (1887) Notes on the birds of Teneriffe. *Ibis* (5)5: 424-435.

von Thanner, R. (1908) Ein Sammelausflug nach La Palma, Hierro und Fuerteventura. *Orn. Jahrb.* 19: 198-215.

von Thanner, R. (1913) Wild und Jagd auf den Kanaren. *Deutsche Jäger-Zeitung* 61: 569-572, 586-589, 600-604, 616-618, 631-633.

Tristram, H. B. (1889) Ornithological notes on the island of Gran Canaria. *Ibis* (6)1: 13-32.

Volsøe, H. (1951) The breeding birds of the Canary Islands, 1. Introduction and synopsis of the species. *Vidensk. Medd. fra Dansk naturh. Foren.* 113: 1-153.

Webb, P. B., Berthelot, S. and Moquin-Tandon, A. (1842) Ornithologie Canarienne. In P. B. Webb and S. Berthelot, *Histoire naturelle des Iles Canaries*, 2, pt. II. Zoologie (Ornithologie) – 1. Paris.

WHITE-TAILED LAUREL PIGEON

Columba junoniae Hartert, 1916

Order COLUMBIFORMES

RARE

Family COLUMBIDAE

Summary Known from laurel forest on Tenerife, La Palma and Gomera in the Canary Islands, this pigeon is relatively common only in parts of La Palma, but well conserved by recent measures.

Distribution The White-tailed Laurel Pigeon is confined to areas of (chiefly laurel) forest that remain on Tenerife, La Palma and Gomera in the Canary Islands (Spain), north-east Atlantic Ocean, its range having contracted with the steady reduction of its habitat (for distribution of remaining laurel forest, see Machado 1976). The species was not known from Tenerife until around 1970 (F. Kämmer *in litt.* 1984) and the information first published in the late 1970s and early 1980s (Conrad 1979, Löhrl 1981). It was then speculated whether its occurrence on Tenerife represented a recent colonisation from La Palma or a chronic ornithological oversight (Löhrl 1981), but there can be little doubt that the latter is the case: there is an unequivocal report by locals of this species ("raboblanco") at Tacoronte a hundred years earlier in 1871 (Godman 1872) – the same name, "rabiblanco" (*sic*), being used for the same bird on Gomera (see Bolle 1857, Meade-Waldo 1889a) – although this affirmation was evidently forgotten amidst subsequent claims that the species was certainly absent from the island (beginning with Reid 1887, Meade-Waldo 1889a; see Remarks). Records are from four areas of Tenerife, the north-west near Erjos (Conrad 1979, Löhrl 1981, K. W. Emmerson *in litt.* 1983), the central north near Palo Blanco, Aguamansa (Agua Mansa) and elsewhere in the Orotava valley (Löhrl 1981, K. W. Emmerson *in litt.* 1983, F. Kämmer *in litt.* 1984), the east-central north above the La Victória and Santa Ursula (K. W. Emmerson *in litt.* 1984), and the north-east at Pico del Inglés on the Anaga peninsula (Löhrl 1981, K. W. Emmerson *in litt.* 1983). On La Palma birds are present in the north-east and north, published localities (from east to north-west) being: the "south slope" of the main caldera (Caldera de Taburiente) west of Santa Cruz (Etchécopar and Hüe 1957); the east-facing outer slope of the caldera (Cullen *et al.* 1952); La Galga (type-locality) (Koenig 1890, Hartert 1916, Volsøe 1951, Fisher 1981); on both outer and inner slopes of Caldera de Taburiente (Conrad 1979); near Los Tilos (Cuyas Robinson 1971, Conrad 1979); near Los Sauces (Etchécopar and Hüe 1957, Conrad 1979); west of Barlovento (Conrad 1979); an unnamed barranco in the north (Lensch 1981); above Garafia in the north-west near the hamlets of Hoja (Hoya) Grande and Machin (von Thanner 1908,1913); birds are also recorded from Fuente Bermeja (Koenig 1890) (position untraced). On Gomera, the species is to be found throughout the extensive area of laurel forest in the central north of the island within the confines of the Garajonay National Park (von Thanner 1913, van den Berg and Bosman 1979, K. W. Emmerson *in litt.* 1983; also Cullen *et al.* 1952). When the first account of this species (at that time not distinguished from the Dark-tailed Laurel Pigeon *Columba bollii*) was published, it was stated to occur in "forests of the western group of islands" (Webb *et al.* 1842), and this seems very likely, although evidence for its

277

occurrence on Gran Canaria and Hierro (the other western islands) is far flimsier than that for the Dark-tailed species (see relevant account). Absence of appropriate food-plants was considered good reason for the absence of this species from Hierro (Meade-Waldo 1890), but its usual food-plants do in fact grow there (Hemmingsen 1963), so that a record of two large, red-breasted pigeons on the island, considered wandering White-tailed Laurel Pigeons from La Palma (Meade-Waldo 1890), seems likely to indicate that a population of the species was in fact formerly resident. There is no evidence whatever of its having occurred on Gran Canaria, other than the early blanket statement (in Webb *et al.* 1842) and the fact that if one species of laurel pigeon lived there it would perhaps be surprising if the other did not. A record from 1402-1404 of "large pigeons with white ends to their tails" on the then locally well-wooded eastern island of Fuerteventura may well have referred to this species (Collar 1983).

Population On Tenerife it is scarce and very local (K. W. Emmerson *in litt.* 1983). Moreover, when observed near Erjos in April 1972 it was commoner than it is today (H.-H. Bergmann *in litt.* 1984), although another observer has found it not uncommon there (M. A. S. Beaman *in litt.* 1984). On La Palma it was originally considered scarcer if more widespread than on Gomera (Meade-Waldo 1889b), but later reports suggested it was locally common (e.g. Cullen *et al.* 1952, Etchécopar and Hüe 1957, Cuyas Robinson 1971), and on the basis of extensive recent research it is now judged fairly common and widespread, locally very common (K. W. Emmerson *in litt.* 1983). On Gomera, where the earliest settlers found and killed näitive pigeons in great quantities (Webb *et al.* 1842, Bolle 1854-1855), it was fairly abundant in steep-sided valleys in 1888 (Meade-Waldo 1889a) but reportedly very rare by 1949 (Cullen *et al.* 1952), and is now considered "not infrequent" in the single large remaining patch of laurel forest on the island, but much less common than the Dark-tailed Laurel Pigeon (K. W. Emmerson *in litt.* 1983; see Population under latter species for comparative records); in certain areas of Gomera, however, and notably at Barranco del Cedro, birds may be "fairly common" (M. A. S. Beaman *in litt.* 1984).

Ecology The ecological separation of this species from the Dark-tailed Laurel Pigeon was originally considered to be at least partly altitudinal, the latter keeping to high forest, the former to lower scrub-covered slopes (Meade-Waldo 1889a), but from the evidence of subsequent records and recent research it is clear that altitude is not the determining factor, rather it is that the species prefers scrubbier areas such as occur both above and below major stands of laurel: thus at the higher levels birds occur in the mixed pine/laurel shrub forest that forms the transition zone between pure laurel and the higher pine forests, birds occasionally even utilising the latter and ranging up to 1,500 and even 2,000 m (K. W. Emmerson *in litt.* 1983; also von Thanner 1908, Cullen *et al.* 1952, Morphy 1964, Conrad 1979); whilst at lower levels they appear to be most frequently found where barrancos form steep slopes and sheer, deep ravines, ledges, rock faces and cliffs, covered in a dense, bushy, mixed vegetation, down to 250 m (K. W. Emmerson *in litt.* 1983; also Meade-Waldo 1889a,b,1893, van den Berg and Bosman 1979, Conrad 1979). On La Palma, they even occur in heavily degraded areas on the edge of cultivations, on which they reportedly feed (K. W. Emmerson *in litt.* 1983). There are several such reports of this species feeding on cultivated fruit and grain (e.g. Meade-Waldo 1889b, Koenig 1890, von Thanner 1913, Cuyas Robinson 1971), and barley and flax have been found in crops of collected specimens (Meade-Waldo 1889a), utilisation of such resources perhaps increasing when natural food-supplies become blighted (Meade-Waldo 1893); however, the chief food appears to be laurel fruits, as in the Dark-tailed Laurel Pigeon (Meade-Waldo 1889a), notably (in La Palma) til *Ocotea foetens* and viñátigo *Persea indica* (Meade-Waldo 1889b), birds spending much time (presumably foraging for fallen fruit) on the ground (Meade-Waldo 1889a, Cullen *et al.* 1952). Breeding was found to occur much later than in the Dark-tailed Laurel Pigeon, beginning in May and lasting throughout the summer (Meade-Waldo 1889a,1893), although there are four clutches in BMNH taken on Gomera in March (NJC; also Bannerman 1963). Clutch-size is one, but unlike the Dark-tailed Laurel Pigeon nests are built on ledges or stumps (Meade-Waldo 1889a,1893, von Thanner 1913); on La Palma nests with two eggs have been reported (Pérez Padrón 1983).

Threats Destruction of the endemic Canarian laurel forests was considered to have been a serious factor in the depletion of birds on both La Palma and Gomera from the earliest times down to the first half of this century (Cullen *et al.* 1952), and deforestation for charcoal was continuing in the 1950s (Hüe and Etchécopar 1958). These factors are, however, no longer a serious cause for concern (K. W. Emmerson *in litt.* 1983).

Conservation Measures Taken Hunting of both the White-tailed and Dark-tailed Laurel Pigeons has been prohibited since 1973, and as of 30 December 1980 under Royal Decree 3181 the species now figure on the list of fully protected Spanish wildlife whose hunting, capture, maintenance in captivity, trading and exportation, are strictly forbidden, as is the taking of their eggs or young (K. W. Emmerson *in litt.* 1983). On Gomera, 3,875 ha of forest, including the best representation of the island's laurel forest, were established as the Garajonay National Park on 25 March 1981 (K. W. Emmerson *in litt.* 1983). On La Palma, 511 ha of laurel forest with a good population of White-tailed Laurel Pigeons have been included in the IUCN network of Man and Biosphere Reserves (K. W. Emmerson *in litt.* 1983). Of the 18,850 ha classified as laurel forest in the western Canary Islands, 7,684 ha are public forest under the jurisdiction of ICONA and are patrolled by forest guards (K. W. Emmerson *in litt.* 1983). Biological studies on both the White-tailed and Dark-tailed Laurel Pigeons began in June 1983 under the provisions of both the Garajonay National Park management plan and the research programme of the Man and Biosphere Reserve on La Palma (K. W. Emmerson *in litt.* 1983).

Conservation Measures Proposed A network of protected areas within the scope of the Spanish Land Use Act has been proposed for the island of La Palma, seven of these areas, totalling some 3,500 ha, encompassing habitat for both this species and the Dark-tailed Laurel Pigeon (K. W. Emmerson *in litt.* 1983). There is an urgent need to clarify the status of the Canary Islands in relation to European legislation: this species, along with the Canarian Black Oystercatcher *Haematopus meadewaldoi*, Dark-tailed Laurel Pigeon, Fuerteventura Stonechat *Saxicola dacotiae* and Blue Chaffinch *Fringilla teydea* (see relevant accounts), should be added to Annex II of the Berne Convention on the Conservation of European Wildlife and Natural Habitats, thereby both confirming that this convention applies to the Canary archipelago and affording important protection to these species and their habitats; moreover, the Canaries must be defined as part of the European territory of Spain prior to the latter's joining the European Community, so that these species can immediately be added to Annex I of the Directive on the Conservation of Wild Birds (EEC/79/409) and thereby further gain from the measures this requires for the protection of their habitats (A. B. Gammell *in litt.* 1984).

Remarks There is a specimen received by BMNH in 1846 labelled "Massina" (NJC), but if this is a locality it cannot be traced even (e.g.) on a contemporary map (Coello 1849).

References

Bannerman, D. A. (1963) *Birds of the Atlantic islands*, 1. Edinburgh and London: Oliver and Boyd.

van den Berg, A. B. and Bosman, C. A. W. (1979) Birding in the Canary Islands. *Dutch Birding* 1: 66-68.

Bolle, C. (1854-1855) Bemerkungen über die Vögel der Canarischen Inseln. *J. Orn.* 2: 447-462; 3: 171-181.

Bolle, C. (1857) Mein zweiter Beitrag zur Vogelkunde der canarischen Inseln. *J. Orn.* 5: 258-292, 305-351.

Coello, F. (1849) Islas Canarias, 1: 280,000. Madrid.

Collar, N. J. (1983) A history of the Houbara in the Canaries. *Bustard Studies* 1: 9-29.

Conrad, R. (1979) Beobachtungen zum Vorkommen der Lorbeertauben auf Teneriffa und La Palma (Kanarische Inseln). *Vogelwelt* 100: 155-156.

Cullen, J. M., Guiton, P. E., Horridge, G. A. and Peirson, J. (1952) Birds on La Palma and Gomera (Canary Islands). *Ibis* 94: 68-84.

Cuyas Robinson, J. (1971) Algunas notas sobre aves observadas en tres visitas a las Islas Canarias. *Ardeola* vol. espec.: 103-153.

Etchécopar, R. D. and Hüe, F. (1957) Nouvelles données sur l'avifaune des îles Canaries recueillies au printemps 1956. *Oiseau et R.F.O.* 27: 309-334.

Fisher, C. T. (1981) Specimens of extinct, endangered or rare birds in the Merseyside County Museums, Liverpool. *Bull. Brit. Orn. Club* 101: 276-285.

Godman, F. C. (1872) Notes on the resident and migratory birds of Madeira and the Canaries. *Ibis* (3)2: 209-224.

Hartert, E. (1916) Notes on pigeons. *Novit. Zool.* 23: 78-88.

Hemmingsen, A. M. (1963) Birds on Hierro and the relation of number of species, and of specific abundances and body weights, to island area. *Vidensk. Medd. fra Dansk naturh. Foren.* 125: 207-236.

Hüe, F. and Etchécopar, R. D. (1958) Un mois de recherches ornithologiques aux îles Canaries. *Terre et Vie* 105: 186-219.

Koenig, A. (1890) Ornithologische Forschungsergebnisse einer Reise nach Madeira und den Canarischen Inseln. *J. Orn.* 38: 257-488.

Lensch, A. (1981) Zum Vorkommen einiger Vogelarten auf der Insel La Palma (Kanaren). *Orn. Mitt.* 33: 229-232.

Löhrl, H. (1981) Zwei extrem gefährdete Tauben des Lorbeerwaldes, *Columba (trocaz) bollii* und *C. junoniae*, auf Teneriffa. *J. Orn.* 122: 173-180.

Machado, A. (1976) Introduction to a faunal study of the Canary Islands' laurisilva, with special reference to the ground-beetles (Coleoptera, Caraboidea). In G. Kunkel, ed. Biogeography and ecology in the Canary Islands. *Monog. Biol.* 30: 347-411.

Meade-Waldo, E. G. (1889a) Notes on some birds of the Canary Islands. *Ibis* (6)1: 1-13.

Meade-Waldo, E. G. (1889b) Further notes on the birds of the Canary Islands. *Ibis* (6)1: 503-520.

Meade-Waldo, E. G. (1890) Further notes on the birds of the Canary Islands. *Ibis* (6)2: 429-438.

Meade-Waldo, E. G. (1893) List of birds observed in the Canary Islands. *Ibis* (6)5: 185-207.

Morphy, M. J. (1964) Ornithological report. Pp. 52-59 in Newcastle-upon-Tyne University Exploration Society 1963 Expedition to La Palma (Canary Islands) Report. Unpublished.

Pérez Padrón, F. (1983) *Las aves de Canarias*. 3rd edition. (Enciclopedia Canaria). Tenerife: ACT.

Reid, S. G. (1887) Notes on the birds of Teneriffe. *Ibis* (5)5: 424-435.

von Thanner, R. (1908) Ein Sammelausflug nach La Palma, Hierro und Fuerteventura. *Orn. Jahrb.* 19: 198-215.

von Thanner, R. (1913) Wild und Jagd auf den Kanaren. *Deutsche Jäger-Zeitung* 61: 569-572, 586-589, 600-604, 616-618, 631-633.

Volsøe, H. (1951) The breeding birds of the Canary Islands, 1. Introduction and synopsis of the species. *Vidensk. Medd. fra Dansk naturh. Foren.* 113: 1-153.

Webb, P. B., Berthelot, S. and Moquin-Tandon, A. (1842) Ornithologie Canarienne. In P. B. Webb and S. Berthelot, *Histoire naturelle des Iles Canaries*, 2, pt. II. Zoologie (Ornithologie) – 1. Paris.

MAROON PIGEON

VULNERABLE

Columba thomensis Bocage, 1888

Order COLUMBIFORMES

Family COLUMBIDAE

Summary This large uncommon forest pigeon, confined to the island of São Tomé, has suffered badly from illegal hunting.

Distribution The Maroon Pigeon is endemic to São Tomé (São Tomé e Príncipe) in the Gulf of Guinea, with nineteenth century records from the adjacent Ilheu das Rolas (= "Dove Island": 0°01'S 6°32'E) (Bocage 1903) where it is now extinct (R. de Naurois *in litt.* 1984). The type-specimen was collected at 100 m (not 1,000 m as in Bannerman 1931a,b) at Angolares (0°08'N 6°39'E) by the south-east coast (Bocage 1888) and the species was found nearby at Roça Granja in 1955 (Frade 1958), but these, the Ilheu das Rolas records and a nineteenth century specimen from Ribeira Peixe, also in the south-east (Bocage 1903), appear to be the only lowland records (save one below). Specimens were obtained at Lake Amélia (0°17'N 6°36'E) in 1928 (Correia 1928-1929, Amadon 1953, M. LeCroy *in litt.* 1984), and three were shot and several others seen around the Pico (highest point of the island: 2,024 m) in 1949, when it was assumed its range could not be more than "a few square miles" (Snow 1950). The species was subsequently found again near the Pico, at Capoeira (0°14'N 6°32'E) south-west of the Pico (Frade 1957), near Monte Café (0°18'N 6°39'E) (Frade 1958) and at Lake Amélia (Frade and dos Santos 1977), both east of the Pico. On this evidence it is chiefly and perhaps now exclusively a species of the montane interior of São Tomé. In the period 1963-1973 the species was found fairly widely above 1,200 m, and what were thought to be young birds were seen as low as 50 m in forest near São Miguel on the west coast, indicating that its range is certainly larger than had been thought in 1949 (R. de Naurois *in litt.* 1984).

Population The statements that this species is "an exceedingly rare bird" (Bannerman 1915) and "possibly the rarest pigeon in existence in West Africa" (Bannerman 1931a) are probably true, at least now, although in 1949 it was known to be absorbing considerable pressure from hunting and was therefore assumed to be "fairly numerous" (Snow 1950). It was still in reasonable numbers in the 1960s, but by 1973 hunting had apparently made it rare (de Naurois 1983, R. de Naurois *in litt.* 1984).

Ecology This pigeon, the largest in West Africa (Bannerman 1931a) and very tame (Snow 1950), inhabits mist-forest (Snow 1950, Frade 1957), sometimes also secondary forest where this has established itself over abandoned plantations at higher levels (Frade 1957). Crops of three specimens (now in BMNH) taken in September 1949 were full of berries of the tree *Schefflera manni*, rarely found below 1,370 m (Snow 1950); their gonads were inactive (NJC), but five of the six birds collected from 26 July to 1 August 1928 had large gonads (M. LeCroy *in litt.* 1984).

Threats The hunting of this species, reported in 1949 (Snow 1950) and outlawed in 1955 (Frade 1958), still continued in the period 1963-1973, when the practice was widespread of lighting fires in clearings in the forest by day, which had the effect of attracting pigeons of several species from over a wide area to perch in nearby trees as easy targets for the hunter (R. de Naurois pers. comm. 1982).

Conservation Measures Taken The species was protected by law in 1955 (Frade 1958) but this had no effect (see Threats).

Conservation Measures Proposed An ICBP project was developed in 1981 to investigate the status, ecology and conservation of the endemic birds of São Tomé e Príncipe, but was unable to proceed in 1982 and 1983. A study of this bird is a component of the project and conservation proposals will follow if the project goes ahead.

Remarks The Maroon Pigeon of São Tomé is a large, long-tailed and mostly unspotted form of the Olive Pigeon *Columba arquatrix*, but there are good precedents for allowing it specific status (e.g. Bannerman 1931a, Goodwin 1970, Snow 1978).

References

Amadon, D. (1953) Avian systematics and evolution in the Gulf of Guinea. The J. G. Correia collection. *Bull. Amer. Mus. Nat. Hist.* 100: 393-451.

Bannerman, D. A. (1915) Report on the birds collected by the late Mr Boyd Alexander (Rifle Brigade) during his last expedition to Africa. Part II. The birds of St.Thomas' Island. *Ibis* (10)3: 89-121.

Bannerman, D. A. (1931a) The Maroon Pigeon of São Tomé. *Ibis* 13(1): 652-654.

Bannerman, D. A. (1931b) *The birds of tropical West Africa*, 2. London: Crown Agents for the Colonies.

Bocage, J. V. B. (1888) Oiseaux nouveaux de l'Ile St.Thomé. *Jorn. Acad. Sci. Lisboa* 12: 229-232.

Bocage, J. V. B. (1903) Contribution à la faune des quatre îles du Golfe de Guinée. IV. Ile de St.Thomé. *Jorn. Acad. Sci. Lisboa* (2)7: 65-96.

Correia, J. G. (1928-1929) Unpublished typescript concerning his São Tomé expedition, held in AMNH.

Frade, F. (1957) New records of non-resident birds, and notes on some resident ones, in São Tomé and Príncipe Islands. Proc. I Pan-Afr. orn. Congr. *Ostrich* suppl. 3: 317-320.

Frade, F. (1958) Aves e mamíferos das ilhas de São Tomé e do Príncipe – notas de sistemática e de protecção à fauna. *Conferência Internacional dos Africanistas ocidentais*. Communicações Zool. e Biol. Anim. 4 (6th session): 137-150.

Frade, F. and dos Santos, J. V. (1977) Aves de S.Tomé e Príncipe. *Garcia de Orta* (Ser. Zool.) 6: 3-18.

Goodwin, D. (1970) *Pigeons and doves of the world.* 2nd edition. London: Trustees of the British Museum (Natural History).

de Naurois, R. (1983) Les oiseaux reproducteurs des îles de São Tomé et Príncipe: liste systématique commentée et indications zoogéographiques. *Bonn. zool. Beitr.* 34: 129-148.

Snow, D. W. (1950) The birds of São Tomé and Príncipe in the Gulf of Guinea. *Ibis* 92: 579-595.

Snow, D. W. ed. (1978) *An atlas of speciation in African non-passerine birds.* London: Trustees of the British Museum (Natural History).

PINK PIGEON   ENDANGERED

Nesoenas mayeri (Prévost, 1843)

Order COLUMBIFORMES   Family COLUMBIDAE

Summary Numbers of this upland forest-dwelling pigeon, endemic to Mauritius, have been critically low in the wild since at least 1960, and all breeding is thought to be currently confined to a single small unprotected grove of trees. However, major achievements in captive breeding in the past eight years have resulted in a zoo stock of around 100 individuals, and an experiment is now under way to establish a new wild population using some of these birds.

Distribution The Pink Pigeon is confined to upland areas of native forest in south-west Mauritius, Indian Ocean. There are no certain records away from this region; a bird taken at Vacoa "prior to 1876" seems to be the most northerly (specimen in UMZC: NJC) although there are reportedly specimens taken in the last century from around Curepipe, Quatre Bornes and above Mahébourg (Temple 1978). The species is considered to have been chronically localised (Temple 1978, Jones in press), although it probably once ranged widely over the forested area between Piton de la Rivière Noire (Black River Peak) and Piton du Milieu in the area roughly circumscribed by the 4,000 mm isohyet (Jones in press). Early this century the species was known to survive in the south-west (Meinertzhagen 1912) and by mid-century was known to be entirely restricted to that area (Rountree *et al.* 1952). In the 1960s to the mid-1970s the upland marshes of Les Mares, the Plaine Champagne scrub, the upland forests of Macabé (Macchabée), Brise Fer and Bel Ombre, the pole forests of the upland plateau and the transitional forests of the south-facing scarp were all utilised (Temple 1978, Jones in press), the core area lying within the 4,500 mm isohyet centring on Mount Cocotte and Les Mares and including Montagne Savanne, Bassin Blanc and Plaine Paul (Jones in press). Following the cutting of Les Mares and Plaine Paul, the focus of distribution has become a 2.5 ha grove of mature exotic Japanese red cedar *Cryptomeria japonica* trees used for both roosting (for part of the year) and nesting, located on the steep south-facing escarpment below Plaine Paul, between Mount Cocotte and Piton Savanne (McKelvey 1976; also Hartley 1977, Jones 1980a). From here birds spread out by day to feed, eastwards along the scarp below Piton Savanne, and westwards along the scarp below Mount Cocotte to Plaine Champagne, the Bel Ombre forest and the northern forested slopes of Piton de la Rivière Noire (McKelvey 1976, Hartley 1977, Jones 1980a,1982a,b, in press, C. G. Jones and A. W. Owadally *in litt.* 1982). The area of contiguous native vegetation and pole forest available to the species in the 1940s through to the 1960s was over 160 km², but is today only 36 km², of which only about 30 km² are actually utilised (Jones in press).

Population This species was considered rare even in the 1830s (Oustalet 1897). The "fine pigeon" reportedly getting scarcer in the Savanne region around 1860 and thought to be the (by then already extinct) Mauritius Blue Pigeon *Alectroenas nitidissima* (Newton 1861) was evidently this species (see Remarks); a few years later the Pink Pigeon was (again) noted to be getting even rarer, with only a small number remaining (Schlegel and Pollen 1868) and before the end of the nineteenth century was feared to be on the verge of extinction (Oustalet 1897). Despite assurances at the start of the present century that the species, though rare, was still quite easily obtained and even said to be increasing (Carié 1904, Meinertzhagen 1912), by 1950 it was again thought "perilously close to extinction" (Rountree 1951), evidence gathered retrospectively suggesting a small but relatively stable population in the 1950s of 40-60 birds which in 1960 were drastically affected (with possibly 50% losses) by two cyclones (Jones in press; also Staub 1971). Field research in 1973-1974 revealed only 25-30 birds, with numbers slowly dwindling and the species appearing "doomed" (Temple 1974a,b, Temple *et al.* 1974); by the end of 1974 the population was "not ... more than 28" (Temple 1975a), "only 29" (Temple 1976b) or "between 27 and 38" (Temple 1978). In February 1975 Cyclone Gervaise reduced the population by nearly 50%, variously reported as leaving only 10-12 birds (Temple 1975b), around 12 (Temple 1976b), 12-15 (Newlands 1975), 15-22 (Temple 1978), or less than 20 (Temple 1976a), breeding success in December raising the number to at least 19 in one account (Temple 1976b), 24 in another (Temple 1976a). In 1976 10 pairs (possibly also a few unpaired individuals) were present and four birds were fledged, but with four adults being taken for captive breeding the total wild population was c. 23 (McKelvey 1976, King 1977; see Remarks). In 1977 the wild population stood at c. 24 (comprising six mated pairs in the *Cryptomeria* grove, probably no more than one pair elsewhere, and six or seven unpaired – probably male – birds, with at least two young hatched during the year) while, following further captures, captive numbers stood at 12, three of which were captive bred (King 1977,1978; also Hartley 1977, S. D. McKelvey *in litt.* 1977 to R. D. Chancellor). In 1978 the wild population, which fledged at least three young (Steele 1979), reportedly stood at c. 30, with 20 in captivity in the government aviaries at Black River, Mauritius, and a further 10 with JWPT (King 1979). In 1979 the *Cryptomeria* grove was estimated to hold 12-20 birds (Jones 1979) and the total number of wild birds prior to Cyclone Claudette and subsequent weather in December 1979/January 1980 was conservatively (now considered generously: C. G. Jones *in litt.* 1984) put at 20-30 (Jones 1980a). In 1980 the wild population was believed halved at 10-15 birds, with only 6-10 birds in the *Cryptomeria* grove (Jones 1980b,1981). In 1981 no more than eight were seen in the grove and, although some breeding success was noted, the wild total was considered 20 at most (Jones 1982a,b). No figures for the wild population in 1982 were given (Jones 1983) but in 1983-1984 it was estimated at 15-20 birds (*ICBP Newsletter* 6,1 [1984]); counts at the *Cryptomeria* grove, January to June 1984, never determined more than 18 birds in total (C. G. Jones and D. M. Todd *in litt.* 1984). Since 1978 the captive breeding programme has continued to prosper and in early 1984 there were 90-100 birds held in Mauritius, Jersey (JWPT), New York (NYZS) and Albuquerque Zoo (U.S.A.) and Vogelpark Walsrode (West Germany) (*ICBP Newsletter* 6,1 [1984]).

Ecology The Pink Pigeon inhabits native evergreen forest and dwarf forest (scrubland), the latter now existing only in remnants on upland heaths and marshes (Procter and Salm 1974, Temple 1974a, Jones 1981), but it currently favours a grove of introduced *Cryptomeria* (see under Distribution), surrounded by degraded native forest and scattered copses of introduced swamp mahogany *Eucalyptus robusta*, for nesting and roosting inside the breeding season (McKelvey 1976, Jones 1980b); outside the breeding season birds are thought to roost singly or in small groups in wind-sheltered valleys or ravines along the south-facing scarp on which the *Cryptomeria* grove is located (Jones in press; also Temple 1978). Prior to the use of this grove for nesting, it has been speculated that the birds nested in either of two natural sites/habitats apparently providing the required shelter, one near *Pandanus* thickets along streams in valleys and ravines (this now replaced by jamrose *Syzygium jambos*), the other in mossy forests on and around Mount Cocotte (this now cyclone-damaged and cut over) (Temple 1978). It is also possible that birds once commonly nested in holes in trees (Jones in press). *Cryptomeria* was first planted in the Pink Pigeon's range in 1918-1920 but is only reported to have been used for nesting by the species since the 1940s or 1950s (Jones in press). Individual birds range widely throughout (and probably utilise the whole of) the species's area of distribution in the course of a year (Temple 1978, C. G. Jones *in litt.* 1984). The species is primarily arboreal and forages in the canopy (Jones 1981 *contra* Meinertzhagen 1912), and is highly agile at the extremities of trees and bushes (Jones in press). Feeding behaviour has been classified as arboreal leaf-feeding and fruit-gathering, ground foraging, and urgent "snack" feeding to fill the crop during incubation; two hours' feeding is sufficient for a 24-hour period (McKelvey 1976), although in the late winter months birds are suspected of spending most of the day foraging (Jones in press). The diet is very catholic, birds taking leaves, young shoots, buds, flowers, fruit and seeds of both native and exotic plants (Jones 1980a, in press), much time (at least formerly: see Threats) being spent feeding on the fruits and flowers of upland dwarf forest plants (Procter and Salm 1974). However, the three major food-plants (flowers, fruits and leaves) appear to be bois maigre *Nuxia verticillata*, bois manioc *Erythrospermum monticolum*, and fandamane *Aphloia theiformis* (Jones in press), other native plants utilised including *Eugenia*, bois d'ébène *Diospyros*, bois cerf *Pittosporum senacia*, bois pigeon *Cordemoya integrifolia*, *Bertiera*, *Gaertnera*, *Mallotus* and "pingo" grass (Newton 1958, Temple *et al.* 1974, Cheke 1975, McKelvey 1976, Staub 1976, Temple 1978); introduced plants utilised include lantana *Lantana camara*, bois d'oiseaux *Litsea glutinosa*, *Homalanthus populifolius* and privet *Ligustrum robustum* var. *walkeri* (McKelvey 1976, C. G. Jones *in litt.* 1984). Birds have also been seen taking pond snails (and to pursue but not catch stranded tadpoles) and, especially before laying, snail shells (McKelvey 1976). Seasonal changes in the availability of food are significant, with a fall-off in the fruits and flowers of the three preferred trees from August to mid-November, when other food also appears generally limited; in early summer (December/January), following the onset of the rains, birds feed much on flowers, while leaves are eaten throughout the year in moderate amounts (Jones in press). Breeding chiefly occurs from October to February (Newton 1958), or November/December to March (Hartley 1977, Staub 1976), though activity may be postponed by bad weather (Hartley 1977) or spread out by repeated nest failures (Temple 1978), being recorded in May and June (Newton 1958, Temple 1976b), with a bird soon to lay in July (Benson 1970-1971). The variation in onset and length of the breeding season is governed by weather conditions and consequent food availability, birds starting to breed the month after the start of the summer rains (Jones in press). There are no special nesting requirements (Cheke 1975); nests are placed 4-16 m up in trees (Temple 1978), and nesting territories in the *Cryptomeria* grove are 800-1,600 m² (Jones in press); of six nests in April 1977, five were in *Cryptomeria*, one in *Diospyros* (Hartley 1977). In one study clutch-size was two; the replacement clutch was also two, but subsequent replacements were one only (McKelvey 1976; also Temple *et al.* 1974, Staub 1976); in later work, clutch-size has been found to be one or two irrespective of clutch number (C. G. Jones *in litt.* 1984). Breeding success is low with only 10-20% of nests resulting in fledged young, with fledged brood-size only 1.1; 0.08-0.15 young fledge per egg laid (Jones in press). Breeding success is greater at the start and end of the breeding season than in the months of peak activity, this probably owing to a lower relative incidence of predation when nests are less clumped (Jones in press). Birds are capable of breeding in their first year (Jones *et al.* in press). In the wild, a male was observed to hybridise (eggs fertile) with a female Madagascar Turtle-dove *Streptopelia picturata* (McKelvey 1976, King 1977). Birds are largely absent from the *Cryptomeria* grove outside the breeding season (Jones 1980a, C. G. Jones *in litt.* 1984). Birds are very tame (Meinertzhagen 1912, Jones 1980a, in press).

Threats A general account of the problems facing endemic forest-dependent birds of Mauritius is given in Threats under Mauritius Kestrel *Falco punctatus*. The most important factors affecting the Pink Pigeon are habitat destruction, late winter food shortages, nest-predation, cyclone (and cyclone-related) mortality, and hunting. The (World Bank financed) clearance in 1971-1974 of half (c. 2,800 ha) of the upland *Sideroxylon-Helichrysum* dwarf forest at Les Mares on Plaine Champagne constituted a major disaster for this species, whose great stronghold this area was (Procter and Salm 1974, Temple 1974a, McKelvey 1976, Hartley 1977, Jones 1980a, in press, Cheke in press). The introduced crab-eating macaque *Macaca fascicularis* was considered responsible for the disappearance of the species as long ago as 1911 (Meinertzhagen 1912), and observations in the 1970s tended to confirm that nest-predation by this mammal is the most critical influence on breeding success (Temple 1974a, McKelvey 1976, Durrell 1977, Hartley 1977, Jones 1982a; but see Conservation Measures Proposed), although the black rat *Rattus rattus* evidently also takes a toll (McKelvey 1976, Jones 1980a, in press), as also does the Indian Mynah *Acridotheres tristis* (Jones in press). Cyclones can now dangerously affect the species not only as a direct cause of mortality (Hartley 1977, Jones 1980a,b) but indirectly by destroying its food supply for several weeks or even months (Temple 1975b,1976a). Although at first food was otherwise not considered limiting (Jones 1980a), studies 1979-1984 have led to the conclusion that food shortages at the end of winter are primarily responsible for limiting the population (Jones in press). Possibly because of the tradition that its flesh was poisonous, hunting did not so seriously affect the Pink Pigeon in past centuries (Oustalet 1897), but was considered to have brought it near extinction by around 1950 (Rountree 1951); several were shot in the early 1970s (Temple 1974a,b,1975a). Additional threats are predation on the ground by introduced mongooses *Herpestes edwardsi* and feral cats (Temple 1975a, McKelvey 1976, Jones in press) and, ironically, nest-predation by another threatened bird species, the Mauritius Cuckoo-shrike *Coracina typica* (McKelvey 1976, Staub 1976; see relevant account); but occasional predation by migrant falcons, e.g. Peregrines *Falco peregrinus* (McKelvey 1976) and possible disturbance at nests by Mauritius Kestrels (McKelvey 1976) are wholly discounted (C. G. Jones *in litt.* 1984). Introduced pigeon species, notably the Madagascar Turtle-dove, are present in Pink Pigeon habitat and while they are basically ground-feeders (on seeds) they may prevent Pink Pigeons from greater exploitation of terrestrial food sources (Jones in press); moreover, the very common introduced Red-whiskered Bulbul *Pycnonotus jocosus* competes for *Nuxia* flowers and this undoubtedly contributes to the premature exhaustion of this resource (Jones in press). Finally, it is possible that inbreeding now plays a part in limiting the population (Jones in press).

Conservation Measures Taken This species has been one of the major concerns of the bird conservation work that began on Mauritius in the early 1970s (for a note on this see Conservation Measures Taken under Mauritius Kestrel). Propagation in captivity to safeguard the Pink Pigeon was first suggested in 1904 (Carié 1904). No success had been achieved by 1911 (Meinertzhagen 1912) but birds were reported to have bred at least once prior to 1976 (Temple 1976a,b) when the present captive breeding programme began (McKelvey 1976, Durrell 1977, Hartley 1977, Jeggo 1977). The success of this programme (chronicled in King 1978,1979, Steele 1979, Jones 1980a,1982a,b, Pasquier 1980) was such that in 1982, despite the distribution of 31 birds to four zoos, it had to be halted temporarily for lack of space (Jones 1983): while the situation in the wild remained critical but roughly stable, 1976-1984, the captive population rose in the same period from zero to around 100 (see Population). This abundance of captive-bred birds has resulted in a project to establish a free-flying population in the Royal Botanical Gardens at Pamplemousses in the north of the island (Pasquier 1980,1982, Jones 1981), this site being chosen for its suitability of habitat (a wide variety of mature trees), freedom from disturbance (in certain areas), lack of monkeys, distance from other suitable habitat (inhibiting birds from wandering) and ease of monitoring (Pasquier 1980): the release of the first pair in this experiment took place in early March 1984 (*On the Edge* no. 47 [1984], *ICBP Newsletter* 6,1 [1984]); and up to June six birds had been released, four survived and a pair had built a nest and were showing signs of breeding (C. G. Jones *in litt.* 1984). The placement of forestry guards at the *Cryptomeria* grove in 1976 reportedly helped reduce predation of nests (McKelvey 1977) but this practice has subsequently been considered ineffective and therefore discontinued (C. G. Jones *in litt.* 1984). The species has long been protected (Meinertzhagen 1912) and in 1974 its remaining native forest habitat received almost complete protection when the Macabé/Bel Ombre Nature Reserve was created through the linking of existing reserves at Petrin, Macabé and Bel Ombre by the addition of Les Mares and Plaine Champagne, forming a large block covering 3,594 ha (Owadally 1976; see map in Procter and Salm 1974). The species is listed on Appendix III of CITES for Mauritius.

Conservation Measures Proposed Protected area status and the strictest protection for the *Cryptomeria* grove where the species breeds (see Distribution) would appear a very desirable step. A long-term plan of planting small, well spaced clumps of *Cryptomeria* in mixed plantations, and certainly the approach of creating commercially viable conservation plantations (see Conservation Measures Proposed under Mauritius Cuckoo-shrike), would probably greatly benefit this species (Jones 1980a, Jones and Owadally 1982, A. S. Cheke pers. comm. 1984). The effect of winter food shortages on the species requires vigorous scientific investigation using marked birds, but a proposal to supplement wild birds' diet in the period from August to mid-November (Jones in press) may render this impossible; in either case, time need not be lost in determining what tree species might be introduced into the plantations referred to above as the best provider of food in the late winter period. Monkey control near actual and potential sites was regarded as essential in the mid-1970s (Temple 1974a, McKelvey 1976, Hartley 1977) and monkey-proofing of trees was considered a realistic proposal (Jones 1979): however, following experiments with dummy nests in the *Cryptomeria* grove to determine the extent of predation by monkeys and rats (Pasquier 1980), and egg-predation studies in 1982-1983 (Jones and Owadally 1982), it appears that monkeys may be less of a problem than has been assumed and protective measures seem unnecessary (see Jones in press). The possibility was raised of managing the wild population by removing eggs, incubating and hatching them safely, and then returning the young to the wild immediately after fledging (Jones 1979), but was evidently transmuted into a procedurally less complex proposal to release captive-bred birds (using radio-telemetry) into the wild population and possibly to introduce birds into another area to establish a new flock (Pasquier 1980). Reintroduction of captive-bred birds into the area of forest between Brise Fer, Mare Longue and Macabé (Macchabée), where the species was formerly found but from which it is now cut off by the pine plantation on Les Mares, is under consideration (Jones in press). Introduction of captive-bred birds to the neighbouring French island of Réunion has been proposed and justified in some detail (a similar pigeon appears to have occurred there formerly, there are no monkeys on the island, native forests are much greater in extent and include many of the same food-plants used in Mauritius, there would be no risk to cultivations and plantations, and there would be no risk to or from other native birds): ideal localities – being quite large and little frequented – for release of birds are Rivière de St.Denis, Takamaka, La Rivière de l'Est, the western part of Plaine de Makes and possibly Rivière des Pluies, each of which could initially support some five pairs, though if the birds were unmolested their natural spread throughout the middle altitude "bois de couleurs" (mixed evergreen forest) is envisaged (Cheke 1975,1978). This proposal has been argued to be biogeographically valid (Temple 1981) and tentatively supported (Moutou 1983), but is currently discountenanced on the grounds that hunting pressure on Réunion is too high (Jones and Owadally 1982): nevertheless, with the continuing success of the captive breeding programme, such an experiment, fully monitored at a suitably undisturbed site and with a well managed publicity campaign, appears an important consideration for the near future. There is a need for a well coordinated plan to ensure the survival of the Pink Pigeon in captivity by proper management of the gene pool and publication of a studbook.

Remarks Concerning the identity of the "fine pigeon" at Savanne around 1860 as *Alectroenas nitidissima*, the copy of *Ibis* (now in the Alfred Newton Library, Department of Zoology, University of Cambridge, U.K.) belonging to Alfred Newton (E. Newton's brother) is marked in his handwriting in the margin "No! Columba mayeri!", presumably as a result of subsequent communication between the brothers. Concerning the number of birds in the wild in 1976, it is not clear from the reports cited whether the four wild birds captured for captive breeding came from the total of 27 (as assumed here) or whether the total in the wild was 27 after their capture (as assumed in Jones in press).

References

Benson, C. W. (1970-1971) The Cambridge collection from the Malagasy region. *Bull. Brit. Orn. Club* 90: 168-172; 91: 1-7.

Carié, P. (1904) Observations sur quelques oiseaux de l'île Maurice. *Ornis* 12: 121-128.

Cheke, A. S. (1975) Proposition pour introduire à la Réunion des oiseaux rares de l'île Maurice. *Info-Nature* no. 12: 25-29.

Cheke, A. S. (1978) Recommendations for the conservation of Mascarene vertebrates. Conservation memorandum no. 3 (arising out of the B.O.U. Mascarene Islands Expedition). Unpublished.

Durrell, G. (1977) *Golden bats and pink pigeons*. London: Collins.

Hartley, J. R. M. (1977) The Mauritius Pink Pigeon *Columba mayeri*. *Dodo* 14: 23-26.

Jeggo, D. (1977) Preliminary notes on the Mauritius Pink Pigeon *Columba mayeri* at the Jersey Zoological Park. *Dodo* 14: 26-30.

Jones, C. G. (1979) Mauritius/Rodrigues conservation project report for January 22nd – June 20th 1979. Unpublished.

Jones, C. G. (1980a) The conservation of the endemic birds and bats of Mauritius and Rodriguez (a progress report and proposal for further activities). Unpublished.

Jones, C. G. (1980b) The conservation of the endemic birds and bats of Mauritius and Rodriguez. Progress report January 1980 – November 1980. Unpublished.

Jones, C. G. (1981) Mauritius: an important lesson in island biology. (A summary of activities and proposals for 1981.) Unpublished.

Jones, C. G. (1982a) The conservation of the endemic birds and bats of Mauritius and Rodrigues. (Annual report 1981, W.W.F. Project 1082.) Unpublished.

Jones, C. G. (1982b) Struggle for survival on tropical islands. *WWF Monthly Report* February: 37-42.

Jones, C. G. (1983) The conservation of the endemic birds and bats of Mauritius and Rodrigues. Annual Report, 1982. Unpublished.

Jones, C. G. (in press) The larger land-birds of Mauritius. In A. W. Diamond, ed. *Studies of Mascarene island birds*. Cambridge: Cambridge University Press.

Jones, C. G. and Owadally, A. W. (1982) Conservation priorities for Mauritius and Rodrigues. Report submitted to ICBP, July. Unpublished.

Jones, C. G., Jeggo, D. F. and Hartley, J. (in press) The maintenance and captive breeding of the Pink Pigeon *Columba mayeri*. *Dodo* 20.

King, W. B. (1977) Notes on a conversation with David McKelvey 31 August 1977. Typescript.

King, W. B. (1978) Mauritius Project 1082. Promotion of conservation. *WWF Yearbook* 1977-1978: 150-151.

King, W. B. (1979) Mauritius Project 1082. Promotion of conservation. *WWF Yearbook* 1978-1979: 137-138.

McKelvey, S. D. (1976) A preliminary study of the Mauritian Pink Pigeon (*Nesoenas meyeri* [*sic*]). *Mauritius Inst. Bull.* 8(2): 145-175.

McKelvey, S. D. (1977) Mauritius Project 1082. Promotion of conservation. *WWF Yearbook* 1976-1977: 181-182.

Meinertzhagen, R. (1912) On the birds of Mauritius. *Ibis* (9)6: 82-108.

Moutou, F. (1983) Propositions pour la réintroduction à la Réunion d'espèces aujourd'hui disparues. *Info-Nature* no. 20: 49-50.

Newlands, W. A. (1975) Letter, 4 October [duplicated to interested parties]. Unpublished.

Newton, E. (1861) Ornithological notes from Mauritius. No. II. A ten days' sojourn at Savanne. *Ibis* 3: 270-277.

Newton, R. (1958) Ornithological notes on Mauritius and the Cargados Carajos Archipelago. *Proc. Roy. Soc. Arts Sci. Mauritius* 2(1): 39-71.

Oustalet, E. (1897) Notice sur la faune ornithologique ancienne et moderne des îles Mascareignes et en particulier de l'île Maurice d'après des documents inédits. *Ann. Sci. Nat. Zool.* (8)3: 1-128.

Owadally, A. W. (1976) *Annual report of the Forestry Service for the year 1974*. Port Louis, Mauritius: L. Carl Achille, Government Printer.

Pasquier, R. F. (1980) Report and management plan on ICBP's project for the conservation of forest birds of Mauritius. Unpublished.

Pasquier, R. F. (1982) Mauritius Project 1082. Conservation of birds of Mauritius. *WWF Yearbook* 1982: 210-211.

Procter, J. and Salm, R. (1974) Conservation in Mauritius 1974. IUCN/WWF consultancy report for Government of Mauritius. Unpublished.

Rountree, F. G. R. (1951) Some aspects of bird-life in Mauritius. *Proc. Roy. Soc. Arts Sci. Mauritius* 1(2): 83-96.

Rountree, F. G. R., Guérin, R., Pelte, S. and Vinson, J. (1952) Catalogue of the birds of Mauritius. *Mauritius Inst. Bull.* 3(3): 155-217.

Schlegel, H. and Pollen, F. P. L. (1868) *Recherches sur la faune de Madagascar et de ses dépendances, d'après les découvertes de François P. L. Pollen et D. C. van Dam*. 2me partie. Mammifères et oiseaux. Leyde.

Staub, F. (1971) Actual situation of the Mauritius endemic birds. *ICBP Bull.* 11: 226-227.

Staub, F. (1976) *Birds of the Mascarenes and Saint Brandon*. Port Louis, Mauritius: Organisation Normale des Enterprises.

Steele, F. N. (1979) Conservation of birds on Mauritius, final report for 1978. Unpublished.

Temple, S. A. (1974a) Appendix 6. The native fauna of Mauritius: 1, the land birds. In J. Procter and R. Salm, Conservation in Mauritius 1974. IUCN/WWF consultancy report for Government of Mauritius. Unpublished.

Temple, S. A. (1974b) Wildlife in Mauritius today. *Oryx* 12: 584-590.

Temple, S. A. (1975a) Project 986: Western Indian Ocean raptores [*sic*] – ecology and conservation. *WWF Yearbook* 1974-1975: 210-212.

Temple, S. A. (1975b) A report on the conservation program in Mauritius, 15 October. Unpublished.

Temple, S. A. (1976a) Project 1082: Mauritius – promotion of conservation. *WWF Yearbook* 1975-1976: 165-166.

Temple, S. A. (1976b) Conservation of endemic birds and other wildlife on Mauritius. A progress report and proposal for future activities. Unpublished.

Temple, S. A. (1978) The life histories and ecology of the indigenous landbirds of Mauritius. Unpublished.

Temple, S. A. (1981) Applied island biogeography and the conservation of endangered island birds in the Indian Ocean. *Biol. Conserv.* 20: 147-161.

Temple, S. A., Staub, J. J. F. and Antoine, R. (1974) Some background information and recommendations on the preservation of the native flora and fauna of Mauritius. Unpublished report to the Government of Mauritius.

BLACK-CHEEKED LOVEBIRD   RARE
Agapornis nigrigenis W. L. Sclater, 1906

Order PSITTACIFORMES   Family PSITTACIDAE
                                                   Subfamily PSITTACINAE

Summary The total range of this very local parrot of mopane woodland amounts to only about 6,000 km², almost exclusively in southern Zambia: despite total legal protection it is not uncommon as a cage-bird and may thus be threatened by trade.

Distribution The Black-cheeked Lovebird is essentially confined to part of the extreme south of Zambia, east of the Machili River to about Livingstone (although probably no longer present in the immediate vicinity of the Victoria Falls partly owing to extensive trapping in the past) and ranging north to Mulanga, Mulobezi and the Nanzhila area of the southern Kafue National Park (Benson 1958, Benson and Irwin 1967). It occurs outside southern Zambia only along the Zambezi River in northern Zimbabwe (Dowsett 1972, Irwin 1981). It possibly occurs in the very northernmost tip of Botswana (C. W. Benson pers. comm. 1982). Its status along the Zambezi in the Caprivi Strip (Namibia) is unclear: a positive report from the area in the 1940s (Leppan 1944) has been questioned (Benson and Irwin 1967), but two specimens dated September 1906 and marked "Caprivi" are known in the Transvaal Museum (C. W. Benson pers. comm. 1982) and a third such specimen has been reported to exist there (Sclater 1909). The species is not now known as far west on the Zambian side of the river; a breeding record from near Sesheke (Zambia) in 1917 (Brooke 1967) is not accepted (James 1970).

Population The species appears to be very local within the range of available habitat, and most recent sightings in Zambia are of small flocks of a few dozen birds only (R. J. Dowsett *in litt*. 1982), although in December 1982 it was found to be reasonably common along the Ngwezi River (the type-locality) (D. R. Aspinwall *in litt*. 1983). In Zimbabwe it is sparse or merely sporadic in occurrence (Dowsett 1972, Irwin 1981). Its population is certainly much less dense than that of the closely related Lilian's Lovebird *Agapornis lilianae* in similar habitat elsewhere in the Zambezi valley and in eastern Zambia (Benson and Irwin 1967). It was formerly far more numerous, and as many as 16,000 were captured in four weeks during 1929, all for the cage-bird market (Moreau 1948).

Ecology The species is confined to medium-altitude deciduous woodland, dominated by mopane *Colophospermum mopane*, but only (or at least chiefly) where this woodland is contiguous with woodland dominated by *Baikiaea plurijuga*, birds keeping to mopane in the dry season but feeding on the young leaves of *Pterocarpus antunesiana* in the *Baikiaea* woodland in the rains (Moreau 1948, R. J. Dowsett *in litt*. 1982; also Benson and Irwin 1967). The species is recorded feeding on seeds of *Rhus quartiniana* and *Syzygium guineense* in riparian growth through mopane, and on grass-seeds *Hyparrhenia* in mopane (Benson and Irwin 1967); it was formerly trapped for trade by being attracted to ripening sorghum in local plots (Moreau 1948). There are breeding records from November and December (Benson *et al.* 1971).

Threats Despite being completely protected by law in Zambia (Dowsett 1971), the Black-cheeked Lovebird is common as a cage-bird and still subject to illegal trapping (R. J. Dowsett *in litt.* 1982). Its current local status appears to indicate that it never recovered (or because of further trapping was never allowed to recover) from the massive exploitation for trade which it endured in the 1920s (see Population above). Hybridisation with Lilian's Lovebird has been achieved in captivity (see Moreau 1948, Smith 1979) and known feral populations of *lilianae* (for example, in the Choma District) might therefore constitute a problem (R. J. Dowsett *in litt.* 1982).

Conservation Measures Taken The Black-cheeked Lovebird is listed on Appendix II of CITES, to which Zambia and Zimbabwe are parties. It has bred well in captivity ever since a few years after first being described (e.g. Phillipps 1908-1909, Smith 1979), but frequent hybridisations (Low 1980) have probably rendered most captive stock impure. For several reasons the habitat of this species makes poor agricultural land and is therefore unlikely to be developed (R. J. Dowsett *in litt.* 1982).

Conservation Measures Proposed A coordinated survey to establish more exactly the status and distribution of the species in the wild is now needed, and should be followed by regular monitoring. A survey of status in captivity is also now desirable, and certain aviculturists might take responsibility for maintaining pure-bred stocks of birds in good numbers, particularly in view of the comments on the mismanagement the Black-cheeked Lovebird has suffered in captivity over the years (see Smith 1979).

Remarks This lovebird is considered by many authorities to be con-specific with Lilian's Lovebird, but there are reasons for treating it as a separate species (see Dowsett and Dowsett-Lemaire 1980), and these are accepted here.

References

Benson, C. W. (1958) Some additions and corrections to *A check list of the birds of Northern Rhodesia. Occ. Pap. Natn. Mus. Southern Rhodesia* 3(22B): 190-197.

Benson, C. W., Brooke, R. K., Dowsett, R. J. and Irwin, M. P. S. (1971) *The birds of Zambia.* London: Collins.

Benson, C. W. and Irwin, M. P. S. (1967) A contribution to the ornithology of Zambia. *Zambia Mus. Pap.* 1.

Brooke, R. K. (1967) Further breeding records from Zambia (no. 6). *Bull. Brit. Orn. Club* 87: 120-122.

Dowsett, R. J. (1971) Bird conservation in Zambia. *ICBP Bull.* 11: 229-233.

Dowsett, R. J. (1972) The type locality of *Agapornis nigrigenis. Bull. Brit. Orn. Club* 92: 22-23.

Dowsett, R. J. and Dowsett-Lemaire, F. (1980) The systematic status of some Zambian birds. *Gerfaut* 70: 151-199.

Irwin, M. P. S. (1981) *The birds of Zimbabwe*. Salisbury, Zimbabwe: Quest Publishing.

James, H. W. (1970) *Catalogue of the birds eggs in the collection of the National Museums of Rhodesia*. Salisbury, Rhodesia: Trustees of the National Museums of Rhodesia.

Leppan, A. W. (1944) Birds of the eastern Caprivi Zipfel. *Ostrich* 15: 20-30.

Low, R. (1980) *Parrots: their care and breeding*. Poole, England: Blandford Press.

Moreau, R. E. (1948) Aspects of evolution in the parrot genus *Agapornis*. *Ibis* 90: 206-239, 449-460.

Phillipps, R. (1908-1909) Breeding of the Black-cheeked Lovebird. *Avicult. Mag.* N.S. 6: 318-329; N.S. 7: 31-36.

Sclater, P. L. (1909) [The Black-faced Lovebird (*Agapornis nigrigenis*).] *Bull. Brit. Orn. Club* 25: 11.

Smith, G. A. (1979) *Lovebirds and related parrots*. London: Paul Elek.

MAURITIUS PARAKEET   ENDANGERED
Psittacula eques (Boddaert, 1783)

Order PSITTACIFORMES   Family PSITTACIDAE
                                                    Subfamily PSITTACINAE

Summary At least four but no more than eleven birds are all that survive of this frugivorous forest-dwelling parrot, endemic to Mauritius (having become extinct on Réunion). No successful nesting has been recorded with certainty since 1976 and birds have consistently evaded capture for the captive breeding that is believed to be the species's last hope.

Distribution The Mauritius Parakeet, now regarded as conspecific with the bird that became extinct on the neighbouring Mascarene island of Réunion (part of France) probably before 1800 (see Cheke in press; also Remarks), is confined to the forested upland slopes and dwarf forest of south-west Mauritius, Indian Ocean, having formerly been much more widespread: nineteenth and early twentieth century records mention Flacq (i.e. the north-eastern lowlands) (Oustalet 1897), the Grande Port district (i.e. eastern forests) (Newton and Newton 1876) and Curepipe (Carié 1904, Meinertzhagen 1912). There is a report that the species was quite commonly encountered in the early 1950s on the Crown Lands Merlo and Petite Merlo, south-west of Piton du Milieu in the middle of Mauritius, suggesting that birds were then ranging over the area between Mare aux Vacoas, Nouvelle France and Piton du Milieu until this area was cleared for tea and forestry between the 1950s and the early 1970s (see Jones in press). Other accounts have suggested that since at least 1950 and at any rate since the early 1970s the species has been confined to the remoter parts of the south-western plateau (Rountree *et al.* 1952, Gill 1971, Procter and Salm 1974, Temple *et al.* 1974, Jones 1980b), the most favoured locality being the Macabé (Macchabée) ridge forest (Temple *et al.* 1974, Newlands 1975b, Jones 1980a). By 1980 its range was considered to be only 40-50 km^2 in extent, embracing Macabé ridge, the head of Grandes Gorges River, the western slopes of Mount Cocotte, the scarp below Plaine Paul, the Bel Ombre forest, Alexandra Falls, the slopes of Piton de la Rivière Noire (Black River Peak) and of Morne Sèche, and near Brise Fer (Jones 1980c,1982a, in press).

Population In 1722 this was evidently one of two species that together formed "an infinity of parrots" on Mauritius (Oustalet 1897) and was still "quite common" in the 1830s (Oustalet 1897). Its numbers were noted to be gradually falling in the 1870s (Newton and Newton 1876) but still reasonably large at the turn of the century (Carié 1904). In the 1950s it was considered perilously close to extinction (Rountree 1951, Newton 1958), and in 1964 it was considered "quite rare" (Gill 1970). Around 1970 there were thought to be roughly 50 pairs left (Staub 1971), while field research 1973-1974 revealed that only around 50 (and no more than 60) birds survived, steadily declining and seemingly doomed (Temple 1974a,b, Temple *et al.* 1974). In 1973 at least seven pairs nested, but only two successfully (Temple *et al.* 1974). In 1974 at least 11 young were raised from six pairs (Temple 1975a,1976a; see Remarks) and an apparently additional "pair" of nestlings was taken for captive breeding (Temple 1975a), censuses 1973-1975 indicating a stable population of 50-60 birds although, on the basis of habitat available, it was thought numbers should have been several times as high (Temple 1975b,1976b). However, the figures given for these years, as well as for 1970 and 1973-1974 above, are considered too high and the result of mistaken impressions of abundance caused by the displacement of birds from clear-felled habitat (C. G. Jones *in litt.* 1984; also A. S. Cheke pers. comm. 1984); and indeed a more detailed account of the censusing that formed the basis of the 1973-1974(-1975) figures indicates that the maximum number was 58, the minimum 32-37, the latter consisting of 11 pairs and some 10-15 unmated birds (Temple 1978). In October 1975 six nest-holes were occupied and eggs laid (Newlands 1975b, Temple 1975b), but in December only two nests were active, both with two young, both young from one nest being taken for captive breeding, the other nest apparently failing (Jones in press). In 1976 three pairs fledged a total of five young and in 1977 there were known to be an additional 18 unpaired males in the population, so that the total number that year was considered perhaps no more than 40 (King 1977,1978; see Remarks). There is no information on breeding activity in 1977 but in mid-1978 the species was judged for the first time to be in greater danger than had been thought, birds having apparently declined rapidly in the previous four or five years (Steele 1978): the largest flock seen in 1978 was of six birds (seen once) (King 1979, Steele 1979), only one pair attempting to breed, without success (Jones 1980b). In 1979 the largest flock-size noted was again six (Jones 1980a) and a preliminary estimate was of a maximum of only 20 birds (Jones 1979; hence Pasquier 1980), two pairs attempting to breed that year but with no evidence of success (Jones 1980a,b). Following heavy cyclonic weather (including Cyclone Claudette) in December 1979 and January 1980, fewer birds were seen (Jones 1980a,c): the total population in 1980 was probably below 10, with a minimum of five seen (Jones 1980c,1981b) and an estimated minimum of six or seven (three or four males, three females), maximum 15 (Jones 1980a,b). In October 1980 a pair (believed the same birds that attempted to nest in 1978) was seen copulating and was thought to have attempted to nest, but with no evidence of success (Jones 1980c,1981a, C. G. Jones *in litt.* 1981 to R. F. Pasquier). In 1981 no more than five or six birds (two males, three females), four of them paired, could be located; one pair attempted to breed, without success (Jones 1981a,1982a,b). In 1982 the population was considered possibly to consist of 3-5 birds, at least 5-10 years old, and to include just one (non-breeding) pair, there being no evidence that year of any breeding activity (Jones 1983, in press). A three-month study of the species, October to December 1983, yielded no evidence of breeding, though a bird with an incomplete collar (i.e. apparently juvenile) was seen on 26 December, and throughout the period no more than four birds (three males, one female) were ever seen clearly at any one time, except once: on 15 December, when at least seven and possibly as many as 11 (identity not absolutely clinched) were seen by four observers on Macabé ridge; even so, probably only two of the birds were female (Ahimaz 1984; also *Flying Free* 2,1 [1984], *ICBP Newsletter* 6,1 [1984], C. G. Jones *in litt.* 1984). These results are, however, open to the interpretation that successful breeding took place in 1983 (A. S. Cheke pers. comm. 1984).

Ecology The species inhabits native upland forest and scrublands (dwarf forest), but also utilises areas of native lowland and middle altitude forest (Jones in press; also Staub 1971) and, at the turn of the century, it was noted even in the "empty lightly wooded country" then existing around Curepipe (Carié 1904) (this latter would have been degraded forest, not a natural habitat: A. S. Cheke pers. comm. 1984). Birds are strictly arboreal, generally keeping to upper branches (Newton and Newton 1876, Jones in press), roosting in sheltered areas (hillsides, ravines), usually in dense and densely foliaged mature stands of trees, ranging over a wide area by day in search of food (Jones 1980b, in press). Those now remaining centre their activities on the Macabé ridge and there favour some of the largest native trees left on Mauritius, e.g. *Canarium mauritianum, Syzygium contractum, Mimusops maxima, Labourdonnaisia* (Jones in press). Birds forage mainly over mid-morning and from mid- to late afternoon, in different areas at different seasons (Jones in press; also Temple 1978). Food is chiefly fruit and flowers, but also leaves, seeds, buds, shoots, twigs and even bark (Jones in press). Birds are highly specialised to feed on native vegetation, needing Sapotaceae and *Eugenia* species, also Burseraceae and *Erythrospermum* (Cheke 1975). Key food species are *Calophyllum* fruits and bois de lait *Tabernaemontana mauritiana*, the birds eating the latex-exuding leaves (Jones in press; also Ahimaz 1984). Other favoured foods are the fruit of bois de natte *Labourdonnaisia glauca*, makak *Mimusops*, bois de pomme *Syzygium glomeratum*, bois manglier *Sideroxylon*, bois maigre *Nuxia verticillata* and bois d'ébène *Diospyros*, but fruits of virtually all indigenous trees are taken (Temple *et al.* 1974, Ahimaz 1984; comprehensive account in Jones in press); the species also used to relish the berries of the introduced tabac marron *Solanum auriculatum* (Carié 1904), which was formerly widespread (A. S. Cheke pers. comm. 1984). Birds eat more leaves in winter, when fruit is scarcer (Jones in press). Breeding generally commences September/October, lasting through till January or February (Temple *et al.* 1974, Temple 1978, Jones in press). Nests are located high (at least 10 m up) in rain-sheltered holes facing away from trade (northerly) winds in the hollow, usually horizontal limbs of old but living emergent native trees, usually *Mimusops*, also *Callophyllum, Canarium* and *Sideroxylon* (Procter and Salm 1974, Temple 1974a,1978, Temple *et al.* 1974, Jones in press). Clutch-size is two, three or four (Jones in press); usually (at least formerly) two young were raised (Temple *et al.* 1974, Staub 1976). Post-fledging dependence is thought to last at least two months (Jones in press). Birds have been reported as both shy (Newton and Newton 1876) and very tame (Meinertzhagen 1912): this depends on season and food supply, hungry birds (August to mid-November) being tamer than well-fed ones (C. G. Jones *in litt.* 1984).

Threats While the reasons for the species's extinction on Réunion remain unknown, it is to be noted that exceptionally high hunting pressure existed in the early years of settlement, and native lowland forest (i.e. that below 1,000 m) all vanished very rapidly, these two factors probably acting in concert to wipe all the birds out (Cheke in press; also A. S. Cheke pers. comm. 1984). A general account of the problems facing the endemic forest-dependent birds of Mauritius is given in Threats under Mauritius Kestrel *Falco punctatus*. Prior to the start of the WWF project in the early 1970s (see Conservation Measures Taken) the decline in the

Mauritius Parakeet was attributed, with varying degrees of certitude, to hunting (Newton 1883, Oustalet 1897, Rountree 1951), habitat loss (birds "retiring before cultivation") (Newton and Newton 1876), the unspecified influence of introduced crab-eating macaques *Macaca fascicularis* (Newton and Newton 1876), and competition from the introduced Ring-necked Parakeet *Psittacula krameri* (Carié 1916, Newton 1958). Three major threats to the species were identified in the early 1970s, namely habitat loss, nest predation by monkeys, and competition for nest-sites from Ring-necked Parakeets and (also introduced) Indian Mynahs *Acrido-theres tristis* (Temple 1974a), although these were subsequently redefined as loss of nest-sites owing to forest degradation, low breeding success owing to both nest predation and nest-site competition, and illegal shooting (Temple 1978). Of all these, habitat loss is agreed upon by subsequent investigators as the single most critical factor: the (World Bank financed) clearance in 1971-1974 of half (c. 2,800 ha) of the upland *Sideroxylon-Helichrysum* dwarf forest at Les Mares on Plaine Champagne for plantation forestry has been blamed for the drastic decline of the species in the course of the rest of the 1970s (Jones 1980a,b, in press, Jones and Owadally 1982). Nest predation by monkeys was reported as the cause of failure of one nest in 1973, the noisiness of birds being noted to facilitate the detection of nests by monkeys (3,500-4,500 of which are estimated in the area of native forest remaining) (Temple *et al.* 1974, Jones 1979,1980b), but examination of records, questioning of local naturalists, and field observations since 1979 have failed to provide evidence that directly implicates monkeys as a cause of breeding failure (Jones in press). Competition for nest-sites from Ring-necked Parakeets was evidently "severe" until the early 1970s (Temple *et al.* 1974, Staub 1976, Temple 1978, Jones 1980b), but the populations of both species have since declined and their ranges no longer greatly overlap (Jones in press); competition for nest-sites from Indian Mynahs, despite their being confined to areas of forest opened up by roads and clearings (Jones 1980a, in press), has been and remains a problem, the only witnessed nesting attempts in both 1980 and 1981 being disrupted by these birds (Jones 1982a,b, in press; also Temple 1978, Pasquier 1982). Intraspecific competition for mates has caused nest failure at least once: the single pair that tried to breed in 1978 deserted after the male was supplanted by an unmated male (King 1979, Steele 1979) and it seems likely that the present predominance of males (see Population) could result in similar disruption in any future breeding attempts (see Jones in press for further interpretation of this issue). While Cyclone Claudette in December 1979 may have caused some direct losses (see Population), Cyclone Gervaise in February 1975 apparently did not (Newlands 1975a, Temple 1975b), though in retrospect birds were thought less common in 1975 than in 1974 (Temple 1978). However, the latter was responsible for toppling eight of 14 known nest trees (Temple 1976b) – in another account 11 of 16 (Temple 1975b) and in another seven of either 13 or 17 (Temple 1978) – yet nest-sites are not considered to limit the population (Jones 1980b); it is a sad coincidence, then, that so high a proportion of nesting attempts in the 1970s and 1980s appear to have been foiled by other hole-nesting birds (see above). That the species has suffered competitive exclusion by the Ring-necked Parakeet has been speculated, with no firm conclusion (Jones 1980a,b, in press). Food shortages at the end of winter, owing not merely to the season but to the gradual degradation of native forest and the competition for and destruction of fruit by black rats *Rattus rattus* and especially monkeys (which tear off and discard large quantities of unripe fruit), are considered probably to have contributed to this species's rarity (Jones 1980a,b,1982a,b, in press). There is the small but distinct danger that hunters may mistake the Mauritius for the Ring-necked Parakeet (Temple *et al.* 1974), and two birds were reportedly shot in 1972 and bullets were found lodged near the nest-cavity entrance of a pair that deserted in 1974 (Temple 1978). Finally, there is the consideration that the remaining birds in the population are too old for any further breeding (hence the absence of breeding activity in recent years).

Conservation Measures Taken This species has been one of the major concerns of the bird conservation work that began on Mauritius in the early 1970s (for a note on this see Conservation Measures Taken under Mauritius Kestrel). On the assumption that monkey predation of nests was seriously affecting reproductive output, 41 monkey-proof nest-boxes were installed in seemingly appropriate locations in native forest between 1974 and 1979 but not one was or has ever been used (Temple 1976b, Jones 1979,1980b,c,1981b,1982a, Staub 1979, Steele 1979). The trunk of the 1978 nest tree was coated with a thick rim of grease to prevent monkeys climbing (Steele 1978). Four birds were taken from nests for captive breeding experiments (two in 1974, two in 1975) but none survived long (Temple 1975a,b, Jones 1980a,b, in press). All subsequent attempts either to capture adults or to obtain eggs or young have failed (Jones 1980b,c, in press, Ahimaz 1984). This species has long been protected (Meinertzhagen 1912) and in 1974 its remaining native forest habitat received almost complete protection when the Macabé/Bel Ombre Nature Reserve was created through the linking of existing reserves at Petrin, Macabé and Bel Ombre by the addition of Les Mares and Plaine Champagne, forming a large block covering 3,594 ha (Owadally 1976; see map in Procter and Salm 1974). The species is listed on Appendix I of CITES, to which Mauritius is a party.

Conservation Measures Proposed As long ago as 1929 it was argued that, in view of the species's impending extinction, "every effort should be made to a secure a breeding stock in order that it may be preserved in captivity" (Tavistock 1929): captive breeding is certainly now regarded as the "best chance" and "only realistic hope" for saving the species (Jones 1980b, in press, Pasquier 1980, Jones and Owadally 1982; resolutions in Pasquier 1981). Control of nest predators and nest-site competitors has been contemplated (Temple 1974a,1976a, King 1978-1979) but never implemented (Jones in press): in view of events in 1980 and 1981 this (or the use of distress-call playback) may be essential if only to buy time for the safe taking of eggs, young or adults for captive breeding. A proposal for the introduction of captive-bred birds to the one small area of habitat suitable on the neighbouring French island of Réunion has been drawn up (Cheke 1975, 1978) but rejected because hunting pressure there is too high (Jones and Owadally 1982, C. G. Jones and A. W. Owadally *in litt.* 1982): but if the projected captive breeding were to prove a success, and if food availability is indeed responsible for depressing numbers in Mauritius, such an experiment, fully monitored and with a well managed publicity campaign, would appear an important future consideration.

Remarks The view that this bird is distinct from the Ring-necked Parakeet has been put forward on both morphological and behavioural grounds (Forshaw and Cooper 1978) and is accepted here; the view that it is not distinct from the extinct form of parakeet on Réunion (see Jones in press; also Cheke in press) is also accepted here, hence the older specific name *eques* replaces the ingenious provisional *echo* bestowed by Newton and Newton (1876) for want of a case that the two forms were identical. Concerning breeding success in 1973 and 1974, data for these two years are (presumably erroneously) reversed but also amplified in Temple (1978). The report (in King 1978) that five Mauritius Parakeets were fledged in (by implication) 1977 in fact refers to 1976.

References

Ahimaz, P. (1984) The Echo Parakeet (*Psittacula [eques] echo*) project report. Draft typescript.

Carié, P. (1904) Observations sur quelques oiseaux de l'île Maurice. *Ornis* 12: 121-128.

Carié, P. (1916) L'acclimatation à l'île Maurice. C.- Oiseaux. *Bull. Soc. Natn. Acclim. Fr.* 63: 107-110, 152-159, 191-198, 245-250, 355-363, 401-404.

Cheke, A. S. (1975) Proposition pour introduire à la Réunion des oiseaux rares de l'île Maurice. *Info-Nature* no. 12: 25-29.

Cheke, A. S. (1978) Recommendations for the conservation of Mascarene vertebrates. Conservation memorandum no. 3 (arising out of the B.O.U. Mascarene Islands Expedition). Unpublished.

Cheke, A. S. (in press) An ecological history of the Mascarene islands. In A. W. Diamond, ed. *Studies of Mascarene island birds*. Cambridge: Cambridge University Press.

Forshaw, J. M. and Cooper, W. T. (1978) *Parrots of the world*. 2nd edition. Melbourne: Lansdowne Editions.

Gill, F. B. (1971) Endemic landbirds of Mauritius Island, Indian Ocean. Unpublished.

Jones, C. G. (1979) Mauritius/Rodrigues conservation project report for January 22nd – June 20th 1979. Unpublished.

Jones, C. G. (1980a) The conservation of the endemic birds and bats of Mauritius and Rodriguez (a progress report and proposal for further activities). Unpublished.

Jones, C. G. (1980b) Parrot on the way to extinction. *Oryx* 15: 350-354.

Jones, C. G. (1980c) The conservation of the endemic birds and bats of Mauritius and Rodriguez. Progress report January 1980 – November 1980. Unpublished.

Jones, C. G. (1981a) Mauritius: an important lesson in island biology. (A summary of activities and proposals for 1981.) Unpublished.

Jones, C. G. (1981b) Mauritius Project 1082. Promotion of conservation. *WWF Yearbook* 1980-1981: 206-212.

Jones, C. G. (1982a) The conservation of the endemic birds and bats of Mauritius and Rodrigues. (Annual report 1981, WWF Project 1082.) Unpublished.

Jones, C. G. (1982b) Struggle for survival on tropical islands. *WWF Monthly Report* February: 37-42.

Jones, C. G. (1983) The conservation of the endemic birds and bats of Mauritius and Rodrigues. Annual Report, 1982. Unpublished.

Jones, C. G. (in press) The larger land-birds of Mauritius. In A. W. Diamond, ed. *Studies of Mascarene island birds*. Cambridge: Cambridge University Press.

Jones, C. G. and Owadally, A. W. (1982) Conservation priorities for Mauritius and Rodrigues. Report submitted to ICBP, July. Unpublished.

King, W. B. (1977) Notes on a conversation with David McKelvey 31 August 1977. Typescript.

King, W. B. (1978) Mauritius Project 1082. Promotion of conservation. *WWF Yearbook* 1977-1978: 150-151.

King, W. B. (1978-1979) *Red data book, 2: Aves*. 2nd edition. Morges, Switzerland: IUCN.

King, W. B. (1979) Mauritius Project 1082. Promotion of conservation. *WWF Yearbook* 1978-1979: 137-138.

Meinertzhagen, R. (1912) On the birds of Mauritius. *Ibis* (9)6: 82-108.

Newlands, W. A. (1975a) Mauritius Conservation Project monthly reports, February – August 1975. Unpublished.

Newlands, W. A. (1975b) Letter, 4 October [duplicated to interested parties]. Unpublished.

Newton, A. and Newton, E. (1876) On the *Psittaci* of the Mascarene islands. *Ibis* (3)6: 281-289.

Newton, E. (1883) Annexe C [Letter to V. Naz, 26 February 1878.] *Trans. Soc. Roy. Arts Sci. Maurice* (NS) 12: 70-73.

Newton, R. (1958) Ornithological notes on Mauritius and the Cargados Carajos Archipelago. *Proc. Roy. Soc. Arts Sci. Mauritius* 2(1): 39-71.

Oustalet, E. (1897) Notice sur la faune ornithologique ancienne et moderne des îles Mascareignes et en particulier de l'île Maurice d'après des documents inédits. *Ann. Sci. Nat. Zool.* (8)3: 1-128.

Owadally, A. W. (1976) *Annual report of the Forestry Service for the year 1974*. Port Louis, Mauritius: L. Carl Achille, Government Printer.

Pasquier, R. F. (1980) Mauritius Project 1082. Endangered bird species. *WWF Yearbook* 1979-1980: 128-129.

Pasquier, R. F. ed. (1981) *Conservation of New World parrots*. [Washington, D.C.:] ICBP Techn. Publ. no. 1.

Pasquier, R. F. (1982) Mauritius Project 1082. Conservation of birds of Mauritius. *WWF Yearbook* 1982: 210-211.

Procter, J. and Salm, R. (1974) Conservation in Mauritius 1974. IUCN/WWF consultancy report for Government of Mauritius. Unpublished.

Rountree, F. G. R. (1951) Some aspects of bird-life in Mauritius. *Proc. Roy. Soc. Arts Sci. Mauritius* 1(2): 83-96.

Rountree, F. G. R., Guérin, R., Pelte, S. and Vinson, J. (1952) Catalogue of the birds of Mauritius. *Mauritius Inst. Bull.* 3(3): 155-217.

Staub, F. (1971) Actual situation of the Mauritius endemic birds. *ICBP Bull.* 11: 226-227.

Staub, F. (1976) *Birds of the Mascarenes and Saint Brandon*. Port Louis, Mauritius: Organisation Normale des Enterprises.

Staub, F. (1979) Mauritius National Section, report 1977-1978. *ICBP Bull.* 13: 188-190.

Steele, F. N. (1978) Conservation of birds on Mauritius, bi-monthly reports, February – November 1978. Unpublished.

Steele, F. N. (1979) Conservation of birds on Mauritius, final report for 1978. Unpublished.

Tavistock, Marquess of (1929) *Parrots and parrot-like birds in captivity*. London: F. V. White.

Temple, S. A. (1974a) Appendix 6. The native fauna of Mauritius: 1, the land birds. In J. Procter and R. Salm, Conservation in Mauritius 1974. IUCN/WWF consultancy report for Government of Mauritius. Unpublished.

Temple, S. A. (1974b) Wildlife in Mauritius today. *Oryx* 12: 584-590.

Temple, S. A. (1975a) Project 986: Western Indian Ocean raptores [*sic*] – ecology and conservation. *WWF Yearbook* 1974-1975: 210-212.

Temple, S. A. (1975b) A report on the conservation program in Mauritius, 15 October. Unpublished.

Temple, S. A. (1976a) Project 1082: Mauritius – promotion of conservation. *WWF Yearbook* 1975-1976: 165-166.

Temple, S. A. (1976b) Conservation of endemic birds and other wildlife on Mauritius. A progress report and proposal for future activities. Unpublished.

Temple, S. A. (1978) The life histories and ecology of the indigenous landbirds of Mauritius. Unpublished.

Temple, S. A., Staub, J. J. F. and Antoine, R. (1974) Some background information and recommendations on the preservation of the native flora and fauna of Mauritius. Unpublished report to the Government of Mauritius.

BANNERMAN'S TURACO   ENDANGERED
Tauraco bannermani (Bates, 1923)

Order CUCULIFORMES   Family MUSOPHAGIDAE

Summary his frugivorous rainforest species is restricted to the Bamenda-Banso Highlands in western Cameroon where it is under very serious threat from forest clearance: it will very probably become extinct unless forest on Mount Oku is preserved.

Distribution Bannerman's Turaco is only known from the Bamenda-Banso Highlands in western Cameroon. The type-specimen was collected in 1922 at 1,830 m in the Banso Mountains north of Kumbo (Bates 1923, Bannerman and Bates 1924). Five specimens were taken in 1925 at Oku (west of Kumbo) and at Lake Bambulue and Santa, both these localities being near Bamenda, and all of them being above 1,830 m (Bannerman 1933). Three birds were collected in 1948 between 1,830 and 2,440 m near Bamenda and birds were also seen in the Oku forests at this time (Serle 1950). In 1967 the species was collected at Lake Oku, 2,100 m (Eisentraut 1973; four specimens in ZFMK: NJC) and in 1974 four birds were taken on Mount Lefo (van den Elzen 1975). In 1984 the ICBP Cameroon Montane Forest Survey found the species on Mount Oku, the Sabga Pass, the Bafut-Ngemba Forest Reserve (including Lake Bambulue), the Bali-Ngemba Forest Reserve and the Bamboutos Mountains (SNS). The species is restricted to montane areas north of the lowland forest block (Louette 1981) where through most of its range it is the only turaco to be found (Eisentraut 1973). Towards the west of the Bamenda Highlands, around Mbengwi and Tinachong, it is replaced by the Guinea Turaco *Tauraco persa* and the two species are sympatric in the Bali-Ngemba Forest Reserve (SNS).

Population The species is common within its very restricted range (SNS).

Ecology This species appears to be restricted to montane forest, especially in ravines and crater rims (Bates 1923, Bannerman 1933, Serle 1950, Eisentraut 1973). It apparently behaves and calls as a typical turaco (Bannerman 1933, Serle 1950, Eisentraut 1973) and eats fruits and berries (Eisentraut 1973). Birds collected in March were in breeding condition (van den Elzen 1975).

Threats All of the forest patches remaining in the Bamenda Highlands are now badly damaged, very small and being rapidly cleared as a result of cultivation, overgrazing by cattle, goats, sheep and horses, wood-cutting and fires (SNS). More extensive areas of forest survive on Mount Oku but even these are being rapidly cleared (SNS).

Conservation Measures Taken None is known, even the forest reserves in which the species occurs being subject to clearance (SNS).

Conservation Measures Proposed The ICBP Cameroon Montane Forest Survey is preparing recommendations for the conservation of forest on Mount Oku, for the consideration of the Cameroon government. Unless this forest is conserved this species along with the Banded Wattle-eye *Platysteira laticincta* (see relevant account) will almost certainly not survive.

Remarks Bannerman's Turaco is most closely related to the Angola Red-crested Turaco *Tauraco erythrolophus* with which it forms a superspecies (Eisentraut 1973, Snow 1978, Louette 1981). Three other threatened bird species, the Green-breasted Bush-shrike *Malaconotus gladiator*, the Banded Wattle-eye and Bannerman's Weaver *Ploceus bannermani* are known from the Bamenda Highlands (see relevant accounts). The Cameroon Mountain Greenbul *Andropadus montanus* (see Appendix C) is also found in the Bamenda Highlands.

References

Bannerman, D. A. (1933) *The birds of tropical West Africa*, 3. London: Crown Agents for the Colonies.

Bannerman, D. A. and Bates, G. L. (1924) On the birds collected in north-western and northern Cameroon and parts of northern Nigeria. Part II. *Ibis* (11)6: 199-277.

Bates, G. L. (1923) [A fine new tauraco.] *Bull. Brit. Orn. Club* 43: 140-141.

Eisentraut, M. (1973) Die Wirbeltierfauna von Fernando Poo und Westkamerun. *Bonn. zool. Monog.* 3.

van den Elzen, R. (1975) Zur Kenntnis der Avifauna Kameruns. *Bonn. zool. Beitr.* 26: 49-75.

Louette, M. (1981) *The birds of Cameroon. An annotated check-list.* Brussels: Verhandeling Wetenschappen, Jaargang 43, no. 163.

Serle, W. (1950) A contribution to the ornithology of the British Cameroons. Part 1. *Ibis* 92: 343-376.

Snow, D. W. ed. (1978) *An atlas of speciation in African non-passerine birds*. London: Trustees of the British Museum (Natural History).

PRINCE RUSPOLI'S TURACO   RARE

Tauraco ruspolii (Salvadori, 1896)

Order CUCULIFORMES   Family MUSOPHAGIDAE

Summary A frugivorous, forest-dwelling species of very limited distribution in southern Ethiopia, possibly commoner and more widespread than hitherto believed, this turaco may be at risk from habitat loss and requires a full study to determine its status, distribution and needs.

Distribution On current knowledge, Prince Ruspoli's Turaco is restricted to a few scattered localities in a single area of southern Ethiopia. The locality for the type-specimen is uncertain, and though Lake Abaya (= Margherita) was originally assumed (Salvadori 1913) there is a strong possibility it was collected at Arero (Araro), central Sidamo province, southern Ethiopia (Moreau 1958). Fifty years later, in 1941-1942, the species was re-discovered at Arero in an isolated patch of forest of only 25 km^2 (Benson 1942, Hall and Moreau 1962), the resulting specimens (in BMNH) being labelled as from 4°48'N 38°50'E at 1,800 m (NJC). In the period 1968-1973, the area north and west of Neghelli (Nagele, Negelli; in Borana) in the upper valleys of the rivers Dawa and Ganale Dorya was found to hold the species: in 1968 and 1971 at and around Wadera (Uaddara), 5°40'N 39°20'E, c. 80 km north-west of Neghelli and c. 120 km north-east of Arero (Erard and Prévost 1970, C. Erard pers. comm. 1983; specimens in MNHN: SNS); in 1971 at a wadi just north of the River Ganale (i.e. in Bale province), c. 25 km north of Neghelli (J. S. Ash *in litt.* 1983); and in 1973 at a locality 27 km west of Neghelli (J. S. Ash *in litt.* 1983). It may also occur in a patch of forest c. 55 km east of Arero (i.e. near Guba) (Hall and Moreau 1962). On present evidence, therefore, it would seem very possible that the species occurs (as speculated in Hall and Moreau 1962) in patches of suitable habitat throughout the dense dendritic drainage system in the upper Dawa valley that extends from Arero and Guba (in the south) north and west of Neghelli (as far north-west as Kibre Mengist [Adola]) at least as far as the adjacent radially drained section of the Ganale Dorya valley, and conceivably north and east into the valleys of the Welmal and Dumale up to Ginir (see War Office 1946, HOGC 1969, TAW 1980). The species has been looked for without success in forest at Yavello (Benson 1945, J. S. Ash *in litt.* 1983) and Mega (Benson 1945), these localities being west-south-west and south-west of Neghelli respectively.

Population Records between 1968 and 1973 have established that this species is commoner than previous evidence had suggested, but information is still too scant to allow confidence concerning its overall abundance. Six birds probably representing four pairs have been recorded in 150 ha of habitat (Erard and Prévost 1970), and 21 birds seen in a day (C. Erard pers. comm. 1983).

Ecology In 1941-1942 at Arero and 1968 at Wadera the species was found in juniper forest with dense evergreen undergrowth at 1,800 m (Benson 1942, Erard and Prévost 1970), but in 1971 it was found in high dense scrub with

Flacourtia (birds there commoner than in juniper) (C. Erard pers. comm. 1983) and in 1971-1973 it was adjudged to be a species of denser mixed woodland, extending into acacia woodland where this was mixed in denser clumps with other tree species along streams and in damp hollows (J. S. Ash *in litt.* 1983): at one locality its habitat was noted as "mixed broad-leaved scrub with scattered acacias (dominant), *Gardenia*, *Ficus* and many other species, 1,275 m", and birds were even found in a large *Ficus* along a dry watercourse in very dry acacia scrub (J. S. Ash *in litt.* 1983; also Gilbert 1971). At Wadera birds were sympatric with the White-cheeked Turaco *Tauraco leucotis* but in different woodland habitats (*ruspolii* in juniper, *leucotis* in broad-leaf) (Erard and Prévost 1970), although at Arero, *leucotis* being absent, it had been assumed that the two were mutually exclusive (Benson 1945). However, the absence of *ruspolii* from certain apparently suitable forests (Benson 1945) indicates some unidentified constraint on its distribution, although because remarkably secretive and elusive (J. S. Ash *in litt.* 1983) it may escape detection, as happened around Neghelli, which was considered a likely area in the 1940s (Benson 1945), prospected unsuccessfully in 1968 (Erard and Prévost 1970) but found to hold birds within 25 km of the town in 1971-1973 (see Distribution). Birds have been seen to eat berries of *Teclea* sp. aff. *nobilis* and of a rubiaceous tree (J. S. Ash *in litt.* 1983; also Gilbert 1971) and though the nest has never been found clutch-size is predicted as two, as in all other congeners (Vincent 1966-1971). Females collected in both October and February had somewhat enlarged gonads (Benson 1945), but those collected in May were not breeding (Erard and Prévost 1970).

Threats The main threat to this species would be through habitat alteration (deforestation can occur in the course of resettlement schemes) but there was no evidence of this in the 1970s (J. S. Ash *in litt.* 1983). However, the juniper forest at Arero only covered 25 km^2 in 1941-1942, and the area 55 km to the east (near Guba) where the species was anticipated was even smaller (Hall and Moreau 1962); the condition of these forests has not subsequently been reported. Against this, the area at Wadera is marked "precipitous ravines and dense forest" (War Office 1946) which implies a degree of invulnerability. The species may, however, be threatened by natural processes (see Remarks).

Conservation Measures Taken None is known.

Conservation Measures Proposed A study of this species is needed to determine its ecological requirements, status and exact distribution, and to prepare sound recommendations for its permanent conservation (see Conservation Measures Proposed under Ethiopian Bush-crow *Zavattariornis stresemanni*).

Remarks This species is apparently relict and has probably suffered in competition with the White-cheeked Turaco (Moreau 1958, Erard and Prévost 1971). Where the two are sympatric, therefore, it is possible that *ruspolii* is very gradually in decline, and that it will ultimately become extinct from natural causes.

References

Benson, C. W. (1942) A new species and ten new races from southern Abyssinia. *Bull. Brit. Orn. Club* 63: 8-19.

Benson, C. W. (1945) Notes on the birds of southern Abyssinia. *Ibis* 87: 489-509.

Erard, C. and Prévost, J. (1970) New facts on the distribution of *Tauraco ruspolii* Salvadori. *Bull. Brit. Orn. Club* 90: 157.

Erard, C. and Prévost, J. (1971) Notes on some Ethiopian birds. *Bull. Brit. Orn. Club* 91: 21-25.

Gilbert, M. G. (1971) Prince Ruspoli's Turaco (*Tauraco ruspolii*). *Ethiopian Wildl. Nat. Hist. Soc. Newsletter* no. 52: 3.

Hall, B. P. and Moreau, R. E. (1962) A study of the rare birds of Africa. *Bull. Brit. Mus. (Nat. Hist.) Zool.* 8: 313-378.

Head Office of Geodesy and Cartography (1969) [Karta Mira] World Map 1:2,500,000, NA-C 37-39 115. Sofia, Bulgaria.

Moreau, R. E. (1958) Some aspects of the Musophagidae. *Ibis* 100: 67-112, 238-270.

Salvadori, T. (1913) On a rare species of touracou (*Turacus ruspolii*). *Ibis* (10)1: 1-2.

The Times Atlas of the World (1980) Comprehensive (sixth) edition. London: Times Books.

Vincent, J. (1966-1971) *Red Data Book, 2. Aves*. Morges, Switzerland: IUCN.

War Office (1946) East Africa, 1:500,000, GSGS 4355, 4th edition.

Coua delalandei (Temminck, 1827)

Order CUCULIFORMES   Family CUCULIDAE

                                                      Subfamily COUINAE

Summary This large terrestrial cuckoo is the only bird (other than the elephantbirds Aepyornithidae) in Madagascar generally believed to have become extinct. There is a very remote possibility that it survives.

Distribution The Snail-eating Coua is known chiefly from Ile de Sainte-Marie off the northern east coast of Madagascar (Sganzin 1840, Ackerman 1841). The species is also repeatedly stated to have occurred on the mainland opposite Ile de Sainte-Marie, especially on the immediately adjacent Pointe-à-Larrée (Milne Edwards and Grandidier 1879, Milon *et al.* 1973; also Hartlaub 1877, Delacour 1932, Rand 1936) and, perhaps owing to its reported survival in the deepest forests of the region between Fito and Maroantsetra (Lavauden 1932), its mainland range has been guessed as "from the head of Antongil Bay southward to Tamatave" (Peters 1940). However, it has been pointed out that "there are no exact records of the provenance of mainland specimens" (Greenway 1967), and indeed it is nowhere clear that any specimen is known to have come from anywhere other than Ile de Sainte-Marie. At least 13 specimens (two each in BMNH and MNHN, one each in MCZ, AMNH, ANSP, RMNH, SMNS, NHMW, Liverpool, Antananarivo and IRSNB: see Remarks) are known to exist (Hartlaub 1860, Delacour 1932, Rand 1936, Greenway 1967, Benson and Schüz 1971, Schifter 1973, Morgan 1975, NJC), the origin of many of which seems likely to have been Ile de Sainte-Marie, as it is recorded that specimens from there were dispersed to various museums (Sganzin 1840). Nevertheless, plate 65 in Milne-Edwards and Grandidier (1876) maps the distribution of this species as the eastern rainforest from the latitude of Tamatave north to that of Ile de Sainte-Marie (but not Ile de Sainte-Marie itself); the authority for such a distribution is not given. A record of the species as a "waterbird" at Lake Alaotra (Baron 1882) is presumably in error.

Population The extinction of this species is probable (as judged in Delacour 1932, Rand 1936, Milon 1952, Greenway 1967) but not certain (*contra* Day 1981). None has been reported with certainty since 1834 (Greenway 1967), although the dates of Ackerman's three-year stay (see Ackerman 1841) are not clear and there are three specimens which could have been collected after this date, though not later than 1837, 1840 or 1850 respectively (Benson and Schüz 1971, Schifter 1973, Morgan 1975). The species was "not very rare" on Ile de Sainte-Marie in 1831-1832 (Sganzin 1840), which may perhaps be the source of the statement in 1860 that it was "not rare on the east coast" (Hartlaub 1860); however, no trace of it could be found during six month's exploration in 1865 and it was therefore judged very rare (Milne Edwards and Grandidier 1879; also Jouanin 1962). Following the failure of the Mission Franco-Anglo-Américaine to find it in 1929-1931, and the failure of the offer of a large reward to the procurer of a specimen in 1932 (see Greenway 1967), it was pronounced probably extinct

(Delacour 1932, Rand 1936). Nevertheless, at just this time a "very reliable native who knew exactly what bird was being referred to" reported that the species still survived on the mainland but was very rare and very shy (Lavauden 1932). Much of the area in question was not visited by the Mission Franco-Anglo-Américaine, and has not apparently been searched subsequently, and it is accepted that the species might conceivably survive in a few remote undisturbed patches (Greenway 1967, Milon *et al.* 1973). Survival on Ile de Sainte-Marie is ruled out as all the original forest has long since been cleared (Lavauden 1932, Daumet 1937, Petter 1963, Keith *et al.* 1974).

Ecology This bird is or was a ground-haunting rainforest-dweller, subsisting on molluscs (Sganzin 1840). An account of its method of breaking snail shells, based on observations in an aviary and apparently also in the wild, has been provided along with brief details of its behaviour and voice (Ackerman 1841).

Threats Habitat destruction was clearly the chief cause of its disappearance from Ile de Sainte-Marie (Lavauden 1932, Petter 1963, Keith *et al.* 1974), and was identified as the chief threat to its existence on the mainland as long ago as 1932 (Lavauden 1932): most of the lowlands between Tamatave and Maroantsetra were devoid of forest at the end of the 1960s (Keith *et al.* 1974). Occasional snaring by natives was reported (Lavauden 1932) and this was presumably quite easy at a time when the species was more numerous, and may have played a part in its decline; it was reportedly hunted as much for feathers as for food (Keith *et al.* 1974). Shell remains at certain localities within the forest may have betrayed the presence of birds to hunters (A. D. Forbes-Watson pers. comm. 1984). A recent account gives a cause of extinction as "introduced rodents" (Day 1981): while there appears to be no direct evidence for this, it is conceivable that rats critically reduced the mollusc fauna in key areas and this indirectly contributed to the species's disappearance (for rats in eastern forests, see Threats under Brown Mesite *Mesitornis unicolor*.)

Conservation Measures Taken None is known.

Conservation Measures Proposed It needs to be properly established, through a reexamination of museum material and records, whether the species occurred on mainland Madagascar. Even if this cannot be done, the ornithological surveys that are needed for other reasons in the Sihanaka and other remaining forests between Fito and Maroantsetra (see Conservation Measures Proposed under Madagascar Serpent Eagle *Eutriorchis astur*) should certainly be weighted towards tracking down evidence of this bird's survival.

Remarks It is to be observed that if the White-breasted Mesite *Mesitornis variegata* went unknown from 1834 to 1929 (see relevant account) and the Yellow-bellied Sunbird-asity *Neodrepanis hypoxantha* from 1929 almost to the present day (but is not extinct: see relevant account), it is certainly conceivable – if less likely – that the Snail-eating Coua could have survived undetected over the same 150-year period. The specimen in IRSNB, whose existence has not previously been announced, was acquired by the museum in 1839 and according to the catalogue it was captured or collected in "Madagascar" in 1832 (P. Devillers pers. comm. 1983), this date perhaps rendering it likely to have come from Sganzin on Ile de Sainte-Marie (see Distribution).

References

Ackerman, M[onsieur].(1841) Note sur le Coua, *Famac-acora* des Malgaches, Hache-escargot (traduction littérale) ou casseur d'escargots. *Rev. Zool.* 4: 209-210.

Baron, R. (1882) From Ambatondrazaka to Fenoarivo. *Antananarivo Annual* no. 6: 75-94.

Benson, C. W. and Schüz, E. (1971) A specimen of *Coua delalandei* (Temminck) (Cuculidae). *Bull. Brit. Orn. Club* 91: 159-160.

Daumet, M. (1937) Sainte-Marie de Madagascar. Son histoire. *Revue de Madagascar* no. 18: 81-110.

Day, D. (1981) *The doomsday book of animals.* London: Ebury Press.

Delacour, J. (1932) Les oiseaux de la Mission Franco-Anglo-Américaine à Madagascar. *Oiseau et R.F.O.* 2: 1-96.

Greenway, J. C. (1967) *Extinct and vanishing birds of the world.* 2nd revised edition. New York: Dover Publications.

Hartlaub, G. (1860) Systematische Uebersicht der Vögel Madagascars. II. Passeres. *J. Orn.* 8: 81-112.

Hartlaub, G. (1877) *Die Vögel Madagascars und der benachbarten Inselgruppen.* Halle.

Jouanin, C. (1962) Inventaire des oiseaux éteints ou en voie d'extinction conservés au Museum de Paris. *Terre et Vie* 109: 257-301.

Keith, S., Forbes-Watson, A. D. and Turner, D. A. (1974) The Madagascar Crested Ibis, a threatened species in an endemic and endangered avifauna. *Wilson Bull.* 86: 197-199.

Lavauden, L. (1932) Etude d'une petite collection d'oiseaux de Madagascar. *Bull. Mus. Natn. Hist. Nat.* (2)4: 629-640.

Milne Edwards, A. and Grandidier, A. (1876) *Histoire physique, naturelle et politique de Madagascar, 13. Histoire naturelle des oiseaux.* Tome II. – Atlas – I. Paris.

Milne Edwards, A. and Grandidier, A. (1879) *Histoire physique, naturelle et politique de Madagascar, 12. Histoire naturelle des oiseaux.* Tome I. Paris.

Milon, P. (1952) Notes sur le genre *Coua. Oiseau et R.F.O.* 22: 75-90.

Milon, P., Petter, J.-J. and Randrianasolo, G. (1973) *Faune de Madagascar, 35. Oiseaux.* Tananarive and Paris: ORSTOM and CNRS.

Morgan, P. J. (1975) A catalogued specimen of *Coua delalandei* (Temminck) (Cuculidae) in Merseyside County Museums, Liverpool. *Bull. Brit. Orn. Club* 95: 62-63.

Peters, J. L. (1940) *Check-list of birds of the world*, 4. Cambridge: Harvard University Press.

Petter, J.-J. (1963) The serious situation in Madagascar. *ICBP Bull.* 9: 95-96.

Rand, A. L. (1936) The distribution and habits of Madagascar birds. *Bull. Amer. Mus. Nat. Hist.* 72: 143-499.

Schifter, H. (1973) A specimen of *Coua delalandei* (Temminck) (Cuculidae) in the Naturhistorisches Museum, Vienna (Austria). *Bull. Brit. Orn. Club* 93: 2-3.

Sganzin, V. (1840) Notes sur les mammifères et sur l'ornithologie de l'île de Madagascar (1831 et 1932). *Mém. Soc. Mus. Hist. Nat. Strasbourg* 3(1), article 3: 1-49.

MADAGASCAR RED OWL
Tyto soumagnei (Milne Edwards, 1878)

INDETERMINATE

Order STRIGIFORMES

Family TYTONIDAE
Subfamily TYTONINAE

Summary This owl is known with certainty from rainforest only in eastern central Madagascar, and has been seen only once in the past 50 years.

Distribution The Madagascar Red Owl inhabits the eastern region of Madagascar in the circle whose diameter runs between Tamatave and Antananarivo. It does not occur "throughout Madagascar" (*contra* Burton 1973). The type-specimen was collected in 1876 on the east coast near Tamatave (Milne Edwards and Grandidier 1879) and a specimen from around Antananarivo (no date) came to the British Museum in 1879 (Sharpe 1879); as this specimen is catalogued as being collected by "Lorimer" (NJC) it presumably cannot be the bird sent back, also in 1879, by Humblot but which is not listed as going to MNHN (Humblot 1882) and indeed cannot be found there (NJC,SNS). There are two other nineteenth century specimens (in BMHN), one from "the upper forest of Eastern Imerina" in March 1893, one from "Merimitatra" (the label also states "between the two forests"), east Madagascar, January 1895 (Wills 1893, NJC); the former area has been cleared of forest (D. A. Turner pers. comm. 1983), but a place bearing the latter name is marked (in Locamus 1900) as a comparatively large settlement (now abandoned or re-named: not in Office of Geography 1955 or on recent maps) east of Anjozorobe, at roughly 18°25'S 48°05'E, on the upper western slopes of the Mangoro valley and thus between the two belts of forest bordering the valley (Sihanaka forest in the east, Angavo escarpment forest in the west). One collector obtained only three birds of this species in 40 years on Madagascar (two of these specimens were destroyed in 1927) (Lavauden 1932); all three were found in Sihanaka forest (Delacour 1932). Two specimens (a pair) were shot in March 1930 at Analamazaotra, near Périnet (Lavauden 1932), and another was taken near Fito, Sihanaka forest, on 15 February 1934 (Allen and Greenway 1935). The only subsequent record has been of a bird in deep mountainous rainforest (1,200-1,800 m) a day's walk from the nearest motorable road, Fierenana district (c. 65 km north of Périnet), in 1973 (King 1978-1979, J. I. Pollock *in litt.* 1983). The species is also reported as occurring on the Masoala peninsula (Milon *et al.* 1973) but evidence for this – although it seems likely – has not been traced.

Population Numbers are unknown, but the species has always appeared to be extremely rare (e.g. Delacour 1932, Lavauden 1932, Milon *et al.* 1973).

Ecology This owl inhabits humid rainforest and is strictly nocturnal, reportedly living in isolated pairs and feeding on frogs caught in clearings (Lavauden 1932). There are no other data, but it is to be observed that at least three specimens have come from localities (Tamatave, Antananarivo and Merimitatra) apparently outside heavily forested areas; however, it is not known to occur in grassland (*contra* Burton 1973).

313

Threats Destruction and disturbance of primary rainforest is the single most serious threat to this and all other rainforest-dependent species in Madagascar (see Threats under Madagascar Serpent Eagle *Eutriorchis astur*).

Conservation Measures Taken The species has been recorded from the area now established as the Périnet-Analamazáotra Special Reserve, which covers 810 ha (Andriamampianina 1981). The Madagascar Red Owl is listed on Appendix I of CITES, to which Madagascar is a party.

Conservation Measures Proposed Immediate and effective protection of as much remaining rainforest as possible would almost certainly guarantee the survival of this and all other rainforest-dependent species in Madagascar; and at least, on current knowledge, complete protection of the intact parts of Sihanaka forest is of extreme importance (see Conservation Measures Proposed under Madagascar Serpent Eagle). Any ornithological work in the other areas from which the species is known, or where it might be expected, should where possible be extended to include searches to locate it.

Remarks Although originally placed in its own genus (*Heliodius*), this species is clearly a small, dark reddish-orange barn owl *Tyto* (Lavauden 1932, Allen and Greenway 1935; also Sharpe 1879).

References

Allen, G. M. and Greenway, J., Jr. (1935) A specimen of *Tyto (Heliodius) soumagnii*. *Auk* 52: 414-417.

Andriamampianina, J. (1981) Les reserves naturelles et la protection de la nature à Madagascar. Pp. 105-111 in P. Oberlé, ed. *Madagascar, un sanctuaire de la nature*. Paris: Lechevalier.

Burton, J. A. ed. (1973) *Owls of the world: their evolution, structure and ecology*. London: Peter Lowe.

Delacour, J. (1932) Les oiseaux de la Mission Franco-Anglo-Américaine à Madagascar. *Oiseau et R.F.O.* 2: 1-96.

Humblot, L. (1882) Rapport sur une mission à Madagascar. *Arch. Miss. Sci. Litt.* (3)8: 153-157.

King, W. B. (1978-1979) *Red data book, 2: Aves*. 2nd edition. Morges, Switzerland: IUCN.

Lavauden, L. (1932) Etude d'une petite collection d'oiseaux de Madagascar. *Bull. Mus. Natn. Hist. Nat.* (2)4: 629-640.

Locamus, P. (1900) Carte de Madagascar, 1: 500,000. Paris.

Milne Edwards, A. and Grandidier, A. (1879) *Histoire physique, naturelle et politique de Madagascar, 12. Histoire naturelle des oiseaux*. Tome I. Paris.

Milon, P., Petter, J.-J. and Randrianasolo, G. (1973) *Faune de Madagascar, 35: Oiseaux*. Tananarive and Paris: ORSTOM and CRNS.

Office of Geography (1955) *Gazetteer no. 2. Madagascar, Réunion and the Comoro Islands*. Washington, D.C.: Department of the Interior.

Sharpe, R. B. (1879) A note on *Heliodius soumagnii*, Grandidier. *Proc. Zool. Soc. Lond.*: 175-176.

Wills, J. (1893) Notes on some Malagasy birds rarely seen in the interior. *Antananarivo Annual* 5 (no. 17): 119-120.

ITOMBWE OWL   INDETERMINATE
Phodilus prigoginei Schouteden, 1952

Order STRIGIFORMES   Family TYTONIDAE
                                                          Subfamily PHODILINAE

Summary This owl is known only from the type-specimen, collected in montane forest in eastern Zaire: subsequent attempts to locate it have been unsuccessful.

Distribution The type-specimen of the Itombwe Owl was collected at Muusi at 2,430 m in the Itombwe Mountains, eastern Zaire, in 1951 (Schouteden 1952). In the mid-1970s a bird, almost certainly this species, was seen on the Rwegura Tea Estate in Burundi (J.-P. Vande weghe pers. comm. 1983), but otherwise there have been no subsequent records (Prigogine 1973). The species is no doubt very elusive and could, therefore, occur on other mountains in central Africa (Hall and Moreau 1962).

Population Numbers are not known. The species is undoubtedly rare since many attempts to locate it between 1952 and 1964 were unsuccessful (Prigogine 1973).

Ecology The only specimen was found at about 14.00 hrs, sleeping in the grass of a mountain forest clearing (Prigogine 1971). No other details are known.

Threats There is a danger of increased forest clearance in the Itombwe Mountains since Kamituga has become an important mining centre, thus increasing the possibility of the area being opened up for larger-scale economic exploitation (Prigogine in press). There is probably a greater danger, however, of clearance around villages higher in the Itombwe Mountains, but there is no recent information on the conservation status of these forests (A. Prigogine *in litt.* 1983).

Conservation Measures Taken None is known other than that the species, along with all Strigiformes, is included on Appendix II of CITES, to which Zaire is a party.

Conservation Measures Proposed A preliminary conservation plan for the forests of the Itombwe Mountains has been prepared (Prigogine in press). It is hoped that this plan will be worked out in some detail and implemented by the Zairean government. A systematic search for this species is needed in the Itombwe Mountains and elsewhere in the central African highlands. Once its distribution is better known it should be possible to recommend the establishment of appropriate forest reserves.

Remarks The only other member of the genus *Phodilus* is the Bay Owl *P. badius* which is widely distributed in South-East Asia (Burton 1973). The two species are, however, less closely related to each other than was once thought to be the case (Prigogine 1973). The forests of the Itombwe Mountains are important for six other threatened bird species (see Remarks under Schouteden's Swift *Schoutedenapus schoutedeni*).

References

Burton, J. A. ed. (1973) *Owls of the world: their evolution, structure and ecology*. London: Peter Lowe.

Hall, B. P. and Moreau, R. E. (1962) A study of the rare birds of Africa. *Bull. Brit. Mus. (Nat. Hist.) Zool.* 8: 313-378.

Prigogine, A. (1971) Les oiseaux de l'Itombwe et de son hinterland, I. *Ann. Mus. Roy. Afr. Centr.* 8°, Sci. Zool. 185: 1-298.

Prigogine, A. (1973) Le statut de *Phodilus prigoginei* Schouteden. *Gerfaut* 63: 177-185.

Prigogine, A. (in press) The conservation of the avifauna of the forests of the Albertine Rift. *Proceedings of the ICBP Tropical Forest Bird Symposium, 1982*.

Schouteden, H. (1952) Un strigidé nouveau d'Afrique noire: *Phodilus prigoginei* nov. sp. *Rev. Zool. Bot. Afr.* 46: 423-428.

SOKOKE SCOPS OWL   ENDANGERED
Otus ireneae Ripley, 1966

Order STRIGIFORMES   Family STRIGIDAE
                                                Subfamily BUBONINAE

Summary Roughly a thousand pairs of this small owl are confined to one lowland forest on the Kenyan coast, portions of which have been destroyed in recent years. Forest destruction remains the major threat to the species.

Distribution The Sokoke Scops Owl is known only from the Sokoke Forest in coastal Kenya where it was discovered when one bird was collected in 1965 (Ripley 1966). By 1979 at least seven further specimens had been taken (Ripley and Bond 1971, Britton and Zimmerman 1979, specimens in NMK and BMNH: SNS). In recent years it has been seen regularly (Britton and Zimmerman 1979). About 111 km^2 of suitable habitat occurs within the Sokoke Forest Reserve (Kelsey and Langton 1984). The owl has also been known in patches of forest to the west and south of the reserve but these areas, which include the type-locality, are being cleared rapidly (Ripley and Bond 1971, Britton and Zimmerman 1979). It might occur well to the north of Sokoke in the Mundane Range near Kiunga, close to the border with Somalia, where suitable habitat is also found (Britton *et al.* in press), but this area has not been explored by ornithologists and is currently inaccessible.

Population Recent population estimates have been of 1,300-1,500 pairs (Britton 1976, Britton and Zimmerman 1979) and 1,000 pairs (Kelsey and Langton 1984). Numbers must be declining as forest clearance continues.

Ecology All records of this species come from *Cynometra-Manilkara* forest on red magarini sands (Britton and Zimmerman 1979, Britton *et al.* in press; see Remarks). In this habitat it occurs at a density of 7-8 pairs per km^2 (Britton and Zimmerman 1979). It avoids lowland rainforest and *Afzelia* forest and also the drier parts of the *Cynometra-Manilkara* forest west of Jilore where the canopy height is less than 4 m (Britton and Zimmerman 1979). The whole of Sokoke Forest has been exploited in the past for valuable timber but the owl appears to have withstood this disturbance (Britton and Zimmerman 1979). Birds are usually seen perched about 3-4 m above the ground and they normally call most frequently for two hours before dawn and for two hours after dusk (Britton and Zimmerman 1979), although some birds call throughout the night (Kelsey and Langton 1984). Stomach contents have included medium-sized Orthoptera, such as "crickets, katydids and a walkingstick", all of which are arboreal leaf-feeding forms, found well above ground (Ripley and Bond 1971).

Threats The major threat is from forest clearance. The areas of forest outside the forest reserve cannot be expected to survive for long (Britton and Zimmerman 1979). Inside the reserve the systematic logging of *Brachylaena hutchinsii* and other valuable timber trees still continues and areas of forest are also

317

being cleared to make way for expanding exotic plantations (Britton and Zimmerman 1979). The species can withstand some habitat disturbance but it seems likely that the continued degradation of the *Cynometra-Manilkara* forest will be detrimental to it (Kelsey and Langton 1984). The felling of *Brachylaena* trees, which are in great demand for the carving industry, is continuing at such a rate that stocks could be exhausted within eight years (Kelsey and Langton 1984). Unfortunately the work of forest officers has been rendered ineffective by shortage of available funds (Kelsey and Langton 1984). It seems that certain conservation regulations have been ignored by people taking advantage of the lack of supervision by officials from the Forestry Department (Kelsey and Langton 1984).

Conservation Measures Taken The Sokoke Forest Reserve covers 400 km^2 (Britton and Zimmerman 1979) though this provides only limited protection for the forest (see Threats above). The Forestry Department of the Kenyan Ministry of Natural Resources has established a 43 km^2 nature reserve inside the forest reserve in which no cutting is permitted (Britton and Zimmerman 1979); there have, however, been several recent reports of large-scale felling inside this nature reserve (Cunningham-van Someren 1981-1982, Kelsey and Langton 1984). The Sokoke Scops Owl is protected by Kenyan law (Britton *et al.* in press) and, along with all Strigiformes, is included on Appendix II of CITES, to which Kenya is a party.

Conservation Measures Proposed It is recommended that the nature reserve area be increased to 60 km^2 and that at least 200 km^2 of forest reserve surrounding the nature reserve be set aside for traditional utilisation only (Britton and Zimmerman 1979, Kelsey and Langton 1984, Britton *et al.* in press). Urgent measures are needed to halt the illegal exploitation that continues inside the existing nature reserve (Kelsey and Langton 1984). All clearance of indigenous woodland and forest at Sokoke should be rapidly phased out (Kelsey and Langton 1984). Timber from *Casuarina* plantations should be used to meet the needs of the local people for purposes such as pole-cutting and firewood: this will require improved production from existing plantations and the setting up of new but peripheral plantations (Kelsey and Langton 1984). Improved facilities for forest officers are urgently needed to enable them to carry out monitoring and enforcement duties (Kelsey and Langton 1984). Better liaison is needed between senior officials of the Forestry Department, based in Nairobi, with the officers in Sokoke, with regular visits to the reserve by the former (Kelsey and Langton 1984). It has been recommended that the forest be developed to facilitate tourism which should provide revenue for the Forestry Department (Kelsey and Langton 1984).

Remarks That the type-specimen of the Sokoke Scops Owl was collected in *Brachystegia* woodland (Britton and Zimmerman 1979) is in error: the net in which it was caught was on red magarini sand (A. D. Forbes-Waston pers. comm. 1984). The species is usually considered to form a superspecies with the West African Cinnamon Scops Owl *Otus icterorhynchus* (Ripley 1966, Snow 1978). Five other threatened bird species, the Sokoke Pipit *Anthus sokokensis*, the East Coast Akalat *Sheppardia gunningi*, the Spotted Ground--thrush *Turdus fischeri*, the

Amani Sunbird *Anthreptes pallidigaster* and Clarke's Weaver *Ploceus golandi* also occur in Sokoke Forest. One species in Appendix C, the Plain-backed Sunbird *Anthreptes reichenowi*, also occurs in Sokoke Forest. In this respect Sokoke Forest is, ornithologically, one of the most important tracts of forest requiring preservation in all Africa.

References

Britton, P. L. (1976) Primary forestland destruction now critical. *Africana* 5(12): 1-2.

Britton, P. L. and Zimmerman, D. A. (1979) The avifauna of Sokoke Forest, Kenya. *J. E. Afr. Nat. Hist. Soc. and Natn. Mus.* 169: 1-15.

Britton, P. L., Stuart, S. N. and Turner, D. A. (in press) East African endangered species. *Proc. V Pan-Afr. orn. Congr.*

Cunningham-van Someren, G. R. ed. (1981-1982) *National Museum of Kenya, Department of Ornithology Museum Avifauna News*: 19,34,63,72.

Kelsey, M. G. and Langton, T. E. S. (1984) The conservation of the Arabuko-Sokoke Forest, Kenya. International Council for Bird Preservation and University of East Anglia. *International Council for Bird Preservation Study Report* no. 4.

Ripley, S. D. (1966) A notable owlet from Kenya. *Ibis* 108: 136-137.

Ripley, S. D. and Bond, G. M. (1971) Systematic notes on a collection of birds from Kenya. *Smithsonian Contrib. Zool.* 111.

Snow, D. W. ed. (1978) *An atlas of speciation in African non-passerine birds.* London: Trustees of the British Museum (Natural History).

GRAND COMORO SCOPS OWL   RARE
Otus pauliani (Benson, 1960)

Order STRIGIFORMES   Family STRIGIDAE
                                     Subfamily BUBONINAE

Summary This small owl, whose population is likely to be small, is as yet known from only two localities in the highest forests of Mount Karthala on Grand Comoro, in the Comoro Islands; the habitat is somewhat vulnerable, and deserves to be fully protected.

Distribution The Grand Comoro Scops Owl is restricted to Grand Comoro, in the Comoro Islands, being known from La Convalescence in the upper reaches of forest on the west side of Mount Karthala, where the type and only specimen was collected and where birds were heard calling in 1958 (Benson 1960) and again in 1981 (M. Louette *in litt.* 1981); and from above Kourani at 1,450 m on the south side of Mount Karthala, where several calling birds were heard in 1983 (M. Louette *in litt.* 1984). The species is presumed to occur in the whole forest/heath integradation zone on the mountain (M. Louette *in litt.* 1984).

Population Numbers are presumably low, since at the time of discovery calling birds were listened for without success elsewhere (Benson 1960).

Ecology Although the species was originally considered restricted to primary montane evergreen forest (Benson 1960, M. Louette *in litt.* 1981), recent records of calling birds indicate that it is a bird of the forest/heath integradation zone on Mount Karthala (M. Louette *in litt.* 1984). The stomach of the single specimen collected held a few beetle remains (Benson 1960).

Threats The restricted range of this species within a notoriously vulnerable habitat (forest on a relatively small island) must be a permanent cause of concern and vigilance for its welfare. There is no habitat destruction at present, but a hiking track now under construction to the crater rim of Mount Karthala will bring many more people to higher elevations and carry the risk of being upgraded as a road, which might then increase the chances of disturbance and destruction of habitat (M. Louette *in litt.* 1984).

Conservation Measures Taken None is known other than that the species, along with all Strigiformes, is included on Appendix II of CITES, to which however the Comoro Islands are not a party.

Conservation Measures Proposed Protected area status, with a concomitant educational programme, for a representative section of the forest and heathland on Mount Karthala would enhance the prospects for survival of this species, the Grand Comoro Flycatcher *Humblotia flavirostris*, the Grand Comoro Drongo *Dicrurus fuscipennis* and the Mount Karthala White-eye *Zosterops mouroniensis* (see relevant accounts).

320

Remarks The discoverer of this form was inclined to consider it a full species, because of its distinct morphology and voice, but deferred to other opinion (see Benson 1960); after further experience of the species of which it was treated as a race (the Madagascar Scops Owl *Otus rutilus*) he re-emphasised the distinctiveness not only of its voice but also of its habitat (montane as opposed to lowland) (see Marshall 1978). The only other person to have heard it also considers it a good species (M. Louette *in litt.* 1981).

References

Benson, C. W. (1960) The birds of the Comoro Islands: results of the British Ornithologists' Union Centenary Expedition 1958. *Ibis* 103b: 5-106.

Marshall, J. T. (1978) Systematics of smaller Asian night birds based on voice. *Orn. Monog.* no. 25.

SEYCHELLES SCOPS OWL   RARE
Otus insularis (Tristram, 1880)

Order STRIGIFORMES   Family STRIGIDAE
                                                               Subfamily BUBONINAE

Summary Although this small forest owl is relatively scarce (80 or more pairs), highly elusive and certainly known from only one island in the Seychelles, it seems unlikely to be declining and a large part of its range has recently been included in a national park: nevertheless some forest exploitation is anticipated which will destroy some of its habitat.

Distribution The Seychelles Scops Owl is known only from the island of Mahé, Seychelles, where its range covers about one-third of the island; virtually all records are from secondary forest between 250 and 600 m altitude (J. Watson *in litt.* 1982). It is assumed formerly to have been distributed throughout highland and lowland forest on Mahé, before all the latter and much of the former were destroyed (Penny 1974). There is no concrete evidence of occurrence on other islands, and attempts to find birds in various parts of Praslin using voice playback, 1976-1978, all failed (J. Watson *in litt.* 1982), but "many local reports" on Praslin have been taken to indicate residence there (Diamond and Feare 1980; see also Penny 1974); one such involved calls, very like those of the species given on Mahé, heard in the Vallée de Mai in August 1976 (Evans 1977). Recent reports from Félicité possibly refer to wanderers from Praslin (Diamond and Feare 1980).

Population This bird remained so little known between its discovery in 1880 and its rediscovery around 1960 that it was omitted from a major review of Seychelles endemic birds in 1940 (Vesey-Fitzgerald 1940), and was pronounced extinct in 1958 (Greenway 1958). A specimen had in fact been collected in March 1940 but its existence, like that of the species, remained widely unrealised until 1960 (Benson 1960). Owing presumably to the sparsity of records even after its rediscovery, it was considered unlikely that more than 20 birds remained (Gaymer *et al.* 1969). However, studies in 1975-1976 established the presence of 12 pairs (distinguished by small constant individual variations in voice) in the Mission area, spaced out regularly at distances of just over 1 km, and extrapolation over the species's known range gives 80+ pairs (Watson 1980, J. Watson *in litt.* 1982), and possibly twice that number (King 1978-1979). It is possible, moreover, that numbers have recovered slightly with secondary forest regeneration (Watson 1981).

Ecology The species is found in remote high (often mist-shrouded) forest, notably in valley heads, in which it is almost exclusively nocturnal (Penny 1968, Watson 1980, J. Watson *in litt.* 1982). The diet is unknown but is expected to consist of large insects, tree-frogs and lizards (Penny 1974): stomachs of specimens have contained grasshoppers, beetle fragments, a lizard, feathers (from preening) and vegetation material (at first misidentified as mammal hairs) (Wilson 1981). The nest-site is unknown, but birds favour "boulder-fields" in forest and spend much time on or close to the ground (J. Watson *in litt.* 1982); subterranean nesting is thus conceivable (Watson 1980). Copulation is accompanied by a high-pitched whistling call; the incidence of this call is highest in October and April, and fledged young have been observed in November and June, suggesting a twice-yearly breeding cycle as in the Seychelles White-eye *Zosterops modestus* from the same habitat (Watson 1980, J. Watson *in litt.* 1982). From an observation of a group of three birds (two adults and one presumed offspring) it seems likely that clutch-size is much reduced, possibly to a single egg (Watson 1979).

Threats New extraction techniques now permit exploitation of the hitherto inaccessible patches of tall woodland in the remoter valley heads, and such sites outside the national park (see below) are no longer secure: logging of the upper Grand Bois valley, where the species is known to exist, is inevitable (Wilson 1981). It was initially feared that the introduced Barn Owl *Tyto alba* could be a competitor (Crook 1960), but this now appears wholly improbable.

Conservation Measures Taken Much of the highland forest where the Seychelles Scops Owl occurs is now incorporated in the Morne Seychellois National Park (Watson 1980). The species, along with all Strigiformes, is included on Appendix II of CITES, to which Seychelles is a party.

Conservation Measures Proposed Information on food and nesting habits of this species is clearly desirable for a fuller understanding of its conservation requirements, and an assessment of the logging schedules for the high forest on Mahé is needed to determine the degree of threat the bird faces from this quarter.

Remarks Voice analysis and comparisons have prompted the consideration that this bird is a race of the Moluccan Scops Owl *Otus magicus* (Marshall 1978), or at least forms a superspecies with it (Keith 1980). This is one of the most remarkable of the many connexions between the avifaunas of the western Indian Ocean and South-East Asia.

References

Benson, C. W. (1960) The birds of the Comoro Islands: results of the British Ornithologists' Union Centenary Expedition 1958. *Ibis* 103b: 5-106.

Crook, J. H. (1960) The present status of certain rare land birds of the Seychelles Islands. Seychelles Government Bulletin.

Diamond, A. W. and Feare, C. J. (1980) Past and present biogeography of central Seychelles birds. *Proc. IV Pan-Afr. orn. Congr.*: 89-98.

Evans, P. G. H. (1977) Aberdeen University Expedition to Praslin, Seychelles, 1976: preliminary report. Unpublished.

Gaymer, R., Blackman, R. A. A., Dawson, P. G., Penny, M. and Penny, C. M. (1969) The endemic birds of Seychelles. *Ibis* 111: 157-176.

Greenway, J. C. (1958) *Extinct and vanishing birds of the world*. New York: American Committee for International Wildlife Protection (Spec. Publ. 13).

Keith, S. (1980) Origins of the avifauna of the Malagasy Region. *Proc. IV Pan-Afr. orn. Congr.*: 99-108.

King, W. B. (1978-1979) *Red data book, 2: Aves*. 2nd edition. Morges, Switzerland: IUCN.

Marshall, J. T. (1978) Systematics of smaller Asian night birds based on voice. *Orn. Monog*. no. 25.

Penny, M. (1968) Endemic birds of the Seychelles. *Oryx* 9: 267-275.

Penny, M. (1974) *The birds of Seychelles and the outlying islands*. London: Collins.

Vesey-Fitzgerald, D. (1940) The birds of the Seychelles. I. The endemic birds. *Ibis* (14)4: 480-489.

Watson, J. (1979) Clutch sizes of Seychelles' endemic land birds. *Bull. Brit. Orn. Club* 99: 102-105.

Watson, J. (1980) The case of the vanishing owl. *Wildlife* 22: 38-39.

Watson, J. (1981) Population ecology, food and conservation of the Seychelles Kestrel (*Falco araea*) on Mahé. Ph.D. thesis, University of Aberdeen.

Wilson, J. R. (1981) Comments upon the ecology and conservation of the Seychelles Scops Owl (*Otus insularis*). Unpublished.

SAO TOME SCOPS OWL   RARE
Otus hartlaubi (Giebel, 1875)

Order STRIGIFORMES   Family STRIGIDAE
                                                  Subfamily BUBONINAE

Summary A fairly widespread but low density species, this owl is confined to forest growth on São Tomé and possibly Príncipe in the Gulf of Guinea.

Distribution The São Tomé Scops Owl is known with certainty only from São Tomé (São Tomé e Príncipe) in the Gulf of Guinea, although there are records of small owls in the north of Príncipe and near the airport (north-central Príncipe) which may refer to this species (see de Naurois 1975). On São Tomé it was recorded in the last century from São Miguel (0°08'N 6°30'E) on the south-west coast, Angolares at 100 m (0°08'N 6°39'E) on the south-east coast, and Roça Minho at 1,000 m (0°16'N 6°38'E) and Roça Saudade (0°17'N 6°38'E), both in the centre of the island (Bocage 1888,1891,1903, Sousa 1888). In 1900 it was found at Ribeira Palma (0°21'N 6°35'E) in the north-west (Salvadori 1903) and, although not reported at the time, at Agua Izé (0°13'N 6°44'E) on the east coast (de Naurois 1975). In 1928 a specimen was collected at Rio Io Grande, just to the south of Angolares (Amadon 1953, de Naurois 1975). In 1949 owls tentatively identified as of this species were seen at Zampalma (0°16'N 6°37'E) (D. W. Snow *in litt.* 1984; hence asterisk in tabulation in Snow 1950). In 1973 and 1974 the species was found in the central-north of the island at Fortunato, Chamiço, Esperança and Lake Amélia (all middle altitude, between Ribeira Palma and Roça Minho), and in the south near the lower reaches of the Rio Caué (de Naurois 1975). Thus the distribution as currently known is roughly a belt north-east of the Pico (highest point) and another (broken) belt across the lower southern slopes of the island.

Population The species is uncommon, occurring at low densities (highest at middle altitudes in the north of the island), but not rare; it has presumably disappeared from plantations at low altitudes (de Naurois 1975).

Ecology In the area where density is highest (Fortunato), habitat consists of secondary forest (not so tall or dense as mist-forest), receiving 1-3 m of rain a year (de Naurois 1975). Stomachs examined held insects (Sousa 1888), young and adult grasshoppers, beetles (chiefly Lucanidae), an adult moth and a few bones (de Naurois 1975). Specimens collected in April, May, October and November all had inactive gonads, but, though fledglings in October indicated a breeding season from the end of August to the start of October, the rainfall pattern suggests most breeding is likely in the period from September to February (de Naurois 1975).

Threats Until the species's ecology is better understood it is difficult to identify the factors that may be responsible for its absence from parts of the island or that may be currently operating against it. Hunting, cats, and the Barn Owl *Tyto alba* have been suggested as excluding it from lowland plantations (de Naurois 1975). Heavy use of pesticides on São Tomé has also been reported in the period

1963-1973 (R. de Naurois pers. comm. 1982) and this would seem a most serious threat, both direct and indirect, to the species.

Conservation Measures Taken None is known other than that the species, along with all Strigiformes, is included on Appendix II of CITES, to which however São Tomé e Príncipe is not a party.

Conservation Measures Proposed An ICBP project was developed in 1981 to investigate the status, ecology and conservation of the endemic birds of São Tomé e Príncipe, but was unable to proceed in 1982 and 1983. A study of this bird is a component of the project and conservation proposals will follow if the project goes ahead.

Remarks This species is remarkable for occurring in two phases (one ochre, the other ochre with white marbling); the absence of ear-tufts or of feathering on the rear of the tarsus has suggested affinities with certain other (mostly Asiatic) scops owls, all tentatively placed in a new sub-genus *Soter* (de Naurois 1975). The species is considered "related to nothing in Africa" (Marshall 1978).

References

Amadon, D. (1953) Avian systematics and evolution in the Gulf of Guinea. The J. G. Correia collection. *Bull. Amer. Mus. Nat. Hist.* 100: 393-451.

Bocage, J. V. B. (1888) Oiseaux nouveaux de l'Ile St.Thomé. *Jorn. Acad. Sci. Lisboa* 12: 229-232.

Bocage, J. V. B. (1891) Oiseaux de l'Ile St.Thomé. *Jorn. Acad. Sci. Lisboa* (2)2: 77-87.

Bocage, J. V. B. (1903) Contribution à la faune des quatre îles du Golfe de Guinée. IV. Ile de St.Thomé. *Jorn. Acad. Sci. Lisboa* (2)7: 65-96.

Marshall, J. T. (1978) Systematics of smaller Asian night birds based on voice. *Orn. Monog.* no. 25.

de Naurois, R. (1975) Le "Scops" de l'Ile de São Tomé *Otus hartlaubi* (Giebel). *Bonn. zool. Beitr.* 26: 319-355.

Salvadori, T. (1903) Contribuzioni alla ornitologia delle isole del Golfo di Guinea. *Mem. Reale Accad. Sci. Torino* (2)53: 1-45.

Snow, D. W. (1950) The birds of São Tomé and Príncipe in the Gulf of Guinea. *Ibis* 92: 579-595.

Sousa, J. A. (1888) Enumeração das aves conhecidas da ilha de S. Thomé seguida da lista das que existem d'esta ilha no Museu de Lisboa. *Jorn. Acad. Sci. Lisboa* 12: 151-159.

USAMBARA EAGLE OWL   RARE
Bubo vosseleri Reichenow, 1908

Order STRIGIFORMES   Family STRIGIDAE
                                           Subfamily BUBONINAE

Summary This large forest owl is known only from the Usambara Mountains, north-eastern Tanzania, where its numbers may lie between 200 and 1,000 and it may be at some risk from forest destruction.

Distribution The Usambara (or Nduk) Eagle Owl is restricted to the East and West Usambara Mountains, north-eastern Tanzania, all records being from altitudes between 900 and 1,500 m (SNS). The forest area within these altitudinal limits has been estimated to be no more than 240 km^2 (van der Willigen and Lovett 1981). All specimens of this owl have come from the Amani area, East Usambaras (e.g. White 1974), where there have been several recent sightings (*Scopus* 5 [1983]: 138). It has also been recorded in recent years on the eastern side of the West Usambaras at Ambangulu Estate (White 1974, Stuart and Turner 1980; also *Scopus* 3 [1980]: 111; 5 [1983]: 138), Balangai Estate (A. Tait pers. comm. 1981) and Mazumbai Forest (Stuart and Hutton 1977, Stuart and van der Willigen 1978, P. J. S. Olney *in litt.* 1982; also *Scopus* 4 [1981]: 108). The species is, however, very elusive (e.g. Moreau 1964, White 1974, Stuart and Hutton 1977), and its occurrence in other rain forests in eastern Tanzania cannot be entirely discounted: an owl which might have been this species was observed in the Nguru Mountains some 200 km to the south-west of the Usambaras, in the 1950s (Moreau 1964).

Population This bird had been recorded on only nine occasions up to 1977 (Stuart and Hutton 1977), but owing to an increased amount of fieldwork there have been at least 10 observations since then (SNS). There were no positive records between 1908, when it was first described (Reichenow 1908), and 1962 (Moreau 1964). Its population, never considered large, must have declined as a result of forest destruction (Stuart and Hutton 1977). The view that the population would certainly be less than 200 birds (King 1978-1979) is now thought pessimistic; a highly optimistic population density of two pairs per km^2 would give a population of less than 500 pairs (SNS).

Ecology This species inhabits evergreen montane forest. However, several young birds have been found on the ground in areas cleared for cardamom (which is generally grown under an intact forest canopy), suggesting that undisturbed forest may not be essential for its survival (White 1974). Nothing is known of the food of this owl (Moreau 1964 *contra* Mackworth-Praed and Grant 1952) nor indeed of its breeding other than that it may occur in holes (see Moreau 1964) and appears to be concentrated around November/February (Moreau 1964, White 1974).

Threats The forests of the Usambaras have suffered considerably, particularly between 1880 and 1935, from clearance for subsistence farming and also, more recently, for tea and cardamom cultivation (though cardamom may not present problems: see Ecology). In an area of 195 km² near Amani, 49% was forested in 1954, compared with only 38% in 1977 (Stuart and Hutton 1977). Two further concerns expressed are the relative scarcity of old trees with holes in which to nest, and possible competition for such sites from the widespread Silvery-cheeked Hornbill *Bycanistes brevis* (White 1974), though both these are now thought unlikely to be significant (SNS).

Conservation Measures Taken Many of the remaining forest areas within the species's range are in forest reserves, which, however, are not always as adequately protected as is desirable (SNS). The species, along with all Strigiformes, is included on Appendix II of CITES, to which Tanzania is a party.

Conservation Measures Proposed A forest conservation plan for the Usambaras is being drawn up, and will shortly be sent to the Tanzanian government for consideration (Stuart in prep.). This species is responsive to calls from captive birds (White 1974) and a population and distribution survey seems feasible using playback techniques, as has been proposed (Moreau 1964).

Remarks The Usambara population of this owl is moderately distinct in its appearance (Moreau 1964; also Olney in press), and (probably) significantly distinct in its calls (White 1974) from Fraser's Eagle Owl *Bubo poensis* which occurs from West Africa east to western Uganda, about 1,500 km distant (Hall and Moreau 1962, 1970). A bird was kept at London Zoo (U.K.) from 1962 (when it was a fledgling) until its death in 1971 (White 1974). Three others, including a definite male and female, are in captivity there now: one is the bird presented in 1971 (White 1974), now (September 1984) nearly 15 years old; the other two are nearly 12 and 10 years old, and were both found as young birds in December/January near Amani (P. J. S. Olney *in litt.* 1982; also Olney in press). Six other threatened bird species occur in the Usambara Mountains (see Remarks under the Usambara Ground Robin *Dryocichloides montanus*).

References

Hall, B.
> P. and Moreau, R. E. (1962) A study of the rare birds of Africa. *Bull. Brit. Mus. (Nat. Hist.) Zool.* 8: 313-378.

King, W. B. (1978-1979) *Red data book, 2. Aves.* 2nd. edition. Morges, Switzerland: IUCN.

Mackworth-Praed, C. W. and Grant, C. H. B. (1952) *African handbook of birds.* Series 1. The birds of eastern and north-eastern Africa, 1. London: Longmans, Green and Co.

Moreau, R. E. (1964) The re-discovery of an African owl *Bubo vosseleri. Bull. Brit. Orn. Club* 84: 47-52.

Olney, P. J. S. (in press) The rare Nduk Eagle Owl *Bubo poensis vosseleri* or *B. vosseleri.* [*Avicult. Mag.*]

Reichenow[, A.] (1908) [Die neue Art *Bubo vosseleri.*] P. 139 in K. Kothe and
O. Haase, Bericht über die 57. Jahresversammlung der Deutschen
Ornithologischen Gesellschaft 1907. *J. Orn.* 56: 122-146.

Stuart, S. N. (in prep.) A forest conservation plan for the Usambara Mountains,
Tanzania.

Stuart, S. N. and Hutton, J. M. eds. (1977) The avifauna of the East Usambara
Mountains, Tanzania. A report compiled by the Cambridge Ornithological
Expedition to East Africa, 1977. Unpublished.

Stuart, S. N. and Turner, D. A. (1980) Some range extensions and other notable
records of forest birds from eastern and northeastern Tanzania. *Scopus* 4: 36-41.

Stuart, S. N. and van der Willigen, T. A. eds. (1978) Report of the Cambridge
Ecological Expedition to Tanzania 1978. Unpublished.

White, G. B. (1974) Rarest eagle owl in trouble. *Oryx* l2: 484-486.

van der Willigen, T. A. and Lovett, J. eds. (1981) Report of the Oxford Expedition
to Tanzania, 1979. Unpublished.

RUFOUS FISHING OWL   RARE
Scotopelia ussheri Sharpe, 1871

Order STRIGIFORMES   Family STRIGIDAE
                                                             Subfamily BUBONINAE

Summary This rarely recorded species is restricted to the rainforest zone of West Africa between Ghana and Sierra Leone. It is probably threatened by forest and mangrove clearance, and also by disturbance and pollution of its presumed riverine habitats.

Distribution The Rufous Fishing Owl is confined to the rainforest zone west of the Dahomey Gap, West Africa. It presumably occurred in suitable places throughout the Upper Guinea forests between Sierra Leone and Ghana though its range must have contracted with habitat destruction. In addition to the records of this species detailed below there was also a bird in the London Zoo in the early 1960s (Thorpe and Griffin 1962); the origin of this specimen is uncertain.

Ghana The type-specimen was collected at Denkera around 1870 (Bannerman 1933) and there is another specimen from this locality in BMNH which was probably collected at about the same time (SNS). The only subsequent record from Ghana is of one collected at Dunkwa in 1941 (Bannerman 1951, Bouet 1961).

Guinea One specimen was collected at N'Zerékoré in 1951 on the Guinean side of Mount Nimba (Hald-Mortensen 1971).

Ivory Coast One captive bird has been seen in a village near Tai in south-western Ivory Coast, and owls have also been seen in the Tai National Park which could have been this species: all these observations took place between 1968 and 1973 (J.-M. Thiollay *in litt.* 1983). In 1983 there was another possible sighting in the Azagny National Park (J.-M. Thiollay *in litt.* 1983).

Liberia Eight specimens of this species have been collected in Liberia, the first on Mount Gallilee in 1888 (Büttikofer 1889). A specimen from Dou reached Chicago Museum in 1948 (Bannerman 1951, Bouet 1961) and two other birds were taken at Harbel and Ganta in 1948 (Rand 1951). Single specimens have been collected more recently, at Suehn in the 1960s (Schouteden 1970), Mount Nimba in 1967 (Colston and Curry-Lindahl in press), Degei in 1973 (Louette 1974) and Duo in 1980 (Louette 1981). In 1981 a nestling from Lofa County was brought to Monrovia Zoo (W. Gatter *in litt.* 1983).

Sierra Leone One bird was captured at Kumrabai-Mamila in 1930 (Bannerman 1931,1933, Bouet 1961). A specimen collected at Petema, near Mongeri, in 1954 is in BMNH (SNS). In 1969 one was seen close to the Ribi River near Newton, immediately to the south of the Freetown Peninsula (G. D. Field pers. comm. 1983). In 1966 a specimen was found in a freezer in the Freetown

University Zoology Laboratory, but it is not known when and where it was collected (G. D. Field pers. comm. 1983).

Population Numbers are not known though the small number of records suggests that it is rare. It is presumably declining with habitat destruction though probably often overlooked owing to its elusive nature.

Ecology Very little is known of the ecology of this species, though the few specimens appear to have been collected in forest along the edges of river and lakes (Bannerman 1933, Rand 1951, Colston and Curry-Lindahl in press). It has also been recorded in mangroves (G. D. Field pers. comm. 1983). It hunts at night and one bird was seen on a perch above a stream in high dark forest (Rand 1951). One specimen was found to have eaten a catfish (Colston and Curry-Lindahl in press).

Threats This species is likely to be threatened by forest and mangrove clearance, both of which are severe in West Africa (Dufresne and Cloutier 1982, Roth 1982, Verschuren 1982,1983, Halle 1983, G. D. Field pers. comm. 1983). There is also severe pollution, resulting from iron ore mining, in the Mano River, bordering Liberia and Sierra Leone, and the Yah River in Liberia (Verschuren 1983) which is presumably detrimental to this species. The locality in which a bird was seen in 1969 in Sierra Leone has now been cleared for rice cultivation (G. D. Field pers. comm. 1983).

Conservation Measures Taken None is known other than that the species, along with all Strigiformes, is included on Appendix II of CITES, to which Ghana, Guinea and Liberia are parties.

Conservation Measures Proposed Surveys are needed to determine whether this species occurs within some of the protected areas of rainforest in West Africa (see Remarks).

Remarks There are several parks and other protected areas in which the Rufous Fishing Owl might occur, as follows.

Ghana Bia National Park covers 30,208 ha; logging is taking place around the borders of the park (IUCN 1977).

Ivory Coast Azagny National Park, 17,000 ha, includes mangroves but is threatened by a high human population outside the park (IUCN 1977).

Banco National Park, 3,000 ha, is threatened by extensions of the Abidjan road system (IUCN 1977).

Marahoue National Park, 100,000 ha, is threatened by "industrial plantations" (IUCN 1977).

Mont Peko National Park, 34,000 ha, suffers encroachment due to a high human population density around the edges (IUCN 1977).

Mount Nimba Strict Nature Reserve, 5,000 ha, is being disturbed by iron ore mining on the Liberian side of the border (IUCN 1977).

N'Zo Fauna Reserve covers 73,000 ha; timber exploitation is permitted (IUCN 1977).

Tai National Park covers 330,000 ha. This is the largest and best preserved patch of primary forest west of the Dahomey Gap (Dufresne and Cloutier 1982, Roth 1982, Halle 1983). Illegal timbering has, however, affected about one-third of the park (Roth 1982). There are, however, plans for its increased protection (Roth 1982, Halle 1983).

Liberia Sapo National Park, 130,000 ha, was recently established (Verschuren 1982,1983). Suitable national parks have also been proposed at Loffa-Mano, 230,000 ha, and Cestos-Senkwen, 145,000 ha (Verschuren 1982,1983). The establishment of other smaller conservation areas has been recommended at Mount Nimba, the Wonegezi Mountains, Cape Mount and the Cavally Valley (Verschuren 1982,1983).

Sierra Leone Representations are being made to the government of Sierra Leone to introduce effective conservation measures in the Gola Forest as a result of WWF/IUCN Elephant Project no. 3039 (G. Merz *in litt.* 1982).

These protected areas are also likely to be of critical importance for six other threatened bird species endemic to rainforest west of the Dahomey Gap: the White-breasted Guineafowl *Agelastes meleagrides*, the Western Wattled Cuckoo-shrike *Campephaga lobata*, the Yellow-throated Olive Greenbul *Criniger olivaceus*, the White-necked Picathartes *Picathartes gymnocephalus*, the Nimba Flycatcher *Melaenornis annamarulae* and the Gola Malimbe *Malimbus ballmanni*, as well as the Yellow-footed Honeyguide *Melignomon eisentrauti*, known also from Cameroon (see relevant accounts). Of these, Tai National Park is known to hold the Guineafowl, the Olive Greenbul, the Cuckoo-shrike, the Flycatcher, and probably the Fishing Owl and the Malimbe; Mount Nimba the Greenbul, the Picathartes, the Flycatcher and at least formerly the Guineafowl; and Gola Forest the Guineafowl, the Greenbul, the Cuckoo-shrike and the Malimbe.

References

Bannerman, D. A. (1931) Account of the birds collected (i) by Mr G. L. Bates on behalf of the British Museum in Sierra Leone and French Guinea; (ii) by Lt. Col. G. J. Houghton, R.A.M.C., in Sierra Leone, recently acquired by the British Museum. Part I. *Ibis* (13)1: 661-697.

Bannerman, D. A. (1933) *The birds of tropical West Africa*, 3. London: Crown Agents for the Colonies.

Bannerman, D. A. (1951) *The birds of tropical West Africa*, 8. London: Crown Agents for the Colonies.

Bouet, G. (1961) *Oiseaux de l'Afrique tropicale*. 2me partie. Paris: Faune de l'Union Française XVII.

Büttikofer, J. (1889) Zoological researches in Liberia. Fourth list of birds. *Notes Leyden Mus.* 11: 113-138.

Colston, P. R. and Curry-Lindahl, K. (in press) The birds of the Mount Nimba region in Liberia. *Bull. Brit. Mus. (Nat. Hist.) Zool.*

Dufresne, A. and Cloutier, A. (1982) Conserving tropical rainforests in West Africa. *WWF Monthly Report* September: 257-262.

Hald-Mortensen, P. (1971) A collection of birds from Liberia and Guinea (Aves). *Steenstrupia* 1: 115-125.

Halle, M. (1983) Timber pressure on last Ivory Coast forest. *WWF News* 22: 2.

IUCN (1977) *World directory of national parks and other protected areas*. Morges, Switzerland: IUCN.

Louette, M. (1974) Contribution to the ornithology of Liberia. Part 3. *Rev. Zool. Afr.* 88: 741-748.

Louette, M. (1981) Contribution to the ornithology of Liberia. Part 5. *Rev. Zool. Afr.* 95: 342-355.

Rand, A. L. (1951) Birds from Liberia. *Fieldiana Zool.* 32: 561-653.

Roth, H. H. (1982) We all want trees – case history of the Tai National Park. 3rd World National Parks Congress, Bali, Indonesia. Unpublished.

Schouteden, H. (1970) Quelques oiseaux du Liberia. *Rev. Zool. Bot. Afr.* 82: 187-192.

Thorpe, W. H. and Griffin, D. R. (1962) The lack of ultrasonic components in the flight noise of owls compared with other birds. *Ibis* 104: 256-257.

Verschuren, J. (1982) Hope for Liberia. *Oryx* 16: 421-427.

Verschuren, J. (1983) Conservation of tropical rain forest in Liberia. Recommendations for wildlife conservation and national parks. Gland, Switzerland: IUCN/WWF.

ALBERTINE OWLET   RARE
Glaucidium albertinum Prigogine, 1983

Order STRIGIFORMES   Family STRIGIDAE
                                                Subfamily BUBONINAE

Summary This rare owl is only known from a few localities in lowland and montane forest in eastern Zaire and Rwanda. Very little is known of its biology or status.

Distribution The Albertine Owlet is known from only five specimens, four from eastern Zaire and one from Rwanda. The species was first collected at 1,120 m at Lundjulu, eastern Zaire, west of Lake Edward, in 1950 (Schouteden 1950, Prigogine 1953). Another specimen was taken at the same locality in 1953 and also in the Nyungwe (Rugege) Forest in Rwanda in the same year (Schouteden 1954). In 1966 a specimen, eventually designated as the type (Prigogine 1983), was taken at 1,690 m at Musangakye in the Itombwe Mountains, north-west of Lake Tanganyika (Prigogine 1971). The most recent record is of a specimen collected in 1981 at about 1,450 m at Munga in the Itombwe Mountains (Prigogine 1983). It is possible that this species is more widely distributed than these few records suggest.

Population Numbers are not known. The small number of collected specimens from an area which has been well explored by ornithologists is an indication that it is rare.

Ecology All specimens of this species have been collected in forest (Schouteden 1950, Prigogine 1971). It has been recorded from both lowland and montane forest (Prigogine in press). The stomach of one bird was found to contain a beetle and a grasshopper (Prigogine 1971).

Threats This species is presumably declining owing to forest clearance: the Nyungwe Forest in Rwanda has been reduced in size (Prigogine in press) and there has been forest clearance in the mountains west of Lake Edward (Prigogine in press) from where this species has been recorded (Prigogine 1953). There is a danger of increased clearance in the Itombwe Mountains since Kamituga has become an important mining centre, thus increasing the possibility of the area being opened up for larger-scale economic exploitation (Prigogine in press). There is probably a greater danger, however, of clearance around villages higher in the Itombwe Mountains, but there is no recent information on the conservation status of these forests (A. Prigogine *in litt.* 1983).

Conservation Measures Taken None is known other than that the species, along with all Strigiformes, is included on Appendix II of CITES, to which Rwanda and Zaire are parties.

Conservation Measures Proposed A preliminary conservation plan for the forests of the Itombwe Mountains has been prepared (Prigogine in press). It is hoped that this plan will be worked out in detail and implemented by the Zairean government. It is also desirable that strict forest conservation measures are introduced in the mountains west of Lake Edward and in Nyungwe Forest (Prigogine in press): the Nyungwe Forest Conservation Project should ensure the preservation of this locality for the species (J.-P. Vande weghe *in litt.* 1983).

Remarks The five known specimens of the Albertine Owlet were once considered to belong to the Chestnut Owlet *Glaucidium castaneum* but a recent study has shown that they constitute a new species (Prigogine 1983). The Chestnut Owlet is now best considered as a subspecies (but with incipient species status: see Appendix E) of the Barred Owlet *G. capense*. Six other threatened bird species occur in the Itombwe Mountains (see Remarks under Schouteden's Swift *Schoutedenapus schoutedeni*). Two other threatened species occur in the Nyungwe Forest, the Kungwe Apalis *Apalis argentea* and Grauer's Swamp Warbler *Bradypterus graueri*; the Albertine Owlet and Grauer's Swamp Warbler are also sympatric in the mountains west of Lake Edward (see relevant accounts).

References

Prigogine, A. (1953) Contribution à l'étude de la faune ornithologique de la région à l'ouest du Lac Edouard. *Ann. Mus. Roy. Congo. Belge* 8°, Sci. Zool. 24: 1-117.

Prigogine, A. (1971) Les oiseaux de l'Itombwe et de son hinterland, 1. *Ann. Mus. Roy. Afr. Centr.* 8°, Sci. Zool. 185: 1-298.

Prigogine, A. (1983) Un nouveau *Glaucidium* de l'Afrique centrale (Aves, Strigidae). *Rev. Zool. Afr.* 97: 886-895.

Prigogine, A. (in press) The conservation of the avifauna of the forests of the Albertine Rift. *Proceedings of the ICBP Tropical Forest Bird Symposium, 1982.*

Schouteden, H. (1950) *Glaucidium castaneum* Reichenow est une bonne espèce (Aves, Strigidae). *Rev. Zool. Bot. Afr.* 44: 135-137.

Schouteden, H. (1954) Quelques oiseaux de la faune Congolaise. *Rev. Zool. Bot. Afr.* 49: 353-356.

SEYCHELLES SWIFTLET   RARE
Collocalia elaphra Oberholser, 1906

Order APODIFORMES   Family APODIDAE
                                                 Subfamily APODINAE

Summary This aerial, insectivorous species, endemic to Seychelles, has a low total population (under 1,000) and its few nest-caves are highly vulnerable to disturbance or vandalism.

Distribution The Seychelles Swiftlet is apparently restricted to the islands of Mahé, Praslin and La Digue in the Seychelles. On all three of these islands birds may be expected to occur anywhere, although there are certain habitat preferences and therefore certain preferred areas (see Ecology). A factor determining distribution (or at least relative abundance) appears to be distribution of nest-caves (see Ecology). On Mahé, no nest-caves are currently known to be used: one near Le Niol reservoir appears to be now unoccupied (Watson 1984), while one in the Glacis district (on the west side of the northern arm of Mahé) is suspected – highest concentrations of birds on Mahé being seen over the boulder fields above Glacis – but not proved (Procter 1972, Watson 1984). Two possible areas for nest-caves on Mahé were identified in the late 1960s, in the mountains above Victoria and between Grand'Anse and Port Glaud (Gaymer *et al.* 1969): of these the former is confirmed by the now disused site at Le Niol (see above), but the latter (on the south-west facing coast in the central section of Mahé) remains to be investigated. On Praslin three nest-caves are known, on Fond Azore and in a river valley at L'Amitié (Evans 1977), and on the southern slopes of Mount Cabris on the Saint Sauveur estate (MacDonald 1978), this last presumably being the site that was earlier reported almost certainly to exist on the Saint Sauveur estate, where entry to confirm nests could not then be made but droppings were seen and echo-locating birds heard (Evans 1977). Nesting near Vallée de Mai, considered possible (Procter 1972), is thus confirmed, as both Fond Azore and Saint Sauveur are immediately to the south of the Vallée de Mai National Park, while L'Amitié is in the far west of Praslin. On La Digue, three "colonies" are known (Watson 1984), these presumably the two found and third reported in 1970 which evidently involved three nest-caves, all at one site in a valley on a west-facing hillside overlooking La Réunion (Procter 1972): in 1977 only two colonies were reported (MacDonald 1978). The species appears to have bred in Félicité but does not now do so (Diamond and Feare 1980, Watson 1984).

Population Although considered "common" (Loustau-Lalanne 1962) or at least "fairly abundant" on Mahé (Vesey-Fitzgerald 1936) and indeed throughout its range (Procter 1970), the species may give the impression of being far commoner than it is, since relatively large flocks occur in traditional areas (Watson 1984). However, the two La Digue colonies studied in 1977 had, at the start of July, only 10 nests (one occupied) and 35 nests (11 occupied) respectively (MacDonald 1978); the colonies on the island number no more than 80 nests in all, and those on Praslin about the same (Watson 1984) or perhaps a few more, 56 nests being counted and

152 birds estimated present at the Mount Cabris colony, 1977 (MacDonald 1978); allowing for undiscovered colonies of comparable size on Mahé, some 250 nests may be expected, and on this basis a population of less than 1,000 birds seems likely (Watson 1984).

Ecology This is an aerial, insectivorous species, and hence present over a wide variety of habitats, e.g. high over mountain forests or low across swampy ground and pools (Penny 1974). On Praslin, although seen everywhere, it is most commonly seen flying over boulder-filled valleys or rocky slopes in the hills (Evans 1977), and similarly on Mahé the most favoured locality is the boulder-fields above Glacis (Watson 1984). Birds have been noted to fly above the forest canopy in the hotter, drier parts of the day, below it in the cooler and more humid periods, presumably in response to flying height of prey (MacDonald 1978). The vast majority of food in boluses brought to feed young was flying ants, Hymenoptera in general forming over 90% of the diet, Diptera about 5% (MacDonald 1978). Although the breeding season is reportedly geared to the start of the south-east monsoon, i.e. from June to November (Penny 1974), the accumulated evidence indicates that the species may breed throughout the year (Cheke in press). Breeding is colonial, nests being built of saliva-cemented lichen or *Casuarina* needles on the roofs of deep caves among boulders (Procter 1970,1972, Mac-Donald 1978); clutch-size is one (MacDonald 1978, Watson 1979). Replacement clutches may be laid within 14 days; and a fresh clutch may appear in a nest within 14 days of a successful fledging, possibly a product of the same parents (MacDonald 1978). Birds are commonly seen in small flocks (Gaymer *et al.* 1969), gathering in larger flocks at certain localities, especially near water (Watson 1984).

Threats The greatest threat to this species is from disturbance or deliberate vandalism at the nest-caves (Watson 1984). Only some half-dozen nest-caves are known, three of them in one general locality, and two further nest-caves appear to have been deserted relatively recently for unknown or unstated reasons (see Distribution). However, occasional visits by ornithologists to one cave on La Digue over about eight years appeared not to have had an effect on the level of occupancy by the birds (Watson 1984). The problem is rather that such visits risk attracting the attention of otherwise uninterested potential vandals to a cave's existence (A. S. Cheke *in litt.* 1984).

Conservation Measures Taken A careful check on nest-caves on La Digue is kept by the island's nature reserve warden and, in the event that birds begin to desert, all inessential visits are to be stopped (Watson 1984).

Conservation Measures Proposed It is recommended that the nest-caves on Praslin be visited as little as possible, and that lockable metal grilles be emplaced at the cave entrances to prevent human access to forestall deliberate or accidental disturbance or destruction (Watson 1984, A. S. Cheke pers. comm. 1984).

Remarks The case for regarding the Seychelles Swiftlet as specifically distinct from the Mascarene Swiftlet *Collocalia francica* (Cheke in press; see Appendix C) is accepted here.

References

Cheke, A. S. (in press) The surviving native land-birds of Mauritius. In A. W. Diamond, ed. *Studies of Mascarene island birds*. Cambridge: Cambridge University Press.

Diamond, A. W. and Feare, C. J. (1980) Past and present biogeography of central Seychelles birds. *Proc. IV Pan-Afr. orn. Congr.*: 89-98.

Evans, P. G. H. ed. (1977) Aberdeen University Expedition to Praslin, Seychelles, 1976: preliminary report. Unpublished.

Gaymer, R., Blackman, R. A. A., Dawson, P. G., Penny, M. and Penny, C. M. (1969) The endemic birds of Seychelles. *Ibis* 111: 157-176.

Loustau-Lalanne, P. (1962) Land birds of the granitic islands of the Seychelles. *Seychelles Soc. Occ. Publ.* 1.

MacDonald, R. A. (1978) The biology of the Seychelles Cave Swiftlet *Aerodramus (francicus) elaphrus*. Pp. 92-112 in P. A. Racey, ed. 1977 Aberdeen University Expedition to the Seychelles Report. Unpublished.

Newton, E. (1867) On the land-birds of the Seychelles archipelago. *Ibis* (2)3: 335-360.

Penny, M. (1974) *The birds of Seychelles and the outlying islands*. London: Collins.

Procter, J. (1970) Conservation in the Seychelles. Report of the Conservation Adviser 1970. [Victoria, Mahé: Government Printer.]

Procter, J. (1972) The nest and the identity of the Seychelles swiftlet *Collocalia*. *Ibis* 114: 272-273.

Vesey-Fitzgerald, D. (1936) Birds of the Seychelles and other islands included within that colony. Victoria (Mahé, Seychelles): Government Printing Office.

Watson, J. (1979) Clutch sizes of Seychelles' endemic land birds. *Bull. Brit. Orn. Club* 99: 102-105.

Watson, J. (1984) Land birds: endangered species on the granitic Seychelles. In D. R. Stoddart, ed. Biogeography and ecology in the Seychelles. *Monog. Biol.* 55: 513-527.

SCHOUTEDEN'S SWIFT   INDETERMINATE
Schoutedenapus schoutedeni (Prigogine, 1960)

Order APODIFORMES   Family APODIDAE
                                                        Subfamily APODINAE

Summary This swift is known only from low and intermediate altitudes to the east and north-east of the Itombwe Mountains in eastern Zaire. Very little is known of its status or habitat requirements.

Distribution Schouteden's Swift was described in 1960 on the basis of two specimens collected in 1959 at Butokolo at 1,470 m on Mount Nyombwe, to the north-east of the main Itombwe Mountain block, in eastern Zaire (Prigogine 1960). It was subsequently reported that another specimen had been collected at Mubandakila on the eastern slopes of the Itombwe Mountains in 1956 (Schouteden 1968, Brooke 1971a), though some other publications make no mention of the species's occurrence at this locality (see Prigogine 1971,1978). It has only been recently confirmed that this specimen belongs to this species (A. Prigogine *in litt.* 1984). The only subsequent records are of two specimens collected, one at Bionga in 1970 and the other at 1,000 m near Kamituga in 1972 (Prigogine 1978). Both of these localities are on the lower eastern slopes of the Itombwe Mountains (Prigogine 1971,1978).

Population Numbers are not known, but the fact that there are only five records of this species in an area which has been well studied by ornithologists suggests that it is rare.

Ecology This species has only been found in forest clearings at low and intermediate elevations (Prigogine in press). The two specimens collected in 1959 were in a flock of about 20 swifts which also included a larger species, probably the Scarce Swift *Schoutedenapus myoptilus* (Prigogine 1960,1971). The specimens collected so far were taken in the months February, June and October (Prigogine 1960,1978, Brooke 1971a), suggesting that the species is resident in the Itombwe area and does not undertake any long-distance movements. Breeding takes place in February or March at the same time as the Scarce Swift in this area (Prigogine 1978).

Threats It is not known to what extent this is a forest-dependent species but since it has always been found near forest it is likely that clearance will adversely affect it. There is a danger of increased clearance in the Itombwe Mountains since Kamituga has become an important mining centre, thus increasing the possibility of the area being opened up for larger-scale economic exploitation (Prigogine in press).

Conservation Measures Taken None is known.

Conservation Measures Proposed A preliminary conservation plan for the forests of the Itombwe Mountains has been prepared (Prigogine in press). It is hoped that this plan will be worked out in detail and implemented by the Zairean government. Further fieldwork is required on Schouteden's Swift to determine what measures would be most appropriate for its conservation.

Remarks The details of the taxonomic history of this species are given in Prigogine (1960) and Brooke (1971a,b). Schouteden's Swift is sympatric with the Scarce Swift, the only other member of its genus (Brooke 1971a,b). The forests of the Itombwe Mountains are important for six other threatened bird species, the Albertine Owlet *Glaucidium albertinum*, Itombwe Owl *Phodilus prigoginei*, African Green Broadbill *Pseudocalyptomena graueri*, Forest Ground-thrush *Turdus oberlaenderi*, Chapin's Flycatcher *Muscicapa lendu* and Rockefeller's Sunbird *Nectarinia rockefelleri* (see relevant accounts).

References

Brooke, R. K. (1971a) Geographical variation and distribution in the swift genus *Schoutedenapus*. *Bull. Brit. Orn. Club* 91: 25-28.

Brooke, R. K. (1971b) Taxonomic history of *Schoutedenapus schoutedeni*. *Bull. Brit. Orn. Club* 91: 93-94.

Prigogine, A. (1960) Un nouveau martinet du Congo. *Rev. Zool. Bot. Afr.* 62: 103-105.

Prigogine, A. (1971) Les oiseaux de l'Itombwe et de son hinterland. Volume I. *Ann. Mus. Roy. Afr. Centr.* 8°, Sci. Zool. 185: 1-298.

Prigogine, A. (1978) Les oiseaux de l'Itombwe et de son hinterland. Volume II. *Ann. Mus. Roy. Afr. Centr.* 8°, Sci. Zool. 223: 1-134.

Prigogine, A. (in press) The conservation of the avifauna of the forests of the Albertine Rift. *Proceedings of the ICBP Tropical Forest Bird Symposium, 1982.*

Schouteden, H. (1968) La faune ornithologique du Kivu 1. Non passereaux. *Doc. Zool. Mus. Roy. Afr. Centr.* 12.

FERNANDO PO SWIFT   INSUFFICIENTLY KNOWN
Apus sladeniae (Ogilvie-Grant, 1904)

Order APODIFORMES   Family APODIDAE
                                            Subfamily APODINAE

Summary This species is known from only ten specimens from Fernando Po, Cameroon, Nigeria and Angola. Very little is known of its status.

Distribution The Fernando Po Swift is known only from a few widely scattered localities in West Africa and one in Angola. It was discovered on Fernando Po (Bioko) Island in Equatorial Guinea in 1903-1904 when six specimens were collected at Fishtown (Ogilvie-Grant 1904, Bannerman 1933). There have been no subsequent records from Fernando Po (Basilio 1963). There is one record from Cameroon where a bird, originally described as a separate species *Apus melanotus* in 1907 (Reichenow 1907), was collected at Bakossi, near Mounts Kupe and Manengouba (de Roo 1970). Sixteen specimens collected in southern Cameroon, probably in the 1940s, and originally assigned to this species (Good 1952) have been shown to be the European Swift *A. apus* (Brooke and Traylor 1967, de Roo 1970). Conversely a Fernando Po Swift collected in 1961 on the Obudu Plateau in eastern Nigeria was originally misidentified as a European Swift (Parker 1971). It has been suggested that the species breeds on Fernando Po and visits the mainland in the non-breeding season (Bannerman 1933). However, it is now known that a population (presumed to be resident) also exists on Mount Môco in Angola, two specimens having been collected there in 1931 and originally misidentified as African Black Swifts *A. barbatus roehli* (Traylor 1960, Brooke 1970).

Population Numbers are not known. The species is very difficult to identify and must, therefore, be often overlooked.

Ecology Virtually nothing is known. Birds collected on Fernando Po in late December and early January were in breeding condition (Ogilvie-Grant 1904, Bannerman 1933).

Threats None is known.

Conservation Measures Taken None is known.

Conservation Measures Proposed Surveys would be helpful, especially on Fernando Po and in Angola, to assess the status of this species and to determine whether conservation action is necessary.

Remarks Although often treated as a subspecies of the African Black Swift, the Fernando Po Swift is now considered a separate species by some authorities (e.g. de Roo 1970, Snow 1978).

References

Bannerman, D. A. (1933) *The birds of tropical West Africa*, 3. London: Crown Agents for the Colonies.

Basilio, A. (1963) *Aves de la Isla de Fernando Poo*. Madrid: Editorial Coculsa.

Brooke, R. K. (1970) Geographical variation and distribution in *Apus barbatus, A. bradfieldi* and *A. niansae* (Aves: Apodidae). *Durban Mus. Novit.* 8: 363-374.

Brooke, R. K. and Traylor, M. A. (1967) *Apus apus apus* in the Cameroons. *Bull. Brit. Orn. Club* 87: 124-125.

Good, A. I. (1952) The birds of French Cameroon. Part 1. *Mem. Inst. Fr. Afr. Noire*, Ser. Nat. Sci. 2: 11-203.

Ogilvie-Grant, W. R. (1904) [Two new species . . . from Fernando Po.] *Bull. Brit. Orn. Club* 14: 55-56.

Parker, R. H. (1971) Fernando Poo Black Swift *Apus barbatus sladeniae* (Ogilvie-Grant) recorded from Nigeria. *Bull. Brit. Orn. Club* 91: 152-153.

Reichenow, A. (1907) Zwei neue afrikanische Arten. *Orn. Monatsber.* 15: 60.

de Roo, A. E. M. (1970) A new race of the African Black Swift *Apus barbatus* (Sclater) from the Republic of Cameroon (Aves: Apodidae). *Rev. Zool. Bot. Afr.* 81: 156-162.

Snow, D. W. ed. (1978) *An atlas of speciation in African non-passerine birds*. London: Trustees of the British Museum (Natural History).

Traylor, M. A. (1960) Notes on the birds of Angola, non-passeres. *Publ. cult. Co. Diam. Angola, Lisboa* no. 51: 129-186.

SHORT-LEGGED GROUND-ROLLER   RARE

Brachypteracias leptosomus (Lesson, 1833)

Order CORACIIFORMES   Family BRACHYPTERACIIDAE

Summary This ground-roller is confined to deep rainforest in the centre and north-east of Madagascar, and is widely considered rare. It is threatened by forest destruction.

Distribution On current limited knowledge, the Short-legged Ground-roller occurs in two discrete general areas of Madagascar, in the north-east (Marojejy to around Maroantsetra) and central-east (chiefly Sihanaka forest). Records from the north-east are from the Marojejy Nature Reserve, September 1972 (Benson *et al.* 1976), around Antanombo Manandriana, one day's march west of Andapa, 1930 (Delacour 1932a, Rand 1932,1936), around "Ambolumaraha-vany" (see Remarks), two days' march north-east of Maroantsetra, 1930 (Delacour 1932a, Rand 1932,1936), and around Bevato, 40 km north-west of Maroantsetra, 1930 (Delacour 1932a, Rand 1932,1936), Maroantsetra (specimen in SMF: NJC), Mananara, November 1876, and Savary (for location of which see Distribution under Brown Mesite *Mesitornis unicolor*), November 1877 to April 1878 (specimens in RMNH: NJC), and from the Masoala peninsula (Turner in press). In the central-east, the species is known from Sihanaka forest (Delacour 1932a), Périnet, August 1982, at 950 m (O. Langrand *in litt.* 1984), the Tamatave region, September 1913 (specimen in SMF: NJC), Fanovana (Delacour 1932a) and the east Imerina forest (Wills 1893, Oberholser 1900), these last two areas having now been cleared (D. A. Turner pers. comm. 1983) as presumably has that around Tamatave. There is also a record from near Ampasimbe (Newton 1863; see Remarks), and a skin in BMNH, undated and labelled "Sambririna": no such locality can be traced (in Office of Geography 1955), but the possibility that "Sambirano" is intended – i.e. the area of humid forest in the far north-west – cannot be ignored. Two other localities, "Ambore" and "Ankoraka Sahamben-drana" (specimens in ZFMK and MNHN respectively: NJC) cannot be traced.

Population This species has been considered commoner than the largely sympatric Scaly Ground-roller *Brachypteracias squamiger* (see relevant account), and over two years 42 specimens were collected or acquired as against 20 of the latter (Delacour 1932a,b). Nevertheless the Short-legged Ground-roller has a somewhat more restricted range and within this has consistently been regarded as rare in some degree (Hartlaub 1877, Milne Edwards and Grandidier 1881, Rand 1936, Lavauden 1937, Milon *et al.* 1973). A recent study has suggested that all ground-rollers have been thought rarer than they are, since their silence and secretive behaviour lead them to be "completely overlooked"; this species is considered "shy though not uncommon" (Turner in press).

Ecology It inhabits heavy rainforest, "frequenting low, wet places where the trees cast a continual shade and the ground-cover of spindly saplings leaves the damp forest floor nearly bare" (Rand 1936). Although it is considered terrestrial,

343

one observation was of a bird that perched on horizontal strands of vines and in small trees, remaining immobile for minutes on end, with short fast flights between perches (Benson *et al.* 1976), another was of a bird which, when flushed from the ground, flew up to a tree and hid behind branches (Dresser 1893), while a recent study suggests it is in fact much the most arboreal of the ground-rollers (Turner in press). It has been reported to scratch at moss and dead leaves with its feet like a gallinaceous bird, to uncover beetles, ants, larvae, millipedes, pill-millipedes, ant-lions, worms and small reptiles (Milne Edwards and Grandidier 1881; hence Milon *et al.* 1973). Of eight stomachs, one held a snake; two, chameleons; one, beetles; two, caterpillars; four, other insects; one, a snail (Rand 1936). Two other stomachs held large ants plus beetle remains (Milon *et al.* 1973) and tenebrionid beetles (Benson *et al.* 1976) respectively. Natives reported it to be a night-feeding bird (Sharpe 1871) and it is said to be at least partly nocturnal (Hildebrandt 1881) and locatable in the early morning and evening (Milne Edwards and Grandidier 1881). It is solitary except in breeding season, when it occurs in pairs (Milne Edwards and Grandidier 1881). Birds breed in December, excavating the nest in a tunnel (c. 1 m) in a bank (Milon *et al.* 1973); they are also reported to nest in holes in trees (Dresser 1893).

Threats Destruction and disturbánce of primary rainforest is the single most serious threat to this and all other rainforest-dependent species in Madagascar (see Threats under Madagascar Serpent Eagle *Eutriorchis astur*).

Conservation Measures Taken The species occurs in the Marojejy Nature Reserve (R.N.I. no. 12), which covers 60,150 ha, and in the Périnet-Analama-zaotra Special Reserve, which covers 810 ha (Andriamampianina 1981).

Conservation Measures Proposed Full protection for all ground-rollers has been called for (Salvan 1970). Immediate and effective protection of as much remaining rainforest as possible would almost certainly guarantee the survival of this and all other rainforest-dependent species in Madagascar; and at least, on current knowledge, complete protection of the intact parts of Sihanaka forest is of extreme importance (see Conservation Measures Proposed under Madagascar Serpent Eagle). Any ornithological work in the other areas from which the species is known, or where it might be expected, should where possible be extended to include searches to locate it. This species requires study to determine the basic aspects of its ecology and whether or not it is migratory: in view of native reports that it hibernates (Dresser 1893), it seems likely that some movement takes place, and an understanding of this may be crucial to its long-term conservation.

Remarks From context, Ampasimbe is evidently the locality on the main road from Antananarivo to Andevoranto, at 18°58'S 48°40'E, well outside the main rainforest block (see Office of Geography 1955, IGNT 1964); however, an earlier map indicates that a small belt of forest, named Madilo, crossed the road near Ampasimbe (see Locamus 1900), though this is presumably now all cleared. "Ambolumarahavary" is presumably identical to "Ambohimarahavary" (see Distribution under Madagascar Serpent Eagle) and is probably, correctly,

"Ambolomirahavavy" (J. T. Hardyman *in litt.* 1984), though in fact none of these names can be traced.

References

Andriamampianina, J. (1981) Les réserves naturelles et la protection de la nature à Madagascar. Pp. 105-111 in P. Oberlé, ed. *Madagascar, un sanctuaire de la nature.* Paris: Lechevalier.

Benson, C. W., Colebrook-Robjent, J. F. R. and Williams, A. (1976) Contribution à l'ornithologie de Madagascar. *Oiseau et R.F.O.* 46: 209-242.

Delacour, J. (1932a) Les oiseaux de la Mission Franco-Anglo-Américaine à Madagascar. *Oiseau et R.F.O.* 2: 1-96.

Delacour, J. (1932b) La Mission Zoologique Franco-Anglo-Américaine à Madagascar. *Bull. Mus. Natn. Hist. Nat.* (2)4: 212-219.

Dresser, H. E. (1893). *A monograph of the Coraciidae, or family of the rollers.* Farnborough, Kent.

Hartlaub, G. (1877) *Die Vögel Madagascars und der benachbarten Inselgruppen.* Halle.

Hildebrandt, J. M. (1881) Skizze zu einem Bilde central-madagassischen Naturlebens im Frühling. *Z. Ges. Erdk. Berlin* 16: 194-203.

Institut Géographique National à Tananarive (1964) Carte de Madagascar, 1: 500,000, Type 1963. Tananarive.

Lavauden, L. (1937) Supplément. A. Milne Edwards and A. Grandidier, *Histoire physique, naturelle et politique de Madagascar, 12. Oiseaux.* Paris: Société d'Editions Géographiques, Maritimes et Coloniales.

Locamus, P. (1900) Carte de Madagascar, 1: 500,000. Paris.

Milne Edwards, A. and Grandidier, A. (1881) *Histoire physique, naturelle et politique de Madagascar, 12. Histoire naturelle des oiseaux.* Tome I. Paris.

Milon, P., Petter, J.-J. and Randrianasolo, G. (1973) *Faune de Madagascar, 35. Oiseaux.* Tananarive and Paris: ORSTOM and CNRS.

Newton, E. (1863) Notes of a second visit to Madagascar. *Ibis* 5: 333-350.

Oberholser, H. C. (1900) Catalogue of a collection of birds from Madagascar. *Proc. U. S. Natn. Mus.* 22: 235-248.

Office of Geography (1955) *Gazetteer no. 2. Madagascar, Réunion and the Comoro Islands.* Washington, D. C.: Department of the Interior.

Rand, A. L. (1932) Mission Franco-Anglo-Américaine à Madagascar: notes de voyage. *Oiseau et R.F.O.* 2: 227-282.

Rand, A. L. (1936) The distribution and habits of Madagascar birds. *Bull. Amer. Mus. Nat. Hist.* 72: 143-499.

Salvan, J. (1970). Remarques sur l'évolution de l'avifauna malgache depuis 1945. *Alauda* 38: 191-203.

Sharpe, R. B. (1871) On the Coraciidae of the Ethiopian Region. *Ibis* (3)1: 270-289.

Turner, D. A. (in press) The ground rollers of Madagascar. *Proc. V Pan-Afr. orn. Congr.*

Wills, J. (1893) Notes on some Malagasy birds rarely seen in the interior. *Antananarivo Annual* 5 (no. 17): 119-120.

SCALY GROUND-ROLLER   RARE

Brachypteracias squamiger Lafresnaye, 1838

Order CORACIIFORMES   Family BRACHYPTERACIIDAE

Summary This ground-roller is confined to deep rainforest in the centre and north-east of Madagascar, and is widely considered rare. It is threatened by forest destruction, by village dogs and by human exploitation for food.

Distribution The Scaly Ground-roller occurs throughout the eastern rainforests of Madagascar. Records are from (north to south) Marojejy (Benson *et al.* 1976), Andapa (Rand 1936), around Maroantsetra (Rand 1936, O. Langrand *in litt.* 1984; see Remarks), "Mointenbato" (Fisher 1981), i.e. Maintimbato, and Savary (for location of both see Distribution under Brown Mesite *Mesitornis unicolor*), December 1877 to April 1878 (specimens in RMNH and MNHN: NJC), the Masoala peninsula (B.-U. Meyburg pers. comm. 1983, Turner in press), the Soamianina (= "Semiang", "Tsimianona") River (type-locality, opposite Ile de Sainte-Marie) (Hartlaub 1877, Milne Edwards and Grandidier 1881), Sihanaka forest (Delacour 1932, Rand 1936), Périnet (Webb 1954), Analamazaotra (specimen in Grenoble: O. Langrand *in litt.* 1984), Rogez (Benson *et al.* 1976), the Tamatave region, July 1912 and October 1913 (specimens in MNHN and SMF: NJC) and south-east Madagascar (Dresser 1893). Its occurrence in the south-east has been entirely overlooked this century, but was substantiated by four specimens (see Dresser 1893). One specimen in BMNH is labelled "Voolaly, S. E. Madagascar" (untraceable) and dated February 1872 (NJC); another in SMF was collected on 8 October 1931 at Emintiminy, south-east Madagascar (NJC), gazetteered as at 24°41'S 46°48'E (Office of Geography 1955) and mapped as on the eastern boundary of the Andohahela Nature Reserve (in IGNT 1964). Of two specimens in BMNH collected by J. Audebert and dated February 1879, one has an illegible label (see Remarks), while the other is from "Antsondririna" (NJC): the only gazetteered locality of this name is in the far north-east, at 13°00'S 49°41'E (Office of Geography 1955), and thus much the most northerly record (if correct) for the species.

Population This species has been widely considered rare in some degree: "very rare" (Sganzin 1840), "quite rare" (Milne Edwards and Grandidier 1881), "everywhere rare" (Rand 1936; also Delacour 1932). Nonetheless, a recent study has suggested that all ground-rollers have been thought rarer than they are, since their silence and secretive behaviour leads them to be "completely overlooked" (Turner in press). The species was seen almost daily on the Masoala peninsula in October 1980 (B.-U. Meyburg pers. comm. 1983).

Ecology The Scaly Ground-roller is a ground-adapted bird of heavy, deep-shaded rainforest with sparse undergrowth (Rand 1936; also Hartlaub 1877, Benson *et al.* 1976), considered the terrestrial counterpart of the somewhat arboreal Short-legged Ground-roller *Brachypteracias leptosomus* (see relevant account); when disturbed, it either flies a few yards or runs a few steps, then stands quietly watching the intruder (Turner in press). Native reports that it is nocturnal (Sharpe 1871) have not been proven; and though several ground-rollers appear to be most active at dusk (Turner in press), recent observations on this species suggested it to be active throughout the day (O. Langrand *in litt.* 1984). Of five stomachs, four contained large terrestrial insects, one a spider (Rand 1936); another held ants and scarabaeid beetles (Benson *et al.* 1976). Prey seen taken includes ground-beetles, ants, caterpillars, centipedes, earthworms, snails, small frogs; Lepidoptera and Diptera are also hawked in flight; whether or not the Short-legged Ground-roller scrapes at the leaf-litter with its feet to uncover its prey, as reported (see relevant account), the Scaly Ground-roller only ever uses its bill for such purposes (O. Langrand *in litt.* 1984). Breeding evidently occurs in September (see Benson *et al.* 1976); a nest-hole probably of this species consisted of a tunnel less than a metre long, with a chamber lined with dead leaves and earthy pellets, built into a bare, sloping bank in deep forest (Benson *et al.* 1976). A nest with young was found on 4 November 1982, 50 km north-west of Maroantsetra at 350 m (O. Langrand *in litt.* 1984).

Threats Destruction and disturbance of primary rainforest is the single most serious threat to this and all other rainforest-dependent species in Madagascar (see Threats under Madagascar Serpent Eagle *Eutriorchis astur*). The species is also threatened by young villagers, who trap birds and catch them in the nest, and by village dogs which also catch birds (O. Langrand *in litt.* 1984).

Conservation Measures Taken The species occurs in the Marojejy Nature Reserve (R.N.I. no. 12), which covers 60,150 ha, and presumably in the Périnet-Analamazaotra Special Reserve, which covers 810 ha, and the Andohahela Nature Reserve (R.N.I. no. 11), which covers 76,020 ha (Andriamampianina 1981).

Conservation Measures Proposed Full protection for all ground-rollers has been called for (Salvan 1970). Immediate and effective protection of as much remaining rainforest as possible would almost certainly guarantee the survival of this and all other rainforest-dependent species in Madagascar; and at least, on current knowledge, complete protection of the intact parts of Sihanaka forest is of extreme importance (see Conservation Measures Proposed under Madagascar Serpent Eagle). Any ornithological work in the other areas from which the species is known, or where it might be expected, should where possible be extended to include searches to locate it.

Remarks For exact localities where the species has been found around Maroantsetra, see Rand (1932). The illegible locality on the Audebert label (see Distribution) is possibly "Ampirina", but no such name has been traced (on Locamus 1900 or in Office of Geography 1955), although it must be fairly close to Antsondririna to have been visited in the same month in 1879.

References

Andriamampianina, J. (1981) Les réserves naturelles et la protection de la nature à Madagascar. Pp. 105-111 in P. Oberlé, ed. *Madagascar, un sanctuaire de la nature*. Paris: Lechevalier.

Benson, C. W., Colebrook-Robjent, J. F. R. and Williams, A. (1976) Contribution à l'ornithologie de Madagascar. *Oiseau et R.F.O.* 46: 209-242.

Delacour, J. (1932) Les oiseaux de la Mission Franco-Anglo-Américaine à Madagascar. *Oiseau et R.F.O.* 2: 1-96.

Dresser, H. E. (1893) *A monograph of the Coraciidae, or family of the rollers*. Farnborough, Kent.

Fisher, C. T. (1981) Specimens of extinct, endangered or rare birds in the Merseyside County Museums, Liverpool. *Bull. Brit. Orn. Club* 101: 276-285.

Hartlaub, G. (1877) *Die Vögel Madagascars und der benachbarten Inselgruppen*. Halle.

Institut Géographique National à Tananarive (1964) Carte de Madagascar, 1: 500,000, Type 1963. Tananarive.

Locamus, P. (1900) Carte de Madagascar, 1: 500,000. Paris.

Milne Edwards, A. and Grandidier, A. (1881) *Histoire physique, naturelle et politique de Madagascar, 12. Histoire naturelle des oiseaux*. Tome I. Paris.

Office of Geography (1955) *Gazetteer no. 2. Madagascar, Réunion and the Comoro Islands*. Washington, D.C.: Department of the Interior.

Rand, A. L. (1932) Mission Franco-Anglo-Américaine à Madagascar: notes de voyage. *Oiseau et R.F.O.* 2: 227-282.

Rand, A. L. (1936) The distribution and habits of Madagascar birds. *Bull. Amer. Mus. Nat. Hist.* 72: 143-499.

Salvan, J. (1970) Remarques sur l'évolution de l'avifauna malgache depuis 1945. *Alauda* 38: 191-203.

Sganzin, V. (1840) Notes sur les mammifères et sur l'ornithologie de l'île de Madagascar (1831 et 1832). *Mém. Soc. Mus. Hist. Nat. Strasbourg* 3(1), article 3: 1-49.

Sharpe, R. B. (1871) On the Coraciidae of the Ethiopian Region. *Ibis* (3)1: 270-289.

Turner, D. A. (in press) The ground rollers of Madagascar. *Proc. V Pan-Afr. orn. Congr.*

Webb, C. S. (1954) *A wanderer in the wind*. London: Hutchinson.

Madagascar Serpent Eagle

White-breasted Guineafowl

Pink Pigeon

Long-tailed Ground-roller

Norman Arlott '84.

African Green Broadbill

Western Wattled Cuckoo-shrike

Mount Kupe Bush-shrike

White-headed Robin-chat

Thyolo Alethe

Rufous-winged Sunbird

Yellow-throated Serin

Golden-naped Weaver

RUFOUS-HEADED GROUND-ROLLER   RARE

Atelornis crossleyi Sharpe, 1875

Order CORACIIFORMES   Family BRACHYPTERACIIDAE

Summary This ground-roller is confined to deep rainforest in the centre and north-east of Madagascar, and is widely considered rare. It is threatened by forest destruction.

Distribution On current limited knowledge, the Rufous-headed Ground-roller occurs in two discrete general areas of Madagascar, in the north-east (Tsaratanana massif, Marojejy Reserve, and Andapa) and central-east (in a circle whose diameter runs from Antananarivo to Tamatave); it has also been recorded in two more southerly general forest areas in south-central Madagascar. Records from the north-east appear to be based on only three specimens, one from Tsaratanana massif at 1,500 m in 1966 (Albignac 1970), one from Ambodifiakarana, in the Marojejy Nature Reserve, at 1,600 m in 1958 (Griveaud 1960, Benson *et al.* 1976), and one from Antanombo Manandriana, one day's march west of Andapa, at around 1,800 m in 1930 (Delacour 1932, Rand 1932,1936). The bird is next recorded some 400 km to the south from the Sihanaka forest (Delacour 1932, Rand 1936), including Didy (Milon *et al.* 1973) and Fito (Benson *et al.* 1976; specimens in MNHN: NJC). Birds have also been seen, collected or acquired from natives in "Forêt Ruanaka" (untraceable: possibly a mistake for "Sianaka") in the Brickaville district, Vohibazaha forest and Lakato forest (specimens in MRAC: NJC), Analamazaotra, and near Périnet (Lavauden 1932, O. Langrand *in litt.* 1984, A. D. Forbes-Watson pers. comm. 1984; see Conservation Measures Taken), Fanovana (Delacour 1932) and the east Imerina forest (Dresser 1893, Rothschild 1895, Oberholser 1900), though this and the forest at Fanovana are now cleared (D. A. Turner pers. comm. 1983). The type-locality, first reported as "Ampas-monhavo" (Sharpe 1875), then "Ampasimanavy" (Milne Edwards and Grandidier 1881), is almost certainly therefore Ampasimaneva, on the Mangoro River, at 19°24'S 48°04'E (see Remarks under Madagascar Serpent Eagle *Eutriorchis astur*). The most southerly records are from south-central Madagascar in "the forest land that lies between the Betsileo and Tanala ... [which] covers the eastern side of the mountains along the edge of the central plateau ... [and] is thick and dense, about fifteen or twenty miles in width" (Deans Cowan 1882) and, in 1984, from the Vondrozo region (O. Langrand pers. comm. 1984).

Population The species is widely considered rare in some degree (Richmond 1897, Lavauden 1932, Rand 1936, Griveaud 1960) but, from the number of skins in one local collection around 1930, it was evidently then "not uncommon" in Sihanaka forest (Rand 1936; also Delacour 1932) and indeed "not rare" at Didy, presumably around 1970 (Milon *et al.* 1973). It was listed as common in the Betsileo/Tanala border forest a century ago (Deans Cowan 1882). A recent study has suggested that all ground-rollers have been thought rarer than they are, since their silence and secretive behaviour lead them to be "completely overlooked"; however this is considered the rarest and least known species (Turner in press), a view endorsed by recent observations (O. Langrand *in litt.* 1984).

Ecology "This bird probably frequents the ground in the heavy forest; one stomach examined contained insect remains" (Rand 1936). It is reported to nest in holes in the ground (Dresser 1893). A not fully grown bird collected in late March (specimen in MNHN: NJC) suggests a December/January breeding season. In central-east Madagascar, the species seemingly disappears during the winter months (May/August) (Dresser 1893), though there are in fact specimens (in BMNH, MNHN and SMNS) from Sihanaka taken in May and August (NJC). There appears to be no other information specifically on this bird, although it has been listed as characteristic of secondary forest dominated by *Ravenala madagascariensis*, such forest mostly occurring from sea-level to 500 m (Lavauden 1937); the basis and validity of this assertion are unknown.

Threats Destruction and disturbance of primary rainforest is the single most serious threat to this and all other rainforest-dependent species in Madagascar (see Threats under Madagascar Serpent Eagle). Two areas of forest where it was known to occur have been felled (see Distribution).

Conservation Measures Taken The species evidently occurs in both the Marojejy Nature Reserve (R.N.I. no. 12), which covers 60,150 ha, and the Tsaratanana Nature Reserve (R.N.I. no. 4), which covers 48,622 ha (Andriamampianina 1981), although its status in both (one record each) appears precarious. Observation of this ground-roller several kilometres from and c. 100 m higher than the Périnet-Analamazaotra Special Reserve has been taken to suggest that the reserve may be too low to be of great value in helping to preserve this species (A. D. Forbes-Watson pers. comm. 1984).

Conservation Measures Proposed Full protection for all ground-rollers has been called for (Salvan 1970). Immediate and effective protection of as much remaining rainforest as possible would almost certainly guarantee the survival of this and all other rainforest-dependent species in Madagascar; and at least, on current knowledge, complete protection of the intact parts of Sihanaka forest is of extreme importance (see Conservation Measures Proposed under Madagascar Serpent Eagle). Any ornithological work in the other areas from which the species is known, or where it might be expected, should where possible be extended to include searches to locate it. This species requires study to determine the basic aspects of its ecology, particularly in relation to its apparent migrations (see Ecology above), an understanding of which is probably crucial to its long-term survival.

References

Albignac, R. (1970) Mammifères et oiseaux du Massif du Tsaratanana. *Mém. ORSTOM* 37: 223-229.

Andriamampianina, J. (1981) Les réserves naturelles et la protection de la nature à

Madagascar. Pp. 105-111 in P. Oberlé, ed. *Madagascar, un sanctuaire de la nature*. Paris: Lechevalier.

Benson, C. W., Colebrook-Robjent, J. F. R. and Williams, A. (1976) Contribution à l'ornithologie de Madagascar. *Oiseau et R.F.O.* 46: 209-242.

Deans Cowan, W. (1882) Notes on the natural history of Madagascar. *Proc. Roy. Phys. Soc. Edinburgh* 7: 133-150.

Delacour, J. (1932) Les oiseaux de la Mission Franco-Anglo-Américaine à Madagascar. *Oiseau et R.F.O.* 2: 1-96.

Dresser, H. E. (1893) *A monograph of the Coraciidae, or family of the rollers*. Farnborough, Kent.

Griveaud, P. (1960) Une mission entomologique au Marojejy. *Naturaliste Malgache* 12: 43-55.

Lavauden, L. (1932) Etude d'une petite collection d'oiseaux de Madagascar. *Bull. Mus. Natn. Hist. Nat.* (2)4: 629-640.

Lavauden, L. (1937) Supplément. A. Milne Edwards and A. Grandidier, *Histoire physique, naturelle et politique de Madagascar, 12. Oiseaux*. Paris: Société d'Editions Géographiques, Maritimes et Coloniales.

Milne Edwards, A. and Grandidier, A. (1881) *Histoire physique, naturelle et politique de Madagascar, 12. Histoire naturelle des oiseaux*. Tome I. Paris.

Milon, P., Petter, J.-J. and Randrianasolo, G. (1973) *Faune de Madagascar, 35. Oiseaux*. Tananarive and Paris: ORSTOM and CNRS.

Oberholser, H. C. (1900) Catalogue of a collection of birds from Madagascar. *Proc. U. S. Natn. Mus.* 22: 235-248.

Rand, A. L. (1932) Mission Franco-Anglo-Américaine à Madagascar: notes de voyage. *Oiseau et R.F.O.* 2: 227-282.

Rand, A. L. (1936) The distribution and habits of Madagascar birds. *Bull. Amer. Mus. Nat. Hist.* 72: 143-499.

Richmond, C. W. (1897) Catalogue of a collection of birds made by Doctor W. L. Abbott in Madagascar, with descriptions of three new species. *Proc. U. S. Natn. Mus.* 19: 677-694.

Rothschild, W. (1895) A new species and genus of rollers. *Novit. Zool.* 2: 479.

Salvan, J. (1970) Remarques sur l'évolution de l'avifauna malgache depuis 1945. *Alauda* 38: 191-203.

Sharpe, R. B. (1875) Contributions to the ornithology of Madagascar. Part IV. *Proc. Zool. Soc. Lond.*: 70-78.

Turner, D. A. (in press) The ground rollers of Madagascar. *Proc. V Pan-Afr. orn. Congr.*

LONG-TAILED GROUND-ROLLER   RARE
Uratelornis chimaera Rothschild, 1895

Order CORACIIFORMES   Family BRACHYPTERACIIDAE

Summary This remarkable terrestrial bird of restricted range within the subdesert region of south-west Madagascar, although numerically safe at present, appears to enjoy no protection whatever.

Distribution The Long-tailed Ground-roller is restricted to a coastal strip between the Mangoky and Fiherenana rivers, south-west Madagascar, ranging up to 80 m altitude (Appert 1968, Milon *et al.* 1973). Most sites known for the species within this area up to 1966 have been listed (see Appert 1968, but also Oustalet 1899, Ménégaux 1907, Bangs 1918), with the conclusion that its distribution coincides with that of *Didierea* woodland (Appert 1968). It therefore has stricter habitat requirements and a lower altitudinal tolerance than the closely sympatric Subdesert Mesite *Monias benschi* (see relevant account). If the altitudinal limit quoted above is accurate, even only roughly, it cannot occur much more than 30 km inland in the southern half of its range (see 100 m contour in Army Map Service 1968), while in the northern half it has not been recorded east of Lake Ihotry (Appert 1968) other than at Mamono village near Ankida (O. Langrand *in litt.* 1984). Moreover, the revelation that some seasonal movement may occur (see Ecology below) suggests that birds range beyond the currently known limits or that they occupy only parts of their known range at any given season. Evidence of its presence beyond the confines of the Mangoky and Fiherenana, e.g. on Montagne de la Table south of Tuléar (Rand 1932; see Remarks), is lacking, and the report that it occurs south to Cap Sainte-Marie (Lavauden 1937) is in error.

Population In the south between Tuléar and Manombo, at the turn of the century, it was found in good numbers mainly at Ambolisatra (Ménégaux 1907), and this area is obviously still important (see Appert 1968). It was found to be fairly common around Lake Ihotry in 1929 (Rand 1932,1936) but was apparently becoming rare there in the 1950s (Griveaud 1960) and was judged to be "extremely rare" from second-hand information in the early 1960s (Petter 1963). In 1968 it was described as "one of the rarest birds in the world" (Appert 1968). A survey (presumably around 1970) concluded that "the total population between Tuléar and Lake Ihotry is not more than 500 pairs, and nearer 250 pairs with an 80% probability" (Milon *et al.* 1973). More recently, a repeated visitor to its area of distribution has suggested that "in areas of undisturbed habitat it is common, and may even be termed locally abundant, particularly in the area of dense *Didierea* woodland some 30 km north of Tuléar" (Turner in press), a judgement supported by another recent observer (O. Langrand *in litt.* 1984).

Ecology The Long-tailed Ground-roller inhabits very arid areas in low, generally fairly dense deciduous woodland, always with (mostly herb- and grass-free) sandy soil (a prerequisite for nesting); it is commonly found in association with the cactus-like *Didierea madagascariensis* and the sporadic *Euphorbia* *stenoclada*, although absent from *Didierea*-covered dunes, which are probably too loose and too little shaded (Appert 1968). It feeds almost exclusively on terrestrial invertebrates (e.g. beetles, grasshoppers, cockroaches, woodlice, caterpillars, ants), typically by rummaging in leaf-litter beneath a bush or tree (Appert 1968; also Oustalet 1899, Rand 1936, Milon *et al.* 1973, and specimen-labels in MNHN: NJC); a low-flying butterfly was also once seen taken (Appert 1968). Birds are active (singing and feeding) at night, at least at times (Appert 1968; also Turner in press); singing occurs commonly in late winter (August/September) (O. Langrand *in litt.* 1984). The species keeps largely to the ground, running powerfully and flying rarely, but typically calls from a low (up to 3 m high) horizontal perch (Appert 1968). Although it is stated to occur in small family groups (Lavauden 1937; hence Petter 1963, Milon *et al.* 1973), this can only happen for a short period in the year, as the species is otherwise reported to occur singly over the southern winter, and always in pairs from the start of the breeding season (October or earlier through to January) (Appert 1968; also Rand 1936). In one area where it was studied (30 km north of Tuléar), birds appeared to be seasonal in occurrence, being present from September to April but generally absent from May to August (Turner in press). The nest-hole is excavated by both birds in flat or slightly sloping ground, with a tunnel extending to up to 120 cm (Appert 1968); a report of nesting in steep riverbanks (Lavauden 1937) has been doubted (Appert 1968; also O. Langrand *in litt.* 1984). Clutches reputedly consist of three or four eggs (Lavauden 1937), this being supported by a record of three juveniles evidently from one brood (Rand 1936).

Threats The restricted range of this species must be a source of permanent concern and vigilance for its welfare; such concern is compounded by its apparently migratory behaviour (see Ecology above), which doubles the risk it faces from any habitat destruction. This species was hunted by herdsmen with blowpipes at the turn of the century (Ménégaux 1907) and natives were trapping birds and digging out nests in the 1950s and 1960s (Griveaud 1960, Appert 1968); trapping by local villagers is still being practised (O. Langrand *in litt.* 1984). Some 20 years ago, the species's habitat was reported to be in a "critical situation ... being more and more broken up and ... in process of rapid extinction" (Petter 1963). Subsequent observers (Appert 1968, Turner in press) have made no reference to such habitat loss, although it is noted that none of this habitat is protected and that at one favoured site (30 km north of Tuléar) some encroachment by villagers is occurring (Turner in press).

Conservation Measures Taken None is known.

Conservation Measures Proposed Full protection for all ground-rollers has been called for (Salvan 1970). Immediate protection of its habitat and protected area status for a representative tract of *Didierea* were formally recommended in 1970 (IUCN 1972). A study to determine the extent and type of habitat destruction reported in the Long-tailed Ground-roller's range (see under Threats) is urgently needed, together with a detailed ecological study of the bird to provide data essential to any strategy for its long-term conservation, particularly in relation to its apparent seasonal movements. Both this and the equally remarkable Subdesert

Mesite, whose ranges are almost exactly coincident, merit conservation by means of a protected area.

Remarks This extraordinary bird occupies a monotypic genus. Concerning its occurence south of Tuléar, a peak named "Mahinia ou Table" and some low hills named "Chaîne de la Table" are indicated as lying behind the coast between the Fiherenana and Onilahy estuaries (in Locamus 1900).

References

Appert, O. (1968) Zur Brutbiologie der Erdracke *Uratelornis chimaera* Rothschild. *J. Orn.* 109: 264-275.

Army Map Service (1968) Tananarive, Africa (Scale 1: 2,000,000). Series 2201, sheet 32, edition 4-AMS. Washington, D.C.

Bangs, O. (1918) [Vertebrata from Madagascar.] Aves. *Bull. Mus. Comp. Zool.* 61: 489-511.

Griveaud, P. (1960) Une mission de recherche de l'I.R.S.M. au lac Ihotry (S. E. Morombe, Province de Tuléar). *Naturaliste Malgache* 12: 33-41.

IUCN (1972) Recommandations: résolutions adoptées par la Conférence. Pp. 12-15 in *C. R. Conférence Internationale sur la Conservation de la Nature et de ses Ressources à Madagascar*. Morges: IUCN (NS) Doc. suppl. no. 36.

Lavauden, L. (1937) Supplément. A. Milne Edwards and A. Grandidier, *Histoire physique, naturelle et politique de Madagascar, 12. Oiseaux*. Paris: Société d'Editions Géographiques, Maritimes et Coloniales.

Locamus, P. (1900) Carte de Madagascar, 1: 500,000. Paris.

Ménégaux, A. (1907) Liste des oiseaux rapportés en 1906 par M. Geay, du sud-ouest de Madagascar. *Bull. Mus. Natn. Hist. Nat.* 13: 104-113.

Milon, P., Petter, J.-J. and Randrianasolo, G. (1973) *Faune de Madagascar, 35. Oiseaux*. Tananarive and Paris: ORSTOM and CNRS.

Oustalet, E. (1899) Note sur le mâle de l'*Uratelornis chimaera*. *Bull. Mus. Natn. Hist. Nat.* 5: 280-282.

Petter, J.-J. (1963) The serious situation in Madagascar. *ICBP Bull.* 9: 95-96.

Rand, A. L. (1932) Mission Franco-Anglo-Américaine à Madagascar: notes de voyage. *Oiseau et R.F.O.* 2: 227-282.

Rand, A. L. (1936) The distribution and habits of Madagascar birds. *Bull. Amer. Mus. Nat. Hist.* 72: 143-499.

Salvan, J. (1970) Remarques sur l'évolution de l'avifauna malgache depuis 1945. *Alauda* 38: 191-203.

Turner, D. A. (in press) The ground rollers of Madagascar. *Proc. V Pan-Afr. orn. Congr.*

WHITE-CHESTED TINKERBIRD   INDETERMINATE

Pogoniulus makawai Benson and Irwin, l965

Order PICIFORMES   Family CAPITONIDAE

Summary This barbet is known only by the type-specimen, from *Cryptosepalum* thicket in north-western Zambia; subsequent attempts to locate it have been unsuccessful.

Distribution The single specimen of the White-chested Tinkerbird was collected in September 1964 some 6 km north of the Mayau (Mayowo) River in the Kabompo District of Zambia (Benson and Irwin 1965a, Dowsett 1980).

Population Numbers are not known, but the species must be at best rare in the region of the type-locality; it is considered a rare relic (Benson and Irwin 1965b). The closely-related Golden-rumped Tinkerbird *Pogoniulus bilineatus* is very numerous in the Mayau area, but in the course of visits in the 1960s (Benson and Irwin 1965b, Oatley 1969) and l970s (Bowen 1980, R. J. Dowsett *in litt.* 1982) to this and other *Cryptosepalum* areas ornithologists have failed to see or hear any tinkerbirds that might be *makawai*.

Ecology The bird was obtained in dense, essentially evergreen, thickets termed mavunda or *Cryptosepalum* (the tree *C. pseudotaxus* being a dominant), and the species was considered probably endemic to this vegetation (Benson and Irwin 1965a), of which there are many hundreds of square kilometres, mostly undisturbed, in the relevant area of north-west Zambia and adjacent Angola (Benson and Irwin 1965b).

Threats None is known. The mavunda thickets are sparsely inhabited by people outside the West Lunga National Park and difficult to clear for agriculture, so the habitat appears not to be threatened (R. J. Dowsett *in litt.* 1982).

Conservation Measures Taken None is known. Much suitable habitat occurs within the West Lunga National Park (R. J. Dowsett *in litt.* 1982).

Conservation Measures Proposed Further attempts are needed to rediscover this species.

Remarks The possibility that the White-chested Tinkerbird is an aberrant individual of the Golden-rumped Tinkerbird is considered not entirely excluded on the limited evidence so far available (Goodwin 1965), and the continuing failure to rediscover *makawai* has reinforced this point (Dowsett and Dowsett-Lemaire 1980), but the latter's validity as a species has been most emphatically reasserted (C. W. Benson pers. comm. 1982).

References

Benson, C. W. and Irwin, M. P. S. (1965a) A new species of tinker-barbet from Northern Rhodesia. *Bull. Brit. Orn. Club* 85: 5-9.

Benson, C. W. and Irwin, M. P. S. (1965b) The birds of *Cryptosepalum* forests, Zambia. *Arnoldia Rhod.* 1(28): 1-12.

Bowen, P. St.J. (1980) The birds of *Cryptosepalum* forest near Mwinilunga. *Bull. Zambian Orn. Soc.* 12: 48-54.

Dowsett, R. J. (1980) Comments on some ornithological type-localities in Zambia. *Zambia Mus. J.* 5: 7-16.

Dowsett, R. J. and Dowsett-Lemaire, F. (1980) The systematic status of some Zambian birds. *Gerfaut* 70: 151-199.

Goodwin, D. (1965) Some remarks on the new barbet. *Bull. Brit. Orn. Club* 85: 9-10.

Oatley, T. B. (1969) Bird ecology in the evergreen forests of north western Zambia. *Puku* 5: 141-180.

YELLOW-FOOTED HONEYGUIDE
Melignomon eisentrauti Louette, 1981

INSUFFICIENTLY KNOWN

Order PICIFORMES

Family INDICATORIDAE

Summary This recently described forest species is known from only a few specimens collected in Cameroon and Liberia and a possible sighting in Ghana. It probably occurs more widely but is likely to have suffered and to continue to suffer from extensive forest clearance in the western part of its range.

Distribution The Yellow-footed Honeyguide has been definitely recorded only in Cameroon and Liberia (Colston 1981, Louette 1981). Although it was not described until 1981 (Louette 1981) the first specimen, provisionally identified as an immature Zenker's Honeyguide *Melignomon zenkeri* (Serle 1959), was collected near Bakebe, at 200 m in Mamfe District, Cameroon, in 1956 (Serle 1965). In the following year another specimen was taken at Malende at 150 m near the north-eastern side of Mount Cameroon (Eisentraut 1963). In Liberia eleven specimens were collected at Yakepa and Grassfield near Mount Nimba between 1965 and 1974 (Forbes-Watson undated, Colston 1981, Colston and Curry-Lindahl in press). The type-specimen was collected 2 km east of Grassfield, near Mount Nimba, in 1980 (Louette 1981). In addition to these specimens an unidentified *Melignomon*, assumed to be this species, was seen in the Kakum Forest Reserve in southern Ghana in 1977 (Macdonald 1980). It is likely that the Yellow-footed Honeyguide has been overlooked and probably occurs more widely in the Upper Guinea forests between Cameroon and Liberia (Colston 1981, Louette 1981), possibly occurring as far west as Sierra Leone.

Population Numbers are not known, though the species must be rare to have avoided detection for so long.

Ecology It is apparently a forest bird (Serle 1959,1965, Macdonald 1980, Colston 1981, Louette 1981, Colston and Curry-Lindahl in press), capable of surviving in secondary forest (Serle 1959, Macdonald 1980). Stomach-contents have been found to consist of insects, yellow wax (or pollen), small fruits and seeds (Colston 1981). A bird collected in Liberia was in breeding condition in March (Louette 1981) and one collected in Cameroon in December was probably nearing breeding condition (Eisentraut 1963). It is presumably a brood parasite like other honeyguides and indirect evidence suggests that the Buff-spotted Woodpecker *Campethera nivosa* and the Brown-eared Woodpecker *C. caroli* might be hosts (Louette 1981).

Threats None is known. Although it can survive in secondary forest (Serle 1959, Macdonald 1980) it is presumably at risk from complete forest clearance, notably in the western part of its range (west of the Dahomey Gap).

Conservation Measures Taken None is known.

Conservation Measures Proposed Surveys are needed to determine whether this species occurs within some of the rainforest national parks in West Africa, especially the large Tai National Park in Ivory Coast and the Korup National Park in Cameroon. Details of the protected areas of rainforest west of the Dahomey Gap and the bird species for which they are or may be important are given in Remarks under Rufous Fishing Owl *Scotopelia ussheri*.

Remarks It has been suggested that the Yellow-footed Honeyguide forms a superspecies with Zenker's Honeyguide (Snow 1978, Colston 1981, Louette 1981), but this view is not universally held (A. D. Forbes-Watson pers. comm. 1984). Zenker's Honeyguide has been seen to the north of Mount Cameroon very close to Malende and so it seems that the two species might be sympatric in this area (A. D. Forbes-Watson pers. comm. 1984). The original descriptions of the Yellow-footed Honeyguide (Colston 1981, Louette 1981) made no mention of the structural differences in the outer tail feathers of the two species; those of the Yellow-footed Honeyguide are emarginated whereas those of Zenker's Honeyguide are rounded (A. D. Forbes-Watson pers. comm. 1984). Several other threatened species occur on Mount Nimba (see Remarks under Rufous Fishing Owl).

References

Colston, P. R. (1981) A newly described species of *Melignomon* [Indicatoridae] from Liberia, West Africa. *Bull. Brit. Orn. Club* 101: 289-291.

Colston, P. R. and Curry-Lindahl, K. (in press) The birds of the Mount Nimba area in Liberia. *Bull. Brit. Mus. (Nat. Hist.) Zool.*

Eisentraut, M. (1963) *Die Wirbeltiere des Kamerungebirges*. Hamburg and Berlin: Paul Parey.

Forbes-Watson, A. D. (undated) Checklist of the birds of Liberia. Non-passeriformes. Unpublished.

Louette, M. (1981) A new species of honeyguide from West Africa. *Rev. Zool. Afr.* 95: 131-135.

Macdonald, M. A. (1980) Further notes on uncommon forest birds in Ghana. *Bull. Brit. Orn. Club* 100: 170-172.

Serle, W. (1959) Note on the immature plumage of the honey-guide *Melignomon zenkeri* Reichenow. *Bull. Brit. Orn. Club* 79: 65.

Serle, W. (1965) A third contribution to the ornithology of the British Cameroons. Part 1. *Ibis* 107: 60-94.

Snow, D. W. ed. (1978) *An atlas of speciation in African non-passerine birds*. London: Trustees of the British Museum (Natural History).

AFRICAN GREEN BROADBILL   RARE
Pseudocalyptomena graueri Rothschild, 1909

Order PASSERIFORMES   Family EURYLAIMIDAE
                                                   Subfamily EURYLAIMINAE

Summary This remarkable forest bird is known from only three mountain ranges, two in eastern Zaire and one in south-western Uganda. There is little recent information on its status.

Distribution The African Green Broadbill is known only from the Itombwe Mountains and the mountains west of Lake Kivu in eastern Zaire, and from the Impenetrable (or Bwindi) forest in south-western Uganda. The type-specimen was collected at 2,000 m in the Itombwe Mountains in 1908, about 80 km west of the Ruzizi Valley (Rothschild 1909). In 1929 seven specimens were taken in the Itombwe Mountains near Luvumba, at 1,950 m on the Lusigi River, on the western slopes of the mountains (Rockefeller and Murphy 1933). Two more birds were seen at the locality in 1933 and three were collected in 1934 (Aspenlind 1935). During the 1940s and 1950s at least 26 specimens were collected in the Itombwe Mountains as follows: 18 from Miki, 1,880-2,040 m, one in 1945, 15 in 1950, and two in 1955; five from Muusi, 2,380-2,480 m, three in 1951, two in 1955; two from Karungu at 1,950 m, one in 1951, one in 1953; and one from Ibachilo, 1,760 m, in 1957 (Prigogine 1971, Chapin 1978; specimens in MRAC and IRSNB: SNS). The species apparently has a rather localised distribution in the Itombwe Mountains (Prigogine 1971). Its overall range in Itombwe is from 1,760 to 2,480 m, 80% of the collected specimens being taken between 1,940 and 2,390 m (Prigogine 1974). It was discovered in the mountains west of Lake Kivu in 1959 when three specimens were collected at Nyawaronga (Prigogine 1971; specimens in MRAC and IRSNB: SNS). There appear to be no subsequent records from Zaire. In 1967 it was discovered in Uganda when a specimen was collected at 2,000 m near the Bwindi Swamp in the Impenetrable Forest (Friedmann and Williams 1968), and in 1969 five more birds were taken in the Bwindi and Ruhizha areas of the forest (Friedmann 1970, Friedmann and Williams 1970).

Population Numbers are not known. It is common in certain parts of the Itombwe Mountains (Prigogine 1971), especially around Miki (Prigogine in press).

Ecology The population of this species in the Impenetrable Forest apparently differs considerably in its ecology from those in eastern Zaire (Friedmann 1970). In the Itombwe Mountains it is usually seen in small groups of 3-10 birds in the middle storey and canopy of the forest edge up to 20 m above the ground (Rockefeller and Murphy 1933, Aspenlind 1935, Prigogine 1971, Chapin 1978). It has also been seen in isolated trees in clearings and fields, and it appears to avoid the densest parts of the forest (Rockefeller and Murphy 1933, Prigogine 1971). The birds fly silently between trees, covering short distances of 10-30 m (Rockefeller and Murphy 1933, Prigogine 1971). They are not shy and even approach human habitations (Aspenlind 1935, Prigogine 1971) but are very difficult to see amongst the foliage of the trees, unless their characteristic call is heard (Prigogine 1971). The birds sometimes join mixed-species parties (Prigogine 1971). They forage for insects in the manner of a woodpecker (Picidae) (Prigogine 1971, Chapin 1978) and have also been seen sallying for insects (Rockefeller and Murphy 1933), though it has been suggested these were display flights (Friedmann 1970). The food consists of fruit and insects (Prigogine 1971). Birds collected in July showed some gonadal enlargement but a full-grown immature bird collected at the same time is suggestive of a prolonged breeding season (Rockefeller and Murphy 1933). The type-specimen is said to have been collected in bamboo forest (Rothschild 1909) and birds collected at Muusi are from within the bamboo zone (Prigogine 1978), but most records are from below the bamboo zone (Rockefeller and Murphy 1933). In the Impenetrable Forest the species lives in the upper portions of the undergrowth of the forest interior, about 2-3 m above the ground (Friedmann 1970). Birds occasionally fly up to the tree-tops from the lower vegetation but they are usually seen in groups of 2-3 birds searching for food, in the manner of waxbills (Estrildidae), especially in Euphorbia trees *Neoboutonia* (Friedmann 1970). They have a slow gliding flight and, as in Itombwe, are not shy (Friedmann 1970). Stomachs of birds collected in the Impenetrable Forest contained seeds, flowers, buds, fruit, beetles, snails and insect larvae (Friedmann 1970).

Threats Forest destruction is presumably detrimental to this species. Forest clearance is known to be taking place in the Impenetrable Forest (K. D. Bishop pers. comm. 1983) and there is a danger of increased clearance in the Itombwe Mountains, thus increasing the possibility of the area being opened up for larger-scale economic exploitation since Kamituga has become an important mining centre (Prigogine in press). There is probably a greater danger, however, of clearance around villages higher in the Itombwe Mountains, but there is no recent information on the conservation status of these forests (A. Prigogine *in litt.* 1983).

Conservation Measures Taken The population in the mountains west of Lake Kivu is presumably in the Kahuzi-Biega National Park and this might prove sufficient to safeguard the species in this area.

Conservation Measures Proposed A preliminary conservation plan for the forests of the Itombwe Mountains has been prepared (Prigogine in press). It is hoped that this plan will be worked out in detail and implemented by the Zairean government. Much stricter conservation measures are also needed for the Impenetrable Forest.

Remarks This extraordinary species was originally thought to be a flycatcher (Rothschild 1909) but has been shown conclusively to be a broadbill, more closely related to the Asian members of the family than to the African genus *Smithornis* (Lowe 1924,1931). The forests of the Itombwe Mountains are important for six other threatened bird species (see Remarks under Schouteden's Swift *Schoutedenapus schoutedeni*). The mountains west of Lake Kivu hold two other threatened bird species, Grauer's Swamp Warbler *Bradypterus graueri* and

Rockefeller's Sunbird *Nectarinia rockefelleri*, while the Impenetrable Forest also holds two other threatened bird species, Grauer's Swamp Warbler and Chapin's Flycatcher *Muscicapa lendu* (see relevant accounts).

References

Aspenlind, L. J. (1935) Huru jag fann Afrikas sällsyntaste fågel, Grauers brednäbb. *Fauna och Flora* 30: 173-179.

Chapin, R. T. (1978) Brief accounts of some central African birds, based on the journals of James Chapin. *Rev. Zool. Afr.* 92: 805-836.

Friedmann, H. (1970) The status and habits of Grauer's Broadbill in Uganda (Aves: Eurylaemidae). *Los Angeles County Mus. Contrib. Sci.* 176.

Friedmann, H. and Williams, J. G. (1968) Notable records of rare and little known birds from western Uganda. *Rev. Zool. Bot. Afr.* 77: 11-36.

Friedmann, H. and Williams, J. G. (1970) Additions to the known avifauna of the Bugoma, Kibale and Impenetrable Forest, West Uganda. *Los Angeles County Mus. Contrib. Sci.* 198.

Lowe, P. R. (1924) On the presence of broadbills (Eurylaemidae) in Africa. *Proc. Zool. Soc. Lond.*: 279-291.

Lowe, P. R. (1931) On the anatomy of *Pseudocalyptomena* and the occurrence of broadbills (Eurylaemidae) in Africa. *Proc. Zool. Soc. Lond.*: 445-461.

Prigogine, A. (1971) Les oiseaux de l'Itombwe et de son hinterland. Volume I. *Ann. Mus. Roy. Afr. Centr.* 8°, Sci. Zool. 185: 1-298.

Prigogine, A. (1974) Contribution à l'étude de la distribution verticale des oiseaux orophiles. *Gerfaut* 64: 75-88.

Prigogine, A. (1978) Les oiseaux de l'Itombwe et de son hinterland. Volume II. *Ann. Mus. Roy. Afr. Centr.* 8°, Sci. Zool. 223: 1-134.

Prigogine, A. (in press) The conservation of the avifauna of the forests of the Albertine Rift. *Proceedings of the ICBP Tropical Forest Bird Symposium, 1982.*

Rockefeller, J. S. and Murphy, C. B. G. (1933) The rediscovery of *Pseudocalyptomena. Auk* 50: 23-29.

Rothschild, W. (1909) Description of a new bird from Africa. *Ibis* (9)3: 690-691.

YELLOW-BELLIED SUNBIRD-ASITY　　　　　　　　INDETERMINATE

Neodrepanis hypoxantha Salomonsen, 1933

Order PASSERIFORMES　　　　　　　　　　Family PHILEPITTIDAE

Summary This Madagascar endemic species, difficult to distinguish from its only congener, is known from 12 specimens collected before 1930, although it was recognised as a species only in 1933. The generally held view that it is unlikely to be extinct, despite extensive forest destruction within its known range, is supported by the discovery of a nesting pair in 1976, but it must be rare at best.

Distribution The Yellow-bellied Sunbird-asity was recognised as a species distinct from the Wattled Sunbird-asity *Neodrepanis coruscans* only in 1933, and no specimens of it have been collected since; it is known only from eastern-central Madagascar, in forests east and perhaps south of Antananarivo, and the Sihanaka forest. Data from the 12 (or 13: see Remarks) currently known specimens, in order of their collection, are as follows:

> one male, no locality or date but prior to October 1879 (Benson 1971);
> one male, central Madagascar, June 1880 (Eck 1968, Benson 1976);
> three males, one female, Andrangoloaka, November 1880 (Stresemann 1937, Salomonsen 1965; also Eck 1968, Benson 1976);
> two males, one female, east of Antananarivo, July 1881 (Salomonsen 1933, Benson 1974);
> one male, "E. Imerina" (near Antananarivo), October/November 1895 (Wetmore 1953);
> one male, Sihanaka forest, 25 February, probably 1925 (Greenway 1967);
> one male, Fito (i.e. Sihanaka forest), August 1929 (Salomonsen 1965).

Andrangoloaka was reported, at second-hand, to be situated high (1,000-1,300 m in one account, 1,400 m in another) on the eastern slopes of the plateau east of Antsirabe, c. 150 km south of Antananarivo, but this settlement and the great majority of surrounding forest no longer exist (Stresemann 1937, Greenway 1967). This information appears without doubt to be wrong, however, since there is or was an "Andrangolaoka" (*sic*) at 19°02'S 47°55'E on the upper slopes of the forested escarpment immediately east of the Mantasoa reservoir east of Antananarivo (Office of Geography 1955; not marked in IGNT 1964): in terms of the other records, this appears no less likely a locality than at Antsirabe, which is well outside the main rainforest belt, and indeed it appears as both "Andrangaloaka" and "Andrangoloaka" on separate nineteenth century maps which show no similar name anywhere near Antsirabe (see Laillet and Superbie 1889, Locamus 1900; also Remarks). The forests around Antananarivo, from the eastern parts of which the type-material came (Salomonsen 1933), no longer exist (Salomonsen 1934; also Wetmore 1953), nor do those at "East Imerina" (D. A. Turner pers. comm. 1983), but the species is expected to survive in Sihanaka forest, to the north-east of the Imerina plateau (Salomonsen 1965, Greenway 1967, Benson 1974). A stand of original forest at Tsinjoarivo, near Antsirabe, was twice identified as a likely site

362

for the species (Lavauden 1937, Greenway 1967; see Remarks), any remaining tiny patches of forest at the former locality of Andrangoloaka could perhaps still have held some birds (Stresemann 1937), and forest east of Anjozorobe (not Ankazobe as reported in King 1978-1979), north-east of Antananarivo, was also considered worth investigating (Lavauden 1937), but whether and in what condition these forests still survive is unknown. The Fierenana district north of Périnet has also been suggested as a possible site for the species (King 1978-1979). In December 1973 and November 1976 birds were seen and photographed (originals and copies with VIREO at ANSP) in forest several kilometres from and c. 100 m higher than the Périnet-Analamazaotra Special Reserve (A. D. Forbes-Watson pers. comm. 1984).

Population Numbers are unknown. While only nineteenth century records, all from the now largely deforested central parts of Madagascar, were known, the species was considered at best very rare and probably extinct, a judgement reinforced by the failure of the Mission Franco-Anglo-Américaine of 1929-1931 to find any (Salomonsen 1933,1934, Lavauden 1937, Stresemann 1937, Wetmore 1953). However, the discovery that birds had been collected in Sihanaka forest in the 1920s has resulted in confident predictions of its survival, albeit in low densities (Salomonsen 1965, Greenway 1967, Benson 1974), and these have been borne out by the 1973 and 1976 sightings even though these were not themselves in Sihanaka (see Distribution). The species was noted for being inexplicably uncommon in the last century around Andrangoloaka (Hildebrandt 1881; see Remarks).

Ecology This species inhabits rainforest; it is regarded as possibly a highland counterpart of the very similar Wattled Sunbird-asity (Wetmore 1953; also Lavauden 1937, A. D. Forbes-Watson pers. comm. 1984), although records from Sihanaka forest indicate possible sympatry between the two species (Benson 1974). It is a nectar-feeder like the Wattled Sunbird-asity; both species assume breeding plumage in September/November (Salomonsen 1965). A pair observed near Périnet in December 1973 were feeding young in a (sunbird-like) nest placed 4-5 m up in thick forest (A. D. Forbes-Watson pers. comm. 1984). The species may inhabit canopy and thus have escaped notice (Benson 1980). However, observations a century ago refer to it feeding at flowering bushes in primary forest clearings, also to its call being a barely audible soft whistle (Hildebrandt 1881; see Remarks). In November 1976 near Périnet a male was observed feeding at *Loranthus* blossom; in December 1973 at the same locality a male was watched flycatching alate termites and feeding them to nestlings (A. D. Forbes-Watson pers. comm. 1984).

Threats Destruction and disturbance of primary rainforest is the single most serious threat to this and all other rainforest-dependent species in Madagascar (see Threats under Madagascar Serpent Eagle *Eutriorchis astur*).

Conservation Measures Taken None is known.

Conservation Measures Proposed Immediate and effective protection of as much remaining rainforest as possible would almost certainly guarantee the survival of this and all other rainforest-dependent species in Madagascar; and at least, on current knowledge, complete protection of the intact parts of Sihanaka forest is of extreme importance (see Conservation Measures Proposed under Madagascar Serpent Eagle). Any ornithological work in the other areas from which the species is known, or where it might be expected, should where possible be extended to include searches to locate it.

Remarks Concerning the number of museum specimens of this species, there is apparently a thirteenth in Sydney, Australia, labelled merely "Antananarivo" (A. D. Forbes-Watson pers. comm. 1984). Along with two other eastern Madagascar forest birds, the Dusky Greenbul *Phyllastrephus tenebrosus* and the Red-tailed Newtonia *Newtonia fanovanae*, the Yellow-bellied Sunbird-asity is thought likely to have been overlooked owing to its sparseness, elusiveness and difficult habitat (Benson 1974). Its validity as a full species has recently been reaffirmed (Benson 1974). The Tsinjoarivo intended as a probable site for the species is most likely that at 19°37'S 47°40'E, i.e. on the edge of the main rainforest belt, and not that at 19°54'S 46°39'E (in Office of Geography 1955). Observations in the last century (Hildebrandt 1881), given under the name of the Wattled Sunbird-asity, appear to refer exclusively to the Yellow-bellied species, reference being made to "brilliant yellow" undersides, only a few specimens being collected (J. M. Hildebrandt was the collector of all four specimens from Andrangoloaka listed under Distribution), and (elsewhere in the paper) Andrangoloaka as the locality in which much fieldwork had been done (and where indeed the paper was written).

References

Benson, C. W. (1971) The Cambridge collection from the Malagasy Region (Part II). *Bull. Brit. Orn. Club* 91: 1-7.

Benson, C. W. (1974) Another specimen of *Neodrepanis hypoxantha. Bull. Brit. Orn. Club* 94: 141-143.

Benson, C. W. (1976) Specimens of *Neodrepanis hypoxantha* in Dresden. *Bull. Brit. Orn. Club* 96: 144.

Benson, C. W. (1980) Fifty years of ornithology in the Malagasy Faunal Region. *Bull. Brit. Orn. Club* 100: 76-80.

Eck, S. (1968) Ein weiteres Exemplar von *Neodrepanis hypoxantha* Salom. (Aves, Philepittidae). *Zool. Abh. Ber. Mus. Tierk. Dresden* 29(16): 229-230.

Greenway, J. C. (1967) *Extinct and vanishing birds of the world.* 2nd revised edition. New York: Dover Publications.

Hildebrandt, J. M. (1881) Skizze zu einem Bilde central-madagassischen Naturlebens im Frühling. *Z. Ges. Erdk. Berlin* 16: 194-203.

Institut Géographique National à Tananarive (1964) Carte de Madagascar, 1: 500,000, Type 1963. Tananarive.

King, W. B. (1978-1979) *Red data book, 2: Aves.* 2nd edition. Morges, Switzerland: IUCN.

Laillet, E. and Superbie, L. (1889) Carte de Madagascar. Paris.

Lavauden, L. (1937) Supplément. A. Milne Edwards and A. Grandidier, *Histoire physique, naturelle et politique de Madagascar, 12. Oiseaux*. Paris: Société d'Editions Géographiques, Maritimes et Coloniales.

Locamus, P. (1900) Carte de Madagascar, 1: 500,000. Paris.

Office of Geography (1955) *Gazetteer no. 2. Madagascar, Réunion and the Comoro Islands*. Washington, D.C.: Department of the Interior.

Salomonsen, F. (1933) [Description of a new sunbird.] *Bull. Brit. Orn. Club* 53: 182-183.

Salomonsen, F. (1934) Les Neodrepanis, genre particulier de soui-mangas malgaches. *Oiseau et R.F.O.* 4: 1-9.

Salomonsen, F. (1965) Notes on the Sunbird-asitys (*Neodrepanis*). *Oiseau et R.F.O.* 35 (no. spéc.): 103-111.

Stresemann, E. (1937) Ein neuer Fund von *Neodrepanis hypoxantha* Salom. *Orn. Monatsber.* 45: 135-136.

Wetmore, A. (1953) A record for *Neodrepanis hypoxantha* of Madagascar. *Auk* 70: 91.

ASH'S LARK   INSUFFICIENTLY KNOWN

Mirafra ashi Colston, 1982

Order PASSERIFORMES   Family ALAUDIDAE

Summary This lark of arid coastal grassy plains, very recently described and as yet known only from a single site in Somalia, requires further investigation to determine its status, distribution and needs.

Distribution Ash's Lark was found on 9 and 10 July 1981 at a site 13 km north of Uarsciek (Warsheikh), itself some 80 km north-east of Moga- dishu, in southern coastal Somalia (Colston 1982). It is not known to occur along the coast south-west of this site, where there have been intensive bird obser- vations, but the coast to the north-east is ornithologically very poorly known, and it could easily be overlooked among the many other larks of the area (J. S. Ash *in litt.* 1983).

Population Six specimens were collected (Colston 1982). Nothing further is known.

Ecology The birds observed were confined to areas of grazed tufted grass on fixed dunes in grassy maritime plain with fossil coral reef outcrops, apparently breeding at the end of the rains in July; males often sang from the tops of small stunted bushes (J. S. Ash *in litt.* 1983).

Threats The apparent restriction of the species's range may be a cause for concern. If an apparent ecological link is established between this species and grazing animals (domestic sheep and goats and wild Speke's Gazelle *Gazella spekei*), loss of domestic stock through drought (such as occurred recently north-east of the type-locality), combined with over-hunting of the gazelle, could reduce grazing and thus adversely alter habitat (J. S. Ash *in litt.* 1983).

Conservation Measures Taken None is known.

Conservation Measures Proposed In view of the very limited knowledge of this species, further fieldwork is needed to determine its range and population, to discover the threats it faces and the best means of countering them. Collection of further specimens should meanwhile not be countenanced.

Remarks Nine other species of lark occur in this area and Ash's Lark could easily be overlooked among two other *Mirafra*, the Red-winged Lark *M. hypermetra hypermetra* and Somali Long-billed Lark *M. somalica rochei* (J. S. Ash *in litt.* 1983). The sympatric Obbia Lark *Calandrella obbiensis*, also endemic to Somalia, is a striking example of an almost totally overlooked species now known to be quite widespread and numerous (see Appendix C).

Reference

Colston, P. R. (1982) A new species of *Mirafra* (Alaudidae) and new races of the Somali Long-billed Lark *Mirafra somalica*, Thekla Lark *Galerida malabarica* and Malindi Pipit *Anthus melindae* from southern coastal Somalia. *Bull. Brit. Orn. Club* 102: 106-114.

DEGODI LARK   INSUFFICIENTLY KNOWN
Mirafra degodiensis Erard, 1975

Order PASSERIFORMES   Family ALAUDIDAE

Summary This lark is only known from two specimens collected together near Bogol Manya in the Degodi region of southern Ethiopia: it requires further investigation to determine its status, distribution and needs.

Distribution The only two specimens of the Degodi Lark were collected on 24 November 1971, 11 km east of "Bogol-Mayo" (evidently Bogol Manya, 4°34'N 41°29'E, in TAW 1980) in the direction of Dolo, at 350 m, in the Degodi region, easternmost Sidamo province, southern Ethiopia (Erard 1975).

Population The species was not recognised as such until the skins were examined in a museum, and nothing was noted at the time of collection concerning the numbers of birds present (see Erard 1975).

Ecology The birds were found on the ground in very light bush consisting of low bushy acacias on bare soil; they had been eating small caterpillars and small orthopterans (Erard 1975).

Threats None is known, except that the range of this species may prove very restricted.

Conservation Measures Taken None is known.

Conservation Measures Proposed Further ornithological fieldwork in the Degodi region is needed to establish the range and status of this species, as well as to ascertain further data on two birds treated in Appendix C, the Somali Short-billed Crombec *Sylvietta philippae* and Salvadori's Serin *Serinus xantholaema*, which both occur in the area (Erard 1974a,b,1975).

Remarks This species is a smaller, noticeably shorter-tailed sibling of Gillett's Lark *Mirafra gilletti* (Erard 1975).

References

Erard, C. (1974a) Notes faunistiques et systématiques sur quelques oiseaux d'Ethiopia. *Bonn. zool. Beitr.* 25: 76-86.

Erard, C. (1974b) Taxonomie des serins à gorge jaune d'Ethiopie. *Oiseau et R.F.O.* 44: 308-323.

Erard, C. (1975) Variation géographique de *Mirafra gilletti*: description d'une espèce jumelle. *Oiseau et R.F.O.* 45: 293-312.

The Times Atlas of the World (1980) Comprehensive (sixth) edition. London: Times Books.

SOUTH AFRICAN LONG-CLAWED LARK INDETERMINATE
Heteromirafra ruddi (Grant, 1908)

Order PASSERIFORMES Family ALAUDIDAE

Summary This species is known from high altitude grasslands in South Africa (Transvaal, Orange Free State, Natal including East Griqualand), Lesotho and perhaps Swaziland. It appears to have disappeared from much of the southern part of its range, owing to habitat degradation.

Distribution In recent years the South African Long-clawed Lark or Rudd's Lark has been reported from the high altitude grasslands of Lesotho, and eastern and north-eastern Orange Free State north to Dullstroom in central Transvaal, South Africa (Brooke in press). In Transvaal it is restricted to the Wakkerstroom, Volksrust, Amersfoort, Ermelo, Carolina, Waterval Boven and Belfast districts (D. G. Allan *in litt.* 1984). It might also occur in western Swaziland (Clancey 1980). It formerly occurred on the eastern and south-eastern grassland slopes of the Drakensberg Mountains (Brooke in press). However, there were no reports of the species in Natal in the 1970s (Cyrus and Robson 1980) and no birds were located during recent surveys of its former range in East Griqualand, Natal (Brooke in press), where it used to occur at Matatiele, Cedarville and Kokstad (Clancey 1980).

Population Numbers are not known. The species is rare and seldom reported and appears to have declined in the southern part of its range (Cyrus and Robson 1980, Brooke in press). It is local everywhere in its Transvaal range (Allan in prep.).

Ecology This species occurs in moist, short, high altitude grasslands, and though it is also reported to forage in old croplands (Brooke in press) this has never been seen by one recent observer (D. G. Allan *in litt.* 1984). In a study of the species in the eastern Transvaal highveld, birds were found to be restricted to higher plateaus between 1,700 and 2,200 m, with short dense *Themeda triandra/ Heteropogon contortus* grassland, especially around the edges of small grassy pans or vleis: food was small insects, and no foraging involved digging with the bill (Allan in prep.). Breeding has been reported in December (Boddam-Whetham 1963), January and February (Allan in prep.), and the clutch-size is three (Allan in prep.; also Brooke in press). It is probably single-brooded (Brooke in press).

Threats This species has probably decreased owing to habitat degradation caused by overgrazing and excessive burning (Brooke in press).

Conservation Measures Taken None is known, other than that the species is fully protected by South African law (Brooke in press).

Conservation Measures Proposed More research is needed to assess its status and distribution and to determine appropriate conservation action.

Remarks The South African Long-clawed Lark forms a superspecies with two other threatened bird species, the Somali Long-clawed Lark *Heteromirafra archeri* and the Sidamo Long-clawed Lark *H. sidamoensis*; these being the only other members of the genus, *Heteromirafra* itself is a threatened taxon.

References

Allan, D. G. (in prep.) Notes on Rudd's Lark in the Transvaal.

Boddam-Whetham, A. D. (1963) Display flight of Rudd's Lark. *Ostrich* 34: 251.

Brooke, R. K. (in press) *The rare and vulnerable birds of South Africa.*

Clancey, P. A. ed. (1980) *S.A.O.S. Checklist of southern African birds.* [Pretoria:] Southern African Ornithological Society.

Cyrus, D. and Robson, N. (1980). *Bird atlas of Natal.* Pietermaritzburg: University of Natal Press.

SOMALI LONG-CLAWED LARK   INDETERMINATE
Heteromirafra archeri Clarke, 1920

Order PASSERIFORMES   Family ALAUDIDAE

Summary This is a secretive grassland species known only from an exceptionally restricted area, at least part of which is now under cultivation, in north-west Somalia: it has been seen only once in the past 60 years, in 1955, when it was very uncommon, and now merits an urgent survey to confirm its existence and determine its needs.

Distribution The Somali Long-clawed Lark is known from the Hargeisa/Buramo area of north-west Somalia along the frontier with Ethiopia. It was originally considered confined to a strip of grassland 25 km long by 8 km wide, at c. 1,500 m, from Jifa Medir ("Jifu Meider", 9°43'N 43°17'E) and Jifa Uri ("Jifu Uri", 9°42'N 43°24'E) south to the Ban Wujaleh (whose centre is at 9°32'N 43°27'E: see Remarks), west of Hargeisa (Archer and Godman 1961; all coordinates read from War Office 1946). However, in April/May 1955 it was found very locally between 15 and 40 km north-west of Buramo (J. G. Williams *in litt.* 1984), i.e. very roughly 100 km north-west of the first site. Its occurrence on the Ethiopian side of the border, east of Jijiga, is not known but anticipated (Archer and Godman 1961, Erard 1975), although this is now a major cereal-growing area (J. S. Ash *in litt.* and pers. comm. 1984). The statement that "its habitat is entirely governed by the extent of the open grasslands and it is only from this centre that it makes forays into the millet fields at Jifa" (Archer and Godman 1961) indicates that even within its tiny range its distribution is patchy. "Jifa" is the type-locality (see Archer and Godman 1961) but is not traceable (on War Office 1946 or in SDGHME 1947), but since under "Localities" (in Archer and Godman 1961) the only two given are "Jifa Uri and the Ban Wujaleh" it is presumably the same as Jifa Uri or, more probably, Jifa Uri and Jifa Medir together. The implication of this (even allowing for the records from north-west of Buramo) is that the Ban Wujaleh (i.e. "Wujaleh grassland") is (or at least was: see Threats) the main and conceivably the only breeding locality for the species.

Population This species has been described as "quite numerous" (Archer and Godman 1961) and "fairly common" (Ash and Miskell 1983) at the Ban Wujaleh, although the latter statement is based on the former and not on any subsequent observations (J. S. Ash *in litt.* and pers. comm. 1984): in other words it has not been seen there since 1922. In the second (previously unpublished) area where it was found in 1955, it was "very uncommon and only a few were seen" (J. G. Williams *in litt.* 1984).

Ecology On the Ban Wujaleh it is restricted to open, fairly short grassland, in which it creeps about very secretively like a mouse or rail (Rallidae), never crossing open ground and only flying when necessary; it occasionally visits millet-fields (Archer and Godman 1961). North-west of Buramo the habitat was "fairly open rocky country with scattered and sparse bush and limited grass cover", the birds skulking in this last and only flying when flushed (J. G. Williams *in litt.* 1984). Food is unrecorded. Nesting was found to occur in June (seven nests in the first week, 1922): the nest is funnel-shaped, extending deep into the roots of a clump of grass, clutch-size three (Archer and Godman 1961).

Threats The extremely restricted range of this species must be a permanent source of concern and vigilance for its welfare. A part of the Ban Wujaleh is now under cultivation as a refugee settlement area (J. S. Ash *in litt.* and pers. comm. 1984) and this must raise grave concern over the bird's status, particularly in view of the tentative conclusion reached under Distribution.

Conservation Measures Taken None is known, other than that the observer of the species in 1955 deliberately refrained from collecting any birds because he considered them too rare (J. G. Williams *in litt.* 1984).

Conservation Measures Proposed If it still survives, this remarkable species merits a detailed study of its ecology and behaviour, on zoogeographical grounds alone, for comparison with the South African Long-clawed Lark *Heteromirafra ruddi* and, if it can be relocated, the Sidamo Long-clawed Lark *H. sidamoensis* (see relevant accounts); but such a study should also be geared to determining the causes of its restricted range, the impact on it of cultivation at the Ban Wujaleh, and the methods for ensuring its conservation. A search for the species in the adjacent area of Ethiopia is long overdue. All such fieldwork must, of course, depend on the political stabilisation of the area.

Remarks "Ban Wujaleh" (see map in Archer and Godman 1961) is evidently the area marked "Wajale" (on War Office 1946), the coordinates for the latter being given above; however, the locality marked as "Wajale" (in TAW 1980) is "Tug Wajale Post" (on War Office 1946) and lies midway on the western edge of the species's known range. The species is remarkable not only for its restricted range, secretive behaviour, structural peculiarities (large head, short tail, very long hind claw) and curious nest, but also because its closest known relative (before the recent discovery of the Sidamo Long-clawed Lark) was the South African Long-clawed Lark, some 4,500 km away. It was this distance which persuaded the original authority to consider the Somali Long-clawed Lark a full species (see Archer and Godman 1961), and this decision has recently been supported by a thorough examination of skins (see Erard 1975). For a sighting of a *Heteromirafra* lark in Kenya, see Remarks under Sidamo Long-clawed Lark; for further commentary, see Remarks under South African Long-clawed Lark.

References

Archer, G. and Godman, E. M. (1961) *The birds of British Somaliland and the Gulf of Aden*, 3. Edinburgh and London: Oliver and Boyd.

Ash, J. S. and Miskell, J. E. (1983) *Birds of Somalia: their habitat, status and distribution. Scopus* Spec. Suppl. 1. Nairobi: Ornithological Sub-Committee, EANHS.

Erard, C. (1975) Une nouvelle alouette du sud de l'Ethiopie. *Alauda* 43: 115-124.

Survey Directorate, General Headquarters Middle East (1947) *East Africa Index Gazetteer, 2 and 2A: Abyssinia, Eritrea, British, French and Italian Somaliland and part of the Sudan*. Cairo (1946): Directorate of Military Survey, The War Office.

The Times Atlas of the World (1980) Comprehensive (sixth) edition. London: Times Books.

War Office (1946) East Africa, 1:500,000, GSGS 4355, 4th edition.

SIDAMO LONG-CLAWED LARK   INDETERMINATE
Heteromirafra sidamoensis (Erard, 1975)

Order PASSERIFORMES   Family ALAUDIDAE

Summary Known from two specimens collected independently near Neghelli in Sidamo province, southern Ethiopia, this species is likely to prove highly restricted in range.

Distribution The type-specimen of the Sidamo Long-clawed Lark was collected on 18 May 1968 less than 2 km south of Neghelli (Nagele, Negelli; in Borana), at 1,450 m, in Sidamo province, southern Ethiopia (Erard 1975). A second specimen (male) was collected 12 km south-east of Neghelli (1-2 km south of the old airport) on 15 April 1974 (J. S. Ash *in litt.* 1983, Ash and Watson in prep.). Similar birds were seen on other occasions in April 1971 and April 1973 at 24 and 48 km south-east (on the track to Filtu) and 48 km south (on the track to Arero) from Neghelli and, although it is not certain that these were Sidamo Long-clawed Larks, these are additional areas that merit searching in the future (Ash and Watson in prep.).

Population Numbers are unknown but the species is considered rare; the type-locality was searched in October/November 1971 without success (Erard 1975).

Ecology The type-specimen was collected in the (seasonally) lush grass of a herbaceous steppe with scattered acacias, i.e. open savanna (Erard 1975). The failure to relocate the species later in the year, when the area was very dry, may indicate its rarity or that some migration occurs. The second specimen was collected in an open area of grassland, 5-6 km in diameter, surrounded by *Acacia/Commiphora* bush: although there was much new grass growing, there were also extensive areas of tall dead grass, some of it forming tussocks (Ash and Watson in prep.). The testes of the second specimen were developed (G. E. Watson and K. L. Pruitt *in litt.* 1984).

Threats None is known, except that – like the other two larks in the genus *Heteromirafra* (see Remarks) – the range of this species is likely to prove very restricted (hence its treatment here as Indeterminate rather than Insufficiently Known, used for the Degodi Lark *Mirafra degodiensis* which is also only known from two specimens). There is, however, "plenty of apparently suitable habitat" (J. S. Ash *in litt.* 1983).

Conservation Measures Taken None is known.

Conservation Measures Proposed Fieldwork is needed to rediscover this species and to determine its range, population and any possible threats it may face (see Conservation Measures Proposed under Ethiopian Bush-crow *Zavattariornis stresemanni*).

Remarks This third species of *Heteromirafra*, though geographically between the two others (the South African and Somali Long-clawed Larks *H. ruddi* and *H. archeri*: see relevant accounts, including Remarks under the former), is quite distinct (Erard 1975). It is to be noted that birds of this genus are believed to have been seen at Isiolo (north of Mount Kenya), Kenya, but that this record had not been published in the absence of a specimen (J. G. Williams pers. comm. 1983).

References

Ash, J. S. and Watson, G. E. (in prep.) A second specimen of *Mirafra (Heteromirafra) sidamoensis* Erard.

Erard, C. (1975) Une nouvelle alouette du sud de l'Ethiopie. *Alauda* 43: 115-124.

BOTHA'S LARK   INDETERMINATE

Spizocorys fringillaris (Sundevall, 1850)

Order PASSERIFORMES   Family ALAUDIDAE

Summary This species, endemic to South Africa, is only known from high altitude grasslands in northern Orange Free State and south-eastern Transvaal. It is rare for unknown reasons and only very seldom reported.

Distribution Botha's Lark is endemic to South Africa and has a very restricted range in the high altitude grasslands west of the Drakensberg watershed (Brooke in press). It occurs from Vredefort in northern Orange Free State locally north-eastwards to Estancia, just west of Breyten, in Transvaal (Brooke in press). In Orange Free State it has been recorded from Vredefort and Leeuwspruit (the type-locality) near Heilbron, and in Transvaal it is restricted to the Standerton, Amersfoort, Bethal, Ermelo and Wakkerstroom districts (Gyldenstolpe 1934, Roberts 1936, Hall and Moreau 1962, Clancey 1963,1980, Brooke in press, D. G. Allan *in litt.* 1984).

Population Numbers are not known. The species has certainly been judged very rare, as shown by the paucity of modern (post-1969) records (Brooke in press), but extrapolation from a crude measure of density (one bird per km^2) suggests an absolute minimum population of 1,000 and possibly up to 20,000 birds (Allan *et al.* 1983). There is no evidence of a population decrease (Brooke in press).

Ecology This species is known only from moist, open *Themeda* grassveld at high altitudes (Hall and Moreau 1962, Brooke in press). Its rarity and limited range are suggestive of strict breeding and foraging requirements (Brooke in press): within hilly sour grassveld near Amersfoort birds have been found patchily distributed in grassland areas on heavily grazed plateaus and upper slopes of hills, not in valley bottoms, vleis, pastures, cultivated lands or rock areas, and food seen taken was small insects (including beetles and moths) (Allan *et al.* 1983). Flocks of about ten birds have been seen (Hall and Moreau 1962) and the clutch-size has been given as three (Brooke in press) although two appears more usual (Allan *et al.* 1983). Breeding has been recorded in November and December (Allan *et al.* 1983).

Threats None is known, other than possibly the development of agriculture within its range (Allan *et al.* 1983) and the fact that the range itself is very restricted.

Conservation Measures Taken None is known, other than that the species is fully protected by South African law (Brooke in press). It might also benefit from the protection afforded to the surroundings of certain large dams in Orange Free State (Brooke in press).

376

Conservation Measures Proposed More research is needed to assess the status and distribution of this species and to determine whether further conservation action is required.

Remarks For many years Botha's Lark was confused with the more widespread and common White-tailed Bush-lark *Mirafra passerina* (Gyldenstolpe 1926) and most publications prior to 1926 which refer to *Spizocorys* (or *Calandrella* or *Alauda*) *fringillaris* are in fact referring to the White-tailed Bush-lark (Hall and Moreau 1962). For details of the systematic position of the species see Maclean (1969); also Allan *et al.* (1983).

References

Allan, D. G., Batchelor, G. R. and Tarboton, W. R. (1983) Breeding of Botha's Lark. *Ostrich* 54: 55-57.

Brooke, R. K. (in press) *The rare and vulnerable birds of South Africa.*

Clancey, P. A. (1963) A further record of Botha's Lark in the Transvaal. *Ostrich* 34: 169-170.

Clancey, P. A. ed. (1980) *S.A.O.S. Checklist of southern African birds.* [Pretoria:] Southern African Ornithological Society.

Gyldenstolpe, N. (1926) Types of birds in the Royal Natural History Museum in Stockholm. *Ark. Zool.* 19A: 1-116.

Gyldenstolpe, N. (1934) The travels and collections of John August Wahlberg, 1810-1856: a pioneer naturalist in South Africa. *Ibis* (13)4: 264-292.

Hall, B. P. and Moreau, R. E. (1962) A study of the rare birds of Africa. *Bull. Brit. Mus. (Nat. Hist.) Zool.* 8: 313-378.

Maclean, G. L. (1969) South African lark genera. *Cimbebasia* ser. A. 1: 79-94.

Roberts, A. (1936) Ornithological notes. *Ann. Transvaal Mus.* 18: 255-269.

RASO LARK ENDANGERED

Alauda razae (Alexander, 1898)

Order PASSERIFORMES Family ALAUDIDAE

Summary Restricted to a part of one very small, arid island (Raso) in the Cape Verde Islands, this ground dwelling bird's population is affected by climate and has recently been judged to be only around 20 pairs, having up to 20 years ago been in a healthy condition.

Distribution The Raso Lark is found only on the uninhabited island of Raso (less correctly, Razo, Raza) in the windward group of the Cape Verde archipelago (Republic of Cape Verde), Atlantic Ocean. Raso is only c. 7 km^2 (Schleich and Wuttke 1983) although the lark formerly chiefly occupied the central and some adjacent areas totalling 1-2 km^2 (de Naurois 1969, R. de Naurois *in litt.* 1983). It is now apparently restricted to an area of c. 1 km^2 in the south-west of the island roughly between Chão Branca and Chão do Castelo (H.-H. Schleich *in litt.* 1983; see map in Schleich and Wuttke 1983). A survey of the island from north to south on 15 June 1981 confirmed that birds were only to be found in the south-west close to the sea (Nørrevang and den Hartog in press).

Population The species was quite common and widespread on Raso when first described (Alexander 1898a), at least 60 being collected there in 1897-1898 (see Remarks); it was reputed to "abound" there in 1951 (Bourne 1955; also Meinertzhagen 1951, but see Remarks), and there was a "pullulement" ("swarm") of adults and juveniles in January 1963 (de Naurois 1969; year corrected from 1962 by R. de Naurois *in litt.* 1983). However, in four subsequent visits a gradual decrease in numbers was noted: in October 1965 the population was estimated to have dropped below 50 pairs, and in March 1968 it was down to less than 40 pairs (de Naurois 1969). Within the period 1979-1982 it was considered nearer only 20 pairs (H.-H. Schleich *in litt.* 1983). On 15 June 1981, after extensive exploration of the island, a flock of about 15-20 birds was eventually found, several and perhaps the majority being immature (Nørrevang and den Hartog in press).

Ecology This species inhabits level plains with mobile volcanic soil and sparse low vegetation; also some sloping ground (de Naurois 1969). Flocks have also been seen feeding among black rocks close to the sea (Alexander 1898a). Food was first reckoned to be grass-seed (Alexander 1898a) and two stomachs contained ants, beetles, seeds, small germinating plants and other vegetable matter, as well as grit (de Naurois 1969). However, the large bill is considered adapted for digging up food, e.g. grubs (Meinertzhagen 1951, Hall 1963), although a claimed observation of this (Meinertzhagen 1951) is now open to doubt (see Remarks) and it has more recently been noted that a bill length difference of 21% exists between the sexes and that their feeding ecology is therefore likely to differ (Burton 1971). There is a suggestion that the species is "adapted to exploit the rich plant and insect life of an isolated sea-bird colony" (Bourne 1966). The frail grass nest (up to three eggs recorded) is made in a small depression in loose stony soil in a patch of grass, under

378

a rock or creeping plant (Alexander 1898b; see photograph in Schleich and Wuttke 1983), but the speculation that it might also be placed low in a dense low shrub (de Naurois 1969) is now discounted (R. de Naurois *in litt.* 1983). Breeding has been reported in April and October (Alexander 1898a,b) and probably occurs from September to April in response to rainfall-dependent vegetation growth; conversely, breeding is greatly inhibited by drought (de Naurois 1969). Some birds seen in mid-June 1981 were very young and had evidently fledged shortly before (Nørrevang and den Hartog in press). Although described as extremely tame (Alexander 1898a, de Naurois 1969), the species had a flushing distance of 10 m in 1981 (Nørrevang and den Hartog in press).

Threats Absence or failure of breeding as a result of drought was blamed for the steady decline in numbers, 1963-1968 (de Naurois 1969). Drought conditions in Cape Verde are known to have continued into the 1970s and were still prevalent in 1981 (A. Nørrevang *in litt.* 1984), and may thus be responsible for the further reduction in numbers that has apparently occurred. Given the low numbers in 1968 and the large number of skins in museum collections (see Remarks), the collection of seven birds in 1970 (Frade 1976) seems to have been a needless risk (and did not even result in published data on gonad condition or stomach contents); further collecting would directly imperil the species. It is possible that competition from the Rufous-backed Sparrow *Passer iagoensis*, apparently more numerous in June 1981 than in the 1960s, may have adversely affected the lark (Nørrevang and den Hartog in press). The suggestion that the birds were formerly more widely distributed in the Cape Verdes but suffered local extinctions when man colonised the archipelago (Bourne 1955) has been discarded (see Bourne 1966), but it is clear that human settlement of Raso could pose serious new threats to the lark. It has already been observed that rats *Rattus* could easily colonise the island and rapidly exterminate the species (King 1978-1979). Its remains have been found in pellets of Barn Owls *Tyto alba* (de Naurois 1969); Kestrels *Falco tinnunculus* and Ravens *Corvus corax* are also present on Raso and seem likely to take a toll of the species (Nørrevang and den Hartog in press).

Conservation Measures Taken None is known.

Conservation Measures Proposed Twenty years ago recommendations were made that Raso should be established as a faunal reserve for the protection of the lark and the giant skink *Macroscincus coctei* (endemic to Raso and neighbouring Branco), and that the lark should be fully protected by law (de Naurois 1964). Action appears not to have been taken on this (the skink is probably extinct: see Schleich 1979, Schleich and Wuttke 1983) and therefore remains highly desirable; certainly no further collecting for museums should be allowed (a view also expressed by Nørrevang and den Hartog in press). A study of this species's biology would provide a better understanding of its conservation requirements, and occasional monitoring would usefully supplement such knowledge.

Remarks This bird was formerly placed in *Spizocorys*, *Calandrella* and even its own genus, *Razocorys*, but is now considered an aberrant skylark *Alauda*

(Hall 1963, Burton 1971). Good series of the species exist in various institutions, e.g. 30 (all collected 28 October – 5 November 1898) in Genoa (Salvadori 1899), 25 (all collected in 1897) in BMNH (D. K. Read pers. comm. 1983), and eight (five collected in 1897) in AMNH (M. LeCroy *in litt.* 1983), plus at least seven in Lisbon (see Threats). A reported observation of this species ("the short time during which I observed *razae*, they were constantly excavating for grubs and not surface-feeding for seeds": Meinertzhagen 1951) appears to be a confusion: the observer's unpublished diaries (Meinertzhagen 1899-1965) indicate that he never visited the Cape Verdes but merely saw them from a ship in 1906, having just previously paid a brief visit to La Palma (Canary Islands) where he had found the Lesser Short-toed Lark *Calandrella rufescens* abundant. It seems highly probable that the remark quoted above and the statement in the same source (Meinertzhagen 1951) that Raso Larks "are abundant" in fact refer to larks seen on La Palma.

References

Alexander, B. (1898a) An ornithological expedition to the Cape Verde Islands. *Ibis* (7)4: 74-118.

Alexander, B. (1898b) Further notes on the ornithology of the Cape Verde Islands. *Ibis* (7)4: 277-285.

Bourne, W. R. P. (1955) The birds of the Cape Verde Islands. *Ibis* 97: 508-556.

Bourne, W. R. P. (1966) Further notes on the birds of the Cape Verde Islands. *Ibis* 108: 425-429.

Burton, P. J. K. (1971) Sexual size dimorphism in *Alauda razae*. *Bull. Brit. Orn. Club* 91: 108-109.

Frade, F. (1976) Aves do arquipélago de Cabo Verde. *Garcia de Orta* Ser. Zool. 5(1): 47-58.

Hall, B. P. (1963) The status of *Spizocorys razae* Alexander. *Bull. Brit. Orn. Club* 83: 133-134.

King, W. B. (1978-1979) *Red data book, 2: Aves.* 2nd edition. Morges, Switzerland: IUCN.

Meinertzhagen, R. (1899-1965) Diaries (76 volumes), held in Rhodes House Library, Oxford.

Meinertzhagen, R. (1951) Review of the Alaudidae. *Proc. Zool. Soc. Lond.* 121: 81-132.

de Naurois, R. (1964) Les oiseaux des îles du Cap-Vert. Suggestions en vue de leur sauvegarde. *Garcia de Orta* 12(4): 609-620.

de Naurois, R. (1969) Notes brèves sur l'avifaune de l'archipel du Cap-Vert. Faunistique, endémisme, écologie. *Bull. Inst. Fond. Afrique Noire* 31, Ser. A(1): 143-218.

Nørrevang, A. and den Hartog, J. C. (in press) Bird observations in the Cape Verde Islands (4-22 June 1981). CANCAP project: contribution to the zoology, botany and paleontology of the Canarian – Cape Verdean region of the North Atlantic Ocean, no. 39. *Courier Forschungsinstitut Senckenberg.*

Salvadori, T. (1899) Collezioni ornitologiche fatte nelle Isole de Capo Verde da Leonardo Fea. *Ann. Mus. Civ. Genova* 40: 283-312.

Schleich, H.-H. (1979) Der Kapverdische Riesenskink, *Macroscincus coctei*, eine ausgestorbene Echse? *Natur u. Mus.* 109: 133-138.

Schleich, H.-H. and Wuttke, M. (1983) Die kapverdischen Eilande Santa Luzia, Branco und Razo – ein Reisebericht. *Natur u. Mus.* 113: 33-44.

WHITE-TAILED SWALLOW   RARE

Hirundo megaensis Benson 1942

Order PASSERIFORMES   Family HIRUNDINIDAE
                                                    Subfamily HIRUNDININAE

Summary The factors restricting this open country species to its small range around Mega and Yavello in southern Ethiopia are unknown and, although it is common, without an understanding of these factors or a measure of protection for its habitat, it must always be considered at some risk.

Distribution The White-tailed Swallow is restricted to an area of very approximately 10,000 km² between and around Yavello (Yabelo) and Mega, Sidamo province, southern Ethiopia. It has been recorded up to 50 km north of Yavello (Benson 1942), 15 km north-north-east of Yavello (J. S. Ash *in litt.* 1983), and 50 km east and south-east of Mega (Benson 1942,1946; but see Remarks) but chiefly between these two towns (Benson 1942,1946, J. S. Ash *in litt.* 1983, C. Erard pers. comm. 1983). The altitudinal range was originally given as 1,220-1,520 m (Benson 1942,1946), but subsequently as 1,220-1,370 m (Hall and Moreau 1962, Urban and Brown 1971), with birds also ranging uncommonly up to 2,400 m (Urban and Brown 1971): it is not known on what evidence these later refinements were made, but in any case it appears that both sets of altitudes were incorrect (see Remarks). There were sight records from highland grasslands (1,800-2,750 m) at Addis Ababa just before 1970 which required confirmation (J. S. Ash *in litt.* 1983, Urban and Brown 1971); no trace of the species was found in the Addis Ababa area in 1969-1977 (J. S. Ash *in litt.* 1983).

Population Within its small range this bird is considered common (Benson 1942,1946) or fairly common (J. S. Ash *in litt.* 1983). In a 60 km stretch of road between Yavello and Mega (from 20 km south of Yavello), 15-20 birds were seen per day, 1971 (C. Erard pers. comm. 1983).

Ecology The species inhabits open, arid, short-grass country with scattered low thorn bushes; it is not associated with buildings (none in this habitat) but is suspected of nesting in holes in tall chimney-stack termitaria common in the area (Benson 1942,1946). Association with these termitaria has been noted subsequently (J. S. Ash *in litt.* 1983, C. Erard pers. comm. 1983), and birds have been seen to feed in the lee of flowering trees (J. S. Ash *in litt.* 1983). They probably breed January/February, as a specimen taken in March had no skull ossification (Benson 1942). Having been noticed in the Yavello/ Mega region throughout the period from June 1941 to March 1942, it is probably not migratory (Benson 1946). The factors restricting this species to its small range are unknown, since apparently suitable habitat occurs elsewhere (e.g. at Neghelli: Benson 1946): south of Mega an escarpment reduces altitude and may represent a natural boundary, but no other features have been identified as possible constraints (Benson 1942, Hall and Moreau 1962); but see Remarks.

Threats No part of the very limited range of this species is known to be protected. It has been pointed out that any development ("range management") scheme between Yavello and Mega, such as those that have been implemented elsewhere in the region (see Threats under Ethiopian Bush-crow *Zavattariornis stresemanni*), might place the bird at risk (J. S. Ash *in litt.* 1983).

Conservation Measures Taken None is known.

Conservation Measures Proposed A study of this species is needed to determine its ecological requirements, status and exact distribution in the Yavello/Mega region, and to prepare sound recommendations for its permanent conservation (see Conservation Measures Proposed under Ethiopian Bush-crow).

Remarks Modern maps show that both Yavello and Mega are at or above 2,000 m, and that the intervening country is at or above 1,500 m (see, e.g., D. Survey [WO and AM] 1962, HOGC 1969, TAW 1980). More interestingly, they also indicate that the 1,500 m contour forms a distinct "peninsula" of high ground protruding south from Yavello to just beyond Mega, with several "islands" of land above 1,500 m to the east of Mega. In the absence of other explanations, it seems possible that there is a precise altitudinal factor at play in determining the limits of this species's range. It seems probable that the localities given as 50 km south-east and 50 km east of Mega (see Distribution) are one and the same, and that the second designation was a correction of the first; at any rate, 50 km east of Mega is on the largest and nearest of the "islands" of ground above 1,500 m in this general region. The species is largely sympatric with the Ethiopian Bush-crow (see relevant sheet), the chief differences being that the latter is also known from 60 km east of Yavello but is not known from 50 km east of Mega.

References

Benson, C. W. (1942) A new species and ten new races from southern Abyssinia. *Bull. Brit. Orn. Club* 63: 8-19.

Benson, C. W. (1946) Notes on the birds of southern Abyssinia. *Ibis* 88: 287-306.

D. Survey (WO and AM) (1962). World 1: 1,000,000, Series 1301, sheet NB-37, 4-GSGS.

Hall, B. P. and Moreau, R. E. (1962) A study of the rare birds of Africa. *Bull. Brit. Mus. (Nat. Hist.) Zool.* 8: 313-378.

Head Office of Geodesy and Cartography (1969) [Karta Mira] World map 1: 2,500,000, NA-C 37-39 115. Sofia, Bulgaria.

The Times Atlas of the World (1980) Comprehensive (sixth) edition. London: Times Books.

Urban, E. K. and Brown, L. H. (1971) *A checklist of the birds of Ethiopia.* Addis Ababa: Haile Selassie I University Press.

SOKOKE PIPIT   VULNERABLE
Anthus sokokensis van Someren, 1921

Order PASSERIFORMES   Family MOTACILLIDAE

Summary This unique forest-dwelling pipit is known from only three lowland forest areas on the East African coast (Kenya, Tanzania). In one of these areas the forest has probably been completely cleared and in another the species is very rare.

Distribution The Sokoke Pipit is known only from three coastal forest sites, one in Kenya and two in Tanzania. Most records of this species come from the type-locality, Sokoke Forest, in Kenya (Turner 1977, Britton and Zimmerman 1979, Britton *et al.* in press) where it is absent only from the impoverished low rainfall habitats in the north-west of the Sokoke Forest Reserve (Britton and Zimmerman 1979). A long series of specimens was collected in Sokoke in 1921, 1923 and 1924 (van Someren 1921,1932). Further specimens were taken in this locality between 1964 and 1970 (Ripley and Bond 1971, and specimens in NMK and BMNH: SNS). In recent years the species has been reported regularly from Sokoke (Britton and Zimmerman 1979). It is also known from the small Gede Forest adjacent to Sokoke (Turner 1977, Britton and Zimmerman 1979). Two specimens were collected 160 km to the south near Moa on the Tanzanian coast in 1931 (Sclater and Moreau 1932). There have been no recent visits by ornithologists to this site but very little coastal forest remains in northern Tanzania and it is unlikely that this patch survives (SNS). The species was found in forest on the Pugu Hills near Dar es Salaam in Tanzania in 1938 (Moreau 1940, and specimen in BMNH: SNS). In 1955 two birds were seen a few miles west of the Pugu Hills near the road from Dar es Salaam to Morogoro (N. R. Fuggles-Couchman *in litt.* 1983). The only other record from the Pugu Hills is of an adult and grown young bird seen in May 1981 (E. O. Willis *in litt.* 1981). It was probably more widespread before the extensive clearance of the coastal forests (Hall and Moreau 1962).

Population Numbers were estimated at 3,000 to 5,000 pairs in the Sokoke Forest Reserve in the late 1970s (Britton and Zimmerman 1979) but perhaps little more than 2,000 pairs in 1983 (Kelsey and Langton 1984), although it has been suggested that both these estimates might be too high (A. D. Forbes-Watson pers. comm. 1984). Numbers occurring in parts of Sokoke outside the forest reserve have not been estimated but many of these areas have now been cleared (Ripley and Bond 1971) and others are unlikely to survive for long (Britton and Zimmerman 1979). It was stated to be rare in the Pugu Hills when it was first discovered there (Moreau 1940) and subsequent fieldwork confirms this impression (Stuart and van der Willigen 1978, N. E. Baker pers. comm. 1981, K. M. Howell pers. comm. 1981, N. R. Fuggles-Couchman *in litt.* 1983). The population at Moa probably no longer survives (Stuart and van der Willigen 1978; SNS).

Ecology In Sokoke Forest where the species has been best studied it is common in dense uncleared forest dominated by *Afzelia cuanzensis* (Britton and

Zimmerman 1979, Kelsey and Langton 1984), contrary to earlier reports which suggested that it preferred forest edges and glades (van Someren 1921,1932, Hall and Moreau 1962). In *Afzelia*-dominated forest, which occupied 50 km^2 inside the Sokoke Forest Reserve in the late 1970s (Britton and Zimmerman 1979) but perhaps only 35 km^2 in 1983 (Kelsey and Langton 1984), the Sokoke Pipit might occur in densities of up to one pair per 2 ha (Britton and Zimmerman 1979). Elsewhere in Sokoke it occurs at lower densities in *Brachystegia* woodland, *Cynometra-Manilkara* forest and lowland rainforest (Britton and Zimmerman 1979, Kelsey and Langton 1984). The forest at the Pugu Hills is not dominated by *Afzelia* trees (Howell 1981) and this might account for the rarity of the species at that locality. The birds seen west of the Pugu Hills in 1955 were on the edge of a thicket, and it is thought that such thickets are relics of the scrubby forest which occurs on the Pugu Hills (N. R. Fuggles-Couchman *in litt.* 1983). The Sokoke Pipit lives mainly on the forest floor (Britton and Zimmerman 1979) and one report records birds feeding on white ants (Sclater and Moreau 1932). When flushed from the ground it usually flies to a high perch (Britton and Zimmerman 1979, Kelsey and Langton 1984). There are no breeding data.

Threats The logging of valuable timber trees in Sokoke Forest continues (Britton and Zimmerman 1979), even within the supposedly inviolate nature reserve (Cunningham-van Someren 1981-1982). Areas of forest are also being cleared for the planting of exotic trees (Britton and Zimmerman 1979). The favoured *Afzelia* forest habitat is being particularly severely disturbed and only about one-third of its area remains in reasonably good condition (Kelsey and Langton 1984). Although the species can tolerate some disturbance to its habitat it is likely that continuing degradation is causing a population decline (Kelsey and Langton 1984). Unfortunately the work of the forest officers at Sokoke has been rendered ineffective by shortage of available funds (Kelsey and Langton 1984). It seems that certain conservation regulations have been ignored by people taking advantage of the lack of supervision by officials from the Forestry Department (Kelsey and Langton 1984). The conservation status of the Pugu Hills is also deteriorating with areas being cleared and cultivated (K. M. Howell *in litt.* 1982); some forest has been cleared for a brick factory and for a kaolin mine (Howell 1981; further details under Conservation Measures Taken).

Conservation Measures Taken The 400 km^2 Sokoke Forest Reserve provides some protection for the forest, though the logging of valuable timber trees and the clearing of forest for plantations are both legal (Britton and Zimmerman 1979). There is a 43 km^2 nature reserve within the forest reserve in which no cutting or exploitation is permitted (Britton and Zimmerman 1979). These regulations are not, however, being observed (Cunningham-van Someren 1981-1982, Kelsey and Langton 1984). A considerable area of *Afzelia* forest, suitable for the Sokoke Pipit, occurs within the nature reserve (Britton and Zimmerman 1979). Pugu Hills are included within the Pugu Forest Reserve but this has not afforded much protection and of the original 22 km^2 of forest, only 10 km^2 remained at the start of the 1980s (Howell 1981).

Conservation Measures Proposed Details of recommendations for the Sokoke Forest are given in Conservation Measures Proposed under Sokoke Scops Owl *Otus ireneae*. The Pugu Forest will survive only if the Tanzanian Forestry Division enforces a much stricter conservation policy (SNS).

Remarks Five other threatened bird species are known from Sokoke Forest (see Remarks under the Sokoke Scops Owl), two of which, the East Coast Akalat *Sheppardia gunningi* and the Spotted Ground Thrush *Turdus fischeri*, are also recorded from the Pugu Hills.

References

Britton, P. L. and Zimmerman, D. A. (1979) The avifauna of Sokoke Forest, Kenya. *J. E. Afr. Nat. Hist. Soc. and Natn. Mus.* 169: 1-15.

Britton, P. L., Stuart, S. N. and Turner, D. A. (in press) East African endangered species. *Proc. V Pan-Afr. orn. Congr.*

Cunningham-van Someren, G. R. ed. (1981-1982) *National Museum of Kenya, Department of Ornithology Museum Avifauna News*: 19,34,63,72.

Hall, B. P. and Moreau, R. E. (1962) A study of the rare birds of Africa. *Bull. Brit. Mus. (Nat. Hist.) Zool.* 8: 313-378.

Howell, K. M. (1981) Pugu Forest Reserve: biological values and development. *Afr. J. Ecol.* 19: 73-81.

Kelsey, M. G. and Langton, T. E. S. (1984) The conservation of the Arabuko-Sokoke Forest, Kenya. International Council for Bird Preservation and University of East Anglia. *International Council for Bird Preservation Study Report* no. 4.

Moreau, R. E. (1940) Distributional notes on East African birds. *Ibis* (14)4: 454-463.

Ripley, S. D. and Bond, G. M. (1971) Systematic notes on a collection of birds from Kenya. *Smithsonian Contrib. Zool.* 111.

Sclater, W. L. and Moreau, R. E. (1932) Taxonomic and field notes on some birds of north-eastern Tanganyika Territory, Part II. *Ibis* (13)2: 656-683.

van Someren, V. G. L. (1921) [New East African forms.] *Bull. Brit. Orn. Club* 41: 120-125.

van Someren, V. G. L. (1932) Birds of Kenya and Uganda, being addenda and corrigenda to my previous paper in *Novitates Zoologicae* XXIX, 1922. *Novit. Zool.* 37: 252-380.

Stuart, S. N. and van der Willigen, T. A. (1978) Report of the Cambridge Ecological Expedition to Tanzania 1978. Unpublished.

Turner, D. A. (1977) Status and distribution of East African endemic species. *Scopus* 1: 2-11,56.

MAURITIUS CUCKOO-SHRIKE   VULNERABLE
Coracina typica (Hartlaub, 1865)

Order PASSERIFORMES   Family CAMPEPHAGIDAE

Summary This insectivorous, forest-dwelling species, endemic to Mauritius, continues to suffer from habitat loss and, more seriously, from very heavy predation of its nests by introduced mammals.

Distribution The Mauritius Cuckoo-shrike is confined to the remaining areas of native forest on Mauritius, Indian Ocean. Since in the 1860s it was found in every part of the island where original forest remained (Pollen 1886), it presumably occurred throughout Mauritius prior to the arrival of man; at the start of this century, it was already confined to the south-western corner of the island (Carié 1904, Meinertzhagen 1912) where it now survives only in and around the Black River Gorges and in the Bel Ombre forest (Procter and Salm 1974, Temple *et al.* 1974, Cheke in press), although the call of the species was thought to have been heard in the Montagnes Bambous in eastern Mauritius in 1973 (Cheke in press; see Remarks).

Population This species's elusiveness (see Ecology) has doubtless been responsible for contradictory statements on its status since as far back as the 1820s, when it was reported as both "common" and "quite rare" (see Oustalet 1897). At the turn of the century it was "very rare" (Carié 1904), twenty years later it was thought the rarest bird on Mauritius and soon to become extinct (Carié 1921), by around 1950 it was (still) "rapidly approaching extinction" (Rountree 1951), but subsequently it was reported locally abundant (and "by no means rare") in the remnants of its habitat (Newton 1958b, Gill 1971b) and still fairly common at Macabé (Macchabée) (Fabian 1970). Preliminary analysis of fieldwork on this species in the early 1970s suggested a population of around 100 pairs (Cheke in press) and this figure was repeated and published without proviso (Temple 1974, Temple *et al.* 1974, King 1978-1979), but full analysis now shows roughly double this quantity: 114 territories were located and, allowing for inaccessible areas and partial coverage of others, the total present in 1974-1975 is estimated to have been 210-220 pairs (Cheke in press). The loss of Les Mares in 1972-1974 may, however, have resulted in abnormally high density at certain localities (since on a revisit in 1978 density had been halved) and, allowing also for the loss of birds at Kanaka forest where they were common (Cheke 1978; see Threats), the present population might now be expected to be 180-190 pairs (Cheke in press).

Ecology The species occurs singly or in pairs (Oustalet 1897, Cheke in press) chiefly in native forest but also in degraded or altered forest in adjacent areas (Oustalet 1897, Newton 1958a, Temple *et al.* 1974, King 1978-1979, Cheke in press), birds reaching high density (16-22 territories per km^2) only in fairly unaltered closed-canopy forest (Cheke in press). Despite the nineteenth century report of its apparent preference for lower altitude forest (Oustalet 1897), the density of birds in areas of remaining good forest was found to fall off rapidly below

450 m where it is drier and warmer (Cheke in press), although the species is present in the lower reaches of Bel Ombre forest at 240 m and is occasionally seen in the Black River Gorges as low as 200 m (C. G. Jones *in litt.* 1984). The species has been reported to favour low forest, e.g. where clearings are becoming overgrown with thickets, and to occur even in relatively open scrubby country (Carié 1921, Gill 1971b); the vicinity of running water may also be important (Carié 1921). Birds were found on the plateau (at Kanaka) in degraded forest interplanted with the commercial evergreens *Eugenia ventenatii* and *Cinnamomum camphora* (Cheke 1978, in press). Birds have been reported to forage in the lower layers of plants (Procter and Salm 1974) but most feeding is done in the canopy (Cheke in press). Birds feed almost exclusively on insects taken from leaves and twigs, chiefly by gleaning, also by hover-feeding and leaf-snatching (Cheke in press; also Gill 1971b, Temple *et al.* 1974). Insects recorded include caterpillars, moths, stick-insects and, mostly, beetles (especially weevils) (Oustalet 1897, Newton 1958a, Staub 1976, Cheke in press); other food items have been berries (Oustalet 1897), a fruit of *Elaendendron orientale* (Cheke in press), a seed (specimen-label in UMZC: NJC) and a half-grown gecko *Phelsuma* (Cheke in press). Pairs appear to keep to well-defined territories (4.5-6 ha in size in the best habitat) throughout the year (Cheke in press), although some association with travelling bird parties, composed chiefly of Mascarene Grey White-eyes *Zosterops borbonicus*, often with Mauritius Fodies *Foudia rubra* and occasionally Mauritius Olive White-eyes *Z. chloronothus*, has been noted (Gill 1971a,b). The breeding season is evidently protracted, activity concentrated in October/November (Pollen 1886) or at least September/December (Temple *et al.* 1974), but direct and indirect evidence indicates that it may continue through until March (Meinertzhagen 1912, Newton 1958a, Cheke in press). Nests are built in forks of trees or against trunks, often poorly concealed (Cheke in press; also Staub 1976), though they are also described as well hidden usually at the top of densely foliaged trees (Pollen 1886, Temple *et al.* 1974); trees used include bois balai *Erythroxylon hypericifolium* (or possibly *Grangeria borbonica*), bois de pomme *Syzygium glomeratum*, Mauritius ebony *Diospyros tessellaria* and bois dur *Securinega durissima* (Cheke in press). Clutch-size is usually two (Pollen 1886, Staub 1976); claims of three (Temple *et al.* 1974) are unsubstantiated (A. S. Cheke pers. comm. 1984). Breeding success is low (see Threats). Birds are very tame (Meinertzhagen 1912) but highly secretive (Newton 1958a, Niven 1965, Temple *et al.* 1974).

Threats A general account of the problems facing the endemic forest-dependent birds of Mauritius is given in Threats under Mauritius Kestrel *Falco punctatus*. The creole name of this species, "merle cuisinier", refers to its former attraction as a table delicacy, birds being much shot even in the breeding season (Newton 1883, Meinertzhagen 1912). Since 1950 two major threats have been identified: habitat loss (Rountree 1951, Temple 1974) and nest predation (Temple 1974, Cheke in press). The (World Bank financed) clearance in 1971-1974 of half (c. 2,800 ha) of the upland *Sideroxylon-Helichrysum* dwarf forest at Les Mares on Plaine Champagne seriously reduced this species's population (Jones 1980, in press, Jones and Owadally 1982, Cheke in press). The most recent loss of habitat has been at Kanaka crater, where clear-felling occurred between 1974 and 1978

(Cheke 1978, in press), and in Crown Land Gouly above Bois Sec, where clear-felling continued up to 1980 (C. G. Jones *in litt.* 1984). Nest predation has been attributed to introduced crab-eating macaques *Macaca fascicularis* and witnessed in black rats *Rattus rattus* (Newton 1876, Temple 1974, Temple *et al.* 1974, Cheke in press, F. Staub *per* C. G. Jones *in litt.* 1984), and may also be perpetrated by introduced Red-whiskered Bulbuls *Pycnonotus jocosus* and Indian Mynahs *Acridotheres tristis* (Temple *et al.* 1974, King 1978-1979, Cheke in press): breeding success was at any rate so low in the early 1970s that it was rare to see the distinctively plumaged young (Temple *et al.* 1974) and every nest that was observed failed (Cheke in press). Red-whiskered Bulbuls and Indian Mynahs may now prevent this species's expansion into disturbed native forest (Jones 1982a,b).

Conservation Measures Taken This species has long been protected by law (Meinertzhagen 1912) and in 1974 its remaining native forest habitat received considerable protection when the Macabé/Bel Ombre Nature Reserve was created throught the linking of existing reserves at Petrin, Macabé and Bel Ombre by the addition of Les Mares and Plaine Champagne, forming a large block covering 3,594 ha (Owadally 1976; see map in Procter and Salm 1974). The report that six pairs were taken to JWPT in 1976 for captive breeding (King 1978-1979) was in error (Cheke 1980).

Conservation Measures Proposed The fact that birds occurred commonly in plantations mixed with depauperate relicts of original native vegetation has given rise to the consideration that, by a carefully chosen mix of evergreen trees (hardwood or tree-crop, with some native species), varied artificial habitats for this and several other threatened endemic species (Mauritius Bulbul *Hypsipetes olivaceus*, Mauritius Olive White-eye and Mauritius Fody) might be created as commercially viable long-term conservation enterprises in many upland areas (Cheke 1978; supported in Jones and Owadally 1982). Reintroduction into suitable unoccupied habitat in the Montagnes Bambous has been suggested (King 1978-1979) but this raises the question of why the bird became extinct there (if it did: see Distribution) and whether the causative factors would still operate. Control of predators, notably monkeys, would benefit the species (Temple 1974). A new census (to be conducted in August/September, when males sing: Gill 1971b) is needed (see Remarks). Work to safeguard this species will now proceed within the framework of the Mauritius Wildlife Research and Conservation Programme (see Conservation Measures Taken under Mauritius Kestrel).

Remarks Apropos the call of the species being heard in the Montagnes Bambous and censusing the species during its song-period, it is to be noted that the Indian Mynah mimics the Mauritius Cuckoo-shrike well, so that caution must be exercised in assigning identity to an unseen singer (C. G. Jones *in litt.* 1984).

References

Carié, P. (1904) Observations sur quelques oiseaux de l'île Maurice. *Ornis* 12: 121-128.

Carié, P. (1921) Le merle cuisinier de l'Ile Maurice (*Lalage rufiventer* Siv.). *Oiseau* 2: 2-5.

Cheke, A. S. (1978) Recommendations for the conservation of Mascarene vertebrates. Conservation memorandum no. 3 (arising out of the B.O.U. Mascarene Islands Expedition). Unpublished.

Cheke, A. S. (1980) [Review of King (1978-1979).] *Ibis* 122: 545.

Cheke, A. S. (in press) The surviving native land-birds of Mauritius. In A. W. Diamond, ed. *Studies of Mascarene island birds*. Cambridge: Cambridge University Press.

Fabian, D. T. (1970) The birds of Mauritius. *Bokmakierie* 22: 16-17, 21.

Gill, F. B. (1971a) Ecology and evolution of the sympatric Mascarene white-eyes, *Zosterops borbonica* and *Zosterops olivacea*. *Auk* 88: 35-60.

Gill, F. B. (1971b) Endemic landbirds of Mauritius Island, Indian Ocean. Unpublished.

Jones, C. G. (1982a) The conservation of the endemic birds and bats of Mauritius and Rodrigues. (Annual report 1981, W.W.F. Project 1082.) Unpublished.

Jones, C. G. (1982b) Struggle for survival on tropical islands. *WWF Monthly Report* February: 37-42.

Jones, C. G. and Owadally, A. W. (1982) Conservation priorities for Mauritius and Rodrigues. Report submitted to ICBP, July. Unpublished.

King, W. B. (1978-1979) *Red data book, 2: Aves*. 2nd edition. Morges, Switzerland: IUCN.

Meinertzhagen, R. (1912) On the birds of Mauritius. *Ibis* (9)6: 82-108.

Newton, A. (1876) On the species of *Hypsipetes* inhabiting Madagascar and the neighbouring islands. *Rowley's Orn. Misc.* 2: 41-52.

Newton, E. (1883) Annexe C [Letter to V. Naz, 26 February 1878]. *Trans. Soc. Roy. Arts Sci. Maurice* (NS) 12: 70-73.

Newton, R. (1958a) Ornithological notes on Mauritius and the Cargados Carajos Archipelago. *Proc. Roy. Soc. Arts Sci. Mauritius* 2(1): 39-71.

Newton, R. (1958b) Bird preservation in Mauritius. *ICBP Bull.* 7: 182-185.

Niven, C. (1965) Birds of Mauritius. *Ostrich* 36: 84-86.

Oustalet, E. (1897) Notice sur la faune ornithologique ancienne et moderne des îles Mascareignes et en particulier de l'île Maurice d'après des documents inédits. *Ann. Sci. Nat. Zool.* (8)3: 1-128.

Owadally, A. W. (1976) *Annual report of the Forestry Service for the year 1974*. Port Louis, Mauritius: L. Carl Achille, Government Printer.

Pollen, F. (1886) On the genus *Oxynotus* of Mauritius and Réunion. *Ibis* (2)2: 275-280.

Procter, J. and Salm, R. (1974) Conservation in Mauritius 1974. IUCN/WWF consultancy report for Government of Mauritius. Unpublished.

Rountree, F. G. R. (1951) Some aspects of bird-life in Mauritius. *Proc. Roy. Soc. Arts Sci. Mauritius* 1(2): 83-96.

Staub, F. (1976) *Birds of the Mascarenes and Saint Brandon*. Port Louis, Mauritius: Organisation Normale des Enterprises.

Temple, S. A. (1974) Appendix 6. The native fauna of Mauritius: 1, the land birds. In J. Procter and R. Salm, Conservation in Mauritius 1974. IUCN/WWF consultancy report for Government of Mauritius. Unpublished.

Temple, S. A., Staub, J. J. F. and Antoine, R. (1974) Some background information and recommendations on the preservation of the native flora and fauna of Mauritius. Unpublished report to the Government of Mauritius.

REUNION CUCKOO-SHRIKE

VULNERABLE

Coracina newtoni (Pollen, 1866)

Order PASSERIFORMES

Family CAMPEPHAGIDAE

Summary This insectivorous forest-dwelling species, endemic to Réunion, is restricted for unknown reasons to one very small and inadequately protected area in the north-west of the island where its habitat is being degraded by deer and where it is at some risk from poachers.

Distribution The Réunion Cuckoo-shrike is confined to a very small area of forest in the north-west of the island of Réunion (part of France) in the Indian Ocean. When first discovered, in the last century, it was present in the heights above La Possession, chiefly in the Dos d'Ane forests, also in the St.-Denis heights and the mountains near Ravine le Frais and Camp Rattaire (see Cheke 1976,1977). It survives today in precisely the same localities: Plaine d'Affouches (adjacent to the Dos d'Ane) and Plaine des Chicots (Ravine le Frais; location of Camp Rattaire not determined), the only difference being that birds now occur at 1,300-1,800 m (Cheke 1976,1977) or up to 1,900 m (Barré 1983) rather than at 800-1,400 m (Schlegel and Pollen 1868; see Remarks). The total area involved is only 16 km^2, but 40% of this holds no birds (Cheke 1976,1977), which explains the recent statement that the species is restricted to just 10 km^2 (Barré 1983). Records from the south-east of the island (Grand Brûlé, St.-Philippe) are open to question (Cheke 1976,1977, in press) and other records require confirmation (see Cheke 1976,1977), notably that of a bird seen at St.-Benoît at 300 m, in the north-east of the island (Milon 1951).

Population At the time of its discovery, this species was "very abundant" (see Cheke 1976,1977), but was later accounted so rare as to be possibly extinct already (Berlioz 1946) or at least on its way to extinction (Milon 1951). Widespread inquiries during a two-month visit in the mid-1960s led to the conclusion that probably no more than 10 pairs survived (Vincent 1966-1971). However, census work conducted over a week in August 1974 (August reportedly being the month in which birds are most vocal and therefore detectable) established the existence of between 43 and 53 territories, and allowed for a calculation of 120 territories (minimum 100, maximum 150) (Cheke 1976,1977). It is assumed that each territory held a pair of birds (Cheke 1976,1977). The population may have been lower in the period from the 1940s to the 1960s, possibly owing to poaching and the major cyclone of January 1948 (Cheke in press), since there is a reliable report that the species increased in the five years prior to 1974 (Cheke 1976,1977, in press; see Conservation Measures Taken). There seems to have been little change since 1974, at least until 1978 (Cheke 1979, in press).

Ecology When first discovered the species was reported to inhabit remote impenetrable forests, preferring thick scrub covering steep slopes (Schlegel and Pollen 1868). Its occurrence then as low as 800 m is assumed to have been in mixed evergreen forest ("bois de couleurs"), but as it was also then noted to feed on palm

390

beetles its retreat to a higher level is attributed to the destruction of palm-trees by poachers (Cheke 1976,1977). Within its present range most territories contain elements of three vegetation-types, tamarin *Acacia heterophylla* forest, mixed evergreen forest, and *Philippia abietina* heath; none is without the two last, but some lower territories lack tamarins (Cheke 1976,1977, in press). Territories appear to be roughly 8 ha in size, 6 ha at lower altitudes (Cheke 1976,1977, in press). Birds occur singly or in pairs (Schlegel and Pollen 1868, Cheke 1976,1977), but sometimes associate with Mascarene Grey White-eyes *Zosterops borbonicus* (Cheke in press); they are generally more silent and canopy-loving than Mauritius Cuckoo-shrikes *Coracina typica* (see relevant account) and are particularly silent and inconspicuous when feeding (Cheke in press). Food is chiefly insects carefully gleaned from leaves, branches and trunks of tamarins, heath, bois de couleurs, bamboo and the lichen on them (Cheke 1976,1977, Barré 1983); items include beetles and their larvae (notably formerly those of *Oryctes* on palms, but native *Oryctes* now appear extinct on Réunion), caterpillars, moths, long-horned (cerambycid) beetles, and often very small insects (Schlegel and Pollen 1868, Pollen 1886, Cheke 1976,1977, in press). Breeding is reported as from late October to early February (Staub 1976), but nest-building can begin as early as August, lasting a month, the laying season continuing until at least January (Cheke in press). The nest is usually placed in a fork near the top of a tree, in one case 13 m up in a patte poule *Euodia obtusifolia* itself 14-15 m high, in another 7 m up in a tan rouge *Weinmannia tinctoria* 8 m high (Cheke 1976,1977, in press). Birds may be double-brooded (Cheke in press). Clutch-size is two (Cheke 1976,1977, in press). Nesting success appears better than in the Mauritius Cuckoo-shrike (Cheke in press).

Threats The habitat in the range of this species is affected by four human activities: deer-hunting, poaching, clearance/reafforestation, and tourism (Cheke 1976,1977). Introduced deer *Cervus timorensis* are maintained in high numbers on the Plaine des Chicots and have largely destroyed all undergrowth and prevented any forest regeneration; moreover, the hunting season extends into October/ November and therefore causes disturbance when birds are breeding (Cheke 1975,1976,1977). A fair amount of poaching occurs, using birdlime, and constitutes a serious risk for a bird of such limited distribution (Cheke 1976,1977). In 1974 the Office National des Forêts was conducting a programme of native forest clearance, replacing it with Japenese red cedar *Cryptomeria japonica*; by that year a fifth of Plaine d'Affouches and all of Plaine des Chicots up to the 1,200 m contour was cleared and replanted, and the present habitat of the species was already being cut, apparently in accordance with a 1968 statement of intent that would have left only enough habitat for c. 15 pairs (Cheke 1976,1977, in press; see Conservation Measures Taken). Black rats *Rattus rattus* are common in the trees at Plaine des Chicots and may have been responsible for taking the young from the first nest ever found, although the predator might also have been the Réunion Harrier *Circus maillardi* (Cheke 1976,1977). The apparent rarity of the Réunion Cuckoo-shrike in the 1950s and 1960s was possibly the result of the highly destructive cyclones of 1944, 1945 and, especially, 1948, and prompts the consideration that any further reduction in habitat would greatly increase the danger of losing the entire species to a single direct hit from a cyclone (Cheke 1976,1977). Pet crab-eating macaques *Macaca fascicularis* are frequently smuggled into Réunion from Mauritius and there is a serious risk that this major pest might become established (Cheke in press). Apparently suitable habitat is still extensive on Réunion and the factors restricting it to one particular area in the north-west are unknown (Cheke 1976,1977, Barré 1983). Its apparent numerical decline may be attributable to the disappearance of palms and their associated *Oryctes* beetles (Cheke 1976,1977), while its current restriction to higher altitudes than formerly might also be the result of (accidently introduced) avian malaria, whose mosquito vector is a lowland species (Cheke 1976,1977).

Conservation Measures Taken A recommendation in 1976 that no more cutting of native forest and replanting with exotics should take place in the Plaine des Chicots and Plaine d'Affouches (Cheke 1976,1977) was agreed to in 1977 (Cheke 1978; also editorial note in Cheke 1977). A proposed road to link the two "plains" to facilitate tourist access would have constituted a great danger to the birds (Cheke 1976,1977) but the idea has been abandoned (editorial note in Cheke 1977). A proposal to introduce wild boar *Sus scrofa* into Plaine des Chicots has not succeeded (Moutou 1983). The presence of a conscientious game-keeper on Plaine des Chicots from 1969 to 1974 was considered to help explain the species's increase during those years (Cheke 1976,1977). This game-keeper now receives a retainer from the local nature protection society (A. S. Cheke pers. comm. 1984).

Conservation Measures Proposed A wardened permanent nature reserve, run by an independent committee, should be established at Plaine des Chicots and Plaine d'Affouches, embracing all the land above 1,300 m as far as the tree-line and, at Plaine d'Affouches, the whole Bras Guillaume valley (Cheke 1976,1977,1978). The number of deer on the Plaine des Chicots should be reduced by two-thirds (or better still removed entirely) to guarantee forest regeneration, enclosures need to be constructed there to study the impact of deer on vegetation, the fence barring deer from Plaine d'Affouches requires maintenance, and deer-hunting should be restricted to the period July/ September (Cheke 1976,1977,1978; also Barré and Barau 1982). The Réunion Cuckoo-shrike needs to be searched for in the following seven areas of forest: the slopes west of Piton Ravine à Malheur on the Dos d'Ane; the Cratère massif near St.-Benoît; the Ste.-Anne heights below the Ligne Domaniale; the heights at St.-Philippe-Tremblet; the Plaine des Merles at Salazie; the Ravines de la Rivière d'Abord, Ravine du Tampon and Bras Jean Payet at Plaine des Cafres; the region along the Ligne Domaniale du Grand Bénard (Cheke 1976,1977, in press).

Remarks Since the birds were originally recorded as "generally" between 800 and 1,400 m (Schlegel and Pollen 1868), it seems unlikely that the population has shifted upwards in altitude, rather that it always occurred up to 1,800 m or so and that it has simply suffered the loss of the birds that formerly occurred between 800 and 1,300 m.

References

Barré, N. (1983) Distribution et abondance des oiseaux terrestres de l'île de la Réunion (Ocean Indien). *Rev. Ecol. (Terre et Vie)* 37: 37-85.

Barré, N. and Barau, A. (1982) *Oiseaux de la Réunion*. St.-Denis [Réunion]: Imprimerie Arts Graphiques Modernes.

Berlioz, J. (1946) *Oiseaux de la Réunion*. Faune de l'Empire Français, IV. Paris: Librairie Larose.

Cheke, A. S. (1975) [Letter.] *Info-Nature* no. 13: 128-129.

Cheke, A. S. (1976) Rapport sur la distribution et la conservation du Tuit-tuit, oiseau rarissime de la Réunion. British Ornithologists' Union Mascarene Islands Expedition Conservation Memorandum no. 2. Unpublished.

Cheke, A. S. (1977) Rapport sur la distribution et la conservation du Tuit-tuit, oiseau rarissime de la Réunion. *Info-Nature* no. 15: 21-38.

Cheke, A. S. (1978) Recommendations for the conservation of Mascarene vertebrates. Conservation memorandum no. 3 (arising out of the B.O.U. Mascarene Islands Expedition). Unpublished.

Cheke, A. S. (1979) The Rodrigues Fody *Foudia flavicans*. A brief history of its decline, and a report on the 1978 expedition. *Dodo* 15 [1978]: 12-19.

Cheke, A. S. (in press) The ecology of the surviving native land-birds of Réunion. In A. W. Diamond, ed. *Studies of Mascarene island birds*. Cambridge: Cambridge University Press.

Milon, P. (1951) Notes sur l'avifaune actuelle de l'île de la Réunion. *Terre et Vie* 98: 129-178.

Moutou, F. (1983) Introduction dans les îles: l'exemple de l'île de la Réunion. *Info-Nature* no. 20: 39-48.

Pollen, F. (1886) On the genus *Oxynotus* of Mauritius and Réunion. *Ibis* (2)2: 275-280.

Schlegel, H. and Pollen, F. P. L. (1868) *Recherches sur la faune de Madagascar et de ses dépendances, d'après les découvertes de François P. L. Pollen et D. C. van Dam*. 2me partie. Mammifères et oiseaux. Leyde.

Staub, F. (1976) *Birds of the Mascarenes and Saint Brandon*. Port Louis, Mauritius: Organisation Normale des Enterprises.

Vincent, J. (1966-1971) *Red data book, 2: Aves*. Morges, Switzerland: IUCN.

WESTERN WATTLED CUCKOO-SHRIKE   VULNERABLE
Campephaga lobata (Temminck, 1824)

Order PASSERIFORMES   Family CAMPEPHAGIDAE

Summary This species is known only from primary lowland rainforest west of the Dahomey Gap where it appears to be very rare. It is presumably seriously threatened by forest destruction.

Distribution The Western Wattled Cuckoo-shrike is confined to the rainforest zone west of the Dahomey Gap, West Africa. The species presumably once occurred in suitable places throughout the Upper Guinea forests between Sierra Leone and Ghana, its range steadily contracting with habitat destruction.

Ghana Two specimens, including the type, are thought to have come from an unspecified locality in Ghana, some time before 1824 (Bannerman 1939). A specimen was collected in the "Interior of Fanti" and reached BMNH in 1875 (Bannerman 1939) and another was taken "in Ashanti", probably near Kumasi, in 1884 (Bannerman 1939). The only subsequent record is of a specimen collected at Mampong in 1935 (Lowe 1937) though there were unconfirmed reports of sightings in western Ghana during the 1970s, when the species was searched for carefully without success (M. A. Macdonald *in litt.* 1982).

Guinea There are no records from Guinea although it might occur, or at least might have occurred, in suitable localities within the forest zone.

Ivory Coast Between 1970 and 1973 the species was observed on two or three occasions in the Tai National Park (J.-M. Thiollay *in litt.* 1983).

Liberia The species was unrecorded in Liberia until 18 specimens were collected in the Mount Nimba area between 1967 and 1971 (Colston and Curry-Lindahl in press). In recent years one was collected near Twedru in Grand Gedeh County and the species was observed on two occasions at this locality (W. Gatter *in litt.* 1983).

Sierra Leone The species was observed in small numbers in the Gola Forest in the 1960s and 1970s (G. D. Field *in litt.* 1983).

Population Numbers are not known, though the small number of records indicates that the species is very rare. In the Gola Forest it is perhaps less rare than in some other localities, since birds were seen on 20 occasions over a period of 62 days (G. D. Field *in litt.* 1983). However, the species is probably easily overlooked and at Mount Nimba more birds were seen after forest clearing started, presumably owing to improved visibility (A. D. Forbes-Watson pers. comm. 1984). It is presumably declining owing to forest destruction.

Ecology Very little is known, though it is almost certainly dependent upon primary forest (G. D. Field *in litt.* 1983, J.-M. Thiollay *in litt.* 1983). In Liberia birds have been seen in riverine rainforest (W. Gatter *in litt.* 1983). One specimen was shot in dense foliage in a "kola" tree along a forest path (Lowe 1937). The diet is known to include caterpillars, grasshoppers and small black seeds (Lowe 1937, Colston and Curry-Lindahl in press). They are usually seen singly or in pairs (G. D. Field *in litt.* 1983). Birds in breeding condition have been collected in February, and August/November (Lowe 1937, Colston and Curry-Lindahl in press) and fully-grown juveniles have been since twice in May (G. D. Field *in litt.* 1983).

Threats This species is threatened by the exploitation and clearance of primary rainforest west of the Dahomey Gap (G. D. Field pers. comm. 1983). The Gola Forest is seriously threatened by timber exploitation (G. D. Field pers. comm. 1983, A. Tye *in litt.* 1983) and the forests around Mount Nimba are being rapidly cleared for timber extraction, iron ore mining and farming (Verschuren 1982,1983, E. O. Willis *per* A. Tye *in litt.* 1983, Colston and Curry-Lindahl in press). The Tai Forest is also suffering from illegal encroachment (Roth 1982, Halle 1983, J.-M. Thiollay *in litt.* 1983). The rate of forest destruction in Africa west of the Dahomey Gap is so severe that any bird species endemic to primary forest in this region must now be considered gravely at risk (see Remarks under Rufous Fishing Owl *Scotopelia ussheri* for the species in question).

Conservation Measures Taken None is known, other than that its occurrence in the Tai National Park in Ivory Coast provides some hope for its survival.

Conservation Measures Proposed Surveys are needed to determine whether this species occurs within some of the protected areas of rainforest in West Africa, other than Tai National Park in Ivory Coast. Details of these protected areas and of the ornithological importance of Tai and Gola Forests and Mount Nimba are given in Remarks under Rufous Fishing Owl.

Remarks This species forms a highly distinctive superspecies with the Eastern Wattled Cuckoo-shrike *Campephaga oriolinus*, which occurs in the rainforest from Cameroon to Zaire (Hall and Moreau 1970). These two forms have been considered to be conspecific (White 1962) but they are very distinct from each other in colouration (Hall and Moreau 1970).

References

Bannerman, D. A. (1939) *The birds of tropical West Africa*, 5. London: Crown Agents for the Colonies.

Colston, P. R. and Curry-Lindahl, K. (in press) The birds of the Mount Nimba region in Liberia. *Bull. Brit. Mus. (Nat. Hist.) Zool.*

Hall, B. P. and Moreau, R. E. (1970) *An atlas of speciation in African passerine birds*. London: Trustees of the British Museum (Natural History).

Halle, M. (1983) Timber pressure on last Ivory Coast forest. *WWF News* 22: 2.

Lowe, W. P. (1937) Report on the Lowe-Waldron expeditions to the Ashanti forests and Northern Territories of the Gold Coast. Part III. *Ibis* (14)1: 830-864.

Roth, H. H. (1982) We all want trees – case history of the Tai National Park. 3rd World National Parks Congress, Bali, Indonesia. Unpublished.

Verschuren, J. (1982) Hope for Liberia. *Oryx* 16: 421-427.

Verschuren, J. (1983) Conservation of tropical rain forest in Liberia. Recommendations for wildlife conservation and national parks. Gland, Switzerland: IUCN/WWF.

White, C. M. N. (1962) *A revised checklist of African shrikes, orioles, drongos, starlings, crows, waxwings, cuckoo-shrikes, bulbuls, accentors, thrushes and babblers*. Lusaka: Department of Game and Fisheries.

PRIGOGINE'S GREENBUL   VULNERABLE
Chlorocichla prigoginei de Roo, 1967

Order PASSERIFORMES   Family PYCNONOTIDAE

Summary This greenbul is known only from patches of forest at intermediate elevations to the north-west of Lake Edward and on the Lendu Plateau west of Lake Mobutu (Lake Albert) in eastern Zaire. It appears to be under serious threat from forest destruction.

Distribution Prigogine's Greenbul was described from a specimen collected at Maboya, north-west of Lake Edward, in eastern Zaire, in 1956 (de Roo 1967). At the time of its description five other specimens were known, three from Maboya collected in 1948, 1949 and 1966 and two from the nearby area of Butembo in 1953 and 1956 (de Roo 1967). Since the description was published another seven specimens have been sent to MRAC: one of these was collected at Butembo in 1956, four from Maboya (three in 1969, one in 1971), one from Kiwira in 1973 and one from Mutaka in 1975 (SNS). The most recent record is of a specimen collected at Kabasha in 1981 (A. Prigogine pers. comm. 1983). All these localities are in a small area between Butembo and Beni, north-west of Lake Edward (Prigogine in press). In 1926 a bird was collected in Djugu Forest on the Lendu Plateau, west of Lake Mobutu (Lake Albert) and was later found to be this species (Prigogine in press, A. Prigogine *in litt.* 1983). This last locality is about 210 km north-east of the Butembo/Beni region. The species appears to have a narrow altitudinal range of 1,300-1,500 m (Prigogine in press).

Population Numbers are not known but the small number of collected specimens from an area which has been well explored by ornithologists is an indication that it is rare.

Ecology This species has been recorded from the dense undergrowth of thickets and small forest patches at intermediate altitudes, including gallery forests along the upper courses of rivers (de Roo 1967, Prigogine 1977, in press, A. Prigogine *in litt.* 1983). It avoids high lowland forest (A. Prigogine pers. comm. 1983). Throughout its range it is sympatric with the very similar Joyful Greenbul *Chlorocichla laetissima* and on one occasion the two species were collected at the same place and on the same day (de Roo 1967).

Threats This species is under severe threat from forest destruction (A. Prigogine *in litt.* 1983). The forest between Butembo and Beni is in small isolated patches in savanna country (de Roo 1967) and, therefore, liable to be cleared (A. Prigogine *in litt.* 1983). This is an area of high human population density where agricultural activities are expanding and large-scale plantations are being established (Prigogine in press). The forest on the Lendu Plateau has apparently also been cleared in many areas (Hall and Moreau 1962).

Conservation Measures Taken None is known.

Conservation Measures Proposed A survey is needed to determine which forest patches, both between Beni and Butembo and on the Lendu Plateau, should be preserved to save this species from extinction (Prigogine in press).

Remarks This species was originally misidentified and thought to be the Joyful Greenbul, a widespread bird in tropical Africa (de Roo 1967). One other threatened bird species occurs on the Lendu Plateau, Chapin's Flycatcher *Muscicapa lendu* (see relevant account).

References

Hall, B. P. and Moreau, R. E. (1962) A study of the rare birds of Africa. *Bull. Brit. Mus. (Nat. Hist.) Zool.* 8: 313-378.

Prigogine, A. (1977) The composition of Itombwe Forest's avifauna. *Bonn. zool. Beitr.* 28: 369-383.

Prigogine, A. (in press) The conservation of the avifauna of the forests of the Albertine Rift. *Proceedings of the ICBP Tropical Forest Bird Symposium, 1982.*

de Roo, A. (1967) A new species of *Chlorocichla* from north-eastern Congo (Aves: Pycnonotidae). *Rev. Zool. Bot. Afr.* 75: 392-395.

APPERT'S GREENBUL RARE
Phyllastrephus apperti Colston, 1972

Order PASSERIFORMES Family PYCNONOTIDAE

Summary This ground-haunting, dry forest bulbul is known with certainty from only two remote unprotected localities in south-west Madagascar, where it is exceptionally rare and faces the danger of destruction of its habitat by fire.

Distribution Appert's Greenbul was first found in a forest 40 km southeast of Ankazoabo, south-west Madagascar, where it was twice seen, on 7 June and 4 September 1962; on the latter date two specimens were collected, from which the species was described ten years later (Colston 1972). Throughout this intervening period the collector never found the bird again during studies over an area of 40,000 km^2 around the Mangoky River (Colston 1972). On 20 August 1974 it was rediscovered in the same patch of forest as in 1962 and a specimen was collected and sent to Antananarivo (O. Appert *in litt.* 1983; for numbers then seen, see Population). A single bird was seen in the nearby Zombitsy forest, east of Sakaraha, in July 1974 (Benson and Irwin 1975), two or three were present the following month (O. Appert *in litt.* 1983), and birds have been consistently seen there subsequently (see below). Two specimens, probably of this species, were collected east of Tuléar ("probably near Sakaraha") and were deposited for a time in Antananarivo, but are now lost (Colston 1972; but see under Distribution and Remarks for Grey-crowned Greenbul *Phyllastrephus cinereiceps*). The sites south-east of Ankazoabo and east of Sakaraha belong to (what was at least in 1963) a fairly unfragmented (but variously named) block of forest (Vohibasia forest, Jarindrano forest, Mangona forest, Zombitsy forest), extending to the north and south of Andranolava and very roughly covering 1,000 km^2 (see IGNT 1964). Nevertheless, despite fieldwork throughout the Zombitsy forest, 1976-1981, the species was always only ever found in the same single area in one corner, only 0.5 km^2 in size (D. A. Turner pers. comm. 1983). A recent (but undated) record of one (seen on the ground) "15 km east of Sakaraha" (O. Langrand *in litt.* 1984) perhaps involves a new (third) site for the species.

Population Numbers are probably very small. Soon after its first description it was considered possibly quite common (Forbes-Watson *et al.* 1973), but subsequent evidence is against this: apart from what is said above under Distribution, it could not be relocated by one observer in the Zombitsy forest in August 1974 (Benson and Irwin 1975) nor was it found at another nearby site east of Sakaraha during five days' fieldwork, 1972-1973 (Benson 1976). From this it would appear that the species is very local and sparse within its small known range. At the corner of the Zombitsy forest where it could always be found, 1976-1981, seven to eight birds were usually to be seen, though once 15; probably 20-30 birds is the maximum for this area (D. A. Turner pers. comm. 1983). In the forest southeast of Ankazoabo on the last occasion the species was seen there (20 August

1974), two groups were encountered, one of two to three and the other of about eight birds (O. Appert *in litt.* 1983).

Ecology The species inhabits dense dry forest, searching for food in the leaf-litter (Colston 1972). Although it is reported to be highly terrestrial, behaving rather like an akalat *Sheppardia*, rarely moving more than 1 m above ground, and always occurring in groups of five to eight (Colston 1972, D. A. Turner pers. comm. 1983), the bird seen in Zombitsy forest in July 1974 was single (though in the company of c. 20 Long-billed Greenbuls *Phyllastrephus madagascariensis*) and kept 1-5 m above ground (Benson and Irwin 1975): indeed, observations in Zombitsy forest in November 1976 were commonly of birds clinging to liana tangles up to 2 m from the ground, in the manner of reed warblers *Acrocephalus* (A. D. Forbes-Watson pers. comm. 1984). Birds have once been seen to go higher in the trees when disturbed, and they may do so habitually at times the forest is more humid (O. Appert *in litt.* 1983). The Zombitsy forest is much greener in the dry season than that south-east of Ankazoabo, retaining some of its leaves (O. Appert *in litt.* 1983).

Threats The highly restricted range of this species must be a source of permanent concern and vigilance for its welfare, and in late 1978 or early 1979 a cyclone destroyed forest as close as 2 km to the single known area in Zombitsy (D. A. Turner pers. comm. 1983); moreover, forest burning in this region has apparently been very serious in recent years (O. Appert *in litt.* 1983).

Conservation Measures Taken None is known.

Conservation Measures Proposed Further fieldwork to determine the range and status of this species is desirable, but protection of the forests from which it is known is perhaps more immediately important. Control of the present forest cutting and burning is essential for ecological stability in the region (O. Appert *in litt.* 1983).

Remarks Study of the Antananarivo specimen, alongside the type, is desirable for absolute confirmation of the validity of the species (Colston 1972).

References

Benson, C. W. (1976) Letter to P. Griveaud, carbon copy held in UMZC.
Benson, C. W. and Irwin, M. P. S. (1975) The systematic position of *Phyllastrephus orostruthus* and *Phyllastrephus xanthophrys*, two species incorrectly placed in the family Pycnonotidae (Aves). *Arnoldia (Rhod.)* 7(17).
Colston, P. R. (1972) A new bulbul from southwestern Madagascar. *Ibis* 114: 89-92.
Forbes-Watson, A. D., Turner, D. A. and Keith, G. S. (1973) Report on bird preservation in Madagascar, part 3. Appendix I. Proposed list of protected Madagascar birds. Report to ICBP, unpublished.
Institut Géographique National à Tananarive (1964) Carte de Madagascar, 1: 500,000, Type 1963. Tananarive.

DUSKY GREENBUL   RARE

Phyllastrephus tenebrosus (Stresemann, 1925)

Order PASSERIFORMES   Family PYCNONOTIDAE

Summary This mysterious bulbul of rainforest undergrowth is known from only eight skins and two adjacent localities (Sihanaka forest and Périnet-Analamazaotra), eastern central Madagascar.

Distribution The Dusky Greenbul was first described from four specimens collected in the Sihanaka forest, eastern Madagascar, of which one was collected in December 1924 (type), one in June 1925 and one in December 1925 (Stresemann 1925, Benson *et al.* 1976, D. K. Read *in litt.* 1983). Two further specimens from Sihanaka forest (undated) were acquired by the Mission Franco-Anglo-Américaine from Herschell-Chauvin around 1930 (Delacour 1932a, Rand 1936), and another was obtained there on 7 April 1929 (Lavauden 1932). A bird was also shot north of Analamazaotra (near Périnet) on 8 May 1929 (Lavauden 1932). A single bird was seen at Périnet on 25 June 1974, one on 23 November 1976 and one on 14 November 1977 (D. A. Turner *in litt.* 1983; also Benson and Irwin 1975). That the species occurs thoughout "forests in the east of Madagascar" (Lavauden 1937) appears an unacceptably sweeping assumption; that it may occur at other sites in the central section of these forests (Milon *et al.* 1973) seems a reasonable hope.

Population Numbers are unknown. This species probably goes unrecorded by combining extreme elusiveness and difficult habitat with general sparseness (Benson 1974). Its rarity has been remarked (Delacour 1932b, Lavauden 1932).

Ecology From existing records (see Distribution) it is confined to humid rainforest. It was judged probably a bird of ground-cover (Rand 1936) and the first observation in life was of a single bird with a pair of White-throated Oxylabes *Oxylabes madagascariensis*, moving through branches c. 2 m above the ground, presumably gleaning insects though it was not actually seen to feed (Benson and Irwin 1975). Subsequent observations confirm it to be an undergrowth species (D. A. Turner pers. comm. 1983). The bird seen in November 1976 was clinging to vertical stems 1-2 m from the ground (A. D. Forbes-Watson pers. comm. 1984).

Threats Destruction and disturbance of primary rainforest is the single most serious threat to this and all other rainforest-dependent species in Madagascar (see Threats under Madagascar Serpent Eagle *Eutriorchis astur*).

Conservation Measures Taken The species occurs in the Périnet-Analamazaotra Special Reserve, which covers 810 ha (Andriamampianina 1981).

Conservation Measures Proposed Immediate and effective protection of as much remaining rainforest as possible would almost certainly guarantee the survival of this and all other rainforest-dependent species in Madagascar; and at least, on current knowledge, complete protection of the intact parts of Sihanaka forest is of extreme importance (see Conservation Measures Proposed under Madagascar Serpent Eagle). Any ornithological work in the other areas from which the species is known, or where it might be expected, should where possible be extended to include searches to locate it.

Remarks The Dusky Greenbul has been treated as a race of the Madagascar Greenbul *Phyllastrephus madagascariensis* (Milon *et al.* 1973) but its validity as a full species has since been reaffirmed (Benson 1974, Benson *et al.* 1976; also Benson and Irwin 1975).

References

Andriamampianina, J. (1981) Les réserves naturelles et la protection de la nature à Madagascar. Pp. 105-111 in P. Oberlé, ed. *Madagascar, un sanctuaire de la nature*. Paris: Lechevalier.

Benson, C. W. (1974) Another specimen of *Neodrepanis hypoxantha*. *Bull. Brit. Orn. Club* 94: 141-143.

Benson, C. W. and Irwin, M. P. S. (1975) The systematic position of *Phyllastrephus orostruthus* and *Phyllastrephus xanthophrys*, two species incorrectly placed in the family Pycnonotidae (Aves). *Arnoldia (Rhod.)* 7(17).

Benson, C. W., Colebrook-Robjent, J. F. R. and Williams, A. (1976) Contribution à l'ornithologie de Madagascar. *Oiseau et R.F.O.* 46: 367-386.

Delacour, J. (1932a) Les oiseaux de la Mission Franco-Anglo-Américaine à Madagascar. *Oiseau et R.F.O.* 2: 1-96.

Delacour, J. (1932b) On the birds collected in Madagascar by the Franco-Anglo-American Expedition, 1929-1931. *Ibis* (13)2: 284-304.

Lavauden, L. (1932) Etude d'une petite collection d'oiseaux de Madagascar. *Bull. Mus. Natn. Hist. Nat.* (2)4: 629-640.

Lavauden, L. (1937) Supplément. A. Milne Edwards and A. Grandidier, *Histoire physique, naturelle et politique de Madagascar, 12. Oiseaux*. Paris: Société d'Editions Géographiques, Maritimes et Coloniales.

Milon, P., Petter, J.-J. and Randrianasolo, G. (1973) *Faune de Madagascar, 35. Oiseaux*. Tananarive and Paris: ORSTOM and CNRS.

Rand, A. L. (1936) The distribution and habits of Madagascar birds. *Bull. Amer. Mus. Nat. Hist.* 72: 143-499.

Stresemann, E. (1925) Eine neue Vogelart aus Madagaskar: *Bernieria tenebrosa* sp.n. *Orn. Monatsber.* 33: 150-151.

GREY-CROWNED GREENBUL

RARE

Phyllastrephus cinereiceps (Sharpe, 1881)

Order PASSERIFORMES

Family PYCNONOTIDAE

Summary This Madagascar bulbul, probably confined to rainforest, remains almost totally unknown, and apparently has been found only twice in the past 50 years.

Distribution The Grey-crowned Greenbul possibly occurs throughout the rainforests of eastern Madagascar, but is known from only a few scattered sites. It was first described from Fianarantsoa, in the southern half of the eastern rainforest belt (Sharpe 1881), and subsequently found in the nearby Ankafana (= Tsarafidy) forest (seven specimens in BMNH, all March 1881: NJC; see Remarks), Sihanaka forest and at Fanovana (Delacour 1932, Rand 1936), though this last area is now cleared (D. A. Turner pers. comm. 1983), and in the Tsaratanana massif (Milon 1957). An observation of the species is reported from "Lambomakandro forest" to the east of Sakaraha in south-west Madagascar (Milon *et al.* 1973), but for a bird previously known only from the humid forest area of the island this record appears somewhat anomalous (see Remarks); if this is discounted, the species has only been recorded twice in the past 50 years, in the Tsaratanana massif (see above) and near Didy, on the western edge of the Sihanaka forest, in May 1971 (A. D. Forbes-Watson pers. comm. 1984).

Population The species was considered uncommon in Sihanaka forest 50 years ago (Delacour 1932) and is known from apparently only a single specimen from Tsaratanana (Milon 1957).

Ecology It inhabits the ground-cover of deep rainforest, gleaning for insects through the low bushes, and associating with the Short-billed Greenbul *Phyllastrephus zosterops* (Rand 1936).

Threats Destruction and disturbance of primary rainforest is the single most serious threat to this and all other rainforest-dependent species in Madagascar (see Threats under Madagascar Serpent Eagle *Eutriorchis astur*).

Conservation Measures Taken The species presumably occurs in the Tsaratanana Nature Reserve (R.N.I. no. 4), which covers 48,622 ha (Andriamampianina 1981).

Conservation Measures Proposed Immediate and effective protection of as much remaining rainforest as possible would almost certainly guarantee the survival of this and all other rainforest-dependent species in Madagascar; and at least, on current knowledge, complete protection of the intact parts of Sihanaka forest is of extreme importance (see Conservation Measures Proposed under Madagascar Serpent Eagle). Any ornithological work in the other areas from which the species is known, or where it might be expected, should where possible be

403

extended to include searches to locate it. The forest at Tsarafidy where this species occurs was identified in 1961 as a place of exceptional interest for its wildlife which certainly deserved complete protection (Griveaud 1961); the species may be expected in the nearby "Nandehizana" forest, if this still survives (for both localities see Conservation Measures Proposed and Remarks under Madagascar Yellowbrow *Crossleyia xanthophrys*).

Remarks It is possible that "Fianarantsoa" was a generalised locality and that the type-material actually came from (the fairly nearby) Tsarafidy forest. The anomalous record of this species from east of Sakaraha, south-west Madagascar, given (in Milon *et al.* 1973) without any further information, may possibly be connected with the two lost specimens thought to be of Appert's Greenbul *Phyllastrephus apperti*, which came from "east of Tuléar, probably near Sakaraha" (Colston 1972; see relevant sheet): two villages named Lambomakandro are situated in the northern parts of the Zombitsy forest (in IGNT 1964), which is one of only two only certain localities for Appert's Greenbul.

References

Andriamampianina, J. (1981) Les réserves naturelles et la protection de la nature à Madagascar. Pp. 105-111 in P. Oberlé, ed. *Madagascar, un sanctuaire de la nature*. Paris: Lechevalier.

Colston, P. R. (1972) A new bulbul from southwestern Madagascar. *Ibis* 114: 89-92.

Delacour, J. (1932) Les oiseaux de la Mission Franco-Anglo-Américaine à Madagascar. *Oiseau et R.F.O.* 2: 1-96.

Griveaud, P. (1961) Un intéressant vestige forestier malgache. *Bull. Acad. Malgache* 39: 9-10.

Institut Géographique National à Tananarive (1964) Carte de Madagascar, 1: 500,000, Type 1963. Tananarive.

Milon, P. (1957) Etude d'une petite collection d'oiseaux du Tsaratanana. *Naturaliste Malgache* 3(2): 167-183.

Milon, P., Petter, J.-J. and Randrianasolo, G. (1973) *Faune de Madagascar, 35. Oiseaux*. Tananarive and Paris: ORSTOM and CNRS.

Rand, A. L. (1936) The distribution and habits of Madagascar birds. *Bull. Amer. Mus. Nat. Hist.* 72: 143-499.

Sharpe, R. B. (1881) On a new genus of Timeliidae from Madagascar, with remarks on some other genera. *Proc. Zool. Soc. Lond.*: 195-197.

YELLOW-THROATED OLIVE GREENBUL
Criniger olivaceus (Swainson, 1837)

VULNERABLE

Order PASSERIFORMES

Family PYCNONOTIDAE

Summary This rarely recorded species is restricted to the rainforest zone of West Africa between Ghana and Senegal. It is probably threatened by forest clearance.

Distribution The Yellow-throated Olive Greenbul is confined to the rainforest zone west of the Dahomey Gap, West Africa. It presumably occurred throughout the Upper Guinea forests between Senegal and Ghana, though its range must have contracted with habitat destruction. The type-specimen (in UMZC) was collected in "West Africa" (Swainson 1837): one author has suggested that it might have come from the Gambia (Bannerman 1936) but the specimen index card is labelled "Sierra Leone" (SNS). Subsequent records of the species are as follows.

Ghana Two specimens were collected at Fanti (Bannerman 1936) probably in the 1870s. The species was searched for intensively in mixed flocks during the 1970s, without success (M. A. Macdonald *in litt.* 1982).

Guinea One specimen was collected at N'Zerékoré in 1930 (Bannerman 1932).

Ivory Coast One was caught in a mist-net in the Tai National Park in 1972 (J.-M. Thiollay *in litt.* 1983).

Liberia Twelve specimens were collected around Mount Nimba in 1965-1968 (Colston and Curry-Lindahl in press). Birds assumed to be this species have been seen at this locality in the last few years (E. O. Willis *per* A. Tye *in litt.* 1983). Another specimen was collected at Sinoe (Greenville) in 1972 (Louette 1974). In recent years the species has been recorded around Tchien and Twedru in the north-east of Grand Gedeh County and there have also been observations in the south of the county (W. Gatter *in litt.* 1983).

Senegal There is a nineteenth century record from Casamance in southern Senegal (Bannerman 1936).

Sierra Leone It is recorded as being moderately common in the Gola Forest in the 1960s and 1970s (Field 1979, G. D. Field pers. comm. 1983). There is also one record around the same time from the Nimini Hills in the south of Kono District (G. D. Field pers. comm. 1983).

Population Numbers are not known, though the fairly small number of records suggest that it is generally rare. It is apparently not uncommon in Grand Gedeh County in Liberia, where it has been seen on about 20 occasions in recent

405

years (W. Gatter *in litt.* 1983), although, at Mount Nimba at least, it appears to occur at a lower density than other species in the genus *Criniger* (A. D. Forbes-Watson pers. comm. 1984). In the Gola Forest birds were seen on 22 occasions over a period of 62 days (G. D. Field pers. comm. 1983). It is presumably declining owing to habitat destruction.

Ecology This species is restricted to primary lowland rainforest (Field 1979, Colston and Curry-Lindahl in press, G. D. Field pers. comm. 1983, W. Gatter *in litt.* 1983) and apparently does not occur in secondary growth (E. O. Willis *per* A. Tye *in litt.* 1983). It is a largely silent bird, usually seen in mixed-species parties (Field 1979, A. Tye *in litt.* 1983). It is mainly insectivorous (Field 1979, Colston and Curry-Lindahl in press) though stomach contents have also been found to include small hard-stoned fruits (Colston and Curry-Lindahl in press). The birds feed at all levels in the forest from the ground stratum to the canopy, searching trunks and branches of trees in the manner of a nuthatch (Sittidae) or a *Phyllastrephus* greenbul (Field 1979). It probably breeds in November (Colston and Curry-Lindahl in press), though one specimen taken in May had small eggs in the ovaries (Bannerman 1932) and a young bird being fed by adults was seen in April (G. D. Field pers. comm. 1983).

Threats This species is threatened by the exploitation and clearance of primary rainforest west of the Dahomey Gap (G. D. Field pers. comm. 1983). The Gola Forest is seriously threatened by timber exploitation (G. D. Field pers. comm. 1983, A. Tye *in litt.* 1983), and the forests around Mount Nimba are being rapidly cleared for timber extraction, iron ore mining and farming (Verschuren 1982,1983, Colston and Curry-Lindahl in press, E. O. Willis *per* A. Tye *in litt.* 1983). The Tai Forest is also suffering from illegal encroachment (Roth 1982, Halle 1983, J.-M. Thiollay *in litt* 1983). The rate of forest destruction in Africa west of the Dahomey Gap is so severe that any bird species endemic to primary forest in this region must now be considered gravely at risk (see Remarks under Rufous Fishing Owl *Scotopelia ussheri* for the species in question).

Conservation Measures Taken None is known, other than that its occurrence in the Tai National Park in Ivory Coast provides some hope for its survival.

Conservation Measures Proposed Surveys are needed to determine whether this species occurs within some of the protected areas of rainforest in West Africa other than Tai National Park in Ivory Coast. Details of these protected areas and of the ornithological importance of the Tai and Gola Forests and Mount Nimba are given in Remarks under Rufous Fishing Owl.

Remarks The taxonomy of the genus *Criniger* in Africa is very complex (Field 1979). The Yellow-throated Olive Greenbul might be closely related to the White-bearded Greenbul *C. ndussumensis* from Cameroon to Zaire (Field 1979) and they have even been considered conspecific (White 1962); this view has not, however, found universal acceptance (Hall and Moreau 1970).

References

Bannerman, D. A. (1932) Account of the birds collected (i) by Mr G. L. Bates on behalf of the British Museum in Sierra Leone and French Guinea; (ii) by Lt. Col. G. J. Houghton, R.A.M.C., in Sierra Leone, recently acquired by the British Museum. Part II. *Ibis* (13)2: 1-33.

Bannerman, D. A. (1936) *The birds of tropical West Africa*, 4. London: Crown Agents for the Colonies.

Colston, P. R. and Curry-Lindahl, K. (in press) The birds of the Mount Nimba region in Liberia. *Bull. Brit. Mus. (Nat. Hist.) Zool.*

Field, G. D. (1979) The genus *Criniger* (Pycnonotidae) in Africa. *Bull. Brit. Orn. Club* 99: 57-59.

Hall, B. P. and Moreau, R. E. (1970) *An atlas of speciation in African passerine birds*. London: Trustees of the British Museum (Natural History).

Halle, M. (1983) Timber pressure on last Ivory Coast forest. *WWF News* 22: 2.

Louette, M. (1974) Contribution to the ornithology of Liberia. Part 3. *Rev. Zool. Afr.* 88: 741-748.

Roth, H. H. (1982) We all want trees – case history of the Tai National Park. 3rd World National Parks Congress, Bali, Indonesia. Unpublished.

Swainson, W. (1837) *Birds of West Africa*, 1. Edinburgh.

Verschuren, J. (1982) Hope for Liberia. *Oryx* 16: 421-427.

Verschuren, J. (1983) Conservation of tropical rain forest in Liberia. Recommendations for wildlife conservation and national parks. Gland, Switzerland: IUCN/WWF.

White, C. M. N. (1962) *A revised checklist of African shrikes, orioles, drongos, starlings, crows, waxwings, cuckoo-shrikes, bulbuls, accentors, thrushes and babblers*. Lusaka: Department of Game and Fisheries.

MAURITIUS BLACK BULBUL   VULNERABLE

Hypsipetes olivaceus Jardine and Selby, 1837

Order PASSERIFORMES   Family PYCNONOTIDAE

Summary This primarily frugivorous forest-dwelling species, endemic to Mauritius, was reduced to some 200 pairs in the mid-1970s and has probably declined further since. Nest predation and competition from introduced birds seem the major threats.

Distribution The Mauritius Black Bulbul is confined to forested areas in the south-west and one area in the east of Mauritius, Indian Ocean. It probably once occurred throughout Mauritius (C. G. Jones and A. W. Owadally *in litt.* 1982) and, since it can in some degree tolerate very degraded forest (see Ecology), until 1950 it was probably present throughout the forest area from the Piton du Fouge (in the far south-west) right up to the Piton du Milieu (in the centre of the island) and the Midlands area south of Curepipe across through the Montagnes Bambous (in the east), since when, however, clearance and further degradation have reduced its range by about half (Cheke in press; also C. G. Jones *in litt.* 1984). The population on Piton du Milieu (Newton 1958a) survived until the early 1970s (C. G. Jones and A. W. Owadally *in litt.* 1982). The main areas where it now survives are: in the native lowland forests extending from Tamarin Gorge along the Magenta escarpment through the lower areas of Black River Gorges, the west-facing slopes of Piton de la Rivière Noire (Black River Peak) to Chamarel and Piton du Fouge; in the native upland forests around the Black River Gorges; on the south-facing escarpment from Bel Ombre to the Montagne Savanne; and on Montagne Lagrave and the Montagnes Bambous (Procter and Salm 1974, Temple *et al.* 1974, Cheke in press, C. G. Jones and A. W. Owadally *in litt.* 1982, C. G. Jones *in litt.* 1984). There was a small, isolated population (two or three pairs) inside the Kanaka crater in May 1983 (C. G. Jones *in litt.* 1984). The species was successfully introduced to Diego Garcia in the Chagos archipelago, central Indian Ocean, but disappeared around 1953 (Cheke in press; see Threats).

Population Formerly this was one of the most widespread and common of Mauritius's endemic birds (Temple *et al.* 1974). Early concern for the species (Newton 1876, Oustalet 1897, Meinertzhagen 1912) was at least partly allayed by various reports indicating that declines had been substantial but not catastrophic (Carié 1904, Rountree 1951, Newton 1958a); in the 1950s it was even judged "locally abundant" in the remnants of its habitat (Newton 1958b) and around 1970 it was "still fairly numerous in dense cover" (Staub 1971). Preliminary impressions from a survey of the species in the south-west forests over the period 1973-1975 led to the assertion that, although numbers had been steadily decreasing in prior years, the total population remained well over 1,000 birds (Temple 1974), but analysis of the data shows that only 72 pairs were then located, yielding a calculated 140 pairs in all for that region (Cheke in press). At least 10 more pairs were present at that time on the Montagne Lagrave and adjacent Montagnes Bambous, the total in these hills being estimated at around 50 pairs (Cheke in press). The breeding

408

population in 1974-1975 was thus only around 200 pairs, with breeding success so low that, even though birds may take two years to mature, the floating population of immatures could hardly have been more than 100, so that the total number of birds then extant was around 500 (Cheke in press). The species appeared to suffer declines as a consequence of Cyclone Gervaise in February 1975 (Temple 1975) and Cyclone Claudette in December 1979 (Jones 1980), and a general decline in recent years has been noted though the population still numbers several hundred (C. G. Jones *in litt.* 1982). There are still "high densities" (guessed at perhaps five pairs per km^2) around Piton du Fouge and Chamarel Peak, but in other west-facing lowland areas density is guessed at only 0.2 pairs per km^2 (C. G. Jones *in litt.* 1984).

Ecology The Mauritius Black Bulbul inhabits native evergreen forest, but apparently shuns closed-canopy growth, preferring trees of irregular height with some openings (Cheke in press). The species also occurs in exotic forest with at least some native vegetation (Cheke in press), and in forest margins, secondary scrub and adjoining exotic plantations and groves (Newton 1958a, Fabian 1970, C. G. Jones *in litt.* 1982), although density in such degraded areas is low at only one or two pairs per km^2 or less (C. G. Jones *in litt.* 1984). Its absence from certain apparently suitable areas is not explicable in terms of climate or vegetation (Cheke in press). Normal density is 4-6 pairs per km^2 (Cheke in press); although this has been taken to imply a home range of something over 12 ha (Temple 1974), birds do not hold exclusive territories but merely have a centre of operations around the nest, and the overlap with other pairs means that home ranges can be as large as 40 ha (Cheke in press). The species is almost entirely arboreal (Newton 1861, Newton 1958a, Cheke in press) and entirely a forest-dweller (Newton 1883), only once recorded outside forest following a cyclone when the individual seen was evidently starving (Jones 1980); however, birds wander within the available habitat outside the breeding season (C. G. Jones *in litt.* 1984). The species is not wholly frugivorous as once believed (Newton 1861,1883) but also eats insects (e.g. caterpillars) by gleaning foliage and branches and by clumsy flycatching, and takes geckos *Phelsuma* (Cheke in press; also Newton 1958a, Temple *et al.* 1974, C. G. Jones *in litt.* 1984). Vegetable diet is primarily small indigenous fruits and seeds, notably those of fandamane *Aphloia theiformis*, various *Eugenia* species, but also those of the exotic invasive privet *Ligustrum robustum* var. *walkeri*, bramble *Rubus roridus* and lantana *Lantana camara* (Temple *et al.* 1974, Staub 1976, Cheke 1978); also flowers, e.g. of *Nuxia verticillata* (Jones 1980, C. G. Jones *in litt.* 1984; exhaustive list in Cheke in press). Breeding reportedly occurs from September to January (Temple *et al.* 1974), though other evidence suggests November to February (Cheke in press); the nest is placed high in a tree (Temple *et al.* 1974) or, usually, in a low bush (Cheke in press); clutch-size is two (Temple *et al.* 1974, Cheke in press). There is a strong possibility that birds do not breed until two years old, so small groups may well be family parties (Cheke in press). Birds usually occur in pairs or small parties (Cheke in press). They are often excessively tame (Newton 1861, Oustalet 1897, Meinertzhagen 1912, Newton 1958a) and often noisy and conspicuous (C. G. Jones *in litt.* 1984), but can also be quiet and furtive, and are then easily overlooked (Newton 1958a, Niven 1965, Fabian 1970), creeping about silently among upper branches, then calling loudly when completely hidden in foliage (Fabian 1970).

Threats A general account of the problems facing the endemic forest-dependent birds of Mauritius is given in Threats under Mauritius Kestrel *Falco punctatus*. The original decline of the Mauritius Black Bulbul is attributed to forest clearance, hunting, and nest predation by introduced crab-eating macaques *Macaca fascicularis* (Newton 1876, C. G. Jones and A. W. Owadally *in litt.* 1982). These three factors, plus two others, still constitute threats of varying intensities to the species. Habitat loss, though a major problem until the early 1970s (see Cheke in press; also Temple 1974, Temple *et al.* 1974), is now considered important only in terms of the steady degradation of native forest by exotic plants (C. G. Jones and A. W. Owadally *in litt.* 1982) (although, from evidence above under Ecology, this seems less of a problem for this bird than perhaps any other threatened Mauritian species). The most recent loss of habitat has been at Kanaka crater, where clear-felling occurred between 1974 and 1978 (Cheke 1978, in press), and on Crown Land Gouly above Bois Sec, where clear-felling continued up to 1980 (C. G. Jones *in litt.* 1984). Hunting of the species as a delicacy was formerly on a massive scale, the birds being especially persecuted around Christmas at the height of the breeding season (Newton 1861,1883, Oustalet 1897, Meinertzhagen 1912) and, despite legal protection (see Conservation Measures Taken), many birds are still caught or shot each year (Temple *et al.* 1974), though this is regarded as an aggravation rather than a serious threat (Cheke in press, C. G. Jones *in litt.* 1984). Nest predation by monkeys, considered a serious threat and much facilitated by the noisy and excitable nature of the birds themselves (Newton 1876, Temple 1974, Temple *et al.* 1974), remains to be confirmed (Cheke in press) but is accepted as very likely (C. G. Jones and A. W. Owadally *in litt.* 1982); black rats *Rattus rattus*, identified as probable nest predators (Cheke in press, C. G. Jones and A. W. Owadally *in litt.* 1982), are reported to have been "observed" as such (McKelvey 1976), and introduced Indian Mynahs *Acridotheres tristis* may also take a toll of nests (Cheke in press). Competition from Indian Mynahs and introduced Red-whiskered Bulbuls *Pycnonotus jocosus* for food has been considered a major threat (Temple 1974), and these two species seem very likely to be preventing any spread of Mauritius Black Bulbuls into exotic secondary (and certain areas of disturbed native) forest (Jones 1982a,b, C. G. Jones and A. W. Owadally *in litt.* 1982; also Cheke in press); the disappearance of the species from Diego Garcia (see Distribution) is attributed to the introduction there of the Indian Mynah (Cheke in press). Finally, the species is evidently vulnerable to the effect of cyclones in the fruiting season (Cheke in press; see Population).

Conservation Measures Taken This species has long been protected by law (Meinertzhagen 1912) and in 1974 a large proportion of its range in south-west Mauritius received protection when the Macabé/Bel Ombre Nature Reserve was created through the linking of existing reserves at Petrin, Macabé and Bel Ombre by the addition of Les Mares and Plaine Champagne, forming a large block covering 3,594 ha (Owadally 1976; see map in Procter and Salm 1974).

Conservation Measures Proposed The creation of habitat by a careful admixture of evergreen trees, on a commercial basis (see Conservation Measures Proposed under Mauritius Cuckoo-shrike *Coracina typica*), might prove beneficial to this species (Cheke 1978; also Jones and Owadally 1982, C. G. Jones and A. W. Owadally *in litt.* 1982). Patches of forest (in addition to those in reserves) should be maintained if possible (Temple 1974) – this surely is most important for the habitat at Montagne Lagrave and Montagnes Bambous, which are reserves for watershed protection but not yet for nature (A. S. Cheke pers. comm. 1984). Stricter enforcement of existing laws protecting this species from being caught or shot was urged in 1974 (Temple *et al.* 1974), as was control of nest predators and food competitors (Temple 1974). The adaptation of birds to the environment on Diego Garcia (see Distribution) prompts the urgent consideration that introduction of some birds to another competitor-free island could be a major contribution to the conservation of the species. Work to safeguard it will now proceed within the framework of the Mauritius Wildlife Research and Conservation Programme (see Conservation Measures Taken under Mauritius Kestrel).

Remarks The view that this species is distinct from the Réunion Black Bulbul *Hypsipetes borbonicus* (see Cheke in press) is accepted here.

References

Carié, P. (1904) Observations sur quelques oiseaux de l'île Maurice. *Ornis* 12: 121-128.

Cheke, A. S. (1978) Recommendations for the conservation of Mascarene vertebrates. Conservation memorandum no. 3 (arising out of the B.O.U. Mascarene Islands Expedition). Unpublished.

Cheke, A. S. (in press) The surviving native land-birds of Mauritius. In A. W. Diamond, ed. *Studies of Mascarene island birds*. Cambridge: Cambridge University Press.

Fabian, D. T. (1970) The birds of Mauritius. *Bokmakierie* 22: 16-17, 21.

Hartlaub, G. (1877) *Die Vögel Madagascars und der benachbarten Inselgruppen.* Halle.

Jones, C. G. (1980) The conservation of the endemic birds and bats of Mauritius and Rodriguez (a progress report and proposal for further activities). Unpublished.

Jones, C. G. (1982a) The conservation of the endemic birds and bats of Mauritius and Rodrigues. (Annual report 1981, WWF Project 1082). Unpublished.

Jones, C. G. (1982b) Struggle for survival on tropical islands. *WWF Monthly Report* February: 37-42.

Jones, C. G. and Owadally, A. W. (1982) Conservation priorities for Mauritius and Rodrigues. Report submitted to ICBP, July. Unpublished.

McKelvey, S. D. (1976) A preliminary study of the Mauritian Pink Pigeon (*Nesoenas meyeri* [*sic*]). *Mauritius Inst. Bull.* 8(2): 145-175.

Meinertzhagen, R. (1912) On the birds of Mauritius. *Ibis* (9)6: 82-108.

Newton, A. (1876) On the species of *Hypsipetes* inhabiting Madagascar and the neighbouring islands. *Rowley's Orn. Misc.* 2: 41-52.

Newton, E. (1861) Ornithological notes from Mauritius. No. II. A ten days' sojourn at Savanne. *Ibis* 3: 270-277.

Newton, E. (1883) Annexe C [Letter to V. Naz, 26 February 1878]. *Trans. Soc. Roy. Arts Sci. Maurice* (NS) 12: 70-73.

Newton, R. (1958a) Ornithological notes on Mauritius and the Cargados Carajos Archipelago. *Proc. Roy. Soc. Arts Sci. Mauritius* 2(1): 39-71.

Newton, R. (1958b) Bird preservation in Mauritius. *ICBP Bull.* 7: 182-185.

Niven, C. (1965) Birds of Mauritius. *Ostrich* 36: 84-86.

Oustalet, E. (1897) Notice sur la faune ornithologique ancienne et moderne des îles Mascareignes et en particulier de l'île Maurice d'après des documents inédits. *Ann. Sci. Nat. Zool.* (8)3: 1-128.

Owadally, A. W. (1976) *Annual report of the Forestry Service for the year 1974.* Port Louis, Mauritius: L. Carl Achille, Government Printer.

Procter, J. and Salm, R. (1974) Conservation in Mauritius 1974. IUCN/WWF consultancy report for Government of Mauritius. Unpublished.

Rountree, F. G. R. (1951) Some aspects of bird-life in Mauritius. *Proc. Roy. Soc. Arts Sci. Mauritius* 1(2): 83-96.

Staub, F. (1971) Actual situation of the Mauritius endemic birds. *ICBP Bull.* 11: 226-227.

Staub, F. (1976) *Birds of the Mascarenes and Saint Brandon.* Port Louis, Mauritius: Organisation Normale des Enterprises.

Temple, S. A. (1974) Appendix 6. The native fauna of Mauritius: 1, the land birds. In J. Procter and R. Salm, Conservation in Mauritius 1974. IUCN/WWF consultancy report for Government of Mauritius. Unpublished.

Temple, S. A. (1975) A report on the conservation program in Mauritius, 15 October. Unpublished.

Temple, S. A., Staub, J. J. F. and Antoine, R. (1974) Some background information and recommendations on the preservation of the native flora and fauna of Mauritius. Unpublished report to the Government of Mauritius.

GABELA HELMET-SHRIKE   INDETERMINATE
Prionops gabela Rand, 1957

Order PASSERIFORMES   Family LANIIDAE
                                                         Subfamily PRIONOPINAE

Summary This helmet-shrike is known only from a small area near Gabela in western Angola. Although there have been very few records it might not be in any immediate danger.

Distribution The type-specimen of the Gabela Helmet-shrike was collected 15 km south of Gabela on the escarpment of western Angola in 1954 (Rand 1957). Two further specimens were taken in 1957, one on the escarpment 19 km south of Gabela and the other at the foot of the escarpment 64 km south of Mumbondo on the Gabela to Muxima road (Hall 1960a). In 1960 two birds were collected at "Londa" (apparently Conda: see Remarks under Gabela Akalat *Sheppardia gabela*), and another at Roça Cassemba, both near Gabela; and the species is recorded from Amboim Forest, also near Gabela (Pinto 1962). The only subsequent records are a sighting of three in dry forest south-west of Chio, July 1972 (Dean 1974), and the collection of one or more specimens south-west of Chio on an unknown date or dates (Dean and Huntley in prep.). All records up to 1960 were from within 40 km of Gabela (Hall and Moreau 1962), but Chio is c. 125 km to the north (in TAW 1980). It has been suggested that the species might occur elsewhere along the escarpment of western Angola though suitable habitat is thought unlikely to cover in total more than a "few hundred square miles" (Hall and Moreau 1962).

Population Numbers are not known. The species has been described as not uncommon in the Amboim Forest (Pinto 1962).

Ecology Most records are from secondary forest on the escarpment at an altitude of 300-900 m (Rand 1957, Heinrich 1958, Hall 1960a, Pinto 1962). It is a canopy bird, apparently able to survive in forest which has been underplanted with coffee (Hall 1960a, Pinto 1962). The specimen taken near the Gabela to Muxima road was in the trees of a dry thicket in an area of mixed thickets and cultivation, well outside the forest area (Hall 1960a). The food consists of insects and larvae (Pinto 1962). Specimens collected in September had enlarged gonads (Pinto 1962). The birds travel in loose groups of 3-5 individuals (Hall 1960a, Pinto 1962).

Threats None is known. It seems possible that the species can withstand extensive modification of its forest habitat (Hall 1960a, Pinto 1962), but its distribution is far too restricted for complacency on this point.

Conservation Measures Taken None is known.

Conservation Measures Proposed A survey is needed to assess the status of this species, identify any threats it faces and recommend appropriate action.

Remarks This bird forms a superspecies with the widespread Retz's Helmet-shrike *Prionops retzii* (Hall and Moreau 1970). The Gabela Helmet-shrike is one of a group of birds endemic to the escarpment zone of western Angola (Hall 1960b), including three other threatened bird species, the Gabela Akalat, Pulitzer's Longbill *Macrosphenus pulitzeri* and Monteiro's Bush-shrike *Malaconotus monteiri*, though this last is also recorded anomalously from Cameroon and possibly Kenya (see relevant accounts).

References

Dean, W. R. J. (1974) Breeding and distributional notes on some Angolan birds. *Durban Mus. Novit.* 10: 109-125.

Dean, W. R. J. and Huntley, M. A. (in prep.) An updated list of the birds of Angola.

Hall, B. P. (1960a) The ecology and taxonomy of some Angolan birds (based on a collection made in 1957). *Bull. Brit. Mus. (Nat. Hist.) Zool.* 6: 367-453.

Hall, B. P. (1960b) The faunistic importance of the scarp of Angola *Ibis* 102: 420-442.

Hall, B. P. and Moreau, R. E. (1962) A study of the rare birds of Africa. *Bull. Brit. Mus. (Nat. Hist.) Zool.* 8: 313-378.

Hall, B. P. and Moreau, R. E. (1970) *An atlas of speciation in African passerine birds*. London: Trustees of the British Museum (Natural History).

Heinrich, G. H. (1958) Zur Verbreitung und Lebensweise der Vögel von Angola. Part 3. *J. Orn.* 99: 399-421.

Pinto, A. A. da R. (1962) As observações de maior destaque das expedições ornitológicas do Instituto de Investigação Científica de Angola. *Bol. Inst. Invest. Cient. Angola* 1: 21-38.

Rand, A. L. (1957) Two new species of birds from Angola. *Fieldiana Zool.* 39: 41-45.

The Times Atlas of the World (1980) Comprehensive (sixth) edition. London: Times Books.

GREEN-BREASTED BUSH-SHRIKE   RARE
Malaconotus gladiator (Reichenow, 1892)

Order PASSERIFORMES   Family LANIIDAE
                                                Subfamily MALACONOTINAE

Summary This insectivorous bird of rainforest canopy is known from only five specimens and a few sight records in western Cameroon and eastern Nigeria. It is a very uncommon bird throughout its range, and its habitat in part of this range is under severe threat.

Distribution The Green-breasted Bush-shrike is known only from a few montane areas in western Cameroon and eastern Nigeria. It was described in 1892 from a specimen collected at 1,000-1,500 m at Buea on the south-eastern slopes of Mount Cameroon (Reichenow 1892). There were no further records until 1948 when a bird was taken near Bambulue in the Bamenda-Banso Highlands at 2,080 m (Serle 1950). In 1950 another was collected near Dikume Balue at 1,520 m in the Rumpi Hills, and in the following year one was shot and another seen at 1,370 m at the type-locality (Serle 1954). In 1961 a bird was collected on the Obudu Plateau at 1,500 m, the first record for Nigeria (Elgood 1965, J. H. Elgood *in litt.* 1983), and there have been a few subsequent field observations from this site (Elgood 1982), the most recent being in 1980 and 1981 (M. Dyer pers. comm. 1983, M. E. Gartshore *in litt.* 1984). In early 1984 the ICBP Cameroon Montane Forest Survey found this species to occur in small numbers between 950 and 1,350 m on the southern slopes of Mount Cameroon and at 1,100-1,950 m on Mount Kupe, 1,400-1,600 m on Mount Nlonako, 1,300 m in the Rumpi Hills, 2,200-2,300 m on Mount Oku, 1,700 m in the Bali-Ngemba Forest Reserve, and 1,750 m in forest between Mbengwi and Tinachong, these last three localities being in the Bamenda Highlands (SNS). This rare species could easily be overlooked and might occur more widely in the mountain forests of Cameroon and Nigeria.

Population The population of this species is likely to be small since it occurs at very low densities throughout its range (SNS).

Ecology All records have been from montane forest, including both primary and old secondary forest (Serle 1950,1954, Elgood 1965,1982). One bird seen in the Obudu Plateau was in a thick clump of secondary growth associated with a cultivated clearing (M. Dyer pers. comm. 1983). In the Bali-Ngemba Forest Reserve one bird was seen in forest underplanted with subsistence crops, suggesting some degree of adaptability to forest exploitation (SNS). It has been seen between two and 20 m above ground (Serle 1950,1954, M. Dyer pers. comm. 1983, SNS), though it is mainly a bird of the canopy (SNS). There is some indirect evidence, from stomach contents, that the species can forage in grassland near forest (Hall and Moreau 1962) but this has not been observed. It is an insectivorous species (Serle 1954, Hall and Moreau 1962), most readily detected by its distinctive, far-carrying call (SNS).

Threats None is known, but it would presumably be at serious risk if forest clearance were to become serious within its range. It is feared that the cattle-ranching development on the Obudu Plateau will lead to an increased demand for firewood with consequent forest clearance (J. H. Elgood *in litt.* 1983). Forest clearance is already very severe throughout the Bamenda Highlands (see Threats under Bannerman's Turaco *Tauraco bannermani*) but the populations further south on Mounts Cameroon, Kupe and Nlonako and the Rumpi Hills are probably more secure for the time being (SNS).

Conservation Measures Taken None is known.

Conservation Measures Proposed The ICBP Cameroon Montane Forest Survey is preparing a forest conservation plan for the Cameroon Highlands for the consideration of the Cameroon government.

Remarks The Green-breasted Bush-shrike is a member of a large superspecies which includes two other threatened species, the Uluguru Bush-shrike *Malaconotus alius* and Monteiro's Bush-shrike *M. monteiri* (see relevant accounts) (Hall and Moreau 1970). Other threatened bird species occur on Mount Cameroon, Mount Kupe and in the Bamenda Highlands (see under the Mount Cameroon Francolin *Francolinus camerunensis*, the Mount Kupe Bush-shrike *M. kupeensis* and Bannerman's Turaco respectively for details of these species). On the Rumpi Hills and Mount Nlonako the Green-breasted Bush-shrike is sympatric with two other threatened bird species, the White-throated Mountain Babbler *Lioptilus gilberti* and the Grey-necked Picathartes *Picathartes oreas* (see relevant accounts) and with three birds in Appendix C, the Cameroon Mountain Greenbul *Andropadus montanus*, the Grey-headed Greenbul *Phyllastrephus poliocephalus* and Ursula's Mouse-coloured Sunbird *Nectarinia ursulae*. On the Obudu Plateau in Nigeria the Green-breasted Bush-shrike is sympatric with the White-throated Mountain Babbler, the Cameroon Mountain Greenbul, the Grey-headed Greenbul and the threatened Bannerman's Weaver *Ploceus bannermani* (see relevant account).

References

Elgood, J. H. (1965) The birds of the Obudu Plateau, Eastern Region of Nigeria. *Nigerian Field* 30: 60-69.

Elgood, J. H. (1982) *The birds of Nigeria*. London: B.O.U. Check-list no. 4.

Hall, B. P. and Moreau, R. E. (1962) A study of the rare birds of Africa. *Bull. Brit. Mus. (Nat. Hist.) Zool.* 8: 313-378.

Hall, B. P. and Moreau, R. E. (1970) *An atlas of speciation in African passerine birds*. London: Trustees of the British Museum (Natural History).

Reichenow, A. (1892) *Laniarius gladiator* Rchw. n. sp. *J. Orn.* 40: 441-442.

Serle, W. (1950) A contribution to the ornithology of the British Cameroons. Part 2. *Ibis* 92: 602-638.

Serle, W. (1954) A second contribution to the ornithology of the British Cameroons. *Ibis* 96: 47-80.

MONTEIRO'S BUSH-SHRIKE   INDETERMINATE
Malaconotus monteiri (Sharpe, 1870)

Order PASSERIFORMES   Family LANIIDAE
                                                     Subfamily MALACONOTINAE

Summary This bush-shrike is known only from the escarpment of western Angola and Mount Cameroon. This is one of the least known bird species in Africa with no recent records.

Distribution Monteiro's Bush-shrike was described in 1870 from a specimen collected along the Rio Dande near Luanda in Angola (Sharpe 1870, Hall 1960a). It was next collected in the early 1900s from Dondo and Ndalo Tando (Ndalotando) in the Angolan escarpment zone (Hall 1960a,b, Hall *et al.* 1966). In 1954 two specimens were collected, one from Mucoso (near Dondo) and one from Gabela (Traylor 1962), both these localities being within the escarpment zone (Hall 1960a,b). An undated record from a further locality, "Bucaso" (mentioned but not traced by Hall 1960b), might refer to "Buçaco" at 12°59'S 14°36'E (Office of Geography 1956), c.250 km south of Gabela. A very similar bird was described from Buea at 1,000 m on Mount Cameroon in 1894 (Reichenow 1894): it was originally named *Laniarius perspicillatus* but is "practically indistinguishable from *monteiri*" and remains the only record of the species from Mount Cameroon (Serle 1954). However, in view of the failure of subsequent observers to find this species on Mount Cameroon, this record must now be open to question. Another apparently similar bird has been collected in the Kakamega Forest in western Kenya (van Someren 1932) but the specimen is now lost (Hall *et al.* 1966, Hall and Moreau 1970).

Population Numbers are not known but the small number of records suggests that the species is very rare, especially on Mount Cameroon which has been well studied by ornithologists.

Ecology Evergreen or gallery forests occur in all the localities in which the species has been recorded and are presumed to be the natural habitat of the bird (Hall 1960a,b, Traylor 1962, Hall *et al.* 1966).

Threats None is known, though forest destruction would presumably be detrimental to the species.

Conservation Measures Taken None is known.

Conservation Measures Proposed A survey is needed to determine the distribution of this species in Angola, to assess the degree of threat to its survival, and to recommend suitable sites for the establishment of nature reserves.

Remarks The taxonomic history of this species is particularly confusing. It has at various times been considered a subspecies of the Grey-headed Bush-

417

shrike *Malaconotus blanchoti* (Hall 1960a,b, Traylor 1962), a colour-morph of the Fiery-breasted Bush-shrike *M. cruentus* (Hall *et al.* 1966) and more recently as a separate species (Hall and Moreau 1970). It forms a superspecies with two other threatened species, the Uluguru Bush-shrike *M. alius* and the Green-breasted Bush-shrike *M. gladiator* (see relevant accounts) (Hall and Moreau 1970). Monteiro's Bush-shrike is one of a group of species whose ranges centre upon the western escarpment of Angola (Hall 1960b), including three other threatened bird species (see Remarks under Gabela Helmet-shrike *Prionops gabela*).

References

Hall, B. P. (1960a) The ecology and taxonomy of some Angolan birds (based on a collection made in 1957). *Bull. Brit. Mus. (Nat. Hist.) Zool.* 6: 367-453.

Hall, B. P. (1960b) The faunistic importance of the scarp of Angola. *Ibis* 102: 420-442.

Hall, B. P. and Moreau, R. E. (1970) *An atlas of speciation in African passerine birds*. London: Trustees of the British Museum (Natural History).

Hall, B. P., Moreau, R. E. and Galbraith, I. C. J. (1966) Polymorphism and parallelism in the African bush-shrikes of the genus *Malaconotus* (including *Chlorophoneus*). *Ibis* 108: 162-182.

Office of Geography (1956) *Gazetteer no. 20. Angola.* Washington, D.C.: Department of the Interior.

Reichenow, A. (1894) Zur Vogelfauna von Kamerun. *J. Orn.* 42: 29-43.

Serle, W. (1954) A second contribution to the ornithology of the British Cameroons. *Ibis* 96: 47-80.

Sharpe, R. B. (1870) On the birds of Angola. Part II. *Proc. Zool. Soc. Lond.*: 142-150.

van Someren, V. G. L. (1932) Birds of Kenya and Uganda, being addenda and corrigenda to my previous paper in *Novitates Zoologicae* XXIX, 1922. *Novit. Zool.* 37: 252-380.

Traylor, M. A. (1962) Notes on the birds of Angola, passeres. *Publ. cult. Co. Diam. Angola, Lisboa* no. 58: 53-142.

ULUGURU BUSH-SHRIKE   RARE
Malaconotus alius Friedmann, 1927

Order PASSERIFORMES   Family LANIIDAE
                                                    Subfamily MALACONOTINAE

Summary This highly elusive, canopy-dwelling bird is restricted to a small area of montane forest in Tanzania. It was rediscovered in 1981 after an absence of records for nearly 20 years; probably its numbers are low but not declining.

Distribution The Uluguru Bush-shrike has been recorded only from Tanzania in the Uluguru Mountain forests over 1,300 m, in an area of probably less than 260 km^2 (Hall and Moreau 1962). The species was discovered in 1926 when two specimens were collected at 1,830 m at Bagilo on the eastern slopes of the mountains (Friedmann 1927, Loveridge 1960). In 1948 one bird was seen in forest above Bunduki on the western slopes of the mountains (J. G. Williams pers. comm. 1983). Between 1952 and 1962 at least 13 specimens were collected, one being labelled "Ulugurus" and the remainder coming from Bagilo, 1,800 m (Britton 1981, Stuart and Jensen 1981, specimen in BMNH: SNS). It appears, therefore, that at least 15 specimens have been collected, not 13 (as stated in Britton 1980). In 1981 the species was seen and heard on both sides of Lupanga Mountain, and on the west escarpment of the Lukwangule Plateau at 2,100 m (Stuart and Jensen 1981, Scharff *et al.* 1982). Another bird was seen at 1,300 m on the eastern side of Lupanga in 1982 (Stuart and Jensen in press, F. P. Jensen *in litt.* 1982).

Population No estimate of numbers has been made. This species is very elusive and several expeditions to the Uluguru Mountains, for example in 1964 (Friedmann and Stager 1964) and 1972 (D. A. Turner pers. comm. 1977), failed to observe it. There were no records between 1927 (when it was discovered) and 1948, nor between 1962 (see Britton 1981) and 1981 (see Stuart and Jensen 1981). After a highly distinctive call was eventually traced to an adult of this species, occurrence of such calls elsewhere suggested that the bird is to be found at very low densities throughout the Uluguru forests above 1,300 m (Stuart and Jensen 1981, in press, Scharff *et al.* 1982, F. P. Jensen *in litt.* 1982).

Ecology The species inhabits the canopy of montane forest above 1,300 m, where it is extremely difficult to see (Scharff *et al.* 1982, F. P. Jensen *in litt.* 1982). One bird was seen in a mixed-species bird party and kept to the densest parts of the foliage (F. P. Jensen *in litt.* 1982). The species has a loud unmistakable call (Stuart and Jensen 1981).

Threats There is very little cutting of the forest at the moment within the altitudinal range of this species and its habitat is not under any immediate threat (Scharff *et al.* 1982, SNS); however, because of its low numbers even minor changes in habitat might adversely affect it, and it should be noted that the lower slopes of the Ulugurus are being exploited steadily by a dense local human population (Scharff *et al.* 1982).

Conservation Measures Taken All the Uluguru forests are within forest reserves which give some measure of protection to the wildlife (Scharff *et al.* 1982).

Conservation Measures Proposed A conservation strategy for the Ulugurus has been drafted with the suggestion to elevate the status of some of the forest to a national nature reserve (Scharff *et al.* 1982).

Remarks The Uluguru Bush-shrike is a member of a large superspecies which includes two other threatened species, the Green-breasted Bush-shrike *Malaconotus gladiator* and Monteiro's Bush-shrike *M. monteiri* (see relevant accounts) (Hall and Moreau 1970). Three other threatened bird species are known from the Ulugurus, Mrs Moreau's Warbler *Bathmocercus winifredae*, the Banded Green Sunbird *Anthreptes rubritorques* and the Tanzanian Mountain Weaver *Ploceus nicolli* (see relevant accounts). There is also another bird endemic to the Ulugurus, Loveridge's Sunbird *Nectarinia loveridgei*, an abundant and adaptable species included in Appendix C. Another bird in Appendix C, the White-winged Apalis *Apalis chariessa*, also occurs in the Uluguru Mountains. Other endemic fauna includes three mammals (one full species, two races), seven reptiles (five full species, two races), eight amphibians (six full species, two races) and a host of invertebrates (Scharff *et al.* 1982).

References

Britton, P. L. (1978) The Andersen collection from Tanzania. *Scopus* 2: 77-85.

Britton, P. L. ed. (1980) *Birds of East Africa: their habitat, status and distribution.* Nairobi: EANHS.

Britton, P. L. (1981) Notes on the Andersen collection and other specimens from Tanzania housed in some West German museums. *Scopus* 5: 14-21.

Friedmann, H. (1927) New birds from Tanganyika Territory. *Proc. New Eng. Zool. Club* 10: 3-7.

Friedmann, H. and Stager, K. F. (1964) Results of the 1964 Cheney Tanganyikan Expedition. Ornithology. *Los Angeles County Mus. Contrib. Sci.* 84.

Hall, B. P. and Moreau, R. E. (1962) A study of the rare birds of Africa. *Bull. Brit. Mus. (Nat. Hist.) Zool.* 8: 313-378.

Hall, B. P. and Moreau, R. E. (1970) *An atlas of speciation in African passerine birds.* London: Trustees of the British Museum (Natural History).

Loveridge, A. (1960) Status of new vertebrates described or collected by Loveridge. *J. E. Afr. Nat. Hist. Soc.* 23: 250-280.

Scharff, N., Stoltze, M. and Jensen, F. P. (1982) The Uluguru Mts., Tanzania. Report of a study-tour, 1981. Unpublished.

Stuart, S. N. and Jensen, F. P. (1981) Further range extensions and other notable records of forest birds from Tanzania. *Scopus* 5: 106-115.

Stuart, S. N. and Jensen, F. P. (in press) The avifauna of the Uluguru Mountains, Tanzania. *Gerfaut.*

MOUNT KUPE BUSH-SHRIKE   INDETERMINATE
Malaconotus kupeensis (Serle, 1951)

Order PASSERIFORMES   Family LANIIDAE
                                                Subfamily MALACONOTINAE

Summary This remarkable and enigmatic shrike is only known from the very restricted rainforest of Mount Kupe in Cameroon where it is rare (apparently from natural causes) and has not been recorded since 1951 despite a recent extensive search.

Distribution This bush-shrike was discovered in 1949 on Mount Kupe, 100 km north-east of Mount Cameroon, in Cameroon (Serle 1951). All records of the species have been at 1,370 m (Serle 1951). The area of forest on Mount Kupe has been estimated to be only 21 km^2 (Hall and Moreau 1962), but the species could conceivably also occur on the nearby Bakossi Mountains and Mount Nlonako, both areas being very poorly known ornithologically.

Population Several unsuccessful searches were made for this species between 1949 when it was discovered and 18 months later in 1951 when it was next recorded (Serle 1951). This suggests that it is very rare in its only known locality: only four specimens have been collected (Hall and Moreau 1962) and there have been no records since 1951. An extensive search in early 1984 by the ICBP Cameroon Montane Forest Survey proved unsuccessful, although a trisyllabic whistle (see Ecology) was heard from an undiscernible singer in the forest canopy on the last day of fieldwork (SNS). If the species survives it must be in very small numbers and an earlier population estimate of 1,200 birds (Hall and Moreau 1962) is likely to be much too high.

Ecology All records of the species have been from primary forest (Serle 1951). In 1949 two birds were seen feeding on insects high in the canopy (Serle 1951). In 1951 a party of three birds, moving about in the branches of smaller trees, 6-9 m above the ground, was collected: the party had not been associating with any other bird species and the stomachs of these birds contained insects (Serle 1951). A distinctive trisyllabic whistle was noted (Serle 1951).

Threats Since the forest cover on which the Mount Kupe Bush-shrike presumably depends has survived, it is likely that the species has declined to very low numbers for natural reasons (SNS).

Conservation Measures Taken None is known. Although Mount Kupe is small, the forest on it has survived owing to the "superstitious dread in which the mountain is held" by the local people (Serle 1950, SNS).

Conservation Measures Proposed Another survey is needed to ascertain the present status of this rare species. In order to be successful, such a survey will probably need to work for several months on Mount Kupe, as well as in the Bakossi

Mountains and Mount Nlonako. The ICBP Cameroon Montane Forest Survey is preparing a preliminary conservation plan for Mount Kupe for the consideration of the Cameroon government.

Remarks This is a very distinctive species with no close relatives in its genus (Hall and Moreau 1970). Three other threatened bird species, the Green-breasted Bush-shrike *Malaconotus gladiator*, the White-throated Mountain Babbler *Lioptilus gilberti* and the Grey-necked Picathartes *Picarthartes oreas*, occur on Mount Kupe (see relevant accounts), as do three species in Appendix C, the Cameroon Mountain Greenbul *Andropadus montanus*, the Grey-headed Greenbul *Phyllastrephus poliocephalus* and Ursula's Mouse-coloured Sunbird *Nectarinia ursulae*.

References

Hall, B. P. and Moreau, R. E. (1962) A study of the rare birds of Africa. *Bull. Brit. Mus. (Nat. Hist.) Zool.* 8: 313-378.

Hall, B. P. and Moreau, R. E. (1970) *An atlas of speciation in African passerine birds.* London: Trustees of the British Museum (Natural History).

Serle, W. (1950) A contribution to the ornithology of the British Cameroons, Part 1. *Ibis* 92: 343-376.

Serle, W. (1951) A new species of shrike and a new race of apalis from West Africa. *Bull. Brit. Orn. Club* 71: 41-43.

SAO TOME FISCAL SHRIKE

Lanius newtoni Bocage, 1891

Order PASSERIFORMES

INDETERMINATE

Family LANIIDAE
Subfamily LANIINAE

Summary This is a little known shrike confined to the southern forested regions of São Tomé and not seen for over 50 years.

Distribution The São Tomé Fiscal Shrike is endemic to São Tomé (São Tomé e Príncipe) in the Gulf of Guinea. It was recorded in the last century from São Miguel and Rio Quija on the south-west coast (Bocage 1891), "Zungui" (untraceable: perhaps N'zumbi, at 0°04'N 6°34'E in Ministério das Colónias 1948, Office of Geography 1962) in the interior of Iogo-Iogo (i.e. far south) (Bocage 1903), and "Zana" (again untraceable) in Angolares, on the south-east coast (Bannerman 1939; see Remarks). In 1928 the species was found again: a female was collected on 29 May at Io Grande in the south-east (this and the area around Lake Amélia subsequently being searched in vain), and between 8 November and 8 December 12 birds (eight males, four females) were collected at Roça Jou (0°07'N 6°30'E) and nearby Rio Quija, three of those at Roça Jou being specifically noted as at 1,060 m and 10 km from the sea (Correia 1928-1929; also M. LeCroy *in litt.* 1984). There are no subsequent records.

Population The species has been reported as "not uncommon" in 1928 (Amadon 1953), but the testimony of the collector is rather that it was "not very common" (Correia 1928-1929). It has not been seen since, and has recently been considered very probably extinct (de Naurois 1983).

Ecology The bird at Io Grande in 1928 was in dense forest on a high hill, those that year at Roça Jou and Rio Quija were in virgin forest (Correia 1928-1929). All had small gonads except two males (November/December), while two females in these months showed traces of juvenile plumage (M. LeCroy *in litt.* 1984). The species is less robust than the African Fiscal Shrike *Lanius collaris* with which it forms a superspecies, and its feeding habits possibly reflect this character (Amadon 1953). The African Fiscal Shrike is a bird of grassland, clearings and cultivations (Bannerman 1939, Hall and Moreau 1970), i.e. the two species are very different in their ecological requirements.

Threats The reasons for this species's long-term rarity are quite unknown. Forest damage (selective felling) and destruction are known to have occurred in lowland areas of the island, notably from around 1890 to 1920 (Bannerman 1915, Correia 1928-1929, Snow 1950, de Naurois 1975, R. de Naurois *in litt.* 1984), and may have affected the bird. Introduced disease and mammalian predators may also have played a part.

Conservation Measures Taken None is known.

423

Conservation Measures Proposed An ICBP project was developed in 1981 to investigate the status, ecology and conservation of the endemic birds of São Tomé e Príncipe, but was unable to proceed in 1982 and 1983. A search for this bird is a component of the project and conservation proposals will follow if the work goes ahead and the species is relocated.

Remarks The record of "a young bird from Zana in Angolares" (Bannerman 1939; see Distribution) is puzzling, since it appears to refer to a specimen originally described as "without indication of sex or locality" (Bocage 1903). Not having been seen in the wild for over 50 years, by CITES criteria this species would now be considered extinct.

References

Amadon, D. (1953) Avian systematics and evolution in the Gulf of Guinea. The J. G. Correia collection. *Bull. Amer. Mus. Nat. Hist.* 100: 393-451.

Bannerman, D. A (1915) Report on the birds collected by the late Mr Boyd Alexander (Rifle Brigade) during his last expedition to Africa. Part II. The birds of St.Thomas' Island. *Ibis* (10)3: 89-121.

Bannerman, D. A. (1939) *The birds of tropical West Africa*, 5. London: Crown Agents for the Colonies.

Bocage, J. V. B. (1891) Oiseaux de l'Ile St.Thomé. *Jorn. Acad. Sci. Lisboa* (2)2: 77-87.

Bocage, J. V. B. (1903) Contribution à la faune des quatre îles du Golfe de Guinée. IV. Ile de St.Thomé. *Jorn. Acad. Sci. Lisboa* (2)7: 65-96.

Correia, J. G. (1928-1929) Unpublished typescript concerning his São Tomé expedition, held in AMNH.

Hall, B. P. and Moreau, R. E. (1970) *An atlas of speciation in African passerine birds*. London: Trustees of the British Museum (Natural History).

Ministério das Colónias (1948) *Atlas de Portugal Ultramarino e das grandes viagens portuguesas de descobrimento e expansão*. Lisboa: Junta das Missões Geográficas e de Investigações Coloniais.

de Naurois, R. (1975) Le "Scops" de l'Ile de São Tomé *Otus hartlaubi* (Giebel). *Bonn. zool. Beitr.* 26: 319-355.

de Naurois, R. (1983) Les oiseaux reproducteurs des îles de São Tomé et Príncipe: liste systématique commentée et indications zoogéographiques. *Bonn. zool. Beitr.* 34: 129-148.

Office of Geography (1962) *Gazetteer no. 63. Rio Muni, Fernando Po, and São Tomé e Príncipe*. Washington, D.C.: Department of the Interior.

Snow, D. W. (1950) The birds of São Tomé and Príncipe in the Gulf of Guinea. *Ibis* 92: 579-595.

VAN DAM'S VANGA   RARE
Xenopirostris damii Schlegel, 1866

Order PASSERIFORMES   Family VANGIDAE

Summary This insectivorous bird of deciduous forest is known this century from a single site (Ankarafantsika) in north-west Madagascar which is, however, a protected area.

Distribution Van Dam's Vanga was originally described from two specimens collected on 9 October 1864 in the forests near Ambassuana (Ambasohana) in the far north-west of Madagascar (Schlegel 1866, Schlegel and Pollen 1868). At least six further specimens were collected at around this time and probably at this locality (given as Pasandava Bay) (Milne Edwards and Grandidier 1885). The generalisation of the type-locality as Pasandava (Ampasindava) Bay (south of Nosy Bé) (e.g. Milne Edwards and Grandidier 1885, Lavauden 1932,1937, Milon *et al.* 1973) or else as "the Sambirano" (Benson *et al.* 1977), i.e. the general region of the river of that name which runs into this bay, is misleading: according to the contemporary map (in Pollen 1868) Ambassuana lay on the river of the same name, some 20 km east of the easternmost part of Pasandava Bay and much closer to Ambara (Ambaro) Bay: it would appear to have been situated at about 13°35'S 48°40'E and a few kilometres east or south of the locality now called Maherivaratra (past which the Ambazoana River flows), and indeed there is an "Ambazoana Bala" marked at roughly this spot in a 1900 map (see Locamus 1900). There have been no further records of the species from the far north-west, but it appears that the Ambazoana valley has never been revisited. The species was rediscovered on 9 October 1928 when a male was collected on the Ankarafantsika plateau, south-east of Majunga, and a juvenile was collected there on 5 July 1930 (Lavauden 1932); the species was found and collected there again in 1969-1971 (Salvan 1970, Forbes-Watson *et al.* 1973) and has been regularly seen subsequently (D. A. Turner pers. comm. 1983, O. Langrand *in litt.* 1984); the area involved in the post-1969 observations is near Lake Ampijoroa (Milon *et al.* 1973, A. D. Forbes-Watson pers. comm. 1984; see Remarks).

Population Although this species was unanimously described as "very rare" (Schlegel and Pollen 1868, Delacour 1932, Lavauden 1932) and even treated as Endangered in King (1978-1979), the most recent observations at Ankarafantsika indicate that it is in fact present in fairly good numbers there, with certainly 50 or more pairs in one relatively small area where the forest is untouched (D. A. Turner pers. comm. 1983).

Ecology It inhabits primary deciduous forest (Delacour 1932, D. A. Turner pers. comm. 1983); it is seen along the edges of woods foraging for insects (Schlegel and Pollen 1868). The stomachs of the first two known specimens contained beetle remains (Schlegel and Pollen 1868). Although described as solitary (Schlegel and Pollen 1868) it was also reported to occur in small groups of six to eight birds (Milne Edwards and Grandidier 1885).

Threats The highly restricted range of this species must be a source of permanent concern and vigilance for its welfare. Deforestation is likely to have affected many areas where it might have been searched for in north-west Madagascar.

Conservation Measures Taken The area where it has been recorded this century partly falls within the Ankarafantsika Nature Reserve (R.N.I. no. 7) (see Andriamampianina 1981).

Conservation Measures Proposed A study of the status and ecology of this bird at Ankarafantsika would help determine where else it might be searched for and what management it might require (besides confirming, for example, that it is resident throughout the year). An investigation of the type-locality (see Distribution) is warranted to establish whether any original tracts of forest remain and whether they still hold populations of this species. All such work should be undertaken in conjunction with studies recommended under Conservation Measures Proposed for the White-breasted Mesite *Mesitornis variegata*.

Remarks Although this species has been considered doubtfully distinct from Lafresnaye's Vanga *Xenopirostris xenopirostris* (see, e.g., Delacour 1932, Appert 1970) and confused with it (see, e.g., Bartlett 1875, Ménégaux 1907), it has been affirmed as a good species (in Lavauden 1932) and this judgement is accepted here. The importance of the Ankarafantsika Nature Reserve as the only locality currently known for the species and the White-breasted Mesite cannot be overstated. However, it is to be noted that (according to IGNT 1964) Ampijoroa is well outside the boundaries of the nature reserve, and right next to the main road from Antananarivo to Majunga.

References

Andriamampianina, J. (1981) Les réserves naturelles et la protection de la nature à Madagascar. Pp. 105-111 in P. Oberlé, ed. *Madagascar, un sanctuaire de la nature*. Paris: Lechevalier.

Appert, O. (1970) Zur Biologie der Vangawürger (Vangidae) Südwest-Madagaskars. *Orn. Beob.* 67: 101-133.

Bartlett, E. (1875) List of the mammals and birds collected by Mr. Waters in Madagascar. *Proc. Zool. Soc. Lond.*: 62-69.

Benson, C. W., Colebrook-Robjent, J. F. R. and Williams, A. (1977) Contribution à l'ornithologie de Madagascar. *Oiseau et R.F.O.* 47: 167-191.

Delacour, J. (1932) Les oiseaux de la Mission Franco-Anglo-Américaine à Madagascar. *Oiseau et R.F.O.* 2: 1-96.

Forbes-Watson, A. D., Turner, D. A. and Keith, G. S. (1973) Report on bird preservation in Madagascar. Part 3, Appendix I. Proposed list of protected Madagascar birds. Report to ICBP, unpublished.

Institut Géographique National à Tananarive (1964) Carte de Madagascar, 1: 500,000, Type 1963. Tananarive.

King, W. B. (1978-1979) *Red data book, 2: Aves*. 2nd edition. Morges, Switzerland: IUCN.

Lavauden, L. (1932) Etude d'une petite collection d'oiseaux de Madagascar. *Bull. Mus. Natn. Hist. Nat.* (2)4: 629-640.

Lavauden, L. (1937) Supplément. A. Milne Edwards and A. Grandidier, *Histoire physique, naturelle et politique de Madagascar, 12. Oiseaux*. Paris: Société d'Editions Géographiques, Maritimes et Coloniales.

Locamus, P. (1900) Carte de Madagascar, 1: 500,000. Paris.

Ménégaux, M. A. (1907) Liste des oiseaux rapportés en 1906 par M. Geay, du sud-ouest de Madagascar. *Bull. Mus. Natn. Hist. Nat.* 13: 104-113.

Milne Edwards, A. and Grandidier, A. (1885) *Histoire physique, naturelle et politique de Madagascar, 12. Histoire naturelle des oiseaux*. Tome I. Paris.

Milon, P., Petter, J.-J. and Randrianasolo, G. (1973) *Faune de Madagascar, 35. Oiseaux*. Tananarive and Paris: ORSTOM and CNRS.

Pollen, F. (1868) *Recherches sur la faune de Madagascar et de ses dépendances, d'après les découvertes de François P. L. Pollen et D. C. van Dam*. 1ère partie. Relation de voyage. Leyde.

Salvan, J. (1970) Remarques sur l'évolution de l'avifaune malgache depuis 1945. *Alauda* 38: 191-203.

Schlegel, H. (1866) [List of the most remarkable species of mammals and birds collected by Messrs Fr. Pollen and D. C. van Dam in Madagascar.] *Proc. Zool. Soc. Lond.*: 419-426.

Schlegel, H. and Pollen, F. P. L. (1868) *Recherches sur la faune de Madagascar et de ses dépendances, d'après les découvertes de François P. L. Pollen et D. C. van Dam*. 2me partie. Mammifères et oiseaux. Leyde.

POLLEN'S VANGA   RARE
Xenopirostris polleni (Schlegel, 1868)

Order PASSERIFORMES   Family VANGIDAE

Summary This insectivorous rainforest bird is known from a wide variety of localities in eastern Madagascar but is everywhere rare.

Distribution The scatter of records for Pollen's Vanga indicates that it is confined to the rainforests of eastern Madagascar. However, the type-locality is the "north-west coast" (Schlegel and Pollen 1868) (attempts to trace anything more precise have been fruitless). If the bird is confined to humid forest, and if the map of the area explored by the original collectors (in Pollen 1868) represents the total area they prospected, then (according to the vegetation map in Rand 1936) the only suitable localities in the north-west are the Montagne d'Ambre or the western parts of the Tsaratanana massif, particularly the Manongarivo massif (west of the Sambirano) (see IGNT 1964). The original three specimens were later described as coming from "north-east" Madagascar (Hartlaub 1877) but this is evidently in error (see Remarks). However, there is a suspected sight record from Marojejy (north-east) in September 1972 (Benson *et al.* 1977) and one was seen at 500 m near Maroantsetra in November 1982 (O. Langrand *in litt.* 1984). All other records except one are from the central parts of eastern Madagascar, listed here from north to south. There are two specimens in BMNH from Fénérive, dated May 1895 (Benson *et al.* 1977, NJC), and twelve in MNHN and MRAC from Sihanaka forest (NJC; also Lavauden 1932), one of these latter actually being taken between Fanovana and Beforona (see Remarks). Specimens are known from both Fanovana (c. 800 m), April 1931 (Delacour 1932, Rand 1932,1936) and August 1932, and Beforona, September 1932 (specimens in Stockholm: C. Edelstam *in litt.* 1983), but forest at least at the former locality no longer exists (D. A. Turner pers. comm. 1983). Individuals have been seen in November 1976, July 1980 and December 1982 at Périnet (D. A. Turner *in litt.* 1983, O. Langrand *in litt.* 1984). Several specimens were reported to have been collected in the forests on the eastern slopes of the great central massif (Milne Edwards and Grandidier 1885), although the only traceable reference to any of these is to one from south-east of Antananarivo, February 1872 (Sharpe 1872; see Remarks); however in UMZC there are three specimens labelled "Imerina, 1891" (Imerina is the whole area around Antananarivo: see Deschamps 1960) and another taken within 60 km of Antananarivo, 1881 (NJC), and presumably all four were from "the forests of the eastern slopes" in central Madagascar. Single adult males were collected at Mahanoro on 1 May and the "Sakales" River (see Remarks) on 15 May 1895 (Richmond 1897). In 1959 a specimen was collected in Tsarafidy forest between Ambohimahasoa and Fianarantsoa (Griveaud 1961), two specimens were collected there ("Forêt d'Amboasary") in January 1961 (Benson *et al.* 1977), two birds were seen (one mist-netted) there in April 1971 (Forbes-Watson *et al.* 1973, D. A. Turner *in litt.* 1983), and a specimen in SMF labelled as Lafresnaye's Vanga *Xenopirostris xenopirostris* and taken at "Amboasary" on 27 October 1931 (NJC) presumably also originates from Tsarafidy. In MNHN there is also a specimen from 30 km north-north-west of Fort

Dauphin in the far south-east of Madagascar, collected on the 26 May 1948 (NJC).

Population Although unanimously regarded as rare (Delacour 1932, Rand 1936, Milon *et al.* 1973) and even as Endangered (in King 1978-1979), it is clear from the evidence above that this species has a much wider range than has often been stated. However, the nineteenth century report of its occurrence in groups (see Ecology) has not been confirmed, which might (conceivably) indicate a greater decline in numbers than that resulting simply from the decline in total forest area. It is evidently only ever present in small numbers wherever it survives.

Ecology Pollen's Vanga is apparently a bird of primary rainforest. It was reported (presumably by a collector in a personal communication) to live in groups of 8-10, to feed on insects, small reptiles and frogs, to fly low and to be tame (Milne Edwards and Grandidier 1885). The MNHN specimen from Fort Dauphin contained a very large spider, a caterpillar and insect remains; it was not in breeding condition (NJC). All sight records given under Distribution (from Maroantsetra, Périnet and Tsarafidy as well as the possible one from Marojejy) were of birds in mixed bird-parties (Benson *et al.* 1977, D. A. Turner *in litt.* 1983. O. Langrand *in litt.* 1984), so it is possible that the groups of 8-10 referred to in the last century were not intended to imply monospecific flocks.

Threats Destruction and disturbance of primary rainforest is the single most serious threat to this and all other rainforest-dependent species in Madagascar (see Threats under Madagascar Serpent Eagle *Eutriorchis astur*). It is not known whether primary forest still occurs in the coastal areas where the species was collected in the last century (Fénérive, Mahanoro, "Sakales" River), but this seems unlikely.

Conservation Measures Taken The species occurs in the Périnet-Analamazaotra Special Reserve, which covers 810 ha, and possibly in the Marojejy Nature Reserve (R.N.I. no. 12), which covers 60,150 ha (Andriamampianina 1981).

Conservation Measures Proposed Immediate and effective protection of as much remaining rainforest as possible would almost certainly guarantee the survival of this and all other rainforest-dependent species in Madagascar; and at least, on current knowledge, complete protection of the intact parts of Sihanaka forest is of extreme importance (see Conservation Measures Proposed under Madagascar Serpent Eagle). Any ornithological work in the other areas from which the species is known, or where it might be expected, should where possible be extended to include searches to locate it. The forest at Tsarafidy where this species occurs was identified in 1961 as a place of exceptional interest for its wildlife which certainly deserved complete protection (Griveaud 1961); the species may be expected in the nearby "Nandehizana" forest, if this still survives (for both localities see Conservation Measures Proposed and Remarks under Madagascar Yellowbrow *Crossleyia xanthophrys*).

Remarks The error concerning the type-material originating from north-east Madagascar arises from the fact that the specimen-labels say "N. O. Madagascar": in both Dutch and German this would signify north-east, and was taken as such by Hartlaub (1877), but the language used on the labels is French ("voyage de Van Dam"), hence "N. O." signifies north-west (specimens in RMNH: NJC). That one of the specimens in MNHN labelled as from Sihanaka should also say "route de Fanovana à Beforona" (i.e. part of the road between Antananarivo and Tamatave) greatly stretches the limits accepted here of the "Sihanaka forest" (see Conservation Measures Proposed under Madagascar Serpent Eagle). "Kinkimauro" was given as the precise locality of the specimen from south-east of Antananarivo (Sharpe 1872), and later repeated as "Kinki-manro" (Hartlaub 1877), but "kinkimavo" was in fact a widespread native name for certain grey birds (Milne Edwards and Grandidier 1885) and it is obvious that the word was written on the specimen's label by the collector and misinterpreted as a site by its recipient. The "Sakales" river cannot be traced but it is evident that the collector was very close to the Sakaleona River (south of Mahanoro) at the time and these are doubtless identical ("Sakales" is obviously a misreading of Sakaleo, a village which in the last century stood at the estuary of the river: see Locamus 1900); both this and the site at Mahanoro have been included in a map of the species's distribution (see Benson *et al.* 1977) although there is no reference to Richmond (1897) as the source. There is a striking similarity between the plumages of the Tylas Vanga *Tylas eduardi* and immature Pollen's Vanga (Sharpe 1870, Benson 1971, Benson *et al.* 1977, O. Langrand *in litt.* 1984) and, as it appears that the two species are sympatric and possibly without differences in habitat, a field study of their relationship has been urged (Benson *et al.* 1977).

References

Andriamampianina, J. (1981) Les réserves naturelles et la protection de la nature à Madagascar. Pp. 105-111 in P. Oberlé, ed. *Madagascar, un sanctuaire de la nature*. Paris: Lechevalier.

Benson, C. W. (1971) The Cambridge collection from the Malagasy Region (Part II). *Bull. Brit. Orn. Club* 91: 1-7.

Benson, C. W., Colebrook-Robjent, J. F. R. and Williams, A. (1977) Contribution à l'ornithologie de Madagascar. *Oiseau et R.F.O.* 47: 41-64, 167-191.

Delacour, J. (1932) Les oiseaux de la Mission Franco-Anglo-Américaine à Madagascar. *Oiseau et R.F.O.* 2: 1-96.

Deschamps, H. (1960) *Histoire de Madagascar*. Paris: Berger-Levrault.

Forbes-Watson, A. D., Turner, D. A. and Keith, G. S. (1973) Report on bird preservation in Madagascar. Part 3, Appendix. Report to ICBP, unpublished.

Griveaud, P. (1961) Un intéressant vestige forestier malgache. *Bull. Acad. Malgache* 39: 9-10.

Hartlaub, G. (1877) *Die Vögel Madagascars und der benachbarten Inselgruppen*. Halle.

Institut Géographique National à Tananarive (1964) Carte de Madagascar, 1: 500,000, Type 1963. Tananarive.

King, W. B. (1978-1979) *Red data book, 2: Aves*. 2nd edition. Morges, Switzerland: IUCN.

Lavauden, L. (1932) Etude d'une petite collection d'oiseaux de Madagascar. *Bull. Mus. Natn. Hist. Nat.* (2)4: 629-640.

Locamus, P. (1900) Carte de Madagascar, 1: 500,000. Paris.

Milne Edwards, A. and Grandidier, A. (1885) *Histoire physique, naturelle et politique de Madagascar, 12. Histoire naturelle des oiseaux.* Tome I. Paris.

Milon, P., Petter, J.-J. and Randrianasolo, G. (1973) *Faune de Madagascar, 35. Oiseaux.* Tananarive and Paris: ORSTOM and CNRS.

Pollen, F. (1868) *Recherches sur la faune de Madagascar et de ses dépendances, d'apres les découvertes de François P. L. Pollen et D. C. van Dam.* 1ère partie. Relation de voyage. Leyde.

Rand, A. L. (1932) Mission Franco-Anglo-Américaine à Madagascar: notes de voyage. *Oiseau et R.F.O.* 2: 227-282.

Rand, A. L. (1936) The distribution and habits of Madagascar birds. *Bull. Amer. Mus. Nat. Hist.* 72: 143-499.

Richmond, C. W. (1897) Catalogue of a collection of birds made by Doctor W. L. Abbott in Madagascar, with descriptions of three new species. *Proc. U. S. Natn. Mus.* 19: 677-694.

Schlegel, H. and Pollen, F. P. L. (1868) *Recherches sur la faune de Madagascar et de ses dépendances, d'après les découvertes de François P. L. Pollen et D. C. van Dam.* 2me partie. Mammifères et oiseaux. Leyde.

Sharpe, R. B. (1870) Contributions to the ornithology of Madagascar. Part I. *Proc. Zool. Soc. Lond.*: 384-401.

Sharpe, R. B. (1872) Contributions to the ornithology of Madagascar. Part III. *Proc. Zool. Soc. Lond.*: 866-869.

SWYNNERTON'S FOREST ROBIN   RARE

Swynnertonia swynnertoni (Shelley, 1906)

Order PASSERIFORMES   Family MUSCICAPIDAE
                                                 Subfamily TURDINAE

Summary Three subspecies of this ground-haunting robin are known from eastern and south-eastern Africa (Zimbabwe, Mozambique and Tanzania), all of which have exceptionally limited distributions. It is confined to middle-altitude and montane forests and depends on the continued survival of these habitats.

Distribution The nominate form of Swynnerton's Forest Robin *S. s. swynnertoni* was discovered in 1905 in Chirinda Forest during the early exploration of the eastern highlands of Zimbabwe (Shelley 1906, Swynnerton 1907,1908). Subsequent studies have shown that the species also occurs in very small forest patches north of Chirinda Forest in the Vumba Highlands (where it occurs on both sides of the Zimbabwe/Mozambique border) and at Stapleford (Benson 1946, Serle 1955, Irwin 1978,1979, M. P. S. Irwin *in litt.* 1983, A. J. Manson *in litt.* 1983). It ranges from 900 to 1,300 m in Chirinda Forest and from 1,400 to 1,700 m in the Vumba Highlands and Stapleford (Irwin 1979,1981, A. J. Manson *in litt.* 1983) but is absent from all other forests in eastern Zimbabwe, including the heavily forested eastern slopes of the Inyanga Highlands (Hall and Moreau 1962, Irwin 1979,1981). The total area occupied by the nominate form has been estimated at not much more than 1,000 ha (Irwin 1979,1981) but recent work in the Vumba Highlands suggests that 3,000 ha is a more likely figure (A. J. Manson *in litt.* 1983). Birds on Mount Gorongosa 115 km to the east in Mozambique have been described as a separate subspecies *S. s. umbratica* (Clancey 1974). This form ranges between 850 and 1,750 m (Pinto 1959, Clancey 1971, J. Burlison *in litt.* 1983) and probably occupies a total range of only a few thousand hectares (Irwin 1979). *S. s. rodgersi* was discovered in 1981 in the Mwanihana Forest on the eastern escarpment of the Uzungwa Mountains in eastern Tanzania (Stuart and Jensen 1981, Jensen and Stuart 1982). In 1984 another population of *rodgersi* was discovered 160 km to the south-west in the forest above Chita, also on the eastern escarpment of the Uzungwa Mountains (F. P. Jensen pers. comm. 1984). This new subspecies has been recorded only between 1,000 and 1,200 m in Mwanihana Forest (F. P. Jensen *in litt.* 1982, Jensen *et al.* in press) and between 1,050 and 1,700 m above Chita (F. P. Jensen pers. comm. 1984) and is separated from the two southern forms by 1,100 km. It is possible that *rodgersi* occurs in other forests on the eastern escarpment of the Uzungwa Mountains but these have not yet been explored by ornithologists. It is certainly absent, however, from the well studied dry forests on the Uzungwa plateau (SNS).

Population Nominate *swynnertoni* is very common in the Chirinda Forest where it has been suggested it might occur at densities of four to six pairs per ha in optimal habitat (Irwin 1979,1981) although this requires confirmation from the study of ringed birds (R. J. Dowsett *in litt.* 1983). It is not uncommon in the

Vumba Highlands (Serle 1955, R. J. Dowsett *in litt.* 1983, A. J. Manson *in litt.* 1983) but probably less abundant than in the Chirinda Forest (Hall and Moreau 1962, Irwin 1979,1981). No detailed population estimates have been made but this race is unlikely to be numerically strong because of its tiny geographical range. *S. s. umbratica* is reported to be numerous on Mount Gorongosa (Clancey 1971, J. Burlison *in litt.* 1983) and its population is probably greater than that of the nominate form (Irwin 1979). *S. s. rodgersi* is known in Mwanihana Forest from only three collected specimens, a few mist-netted birds and one sight record (F. P. Jensen *in litt.* 1982, Jensen *et al.* in press). It is certainly a low-density bird in Mwanihana Forest and apparently restricted to a narrow altitudinal range (F. P. Jensen *in litt.* 1982, Jensen *et al.* in press). However, at Chita this subspecies has a wider altitudinal range (see Distribution), and also appears to be commoner, since 17 birds were netted there in only a few weeks (F. P. Jensen pers. comm. 1984). It will not be possible to make an estimate of its population until its distribution in the escarpment forests of the Uzungwas is better known.

Ecology The species inhabits the ground stratum of middle altitude and montane evergreen forest (Swynnerton 1907,1908, Serle 1955, Cooper 1970, Clancey 1971, Borrett 1973, Irwin 1981, J. Burlison *in litt.* 1983, A. J. Manson *in litt.* 1983), sometimes preferring areas where *Dracaena fragrans* dominates the undergrowth (Swynnerton 1907,1908). The birds like areas of bare forest floor with thick layers of detritus (J. Burlison *in litt.* 1983, A. J. Manson *in litt.* 1983). They are rarely seen more than 2 m above the ground (J. Burlison *in litt.* 1983). The diet of the nominate race has been studied in some detail: it eats insects, (Coleoptera and Hymenoptera, especially larvae), woodlice and ants, occasionally also small fruits (Swynnerton 1908, Oatley 1970, Dick 1981). Its breeding habits are well known (Swynnerton 1907,1908, A. J. Manson *in litt.* 1983). Most nests are placed on *Dracaena* plants, in branch forks, on stumps, or against tree-trunks, supported by vines, almost always less than 3 m from the ground (Swynnerton 1907,1908, A. J. Manson *in litt.* 1983). The nest is cup-shaped and two eggs are laid (Swynnerton 1907,1908). It breeds from October to January (Irwin 1981) and feeds on the forest floor (Swynnerton 1907, Cooper 1970, Irwin 1981, J. Burlison *in litt.* 1983, A. J. Manson *in litt.* 1983). Swynnerton's Forest Robin is sympatric with the White-starred Forest Robin *Pogonocichla stellata* throughout the former's range but there is some degree of ecological segregation between the two species (Hall and Moreau 1970, Dick 1981), the latter taking a higher proportion of flying insects, especially Lepidoptera and perhaps larger food items (Dick 1981). A more likely potential competitor with Swynnerton's Forest Robin is Sharpe's Akalat *Sheppardia sharpei*, which appears to be very similar in behaviour and ecology (Irwin and Clancey 1974, R. J. Dowsett *in litt.* 1981, F. P. Jensen *in litt.* 1982). In Mwanihana Forest, where the two species are sympatric, Sharpe's Akalat is very common and Swynnerton's Forest Robin rare (F. P. Jensen *in litt.* 1982). At Chita, where Swynnerton's Forest Robin is more numerous, it is nevertheless greatly outnumbered by Sharpe's Akalat (F. P. Jensen pers. comm. 1984). It is possible that the latter has displaced the former through much of eastern Tanzania and northern Malawi. Swynnerton's Forest Robin has been seen in bird parties in Chirinda Forest, associating in particular with Stripe-cheeked Greenbuls *Andropa-*

dus milanjensis and White-tailed Crested Flycatchers *Trochocercus albonotatus* (Cooper 1970). On Mount Gorongosa, however, it does not appear to be a regular member of bird parties (J. Burlison *in litt.* 1983).

Threats The main threat is from forest clearance; evidence of encroachment by local farmers on the edges of Chirinda Forest in the past, and in the Vumba Mountains is, therefore, particularly alarming (Borrett 1973, A. J. Manson *in litt.* 1983). There has also been encroachment by shifting cultivators on Mount Gorongosa (J. Burlison *in litt.* 1983) and exploitation of valuable timber trees continues in Mwanihana Forest and elsewhere in the Uzungwa Mountains (Rodgers and Homewood 1982).

Conservation Measures Taken The Chirinda Forest forms part of the Gungunyana Forest Reserve which is at present receiving adequate safeguards (M. P. S. Irwin *in litt.* 1983). In the Vumba Mountains about 1,600 ha of forest is protected, not all of which is suitable for this species (A. J. Manson *in litt.* 1983). On Mount Gorongosa the Mozambique government has attempted to limit human habitation and cultivation to below 600 m though this has been difficult to implement (J. Burlison *in litt.* 1983). Probably the entire population of the race *rodgersi* is within forest reserves, which give some measure of protection to wildlife (SNS).

Conservation Measures Proposed In Zimbabwe, present conservation policies are probably adequate (M. P. S. Irwin *in litt.* 1983). It is hoped that a reserve will be created on Mount Gorongosa to safeguard the forests there (J. Burlison *in litt.* 1983). In Tanzania the range of *rodgersi* needs to be more accurately documented. The proposed Mwanihana National Park, if gazetted, would safeguard this subspecies (Rodgers and Homewood 1982) but it is not known whether the Tanzanian government will implement this recommendation (W. A. Rodgers *in litt.* 1983).

Remarks Swynnerton's Forest Robin has been placed in the genus *Pogonocichla* by some authorities (Hall and Moreau 1962,1970). The resemblance between it and *Pogonocichla* is now regarded as superficial and it is best placed in the monotypic genus *Swynnertonia* (Irwin and Clancey 1974). Swynnerton's Forest Robin certainly has no very close relatives but it is probably closest to Sharpe's Akalat *Sheppardia sharpei* (R. J. Dowsett *in litt.* 1981, F. P. Jensen *in litt.* 1982). The forest avifaunas of eastern Zimbabwe include two other rare species, the Forest Prinia *Prinia robertsi* and the Chirinda Apalis *Apalis chirindensis* (Irwin 1979), the latter also occuring on Mount Gorongosa (see Appendix C). In Mwanihana Forest Swynnerton's Forest Robin occurs alongside five other threatened bird species (see Remarks under the Rufous-winged Sunbird *Nectarinia rufipennis*).

References

Benson, C. W. (1946) A visit to the Vumba Highlands, Southern Rhodesia. *Ostrich* 17: 280-296.

Borrett, R. (1973) To Swynnerton's forest. *Bokmakierie* 2: 38-41.

Clancey, P. A. (1971) *A handlist of the birds of southern Moçambique.* Lourenço Marques: Instituto de Investigação Científica de Moçambique.

Clancey, P. A. (1974) Subspeciation studies in some Rhodesian birds. *Arnoldia (Rhod.)* 6(28).

Cooper, J. (1970) Swynnerton's Robin and bird parties on Mount Selinda. *Honeyguide* no. 62: 32.

Dick, J. A. (1981) A comparison of foods eaten by Swynnerton's Robin and Starred Robin in Chirinda Forest. *Ostrich* 52: 251-253.

Hall, B. P. and Moreau, R. E. (1962) A study of the rare birds of Africa. *Bull. Brit. Mus. (Nat. Hist.) Zool.* 8: 313-378.

Hall, B. P. and Moreau, R. E. (1970) *An atlas of speciation in African passerine birds.* London: Trustees of the British Museum (Natural History).

Irwin, M. P. S. (1978) Endangered Rhodesian birds. *Rhod. Sci. News* 12: 150-151.

Irwin, M. P. S. (1979) The Zimbabwe-Rhodesian and Moçambique highland avian endemics: their evolution and origins. *Honeyguide* no. 99: 5-11.

Irwin, M. P. S. (1981) *The birds of Zimbabwe.* Salisbury, Zimbabwe: Quest Publishing.

Irwin, M. P. S. and Clancey, P. A. (1974) A re-appraisal of the generic relationships of some African forest-dwelling robins. *Arnoldia (Rhod.)* 6(34).

Jensen, F. P. and Stuart, S. N. (1982) New subspecies of forest birds from Tanzania. *Bull. Brit. Orn. Club* 102: 95-99.

Jensen, F. P., Stuart, S. N. and Brogger-Jensen, S. (in press) Altitudinal distribution of the avifauna of the Mwanihana Forest, Tanzania. *Gerfaut.*

Oatley, T. B. (1970) Observations on the food and feeding habits of some African robins (Aves: Turdinae). *Ann. Natal Mus.* 20: 293-327.

Pinto, A. A. da R. (1959) Um esbôço da avifauna sedentária da região da Gorongoza, Moçambique. Proc. I Pan-Afr. orn. Congr. *Ostrich* suppl. 3: 98-125.

Rodgers, W. A. and Homewood, K. M. (1982) Biological values and conservation prospects for the forests and primate populations of the Uzungwa Mountains, Tanzania. *Biol. Conserv.* 24: 285-304.

Serle, W. (1955) Miscellaneous notes on the birds of the Eastern Highlands of Southern Rhodesia. *Ostrich* 26: 115-127.

Shelley, G. E. (1906) [New species from a collection of birds obtained in Gazaland.] *Bull. Brit. Orn. Club* 16: 125-126.

Stuart, S. N. and Jensen, F. P. (1981) Further range extensions and other notable records of forest birds from Tanzania. *Scopus* 5: 106-115.

Swynnerton, C. F. M. (1907) On the birds of Gazaland, Part 1. *Ibis* (9)1: 30-74.

Swynnerton, C. F. M. (1908) Further notes on the birds of Gazaland, Part 1. *Ibis* (9)2: 1-107.

GABELA AKALAT   INDETERMINATE
Sheppardia gabela (Rand, 1957)

Order PASSERIFORMES   Family MUSCICAPIDAE
                                                          Subfamily TURDINAE

Summary This akalat is known only from the understorey of forest patches near Gabela on the escarpment of western Angola. There is no recent information on its status, but there is good evidence that its habitat has been substantially removed.

Distribution The Gabela Akalat was discovered in 1954 when five specimens were collected 15 km south of Gabela (Rand 1957, Heinrich 1958). In 1960 two specimens were collected at "Londa" (apparently Conda: see Remarks), near Gabela, and another two at Assango, 35 km south of Gabela (Pinto 1962). The only subsequent record is from Conde (distinct from Conda), near (east of) Gabela in the early 1970s (Dean and Huntley in prep.). It has been suggested that the species might occur in other relict patches of forest on the escarpment of western Angola but suitable habitat is thought to cover in total no more than a "few hundred square miles" (Hall and Moreau 1962).

Population Numbers are not known.

Ecology All records have come from patches of primary and secondary forest (Rand 1957, Heinrich 1958, Pinto 1962). It appears to be a bird of the forest understorey where the undergrowth is densest (Heinrich 1958, Pinto 1962). The species is most easily seen in the mornings and evenings when the birds come to the forest edge in the vicinity of clearings and coffee plantations; during the hot part of the day they withdraw into the forest interior (Pinto 1962). The birds are very shy and difficult to observe, often remaining motionless for a long time (Pinto 1962). They take their prey from leaves and branches and are probably exclusively insectivorous (Pinto 1962). Specimens collected in September had enlarged gonads (Pinto 1962).

Threats There is no recent information on the conservation status of this species but it is likely to be threatened by forest clearance. It is known that coffee has been planted under the canopy in many of the forest patches around Gabela, destroying the undergrowth in which this species lives (Hall and Moreau 1962).

Conservation Measures Taken None is known.

Conservation Measures Proposed A survey is urgently needed to determine the conservation status of this species and to recommend which forest sites should be preserved to ensure its survival.

Remarks Although originally described as a flycatcher *Muscicapa gabela* (Rand 1957) there is strong evidence that this species is an akalat in the genus

Sheppardia (Hall 1961). This diagnosis is supported by field observations (Pinto 1962). Recently some reservations have been expressed on this arrangement (Irwin and Clancey 1974) and one author places it in a subgenus *Gabelatrix* within *Sheppardia* (Clancey 1977). This is one of a group of birds endemic to the escarpment zone of western Angola (Hall 1960) including three other threatened species (see Remarks under Gabela Helmet-shrike *Prionops gabela*). The locality given as "Londa" throughout Pinto (1962) is referred to (without comment on the disparity) as "Conda" by A. A. da Rosa Pinto (*in litt.* 1983), this locality being due south of Gabela.

References

Clancey, P. A. (1977) Miscellaneous taxonomic notes on African birds. 50. *Durban Mus. Novit.* 11: 247-264.

Dean, W. R. J. and Huntley, M. A. (in prep.) An updated list of the birds of Angola.

Hall, B. P. (1960) The faunistic importance of the scarp of Angola. *Ibis* 102: 420-442.

Hall, B. P. (1961) Is *Muscicapa gabela* an Akalat? *Bull. Brit. Orn. Club* 81: 45-46.

Hall, B. P. and Moreau, R. E. (1962) A study of the rare birds of Africa. *Bull. Brit. Mus. (Nat. Hist.) Zool.* 8: 313-378.

Heinrich, G. H. (1958) Zur Verbreitung und Lebensweise der Vögel von Angola. Part 2. *J. Orn.* 99: 322-362.

Irwin, M. P. S. and Clancey, P. A. (1974) A re-appraisal of the generic relationships of some African forest-dwelling robins (Aves: Turdidae). *Arnoldia (Rhod.)* 34(6).

Pinto, A. A. da R. (1962) As observações de maior destaque das expedições ornitológicas do Instituto de Investigação Científica de Angola. *Bol. Inst. Invest. Cient. Angola* 1: 21-38.

Rand, A. L. (1957) Two new species of birds from Angola. *Fieldiana Zool.* 39: 41-45.

EAST COAST AKALAT   RARE
Sheppardia gunningi Haagner, 1909

Order PASSERIFORMES   Family MUSCICAPIDAE
                                                              Subfamily TURDINAE

Summary This is an extremely local forest bird from eastern and southern Africa (Kenya, Tanzania, Mozambique and Malawi). The two coastal subspecies (*gunningi* and *sokokensis*) have been reported as fairly common at a very few localities, as has *bensoni* from Malawi, but all three are threatened by habitat destruction.

Distribution The East Coast Akalat is known from three isolated subspecies: nominate *gunningi* from coastal southern Mozambique; *sokokensis* from coastal Kenya and Tanzania; and *bensoni* from Malawi. The nominate form was discovered in 1908 at Dondo (= Mzimbiti) when one specimen was collected (Haagner 1909, Sheppard 1909). It appears that there were other early records from nearby at Beira (Sofala) (Clancey 1971). Four birds were collected at the type-locality in 1946 (Benson 1946,1947) as were another eight in 1968 (Clancey 1969). In 1962 its known range was extended northwards when three were collected at Chineziwa (Chiniziua) and birds were also heard as far north as the Zambezi River (Irwin 1963). The most recent report of this subspecies is of two sightings, probably in the late 1970s, in the Inhamitanda Forest between Beira and the Zambezi River (J. Burlison *in litt.* 1983). The subspecies *sokokensis* was discovered in 1921 when three specimens were collected in the Sokoke Forest in coastal Kenya (van Someren 1921). By 1932 several more had been taken in the type-locality and also at Rabai to the south (van Someren 1932). Further specimens were collected in the Sokoke Forest between 1964 and 1966 (Ripley and Bond 1971) and in recent years there have been regular reports of the species from this site (Britton and Zimmerman 1979, Kelsey and Langton 1984). The bird also occurs on the Shimba Hills, where it had been discovered by 1946 (Benson 1946) and at Shimoni (Britton 1980); the status of the species at these two localities appears to be poorly documented, though a bird was seen in the Shimba Hills forest in 1983 (Kelsey and Langton 1984). In 1962 the known range of this subspecies was extended 160 km to the north when a specimen was collected at Makeri on the lower Tana River (Keith 1968). Birds were also mist-netted nearby around Garsen in 1972 (Andrews *et al.* 1975). In Tanzania *sokokensis* is known only from the Pugu Hills near Dar es Salaam where one bird was collected at 300 m in 1938 (Moreau 1940, specimen in BMNH: SNS). Further birds were collected in this locality in 1947 and 1949 (specimens in BMNH: SNS) and one bird was seen in 1955 (N. R. Fuggles-Couchman *in litt.* 1983). In 1961 seven specimens were collected in the "Pugu Hills", though this locality was said to be 80 km south of Dar es Salaam (Ripley and Heinrich 1966); if the stated distance is correct then these birds were collected at a different site from the area called the Pugu Hills by most authors, which is 20 km west of Dar es Salaam (Howell 1981). Since 1978 the species has been recorded regularly in the Pugu Hills (Stuart and van der Willigen 1978, Stuart and Turner 1980, N. E. Baker *in litt.* 1983). It is, however, certainly absent from apparently

438

suitable habitats in the foothills of the Usambara and Uluguru Mountains (Stuart and van der Willigen 1978). A probable sight record in 1932 from Netia in coastal northern Mozambique (Benson 1946) is geographically intermediate between the nominate form and *sokokensis*. The subspecies *bensoni* was discovered in 1938 when six specimens were collected at 500 m near Nkhata Bay in Malawi (Kinnear 1938, Benson 1940). Another specimen was taken at Chintheche, 600 m, in the same year (Benson 1940) and in 1940 one was collected at 1,220 m 48 km south-west of Chintheche near Kurirwi (Benson 1942). More recently the species has been found at Kalwe Bay and Nkhata Bay in 1980 (Dowsett 1980). In 1982 and 1983 an extensive ornithological survey found this subspecies to be more widespread than was hitherto believed, ranging through the Nkhata Bay District (which includes the old Chintheche District) from Choma Mountain in the north, south to Kuwilwe and west to near Chikangawa (R. J. Dowsett *in litt.* 1983). Localities include the Viphya Plateau, Kalwe and Mkuwadzi and the species ranges from the shore of Lake Malawi at 475 m up to 1,750 m on Choma Mountain (R. J. Dowsett *in litt.* 1983). It might be seasonal at the highest altitudes, moving to lower levels in the non-breeding season (R. J. Dowsett *in litt.* 1983).

Population Numbers are not known. There are a few localities where this skulking species has been found fairly common, notably at Dondo (Clancey 1969), the Pugu Hills (Stuart and van der Willigen 1978, Stuart and Turner 1980, N. E. Baker *in litt.* 1983) and the Sokoke Forest, where it might be seasonal (Britton and Zimmerman 1979, Kelsey and Langton 1984). In Malawi it is common through most of its range, occurring at densities of one pair per ha at high altitudes and at even greater densities in the lakeshore forests where it approaches two pairs per ha (R. J. Dowsett *in litt.* 1983). One tiny population of about six pairs in the 7.5 ha forest on Choma Mountain is apparently viable and long-established (R. J. Dowsett *in litt.* 1983).

Ecology The species inhabits the ground stratum of dense evergreen forest (Benson 1940,1942,1946, Irwin 1963, Clancey 1969,1971, Andrews *et al.* 1975, Benson and Benson 1977, Stuart and van der Willigen 1978, Britton and Zimmerman 1979, Britton 1980, N. E. Baker *in litt.* 1983, R. J. Dowsett *in litt.* 1983). In the Sokoke Forest it occurs mainly in lowland rainforest, though there are records from *Cynometra-Manilkara* forest, *Cynometra* thicket and *Afzelia* forest (Britton and Zimmerman 1979, Kelsey and Langton 1984). It is apparently mainly solitary though the nominate race has been recorded feeding in association with the Red-capped Robin-chat *Cossypha natalensis* and the Eastern Bearded Scrub Robin *Cercotrichas quadrivirgata* (Clancey 1969). The species feeds to a large extent on the ground, taking beetles, ants, grasshoppers, lepidopterous larvae and probably other insects (Irwin 1963, Ripley and Heinrich 1966, Clancey 1969, Britton and Zimmerman 1979, R. J. Dowsett *in litt.* 1983). There is some evidence that the East Coast Akalat competes with the White-starred Forest Robin *Pogonocichla stellata*, at least in Malawi (R. J. Dowsett *in litt.* 1983). The two species are completely allopatric within their breeding ranges (R. D. Dowsett *in litt.* 1983).

Threats The habitat of this species is under pressure throughout its range, even within forest reserves (Clancey 1969, Ripley and Bond 1971, Stuart and van der Willigen 1978, Britton and Zimmerman 1979, Benson 1980, Howell 1981, K. M. Howell *in litt.* 1982, J. Burlison *in litt.* 1983, R. J. Dowsett *in litt.* 1983). Much of the forest around Dondo has been destroyed to make way for sugarcane plantations (Clancey 1969, P. A. Clancey *in litt.* 1983). Other coastal forests in southern Mozambique are threatened by shifting cultivation (J. Burlison *in litt.* 1983). Considerable forest clearance is taking place in the Sokoke Forest, even within the supposedly inviolate nature reserve (Cunningham-van Someren 1981-1982, Kelsey and Langton 1984). Unfortunately the work of forest officers at Sokoke has been rendered ineffective by shortage of available funds (Kelsey and Langton 1984). It seems that certain conservation regulations have been ignored by people taking advantage of the lack of supervision by officials from the Forestry Department (Kelsey and Langton 1984). Other areas of coastal forest are being destroyed in Kenya (Britton 1976) and the situation is particularly serious in the Pugu Hills in Tanzania where substantial cutting is taking place (K. M. Howell *in litt.* 1982) and at the start of the 1980s only 10 km^2 of forest survived in an original reserve area of 22 km^2 (Howell 1981). In Malawi much suitable forest has already been cleared and some areas, such as Mkuwadzi and Kalwe are still under considerable threat (R. J. Dowsett *in litt.* 1983).

Conservation Measures Taken The species occurs in several forest reserves in coastal Mozambique, Tanzania and Kenya but nearly all of these appear to be very poorly protected (van Someren 1932, Clancey 1969, Ripley and Bond 1971, Britton 1976, Stuart and van der Willigen 1978, Britton and Zimmerman 1979, Howell 1981, K. M. Howell *in litt.* 1982, J. Burlison *in litt.* 1983, R. J. Dowsett *in litt.* 1983). If the nominate form is found to occur in the recently established Marromeu Wildlife Utilisation Area in southern Mozambique, then its future will be much more secure (J. Burlison *in litt.* 1983). The race *bensoni* occurs in several protected areas, some of which are well conserved (Britton 1980). An important population survives in the South Viphya Forest Reserve, where the remnant riparian evergreen forest is surrounded by a pine plantation (R. J. Dowsett *in litt.* 1983); as a result protection from felling and fire is very good (R. J. Dowsett *in litt.* 1983). Moreover, a potentially damaging plantation scheme within the range of *bensoni* has now been abandoned (R. J. Dowsett *in litt.* 1983).

Conservation Measures Proposed Much more adequate conservation measures are needed to preserve forests throughout the range of this species. Particularly important sites include the Inhamitanda Forest in southern Mozambique, the Pugu Hills in Tanzania and the Sokoke Forest in Kenya. Details of recommendations for the Sokoke Forest are given in Conservation Measures Proposed under Sokoke Scops Owl *Otus ireneae*. However, the species can survive in tiny patches of forest (R. J. Dowsett *in litt.* 1983) and these should also be preserved.

Remarks Five other threatened bird species occur in the Sokoke Forest (see Remarks under the Sokoke Scops Owl). Two other threatened bird species are recorded from the Pugu Hills, the Sokoke Pipit *Anthus sokokensis* and the Spotted Ground-thrush *Turdus fischeri*. In the forests of the lower Tana River the East Coast Akalat is sympatric with a bird treated in Appendix C, the White-winged Apalis *Apalis chariessa*.

References

Andrews, P., Groves, C. P. and Horne, J. F. M. (1975) Ecology of the lower Tana River flood plain (Kenya). *J. E. Afr. Nat. Hist. Soc. and Natn. Mus.* 151: 1-31.

Benson, C. W. (1940) Further notes on Nyasaland birds (with particular reference to those of the Northern Province), Part III. *Ibis* (14)4: 583-629.

Benson, C. W. (1942) Additional notes on Nyasaland birds, Part II. *Ibis* (14)6: 299-337.

Benson, C. W. (1946) Notes on eastern and southern African birds. *Bull. Brit. Orn. Club* 67: 28-33.

Benson, C. W. (1947) The birds of Mzimbiti, near Beira, Portuguese East Africa. *Ostrich* 28: 125-128.

Benson, C. W. (1980) Man-induced changes in Malawi birds. *Proc. IV Pan-Afr. orn. Congr.*: 373-381.

Benson, C. W. and Benson, F. M. (1977) *The birds of Malawi*. Limbe, Malawi: Montfort Press.

Britton, P. L. (1976) Primary forestland destruction now critical. *Africana* 5(12): 1-2.

Britton, P. L. ed. (1980) *Birds of East Africa: their habitat, status and distribution*. Nairobi: EANHS.

Britton, P. L. and Zimmerman, D. A. (1979) The avifauna of Sokoke Forest, Kenya. *J. E. Afr. Nat. Hist. Soc. and Natn. Mus.* 169: 1-15.

Clancey, P. A. (1969) The status of Gunning's Robin. *Ostrich* 40: 19-20.

Clancey, P. A. (1971) *A handlist of the birds of southern Moçambique*. Lourenço Marques: Instituto de Investigação Científica de Moçambique.

Cunningham-van Someren, G. R. ed. (1981-1982) *National Museum of Kenya, Department of Ornithology Museum Avifauna News*: 19,34,63,72.

Dowsett, R. J. ed. (1980) Nyala records. *Nyala* 7: 145-152.

Haagner, A. (1909) Descriptions of two new species of flycatchers from Portuguese South-east Africa. *Ann. Transvaal Mus.* 1: 179-180.

Howell, K. M. (1981) Pugu Forest Reserve: biological values and development. *Afr. J. Ecol.* 19: 73-81.

Irwin, M. P. S. (1963) Systematic and distributional notes on southern African birds. *Durban Mus. Novit.* 7: 1-26.

Keith, S. (1968) Notes on birds of East Africa, including additions to the avifauna. *Amer. Mus. Novit.* 2321.

Kelsey, M. G. and Langton, T. E. S. (1984) The conservation of the Arabuko-Sokoke Forest, Kenya. International Council for Bird Preservation and University of East Anglia. *International Council for Bird Preservation Study Report* no. 4.

Kinnear, N. B. (1938) [A new species of *Sheppardia*.] *Bull. Brit. Orn. Club* 58: 138-139.

Moreau, R. E. (1940) Distributional notes on East African birds. *Ibis* (14)4: 454-463.

Ripley, S. D. and Bond, G. M. (1971) Systematic notes on a collection of birds from Kenya. *Smithsonian Contrib. Zool.* 111.

Ripley, S. D. and Heinrich, G. H. (1966) Comments on the avifauna of Tanzania, I. *Postilla* 96.

Sheppard, P. A. (1909) A list of, and notes on, birds collected and observed in the District of Beira, Portuguese S. E. Africa. *J. S. Afr. Orn. Union* 5: 24-49.

van Someren, V. G. L. (1921) [New East African forms.] *Bull. Brit. Orn. Club* 41: 120-125.

van Someren, V. G. L. (1932) Birds of Kenya and Uganda, being addenda and corrigenda to my previous paper in "*Novitates Zoologicae*" XXIX, 1922. *Novit. Zool.* 37: 252-380.

Stuart, S. N. and Turner, D. A. (1980) Some range extensions and other notable records of forest birds from eastern and northeastern Tanzania. *Scopus* 4: 36-41.

Stuart, S. N. and van der Willigen, T. A., eds (1978) Report of the Cambridge Ecological Expedition to Tanzania 1978. Unpublished.

WHITE-HEADED ROBIN-CHAT
Cossypha heinrichi Rand, 1955

INDETERMINATE

Order PASSERIFORMES

Family MUSCICAPIDAE
Subfamily TURDINAE

Summary This undergrowth-haunting chat is known only from one area in northern Angola and a few forest patches 500 km to the north in western Zaire, and possibly as far north as the equator. It remains very little known and might be more widely distributed than these records suggest.

Distribution The White-headed Robin-chat is known from very restricted areas in Angola and Zaire. It was discovered in 1954 when three specimens were collected 30 km north-east of Duque de Bragança in northern Angola (Rand 1955, Heinrich 1958). Another nine specimens were taken, and observations made, at the same locality in 1957 (Ripley and Heinrich 1966). In 1975 the species was discovered in western Zaire in the Bombo-Lumene Nature Reserve (4°30'S 16°08'E) 500 km north of the Angola locality, one specimen being collected and at least another five (including two parents and a newly fledged young) seen (Harrison 1977). Birds were found subsequently at four other sites within 15 km of Bombo-Lumene, and a bird "almost certainly of this species was glimpsed 550 km north-northeast near Mbandaka (on the equator, 18°24'E)" (Harrison 1977). In 1980 another three specimens were collected at Nkiene near Bombo-Lumene (Louette 1981). The range of this species is clearly very imperfectly known and may well be more extensive than the records above suggest.

Population Numbers are not known, but the scarcity of records of the species suggests that it is rare.

Ecology In Angola the species has been found in the dense undergrowth of gallery forests along rivers and brooks (Heinrich 1958, Ripley and Heinrich 1966). The birds occasionally visit surrounding savanna areas in pursuit of driver (doryline) ants (Ripley and Heinrich 1966). In Zaire the species is recorded from the undergrowth of isolated patches of "thick tropical forest (not gallery forest)" in the savanna, these patches ranging in size from 1 ha to 325 ha (Harrison 1977). The species is apparently very elusive in the understorey, keeping to the forest floor and the undergrowth up to a height of 4 m (Ripley and Heinrich 1966, Harrison 1977). It is insectivorous, feeding especially on driver ants (Ripley and Heinrich 1966). One party of four birds was seen feeding on ants on the branch of a tree, while the stomach of a specimen held fragments of beetles and ants (Harrison 1977). The presence of juvenile birds suggests two breeding seasons in Angola, in February and October (Ripley and Heinrich 1966). In Zaire breeding takes place between September and November, at the start of the rainy season (Harrison 1977, Louette 1981).

Threats None is known. Forest destruction would presumably be detrimental to this species, and the sizes of the forest patches from which it is known in Zaire are disconcertingly tiny.

443

Conservation Measures Taken None is known other than that one of the small forest patches from which the species is known (Bombo-Lumene) is a nature reserve.

Conservation Measures Proposed A survey is needed to determine the distribution of this species and to assess the degree of threat to its survival. If it is in serious danger it will be necessary to recommend suitable sites for the establishment of nature reserves.

Remarks The White-headed Robin-chat apparently has no close relatives, though it is perhaps nearest to the White-crowned Robin-chat *Cossypha albicapilla* (Rand 1955, Hall and Moreau 1962). At Nkiene it is sympatric with three other robin-chats, Snowy-headed *C. niveicapilla*, White-browed *C. heuglini* and Red-capped *C. natalensis* (Louette 1981).

References

Hall, B. P. and Moreau, R. E. (1962) A study of the rare birds of Africa. *Bull. Brit. Mus. (Nat. Hist.) Zool.* 8: 313-378.

Harrison, I. D. (1977) Extension of range of the White-headed Robin-chat *Cossypha heinrichi. Bull. Brit. Orn. Club* 97: 20-21.

Heinrich, G. H. (1958) Zur Verbreitung und Lebensweise der Vögel von Angola. Part 2. *J. Orn.* 99: 322-362.

Louette, M. (1981) Sur quelques specimens nouveaux de *Cossypha heinrichi* du Zaire (Aves, Turdinae). *Rev. Zool. Afr.* 95: 356-358.

Rand, A. L. (1955) A new species of thrush from Angola. *Fieldiana Zool.* 34: 327-329.

Ripley, S. D. and Heinrich, G. H. (1966) Additions to the avifauna of northern Angola. II. *Postilla* 95.

DAPPLED MOUNTAIN ROBIN   RARE
Modulatrix orostruthus (Vincent, 1933)

Order PASSERIFORMES   Family MUSCICAPIDAE
                                             Subfamily TURDINAE

Summary This is a highly elusive, very low density species, and the known range of all three subspecies consists of several small, well separated patches of montane forest in eastern Africa.

Distribution The Dappled Mountain Robin is known only from three isolated subspecies, one in Mozambique and two in Tanzania. The nominate subspecies is known only from the type specimen collected in 1932 at 1,465 m on Namuli Mountain in northern Mozambique, when a second bird was seen (Vincent 1933,1935). There appear to have been no subsequent visits to this area by ornithologists. The subspecies *M. o. amani* occurs in the East Usambara Mountains of north-eastern Tanzania, 1,150 km north of Namuli where the type-specimen was collected in 1935 (Sclater and Moreau 1935, Moreau and Moreau 1937). This subspecies was not recorded again until four were collected in 1962 and another two were taken in 1963 (Ripley and Heinrich 1966, Keith 1968). Two were collected in 1966 and two more were ringed and released in 1973, one of these being recaptured in the following year (Benson and Irwin 1975). Between 1977 and 1981 a further ten birds were mist-netted and released (SNS). It has only been located in the immediate vicinity of Amani at 900 m, though it might occur throughout the East Usambara forests between 800 and 1,100 m, which would indicate a range of 100 km² (van der Willigen and Lovett 1981). Two specimens supposedly taken at 1,200 m near Amani in 1962 (Ripley and Heinrich 1966) were probably collected at 900 m (SNS). A third subspecies, *M. o. sanjei*, recently described, was discovered when the type-specimen was netted in Mwanihana Forest on the eastern escarpment of the Uzungwa Mountains, at 1,250 m, in eastern Tanzania in 1981 (Stuart and Jensen 1981, Jensen and Stuart 1982). In 1982 two more birds were mist-netted at 1,400 and 1,600 m in the same forest, one of these birds being collected (Jensen *et al.* in press). In 1984 another population, presumably of *sanjei*, was discovered 160 km south-west along the eastern escarpment of the Uzungwa Mountains at 1,450-1,700 m in the forest above Chita (F. P. Jensen pers. comm. 1984). Mwanihana and Chita forests are located geographically between Namuli and Amani, where the other two subspecies occur, and the existence of the species in this region fulfils a prediction made in 1977 (Stuart and Hutton 1977). Moreover, if the explanation for the species's disjunct distribution is valid (Stuart 1981, see Remarks), it could possibly yet be found in a few other places where the Spot-throat *Modulatrix stictigula* is rare or absent (Stuart 1981); however, at Chita both species are fairly common and sympatric (F. P. Jensen pers. comm. 1984).

Population All evidence points to this being a very low density species (Vincent 1935, Moreau and Moreau 1937, Stuart and Hutton 1977, Stuart and Jensen 1981, van der Willigen and Lovett 1981) except at Chita (see below). The population of nominate *orostruthus* is not known, but is likely to be very small. For

445

amani an earlier estimate of four birds occupying 1.6 km^2 (cited in King 1978-1979), yielding a guessed-at total of 85-200 birds in the East Usambaras (Stuart and Hutton 1977), is now known to be too pessimistic, but its population would still be only a few hundred individuals if it proved to be restricted to the vicinity of Amani (SNS). If it is spread throughout the East Usambara forests then there are likely to be several thousand (SNS). The population of *sanjei*, being only very recently discovered, cannot be estimated. A period of intensive mist-netting, however, suggested that it occurs at a low density in Mwanihana Forest (Jensen *et al.* in press) but it seems to be considerably more common at Chita, where 13 birds were mist-netted in a few weeks (F. P. Jensen pers. comm. 1984).

Ecology This species is restricted to evergreen rain forest, apparently at intermediate elevations (Vincent 1933,1935, Sclater and Moreau 1935, Ripley and Heinrich 1966, Stuart and Hutton 1977, Stuart and van der Willigen 1978, Stuart 1981, Stuart and Jensen 1981, van der Willigen and Lovett 1981, Jensen and Stuart 1982, Jensen *et al.* in press). Circumstantial evidence suggests that it feeds on the ground (Stuart 1981). Virtually nothing else is known of the species, though stomach contents indicate its diet consists of insects (Stuart 1981); it has only very rarely been observed in the field (Stuart 1981). Birds with brood patches have been caught at Amani in November (SNS) and a juvenile was mist-netted at Chita in the same month (F. P. Jensen pers. comm. 1984).

Threats None is known on Namuli Mountain. Much of the forest understorey in the East Usambaras has been cleared for growing cardamom in recent years (Stuart and Hutton 1977, Stuart and van der Willigen 1978, van der Willigen and Lovett 1981, Rodgers and Homewood 1982a, Stuart in prep.). The species cannot survive in such a modified habitat (Stuart and Hutton 1977, Stuart and van der Willigen 1978). The forests of the eastern Uzungwa escarpment have so far suffered less encroachment (Rodgers and Homewood 1982b). The disjunct dpstribution of the species may be due to natural factors (see Remarks).

Conservation Measures Taken None is known for nominate *orostruthus*. Some but not all of the forest in the Amani area, and probably the entire range of *sanjei*, is in forest reserves, which provide some measure of protection to wildlife (Rodgers and Homewood 1982a,b, Stuart in prep., SNS).

Conservation Measures Proposed A survey of Namuli Mountain is needed to ascertain the status of nominate *orostruthus* (and several other birds: see Remarks), and to recommend appropriate conservation measures. For *amani*, a thorough survey should be undertaken to find out how widely spread it is in the East Usambaras; a forest conservation plan for the Usambaras is being prepared for the consideration of the Tanzanian government (Stuart in prep.). Immediate follow-up work is needed to delimit the range of *sanjei*. It has been suggested that part of the forest in the eastern Uzungwa Mountains be included in a new park, the Mwanihana National Park (Rodgers and Homewood 1982b), but it is not known whether the Tanzanian government will implement this proposal (W. A. Rodgers *in litt.* 1983).

Remarks When discovered, the species was placed in the genus *Phyllas-trephus* (Pycnonotidae) but a reappraisal in 1975 suggested it to be a thrush rather than a bulbul (Benson and Irwin 1975). It has also been suggested that the fragmented range of this species is due to competition with the Spot-throat and with the Pale-breasted Illadopsis *Trichastoma rufipennis* (Stuart 1981), and the strong interlocking of the ranges of Dappled Mountain Robin and Spot-throat clearly supports their grouping in one genus (Stuart 1981). In Mwanihana Forest, however, the Dappled Mountain Robin and the Spot-throat are sympatric over an altitudinal range of 300 m (Jensen *et al.* in press). The importance of the three forests where this species occurs cannot be overstated. One other threatened bird species, the Thyolo Alethe *Alethe choloensis*, also occurs on Namuli Mountain, as well as a very distinct subspecies of the Bar-throated Apalis, the Namuli Apalis *Apalis (thoracica) lynesi*, included in Appendix E. Six other threatened bird species occur in the Usambaras and six more such species occur in the Uzungwas (see Remarks under the Usambara Ground Robin *Dryocichloides montanus* and the Iringa Ground Robin *D. lowei* respectively). The Dappled Mountain Robin might occur on the little known Chiperone Mountain, Mozambique, and possibly on Mulanje and Thyolo Mountains in Malawi, all of which are relatively close to Namuli Mountain (Benson and Benson 1977, C. W. Benson pers. comm. 1982). It might, however, be noted that by CITES criteria the nominate race would be treated as extinct.

References

Benson, C. W. and Benson, F. M. (1977) *The birds of Malawi*. Limbe, Malawi: Montfort Press.

Benson, C. W. and Irwin, M. P. S. (1975) The systematic position of *Phyllastrephus orostruthus* and *Phyllastrephus xanthophrys*, two species incorrectly placed in the family Pycnonotidae (Aves). *Arnoldia (Rhod.)* 7(17).

Jensen, F. P. and Stuart, S. N. (1982) New subspecies of forest birds from Tanzania. *Bull. Brit. Orn. Club* 102: 95-99.

Jensen, F. P., Stuart, S. N. and Brogger-Jensen, S. (in press) Altitudinal distribution of the avifauna of the Mwanihana Forest, Tanzania. *Gerfaut*.

Keith, S. (1968) Notes on East African birds, including additions to the avifauna. *Amer. Mus. Novit.* 2321.

King, W. B. (1978-1979) *Red data book, 2: Aves*. 2nd edition. Morges, Switzerland: IUCN.

Moreau, R. E. and Moreau, W. M. (1937) Biological and other notes on some East African birds. Part 2. *Ibis* (14)1: 321-345.

Ripley S. D. and Heinrich, G. H. (1966) Comments on the avifauna of Tanzania 1. *Postilla* 96.

Rodgers, W. A. and Homewood, K. M. (1982a) Species richness and endemism in the Usambara mountain forests, Tanzania. *Biol. J. Linn. Soc.* 18: 197-242.

Rodgers, W. A. and Homewood, K. M. (1982b) Biological values and conservation prospects for the forest and primate populations of the Uzungwa Mountains, Tanzania. *Biol. Conserv.* 24: 285-304.

Sclater, W. L. and Moreau, R. E. (1935) [One new species and five new subspecies (from) the central northern highlands of Tanganyika Territory.] *Bull. Brit. Orn. Club* 56: 10-19.

Stuart, S. N. (1981) An explanation for the disjunct distributions of *Modulatrix orostruthus* and *Apalis* (or *Orthotomus*) *moreaui*. *Scopus* 5: 1-4.

Stuart, S. N. (in prep.) A forest conservation plan for the Usambara Mountains, Tanzania.

Stuart, S. N. and Hutton, J. M. eds. (1977) The avifauna of the East Usambara Mountains, Tanzania. A report compiled by the Cambridge Ornithological Expedition to East Africa, 1977. Unpublished.

Stuart, S. N. and Jensen, F. P. (1981) Further range extensions and other notable records of forest birds from Tanzania. *Scopus* 5: 106-115.

Stuart, S. N. and van der Willigen, T. A. eds. (1978) Report of the Cambridge Ecological Expedition to Tanzania 1978. Unpublished.

Vincent, J. (1933) [Four new species and eighteen new subspecies ... collected during the recent Portuguese East African Expedition.] *Bull. Brit. Orn. Club* 53: 129-149.

Vincent, J. (1935) The birds of northern Portuguese East Africa. Comprising a list of, and observations on, the collections made during the British Museum Expedition of 1931-32. Part VII. *Ibis* (13)5: 355-397.

van der Willigen, T. A. and Lovett, J. eds. (1981) Report of the Oxford Expedition to Tanzania 1979. Unpublished.

USAMBARA GROUND ROBIN   RARE

Dryocichloides montanus (Reichenow, 1907)

Order PASSERIFORMES   Family MUSCICAPIDAE
                                                       Subfamily TURDINAE

Summary Although recently discovered to be numerically strong, this ground-haunting, insectivorous species remains restricted to part of a single mountain range (the West Usambaras) in Tanzania which is suffering from clearance of its natural forest for softwood plantations.

Distribution The Usambara Ground Robin is confined to the West Usambara Mountains in Tanzania above 1,600 m at Shume, Shagayu and Mazumbai; this is a forested area of no more than 140 km^2 (van der Willigen and Lovett 1981). The species was described in 1907 on the basis of a specimen from "Usambara" (Reichenow 1907). In 1931 another six specimens were collected and several birds were seen between 1,700 and 1,950 m in the Shume and Shagayu forests in the West Usambaras (Sclater and Moreau 1933; specimens in NMK and BMNH: SNS). The species was not recorded again until 1962 when eight specimens were collected near Shume at 2,100 m (Ripley and Heinrich 1966). Another bird was taken at Shume in 1966 (specimen in NMK: SNS). In 1977 the species was seen at Mazumbai in the West Usambaras (Stuart and Turner 1980) and three other birds were mist-netted at this site down to 1,600 m between 1978 and 1980 (Stuart and van der Willigen 1978, Stuart and Turner 1980, SNS). Between 1979 and 1981 many birds were seen and mist-netted in the Shume Forest at 1,800-2,200 m (Stuart and Turner 1980, van der Willigen and Lovett 1981, SNS). Birds were also seen in the Shagayu Forest at 2,000 m in 1981 (SNS). The supposed East Usambara specimen, collected in 1966 (see Stuart and Hutton 1977), has been investigated and found to have been collected in Shume (SNS); a doubtful 1931 specimen from the East Usambaras (Stuart and Hutton 1977, Stuart and van der Willigen 1978) is now known to have been a misidentification (SNS).

Population Although it is very rare through some of its range, e.g. at Mazumbai, which is at its lower altitudinal limit, and its population was once thought to be only a few hundred individuals (Stuart and van der Willigen 1978), recent work has shown the populations in the Shume and Shagayu forests, whose combined area above 1,600 m is 90 km^2, to be at very high densities (2-3 individuals per ha) and a conservative estimate of the total population would be 28,000 birds (van der Willigen and Lovett 1981).

Ecology This bird inhabits the floor of dark, shaded, mature, evergreen cloud-forest with plenty of leaf-litter, at altitudes above 1,600 m (Sclater and Moreau 1933, Ripley and Heinrich 1966, Turner 1977, Stuart and van der Willigen 1978, van der Willigen and Lovett 1981). Contrary to an earlier report (Stuart and van der Willigen 1978) this species can tolerate a considerable amount of disturbance to its forest habitat, providing the canopy cover remains good (van der Willigen and Lovett 1981, SNS); however it appears to be absent from the

Juniperus-dominated forest in the extreme west of the West Usambaras (SNS). Although the birds spend much time feeding on the forest floor they also perch in low vegetation, occasionally as high as 2 m above the ground (Sclater and Moreau 1933, Ripley and Heinrich 1966, SNS). They are often seen following swarms of driver (doryline) ants (Sclater and Moreau 1933, Ripley and Heinrich 1966, Willis 1981, SNS), though they probably feed mainly on small insects flushed by the ants rather than on the ants themselves (Willis 1981). The birds are tame and as many as 12 have been seen at one ant swarm (Sclater and Moreau 1933, Ripley and Heinrich 1966, SNS). The breeding season lasts from October to March (SNS) though the nest and eggs have not been described.

Threats The forest in which this species lives is slowly being replaced by softwood plantations, and being degraded by excessive harvesting of camphor trees *Ocotea usambarensis* (Stuart in prep.).

Conservation Measures Taken Nearly all this bird's range is within government forest reserves, which provide some measure of protection for wildlife (Stuart in prep.). There is, however, nothing to prevent softwood trees being planted within the forest reserves at the expense of the natural forest, as is happening (Stuart in prep.).

Conservation Measures Proposed A forest conservation proposal for the Usambara Mountains is being prepared for consideration by the Tanzanian government (Stuart in prep.).

Remarks The generic relationships of many African robins are obscure but the Usambara Ground Robin is now usually placed in the genus *Dryocichloides* (Irwin and Clancey 1974). The species is closely related to another threatened bird species, the Iringa Ground Robin *Dryocichloides lowei*, and has even been regarded as conspecific with it (Ripley and Heinrich 1966). This is not, however, generally accepted (see Hall and Moreau 1970, Stuart and Hutton 1977, Turner 1977). Six other threatened bird species occur in the Usambaras, these being the Usambara Eagle Owl *Bubo vosseleri*, the Dappled Mountain Robin *Modulatrix orostruthus*, the Long-billed Apalis *Apalis moreaui*, the Amani Sunbird *Anthreptes pallidigaster*, the Banded Green Sunbird *A. rubritorques* and the Tanzanian Mountain Weaver *Ploceus nicolli*. The Usambara Mountains are also an important area for other threatened animal species (for details see Wells *et al.* 1983).

References

Hall, B. P. and Moreau, R. E. (1970) *An atlas of speciation in African passerine birds*. London: Trustees of the British Museum (Natural History).
Irwin, M. P. S. and Clancey, P. A. (1974) A re-appraisal of the generic relationships of some African forest-dwelling robins (Aves: Turdidae). *Arnoldia (Rhod.)* 6(34).
Reichenow, A. (1907) Neue Vogelarten. *Orn. Monatsber.* 15: 29-31.
Ripley, S. D. and Heinrich, G. H. (1966) Comments on the avifauna of Tanzania 1. *Postilla* 96.

Sclater, W. L. and Moreau, R. E. (1933) Taxonomic and field notes on some birds of north-eastern Tanganyika Territory, Part III. *Ibis* (13)1: 1-33.

Stuart, S. N. (in prep.) A forest conservation plan for the Usambara Mountains, Tanzania.

Stuart, S. N. and Hutton, J. M. eds. (1977) The avifauna of the East Usambara Mountains, Tanzania. A report compiled by the Cambridge Ornithological Expedition to East Africa, 1977. Unpublished.

Stuart, S. N. and Turner, D. A. (1980) Some range extensions and other notable records of forest birds from eastern and northeastern Tanzania. *Scopus* 4: 36-41.

Stuart, S. N. and van der Willigen, T. A. eds. (1978) Report of the Cambridge Ecological Expedition to Tanzania 1978. Unpublished.

Turner, D. A. (1977) Status and distribution of the East African endemic species. *Scopus* 1: 2-11,56.

Wells, S. M., Pyle, R. M. and Collins, N. M. (1983) *The IUCN invertebrate red data book*. Gland, Switzerland: IUCN.

van der Willigen, T. A. and Lovett, J. eds. (1981) Report of the Oxford Expedition to Tanzania 1979. Unpublished.

Willis, E. O. (1981) A preliminary survey of African ant-following birds. Unpublished report to the National Geographic Society.

IRINGA GROUND ROBIN   RARE
Dryocichloides lowei (Grant and Mackworth-Praed, 1941)

Order PASSERIFORMES   Family MUSCICAPIDAE
                                             Subfamily TURDINAE

Summary Endemic to six patches of mainly dry montane forest in southern Tanzania, this ground-haunting, insectivorous species depends for its survival on more effective forest conservation.

Distribution The Iringa Ground Robin is a seldom recorded species known from only six forest patches in the Southern Highlands and Uzungwa Mountains in southern Tanzania. All records have been from above 1,450 m. The type was collected in Njombe Forest, 12 km south of Njombe, on the eastern side of the Southern Highlands in 1931 (Lynes 1934, Grant and Mackworth-Praed 1941). Subsequent collecting expeditions located the species at Uwemba, 2,000 m, 20 km south of Njombe in 1950 (Britton 1981) and Mdando Forest, 2,450 m, in the Livingstone Mountains, 48 km south of Njombe in 1962 (Ripley and Heinrich 1966). The species was discovered 150 km to the north-east at 2,100 m in Dabaga Forest in the Uzungwa Mountains in 1962 (Ripley and Heinrich 1966), and since 1979 it has been recorded in forest patches on the Mufindi Tea Estate, including the nearby Kigogo Forest, in the Uzungwa Mountains down to 1,500 m (van der Willigen and Lovett 1981, Willis 1981, A. J. Beakbane *in litt.* 1983, E. M. Boswell *in litt.* 1983, SNS). This site is about half-way between Dabaga and Njombe. It is not clear how far to the west the bird occurs in the Southern Highlands, or to the north and east in the Uzungwa Mountains. It seems to avoid areas of high rainfall and is, therefore, absent from the rainforests on Mount Rungwe in the Southern Highlands (F. P. Jensen *in litt.* 1980) and from Mwanihana Forest in the Uzungwa Mountains (Jensen *et al.* in press), being replaced in these forests by Sharpe's Akalat *Sheppardia sharpei*. However, in 1984 the species was discovered in very small numbers in a wetter forest type at Chita, 1,450-1,700 m, on the eastern escarpment of the Uzungwa Mountains between Mufindi and Dabaga (F. P. Jensen pers. comm. 1984). At Dabaga and Uwemba, both areas of intermediate rainfall, the two species are sympatric (Ripley and Heinrich 1966, Britton 1981). They are also sympatric at Chita (F. P. Jensen pers. comm. 1984). In 1979 a brief investigation of Luhombero Mountain in the Uzungwas, 90 km north-east of Dabaga and only 30 km west of Mwanihana Forest, located Sharpe's Akalat but not the Iringa Ground Robin (D. C. Moyer *in litt.* 1982): this suggests that the latter does not occur in the proposed Mwanihana National Park (Rodgers and Homewood 1982).

Population Except for the records from Mufindi, where it appears to be fairly common (van der Willigen and Lovett 1981, Willis 1981), there is no information on the abundance of this species. The area of the dry plateau forests is probably not very great, at least in the Uzungwa Mountains (Rodgers 1981, Rodgers and Homewood 1982) and so the population of the species similarly might not be very great. Although the species is fairly common at Mufindi it probably occurs at lower densities than its allospecies, the Usambara Ground Robin *Dryocichloides montanus*, in the Usambaras (SNS; see relevant account). At Chita it is rare, being greatly outnumbered by Sharpe's Akalat (F. P. Jensen pers. comm. 1984).

Ecology The Iringa Ground Robin inhabits the ground stratum of dry montane forest (Ripley and Heinrich 1966, van der Willigen and Lovett 1981, Willis 1981) where it regularly follows swarms of driver (doryline) ants, feeding on insects flushed by them (Ripley and Heinrich 1966, Willis 1981). It is unable to survive in the areas of montane grassland and cultivation which are replacing the forest, but it can tolerate some degree of forest disturbance (van der Willigen and Lovett 1981, SNS).

Threats The forested area in the Uzungwa Mountains is being reduced as a result of both fires and human exploitation (Rodgers 1981, Rodgers and Homewood 1982). There is no recent information on the status of forest conservation in the Southern Highlands, but there is every likelihood that fire and clearance are also resulting in forest fragmentation there.

Conservation Measures Taken Most of the forests which this species inhabits are within forest reserves, which provide some measure of protection to wildlife (SNS).

Conservation Measures Proposed More work is required to document the range of this species, in particular to determine whether it occurs inside the proposed Mwanihana National Park. A survey of the status of forest conservation in the Southern Highlands is also needed. Measures aimed at controlling the frequency of fires in the montane grasslands would reduce the attrition and fragmentation of the dry plateau forests. This would involve encouraging local farmers not to burn during the dry season.

Remarks This species is remarkably similar to Sharpe's Akalat and the type-specimen was originally assigned to this latter species (Lynes 1934, Grant and Mackworth-Praed 1941). This similarity – which has probably led to the former being under-recorded – is, however, purely superficial (SNS) and the Iringa Ground Robin's closest relative is the threatened Usambara Ground Robin: it has even been suggested that these two birds are conspecific (Ripley and Heinrich 1966) but this view is not generally accepted (Hall and Moreau 1970, Turner 1977). Six other threatened bird species occur in the Uzungwa Mountains, Swynerton's Forest Robin *Swynnertonia swynnertoni*, the Dappled Mountain Robin *Modulatrix orostruthus*, Mrs Moreau's Warbler *Bathmocercus winifredae*, the Banded Green Sunbird *Anthreptes rubritorques*, the Rufous-winged Sunbird *Nectarinia rufipennis* and the Tanzanian Mountain Weaver *Ploceus nicolli* (all six of these occurring in Mwanihana Forest: see Remarks under Rufous-winged Sunbird). Two species in Appendix C, the White-winged Apalis *Apalis chariessa* and Moreau's Sunbird *Nectarinia moreaui*, also occur in the Uzungwas. In the Southern Highlands and the Uzungwa Mountains a very distinct subspecies of the Thick-billed Seed-eater *Serinus (burtoni) melanochrous* occurs (see Appendix E).

References

Britton, P. L. (1981) Notes on the Andersen collection and other specimens from Tanzania housed in some West German museums. *Scopus* 5: 14-21.

Britton, P. L., Stuart, S. N. and Turner, D. A. (in press) East African endangered species. *Proc. V Pan-Afr. orn. Congr.*

Grant, C. H. B. and Mackworth-Praed, C. W. (1941) A new Alethe from Tanganyika Territory. *Bull. Brit. Orn. Club* 61: 61.

Hall, B. P. and Moreau, R. E. (1970) *An atlas of speciation in African passerine birds.* London: Trustees of the British Museum (Natural History).

Jensen, F. P., Stuart, S. N. and Brogger-Jensen, S. (in press) Altitudinal distribution of the avifauna of the Mwanihana Forest, Tanzania. *Gerfaut.*

Lynes, H. (1934) Contributions to the ornithology of southern Tanganyika Territory. *J. Orn.* 82 suppl.: 1-147.

Ripley, S. D. and Heinrich, G. H. (1966) Comments on the avifauna of Tanzania. I. *Postilla* 96.

Rodgers, W. A. (1981) An aerial survey of natural forest conservation status in the Uzungwa Mountains, southern Tanzania. Unpublished.

Rodgers, W. A. and Homewood, K. M. (1982) Biological values and conservation prospects for the forests and primate populations of the Uzungwa Mountains, Tanzania. *Biol. Conserv.* 24: 285-304.

Turner, D. A. (1977) Status and distribution of the East African endemic species. *Scopus* 1: 2-11,56.

van der Willigen, T. A. and Lovett, J. C. eds. (1981) Report of the Oxford Expedition to Tanzania, 1979. Unpublished.

Willis, E. O. (1981) A preliminary survey of African ant-following birds. Unpublished report to the National Geographical Society.

THYOLO ALETHE
Alethe choloensis Sclater, 1927

ENDANGERED

Order PASSERIFORMES

Family MUSICAPIDAE
Subfamily TURDINAE

Summary This ground-haunting, insectivorous species is confined to some of the remaining very small patches of highland forest in southern Malawi and adjacent Mozambique east of the Shire valley. Several such forest patches have been cleared relatively recently, and habitat destruction on several other mountains is continuing apace.

Distribution The Thyolo Alethe is known only from 13 areas of sub-montane evergreen forest east of the Shire valley in southern Malawi, most of them now tiny, and two such areas in northern Mozambique (Vincent 1935, Benson 1950, Dowsett 1981a,b, R. J. Dowsett *in litt.* 1984). In Malawi it occurs in every area of suitable habitat within its range (R. J. Dowsett *in litt.* 1984). There are recent (post-1970) records from Mounts Thyolo (formerly Cholo), Zomba, Chiradzulu (or Lisau), Soche, Chikala, Mulanje, Mangochi, Bangwe, Michese, Malabvi, Ndirande, Malosa and Mapalamba all in southern Malawi (Jackson 1971, Johnston-Stewart 1977,1982, Stead 1978, Dowsett and Hunter 1980, Hunter 1980, Dowsett 1981a,b, Willis 1981, R. J. Dowsett *in litt.* 1984) but it is presumably now extinct in the nearby Mpingwe and Nansadi forests which had been completed felled by the 1980s (Stead 1978, Dowsett 1981a). There is no recent information on its status in northern Mozambique (R. J. Dowsett and F. Dowsett-Lemaire *in litt.* 1982). The species was discovered in 1926 on Thyolo Mountain (Sclater 1927) and three further specimens were collected at this site between 1,250 and 1,370 m in 1932 (Vincent 1935). Another three birds were taken on Thyolo in 1933, all at 1,370 m (specimens in BMNH: SNS) and field observations were made here between 1944 and 1946 (Benson and Benson 1947, Benson 1948). More recent investigations, since 1971, have produced regular sightings of the species on Thyolo, from 1,150 m up to the peak at 1,460 m (Johnston-Stewart 1977,1982, Willis 1981) but it is apparently absent from the isolated, lower altitude (1,050 m) riparian forests to the east of the mountain (Johnston-Stewart 1982). The species was first discovered on Mulanje Mountain in 1936 when two birds were collected at 1,070 m on the escarpment (Benson 1940). Another specimen was collected at 915 m at the same locality in 1944 (specimen in BMNH: SNS). In 1970 another two birds were taken at Ruo, 915 m, on Mulanje (Jackson 1971). More recent fieldwork has shown that the species breeds at 1,000 to 1,800 m on Mulanje, moving down to 600 m in the non-breeding season (R. J. Dowsett *in litt.* 1984). One survey, in 1974, of the forest above 1,800 m failed to locate the species (Penry and Talbot 1975). In 1936 one specimen was collected on Mangochi Mountain at 1,530 m (Benson 1940) and birds were seen at this locality in 1972 (Dowsett and Hunter 1980) and again in 1983 (R. J. Dowsett *in litt.* 1984). The species was collected on Chikala Mountain between 1944 and 1946 (Benson and Benson 1947) and also at Chiradzulu around the same time (Benson and Benson 1947, Benson 1948, specimens in BMNH: SNS). There have been recent field observations at this site (Dowsett 1981a), including some in 1981 at 1,550 m on Chiradzulu (Willis 1981) and at both sites in 1983 (R. J. Dowsett *in litt.* 1984). Between 1944 and 1946 the species was found on Mpingwe Mountain and in Nansadi Forest (Benson and Benson 1947, Benson 1948) though it is most unlikely that these populations still survive (Stead 1978, Dowsett 1981a; see above). Recent records of the species from Zomba Mountain up to 1,900 m (Stead 1978, R. J. Dowsett *in litt.* 1984), including one in 1980 (Hunter 1980) and several in 1983 (R. J. Dowsett *in litt.* 1984), are probably merely the result of increased fieldwork rather than immigration (Dowsett 1981a; see Stead 1978). In 1981 the species was discovered for the first time on Bangwe Mountain (Dowsett 1981b) and in 1983 on Michese, Malabvi, Ndirande, Malosa and Mapalamba (R. J. Dowsett *in litt.* 1984). The Thyolo Alethe was discovered in Mozambique in 1932 when two specimens were collected at 1,700 m on Namuli Mountain and described as a separate subspecies *A. c. namuli* (Vincent 1933,1935). The only other record of the species from Mozambique is of two specimens, belonging to the nominate form, collected at 1,530 and 1,830 m in 1950 on Chiperone Mountain (Benson 1950, and specimens in BMNH: SNS), which is very close to Mulanje Mountain in Malawi.

Population The population in Malawi is in the order of 1,500 pairs, with 1,000 on Mulanje, 200 on Thyolo and 300 in the remaining 11 sites (R. J. Dowsett *in litt.* 1983,1984). Breeding densities of the Thyolo Alethe vary locally from one pair per 2-3 ha to one pair per 5 ha (R. J. Dowsett *in litt.* 1984). There is no recent information on the status of this species in Mozambique.

Ecology Habitat has been given as the ground stratum of tall evergreen forest (Sclater 1927, Vincent 1935, Benson 1940, Benson and Benson 1947,1977, Johnston-Stewart 1977,1982, Dowsett and Hunter 1980, Willis 1981, R. J. Dowsett and F. Dowsett-Lemaire *in litt.* 1982), lacking any shrubby understorey (R. J. Dowsett and F. Dowsett-Lemaire *in litt.* 1982), but the species also inhabits forest with dense thicket undergrowth on rare occasions (Vincent 1935, C. W. Benson pers. comm. 1982, R. J. Dowsett *in litt.* 1984). In the non-breeding season birds can be seen in groups of 4-5, often following *Dorylus* ant swarms (Vincent 1933,1935, Johnston-Stewart 1977,1982, Willis 1981, R. J. Dowsett *in litt.* 1984). Their foraging behaviour around ant swarms has been described and they probably feed mainly on insects flushed by the ants (Willis 1981, Johnston-Stewart 1982). When ants are not present the birds are generalised foragers on the ground (Willis 1981) and have been noted as feeding on small beetles (Vincent 1933,1935). Breeding is thought to start in September and on Thyolo young birds have been seen between December and February, and occasionally as late as April (Johnston-Stewart 1982), though these were apparently not accurately aged (R. J. Dowsett *in litt.* 1984). The species makes limited seasonal altitudinal movements (C. W. Benson pers. comm. 1982, R. J. Dowsett *in litt.* 1984; see Distribution).

Threats The sub-montane forests on Mulanje and Thyolo, the two most important localities, are threatened by clearance and encroachment (Johnston-Stewart 1977,1982, N. G. B. Johnston-Stewart *per* R. J. Dowsett and F. Dowsett-Lemaire *in litt.* 1982, Dowsett 1981a,b, Willis 1981, R. J. Dowsett *in litt.* 1983).

Most of the other mountain forests in Malawi where the species has been seen since 1970 are under similar pressure, only Zomba and Malosa having viable populations and receiving reasonable protection (R. J. Dowsett *in litt.* 1984). There is no recent information on the conservation status of the Namuli and Chiperone forests in Mozambique.

Conservation Measures Taken None is known.

Conservation Measures Proposed The status of this species throughout its range in southern Malawi was studied in 1983 and 1984, and recommendations will be made to the appropriate authorities regarding its protection (R. J. Dowsett and F. Dowsett-Lemaire *in litt.* 1984).

Remarks One other threatened bird species, the Spotted Ground-thrush *Turdus fischeri*, occurs on Mounts Thyolo, Chiradzulu, Soche and Mulanje, and another, the Dappled Mountain Robin *Modulatrix orostruthus*, occurs on Namuli Mountain (see relevant accounts). One highly distinct subspecies, mentioned in Appendix E, the Thyolo Green Barbet *Stactolaema (olivacea) belcheri*, is only found on these two mountains. Another very distinct subspecies included in Appendix E, the Namuli (Bar-throated) Apalis *Apalis (thoracica) lynesi*, is endemic to Namuli. The Thyolo Alethe also overlaps with an Appendix C species, the White-winged Apalis *Apalis chariessa*, in several localities.

References

Benson, C. W. (1940) Further notes on Nyasaland birds (with particular reference to those of the Northern Province), Part III. *Ibis* (14)4: 583-629.

Benson, C. W. (1948) Evergreen forests near Blantyre: comparative variety of birds species. *Nyasaland J.* 1(2): 45-52.

Benson, C. W. (1950) A collection from Chiperoni Mountain, Portuguese East Africa. *Bull. Brit. Orn. Club* 70: 51.

Benson, C. W. (1980) Man-induced changes in Malawi birds. *Proc. IV Pan-Afr. orn. Congr.*: 373-381.

Benson, C. W. and Benson, F. M. (1947) Some breeding and other records from Nyasaland. *Ibis* 89: 279-290.

Benson, C. W. and Benson, F. M. (1977) *The birds of Malawi.* Limbe, Malawi: Montfort Press.

Dowsett, R. J. (1981a) The past and present distribution of montane birds in Malawi. *Nyala* 7: 25-45.

Dowsett, R. J. ed. (1981b) Nyala Records. *Nyala* 7: 157-166.

Dowsett, R. J. and Hunter, N. D. (1980) Birds and mammals of Mangochi Mountain, Malawi. *Nyala* 6: 5-18.

Hunter, N. D. (1980) Nyala records: record editor's comments. *Nyala* 6: 72-74.

Jackson, H. D. (1971) Ornithological results of the 1970 National Museums of Rhodesia Expedition to Malawi. *Arnoldia (Rhod.)* 5(12).

Johnston-Stewart, N. G. B. (1977) Birds of Thyolo District. *Nyala* 3: 67-96.

Johnston-Stewart, N. G. B. (1982) Evergreen forest birds in upper Thyolo. *Nyala* 8: 69-84.

Penry, E. H. and Talbot, J. N. (1975) Notes on the birds of the higher altitudes of Mulanje Mountain, Malawi. *Honeyguide* no. 82: 15-25.

Sclater, W. L. (1927) [Three new African birds.] *Bull. Brit. Orn. Club* 47: 85-87.

Stead, D. E. (1978) The birds of the montane evergreen forests of southern Malawi. *Nyala* 6: 5-18.

Vincent, J. (1933) [Four new species and eighteen new subspecies ... collected during the recent Portuguese East African Expedition.] *Bull. Brit. Orn. Club* 53: 129-149.

Vincent, J. (1935) The birds of northern Portuguese East Africa. Comprising a list of, and observations on, the collections made during the British Museum Expedition of 1931-32, Part VIII. *Ibis* (13)5: 485-529.

Willis, E. O. (1981) A preliminary survey of African ant-following birds. Unpublished report to the National Geographical Society.

SEYCHELLES MAGPIE-ROBIN   ENDANGERED
Copsychus sechellarum A. Newton, 1865

Order PASSERIFORMES   Family MUSCICAPIDAE
                                             Subfamily TURDINAE

Summary Only 26 individuals of this ground-foraging chat were in existence at October 1983, all but one of which were confined to Frégate Island (2 km^2) in the Seychelles. An attempted reintroduction to Aride (Seychelles) in 1978 and 1979 was unsuccessful (one survivor), while on Frégate almost all recruitment subsequently ceased owing apparently to predation by feral cats on young birds. A cat eradication campaign, begun in 1981 and completed in 1982, coincided initially with greatly improved survival of young birds but, mainly for lack of habitat but also perhaps through competition from and nest-predation by introduced Indian Mynahs *Acridotheres tristis*, the population has since shown little sign of returning to the level it had before the cat population began to grow.

Distribution The Seychelles Magpie-robin is currently confined to Frégate Island (though with one introduced bird surviving on Aride Island) in the Seychelles. It was formerly known from Mahé and its satellite islands, plus Praslin, Marianne, La Digue and Aride; evidence of its occurrence on Félicité, as reported (Loustau-Lalanne 1962, Honneger 1966, Gaymer *et al.* 1969, High 1974), appears non-existent (this view is also taken in Diamond and Feare 1980). Extinction on Mahé presumably took place during the 1870s (see Newton 1867, Watson 1978); there is unequivocal evidence of its occurrence on at least one Mahé satellite (L'Ile du Sud-est) in 1768 (Lionnet 1980) and the original description of the species mentions its presence on "a small islet quite close to Mahé" (Newton 1865), but there are no subsequent references. The species was becoming scarce on Praslin in 1867, evidently owing to cat predation (Newton 1867), and soon after being considered extinct on the island it was reported to have been reintroduced there from La Digue (Pike 1872); there are no modern records, and the statement that it survived on Praslin after World War II, possibly into the 1950s and even to the present (Penny 1974), appears wholly unfounded. Although rats *Rattus* and cats abounded on La Digue in 1867 (Newton 1867), the species was still common there shortly afterwards (Hartlaub 1877, Vesey-Fitzgerald 1936) but was not reported from the island subsequently. It was common on Marianne in 1867, but died out there during the 1930s (Vesey-Fitzgerald 1940), though another report implies it survived till around 1948 (Crook 1960). In 1868 18-20 adults were encountered on Aride, each pair being accompanied by two immature birds (Hartlaub 1877), and 24 specimens were collected presumably on a single visit to the island in the 1870s (Oustalet 1878), but the species became extinct there only in the 1930s (Vesey-Fitzgerald 1940): cats became established on (and temporarily overran) the island in the 1920s (Ridley and Percy 1958) and although they were quickly killed off, circumstances prevented the recovery of the evidently depleted Magpie-robin population (Todd 1982). At some stage prior to August 1892 Magpie-robins were successfully introduced to Alphonse (Ridgway 1896), a coralline island in the Amirantes c. 400 km south-west of central Seychelles, which by 1940 was considered to be the species's stronghold (Vesey-Fitzgerald 1940); however, cats were taken there in the 1950s (Watson 1978), and a three-day intensive search in 1965 (Gaymer *et al.* 1969) and further visits in 1974 (A. W. Diamond pers. comm. 1982) and 1977 (Watson 1978) failed to locate any birds. It is possible (but unlikely) that Magpie-robins were also liberated on Aldabra prior to 1878 (see Diamond 1981). When the species was first found on Frégate in 1871, the owner prevented collection of a specimen on the grounds of rarity (Pike 1872), yet in 1873 the inhabitants were said to snare the birds, which were common (Vesey-Fitzgerald 1936; also Hartlaub 1877); by 1940, apart from Alphonse, it (probably) survived only on this island (Vesey-Fitzgerald 1940). Its distribution there was subsequently found to be largely restricted to the eastern and small western coastal "plateaus", which comprise only 30 ha (14.3%) of the island's land area (210 ha, not 700 ha as given in Wilson and Wilson 1976,1978) (Watson 1978; also High 1974). The construction of an airstrip on part of the eastern plateau in the mid-1970s did not result in a feared reduction in the species's range (Wilson and Wilson 1976,1978).

Population On Frégate in the last century the species was reported to be "widespread and very numerous" (Hartlaub 1877). The first attempt at a census there, in 1959, yielded "only ten pairs (20 birds)" (Crook 1960); soon after, c. 30 were reported present (Loustau-Lalanne 1962), but in 1964 there were not more than 15-20 (Honneger 1966) while in 1965 a mere eight birds (including two "young") could be found, with 12-15 estimated maximum (Penny 1968, Gaymer *et al.* 1969). However, in 1967 nine (Gaymer *et al.* 1969) or 15 birds (Penny 1968) were counted, suggesting a maximum of not more than 20; during a brief visit in June 1970 16 were seen and a total of 25 guessed at (Procter 1970); and in May 1973 38 birds were found, 34 of which were in the eastern plateau area (High 1974). In May 1976 34 birds (20 adults, 12 juveniles and two fledglings) were counted in 10 territorial groups, this considered the maximum possible for the habitat available (Wilson and Wilson 1976,1978). However, a maximum of 41 birds was present during one year's study of the species, July 1977 to July 1978, with groups established in 12-13 territories and each territory occupied by only one breeding pair, with up to six birds to a group (Watson 1978). In April 1978, just prior to the transfer of six birds to Aride, there were 39 birds (including 10 juveniles) in 12 territories; in April 1979, just prior to a second transfer of four birds, there were 38 (including 11 juveniles) in 11 territories (Watson 1978, Watson and Trowbridge 1979). However, by October 1980 there were only 27 (including two juveniles) in nine territories (Watson 1982) and in February 1981 these had fallen to 24 (including two juveniles) in the same nine territories (Todd 1982). This decline was attributed to (a) reduction in agriculture causing the loss of suitable habitat in two territories and (b) increased predation by feral cats on young birds causing almost nil recruitment since May 1979 (J. Watson *in litt.* and pers. comm. 1982; see Threats). At the start of a cat eradication programme in July 1981 21 birds were alive (three adults and the two February juveniles had died, and two new juveniles were present): during August three more adults died while two more young fledged, reducing the total to 20, but thereafter no more adults died and the population at the end of March 1982 stood at 24 (including eight juveniles) in the same nine territories, with a single male surviving on Aride (Todd 1982). In

October 1982 a minimum of 24 birds was present in nine territories, including three subadults and two fledged young (Watson 1982). In February 1983 during a week's survey only 18-19 birds could be found in 10 territories, all birds seen being in adult plumage, indicating (a) the loss of the two young seen in October 1982 and (b) no successful breeding since then; moreover, the three subadults from the previous October were suspected of being the other birds that had disappeared (Warman and Warman 1983). In June 1983 21 birds were counted in 10 territories and in October these held 24 birds (including five subadults) plus one nestling, this last fledging successfully in a territory which had been provided with a water-tank in February (see Conservation Measures Taken), the first time in over six years that a young bird was known to be reared to fledging at that site (Watson 1983; also Laboudallon 1983). The single male on Aride was still alive in December 1983 (Ch. Imboden pers. comm. 1984). In late July 1984 there were 25 birds (including one juvenile) present in 11 territories, and three occupied nests were found, one with a nestling and two with an egg each (Laboudallon 1984).

Ecology The species's habitat requirements were first assessed in a short study which found that, for feeding, large trees providing low perches in shade and open ground with sparse or no herb layer were needed (i.e. groves of sangdragon *Pterocarpus indicus* and breadfruit *Artocarpus altilis*, with other trees scattered singly, mixed with cultivated plots, tracks and open ground around houses), while for breeding bases of coconut fronds or rotted-out tree holes were used (Wilson and Wilson 1976). In a later, longer study, feeding habitat was determined more exactly as herb-free ground-layer of two types, bare earth and leaf-litter, associated with four main island habitats (vegetable gardens and mature plateau woodland on the deep rich soils of the coastal plateaus, and *Pterocarpus* woodland and cashew woodland on the poorer shallow hill soils); while of 41 nesting attempts observed, 38 occurred in crowns of coconut palms *Cocos nucifera* and three in holes in trees (Watson 1978). Notwithstanding that the species formerly occurred on Aride (as dry as its name implies), standing water may be important for the species, as two of the least successful territories on Frégate were also those without access to fresh water, yet successful breeding took place in one within a year of a water-tank being installed in it (see Population, Conservation Measures Taken). Most prey is small invertebrates inhabiting the upper layers of soil and leaf-litter, including cockroaches (especially *Pycnoscelus indicus*), scorpions, termites, earwigs, the giant millipede *Scaphiostreptus madacassus* (small specimens), the giant tenebrionid beetle *Polposipus herculeanus* (endemic to Frégate: see Remarks), and the yellow hornet *Polistes olivaceus*; vertebrates include four species of skink and two of gecko; fruit is also taken (Watson 1978; other data in Newton 1867, Loustau-Lalanne 1962, Gaymer *et al.* 1969, Diamond 1973, High 1974). Birds reintroduced to Aride (which has a large seabird colony) (see Conservation Measures Taken) fed substantially on young geckos in banana plantations, eggs of the Black Noddy *Anous tenuirostris*, and fish dropped by seabirds feeding their young; less time was spent in foraging than on Frégate, possibly as a result of these abundances (Hellawell 1979). Giant tortoises *Geochelone gigantea* are present in the two hill soil habitats on Frégate, and Magpie-robins commonly forage in their tracks, notably when the ground is dry (Watson 1978). Breeding occurs year-round with evidence of peaks around September and April: clutch-size is always one, incubation period (timed once) being 20 days (Watson 1978). Chicks leave the nest at c. 15 days, but can first fly weakly only at 18-19 days, strongly at 25 days; although they keep to low vegetation in this period, they call loudly and insistently and are thus very easy to locate (Watson 1978). Fledging success 1977-1978 was 30-40%; at least 90% of all nesting failures occurred during incubation or before nestlings were a week old; the skink *Mabuya wrightii* was probably the chief nest-predator; less likely causes of loss might have been Indian Mynahs *Acridotheres tristis* and the tree snake *Lycognathophis sechellensis* preying on eggs, and feral cats (then considered too few in number to pose a serious threat) preying on young newly out of the nest (Watson 1978), though in 1981-1982 skinks were considered less of a threat than Indian Mynahs, which were twice suspected of direct interference with nests and probably predation of their contents (Todd 1982). Thirteen young fledged 1977-1978, representing 1.1 young per pair; overall first-year mortality was 52%, adult mortality tentatively put at 8.3% per year, and mean adult life expectancy at one year calculated from this as a further 8.1 years; on the basis of these data, 4-5 young reared in the period would have been surplus to the population (Watson 1978). From a follow-up study in 1979, first-year mortality was put at 55.5%, adult mortality 8.9% per year, and mean adult life expectancy 10.7 years (see Remarks); annual surplus production was re-calculated as 3.7 (Watson and Trowbridge 1979). Birds less than three months old tend to remain on the parental territory; birds older than this are more likely to occur on a non-parental territory (i.e. territorial groups are not families) (Watson 1978). When five adults were removed (for transfer to Aride) from hill-site territories, four of the vacancies were filled within two months by non-breeding surplus birds in other groups, mostly from plateau sites (where group sizes are larger); first breeding has occurred at just over 12 months (Watson 1978).

Threats Very strong circumstantial and indirect evidence indicates that cats were responsible for the extinction of the Seychelles Magpie-robin on some other islands (see Distribution) and for the post-1979 decline on Frégate (see Conservation Measures Taken), probably mostly by preying on non- or weak fliers just out of the nest (see Ecology). Agricultural desuetude on the main plateau since 1979 has resulted in a rich herbaceous cover on much previous feeding habitat, and hence the loss of two territories (Watson 1982, Warman and Warman 1983). In late 1982 severe storms brought down many trees that had provided several feeding areas (Warman and Warman 1983; also Todd 1983). Apart from these factors and the nest-predators mentioned under Ecology, Indian Mynahs are possible food competitors (Newton 1867, High 1974) and one was blamed for the death in 1982 of a fully fledged juvenile during a dispute (Todd 1982); and the absence of rats, which have been suspected of causing local Magpie-robin extinctions, is considered a vital requisite for survival (Vesey-Fitzgerald 1940, Watson 1978, Todd 1982). There are reportedly no Barn Owls *Tyto alba* on the island and the Cattle Egret *Bubulcus ibis*, a possible threat, no longer exists there (Todd 1982). The statement that Magpie-robins were formerly favourite cage-birds (Foster-Vesey-Fitzgerald 1953) lends support to the view, otherwise apparently unsubstantiated, that extinctions on other islands were the result of capture, keeping and selling as rarity-value cage-birds (Honneger 1966); it may be noted that the type-specimen was a cage-bird (Newton 1865), and birds held in captivity even for short periods readily begin singing (Todd 1982, D. M. Todd *in litt.* 1982).

Conservation Measures Taken Following the report that cats had recently become established on Frégate and that the Magpie-robin was "in imminent danger of extinction" (Crook 1960), a government campaign resulted in 86 (in another report 91) cats (including domestic pets) being destroyed in 1960 (Todd 1982, D. M. Todd in *litt.* 1982). Thereafter cats as well as rats have been stringently excluded from the island, and a bounty system on each cat subsequently destroyed was operated by successive owners (Penny 1968, Watson 1978, Todd 1982). An outbreak of feline enteritis in Seychelles occurred in 1965-1966 and there may be a connexion between this and the notable recovery of Magpie-robins from their apparent all-time low in 1965 (Todd 1982). A strict ban on agricultural chemicals was in force in 1973 (Diamond 1973) and was recommended to remain so (ICBP 1976), although it was later reported that the islanders (merely) do not grow produce "requiring heavy doses of pesticides" (Watson 1978); this appears in keeping with the island's traditional undemanding management regime, which strongly favours all wildlife there (Procter 1970). WWF Project 1590 (see Watson 1978) was developed by ICBP as a result of the concern expressed at the IV Pan-African Ornithological Congress (Mahé, Seychelles), November 1976, for the future safety of the Magpie-robin and the Seychelles Black Paradise Flycatcher *Terpsiphone corvina* (see relevant account): its fundamental aim was to establish the status, needs and principal biological details of the two species. Since, however, the 12(-13) territories present during the resulting fieldwork, 1977-1978, covered all suitable feeding habitat on Frégate (Watson 1978), and given the appropriate conditions on Aride (it formerly held Magpie-robins; is rat- and cat-free; and runs as a nature reserve), in April 1978 six birds (five adults and one juvenile) were flown to Aride and released (Watson 1978, Hellawell 1979). The juvenile (female) disappeared immediately and two adult males within five months (possibly through the unauthorised use of domestic insecticides), although one of them was first involved in two breeding attempts: from the second of these, after his disappearance, a chick hatched but did not survive, though cared for by the sole remaining male, who had himself attempted unsuccessfully to breed with the other adult female in mid-August but who now formed a bond with the widowed female; this new pair attempted to nest again in October but the results are not known (Hellawell 1979). This pair was still present in March 1979 but the other female had disappeared; in April two more adult pairs were transferred to Aride from Frégate (Watson and Trowbridge 1979). No monitoring or rapid follow-up was possible but there is evidence that at least two chicks were fledged (Todd 1982). However in September 1980 only the last male from the 1978 transfer survived (J. Watson *in litt.* and pers. comm. 1982); he was still present in December 1983 (see Population). On Frégate, meanwhile, a rapidly accelerating growth in the feral cat population is now believed to have started from around the time of the second transfer to Aride (i.e. April 1979), resulting in the collapse of recruitment reported under Population. In July 1981 an ICBP project, drawing on New Zealand Wildlife Service expertise, began operation to eradicate these animals completely from

Frégate: 51 cats were definitely killed, three more probably, and two found dead; by early 1982 Magpie-robin recruitment had risen to its highest proportionate level on record (Todd 1982), and by October 1982 the island was believed free of cats (Watson 1982), no sign being seen during subsequent monitoring (Laboudallon 1983, Warman and Warman 1983, Watson 1983). A proposal to provide standing water in two territories using water-tanks with perches (Todd 1982; also Watson 1983) was carried out in February 1983 (Warman and Warman 1983), and successful breeding at one site ensued within the year (see Population). A policy to encourage tourism on Frégate from 1983 onwards was felt likely to encourage more vegetable growing on the island and thus result in the restoration of feeding habitat for the species (Watson 1982) but there was no evidence of an increase in gardening in February 1983 (Warman and Warman 1983).

Conservation Measures Proposed Many proposals have been put forward in the last two decades, not all now relevant. A series of recommendations was made for the continuation and extension of present agricultural conditions on Frégate (Watson 1978) but was not taken up (see Threats). Comprehensive proposals have now been drawn up for the active management of these and other areas (extensive tree planting, immediate clearance of herb layer, etc.) with the aim of restoring and even surpassing the maximum number of birds present in 1977-1978 (Todd 1982,1983); in particular, clearance of the herb layer has been urgently recommended (Warman and Warman 1983). Monitoring of the Magpie-robin population and its relations with the Indian Mynahs is essential, and the possibility of eradicating Indian Mynahs entirely from Frégate requires serious investigation in the light of recent evidence (see Ecology and Threats). The discouraging of inhabitants and visitors from disturbing nesting birds remains important (Wilson and Wilson 1976,1979, Todd 1982). Siting any new houses in locations away from present buildings might encourage pairs to become established in the vicinity (Wilson and Wilson 1976). A close check needs to be kept on pesticides used on the island; cats must continue to be eliminated (if present) and excluded from the island, and stricter precautions need to be taken to prevent the accidental introduction of rats (Todd 1982). A prescriptive management plan for the whole island has been called for (Warman and Warman 1983). Once the population has regenerated and stabilised, a strategy for future reintroductions and captive propagation must be adopted and implemented; this issue is currently under review by ICBP.

Remarks As noted under Ecology, Frégate is also the only locality for the remarkable giant tenebrionid beetle, a species regarded as threatened because of the restriction of its range (rats presumably wipe it out at once) (Wells *et al.* 1983): the conservation of both beetle and bird can and should proceed together, both being particularly attached (e.g.) to sangdragon groves (Lloyd 1971). Concerning mean adult life expectancy, the figure of 10.7 years cited by Watson and Trowbridge (1979) seems to be in error, since calculation from adult mortality of 8.9% per year yields a figure of a further 7.2 years at one year (M. D. Jenkins pers. comm. 1984).

References

Crook, J. H. (1960) The present status of certain rare land birds of the Seychelles Islands. Seychelles Government Bulletin.

Diamond, A. W. (1973) Report on a visit to Frigate Island, L'Ilot and Ste.Marie, 17-20 November 1973. Cousin Island Research Station, Techn. Rep. 4. ICBP, unpublished.

Diamond, A. W. and Feare, C. J. (1980) Past and present biogeography of central Seychelles birds. *Proc. IV Pan-Afr. orn. Congr.*: 89-98.

Diamond, E. P. (1981) An early report of the flora and fauna of the Aldabra group. *Atoll Res. Bull.* no. 255: 1-10.

Foster-Vesey-Fitzgerald, D. (1953) Wild life in Seychelles. *Oryx* 2: 28-32.

Gaymer, R., Blackman, R. A. A., Dawson, P. G., Penny, M. and Penny, C. M. (1969) The endemic birds of Seychelles. *Ibis* 111: 157-176.

Hartlaub, G. (1877) *Die Vögel Madagascars und der benachbarten Inselgruppen.* Halle.

Hellawell, C. (1979) The Magpie Robin on Aride. Unpublished.

High, J. (1974) Seychelles Magpie Robin: coming back from the brink of extinction? *Wildlife* 16: 61.

Honneger, R. E. (1966) Ornithologische Beobachtungen von den Seychelles. *Natur u. Mus.* 96: 481-488.

ICBP (1976) Bird preservation in the Seychelles. Fifth report on Cousin Island Nature Reserve and other islands 1973-1976. [London: ICBP.]

Laboudallon, V. (1983) Magpie Robin (*Copsychus sechellarum*) on Frégate Island. Unpublished.

Laboudallon, V. (1984) Visit to Frégate Island, Rep. of Seychelles, 22 to 25 July 1984. Report to the International Council for Bird Preservation.

Lionnet, G. (1980) Les oiseaux observés aux Seychelles en 1768 au cours de l'expédition Marion-Dufresne. *Proc. IV Pan-Afr. orn. Congr.*: 65-69.

Lloyd, D. E. B. (1971) Survey of the Giant Tenebrionid Beetle *Pulposipes [sic] herculeanus* on Frigate Island, November 1971. Cousin Island Research Station, Techn. Rep. 2. ICBP, unpublished.

Loustau-Lalanne, P. (1962) Land birds of the granitic islands of the Seychelles. *Seychelles Soc. Occ. Publ.* 1.

Newton, A. (1865) On an apparently undescribed bird from the Seychelles Islands. *Ibis* (2)1: 331-337.

Newton, E. (1867) On the land-birds of the Seychelles archipelago. *Ibis* (2)3: 335-360.

Oustalet, M. E. (1878) Etude sur la faune ornithologique des Iles Seychelles. *Bull. Soc. Philomath. Paris* (7)2: 161-206.

Penny, M. (1968) Endemic birds of the Seychelles. *Oryx* 9: 267-275.

Penny, M. (1974) *The birds of Seychelles and the outlying islands.* London: Collins.

Pike, N. (1872) A visit to the seychelles Islands. *Trans. Roy. Soc. Arts Sci. Mauritius* N.S. 6: 83-143.

Procter, J. (1970) Conservation in the Seychelles. Report of the conservation adviser. [Victoria, Mahé: Government Printer.]

Ridgway, R. (1896) On birds collected by Doctor W. L. Abbott in the Seychelles, Amirantes, Gloriosa, Assumption, Aldabra, and adjacent islands, with notes on habits, etc., by the collector. *Proc. U. S. Natn. Mus.* 18 [1895]: 509-546.

Ridley, M. W. and Percy, Lord R. (1958) The exploitation of sea birds in Seychelles. Colonial Research Studies no. 25. London: Colonial Office.

Todd, D. M. (1982) Seychelles Magpie Robin: cat eradication on Frégate Island. International Council for Bird Preservation Emergency Project. Unpublished.

Todd, D. M. (1983) Seychelles Magpie Robin *Copsychus sechellarum* – proposals for improving the feeding habitat on Frégate Island, Seychelles. Unpublished.

Vesey-Fitzgerald, D. (1936) Birds of the Seychelles and other islands included within that colony. Victoria (Mahé), Seychelles: Government Printing Office.

Vesey-Fitzgerald, D. (1940) The birds of the Seychelles. I. The endemic birds. *Ibis* (14)4: 480-489.

Warman, C. and Warman, S. (1983) Visit to Frégate Island, Seychelles – 25th February to lst March 1983. Report to the International Council for Bird Preservation. Unpublished.

Watson, J. (1978) The Seychelles Magpie Robin (*Copsychus sechellarum*). World Wildlife Fund Project 1590: Endangered land birds, Seychelles. Final report 1 (a). Unpublished.

Watson, J. (1982) Report on a visit to Seychelles, 18 October – 10 November 1982. Manuscript.

Watson, J. (1983) Results of a survey of Magpie Robins on Frigate, 3-10 October 1983. Unpublished.

Watson, J. and Trowbridge, B. J. (1979) The Seychelles Magpie Robin *Copsychus sechellarum*. World Wildlife Fund Project 1590. Endangered land birds, Seychelles. Final report 2 (a). Unpublished.

Wells, S. M., Pyle, R. M. and Collins, N. M. (1983) *The IUCN invertebrate red data book*. Gland, Switzerland: IUCN.

Wilson, J. and Wilson, R. (1976) A survey of the Seychelles Magpie Robin on Frigate Island, May 1976. Cousin Island Research Station, Techn. Rep. 7. ICBP, unpublished.

Wilson, J. and Wilson, R. (1978) Observations on the Seychelles Magpie Robin *Copsychus seychellarum* [*sic*]. *Bull. Brit. Orn. Club* 98: 15-21.

FUERTEVENTURA STONECHAT

Saxicola dacotiae (Meade-Waldo, 1889)

RARE

Order PASSERIFORMES

Family MUSCICAPIDAE
Subfamily TURDINAE

Summary This insectivorous, scrub-haunting chat is confined to the large arid island of Fuerteventura in the Canary Islands, where it is widely but very locally distributed, and probably has a low total population which may be diminishing as tourist facilities develop on the island.

Distribution The Fuerteventura Stonechat is endemic to Fuerteventura, in the eastern group of Canary Islands (Spain), where it occurs throughout the island but very locally, entirely as determined by suitable habitat, most of which is relatively close to the coastline (von Thanner 1914, Volsøe 1951, Bannerman 1963, Shirt 1983, Collins in press; see Ecology): most birds are in the southern half of the island (Shirt 1983, Collins in press). The species was originally considered restricted to (and thinly distributed in) the southern half of the island (Meade-Waldo 1893, von Thanner 1905), and subsequently judged to be absent at least from the west on account of the strong winds there (Polatzek 1908-1909), but by 1914 it had been found to occur from Corralejo in the far north to the Jandía peninsula in the far south (von Thanner 1914) and from Barranco de Rio Cabras in the east (Polatzek 1908-1909) to Barranco de la Peña in the west (Bannerman 1914), as well as at several sites in the interior extending from La Oliva in the north (Polatzek 1908-1909, Bannerman 1914) to Tuineje in the south (Meade-Waldo 1889a). Whether this extension in distribution represented a spread by the bird itself or merely reflected improved ornithological coverage of the island is unclear (see also under Population). Localities other than those above that are known for the species include Rio de las Palmas (von Thanner 1905), Casillas del Angel and environs (Polatzek 1908-1909), Antigua, the beach at Gran Tarajal, and between Tuineje and Pozo Negro (Bannerman 1914), the (old) airport near Puerto del Rosário (Hüe and Etchécopar 1958), Barranco de la Torre (Hemmingsen 1958), the reservoir at Los Molinos (Collins in press), a barranco west of the Cuchillas del Palo in western Jandía (J. Heinze *in litt.* 1978) and Punta Junquilla, north-west Jandía (Vicente 1961); a substantial number of other sites are known (D. B. Shirt pers. comm. 1979, D. R. Collins pers. comm. 1981, B. Phillips *in litt.* 1984; and see, e.g., Pérez Padrón and Bacallado 1972, Pérez Padrón 1983). The species appears sedentary and there are records that confirm its presence in localities between years, decades and centuries, e.g. at Tuineje (Meade-Waldo 1889a, Bannerman 1963), La Oliva (Polatzek 1908-1909, Bannerman 1914, van den Berg and Bosman 1979, D. R. Collins pers. comm. 1981), Barranco de la Peña (Bannerman 1914, Hooker 1958, J. Heinze *in litt.* 1978). Although the species has never been recorded from Lanzarote, despite repeated searches (e.g. Meade-Waldo 1890, Etchécopar and Hüe 1957, Hüe and Etchécopar 1958, Shirt 1983), specimens of it were found and collected in June 1913 on the small islands of Montaña Clara and Alegranza, to the north of Lanzarote, and determined as a new race *murielae* (Bannerman 1914, 1919-1920, 1922, 1963): it was concluded that the species was resident on Alegranza (this being supported by local testimony) and a presumed occasional breeder (having crossed from Alegranza) on Montaña Clara (Bannerman 1963), but extensive searches in 1956 of Graciosa and Montaña Clara (Etchécopar and Hüe 1957, Hüe and Etchécopar 1958), in 1970 of Graciosa, Montaña Clara and Alegranza (Lovegrove 1971), in April 1981 of Alegranza (H.-H. Bergmann *in litt.* 1984) and at an unspecified date of Alegranza and Montaña Clara (Pérez Padrón 1983) could not relocate the bird, nor find anyone who knew it. The (admitted) anomaly of these records is compounded by doubt as to the validity of the racial distinctness of the birds involved (see Bannerman 1963), by the fact that it is nowhere entirely clear that the original authority – who did not visit Alegranza – ever personally saw any of the birds alive (see Bannerman 1914, 1919-1920, 1922, 1963), and by his own (unadmitted) confusion as to the fate of the birds on Montaña Clara, which were first expected to have flown straight to "the mainland" (i.e., apparently – from context – the coast of Africa) or else Alegranza (Bannerman 1919-1920), then confidently believed to have flown to Alegranza (also Bannerman 1919-1920), and later (Alegranza being ruled out because of headwinds) considered to have crossed to Graciosa and thence perhaps to Lanzarote (Bannerman 1963); for a possible explanation of these records, see Population. The consideration that a population of this species might inhabit the Sous in southern Morocco, adjacent to the eastern Canaries (Tristram 1890, Meade-Waldo 1893, Bannerman 1919-1920), has been shown to be mistaken (Volsøe 1951).

Population An extensive general survey of the avifauna of Fuerteventura in March and April 1979 encountered up to 35 pairs, at least 15 of which had young; the highest densities were in barrancos in the south, with a maximum of 18-19 birds (nine adults and nine or ten juveniles) in a 2 km stretch of one barranco (Shirt 1983). In January 1982 11 pairs were found in one barranco on Jandía (H. Löhrl *in litt.* 1984). In Barranco de la Peña in 1913 birds were "plentiful" (Bannerman 1914), even "literally teeming" (Bannerman 1922), and this locality still holds birds (Hooker 1958, J. Heinze *in litt.* 1978, Collins in press). Altogether, a reasoned guess might be of a total population of 50-150 pairs (a view shared by D. R. Collins *in litt.* 1984). Although it seems highly improbable that the species was confined to the south and south-east at the time of its discovery and then expanded in numbers and range through the rest of the island, some early observers were quite categorical that it was not in certain areas in the years 1902-1904 where it was subsequently discovered (see Polatzek 1908-1909, von Thanner 1908), while by 1914 it was concluded that the distribution must be stable because there was no further habitat available (von Thanner 1914): if these and other fragments of evidence are construed to imply that numbers expanded from before or around 1900 to saturation levels before or around 1914 (the evidence for expansion is marshalled most thoroughly in Bannerman 1914), it is possible to consider that the birds seen in 1913 on Montaña Clara and Alegranza had relatively recently dispersed from Fuerteventura, in which case their taxonomic status must again fall in doubt. A presumed family party of four or five birds comprises the 1913 record from Montaña Clara (two collected, the rest immediately disappearing), while on Alegranza birds were in parties of three to five and "everywhere decidedly plentiful" (ten collected) (Bannerman 1914,1919-1920,1922,1963), though the total population on these two islands must have been small, the combined area available being at most 13 km² (Volsøe 1951). That the population on Fuerteventura may be subject to fluctuations or displacement is supported by the finding in April 1984 that very few birds were present in known sites for the species (*ICBP Newsletter* 6,2 [1984]).

Ecology In the 1979 survey and analysis, birds were found to prefer rocky hillsides, edges of malpais (lava-flows), barrancos (watercourses) and cultivations near slopes (Shirt 1983), and subsequent observations have determined that the common characteristics in habitat are rocky slopes and reasonably developed scrub (typically aulaga *Launaea arborescens*, saltwort *Salsola vermiculata*, box-thorn *Lycium intricatum*, with the succulent spurge *Euphorbia obtusifolia* and ragwort *Senecio kleinia*), birds also locally occurring on the south coast seashore (where the scrub is dominated by *S. vermiculata* and the glasswort *Salicornia fruticosa*) and around a few areas of permanent water (Collins in press). These findings largely bear out old accounts, e.g. "distributed wherever there was a little cover, especially frequenting the small barrancos on the low hills" (Meade-Waldo 1893; see also Meade-Waldo 1889b, von Thanner 1905, Polatzek 1908-1909, Bannerman 1914). On Jandía, December 1976, a pair was found in a barranco dominated by *Launaea arborescens* and the threatened spurge *Euphorbia handiensis* (J. Heinze *in litt.* 1978). Also on Jandía, the species was found to be common in one barranco where males used bushes of the tobacco *Nicotiana glauca* as look-out perches, but absent from an adjacent barranco where no vegetation grew (H. Löhrl *in litt.* 1984). Birds are notably tame (Meade-Waldo 1893, von Thanner 1905), and may sometimes live close to human dwellings (von Thanner 1905), their look-out perches including bushes, walls, stones (von Thanner 1905) and even roof-tops (Bannerman 1963). From such look-outs they fly out to catch insects in the air or on the ground (Polatzek 1908-1909, Bannerman 1914, Hemmingsen 1958); food is chiefly flies (Cabrera y Diaz 1893, Polatzek 1908-1909) and a large soft-bodied fly species has been noted as especially preferred (von Thanner 1905). Centipedes, caterpillars and small Hymenoptera are also important and, when birds are feeding their young, food caught on the ground appears to predominate (D. R. Collins *in litt.* 1984); beetles and spiders also compose the diet (Pérez Padrón 1983). Breeding has always been noted to occur very early in the year, at least in some pairs, with fledging as early as mid-February (Meade-Waldo 1889b, von Thanner 1910), and recent study shows that onset of breeding is related to the first heavy rains of winter, birds at once starting to sing and prospect for nest-sites (Collins in press) although, in general, most egg-laying occurs in February and March (von Thanner 1905, Polatzek 1908-1909, Collins in press). Nests are hidden away in holes in rocks (e.g. in sides of barrancos) or low walls, on the ground under stones, in cactus thickets or under shrubs (notably *Lycium intricatum*) or bushy grasses, and usually on slopes (Meade-Waldo 1889b, von Thanner 1905,1910, Polatzek 1908-1909, Bannerman 1963, Collins in press). Clutch-size is two to five, three (to four) most usual (Meade-Waldo 1889b, von Thanner 1905,1912, Polatzek 1908-1909, Collins in press). In 1979, of 12 pairs whose young were accurately counted, five had one young, four had two and three had three (Shirt 1983). Breeding in May – adult and young collected 24 May (Polatzek 1908-1909), pair feeding young, 21 May (Witt 1971) – has been considered to refer to a second brood and second broods are considered unusual (Bannerman 1963), but there was one proven instance in 1980, where a second nest, only 20-30 m from the first, hatched young (on 5 April) only 23 days after the previous brood fledged (Collins in press). In Alegranza birds were seen chiefly in barren stony country with low hills covered with *Euphorbia* and other vegetation, still apparently in family parties in June (Bannerman 1914,1963).

Threats If it is accepted that birds on Montaña Clara and Alegranza were resident there and constituted a valid subspecies, then the unexplained (and now quite certain) extinction of this population is the greatest loss yet sustained by the species and the clearest indication that it is vulnerable to some unidentified threat. On Fuerteventura three introduced mammals are likely to augment natural predation rates by indigenous birds: cats may restrict numbers near villages, and rats *Rattus* and vagrant hedgehogs *Erinaceus algirus*, which both appear common, probably take eggs (Collins in press). Tourist and general development has resulted in a small overall loss of habitat, e.g. the species no longer occurs at Gran Tarajal where a holiday complex now stands, though such development is not considered a serious threat (Collins in press). It is to be observed, nonetheless, that improved tourist facilities are rendering the species ever more accessible to Europeans on holiday, and this presents a small danger of disturbance by birdwatchers and an unquantifiable but possibly quite serious danger of exploitation by egg-collectors; in these respects it is important to follow the fate of those birds whose exact location was recently revealed for the benefit of birdwatching tourists (van den Berg and Bosman 1979). The only other currently identifiable threat is the long-term and evidently continuing dessication of Fuerteventura, which 500 years ago was lush and well-wooded in places (see Collar 1983).

Conservation Measures Taken This species is fully protected by law under Royal Decree 3181, 30 December 1981 (K. W. Emmerson *in litt.* 1984). It is to be noted that the name of the barranco with the maximum count of birds in 1979 (Shirt 1983) was deliberately suppressed and that the original collector and authority deliberately refrained from taking a female that was feeding young (Meade-Waldo 1889b).

Conservation Measures Proposed Protected area status for several major barrancos holding the species on Fuerteventura is desirable (on Jandía the sites could also protect the remaining stands of *Euphorbia handiensis*). Exceedingly harsh (and well advertised) penalties for the taking of eggs would also seem appropriate. An accurate and thorough assessment of numbers and distribution is needed in order to monitor long-term trends. The need for and potential benefits of clarifying the status of the Canaries in relation to European legislation are stated in Conservation Measures Proposed under White-tailed Laurel Pigeon *Columba junoniae*.

Remarks The view that the Fuerteventura Stonechat is but a well-marked subspecies of the widespread Stonechat *Saxicola torquata* (Volsøe 1951) has been vigorously opposed, although the connexion between the two is quite certain

(Bannerman 1963). The variability of plumage noted in this species (von Thanner 1905, Polatzek 1908-1909, Volsøe 1951, Shirt 1983) also occurs in another island offshoot of *S. torquata*, the Réunion Stonechat *S. tectes* (see Cheke 1975).

References

Bannerman, D. A. (1914) An ornithological expedition to the eastern Canary Islands. *Ibis* (10)2: 38-90, 228-293.

Bannerman, D. A. (1919-1920) List of the birds of the Canary Islands, with detailed reference to the migratory species and the accidental visitors. *Ibis* (11)1: 84-131, 291-321, 457-495, 708-764; (11)2: 97-132, 323-360, 519-569.

Bannerman, D. A. (1922) *The Canary Islands: their history, natural history and scenery*. London and Edinburgh: Gurney and Jackson.

Bannerman, D. A. (1963) *Birds of the Atlantic islands*, 1. Edinburgh and London: Oliver and Boyd.

van den Berg, A. B. and Bosman, C. A. W. (1979) Birding in the Canary Islands. *Dutch Birding* 1: 66-68.

Cabrera y Diaz, A. (1893) Catálogo de las aves del archipiélago canario. *Ann. Soc. Esp. Hist. Nat.* 22: 151-220.

Cheke, A. (1975) Pourquoi le "tec-tec" est-il si variable? *Info-Nature, Ile Réunion* 13: 88-89.

Collar, N. J. (1983) A history of the Houbara in the Canaries. *Bustard Studies* 1: 9-29.

Collins, D. R. (in press) Observations on the Canary Islands Chat *Saxicola dacotiae*. *Brit. Birds*.

Etchécopar, R. D. and Hüe, F. (1957) Nouvelles données sur l'avifaune des îles Canaries recueillies au printemps 1956. *Oiseau et R.F.O.* 27: 309-334.

Hemmingsen, A. M. (1958) Field observations of birds in the Canary Islands. *Vidensk. Medd. fra Dansk naturh. Foren.* 120: 189-206.

Hooker, T. (1958) Birds seen on the eastern Canary Island of Fuerteventura. *Ibis* 100: 446-449.

Hüe, F. and Etchécopar, R. D. (1958) Un mois de recherches ornithologiques aux îles Canaries. *Terre et Vie* 105: 186-219.

Lovegrove, R. (1971) B.O.U. supported expedition to northeast Canary Islands, July – August 1970. *Ibis* 113: 269-272.

Meade-Waldo, E. G. (1889a) Notes on some birds of the Canary Islands. *Ibis* (6)1: 1-13.

Meade-Waldo, E. G. (1889b) Further notes on the birds of the Canary Islands. *Ibis* (6)1: 503-520.

Meade-Waldo, E. G. (1890) Further notes on the birds of the Canary Islands. *Ibis* (6)2: 429-438.

Meade-Waldo, E. G. (1893) List of birds observed in the Canary Islands. *Ibis* (6)5: 185-207.

Pérez Padrón, F. (1983) *Las aves de Canarias*. 3rd edition. (Enciclopedia Canaria). Tenerife: ACT.

Pérez Padrón, F. and Bacallado Aránega, J. J. (1972) Observaciones ornitológicas en la Isla de Fuerteventura. *Vieraea* 2: 52-56.

Polatzek, J. (1908-1909) Die Vögel der Canaren. *Orn. Jahrb.* 19: 81-119, 161-197; 20: 1-24, 117-134, 202-210.

Shirt, D. B. (1983) The avifauna of Fuerteventura and Lanzarote. *Bustard Studies* 1: 57-68.

von Thanner, R. (1905) Ein Sammelausflug nach Fuerteventura. *Orn. Jahrb.* 16: 50-66.

von Thanner, R. (1908) Ein Sammelausflug nach La Palma, Hierro und Fuerteventura. *Orn. Jahrb.* 19: 198-215.

von Thanner, R. (1910) Ornithologische Notizen, Fuerteventura betreffend. *Orn. Jahrb.* 21: 226-229.

von Thanner, R. (1912) Von den Kanaren. *Orn. Jahrb.* 23: 221-228.

von Thanner, R. (1914) Bemerkungen und Berichtigungen über die Verbreitung einzelner Vogelarten auf den Kanaren. *Orn. Jahrb.* 25: 86-94.

Tristram, H. B. (1890) Notes on the island of Palma in the Canary group. *Ibis* (6)2: 67-76.

Vicente, R. O. (1961) Aves observadas nas imediações do Faro de Jandía, Ilha de Fuerteventura (Canarias). *Ardeola* 7: 241-247.

Volsøe, H. (1951) The breeding birds of the Canary Islands, 1. Introduction and synopsis of the species. *Vidensk. Medd. fra Dansk naturh. Foren.* 113: 1-153.

Witt, H. -H. (1971) Ornithologische Beobachtungen auf den Kanaren. *Orn. Mitt.* 23: 145-148.

BENSON'S ROCKTHRUSH

Monticola bensoni Farkas, 1971

INSUFFICIENTLY KNOWN

Order PASSERIFORMES

Family MUSCICAPIDAE
Subfamily TURDINAE

Summary This recently described rock-haunting thrush is possibly quite widespread but as yet is known only from a few dry rocky areas in south-west Madagascar.

Distribution Benson's Rockthrush was recently described from two old specimens collected by "Zaast" at an unknown time in an intraceable locality ("Ankarefu, Antinosy Cy") in "south-west" Madagascar (Farkas 1971). In 1962 birds were discovered and recognised as a new species at several localities in the Mangoky River region and the northern Isalo massif, and found again in 1969 and 1970 in the latter locality and at a single site between Ihosy and Zazafotsy (east of the northern Isalo massif) (Farkas 1971). In August 1969 and June 1971 the species was found 150 km south of the northern Isalo massif (D. A. Turner *in litt.* 1983). On 10 July 1977 two birds were observed on telephone wires along the main road running through the Zombitsy Forest Reserve near Sakaraha (D. A. Turner *in litt.* 1983). Excluding the records from "Antinosy County" (southern Madagascar; but see Remarks), all sightings are from between the Mangoky and Onilahy Rivers, south-west Madagascar, but the distribution of the species has been anticipated as covering one-fifth of the island, from "at least" the eastern fringes of the Bemaraha plateau in the central-west to "Antinosy County" in the south (see map in Farkas 1971, also under Remarks); it should however be noted that localised distribution, despite more extensive and apparently similar habitat, is a characteristic of several threatened Madagascar birds (e.g. Subdesert Mesite *Monias benschi*, Appert's Greenbul *Phyllastrephus apperti*) and a wider range for this species cannot be assumed with confidence. In the Mangoky region birds were only seen in winter (June/July) and in different habitat (see Ecology), and it seems likely that some local migration occurs at this season (Farkas 1971).

Population Numbers are unknown. At least six males (some paired) were found along a 2 km stretch of road in one locality (Farkas 1971), so the population density is probably fairly high and stable in suitable habitat. Nevertheless, on present information it remains possible that total numbers are very small (Forbes-Watson *et al.* 1973).

Ecology This is the only rock-inhabiting *Monticola* in Madagascar, apparently preferring huge rocks and extended cliff faces rising steeply out of open rolling hillsides, birds keeping mostly to rocks, occasionally visiting thin bushes, small trees, etc., but retreating to high rocks in alarm; food is insects sometimes caught in flight (Farkas 1971). Display-flights are performed from the highest available rock-peaks, the song being loud, clear, attractive; territories may be as close as 200 m and the species is probably double-brooded or else a late summer breeder (Farkas 1971). In winter, some birds are found in dry riverbeds, rocky

473

canyons, hill slopes with huge boulders, all with scattered bushes and trees (Farkas 1971); the birds on wires by the roadside in dry forest at Zombitsy were also presumably wintering (D. A. Turner *in litt.* 1983).

Threats None is known, but the population could prove to be extremely low and restricted.

Conservation Measures Taken The Isalo massif is protected as a national park (Andriamampianina 1981). It is to be noted that the original authority did not collect any new specimens but used one of the two old skins for the type (Farkas 1971).

Conservation Measures Proposed Studies are needed to determine the extent of this species's breeding and wintering range, undertaken in the course of other fieldwork in the general region of and at increasing distances from the Isalo massif.

Remarks Although treated as a race of the "Madagascar Rockthrush" *Pseudocossyphus imerinus* (Milon *et al.* 1973), the status of Benson's Rockthrush as a valid species has been reaffirmed (see Benson *et al.* 1977). The map in Farkas (1971) shows "Antinosy [*sic*] County" in the far south of Madagascar; however, maps in Deschamps (1960) also show that the Antanosy people occupied and still occupy the extreme south-east part of southern Madagascar, south and east of the area shown by Farkas. While it is still possible that Benson's Rockthrush occurs in the southern area shaded by Farkas (1971), e.g. in the Ivakoany massif, the maps in Deschamps (1960) show an area of south-west Madagascar, across the Onilahy River at the southernmost end of the Isalo massif, colonised by "Antanosy émigrés", and this seems more likely to be the type-locality of the species (the "Cy" on the type's specimen-label probably signifies "country" rather than the assumed "County", hence something less institutionalised and fixed). Moreover, of 11 gazetteered localities under the name "Ankarefo" ("Ankarefu" is not listed) in Office of Geography (1955), only one falls into either area of Antanosy people as marked by Deschamps, this being just north of Betroka at 23°06'S 46°06'E, some 100 km east of the Isalo massif.

References

Andriamampianina J. (1981) Les réserves naturelles et la protection de la nature à Madagascar. Pp. 105-111 in P. Oberlé, ed. *Madagascar, un sanctuaire de la nature*. Paris: Lechevalier.

Benson, C. W., Colebrook-Robjent, J. F. R. and Williams, A. (1977) Contribution à l'ornithologie de Madagascar. *Oiseau et R.F.O.* 47: 41-64.

Deschamps, H. (1960) *Histoire de Madagascar*. Paris: Berger-Levrault.

Farkas, T. (1971) *Monticola bensoni*, a new species from south-western Madagascar. *Ostrich* Suppl. 9: 83-90.

Forbes-Watson, A. D., Turner, D. A. and Keith, G. S. (1973) Report on bird preservation in Madagascar, part 3, Appendix I. Proposed list of protected Madagascar birds. Report to ICBP, unpublished.

Milon, P., Petter, J.-J. and Randrianasolo, G. (1973) *Faune de Madagascar, 35. Oiseaux*. Tananarive and Paris: ORSTOM and CRNS.

Office of Geography (1955) *Gazetteer no. 2. Madagascar, Réunion and the Comoro Islands*. Washington, D.C.: Department of the Interior.

FOREST GROUND-THRUSH   RARE

Turdus oberlaenderi (Sassi, 1914)

Order PASSERIFORMES   Family MUSCICAPIDAE
                                                   Subfamily TURDINAE

Summary This ground-thrush is known only from a few localities in low and middle altitude forest in eastern Zaire and from the Bwamba Forest in western Uganda (where it is possibly now extinct). There is little recent information on its status.

Distribution The Forest Ground-thrush is restricted to a few places in eastern Zaire and the Bwamba forest in Uganda (where it may no longer occur). It was discovered in 1910 when two specimens were collected in the Ituri Forest between Beni and Mawambi, in eastern Zaire (Sassi 1914,1915,1916). In 1925 a bird was taken at Bondo Mabe, near Arebi, just south of Watsa on the northern edge of the Ituri Forest (Schouteden 1936,1963). Two specimens were collected in the early 1950s in the Semliki valley to the west of Mount Rwenzori, one at Biangolo and one from Muntule on Mount Hoyo (Prigogine 1965,1980a). The only other records from Zaire are five specimens collected in the low and middle altitude forests on the western slopes of the Itombwe Mountains (Prigogine 1971,1978). One of these specimens was collected at Kakanda at 1,240 m in 1956, two at Kamituga in 1966, and two at Nyamupe at 1,420 m in 1970 (Prigogine 1971,1978, A. Prigogine *in litt.* 1983; specimens in MRAC: SNS). In Uganda the species has been recorded from the Bwamba Forest on the east side of the Semliki valley, all six specimens being collected in July (Friedmann and Williams 1968,1971, Keith 1968, Keith and Twomey 1968). One of these was collected in 1960 (Keith and Twomey 1968), four in 1963 (Keith 1968) and one at 700 m at Ntandi in 1967 (Friedmann and Williams 1968,1971). The fact that all these birds were collected in the same month suggests that the species makes small-scale migratory movements along the east of its range. The species is restricted to low and middle altitudes (Prigogine 1980a, in press). In the Rwenzori/Semliki area it ranges from 700 to 1,300 m and in the Itombwe Mountains from 1,080 to 1,420 m (Prigogine 1980a,b).

Population Numbers are not known. The small number of specimens collected is an indication that it is rare.

Ecology All records of this species have been from lowland and transition forest (Keith 1968, Prigogine 1971,1980b, in press). In Bwamba Forest the birds have been found on the forest floor in big "ironwood" stands where the undergrowth is fairly open, avoiding the denser areas of tangled secondary growth and singing from the mid-stratum, 7-10 m above the ground (Keith 1968). In the Itombwe Mountains fledglings have been found in March and September (Prigogine 1971,1978). The food consists of slugs and caterpillars (Prigogine 1978). The species is sympatric with the related Orange Ground-thrush *Turdus gurneyi* in Itombwe Forest (Prigogine 1965,1980a).

476

Threats This species is presumably declining due to forest clearance. The Bwamba Forest in western Uganda has already been largely destroyed (S. K. Eltringham pers. comm. 1982, K. D. Bishop pers. comm. 1983) and so this species might now be endemic to Zaire. Forest clearance was also noted as taking place around Oisha, 24 km north of Beni, in 1983, well within the range of this species (A. Prigogine *in litt.* 1983). There is a danger of increased clearance in the Itombwe Mountains since Kamituga (from where this species has been collected) has become an important mining centre, thus increasing the possibility of the area being opened up for larger-scale economic exploitation (Prigogine in press).

Conservation Measures Taken This species occurs in the Virunga National Park on the west bank of the Semliki valley but none of the other localities in which it occurs is protected.

Conservation Measures Proposed It is hoped that the northern part of the Virunga National Park will be extended westwards to include the eastern part of the Ituri Forest (Prigogine in press). A preliminary conservation plan for the forests of the Itombwe Mountains has been prepared (Prigogine in press). It is hoped that this plan will be worked out in detail and implemented by the Zairean government.

Remarks The Ituri Forest is important for three other threatened bird species (see Remarks under Nahan's Francolin *Francolinus nahani*). The forests of the Itombwe Mountains are important for six other threatened bird species (see Remarks under Schouteden's Swift *Schoutedenapus schoutedeni*).

References

Friedmann, H. and Williams, J. G. (1968) Notable records of rare and little-known birds from western Uganda. *Rev. Zool. Bot. Afr.* 77: 11-36.

Friedmann, H. and Williams, J. G. (1971) The birds of the lowlands of Bwamba, Toro Province, Uganda. *Los Angeles County Mus. Contrib. Sci.* 211.

Keith, S. (1968) Notes on birds of East Africa, including additions to the avifauna. *Amer. Mus. Novit.* 2321.

Keith, S. and Twomey, A. (1968) New distributional records of some East African birds. *Ibis* 110: 537-548.

Prigogine, A. (1965) Notes sur les *Geokichla* de la République du Congo. *Rev. Zool. Bot. Afr.* 71: 230-244.

Prigogine, A. (1971) Les oiseaux de l'Itombwe et de son hinterland. Volume 1. *Ann. Mus. Roy. Afr. Centr.* 8°, Sci. Zool. 185: 1-298.

Prigogine, A. (1978) Les oiseaux de l'Itombwe et de son hinterland. Volume 2. *Ann. Mus. Roy. Afr. Centr.* 8°, Sci. Zool. 223: 1-134.

Prigogine, A. (1980a) Etude de quelques contacts secondaires au Zaire oriental. *Gerfaut* 70: 305-384.

Prigogine, A. (1980b) The altitudinal distribution of the avifauna in the Itombwe Forest (Zaire). *Proc. IV Pan-Afr. Orn. Congr.*: 169-184.

Prigogine, A. (in press) The conservation of the avifauna of the forests of the Albertine Rift. *Proceedings of the ICBP Tropical Forest Bird Symposium, 1982.*

Sassi, M. (1914) Einige neue Formen der innerafrikanischen Ornis aus der Kollektion Grauer. *Anz. K. Akad. Wiss. Wien* 51: 308-312.

Sassi, M. (1915) Einige neue Formen der innerafrikanischen Ornis aus der Kollektion Grauer. *J. Orn.* 63: 112-118.

Sassi, M. (1916) Beitrag zur Ornis Zentralafrikas. *Ann. k. k. Naturh. Hofmus. Wien* 30: 239-306.

Schouteden, H. (1936) Contribution à la faune ornithologique du Nord-Est Congo Belge. *Ann. Mus. Roy. Congo Belge* Zool. Ser. 4, 1: 41-156.

Schouteden, H. (1963) La faune ornithologique des districts du Bas-Uele et du Haut-Uele. *Doc. Zool. Mus. Roy. Afr. Centr.* 4.

KIBALE GROUND-THRUSH   INDETERMINATE
Turdus kibalensis (Prigogine, 1978)

Order PASSERIFORMES   Family MUSCICAPIDAE
                                                              Subfamily TURDINAE

Summary Known only from Kibale Forest, western Uganda, and not reported since its discovery despite continuing biological fieldwork there, this ground-thrush may now be threatened by loss of mature forest in Kibale, which has been substantial over the past three decades.

Distribution The Kibale Ground-thrush is only known from Kibale Forest, western Uganda. Two adult males were collected in 1966 at 1,525 m on the edge of the Kibale Forest near Fort Portal (Prigogine 1978, D. A. Turner *in litt.* 1983). The species either has a very restricted distribution within Kibale or occurs at very low densities, since biologists' bird-lists, representing more than 22 man-years of fieldwork in Kibale dating back to 1970, include all the secretive, ground-dwelling Turdinae known from Kibale except any ground-thrushes (J. P. Skorupa *in litt.* 1982). That it is of seasonal occurrence in Kibale requires consideration (the specimens collected were in non-breeding state: Friedmann and Williams 1968), but this is regarded as improbable (J. P. Skorupa *in litt.* 1982).

Population Numbers are not known, though the evidence given above suggests that it is a very low density species.

Ecology In the original description it was considered a montane species, apparently because certain other typically montane species inhabit Kibale (Prigogine 1978); however, this need not be so since a good number of typically lowland bird species also occur in the forest (J. P. Skorupa *in litt.* 1982). The two specimens were collected in a patch of thick secondary forest and were together in the same mist-net (D. A. Turner *in litt.* 1983).

Threats Approximately the northern third of Kibale has been selectively felled for timber (Struhsaker 1972), and approximately the southern third has been lost to agricultural encroachment (Struhsaker 1981), so that only c. 185 km^2 of forest remain intact (J. P. Skorupa *in litt.* 1982). However, owing to altitudinal, edaphic and historical factors, on average only 60% of any given area within Kibale consists of high forest (Wing and Buss 1970). Since the only two specimens were collected in secondary forest it is possible that the species can withstand some forest exploitation.

Conservation Measures Taken Reserve status conferred in 1932 established sole government rights to exploit timber in Kibale; the reserve covers 550 km^2 of land but, as noted under Threats, undisturbed forest currently exists over only 185 km^2 (Kingston 1967, J. P. Skorupa *in litt.* 1982). However, within this latter area a nature reserve now covers 60 km^2 and is protected from all human interference other than paths for (non-experimental) scientific research (Kingston

1967, Struhsaker 1972, J. P. Skorupa *in litt.* 1982). NYZS has sponsored major project work in Kibale Forest (see Struhsaker 1972).

Conservation Measures Proposed Fieldwork is needed to confirm the survival of this species and to provide information on its status, distribution and ecology. Fuller protection of all 185 km² of undisturbed forest in Kibale is greatly needed.

Remarks Although not a highly distinctive species (Prigogine 1978, D. A. Turner *in litt.* 1983), its restriction to Kibale is a major consideration in the case for greater safeguards on the forest, which has been identified as one of the five most important forests for wildlife in Uganda (Kingdon 1973). Since 1970, when Kibale's avifauna was considered well known (Friedmann and Williams 1970), over 80 bird species have been added to the forest's list, which in 1982 stood at c. 290 (J. P. Skorupa *in litt.* 1982).

References

Friedmann, H. and Williams, J. G. (1968) Notable records of rare or little-known birds from western Uganda. *Rev. Zool. Bot. Afr.* 77: 11-36.

Friedmann, H. and Williams, J. G. (1970) Additions to the known avifauna of the Bugoma, Kibale and Impenetrable Forests, West Uganda. *Los Angeles County Mus. Contrib. Sci.* 198.

Kingdon, J. (1973) Endemic mammals and birds of western Uganda: measuring Uganda's wealth and a plea for supra-economic values. *Uganda J.* 37: 1-7.

Kingston, B. (1967) Working plan for Kibale and Itwara Central Forest Reserves, Toro District, Uganda. Entebbe: Uganda Forest Department.

Prigogine, A. (1978) A new ground-thrush from Africa. *Gerfaut* 68: 482-492.

Struhsaker, T. T. (1972) Rain-forest conservation in Africa. *Primates* 13: 103-109.

Struhsaker, T. T. (1981) Forest and primate conservation in East Africa. *Afr. J. Ecol.* 19: 99-114.

Wing, L. D. and Buss, I. O. (1970) *Elephants and forests.* Washington D.C.: Wildlife Society (Wildlife Monographs no. 19).

SPOTTED GROUND-THRUSH   RARE
Turdus fischeri Hellmayr, 1901

Order PASSERIFORMES   Family MUSCICAPIDAE
                                                    Subfamily TURDINAE

Summary A remarkably elusive and very poorly known thrush of the forest floor, requiring deep shade and deep leaf-litter, this relict species has one of the most extraordinary distributions of any African bird. Its two migratory coastal subspecies (*fischeri* in East Africa and *natalicus* in South Africa) have been reported as fairly common at a very few localities each; of the two resident inland subspecies, *belcheri* is known from only four localities in Malawi and numbers 30-40 pairs, *maxis* by a single specimen from southernmost Sudan, while another single specimen of uncertain racial affinities is known from Zaire. Despite recent forest protection in South Africa, the forest habitats of all populations are vulnerable and in some cases already disappearing, yet the breeding grounds of nominate *fischeri* remain completely unknown.

Distribution The Spotted Ground-thrush is evidently a relict species (Clancey 1955a). The small nominate *fischeri* is known only as a non-breeding visitor (late March to late November, mainly May to October) to coastal forests in Kenya, showing clear preference for the tiny remaining patches of coral rag forest at Gede Ruins, Diani (= Jadini) and Shimoni, with a much smaller but regular presence in Sokoke Forest (Britton and Rathbun 1978, Britton 1980, Britton *et al.* 1980, J. G. Williams *in litt.* 1983). There are a few records (some ancient) from other coastal forests, Lamu, Kipini, Mambrui, Bamburi and most recently Mrima (Britton 1980, Britton *et al.* 1980). On 27 April 1982 a bird was reported from Kibwezi Forest, well inland at 2°26'S 37°53'E (Cunningham-van Someren 1982), but this record should perhaps be considered provisional as it is currently unverified. There are just two records from coastal Tanzania, Pangani on 21 August 1883 (Hellmayer 1901), Pugu Hills in the 1970s (SNS; both in Britton 1980); the species appears to be absent from the Usambara and Uluguru foothills (SNS). Two remarkable further records from south-western Tanzania, at Ufipa (8°00'S 31°30'E) and Mbeya (8°54'S 33°27'E) in August 1938, have recently come to light (Cunningham-van Someren 1980; coordinates for these – and all other East African – sites in Britton 1980); these two records are not, however, backed by extant specimens (the localities are within the range of the very similar Ground-scraper Thrush *Turdus litsipsirupa*) and it is best to consider them provisional. If valid they probably refer to birds racially closer to those from Malawi and southern Zaire (see below). Where nominate *fischeri* breeds is unknown, but coastal forests in northern Mozambique are proposed as perhaps the likeliest possibility (C. W. Benson pers. comm. 1982; see also Ecology). The southern form *natalicus* is restricted to patches of coastal forest in eastern South Africa from around East London (Cape Province) north to Lake St.Lucia (Natal) (Clancey 1964, Siegfried *et al.* 1976). There are records of breeding in Natal and KwaZulu north to Ngoye (Umgoye) Forest, November/December (Liversidge 1957, Clancey 1964, I. F. Garland *per* R. J. Dowsett *in litt.* 1982), birds being recorded all year round just south of Durban and in the Mtunzini/Ngoye area (Cyrus and Robson 1980), and breeding in the latter being noted in December 1980 (W. R. J. Dean *in litt.* 1984); nevertheless the bulk of the population apparently breeds in the southern parts of the range below Durban, particularly in the Port St.Johns (Pondoland) region on the Transkei coast (e.g. Mgqeleni and Lusikisiki districts), birds being present from mid-August/September through till around April (though earlier reported resident: Shortridge and Sclater 1904), when most (if not all) migrate north at night (over Durban, with some resulting casualties) to the forested coastal districts of Natal from Durban north to KwaZulu for the austral winter (Roberts 1926, Benson 1950, Chiazzari 1952, Clancey 1955a,b,1957a,b, Quickelberge 1969, Brooke in press, specimen in ZFMK: NJC). There are older records from as far south as Port Elizabeth (Benson 1950) but these are now regarded as unacceptable (Brooke in press) and in any case with the destruction of coastal forests from the eastern Cape Province northwards the species's range has (or would have) presumably contracted accordingly (Siegfried *et al.* 1976): but although records from around East London are reported as being in winter and regarded as possibly of southward-moving birds from Transkei rather than ones locally breeding (Brooke in press), one specimen from Gonubie by East London was obtained on 6 August 1970, and another at Mazeppa Bay (32°28'S 28°40'E on TSO 1965) on 18 September 1970, with a sight record in Dwesa Forest (north-east of Mazeppa Bay) in September 1977 (C. J. Vernon *per* R. W. Markham *in litt.* 1983). The isolated inland form *belcheri* is now known from Mounts Soche, Thyolo, Lisau (or Chiradzulu) and (the south-east slopes of) Mulanje (up to at least 1,500 m) in southern Malawi; apart from perhaps local vertical movements, the population would appear probably resident, although wing-measurements show a close affinity with migratory *natalicus*, suggesting the separation of the two forms may be recent (Benson 1950,1952, Nikolaus 1982, R. J. Dowsett *in litt.* 1982,1983). Neighbouring mountains in Mozambique may also hold *belcheri* (Benson 1952). A single bird collected at Lusinga, 8°56'S 27°12'E, at 1,700 m in Upemba National Park, Zaire, 7 October 1973, was considered likely to represent a population breeding there (Benson and Benson 1975); although apparently too close to *belcheri* to warrant separation (Benson and Benson 1975), its wing measurements are distinct (Nikolaus 1982). The newly discovered form *maxis* is known from a single specimen collected at 1,250 m in October 1979 in the Lotti Forest on the south-western slopes of the Imatong Mountains, South Sudan; on available evidence, it probably breeds at the start of the rains in April and is sedentary, but undertakes local seasonal vertical movements (Nikolaus 1982).

Population Despite two sight records (Benson 1950,1954), nominate *fischeri* was considered probably extinct in the mid-1950s (Mackworth-Praed and Grant 1955). Its survival was conclusively established in 1964 (Keith and Twomey 1968). However, it remains extremely rare and is only seasonally common at three sites (see above): although in one study (Britton and Rathbun 1978) it was probably the third and in another (Bennun 1983) the second most numerous bird on the forest floor at Gede, May to October, the area involved is only 44 ha so that an estimated density there of 1.5-2 birds per ha, 1983, indicated a population of only 60-80 birds, and the other two forests are comparably tiny (Bennun 1983; also

Kelsey and Langton 1984). Sokoke Forest still covers nearly 40,000 ha, however, and so may conceivably support a sizeable population of birds living at a much lower density (Bennun 1983). Investigations in the 1950s indicated that the South African form *natalicus*, though never plentiful (Shortridge and Sclater 1904, Winterbottom and Hare 1947), had been under-recorded and was apparently still present in reasonable numbers in both summer and winter habitats, and in no danger of extinction (Benson 1950, Clancey 1955a,b). A later study concluded that it was still safe in its Pondoland breeding area, but that it was possibly in decline as forest disturbance and destruction would be shrinking its range (Quickelberge 1969). The following year (1970) it was described as rare in coastal forest at Port St.Johns, Pondoland (McCulloch *et al.* 1970). In 1976 no evidence for a decline could be shown and the *natalicus* population was thought perhaps the only viable one remaining (Siegfried *et al.* 1976). *T. f. belcheri* was considered possibly extinct when first described (Benson 1950), but recent sightings suggest that total numbers are in the order of 30-40 pairs (R. J. Dowsett *in litt.* 1982,1983). Despite three years' fieldwork in the Imatongs, *maxis* was only found once and must be rare at best (Nikolaus 1982).

Ecology Birds inhabit the less disturbed parts of luxuriant moist evergreen forest, not much above sea-level in South Africa but at c. 1,300-1,600 m in Malawi (Quickelberge 1969, R. J. Dowsett *in litt.* 1982,1983). On their breeding grounds, Pondoland, they are confined purely to larger forests and are still further restricted within each, favouring the narrow strips on either side of small streams at the bottom of valleys and the basal portions of the steep adjoining slopes, these being most deeply shaded with the thickest and dampest leaf-litter, and with only sparse undergrowth: birds there are usually solitary or in pairs, keeping to darker parts of the forest on the ground or in the lower branches of leafy trees; they are always inconspicuous, though delivering a rich song at dawn and dusk in the upper branches (Chiazzari 1952). Migratory populations may evidently use moist bushland and thicket (*natalicus* even turning up in shady gardens) at least on passage (Clancey 1964, Lawson 1971, Britton 1980, Brooke in press), and some *natalicus* are known to winter in coastal dune-forest at Mtunzini (KwaZulu) (Garland 1967); otherwise they appear to winter in taller forests on the coast (Clancey 1964, Oatley 1966), which for nominate *fischeri* are preferentially on coral rag (Britton 1980). The Kenyan coral rag forests (Gede, Diani, Shimoni) "lack the thick and diverse undergrowth layer characteristic of lowland rain forest in coastal Kenya" (Britton *et al.* 1980), and it is this factor (not the three possible explanations offered in Britton and Rathbun 1978) that is considered to explain the relatively high densities of birds they hold (Bennun 1983): in Gede (as in Pondoland) birds showed a distinct preference for more deeply shaded areas with thicker leaf-litter and more open understorey, though apparently utilising adjacent denser undergrowth as refuges (Bennun 1983; also Kelsey and Langton 1984). Birds wintering at Gede moved and foraged within a very circumscribed home range, two of which were calculated as 1,360 m^2 and 1,374 m^2 (Bennun 1983); although no territorialism was observed in this study, squabbling between two birds when one approached another feeding on ants has been witnessed at Diani, on a day when all observations were somewhat anomalously made outside the forest proper, e.g. on leaf-strewn roads and waste ground (Burrell *et al.* 1976). Birds forage in typical thrush fashion, scratching up the leaves and stabbing at discovered prey with the bill (Chiazzari 1952, Bennun 1983). Food is known from stomach-contents to include seeds, fruit, grubs, insects and small millipedes *Prionopetalum* (Chiazzari 1952, Britton and Rathbun 1978, Britton and Zimmerman 1979); land-molluscs are also named (Clancey 1964). Birds at Gede were solitary feeders and appeared to avoid ant-columns or bird parties foraging at them (Bennun 1983), yet a century earlier birds in forest at Kipini were frequently in pairs and particularly noted to keep near ant nests (Fischer 1879). Birds at Gede were largely silent (Bennun 1983) but those at Kipini sang, rarely (Fischer 1879), as do those at Diani, sometimes in response to (but with a voice distinct from) tape-recordings of *natalicus* (Kelsey and Langton 1984). Breeding occurs in November/January, South Africa, clutch-size being three and birds probably single-brooded (Roberts 1926, Liversidge 1957, Brooke in press); one nest was 1.5 m up in the coppiced stump of a small forest tree (W. R. J. Dean *in litt.* 1984). In Malawi, the only nest found held two eggs, November (Benson 1950). Data on migration are given under Distribution; however, in support of the possibility that nominate *fischeri* winters in northern Mozambique it has been pointed out that, while birds are rainy season visitors to coastal Kenya (the south-east monsoon extending from April to November), the period of maximum rainfall (80% of annual total) in northern Mozambique is from November to March (Bennun 1983). The elusiveness of the species is partly attributable to its habit of remaining stock-still when disturbed, on one occasion doing so for six minutes (Bennun 1983).

Threats In Kenya, the coral rag forests utilised by the species are so small in area that they must be considered permanently at risk: the future of Diani seems particularly insecure (Kelsey and Langton 1984). Inability in 1983 to find more than one subadult bird of this species has led to the speculation that breeding success in recent years has been reduced, perhaps by habitat destruction on the unknown breeding grounds (Bennun 1983, Kelsey and Langton 1984). In the Sokoke Forest logging is taking place even within the supposedly inviolate nature reserve (Cunningham-van Someren 1981-1982, Kelsey and Langton 1984); for further details see Threats under Sokoke Scops Owl *Otus ireneae*. Although remaining forests in Pondoland were relatively undisturbed over a decade ago (Quickelberge 1969), the long-term future of such forests in parts of South Africa must remain a matter of concern, as high human population levels in the "homelands" exert increasing pressure: in coastal Natal and KwaZulu the growing of sugar-cane has resulted in the destruction of large areas of coastal forest (R. J. Dowsett *in litt.* 1982,1983). This was already happening in the early 1950s around Durban (Chiazzari 1952), where *natalicus* was reported formerly to have bred (Liversidge 1957, Moreau 1966, Lawson 1971), the lights of the city of Durban itself providing a considerable distraction to migrating birds, which are frequently killed in collisions (Clancey 1955a,1957a, Brooke in press). To the south-west, the future of forests around East London and King William's Town has been regarded as hopeless, owing to the pressure of local exploitation (Poduschka 1980,1982). In Malawi three of the four localities for *belcheri* are in forests that are under very heavy pressure from clearing for firewood and agriculture (maize gardens), and prospects for their survival are very poor, while the fourth, Mount Lisau (near the heavily populated Chiradzulu), is likely to come under such pressure in the near future (Dowsett 1981, R. J. Dowsett *in litt.* 1982,1983). Forest destruction in the Imatongs appears such that, in the absence of protective measures, *maxis* could become extinct before anything further is learned about it (Nikolaus 1982).

Conservation Measures Taken In Natal, a Wildlife Society of Southern Africa campaign has resulted in most remnant coastal dune and coastal escarpment forests becoming (and the remainder soon to become) nature conservation areas, while on the Transkei coast four nature reserves – Mkambati (at Umtentu), Mount Thesiger (by Port St.Johns), Hluleka (500 ha, south of Port St.Johns) and Dwesa (4,000 ha, still further south) – have been established and afford the species complete protection, with a projected Pondoland Coast National Park to cover the region between Mount Thesiger and Mkambati (K. H. Cooper *in litt.* 1983; also WSSA 1977, van Rensburg 1982). A suggestion that census-work, ecological studies and a ringing project on nominate *fischeri* at Gede would be feasible and worthwhile (Collar 1982) has been followed up (Bennun 1983) as part of a major initiative to assess and promote the conservation of the adjacent Sokoke Forest, where the species also occurs (see Kelsey and Langton 1984). There is a 43 km² nature reserve within the forest reserve at Sokoke in which no cutting or exploitation is permitted (Britton and Zimmerman 1979), though these regulations are not being observed (Cunningham-van Someren 1981-1982, Kelsey and Langton 1984). The anticipated population in Zaire presumably permanently inhabits the Upemba National Park (see Distribution).

Conservation Measures Proposed A survey of the distribution and numerical status of *natalicus* has been called for (Siegfried *et al.* 1976) but appears not yet to have been undertaken. Continuation of the census-work, ecological studies, and ringing project to determine age-structure and mortality in nominate *fischeri* is needed at Gede, Kenya; it is most desirable that the breeding area(s) of this race are soon discovered. Details of recommendations for the Sokoke Forest are given in Conservation Measures Proposed under Sokoke Scops Owl. Outside South Africa, (and excluding Zaire), the patches of forest where the thrush is known to occur are extremely small and its survival depends on the permanent and complete conservation of forests at Mounts Thyolo, Lisau, Mulanje and Soche (Malawi), at Gede, Diani, Shimoni, Sokoke and Mrima (Kenya), and on the Imatong Mountains (South Sudan), whose combined total area (excluding Sokoke) is still only a few km²; the biological importance of some of these areas is indicated below.

Remarks The forest patches referred to in the previous sentence are remarkable for holding a wide variety of rare and endemic wildlife: threatened birds for which the survival of Sokoke Forest is crucial are listed in Remarks under Sokoke Scops Owl, and those dependent on the montane forests of southern Malawi in Remarks under Thyolo Alethe *Alethe choloensis*, while perhaps the most remarkable threatened animal with which the Spotted Ground-thrush apparently shares its breeding habitat in Pondoland and southward is the giant golden mole

Chrysospalax trevelyani (see Poduschka 1980,1982). It should be noted that *T. fischeri* also features in the literature as *Geokichla guttata*, *Zoothera guttata* and *Psophocichla guttata*, and under the vernacular names "Natal Thrush" and "Spotted Forest Thrush".

References

Bennun, L. (1983) The Spotted Ground Thrush at Gedi in coastal Kenya. University of Cambridge (Zoology) Long Vacation Project (undergraduate dissertation). Unpublished manuscript.

Benson, C. W. (1950) Some notes on the Spotted Forest Thrush *Turdus fischeri*. *Ostrich* 21: 58-61.

Benson, C. W. (1952) A further note on the Spotted Forest Thrush *Turdus fischeri*. *Ostrich* 23: 48.

Benson, C. W. (1954) The status of *Turdus fischeri belcheri* Benson, "Ostrich", 1950, p. 58. *Bull. Brit. Orn. Club* 74: 88-90.

Benson, C. W. and Benson, F. M. (1975) Studies of some Malawi birds. *Arnoldia (Rhod.)* 7(32).

Britton, P. L. ed. (1980) *Birds of East Africa: their habitat, status and distribution*. Nairobi: EANHS.

Britton, P. L. and Rathbun, G. B. (1978) Two migratory thrushes and the African Pitta in coastal Kenya. *Scopus* 2: 11-17.

Britton, P. L. and Zimmerman, D. A. (1979) The avifauna of Sokoke Forest, Kenya. *J. E. Afr. Nat. Hist. Soc. and Natn. Mus.* no. 169.

Britton, P. L., Britton, H. A. and Coverdale, M. A. C. (1980) The avifauna of Mrima hill, south Kenya coast. *Scopus* 4: 73-78.

Britton, P. L., Stuart, S. N. and Turner, D. A. (in press) East African endangered species. *Proc. V Pan-Afr. orn. Congr.*

Brooke, R. K. (in press) *The rare and vulnerable birds of South Africa*.

Burrell, J. H., Abel, R. and Abel, Mrs (1976) A not so "extinct" thrush on the Kenya coast. *EANHS Bull.* March/April: 32-33.

Chiazzari, W. L. (1952) Some observations on the Natal Spotted Forest Thrush *Turdus fischeri natalicus*. *Ostrich* 23: 49-50.

Clancey, P. A. (1955a) Further as to the present status of (*Turdus fischeri natalicus*) [*sic*]. *Ostrich* 26: 164-165.

Clancey, P. A. (1955b) Results of the Durban Museum ornithological expedition to Pondoland in August, 1954. *Durban Mus. Novit.* 4(13): 187-214.

Clancey, P. A. (1957a) Further records of the Spotted Thrush being killed on migration. *Ostrich* 28: 126-127.

Clancey, P. A. (1957b) Some further records of the Spotted Thrush on migration. *Ostrich* 28: 237.

Clancey, P. A. (1964) *The birds of Natal and Zululand*. Edinburgh and London: Oliver and Boyd.

Collar, N. J. (1982) Extracts from the red data book for the birds of Africa and associated islands. Cambridge: ICBP, unpublished.

Cunningham-van Someren, G. R. ed. (1980) *National Museum of Kenya Division of Natural Sciences, Department of Ornithology Newsletter* no. 50 (May): 106.

Cunningham-van Someren, G. R. ed. (1981-1982) *National Museum of Kenya, Department of Ornithology Museum Avifauna News*: 19,34,63,72.

Cunningham-van Someren, G. R. ed. (1982) *National Museum of Kenya, Department of Ornithology Museum Avifauna News* (April): 49,51.

Cyrus, D. and Robson, N. (1980) *Bird atlas of Natal*. Pietermaritzburg: University of Natal Press.

Dowsett, R. J. (1981) The past and present distribution of montane birds in Malawi. *Nyala* 7: 25-45.

Fischer, G. A. (1879) Briefliche Reiseberichte aus Ost-Afrika. IV. *J. Orn.* 27: 275-304.

Garland, I. F. (1967) List of birds on the farm Twinstreams, Mtunzini District, Zululand. *S. Afr. Avifauna Ser.* no. 46.

Hellmayer [*sic*], E. (1901) Ueber *Turdus guttatus* Vig. *Orn. Monatsber.* 9: 53-54.

Keith, S. and Twomey, A. (1968) New distributional records for some East African birds. *Ibis* 110: 537-548.

Kelsey, M. G. and Langton, T. E. S. (1984) The conservation of the Arabuko-Sokoke Forest, Kenya. International Council for Bird Preservation and University of East Anglia. *International Council for Bird Preservation Study Report* no. 4.

Lawson, W. J. (1971) Check list of the birds of Durban. *S. Afr. Avifauna Ser.* no. 73.

Liversidge, R. (1957) A note on the Natal Thrush *Turdus fischeri*. *Ostrich* 28: 179-180.

Mackworth-Praed, C. W. and Grant, C. H. B. (1955) *African handbook of birds*, Series 1. The birds of eastern and north-eastern Africa, 2. London: Longmans, Green and Co.

McCulloch, D., Skead, C. J. and Winterbottom, J. M. (1970) The birds of Port St.Johns. *S. Afr. Avifauna Ser.* no. 71.

Moreau, R. E. (1966) *The bird faunas of Africa and its islands*. London: Academic Press.

Nikolaus, G. (1982) A new race of the Spotted Ground Thrush *Turdus fischeri* from South Sudan. *Bull. Brit. Orn. Club* 102: 45-47.

Oatley, T. B. (1966) Competition and local migration in some African Turdidae. Proc. II Pan-Afr. orn. Congr. *Ostrich* suppl. 6: 409-418.

Poduschka, W. (1980) Notes on the Giant Golden Mole *Chrysospalax trevelyani* Günther, 1875 (Mammalia: Insectivora) and its survival chances. *Z. Säugetierk.* 45: 193-206.

Poduschka, W. (1982) The giant golden mole. *Oryx* 16: 232-234.

Quickelberge, C. D. (1969) Notes on the Spotted Thrush *Turdus fischeri*. *Ostrich* 40: 133-134.

van Rensburg, T. (1982) Conservation in the Transkei. *Environment RSA* 9(11): 1-3.

Roberts, A. (1926) Descriptions of some S. African birds' eggs. *Ann. Transvaal Mus.* 11: 226-244.

Shortridge, G. C. and Sclater, W. L. (1904) On a collection of birds from the neighbourhood of Port St.Johns, in Pondoland. *Ibis* (8)4: 173-208.

Siegfried, W. R., Frost, P. G. H., Cooper, J. and Kemp, A. C. (1976) South African red data book – Aves. Pretoria: South African National Scientific Programmes Report no. 7.

TSO (1965) South Africa 1: 250,000 Topo-cadastral: sheet 3228 Kei Mouth. Pretoria: Government Printer.

Wildlife Society of Southern Africa (1977) A preliminary survey of the Transkei Coast undertaken to identify nature conservation priorities and high density recreation areas. Unpublished.

Winterbottom, J. M. and Hare, H. L. (1947) On the birds of Port St.Johns, Pondoland. *Ostrich* 18: 86-102.

TAITA THRUSH   ENDANGERED
Turdus helleri (Mearns, 1913)

Order PASSERIFORMES   Family MUSCICAPIDAE
                                                       Subfamily TURDINAE

Summary An almost wholly unknown bird, this ground-dwelling forest thrush is apparently confined to the Taita Hills and Mount Kasigau in south-east Kenya. Available habitat in the Taita Hills covers less than 5 km^2 and is under serious threat of destruction.

Distribution The Taita Thrush is confined to natural forest on the Taita Hills and Mount Kasigau in south-east Kenya, with one record from Mount Kilimanjaro c. 100 km to the west. Natural forest on the Taita Hills now covers less than 5 km^2 (Turner 1979, Collins and Clifton in press, Collins and Morris in press) and occurs in just three patches, Mbololo, Ngangao and Ronge, of which only Mbololo is of any extent (4 km^2) and moderately intact (see Threats). Since the Taita Thrush only occurs above 1,500 m (Hall and Moreau 1962) – although the type-specimen was reportedly from 1,200 m (Mearns 1913) – and as the other patches of forest are so small and damaged, it is likely that Mbololo is not only the type-locality (see Mearns 1913) but also now the main locality for the species in the Taita Hills (as stated in Cunningham-van Someren 1981). Birds were, however, seen in Ngangao in 1965 (Vincent 1966-1971), 1973, 1974, 1978 and 1981 (D. A. Turner *in litt.* 1984). The Taita Thrush has also been recorded from Mount Kasigau, south-east of the Taita Hills (J. G. Williams *in litt.* 1984). A bird was reported from the lower slopes of Mount Kilimanjaro, Tanzania (c. 2,000 m) on 20 February 1956 (Bednall 1958), though this was probably "a straggler" (Hall and Moreau 1962) or a mistaken identification (H. Grossmann pers. comm. 1984) but see Remarks.

Population Numbers are unknown. On the Taita Hills the bird has been called "uncommon" (Britton 1980), or "in fairly small numbers" (D. A. Turner *in litt.* 1984), this presumably referring to the density at which it occurs and not merely the restriction of its range. In 1953 two or three birds were seen on Mbololo, and in 1965 several – supposedly about eight – were seen on Ngangao (Vincent 1966-1971). On Mount Kasigau it is reported to be common (J. G. Williams *in litt.* 1984).

Ecology The species is described as a bird of ground-stratum of the forest interior (Britton 1980) where it forages in leaf litter (D. A. Turner *in litt.* 1984). The specimen seen on Kilimanjaro was observed to fly down from a banana tree to a vegetable patch where it pecked at the ground in typical thrush *Turdus* fashion (Bednall 1958). Three specimens in BMNH, collected in November (1937) at 1,600 to 1,725 m, were all in breeding condition (SNS). The type-specimen at 1,200 m was also collected in November (1911) (Mearns 1913). Clutch-size is expected to be 2-3 (Vincent 1966-1971).

Threats The Taita Hills support an ever-increasing human population (Turner 1979, Collins and Clifton in press); the steep slopes were originally completely forested but have now mostly been cleared for fuel and agriculture (Collins and Morris in press). Under Forest Department procedures, natural areas gazetted as "National Forest" are ones that can be felled and re-planted with exotics (Collins and Clifton in press): one important area of natural forest, Chawia (which included the forests on Bura Bluff), has been lost in the past 20 years in this way (Collins and Clifton in press, Collins and Morris in press), and of the three remaining areas two, Mbololo and Ngangao (0.5 km²), are listed for early gazetting as National Forests (Collins and Clifton in press) and the third, Ronge, was long since cut over so that now only 20% of its 3 km² is natural forest (Collins and Clifton in press). Both Mbololo and Ngangao are under constant pressure for building timber and firewood (Collins and Clifton in press, Collins and Morris in press). The forest on Mount Kasigau is very inaccessible and might, therefore, be under little immediate threat (J. G. Williams *in litt.* 1984).

Conservation Measures Taken None is known.

Conservation Measures Proposed Nothing has yet been done to conserve natural forest on the Taita Hills (Collins and Morris in press). Mbololo and Ngangao "should now be set aside as immutable and fully protected sanctuaries" (Collins and Clifton in press; also Cunningham-van Someren 1982): both forests currently stabilise soils and their destruction would aggravate the already serious problem of erosion in the Taita Hills, while their area is too insignificant and the terrain too steep to be of value in the production of commercial timber, so if further plantation is considered important it should be concentrated on the deforested and derelict lands at lower altitudes (Collins and Clifton in press). The Forest Department currently manages both Ngangao and Mbololo and is in the process of gazetting them as National Forests (Collins and Morris in press). Although a small nature reserve is planned for Mbololo, gazetting offers no guarantee of legal protection (Collins and Morris in press). A comprehensive faunal survey of the remaining natural forests on the Taita Hills is desirable to reaffirm their known biological uniqueness (see Remarks) and an educational programme for the local people merits consideration. A study to determine the population, ecology and conservation needs of the Taita Thrush is urgent in view of the continuing erosion of its habitat, but should if possible form part of the wider faunal survey suggested above. A survey of the species on Mount Kasigau to confirm its status there is also required.

Remarks The remaining natural forest on the Taita Hills holds a remarkably rich endemic fauna and flora, including (at species level) the back-fanged colubrid snake *Amblyodipsas teitana*, the caecilian *Afrocaecilia teitana*, the Taita glider butterfly *Cymothoe teita*, the Taita African violet *Saintpaulia teitensis* and the tree *Memecylon teitense* (for further taxa and information, see Cunningham-van Someren 1982, Collins and Clifton in press, Collins and Morris in press). Two incipient bird species occur there, the Taita (Bar-throated) Apalis *Apalis (thoracica) fascigularis* and the Taita (Montane) White-eye *Zosterops (poliogaster)*

489

silvanus (see Appendix E). The Taita Thrush has commonly been treated as a melanistic race of the Northern Olive Thrush *Turdus abyssinicus* (e.g. in Britton 1980), but it is believed by some to be sufficiently well marked to be accorded specific status (Hall and Moreau 1962, D. W. Snow pers. comm. 1984); moreover, it is believed to have a very different song, and the case would be complete if it were resident on Kilimanjaro where the Olive Thrush is known to be present (Hall and Moreau 1962). The Kilimanjaro forests have, however, been well explored by ornithologists and its presence there is considered extremely unlikely (H. Grossmann pers. comm. 1984, D. A. Turner *in litt.* 1984).

References

Bednall, D. K. (1958) Heller's Thrush on Kilimanjaro. *J. E. Afr. Nat. Hist. Soc.* 23(2)[no.99]: 17.

Britton, P. L. ed. (1980) *Birds of East Africa: their habitat, status and distribution.* Nairobi: EANHS.

Collins, N. M. and Clifton, M. P. (in press) Threatened wildlife of the Taita Hills. *Swara.*

Collins, N. M. and Morris, M. G. (in press) *The IUCN swallowtail red data book.* Gland, Switzerland: IUCN.

Cunningham-van Someren, G. R. (1981) National Museum of Kenya, Division of Natural Sciences: Conservation Status Report No. 2, Part 1. Avifauna. Unpublished.

Cunningham-van Someren, G. R. (1982) Review of habitat status of some important biotic communities in Kenya. Division of Natural Sciences, National Museum Kenya. Unpublished.

Hall, B. P. and Moreau, R. E. (1962) A study of the rare birds of Africa. *Bull. Brit. Mus. (Nat. Hist.) Zool.* 8: 313-378.

Mearns, E. A. (1913) Descriptions of four new African thrushes of the genera *Planesticus* and *Geocichla*. *Smithsonian Misc. Coll.* 61, no. 10.

Turner, D. A. (1979) Greenbuls of the Taita Hills, S. E. Kenya. *Scopus* 3: 27-28.

Vincent, J. (1966-1971) *Red data book, 2: Aves.* Morges, Switzerland: IUCN.

HINDE'S PIED BABBLER   VULNERABLE
Turdoides hindei (Sharpe, 1900)

Order PASSERIFORMES   Family MUSCICAPIDAE
                                                  Subfamily TIMALIINAE

Summary This species is restricted to a small area of Kenya south and east of Mount Kenya, where it is a bird of secondary vegetation and open woodland on steep-sided valleys and along gullies. There is evidence of a considerable contraction in range during this century.

Distribution Hinde's Pied Babbler, endemic to Kenya, has been recorded from an area of 17,500 km^2 to the south and east of Mount Kenya (Plumb 1979). Since 1971 most records of the species have been from a small area of 1,050 km^2 between Runyenge and Saba Saba, centred on Embu (Plumb 1979). However, there have been several records of the species from the Potha Estate near Machakos (J. G. Williams *in litt.* 1983, Lewis 1984), most recently in 1984 (A. D. Lewis *in litt.* 1984). This locality is 65 km south of the main centre of distribution around Saba Saba and Embu (Lewis 1984). Its distribution seems to be linked to the river systems of the upper Tana (Plumb 1979, Lewis 1984). The apparent contraction of range might not be real as the species is easily overlooked (Lewis 1984), and further exploration might show the species to occur in some sites from which it has not yet been recorded, especially in the little known river valleys south of Mount Kenya (Plumb 1979). Localities from which the species has been collected but in which it might now be absent include Athi River (the type-locality, last recorded in 1900), Ol Donyo Sabuk (Ol Doinyo Sapuk) (last recorded in 1970 despite subsequent exploration), Thika River (last recorded in 1949), the confluence of the Thika and Tana Rivers (last recorded in 1912), Kitui (last recorded in 1961), Ruiru (last recorded in 1956), Nziu River (last recorded in 1932), Chuka (last recorded in 1944), Meru (last recorded in 1944) and Marung'a (Fort Hall) where one group was seen regularly between 1957 and 1964 (Sharpe 1900, van Someren 1922, Friedmann 1930, Plumb 1979, Lewis 1983, A. D. Forbes-Watson pers. comm. 1984); it could, however, survive in the little known areas to the east of its range, such as Kitui and Nziu (Lewis 1984). The species has a fairly narrow altitudinal range, between 1,070 and 1,700 m (Blencowe 1960, Plumb 1979, Lewis 1983).

Population No detailed censuses have been carried out but the species is known to be relatively common within its very restricted area of distribution around Embu (Blencowe 1960, Plumb 1979). It was described as being quite common at Ruiru in the early 1950s and as being common at Kitui in 1960/1961 (Lewis 1983). In 1978 it was known from 23 sites, nearly all of these holding only one party of up to eight birds, making a known population of only 200 birds (W. J. Plumb *in litt.* 1983). However, the species doubtless occurs in many more inaccessible locations, possibly over a wider area than has hitherto been realised (Lewis 1984). This suggests a total population in thousands rather than hundreds.

491

Ecology Hinde's Pied Babbler occurs in river valleys where it prefers secondary growth in which some trees remain, particularly in areas where the alien *Lantana* is established (Plumb 1979, Britton 1980). This habitat preference tends to restrict the species to steep-sided valleys which either defy cultivation or have been allowed to revert to bushy growth (Plumb 1979). It is likely that the species has adapted to the *Lantana* habitat relatively recently, following the clearance of its original habitat on rocky hillsides and valleys, dominated by *Combretum*, *Terminalia*, *Croton*, *Cussonia*, *Cassia* and *Commiphora* (G. R. Cunningham-van Someren *in litt.* 1983). The species has also been recorded, less commonly, in drier open woodland where it frequents bushy streams and gullies in preference to more open areas (Plumb 1979, Lewis 1984). The birds prefer the interior of thickets but sometimes perch in exposed positions on riparian trees for several minutes at a time (Lewis 1984). Birds collected at Ol Donyo Sabuk in 1970 were in acacia bush, though the species may no longer occur there (Plumb 1979, see Distribution). Hinde's Pied Babbler behaves as a typical babbler, occurring in parties of six to eight, which are highly sedentary within a small area (Plumb 1979, D. A. Turner *in litt.* 1983). It has been suggested that this species occurs in isolated groups with little or no interchange between populations in different valleys (Plumb 1979). Considerable inbreeding may occur, hence the occasional occurrence of partial albinism in this species and the wide variation in plumage (Plumb 1979). Birds remain silent for long periods of time though they often make loud babbling calls when on the move (Plumb 1979). When they are skulking and silent they are extremely difficult to detect, which suggests that they are easily overlooked (Lewis 1984, A. D. Lewis *in litt.* 1984). Mutual preening has been observed and birds remain in parties during the breeding season (van Someren 1932, Plumb 1979). There are a few breeding records for February, April and September (van Someren 1932, Blencowe 1960, Plumb 1979). Hinde's Pied Babbler has also been recorded as a host for the Black-and-White Cuckoo *Clamator jacobinus* (Plumb 1979, Lewis 1983).

Threats Inbreeding, if taking place, might result in a reduction in the fertility of the species (Plumb 1979). It is also possible that collecting of specimens has contributed to the contraction of the range (Plumb 1979, W. J. Plumb *in litt.* 1983). However, the main cause of its apparent decline is probably the clearance of *Lantana* habitat for maize cultivation (G. R. Cunningham-van Someren *in litt.* 1983, W. J. Plumb *in litt.* 1983, D. A. Turner *in litt.* 1983). In some areas around Embu, such as Kianyaga, this clearance is proceeding at an alarming rate (D. A. Turner *in litt.* 1983). It is also possible that habitats have been destroyed by rice irrigation schemes and by dams along the Tana River (G. R. Cunningham-van Someren *in litt.* 1983).

Conservation Measures Taken None is known.

Conservation Measures Proposed Further collecting of this species should be prohibited and more work is needed to delimit its range and assess its status more accurately. Efforts should be made to preserve areas of *Lantana* habitat in order to safeguard the species, and a study of its biology is desirable to determine any other factors responsible for its decline.

Remarks It has been suggested that Hinde's Pied Babbler is a hybrid between the Northern Pied Babbler *Turdoides hypoleucos* and the Arrow-marked Babbler *T. jardinei* (Hall and Moreau 1962,1970, Turner 1977). Several studies, however, do not support this contention (van Someren 1932, Plumb 1979, G. R. Cunningham-van Someren *in litt.* 1983, D. A. Turner *in litt.* 1983).

References

Blencowe, E. J. (1960) Hinde's Pied Babbler in Embu District. *J. E. Afr. Nat. Hist. Soc.* 23: 248.

Britton, P. L. ed. (1980) *Birds of East Africa: their habitat, status and distribution.* Nairobi: EANHS.

Friedmann, H. (1930) Birds collected by the Childs Frick expedition to Ethiopia and Kenya Colony. Part 2 – Passeres. *Bull. U. S. Natn. Mus.* 153: 1-506.

Hall, B. P. and Moreau, R. E. (1962) A study of the rare birds of Africa. *Bull. Brit. Mus. (Nat. Hist.) Zool.* 8: 313-378.

Hall, B. P. and Moreau, R. E. (1970) *An atlas of speciation in African passerine birds.* London: Trustees of the British Museum (Natural History).

Lewis, A. D. (1983) Old records of some scarce or little-known species from Kenya. *Scopus* 7: 89-90.

Lewis, A. D. (1984) Hinde's Pied Babbler *Turdoides hindei* south of Machakos, Kenya. *Scopus* 8: 48-49.

Plumb, W. J. (1979) Observations on Hinde's Babbler *Turdoides hindei. Scopus* 3: 61-67.

Sharpe, R. B. (1900) [Several new species of bird from Africa.] *Bull. Brit. Orn. Club* 11: 28-29.

van Someren, V. G. L. (1922) Notes on the birds of East Africa. *Novit. Zool.* 29: 1-246.

van Someren, V. G. L. (1932) Birds of Kenya and Uganda, being addenda and corrigenda to my previous paper in "Novitates Zoologicae", XXIX, 1922. *Novit. Zool.* 37: 252-380.

Turner, D. A. (1977) Status and distribution of East African endemic species. *Scopus* 1: 2-11,56.

WHITE-THROATED MOUNTAIN BABBLER   RARE

Lioptilus gilberti (Serle, 1949)

Order PASSERIFORMES   Family MUSCICAPIDAE
                                             Subfamily TIMALIINAE

Summary This insectivorous, canopy-haunting species is known from only a few localities in western Cameroon and eastern Nigeria. Although common where it occurs it is only occasionally found outside primary montane forest.

Distribution The White-throated Mountain Babbler has only been found in a few montane localities in western Cameroon and eastern Nigeria. The type-specimen was collected in 1948 at 1,520 m on Mount Kupe (Serle 1949). Further fieldwork carried out between 1949 and 1951 showed the species to occur between 1,370 and 2,130 m on Mount Kupe (Serle 1954) and there are 23 specimens from this locality in the BMNH (SNS). In 1984 the ICBP Cameroon Montane Forest Survey recorded the species down to 950 m on the western slopes of Mount Kupe (SNS). In 1950 the species was discovered in the Rumpi Hills near Dikume Balue where 12 specimens were collected between 1,220 and 1,520 m (Serle 1954). In 1984 birds were observed in the Rumpi Hills between 1,100 and 1,700 m (SNS). Further to the north four birds were taken at Foto near Dschang at 1,670 m in 1957 (Serle 1965). In 1984 the ICBP Cameroon Montane Forest Survey discovered the species on Mount Nlonako, north-east of Mount Kupe, at an elevation of 1,600-1,800 m (SNS). In Nigeria the species is only known from the Obudu Plateau at 1,520 m where it was discovered in 1953 when six specimens were collected (Serle 1957); the species has been seen regularly at this site since then (Elgood 1965,1982, M. Dyer pers. comm. 1983, M. E. Gartshore pers. comm. 1983).

Population Numbers are not known, but the species is common where it occurs (Serle 1949,1954, Elgood 1982, SNS).

Ecology This species is restricted to montane forest (Serle 1949, 1950, 1954, 1957, 1965, Elgood 1965, 1982). It is usually found only in primary forest, although it is occasionally seen in mature secondary growth (Serle 1954). The birds travel through forest in small flocks (Serle 1949, 1950, 1954, Elgood 1982) sometimes as large as 10-12 birds (Serle 1950, Elgood 1982). These flocks are very vocal and active as the birds hop and fly from branch to branch (Serle 1949, 1954). It is generally a species of the canopy, occasionally descending into the forest mid-stratum (Serle 1949, 1954) or even the ground-stratum (M. Dyer pers. comm. 1983, M. E. Gartshore pers. comm. 1983). White-throated Mountain Babblers are usually closely associated with flocks of the Grey-headed Greenbul *Phyllastrephus poliocephalus* (see Appendix C) and sometimes also Tullberg's Woodpecker *Campethera tullbergi*, Elliot's Woodpecker *Mesopicos ellioti*, the White-bellied Flycatcher *Trochocercus albiventris*, the Drongo *Dicrurus adsimilis* and Waller's Chestnut-winged Starling *Onychognathus walleri* (Serle 1950, 1954). The species is mainly insectivorous and the birds search for food in moss, epiphytes and crevices in bark (Serle 1954, M. Dyer pers. comm. 1983, M. E. Gartshore pers. comm.

494

1983). Breeding activity has been noted in June (Serle 1954,1957) and juveniles have been seen between November and January (Serle 1954).

Threats None is known. This species appears to be dependent on primary montane forest and has a very restricted distribution, and thus could be at risk should forest exploitation become a serious problem. At present the forest is still adequately preserved on Mount Kupe, the Rumpi Hills and Mount Nlonako (SNS).

Conservation Measures Taken None is known.

Conservation Measures Proposed The ICBP Cameroon Montane Forest Survey is preparing a forest conservation plan for the Cameroon Highlands for the consideration of the Cameroon government.

Remarks The White-throated Mountain Babbler is sometimes considered to form a superspecies with the Red-collared Flycatcher-babbler *Lioptilus rufocinctus* and Chapin's Flycatcher-babbler *L. chapini*, both of which occur in eastern Zaire (Hall and Moreau 1970) and are included in Appendix C. It is, however, a very distinct species and has sometimes been considered to belong to a monotypic genus *Kupeornis* (Serle 1949, M. Eisentraut *in litt.* 1983). For details of threatened bird species occurring on Mount Kupe see under the Mount Kupe Bush-shrike *Malaconotus kupeensis*; for details of rare species on the Rumpi Hills, Mount Nlonako and the Obudu Plateau see under the Green-breasted Bush-shrike *M. gladiator*.

References

Elgood, J. H. (1965) The birds of the Obudu Plateau, Eastern Region of Nigeria. *Nigerian Field* 30: 60-69.

Elgood, J. H. (1982) *The birds of Nigeria*. London: B.O.U. Check-list no. 4.

Hall, B. P. and Moreau, R. E. (1970) *An atlas of speciation in African passerine birds*. London: Trustees of the British Museum (Natural History).

Serle, W. (1949) A new genus and species of babbler and new races of a wood-hoopoe, swift, barbet, robin-chat, scrub-warblers and apalis from West Africa. *Bull. Brit. Orn. Club* 69: 50-56.

Serle, W. (1950) A contribution to the ornithology of the British Cameroons. Part 2. *Ibis* 92: 602-638.

Serle, W. (1954) A second contribution to the ornithology of the British Cameroons. *Ibis* 96: 47-80.

Serle, W. (1957) A contribution to the ornithology of the Eastern Region of Nigeria. Part 2. *Ibis* 99: 628-685.

Serle, W. (1965) A third contribution to the ornithology of the British Cameroons. Part 1. *Ibis* 107: 60-94.

MADAGASCAR YELLOWBROW

INDETERMINATE

Crossleyia xanthophrys (Sharpe, 1875)

Order PASSERIFORMES

Family MUSCICAPIDAE
Subfamily TIMALIINAE

Summary This distinctive species is confined to Madagascar's rainforests, where it has been seen only twice in the past 50 years.

Distribution The Madagascar Yellowbrow is known from rainforest in central eastern Madagascar, with one record from the north. It was first described from a single bird collected on the "east coast" of Madagascar (Milne Edwards and Grandidier 1881). Subsequently it was widely collected but very poorly documented in the literature. Published records before 1930 are of three specimens from Fianarantsoa received in BMNH in 1880 (Sharpe 1881; NJC), the species as common in Ankafana (= Tsarafidy) and "Nandehizana" forests, also around 1880 (Deans Cowan 1882; see Remarks), a specimen presumably from the eastern Imerina forests in the 1890s (Oberholser 1900), and a "considerable number of skins" (at least eighteen) procured by one collector from Sihanaka forest (Delacour 1932, Rand 1932). In BMNH there are in fact six specimens from Ankafana (which may well be the locality intended by "Fianarantsoa", which is fairly nearby) and six also from Sihanaka, in MNHN there are 12 from Sihanaka, and in BMNH and MRAC together there are also two from Brickaville district, 1925, six from Andevoranto forest, 1925, four from Lakato forest, 1924-1925, and one from "Betsileo", undated (NJC,SNS), "Betsileo" indicating south-central Madagascar (see map in Deschamps 1960, also Locamus 1900). Despite this relative wealth of records, since 1930 there have been only two: one in the Tsaratanana massif in the north in 1966 (Albignac 1970) and one at Périnet east of Antananarivo in July 1968 (Benson and Irwin 1975).

Population Along with the Yellow-bellied Sunbird-asity *Neodrepanis hypoxantha*, Dusky Greenbul *Phyllastrephus tenebrosus* and Red-tailed Newtonia *Newtonia fanovanae*, this species is considered difficult to observe because of its elusiveness, sparseness, and difficult habitat (Benson 1974, Benson and Irwin 1975). That one particular collector should have obtained a "considerable number" of specimens probably only reflects the time-period over which his collections were made (40 years in one account: see Distribution under Madagascar Red Owl *Tyto soumagnei*) and, perhaps, the hunting techniques of the natives from whom most of his ornithological material was acquired (see Rand 1932).

Ecology General "habits" were considered likely to prove similar to the Grey-crowned Oxylabes *Oxylabes cinereiceps*, which is a bird of ground-cover in heavy forest and gleans for insects through low bushes (Rand 1932). The bird seen in 1968 was in undergrowth on the edge of evergreen forest (Benson and Irwin 1975).

Threats Destruction and disturbance of primary rainforest is the single most serious threat to this and all other rainforest-dependent species in Madagascar

496

(see Threats under Madagascar Serpent Eagle *Eutriorchis astur*). The forest in eastern Imerina is now all cleared (D. A. Turner pers. comm. 1983), and it seems unlikely that forest near the coast at Brickaville or Andevoranto would now be extant.

Conservation Measures Taken The species has been recorded from the Tsaratanana Nature Reserve (R.N.I. no. 4), which covers 48,622 ha, and the Périnet-Analazamaotra Special Reserve, which covers 810 ha (Andriamampianina 1981).

Conservation Measures Proposed Immediate and effective protection of as much remaining rainforest as possible would almost certainly guarantee the survival of this and all other rainforest-dependent species in Madagascar; and at least, on current knowledge, complete protection of the intact parts of Sianaka forest is of extreme importance (see Conservation Measures Proposed under Madagascar Serpent Eagle). Any ornithological work in the other areas from which the species is known, or where it might be expected, should where possible be extended to include searches to locate it. The forest at Tsarafidy where this species occurs was identified in 1961 as a place of exceptional interest for its wildlife which certainly deserved complete protection (Griveaud 1961); protection for "Nandehizana" forest, if it survives, is also merited, and a survey to relocate and evaluate this forest is warranted (see Remarks).

Remarks Tsarafidy (i.e. Ankafana) forest, north of Fianarantsoa, is important not only for this species but also for Pollen's Vanga *Xenopirostris polleni* and the Grey-crowned Greenbul *Phyllastrephus cinereiceps* (see relevant accounts), Pitta-like Ground-roller *Atelornis pittoides* and Brown Emu-tail *Dromaeocercus brunneus* (see Appendix C), as well as many rare lemurs, invertebrates and plants (Deans Cowan 1882, Griveaud 1961). The location of "Nandehizana" forest, also of substantial importance (see Deans Cowan 1882), has not hitherto been traced, but there is a Nandihizina marked on an old map (see Locamus 1900) somewhat to the north of what is now called Tsarafidy, and which on a modern map would be located at 20°47'S 47°10'E, i.e. the block of forest straddling the road between Ambositra and Ambohimahasoa (in IGNT 1964). A taxonomic reassessment of this bird has judged it to be a babbler (Timaliinae) not a bulbul (Pycnonotidae) (Benson and Irwin 1975), and it now reoccupies the monotypic genus created for it in 1877 (Hartlaub 1877), being aberrant enough possibly to require placing in a separate tribe, the Crossleyini (Irwin 1983).

References

Albignac, R. (1970) Mammifères et oiseaux du Massif du Tsaratanana. *Mém. ORSTOM* 37: 223-229.
Andriamampianina, J. (1981) Les réserves naturelles et la protection de la nature à Madagascar. Pp. 105-111 in P. Oberlé, ed. *Madagascar, un sanctuaire de la nature*. Paris: Lechevalier.
Benson, C. W. (1974) Another specimen of *Neodrepanis hypoxantha*. *Bull. Brit. Orn. Club* 94: 141-143.

Benson, C. W. and Irwin, M. P. S. (1975) The systematic position of *Phyllastrephus orostruthus* and *Phyllastrephus xanthophrys*, two species incorrectly placed in the family Pycnonotidae (Aves). *Arnoldia (Rhod.)* 7(17).

Deans Cowan, W. (1882) Notes on the natural history of Madagascar. *Proc. Roy. Phys. Soc. Edinburgh* 7: 133-150.

Delacour, J. (1932) La Mission Zoologique Franco-Anglo-Américaine à Madagascar. *Bull. Mus. Natn. Hist. Nat.* (2)4: 212-219.

Deschamps, H. (1960) *Histoire de Madagascar*. Paris: Berger-Levrault.

Griveaud, P. (1961) Un interresant vestige forestier malgache. *Bull. Acad. Malgache* 19: 677-694.

Hartlaub, G. (1877) *Die Vögel Madagascars und den benachbarten Inselgruppen*. Halle.

Institut Géographique National à Tananarive (1964) Carte de Madagascar, 1: 500,000, Type 1963. Tananarive.

Irwin, M. P. S. (1983) The Malagasy species of Timaliidae (Babblers). *Honeyguide* no. 116: 26-31.

Locamus, P. (1900) Carte de Madagascar, 1: 500,000. Paris.

Milne Edwards, A. and Grandidier, A. (1881) *Histoire physique, naturelle et politique de Madagascar, 12. Histoire naturelle des oiseaux*. Tome II. Paris.

Oberholser, H. C. (1900) Catalogue of a collection of birds from Madagascar. *Proc. U. S. Natn. Mus.* 22: 235-248.

Rand, A. L. (1932) Mission Franco-Anglo-Américaine à Madagascar. Notes de voyage. *Oiseau et R.F.O.* 2: 227-282.

Sharpe, R. B. (1881) On a new genus of Timeliidae from Madagascar, with remarks on some other genera. *Proc. Zool. Soc. Lond.*: 195-197.

WHITE-NECKED PICATHARTES   VULNERABLE
Picathartes gymnocephalus (Temminck, 1825)

Order PASSERIFORMES   Family MUSCICAPIDAE
                                                Subfamily PICATHARTINAE

Summary This remarkable ground-haunting bird is restricted to the Upper Guinea forest zone from Togo to Sierra Leone, where it breeds in small colonies in caves and on rock faces under a rainforest cover. It is threatened by forest clearance, hunting and collecting for zoos.

Distribution The White-necked Picathartes (or White-necked Rockfowl) occurs in suitable places throughout the remaining fragments of the rainforest zone of the Upper Guinea region in Ghana, Ivory Coast, Liberia, Sierra Leone and Guinea, but is possibly extinct in Togo. The type-specimen is thought to have come from the "English possessions on the Guinea coast" (Temminck and Meiffren Laugier de Chartrouse 1825), possibly Sierra Leone (Sharpe 1872). In addition to the localities mentioned below there is a specimen in IRSNB from "Sénégambie" collected in 1886 (NJC): the exact provenance of this bird is not at all clear and the species has never otherwise been recorded from either Senegal or Gambia.

Ghana Nineteenth century localities for the species are "Ghana", 1872 (specimens in RMNH: NJC), Denkera in the early 1870s (Sharpe 1872, Ussher 1874) and in or before 1891 (specimen in BMNH: SNS), Abetifi, 1877 (specimen in SMNS: NJC), Fantee in or before 1891 (specimen in SMF: NJC) and Kumasi, Ashanti, in or before 1900 (specimen in BMNH: SNS; but see Bannerman 1948). The species was not recorded again in Ghana until 1953 when a colony was found 10 km north of the Opon Valley railway station (Grimes and Gardiner 1963). Other colonies were located at Fumso, 80 km north of Cape Coast, in the mid-1950s (McArdle 1958) and at Kwahu Tafo, east of Mpraeso in 1958 (Grimes and Darku 1968). Subsequent exploration has located several more sites, especially around Mpraeso (where eight colonies were found by forest guards drawing farm boundaries within a forest reserve), Abetifi, Bekwai (south of this town) and Kumasi (north-west of this town) (Sutton 1965, Grimes and Darku 1968). It is now clear that the main Ghanaian population of this species occurs along the Kwahu escarpment between Mampong Ashanti and the Akwapim Hills and also in several places south and south-west of the escarpment area (Grimes and Darku 1968). Some old nests discovered on the southern slopes of the Akwapim Hills, 24 km north of Accra, were probably long abandoned due to replacement of the forest by agricultural land (Grimes and Darku 1968). All known Ghanaian colonies are near footpaths and so there are probably many unlocated sites (L. G. Grimes *in litt.* 1977 to W. B. King).

Guinea Five birds were collected in Guinea near the border with Sierra Leone in 1965 (specimens in ZFMK: NJC). A few nests of the species were found inside Guinea just north of Mount Nimba in 1968 (A. D. Forbes-Watson pers.

499

comm. 1984). A bird, possibly this species, was seen in 1980 on Kakoulima Hill, 80 km north-east of Conakry (Richards 1982).

Ivory Coast A small colony was found at the foot of Mount Nimba in 1968 (Brunel and Thiollay 1969). The only other published record is of single birds seen at Lamto (apparently a long way from suitable breeding sites), one in 1981 and one in 1982 (Prendergast 1983). One recent review notes the species as occurring in "south-western Ivory Coast" (Thiollay in press).

Liberia An old undated specimen (probably nineteenth century), collected in "Liberia" is now in MNHN (SNS). There were no subsequent records until 1964 when several specimens were collected in the mountainous area near Zorzor (Grimes and Darku 1968). Up to 32 birds, presumably of Liberian origin, were exhibited in Monrovia Zoo between 1966 and 1970 (*Internat. Zoo Yearbook* 6-11 [1966-1971]). During the 1960s single specimens were collected at Geatown in Grand Gedeh County and Fassawalazu, Wainjama and Zowolo in Lofa County (Schouteden 1970). Two birds were collected at 600 m in the foothills of Mount Nimba, one in 1967 and the other in 1968, and one nest was found (Colston and Curry-Lindahl in press). A bird was also taken at an unspecified Liberian locality in 1974 or 1975 (Louette 1978) and another was collected in Lofa County in 1979 (Louette 1981). In recent years two colonies have been observed in Grand Gedeh County and one in Nimba County, though there are apparently several other more inaccessible colonies (W. Gatter *in litt.* 1983). The status of the species in Lofa County is now uncertain following the severe disturbance of many of the colonies by animal dealers (W. Gatter *in litt.* 1983). Another colony near Tchien was disturbed by dealers in 1982 (W. Gatter *in litt.* 1983). Mining activites resulted in the destruction of colonies at Bong in the early 1970s and at Mount Nimba more recently (W. Gatter *in litt.* 1983). Nevertheless it seems that this species is still quite widely distributed in Liberia.

Sierra Leone One specimen was collected in the Peninsular Forest 32 km south of Freetown in 1912 (Kelsall 1914). Another was taken nearby in Sugarloaf Forest, Peninsula, in 1913 (Bannerman 1932) and in 1937 six birds were seen in the Peninsular Forest Reserve (Walker 1939). The species was seen at Mabonto in the foothills at the western edge of the north-eastern plateau of Sierra Leone in 1927, though by 1954 this area was deforested and the birds had gone (Glanville 1954). In 1950 the species was discovered in several places along the southern edge of the plateau and four specimens were collected at Mongheri (Glanville 1954, Yealland 1965). About the same time it was located south of Kono, near Waoma, probably also near the southern slopes of the plateau, and a specimen was taken in the Tunkia Chiefdom near the Liberian border (Glanville 1954). A bird captured at Mongheri in 1954 and taken to London Zoo was the first live specimen to be exhibited outside Africa (Attenborough 1955). By the mid-1960s the species was known to be well distributed in the western, southern and eastern provinces of Sierra Leone with up to 30 colonies located (Grimes and Darku 1968). In the late 1970s the main centres of the population were in the Loma and Tingi Hills (north-east plateau) and in the Peninsular Forest outside Freetown (G. D. Field pers.

comm. 1983). The species is also likely to occur in other less well known areas, such as the Tama/Tonkoli forests west of Kono and the Kangari Hills north of Bo (G. D. Field pers. comm. 1983).

Togo The only records are of a nesting colony discovered at Apotsi in south-western Togo in 1894; it was also noted from Leglebi, presumably at the same time (Bannerman 1948). These localities are apparently on the extreme eastern edge of the species's natural range and it is possible that it no longer survives in Togo.

Population No detailed estimates of population are available but the species is clearly very local and uncommon on account of its highly specialised habitat requirements (e.g. Glanville 1954, Attenborough 1955, Grimes and Gardiner 1963, Yealland 1965, Grimes and Darku 1968, Thiollay in press). The species is for example apparently very rare in Ivory Coast owing to shortage of suitable habitat (J.-M. Thiollay *in litt.* 1983). Because the bird is so secretive and nests in inaccessible locations it is probably, however, less threatened than has sometimes been supposed (Glanville 1954, Grimes and Gardiner 1963, Grimes and Darku 1968). There is some (though slight) evidence of a population decline: one abandoned nesting-site was discovered 24 km north of Accra (Grimes and Darku 1968) and in Sierra Leone there are apparently no large colonies left (G. D. Field pers. comm. 1983). Although there have been no censuses of this species one informed guess put the Ghanaian population at 200-300 pairs (in King 1978-1979).

Ecology Most records of this species are from rocky ground under a rainforest canopy (Ussher 1874, Walker 1939, Bannerman 1948, Glanville 1954, Attenborough 1955, McArdle 1958, Grimes 1963,1964, Grimes and Gardiner 1963, Sutton 1965, Yealland 1965, Grimes and Darku 1968, Brunel and Thiollay 1969, Richards 1982, Colston and Curry-Lindahl in press, Thiollay in press). It is most numerous in forest in hilly country where there are probably more suitable breeding sites (Glanville 1954, Grimes and Darku 1968, G. D. Field pers. comm. 1983) but records from riverine forest near Lamto, Ivory Coast, suggest that birds occasionally wander considerable distances from their preferred breeding habitat (Prendergast 1983). The species can tolerate some disturbances to primary forest (Grimes and Darku 1968, L. G. Grimes *in litt.* 1977 to W. B. King, G. D. Field pers. comm. 1983). One well studied colony at Aduamoah, near Mpraeso, Ghana, still survived in 1978 (M. A. Macdonald *in litt.* 1982), even though the forest bordering the nesting-site was clear-felled in 1965 (Grimes and Darku 1968). Another Ghanaian colony at Fumso throve in forest completely surrounded by a cocoa plantation (McArdle 1958) and in Sierra Leone some colonies survive in tiny forest patches (G. D. Field pers. comm. 1983). The food consists of snails, beetles, cockroaches, grasshoppers, earwigs, *Dorylus* ants and other insects, taken from the ground (Lowe 1938, Walker 1939), and the species is known to join mixed bird parties following ant trails (Walker 1939, G. D. Field pers. comm. 1983). The birds nest singly or in colonies of 2-5 pairs (Glanville 1954, Grimes and Gardiner 1963, Grimes 1964, Grimes and Darku 1968, Brunel and Thiollay 1969, Colston and Curry-Lindahl in press), sometimes probably more (G. D. Field pers. comm.

1983). They nest on overhanging cliffs or in caves, the nests being made of mud and plant fibres and situated 2-6 m above the ground (Attenborough 1955, McArdle 1958, Grimes 1963, Grimes and Gardiner 1963, Sutton 1965, Yealland 1965, Grimes and Darku 1968, Colston and Curry-Lindahl in press). The normal clutch-size is two (Glanville 1954, Grimes 1964, Grimes and Darku 1968, Brunel and Thiollay 1969). Most pairs are probably double-brooded (Grimes 1964, Grimes and Darku 1968) and breeding occurs at times of peak rainfall (Glanville 1954, Grimes 1964, Grimes and Darku 1968). In Ghana there are two peaks in breeding activity each year, in March/June and September/November, each coinciding with a rainfall peak (Grimes and Darku 1968). In Sierra Leone, where there is a single wet season, breeding takes place from April to October (Glanville 1954). There are always more nests than pairs of birds in a colony, partly because each pair uses one nest for breeding and another for roosting (Glanville 1954, Grimes 1964, Grimes and Darku 1968). When disturbed the birds often hop rapidly away through the undergrowth, rather than flying (Walker 1939, Prendergast 1983).

Threats This species has declined mainly as a result of forest clearance (Grimes and Darku 1968, L. G. Grimes *in litt.* 1977 to W. B. King, G. D. Field pers. comm. 1983): the rate of forest destruction in Africa west of the Dahomey Gap is so severe that any bird species endemic to primary forest in this region must now be considered gravely at risk (see Remarks under Rufous Fishing Owl *Scotopelia ussheri* for the species in question). The species is also suffering from hunting and collecting for zoos (see under Remarks for details of the captive population). In Liberia animal dealers collected adult and juvenile birds, disturbing and destroying many colonies (W. Gatter *in litt.* 1983; see Distribution). Nearly all these birds died within the first 24 hours (W. Gatter *in litt.* 1983). Hunting pressure is probably not very severe because the bird has little food value and tends to occur in very inaccessible localities (Glanville 1954); nevertheless some adults are killed or trapped and young taken from nests by people primarily catching bats (J.-M. Thiollay *in litt.* 1982). In Ivory Coast the birds are sometimes hunted deliberately and traps are placed on the cave floor, in the cave entrance or on the birds' nests (J.-M. Thiollay *in litt.* 1983).

Conservation Measures Taken None is known in Togo, Ivory Coast, Liberia, Sierra Leone or Guinea. In Ghana the species has been fully protected by law since 1961 (Grimes and Gardiner 1963) and several of the known colonies along the Kwahu escarpment are in forest reserves (Grimes and Darku 1968). In 1965 a local farmer clear-felled the forest bordering the well known nesting-site at Aduamoah near Mpraeso, but as a result of pressure from conservationists this area was not cultivated but allowed to regenerate (Grimes and Darku 1968). The colony was still in existence 13 years later (M. A. Macdonald *in litt.* 1982). The species is listed on Appendix I of CITES, to which Ghana, Guinea and Liberia are parties. Captive breeding has not been shown to be a conservation tool for this species and is treated under Remarks.

Conservation Measures Proposed Strict protection of forest in the breeding areas of the species is essential for its survival. Probably the most critical areas are the Kwahu escarpment in Ghana, the Mount Nimba area of Ivory Coast, Liberia and Guinea, other hilly areas in northern Liberia and southern Guinea, and the Loma and Tingi Hills and the area behind Freetown in Sierra Leone. Unfortunately the species has not been found in the large Tai National Park in south-western Ivory Coast (Thiollay in press), probably because there is little suitable breeding habitat (for details of other protected areas of rainforest west of the Dahomey Gap, the other threatened bird species they might or do contain, and the ornithological importance of Mount Nimba, see Remarks under Rufous Fishing Owl). In view of the difficulty of breeding this species in captivity (see under Remarks) it would be most desirable for the countries in which this species occurs to prohibit its export to zoos in Europe and North America. It is also to be hoped that Guinea, Ivory Coast, Liberia, Sierra Leone and Togo will follow Ghana in providing complete legal protection for this species.

Remarks The White-necked Picathartes forms a superspecies with another threatened species and the only other member of its genus, the Grey-necked Picathartes *Picathartes oreas* (Hall and Moreau 1970) of Cameroon and Gabon. The two species of *Picathartes* are very unusual among birds in that they breed in caves (Brosset 1965, Chopard 1966). The taxonomic position of the genus *Picathartes* has long been disputed. The White-necked Picathartes was originally described as a crow *Corvus gymnocephalus* (Temminck and Meiffren Laugier de Chartrouse 1825) but was soon transferred to a new genus (*Picathartes*) (Lesson 1828) though it was still included in the Corvidae. One more recent authority has supported this possible corvid relationship (Serle 1952) though another transferred the genus to the starlings (Sturnidae) on anatomical grounds (Lowe 1938). Most workers, however, now consider *Picathartes* to be aberrant babblers (Muscicapidae: Timaliinae) possibly warranting their own subfamily (as treated here) (Amadon 1943, Delacour and Amadon 1951, Beecher 1953, Sibley 1970,1973, Olson 1979). Some authors have also considered the genus to have an Asiatic origin (Lowe 1938, Olson 1979). One objection to considering *Picathartes* as babblers is their habit of indirect head-scratching (all other babblers being direct head-scratchers) (Simmons 1957,1961).

Birds in captivity The first specimen of the White-necked Picathartes to be exhibited alive outside Africa was in London Zoo in 1955 (Attenborough 1955, Yealland 1965). The species is now well represented in several of the world's major zoos, details of the captive population between 1964 and 1981 being given in the table below (data compiled from *Internat. Zoo Yearbook* 5-22 [1965-1982]).

The number of White-necked Picathartes in zoological collections between 1964 and 1981

Zoo	1964	1965	1966	1967	1968	1969	1970	1971	1972
1				3	3	3	3	3	7(4)
2	2	2	2	2	2	2	1	3	1
3							1	1	
4			2	2	2	2	2	2	2
5									2
6						2	1		
7									8
8									
9									
10	5	7(1)	5	7(1)	6	4(1)	4	6(1)	4
11			2	3	3	1	1	1	1
12			4	3	3	3	3	3	3
13			2	16	32	32	?		
14	1	1			6	6	6	4	3
15				2	2	2		4	4
16								1	1
17			2	3	4	1			
18								2	6
19			1	1	1	1	1	2	
20									
21						5	5	4	9
22									7
23	1		1	3	3	3	2	2	2
24		2	2	3	2	1			
TOTAL	9	12(1)	23	48(1)	69	68(1)	30	38(1)	60(4)

Key to table: Figures not in brackets are the total number of White-necked Picathartes in a given zoo in a given year. Figures in brackets refer to birds bred and reared in captivity. The code for the zoos is as follows:

1. Amsterdam, Netherlands
2. Antwerp, Belgium
3. Baltimore, U.S.A.
4. Chicago Brookfield, U.S.A.
5. Cincinnati, U.S.A.
6. Cologne, West Germany
7. Copenhagen, Denmark
8. Denver, U.S.A.
9. Fort Worth, U.S.A.
10. Frankfurt, West Germany
11. Los Angeles, U.S.A.
12. Memphis, U.S.A.
13. Monrovia, Liberia
14. NYZS (Bronx Zoo), U.S.A.
15. Philadelphia, U.S.A.
16. Rotterdam, Netherlands
17. St.Louis, U.S.A.
18. San Antonio, U.S.A.
19. Tampa, U.S.A.
20. Vienna, Austria
21. Walsrode, West Germany
22. Washington NZP, U.S.A.
23. Wassenaar, Netherlands
24. West Berlin, West Germany

Zoo	1973	1974	1975	1976	1977	1978	1979	1980	1981
1	6(3)	6(3)	5(2)	5(2)	4(4)	2(2)	1(1)	1	
2	6	2	2	1	1	8	5	3	3
3	1								
4	2	2	1	1					
5									
6		1	1	4	4	4	4	4	
7	8	4	3	8	4	2	5	4	2
8				2	2	2	2	2	
9		2							
10	3(2)	2	3(2)	3(2)	3(2)	3(2)	3(2)	2(2)	3(2)
11									
12	3	3	3	?	2	2	1	1	
13									
14	3	2							
15	3	3	3	2	2	1			
16	2	1	1	1	1	1	8	7	5
17									
18	11	11	11	8	8	8	6	6(1)	7(1)
19									
20				3	3	3	3	3	3
21	?	8	11	?	3	1	1	1	?
22	6	4	2	2			2	1	3
23	3								
24									
TOTAL	57(5)	51(3)	46(4)	40(4)	37(6)	37(4)	41(3)	35(3)	26(3)

It can be seen from the table that attempts to establish a stable captive breeding programme have failed and the great majority of White-necked Picathartes imported into Europe and North America have died within a few years, leaving no offspring. Successful breeding has taken place only at Amsterdam (three times), Frankfurt (six times) and San Antonio (once); for details of successful captive breeding see Faust (1970) and Dekker (1971-1972,1973). It is not possible, from the information given in the table, to calculate an exact figure for the number of birds exported from Africa up to 1981 because some specimens have been loaned between zoos in order to facilitate breeding programmes; it is likely, however, that approximately 130 birds have been exported up to 1981. Clearly restrictions on this trade are needed. It is not known with certainty which countries are exporting this species, but it seems unlikely that many of the birds have come from Ghana (L. G. Grimes *in litt.* 1977 to W. B. King), so most will probably have originated from Sierra Leone, Liberia and Ivory Coast.

References

Amadon, D. (1943) The genera of starlings and their relationships. *Amer. Mus. Novit.* 1247.

Attenborough, D. (1955) Expedition to Sierra Leone. *Zoo Life* 10: 11-20.

Bannerman, D. A. (1932) Account of the birds collected (i) by Mr G. L. Bates on behalf of the British Museum in Sierra Leone and French Guinea; (ii) by Lt.-Col. G. J. Houghton, R.A.M.C., in Sierra Leone, recently acquired by the British Museum. Part III. *Ibis* (13)2: 218-261.

Bannerman, D. A. (1948) *The birds of tropical West Africa*, 6. London: Crown Agents for the Colonies.

Beecher, W. J (1953) A phylogeny of the oscines. *Auk* 70: 270-333.

Brosset, A. (1965) Un oiseau africain troglophile: *Picathartes orea* [*sic*]. *Ann. Speleol.* 2: 425-429.

Brunel, J. and Thiollay, J.-M. (1969). Liste préliminaire des oiseaux de Côte d'Ivoire. Deuxième partie. *Alauda* 37: 315-337.

Chopard, L. (1966) Un oiseau cavernicole du Gabon. *Science, Progrès, Nature* 3379: 410-411.

Colston, P. R. and Curry-Lindahl, K. (in press) The birds of the Mount Nimba region in Liberia. *Bull. Brit. Mus. (Nat. Hist.) Zool.*

Dekker, D. (1971-1972) Weisshals-Stelzenkrähen (*Picathartes gymnocephalus*). *Z. Kölner Zoo* 14: 155-161.

Dekker, D. (1973) Hatching the White-necked Bald Crow *Picathartes gymnocephalus* at Amsterdam Zoo. *Internat. Zoo Yearbook* 13: 120-121.

Delacour, J. and Amadon, D. (1951) The systematic position of *Picathartes*. *Ibis* 93: 60-62.

Faust, I. (1970) Brut und Aufzucht einer Weisshals-Stelzenkrähe (*Picathartes gymnocephalus* Temminck) in Zoologische Garten Frankfurt am Main. *Zool. Garten* 38: 30-36.

Glanville, R. R. (1954) *Picathartes gymnocephalus* in Sierra Leone. *Ibis* 96: 481-484.

Grimes, L. G. (1963) Some observations on *Picathartes gymnocephalus*. *Nigerian Field* 28: 63-65.

Grimes, L. G. (1964) Some notes on the breeding of *Picathartes gymnocephalus* in Ghana. *Ibis* 106: 258-260.

Grimes, L. G. and Darku, K. (1968) Some recent breeding records of *Picathartes gymnocephalus* in Ghana and notes on its distribution in West Africa. *Ibis* 110: 93-99.

Grimes, L. G. and Gardiner, N. (1963). Looking for *Picathartes gymnocephalus* in Ghana. *Nigerian Field* 28: 55-63.

Hall, B. P. and Moreau, R. E. (1970) *An atlas of speciation in African passerine birds*. London: Trustees of the British Museum (Natural History).

Kelsall, H. J. (1914) Notes on a collection of birds from Sierra Leone. *Ibis* (10)2: 192-228.

Lesson, R. P. (1828) *Manuel d'ornithologie ou description des genres et des principales espèces d'oiseaux*, 1. Paris.

Louette, M. (1978) Contribution to the ornithology of Liberia (Part 4). *Rev. Zool. Afr.* 92: 639-643.

Louette, M. (1981) Contribution to the ornithology of Liberia (Part 5). *Rev. Zool. Afr.* 95: 342-355.

Lowe, P. R. (1938) Some anatomical and other notes on the systematic position of *Picathartes*, together with some remarks on the families Sturnidae and Eulabetidae. *Ibis* (14)2: 254-269.

McArdle, T. D. (1958) The Bare-headed Rockfowl *Picathartes gymnocephalus*. *Nigerian Field* 28: 55-63.

Olson, S. L. (1979) *Picathartes* – another West African forest relict with possible Asian affinities. *Bull. Brit. Orn. Club* 99: 112-113.

Prendergast, H. D. V. (1983) New records from the Lamto region, Ivory Coast. *Malimbus* 5: 56.

Richards, D. K. (1982) The birds of Conakry and Kakulima, Democratic Republic of Guinea. *Malimbus* 4: 93-103.

Schouteden, H. (1970) Quelques oiseaux du Liberia. *Rev. Zool. Bot. Afr.* 82: 187-192.

Serle, W. (1952) The affinities of the genus *Picathartes* Lesson. *Bull. Brit. Orn. Club* 72: 2-6.

Sharpe, R. B. (1872) On recent collections of birds from the Fantee Country in western Africa. *Ibis* (3)2: 66-74.

Sibley, C. G. (1970) A comparative study of the egg-white proteins of passerine birds. *Bull. Peabody Mus. Nat. Hist.* 32: 1-131.

Sibley, C. G. (1973) The relationships of *Picathartes*. *Bull. Brit. Orn. Club* 93: 23-25.

Simmons, K. E. L. (1957) The taxonomic significance of the head-scratching methods of birds. *Ibis* 99: 178-181.

Simmons, K. E. L. (1961) Problems of head-scratching in birds. *Ibis* 103a: 37-49.

Sutton, R. W. W. (1965) Notes on birds seen in Ghana in 1964. III: birds noted on a 15,000 mile tour of Ghana. *Bull. Nigerian Orn. Soc.* 2: 102-107.

Temminck, C. J. and Meiffren Laugier de Chartrouse, Baron (1825) *Nouveau recueil de planches coloriées d'oiseaux*, Livraison 55. Paris.

Thiollay, J.-M. (in press) The West African forest avifauna: a review. *Proceedings of the ICBP Tropical Forest Bird Symposium, 1982.*

Ussher, H. T. (1874) Notes on the ornithology of the Gold Coast. *Ibis* (3)4: 43-75.

Walker, G. R. (1939) Notes on the birds of Sierra Leone. *Ibis* (14)3: 401-450.

Yealland, J. J. (1965) *Picathartes*. *Zoo Life* 10: 9-10.

GREY-NECKED PICATHARTES   RARE
Picathartes oreas Reichenow, 1899

Order PASSERIFORMES   Family MUSCICAPIDAE
                                               Subfamily PICATHARTINAE

Summary This remarkable ground-haunting bird is restricted to southern Cameroon, north-eastern Gabon and possibly Equatorial Guinea where it breeds in small colonies in caves and on rock faces under a rainforest cover. It is threatened by forest clearance, hunting and collecting for zoos.

Distribution The Grey-necked Picathartes (or Grey-necked Rockfowl) occurs only in southern Cameroon (mainly the south-west) and north-eastern Gabon, possibly also Equatorial Guinea. Its range covers approximately 40,000 km² (Thiollay in press).

Cameroon The type-specimen was collected near Victoria at the foot of Mount Cameroon (Reichenow 1899). At one time there was some doubt as to whether Victoria was the correct type-locality (Bannerman 1948) but in 1957 another specimen was collected at Man-of-War Bay, near Victoria (Serle 1965). Soon after the type was described the species was found in the hills around Efulen in southern Cameroon (Sharpe 1904) and in 1902 seven specimens were collected there (Sharpe and Bates 1908). The nest and eggs of the bird were also discovered and in 1905 another specimen was collected at the same locality (Sharpe and Bates 1908). Further birds have been taken at Efulen, one in 1929 (specimen in MNHN: SNS), and two in 1949 (Kieffer 1953). Elsewhere in south-western Cameroon the species was discovered (mainly in the 1930s and 1940s) at Kribi, where nesting was also observed (Bannerman 1948), Landji (near Nko'olong, north of Kribi on the coast), Lolodorf (inland up the Lakoundji River), Melan (near Lolodorf) and at Ekoukoua Nkok (near Campo on the border with Equatorial Guinea) (Reis 1945, Good 1953). In 1950 abandoned nests of this species were found at Nyabessan (between Campo and Ambam near the border with Equatorial Guinea) and in 1951 a colony was located near Messaména at "Schuan" (Kieffer 1953) (possibly the same as Chouam: M. Louette *in litt.* 1983). Since Messaména is considerably to the east of all other known sites for the species in Cameroon, some doubt has been expressed as to the accuracy of this report (Louette 1981); Messaména is not, however, as far east as Belinga, from where the species is known in Gabon (see below) so this doubt might not be warranted. In 1968 the species was discovered in the Yaoundé area and one specimen was collected (Germain *et al.* 1973). A pair was taken from a nest nearby at the foot of Mount Kala in 1970 and the bird was also reported from the slopes of Mount Mbou-Minkoum, north-west of Yaoundé (Germain *et al.* 1973). There have been several records of this species from around Yaoundé in 1983 and 1984, including breeding records (J.-P. Decoux pers. comm. 1984). In the former British Cameroons, near the Nigerian border, this species has been found in several places apart from the type-locality. Seven specimens were collected near Mamfe around the upper reaches of the Cross River between 1949 and 1951 (Serle 1954) and ten colonies were discovered (Serle 1952b). Other ornithologists located the species in the Mamfe area in the 1950s and 1960s (Golding 1968,iEisentraut 1973). In 1951 a specimen was collected and another seen at about 1,050 m on Mount Kupe, above Nyassosso, and others were seen near the mountain summit at about 2,100 m (Serle 1954). The species was found again on the summit of Mount Kupe in 1984 during the ICBP Cameroon Montane Forest Survey (F. P. Jensen pers. comm. 1984). In 1948 it was found 14 km from Kumba and one captured bird was taken to London Zoo (Webb 1949). The species has been seen in Meme Division north of Mount Cameroon, near Kumba, in 1971, 1973, 1974 and 1984 (Moore 1974, A. Moore *in litt.* 1983, SNS). There was also a report in 1975 of a colony near Mbonge, 50 km west of Kumba (A. Moore *in litt.* 1983). A bird was netted at Dikume Balue in the Rumpi Hills around in 1967 (A. Moore *per* W. Serle *in litt.* 1983, A. Moore *in litt.* 1983) and nests were seen at this locality in 1984 (M. E. Gartshore pers. comm. 1984). Elsewhere in western Cameroon the species has been recorded during 1983 and 1984 in the course of the ICBP Cameroon Montane Forest Survey on the southern slopes of Mount Cameroon at 450-950 m (H. Tye pers. comm. 1984, SNS) and at 1,250 m on Mount Nlonako (F. P. Jensen pers. comm. 1984). There have also been reports in recent years from the Korup National Park near the Nigerian border (J. S. Gartlan pers. comm. 1984, J. Thomas pers. comm. 1984). With the exception of the Messaména record, all reports of the species have been from within 200 km of the coast; it ranges from near the Nigerian border in the north to the frontier with Equatorial Guinea in the south (Louette 1981).

Equatorial Guinea The Grey-necked Picathartes is reported to occur in Equatorial Guinea (Hall and Moreau 1962, Louette 1981) but it has not been possible to trace any definite records or specimens from this country; nevertheless the species almost certainly occurs there since it has been found very nearby in Cameroon and Gabon.

Gabon In 1963 this species was discovered in Gabon when six colonies were located in the Belinga area (Brosset 1965a,b). It is also known to occur at Oyem near the border with Equatorial Guinea (A. Brosset pers. comm. 1983). One bird collected at Mouila in southern Gabon was probably a wanderer (A. Brosset pers. comm. 1983).

Population No detailed estimates are available but the species is clearly local on account of its highly specialised habitat requirements (Webb 1949, Serle 1952b,1954, Good 1953, Hall and Moreau 1962, Brosset 1965a,b, Golding 1968, Thiollay in press, A. Brosset pers. comm. 1983). Nevertheless it appears that the species is not uncommon in suitable areas (SNS). Because the bird is so secretive and nests in inaccessible locations it is probably less threatened than has sometimes been supposed (Good 1953, Kieffer 1953, Golding 1968, A. Brosset pers. comm. 1983). In the former British Cameroons it is probably commoner around Mamfe than around Kumba and Mount Kupe (Serle 1952a). At Mamfe ten colonies were discovered, separated from each other by walks lasting 15 minutes to three hours (Serle 1952b). Each colony had 4-8 nests, not all in use (Serle 1952b). In Gabon the species is reported as common in caves around Belinga and Oyem but the total

Gabonese population is probably low as only a few suitable nesting areas exist (A. Brosset pers. comm. 1983). There is no direct evidence of a population decline but trapping of birds is certainly taking place (Webb 1949, Kieffer 1953, Golding 1968, Germain *et al.* 1973, Thiollay in press, A. Brosset pers. comm. 1983). The populations in eastern Gabon have not declined over the last 20 years (A. Brosset pers. comm. 1983).

Ecology Most records of this species are from rocky ground and caves under a rainforest canopy (Sharpe and Bates 1908, Bannerman 1948, Webb 1949, Serle 1952a,b,1954, Kieffer 1953, Brosset 1965a,b, Golding 1968, Eisentraut 1973, Germain *et al.* 1973, Moore 1974, A. Brosset pers. comm. 1983) though the record of a bird from Mouila in southern Gabon suggests that some wandering takes place (A. Brosset pers. comm. 1983). Although most colonies have been found in primary rainforest (Kieffer 1953, Brosset 1965a,b) there is no reason to suppose that they cannot withstand some forest disturbance, provided that complete clearance does not take place (see also under the White-necked Picathartes *Picarthates gymnocephalus*). The birds sometimes perch in low vegetation but are rarely seen much more than 2 m above the ground (Moore 1974). The food consists of tiny snails, grasshoppers, earwigs, cockroaches, beetles, *Dorylus* ants, termites, other large insects and small vertebrates (Sharpe and Bates 1908, Lowe 1938, Kieffer 1953, Brosset 1965a,b). In Gabon the birds leave their caves soon after dawn in pairs or small groups to forage on the forest floor usually within 100 to 200 m of the caves (Brosset 1965a,b). Around midday they return to the caves to rest but they resume feeding later in the afternoon (Brosset 1965a,b). The birds nest in colonies of up to ten birds (Brosset 1965a,b) with 12 nests, including old ones (Kieffer 1953). On Mount Cameroon, where there is an abundance of suitable nesting sites, the species appears not to be a colonial breeder (H. Tye pers. comm. 1984). Nesting sites are on overhanging cliffs (Sharpe and Bates 1908, Reis 1945, Webb 1949, Serle 1952a,b, Kieffer 1953) or in small caves (Brosset 1965a,b, A. Brosset pers. comm. 1983). At Mamfe it breeds on the same sandstone cliffs as the uncommon Bates's Swift *Apus batesi* (Serle 1954). In Gabon the birds share the caves with huge colonies of bats (Brosset 1965a,b). The nests are made of mud and plant fibres and situated 1.3-8 m above the ground (Sharpe and Bates 1908, Reis 1945, Serle 1952b, Kieffer 1953, Brosset 1965a,b, H. Tye pers. comm. 1984). One nest has also been found in a hollow in a burnt-out log (Reis 1945). The normal clutch-size is two (Serle 1952b, Brosset 1965a,b) and it is possible that the whole colony assists in incubation and the rearing of the young (Brosset 1965a,b). It seems that only one bird is normally reared per nest (Brosset 1965a,b). At Mamfe nest building starts in March and breeding coincides with the wet season from May to October (Serle 1952b,1981). Breeding has also been noted in April near Yaoundé (Germain *et al.* 1973), in November at "Schuan" near Messaména (Kieffer 1953), in December and January on Mount Cameroon (H. Tye pers. comm. 1984), in August near Kumba (A. Moore *in litt.* 1983), and a bird collected near Victoria in July was in breeding condition (Serle 1965). At Belinga in Gabon breeding has been noted between November and May, though there is not a consistent annual breeding cycle (Brosset 1965a,b, A. Brosset pers. comm. 1983). Breeding success is very low and the birds are sensitive to disturbance (A. Brosset pers. comm. 1983, H. Tye pers. comm. 1984). At Mamfe the birds are thought to use one of their breeding colonies as a communal roost; up to 50 birds apparently spend the night in the lower branches of small trees of the foot of the breeding cliff (Serle 1952b). By contrast birds at Belinga roost in their nesting caves on ledges and in old nests (Brosset 1965a,b). At Meme they appear to leave the cliffs outside the breeding season (Moore 1974) although at Belinga they appear to stay near caves throughout the year (Brosset 1965a,b). The species is very elusive and is particularly difficult to find at its feeding grounds if these are at any distance from the breeding sites (Serle 1952a): when disturbed the birds rapidly hop away through the undergrowth (Kieffer 1953, H. Tye pers. comm. 1984).

Threats Like the White-necked Picathartes, this species (which is similar in its biology) is presumably at risk from forest clearance (*contra* the statement in King 1978-1979). There is no record of this species surviving in areas where the forest has been destroyed and one report specifically noted that the bird was absent from the cleared areas around the Dja River in southern Cameroon (Bates 1909). The forests of north-eastern Gabon are unprotected and there are plans to exploit them once they become accessible through a railway which is at present under construction (Thiollay in press). The species is certainly hunted in some areas for food (Webb 1949, Kieffer 1953, Golding 1968, Germain *et al.* 1973, A. Moore *per* W. Serle *in litt.* 1983, A. Moore *in litt.* 1983). The Bulu people around Efulen are known to trap the bird while the Badjue tribe at "Schuan" do not hunt it (Kieffer 1953). Some adults are killed or trapped and young taken from nests by people primarily catching bats (J.-M. Thiollay *in litt.* 1982). Several birds are also known to have been captured at Oyem in Gabon and exported to West German zoos (see under Remarks for details of the captive population) (A. Brosset pers. comm. 1983). One bird netted at Dikume Balue in Cameroon by an animal dealer died after a few days (A. Moore *per* W. Serle *in litt.* 1983).

Conservation Measures Taken None is known in Gabon and Equatorial Guinea. In Cameroon the species occurs in the recently established Korup National Park, south of Mamfe (for details of this park see *Sumbu* 1 [1982]: 2-12). The species is listed on Appendix I of CITES, to which Cameroon is a party. Captive breeding has not been shown to be a conservation tool for this species and is treated under Remarks.

Conservation Measures Proposed Surveys are needed to ascertain whether viable populations of this species occur in the Korup National Park, and also in the proposed Dja National Park in southern Cameroon (see *Sumbu* 1 [1982]: 2-12). It is to be hoped that a national park will be established in north-eastern Gabon to protect this and other forest species. Cameroon, Gabon and Equatorial Guinea should also take the necessary steps to protect this species from hunters and collectors.

Remarks In the mountains of western Cameroon this species is sympatric with several other threatened birds, these being the Mount Cameroon Francolin *Francolinus camerunensis*, the Green-breasted Bush-shrike *Malaconotus gladiator*, the Mount Kupe Bush-shrike *M. kupeensis* and the White-throated Mountain Babbler *Lioptilus gilberti* (see relevant accounts). For details of the systematic position and unusual cave-dwelling habits of the genus *Picathartes*, see Remarks under White-necked Picathartes. The first Grey-necked Picathartes to be exhibited alive outside Africa was taken to London Zoo in 1949 (Webb 1949). The species has always been rarer in zoological collections than the White-necked Picathartes, details of the captive population between 1969 and 1981 being given in the table below (data compiled from *Internat. Zoo Yearbook* 9-22 [1969-1982]).

The number of Grey-necked Picathartes in zoological collections between 1969 and 1981

Zoo	1969	1970	1971	1972	1973	1974	1975	1976	1977
1	3	4	3	5(3)	5(3)	3(2)	3(2)	3(2)	3(?)
2		6	5	5	?	2	2	?	
3		1	1	1	1	1			
TOTAL	3	11	9	11(3)	6(3)	6(2)	5(2)	3(2)	3(2)

Zoo	1978	1979	1980	1981
1	3(2)	3(2)	3(2)	5(4)
2				
3				
TOTAL	3(2)	3(2)	3(2)	5(4)

Key to table: Figures not in brackets are the total number of Grey-necked Picathartes in a given zoo in a given year. Figures in brackets refer to birds bred and reared in captivity. The code for the zoos is as follows:

    1. Frankfurt, West Germany
    2. Walsrode, West Germany
    3. Wassenaar, Netherlands

Successful captive breeding of this species has only taken place at Frankfurt (see Faust 1971). It is too early to know if a stable captive breeding programme can be established but, in view of the disappointing results of the White-necked Picathartes breeding programmes, this seems unlikely.

References

Bannerman, D. A. (1948) *The birds of tropical West Africa*, 6. London: Crown Agents for the Colonies.

Bates, G. L. (1909) Field notes on the birds of southern Kamerun, West Africa. *Ibis* (9)3: 1-74.

Brosset, A. (1965a) La biologie de *Picathartes orea* [*sic*]. *Biologia Gabonica* 39: 188-190.

Brosset, A. (1965b) Un oiseau africain troglophile: *Picathartes orea* [*sic*]. *Ann. Speleol.* 2: 425-429.

Eisentraut, M. (1973) Die Wirbeltierfauna von Fernando Poo und Westkamerun. *Bonn. zool. Monogr.* 3.

Faust, R. (1971) Welt-Erstzucht von Blaustirn-Stelzenkrähen (*Picathartes oreas*). *Gefied. Welt* 95: 240.

Germain, M., Dragesco, J., Roux, F. and Garcin, H. (1973) Contribution à l'ornithologie du Sud-Cameroun. II Passeriformes. *Oiseau et R.F.O.* 43: 212-259.

Golding, R. R. (1968) A la recherche d'oiseaux des rochers à tête dénudée (*Picathartes*). *Zoo Antwerp* 33: 148-151.

Good, A. I. (1953) The birds of French Cameroon. Part II. *Mém. Inst. Fr. Afr. Noire*, Ser. Sci. Nat. 3: 1-269.

Hall, B. P. and Moreau, R. E. (1962) A study of the rare birds of Africa. *Bull. Brit. Mus. (Nat. Hist.) Zool.* 8: 313-378.

Kieffer, C. (1953) Quelques observations sur le *Picathartes oreas* Rchw. *Oiseau et R.F.O.* 23: 142-144.

King, W. B. (1978-1979) *Red data book, 2. Aves.* 2nd edition. Morges, Switzerland: IUCN.

Louette, M. (1981) *The birds of Cameroon. An annotated check-list.* Brussels: Verhandeling Wetenschappen, Jaargang 43, no. 163.

Lowe, P. R. (1938) Some anatomical and other notes on the systematic position of the genus *Picathartes*, together with some remarks on the families Sturnidae and Eulabetidae. *Ibis* (14)2: 254-269.

Moore, A. (1974) Cameroon Bare-headed Rock-fowl. *Nigerian Field* 39: 188-190.

Reichenow, A. (1899) Neu entdeckte Arten von Kamerun. *Orn. Monatsber.* 7: 40-41.

Reis, J. A. (1945) Les oiseaux du Cameroun Français. *Bull. Soc. Etude Cameroun* 11: 17-55.

Serle, W. (1952a) The Lower Guinea Bare-headed Crow (*Picathartes oreas* Reichenow). *Nigerian Field* 17: 131-132.

Serle, W. (1952b) The affinities of the genus *Picathartes* Lesson. *Bull. Brit. Orn. Club* 72: 2-6.

Serle, W. (1954) A second contribution to the ornithology of the British Cameroons. *Ibis* 96: 47-80.

Serle, W. (1965) A third contribution to the ornithology of the British Cameroons. Part 2. *Ibis* 107: 230-256.

Serle, W. (1981) The breeding seasons of birds in the lowland forest and in the montane forest of West Cameroon. *Ibis* 123: 62-74.

Sharpe, R. B. (1904) On further collections of birds from the Efulen District of Camaroon, West Africa. Part II. *Ibis* (8)4: 591-638.

Sharpe, R. B. and Bates, G. L. (1908) On further collections of birds from the Efulen District of Cameroon, West Africa, with notes by the collector. Part VI. *Ibis* (9)2: 317-357.

Thiollay, J.-M. (in press) The West African forest avifauna: a review. *Proceedings of the ICBP Tropical Forest Bird Symposium, 1982.*

Webb, C. S. (1949) Some notes on the Grey-necked Picathartes (*Picathartes oreas*). *Avicult. Mag.* 55: 149-154.

GRAUER'S SWAMP WARBLER   VULNERABLE
Bradypterus graueri Neumann, 1908

Order PASSERIFORMES   Family MUSCICAPIDAE
                                                          Subfamily SYLVIINAE

___

Summary This warbler is known only from a few highland swamps in eastern Zaire, south-western Uganda, Rwanda and northern Burundi. Although it is common where it occurs it is in severe danger from swamp drainage.

Distribution Grauer's Swamp Warbler is restricted to highland swamps in the mountains around Lakes Kivu and Edward, in eastern Zaire, south-western Uganda, Rwanda and northern Burundi. The type-specimen was collected in Rwanda in 1907 at 2,200 m in the lower spurs of the western Kivu Volcanoes below Mount Sabyinyo (Neumann 1908, Chapin 1953, Schouteden 1966). The next record was of a bird collected in 1927 10 km south of Lubero, just south of Mount Mapanda in the mountains west of Lake Edward in eastern Zaire (Chapin 1953). In the 1950s three more birds were collected west of Lake Edward at 2,200 m, north of Alimbongo (Chapin 1973). In the mountains west of Lake Kivu the species has been collected at Nyawaronga, 2,180 m, in 1959, at Mumba, 2,240-2,270 m, in 1967, and in the Kahuzi Swamp, 2,280-2,370 m, in 1969 and 1970 (Schouteden 1969, Chapin 1973, A. Prigogine pers. comm. 1983). Observations of the species were made in the Kahuzi-Biega National Park, west of Lake Kivu, in 1978 (C. Carter *in litt.* 1984). Three specimens (no date given) have been collected at Mukohole in the Nyungwe (Rugege) Forest, Rwanda (Schouteden 1966, Chapin 1973) and it has also been found in the Kamiranzovu Swamp in the same forest in recent years (J.-P. Vande weghe pers. comm. 1983). In 1978 a specimen was collected nearby at Tshava, 2,250 m (A. Prigogine *in litt.* 1983). Further recent exploration in northern Rwanda has located the species in the Rugezi Swamp (J.-P. Vande weghe pers. comm. 1983) and in the marshes between the Virunga Volcanoes, though it probably no longer occurs in the type-locality itself (J. R. Wilson *in litt.* 1983,1984). In 1978 a specimen was collected in Burundi between Teza and the Rwandan border and a bird was observed at this locality in 1982 (A. Prigogine *in litt.* 1983, J.-P. Vande weghe *in litt.* 1984). The species was discovered in Uganda in 1967 when 12 birds were collected in the Bwindi Swamp at 2,000 m in the Impenetrable (Bwindi) Forest (Friedmann and Williams 1968). A further nine specimens were collected in the Bwindi Swamp and the nearby Ruhizha Swamp in 1969 (Friedmann and Williams 1970). This species is absent from many apparently suitable sites, most notably in the Itombwe Mountains (A. Prigogine pers. comm. 1983). The most important site for it is probably the Rugezi Swamp in northern Rwanda, which covers 8,000 ha (J.-P. Vande weghe pers. comm. 1983; but see Threats). Other swamps in which the species occurs, such as the Kamiranzovu Swamp which covers 100-200 ha, are very small (J.-P. Vande weghe pers. comm. 1983). The total area suitable for the species in Rwanda, where it occurs from 1,950 to 2,600 m, has been estimated at only about 9,000 ha (Vande weghe 1983), while in Burundi probably only 50-100 ha of suitable habitat survives (J.-P. Vande weghe *in litt.* 1984). One account has estimated the total range of the species at no more than "a few square miles" (Hall and Moreau 1970).

Population The species is common where it occurs (Friedmann and Williams 1968,1970, A. Prigogine pers. comm. 1983, J.-P. Vande weghe pers. comm. 1983, J. R. Wilson *in litt.* 1983) but the total population cannot be very large because of its very restricted distribution. Nevertheless the population in the Kamiranzovu Swamp is probably about 3,000 birds (J.-P. Vande weghe *in litt.* 1984). The total population in Burundi probably numbers fewer than 100 pairs (J.-P. Vande weghe *in litt.* 1984).

Ecology This species is restricted to highland swamps (Neumann 1908, Chapin 1953, Hall and Moreau 1962,1970, Friedmann and Williams 1968,1970) where it inhabits a great variety of swamp vegetation-types: it occurs in short grass swamps with *Sphagnum*, *Xyris* and *Lobelia mildbeadtiana*, in swamps with medium-sized sedges such as *Cyperus latifolius* or *C. denudatus*, *Juncus* and ferns, in long grass swamps with *Miscanthidium violaceum* and in swamps with dense scrubby vegetation composed of strands of *Myrica kandtiana*, *Erica kingaensis*, *Vaccinium stanleyi*, *Syzygium cordatum* and *Hypericum revolutum* (Vande weghe 1983). In the Nyungwe Forest it occurs in tiny swamps, surrounded by forest, suggesting that the species can penetrate forest along small watercourses (Vande weghe 1983). In northern Rwanda it survives at great distances from forest and so it cannot be considered a forest species (Vande weghe 1983), as has been suggested (Prigogine 1978). It feeds in the lower strata of the vegetation but sings on higher stems and twigs (Vande weghe 1983). A specimen collected in March was in breeding condition (Chapin 1953). Outside the breeding season it has been seen in flocks of 10-12 birds (Vande weghe 1983).

Threats There are plans to drain the large Rugezi Swamp and to plant the area with tea (Vande weghe 1983, J.-P. Vande weghe pers. comm. 1983). The Kamiranzovu Swamp in the Nyungwe Forest may be drained for gold exploration (J.-P. Vande weghe pers. comm. 1983). There are also plans to construct adductions to bring water from the marshes around the Virunga Volcanoes to nearby villages: if the construction of these adductions is not properly controlled the swamps might dry out (J. R. Wilson *in litt.* 1983). Forest clearance is known to be taking place in the Impenetrable Forest (K. D. Bishop pers. comm. 1983) and this may affect the future of Bwindi Swamp.

Conservation Measures Taken The Kahuzi Swamp is protected in the Kahuzi-Biega National Park (A. Prigogine pers. comm. 1983). The Virunga Volcanoes National Park in Rwanda includes several sites for this species, but the conservation of these swamps is by no means secure (see Threats above).

Conservation Measures Proposed More adequate conservation measures are required to safeguard the montane swamp habitat of this species. Although the Rugezi Swamp in Rwanda must contain a large proportion of the total population of this species, it is probably not possible to protect it, since human pressure on the land is very great (J.-P. Vande weghe *in litt.* 1984). However, the Nyungwe Forest Conservation Project has recently been established and it is hoped that this will conserve the Kamiranzovu Swamp and many other small swamps where the species occurs (Vande weghe 1983, J.-P. Vande weghe *in litt.* 1984).

Remarks Grauer's Swamp Warbler forms a superspecies with another threatened species, the Dja River Warbler *Bradypterus grandis* (see relevant account), and with the White-winged Warbler *B. carpalis* (see Appendix C) (Hall and Moreau 1970, Chapin 1973; but see Vande weghe 1983). A total of five other threatened bird species occurs in the Nyungwe Forest, the Impenetrable Forest and in the mountains west of Lake Kivu and Lake Edward (see Remarks under the Albertine Owlet *Glaucidium albertinum* and the African Green Broadbill *Pseudocalyptomena graueri*). The Rugezi Swamp and the Virunga Volcanoes are important sites for one other threatened bird species, the Papyrus Yellow Warbler *Chloropeta gracilirostris* (see relevant account).

References

Chapin, J. P. (1953) The birds of the Belgian Congo. Part 3. *Bull. Amer. Mus. Nat. Hist.* 75A.

Chapin, R. T. (1973) Observations on *Bradypterus carpalis* and *Bradypterus graueri. Bull. Brit. Orn. Club* 93: 167-170.

Friedmann, H. and Williams, J. G. (1968) Notable records of rare and little-known birds from western Uganda. *Rev. Zool. Bot. Afr.* 77: 11-36.

Friedmann, H. and Williams, J. G. (1970) Additions to the known avifaunas of the Bugoma, Kibale, and Impenetrable Forests, West Uganda. *Los Angeles County Mus. Contrib. Sci.* 198.

Hall, B. P. and Moreau, R. E. (1962) A study of the rare birds of Africa. *Bull. Brit. Mus. (Nat. Hist.) Zool.* 8: 313-378.

Hall, B. P. and Moreau, R. E. (1970) *An atlas of speciation in African passerine birds.* London: Trustees of the British Museum (Natural History).

Neumann, O. (1908) [New African birds.] *Bull. Brit. Orn. Club* 21: 54-57.

Prigogine, A. (1978) Les oiseaux de l'Itombwe et de son hinterland. Volume II. *Ann. Mus. Roy. Afr. Centr.* 8°, Sci. Zool. 223: 1-298.

Schouteden, H. (1966) La faune ornithologique du Rwanda. *Doc. Zool. Mus. Roy. Afr. Centr.* 10.

Schouteden, H. (1969) La faune ornithologique du Kivu II. Passereaux. *Doc. Zool. Mus. Roy. Afr. Centr.* 15.

Vande weghe, J.-P. (1983) Sympatric occurrence of the White-winged Warbler *Bradypterus carpalis* and Grauer's Rush Warbler *B. graueri* in Rwanda. *Scopus* 7: 85-88.

DJA RIVER WARBLER   INSUFFICIENTLY KNOWN
Bradypterus grandis Ogilvie-Grant, 1917

Order PASSERIFORMES   Family MUSCICAPIDAE
                                                            Subfamily SYLVIINAE

Summary This apparently rare species is known from only a few localities in southern Cameroon and Gabon. It is a bird of dense undergrowth and might be commoner than the few records suggest.

Distribution The Dja River Warbler is known only from a few localities in southern Cameroon and Gabon. The type-specimen was collected at Bitye, at 600 m on the Dja River, southern Cameroon, in 1914 (Ogilvie-Grant 1917). There were no further records until 1951 when two specimens were collected at Mbigou on Mount Du Chaillu, at 700 m, in Gabon (Rand *et al.* 1959). Another Gabon specimen was taken at Mimongo, 800 m, in the following year (Rand *et al.* 1959). In the 1950s three further specimens from Gabon, all badly preserved, were discovered in a museum, but the exact localities in which they were collected are not known (Rand *et al.* 1959). The only more recent record is of a bird caught at Makoukou Airport in north-eastern Gabon around 1970: this bird, which was probably released, was thought to be a vagrant (A. Brosset pers. comm. 1983).

Population Numbers are not known. The paucity of records is an indication that it is rare, though it probably occurs in areas where there is little ornithological activity.

Ecology Very little is known about this species. The type-specimen was found in a dense growth of tall *Pennisetum* grass (Bates 1930, Bannerman 1939) and the Gabonese birds were in dense low growth of recently abandoned plantations (Rand *et al.* 1959). The birds keep near the ground and are very difficult to see, a beautiful song usually being the only clue to their presence (Rand *et al.* 1959).

Threats None is known. It appears not to be a forest species and so might even increase with forest clearance.

Conservation Measures Taken None is known, although the type-locality might be within the proposed Dja National Park.

Conservation Measures Proposed A survey is needed to assess the present status of this little known species and to determine whether any conservation action is required.

Remarks The Dja River Warbler forms a superspecies with another threatened species, Grauer's Swamp Warbler *Bradypterus graueri* (see relevant account), and with the White-winged Warbler *B. carpalis* (see Appendix C) (Hall and Moreau 1970, Chapin 1973; but see Vande weghe 1983).

517

References

Bannerman, D. A. (1939) *The birds of tropical West Africa*, 5. London: Crown Agents for the Colonies.

Bates, G. L. (1930) *Handbook of the birds of West Africa*. London: John Bale, Sons and Danielsson.

Chapin, R. T. (1973) Observations on *Bradypterus carpalis* and *Bradypterus graueri*. *Bull. Brit. Orn. Club* 93: 167-170.

Hall, B. P. and Moreau, R. E. (1970) *An atlas of speciation in African passerine birds*. London: Trustees of the British Museum (Natural History).

Ogilvie-Grant, W. R. (1917) Remarks on some recent collections of birds made by Mr G. L. Bates in Cameroon. *Ibis* (10)5: 72-90.

Rand, A. L., Friedmann, H. and Traylor, M. A. (1959) Birds from Gabon and Moyen Congo. *Fieldiana Zool.* 41: 221-411.

Vande weghe, J.-P. (1983) Sympatric occurrence of the White-winged Warbler *Bradypterus carpalis* and Grauer's Rush Warbler *B. graueri* in Rwanda. *Scopus* 7: 85-88.

RODRIGUES WARBLER   ENDANGERED
Acrocephalus rodericanus (A. Newton, 1865)

Order PASSERIFORMES   Family MUSCICAPIDAE
                                                  Subfamily SYLVIINAE

Summary The clearance and disturbance of this species's dense thicket habitat on the island of Rodrigues in the Indian Ocean, coupled with the impact of cyclones in the past two decades, has left a population of only some 20-25 pairs: habitat creation and conservation are urgently needed. Recent evidence that black rats *Rattus rattus* are now on Rodrigues appears to make the situation highly critical.

Distribution The Rodrigues Warbler is confined to a few valleys in the centre of the island of Rodrigues (part of Mauritius) in the Indian Ocean. When first discovered, the species was recorded from west of Port Mathurin in the north of the island, and from Plaine Corail in the south-west (Newton 1865; also Cheke in press), but there have been no further records from these areas. The centre of distribution is now the northwards-running Cascade Pigeon valley (above Port Mathurin), particularly in its upper reaches around La Source: of a total of 24 sites on the island where individuals or pairs were encountered in 1974, 12 were in this valley where they covered about 24 ha of habitat (Cheke 1974, in press; also Vinson 1964, Gill 1967, Cheke 1980, Jones 1983, C. G. Jones *in litt.* 1982), the other 12 also being in valleys radiating from Mont Lubin (adjacent to La Source), the general localities being Gros Mangue/Solitude, Mont Limon, St.Gabriel, Petit Gabriel and Mont Malartic (Cheke 1974). By 1978 the last four localities had been abandoned (Cheke 1979a) and although St.Gabriel held a bird again in 1979 (Mungroo 1979) it did not in 1982 (Jones 1983), so that the only other certain area for the species outside the Cascade Pigeon valley is the parallel Rivière Bambous valley immediately to the east, from Solitude and Vangar upstream to Gros Mangue and Citronelle (Jones 1983, C. G. Jones *in litt.* 1982; for a complete account of distribution and population trends over the past century see Cheke in press). In April 1983, however, though still absent from St.Gabriel, Petit Gabriel and Mont Malartic, the species was found on Grande Montagne, some 2 km east of La Source (C. G. Jones *in litt.* 1984), and in February 1984 birds were seen on Mont Malartic and Montagne Cimitière, respectively 1 km and 2 km west of La Source (W. Strahm *per* C. G. Jones *in litt.* 1984).

Population The species was assumed to be "exceedingly common" when first discovered (Newton 1865), although only four birds appear to have been encountered; at any rate, it was "very common" a decade later (Slater c. 1875). It was not rare in 1930 (Vinson 1964), but by the 1960s it was considered so rare as to be on the brink of extinction (Vinson 1964, Gill 1967). In the early 1970s the population was considered not more than 30 (Gomy 1973), but in 1974 the first comprehensive census concluded that it was in the order of 20-25 pairs (Cheke 1974). Contrary to expectations (based on the absence of cyclones since 1974), an incomplete survey in September 1978 showed a retreat from former "outlying" areas (see Distribution), though numbers were still around 20-25 pairs (Cheke 1979a), while Cyclone Celine II in February 1979 reduced them to eight pairs (not nine as in Cheke 1979a) and one single bird (Mungroo 1979). In October/ November 1981 only seven birds were seen (two pairs and a trio), all in Cascade Pigeon, with at least one bird heard in Solitude, and an estimated total of 10 pairs was reported (Carroll 1981,1982; also Jones 1982a,b,1983). In February/March 1982 densities of birds were noted to be highest at La Source and in the forest south-west of Citronelle (Jones 1983), and the population was estimated at, once more, 20-25 pairs (C. G. Jones *in litt.* 1982). A survey in early April 1983 yielded the following results: 21 birds were counted (29-48 estimated), eight (8-12 estimated) at Cascade Pigeon, six (10-12 estimated) at La Source, four (8-12 estimated) at Solitude, one (less than five estimated) at Sygangue, one (less than five estimated) at Mont Limon, and one (less than five estimated) at Grande Montagne (C. G. Jones *in litt.* 1984).

Ecology At the time of the species's discovery Rodrigues was already very heavily degraded, but from the discoverer's very imprecise narrative it would appear that birds were to be found in habitat as different as flat areas of rock with "some stunted shrubs" to relatively tall (c. 20 m high) forest (see Newton 1865). In the early 1970s the species was reported to inhabit the remnants of native forest (Staub 1973) and to have adapted to copses of the introduced jamrose *Syzygium jambos* and young mango *Mangifera indica* (Gomy 1973, Staub 1973). In February 1974, however, except for one individual seen regularly in a mahogany *Swietenia mahogani* plantation, all birds found were in dense, 2.5-10 m high jamrose-dominated thicket, apparently preferring areas with clearings and glades or perhaps even entirely avoiding the densest continuous stands of jamrose (Cheke 1974, 1978b, in press). In early 1982 birds were chiefly found in jamrose as in 1974; at Gros Mangue, they were also in wooded areas of mango with an understorey of guava *Psidium cattleianum*, jamrose and other species and, south of Vangar, in almost pure stands of tecoma *Tabebuia pallida* (C. G. Jones *in litt.* 1982), this again being similar to 1974 findings (A. S. Cheke pers. comm. 1984). Birds are exclusively insectivorous, hopping nimbly from branch to branch gleaning from leaves and twigs, rarely flying further than 10(-30) m at a time (Slater c. 1875, Gomy 1973, Staub 1973, Cheke 1978b); food observed taken includes planthopper (Homoptera) larvae and caterpillars (Cheke in press). The breeding season perhaps extends from September/October through to March, possibly normally with two broods (Cheke in press). Guava appears preferred for the nest-site (Cheke in press). Clutch-size is three but usually only one young is raised (Gomy 1973, Staub 1973, Cheke 1974, in press); in the last century up to five eggs were reported laid (Slater c. 1875). Birds can be tame and inquisitive (Gomy 1973, Staub 1973) but are also secretive and inconspicuous (Staub 1973, Cheke 1974), and the ease with which they can be found is evidently dependent on season (Cheke 1974, C. G. Jones *in litt.* 1984).

Threats Three factors appear to influence this species adversely: habitat destruction, habitat disturbance, and cyclones (Cheke in press); nest predation by black rats *Rattus rattus* is now also to be expected (see below). The jamrose with which birds are now so strongly associated was introduced to Rodrigues in the 1880s and, being planted extensively for watershed protection, reached its maximum coverage from 1910 to around 1955, but from 1955 to 1968 large areas of this and other tree cover were cut down and fragmented (Cheke 1974, in press); the remaining jamrose was considered threatened in the early 1970s (Gomy 1973). In 1974, to relieve the plight of livestock dying from prolonged drought, permission was given to graze cattle and goats in forest land, but revocation of this permission was subsequently impossible to enforce, so that undergrowth was heavily affected and habitat drastically impaired (Cheke 1979a). Illegal woodcutting, although possibly benefiting the species on a limited scale by making clearings (Cheke 1974), was noted to have increased sharply between 1974 and 1978 (Cheke 1979a) and is a disturbance to nesting birds (Cheke 1974); the absence of birds from apparently suitable habitat near dwellings is attributed to the disturbance factor (Cheke 1974). In 1968 Cyclone Monique nearly eradicated the species (Staub 1973), in early 1973 four cyclones in succession evidently had a major effect (Gomy 1973, Cheke 1974, in press), and in 1979 Cyclone Celine II is thought to have reduced the population by two-thirds (Cheke 1980): its present distribution on the northern slopes is possibly related to the degree of protection they provide in the absence of the more cyclone-resistant native vegetation (Cheke in press). The colonisation of Rodrigues by the black rat, a notorious nest predator of arboreal birds, has been warned against (Cheke 1979b), but the species has recently been recorded from the island (C. G. Jones *per* A. S. Cheke pers. comm. 1984). The possibility of pet crab-eating macaques *Macaca fascicularis* being brought to the island and escaping is a real threat (A. S. Cheke pers. comm. 1984).

Conservation Measures Taken Legal protection for this bird, called for (in Staub 1973, Cheke 1974,1978a), has recently been given (C. G. Jones *in litt.* 1984). It is listed on Appendix III of CITES for Mauritius.

Conservation Measures Proposed A suggestion to subsidise paraffin in order to reduce pressure on jamrose thickets from woodcutters (Cheke 1974, 1978b) is believed not to have been acted on (W. Strahm *in litt.* 1984). The declaration and fencing-off of La Source and Cascade Pigeon as protected areas was considered urgent over a decade ago (Staub 1973). Planting of jamrose thicket for watershed protection and to extend the species's habitat has been urged (Cheke 1974,1978a), and a detailed and comprehensive set of suggestions and management proposals in respect of this and other factors (e.g. disturbance) ultimately bearing on the species's conservation, but giving due consideration to the needs of local people, has been put forward in anticipation that their implementation would result in the population stabilising at 50-100 pairs (Cheke 1978b; also Cheke 1974). The formal protection and active conservation of the important relic of native forest at Cascade St.Louis, the rich sheltered vegetation in Anse Quitor, and the upland forest at Grande Montagne would result in habitats that could be restocked with the Rodrigues Warbler and Rodrigues Fody *Foudia flavicans* (Cheke 1974,1978b). Introduction of several pairs to Réunion, where there are very large areas of jamrose, requires consideration as an emergency if a decline occurs or as an experiment if there is an increase (Cheke 1974,1975); for reflections on appropriate conditions for such an introduction, see Conservation Measures Proposed under Mauritius Fody *F. rubra*. Work to safeguard this species will now proceed within the framework of the Mauritius Wildlife Research and Conservation Programme (see Conservation Measures Taken under Mauritius Kestrel *Falco punctatus*).

Remarks The Rodrigues Warbler is closely allied to the Seychelles Warbler *Acrocephalus sechellensis* (A. S. Cheke pers. comm. 1984): restitution of the genus *Bebrornis* for the latter (see Remarks in the relevant account) would imply the same for the former.

References

Carroll, J. B. (1981) The wild status and behaviour of the Rodrigues fruit bat *Pteropus rodricensis*. A report of the 1981 field study. *Dodo* 18: 20-29.

Carroll, J. B. (1982) Rodrigues. *On the Edge (Wildlife Preservation Trust Jersey Newsletter)* no. 43.

Cheke, A. S. (1974) British Ornithologists' Union Mascarene Islands Expedition: Report on Rodrigues. Unpublished.

Cheke, A. S. (1975) Proposition pour introduire à la Réunion des oiseaux rares de l'île Maurice. *Info-Nature* no. 12: 25-29.

Cheke, A. S. (1978a) Recommendations for the conservation of Mascarene vertebrates. Conservation memorandum no. 3 (arising out of the B.O.U. Mascarene Islands Expedition). Unpublished.

Cheke, A. S. (1978b) Habitat management for conservation in Rodrigues (Indian Ocean). Conservation memorandum no. 4 (arising out of the B.O.U. Mascarene Islands Expedition). Unpublished.

Cheke, A. S. (1979a) The Rodrigues Fody *Foudia flavicans*. A brief history of its decline, and a report on the 1978 expedition. *Dodo* 15 [1978]: 12-19.

Cheke, A. S. (1979b) The threat to the endemic birds of Rodrigues (Indian Ocean) from the possible introduction of ship rats *Rattus rattus* from vessels coming alongside the proposed new wharf at Port Mathurin. Conservation memorandum no. 5 (arising out of the British Ornithologists' Union Mascarene Islands Expedition). Unpublished.

Cheke, A. S. (1980) Urgency and inertia in the conservation of endangered island species, illustrated by Rodrigues. *Proc. IV Pan-Afr. orn. Congr.*: 355-359.

Cheke, A. S. (in press) Observations on the surviving endemic birds of Rodrigues. In A. W. Diamond, ed. *Studies of Mascarene island birds*. Cambridge: Cambridge University Press.

Gill, F. B. (1967). Birds of Rodriguez Island (Indian Ocean). *Ibis* 109: 383-390.

Gomy, Y. (1973) Voyage en île d'amertume. *Info-Nature* no. 9: 72-99.

Jones, C. G. (1982a) The conservation of the endemic birds and bats of Mauritius and Rodrigues. (Annual report 1981, WWF Project 1082). Unpublished.

Jones, C. G. (1982b) Struggle for survival on tropical islands. *WWF Monthly Report* February: 37-42.

Jones, C. G. (1983) The conservation of the endemic birds and bats of Mauritius and Rodrigues. Annual Report, 1982. Unpublished.

Mungroo, Y. (1979) Report of post Cyclone Celine II survey of the endemic passeriformes, and bats and sea birds of Rodrigues. Unpublished.

Newton, E. (1865) Notes of a visit to the island of Rodriguez. *Ibis* (2)1: 146-154.

Slater, H. H. (c. 1875) Notes on the birds of Rodrigues. Manuscript in the Alfred Newton Library, Department of Zoology, University of Cambridge.

Staub, F. (1973) Birds of Rodriguez Island. *Proc. Roy. Soc. Arts Sci. Mauritius* 4(1): 17-59.

Vinson, J. (1964) Quelques remarques sur l'île Rodrigue et sur sa faune terrestre. *Proc. Roy. Soc. Arts Sci. Mauritius* 2(3): 263-277.

SEYCHELLES WARBLER   RARE
Acrocephalus sechellensis (Oustalet, 1877)

Order PASSERIFORMES   Family MUSCICAPIDAE
                                                  Subfamily SYLVIINAE

Summary This insectivorous warbler is restricted to one tiny island, Cousin, in the Seychelles where, following ICBP management of the island as a nature reserve and the associated recovery of much of its natural vegetation, it is now relatively common, some 250-300 birds being present in 1981; but until it is properly established on a second island it must be considered permanently at risk.

Distribution The Seychelles Warbler is confined to the tiny (27 ha) island of Cousin in the Seychelles, records of the species there dating from 1888 (Diamond 1980). It was initially reported from Marianne and Cousine (Oustalet 1878) although it subsequently disappeared from both (it may once also have been on Mahé: see Lionnet 1980). Ten years before the species was found for science, on Marianne, this island faced impending wholesale clearance of native forest for replanting with coconuts (Newton 1967). It is not clear when this occurred, but neither this bird nor the Chestnut-flanked White-eye *Zosterops (mayottensis) semiflavus*, only certainly known from Marianne, appears to have been recorded there beyond the 1870s (for the latter see Greenway 1967). The early records from Cousine may or may not have been in error for Cousin (Gaymer *et al.* 1969, Diamond 1980). Around 1960 six birds were reportedly introduced to Cousine (Penny 1974) (this undocumented event appears to have been a remarkable risk given the population believed to exist at the time), but subsequent occasional sightings on this island need not have been of survivors or descendants since some birds on Cousin may disperse: thus one was seen on Cousine in 1970 (Penny 1974), taped song playback revealed three in 1972, none in 1973 and most of 1974, then two in December 1974 showing signs of breeding (Diamond 1980), none in 1977 (M. C. Garnett pers. comm. 1982) and a single bird in January 1982 (N. J. Phillips and V. E. Wood *in litt.* 1982). In 1970 there were reports of this species on Félicité (Procter 1970).

Population Birds were regarded as rare on Cousin as recently as 1938 (Vesey-Fitzgerald 1940), though apparently more numerous in 1953, when the species was pronounced "in no danger of extinction" (Foster-Vesey-Fitzgerald 1953). In 1959, 30 birds were counted (Crook 1960) and in 1965 it was estimated that about 50 adults were present (Penny 1967, Gaymer *et al.* 1969). Habitat management from 1968 resulted in a steady increase in numbers until an estimated 274 (250-300) birds were present in about 120 territories in January 1975 (Diamond 1975,1980). The first full census since then, conducted in March 1981, revealed 288 birds in 128 territories; although this suggested a stabilised population and an island carrying capacity of under 300, there had been considerable changes in territory size and distribution since the mid-1970s, with numbers increasing and decreasing in different habitats, so that no true stabilisation had occurred (Bathe and Bathe 1982a). A census conducted in late April and early May 1982 indicated that the number of territories was between 60 and 65 and the number of birds was 157, plus perhaps six more (Phillips 1982): this was regarded as a fairly complete census and certainly indicated a decrease in total numbers (N. J. Phillips *in litt.* 1984).

Ecology The main habitat requirement of this species appears to be scrub and the tall scrub-like vegetation probably represented by mature woodland dominated by *Pisonia grandis* (Bathe and Bathe 1982a, Phillips and Wood 1983). Scrub has been considered optimal habitat on the grounds that territory sizes, generally ranging from 600 m^2 (though as low as 280 m^2 in mangrove: Sorensen 1982) to 8,800 m^2, were inversely correlated with the amount of scrub present and positively correlated with tree cover (Bathe and Bathe 1982a); this analysis was, however, extended and reinterpreted to suggest that density in scrubby areas could be explained simply in terms of the amount of foliage present, and that truly mature *Pisonia* woodland would prove to be optimal habitat for the species, since it probably forms not a closed canopy as had been thought (see Threats) but "a kind of three-dimensional network of living wood of all ages with a wide range of diameter, height and spacing", with large amounts of dead wood on the ground, open canopy, and foliage at all levels down to the ground (Phillips and Wood 1983). Although the species holds year-round all-purpose group territories, generally with three birds involved but up to eight recorded, individual birds always forage alone within the territory (Sorensen 1982; also Diamond 1980). In a year-round study, 29 tree species and 16 herbs were utilised by foraging birds, but 95% of all such observations involved only 10 plant species, the first four of these being (in order) the trees *Pisonia grandis*, *Morinda citrifolia*, *Casuarina equisetifolia*, and the herb *Achyranthes aspera* (Bathe and Bathe 1982b); *Morinda* was earlier identified as the most preferred plant, followed by *Pisonia* (Lloyd 1973). The species is very largely insectivorous, with a relatively restricted diet: during a year, only 42 species were found to have been taken, of which seven (an ant, four hemipteran bugs, a beetle and a bee) formed 56% of all (628) invertebrates extracted from vomitus (Bathe and Bathe 1982b). Of the samples taken, 81% held remains of bugs, three species being involved, each showing a high level of host specificity (one confined to *Pisonia*, one to *Achyranthes*, and one commonest on *Morinda*), and 62% of samples held eggs of (probably) the shield bug *Bathycoelia*, common in *Morinda* (Bathe and Bathe 1982b). Spiders and occasionally very small skinks and geckos have also been noted as prey (Lloyd 1973). Birds mostly (c. 95% of feeding records in two studies) glean food from foliage and twigs, rarely from bark, chiefly on the undersides of leaves, prey being caught in jumps or short flights, very rarely also by fly-catching away from vegetation or feeding on the ground (Lloyd 1973, Bathe and Bathe 1982b). Birds spend 40% of feeding time below 4 m, even though only 14% of foliage occurs there (Bathe and Bathe 1982a,b); they have also been noted to prefer particular parts of their territories, presumably indicating a patchy food resource but with a predictably steady replenishment rate, e.g. anthills, termitaria (Sorensen 1982). There is little variation in feeding sites during the day, but an early morning peak in use of *Morinda* and an afternoon and pre-dusk concentration in *Achyranthes* have been noted (Lloyd 1973). Increased feeding activity in April/May and October/November corresponded with periods when most birds were provisioning young (Bathe and Bathe 1982b). Indeed, annual peaks in production of juveniles in April and September/October suggested a link between timing of breeding and rainfall, the former (specifically hatching) being geared to peak production of insects consequent upon the latter (Diamond 1980). However, continuing studies have suggested a lack of seasonality in the timing of breeding which, if the case, implies that birds attempt to breed whenever physiologically capable and that it is variation in breeding success, not in numbers of birds starting to breed, that results in fledging peaks (Phillips 1984). Seasonal defoliation by salt-spray on opposite sides of the island (in the south-east by the trade wind, April to October, in the north-west by the monsoon, November to March) affects breeding success, significantly more birds fledging each season from the half of the island in the lee of the prevailing wind, and a significant correlation exists between fledging frequency and foliage production three months earlier, leeward trees being more densely leaved and growing faster (Phillips 1984; also Phillips and Wood 1983). Nests may be as high as 20 m in the vegetation (Bathe and Bathe 1982a); clutch-size is almost always one, rarely two (Diamond 1980), almost invariably only one young fledging and remaining within the territory until independent (Phillips 1984).

Threats The single serious threat to the species on Cousin was recently thought to be that constituted by the management plan's aim to allow natural *Pisonia* woodland to regenerate through the island's extensive coconut plantation (see Conservation Measures Taken): as scrub was believed (with good reason) to be the optimal habitat (see Ecology), the steady growth of the understorey towards climax and eventual domination by *Pisonia* was viewed as a threat since older, closed-canopy *Pisonia* (mistakenly considered mature) held far fewer birds than *Pisonia* scrub and moreover excluded *Morinda* and reduced herb cover (Bathe and Bathe 1982a,b). It was postulated that giant tortoises *Geochelone gigantea* might have been responsible for maintaining scrub conditions on the island by browsing and trampling, and it was at any rate considered imperative not to allow total regeneration of *Pisonia* to occur (Bathe and Bathe 1982b; hence *New Scientist* 95 [19 August 1982]: 486). However, the first generation of natural trees since the coconut plantation was abandoned is now starting to shed large branches, partially uproot in strong winds and rain, and produce stolon-like branching and secondary growth, suggesting that the currently developing closed-canopy *Pisonia* is only transitional, that truly mature *Pisonia* resembles "tall scrub" in form, and that therefore Seychelles Warbler numbers will increase to their maximum in this habitat (Phillips and Wood 1983; see Ecology). Despite the relative security the island now enjoys (see Conservation Measures Taken), Cousin is too small and the risk of accidental introduction of predators, notably rats *Rattus*, too permanent for this warbler to be considered safe, and its "Out of Danger" status (King 1978-1979) is here withdrawn until it is safely established on a second island.

Conservation Measures Taken Cousin Island was approved as a Strict Nature Reserve by the Seychelles Government in 1975, having been acquired and managed as a nature reserve since 1968 by ICBP (see Barclay-Smith 1971, Diamond 1975). Since 1965 and especially since 1968, extensive woodland scrub has been allowed to grow up under the coconut groves which have covered much of the island for most of the century: the coconuts have been gathered, thus inhibiting regeneration, with the result that the understorey of native shrubs and trees which had been removed by former owners is once more developing (Diamond 1975; also Lloyd 1973; see Ecology, Threats). The only introduced predator on the island is the Barn Owl *Tyto alba* which is regularly controlled but periodically re-invades Cousin from nearby Praslin (Diamond 1975).

Conservation Measures Proposed If it is accepted that the maturation of *Pisonia* does not constitute a threat to the species but by contrast will offer it optimal habitat (see Ecology, Threats), at least half the "plateau" on Cousin should be left to regenerate without any further management (Phillips and Wood 1983). To maximise breeding success and population size, seasonal defoliation on the island (see Ecology) should be minimised, something best achieved by allowing mature *Casuarina* – whose observed importance to the species (see Ecology) may simply reflect the absence of more suitable plants – to die off along the coast without replacement, and thus letting the hedge-like, salt-resistant *Scaevola taccadae* cover these areas and provide a continuous screen (Phillips 1984). Continuation of the control of Barn Owls and of measures designed to exclude other predators, especially rats and cats, is essential (Diamond 1975; also Diamond and Feare 1980), though there is no evidence of Barn Owls killing warblers (N. J. Phillips and V. E. Wood *in litt.* 1982). Establishment of the warbler on another island is an important long-term safeguard, proposed in King (1978-1979); however, the presence of suitable habitat and the absence of cats and rats are amongst the conditions needed on any island before introduction can take place, while the limited diet referred to above (under Ecology) is a consequence of the limited insect fauna of Cousin, not of an inherent requirement, and considerations of diet would almost certainly not apply on candidate islands for introduction (G. M. Bathe and H. V. Bathe *in litt.* 1982).

Remarks Despite a recent merging of the genus *Bebrornis* in *Acrocephalus* (Diamond 1980), the Seychelles Warbler shows "important ecological and structural differences" from *Acrocephalus* such that *Bebrornis* may need to be retained (Phillips and Wood 1983). The species is interesting for several reasons other than its restricted range: in optimal habitat, it has the smallest territory of its kind of any passerine (Diamond 1980), and its solitariness and lack of spatial organisation are unique among species of cooperatively breeding birds studied to date (Sorensen 1982).

References

Barclay-Smith, P. (1971) Preservation of endangered species in the Indian Ocean. Report on measures taken in the Seychelles group of islands. *ICBP Bull.* 11: 170-173.

Bathe, G. M. and Bathe, H. V. (1982a) Territory size and habitat requirement of the Seychelles Brush Warbler *Acrocephalus (Bebrornis) sechellensis*. Cousin Island Research Station, Techn. Rep. 18. ICBP, unpublished.

Bathe, H. and Bathe, G. (1982b) Feeding studies of three endemic landbirds, *Acrocephalus (= Bebrornis) sechellensis* (Seychelles Brush Warbler), *Foudia sechellarum* (Seychelles Fody), and *Nectarinia dussumieri* (Seychelles Sunbird), on Cousin Island, Seychelles, with implications for their conservation through vegetation management. Unpublished.

Crook, J. H. (1960) The present status of certain rare land birds of the Seychelles islands. Seychelles Government Bulletin.

Diamond, A. W. (1975) Cousin Island Nature Reserve management plan 1975-1979. London: ICBP.

Diamond, A. W. (1980) Seasonality, population structure and breeding ecology of the Seychelles Brush Warbler *Acrocephalus sechellensis*. *Proc. IV Pan-Afr. orn. Congr.*: 253-266.

Diamond, A. W. and Feare, C. J. (1980) Past and present biogeography of central Seychelles birds. *Proc. IV Pan-Afr. orn. Congr.*: 89-98.

Foster-Vesey-Fitzgerald, D. (1953) Wild life in Seychelles. *Oryx* 2: 28-32.

Gaymer, R., Blackman, R. A. A., Dawson, P. G., Penny, M. and Penny, C. M. (1969) The endemic birds of Seychelles. *Ibis* 111: 157-176.

Greenway, J. C. (1967) *Extinct and vanishing birds of the world*. 2nd revised edition. New York: Dover Publications.

King, W. B. (1978-1979) *Red data book, 2: Aves*. 2nd edition. Morges, Switzerland: IUCN.

Lionnet, G. (1980) Les oiseaux observés aux Seychelles en 1768 au cours de l'expédition Marion-Dufresne. *Proc. IV Pan-Afr. orn. Congr.*: 65-69.

Lloyd, D. E. B. (1973) Habitat utilisation by land birds of Cousin Island, and the Seychelles (incomplete). Cousin Island Research Station, Techn. Rep. 5. ICBP, unpublished.

Newton, E. (1867) On the land-birds of the Seychelles archipelago. *Ibis* (2)3: 335-360.

Oustalet, M. E. (1878) Etude sur la faune ornithologique des Iles Seychelles. *Bull. Soc. Philomath. Paris* (7)2: 161-206.

Penny, M. (1967) A new sanctuary in the Seychelles. *Oryx* 9: 214-216.

Penny, M. (1974) *The birds of Seychelles and the outlying islands*. London: Collins.

Phillips, J. (1982) Forty-sixth report of the Scientific Administrator, 1st April – 30th June 1982, Cousin Island, Seychelles. ICBP British Section, unpublished.

Phillips, N. J. (1984) Seasonal and locational differences in the breeding success of the Seychelles Brush Warbler *Bebrornis sechellensis*. Cousin Island Research Station, Techn. Rep. 34. ICBP, unpublished.

Phillips, N. J. and Wood, V. E. (1983) Cousin Island's vegetation: past, present and future. Cousin Island Research Station, Techn. Rep. 33. ICBP, unpublished.

Procter, J. (1970) Conservation in the Seychelles. Report of the conservation adviser. [Victoria, Mahé: Government Printer.]

Sorensen, A. E. (1982) The spatial distribution and foraging behaviour of the Seychelles Brush Warbler *Acrocephalus (Bebrornis) sechellensis*. Cousin Island Research Station, Techn. Rep. 21. ICBP, unpublished.

Vesey-Fitzgerald, D. (1940) The birds of the Seychelles. I. The endemic birds. *Ibis* (14)4: 480-489.

ALDABRA WARBLER   ENDANGERED
Nesillas aldabranus Benson and Penny, 1968

Order PASSERIFORMES   Family MUSCICAPIDAE
                                                              Subfamily SYLVIINAE

Summary On current knowledge this is almost certainly the rarest, most restricted and most highly threatened species of bird in the world: it is found only in a 10 ha strip of coastal vegetation on Aldabra (Seychelles), western Indian Ocean, where in the past decade no more than five birds have been seen and, since 1977, only two. Further suitable habitat may cover no more than another 10 ha, but in any case now faces destruction by tortoises and goats, while rat predation on nests is perhaps the single most important factor in the species's exceptional rarity.

Distribution The Aldabra Warbler is restricted to a tiny part of Aldabra, an outlying atoll of the Seychelles. Since its recent discovery (Benson and Penny 1968) it has – save for one record (see below) – always been confined to an area of 10 ha, consisting of a 50 m wide strip along the north coast of Middle Island (= Ile Malabar), Aldabra, running east for 2 km from the west end at Passe Gionnet (Prys-Jones 1979). Specific searches on Ile Polymnie and at the east end of Middle Island were fruitless, as was a general survey of land birds over the greater part of the atoll (Benson and Penny 1968). Subsequent habitat analysis at the one known site indicated that the species's maximum likely distribution is bounded by the same 50 m strip extending a total of 9 km along the coast, giving an area of 45 ha (Prys-Jones 1979). However, since around 1976 goats and giant tortoises *Geochelone gigantea* have penetrated, and probably degraded, this vegetation from the east at least as far as Opark, only 5 km east of Passe Gionnet, so that apparently suitable habitat, covering 25 ha, exists only between these two last-named sites (Hambler *et al.* in prep.). An old nest, possibly of this species, was found just west of Opark in September 1983 (Hambler *et al.* in prep.). However, on 1 September 1981 an unseen bird was heard by two observers near Anse Petit Grabeau (beyond the eastern end of the 9 km stretch mentioned above), and was identified as an Aldabra Warbler after a tape-recording of its calls was subsequently listened to (Hambler *et al.* in prep.; see Remarks).

Population Following the collection of the first two specimens (a presumed pair) and a nest in December 1967 and January 1968 (Benson and Penny 1968) this species was not seen again until April 1974 (Prys-Jones 1979). Subsequently a medium-term study was able to identify only five individuals, three males and two females: in 1974-1975 the females paired with a male each, and at least one developed a brood-patch, but no young were ever detected, while after November 1975 only unmated males were found, and in February 1977 only two males were certainly known to survive (Prys-Jones 1979). In October 1983 one of these males was seen on three occasions close to the area where it had previously mostly been found, and a bird was heard 1 km away at the Gionnet channel (Hambler *et al.* 1983, Hambler *et al.* in prep.). Extrapolation from the results of studies in the known area of distribution in the 1970s indicated a maximum of 25 birds in the 9 km stretch of habitat then considered suitable, but for various reasons this figure was considered highly optimistic (Prys-Jones 1979). If suitable habitat now extends only 5 km (see Distribution), the maximum population would be only 13; it is to be noted, however, that no birds were ever found at Opark during the 1974-1977 study (Prys-Jones 1979).

Ecology The area used by the species consists of dense tall scrub, up to c. 5 m high, dominated by *Pandanus tectorius, Pemphis acidula, Sideroxylon inerme, Dracaena reflexa* and *Mystroxylon aethiopicum* (Benson and Penny 1971). A number of factors, in combination, distinguish this area from any other on Aldabra: (a) extremely dense, closed-canopy vegetation, with a considerable leaf-litter and/or soil layer; (b) large, dense stands of almost pure *Pandanus* (with which the species is positively associated; but see Remarks), these being used for foraging and probably offering relatively good protection to nests against rats *Rattus*; (c) a high abundance of *Dracaena reflexa*, much used for foraging; and (d) a total absence of both goats and tortoises, which elsewhere on Aldabra may be responsible for disturbing and opening up areas of dense scrub (Prys-Jones 1979). A further feature of the Gionnet area is a high rainfall relative to the rest of Aldabra, which may influence invertebrate abundance there (Hambler *et al.* in prep.). Birds are extremely difficult to observe, being generally silent and foraging largely below 1.5 m (Prys-Jones 1979). Food, consisting entirely of small invertebrates up to 30 mm in length, is known to include small spiders and beetles, moths, winged ants, bugs and caterpillars, possibly also grasshoppers (Benson and Penny 1968, Prys-Jones 1979). Territories are c. 0.75 ha, but apparently up to 1.5 ha, occupied year-round; breeding probably occurs from October to January (Prys-Jones 1979). A nest with a full clutch of three, 1967, was 0.6 m above ground in leaf-bases of young *Pandanus* scrub; two empty nests, 1968, were respectively 3.2 m up in a thicket between stems of *Mystroxylon* and 1.5 m up between forking stems of *Pemphis* (Benson and Penny 1968).

Threats Cats and black rats *Rattus rattus* are present on Middle Island, the former still in very low numbers, the latter ubiquitous: very high nest-predation on Aldabra passerines is mostly attributed to rats (Prys-Jones 1979) and it seems very probable that rats are the main cause of the critical condition of the Aldabra Warbler. Rats are now eating the bark and killing branches of *Mystroxylon* and *Sideroxylon*, apparently a new phenomenon (Hambler *et al.* in prep.). Moreover, tortoises have started and goats seem likely soon to start to penetrate west of Opark, the latter in particular posing a very serious threat to the vegetation (Hambler *et al.* in prep.), their numbers on Aldabra having quintupled between 1977 and 1982 (Newing *et al.* 1984).

Conservation Measures Taken Proposals to develop Aldabra as a military air base were dropped in 1967 (Stoddart 1968). The Royal Society of London took over the lease and opened a research station there in 1971 (Stoddart 1979). Since March 1980 the research station has been run by the Seychelles Islands Foundation, in September 1981 the island was designated a Special Reserve, and in December 1982 it was added to the World Heritage Site list (Stoddart and Ferrari 1983). The

Aldabra Warbler was studied over 27 months from July 1974 to February 1977 with a view to identifying its status and needs (Prys-Jones 1979). A resulting proposal that no east-west paths should be cut which might permit westward encroachment by goats or tortoises has been adopted (C. W. D. Gibson pers. comm. 1982).

Conservation Measures Proposed The elimination of goats from Middle Island is regarded as urgent and control measures are being planned (C. Hambler *in litt.* 1983). Both rat eradication and the creation of further suitable areas for Brush Warblers have been accepted as unfeasible (the former at least currently), but further investigation has been urged both of the remaining suspected area of distribution and of other places – such as the densely vegetated, little known region in the south-west corner of South Island (= Grande Terre) – where the species might conceivably occur (Prys-Jones 1979; see Remarks).

Remarks Suitable habitat for the species as defined under Ecology now ends at Opark, since *Dracaena* is lost east of this site, and the vegetation is more open and differently composed (Hambler *et al.* in prep.). The 1981 record (see Distribution) was in a patch of fairly thick mixed scrub adjacent to some pure *Pemphis* scrub: if birds are resident in this vegetation, other such habitat is available, probably becoming more suitable westward towards Opark (C. Hambler *in litt.* 1983). However, if birds are to be found elsewhere than in the habitat defined under Ecology, they are most likely to be further inland between Gionnet and Opark, as far as the pure *Pemphis* scrub: this area does not hold *Pandanus*, but the measure used to establish the importance to the species of this plant (in Prys-Jones 1979) was possibly not sensitive enough to be confident of the finding (Hambler *et al.* in prep.). South Island could conceivably harbour birds if their habitat requirements are less stringent than appears, but mixed scrub there is rapidly being degraded (Hambler *et al.* in prep.).

References

Benson, C. W. and Penny, M. J. (1971) The land birds of Aldabra. *Phil. Trans. Roy. Soc. Lond.* B 260: 417-527.

Benson, C. W. and Penny, M. J. (1968) A new species of warbler from the Aldabra Atoll. *Bull. Brit. Orn. Club* 88: 102-108.

Hambler, C., Hambler, K. and Newing, J. (1983) Cambridge Aldabra Rail and Brush Warbler Expedition, 1983, preliminary report. Unpublished.

Hambler, C., Hambler, K. and Newing, J. M. (in prep.) Some observations on *Nesillas aldabranus* – the endangered brush warbler of Aldabra Atoll.

Newing, T., Daly, K. and Hambler, K. (1984) Southampton University Expedition to Aldabra 1982, final report. Unpublished.

Prys-Jones, R. P. (1979) The ecology and conservation of the Aldabra brush warbler *Nesillas aldabranus*. *Phil. Trans. Roy. Soc. Lond.* B 286: 211-224.

Stoddart, D. R. (1968) The Aldabra affair. *Biol. Conserv.* 1: 63-69.

Stoddart, D. R. (1979) Aldabra and the Aldabra Research Station. *Phil. Trans. Roy. Soc. Lond.* B 286: 3-10.

Stoddart, D. R. and Ferrari, J. D. M. (1983) Aldabra atoll: a stunning success story for conservation. *Nature and Resources* 19(1): 20-28.

PAPYRUS YELLOW WARBLER   RARE

Chloropeta gracilirostris Ogilvie-Grant, 1906

Order PASSERIFORMES   Family MUSCICAPIDAE
                                                   Subfamily SYLVIINAE

Summary This rare warbler is known chiefly from papyrus swamps, but occasionally other marshy habitats, in areas of high rainfall in Burundi, Kenya, Rwanda, Uganda, Zaire and Zambia. It is threatened by attempts to drain and exploit papyrus swamps.

Distribution The Papyrus Yellow Warbler has a patchy distribution and comprises two subspecies. The nominate form occurs in western Uganda, western Kenya, Rwanda, Burundi and eastern Zaire. *C. g. bensoni* is restricted to Lake Mweru at the mouth of the Luapula River, on the border of southern Zaire and northern Zambia.

Burundi This species was discovered in Burundi in 1979 near Karuzi, and subsequently in the Ndurumu Valley, in the centre of the country (Vande weghe 1981).

Kenya The species is known in Kenya from Lake Kanyaboli (part of the Yala Swamp) in the west of the country, where it was discovered in 1969 (Britton and Harper 1969) and where it was subsequently seen on several occasions between 1969 and 1972 (Britton 1978). It has also recently been recorded from the extensive papyrus swamps at Kendu Bay in Lake Victoria, and it is believed that the species may prove more widespread in Lake Victoria's fringing papyrus, which are little explored ornithologically (D. A. Turner *in litt.* 1983).

Rwanda Exploration between 1969 and 1981 has located the species in northern Rwanda around Lakes Luhondo and Bulera at 1,750 and 1,860 m respectively and in the nearby Rugezi and Mulindi swamps at 2,050 and 1,850 m (Vande weghe 1981). It has also been found in central, southern and south-eastern Rwanda in the Akanyaru Swamp and in the Kagogo and Kibaya valleys but it is absent from the Akagera National Park (Vande weghe 1981).

Uganda The type-specimen was collected at Muhokya (Mokia) at 1,000 m on the south-eastern slopes of Mount Rwenzori in 1906, near Lake George (Ogilvie-Grant 1906,1910, Chapin 1953). There were no subsequent records until 1927 when birds were collected on the shores of Lakes Edward, Bunyonyi (at 2,000 m) and Mutanda (at 1,800 m) (Chapin 1953). There have been unconfirmed sight records from the southern end of Lake Mobutu (Lake Albert) (Chapin 1953) but there appears to be no recent information on the status of this species in Uganda.

Zaire Both subspecies are recorded (Schouteden 1957): the nominate form was collected at Kabare on the shores of Lake Edward in 1927 (Chapin 1953,

Schouteden 1954-1955) and in the early 1930s four specimens were collected at Kibga, 2,400 m, south of Mount Visoke, in the Virunga Volcanoes (Schouteden 1938); the race *bensoni* is known from Nkole on the Luapula River at the southern end of Lake Mweru, where three specimens were collected in 1938 (Chapin 1953). There is no recent information on the status of the species in Zaire.

Zambia Six specimens of the race *bensoni* were collected on the Zambian side of the Luapula River in 1953 (Amadon 1954) and it was noted again in the same locality in 1964 (Keith and Vernon 1966,1969) and also during the last few years (D. R. Aspinwall *in litt.* 1983). It apparently does not occur around Lake Mweru itself but rather along the Luapula River, especially about 3 km upstream from the mouth of the river (Keith and Vernon 1969, Benson *et al.* 1971).

Population No detailed estimates have been made. In Burundi there is little information but the species is apparently rare (Vande weghe 1981). In Kenya the species was recorded on nine out of 15 monthly visits to Lake Kanyaboli (Britton 1978). In Rwanda it was recorded on over 75% of monthly surveys at the Rugezi and Mulindi swamps, between 25 and 75% of monthly surveys at the Akanyaru Swamp, and less than 25% of such surveys in the Kagogo valley (Vande weghe 1981). It is also described as plentiful around Lakes Bulera and Luhondo but much less common in the Kibaya valley (Vande weghe 1981). Although the density of the species is high at Rugezi, Mulindi, Bulera and Luhondo, the population in these areas must be small because suitable habitat is very restricted (J.-P. Vande weghe pers. comm. 1983). The Akanyaru Swamp, where density is much lower, probably has a much larger population because it covers a huge area (J.-P. Vande weghe pers. comm. 1983). In Uganda and Zaire numbers are not known. In Zambia it is fairly common in papyrus 3 km upstream from the mouth of the Luapula River (Keith and Vernon 1969).

Ecology This species is largely restricted to papyrus swamps (Chapin 1953, Keith and Vernon 1966,1969, Britton and Harper 1969, Benson *et al.* 1971, Britton 1978, Vande weghe 1981, D. R. Aspinwall *in litt.* 1983) where it is most frequent at high altitudes and in areas of high rainfall (Vande weghe 1981). The Rugezi and Mulindi swamps, where it is plentiful, are at altitudes of 2,050 and 1,850 m and have mean annual rainfalls of 1,200 and 1,050 mm respectively (Vande weghe 1981). The Akanyaru Swamp and the Kagogo valley, where it is less common, are both at 1,350 m, and have mean annual rainfalls of 1,050 and 1,000 mm respectively (Vande weghe 1981). It is absent from the Akagera National Park (altitude 1,300 m, mean annual rainfall 800 mm) and also many apparently suitable localities in western Tanzania and south-eastern Zaire, probably because the mean annual rainfall is less than 1,000 mm in these areas (Vande weghe 1981). It has been suggested that the species is in competition with the African Reed Warbler *Acrocephalus baeticatus*, which is usually found in swamps at lower altitudes and in drier areas (Vande weghe 1981). The two species have extraordinarily complementary distributions in Rwanda and Burundi, though they do overlap in small numbers in the Akanyaru Swamp and in the Kibaya and Kagogo valleys (Vande weghe 1981). They are also sympatric at Lake Kanyaboli and at the mouth of the Luapula River, though the African Reed Warbler is uncommon at both of these sites (Benson *et al.* 1971, Britton 1978). In Rwanda and Burundi the Papyrus Yellow Warbler forages in the middle and upper strata of papyrus (Vande weghe 1981) but in Zambia it apparently keeps to lower levels (Keith and Vernon 1966). Although it is normally considered an endemic to papyrus swamps it does occur in considerable numbers in other marshy habitats around Lakes Luhondo (at 1,750 m) and Bulera (at 1,860 m) in northern Rwanda (Vande weghe 1981). It is, however, restricted to papyrus swamps at lower altitudes and in the drier parts of its range (Vande weghe 1981), the race *bensoni* being apparently confined to papyrus growing in deep water (Keith and Vernon 1969). In Uganda and Zaire birds have been seen hopping from stem to stem in the papyrus (Chapin 1953) and in Zambia they apparently do not have a regular singing perch but sing as they move about low down in the vegetation (Keith and Vernon 1966). The diet consists of tiny insects (Chapin 1953). One bird collected at Lake Kanyaboli in June was in breeding condition (Britton and Harper 1969).

Threats This species is threatened by the draining of swamps and the cutting of papyrus: Lake Kanyaboli is threatened by a large land reclamation and irrigation scheme which might cut off the water supply to the lake (G. R. Cunningham-van Someren *in litt.* 1983), there are plans to drain the large Rugezi Swamp in northern Rwanda and to plant the area with tea (J.-P. Vande weghe pers. comm. 1983), and there are schemes being introduced to cut papyrus for fuel (Jones 1983). The areas of papyrus along the lower Luapula River in Zambia are apparently under no immediate threat (D. R. Aspinwall *in litt.* 1984).

Conservation Measures Taken This species probably occurs within the Rwenzori National Park in Uganda and the Virunga National Park in Zaire.

Conservation Measures Proposed Particularly important sites for which effective conservation is urgently needed are Lakes Bunyoni and Mutanda in Uganda, Lake Kanyaboli in Kenya, the Akanyaru Swamp in Rwanda, and the mouth of the Luapula River in Zaire and Zambia. A survey of the birds (notably this species) of western Kenyan papyrus swamps was scheduled for 1984 (D. A. Turner *in litt.* 1983). A survey is also needed to assess the present status of this species in Uganda and Zaire. It is also to be hoped that papyrus-cutting schemes will be subject to careful guidelines that limit ecological damage.

Remarks This species has been placed in a monotypic genus *Calamonastides* (Grant and Mackworth-Praed 1940), though subsequent authorities have included it in *Chloropeta* (Chapin 1953, Benson *et al.* 1971). The Papyrus Yellow Warbler is the most threatened of the birds endemic to papyrus swamps in Africa. One bird sometimes associated with papyrus, the Shoebill *Balaeniceps rex*, is treated here as a Species of Special Concern, while several others are included in Appendix C. The Papyrus Yellow Warbler is sympatric with the Shoebill in several areas and also with another threatened bird species, Grauer's Swamp Warbler *Bradypterus graueri* (which is not a papyrus endemic), in the Rugezi Swamp and around the Virunga Volcanoes (see relevant accounts).

References

Amadon, D. (1954) A new race of *Chloropeta gracilirostris* Ogilvie-Grant. *Ostrich* 25: 140-141.

Benson, C. W., Brooke, R. K., Dowsett, R. J. and Irwin, M. P. S. (1971) *The birds of Zambia*. London: Collins.

Britton, P. L. (1978) Seasonality, density and diversity of birds of a papyrus swamp in western Kenya. *Ibis* 120: 450-466.

Britton, P. L. and Harper, J. F. (1969) Some new distributional records for Kenya. *Bull. Brit. Orn. Club* 89: 162-165.

Chapin, J. P. (1953) The birds of the Belgian Congo. Part 3. *Bull. Amer. Mus. Nat. Hist.* 75A.

Grant, C. H. B. and Mackworth-Praed, C. W. (1940) A new genus of African swamp warbler. *Bull. Brit. Orn. Club* 60: 91-92.

Jones, M. B. (1983) Papyrus: a new fuel for the Third World. *New Scientist* 99, 11 August: 418-421.

Keith, S. and Vernon, C. (1966) Notes on African warblers of the genus *Chloropeta* Smith. *Bull. Brit. Orn. Club* 86: 115-120.

Keith, G. S. and Vernon, C. J. (1969) Bird notes from northern and eastern Zambia. *Puku* 5: 131-139.

Ogilvie-Grant, W. R. (1906) [New species from Ruwenzori.] *Bull. Brit. Orn. Club* 19: 32-33.

Ogilvie-Grant, W. R. (1910) Ruwenzori Expedition Reports 16. Aves. *Trans. Zool. Soc. Lond.* 19: 253-453.

Schouteden, H. (1938) Oiseaux. *Exploration du Parc National Albert, Mission G. F. de Witte (1933-1935)* 9: 1-198.

Schouteden, H. (1954-1955) De Vogels van belgisch Congo en van Ruanda-Urundi, 3. *Ann. Mus. Roy. Congo Belge*, Zool. (4)4: 1-524.

Schouteden, H. (1957) Faune du Congo Belge et du Ruanda-Urundi. IV. Oiseaux passereaux (1). *Ann. Mus. Roy. Congo Belge* 8°, Sci. Zool. 29: 1-434.

Vande weghe, J.-P. (1981) L'avifaune des papyraies au Rwanda et au Burundi. *Gerfaut* 71: 489-536.

TANA RIVER CISTICOLA
Cisticola restricta Traylor, 1967

Order PASSERIFORMES

INSUFFICIENTLY KNOWN

Family MUSCICAPIDAE
Subfamily SYLVIINAE

Summary This warbler is known from a small number of specimens, all collected in the lower Tana River basin in eastern Kenya. Recent attempts to locate the species in the field have been unsuccessful; it may occur in Somalia.

Distribution The Tana River Cisticola is found in the lower Tana River basin in eastern Kenya, near the coast (Traylor 1967, Britton 1980). The type-specimen was collected in 1932 at Karawa and other early records are from Mnazinia (presumably the "Mnazini" in TAW 1980), Sangole and Ijara (Traylor 1967). In the 1960s some specimens were collected south of Garissa (J. G. Williams *in litt.* 1983) and in 1967 two specimens were collected a few kilometres south of Garsen (specimens in BMNH: SNS); in 1972 another was taken in the type-locality (G. R. Cunningham-van Someren *in litt.* 1983). All recent attempts to locate the bird within its Kenyan range have been unsuccessful and it has been suggested that the main population is within southern Somalia where there have been observations of birds which might be this species (Lewis 1982).

Population Numbers are not known.

Ecology The species inhabits semi-arid sandy *Acacia* bushland (Britton 1980, J. G. Williams *in litt.* 1983, and specimen labels in BMNH: SNS). In the field it is similar to the Ashy Cisticola *Cisticola cinereola* but it has a less strident call (J. G. Williams *in litt.* 1983).

Threats It is not known what effects the building of dams on the Tana River will have on the adjacent bushland habitat (P. L. Britton *in litt.* 1983, G. R. Cunningham-van Someren *in litt.* 1983) but there is no reason to believe that such developments will be detrimental to the species (P. L. Britton *in litt.* 1983, J. G. Williams *in litt.* 1983).

Conservation Measures Taken None is known.

Conservation Measures Proposed A more thorough attempt to discover the distribution and habitat requirements of the species is required in both Kenya and Somalia.

Remarks The first six specimens of the Tana River Cisticola were originally thought to be examples of the Ashy Cisticola, but were subsequently found to belong to a new species (Traylor 1967). Although it is superficially similar to the Ashy Cisticola its relationships are probably closer to the Rattling Cisticola *Cisticola chiniana* or the Wailing Cisticola *C. lais distincta* (Traylor 1967).

References

Britton, P. L. (1980) *Birds of East Africa: their habitat, status and distribution*. Nairobi: EANHS.

Lewis, A. D. (1982) Field identification of the genus *Cisticola* (Aves) in Kenya: Part 3. *EANHS Bull.* March/April: 28-37.

The Times Atlas of the World (1980) Comprehensive (sixth) edition. London: Times Books.

Traylor, M. A. (1967) A new species of Cisticola. *Bull. Brit. Orn. Club* 87: 45-48.

RIVER PRINIA   INSUFFICIENTLY KNOWN
Prinia "fluviatilis" Chappuis, 1974

Order PASSERIFORMES   Family MUSCICAPIDAE
                                             Subfamily SYLVIINAE

Summary This recently discovered species, for which a full description is awaited, is known only from waterside vegetation in a few localities shared between Niger, Chad and northern Cameroon. Nothing is known of its status.

Distribution The River Prinia has been found only in a few localities in Niger, Chad and northern Cameroon. Two birds were found south of Gao in Niger in 1969 (Chappuis 1974). Two more birds were located near N'Djamena, in Chad, along the edge of the Chari River in 1972 (Chappuis 1974). Another bird was found around the same time in Chad in the area south of Lake Chad (Chappuis 1974). Birds have also been located south of Lake Chad in northern Cameroon (Louette 1981). The distribution of this species is still very imperfectly known (Louette 1981).

Population Numbers are not known.

Ecology All records of this species have been from waterside vegetation, usually along water-courses (Chappuis 1974). Unlike the related Tawny-flanked Prinia *Prinia subflava* this species is never associated with trees (Chappuis 1974). The River Prinia is a very active species and its song is completely different from that of the Tawny-flanked Prinia (Chappuis 1974).

Threats None is known.

Conservation Measures Taken None is known.

Conservation Measures Proposed A survey is needed to assess the taxonomic and conservation status of this species and to determine whether conservation action is needed.

Remarks The original description of this species unfortunately failed to designate a type-specimen or a type-locality (Mayr and Vuilleumier 1983). A full description of it is also awaited (Louette 1981).

References

Chappuis, C. (1974) Illustration sonore de problèmes bioacoustiques posés par les oiseaux de la zone éthiopienne, deuxième partie. *Alauda* 42: 467-500.
Louette, M. (1981) *The birds of Cameroon. An annotated check-list*. Brussels: Verhandeling Wetenschappen, Jaargang 43, no. 163.
Mayr, E. and Vuilleumier, F. (1983) New species of birds described from 1966 to 1975. *J. Orn.* 124: 217-232.

KARAMOJA APALIS
Apalis karamojae (van Someren, 1921)

Order PASSERIFORMES

INSUFFICIENTLY KNOWN

Family MUSCICAPIDAE
Subfamily SYLVIINAE

Summary This is a very little known warbler recorded from only a few places in north-eastern Uganda and northern Tanzania. The species is clearly rare but further research might show it to be in no immediate danger.

Distribution The Karamoja Apalis was discovered at Mount Kamalinga in Karamoja District, Uganda, where three specimens were collected in 1919 (van Someren 1921a,b,1922). The next specimen was taken in 1931 at Napiananya, Karamoja, in 1931 (specimen in BMNH: SNS). This locality, also written "Napianyenya", is at 1°52'N 34°35'E (Office of Geography 1964), 50 km from Mount Kamalinga at the foot of Mount Kadam (sometimes called Kaduma or Debasien), a locality mentioned for this species by some authors (Hall and Moreau 1962, White 1962, Britton 1980). In 1958 a specimen was collected at the foot of Mount Moroto, 80 km north of the type-locality, also in Karamoja (specimen in NMK: Hall and Moreau 1962, G. R. Cunningham-van Someren *in litt.* 1983), and another was taken at the same locality in the early 1960s (J. G. Williams pers. comm. 1983). The only subsequent record from Uganda is of five birds seen (including one collected, now in BMNH: SNS) at Kanatorok in Kidepo Valley National Park, 160 km north of Mount Moroto, in 1966 (Elliott 1972). In 1961 a separate population was discovered (three specimens collected) at Itumba on the Wembere Steppe in the Sukumaland area of northern Tanzania, 120 km east-south-east of Nzega and 720 km south of the Karamoja population (Hall and Moreau 1962, G. R. Cunningham-van Someren *in litt.* 1983, B. W. H. Stronach *in litt.* 1983). Another specimen was collected nearby at Ngongoro in 1962 (specimen in BMNH: SNS). Several field observations have been made on this Sukumaland population (J. F. Reynolds *in litt.* 1983, B. W. H. Stronach *in litt.* 1983). In the late 1970s and early 1980s the species was seen over a wider area between Nzega and Igunga, south to Ndala (R. K. Walton *in litt.* 1983). There is also an unconfirmed record of this bird from Ndutu in the south of the Serengeti National Park, 230 km north-north-east of the Wembere Steppe (G. R. Cunningham-van Someren *in litt.* 1983).

Population Numbers are not known. The very few records from Uganda suggest it must be rare there, but it is reported as not uncommon in suitable parts of the Wembere Steppe in Tanzania (J. F. Reynolds *in litt.* 1983, B. W. H. Stronach *in litt.* 1983) and also at Nzega (R. K. Walton *in litt.* 1983).

Ecology Very little is known of the ecology of this species in Uganda. The Mount Moroto specimens probably came from areas of thick bush and small trees, especially along seasonal watercourses (Hall and Moreau 1962). In Kidepo Valley National Park a small flock of five birds was seen low in dwarf acacia (Elliott 1972). In Tanzania the species has been found in areas of *Acacia kirkii*, *A. drepanolobium*

539

and *A. mellifera* intermingled with *Commiphora ugogensis* on seasonally inundated ground along the edge of the Wembere River (Hall and Moreau 1962, J. F. Reynolds *in litt.* 1983, B. W. H. Stronach *in litt.* 1983, R. K. Walton *in litt.* 1983). This habitat stretches in a very narrow band for about 175 km and it is likely that the Karamoja Apalis occurs through the entire length of the band (B. W. H. Stronach *in litt.* 1983). It also occurs in dense bushy growth, especially on hard, imperfectly drained sodic soils (R. K. Walton *in litt.* 1983). The species apparently travels in foraging parties (J. F. Reynolds *in litt.* 1983). Details of its breeding are unknown.

Threats None is known in Uganda. In Tanzania there has been a massive human population increase in Sukumaland and the species is therefore likely to be threatened by habitat changes (R. K. Walton *in litt.* 1983). There has been much wood-cutting and cattle-grazing throughout this area, almost certainly detrimental to the species (R. K. Walton *in litt.* 1983). It has been suggested that the Karamoja and the Sukumaland populations of this species have become separated in recent times by extensive clearance and cultivation around the shore of Lake Victoria (Hall and Moreau 1962, Turner 1977); however, the two are subspecifically distinct (see Remarks).

Conservation Measures Taken None is known other than that the Kidepo Valley National Park provides some hope for the species's long-term security.

Conservation Measures Proposed A survey is needed to assess the status of this species in Uganda and Tanzania. It may be necessary to recommend the creation of a nature reserve to protect the Tanzanian population.

Remarks The Karamoja Apalis is a very distinct species with no close relatives (Hall and Moreau 1962). The Tanzanian birds are much darker than those in Uganda (Hall and Moreau 1962) and represent an undescribed subspecies (Stuart and Collar in press).

References

Britton, P. L. ed. (1980) *Birds of East Africa: their habitat, status and distribution.* Nairobi: EANHS.

Elliott, C. C. H. (1972) An ornithological survey of Kidepo National Park, northern Uganda. *J. E. Afr. Nat. Hist. Soc. and Natn. Mus.* 129: 1-31.

Hall, B. P. and Moreau, R. E. (1962) A study of the rare birds of Africa. *Bull. Brit. Mus. (Nat. Hist.) Zool.* 8: 313-378.

Office of Geography (1964) *Gazetteer no. 82. Uganda.* Washington, D. C.: Department of the Interior.

van Someren, V. G. L. (1921a) [New East African forms.] *Bull. Brit. Orn. Club* 41: 120-125.

van Someren, V. G. L. (1921b) On a collection of birds from Turkanaland. *J. E. Afr. Uganda Nat. Hist. Soc.* 16: 3-38.

van Someren, V. G. L. (1922) Notes on the birds of East Africa. *Novit. Zool.* 29: 1-246.

Stuart, S. N. and Collar, N. J. (in press) Subspeciation in the Karamoja Apalis *Apalis karamojae*. *Bull. Brit. Orn. Club*.

Turner, D. A. (1977) Status and distribution of East African endemic species. *Scopus* 1: 2-11,56.

White, C. M. N. (1962) A check-list of Ethiopian Muscicapidae (Sylviinae), Part III. *Occ. Pap. Natn. Mus. S. Rhod.* 26B: 695-738.

KUNGWE APALIS

RARE

Apalis argentea Moreau, 1941

Order PASSERIFORMES

Family MUSCICAPIDAE
Subfamily SYLVIINAE

Summary This warbler is known only from a few isolated forest areas in western Tanzania, eastern Zaire, Rwanda and Burundi. It appears to be in danger from forest clearance through most of its range.

Distribution The nominate subspecies of the Kungwe Apalis is restricted to the area around Mahale (or Kungwe) Mountain in western Tanzania, whereas *A. a. eidos* occurs on Idjwi Island in Lake Kivu, eastern Zaire, the Nyungwe (or Rugege) Forest in Rwanda and the Bururi Forest in Burundi. The nominate subspecies was discovered in 1940 when a specimen was collected in montane forest above Ujamba on Mahale Mountain (Moreau 1941). Between 1949 and 1951 four birds originally identified as the Grey Apalis *Apalis cinerea* were collected at 1,830 m on Mahale Mountain (F. P. Jensen *in litt.* 1983). One of these, now in ZMK, is certainly the Kungwe Apalis (F. P. Jensen *in litt.* 1983) and it is likely that the other three are also since the Grey Apalis has never been recorded from the Mahale area (Britton 1980). In 1958 two more specimens were collected, and a few birds seen, in the same locality at 2,000 m (Ulfstrand 1960, Ulfstrand and Lamprey 1960). The altitudinal range of the species on Mahale Mountain is said to be from 1,800 to 2,200 m (Britton 1980), this information presumably being based on unpublished records of the species. To the north-east of the main Mahale Mountain block, three specimens were collected at 1,300 m along the Lukolansala River, a tributary of the upper Nyamanzi River, in 1943 (specimens in BMNH: SNS). Also in 1943 a specimen was taken to the east of Mahale, 64 km north-east of Karema, on the Katuma River at 1,200 m, near Mpanda (specimen in BMNH: SNS). The race *eidos* was discovered in 1939 when eight birds were collected on Idjwi Island, in Lake Kivu, eastern Zaire (Peters and Loveridge 1942). There have been many subsequent records of this species from Idjwi Island up to 1969 (Prigogine 1967,1973), including 17 specimens in MRAC (SNS). On Idjwi Island the species occurs between 1,510 and 2,000 m (Prigogine 1967). In 1953 *eidos* was found in the Nyungwe Forest, Rwanda (specimen in MRAC: SNS) and it was rediscovered at this locality in 1972, when field observations were made at 1,900 – 2,000 m on two occasions (Vande weghe 1974). It is now known to be restricted to only a few hundred hectares on the northern edge of the western part of Nyungwe Forest (J.-P. Vande weghe pers. comm. 1983), around Uwinka and the Nyirabanda valley (Vande weghe 1974), and Cyaruga (from where there is a specimen in IRSNB: SNS). There are also recent records from the Bururi Forest in Burundi, where only 10 ha of suitable habitat survive (J.-P. Vande weghe pers. comm. 1983).

Population Numbers are not known. Very little information is available on the abundance of the nominate subspecies. The race *eidos* is reported to be common on Idjwi Island and locally common in the extreme north-western corner of Nyungwe Forest (Prigogine 1967, in press, J.-P. Vande weghe *in litt.* 1983).

Ecology On Mahale Mountain this species is known from forest and forest edges with bamboo (Moreau 1941, Ulfstrand 1960, Britton 1980, F. P. Jensen *in litt.* 1983) where it keeps to the canopy (Moreau 1943): on one occasion a flock of 5-6 birds was seen, moving quickly through the vegetation (Ulfstrand 1960). It is apparently shy and difficult to approach (Moreau 1943, Ulfstrand 1960). Along the Lukolansala and Katuma Rivers it is also found in forest, according to BMNH specimen-labels (SNS). The race *eidos* occurs in groups of 4-6 (exceptionally 12-20) individuals in the middle and canopy strata of primary forest, e.g. on Idjwi Island (Prigogine 1967, J.-P. Vande weghe *in litt.* 1983). In Nyungwe and Bururi Forests it occurs only in dry forest, hence its very restricted distribution in both these areas (J.-P. Vande weghe pers. comm. 1983). In Nyungwe Forest it has been seen in secondary vegetation and in isolated trees (Vande weghe 1974). On Idjwi Island no congeners are present (Prigogine 1967) but in Nyungwe Forest it has been seen in a mixed-species flock with the Masked Apalis *Apalis binotata*, the Grey Apalis and the Black-throated Apalis *A. jacksoni* (Vande weghe 1974, J.-P. Vande weghe *in litt.* 1983). Breeding probably takes place on Idjwi Island in June and July (Prigogine 1967).

Threats This species is presumably under threat from forest clearance. It is known that many of the forests in the valleys around Mahale Mountain and Mpanda have been destroyed (J. Kielland pers. comm. 1981). The forest on Idjwi Island is also threatened with clearance (A. Prigogine *in litt.* 1983) and the tiny areas of dry forest at Nyungwe and Bururi are at risk from fire and cutting (J.-P. Vande weghe pers. comm. 1983).

Conservation Measures Taken None is known.

Conservation Measures Proposed The Tanzanian government is planning to establish a national park on Mahale Mountain (W. A. Rodgers pers. comm. 1981), which should be sufficient to safeguard the nominate subspecies. The Nyungwe Forest Conservation Project should ensure the preservation of the small area there in which the race *eidos* occurs (J.-P. Vande weghe *in litt.* 1983).

Remarks Although the two forms of this bird were once considered separate species, they are now judged conspecific (Hall and Moreau 1970). Two other threatened bird species are known from the Nyungwe Forest (see Remarks under Albertine Owlet *Glaucidium albertinum*).

References

Britton, P. L. ed. (1980) *Birds of East Africa: their habitat, status and distribution.* Nairobi: EANHS.

Hall, B. P. and Moreau, R. E. (1970) *An atlas of speciation in African passerine birds.* London: Trustees of the British Museum (Natural History).

Moreau, R. E. (1941) New races of Pink-footed Puffback and Brown-chested Alethe and a new species of bush-warbler from eastern Africa. *Bull. Brit. Orn. Club* 61: 45-47.

Moreau, R. E. (1943) A contribution to the ornithology of the east side of Lake Tanganyika. *Ibis* 85: 377-412.

Peters, J. L. and Loveridge, A. (1942) Scientific results of a fourth expedition to forested areas in east and central Africa. *Bull. Mus. Comp. Zool.* 89: 217-275.

Prigogine, A. (1967) La faune ornithologique de l'île Idjwi. *Rev. Zool. Bot. Afr.* 75: 249-274.

Prigogine, A. (1973) La faune ornithologique de l'île Idjwi (addendum). *Rev. Zool. Bot. Afr.* 87: 189-194.

Prigogine, A. (in press) The conservation of the avifauna of the forests of the Albertine Rift. *Proceedings of the ICBP Tropical Forest Bird Symposium, 1982*.

Ulfstrand, S. (1960) The juvenile plumage of *Apalis argentea* Moreau 1941 and a note on the habitat of the species. *Bull. Brit. Orn. Club* 80: 2-3.

Ulfstrand, S. and Lamprey, H. (1960) On the birds of the Kungwe-Mahari area in western Tanganyika Territory. *J. E. Afr. Nat. Hist. Soc.* 23: 223-232.

Vande weghe, J.-P. (1974) Additions et corrections à l'avifaune du Rwanda. *Rev. Zool. Afr.* 81: 81-98.

KABOBO APALIS   RARE

Apalis kaboboensis Prigogine, 1955

Order PASSERIFORMES   Family MUSCICAPIDAE

                                                           Subfamily SYLVIINAE

Summary This warbler is known only from montane forest on Mount Kabobo, west of Lake Tanganyika, in eastern Zaire. There is no recent information on its status.

Distribution The Kabobo Apalis was discovered in 1954 in montane forest on Mount Kabobo at 1,660 m (Prigogine 1955). A total of at least 24 birds was collected on the mountain between 1954 and 1957 (specimens in MRAC, IRSNB and BMNH: SNS) but there appear to have been no subsequent visits to this area by ornithologists. The species has been recorded between 1,600 and 2,480 m (Prigogine 1955,1960, in press). It is unlikely to be found on neighbouring mountain ranges, since these are occupied by a related species, the Chestnut-throated Apalis *Apalis porphyrolaema* (Hall and Moreau 1962).

Population Numbers are not known. This species is reported to be common on Mount Kabobo (Prigogine in press) though the area it occupies is probably less than 2,000 km^2 (A. Prigogine *in litt.* 1983).

Ecology Very little is known about the ecology of this species. It occurs in the canopy of montane forest (Prigogine 1955). Five other members of its genus occur on the mountain (Prigogine 1960).

Threats None is known. Forest destruction would presumably be detrimental to the species, but there is no recent information on the conservation status of the Mount Kabobo forests (Prigogine in press).

Conservation Measures Taken None is known.

Conservation Measures Proposed A nature reserve or national park should be established on Mount Kabobo (Prigogine in press).

Remarks Although sometimes believed to be a subspecies of the Chestnut-throated Apalis (Hall and Moreau 1970) it is considered that the Kabobo Apalis has diverged sufficiently to deserve specific status (Prigogine 1955,1960, in press).

References

Hall, B. P. and Moreau, R. E. (1962) A study of the rare birds of Africa. *Bull. Brit. Mus. (Nat. Hist.) Zool.* 8: 313-378.

Hall, B. P. and Moreau, R. E. (1970) *An atlas of speciation in African passerine birds*. London: Trustees of the British Museum (Natural History).

Prigogine, A. (1955) Une nouvelle fauvette du genre *Apalis* du Congo Belge. *Rev. Zool. Bot. Afr.* 51: 240-242.

Prigogine, A. (1960) La faune ornithologique du massif du Mont Kabobo. *Ann. Mus. Roy. Congo Belge* 8°, Sci. Zool. 85: 1-46.

Prigogine, A. (in press) The conservation of the avifauna of the forests of the Albertine Rift. *Proceedings of the ICBP Tropical Forest Bird Symposium, 1982.*

Order PASSERIFORMES

Family MUSCICAPIDAE
Subfamily SYLVIINAE

Summary This is a low-density species with two subspecies known from widely separated montane forests in Tanzania and Mozambique. It is mainly a bird of forest clearings and edges but it is still vulnerable to forest destruction.

Distribution The Long-billed Apalis is known only from two localities, one in Tanzania and one in Mozambique. The nominate race is known from the forests of the East Usambara Mountains in north-eastern Tanzania at 900 to 1,050 m (SNS). It was originally discovered at Amani in 1930 (Sclater 1931, Sclater and Moreau 1933) but has now been recorded in several parts of the East Usambara plateau, but only within a narrow altitudinal range (Stuart and Hutton 1977, SNS). At least seven birds were collected between 1930 and 1932 (specimens in BMNH: SNS) but it appears that no further records were documented until 1972 when some birds were seen and heard near Amani (R. J. Stjernstedt *in litt.* 1977). Since 1977 the nominate race has been recorded more frequently owing to increased fieldwork (Stuart and Hutton 1977, Stuart and van der Willigen 1978, D. A. Turner pers. comm. 1977, SNS). The race *sousae* is known only from seven specimens collected in 1945 on the Njesi Plateau at 1,650 m in northern Mozambique, 1,050 km south of the Usambaras (Benson 1945,1946). There have been no subsequent visits to this area by ornithologists. It has been suggested that the species has become extinct on the mountains between the East Usambaras and the Njesi Plateau owing to competition with other birds (Stuart 1981), though there may be some undiscovered intervening populations (see Remarks).

Population Nominate *moreaui* is known to be a low-density bird but no population estimates have been made. About 110 km^2 of forest still survived in the East Usambaras in 1979 within the altitudinal range of this subspecies (van der Willigen and Lovett 1981). The population of *sousae* is not known but the securing of seven specimens in two weeks (Benson 1946) suggests that it might occur at a higher density than the nominate subspecies. The area of forest on the Njesi Plateau is, however, probably less than 25 km^2 (Hall and Moreau 1962).

Ecology The habitat of the nominate form was originally described as the "undergrowth of dense forests" (Sclater and Moreau 1933). All recent records, however, have been from clearings and the forest edge in dense undergrowth (Stuart and Hutton 1977, SNS), occasionally at a considerable distance from forest (Stuart and Hutton 1977). Its natural habitat is probably clearings where trees have fallen, and such habitats have probably increased with the fragmentation of the forests and the felling of valuable timber trees (Stuart and Hutton 1977, SNS). The species is, however, very scarce and is often absent from large areas of apparently suitable habitat (SNS). *A. m. sousae*, in contrast to the nominate form, is reported to inhabit the forest canopy (Benson 1946), but this might be mistaken (Hall and

Moreau 1970, C. W. Benson *in litt.* 1980). It has been suggested, however, that this subspecies has avoided competition with the Red-capped Forest Warbler *Orthotomus metopias* by living in the canopy (Stuart 1981). The Long-billed Apalis is a very secretive species and would be very difficult to find were it not for its distinctive call (Sclater and Moreau 1933, Stuart and Hutton 1977, R. J. Stjernstedt *in litt.* 1977, D. A. Turner pers. comm. 1977, SNS). It has occasionally been seen in mixed-species parties (Stuart and Hutton 1977) and its food consists of insects (Sclater and Moreau 1933). There are no breeding data.

Threats It is clear that both subspecies would be adversely affected by widespread forest destruction but there is no recent information on the state of forest conservation on the Njesi Plateau. The rapid clearance of the East Usambara forests for cardamom plantations and of areas of undergrowth outside the forests for subsistence cultivation and *Eucalyptus* plantations (Rodgers and Homewood 1982, Stuart in prep.) poses a serious threat to the nominate subspecies (SNS).

Conservation Measures Taken Some of the forests in the East Usambaras are in forest reserves but those outside reserves are being cleared rapidly (Rodgers and Homewood 1982, Stuart in prep.; see Threats above). No conservation measures are known for the Njesi Plateau.

Conservation Measures Proposed A forest conservation proposal for the Usambaras is being prepared for the consideration of the Tanzanian government (Stuart in prep.). A survey of the Njesi Plateau is required to ascertain the status of *A. m. sousae* and to recommend appropriate conservation measures.

Remarks Many authors have considered that this species is not an *Apalis* warbler but a tailorbird in the genus *Orthotomus* (White 1960, Hall and Moreau 1962,1970, Fry 1976, Stuart 1981). All species of tailorbirds sew leaves together to make their nests, so this taxonomic judgement cannot be confirmed until the nest of the Long-billed Apalis is discovered. It has been suggested that the disjunct range of the species is due to unsuccessful competition with the Red-capped Forest Warbler and the Grey-backed Camaroptera *Camaroptera brachyura* (Stuart 1981). It may be that all three of these species belong in the same genus (Fry 1976). Attempts to locate the Long-billed Apalis in the middle altitude forests of the Nguru, Uluguru and Uzungwa Mountains in eastern Tanzania, where it might occur, have not so far been successful (SNS). Six other threatened bird species occur in the Usambaras (see Remarks under the Usambara Ground Robin *Dryocichloides montanus*).

References

Benson, C. W. (1945) A new race of the Long-billed Forest Warbler from Northern Portuguese East Africa. *Bull. Brit. Orn. Club* 66: 19.

Benson, C. W. (1946) A collection from near Unangu, Portuguese East Africa. *Ibis* 88: 240-241.

Fry, C. H. (1976) On the systematics of African and Asian tailor-birds (Sylviinae). *Arnoldia (Rhod.)* 8(6).

Hall, B. P. and Moreau, R. E. (1962) A study of the rare birds of Africa. *Bull. Brit. Mus. (Nat. Hist.) Zool.* 8: 313-378.

Hall, B. P. and Moreau, R. E. (1970) *An atlas of speciation in African passerine birds.* London: Trustees of the British Museum (Natural History).

Rodgers, W. A. and Homewood, K. M. (1982) Species richness and endemism in the Usambara mountain forests, Tanzania. *Biol. J. Linn. Soc.* 18: 197-242.

Sclater, W. L. (1931) [Three new birds from Amani Forest, in the Usambara District of Tanganyika.] *Bull. Brit. Orn. Club* 51: 109-112.

Sclater, W. L. and Moreau, R. E. (1933) Taxonomic and field notes on some birds of north-eastern Tanganyika Territory, Part III. *Ibis* (13)3: 1-33.

Stuart, S. N. (1981) An explanation for the disjunct distributions of *Modulatrix orostruthus* and *Apalis* (or *Orthotomus*) *moreaui*. *Scopus* 5: 1-4.

Stuart, S. N. (in prep.) A forest conservation plan for the Usambara Mountains, Tanzania.

Stuart, S. N. and Hutton, J. M. eds. (1977) The avifauna of the East Usambara Mountains, Tanzania. A report compiled by the Cambridge Ornithological Expedition to East Africa 1977. Unpublished.

Stuart, S. N. and van der Willigen, T. A. eds. (1978) Report of the Cambridge Ecological Expedition to Tanzania 1978. Unpublished.

White, C. M. N. (1960) Further notes on African warblers. *Bull. Brit. Orn. Club* 80: 147-152.

van der Willigen, T. A. and Lovett, J. C. eds. (1981) Report of the Oxford Expedition to Tanzania 1979. Unpublished.

MRS MOREAU'S WARBLER

RARE

Bathmocercus winifredae (Moreau, 1938)

Order PASSERIFORMES

Family MUSCICAPIDAE
Subfamily SYLVIINAE

Summary Known from three restricted areas of mountain forest in eastern Tanzania. The species is not in immediate danger but more effective conservation of its forest habitat is required.

Distribution Mrs Moreau's Warbler is known only from three mountain ranges in eastern Tanzania. The species was discovered in Kinole Forest in the Uluguru Mountains in 1937 (Moreau 1938) and the many subsequent records show it to be distributed throughout the mountains, from 1,350 up to at least 2,350 m (Moreau 1946, Williams 1951, Friedmann and Stager 1964, Turner 1977, Scharff *et al.* 1982, Stuart and Jensen in press, and specimens in ZMK [F. P. Jensen *in litt.* 1983] and NMK and BMNH: SNS). It is, however, uncommon below 1,650 m (Moreau 1946). The species was discovered at Mandege in the Ukaguru Mountains in 1964 (Friedmann and Stager 1964) and further observations were made at this locality in 1978 (Stuart and van der Willigen 1978). All Ukaguru records are from between 1,500 and 1,650 m but the forests have not been explored ornithologically at higher altitudes (SNS). In 1982 the species was discovered in the Mwanihana Forest on the eastern escarpment of the Uzungwa Mountains where it has been recorded between 1,300 and 1,700 m (Jensen *et al.* in press, F. P. Jensen *in litt.* 1982). It is possible that it occurs in other forests on the wet eastern escarpment of the Uzungwas but an attempt to locate birds on the escarpment at Chita, 160 km south-west of Mwanihana Forest, in 1984 was not successful (F. P. Jensen pers. comm. 1984). It is almost certainly absent from the dry plateau forests which have been well studied by ornithologists (Jensen *et al.* in press). It may also occur in the forests of the Rubeho Mountains, between the Uzungwas and the Ukagurus, but these are unknown ornithologically.

Population The species is described as fairly common in the Ulugurus (Friedmann and Stager 1964, Turner 1977, Stuart and van der Willigen 1978, Stuart and Jensen in press), especially above 1,650 m (SNS). It is common in the Ukagurus (Stuart and van der Willigen 1978) and fairly common in Mwanihana Forest (Jensen *et al.* in press, F. P. Jensen *in litt.* 1982). No population estimate can be made until its distribution is better known.

Ecology Mrs Moreau's Warbler prefers the understorey of montane forest, especially natural clearings where the undergrowth is very dense (Williams 1951, Stuart and van der Willigen 1978). It occurs in wet forests in the Ulugurus and Uzungwas and in dry forests in the Ulugurus and Ukagurus (Moreau 1946, Hall and Moreau 1962, Stuart and van der Willigen 1978). It is unclear why it avoids the dry plateau forests of the Uzungwas. The breeding season is from October to March (Williams 1951, Friedmann and Stager 1964) but the nest and eggs are undescribed. It feeds on a wide variety of insects and other invertebrates, especially weevils

550

(Curculionidae) which it takes from the undergrowth and from the ground (Williams 1951, Friedmann and Stager 1964). Birds seem to travel through the undergrowth in pairs (Williams 1951, Stuart and van der Willigen 1978), constantly on the move, and occasionally moving up to 6 m above the ground (Stuart and van der Willigen 1978). The extraordinary song (Moreau 1946, Williams 1951) is usually delivered as a duet (Stuart and van der Willigen 1978).

Threats The species is certainly vulnerable to forest clearance, which is taking place in the Ulugurus (Scharff *et al.* 1982). Parts of the Ukaguru forests have also been cleared for softwood plantations (Stuart and van der Willigen 1978). Some forest exploitation is also taking place in the forests of the eastern escarpment of the Uzungwa Mountains (Rodgers and Homewood 1982).

Conservation Measures Taken Probably the entire population of this species is within forest reserves, which give some measure of protection to wildlife (SNS).

Conservation Measures Proposed A conservation strategy for the Ulugurus has been drafted with the proposal to elevate the status of the forest to a national nature reserve (Scharff *et al.* 1982). It has also been suggested that the Mwanihana Forest in the Uzungwas be included in a new national park (Rodgers and Homewood 1982). Further work is needed to determine the distribution of this species. If it is found to occur throughout the escarpment forests of the Uzungwas and in the Rubeho Mountains it could no longer be regarded as threatened.

Remarks Although at one time placed in the monotypic genus *Scepomycter* (Grant and Mackworth-Praed 1941) this species is now generally placed in the genus *Bathmocercus* forming a superspecies with the Rufous Warblers *B. cerviniventris* and *B. rufus* (Hall and Moreau 1970). Three other threatened bird species occur in the Ulugurus and six such species occur in the Uzungwas (see emarks under the Uluguru Bush-shrike *Malaconotus alius* and the Iringa Ground Robin *Dryocichloides lowei* respectively). In the Ukagurus one species in Appendix C occurs, Moreau's Sunbird *Nectarinia moreaui*.

References

Friedmann, H. and Stager, K. E. (1964) Results of the 1964 Cheney Tanganyikan Expedition. Ornithology. *Los Angeles County Mus. Contrib. Sci.* 84.

Grant, C. H. B. and Mackworth-Praed, C. W. (1941) A new genus of red-capped warbler from Tanganyika Territory. *Bull. Brit. Orn. Club* 62: 30.

Hall, B. P. and Moreau, R. E. (1962) A study of the rare birds of Africa. *Bull. Brit. Mus. (Nat. Hist.) Zool.* 8: 313-378.

Hall, B. P. and Moreau, R. E. (1970) *An atlas of speciation in African passerine birds.* London: Trustees of the British Museum (Natural History).

Jensen, F. P., Stuart, S. N. and Brogger-Jensen, S. (in press) Altitudinal distribution of the avifauna of the Mwanihana Forest, Tanzania. *Gerfaut.*

Moreau, R. E. (1938) [A new *Artisornis*.] *Bull. Brit. Orn. Club* 58: 139.

Moreau, R. E. (1946) The adult of Mrs Moreau's Warbler. *Bull. Brit. Orn. Club* 66: 44.

Rodgers, W. A. and Homewood, K. M. (1982) Biological values and conservation prospects for the forests and primate populations of the Uzungwa Mts., Tanzania. *Biol. Conserv.* 24: 285-304.

Scharff, N., Stoltze, M. and Jensen, F. P. (1982) The Uluguru Mts., Tanzania. Report of a study tour, 1981. Unpublished.

Stuart, S. N. and Jensen, F. P. (in press) The avifauna of the Uluguru Mountains, Tanzania. *Gerfaut.*

Stuart, S. N. and van der Willigen, T. A. (1978) Report of the Cambridge Ecological Expedition to Tanzania 1978. Unpublished.

Turner, D. A. (1977) Status and distribution of East African endemic species. *Scopus* 1: 2-11,56.

Williams, J. G. (1951) Notes on *Scepomycter winifredae* and *Cinnyris loveridgei*. *Ibis* 93: 469-470.

TURNER'S EREMOMELA   RARE
Eremomela turneri (van Someren, 1920)

Order PASSERIFORMES   Family MUSCICAPIDAE
                                                 Subfamily SYLVIINAE

Summary This rare forest warbler has a patchy distribution in western Kenya, south-western Uganda and eastern Zaire. There is little recent information on its status.

Distribution Turner's Eremomela is known only from a few localities in western Kenya, south-western Uganda and eastern Zaire. The type-specimen was collected in 1915 along the Yala River in western Kenya (van Someren 1920) and most subsequent Kenyan records have been from 1,500-1,700 m in Kakamega Forest (Tennent 1965, Ripley and Bond 1971, Zimmerman 1972, Britton 1980) through which the Yala River flows. Birds have been collected at Kakamega in 1961-1962 (specimens in NMK: G. R. Cunningham-van Someren *in litt.* 1983), 1964-1966 (see Ripley and Bond 1971, Zimmerman 1972) and 1970 (specimen in BMNH: SNS). In 1982 a small party of birds was seen in the nearby South Nandi Forest (M. A. Macdonald *in litt.* 1982). The only Uganda record is of one collected in 1911 in Nyondo Forest, near Kayonsha, just east of the Rutshuru valley in the extreme south-west of the country near the Zaire border (Chapin 1953). In 1950 the species was discovered in Zaire in the south-eastern corner of the equatorial forest belt (Prigogine 1958). Birds from this area have been described as a separate subspecies *E. t. kalindei* and it is likely that the Ugandan bird is also referable to this race (Prigogine 1958). Zaire specimens (in MRAC and IRSNB) have been collected at Mazali in 1950, Abyaloze in 1953, Makayobo in 1953, Kalima (two), 590 m, in 1954, and Kailo (four), 470 m, in 1956-1958 (SNS). In June 1978 one bird was observed 50 km north of Beni (C. Carter *in litt.* 1984). This observation is considerably further to the north than all previous records from Zaire, though it is not far from Nyondo Forest in Uganda.

Population Numbers are not known. Although one report refers to this species being uncommon in Kakamega Forest (Britton 1980) it is usually considered to be locally common in suitable areas (Tennent 1965, A. W. Diamond pers. comm. 1983, F. R. Lambert *in litt.* 1983, D. A. Turner *in litt.* 1983). In 1963 three birds were recorded in a 20 ha survey area in Kakamega, with two birds on the same plot in 1965 and three in 1966 (Zimmerman 1972). However, this survey was carried out in closed forest whereas the species is most frequent in more open habitats along the forest edge (A. W. Diamond pers. comm. 1983).

Ecology The species occurs mainly along streams and in forest edges and clearings, "native plantations" and second growth (Prigogine 1958, Zimmerman 1972, Britton 1980, A. W. Diamond pers. comm. 1983). It usually keeps to the tops of trees (Prigogine 1958, Zimmerman 1972, F. R. Lambert *in litt.* 1983, D. A. Turner *in litt.* 1983) and if it occurs in primary forest it is not likely to be easily visible (Zimmerman 1972). In Zaire, birds have been noted in small flocks of 10-15

(Prigogine 1958) and in Kakamega Forest they are usually seen in groups of 3-6, commonly feeding alongside the Buff-throated Apalis *Apalis rufogularis* (F. R. Lambert *in litt.* 1983). The closely related Brown-crowned Eremomela *Eremomela badiceps*, which overlaps with Turner's Eremomela in Zaire, feeds at lower levels in the vegetation (Prigogine 1958). The food consists of caterpillars and other insects, and birds in breeding condition have been collected in February and August (Prigogine 1958, Zimmerman 1972). The Brown-crowned Eremomela breeds at the same time of year (Prigogine 1958).

Threats Although this is a species of forest edges and clearings it is likely that forest clearance will be detrimental to its survival. There has been considerable encroachment of the forest at Kakamega (Diamond 1979), where the most serious problems are caused by cattle grazing and the removal, usually illegally, of saplings, timber and firewood (Cords 1982); but see Conservation Measures Taken and Conservation Measures Proposed.

Conservation Measures Taken A small area of the Kakamega Forest, south of the Yala River, has been set aside as a national reserve (G. R. Cunningham-van Someren *in litt.* 1983), and the northern part of the forest (9,698 ha) was declared a national park in 1983 (IUCN in press).

Conservation Measures Proposed Effective forest conservation measures are required at Kakamega, and around Kailo in Zaire. Some preliminary conservation recommendations for the Kakamega Forest have been prepared (Cords 1982) but it is not clear whether these are entirely fulfilled by the national park that now exists there. A survey is also needed to ascertain the present status of this species in eastern Zaire and Uganda.

Remarks Turner's Eremomela was once considered a subspecies of the Brown-crowned Eremomela until the two forms were found to be sympatric around Kailo in eastern Zaire (Prigogine 1958). In the Kakemega Forest it is sympatric with one other threatened bird species, Chapin's Flycatcher *Muscicapa lendu* (see relevant account).

References

Britton, P. L. ed. (1980) *Birds of East Africa: their habitat, status and distribution.* Nairobi: EANHS.

Chapin, J. P. (1953) The birds of the Belgian Congo. Part 3. *Bull. Amer. Mus. Nat. Hist.* 75A.

Cords, M. (1982) A report on harmful exploitation of indigenous forest in Kakamega. Unpublished.

Diamond, A. W. (1979) Kakamega. Is there a way to stop the rot? *Swara* 2(1): 25-26.

IUCN (in press) *The IUCN directory of Afrotropical protected areas.* Cambridge (U.K.) and Gland (Switzerland): IUCN Conservation Monitoring Centre and Commission on National Parks and Protected Areas.

Prigogine, A. (1958) The status of *Eremomela turneri* van Someren and the description of a new race from the Belgian Congo. *Bull. Brit. Orn. Club* 78: 146-148.

Ripley, S. D. and Bond, G. M. (1971) Systematic notes on a collection of birds from Kenya. *Smithsonian Contrib. Zool.* 111.

van Someren, Dr [V. G. L.] (1920) [New species and subspecies from East Africa and Uganda.] *Bull. Brit. Orn. Club* 40: 91-96.

Tennent, J. R. M. (1965) Notes on the birds of Kakamega Forest. *J. E. Afr. Nat. Hist. Soc. and Natn. Mus.* 25: 95-100.

Zimmerman, D. A. (1972) The avifauna of the Kakamega Forest, including a bird population study. *Bull. Amer. Mus. Nat. Hist.* 149: 255-399.

PULITZER'S LONGBILL

Macrosphenus pulitzeri Boulton, 1931

INDETERMINATE

Order PASSERIFORMES

Family MUSCICAPIDAE
Subfamily SYLVIINAE

Summary This warbler is known only from two forest areas on the escarpment of western Angola. There is no recent information on its status.

Distribution The type-specimen of Pulitzer's Longbill was collected at Chingoroi in the Camucuio Range in 1930 (Boulton 1931). The next specimen was taken 20 km from Chingoroi in 1960 and there were a few subsequent field observations from this area (Pinto 1962), and a specimen was taken at Caiundi at 1,030 m in October 1970 (J. N. Novais *in litt.* 1984). Another bird was collected 8 km from Vila Nova do Seles, about 180 km north of Chingoroi, in 1960 (Pinto 1962). In October 1974 a bird was taken at "Canjala (Egito), Benguela" at 300 m (J. N. Novais *in litt.* 1984; see Remarks). It has been suggested that the species might occur in other relict patches of forest on the escarpment of western Angola but all the forests in which it occurs are thought unlikely to cover more than a "few hundred square miles" (Hall and Moreau 1962).

Population Numbers are not known. In 1960 it was described as very rare at Vila Nova do Seles but slightly less so at Chingoroi (Pinto 1962).

Ecology All records are from "dry evergreen forest" (Hall and Moreau 1962) and "secondary forest" (Pinto 1962). The birds are difficult to observe, often hidden in the dense foliage of the trees (Pinto 1962). They are very restless as they search for insects at a very low (almost ground-) level in the forest (Pinto 1962). The type-specimen, which was collected in December (Boulton 1931), had an egg in its oviduct (Pinto 1962).

Threats There is no recent information on the conservation status of this species but it seems likely to be threatened by forest clearance; however, it has been speculated that it might be able to survive in coffee plantations (A. A. da R. Pinto *in litt.* 1983).

Conservation Measures Taken None is known.

Conservation Measures Proposed A survey is urgently needed to determine the conservation status of this species and to recommend which forest sites should be preserved to ensure its survival.

Remarks Pulitzer's Longbill forms a superspecies with the Grey Longbill *Macrosphenus concolor*, which ranges from Sierra Leone to Uganda (Hall and Moreau 1962,1970). This species is one of a group of birds endemic to the escarpment zone of western Angola (Hall 1960) including three other threatened bird species (seee Remarks under Gabela Helmet-shrike *Prionops gabela*). The specimen taken at Canjala is presumably that referred to by A. A. da R. Pinto (*in litt.* 1983) as the "recent capture at Balabaia, Egito".

References

Boulton, R. (1931) New species and subspecies of African birds. *Ann. Carnegie Mus.* 21: 43-56.

Hall, B. P. (1960) The faunistic importance of the scarp of Angola. *Ibis* 102: 420-442.

Hall, B. P. and Moreau, R. E. (1962) A study of the rare birds of Africa. *Bull. Brit. Mus. (Nat. Hist.) Zool.* 8: 313-378.

Hall, B. P. and Moreau, R. E. (1970) *An atlas of speciation in African passerine birds.* London: Trustees of the British Museum (Natural History).

Pinto, A. A. da R. (1962) As observações de maior destaque das expedições ornitológicas do Instituto de Investigação Científica de Angola. *Bol. Inst. Invest. Cient. Angola* 1: 21-38.

SAO TOME SHORT-TAIL
Amaurocichla bocagii Sharpe, 1892

INDETERMINATE

Order PASSERIFORMES

Family [MUSCICAPIDAE]
Subfamily [SYLVIINAE]

Summary This is a remarkable little forest bird of puzzling affinities and apparently tree-creeping and ground-haunting habits, confined to the island of São Tomé and not seen for over 50 years.

Distribution The São Tomé Short-tail is endemic to São Tomé (São Tomé e Príncipe) in the Gulf of Guinea. All records are from a small section bordering the west coast of the island, from Binda (0°13'N 6°28'E) south to Juliana de Sousa (0°12'N 6°28'E), São Miguel and Rio Quija (both 0°08'N 6°30'E) (Sharpe 1892, Bocage 1903, de Naurois in press; coordinates derived from Centro de Geográfia do Ultramar 1968). Three specimens were collected at the first three localities, 1890-1891, and three more were collected in 1928, two on 4 December and one on 8 December, all at Rio Quija (Correia 1928-1929; data on AMNH specimen-labels from R. F. Pasquier *in litt.* 1984). There are no subsequent records.

Population This has presumably always been a rare and localised species, though evidently also exceptionally elusive. Although it has been considered very probably extinct (de Naurois 1983) there are grounds for optimism that it may survive since much habitat is intact (de Naurois in press).

Ecology Examination of the 1928 material suggested the species to be "a long-legged, weak-flying denizen of the undergrowth" (Amadon 1953). The collector of these specimens actually thought them rails (Rallidae), finding the first in virgin forest "on small stones in the centre of the creek ... just at the head of the Rio Quija ... looking for something in the sand", the second flushing briefly (at the shot that killed the first) to land "on a dry limb right among the stones" (these two were a male and a female and perhaps paired), the third being collected four days later near the same spot but "on the mud ground" (Correia 1928-1929; English adapted by NJC). Since the birds were only found during or just after rain (the locality being visited several times when dry with no trace of them) it was speculated that they only came out in rainy weather (Correia 1928-1929). It has recently been established, moreover, that the original collector observed it creeping along branches like a tree-creeper (Certhiidae), and this appears to be confirmed by the abraded vanes and projecting shafts on the tails of some extant specimens (de Naurois in press).

Threats The reasons for this species's long-term rarity are quite un-known. Forest damage (selective felling) and destruction are known to have occurred in lowland areas of the island, notably from around 1890 to 1920 (Bannerman 1915, Correia 1928-1929, Snow 1950, de Naurois 1975, R. de Naurois *in litt.* 1984), and may have affected the bird. Introduced disease and mammalian predators may also have played a part.

Conservation Measures Taken None is known.

Conservation Measures Proposed An ICBP project was developed in 1981 to investigate the status, ecology and conservation of the endemic birds of São Tomé e Príncipe, but was unable to proceed in 1982 and 1983. A search for this bird is a component of the project and conservation proposals will follow if the work goes ahead and the species is relocated.

Remarks The São Tomé Short-tail is an extraordinary bird, combining characters in such a way as to be unclassifiable on present material. If it is not an aberrant warbler (Sylviinae), as tentatively treated here, or babbler (Timaliinae, both in the Muscicapidae) (see Amadon 1953), it has recently been suggested that its affinities may lie with certain South American families such as the woodhewers (Dendrocolaptidae) and ovenbirds (Furnariidae)), in particular the White-throated Treerunner *Pygarrhichas albogularis* (Furnariidae) (de Naurois in press). Not having been seen in the wild for over 50 years, by CITES criteria the São Tomé Short-tail would now be considered extinct.

References

Amadon, D. (1953) Avian systematics and evolution in the Gulf of Guinea. The J. G. Correia collection. *Bull. Amer. Mus. Nat. Hist.* 100: 393-451.

Bannerman, D. A. (1915) Report on the birds collected by the late Mr Boyd Alexander (Rifle Brigade) during his last expedition to Africa. Part II. The birds of St.Thomas' Island. *Ibis* (10)3: 89-121.

Bocage, J. V. B. (1903) Contribution à la faune des quatre îles du Golfe de Guinée. IV. Ile de St.Thomé. *Jorn. Acad. Sci. Lisboa* (2)7: 65-96.

Centro de Geográfia do Ultramar (1968) *Relação dos nomes geográficos de S. Tomé e Príncipe*. Lisboa: Junta de Investigações do Ultramar.

Correia, J. G. (1928-1929) Unpublished typescript concerning his São Tomé expedition, held in AMNH.

de Naurois, R. (1975) Le "Scops" de l'Ile de São Tomé *Otus hartlaubi* (Giebel). *Bonn. zool. Beitr.* 26: 319-355.

de Naurois, R. (1983) Les oiseaux reproducteurs des îles de São Tomé et Príncipe: liste systématique commentée et indications zoogéographiques. *Bonn. zool. Beitr.* 34: 129-148.

de Naurois, R. (in press) Une énigme ornithologique: *Amaurocichla bocagii* Sharpe 1892 (Ilha de São Tomé, Golfe de Guinée).

Sharpe, R. B. (1892) Descriptions of some new species of timeliine birds from West Africa. *Proc. Zool. Soc. Lond.*: 227-228.

Snow, D. W. (1950) The birds of São Tomé and Príncipe in the Gulf of Guinea. *Ibis* 92: 579-595.

NIMBA FLYCATCHER INDETERMINATE

Melaenornis annamarulae Forbes-Watson, 1970

Order PASSERIFORMES Family MUSCICAPIDAE
Subfamily MUSCICAPINAE

Summary This species is known only from lowland rainforest at the foot of Mount Nimba in Liberia and from the Tai National Park in south-western Ivory Coast. It has not, so far, been discovered elsewhere in West Africa and must therefore be very rare.

Distribution The Nimba Flycatcher is known from a single locality each in Liberia and Ivory Coast. It was discovered in 1967 at the foot of Mount Nimba in Liberia (Forbes-Watson 1970) and 12 specimens were collected at this locality between 1967 and 1971 (Colston and Curry-Lindahl in press). The only other record is of one collected in the Tai National Park in south western Ivory Coast in 1976 (specimen in MNHN: SNS). The species is likely to occur elsewhere in Liberia and Ivory Coast, and possibly also in Sierra Leone and Guinea, but so far searches have not been successful (G. D. Field pers. comm. 1983, W. Gatter *in litt.* 1983). It has been suggested that the species is restricted to the northern part of the forest zone (W. Gatter *in litt.* 1983).

Population Numbers are not known, though the small number of records indicates that it is very rare. Apart from the 12 specimens collected at Mount Nimba between 1967 and 1971 about 20 other individuals were seen during the same period (Forbes-Watson 1970, Colston and Curry-Lindahl in press). The species is probably easily overlooked and at Mount Nimba more birds were seen after forest clearing started, presumably owing to improved visibility (A. D. Forbes-Watson pers. comm. 1984).

Ecology This is a species of the interior of primary lowland forest, generally keeping 30 m and more above ground; it has never been seen below 20 m (Forbes-Watson 1970). It does not occur in the higher altitude forests of Mount Nimba (Forbes-Watson 1970). The species is usually seen in groups of 4-6 birds, though occasionally in pairs, often remaining in one general vicinity for several days (Forbes-Watson 1970). These groups are not very active but move slowly through the treetops, occasionally giving loud, strident calls (Forbes-Watson 1970). Food consists of insects caught on the wing or taken occasionally from crevices and moss on the branches of forest trees (Forbes-Watson 1970). Breeding is believed to take place during the wet season in July and August (Forbes-Watson 1970).

Threats The forests around Mount Nimba are being rapidly cleared for timber extraction, iron ore mining and farming (Verschuren 1982,1983, Colston and Curry-Lindahl in press, E. O. Willis *per* A. Tye *in litt.* 1983). The Tai Forest is also suffering from illegal encroachment (Roth 1982, Halle 1983, J.-M. Thiollay *in litt.* 1983). The rate of forest destruction in Africa west of the Dahomey Gap is so severe that any bird species endemic to primary forest in this region must now be considered gravely at risk (see Remarks under Rufous Fishing Owl *Scotopelia ussheri* for the species in question).

Conservation Measures Taken None is known, other than that the record of the species's occurrence within the Tai National Park in Ivory Coast provides some hope for its survival.

Conservation Measures Proposed Further studies are needed in Liberia, Ivory Coast and neighbouring countries to determine the distribution and status of this species, especially within protected areas of rainforest. Details of such protected areas and of the ornithological importance of Mount Nimba and Tai Forest are given in Remarks under Rufous Fishing Owl.

Remarks The Nimba Flycatcher is very distinct with no close relatives in its genus (Forbes-Watson 1970). Both its call and silhouette are apparently reminiscent of the Square-tailed Drongo *Dicrurus ludwigii* and it has been suggested that confusion between the two species has led to the former being overlooked (Forbes-Watson 1970).

References

Colston, P. R. and Curry-Lindahl, K. (in press) The birds of the Mount Nimba region in Liberia. *Bull. Brit. Mus. (Nat. Hist.) Zool.*

Forbes-Watson, A. D. (1970) A new species of *Melaenornis* (Muscicapinae) from Liberia. *Bull. Brit. Orn. Club* 90: 145-148.

Halle, M. (1983) Timber pressure on last Ivory Coast forest. *WWF News* 22: 2.

Roth, H. H. (1982) We all want trees – case history of the Tai National Park. 3rd World National Parks Congress, Bali, Indonesia. Unpublished.

Verschuren, J. (1982) Hope for Liberia. *Oryx* 16: 421-427.

Verschuren, J. (1983) Conservation of tropical rain forest in Liberia. Recommendations for wildlife conservation and national parks. Gland, Switzerland: IUCN/WWF.

CHAPIN'S FLYCATCHER   RARE

Muscicapa lendu (Chapin, 1932)

Order PASSERIFORMES   Family MUSCICAPIDAE
                                          Subfamily MUSCICAPINAE

Summary This flycatcher is known with certainty only from two mountain ranges in eastern Zaire, one forest in south-western Uganda and one small area in western Kenya. It might occur more widely, but it is rare throughout its range.

Distribution Chapin's Flycatcher is only known from the Lendu Plateau and Itombwe Mountains in eastern Zaire, the Impenetrable (or Bwindi) Forest in south-western Uganda and the Kakamega and North Nandi Forests in western Kenya. The type-specimen was collected in 1926 at Djugu, 1,650 m, on the Lendu Plateau, west of Lake Mobutu (Lake Albert) (Chapin 1932). There have been no subsequent records from this area. In 1954 the species was discovered in the Itombwe Mountains (Prigogine 1957). Eleven specimens are now known from this area (Prigogine 1971) as follows: nine from Ibachilo, 1,750-1,820 m, in 1956-1958; one from Milanga, 1,700 m, in 1957; and one from Butokolo, north-west of the main Itombwe block, 1,470 m, in 1959 (Prigogine 1957,1971; specimens in MRAC and IRSNB: SNS). These Itombwe birds form a distinct subspecies, *M. l. itombwensis* (Prigogine 1957), and occur in only a narrow altitudinal range between 1,470 and 1,820 m (Prigogine 1980). In 1960 a specimen of the nominate form was collected in the Impenetrable Forest in south-western Uganda at 1,500 m (Keith and Twomey 1958). Nominate birds were also discovered in the Kakamega Forest in western Kenya, one specimen being collected in 1963 and three in 1965 (Ripley and Bond 1971). A bird almost certainly this species was seen in Kakamega Forest in 1965 (Zimmerman 1972), since when there have a few other sight records from this locality, the most recent published case being of one in 1981 (*Scopus* 5 [1981]: 143). The species has also been seen in the nearby North Nandi Forest (Britton 1980), where one was collected in 1978 at 2,130 m (G. R. Cunningham-van Someren *in litt.* 1983). The altitudinal range of the species in western Kenya is from 1,600 to 2,150 m (Britton 1980). In addition to these confirmed records, a pair of birds, almost certainly this species and probably belonging to the nominate race, was seen near Bunyole, at 2,100 m, north-west of Lake Kivu, in eastern Zaire in 1957 (Chapin 1978).

Population Numbers are not known. The species is clearly very rare on the Lendu Plateau, since it has eluded several attempts to relocate it (Prigogine 1957). It is also described as rare in the Itombwe Mountains (Prigogine 1971) and in its Kenyan and Ugandan sites (Britton 1980): in Kakamega Forest the species has been seen on only two occasions in over 50 visits in recent years (D. A. Turner *in litt.* 1983).

Ecology All records of this species are from montane forest above about 1,500 m (Chapin 1932, Prigogine 1957,1971, Keith and Twomey 1968, Keith *et al.* 1969, Zimmerman 1972, Britton 1980, G. R. Cunningham-van Someren *in litt.*

1983). In the Itombwe Mountains birds occur in groups of 2-4, sometimes in mixed-species flocks, high in the forest canopy (Prigogine 1957,1971). They are usually seen in the tree-tops, on branches with little foliage (Prigogine 1957,1971). Breeding takes place in March and September, perhaps also in January and February (Prigogine 1971). One pair, almost certainly this species, had a nest over a pond in June (Chapin 1978). In the Itombwe Mountains it does not overlap with the related Olivaceous Flycatcher *Muscicapa olivacens* which occurs up to 1,050 m in the foothills (Prigogine 1980).

Threats This species is probably suffering as a result of forest clearance, which is known to be taking place especially in the Impenetrable Forest (K. D. Bishop pers. comm. 1983), the Kakamega Forest (Diamond 1979, Cords 1982), and the North Nandi Forest (G. R. Cunningham-van Someren *in litt.* 1983). The most serious problems in Kakamega are caused by cattle grazing and the removal, usually illegally, of saplings, timber and firewood (Cords 1982); but see Conservation Measures Taken and Conservation Measures Proposed. The forest on the Lendu Plateau has apparently also been cleared in many areas (Hall and Moreau 1962) and there is a danger of increased clearance in the Itombwe Mountains since Kamituga has become an important mining centre, thus increasing the possibility of the area being opened up for larger-scale exploitation (Prigogine in press). There is probably a greater danger, however, of clearance around villages higher in the Itombwe Mountains, but there is no recent information on the conservation status of these forests (A. Prigogine *in litt.* 1983).

Conservation Measures Taken A small area of the Kakamega Forest, south of the Yala River, has been set aside as a national reserve (G. R. Cunningham-van Someren *in litt.* 1983), and the northern part of the forest (9,698 ha) was declared a national park in 1983 (IUCN in press).

Conservation Measures Proposed Much stricter forest conservation measures need to be introduced throughout the range of this species. Some preliminary conservation recommendations for the Kakamega Forest have been prepared (Cords 1982) but it is not clear whether these are entirely fulfilled by the national park that now exists there. A preliminary conservation plan for the Itombwe Mountain forests has been prepared (Prigogine in press). It is hoped that this plan will be worked out in detail and implemented by the Zairean government. Further fieldwork is also required to determine the distribution of this species more accurately in eastern Zaire and to identify the forest patches (e.g. on the Lendu Plateau) that should be preserved for the sake of this species.

Remarks Details of the taxonomic history of this species are given in Prigogine (1957), Hall and Moreau (1962), Keith and Twomey (1968), Ripley and Bond (1971) and Chapin (1978). The forests of the Itombwe Mountains are important for six other threatened bird species species (see Remarks under Schouteden's Swift *Schoutedenapus schoutedeni*). The Impenetrable Forest is important for two other threatened bird species (see Remarks under African Green Broadbill *Pseudocalyptomena graueri*). On both the Lendu Plateau and in the

Kakamega Forest Chapin's Flycatcher is sympatric with one other threatened bird species, respectively Prigogine's Greenbul *Chlorocichla prigoginei* and Turner's Eremomela *Eremomela turneri*: see relevant accounts).

References

Britton, P. L. ed. (1980) *Birds of East Africa: their habitat, status and distribution.* Nairobi: EANHS.

Chapin, J. P. (1932) Fourteen new birds from tropical Africa. *Amer. Mus. Novit.* 570.

Chapin, R. T. (1978) Brief accounts of some central African birds, based on the journals of James Chapin. *Rev. Zool. Afr.* 92: 805-836.

Cords, M. (1982) A report on harmful exploitation of indigenous forest in Kakamega. Unpublished.

Diamond, A. W. (1979) Kakamega. Is there a way to stop the rot? *Swara* 2(1): 25-26.

Hall, B. P. and Moreau, R. E. (1962) A study of the rare birds of Africa. *Bull. Brit. Mus. (Nat. Hist.) Zool.* 8. 313-378.

Keith, S. and Twomey, A. (1968) New distributional records of some East African birds. *Ibis* 110: 537-548.

Keith, S., Twomey, A., Friedmann, H. and Williams, J. (1969) The avifauna of the Impenetrable Forest, Uganda. *Amer. Mus. Novit.* 2389.

IUCN (in press) *The IUCN directory of Afrotropical protected areas.* Cambridge (U.K) and Gland (Switzerland): IUCN Conservation Monitoring Centre and Commission on National Parks and Protected Areas.

Prigogine, A. (1957) La redécouverte de *Muscicapa lendu* (Chapin). *Rev. Zool. Bot. Afr.* 55: 405-410.

Prigogine, A. (1971) Les oiseaux de l'Itombwe et de son hinterland. Volume 1. *Ann. Mus. Roy. Afr. Centr.* 8°, Sci. Zool. 185: 1-298.

Prigogine, A. (1980) The altitudinal distribution of the avifauna in the Itombwe Forest (Zaire). *Proc. IV Pan-Afr. orn. Congr.*: 169-184.

Prigogine, A. (in press) The conservation of the avifauna of the forests of the Albertine Rift. *Proceedings of the ICBP Tropical Forest Bird Symposium, 1982.*

Ripley, S. D. and Bond, G. M. (1971) Systematic notes on a collection of birds from Kenya. *Smithsonian Contrib. Zool.* 111.

Zimmerman, D. A. (1972) The avifauna of Kakamega Forest, western Kenya, including a bird population study. *Bull. Amer. Mus. Nat. Hist.* 149: 255-399.

GRAND COMORO FLYCATCHER   RARE

Humblotia flavirostris Milne Edwards and Oustalet, 1887

Order PASSERIFORMES   Family MUSCICAPIDAE
                                                                Subfamily MUSCICAPINAE

Summary This is a distinctive flycatcher in its own genus, confined to forest and heath on Mount Karthala, Grand Comoro, in the Comoro Islands; the habitat is somewhat vulnerable, and deserves to be fully protected.

Distribution The Grand Comoro Flycatcher is restricted to Grand Comoro, in the Comoro Islands. In 1958 it was found at Nioumbadjou and La Convalescence, and appeared entirely confined to Mount Karthala (southern half of the island), never being seen at La Grille in the north (Benson 1960). In 1981 it was found above 1,000 m on Mount Karthala (M. Louette *in litt.* 1981).

Population Considered uncommon in 1958 (Benson 1960) and not seen at all at Nioumbadjou in 1965, despite searches (Forbes-Watson 1969), the species was, however, present in fair numbers above 1,000 m in 1981 (M. Louette *in litt.* 1981), and in 1983 it was found from at least 800 m up to the forest/heath integradation zone, being decidedly common in this latter area (M. Louette *in litt.* 1984).

Ecology Although once believed to be strictly confined to interior evergreen forest, never being seen in clearings (Benson 1960), it has been found in recent studies to occur in pure stands of *Philippia* heath above the forest belt (M. Louette *in litt.* 1984). It feeds in short aerial sorties from a perch in typical *Muscicapa* flycatcher manner, remaining independent of mixed species flocks (Benson 1960). Stomachs invariably held insects, including beetles, hemiptera and a dragonfly (Benson 1960). Breeding is presumed to occur in October and November (Benson 1960), though no such activity was noted in October 1983 (M. Louette *in litt.* 1984). Birds are most active early in the morning and late in the afternoon (M. Louette *in litt.* 1984).

Threats The restricted range of this species within a notoriously vulnerable habitat (forest on a relatively small island) must be a permanent cause of concern and vigilance for its welfare. At present the habitat is unaffected, although there is some cutting of the lower forest for local use (M. Louette *in litt.* 1981, R. Potvliege *in litt.* 1983). A road now under construction to take cars to the crater rim on Mount Karthala will, however bring many more people to higher elevations and increase the risk of habitat destruction (M. Louette *in litt.* 1984).

Conservation Measures Taken None is known.

Conservation Measures Proposed Protected area status, with a con- comitant educational programme, for a representative section of the forest and heathland on Mount Karthala would enhance the prospects for survival of this species, the Grand Comoro Scops Owl *Otus pauliani*, the Grand Comoro Drongo *Dicrurus fuscipennis* and the Mount Karthala White-eye *Zosterops mouroniensis* (see relevant sheets).

Remarks This species is the only member of the genus *Humblotia*.

References

Benson, C.W. (1960) The birds of the Comoro Islands: results of the British Ornithologists' Union Centenary Expedition 1958. *Ibis* 103b: 5-106.
Forbes-Watson, A.D. (1969) Notes on birds observed in the Comoros on behalf of the Smithsonian Institution. *Atoll Res. Bull.* no. 128.

RED-TAILED NEWTONIA

Newtonia fanovanae Gyldenstolpe, 1933

INDETERMINATE

Order PASSERIFORMES

Family MUSCICAPIDAE
Subfamily MUSCICAPINAE

Summary This flycatcher is known only from a single specimen from a forest, now cleared, in eastern central Madagascar. If it is not an invalid taxon based on an aberrant bird, it is either greatly overlooked, genuinely rare, or extinct.

Distribution The type and only specimen (adult, sex unknown) of the Red-tailed Newtonia was collected in the Fanovana forest, eastern central Madagascar, in December 1931 (Gyldenstolpe 1933). Although its late discovery may reflect a very limited area of distribution (Gyldenstolpe 1933) it probably inhabits "the forest of the central part of the Humid East" (Rand 1936) and may occur in the Sihanaka forest (Salomomsen 1965) and at Périnet (Benson *et al.* 1977), although observations at Périnet in recent years have failed to find it (D. A. Turner pers. comm. 1983).

Population Numbers are unknown, but the species is regarded as probably sparse (Benson 1974).

Ecology The ecology of this species is wholly unknown, other than that it must, as a flycatcher, be insectivorous. It has been speculated, on the basis of the plumage and ecological characters of its congeners, that the species may frequent the canopy of evergreen forest, in which it could be easily overlooked, especially if in any case uncommon (Benson 1974, Benson *et al.* 1977). Such speculation matches the contention that the species is a mimic of the female Red-tailed Vanga *Calicalicus madagascariensis* (see Remarks), since the latter is a bird of forest canopy (Milon *et al.* 1973, Benson *et al.* 1977).

Threats Destruction and disturbance of primary rainforest is the single most serious threat to this and all other rainforest-dependent species in Madagascar (see Threats under Madagascar Serpent Eagle *Eutriorchis astur*). The forest at Fanovana is now completely cleared (D. A. Turner pers. comm. 1983).

Conservation Measures Taken None is known.

Conservation Measures Proposed Protection of as much remaining rainforest as possible is the primary need; further study at certain sites, especially Périnet, to establish the continued existence and likely requirements of this species, is desirable.

Remarks Not having been seen for over 50 years, by CITES criteria the Red-tailed Newtonia could be treated as extinct. However, along with two other eastern Madagascar forest birds, the Yellow-bellied Sunbird-asity *Neodrepanis* hypoxantha and the Dusky Greenbul *Phyllastrephus tenebrosus*, it is thought likely to have been overlooked owing to its sparseness, elusiveness and difficult habitat (Benson 1974, Benson *et al.* 1977). Its validity as a full species has recently been reaffirmed (Benson *et al.* 1977), the possibility that it is an aberrant female Red-tailed Vanga (Forbes-Watson *et al.* 1973) being rejected on the grounds of its slender *Newtonia* bill, the Vanga having a short, stout bill and also differing in its larger, heavier size, black lower mandible, pale lores, and conspicuous broad (not narrow) white eye-ring (G. S. Keith *in litt.* 1983); nevertheless, the similarity in the plumage between the two is so "incredibly close...that this must be a case of mimicry" (C. Edelstam *in litt.* 1983).

References

Benson, C. W. (1974) Another specimen of *Neodrepanis hypoxantha. Bull. Brit. Orn. Club* 94: 141-143.

Benson, C. W., Colebrook-Robjent, J. F. R. and Williams, A. (1977) Contribution à l'ornithologie de Madagascar. *Oiseau et R.F.O.* 47: 41-64.

Forbes-Watson, A. D., Turner, D. A. and Keith, G. S. (1973) Report on bird preservation in Madagascar. Part 3, Appendix I. Proposed list of protected Madagascar birds. Report to ICBP, unpublished.

Gyldenstolpe, N. (1933) A remarkable new flycatcher from Madagascar. *Ark. Zool.* 25B (2): 1-3.

Milon, P., Petter, J.-J. and Randrianasolo, G. (1973) *Faune de Madagascar, 35: Oiseaux*. Tananarive and Paris: ORSTOM and CRNS.

Rand, A. L. (1936) The distribution and habits of Madagascar birds. *Bull. Amer. Mus. Nat. Hist.* 72: 143-499.

Salomonsen, F. (1965). Notes on the Sunbird-asitys (*Neodrepanis*). *Oiseau et R.F.O.* 35 (no. spéc.): 103-111.

BANDED WATTLE-EYE   ENDANGERED
Platysteira laticincta Bates, 1926

Order PASSERIFORMES   Family MUSCICAPIDAE
                                               Subfamily PLATYSTEIRINAE

Summary This flycatcher is known only from patches of montane forest in the Bamenda Highlands, western Cameroon, which are being rapidly cleared; it will very probably become extinct unless forest on Mount Oku is preserved.

Distribution The Banded Wattle-eye is known only from the Bamenda Highlands in Cameroon, where it was discovered at 1,830 m on Mount Oku in 1925 (Bates 1926). In the late 1940s, 13 specimens were collected near Bamenda, four at Ndu (near Kumbo) and one at Mount Oku (Serle 1950). There were no further records until 1974, when two females were collected in March on Mount Lefo, south of Bamenda (van den Elzen 1975). In 1984 when the ICBP Cameroon Montane Forest Survey located the species at 2,100-2,450 m on Mount Oku, 2,100 m at Lake Bambulue, 1,850 m at the Sabga Pass and 1,750 m in the Bali-Ngemba Forest Reserve (SNS). At lower altitudes the species is replaced by the Scarlet-spectacled Wattle-eye *Platysteira cyanea* (Hall and Moreau 1962), though the two species are sympatric at the Sabga Pass and in the Bali-Ngemba Forest Reserve (SNS).

Population Although very restricted in distribution, this species is reasonably common where it occurs (SNS).

Ecology It occurs singly or in pairs in high montane forest, from the ground stratum to the canopy top (Bates 1926, Serle 1950). In the Bali-Ngemba Forest Reserve it has been seen in forest underplanted with subsistence crops (SNS). A bird in breeding condition has been collected in September (Serle 1950) and juveniles have been recorded in October (Serle 1950) and March (SNS). It is a much quieter species than the Scarlet-spectacled Wattle-eye (Serle 1950, SNS).

Threats All of the forest patches remaining in the Bamenda Highlands are now badly damaged, very small and being rapidly cleared as a result of cultivation, overgrazing by cattle, goats, sheep and horses, wood-cutting and fires (SNS). More extensive areas of forest survive on Mount Oku, but even these are being rapidly cleared (SNS).

Conservation Measures Taken None is known, even the forest reserve in which the species occurs being subject to clearance (SNS).

Conservation Measures Proposed The ICBP Cameroon Montane Forest Survey is preparing recommendations for the conservation of forest on Mount Oku for the consideration of the Cameroon government. Unless this forest is conserved the species along with Bannerman's Turaco *Tauraco bannermani* (see relevant account) will almost certainly not survive.

Remarks The Banded Wattle-eye is most closely related to the Black-throated Wattle-eye *Platysteira peltata* of eastern, central and southern Africa (Hall and Moreau 1962,1970) and the two forms are sometimes considered to be conspecific (Hall and Moreau 1970). They differ greatly in their habitat requirements, however, the Black-throated Wattle-eye normally occurring in fringing forest and scrub, usually at low altitudes (Hall and Moreau 1962,1970). Details of other threatened species occurring in the Bamenda Highlands are given in Remarks under Bannerman's Turaco.

References

Bates, G. L. (1926) New birds from the mountains of N. W. Cameroon. *Bull. Brit. Orn. Club* 46: 87-93.

van den Elzen, R. (1975) Zur Kenntnis der Avifauna Kameruns. *Bonn. zool. Beitr.* 26: 49-75.

Hall, B. P. and Moreau, R. E. (1962) A study of the rare birds of Africa. *Bull. Brit. Mus. (Nat. Hist.) Zool.* 8. 313-378.

Hall, B. P. and Moreau, R. E. (1970) *An atlas of speciation in African passerine birds.* London: Trustees of the British Museum (Natural History).

Serle, W. (1950) A contribution to the ornithology of the British Cameroons. Part 2. *Ibis* 92: 602-638.

SEYCHELLES BLACK PARADISE FLYCATCHER   RARE
Terpsiphone corvina (E. Newton, 1867)

Order PASSERIFORMES   Family MUSCICAPIDAE
                                        Subfamily MONARCHINAE

Summary The one certainly viable population (c. 60 individuals) of this Seychelles endemic occurs on La Digue; very small numbers occur on Praslin and possibly Félicité. Mature stands of indigenous *Calophyllum* and *Terminalia* dictate its distribution. A special reserve has been established to protect a small part of the La Digue population.

Distribution The Seychelles Black Paradise Flycatcher is chiefly known from the island of La Digue, in the Seychelles. It was first described from specimens at a small colony in north-east Praslin (Newton 1867), possibly the same as that which may survive there at present, where two males, a female, and three disused nests were found, 1978 (Watson 1981). It has been reported from (and collected on) Marianne, but not since 1936 (Oustalet 1878, Ridgway 1896, Vesey-Fitzgerald 1936, Watson 1981). Birds were present on Félicité in 1906 (Nicoll 1906) and during the 1930s (Vesey-Fitzgerald 1936,1940a); a single female was seen there in 1976 (Watson 1981). A record from Curieuse (Loustau-Lalanne 1962) is in error (Watson 1981). The species was first found on La Digue in 1871 (Pike 1872) and collected there in 1890 (Ridgway 1896); since 1940 (Vesey-Fitzgerald 1940a) this island has been recognised as the single stronghold of the species, with the whole population distributed on five coastal "plateaus", in particular the large (162 ha) western plateau with its 64 ha of *Calophyllum/Terminalia* woodland (Watson 1977,1981). The fact that this type of woodland, with which the flycatcher is so closely associated, constituted the original forest on coastal lowlands throughout Seychelles (Vesey-Fitzgerald 1940b) suggests the species would have been very widespread in the archipelago before colonisation by man in 1744.

Population Birds of this species on Praslin have always been very few (Newton 1867, Pike 1872, Vesey-Fitzgerald 1936, Watson 1981), but they were reported to be "tolerably common" on La Digue and Félicité in 1936 (Vesey-Fitzgerald 1936), with "plenty" on the former in 1959 (Crook 1960). Twenty-eight birds were counted on La Digue in February 1965 (Penny 1968, Gaymer *et al.* 1969), 29-31 in April 1969, though 45 (not more than 50) were then considered likely (Fayon 1971), and 50-80 (or 80-90) were considered likely, 1971 (Beamish 1972, Frädrich 1972); 29 pairs plus three non-breeding birds were present, 1977-1978, with probably only 5-10 birds elsewhere on Praslin and Félicité, giving a total population of probably 70-80 individuals (Watson 1981).

Ecology The species's association with takamaka *Calophyllum inophyllum* and badamier *Terminalia catappa* woodland has long been recognised (Loustau-Lalanne 1962, Gaymer *et al.* 1969, Beamish 1972, Fraser 1972), and its predilection for marshy areas noted earlier still (Newton 1867, Vesey-Fitzgerald 1940a, Foster-Vesey-Fitzgerald 1953, Loustau-Lalanne 1962). In 1977-1978, nesting territories occurred exclusively in *Calophyllum/Terminalia* woodland; moreover, density of territories increased significantly with proximity to freshwater marsh or drainage systems, probably because of increased abundance of insect food near waterbodies (Watson 1981). Birds feed on a variety of insects, some of which, e.g. dragonflies and mosquitoes, are dependent on freshwater for breeding (Watson 1981). Sexes showed a significant vertical separation of feeding niche, the all-dark males hunting more in low-level, deeper shade areas, the counter-shaded females keeping to the higher, lighter layers of canopy; thus at one site where only females were present, lack of males appeared attributable to lack of low-level, high-shade vegetation (Watson 1981). Nests are typically sited on the outer, downward-hanging branchlets of *Calophyllum* or *Terminalia* at the edge of a clearing (Gaymer *et al.* 1969, Beamish 1972, Fraser 1972). In 1977-1978, 94% of nests (n=96) were built in these trees, 60% at a height of 3-5 m; nesting success was low, with only 17% of nesting attempts (n=90) and only 24% of nests with eggs (n=52) resulting in fledged young (former figure probably too high) (Watson 1981). Clutch-size is invariably one (Beamish 1972, Fraser 1972, Watson 1981). Breeding occurs year-round, but 75% of all nesting attempts, 1977-1978, occurred from November to April, the period of the north-west monsoon (Watson 1981). Although there is little evidence of alarm at various forms of human disturbance shown by nesting birds (Fraser 1972), nests situated more than 5 m from a footpath or road were more than twice as successful as nests less than 5 m from them (Watson 1981; see also Penny 1968, Gaymer *et al.* 1969).

Threats The fairly precise habitat requirements of this bird and the destruction of such habitat throughout Seychelles (see Distribution, Ecology) indicates the relative precariousness of the present situation: any loss of habitat on La Digue would be extremely serious for such a small population. Disturbance at nests is evidently a detrimental factor (see Ecology).

Conservation Measures Taken In 1964-1965, self-sustaining popular interest in the species on La Digue was actively fostered (Penny 1968) and since around 1970 a warden has overseen its protection there (Beamish 1972, Watson 1981). Scientific research in 1977-1978 to establish its numbers and requirements was funded by WWF and administered by ICBP (Watson 1981), and a resulting recommendation, that a key area of *Calophyllum/Terminalia* woodland be established as a nature reserve for the species (Watson 1981), has been acted upon (J. Watson *in litt.* 1982).

Conservation Measures Proposed On La Digue, replanting of *Calophyllum/Terminalia* in plateau areas is urged, not only to assist the flycatcher but to ensure the survival of the local ship-building industry (Watson 1981). The freshwater marsh north of L'Union on the western plateau needs strict conservation, including a ban on insecticides (Watson 1981). A complete census was required in 1982-1983 during the north-west monsoon to check against population changes (Watson 1981) but appears not to have been undertaken. Introduction of the species to a rat- and cat-free island was considered important in 1962 (Loustau-Lalanne 1962), but rats *Rattus* and cats abound on the western plateau of La Digue, where the birds' siting of nests appears to prevent predation by mammals or reptiles; nevertheless, to increase the population and to guarantee against unforeseen events, it is recommended that the extensive plateau at Baie La Raie, Curieuse, be replanted with *Calophyllum/Terminalia* woodland with a view to future introduction of the species to the island (Watson 1981).

References

Beamish, T. (1972) The Paradise Flycatcher, Seychelles. *Biol. Conserv.* 4: 311-313.

Crook, J. H. (1960) The present status of certain rare land birds of the Seychelles Islands. Seychelles Government Bulletin.

Fayon, M. (1971) The plight of the Paradise Flycatcher. *J. Seychelles Soc.* 7: 8-11.

Foster-Vesey-Fitzgerald, D. (1953) Wild life in Seychelles. *Oryx* 2: 28-32.

Frädrich, H. (1972) Beitrag zur Avifauna der Seychellen und anderer Inseln der westlichen Indischen Ozeans. *Sitzungsber. Ges. Naturforsch. Freunde Berlin* 12(1-2): 132-145.

Fraser, W. (1972) Notes on *Terpsiphone corvina*. *Ibis* 114: 399-401.

Gaymer, R., Blackman, R. A. A., Dawson, P. G., Penny, M. and Penny, C. M. (1969) The endemic birds of Seychelles. *Ibis* 111: 157-176.

Loustau-Lalanne, P. (1962) Land birds of the granitic islands of the Seychelles. *Seychelles Soc. Occ. Publ.* 1.

Newton, E. (1867) On the land-birds of the Seychelles archipelago. *Ibis* (2)3: 335-360.

Nicoll, M. J. (1906) On the birds collected and observed during the voyage of the "Valhalla", R.Y.S., from November 1905 to May 1906. *Ibis* (8)6: 666-712.

Oustalet, M. E. (1878) Etude sur la faune ornithologique des Iles Seychelles. *Bull. Soc. Philomath. Paris* (7)2: 161-206.

Penny, M. (1968) Endemic birds of the Seychelles. *Oryx* 9: 267-275.

Pike, N. (1872) A visit to the Seychelles Islands. *Trans. Roy. Soc. Arts Sci. Mauritius* N.S. 6: 83-143.

Ridgway, R. (1896) On birds collected by Doctor W. L. Abbott in the Seychelles, Amirantes, Gloriosa, Assumption, Aldabra, and adjacent islands, with notes on habits, etc., by the collector. *Proc. U. S. Natn. Mus.* 18 [1895]: 509-546.

Vesey-Fitzgerald, D. (1936) Birds of the Seychelles and other islands included within that colony. Victoria (Mahé), Seychelles: Government Printing Office.

Vesey-Fitzgerald, D. (1940a) The birds of the Seychelles. I. The endemic birds. *Ibis* (14)4: 480-489.

Vesey-Fitzgerald, D. (1940b) On the vegetation of the Seychelles. *J. Ecol.* 28: 465-483.

Watson, J. (1977) The Seychelles Paradise Flycatcher (*Terpsiphone corvina*). Progress report 2 [to ICBP]. Unpublished.

Watson, J. (1981) The Seychelles Black Paradise Flycatcher (*Terpsiphone corvina*) on La Digue. World Wildlife Fund Project 1590: Endangered landbirds, Seychelles. Final report 1 (b). Unpublished.

ALGERIAN NUTHATCH   RARE
Sitta ledanti Vielliard, 1976

Order PASSERIFORMES   Family SITTIDAE
                                                          Subfamily SITTINAE

Summary A forest species apparently dependent on insects in summer and seeds in winter, and with a need for standing dead wood in which to nest, this recently described bird is confined to a single mountain (Mont Babor, a national park) in Algeria, had a population in 1982 of around 80 pairs (though the level may fluctuate with annual conditions), is threatened in the long term by loss of habitat but can be saved by the implementation of management proposals aimed chiefly at safeguarding existing forest.

Distribution The Algerian Nuthatch is confined to forest on Mont Babor (Djebel Babor, roughly 36°30'N 5°30'E), which rises to 2,000 m and is situated c. 20 km from the coast in the Petite Kabylie region of northern Algeria (Burnier 1976, Heim de Balsac 1976, Vielliard 1976a,b,1977,1978, Ledant 1977). Forest covers less than 13 km² on Mont Babor but optimum habitat for the species, concentrated at upper levels round the peak, covers less than 2.5 km² (Ledant *et al.* in press; also Vielliard 1978, Gatter and Mattes 1979). Searches of relict woods on the nearby Djebel Tababor in 1977 and 1982, and of Djebel Takoucht in 1982, yielded no birds, although the species was probably present on the former before fire degraded the habitat (Ledant and Jacobs 1977, Ledant *et al.* in press).

Population Following the species's discovery in 1975, successive investigations of its status and distribution culminated in an estimate that c. 80 pairs were present in May 1982 (Ledant *et al.* in press). Originally, in July 1976, only nine pairs were found and no more than 12 believed present (Vielliard 1976a,b,1978, Ledant 1977), and the habitat was considered incapable of holding more than some 20 pairs (Vielliard 1977). Then in June 1977 8-10 pairs were counted in the same area as the previous year but another "dozen" pairs, not systematically censused, were found lower down (Ledant and Jacobs 1977), the total being reported elsewhere as 16 pairs found and 20 estimated (Vielliard 1978,1980, Ledant *et al.* in press). In March and June 1978, 54 territories were considered to have been found and a total of 70 was estimated (Gatter and Mattes 1979). These findings were reinterpreted as indicating only 25-30 pairs in 1978 (Vielliard 1980), and the change in numbers was considered probably the result of a real increase in birds (Gatter and Mattes 1979, Vielliard 1980, Ledant 1981, Ledant *et al.* 1981), imprecise censusing (Ledant 1981, Ledant *et al.* 1981), and over-optimistic interpretation of data by the 1978 observers (Ledant 1981). Nevertheless, the results of the 1982 survey (see above, and under Ecology) tend to vindicate the original assertions derived from the 1978 survey.

Ecology The Djebel Babor forms a sharp high ridge whose proximity to the sea gives it a very humid and cold winter climate, with an annual precipitation of some 200-240(-250) cm, most of which falls as snow that can lie 2(-4) m thick on the ground and last from November to April/May, while the period from

July/August to October is dry, with a Mediterranean climate (Vielliard 1976b,1978, Ledant 1977, Gatter and Mattes 1979, Ledant *et al.* in press, J.-P. Ledant *in litt.* 1984). Important early studies of the species and its ecology (Ledant 1977, Ledant and Jacobs 1977, Vielliard 1978, and especially Gatter and Mattes 1979) are now modified and amplified by the results of work in 1982 (Ledant *et al.* in press) suggesting that the three major factors affecting density are diversity of tree species (winter seed supplies are more certain in forest with a good mix of trees; see also Gatter and Mattes 1979), the size and age of trees (volume of dead wood and quantity of epiphytic growth are important) and altitude (which influences epiphytic growth; also Gatter and Mattes 1979). Six forest-types have been identified on Babor: (a) low coppiced evergreen oak *Quercus ilex* forest, rising only to c. 1,200 m, higher in the west (Algerian Nuthatch absent from this type); (b) deciduous oak *Q. faginea* forest, rich in cedar *Cedrus atlantica* and with some maple *Acer obtusatum*, service *Sorbus terminalis* and *S. aria*, holly *Ilex aquifolium* and yew *Taxus baccata*, from 1,200 to 1,650 m; (c) oak/fir forest, as for deciduous oak forest but with the Algerian fir *Abies numidica* (endemic to Mont Babor) forming 36% of large trees (oak 36%, cedar 27%) and with groups of poplar *Populus tremula*, from 1,650 to 1,800 m; (d) summit forest, as for oak/fir forest but with a higher proportion of old trees and different quantities of large species (77% cedar, 12% fir, 11% oak), plus yews; (e) cedar forest, greatly dominated by the one species, occurring in areas once burnt or of shallow soil; (f) mixed cedar, intermediate between cedar forest and summit forest (87% cedar, 10% oak, 3% fir) in one area to the east of the summit (Ledant *et al.* in press). The surface area of all but the first of these forest-types, the density of pairs of Algerian Nuthatches in them, and hence the total number of pairs of the species, all as at May 1982, have been tabulated as follows (in Ledant *et al.* in press).

Forest-type	Area in ha	Pairs/100 ha	Numbers of pairs
Summit forest	38	30	11.4
Mixed cedar	20	15	3
Oak/fir	170	12	20.4
Deciduous oak (above 1,800 m)	80	10	8
Deciduous oak (below 1,800 m)	680	5	34
Cedar	280	2	5.6
TOTAL	1,268		82

Owing however to variable severity of winters (as discussed in Vielliard 1978), the annual variations in seed production between and within tree species (notably cedars and oaks, as discussed in Gatter and Mattes 1979), and the probable variation in breeding success in different forest-types, the figures concerning the Nuthatch tabulated here cannot represent constants; moreover, the importance of forest-types may vary with season, cedar (e.g.) being extensively used in years of heavy mast (Gatter and Mattes 1979). In winter (March), birds were seen feeding only on tree-trunks and larger branches, the latter commonly swathed in moss and lichen, and four feeding methods were noted: gathering small items from all surfaces; prizing off bark; hacking bark loose (these three all for small invertebrates or their eggs); and storing and retrieving seeds in moss- and lichen-covered branches (Gatter and Mattes 1979). In summer, birds show a marked preference for foraging in the new leaves, old blossoms and especially twigs of deciduous oaks, where they find geometrid caterpillars plentiful (though probably not each year: J.-P. Ledant *in litt.* 1984), other food in the nesting period being noctuid caterpillars, beetles, spiders, Dermaptera, winged Hymenoptera, and conifer (cedar and fir) seeds, these last evidently important for feeding young (Gatter and Mattes 1979; also Ledant and Jacobs 1977, Le Fur 1981). This tit-like use of thin outer branches (in summer) is a habit the species shares with its closest relatives, the Corsican Nuthatch *Sitta whiteheadi* and Krüper's Nuthatch *S. krueperi*, although unlike them it does not fly-catch (Ledant and Jacobs 1977, Ledant 1978); seeds of yew were also noted as food in 1982 and were the main food in September 1981 (Ledant *et al.* 1984, in press, J.-P. Ledant *in litt.* 1984). Most nest-holes are located in the dead wood of fir, but also cedar and oak, 3-15 m up (Ledant and Jacobs 1977, Vielliard 1978, Gatter and Mattes 1979). Clutch-size is unknown, but young fledged are never more than three, and usually two (Ledant and Jacobs 1977), although four fledged young are mentioned in the original description (Vielliard 1976a). Season varies slightly with conditions, birds breeding late and synchronously in 1976 (Vielliard 1976b), earlier and asynchronously in 1977 (Ledant and Jacobs 1977), with breeding still in progress, July, in 1981 (Fosse and Vaillant 1982) but apparently over by July in 1982 (van den Berg 1982). A juvenile-like bird in November suggested a second brood (Ledant and Jacobs 1977). In winter birds are to be found in the same areas as those in which they breed, but will also join mixed bird parties (Ledant and Jacobs 1977, Jacobs *et al.* 1978). Birds are evidently strictly sedentary, and winter conditions on Babor must cause serious mortality even if they descend the slopes (Vielliard 1976b,1978); presumably, however, mortality is most acute in severe winters that follow a major failure in mast production, since the caching behaviour of the species ought otherwise to counteract the effects of bad weather alone.

Threats The threats to this species have been generalised as of three types: reduction of forested area by fire, pasturage and wood-cutting; replacement of mixed forest by cedar in the wake of fire; and decrease in diversity of woody species as a consequence of long-term pasturage (Ledant *et al.* in press). The major area of concern is the summit forest and adjacent mixed cedar forest, the most preferred habits of the Algerian Nuthatch, both of which have been seriously diminished by fire and suffer from chronic lack of regeneration owing chiefly to high-intensity pasturage (Ledant *et al.* in press). Excessive pasturage has been recognised as a serious problem ever since the discovery of the species (Ledant 1977, Vielliard 1978, Gatter and Mattes 1979): the disappearance of the lion *Panthera leo* towards the end of the last century and the leopard *P. pardus* around 1960 has abetted the increase of summer grazing and browsing by cattle, sheep and goats on Mont Babor this century (Ledant *et al.* in press), and the loss of these predators is presumably responsible for the very high numbers of wild boar *Sus scrofa* that now cause the destruction of much young vegetation (Gatter and Mattes

1979; also Ledant *et al.* in press). However, the presence of the northern jackal *Canis aureus* requires that small livestock be taken off the mountain each day, which itself has resulted in erosion in some areas (Ledant 1981). Fire has ravaged Mont Babor several times in the past century, notably in 1867-1868, 1917, and the period 1954-1962 (Vielliard 1977,1978, Ledant 1981): generally either cedar monopolises the burnt-over ground (Ledant 1977, Ledant *et al.* in press) or the area may fail to regenerate under pressure from soil erosion, pasturage and/or wood-cutting (as, e.g., occurred – in one account probably as a consequence of napalm usage during the Algerian War of Liberation – on the adjacent Mont Tababor: see Vielliard 1978, Ledant 1981). On Mont Babor, a 1959 map shows a large oak wood on the southern slope which today is bare and stony (Ledant 1981). Wood-cutting has been for local use only but is significant at lower levels (Ledant 1981, Ledant *et al.* in press); removal of dead trees as part of the forest's management was, however, recommended just prior to the Nuthatch's discovery (Ledant and Jacobs 1977). The construction of a motorable track up into the mountain in the 1970s has led to erosion along its length and to fears on the grounds of disturbance from excessive numbers of visitors and hunters, facilitation of access by museum and other collectors and by lorries (instead of mules and donkeys) for the transportation of wood, and a greatly increased risk of fire through all consequent increases in human presence (Ledant 1981; also Burnier 1976); moreover, the construction of further tracks had been recommended just prior to the Nuthatch's discovery (Ledant and Jacobs 1977). The most serious natural threat to the species is presumably the combination of very poor seed production in the autumn and particularly intense and protracted snow conditions the following winter (see Ecology above). Possible natural predators (at least on eggs and nestlings) are the Barbary macaque *Macaca sylvanus* (common), oak dormouse *Eliomys quercinus* (presence unconfirmed), North African weasel *Mustela (nivalis) numidica*, Great Spotted Woodpecker *Dendrocopus major* (rare) and Jay *Garrulus glandarius* (common) (Vielliard 1976b,1978, Gatter and Mattes 1979).

Conservation Measures Taken Collection of specimens for the original description was limited to a pair whose four young were first allowed to become independent (Vielliard 1976a,1978), and an appeal was made to museums to abstain from seeking to collect further specimens (Géroudet 1976, Vielliard 1976a). Mont Babor has had national park status since 1931, and in the period 1954-1962 it was defended to prevent its use as a refuge by nationalists, while in 1981 wardening was increased and goats and sheep (but not cattle) were thereafter excluded (Ledant *et al.* in press). A suggestion to provide bottled gas for local inhabitants to reduce their need for firewood (Ledant 1981) has been taken up and wood-cutting is already waning (Ledant *et al.* in press). The call to clarify the Algerian Nuthatch's ecology (Vielliard 1978) has to a large degree been answered by important studies in 1978 (Gatter and Mattes 1979) and 1982 (Ledant *et al.* in press). Some further measures have now been taken (see Conservation Measures Proposed).

Conservation Measures Proposed A series of measures is needed to counter deforestation, to favour the maintenance of old trees and species diversity, and to promote regeneration and soil stability, all without alienating the local community (Vielliard 1978, Ledant 1981, Ledant *et al.* in press). The following proposals have been made, some of which (b, e, j, k: J.-P. Ledant *in litt.* 1984) have already been accepted by the forestry services: (a) adoption of a general policy not to encourage tourism to the point where alterations to the forest and its environs are necessary to cater for the volume of interested visitors or where the lives of local people are affected; (b) reduction of pasturage in summit and mixed cedar forest, e.g. by planting forage outside the forest and by the rotational exclusion of livestock from particular areas; (c) study of vegetation to determine means of integrating long-term conservation management with the short-term interests of the forest's traditional users; (d) negotiation with local people to reduce wood-cutting in exchange for compensations; (e) no further cutting by the forest services and especially no removal of dead trees; (f) establishment of plantations outside the present forest perimeter to alleviate pressure for firewood; (g) modification of present wood-cutting techniques; (h) restoration and reafforestation of track slopes; (i) reafforestation of the southern slopes of Mont Babor; (j) no further construction of tracks for access; (k) closure of existing track to all but forest service vehicles; (l) provision of foresters with fire-surveillance, -alarm and -fighting equipment and vehicles (Ledant 1981, Ledant *et al.* in press). In addition to these, the reduction of wild boar has been urged (Gatter and Mattes 1979). The population dynamics of the Algerian Nuthatch, and in particular the causes of mortality, as well as the conditions maintaining its environment, have been proposed as subjects for study (Vielliard 1978). The whole forest area on Babor is proposed as a nature reserve, which will confer stricter protection on the area, e.g. building will be forbidden (M. Smart *in litt.* 1984).

Remarks The Djebel Babor is a site of outstanding natural value in Algeria. Four species of plant, most notably the Algerian fir, are wholly endemic to the mountain, and several others occur at only one or two other localities; moreover, it is the only site in all Africa for five plant species, and another four occur in only one other locality on the continent (Vielliard 1978). It holds "important entomological surprises", though these are unspecified (Di Carlo 1976). It is one of the few localities where the Barbary macaque thrives and is the most recently named site in Algeria for the leopard (Ledant 1981). The forest benefits the reservoir at Eghil Emda, and provides local people with water, provender and firewood (Ledant 1981). The discovery as late as the mid-1970s of a species new to science within the western Palearctic region was a truly remarkable event with considerable biogeographical interest (see Burnier 1976, Heim de Balsac 1976, Vielliard 1976b,1980, Ledant 1978; popular article with photographs in van den Berg 1984).

References

van den Berg, A. B. (1982) Plumages of Algerian Nuthatch. *Dutch Birding* 4: 98-100.

van den Berg, A. B. (1984) De Algerijnse Boomklever een nieuwe soort. *Vogels* 4 (no. 23): 174-177.

Burnier, E. (1976) Une nouvelle espèce de l'avifaune paléarctique: la Sittelle kabyle *Sitta ledanti. Nos Oiseaux* 33: 337-340.

Di Carlo, E. A. (1976) La scoperta di una nuova specie dell'avifauna paleartica: il Picchio muratore magrebino *Sitta ledanti* Vielliard. *Riv. ital. Orn.* 46: 243-247.

Fosse, A. and Vaillant, G. (1982) A propos de la couleur de la calotte chez la Sittelle kabyle (*Sitta ledanti*). *Alauda* 50: 228.

Gatter, W. and Mattes, H. (1979) Zur Populationsgrösse und Okologie des neuentdeckten Kabylienkleibers *Sitta ledanti* Vielliard 1976. *J. Orn.* 120: 390-405.

Géroudet, P. (1976) A propos de la Sittelle kabyle. *Nos Oiseaux* 33: 340-342.

Heim de Balsac, H. (1976) Commentaires sur la découverte d'un élément imprévu de la faune palearctique. *Alauda* 34: 353-355.

Jacobs, P., Mahler [*sic*; correctly, Malher], F. and Ochando, B. (1978) A propos de la couleur de la calotte chez la Sittelle kabyle (*Sitta ledanti*). *Aves* 15: 149-153.

Ledant, J.-P. (1977) La Sittelle kabyle (*Sitta ledanti* Vielliard), espèce endémique montagnarde récemment découverte. *Aves* 14: 83-85.

Ledant, J.-P. (1978) Données comparées sur la Sittelle corse (*Sitta whiteheadi*) et sur la Sittelle kabyle (*Sitta ledanti*). *Aves* 15: 154-157.

Ledant, J.-P. (1981) Conservation et fragilité de la forêt de Babor, habitat de la Sittelle kabyle. *Aves* 18: 1-9.

Ledant, J.-P. and Jacobs, P. (1977) La Sittelle kabyle (*Sitta ledanti*): données nouvelles sur sa biologie. *Aves* 14: 233-242.

Ledant, J.-P., Jacob, J.-P., Jacobs, P., Malher, F., Ochando, B. and Roché, J. (1981) Mise à jour de l'avifaune algérienne. *Gerfaut* 71: 295-398.

Ledant, J.-P., Jacobs, P. and Ochando, B. (1984) Dynamique de l'if (*Taxus baccata*) au Mont Babor. *Bull. Forestière Conserv. Nat.* (INA, Alger) 6: 27-29.

Ledant, J.-P., Jacobs, P., Ochando, B. and Renault, J. (in press) Dynamique de la forêt du Mont Babor et préférences écologiques de la Sittelle kabyle (*Sitta ledanti*). [*Biol. Conserv.*]

Le Fur, R. (1981) Notes sur l'avifaune algérienne, 2. *Alauda* 49: 295-299.

Vielliard, J. (1976a) La Sitelle [*sic*] kabyle. *Alauda* 44: 351-352.

Vielliard, J. (1976b) Un nouveau témoin rélictuel de la spécification dans la zone méditerranéenne: *Sitta ledanti* (Aves: Sittidae). *C. R. Acad. Sci. Paris* 283D: 1193-1195.

Vielliard, J. (1977) La Sittelle kabyle, un témoin de l'évolution. *La Recherche* no. 84: 1104-1105.

Vielliard, J. (1978) Le Djebel Babor et sa Sittelle *Sitta ledanti* Vielliard 1976. *Alauda* 46: 1-42.

Vielliard, J. (1980) Remarques complémentaires sur la Sittelle kabyle *Sitta ledanti* Vielliard 1976. *Alauda* 48: 139-150.

AMANI SUNBIRD   RARE

Anthreptes pallidigaster Sclater and Moreau, 1935

Order PASSERIFORMES   Family NECTARINIIDAE

Summary This sunbird is confined to two small areas of forest in East Africa (Kenya, Tanzania). Habitat destruction constitutes the principal threat to the species.

Distribution The Amani Sunbird has been recorded in two localities: up to 900 m in the East Usambara Mountains, north-eastern Tanzania, where its habitat covers no more than 130 km^2 (van der Willigen and Lovett 1981); and, 320 km to the north, in the coastal lowland Sokoke Forest, Kilifi District, Kenya, where it occupied no more than 70 km^2 in the late 1970s (Hall and Moreau 1962, Turner 1977, Britton and Zimmerman 1979). This area of suitable habitat in Sokoke had decreased to 67 km^2 by 1983 (Kelsey and Langton 1984). The species was discovered in 1935 when three birds were collected at 500 m, 7 km to the east of Amani in the foothills of the East Usambara Mountains (Sclater and Moreau 1935). Birds were also seen and collected at Amani itself, 900 m, in the same year (Moreau and Moreau 1937). In 1966 five specimens were collected at Amani (specimens in NMK: SNS) and there have been several sight records of the bird in the East Usambaras in the 1970s and 1980s (D. A. Turner pers. comm. 1977, Stuart and Turner 1980, SNS). The exact date of the species's discovery in the Sokoke Forest appears not to be published, though it had certainly been recorded by 1955 (Mackworth-Praed and Grant 1955). Several specimens were collected there between 1964 and 1966 (Ripley and Bond 1971) and in subsequent years the species has been recorded regularly (Turner 1977, Britton and Britton 1978, Britton and Zimmerman 1979, Kelsey and Langton 1984, Britton *et al.* in press). Being unobtrusive and diminutive, it is possible that the species occurs undetected in other remnant patches of lowland coastal forest in East Africa, but all these are acutely threatened with destruction (Britton 1976, Stuart and Hutton 1977, Stuart and van der Willigen 1978).

Population In the East Usambaras flocks of up to 18 have been seen near Amani (Moreau and Moreau 1937), but the species is generally uncommon in this locality (Stuart and Hutton 1977). Its local movements in the East Usambaras are not clearly understood, making it difficult to determine its status there (Moreau and Moreau 1937, D. A. Turner pers. comm. 1977). The Sokoke Forest population in the 1970s was estimated at 2,900-4,700 pairs (Britton and Britton 1978, Britton and Zimmerman 1979).

Ecology The Amani Sunbird is apparently largely a lowland coastal forest species, keeping much to the canopy (Moreau and Moreau 1937, Turner 1977, Stuart and Hutton 1977). In the East Usambaras it occurs in forests on the lower slopes and foothills (Moreau and Moreau 1937, Stuart and Hutton 1977, D. A. Turner pers. comm. 1977). Birds have been seen in flocks of up to 18 (Moreau and Moreau 1937) but generally occur singly or in pairs (Stuart and

Hutton 1977, Britton and Britton 1978, Kelsey and Langton 1984). They sometimes join mixed-species parties (Stuart and Hutton 1977, Britton and Britton 1978, D. A. Turner pers. comm. 1977). In the Sokoke Forest this is a bird of *Brachystegia* woodland, rather than forest (Turner 1977, Britton and Britton 1978, Britton and Zimmerman 1979, Kelsey and Langton 1984, J. G. Williams *in litt.* 1983), although secondary forest in the East Usambaras may be structurally similar to this (Stuart and Hutton 1977). Birds have been seen feeding at *Loranthus* blossoms in the Sokoke Forest and at *Erythrina* blossoms at Amani (J. G. Williams *in litt.* 1983). Breeding has been noted in the Sokoke Forest in March, May, June, September and October (Britton and Britton 1978) and a pair have been observed displaying in the East Usambaras in August (Stuart and Hutton 1977).

Threats This species is under threat from habitat destruction in both the East Usambaras and the Sokoke Forest (Stuart and Hutton 1977, Kelsey and Langton 1984). In a 195 km^2 area around Amani, 49% was forested in 1954 compared with only 38% in 1977 (Stuart and Hutton 1977). In the Sokoke Forest areas of suitable habitat outside the forest reserve cannot be expected to survive for long (Britton and Zimmerman 1979). Inside the reserve the systematic logging of *Brachystegia speciformis* still continues (Britton and Zimmerman 1979, Kelsey and Langton 1984). At the present rate of cutting the *Brachystegia* woodland would all be felled within the next 20 years (Kelsey and Langton 1984). Illegal cutting is taking place in the supposedly inviolate Sokoke Nature Reserve (Cunningham-van Someren 1981-1982, Kelsey and Langton 1984). Unfortunately the work of the forest officers at Sokoke has been rendered ineffective by shortage of available funds (Kelsey and Langton 1984). It seems that certain conservation regulations have been ignored by people taking advantage of the lack of supervision by officials from the Forestry Department (Kelsey and Langton 1984).

Conservation Measures Taken Much of the East Usambara habitat of this species is in forest reserves, but there is still danger from expanding teak and cardamom plantations (SNS). Within the 400 km^2 of the Sokoke Forest Reserve, a 43 km^2 tract, which contains part of the habitat of this species, is a nature reserve in which no cutting or disturbance is permitted (Britton 1976, Britton and Zimmerman 1979; but see under Threats above).

Conservation Measures Proposed A forest conservation proposal for the Usambaras is being prepared for consideration by the Tanzanian government (Stuart in prep.). Details of recommendations for the Sokoke Forest are given in Conservation Measures Proposed under Sokoke Scops Owl *Otus ireneae*.

Remarks Six other threatened bird species occur in the Usambara forests and five more such species occur in Sokoke Forest (see Remarks under the Usambara Ground Robin *Dryocichloides montanus* and Sokoke Scops Owl respectively).

References

Britton, P. L. (1976) Primary forestland destruction now critical. *Africana* 5(12): 1-2.

Britton, P. L. and Britton, H. A. (1978) Notes on the Amani Sunbird *Anthreptes pallidigaster* including a description of the nest and eggs. *Scopus* 2: 102-103.

Britton, P. L. and Zimmerman, D. A. (1979) The avifauna of Sokoke Forest, Kenya. *J. E. Afr. nat. Hist. Soc. and Natn. Mus.* 169: 1-15.

Britton, P. L., Stuart, S. N. and Turner, D. A. (in press) East African endangered species. *Proc. V Pan-Afr. orn. Congr.*

Cunningham-van Someren, G. R. ed. (1981-1982) *National Museum of Kenya, Department of Ornithology Museum Avifauna News*: 19,34,63,72.

Hall, B. P. and Moreau, R. E. (1962) A study of the rare birds of Africa. *Bull. Brit. Mus. (Nat. Hist.) Zool.* 8: 313-378.

Kelsey, M. G. and Langton, T. E. S. (1984) The conservation of the Arabuko-Sokoke Forest, Kenya. International Council for Bird Preservation and University of East Anglia. *International Council for Bird Preservation Study Report* no. 4.

Mackworth-Praed, C. W. and Grant, C. H. B. (1955) *African handbook of birds.* Series 1. Birds of eastern and north-eastern Africa, 2. London: Longmans, Green and Co.

Moreau, R. E. and Moreau, W. M. (1937) Biological and other notes on some East Africa birds, Part 2. *Ibis* 14(1): 321-345.

Ripley, S. D. and Bond, G. M. (1971) Systematic notes on a collection of birds from Kenya. *Smithsonian Contrib. Zool.* 111.

Sclater, W. L. and Moreau, R. E. (1935) [One new species and five new subspecies (from) the central northern highlands of Tanganyika Territory.] *Bull. Brit. Orn. Club* 56: 10-19.

Stuart, S. N. (in prep.) A forest conservation plan for the Usambara Mountains, Tanzania.

Stuart, S. N. and Hutton, J. M. eds. (1977) The avifauna of the East Usambara Mountains, Tanzania. A report compiled by the Cambridge Ornithological Expedition to East Africa, 1977. Unpublished.

Stuart, S. N. and Turner, D. A. (1980) Some range extensions and other notable records of forest birds from eastern and northeastern Tanzania. *Scopus* 4: 36-41.

Stuart, S. N. and van der Willigen, T. A. (1978) Report of the Cambridge Ecological Expedition to Tanzania 1978. Unpublished.

Turner, D. A. (1977) Status and distribution of the East African endemic species. *Scopus* 1: 2-11,56.

van der Willigen, T. A. and Lovett, J. eds. (1981) Report of the Oxford Expedition to Tanzania 1979. Unpublished.

BANDED GREEN SUNBIRD   RARE

Anthreptes rubritorques Reichenow, 1905

Order PASSERIFORMES   Family NECTARINIIDAE

Summary This species is known from four forest areas in eastern Tanzania. In only one of these localities is it at all common and this is the area where it is most threatened by forest destruction.

Distribution The Banded Green Sunbird is a middle-altitude species known from the Usambara, Nguru, Uluguru and Uzungwa Mountains in eastern Tanzania. Most records come from the Usambara Mountains, where it is fairly common in and around the forests between 750 and 1,200 m and in much smaller numbers up to 1,500 m (Stuart and Turner 1980, Stuart and Jensen 1981). The bulk of the population is probably on the East Usambara plateau and the south-western corner of the West Usambaras (SNS). The type-specimen, however, was collected at Mlalo in the north-west of the West Usambaras and described in 1905 (Reichenow 1905); there have been no subsequent records from this area. In the early 1930s field observations were made on the species around Amani in the East Usambaras and several birds were collected (Sclater and Moreau 1933, Moreau and Moreau 1937, and specimens in NMK and BMNH: SNS). Further specimens were taken in 1966 from Amani (in NMK: SNS) and since the early 1970s the species has been regularly reported from the East Usambaras (Stuart and Hutton 1977, Stuart and van der Willigen 1978, Turner 1978, Stuart and Turner 1980) including one record as low as 750 m at Magrotto in 1981 (Stuart and Jensen 1981). In the West Usambaras it was discovered at Mazumbai, 1,500 m, in 1977 (Stuart and van der Willigen 1978, Turner 1978) and there have been a few subsequent records from this site (Stuart and Jensen 1981). Other recent West Usambara records have come from Ambangulu, 1,200 m, and Dindira, 1,000 m, in the south-west of the mountains (Stuart and Turner 1980, SNS). In the Nguru Mountains it is known up to 1,600 m on the eastern slopes from only five collected specimens in the 1940s and 1950s (Britton 1980,1981, P. L. Britton pers. comm. 1982, and specimen in BMNH: SNS) and from a few sight records, probably in the late 1940s (J. G. Williams pers. comm. 1983). It appears to be very uncommon at this locality and a search for the species in 1978 was unsuccessful (Stuart and van der Willigen 1978). In the Uluguru Mountains the species is also known from only five specimens, all collected on the eastern slopes by T. Andersen (Britton 1981) during the 1950s (P. L. Britton pers. comm. 1982). Two of these specimens were stated to have been collected as low as 900 m and one as high as 1,800 m (Britton 1978,1981) but Andersen is considered often inaccurate in estimations of altitude (Stuart and Jensen in press) and it seems unlikely that he collected this species above 1,600 m. Other ornithological exploration in the Ulugurus has not detected the bird, so it appears very rare there (Sclater and Moreau 1933, F. P. Jensen *in litt.* 1982). In the Uzungwa Mountains the species is known from a sight record in 1982 of a small flock at 1,000 m in Mwanihana Forest (Jensen *et al.* in press, F. P. Jensen *in litt.* 1982) and a single male seen at 850 m at the same locality in 1984 (SNS). It seems to be very rare at this site but it may also occur in other forests on the eastern escarpment of the Uzungwas. However, an attempt in 1984 to locate the species 160 km south-west of Mwanihana Forest on the Uzungwa escarpment above Chita was unsuccessful (F. P. Jensen pers. comm. 1984).

Population The populations in the Nguru, Uluguru and Uzungwa Mountains are probably very small and possibly vestigial (SNS), although one report describes the species as common at flowering trees in the Nguru foothills (J. G. Williams pers. comm. 1983). Greater numbers probably exist in the Usambaras where it occurs at a much higher density (SNS). Population estimates are, however, very difficult to make because birds move around erratically in search of fruiting trees, where they may gather in flocks of up to 60 (Stuart and Hutton 1977, Turner 1978, Britton 1980). In 1979 there was about 200 km^2 of forest within the altitudinal range of this species in the Usambaras (van der Willigen and Lovett 1981).

Ecology The Banded Green Sunbird inhabits the canopy of middle altitude rainforest between 750 and 1,600 m (Sclater and Moreau 1933, Moreau and Moreau 1937, Stuart and Hutton 1977, Stuart and van der Willigen 1978, Britton 1980, van der Willigen and Lovett 1981); there are no records from dry forests in any of the four mountain ranges where it occurs (SNS). The species is usually found in the tops of tall trees and can adapt to secondary habitats in which some forest trees survive (Stuart and Hutton 1977, Stuart and van der Willigen 1978, Turner 1978, van der Willigen and Lovett 1981). It is probably, however, dependent on the forest environment (van der Willigen and Lovett 1981), leaving the forest only when suitable trees that grow outside it, such as *Casearia battiscombei*, are in fruit (Turner 1978). The food consists of nectar and small berries, including those of *Macaranga kilimandscharica* (Sclater and Moreau 1933, Moreau 1935). Birds have also been seen feeding in flowering *Erythrina* trees (J. G. Williams pers. comm. 1983). The birds often nest in exotic trees planted near the forest (Moreau and Moreau 1937). One nest was observed in a very open situation in August 1977 but was subsequently destroyed (Stuart and Hutton 1977); others have been observed on the forest edge in January, October and November (Moreau and Moreau 1937, SNS). Although sometimes seen in pairs, birds often gather in flocks of up to 60 (Stuart and Hutton 1977, Turner 1978, Britton 1980).

Threats Forest clearance, especially for cardamom plantations, is very severe throughout the range of this species in the Usambaras (van der Willigen and Lovett 1981, Rodgers and Homewood 1982b, Stuart in prep.) and although it may well survive in some of the new secondary habitats in the short term, its long-term survival is not assured (SNS). The apparently tiny populations in the Ngurus, Ulugurus and Uzungwas may not be so threatened but even there some clearance is taking place (Rodgers and Homewood 1982a, Scharff *et al.* 1982).

Conservation Measures Taken The populations in the Nguru, Uluguru and Uzungwa Mountains are almost entirely within forest reserves, which provide some measure of protection to wildlife (Rodgers and Homewood 1982a, Scharff *et al.* 1982, SNS). Some of the Usambara population is also within forest reserves but a large part is on public land where forest destruction is very serious (van der Willigen and Lovett 1981, Rodgers and Homewood 1982b, Stuart in prep.).

Conservation Measures Proposed A forest conservation proposal for the Usambaras is being prepared for the consideration of the Tanzanian government (Stuart in prep.). The population in the Uzungwas would be safeguarded if the proposed Mwanihana National Park were to be gazetted (Rodgers and Homewood 1982a) but it is not known whether the Tanzanian government will implement this recommendation (W. A. Rodgers *in litt.* 1983). Stricter forest conservation measures are also needed in the Uluguru Mountains and it has been suggested that a national nature reserve be established (Scharff *et al.* 1982).

Remarks The Banded Green Sunbird is a member of a superspecies which also includes the Green Sunbird *Anthreptes rectirostris*, which ranges widely through the forests of West and Central Africa. The Banded Green Sunbird is very isolated from its allospecies and is considered to have diverged to the specific level (Hall and Moreau 1970). Six other threatened bird species occur in the Usambaras, three more in the Ulugurus and six more in the Uzungwas (see Remarks under Usambara Ground Robin *Dryocichloides montanus*, Uluguru Bush-shrike *Malaconotus alius* and Iringa Ground Robin *D. lowei* respectively). In the Ngurus one species treated in Appendix C occurs, Moreau's Sunbird *Nectarinia moreaui*.

References

Britton, P. L. (1978) The Andersen Collection from Tanzania. *Scopus* 2: 77-85.

Britton, P. L. ed. (1980) *Birds of East Africa: their habitat, status and distribution.* Nairobi: EANHS.

Britton, P. L. (1981) Notes on the Andersen Collection and other specimens from Tanzania housed in some West German museums. *Scopus* 5: 14-21.

Hall, B. P. and Moreau, R. E. (1970) *An atlas of speciation in African passerine birds.* London: Trustees of the British Museum (Natural History).

Jensen, F. P., Stuart, S. N. and Brogger-Jensen, S. (in press) Altitudinal distribution of the avifauna of the Mwanihana Forest, Tanzania. *Gerfaut.*

Moreau, R. E. (1935) A synecological study of Usambara, Tanganyika Territory, with particular reference to birds. *J. Ecol.* 23: 1-43.

Moreau, R. E. and Moreau, W. M. (1937) Biological and other notes on some East African birds, Part II. *Ibis* (14)1: 321-345.

Reichenow, A. (1905) Beschreibung neuer Arten. *Orn. Monatsber.* 13: 179-182.

Rodgers, W. A. and Homewood, K. M. (1982a) Biological values and conservation prospects for the forests and primate populations of the Uzungwa Mountains, Tanzania. *Biol. Conserv.* 24: 285-304.

Rodgers, W. A. and Homewood, K. M. (1982b) Species richness and endemism in the Usambara mountain forests, Tanzania. *Biol. J. Linn. Soc.* 18: 197-242.

Scharff, N., Stoltze, M., and Jensen, F. P. (1982) The Uluguru Mts., Tanzania. Report of a study-tour, 1981. Unpublished.

Sclater, W. L. and Moreau, R. E. (1933) Taxonomic and field notes on some birds of north-eastern Tanganyika Territory, Part V. *Ibis* (13)3: 399-440.

Stuart, S. N. (in prep.) A forest conservation plan for the Usambara Mountains, Tanzania.

Stuart, S. N. and Hutton, J. M. eds. (1977) The avifauna of the East Usambara Mountains, Tanzania. A report compiled by the Cambridge Ornithological Expedition to East Africa 1977. Unpublished.

Stuart, S. N. and Jensen, F. P. (1981) Further range extensions and other notable records of forest birds from Tanzania. *Scopus* 5: 106-115.

Stuart, S. N. and Jensen, F. P. (in press) The avifauna of the Uluguru Mountains, Tanzania. *Gerfaut.*

Stuart, S. N. and Turner, D. A. (1980) Some range extensions and other notable records of forest birds from Tanzania. *Scopus* 4: 36-41.

Stuart, S. N. and van der Willigen, T. A. eds. (1978) Report of the Cambridge Ecological Expedition to Tanzania 1978. Unpublished.

Turner, D. A. (1978) Interim report on the endangered birds of the Usambara Mountains. Unpublished.

van der Willigen, T. A. and Lovett, J. C. eds. (1981) Report of the Oxford Expedition to Tanzania 1979. Unpublished.

RUFOUS-WINGED SUNBIRD
Nectarinia rufipennis Jensen, 1983

RARE

Order PASSERIFORMES

Family NECTARINIIDAE

Summary This very recently discovered species is known from only one mountain forest area in eastern Tanzania. It is a bird of the forest interior and would decline if forest clearance started there.

Distribution The Rufous-winged Sunbird is known only from the Mwanihana Forest on the eastern escarpment of the Uzungwa Mountains in eastern Tanzania (Jensen 1983). It was discovered in 1981 when one male bird was mistnetted at 1,000 m (Stuart and Jensen 1981, Jensen 1983). The first female was netted a few weeks later in the same year, also at 1,000 m (Stuart and Jensen 1981, Jensen 1983). Subsequent studies in 1982 and 1983 have shown that the species occurs from 600 m to 1,700 m in Mwanihana Forest (Jensen *et al.* in press, F. P. Jensen *in litt.* 1982, A. J. Beakbane *in litt.* 1983). It might also occur in some other rainforests on the eastern escarpment of the Uzungwas which still cover a considerable area (Rodgers and Homewood 1982). However, a thorough search for the species at Chita, 160 km to the south-west of Mwanihana Forest along the Uzungwa escarpment, in 1984, proved fruitless (F. P. Jensen pers. comm. 1984). This suggests that the range of the Rufous-winged Sunbird may prove to be very small. The species is almost certainly absent from the dry plateau forests of the Uzungwas, which have been well explored by ornithologists (Stuart *et al.* 1981, SNS).

Population No population estimates can be made until the distribution of this species in the escarpment forests of the Uzungwa Mountains is better known. In Mwanihana Forest it is uncommon below 1,000 m but much more numerous above 1,500 m (Jensen *et al.* in press, F. P. Jensen *in litt.* 1982).

Ecology The Rufous-winged Sunbird is recorded from forest interior, feeding mainly 2-8 m from the ground, though it has occasionally been seen up to 30 m in the canopy (Jensen 1983, Jensen *et al.* in press, F. P. Jensen *in litt.* 1982). Birds have been noted feeding on the nectar of the flowers of an undergrowth shrub *Achryspermum radicans* (A. J Beakbane *in litt.* 1983). The species is particularly aggressive to other sunbirds, especially the Olive Sunbird *Nectarinia olivacea* and Moreau's Sunbird *N. moreaui* (F. P. Jensen *in litt.* 1982).

Threats Some felling of valuable timber trees is taking place in Mwanihana Forest and also elsewhere on the eastern escarpment of the Uzungwa Mountains (Rodgers and Homewood 1982, A. J. Beakbane *in litt.* 1983, SNS).

Conservation Measures Taken Most of the range of this species is likely to be within forest reserves, which provide some measure of protection for wildlife (SNS).

Conservation Measures Proposed It has been suggested that the Mwanihana Forest be included within a new national park (Rodgers 1982, Rodgers and Homewood 1982). If this national park is gazetted the future of this very restricted species will probably be assured.

Remarks This distinctive new species has no close relatives (Jensen 1983) and occurs in an area of particular biological and conservation importance. Five other threatened bird species are known to occur in Mwanihana Forest, Swynnerton's Forest Robin *Swynnertonia swynnertoni*, the Dappled Mountain Robin *Modulatrix orostruthus*, Mrs Moreau's Warbler *Bathmocercus winifredae*, the Banded Green Sunbird *Anthreptes rubritorques* and the Tanzanian Mountain Weaver *Ploceus nicolli*. The national park proposed for Mwanihana would also include a large area of dry plateau forest, where another threatened species, the Iringa Ground Robin *Dryocichloides lowei*, might well occur. In addition, two species listed in Appendix C, the White-winged Apalis *Apalis chariessa* and Moreau's Sunbird *Nectarinia moreaui*, also occur in Mwanihana Forest.

References

Jensen, F. P. (1983) A new species of sunbird from Tanzania. *Ibis* 125: 447-449.

Jensen, F. P., Stuart, S. N. and Brogger-Jensen, S. (in press) Altitudinal distribution of the avifauna of the Mwanihana Forest, Tanzania. *Gerfaut*.

Rodgers, W. A. (1982) WWF/IUCN Tropical Forests and Primates Programme, Tanzania. Gland, Switzerland: WWF/IUCN.

Rodgers, W. A. and Homewood, K. M. (1982) Biological values and conservation prospects for the forests and primate populations of the Uzungwa Mountains, Tanzania. *Biol. Conserv.* 24: 285-304.

Stuart, S. N., Howell, K. M., van der Willigen, T. A. and Geertsema, A. A. (1981) Some additions to the forest avifauna of the Uzungwa Mountains, Tanzania. *Scopus* 5: 46-50.

Stuart, S. N. and Jensen, F. P. (1981) Further range extensions and other notable records of forest birds from Tanzania. *Scopus* 5: 106-115.

MARUNGU SUNBIRD   ENDANGERED

Nectarinia prigoginei (Macdonald, 1958)

Order PASSERIFORMES   Family NECTARINIIDAE

Summary This nectar-feeding species is only known from riparian forest patches in the Marungu Highlands of south-eastern Zaire. The available habitat is very restricted in area and being cleared rapidly; the bird is, therefore, in considerable danger.

Distribution The Marungu Sunbird was discovered in 1926 when three specimens were collected at Matafali (1,900 m), Sambwe (1,860 m) and Pande (1,860 m) in the Marungu Highlands in south-eastern Zaire (Chapin 1954). Three specimens were collected at Kasiki (2,020-2,280 m) in 1931 (Schouteden 1949) and another eight along the Lufuko River (1,900 m) in 1972, all in the Marungu Highlands (Dowsett and Prigogine 1974, Benson and Prigogine 1981). Several others were seen along the Lufuko River in 1971 and 1972 (R. J. Dowsett *in litt.* 1983, R. J. Stjernstedt *per* R. J. Dowsett *in litt.* 1983).

Population Numbers are not known but birds were noted as common on the edge of riparian forest along the Lufuko River in 1972 (Dowsett and Prigogine 1974).

Ecology The first three specimens "were found in a thick tangle and in a cornfield, not far from streams" (Chapin 1954). In 1972, however, the species was found on the edge of riparian forest (Dowsett and Prigogine 1974) and this is probably the more usual habitat (Benson and Prigogine 1981). No further data are available, but *Nectarinia* sunbirds are typically nectar-feeders.

Threats The riparian forest on which this species probably depends and which covers only a very small area of the Marungu Highlands is under severe threat from timber-felling and from the erosion of stream banks resulting from overgrazing by cattle (Dowsett and Prigogine 1974).

Conservation Measures Taken None is known.

Conservation Measures Proposed Fieldwork is needed to assess the status of this species, and to determine the extent and condition of the remaining forest patches in the Marungu Highlands. Nature reserves should then be established in suitable areas where timber-felling and cattle-grazing could be prohibited.

Remarks The Marungu Sunbird has had a confusing taxonomic history (see Macdonald 1958, Clancey and Irwin 1978, Prigogine 1979, Benson and Prigogine 1981). It has several characters apparently shared with the Eastern Double-collared Sunbird *Nectarinia mediocris* and Stuhlmann's Double-collared Sunbird *N. stuhlmanni*, and is possibly of hybrid origin (Benson and Prigogine 1981).

References

Benson, C. W. and Prigogine, A. (1981) The status of *Nectarinia afra prigoginei* (Macdonald). *Gerfaut* 71: 47-57.

Chapin, J. P. (1954) The birds of the Belgian Congo. Part 4. *Bull. Amer. Mus. Nat. Hist.* 75B.

Clancey, P. A. and Irwin, M. P. S. (1978) Species limits in the *Nectarinia afra/N. chalybea* complex of African double-collared sunbirds. *Durban. Mus. Novit.* 11(20): 331-351.

Dowsett, R. J. and Prigogine, A. (1974) The avifauna of the Marungu Highlands. *Hydrobiological survey of the Lake Bangweulu Luapula River basin* 19: 1-67.

Macdonald, J. D. (1958) Note on *Cinnyris manoensis* Reichenow. *Bull. Brit. Orn. Club* 78: 7-9.

Prigogine, A. (1979) Subspecific variation of Stuhlmann's Double-collared Sunbird, *Nectarinia stuhlmanni*, around the Albertine Rift. *Gerfaut* 69: 225-238.

Schouteden, H. (1949) Contribution à l'étude de la faune ornithologique du Katanga (Congo Belge). *Rev. Zool. Bot. Afr.* 42: 158-174.

ROCKEFELLER'S SUNBIRD   RARE
Nectarinia rockefelleri (Chapin, 1932)

Order PASSERIFORMES   Family NECTARINIIDAE

Summary This nectar-feeding species is restricted to high montane forest and afro-alpine moorland in three mountain ranges in eastern Zaire. Although its distribution covers a tiny area and it has been recorded only once since 1953, further research may show that it is not in any immediate danger.

Distribution Rockefeller's Sunbird was discovered in 1929 when two specimens were collected at about 2,750 m on Mount Kandashomwa in the Itombwe Mountains, north-west of Lake Tanganyika in eastern Zaire (Chapin 1932). Eleven further specimens have been collected from the Itombwe Mountains as follows: one from Ngusa, 2,240 m, in 1950; six from Mount Mohi, 2,960-3,300 m, from 1951 to 1953; two from Lake Lungwe, 2,680 m, in 1951 and 1953; one from Nzombe, 2,050 m, in 1953; and one from Muusi, 2,540 m, in 1963 (Prigogine 1971,1980a, and specimens in MRAC and IRSNB: SNS). With the exception of Ngusa and Nzombe, all these localities are in the Mount Kandashomwa area at the northern end of the Itombwe Mountain block (Prigogine 1980a); Ngusa and Nzombe are about 35 km to the south-west of Mount Kandashomwa, and at lower altitudes. Rockefeller's Sunbird appears not to occur in the southern part of the Itombwe Mountains (Prigogine 1980a). In 1942 the species was discovered 80 km north of Itombwe on Mount Kahusi, west of Lake Kivu, at 3,000 m (Hendrickx and Massart-Lis 1952). Another specimen was collected very nearby on Mount Kabushwa at 3,200 m in 1951 (Hendrickx and Massart-Lis 1952). In April 1978 one male bird was seen clearly on Mount Karisimbi north of Lake Kivu (A. D. Forbes-Watson pers. comm. 1984). All records of the species (save this last for which the altitude is not certainly known) are from between 2,050 and 3,300 m (Prigogine 1974,1980b) and its range has been estimated to cover only 250 km^2 (Hall and Moreau 1962). A sight record of two at Rwegura in Burundi in 1975 (Gaugris 1976) requires confirmation (Gaugris *et al.* 1981).

Population Numbers are not known. The species is reported to be common, at least in parts of its small range (Chapin 1954, Prigogine 1980a).

Ecology Although it occurs in montane forest down to 2,050 m (Prigogine 1974,1980b), this is mainly a species of galleries in bamboo forest at higher altitudes (Chapin 1954, Prigogine 1980a). The birds apparently prefer the thickets along streams, rather than the bamboo forest itself (Chapin 1954). They have also been found in heather (Hendrickx and Massart-Lis 1952), presumably in afro-alpine vegetation. They occur alone or in pairs at mid-height in trees, sometimes joining mixed-species parties (Prigogine 1971). The species is sympatric with the closely related Regal Sunbird *Nectarinia regia* on Mount Kahuzi (Hendrickx and Massart-Lis 1952) and the two species overlap between 2,050 and 2,380 m in the Itombwe Mountains (Prigogine 1974,1980a,b).

Threats This species would presumably be threatened if forest destruction became serious within its restricted range, although this may not be immediately likely given the very high altitudes involved. There is, however, a danger from clearance around villages in the upper reaches of the Itombwe Mountains, but there is no recent information on the conservation status of these forests (A. Prigogine *in litt.* 1983).

Conservation Measures Taken None is known, other than that the Kahuzi-Biega National Park, west of Lake Kivu (Prigogine in press), might prove sufficient to safeguard the species.

Conservation Measures Proposed A preliminary conservation plan for the forests of the Itombwe Mountains has been prepared (Prigogine in press). It is hoped that this plan will be worked out in detail and implemented by the Zairean government. Further work is also required to determine what threats, if any, Rockefeller's Sunbird is facing.

Remarks The forests of the Itombwe Mountains are important for six other threatened bird species (see Remarks under Schouteden's Swift *Schoutedenapus schoutedeni*). Two other threatened bird species occur in the mountains west of Lake Kivu (see Remarks under the African Green Broadbill *Pseudocalyptomena graueri*).

References

Chapin, J. P. (1932) Fourteen new birds from tropical Africa. *Amer. Mus. Novit.* 570.

Chapin, J. P. (1954) The birds of the Belgian Congo. Part 4. *Bull. Amer. Mus. Nat. Hist.* 75B.

Gaugris, Y. (1976) Additions à l'inventaire des oiseaux du Burundi (Decembre 1971 – Decembre 1975). *Oiseau et R.F.O.* 46: 273-289.

Gaugris, Y., Prigogine, A. and Vande weghe, J.-P. (1981) Additions et corrections à l'avifaune du Burundi. *Gerfaut* 71: 3-39.

Hall, B. P. and Moreau, R. E. (1962) A study of the rare birds of Africa. *Bull. Brit. Mus. (Nat. Hist.) Zool.* 8: 313-378.

Hendrickx, F. L. and Massart-Lis, Y. (1952) *Cinnyris rockefelleri* Chapin. *Ibis* 94: 531-532.

Prigogine, A. (1971) Les oiseaux de l'Itombwe et de son hinterland. Volume I. *Ann. Mus. Roy. Afr. Centr.* 8°, Sci. Zool. 185: 1-298.

Prigogine, A. (1974) Contribution à l'étude de la distribution verticale des oiseaux orophiles. *Gerfaut* 64: 75-88.

Prigogine, A. (1980a) Etude de quelques contacts secondaires au Zaire oriental. *Gerfaut* 70: 305-384.

Prigogine, A. (1980b) The altitudinal distribution of the avifauna in the Itombwe Forest (Zaire). *Proc. IV Pan-Afr. Orn. Congr.*: 169-184.

Prigogine, A. (in press) The conservation of the avifauna of the forests of the Albertine Rift. *Proceedings of the ICBP Tropical Forest Bird Symposium, 1982.*

SAO TOME WHITE-EYE   INDETERMINATE
Zosterops ficedulinus Hartlaub, 1866

Order PASSERIFORMES   Family ZOSTEROPIDAE

Summary This small forest-dwelling white-eye is confined to the islands of São Tomé and Príncipe, and has declined on both in the past century, seriously on Príncipe, worryingly on São Tomé.

Distribution The São Tomé White-eye is confined to São Tomé and Príncipe (São Tomé e Príncipe) in the Gulf of Guinea. On São Tomé the species (race *feae*) has been recorded from Santa Cruz/Poto (roughly 0°20'N 6°40'E), Bom Retiro (0°20'N 6°39'E), Vista Alegre (0°19'N 6°41'E) and Agua Creola (Agua Crioula, 0°19'N 6°42'E) in the north-east, Ribeira Palma (0°21'N 6°35'E) in the north-west, Binda (0°13'N 6°28'E) in the far west, Rio Quija (0°08'N 6°30'E) in the south-west, Agua Izé (0°13'N 6°44'E) in the far east, Io Grande near Angolares (0°08'N 6°39'E) in the south-east, Nova Moca (0°17'N 6°38'E) in the north-central region, and "Zalma" (untraceable, but "Zampalma" is at 0°16'N 6°37'E, also in the north-central region) (Bocage 1903, Salvadori 1903, Bannerman 1915, Correia 1928-1929, Frade and dos Santos 1977). On Príncipe the nominate race *ficedulinus* was originally found on the hilly parts of the interior with few on lower ground (Dohrn 1866, Keulemans 1866), birds being collected at "Sindy" (Bocage 1903) (evidently Sundi, at 1°40'N 7°23'E, i.e. the north-west), Bahía do Oeste (untraceable but presumably in the west) (Salvadori 1903) and Mesa (1°35'N 7°21'E) in the south-west, at 500 m (de Naurois 1983; all coordinates derived from Centro de Geográfia do Ultramar 1968). In 1928 it was described as living "all over" São Tomé (Correia 1928-1929).

Population The species was common on São Tomé in the late 1920s (Correia 1928-1929, Amadon 1953) but by the 1960s and 1970s it was uncommon (de Naurois 1983). On Príncipe it was fairly common in the higher parts of the island when first discovered (Keulemans 1866) but only two (three in Correia 1928-1929) specimens were collected in the late 1920s (Amadon 1953) and it is now certainly rare there (de Naurois 1983).

Ecology On São Tomé birds inhabit dense and degraded forest at high and middle altitudes (de Naurois 1983); nevertheless, all localities named under Distribution are at 350 m or below, except for Nova Moca and Zampalma, which are at c. 1,000 m (but even these latter are on relatively gentle sloping ground below the main mountainous region of the island) (data here are derived from examination of Ministério das Colónias 1948). On Príncipe it is (or was) a bird of uninhabited forest (Keulemans 1866), though in 1928 it was noted to occur in the tops of the highest trees in plantations (Correia 1928-1929). On São Tomé, too, it occurs in the tops of tall trees in small flocks, flying very fast between trees (Correia 1928-1929, R. de Naurois pers. comm. 1982). Birds eat insects and berries (Keulemans 1866) and have been seen gleaning food from leaves (Correia 1928-1929). They breed from September onwards, placing the nest between branches;

clutch-size is 3-5 (Keulemans 1866). Birds form monospecific flocks on Príncipe, sometimes consorting with the Príncipe Speirops *Speirops leucophaeus* (Keulemans 1866); on São Tomé their habits are the same as the Black-capped Speirops *S. lugubris* (Salvadori 1903).

Threats None is known; however the better documented plight of two other forest-dependent island congeners, the Mauritius White-eye *Zosterops chloronothus* and the Seychelles White-eye *Z. modestus* (see relevant accounts), is an indication that the evident decline in this species since its first discovery may reflect a serious problem. Habitat destruction on Príncipe has been extensive (see Bannerman 1914); on São Tomé all named localities now fall within cacau-growing areas except the upper reaches of Rio Quija and Io Grande, which are still forested, Nova Moca, which is a plantation, and Zampalma, which appears to be in forest (but which is not a certain locality: see Distribution) (data here are from de Carvalho Rodrigues 1974).

Conservation Measures Taken None is known.

Conservation Measures Proposed An ICBP project was developed in 1981 to investigate the status, ecology and conservation of the endemic birds of São Tomé e Príncipe, but was unable to proceed in 1982 and 1983. A study of this bird is a component of the project and conservation proposals will follow if the project goes ahead.

References

Amadon, D. (1953) Avian systematics and evolution in the Gulf of Guinea. The J. G. Correia collection. *Bull. Amer. Mus. Nat. Hist.* 100: 393-451.

Bannerman, D. A. (1914) Report on the birds collected by the late Mr Boyd Alexander (Rifle Brigade) during his last expedition to Africa. Part I. The birds of Prince's Island. *Ibis* (10)2: 596-631.

Bannerman, D. A. (1915) Report on the birds collected by the late Mr Boyd Alexander (Rifle Brigade) during his last expedition to Africa. Part III. The birds of St.Thomas' Island. *Ibis* (10)3: 89-121.

Bocage, J. V. B. (1903) Contribution à la faune des quatre îles du Golfe de Guinée. IV. Ile de St.Thomé. *Jorn. Acad. Sci. Lisboa* (2)7: 65-96.

de Carvalho Rodrigues, F. M. (1974) *S.Tomé e Príncipe sob o ponto de vista agrícola*. Estudos, Ensaios e Documentos 130A. Lisboa: Junta de Investigações Científicas do Ultramar (Cartas Agrícolas).

Centro de Geográfia do Ultramar (1968) *Relãçao dos nomes geográficos de S.Tomé e Príncipe*. Lisboa: Junta de Investigações do Ultramar.

Correia, J. G. (1928-1929) Unpublished typescript concerning his São Tomé expedition, held in AMNH.

Dohrn, H. (1866) Synopsis of the birds of Ilha do Príncipe, with some remarks on their habits and descriptions of new species. *Proc. Zool. Soc. Lond.*: 324-332.

Frade, F. and dos Santos, J. V. (1977) Aves de S.Tomé e Príncipe. *Garcia de Orta* (Ser. Zool.) 6: 3-18.

Keulemans, J. G. (1866) Opmerkingen over de vogels van de Kaap-verdische Eilanden en van Prins-eiland (Ilha do Príncipe) in de Bogt van Guinea gelagen. *Nederl. Tijdschr. Dierk.* 3: 363-401.

Ministério das Colónias (1948) *Atlas de Portugal Ultramarino e das grandes viagens portuguesas de descobrimento e expansão*. Lisboa: Junta das Missões Geográficas e de Investigações Coloniais.

de Naurois, R. (1983) Les oiseaux reproducteurs des îles de São Tomé et Príncipe: liste systématique commentée et indications zoogéographiques. *Bonn. zool. Beitr.* 34: 129-148.

Salvadori, T. (1903) Contribuzioni alla ornitologia delle isole del Golfo di Guinea. *Mem. Reale Accad. Sci. Torino* (2)53: 1-45.

SEYCHELLES WHITE-EYE   ENDANGERED
Zosterops modestus E. Newton, 1867

Order PASSERIFORMES   Family ZOSTEROPIDAE

Summary The rapid and proportionately massive decrease in this species since 1975-1976 is as unexplained as its confinement to three tiny areas of mixed secondary forest on one island, Mahé, in the Seychelles. Nothing positive can apparently be done for it and, on present evidence, it will possibly very shortly become extinct.

Distribution Apart from a (now lost) specimen registered as collected on Marianne in 1879 (Diamond and Feare 1980), the Seychelles White-eye is known only from Mahé, Seychelles. It was first found near Forêt Niol (see Remarks) and behind Victoria (Newton 1867), and subsequently on the Cascade estate (Nicoll 1906); the first general assessment of its distribution on Mahé indicated its presence throughout the central massif between the 300 and 600 m contours (Vesey-Fitzgerald 1940). Since its "rediscovery" around 1960 it appears to have remained largely confined to three general localities, each less than 5 km^2 in extent, at La Misère, Mission and Rochon (J. Watson *in litt.* 1981,1982). It is possible that as yet undiscovered populations exist in other localities (Wilson 1981).

Population Earlier reports refer to birds being "tolerably plentiful" in a grove of clove-trees (Newton 1867), "fairly abundant" on one estate (Nicoll 1906), and "not infrequent" in the central parts of Mahé (Vesey-Fitzgerald 1940). However, there was a gap in observations for c. 20 years to around 1960, leading first to the conclusion that the species had become extinct (Crook 1961), then to the opinion that it had undergone a "decline and apparent recovery" (Gaymer *et al.* 1969); this view is not supported by valid evidence (Feare 1975). In 1975-1976, populations of 20-30 birds were considered present at both La Misère and Mission, with perhaps 2-3 pairs at Rochon, giving a guessed-at total population of under 100; but in 1979-1980 it was very difficult to find more than one or two birds at the first two localities, while the third was not visited (J. Watson *in litt.* 1981,1982). In October 1982 a pair was found at Mission and it was considered possible that 5-6 pairs might exist in that general region (J. Watson *in litt.* 1981,1982).

Ecology The species inhabits mixed secondary forest above 300 m, especially where certain tall trees, including *Albizia falcataria* and *Pterocarpus indica*, have an underlying or adjacent scrub layer partly composed of the same species; most feeding is considered to be done in this scrub layer, usually below 3 m (Feare 1975), but foraging has also been seen consistently to occur in the tops of *Calophyllum* and other trees, birds hopping along branches to search amongst leaves and into bark crevices (Greig-Smith 1978,1979, Wilson 1981). Of 16 tree species in which feeding was noted, 1975-1976, only two were indigenous and were used in only 3% of observations (J. Watson *in litt.* 1981,1982). Birds are largely insectivorous, taking (e.g.) mealy bugs *Coccus*, caterpillars, possibly ants; also berries of *Lantana camara* (Feare 1975, Greig-Smith 1978, Wilson 1981). Breeding, which can be co-operative, occurs at the start and end of the north-west monsoon (October/November and February/March); two eggs are laid (Greig-Smith 1979, Watson 1979, J. Watson *in litt.* 1981,1982). The choice of nest-sites in dense foliage of broad-leaved trees, possibly to reduce risk of rain-damage, may contribute to the species's present restricted distribution, which may also be affected by aggressive interference, shown by Seychelles Bulbuls *Hypsipetes crassirostris* and (introduced) Madagascar Fodies *Foudia madagascariensis*, and very probably also by from (introduced) Indian Mynahs *Acridotheres tristis* (Greig-Smith 1979).

Threats The factors (other than the "natural" ones mentioned under Ecology) adversely influencing the numbers of this species remain wholly unclear: habitat of the type known to be used is extensive on Mahé (Wilson 1981). Unfortunately, birds occur in localities with (now) considerable human activity: since the late 1970s two trees known to have been used for nesting have been felled to make way for power-lines, and the Mission area is of great importance for both forestry and commercial tea-growing, the latter likely to be entirely incompatible with the species's conservation (Wilson 1981).

Conservation Measures Taken The whole of the Mission population is within the Morne Seychellois National Park (J. Watson *in litt.* 1981,1982), though this does not protect it from land-use changes (see Threats); the other two populations are at its periphery and are likely to range outside it (J. Watson *in litt.* 1981,1982).

Conservation Measures Proposed There is an urgent need to determine the species's status more exactly, and to investigate the reasons for its extraordinarily restricted distribution (J. Watson *in litt.* 1981,1982).

Remarks The Chestnut-flanked White-eye *Zosterops (mayottensis) semiflavus*, another Seychelles endemic, became extinct on Marianne presumably as a result of wholesale habitat clearance (see Distribution under Seychelles Warbler *Acrocephalus sechellarum*). It is conceivable, however, from context, that the birds seen near Forêt Niol in 1867 were, in fact, specimens of the Chestnut-flanked White-eye (see Newton 1867).

References

Crook, J. H. (1961) The fodies (Ploceinae) of the Seychelles Islands. *Ibis* 103a: 517-548.

Diamond, A. W. and Feare, C. J. (1980) Past and present biogeography of central Seychelles birds. *Proc. IV Pan-Afr. orn. Congr.*: 89-98.

Feare, C. J. (1975) Observations on the Seychelles White-eye *Zosterops modesta*. *Auk* 92: 615-618.

Gaymer, R., Blackman, R. A. A., Dawson, P. G., Penny, M. and Penny, C. M. (1969) The endemic birds of Seychelles. *Ibis* 111: 157-176.

Greig-Smith, P. W. (1979) Observations of nesting and group behaviour of Seychelles White-eyes *Zosterops modesta*. *Ibis* 121: 344-348.

Greig-Smith, P. W. (1978) Imitative foraging in mixed-species flocks of Seychelles birds. *Ibis* 120: 233-235.

Newton, E. (1867) On the land-birds of the Seychelles archipelago. *Ibis* (2)3: 335-360.

Nicoll, M. J. (1906) On the birds collected and observed during the voyage of the "Valhalla", R.Y.S., from November 1905 to May 1906. *Ibis* (8)6: 666-712.

Vesey-Fitzgerald, D. (1940) The birds of the Seychelles. I. The endemic birds. *Ibis* (14)4: 480-489.

Watson, J. (1979) Clutch sizes of Seychelles' endemic land birds. *Bull. Brit. Orn. Club* 99: 102-105.

Wilson, J. R. (1981) A résumé of the information on the ecology of the Seychelles White-eye (*Zosterops modesta*) and comments on its conservation. Unpublished.

MOUNT KARTHALA WHITE-EYE   RARE
Zosterops mouroniensis Milne Edwards and Oustalet, 1885

Order PASSERIFORMES   Family ZOSTEROPIDAE

Summary There is evidence for a slight contraction of range and decline in numbers in this small fruit- and insect-eating bird, now restricted to the single small area of *Philippia* heath at the top of Mount Karthala on Grand Comoro, Comoro Islands; its habitat deserves to be fully protected.

Distribution The Mount Karthala White-eye is restricted to Grand Comoro, in the Comoro Islands, where it is confined to the heath zone on Mount Karthala from 1,700 m to the summit above 2,600 m (Benson 1960); the total area involved is evidently very small, and may have contracted (see Population).

Population In 1958 the species was common, and was even found in evergreen forest at 1,700 m (Benson 1960); at the start of the 1980s it was considered to be "not uncommon but localised", and only to be found in the heath zone (M. Louette *in litt.* 1984).

Ecology It inhabits *Philippia* heath, which grows up to 5 m tall in its lower reaches from around 1,700 m, but less than half this height at the summit of Mount Karthala; there are few other plants in the heath zone, all very stunted (Benson 1960). Birds have been noted in the uppermost reaches of the evergreen forest adjacent to the heath zone, but not recently (see Population). Food of birds collected in September was mainly small purple berries, with some insects (including one caterpillar) (Benson 1960). Ten of 11 males collected in September were in or near breeding condition, and a nest with three eggs was found 4 m above ground and 1 m from the top of a *Philippia* bush (Benson 1960).

Threats The restriction of this species to the top of one mountain is not a cause for concern if its habitat remains unaltered, as seems very likely. Nevertheless, a hiking track now under construction to the crater rim of Mount Karthala will bring many more people to higher elevations and carry the risk of being upgraded as a road, which might then increase the chances of disturbance and destruction of habitat (M. Louette *in litt.* 1984). Mount Karthala is an active volcano and in 1958 large patches of heath near the summit had been burnt, probably as a result of volcanic activity (Benson 1960); the species is evidently at permanent risk from a serious eruption.

Conservation Measures Taken None is known.

Conservation Measures Proposed Protected area status, with a concomitant educational programme, for a representative section of the forest and heathland on Mount Karthala would enhance the prospects for survival of this species, the Grand Comoro Scops Owl *Otus pauliani*, the Grand Comoro

Flycatcher *Humblotia flavirostris* and the Grand Comoro Drongo *Dicrurus fuscipennis* (see relevant accounts).

Reference

Benson, C. W. (1960) The birds of the Comoro Islands: results of the British Ornithologists' Union Centenary Expedition 1958. *Ibis* 103b: 5-106.

MAURITIUS OLIVE WHITE-EYE   VULNERABLE
Zosterops chloronothus (Vieillot, 1817)

Order PASSERIFORMES   Family ZOSTEROPIDAE

Summary This small forest-dwelling nectar-feeding bird, endemic to Mauritius, has suffered until very recently from habitat clearance, and there are now probably only some 275 pairs of birds remaining. Provision of food-plants and some habitat creation are needed.

Distribution The Mauritius Olive White-eye is confined to upland areas of south-west Mauritius, Indian Ocean, and to two upland areas in the centre of the island, with records from elsewhere reflecting its restless, wandering behaviour, at least when not breeding (see Ecology). The centre of distribution is in the south-west in and around Plaine Champagne, Alexandra Falls, Mount Cocotte and Montagne Savanne, with fewer birds as far south as Bel Ombre and Combo (Gill 1971, Temple 1974a, Temple *et al.* 1974, Cheke in press). Although it was recorded in the 1940s from Le Pouce above Port Louis (J. Vinson *per* C. G. Jones *in litt.* 1984) and in the 1930s from the eastern uplands of Montagnes Bambous and Montagne Blanche, it is not known whether birds ever bred in these areas, and they do not now occur there (Cheke in press); however, in the centre of the island an apparently isolated population is present on Montagne Lagrave and birds are still occasionally recorded from Piton du Milieu as they were in the 1950s (Newton 1958, Cheke in press, C. G. Jones *in litt.* 1984), but the clearance of large tracts of dwarf forest since 1950 has resulted in considerable range contraction (Cheke in press), with records of birds in town gardens (Newton 1958, Niven 1965, Gill 1971, Temple *et al.* 1974) now rare or non-existent (Cheke in press).

Population In the last century this species was "not very common" (Clark 1859) and throughout this century it has generally been considered rare (Meinertzhagen 1912, Newton 1958, Gill 1971, Staub 1971) and, at worst, seriously threatened with extinction (Rountree 1951, Temple 1974a,b). In 1964 it was commonest near Mount Cocotte and on Plaine Champagne where up to 10 birds per day were encountered, and it was expected to prove commoner than realised on account of its feeding behaviour and general elusiveness (Gill 1971; see Ecology); in 1970 it was indeed found in larger numbers than expected and even thought to be recovering (Staub 1971). However, at least partly owing to the destruction of 800 ha of habitat, a marked decrease in the years prior to 1974 was noted, numbers being put at less than 1,000 birds (Temple 1974a,b). The likely population in 1974-1975 was around 350 pairs, but as probably many of these had recently been displaced by continuing habitat clearance the numbers at (what is nonetheless) the centre of distribution were probably above its long-term carrying capacity, so the present population is likely to be nearer 275 pairs, as observations in 1978 and subsequently have tended to show (Cheke in press).

Ecology The Mauritius Olive White-eye inhabits upland native forests including dwarf forest (Procter and Salm 1974, Temple *et al.* 1974, Cheke in press),

601

being found in canopy or near ground level (Fabian 1970), its most important requirements being a good supply of nectar-producing flowers (Temple 1974a) and sufficient rainfall, since it rarely occurs in forest outside the 4,000 mm isohyet except above the southern scarp at Bel Ombre and Combo (Cheke in press); however, it may be found "in all forms of vegetation", even gardens (Newton 1958, Temple 1974a), albeit at greatly reduced densities (see Cheke in press), and evidently for the most part not permanently; the grove of Japanese red cedar *Cryptomeria japonica* below Plaine Paul important for the Pink Pigeon *Nesoenas mayeri* (see relevant account) is a frequent locality (Jones 1980). Food is nectar and insects, the bird using its long thin bill either to probe or to pierce flowers, and gleaning insects mostly from foliage, more rarely from bark, sometimes fly-catching (Temple *et al.* 1974, Cheke in press); because plants in bloom are often widely separated, birds are constantly on the move and travel long distances, appearing suddenly, feeding briefly, then moving on (Gill 1971, Temple *et al.* 1974). Food-plants (not necessarily native) include *Eugenia* species, especially those with flowers on the trunk or branches (comprehensive list in Cheke in press). The breeding season begins from September to November (Carié 1904), although more recent research suggests it lasts from October to January or early February (Temple *et al.* 1974, Cheke in press). The nest is well concealed in a thick bush, often close to the ground (Temple *et al.* 1974). Clutch-size is two (Hartlaub 1877, Temple *et al.* 1974, Staub 1976, Cheke in press), rarely three (Carié 1904). Birds have large overlapping home ranges and defend only a small area around the nest or a particular plant in flower against conspecifics and Grey White-eyes *Zosterops borbonicus* (Cheke in press). They keep regularly to their home ranges only during the breeding season, wandering widely in search of flowers at other times (Cheke in press), when they may associate loosely with bird parties composed chiefly of Grey White-eyes (Gill 1971; also Niven 1965). Birds are commonly found in pairs, sometimes in family parties of four or five birds, never more than six (Carié 1904, Newton 1958); although sometimes remarkably tame (Meinertzhagen 1912, Fabian 1970), they are also secretive and can be easily overlooked (Newton 1958, Gill 1971, Temple *et al.* 1974), particularly as a result of their feeding behaviour (see above).

Threats A general account of the problems facing the endemic forest-dependent birds of Mauritius is given in Threats under Mauritius Kestrel *Falco punctatus*. Around 1950 loss of forest was identified as the major cause of this species's decline (Rountree 1951), but it was at that time that the critical phase of habitat destruction was just beginning: the clearance of scrubby forests at the Midlands and Mare aux Vacoas started around then (Cheke in press), culminating in the loss of those at Grand Bassin and Parc aux Cerfs (Procter and Salm 1974, Temple 1974a,b, Temple *et al.* 1974, Cheke in press); moreover, the (World Bank financed) clearance in 1971-1974 of half (c. 2,800 ha) of the upland *Sideroxylon-Helichrysum* dwarf forest at Les Mares on Plaine Champagne for plantation forestry seriously reduced this species's population (Jones 1980, Cheke in press). The most recent loss of habitat has been at Kanaka crater, where clear-felling occurred between 1974 and 1978 (Cheke 1978, in press), and in Crown Land Gouly above Bois Sec, where clear-felling continued up to 1980 (C. G. Jones *in litt* 1984).

The introduced Red-whiskered Bulbul *Pycnonotus jocosus* has been blamed for taking both eggs and adults (Carié 1916). Introduced crab-eating macaques *Macaca fascicularis*, mongooses *Herpestes edwardsi* and black rats *Rattus rattus* are also stated to destroy eggs and nestlings (Temple *et al.* 1974; also Cheke in press).

Conservation Measures Taken This species has long been protected by law (Meinertzhagen 1912) and in 1974 its remaining native forest habitat received considerable protection when the Macabé/Bel Ombre Nature Reserve was created through the linking of existing reserves at Petrin, Macabé and Bel Ombre by the addition of Les Mares and Plaine Champagne, forming a large block covering 3,594 ha (Owadally 1976; see map in Procter and Salm 1974).

Conservation Measures Proposed The creation of habitat by a careful admixture of evergreen trees, on a commercial basis (see Conservation Measures Proposed under Mauritius Cuckoo-shrike *Coracina typica*), might prove beneficial to this species (Cheke 1978). Since the closely related Réunion Olive White-eye *Zosterops olivaceus* feeds extensively on nectar of *Hypericum lanceolatum* (extinct on Mauritius) and on the introduced but apparently harmless *Fuchsia magellanica*, the establishment of these plants in depauperate marginal forest areas would seem likely to boost food resources for the Mauritius Olive White-eye (Cheke 1978; also Jones and Owadally 1982); the bottlebrush *Callistemon citrinus*, widely planted on Mauritius, is used by the bird and would no doubt also become staple if planted in suitable areas (Jones 1980). Modification of a general policy of roadside planting has been urged in favour of nectar-producing species (Temple 1974a). Work to safeguard this species will now proceed within the framework of the Mauritius Wildlife Research and Conservation Programme (see Conservation Measures Taken under Mauritius Kestrel).

Remarks The view that this bird is distinct at specific level from the Réunion Olive White-eye (Gill 1970) is accepted here. It possesses much the longest bill and tongue of all the white-eyes (Zosteropidae) (Cheke in press).

References

Carié, P. (1904) Observations sur quelques oiseaux de l'île Maurice. *Ornis* 12: 121-128.

Carié, P. (1916) L'acclimatation à l'île Maurice. C.- Oiseaux. *Bull. Soc. Natn. Acclim. Fr.* 63: 107-110, 152-159, 191-198, 245-250, 355-363, 401-404.

Cheke, A. S. (1978) Recommendations for the conservation of Mascarene vertebrates. Conservation memorandum no. 3 (arising out of the B.O.U. Mascarene Islands Expedition). Unpublished.

Cheke, A. S. (in press) The surviving native land-birds of Mauritius. In A. W. Diamond, ed. *Studies of Mascarene island birds*. Cambridge: Cambridge University Press.

Clark, G. (1859) A ramble round Mauritius with some excursions in the interior of that island; to which is added a familiar description of its fauna and some subjects of its fauna. Pp. I-CXXXII in *The Mauritius register: historical, official and commercial, corrected to the 30th June 1859*. Port Louis: L. Channell.

Fabian, D. T. (1970) The birds of Mauritius. *Bokmakierie* 22: 16-17, 21.

Gill, F. B. (1970) The taxonomy of the Mascarene Olive White-eye, *Zosterops olivacea* (L.). *Bull. Brit. Orn. Club* 90: 81-82.

Gill, F. B. (1971) Ecology and evolution of the sympatric Mascarene white-eyes, *Zosterops borbonica* and *Zosterops olivacea*. *Auk* 88: 35-60.

Hartlaub, G. (1877) *Die Vögel Madagascars und der benachbarten Inselgruppen.* Halle.

Jones, C. G. (1980) The conservation of the endemic birds and bats of Mauritius and Rodriguez (a progress report and proposal for further activities). Unpublished.

Jones, C. G. and Owadally, A. W. (1982) Conservation priorities for Mauritius and Rodrigues. Report submitted to ICBP, July. Unpublished.

Meinertzhagen, R. (1912) On the birds of Mauritius. *Ibis* (9)6: 82-108.

Newton, R. (1958) Ornithological notes on Mauritius and the Cargados Carajos Archipelago. *Proc. Roy. Soc. Arts Sci. Mauritius* 2(1): 39-71.

Niven, C. (1965) Birds of Mauritius. *Ostrich* 36: 84-86.

Owadally, A. W. (1976) *Annual report of the Forestry Service for the year 1974.* Port Louis, Mauritius: L. Carl Achille, Government Printer.

Procter, J. and Salm, R. (1974) Conservation in Mauritius 1974. IUCN/WWF consultancy report for Government of Mauritius. Unpublished.

Rountree, F. G. R. (1951) Some aspects of bird-life in Mauritius. *Proc. Roy. Soc. Arts Sci. Mauritius* 1(2): 83-96.

Staub, F. (1971) Actual situation of the Mauritius endemic birds. *ICBP Bull.* 11: 226-227.

Staub, F. (1976) *Birds of the Mascarenes and Saint Brandon.* Port Louis, Mauritius: Organisation Normale des Enterprises.

Temple, S. A. (1974a) Appendix 6. The native fauna of Mauritius: 1, the land birds. In J. Procter and R. Salm, Conservation in Mauritius 1974. IUCN/WWF consultancy report for Government of Mauritius. Unpublished.

Temple, S. A. (1974b) Wildlife in Mauritius today. *Oryx* 12: 584-590.

Temple, S. A., Staub, J. J. F. and Antoine, R. (1974) Some background information and recommendations on the preservation of the native flora and fauna of Mauritius. Unpublished report to the Government of Mauritius.

FERNANDO PO SPEIROPS   RARE
Speirops brunneus (Salvadori, 1903)

Order PASSERIFORMES   Family ZOSTEROPIDAE

Summary This rarely recorded white-eye is restricted to the very small area of open forest and bush on the higher parts of Pico de Santa Isabel on Fernando Po Island, Equatorial Guinea. There is no recent information on its status or on that of its habitat.

Distribution The Fernando Po Speirops is only known from the higher slopes of Pico de Santa Isabel, above 1,900 m, on Fernando Po (Bioko) Island, Equatorial Guinea. The type-specimen was collected at 2,400 m in 1894 (Salvadori 1903, Basilio 1963), not in 1903, as stated in Vincent (1966-1971). There were no further records until 1940 when three specimens were collected, two of these being at 2,000 m (Wolff-Metternich and Stresemann 1956), no altitude being given for the third (Stresemann 1948) (this third specimen was mistakenly stated to have been collected in 1948 in Vincent 1966-1971). Other birds were collected in 1947 and 1957 (Basilio 1963), not in 1955 as stated in Vincent (1966-1971). In 1966 15 birds were collected, 14 at 2,100 m and one at 2,700 m (Eisentraut 1968,1973). Also in late 1966 and early 1967 field observations were made of the species on Pico de Santa Isabel above 1,900 m (Wells 1968, D. R. Wells *in litt.* 1983). It is apparently absent from the southern mountains of Fernando Po (Wells 1968).

Population Numbers are not known. It is apparently quite common on the higher slopes of the mountain (M. Eisentraut *in litt.* 1983, D. R. Wells *in litt.* 1983) but the area which it inhabits is tiny (Wells 1968).

Ecology This species occurs in fairly open "lichen forest" above 1,900 m, not in the "moss forest" which occurs at lower altitudes (Wells 1968, D. R. Wells *in litt.* 1983). It prefers the more open areas, especially the edges of forest clearings (Eisentraut 1968,1973, Wells 1968), and is found in bush and tree savanna above the forest line (M. Eisentraut *in litt.* 1983). The birds occur in small flocks (D. R. Wells *in litt.* 1983) and two specimens were taken from a group of four birds (Wolff-Metternich and Stresemann 1956). They eat insects and berries; birds in breeding condition have been collected in October and December from which it was deduced that breeding takes place at the beginning of the dry season (Eisentraut 1973).

Threats None is known. Extensive forest clearance could be a threat to the species, and though it also occurs in the montane heathland this covers only a very small area indeed (D. R. Wells *in litt.* 1983).

Conservation Measures Taken None is known.

Conservation Measures Proposed A survey is needed to assess the status of this species and to determine whether conservation action is needed.

Remarks The Fernando Po Speirops is the only species of bird endemic to Fernando Po (Amadon 1953, Amadon and Basilio 1957). It forms a superspecies with the two other members of its genus, the Black-capped Speirops *Speirops lugubris* of Mount Cameroon and São Tomé and the Príncipe Speirops *S. leucophaeus* of Príncipe (Amadon 1953, Amadon and Basilio 1957, Eisentraut 1968,1973, Hall and Moreau 1970).

References

Amadon, D. (1953) Avian systematics and evolution in the Gulf of Guinea. The J. G. Correia Collection. *Bull. Amer. Mus. Nat. Hist.* 100: 393-452.

Amadon, D. and Basilio, A. (1957) Notes on the birds of Fernando Poo Island, Spanish Equatorial Africa. *Amer. Mus. Novit.* 1846.

Basilio, A. (1963) *Aves de la Isla de Fernando Poo*. Madrid: Editorial Coculsa.

Eisentraut, M. (1968) Beitrag zur Vogelfauna von Fernando Poo und Westkamerun. *Bonn. zool. Beitr.* 19: 49-68.

Eisentraut, M. (1973) Die Wirbeltierfauna von Fernando Poo und Westkamerun. *Bonn. zool. Monog.* 3.

Hall, B. P. and Moreau, R. E. (1970) *An atlas of speciation in African passerine birds*. London: Trustees of the British Museum (Natural History).

Salvadori, T. (1903) Caratteri di due nuove specie di uccelli di Fernando Po. *Boll. Mus. Torino* 18(442): 1.

Stresemann, E. (1948) A small contribution to the ornithology of Fernando Po. *Ibis* 90: 334-335.

Wells, D. R. (1968) Zonation of bird communities on Fernando Poo. *Bull. Nigerian Orn. Soc.* 5: 71-87.

Wolff-Metternich, G. F. and Stresemann, E. (1956) Biologische Notizen über Vögel von Fernando Po. *J. Orn.* 97: 274-290.

GOUGH BUNTING   RARE
Rowettia goughensis (Eagle Clarke, 1905)

Order PASSERIFORMES   Family EMBERIZIDAE
                                                      Subfamily EMBERIZINAE

Summary This omnivorous bird is endemic to Gough Island in the South Atlantic Ocean where it may only number some 200 pairs and is permanently at risk from introduction of mammalian predators, especially while a weather station on the island remains manned.

Distribution The Gough Bunting is restricted to Gough Island in the Tristan da Cunha group (a dependency of the British Crown Colony of St.Helena), South Atlantic Ocean; it has been recorded throughout the island up to 600 m (Wilkins 1923, Ripley 1954, Holdgate 1958, Wace and Holdgate 1976).

Population This species appears always to have been considered in good numbers (Verrill 1895, Wilkins 1923, Elliott 1953, Holdgate 1958, Elliott 1969) and one guess in the 1950s put the total population at about 2,000 birds (Holdgate 1957). However, birds were not particularly common, October/November 1974, when (on the basis of breeding density given under Ecology) the total population was estimated at only about 200 pairs (Richardson in press). Subsequently the only reports are that birds are "abundant" on the island (Voisin 1979) and were "not uncommon" in late 1980 around the meteorological station (Clancey 1981).

Ecology There are three vegetation-types on Gough occurring below 600 m, namely: tussock-grass (*Spartina* and *Poa*) on cliffs and penguin rookeries; fern-bush where thickets of the island-tree *Phylica arborea* grow amongst dwarf tree-ferns *Blechnum* to form a dense tangle of vegetation up to c. 300 m; and, above this, a zone of wet heath vegetation with low creeping plants, tufted grasses, sedges and moss up to c. 600 m (Wace and Holdgate 1976). The species's preference of vegetation-types is unknown, but observers have repeatedly noted birds close to or on the seashore where they forage almost to the tide-line amongst the boulders, stranded wood and seaweed (Eagle Clarke 1905, Elliott 1957, Holdgate 1958, Elliott 1969, Clancey 1981). Birds are reported to favour the edge of sea-cliffs (Clancey 1981) and to be most abundant along coasts and on "open upper ground" (Holdgate 1958), although another report noted birds somewhat less plentiful at higher levels (Wilkins 1923). The species is certainly not dependent on woodland and feeds almost invariably on the ground (Elliott 1953,1957). It is apparently omnivorous, taking a "multitude" of foods, invertebrates, fruits and seeds, meat off dead seabirds and broken seabird eggs, and visiting dustbins and even hopping into camp kitchens for scraps (Richardson in press; also Holdgate 1958, Elliott 1970). On the seashore small sandhoppers *Orchestia* have been noted as chief prey (Holdgate 1958) but kelp flies and other invertebrates are also taken in numbers (Wilkins 1923, Elliott 1969, Richardson in press). Inland, birds have been seen to take flies on rocks beside a stream (Wilkins 1923) and to hawk flies across the face of a waterfall (Holdgate 1958), also to take the flowers and seeds of

607

the tea-plant *Chenopodium tomentosum* and tussock-grass (Wilkins 1923), "grass seeds" (Holdgate 1958, Richardson in press), sedge fruit (Holdgate 1958), and crowberries *Empetrum* (Holdgate 1958), this last presumably being the small berry-bearing mountain plant on which birds were observed to feed "very largely" in September/October 1983 (R. W. Furness *in litt.* 1984). Nesting occurs in September/October (Voisin 1979, Clancey 1981, Williams and Imber 1982, Richardson in press). Of nine occupied nests, 1979, two were in open upland areas sunk in scrapes beneath overhanging tufts of *"Cyperus"* sedge, two were in lower gorges and placed 2-3 m above ground (one in a cleft in a bare rock-face, one on a ledge in a fern-covered rock-face), and five at lower altitudes were in clumps of fern *Elaphoglossum* (two), a tree-fern, the roots of a fallen island-tree, and tussock-grass (Williams and Imber 1982; see also Voisin 1979, Clancey 1981). Clutch-size is two (Voisin 1979, Williams and Imber 1982). Density of birds in the breeding season in two areas of the island (Long Beach and the south-east quadrant) was approximately four adults per km^2 (Richardson in press). Birds appear highly sedentary: those colour-ringed at the Glen (on the east side) rarely moved far away from this area, although young birds are harried away by territorial birds and therefore presumably wander more extensively (Holdgate 1958). Birds have always been considered very tame (Verrill 1895, Wilkins 1923, Elliott 1969), examining observer's shoes and turn-ups for invertebrates (Elliott 1969) and pecking at socks for seeds (Holdgate 1958), yet they are less approachable away from human habitation (Elliott 1969) and are even considered less approachable than *Nesospiza* buntings on Nightingale and Inaccessible Islands in the same island group (Richardson in press; see relevant accounts).

Threats Although it has been stated that this bird "could not be easily brought to extinction", implicitly because not dependent on woodland (Elliott 1953), there seems little doubt that the single and very real threat to the species is the risk of mammalian predators, especially rats *Rattus* and cats, becoming established on Gough, a threat that has substantially increased since the establishment of a permanently manned weather station on the island in 1955 (Holdgate 1957, Bourne 1981): a dead rat was found in a packing-case in 1967 (Elliott 1969) and another on the Gough supply ship in 1974 (Richardson in press), and rats were thought to have been seen alive and wild on the island in 1983 (R. W. Furness *in litt.* 1984). Even the one known introduced rodent, the house mouse *Mus musculus*, appears to eat the eggs of smaller birds on Gough (Bourne 1981) and so presumably may affect this species. The endemic Gough Moorhen *Gallinula comeri* (see relevant account) harries buntings (Richardson in press) and is even reported occasionally to prey on them (M. K. Swales *in litt.* 1984).

Conservation Measures Taken In 1976 Gough Island was declared a wildlife reserve and the unauthorised collection of birds or importation of exotic live animals was prohibited (see Wace and Holdgate 1976). At least one live specimen of the Gough Bunting has been brought back to Europe (Liang-Sheng 1957) but apparently no captive colony was established.

Conservation Measures Proposed Following the discovery of the dead rat in 1967 (see Threats) stronger measures were considered necessary at the Gough weather station's packing warehouse in Cape Town (Elliott 1969) and such vigilance must always be exercised while the station remains on the island. Indeed, whether the very recent record of rats on the island (see Threats) is confirmed or not, the interests of wildlife require that permission to man this weather station be rescinded at the earliest moment. There are no suitable (rat-free) islands in the South Atlantic to which birds could be introduced to establish a second, reserve population, but if rats are proven to be established on Gough emergency action may be necessary to develop a captive colony of birds.

Remarks This bird was originally considered to be two species because the plumage of both first- and second-year birds is rufous with black streaks, while older birds are olive-green with a black throat (see Eagle Clarke 1905, Lowe 1923). The species occupies the monotypic genus *Rowettia* (see Lowe 1923) although it is considered close to the South American genus *Melanodera* (Rand 1955) and has even been placed in it (Greenway 1967), while its morphological distinctiveness from *Nesospiza* has been questioned (Abbott 1978) despite a report of its behavioural dissimilarity (in Elliott 1957). It is host to a cestode believed endemic to Gough Island (Liang-Sheng 1957). A view of Gough as an island of major biological importance is given in Remarks under Gough Moorhen.

References

Abbott, I. (1978) The significance of morphological variation in the finch species on Gough, Inaccessible and Nightingale Islands, South Atlantic Ocean. *J. Zool., Lond.* 184: 119-125.

Bourne, W. R. P. (1981) Fur seals return to Gough Island. *Oryx* 16: 46-47.

Clancey, P. A. (1981) On birds from Gough Island, central South Atlantic. *Durban Mus. Novit.* 12(17): 187-200.

Eagle Clarke, W. (1905) Ornithological results of the Scottish National Antarctic Expedition. – I. On the birds of Gough Island, South Atlantic Ocean. *Ibis* (8)5: 247-268.

Elliott, C. C. H. (1969) Gough Island. *Bokmakierie* 21: 17-19.

Elliott, C. C. H. (1970) Additional notes on the sea-birds of Gough Island. *Ibis* 112: 112-114.

Elliott, H. F. I. (1953) The fauna of Tristan da Cunha. *Oryx* 2: 41-53.

Elliott, H. F. I. (1957) A contribution to the ornithology of the Tristan da Cunha group. *Ibis* 99: 545-586.

Greenway, J. C. (1967) *Extinct and vanishing birds of the world.* 2nd revised edition. New York: Dover Publications.

Holdgate, M. W. (1957) Gough Island – a possible sanctuary. *Oryx* 4: 168-175.

Holdgate, M. W. (1958) *Mountains in the sea.* London: Macmillan.

Liang-Sheng, Y. (1957) A new species of *Anomotaenia* (Cestoda) from the Gough Island Bunting, *Rowettia goughensis*. *Proc. Zool. Soc. Lond.* 128: 297-300.

Lowe, P. R. (1923) Notes on some land birds of the Tristan da Cunha group collected by the "Quest" Expedition. *Ibis* (11)5: 511-529.

Rand, A. L. (1955) The origin of the land birds of Tristan da Cunha. *Fieldiana Zool.* 37: 139-166.

Richardson, M. E. (in press) Aspects of the ornithology of the Tristan da Cunha group. *Cormorant.*

Ripley, S. D. (1954) Birds from Gough Island. *Postilla* 19.

Verrill, G. E. (1895) On some birds and eggs collected by Mr Geo. Comer at Gough Island, Kerguelen Island, and the Island of South Georgia. *Trans. Connecticut Acad. Arts Sci.* 9: 430-478.

Voisin, J.-F. (1979) The nest and eggs of the Gough Island Bunting. *Ostrich* 50: 122-124.

Wace, N. M. and Holdgate, M. W. (1976) *Man and nature in Tristan da Cunha.* Morges, Switzerland: IUCN (Monograph no. 6).

Wilkins, G. H. (1923) Report on the birds collected during the voyage of the "Quest" (Shackleton-Rowett Expedition) to the southern Atlantic. *Ibis* (11)5: 474-511.

Williams, A. J. and Imber, M. J. (1982 [published 1984]) Ornithological observations at Gough Island in 1979, 1980 and 1981. *S. Afr. J. Antarctic Res.* 12: 40-45.

TRISTAN BUNTING

Nesospiza acunhae Cabanis, 1873

Order PASSERIFORMES   Family EMBERIZIDAE
                                                          Subfamily EMBERIZINAE

Summary This bunting is restricted to but widespread on Inaccessible and Nightingale (also Middle and Stoltenhoff) Islands in the Tristan da Cunha group, and despite a population of at least several thousand it remains at risk from the introduction of rats, cats and alien plants, having long since become extinct on Tristan da Cunha itself.

Distribution The Tristan Bunting is confined to Nightingale and Inaccessible Islands (3 km² and 16 km² respectively) in the Tristan da Cunha group (a dependency of the British Crown Colony of St.Helena), South Atlantic Ocean; also to the tiny Middle and Stoltenhoff Islands immediately adjacent to Nightingale Island. The species occurs throughout these islands (Hagen 1952, Wace and Holdgate 1976, Richardson in press). It was formerly found on the main island of Tristan da Cunha, "over the whole island", but is now extinct there (Hagen 1952, Stresemann 1953; but see Conservation Measures Proposed).

Population Throughout the present century this species has been abundant on both Nightingale and Inaccessible Islands (Wilkins 1923, Broekhuysen and Macnae 1949, Hagen 1952, Elliott 1953, Wace and Holdgate 1976). In the early 1970s an estimated 500-1,000 pairs were present on Nightingale, 40-80 pairs on Middle, and 20-40 pairs on Stoltenhoff, while the population on Inaccessible was considered probably to consist of 500-1,000 pairs (Richardson in press). However, from general observations, 1982-1983, at least 5,000 birds (divided equally between the two morphs: see Ecology, Remarks) were estimated present on Inaccessible (M. W. Fraser *in litt.* 1984). On Tristan da Cunha the species was "plentiful" in 1817 (therefore presumably in thousands), uncommon by 1852, and extinct by 1873 (Hagen 1952, Wace and Holdgate 1976, Bourne and David 1981).

Ecology The preferred habitat of this bird appears to be tussock-grass *Spartina arundinacea* (Wilkins 1923, Hagen 1952). This habitat dominates Nightingale, Middle and Stoltenhoff Islands (Wace and Holdgate 1976). On Inaccessible, where coastal tussock-grass is replaced on the peaty plateau by fernbush *Blechnum* and island-tree *Phylica arborea* thickets (Wace and Holdgate 1976), the species occurs throughout but birds in these two main vegetation-types appear morphologically distinct, with "bright" birds on the plateau, where they are common, and "dull" ones in the tussock-grass of coastal strips, where they are abundant, with up to 10 pairs per ha (M. W. Fraser *in litt.* 1984; see Remarks). Birds on Nightingale have been considered mainly insect-eaters, those on Inaccessible mainly seed-eaters (Elliott 1957). On Inaccessible, "bright" birds of the plateau fed more extensively in *Phylica* than "dull" ones, though this was a function of availability of resources; in *Phylica*, birds fed slowly and methodically, in the manner of Grosbeak Buntings *Nesospiza wilkinsi* (see relevant account)

611

(M. W. Fraser *in litt.* 1984). "Dull" birds fed most commonly on flowers and seed-heads of *Spartina* and its associated insects, but also foraged on open ground amongst short vegetation such as *Empetrum* and *Blechnum*, on *Rumex* seeds scattered on the boulder beach, and amongst rocks exposed at low tide; food brought to young included grubs and caterpillars but was presumed to be mostly regurgitated *Spartina* seeds (M. W. Fraser *in litt.* 1984). Birds have been reported (without consideration to island) to feed on flies, beetles and other small invertebrates, tussock- and other grass seeds, and seeds of berries (*Nertera, Empetrum*), birds in *Phylica* on Nightingale mostly foraging in lower vegetation or on the ground, examining lichen on trunks probably for insects (Wilkins 1923, Hagen 1952). Stomach contents of birds from Middle and Stoltenhoff Islands included beetles, moth larvae, other insect remains, and tussock-grass seeds (Richardson in press). The breeding season has been found to extend from November to January (Hagen 1952, Elliott 1957) or early February (Richardson in press), but most recently, in 1982-1983, displaying and nest-building was observed in mid-October, yet by mid-February, though fledged young were much in evidence, birds still had nests with eggs (M. W. Fraser *in litt.* 1984). Nests are well concealed either on the ground amongst *Spartina* stems or in *Spartina/Blechnum* mix, or up to 1 m above the ground in sloping or horizontal bent-over tussock bundles, with clutch-size one or two (M. W. Fraser *in litt.* 1984; also Elliott 1957). The incubation period of one egg was 18 days; the nestling period of one chick (not from the egg above) was 19 days (M. W. Fraser *in litt.* 1984). Some nests are abandoned after especially cold, wet weather; eggs and young are much eaten by Tristan Thrushes *Nesocichla eremita* (see Appendix C) and adults fall prey to Tristan Great Skuas *Catharacta skua hamiltoni*, birds invariably giving the alarm at the presence of these seabirds (M. W. Fraser *in litt.* 1984). Birds live in pairs or family parties without flocking (Hagen 1952) and are very tame (Wilkins 1923).

Threats The extinction of this species on Tristan da Cunha within 56 years or less of its having been common and widespread there is clear evidence of its vulnerability to altered conditions: the causes of extinction are not clear, although the almost complete extermination of tussock-grass – extensive burning of which took place in 1824 (Abbott 1978) – is perhaps chiefly responsible (Hagen 1952). Mammalian predators may also have played a major part (Elliott 1957). The main threat to the species now is certainly the risk of mammalian predators (rats and cats) becoming established on one or both islands: see Threats under Inaccessible Rail *Atlantisia rogersi* for further documentation of this threat, and for information on risks from other mammals, fire, and the invasive exotic New Zealand flax *Phormium tenax*.

Conservation Measures Taken Much has been done since 1950 to establish principles for the management of Inaccessible and its wildlife and to foster understanding of these principles by the Tristan islanders, resulting in a new conservation ordinance in 1976 (see Elliott 1953, Wace and Holdgate 1976).

Conservation Measures Proposed Protected area status for Inaccessible Island has at least twice been urged (Broekhuysen 1957, Flint 1967) and, although the articles of the 1976 ordinance provide important protection for the island (see Wace and Holdgate 1976), more formal and concrete recognition of its importance to wildlife and science is still desirable (a view fully endorsed by the Denstone Expedition to Inaccessible: M. K. Swales *in litt.* 1984). A search of Tristan da Cunha itself is advocated, since there is a very remote possibility that the species survives there (M. W. Fraser *in litt.* 1984).

Remarks Birds on Inaccessible have recently been reported to occur in three plumage types, two of which are separated by distribution and vegetation-type – bright-coloured birds (both sexes, producing bright-coloured young) living exclusively (no overlap) in *Blechnum* ferns and *Phylica* scrub on the summit plateau, and dull-coloured ones only in the uniform tussock-grass and scattered *Phylica* of the lower slopes; a small sample yielded no biometric differences, but the song and calls of the "bright" birds appeared harsher than those of the "dull" ones (Fraser 1983, M. W. Fraser *in litt.* 1984; also "Denstone Expedition to Inaccessible Island", *Denstonian* Supplement, Autumn 1983: 48; *Bull. Brit. Orn. Club* 104 [1984]: 3). In addition, a bird seen briefly and only once on the plateau at North Point combined the characters of the Grosbeak Bunting (colour, bill shape) and the Tristan Bunting (overall size) (M. W. Fraser *in litt.* 1984). Whether or not these findings result in some taxonomic revision of the Inaccessible birds, they constitute a remarkable biological discovery concerning variation within a population of so small a total range. The taxonomy of this species is already complicated by the fact that the only known specimen from Tristan da Cunha is also the type of the species, so that while birds on Nightingale have been distinguished from those on Inaccessible under the name *questi*, those on Inaccessible have had to remain as nominate *acunhae* for lack of comparative material (see Hagen 1952); birds on Middle and Stoltenhoff Islands appear inseparable in both morphology and behaviour from those on Nightingale (Richardson in press). The only other member of the genus, the Grosbeak Bunting, is similarly confined to Nightingale and Inaccessible (see Remarks in the relevant account for further evidence of the ornithological importance of these two islands).

References

Abbott, I. (1978) The significance of morphological variation in the finch species on Gough, Inaccessible and Nightingale Islands, South Atlantic Ocean. *J. Zool., Lond.* 184: 119-125.

Bourne, W. R. P. and David, A. C. F. (1981) Nineteenth century bird records from Tristan da Cunha. *Bull. Brit. Orn. Club* 101: 247-256.

Broekhuysen, G. J. (1957) Note. *Oryx* 4: 175-176.

Broekhuysen, G. J. and Macnae, W. (1949) Observations on the birds of Tristan da Cunha Islands and Gough Island in February and early March, 1948. *Ardea* 37: 97-113.

Elliott, H. F. I. (1953) The fauna of Tristan da Cunha. *Oryx* 2: 41-53.

Elliott, H. F. I. (1957) A contribution to the ornithology of the Tristan da Cunha group. *Ibis* 99: 545-586.

Flint, J. H. (1967) Conservation problems on Tristan da Cunha. *Oryx* 9: 28-32.

Fraser, M. W. (1983) The Denstone Expedition to Inaccessible Island. *Cormorant* 11: 69-73.

Hagen, Y. (1952) *Birds of Tristan da Cunha*. Results of the Norwegian Scientific Expedition to Tristan da Cunha 1937-1938, no. 20. Oslo: Norske Videnskaps-Akademi.

Richardson, M. E. (in press) Aspects of the ornithology of the Tristan da Cunha group. *Cormorant*.

Stresemann, E. (1953) Birds collected by Capt. Dugald Carmichael on Tristan da Cunha 1816-1817. *Ibis* 95: 146-147.

Wace, N. M. and Holdgate, M. W. (1976) *Man and nature in Tristan da Cunha*. Morges, Switzerland: IUCN (Monograph no. 6).

Wilkins, G. H. (1923) Report on the birds collected during the voyage of the "Quest" (Shackleton-Rowett Expedition) to the southern Atlantic. *Ibis* (11)5: 474-511.

GROSBEAK BUNTING   RARE
Nesospiza wilkinsi Lowe, 1923

Order PASSERIFORMES   Family EMBERIZIDAE
                                              Subfamily EMBERIZINAE

Summary This large seed-eating bunting is restricted to areas of woodland on Inaccessible and Nightingale Islands in the Tristan da Cunha group, with a total population in the low hundreds; it is at permanent risk from the introduction of rats, cats and alien plants, and from loss of its woodland habitat.

Distribution The Grosbeak Bunting is confined to woodland on Nightingale and Inaccessible Islands (3 km^2 and 16 km^2 respectively) in the Tristan da Cunha group (a dependency of the British Crown Colony of St.Helena), South Atlantic Ocean: most woodland on Nightingale is in the central parts of the island, while on Inaccessible it is largely concentrated in the north-east and south-east sides on the lower upland slopes, but with several isolated patches, e.g. at Blenden Hall (M. K. Swales *in litt.* 1984; see also Broekhuysen and Macnae 1949, Elliott 1953,1957, Wace and Holdgate 1976).

Population A census of the nominate race *wilkinsi* on Nightingale, April 1950, revealed some 30 pairs with 30 young of the year (Elliott 1957), though possibly up to 40 pairs were present (Elliott 1953); the race *dunnei* on Inaccessible was then considered sparse (Elliott 1953) and probably not more numerous than nominate *wilkinsi*, despite Inaccessible's greater size (Elliott 1957). Subsequently, the same observer suggested 70-120 *wilkinsi* and 40-90 *dunnei* (Vincent 1966-1971, also King 1978-1979), i.e. a world total of 110-210 birds: the woodlands holding the species had apparently never been more than twice as extensive as they were around 1950, so the two races could never have had more than 200-300 birds apiece (Elliott 1957). There were still around 30 pairs on Nightingale in 1974, when *Phylica* woodland covered approximately 20 ha (Richardson in press). However, a recent re-assessment (in 1982-1983) gives a more promising account of the situation on Inaccessible (*contra* the report in *Bull. Brit. Orn. Club* 104 [1984]: 3): a minimum of one pair per 2 ha of *Phylica* woodland was found at Blenden Hall and, assuming this had no characteristics not found in the rest of the island's *Phylica* cover, which extends in total over c. 4.5 km^2, a population in the order of 200 pairs is to be anticipated (M. W. Fraser *in litt.* 1984). This may at least in part be due to the increase in extent of habitat in the past 35 years (see Conservation Measures Taken). Populations on both islands probably vary with season, suffering most in winter when competition with other land-birds for certain food-items (e.g. *Empetrum* seeds) may become critical (M. K. Swales *in litt.* 1984). Populations may also fluctuate over larger periods of time owing to natural and man-induced damage to *Phylica* woodland (H. F. I. Elliott *in litt.* 1984; see Threats).

Ecology This is a woodland species, specialising on the seeds of the island-tree *Phylica arborea* which forms groves on both Nightingale and Inaccessible (Elliott 1953,1957). Birds keep largely to these groves, climbing among branches like a crossbill *Loxia* (Fringillidae), methodically testing the *Phylica* berries in their bills, and only breaking off, husking and eating the blackest (presumably ripest) ones (Elliott 1957, M. W. Fraser *in litt.* 1984; also Wilkins 1923, Hagen 1952). Although birds are reported as only wandering rarely to tussock-grass *Spartina* and cranberry *Empetrum* areas (Elliott 1957), on Inaccessible in 1958-1959 birds were collected in tussock (Voous 1962) and in 1982-1983 up to six birds were seen foraging in tussock, one habitually, another being witnessed slowly and deliberately picking insects off the undersides of *Rumex* leaves and burrowing deep into the tussock (M. W. Fraser *in litt.* 1984). Moreover, on Nightingale food has been found to comprise *Phylica* and *Nertera* seeds, the latter indicating that birds must forage in low vegetation (Hagen 1952, Richardson in press); and on Inaccessible food has also been noted to consist of *Empetrum* and perhaps *Spartina* seeds, with fragments of insects and caterpillars (Hagen 1952; also Elliott 1957), while young birds were apparently fed chiefly on *Empetrum* seeds (Elliott 1957). From specimens collected in February 1938 the breeding season was judged probably to be in the austral spring (Hagen 1952), but subsequent observations (on Nightingale) indicated a later period, December to February, with a record of a fledged young being fed by (apparently three) different females as late as 4 April (Elliott 1953,1957). Nests were in clumps of vegetation near ground-level, clutch-size being two (Elliott 1957). On Inaccessible, 1982-1983, males were holding territories from the start of November, two recently fledged young being seen in January; as males were still singing in February the species may produce second broods (M. W. Fraser *in litt.* 1984, M. K. Swales *in litt.* 1984). In the breeding season (at least), subadult birds possibly form a mobile component of the population: of 10 birds marked at Blenden Hall, only one was seen again (M. W. Fraser *in litt.* 1984; also "Denstone Expedition to Inaccessible Island", *Denstonian* Supplement, Autumn 1983: 48).

Threats The two main threats to this species are the risk of mammalian predators (rats *Rattus* and cats) becoming established on one or both of the islands, and of the disappearance of its woodland habitat. Mammalian predators could easily exploit the species when nesting; see Threats under Inaccessible Rail *Atlantisia rogersi* for further documentation of this threat, and for information on risks from other mammals, fire, and the invasive exotic New Zealand flax *Phormium tenax*. Although *Phylica* regenerates rapidly, woodland on both islands is liable to extensive storm damage, temporarily reducing food-supply: a considerable acreage on Nightingale was lost around 1950 in this way (Elliott 1953,1957), while in 1974 about a hectare of the estimated 20 ha of *Phylica* on Nightingale was unwittingly destroyed during operations to control New Zealand flax (Richardson in press).

Conservation Measures Taken Much has been done since 1950 to establish principles for the management of Inaccessible and its wildlife and to foster understanding of these principles by the Trisan islanders, resulting in a new conservation ordinance in 1976 (see Elliott 1953, Wace and Holdgate 1976). The removal of domestic stock from Inaccessible in the 1950s (see Wace and Holdgate 1976), partly dictated by conservation considerations (King 1978-1979), is presumably responsible for the present rapid extension of *Phylica* woodland on the plateau (and thus for the apparent increase in number of birds: see Population), although a succession of mild winters (*Phylica* is not frost-hardy) may have been of equal importance (M. K. Swales *in litt.* 1983).

Conservation Measures Proposed Protected area status for Inaccessible Island has at least twice been urged (Broekhuysen 1957, Flint 1967) and, although the articles of the 1976 ordinance provide important protection for the island (see Wace and Holdgate 1976), more formal and concrete recognition of its importance to wildlife and science is still desirable (a view fully endorsed by the Denstone Expedition to Inaccessible: M. K. Swales *in litt.* 1984). Scientific collection of this species requires the strictest control (Wace and Holdgate 1976).

Remarks This strikingly large-billed bird, though claimed as a fringillid (Roberts and Kirby 1948), has been determined as a *Nesospiza* and hence more likely an emberizid (Rand 1955; also Swales 1971). The only other member of the genus, the Tristan Bunting *N. acunhae*, is similarly confined to Nightingale and Inaccessible (see relevant account). "These birds are of singular interest because they seem to present a case of evolutionary divergence paralleling in miniature that of the Galápagos finches studied by Darwin" (Wace and Holdgate 1976). The Tristan Thrush *Nesocichla eremita* is also on both islands and on Tristan da Cunha itself (see Appendix F). Inaccessible is also important as the only home of the Inaccessible Rail (see relevant account) and for seabird colonies of exceptional importance (Broekhuysen and Macnae 1949, Hagen 1952, Elliott 1953,1957, Flint 1967, Wace and Holdgate 1976). All these factors reinforce the case for protected area status for Inaccessible.

References

Broekhuysen, G. J. (1957) Note. *Oryx* 4: 175-176.

Broekhuysen, G. J. and Macnae, W. (1949) Observations on the birds of Tristan da Cunha Islands and Gough Island in February and early March, 1948. *Ardea* 37: 97-113.

Elliott, H. F. I. (1953) The fauna of Tristan da Cunha. *Oryx* 2: 41-53.

Elliott, H. F. I. (1957) A contribution to the ornithology of the Tristan da Cunha group. *Ibis* 99: 545-586.

Flint, J. H. (1967) Conservation problems on Tristan da Cunha. *Oryx* 9: 28-32.

Hagen, Y. (1952) *Birds of Tristan da Cunha*. Results of the Norwegian Scientific Expedition to Tristan da Cunha 1937-1938, no. 20. Oslo: Norske Videnskaps-Akademi.

King, W. B. (1978-1979) *Red data book, 2: Aves*. 2nd edition. Morges, Switzerland: IUCN.

Rand, A. L. (1955) The origin of the land birds of Tristan da Cunha. *Fieldiana Zool.* 37: 139-166.

Richardson, M. E. (in press) Aspects of the ornithology of the Tristan da Cunha group. *Cormorant*.

Roberts, A. and Kirby, J. (1948) On a collection of birds and eggs from Tristan d'Acunha Islands, made by John Kirby. *Ann. Transvaal Mus.* 21: 55-62.

Swales, M. K. (1971) A preliminary study on the application of the internal structure of feather barbs to avian taxonomy. Proc. III Pan-Afr. orn. Congr. *Ostrich* suppl. 8: 55-66.

Vincent, J. (1966-1971) *Red data book, 2: Aves*. Morges, Switzerland: IUCN.

Voous, K. H. (1962) Notes on a collection of birds from Tristan da Cunha and Gough Island. *Beaufortia* 9 (no. 99): 105-114.

Wace, N. M. and Holdgate, M. W. (1976) *Man and nature in Tristan da Cunha*. Morges, Switzerland: IUCN (Monograph no. 6).

Wilkins, G. H. (1923) Report on the birds collected during the voyage of the "Quest" (Shackleton-Rowett Expedition) to the southern Atlantic. *Ibis* (11)5: 474-511.

BLUE CHAFFINCH   RARE
Fringilla teydea Webb, Berthelot and Moquin-Tandon, 1842

Order PASSERIFORMES   Family FRINGILLIDAE
                                                    Subfamily FRINGILLINAE

Summary This celebrated Canary Island endemic species is confined to pine forests on Tenerife and Gran Canaria, its range and numbers in the latter island being relatively small and decreasing. Statements concerning its safety have been remarkably conflicting, and it was at one period heavily over-collected, so that its inclusion here is in part a matter of precaution and clarification.

Distribution The Blue Chaffinch is confined to the pine forest regions of Tenerife (nominate *teydea*) and Gran Canaria (race *polatzeki*), Canary Islands (Spain). On Tenerife, it has been reported from "all the pine forests" (Meade-Waldo 1983; also von Thanner 1910). The distribution of these forests was reported to have remained unchanged in the hundred years to 1947 (Lack and Southern 1949) and apparently still is so (see sketch-map in Pérez Padrón 1981), although another account refers to and maps the major fragmentation of the pine belt that existed in 1949, when replanting was planned (see Martín *et al.* in press). At any rate, published records from specified localities suggest variation in the utilisation of areas of forest by the species, and are given here for reference and according to general position (north, north-east, or south). In the north, records (west to east) are from above Icod de los Viños (Koenig 1890), La Guancha (Godman 1872, Koenig 1890), Icod el Alto (Koenig 1890), and near El Portillo (van den Berg and Bosman 1979, H.-H. Bergmann *in litt.* 1984); Icod de los Viños must be near the species's western limits as pine is replaced by laurel further west (M. A. S. Beaman *in litt.* 1984). In the north-east, records on the north side of the main ridge are from above Agua Mansa (Aguamansa) (Lack and Southern 1949) and Santa Ursula (breeding proved) (Koenig 1890, Bannerman 1963), on the ridge itself in a small area above (to south of) La Esperanza (S. J. Broyd *per* J. S. M. Albrecht *in litt.* 1984), and on the south side from above Arafo (probably) (Hemmingsen 1958) and Guimar (Bannerman 1963); fieldwork in the 1970s showed the species to be widespread throughout the main ridge of Tenerife from La Esperanza south-west to the Mirador Ortuno (east of and above La Orotava), birds petering out on the upper part of the ridge between the Mirador Ortuno and El Portillo (M. A. S. Beaman *in litt.* 1984). In the south, the extensive pine forests around and above Vilaflor (Chasna), the type-locality, are recognised as a major locality for the species (e.g. Koenig 1890, von Thanner 1903, Polatzek 1908-1909), have produced most published records (Webb *et al.* 1842, Godman 1872, von Thanner 1903, Lack and Southern 1949, Volsøe 1951, Hemmingsen 1958), and continue to hold a reasonably dense population (M. A. S. Beaman *in litt.* 1984, H.-H. Bergmann *in litt.* 1984, H. Löhrl *in litt.* 1984); however, the only other published localities in the south are Boca de Tauce, i.e. north-west of Vilaflor (Volsøe 1951), and the Casa Forestal on Pico de Teide, i.e. north-east of Vilaflor (Hüe and Etchécopar 1958), although there are specimens in NHMW from Granadilla, east of Vilaflor and somewhat below the pine belt, May 1914, and from Adeje, west of Vilaflor and

619

well below the pine belt, February 1904 (H. Schifter *in litt.* 1984). On this evidence, there are large tracts of pines both west and east of Vilaflor from which there are no certain records, although two localities, Estancia de los Alemanos (Bolle 1854-1855) and La Sorriba (from which the species was only known by repute) (Gurney 1927), have not been traced; fieldwork in the 1970s has shown that indeed birds are generally not to be found in this southern part of the island outside the Vilaflor/Boca de Tauce region, and searches north and west of Guia de Isora (on the western slopes of Pico de Teide) in what is poor quality pine forest drew blanks (M. A. S. Beaman *in litt.* 1984). Many sites – e.g. "Icod", La Guancha, Agua Mansa, La Esperanza, Vilaflor – can be searched without success (Reid 1887, von Thanner 1903, Lack and Southern 1949, Volsøe 1951, Mountfort 1960, Witt 1971), the birds being easily overlooked (H.-H. Bergmann *in litt.* 1984) or possibly showing seasonal displacements. Although the species was first encountered on Las Cañadas plateau and consequently believed to be endemic to Pico de Teide above the tree-line (hence its scientific name) (Webb *et al.* 1842), its occurrence on the open parts of the mountain is evidently only occasional (see Ecology). On Gran Canaria, it is known chiefly from the extensive Pinar de Pajonales (Pajonales pine forest) above Mogan in the south-west, and was long considered exclusive to this area (Polatzek 1908-1909, von Thanner 1910, Bannerman 1912, Volsøe 1951), but in 1957 it was found nesting in the relatively young Pinar de Tamadaba (Tamadaba pine forest) in the north-west (Hemmingsen 1958), while there is an anomalous but reliable record, dating from 1910, of two birds at Teror (well away from pine forest) in the north of the island (Bannerman 1963). The other major pine forest other than Pajonales and Tamadaba is around San Bartolomé de Tirajana (Hemmingsen 1958) where the species has been looked for without success (Bannerman 1912). The Pinar de Pajonales is evidently now somewhat fragmented – e.g. now mapped as Pinar de Inagua and Pinar de Ojeda (Firestone Hispania 1972) – and the distribution of this species within it appears always to have been variable (von Thanner 1910, Bannerman 1912). Its reported occurrence in the pine forests on La Palma (Koenig 1890) has never been substantiated, although habitat there is clearly still extensive (see sketch-map in Pérez Padrón 1981). A vagrant, race undetermined, was observed on 18 October 1967 in north-west Lanzarote (Trotter 1970).

Population From a complete reading of available sources, it appears that by moving about and/or being patchily distributed or concentrated within its pine forest habitat this species has given differing impressions of its abundance to different observers. The following chronological compilation, also reflecting observers' fears apropos habitat destruction and hunting, indicates the variation in published assessments of its status: on Tenerife, not very common (Godman 1872), not even heard (Reid 1887), reportedly rare (Hartwig 1886), days considered numbered (Meade-Waldo 1889a; also Koenig 1890), not rare in a few places but surprisingly not commoner (Meade-Waldo 1889b), holding its own and in one place increasing (Meade-Waldo 1893), near rapid extinction (Cabrera y Diaz 1893), now rather rare (Hartert 1901), not so rare as generally believed (Polatzek 1908-1909), destined for extinction unless steps taken (Gurney 1927), not uncommon and not yet in danger of extinction (Lack and Southern 1949), still rather common above Vilaflor (Volsøe 1951), on the way to recovery and relatively common (Etchécopar and Hüe 1957), much less numerous than previous reports suggest (Mountfort 1960), on the brink of extinction (Cuyas Robinson 1971, Bacallado 1976); on Gran Canaria, common only in one small area and therefore altogether very rare (von Thanner 1910), where common in 1911 none found in 1912 (von Thanner 1912), probably not so near extinction as presumed (Volsøe 1951), on the brink of extinction (Cuyas Robinson 1971, Bacallado 1976). Recent studies have, indeed, shown that Blue Chaffinch density within pine forest varies with understorey composition (see Ecology) and that forest and understorey conditions have varied over the past century (pine forest once girdled the entire main peak of Tenerife but became badly fragmented, causing a serious decline in the birds; substantial replanting has led to a slow but steady recovery in their numbers on the island) (Martín *et al.* in press); hence some of the judgements quoted above may not have been so wildly inaccurate as they perhaps appear. In a 125-minute line transect through pine forest, 23 March 1947, ten birds were counted, the species thus figuring as the third commonest bird in this habitat (Lack and Southern 1949). In the 1970s birds were fairly common (locally common) in all areas with large pines along the section of the Tenerife main ridge from La Esperanza to around the Mirador Ortuno, and certainly commoner than in the Vilaflor area (M. A. S. Beaman *in litt.* 1984; also Martín 1979). On Gran Canaria in spring 1978 only one pair could be found in the Pinar de Tamadaba, and song was heard in Pinar de Pajonales: the race *polatzeki* is thus considered in clear decline and in a precarious condition (Martín *et al.* in press), although the species is still (1984) present but local in both tracts of forest (G. Diaz *per* K. W. Emmerson *in litt.* 1984).

Ecology The Blue Chaffinch is almost exclusive to stands of the endemic Canarian pine *Pinus canariensis*, which on Tenerife range from c. 1,200 to 2,000 m (Polatzek 1908-1909, Volsøe 1951, Pérez Padrón 1981) and on Gran Canaria from c. 700 to 1,200 m (Polatzek 1908-1909, Bannerman 1912), birds only occasionally leaving this habitat to feed in adjacent areas above (up to 2,200 m) and below the pine zone and, rarely (e.g. in snowy or foggy weather), coming into gardens and orchards within or near the pine zone (Koenig 1890, von Thanner 1903, Polatzek 1908-1909, Hemmingsen 1958, Volsøe 1951, Pérez Padrón 1981). Within pine forest on Tenerife birds are also found in tree-heath *Erica arborea* and laurels (Meade-Waldo 1889a); they also now occur in areas where the introduced pine *P. radiata* borders or mingles with Canarian pine, but is virtually absent from pure plantations of *P. radiata* (A. Martín and K. W. Emmerson *in litt.* 1984). On Gran Canaria, the only site where the abundance of birds matched that on Tenerife was near a spring where the strongest, finest pines grew and had a rich undergrowth, birds using the latter for both cover and food (von Thanner 1910), but, although loss of undergrowth is evidently considered deleterious to the species (see Threats), on Tenerife a healthy population was found in the south between 1,600 and 1,800 m in sparse forest with neither undergrowth nor regrowth and bearing no resemblance to its original condition (Polatzek 1908-1909). Nevertheless, recent studies show that four types of undergrowth exist in natural pine forest on the northern side of the island, (a) with faya *Myrica faya* and tree-heath, (b) with tree-heath, (c) with escobon *Chamaecytisus proliferus* and (d) with codeso *Adenocarpus viscosus* and retama *Spartocytisus supranubius*, while in the southern pine forests the undergrowth (if any) consists largely of escobon; the Blue Chaffinch shows a great preference for pine with understorey of escobon, since escobon sustains caterpillars much exploited for feeding the young (Martín *et al.* in press). Territories of birds in pine with escobon understorey were 3 ha in extent (Martín *et al.* in press). The presence of mature pines is evidently important for the species, since they are noted as major sources of insect food (Polatzek 1908-1909) and must produce greater crops of pine cones, birds generally being found on the ground in the early morning and late afternoon where good quantities of ripe cones have fallen (Koenig 1890); birds are also found wherever the Great Spotted Woodpecker *Dendrocopus major* (von Thanner 1903, Polatzek 1908-1909, Bannerman 1963) and to a lesser degree the Blue Tit *Parus caeruleus* occur (Polatzek 1908-1909; but see von Thanner 1910), presumably the maturity of the trees again being the common factor. Although patches of such trees may be traditional sites for the species, birds evidently move about considerably within the forest (Bannerman 1912), in winter (young birds in particular) travelling about in small parties of up to eight, occasionally associating with the Chaffinch *Fringilla coelebs* (Meade-Waldo 1889a, Koenig 1890, Lack and Southern 1949), in high summer flying to drink at the few accessible remaining sources of water (Koenig 1890, Polatzek 1908-1909). The habits of the two races are considered identical (Polatzek 1908-1909, von Thanner 1910); in the best locality on Gran Canaria, birds have been noted to live quietly, perching for long periods without moving when not feeding or flying to drink (von Thanner 1910). On Tenerife they have been found to be extremely tame, even coming into a hide to feed on birdseed or butterflies released from the fingers of the observer (Meade-Waldo 1889a,b). Food is chiefly pine seeds (which the bill is adapted to crush: Volsøe 1951) and insects, the former taken from open cones on trees and ground, the latter hawked in the air and hunted in bark and on the ground (Meade-Waldo 1889b); pine needles are also sometimes taken (Polatzek 1908-1909), and the seeds of "forget-me-not" (presumably *Myosotis latifolia*) (Meade-Waldo 1889b), chick-weed *Stellaria media* (von Thanner 1910), bean-trefoil *Adenocarpus viscosus* (Koenig 1890, Pérez Padrón 1981), brambles *Rubus* (Pérez Padrón 1981), possibly the fruit of faya (since birds have been seen on the ground beneath faya understorey) (Martín *et al.* in press) and, outside the pines, reportedly retama (Godman 1872, Koenig 1890); insects include adult *Dasichyra fortunata* (Lyman-triidae) (Pérez Padrón 1981), Lepidoptera in general and heterocerid beetles (Cabrera y Diaz 1893), larvae of wood-boring beetles (Pérez Padrón 1983), and a tenebrionid beetle has been seen taken (Koenig 1890). A collector who considered it easier to shoot his specimens on the ground found their stomachs almost exclusively full of pine seeds (Koenig 1890), whereas another considered it easier to shoot birds in trees as they were then more active, in the pursuit of insects (Polatzek 1908-1909), and it may generally be that most seeds are foraged from the ground and most insects taken in trees. Young birds are fed on both (von Thanner 1903), though a recent study indicates that food brought to young is chiefly invertebrates and their larvae, including tenebrionid beetles, the weevil *Brachy-deres sculpturatus*, bush-crickets, the ant-lion *Formicaleo catta* and, amongst the Lepidoptera (apart from *Dasichyra fortunata*), *Macroglossum stellatarum* (Sphing-idae), *Noctua pronuba*, *N. noacki*, *Cucullia canariensis* and *Brionycta pineti opulenta* (Noctuidae) (Martín *et al.* in press). Although males may sing, show gonadal development and pair with females early (Meade-Waldo 1889b, Koenig 1890, Lack and Southern 1949), breeding occurs very late, the earliest of 18 nests in 1889 to contain a completed clutch being around 24-25 June (Meade-Waldo 1889b), while in 1902-1903 eight completed clutches were taken between 13 June and 25 August, the later nests attributable to first-year (still immature-plumaged) birds (von Thanner 1903); earliest clutches have been in the second half of May (von Thanner 1910). On Gran Canaria birds were claimed to breed in March (Polatzek 1908-1909) but this is either anomalous or merely assumed from gonadal condition; breeding may, however, occur earlier because of lower altitude (von Thanner 1910), and a prediction that *polatzeki* builds in May and lays in late May (Bannerman 1912) has been supported by observations (Hemmingsen 1958), though the eggs of this race apparently remain unknown (Bannerman 1963). Nests are placed at varying heights (2-14 m) in small or large pines, against the trunk, at the end of branches, etc. (Meade-Waldo 1889a,b, von Thanner 1903,1905). A report of nests in retama (outside the pine zone) (Godman 1872) is mistaken (Koenig 1890); a report of occasional nests in tree-heath and laurel (Volsøe 1951) is apparently unsupported. Clutch-size is normally two (Meade-Waldo 1889b, von Thanner 1903), although apparently rarely one (von Thanner 1903, also Martín *et al.* in press). There is no second brood unless (perhaps) the first attempt fails early (Meade-Waldo 1889b; also von Thanner 1903). The family stays together till late autumn (von Thanner 1903).

Threats This species is not currently known to be at risk, although one of its two populations (*polatzeki* on Gran Canaria) evidently is (see Population), and the bird's total insular range is small. In the past, two major threats – hunting and habitat destruction – have been identified as the basis for fears about its ultimate survival. About a century ago the market in specimens was so great that shooting on a large scale by local people was considered likely to exterminate it (Meade-Waldo 1889a; also Koenig 1890, Cabrera y Diaz 1893), but this did not discourage one collector from killing 76 on Gran Canaria in 1909 and 122 on Tenerife over a period of years (von Thanner 1910), the admission of which caused a considerable wrangle (Ogilvie-Grant 1910, Bannerman 1912, von Thanner 1912,1913,1914) which in turn probably resulted in much greater awareness of the species and its plight. Collecting was defended, just prior to this outcry, on the grounds that an area emptied of birds is quickly replenished by stocks from elsewhere and that in any case the market was at that time tailing off [!], while the taking of eggs was considered to do negligible harm (Polatzek 1908-1909). Pine forest destruction was mentioned as a direct threat to the species at a time when, paradoxically, the same observer found pine stands to be still extensive (Gurney 1927); subsequently it was the removal of undergrowth for packing and litter which was considered more insidious (Lack and Southern 1949, Volsøe 1951); however, in 1960 "the process of denuding the slopes of Mount Teide" was noted with alarm (Mountfort 1960). On Gran Canaria in 1888 the species was missed in the Pinar de Pajonales, which was recorded as regenerating after being "recklessly destroyed" (Tristram 1889): possibly the species was at that stage in very low numbers in the forest. Piping of water from permanent sources in the mountains may now be reducing the number of drinking places in high summer (Bannerman 1963). Until at least 1956 the species was commonly kept as a cage-bird on Tenerife (Etchécopar and Hüe 1957, Hüe and Etchécopar 1958). The only proven natural enemy is the Sparrowhawk *Accipiter nisus* (Meade-Waldo 1889b), present on both Tenerife and Gran Canaria (see especially Koenig 1890, von Thanner 1913,1914), but now in such low numbers in pine forest on Tenerife as to have no influence on Blue Chaffinch numbers (Martín *et al.* in press). A Kestrel *Falco tinnunculus* was suspected of plundering one nest on Gran Canaria (Hemmingsen 1958).

Conservation Measures Taken The species is fully protected by law under Royal Decree 3181, 30 December 1980 (K. W. Emmerson *in litt.* 1984). Replanting of *Pinus canariensis* on Tenerife in the mid-1950s led to several tens of thousands of hectares being reafforested, and this was considered to be instrumental in the maintenance of good numbers of Blue Chaffinches (Etchécopar and Hüe 1957). It is to be noted that the first finder of nests, with remarkable consideration for his time, not only restricted himself to taking seven (of 18 inspected) but, having established that Sparrowhawks killed this species, destroyed several nests of the former so as to counterbalance the loss of nests caused by himself (Meade-Waldo 1889b), his action apparently resulting in a small increase in one area (Meade-Waldo 1893).

Conservation Measures Proposed Following studies of this species in recent years, it has been urged that the pine replanting policy be maintained, undergrowth clearance prohibited, nature reserves created and the race *polatzeki* included in a list (which is not specified) of protected species (Martín *et al.* in press). Continued study of the year-round ecology of this species on both islands is needed to determine what further action is necessary or feasible to improve its numbers and distribution. The need for and potential benefits of clarifying the status of the Canaries in relation to European legislation are stated in Conservation Measures Taken under White-tailed Laurel Pigeon *Columba junoniae*.

References

Bacallado, J. J. (1976) Notas sobre la distribución y evolución de la avifauna canaria. In G. Kunkel, ed. Biogeography and ecology in the Canary Islands. *Monog. Biol.* 30: 413-431.

Bannerman, D. A. (1912) The birds of Gran Canaria. *Ibis* (9)6: 557-627.

Bannerman, D. A. (1963) *Birds of the Atlantic islands*, 1. Edinburgh and London: Oliver and Boyd.

van den Berg, A. B. and Bosman, C. A. W. (1979) Birding in the Canary Islands. *Dutch Birding* 1: 66-68.

Bolle, C. (1854-1855) Bemerkungen über die Vögel der canarischen Inseln. *J. Orn.* 2: 447-462; 3: 171-181.

Cabrera y Diaz, A. (1893) Catálogo de las aves del archipiélago canario. *Ann. Soc. Esp. Hist. Nat.* 22: 151-220.

Cuyas Robinson, J. (1971) Algunas notas sobre aves observadas en tres visitas a las Islas Canarias. *Ardeola* vol. espec.: 103-153.

Etchécopar, R. D. and Hüe, F. (1957) Nouvelles données sur l'avifaune des îles Canaries recueillies au printemps 1956. *Oiseau et R.F.O.* 27: 309-334.

Firestone Hispania (1972) Islas Canarias Mapa Turistico. 1: 150,000, 6-0472. San Sebastian.

Godman, F. C. (1872) Notes on the resident and migratory birds of Madeira and the Canaries. *Ibis* (3)2: 209-224.

Gurney, G. H. (1927) Notes on birds observed at Orotava, Tenerife. *Ibis* (12)3: 634-644.

Hartert, E. (1901) [Aus den Wanderjahren eines Naturforschers. Reisen und Forschungen in Afrika, Asien und Amerika, 5.] Die Fauna der Canarischen Inseln. *Novit. Zool.* 8: 304-335.

Hartwig, W. (1886) Die Vögel Madeiras. *J. Orn.* 34: 452-486.

Hemmingsen, A. M. (1958) Field observations of birds in the Canary Islands. *Vidensk. Medd. fra Dansk naturh. Foren.* 120: 189-206.

Hüe, F. and Etchécopar, R. D. (1958) Un mois de recherches ornithologiques aux îles Canaries. *Terre et Vie* 105: 186-219.

Koenig, A. (1890) Ornithologische Forschungsergebnisse einer Reise nach Madeira und den Canarischen Inseln. *J. Orn.* 38: 257-488.

Lack, D. and Southern, H. N. (1949) Birds on Tenerife. *Ibis* 91: 607-626.

Martín, A. (1979) Contribución al estudio de la avifauna canaria: la biología del Pinzón Azul del Teide (*Fringilla teydea teydea* Moquin-Tandon). Memoria de Licenciatura, Universidad de La Laguna, Tenerife.

Martín, A., Bacallado, J. J. and Emmerson, K. W. (in press) Contribución al estudio de la avifauna canaria: la biología del Pinzón Azul del Teide (*Fringilla teydea teydea* Moquin-Tandon). II Reunión Iberoamericana de Conservación y Zoología de Vertebrados, 15-20 June 1980, Cáceres, Spain.

Meade-Waldo, E. G. (1889a) Notes on some birds of the Canary Islands. *Ibis* (6)1: 1-13.

Meade-Waldo, E. G. (1889b) Further notes on the birds of the Canary Islands. *Ibis* (6)1: 503-520.

Meade-Waldo, E. G. (1893) List of birds observed in the Canary Islands. *Ibis* (6)5: 185-207.

Mountfort, G. (1960) Notes on the birds of Tenerife. *Ibis* 102: 618-619.

Ogilvie-Grant, W. R. (1910) [Record of remarks.] *Bull. Brit. Orn. Club* 25: 119.

Pérez Padrón, F. (1981) Las aves del pinar canario. *Vida Silvestre* no. 40: 258-263.

Pérez Padrón, F. (1983) *Las aves de Canarias*. 3rd edition. (Enciclopedia Canaria). Tenerife: ACT.

Polatzek, J. (1908-1909) Die Vögel der Canaren. *Orn. Jahrb.* 19: 81-119, 161-197; 20: 1-24, 117-134, 202-210.

Reid, S. G. (1887) Notes on the birds of Teneriffe. *Ibis* (5)5: 424-435.

von Thanner, R. (1903) Beobachtungen aus den Pinienwäldern Tenerife's. *Orn. Jahrb.* 14: 211-217.

von Thanner, R. (1905) Notizen aus Tenerife. *Orn. Jahrb.* 16: 211-214.

von Thanner, R. (1910) Beiträge zur Ornis Gran Canaria's. *Orn. Jahrb.* 21: 81-101.

von Thanner, R. (1912) Von den Kanaren. *Orn. Jahrb.* 23: 221-228.

von Thanner, R. (1913) [Letter.] *Ibis* (10)1: 330-332.

von Thanner, R. (1914) Bemerkungen und Berichtigungen über die Verbreitung einzelner Vogelarten auf den Kanaren. *Orn. Jahrb.* 25: 86-94.

Tristram, H. B. (1889) Ornithological notes on the island of Gran Canaria. *Ibis* (6)1: 13-22.

Trotter, W. D. C. (1970) Observations faunistiques sur l'île de Lanzarote (Canaries). *Oiseau et R.F.O.* 40: 160-170.

Volsøe, H. (1951) The breeding birds of the Canary Islands, 1. Introduction and synopsis of the species. *Vidensk. Medd. fra Dansk naturh. Foren.* 113: 1-153.

Webb, P. B., Berthelot, S. and Moquin-Tandon, A. (1842) Ornithologie Canarienne. In P. B. Webb and S. Berthelot, *Histoire naturelle des Iles Canaries*, 2, pt. II. Zoologie (Ornithologie) – 1. Paris.

Witt, H.-H. (1971) Ornithologische Beobachtungen auf den Kanaren. *Orn. Mitt.* 23: 145-148.

YELLOW-THROATED SERIN

Serinus flavigula Salvadori, 1888

Order PASSERIFORMES

INDETERMINATE

Family FRINGILLIDAE
Subfamily CARDUELINAE

Summary Known from three century-old specimens taken in one relatively small area of Shoa province, eastern Ethiopia, this small finch needs to be searched for at its original localities and to the north and east of them.

Distribution The Yellow-throated Serin is known from three specimens, collected at Kolla di Aigaber (9°36'N 40°04'E), 16 October 1880, Ambokarra (9°31'N 40°09'E), 17 May 1885, and Malca-Ghebdu ("Melka Jebdu Shet'" [*shet'* = stream] is at 9°34'N 39°53'E in DMA 1982), 19 February 1886, all in Shoa province, Ethiopia (Salvadori 1884,1888, Erard 1974). These three localities are close together at the foot of the eastern escarpment of the West Highlands (east of and below Ankober); Malca-Ghebdu, previously untraced (Erard 1974), is from the coordinates above c.20 km east of Ankober. Other areas where the species might occur are mentioned under Conservation Measures Proposed.

Population There is no record of the numbers of birds seen at the time the specimens were collected.

Ecology The known localities are in relatively arid habitat (Erard 1974).

Threats None is known, except that the range of this species is likely to prove very restricted.

Conservation Measures Taken None is known.

Conservation Measures Proposed Fieldwork is needed to rediscover this species and to determine its range, population and any possible threats it may face. Such work could perhaps be combined with study of the Ankober Serin *Serinus ankoberensis* (see relevant account) in the adjacent highlands. However, it has been suggested that searches should be conducted to the north and east of the known localities, in the extreme north of Harar province and in Wollo (Welo) province (Erard 1974).

Remarks A recent revaluation of the problematic *Serinus* forms from Ethiopia has concluded that *flavigula* is a good species, but close to the Yellow-rumped Serin *Serinus xanthopygius*; it is represented only by the three specimens from the 1880s (Erard 1974). Not having been seen in the wild for over 50 years, by CITES criteria the Yellow-throated Serin may be considered extinct, one of only two bird species endemic to the African continent in this situation, the other being the Golden-naped Weaver *Ploceus aureonucha* (see relevant account).

References

DMA (1982) *Gazetteer of Ethiopia*. Washington, D.C.: Defense Mapping Agency.

Erard, C. (1974) Taxonomie des serins à gorge jaune d'Ethiopie. *Oiseau et R.F.O.* 44: 308-323.

Salvadori, T. (1884) Spedizione Italiana nell'Africa Equatoriale. Risulti zoologici. Ucelli della Scioa e della regione fra Zelia e la Scioa. *Ann. Mus. Civ. Genova* (2)1: 7-276.

Salvadori, T. (1888) Catalogo di una collezione di uccelli dello Scioa fatta dal Dott. Vicenzo Ragazzi negli anni 1884, 1885, 1886. *Ann. Mus. Civ. Genova* (2)6: 185-326.

ANKOBER SERIN   RARE

Serinus ankoberensis Ash, 1979

Order PASSERIFORMES   Family FRINGILLIDAE

Subfamily CARDUELINAE

Summary This is a small, cliff-frequenting, montane finch, very recently described and as yet known only from a single small area in Ethiopia; the population is likely to prove small, and fieldwork is needed to provide more background data on the species.

Distribution The Ankober Serin was first discovered in November 1976 at a site 3 km north of Ankober (9°36'N 39°46'E), along the top edge of the extreme eastern escarpment of the West Highlands (Shoa Province) of Ethiopia, and on various occasions up to April 1977 relocated there and at a site 4 km further north, at altitudes from 2,980 to 3,110 m (Ash 1979). It was subsequently found in what was considered the same area (about 8 km from Ankober near Mount Mabrate at 3,000 m) on 19 January 1981 (J. Alamargot *in litt.* 1983). Bird observations at similar sites and altitudes in many other parts of Ethiopia have produced no record of this species (J. Alamargot *in litt.* 1983).

Population Numbers are unknown, but conceivably very small; a flock of 15 or so was seen in November 1976 and January 1977 (Ash 1979). Two flocks totalling about 50 birds were seen on 19 January 1981 (J. Alamargot *in litt.* 1983).

Ecology The species inhabits broken cliff-tops (sheer rockfaces interspersed with areas of steep vegetated slopes and earth banks); birds were seen to spend much time on rock surfaces, often clinging to vertical stone faces and bare earth banks, and to alight on no vegetation other than grass (Ash 1979). They were gregarious, and fed on grass and other seeds (Ash 1979). A nest (clutch-size three) was found, February/March, inside a vertical hole on the underside of an overhanging earth bank; breeding also appeared to have taken place in September/October (Ash 1979).

Threats None is known, but the apparent restriction of the species's range is a general cause for concern.

Conservation Measures Taken The collector deliberately restricted himmself to two specimens (Ash 1979).

Conservation Measures Proposed Further fieldwork is needed to determine the species's range, population, and any possible threats it may face. Such work could perhaps be combined with searches for and studies of the Yellow-throated Serin *Serinus flavigula* in the adjacent lowlands (see relevant account).

Remarks The creamy, streaky plumage of this species makes it difficult to locate, and it may yet be found to occur in previously watched areas of Ethiopia, though not commonly (J. Alamargot *in litt.* 1983). Several other Ethiopian endemic *Serinus* species remain little known, and apparently confined to very small areas, including the Yellow-throated Serin and Salvadori's Serin *S. xantholaema* (see Appendix C), with one and possibly another undescribed species (of *Serinus*) from southern and central Ethiopia respectively (Ash 1979).

Reference

Ash, J. S. (1979) A new species of serin from Ethiopia. *Ibis* 121: 1-7.

SAO TOME GROSBEAK
Neospiza concolor (Bocage, 1888)

Order PASSERIFORMES

INDETERMINATE

Family FRINGILLIDAE
Subfamily CARDUELINAE

Distribution The São Tomé Grosbeak is endemic to São Tomé (São Tomé e Príncipe) in the Gulf of Guinea. Records are from only three localities, Angolares (São João dos Angolares, 0°08'N 6°39'E) on the south-east coast in 1888, and São Miguel and Rio Quija (both 0°08'N 6°30'E) on the south-west coast in 1890 (Bocage 1888,1891; coordinates derived from Centro de Geográfia do Ultramar 1968), a total of three specimens being collected (see Remarks).

Population The species has been considered rare and localised since the time of its discovery (Bocage 1891), although it is to be noted that the local inhabitants had a name (*enjolo*) for it (Bocage 1888). It was searched for in vain at Rio Quija in 1928 (Correia 1928-1929). The possibility of it being extinct was first raised in 1950 (Snow 1950) and was reinforced after fruitless searches, 1963-1973 (de Naurois 1975b). It was recently listed as "very probably extinct" (de Naurois 1983) and indeed treated as extinct in King (1978-1979), but there is still a faint hope that it survives (R. de Naurois *in litt.* 1983).

Ecology The species inhabits forests (Bocage 1891). There is no further information.

Threats The reasons for this species's long-term rarity are quite unknown. Forest damage (selective felling) and destruction are known to have occurred, notably from around 1890 to 1920 (Bannerman 1915, Correia 1928-1929, Snow 1950, de Naurois 1975a, R. de Naurois *in litt.* 1984), and may have affected the bird. Introduced disease and mammalian predators may also have played a part.

Conservation Measures Taken None is known.

Conservation Measures Proposed An ICBP project was developed in 1981 to investigate the status, ecology and conservation of the endemic birds of São Tomé e Príncipe, but was unable to proceed in 1982 and 1983. A search for this bird is a component of the project and conservation proposals will follow if the work goes ahead and the species is relocated.

Remarks As made clear under Distribution, Rio Quija does not flow through Angolares (*contra* Bannerman 1949, Greenway 1967) and three specimens were originally collected, not two (*contra* Moreau 1960, Amadon 1965). However, a fire in the Bocage Museum, Lisbon, in 1975 almost certainly means that only a single specimen now survives, in BMNH (R. de Naurois *in litt.* 1983). Although originally considered a grosbeak-weaver *Amblyospiza* (Ploceidae) (Bocage 1888), the tide of opinion has this century run in favour of this species being a true finch (Fringillidae), probably closest to *Poliospiza* (Salvadori 1903, Amadon 1953,1965, de Naurois 1975b, de Naurois and Wolters 1975). Not having been seen in the wild for over 50 years, by CITES criteria this species would now be considered extinct.

References

Amadon, D. (1953) Avian systematics and evolution in the Gulf of Guinea. The J. G. Correia collection. *Bull. Amer. Mus. Nat. Hist.* 100: 393-451.

Amadon, D. (1965) Position of the genus *Neospiza* Salvadori. *Ibis* 107: 395-396.

Bannerman, D. A. (1915) Report on the birds collected by the late Mr Boyd Alexander (Rifle Brigade) during his last expedition to Africa. Part II. The birds of St.Thomas' Island. *Ibis* (10)3: 89-121.

Bannerman, D. A. (1949) *The birds of tropical West Africa*, 7. London: Crown Agents for the Colonies.

Bocage, J. V. B. (1888) Oiseaux nouveaux de l'Ile St.Thomé. *Jorn. Acad. Sci. Lisboa* 12: 229-232.

Bocage, J. V. B. (1891) Oiseaux de l'Ile St.Thomé. *Jorn. Acad. Sci. Lisboa* (2)2: 77-87.

Centro de Geográfia do Ultramar (1968) *Relação dos nomes geográficos de S.Tomé e Príncipe.* Lisboa: Junta de Investigações do Ultramar.

Correia, J. G. (1928-1929) Unpublished typescript concerning his São Tomé expedition, held in AMNH.

Greenway, J. C. (1967) *Extinct and vanishing birds of the world.* 2nd revised edition. New York: Dover Publications.

King, W. B. (1978-1979) *Red data book, 2. Aves.* 2nd edition. Morges, Switzerland: IUCN.

Moreau, R. E. (1960) Conspectus and classification of the ploceine weaver-birds. *Ibis* 102: 298-321.

de Naurois, R. (1975a) Le "Scops" de l'Ile de São Tomé *Otus hartlaubi* (Giebel). *Bonn. zool. Beitr.* 26: 319-355.

de Naurois, R. (1975b) Les Carduelinae des îles de São Tomé et Príncipe (Golfe de Guinée). *Ardeola* 21: 903-931.

de Naurois, R. (1983) Les oiseaux reproducteurs des îles de São Tomé et Príncipe: liste systématique commentée et indications zoogéographiques. *Bonn. zool. Beitr.* 34: 129-148.

de Naurois, R. and Wolters, H. E. (1975) The affinities of the São Tomé Weaver *Textor grandis* (Gray, 1844). *Bull. Brit. Orn. Club* 95: 122-126.

Salvadori, T. (1903) Contribuzioni alla ornitologia delle isole del Golfo di Guinea. *Mem. Reale Accad. Sci. Torino* (2)53: 1-45.

Snow, D. W. (1950) The birds of São Tomé and Príncipe in the Gulf of Guinea. *Ibis* 92: 579-595.

WARSANGLI LINNET

RARE

Acanthis johannis (Clarke, 1919)

Order PASSERIFORMES

Family FRINGILLIDAE
Subfamily CARDUELINAE

Summary Known only from five sites (numerous in only one) in two small areas of the northern Somalia highlands, this seed-eater occurs in both open country and juniper forest although its essential needs are unclear: until these are elucidated, the threats it faces cannot be understood or remedied.

Distribution The Warsangli Linnet is endemic to the main mountainous range (labelled "Jebel Warsangeli" in the west and "Al Mado" in the east in DMAAC 1979) bordering the Gulf of Aden in the central part of northern Somalia, and is known there from only five sites in two well separated areas. The principal site is the Daloh Forest Reserve (10°45'N 47°15'E), c. 17 km north of Erigavo in the western part of the Jebel Warsangli: although this site and the area around Erigavo was prospected for the species without success in January 1949 (Meinertzhagen 1948-1949), three specimens were collected there in August and October 1955 (Williams 1956, Archer and Godman 1961), and five in April 1956 (specimens in BMNH: SNS), and it is evident that sightings of the species in small flocks were frequent in these years at this locality. It was found commonly there and in an adjacent gorge in May 1979 (Ash and Miskell 1981). There are also two specimens from Tagair (10°45'N 47°24'E, i.e. 15 km east of Daloh, though reportedly "14 miles [23 km] north of Erigavo"), collected 26 July 1956 (Williams 1957; SNS) and 27 July 1957 (Ash and Miskell 1981), and birds were seen at this locality in late May 1956 (Clarke 1968). A report that the species occurs at Bukh (Bakh, Bokh) (10°36'N 47°12'E), west (not north-west as in Archer and Godman 1961) of Erigavo (Williams 1956) remains to be confirmed. All other records are from three close localities in the eastern part of the mountain range ("Al Mado"). The type-locality is Mush Aled (Musha Aled, Mas Aled) (11°00'N 48°19E), where three birds were shot (only one preserved) from a flock of 25-30 in February 1919 (Archer and Godman 1961). Searches of this locality in March 1919 and May 1980 produced no records, but on the latter date three birds were seen at Moon (11°01'N 48°26'E) and one at Ragad (10°59'N 48°31'E) (Ash and Miskell 1981). Exploration of the discrete mountainous block east of Bosaso (= Bender Cassim, 11°17'N 49°11'E) produced no records, but there appeared to be no suitable habitat (too arid and bare) (Ash and Miskell 1981). On this evidence, the view that the species's range extends "from the Warsangli country to the high ranges of the Mijjertein ["Migiurtinia" in TAW 1980] in the neighbourhood of Cape Guardafui" and that its stronghold is in this latter region (Archer and Godman 1961) must now be seriously doubted. However, the species probably extends along some 250 km of escarpment, in a very narrow strip a few kilometres wide between 1,200 and 2,400 m, from 100 km east of Mush Aled west to Daloh (Ash and Miskell 1981). Indeed it seems equally likely that it occurs along the escarpment that continues, more indentedly, east and south of Daloh (i.e. the western end of the Jebel Warsangli); nevertheless doubts must remain about the continuity of its distribution in this range and about its numerical status everywhere except Daloh (see Remarks).

Population The species was not found at and near Daloh during several days' exploration and collecting in January 1949 (Meinertzhagen 1948-1949), but was evidently in good numbers there (at least seasonally) in 1955-1957) (see Distribution; this view also taken in Vincent 1966-1971), and was "one of the commonest small birds" there in May 1979, with up to 100 being seen in a morning within a 2-3 km radius, although only males were ever seen and only for part of the day (Ash and Miskell 1981). All birds seen at Tagair in May 1956 appeared also to be males (G. C. Clarke *per* J. S. Ash *in litt.* 1984). The original collector's memory was that the species was common at Mush Aled during his brief visit in February 1919, but no birds could be found there the following month (Archer and Godman 1961) or in May 1980 (Ash and Miskell 1981), and a total of only four could be found on the last-named date in the area stretching 30 km to the east (Ash and Miskell 1981; see Distribution). The basis for the view that "numbers may have increased in recent years" (Ash and Miskell 1981) is not entirely certain, and indeed it is possible to suggest that a decline may be in progress (see Remarks).

Ecology At Daloh, the species occurs (for at least part of the day and over at least part of the year: records from April to October) in the rocky evergreen forest zone at 1,800-2,100 m, which in 1955 consisted chiefly of *Juniperus procera*, *Olea chrysophylla*, *Dodonaea viscosa*, *Cadia purpurea* and *Sideroxylon*, and which in 1979 was "degraded, ... with ... many open areas due to felling, damage by fire, and cattle-grazing" though also in places with "a fairly dense under-storey, composed particularly of thickets of a shrubby species of *Salvia*" (Ash and Miskell 1981). Apart from one bird feeding on low grass seeds, all observations of birds eating in 1979 involved the green seeds of this *Salvia* thicket (Ash and Miskell 1981) which, however, was in more open areas and not dependent on shade (J. S. Ash *in litt.* 1984). Feeding on grass and *Salvia* seeds was also noted in 1956 (Clarke 1968, G. C. Clarke *per* J. S. Ash *in litt.* 1984). In the period July to October 1955 it was thought birds were only visiting the forest to drink (birds only present 0630-0930 hrs) and the stomachs of the three specimens then collected contained quartz particles and grass seeds (Williams 1956). In May 1956 at Tagair birds were seen to fly in to drink at a well in small parties, apparently throughout the day, although after a fall of rain the numbers visiting the well in subsequent days dropped sharply (Clarke 1968). The flock from which the type was secured had been feeding in rather open scrub on the side of a ravine (Archer and Godman 1961), the bird seen at Ragad flew up from a sheer cliff face (Ash and Miskell 1981), while the habitat at Bukh (see Distribution) is open rocky grassland with springs and *Euphorbia* (Williams 1956). It therefore seems certain that the species utilises both open rocky country and forest, although what is optimal for it is not clear; the view that "forest destruction could be a contributory factor actually favouring the species, since it opens up denser stands of relatively close canopy forest" may be correct but is not necessarily ground for optimism (see Remarks). Birds are gregarious (see Williams 1956, Ash and Miskell 1981). Nests (so far undiscovered) are according to local report placed "in the hollows formed below branches on the trunks of junipers" (see Ash and Miskell 1981), but the lack of any sightings of females at Daloh in May 1979 suggested they may have then been incubating eggs some distance away (Ash and Miskell 1981); it would therefore perhaps be surprising if they were doing so within the forest zone. Males were in breeding condition in May 1979 (Ash and Miskell 1981), and the only known juvenile is from late July (Williams 1957).

Threats If the species is to any extent forest-dependent (see Remarks), degradation at Daloh may pose a problem. It is to be noted that there is no juniper forest around Mush Aled or Ragad but that the area "may well have been forested in the recent past" (Ash and Miskell 1981); moreover, a road through the eastern end of the species's projected range (between Bosaso and Ragad) "will make areas of juniper forest more easily accessible" (Ash and Miskell 1981).

Conservation Measures Taken None is known.

Conservation Measures Proposed Much further work is needed to determine the status, distribution and breeding biology of the species (Ash and Miskell 1981). Any such work should aim to provide key information on habitat requirements through the annual cycle, and to document the exploitation of forest resources throughout the Jebel Warsangli and Al Mado range (see Remarks).

Remarks The tentative optimism in the recent account of this species's status (Ash and Miskell 1981; not echoed in the Introduction to Ash and Miskell 1983) is based on several points which appear open to reinterpretation. The numbers found at Daloh in 1979 are evidently considered likely to have been higher than those in the 1950s; however, the previous observer there was a non-ornithologist, whose records would inevitably be less full, yet which even so can be judged to imply that the species was then reasonably common. The attribution of a fairly extensive if still putative range (see Distribution) does not, of course, imply uniformity of density of birds within it, as indeed the paucity of records (and of numbers of birds) from the three eastern sites bears out. This range is anticipated from the reported presence of "much suitable habitat" between Mush Aled and Daloh but, as noted under Ecology, a full understanding of this species's habitat preferences is lacking. On the basis of existing records, it would appear that density increases with amount and proximity of forest. Even if partial forest destruction confers certain benefits on the species, the subsequent total destruction would seem likely to be highly detrimental. It is possible that in areas where forest is cleared (as may have happened recently around Mush Aled, and as appears to be happening at Daloh and about to happen east of Ragad) local populations of the species decline or completely disappear, so that its distribution is currently becoming ever more disjunct and precarious.

References

Archer, G. and Godman, E. M. (1961) *The birds of British Somaliland and the Gulf of Aden*, 4. Edinburgh and London: Oliver and Boyd.

Ash, J. S. and Miskell, J. E. (1981) Present abundance of the Warsangli Linnet *Acanthis johannis. Bull. Brit. Orn. Club* 101: 396-398.

Ash, J. S. and Miskell, J. E. (1983) *Birds of Somalia: their habitat, status and distribution. Scopus* Spec. Suppl. 1. Nairobi: Ornithological Sub-Committee, EANHS.

Clarke, G. C. (1968) Somali bird notes. Manuscript.

DMAAC (1979) Tactical Pilotage Chart, 1:500,000. K-6D, 3rd edition. Missouri: Defense Mapping Agency Aerospace Center, St.Louis Air Force Station.

Meinertzhagen, R. (1948-1949) Diary, volume 58 (76 volumes held in Rhodes House Library, Oxford).

The Times Atlas of the World (1980) Comprehensive (sixth) edition. London: Times Books.

Vincent, J. (1966-1971) *Red data book, 2. Aves.* Morges, Switzerland: IUCN.

Williams, J. G. (1956) The re-discovery of *Warsanglia johannis. Ibis* 98: 531-532.

Williams, J. G. (1957) The juvenile plumage of *Warsanglia johannis. Bull. Brit. Orn. Club* 77: 157.

ANAMBRA WAXBILL   INSUFFICIENTLY KNOWN
Estrilda poliopareia Reichenow, 1902

Order PASSERIFORMES   Family ESTRILDIDAE

Summary This waxbill is known only from a few riverine grassland localities in southern Nigeria. Although only rarely recorded it is probably under no immediate threat.

Distribution The Anambra Waxbill appears to be restricted to a few localities in southern Nigeria. The type-specimen was described in 1902 from "Congo" (Reichenow 1902) though this was almost certainly a mistake (Chapin 1950). The species was first reported from Nigeria in 1907 when a specimen was taken at Agoulerie on Anambra Creek on the lower Niger River (Heinroth 1907). In 1954 ten birds were collected 30 km to the south-west on the Niger sandbank at Onitsha (Serle 1957). There have been subsequent sight records at Forcados on the western edge of the Niger Delta and at Badagri in extreme south-western Nigeria near the border with Benin (Elgood 1982).

Population Numbers are not known. The species was reported to be common at Onitsha in 1954 (Serle 1957) and might, therefore, be largely overlooked within its small range.

Ecology This species is known from long grass and herbage along rivers and on lagoon sandbanks (Serle 1957, Elgood 1982). The birds live in small flocks of up to 20 birds or more, which frequently merge and split (Serle 1957). They are especially fond of very tall rank elephant grass (presumably *Pennisetum*) (W. Serle *in litt.* 1983). They feed on seeds which are taken directly from plants, not from the ground, and frequently sidle up and down grass stems (Serle 1957). One bird collected in June was coming into breeding condition (Serle 1957). The birds utter a variety of nondescript estrildid calls and large flocks are audible at a considerable distance (W. Serle *in litt.* 1983). Much of the habitat of the species is liable to flooding and so the birds must make some small-scale movements (W. Serle *in litt.* 1983).

Threats None is known.

Conservation Measures Taken None is known.

Conservation Measures Proposed A survey is needed to assess the status of this species and to determine whether any threat to its survival exists.

Remarks It is possible that the Anambra Waxbill is conspecific with the widespread Fawn-breasted Waxbill *Estrilda paludicola* (Goodwin 1982).

References

Chapin, J. P. (1950) A new race of *Estrilda paludicola* from the Congo River. *Bull. Brit. Orn. Club* 70: 23-25.

Elgood, J. H. (1982) *The birds of Nigeria.* London: B.O.U. Check-list no. 4.

Goodwin, D. (1982) *Estrildid finches of the world.* Oxford and London: British Museum (Natural History) and Oxford University Press.

Heinroth, O. (1907) Deutsche Ornithologische Gesellschaft. Bericht über die September-Sitzung 1907. *J. Orn.* 55: 622-624.

Reichenow, A. (1902) Neue afrikanische Arten. *Orn. Monatsber.* 10: 184-185.

Serle, W. (1957) A contribution to the ornithology of the Eastern Region of Nigeria. Part 2. *Ibis* 99: 628-685.

BLACK-LORED WAXBILL
Estrilda nigriloris Chapin, 1928

Order PASSERIFORMES

INSUFFICIENTLY KNOWN

Family ESTRILDIDAE

Summary This waxbill is known only from a restricted area in southern Zaire around the Lualaba River and Lake Upemba where it is very little studied; it might not be seriously threatened.

Distribution The Black-lored Waxbill was discovered in 1927 at Kiabo on the banks of the Lualaba River (Chapin 1928). It was collected subsequently at Sombe in 1949 and Kaleka in 1950, about 14 km south of the type-locality on the Lualaba River (Chapin 1954, Schouteden 1971; and specimens in MRAC: SNS). There is another record from Mabwe in 1948 on the eastern shore of Lake Upemba (Verheyen 1953; specimen in IRSNB: SNS). There appear, however, to be no records of the species since 1950. Its total range has been estimated at less than 2,600 km^2 (Hall and Moreau 1962).

Population Numbers are not known. It may not be uncommon within its limited range since the first specimens were collected from a flock of 20-30 birds (Chapin 1928,1954).

Ecology It has been found around the Lualaba River and Lake Upemba in level grassy plains with tall grasses and bushes (Chapin 1928,1954, Lippens and Wille 1976, Goodwin 1982). It is known to occur in small flocks (Chapin 1928,1954).

Threats None is known.

Conservation Measures Taken Most of the population of this species is probably within the Upemba National Park (see Verheyen 1953) and so it may not be seriously threatened.

Conservation Measures Proposed A survey is needed to determine the distribution, population and habitat requirements of this very rarely recorded bird and to ascertain whether it is a species distinct from the Common Waxbill *Estrilda astrild*.

Remarks The Black-lored Waxbill is generally considered to form a superspecies with the Common Waxbill with which it appears to be allopatric (Chapin 1928,1954, Hall and Moreau 1970, Lippens and Wille 1976); no intermediates between the two birds have ever been found (Lippens and Wille 1976).

References

Chapin, J. P. (1928) A new species of waxbill (*Estrilda*) from southeastern Congo. *Amer. Mus. Novit.* 308.

Chapin, J. P. (1954) The birds of the Belgian Congo. Part 4. *Bull. Amer. Mus. Nat. Hist.* 75B.

Goodwin, D. (1982) *Estrildid finches of the world*. London: British Museum (Natural History) and Oxford University Press.

Hall, B. P. and Moreau, R. E. (1962) A study of the rare birds of Africa. *Bull. Brit. (Nat. Hist.) Zool.* 8: 313-378.

Hall, B. P. and Moreau, R. E. (1970) *An atlas of speciation in African passerine birds*. London: Trustees of the British Museum (Natural History).

Lippens, L. and Wille, H. (1976) *Les oiseaux du Zaire*. Tielt, Belgium: Lannoo.

Schouteden, H. (1971) La faune ornithologique de la Province du Katanga. *Doc. Zool. Mus. Afr. Centr.* 17.

Verheyen, R. (1953) Oiseaux. *Exploration du Parc National de l'Upemba, Mission G. F. de Witte (1946-1949)* 19.

BANNERMAN'S WEAVER   VULNERABLE

Ploceus bannermani Chapin, 1932

Order PASSERIFORMES   Family PLOCEIDAE
                                                  Subfamily PLOCEINAE

Summary This forest-edge species is known only from a few montane areas in western Cameroon and eastern Nigeria, and while still not uncommon where it occurs its habitat is steadily disappearing.

Distribution Bannerman's Weaver has only been recorded in a few localities in western Cameroon and eastern Nigeria. The species was described from three specimens collected in 1930, two near Dschang at the southern end of the Bamenda-Banso Highlands and one from near N'kongsamba probably on Mount Manengouba (Chapin 1932). An originally misidentified specimen was collected at Ninong on Mount Manengouba in 1909 (Chapin 1932) and in 1948 four specimens were collected, one each from Paola village on Mount Manengouba, Bamenda, Lake Oku, and 7 km west of Oku (Serle 1950, and examination of specimen-labels in BMNH: SNS). These localities are at altitudes of between 1,520 and 2,280 m (Serle 1950). One bird was collected and another seen further north in the Bamenda Highlands at Wum Crater Lake, 1,100 m, in 1953 (Serle 1965). In 1966 five specimens were collected around Lake Manengouba, 1,800-2,100 m, and two were taken at Lake Oku, 2,100 m, in the following year (Eisentraut 1973, and examination of specimen-labels in ZFMK: NJC). In 1984 the ICBP Cameroon Montane Forest Survey recorded the species on Mount Manengouba, Mount Oku, the Bafut-Ngemba Forest Reserve, the Bamboutos Mountains and in an area of forest between Mbengwi and Tinachong, all these areas with the exception of Mount Manengouba being in the Bamenda Highlands (SNS). Bannerman's Weaver was discovered on the Obudu Plateau in Nigeria in 1974 (Elgood 1982). Birds were seen at this locality on ten occasions between November 1976 and June 1977, and 12 pairs were counted and one bird collected in 1980 (Elgood 1982, M. Dyer pers. comm. 1983, M. E. Gartshore pers. comm. 1983). In 1981 one bird was mist-netted at Maisamari on the Mambila Plateau in eastern Nigeria (M. Dyer pers. comm. 1983, M. E. Gartshore pers. comm. 1983). This record represents a considerable range extension to the north-east.

Population Numbers are not known. One report describes the species as being scarce (Serle 1950) but it is not uncommon on Mount Manengouba (Eisentraut 1973, SNS), Mount Oku (SNS) and the Obudu Plateau (Elgood 1982, M. Dyer pers. comm. 1983, M. E. Gartshore pers. comm. 1983).

Ecology This species occurs in trees and shrubs on the edge of montane forest and in dense shrubbery in the more open parts of such forest (Serle 1950,1965, Elgood 1982, SNS). It is not a true forest interior species and it has been found in bushy habitats around Lake Manengouba (Eisentraut 1973). On the Obudu Plateau it occurs along the edges of thin strips of forest in deep ravines and the bird from the Mambila Plateau was in a tiny strip of gallery forest, only a few trees wide (M. Dyer pers. comm. 1983, M. E. Gartshore pers. comm. 1983). Breeding has been noted in December and January at Lake Manengouba: the nests are attached to thorn-bushes about 2.5-3 m above the ground and two that were examined each contained two eggs (Eisentraut 1973). Birds sometimes occur in small parties (Serle 1950).

Threats The habitats of this species (both the forests and the surrounding areas of dense shrubbery) are under threat in Cameroon. All of the forest patches remaining in the Bamenda Highlands are now badly damaged, very small and being rapidly cleared as a result of cultivation, overgrazing by cattle, sheep, goats and horses, wood-cutting and fires (SNS). Even the more extensive areas of forest, such as on Mount Oku and also Mount Manengouba, are being rapidly cleared (SNS). Although forest destruction may even benefit the species in the short term by providing more open habitat, as this in turn is degraded to grassland the birds will entirely disappear (SNS).

Conservation Measures Taken None is known, even the forest reserves in which the species occurs being subject to clearance (SNS).

Conservation Measures Proposed The ICBP Cameroon Montane Forest Survey is preparing recommendations for the conservation of forest on Mount Oku and Mount Manengouba for the consideration of the Cameroon government.

Remarks Bannerman's Weaver is a distinct species without any obvious close relatives (Hall and Moreau 1970). For details of other threatened bird species occurring in the Bamenda Highlands and the Obudu Plateau see Remarks under Bannerman's Turaco *Tauraco bannermani* and the Green-breasted Bush-shrike *Malaconotus gladiator* respectively. One species in Appendix C, the Cameroon Mountain Greenbul *Andropadus montanus*, also occurs on Mount Manengouba.

References

Chapin, J. P. (1932) Fourteen new birds from tropical Africa. *Amer. Mus. Novit.* 570.

Eisentraut, M. (1973) Die Wirbeltierfauna von Fernando Poo und Westkamerun. *Bonn. zool. Monog.* 3.

Elgood, J. H. (1982) *The birds of Nigeria*. London: B.O.U. Check-list no. 4.

Hall, B. P. and Moreau, R. E. (1970) *An atlas of speciation in African passerine birds*. London: Trustees of the British Museum (Natural History).

Serle, W. (1950) A contribution to the ornithology of the British Cameroons. Part 2. *Ibis* 92: 602-638.

Serle, W. (1965) A third contribution to the ornithology of the British Cameroons. Part 2. *Ibis* 107: 230-246.

BATES'S WEAVER   RARE
Ploceus batesi (Sharpe, 1908)

Order PASSERIFORMES   Family PLOCEIDAE
                                                     Subfamily PLOCEINAE

Summary This rare weaver is known only from a few localities in lowland rainforest in southern Cameroon. It is very rarely recorded and would presumably be in severe danger if forest clearance were to become a serious problem within its range.

Distribution Bates's Weaver is only known from the forests of southern Cameroon. The type-specimen was collected near the Dja River in 1906 (Sharpe and Bates 1908). In 1908 another specimen was taken nearby at Kumangola (Ogilvie-Grant 1910, Sharpe 1910) and in the following year four birds were collected at Bitye (Bannerman 1949), also near the Dja River. The known range was extended westwards when a specimen was taken at Lolodorf (Bannerman 1949), this bird being presented to BMNH in 1923 (SNS). Other specimens were collected at Lolodorf and Sangmélima, probably during the 1940s (Good 1953). In AMNH and Berlin Museum there are specimens from Molundu (Louette 1981), though details of these appear not to be published. In 1978 a pair was seen in March and again in April at Tissongo in the Douala-Edea Forest Reserve, near the coast, just south of the Sanaga River (P. A. Agland pers. comm. 1984). The only other recent record is of a bird seen near Victoria, at the foot of Mount Cameroon, in 1979, a record which represents a considerable extension of the known range to the west (Taylor 1981).

Population Numbers are not known. It appears to be a very scarce species, only occasionally recorded (Bates 1930, Bannerman 1949, Good 1953, Taylor 1981).

Ecology This species is only known from lowland rainforest (Bates 1930, Bannerman 1949, Good 1953, Taylor 1981). Birds have been seen singly (Taylor 1981), in pairs (Good 1953), and once in a mixed-species party of insectivorous birds (Bates 1930, Bannerman 1949). The diet consists of insects (Bates 1930, Bannerman 1949) and one bird was seen moving in a zig-zag manner up a creeper-covered tree-trunk, apparently searching for insects (Taylor 1981).

Threats None is known, though the species would presumably be at serious risk if forest clearance were to become extensive within its range.

Conservation Measures Taken Bates's Weaver presumably occurs within the proposed Dja National Park in southern Cameroon.

Conservation Measures Proposed A survey is needed to determine the status of the species and to confirm its presence in the proposed Dja National Park. It is to be hoped that the Dja Forest will soon be officially declared a national park.

Remarks This rare species has no close relatives (Hall and Moreau 1970).

References

Bannerman, D. A. (1949) *The birds of tropical West Africa*, 7. London: Crown Agents for the Colonies.

Bates, G. L. (1930) *Handbook of the birds of West Africa*. London: John Bale, Sons and Danielsson.

Good, A. I. (1953) The birds of French Cameroon. Part II. *Mém. Inst. Fr. Afr. Noire*, Ser. Nat. Sci. 3: 7-269.

Hall, B. P. and Moreau, R. E. (1970) *An atlas of speciation in African passerine birds*. London: Trustees of the British Museum (Natural History).

Louette, M. (1981) *The birds of Cameroon. An annotated check-list*. Brussels: Verhandeling Wetenschapen, Jaargang 43, no. 163.

Ogilvie-Grant, W. R. (1910) Note on a rare weaver-bird (*Othyphantes batesi*). *Ibis* (9)4: 435.

Sharpe, R. B. (1910) [The hitherto unknown male of Bates's Weaver-finch.] *Bull. Brit. Orn. Club* 25: 41.

Sharpe, R. B. and Bates, G. L. (1908) On further collections of birds from the Efulen District of Cameroon, West Africa. Part VI. *Ibis* (9)2: 317-357.

Taylor, P. B. (1981) Bates's Weaver *Ploceus batesi* near Victoria, and other observations from western Cameroun. *Malimbus* 3: 49-50.

BLACK-CHINNED WEAVER   INSUFFICIENTLY KNOWN
Ploceus nigrimentum Reichenow, 1904

Order PASSERIFORMES   Family PLOCEIDAE
                                                                   Subfamily PLOCEINAE

Summary This weaver is known only from two widely separated areas, one in Angola and one in Congo, and there are no very recent records.

Distribution The type-specimen of the Black-chinned Weaver was described from Galanga in the Bailundu (Bailundo) Highlands of western Angola (Reichenow 1904). Subsequently a few specimens were taken nearby at Mombolo (Chapin 1954, Hall and Moreau 1962), available evidence suggesting that these were collected in 1927 (Traylor 1960). The species has more recently (at least before 1973) been recorded in the higher elevations of Huambo province (Dean and Huntley in prep.), this straddling the central part of the Bailundu Highlands. The only other record is of five birds seen, including one collected, at Djambala on the Baleke Plateau in Congo in November 1951, 1,050 km to the north of the Angola localities (Rand *et al.* 1959, Hall and Moreau 1962). The Angola localities are at an elevation of over 1,500 m and Djambala is at 750 m, suggesting that this is a species of reasonably high altitudes (Hall and Moreau 1962). It is likely that it occurs in intervening localities between the Bailundu Highlands and Djambala, such as north-western Angola north of the Cuanza River and the western parts of Zaire (Traylor 1960).

Population Numbers are not known though birds are apparently rare in the Bailundu Highlands (Traylor 1963).

Ecology At Djambala the birds were seen in the tops of low trees in savanna and were very shy (Rand *et al.* 1959). There is no habitat information on this species in Angola but there is montane forest, woodland and grassland in the localities where it has been collected (Hall and Moreau 1962). It is probably, however, a non-forest bird (Moreau 1960). There is no information on its behaviour or breeding.

Threats None is known.

Conservation Measures Taken None is known.

Conservation Measures Proposed A survey is needed to determine the distribution of this species and to assess its habitat requirements. If it is under any threat it will be necessary to recommend appropriate conservation measures.

Remarks The Black-chinned Weaver forms a superspecies with the Baglafecht Weaver *Ploceus baglafecht* and Bertram's Weaver *P. bertrandi*, both of which are more widespread in eastern Africa (Hall and Moreau 1970).

References

Chapin, J. P. (1954) The birds of the Belgian Congo. Part 4. *Bull. Amer. Mus. Nat. Hist.* 75B.

Dean, W. R. J, and Huntley, M. A. (in prep.) An updated list of the birds of Angola.

Hall, B. P. and Moreau, R. E. (1962) A study of the rare birds of Africa. *Bull. Brit. Mus. (Nat. Hist.) Zool.* 8: 313-378.

Hall, B. P. and Moreau, R. E. (1970) *An atlas of speciation in African passerine birds.* London: Trustees of the British Museum (Natural History).

Moreau, R. E. (1960) Conspectus and classification of the ploceine weaver-birds. *Ibis* 102: 298-321.

Rand, A. L., Friedmann, H. and Traylor, M. A. (1959) Birds of Gabon and Moyen Congo. *Fieldiana Zool.* 41: 221-411.

Reichenow, A. (1904) *Die Vögel Afrikas*, 3. Neudamm: J. Neumann.

Traylor, M. A. (1960) Notes on the birds of Angola, non-passeres. *Publ. cult. Co. Diam. Angola, Lisboa* no. 51: 129-186.

Traylor, M. A. (1963) Check-list of Angolan birds. *Publ. cult. Co. Diam. Angola, Lisboa* no. 61.

LOANGO SLENDER-BILLED WEAVER
Ploceus subpersonatus (Cabanis, 1876)

Order PASSERIFORMES

INSUFFICIENTLY KNOWN

Family PLOCEIDAE
Subfamily PLOCEINAE

Summary This weaver is known only from the coastal strip from Gabon to the mouth of the Zaire River. There are few recent records.

Distribution The type-specimen of the Loango Slender-billed Weaver was described from Chinchoxo ("Tschintschoscho") in Cabinda in 1876 (Cabanis 1876, Reichenow 1904). At least two further specimens were collected at Landana in Cabinda (Reichenow 1904), in 1876 (Sharpe and Bouvier 1876) and in 1883 (specimen in BMNH: SNS). The only subsequent record from Cabinda is of two birds collected at Chiloango in 1969 (Pinto 1972). In coastal Zaire a bird almost certainly of this species was seen at Boma in 1915 and another was collected between Moanda and Vista in 1945 (Chapin 1954). Four birds were collected at Fernan Vaz in coastal Gabon in 1951 (Rand *et al.* 1959), representing an extension of the known range 550 km to the north. The species presumably also occurs in coastal Congo between Gabon and Cabinda but there are no records.

Population Numbers are not known but the paucity of records suggests that the species is rare (a view shared by A. A. da R. Pinto *in litt.* 1983).

Ecology This species is very little known. It has been reported from secondary growth (Rand *et al.* 1959), floating grass at a lake border (Rand *et al.* 1959), the edge of a papyrus swamp (Chapin 1954) and in a coconut-palm (Chapin 1954). The birds in 1969 were in scattered trees along the margins of the Chiloango River near its source (A. A. da R. Pinto *in litt.* 1983). There is no information on its behaviour or breeding.

Threats None is known.

Conservation Measures Taken None is known.

Conservation Measures Proposed A survey is needed to determine the distribution of this species and to assess its habitat requirements. If it is under any threat it will be necessary to recommend appropriate conservation measures.

Remarks The Loango Slender-billed Weaver forms a superspecies with the Slender-billed Weaver *Ploceus pelzelni* and the Little Weaver *P. luteolus*, both of which are widely distributed in Africa (Hall and Moreau 1970).

References

Cabanis, J. (1876) [Ein neuer ... Webervogel.] *J. Orn.* 24: 92.

Chapin, J. P. (1954) The birds of the Belgian Congo. Part 4. *Bull. Amer. Mus. Nat. Hist.* 75B.

Hall, B. P. and Moreau, R. E. (1970) *An atlas of speciation in African passerine birds.* London: Trustees of the British Museum (Natural History).

Pinto, A. A. da R. (1972) Contribuição para o estudo da avifauna do Distrito de Cabinda (Angola). *Mem. Trab. Inst. Cient. Angola* no. 10.

Rand, A. L., Friedmann, H. and Traylor, M. A. (1959) Birds of Gabon and Moyen Congo. *Fieldiana Zool.* 41: 221-411.

Reichenow, A. (1904) *Die Vögel Afrikas*, 3. Neudamm: J. Neumann.

Sharpe, R. B. and Bouvier, A. (1876) Etudes d'ornithologie africain. *Bull. Soc. Zool. France* 1: 36-53.

LAKE LUFIRA WEAVER
Ploceus ruweti Louette and Benson, 1982

Order PASSERIFORMES

INSUFFICIENTLY KNOWN

Family PLOCEIDAE
Subfamily PLOCEINAE

Summary This newly described weaver is known only from swamps bordering Lake Lufira in southern Zaire; there is no recent information on its status.

Distribution The Lake Lufira Weaver is known only from swamps bordering Lake Lufira (or Lake Tshangalele) in southern Zaire (Louette and Benson 1982). The type was collected in 1960 but has only recently been recognised as a distinct species (Louette and Benson 1982; see Remarks). There appear to be no subsequent observations of the species, presumably owing to the lack of ornithological fieldwork in the area. Birds in non-breeding plumage observed and collected in the early 1960s at Lake Dilolo, Moxico District, eastern Angola, 550 km to the west of Lake Lufira, were tentatively assigned to the Vitelline Masked Weaver *Ploceus velatus tahatali* (Pinto 1965); one of the specimens collected at this locality had some orange on the breast (Pinto 1965) and it was therefore thought that the Dilolo birds might represent an isolated population of the Lake Lufira Weaver (C. W. Benson pers. comm. 1982), but recent examination of these specimens has shown that this is not the case (Louette 1984).

Population The species was reported as common in 1960 around Lake Lufira (Ruwet 1965).

Ecology It lives in reedbeds of *Phragmites* and *Typha*, interspersed with bushes and *Sesbania leptocarpa* (Ruwet 1965). The breeding season lasts from January to April (Ruwet 1964,1965) and colonies vary in size from three to 20 nests (Ruwet 1965). Birds normally raise two broods in a breeding season (Ruwet 1965).

Threats None is known other than that it has been found only in a very restricted area.

Conservation Measures Taken None is known.

Conservation Measures Proposed A survey is needed to determine the distribution of the Lake Lufira Weaver more accurately in southern Zaire and to establish whether there are any threats to its survival.

Remarks This recently described species was originally mistaken for the Yellow-backed Weaver *Ploceus melanocephalus* (Ruwet 1964,1965). A recent taxonomic study has, however, shown that the Lake Lufira birds belong to a distinct species, closely related to two other swamp-dwelling species, the Tanganyika Masked Weaver *P. reichardi* and the Katanga Masked Weaver *P. katangae* (Louette and Benson 1982).

References

Louette, M. and Benson, C. W. (1982) Swamp-dwelling weavers of the *Ploceus velatus/vitellinus* complex, with the description of a new species. *Bull. Brit. Orn. Club* 102: 24-31.

Louette, M. (1984) The identity of swamp-dwelling weavers in northeast Angola. *Bull. Brit. Orn. Club* 104: 22-24.

Pinto, A. A. da R. (1965) Contribuição para o conhecimento da avifauna da região nordeste do distrito do Moxico, Angola. *Bol. Inst. Invest. cient. Angola* 1(2): 153-249.

Ruwet, J.-C. (1964) La périodicité de la reproduction chez les oiseaux du Katanga. *Gerfaut* 54: 84-110.

Ruwet, J.-C. (1965) Notes écologiques et éthologiques sur les oiseaux des plaines de la Lufira supérieure (Katanga) III. *Rev. Zool. Bot. Afr.* 72: 389-427.

CLARKE'S WEAVER
Ploceus golandi (Clarke, 1913)

Order PASSERIFORMES

ENDANGERED

Family PLOCEIDAE
Subfamily PLOCEINAE

Summary This elusive species is known only from one area of forest (Sokoke) on the Kenyan coast which is threatened by excessive logging. It might migrate away from the Kenyan coast at some times of the year but any such movements are not understood.

Distribution Clarke's Weaver is known only from the area between Kilifi Creek and the Sabaki River, in and around the Sokoke Forest in coastal Kenya (Britton *et al.* in press), from where it was described in 1913 (Clarke 1913). The species was found there again in 1955 when one bird was collected from a flock of 20 birds (Williams 1957) and in 1958 more flocks were seen and six more specimens obtained (Clancey and Williams 1959). Five birds were collected in 1964 (Ripley and Bond 1971), since when it has been recorded regularly from Sokoke Forest (*Scopus* 1 [1977]: 124; 3 [1979]: 114; 4 [1980]: 113, Britton and Zimmerman 1979, Kelsey and Langton 1984, Taylor 1984, and specimens in NMK and BMNH: SNS). The species might be migratory since most birds have been recorded between August and October, though there are records from April (Clancey and Williams 1959, *Scopus* 3 [1979]: 114; 6 [1982]: 119, Taylor 1984), July (*Scopus* 4 [1980]: 113), November (*Scopus* 2 [1978]: 116; 3 [1979]: 114; 4 [1980]: 113; 5 [1981]: 145) and December (*Scopus* 1 [1977]: 124; 7 [1983]: 120). If many of the birds do migrate away from Sokoke seasonally, there is no information as to where they might go (Britton 1980, Taylor 1984, Britton *et al.* in press).

Population Numbers have been estimated at 1,000 to 2,000 pairs but the numbers of this species are difficult to count accurately because of its flocking habits (Britton *et al.* in press).

Ecology Clarke's Weaver has been recorded in all forest habitats within Sokoke Forest though it is commonest in *Brachystegia* woodland (Britton and Zimmerman 1979, Britton 1980, Kelsey and Langton 1984, Britton *et al.* in press), where it forms noisy flocks of 5-30, occasionally up to 100 birds, often with Retz's Helmet-shrike *Prionops retzii* and the Chestnut-fronted Helmet-shrike *P. scopifrons* (Britton and Zimmerman 1979). Birds have also been seen in single-sex flocks (Clancey and Williams 1959). It has been suggested that the species is not migratory but tends to be seen mainly during the period between August and October because it forms flocks at this time (Britton *et al.* in press). During the remainder of the year it might be overlooked, presumably nesting at low densities in the tops of tall trees (Britton *et al.* in press). However, the complete lack of records from January to March, the most likely breeding season, suggests that it nests away from the Sokoke Forest (Taylor 1984). One April record was of a pair, possibly nesting nearby (*Scopus* 3 [1979]: 114) and juveniles have been seen in April, suggesting breeding in February (Taylor 1984), but nesting sites are unknown (Taylor 1984,

651

Britton *et al.* in press). The food consists of cockchafers, beetles and Lepidoptera larvae, all obtained high up in the trees (Clancey and Williams 1959).

Threats The main threat to this species is forest clearance (Kelsey and Langton 1984). Areas of forest outside the Sokoke Forest Reserve are being cleared and cannot be expected to survive for long (Britton and Zimmerman 1979). Some forest patches in which this weaver is known to have occurred have been cleared (Ripley and Bond 1971). Inside the forest reserve valuable timber trees, such as *Brachystegia speciformis*, are still being logged and areas of forest are being cleared for the planting of exotic trees (Britton and Zimmerman 1979, Kelsey and Langton 1984). At the present rate of cutting the favoured *Brachystegia* woodland habitat could all be felled within the next 20 years (Kelsey and Langton 1984). Logging is also taking place within the supposedly inviolate nature reserve (Cunningham-van Someren 1981-1982, Kelsey and Langton 1984). Unfortunately the work of the forest officers at Sokoke has been rendered ineffective by shortage of available funds (Kelsey and Langton 1984). It seems that certain conservation regulations have been ignored by people taking advantage of the lack of supervision by officials from the Forestry Department (Kelsey and Langton 1984).

Conservation Measures Taken The 400 km^2 Sokoke Forest Reserve provides some protection for the forest, though the logging of valuable timber trees and the clearing of forest for plantations are both legal (Britton and Zimmerman 1979). There is a 43 km^2 nature reserve within the forest reserve in which no cutting or disturbance is permitted (Britton and Zimmerman 1979; but see under Threats above). The nature reserve includes a considerable area of the favoured *Brachystegia* woodland habitat (Britton and Zimmerman 1979).

Conservation Measures Proposed Details of recommendations for the Sokoke Forest are given in Conservation Measures Proposed under Sokoke Scops Owl *Otus ireneae*.

Remarks Clarke's Weaver forms a superspecies with Weyns's Weaver *Ploceus weynsi* of Central Africa (Clancey and Williams 1959, Hall and Moreau 1970). Five other threatened bird species are known from the Sokoke Forest (see Remarks under Sokoke Scops Owl).

References

Britton, P. L. ed. (1980) *Birds of East Africa: their habitat, status and distribution.* Nairobi: EANHS.

Britton, P. L. and Zimmerman, D. A. (1979) The avifauna of Sokoke Forest, Kenya. *J. E. Afr. Nat. Hist. Soc. and Natn. Mus.* 169: 1-15.

Britton, P. L., Stuart, S. N. and Turner, D. A. (in press) East African endangered species. *Proc. V Pan-Afr. orn. Congr.*

Clancey, P. A. and Williams, J. G. (1959) On the unknown female dress and specific relationships of *Ploceus golandi* (Clarke). *Ibis* 101: 247-248.

Clarke, S. R. (1913) [A short account of a shooting expedition ... to the Lorian, British East Africa.] *Bull. Brit. Orn. Club* 31: 31-33.

Cunningham-van Someren, G. R. ed. (1981-1982) *National Museum of Kenya, Department of Ornithology Museum Avifauna News*: 19,34,63,72.

Hall, B. P. and Moreau, R. E. (1970) *An atlas of speciation in African passerine birds*. London: Trustees of the British Museum (Natural History).

Kelsey, M. G. and Langton, T. E. S. (1984) The conservation of the Arabuko-Sokoke Forest, Kenya. International Council for Bird Preservation and University of East Anglia. *International Council for Bird Preservation Study Report* no. 4.

Ripley, S. D. and Bond, G. M. (1971) Systematic notes on a collection of birds from Kenya. *Smithsonian Contrib. Zool.* 111.

Taylor, P. B. (1984) Recent Kenya records of Clarke's Weaver *Ploceus golandi* and an indication of its breeding season. *Scopus* 8: 28-29.

Williams, J. G. (1957) The re-discovery and status of *Ploceus golandi*. *Ibis* 99: 123-124.

GOLDEN-NAPED WEAVER

INDETERMINATE

Ploceus aureonucha (Sassi, 1920)

Order PASSERIFORMES

Family PLOCEIDAE
Subfamily PLOCEINAE

Summary This weaver is known only from a small part of the Ituri Forest, north of Beni in eastern Zaire, where forest clearance is taking place. It is very rare and has not been recorded since 1926.

Distribution All records of the Golden-naped Weaver have been from within a small triangle of the Ituri Forest, eastern Zaire, between Mawambi, Irumu and Beni (Chapin 1954). The species was discovered in 1910 when three specimens were collected between Beni and Mawambi in the Ituri Forest (Sassi 1920,1924). A specimen collected at Ukaika in the same year (Sassi 1920,1924) proved to be a misidentified Yellow-legged Weaver *Ploceus flavipes* (Sassi 1924, Chapin 1954; see relevant account). In 1921 a specimen was collected and a few others seen at Campi ya Wambuti, west of Irumu (Gyldenstolpe 1924). In September 1926 one was collected 48 km south of Irumu on the road to Beni and five days later two were taken from a flock of 20-25 young birds 8 km north of Beni (Chapin 1954). There have been no subsequent records.

Population Numbers are not known. This species is clearly very rare since it has eluded detection by many ornithologists who have visited the Ituri Forest.

Ecology This species is restricted to the canopy of lowland rainforest (Gyldenstolpe 1924, Chapin 1954). Most records are from dense primary forest (Gyldenstolpe 1924, Chapin 1954) although on one occasion a party of 20-25 young birds was recorded from old secondary growth in which many tall trees remained standing (Chapin 1954). It is possible that the species is usually found in parties since in 1921 a small group was seen climbing in the branches of a medium-sized tree (Gyldenstolpe 1924). The food consists of fruit and insects (Chapin 1954). An adult in breeding condition has been collected in September although independent juveniles have also been found in the same month (Chapin 1954).

Threats This species is probably in severe danger from forest clearance which in 1983 was noted as taking place around Oisha, 24 km north of Beni, and well within the range of this species (A. Prigogine *in litt.* 1983).

Conservation Measures Taken None is known.

Conservation Measures Proposed The Golden-naped Weaver can probably only be saved from extinction if the northern part of the Virunga National Park is extended westwards to include the eastern part of the Ituri Forest (Prigogine in press). A survey is also needed to ascertain whether the species does in fact still survive.

Remarks Not having been seen in the wild for over 50 years, by CITES criteria the Golden-naped Weaver may be considered extinct, one of only two bird species endemic to the African continent in this situation, the other being the Yellow-throated Serin *Serinus flavigula* (see relevant account). However, since suitable habitat survives within its known range it is likely still to survive. The Ituri Forest is important for three other threatened bird species (see Remarks under Nahan's Francolin *Francolinus nahani*).

References

Chapin, J. P. (1954) The birds of the Belgian Congo. Part 4. *Bull. Amer. Mus. Nat. Hist.* 75B.

Gyldenstolpe, N. (1924) Zoological results of the Swedish Expedition to Central Africa 1921. Vertebrata I. Birds. *Kungl. Svenska Vetensk. Akad. Handl.* Ser. 3, 1(3): 1-326.

Prigogine, A. (in press) The conservation of the avifauna of the forests of the Albertine Rift. *Proceedings of the ICBP Tropical Forest Bird Symposium, 1982.*

Sassi, M. (1920) Zwei neue Weber aus Mittelafrika. *Orn. Monatsber.* 28: 81.

Sassi, M. (1924) Beitrag zur Ornis Zentralafrikas III. *Ann. Naturhist. Mus. Wien* 38: 20-81.

YELLOW-LEGGED WEAVER   VULNERABLE
Ploceus flavipes (Chapin, 1916)

Order PASSERIFORMES   Family PLOCEIDAE
                                                      Subfamily PLOCEINAE

Summary This weaver is known only from the Ituri Forest in eastern Zaire where it appears to be rare. It has not been recorded since 1953.

Distribution The Yellow-legged Weaver is, like the Golden-naped Weaver *Ploceus aureonucha* (see relevant account), restricted to the Ituri Forest in eastern Zaire, but is more widely distributed. The type-specimen was collected at Avakubi on the Ituri River in 1913 (Chapin 1916). An earlier specimen, collected to the south-east at Ukaika in 1910 (Sassi 1920,1924), was originally misidentified as a Golden-naped Weaver (Stresemann 1925). In 1921 two specimens were collected at Campi ya Wambuti and one was taken at Simbo (Gyldenstolpe 1924). Both these localities are close to each other, to the west of Irumu (Gyldenstolpe 1924). Single specimens have been collected at Bilolo in 1950, Tungudu in the Semliki valley in 1952 and at Makayobe near the Djuma River in 1953 (Progogine 1960), but there appear to be no subsequent records. Its total range is or was probably about 7,500 km^2 (Hall and Moreau 1962).

Population Numbers are not known, but the paucity of records is an indication that it is rare.

Ecology The species appears to be restricted to lowland rainforest where it is found in the tops of tall and medium-sized trees (Gyldenstolpe 1924, Chapin 1954). The stomach of one bird was found to contain small caterpillars (Chapin 1954). A specimen in September had developing eggs in its oviduct (Chapin 1954).

Threats The species is presumably under threat from forest clearance which in 1983 was noted as taking place around Oisha, 24 km north of Beni and well within the range of this species (A. Prigogine *in litt.* 1983).

Conservation Measures Taken None is known.

Conservation Measures Proposed The Yellow-legged Weaver would be best protected if the northern part of the Virunga National Park were extended westwards to include the eastern part of the Ituri Forest (Prigogine in press). A survey is also needed to ascertain the present status of the species.

Remarks This species is sometimes placed in the genus *Malimbus* (Chapin 1916) or in a monotypic genus *Rhinoploceus* (Gyldenstolpe 1924). The Ituri Forest is important for three other threatened bird species (see Remarks under Nahan's Francolin *Francolinus nahani*).

References

Chapin, J. P. (1916) Four new birds from the Belgian Congo. *Bull. Amer. Mus. Nat. Hist.* 35: 23-29.

Chapin, J. P. (1954) The birds of the Belgian Congo. Part 4. *Bull. Amer. Mus. Nat. Hist.* 75B.

Gyldenstolpe, N. (1924) Zoological results of the Swedish Expedition to Central Africa 1921. Vertebrata I. Birds. *Kungl. Svenska Vetensk. Akad. Handl.* Ser. 3, 1(3): 1-326.

Hall, B. P. and Moreau, R. E. (1962) A study of the rare birds of Africa. *Bull. Brit. Mus. (Nat. Hist.) Zool.* 8: 313-378.

Prigogine, A. (1960) Le mâle de *Ploceus flavipes* (Chapin). *Rev. Zool. Bot. Afr.* 61: 364-365.

Prigogine, A. (in press) The conservation of the avifauna of the forests of the Albertine Rift. *Proceedings of the ICBP Tropical Forest Bird Symposium, 1982.*

Sassi, M. (1920) Zwei neue Weber aus Mittelafrika. *Orn. Monatsber.* 28: 81.

Sassi, M. (1924) Beitrag zur Ornis Zentralafrikas III. *Ann. Naturhist. Mus. Wien* 38: 20-81.

Stresemann, E. (1925) *Ploceus flavipes* (Chapin). *Orn. Monatsber.* 33: 89-90.

TANZANIAN MOUNTAIN WEAVER   RARE
Ploceus nicolli Sclater, 1931

Order PASSERIFORMES   Family PLOCEIDAE
                                                    Subfamily PLOCEINAE

Summary This forest species is restricted to three Tanzanian mountain ranges, where it is elusive and occurs at low densities. In the Usambara Mountains it is under some threat from forest destruction.

Distribution The population of the Tanzanian Mountain Weaver representing the nominate subspecies inhabits the East and West Usambara Mountains in north-eastern Tanzania (Sclater 1931), from 900 to 2,200 m, though there are no recent records from below 1,350 m, despite much fieldwork in this area (van der Willigen and Lovett 1981, D. A. Turner pers. comm. 1980). The species was discovered in 1931 when three specimens were collected at 900 m at Amani in the East Usambaras and one was taken at Lushoto in the West Usambaras, at 1,370 m (Sclater 1931, Sclater and Moreau 1933). There were also a few sight records around the same time (Sclater 1931, Sclater and Moreau 1933). There were no further records until 1962 when nine specimens were taken between 1,700 and 2,100 m in three West Usambara localities, Lushoto, Manolo and Shume (Ripley and Heinrich 1966). Since 1977 there have been several field observations at Mazumbai, 1,500 m in the West Usambaras (Stuart and van der Willigen 1978, Stuart and Turner 1980, van der Willigen and Lovett 1981, D. A. Turner pers. comm. 1980) and in 1981 there were also records from Shume up to 2,200 m and Balangai at 1,400 m, also in the West Usambaras (Stuart and Jensen 1981, SNS). Birds representing a newly described subspecies, *P. n. anderseni*, occur in the Uluguru Mountains, and in Mwanihana and Chita forests on the eastern escarpment of the Uzungwa Mountains, in east-central Tanzania (Stuart and Jensen 1981, Franzmann 1983, F. P. Jensen pers. comm. 1984). The Uluguru population is known from two specimens and one sighting (Ripley and Heinrich 1966, Britton 1980, Stuart and Jensen 1981, Franzmann 1983). One of these specimens was collected at 1,500-1,800 m in 1952 (Franzmann 1983) and the other was taken at 1,600 m in 1961 (Ripley and Heinrich 1966). The field observation was of a bird at 1,350 m in Kinole Forest in 1981 (Stuart and Jensen 1981). The Mwanihana Forest birds are known from several sightings in 1981-1982 from 1,100 to 1,700 m (Stuart and Jensen 1981, Franzmann 1983, Jensen *et al.* in press) and in 1984 a pair was seen on several occasions at 1,500 m in the forest above Chita (F. P. Jensen pers. comm. 1984).

Population Although this weaver has never been known to be numerous, a decline is believed to have taken place in the lower elevations of its range in the Usambaras (Stuart and Turner 1980). The original collector saw it on only six occasions during his first three years of residence at Amani (Sclater and Moreau 1933). It is now considered possibly extinct in the East Usambaras, where despite much searching it has apparently not been reported since the 1930s (Stuart and Hutton 1977, van der Willigen and Lovett 1981): the report (in van der Willigen and Lovett 1981) that a bird was seen there in 1963 is in error (D. A. Turner pers. comm. 1980). There have been a number of sightings in the West Usambaras since 1977, but very few considering the amount of fieldwork that has been done there; it must be a very low density bird, though population estimates can only be guesses (SNS). The population at Mazumbai is estimated at 10 pairs in a total area of 400 ha (Stuart and Turner 1980). The population of the new subspecies is impossible to judge, it being known from just two specimens and a few sightings (Ripley and Heinrich 1966, Britton 1980, Stuart and Jensen 1981, Franzmann 1983, Stuart and Jensen 1983, Jensen *et al.* in press). Like the nominate subspecies, however, it appears to be a very low density bird, at least in the Ulugurus (Stuart and Jensen in press). In the Mwanihana Forest the species appears to be more numerous than in either the Usambaras or Ulugurus, though even here it is not common (F. P. Jensen *in litt.* 1983). The rarity of both races may be the result of competition with the much commoner forest-dwelling Dark-backed Weaver *Ploceus bicolor* (Stuart and Hutton 1977).

Ecology Canopy of montane evergreen forest (Sclater and Moreau 1933, Stuart and Hutton 1977, Stuart and van der Willigen 1978, Britton 1980, van der Willigen and Lovett 1981, Franzmann 1983, D. A. Turner pers. comm. 1980). Birds have also been seen on the forest edge, in plantations and in isolated trees in cultivated areas (Sclater 1931, Sclater and Moreau 1933, van der Willigen and Lovett 1981, D. A. Turner pers. comm. 1980, SNS) but always within 100 m of the forest (Sclater and Moreau 1933, SNS). They are usually seen in mixed-species parties, often with Dark-backed Weavers, and often hang upside-down on branches like tits (Paridae) (Stuart and Hutton 1977, van der Willigen and Lovett 1981, D. A. Turner pers. comm. 1980). The diet consists of insects (Sclater and Moreau 1933).

Threats In the Usambaras the forest has been seriously reduced by clearing for subsistence agriculture, tea, cardamom and softwood plantations (Stuart and Hutton 1977, Stuart and van der Willigen 1978, van der Willigen and Lovett 1981, Rodgers and Homewood 1982b, Stuart in prep.). The forests of the Ulugurus and the eastern Uzungwa escarpment have so far suffered less encroachment (Scharff *et al.* 1982, Rodgers and Homewood 1982a).

Conservation Measures Taken Most of the remaining populations of both subspecies are in forest reserves, which provide some measure of protection to wildlife (Rodgers and Homewood 1982a,b, Scharff *et al.* 1982, Stuart in prep., SNS).

Conservation Measures Proposed A conservation proposal for the Usambara forests is being prepared for consideration by the Tanzanian government (Stuart in prep.). The forests occupied by the subspecies *anderseni* are under less imminent threat, at least at the altitudes at which this species occurs, but encroachment is nevertheless taking place (Rodgers and Homewood 1982a, Scharff *et al.* 1982). It has been suggested that a national nature reserve be established in the Uluguru forests (Scharff *et al.* 1982) and that the Mwanihana Forest in the eastern Uzungwa Mountains be included in a new park, the Mwanihana National Park (Rodgers and Homewood 1982a). It is not clear whether the Tanzanian government will implement these proposals (W. A. Rodgers *in litt.* 1983).

Remarks The case has been made for regarding *P. nicolli* as a species separate from the Olive-headed Golden Weaver *Ploceus olivaceiceps* (Franzmann 1983; also Stuart and Hutton 1977, Stuart and van der Willigen 1978). Six other threatened bird species occur in the Usambaras, three more such species occur in the Ulugurus and six more in the Uzungwas (see Remarks under the Usambara Ground Robin *Dryocichloides montanus*, the Uluguru Bush-shrike *Malaconotus alius* and the Iringa Ground Robin *D. lowei* respectively).

References

Britton, P. L. ed. (1980) *Birds of East Africa: their habitat, status and distribution.* Nairobi: EANHS.

Franzmann, N.-E., (1983) A new subspecies of the Usambara Weaver *Ploceus nicolli. Bull. Brit. Orn. Club* 103: 49-51.

Jensen, F. P., Stuart, S. N. and Brogger-Jensen, S. (in press) Altitudinal distribution of the avifauna of the Mwanihana Forest, Tanzania. *Gerfaut.*

Ripley, S. D. and Heinrich, G. H. (1966) Comments on the avifauna of Tanzania 1. *Postilla* 96.

Rodgers, W. A. and Homewood, K. M. (1982a) Biological values and conservation prospects for the forests and primate populations of the Uzungwa Mountains, Tanzania. *Biol. Conserv.* 24: 285-304.

Rodgers, W. A. and Homewood, K. M. (1982b) Species richness and endemism in the Usambara mountain forests, Tanzania. *Biol. J. Linn. Soc.* 18: 197-242.

Scharff, N., Stoltze, M. and Jensen, F. P. (1982) The Uluguru Mts., Tanzania. Report of a study-tour, 1981. Unpublished.

Sclater, W. L. (1931) [A new African weaver.] *Bull. Brit. Orn. Club* 52: 26-27.

Sclater, W. L. and Moreau, R. E. (1933) Taxonomic and field notes on some birds of north-eastern Tanganyika Territory, Part V. *Ibis* 13(3): 399-440.

Stuart, S. N. (in prep.) A forest conservation plan for the Usambara Mountains, Tanzania.

Stuart, S. N. and Hutton, J. M. eds. (1977) The avifauna of the East Usambara Mountains, Tanzania. A report compiled by the Cambridge Ornithological Expedition to East Africa, 1977. Unpublished.

Stuart, S. N. and Jensen, F. P. (1981) Further range extensions and other notable records of forest birds from Tanzania. *Scopus* 5: 106-115.

Stuart, S. N. and Jensen, F. P. (in press) The avifauna of the Uluguru Mountains, Tanzania. *Gerfaut.*

Stuart, S. N. and Turner, D. A. (1980) Some range extensions and other notable records of forest birds from eastern and northeastern Tanzania. *Scopus* 4: 36-41.

Stuart, S. N. and van der Willigen, T. A. (1978) Report of the Cambridge Ecological Expedition to Tanzania 1978. Unpublished.

van der Willigen, T. A. and Lovett, J. eds. (1981) Report of the Oxford Expedition to Tanzania 1979. Unpublished.

IBADAN MALIMBE
Malimbus ibadanensis Elgood, 1958

ENDANGERED

Order PASSERIFORMES

Family PLOCEIDAE
Subfamily PLOCEINAE

Summary This weaver is known only from a restricted area in south-western Nigeria, mainly along the interface between forest and savanna. Having a very restricted known range subject to massive habitat destruction, it is almost certainly endangered.

Distribution The Ibadan Malimbe is endemic to Nigeria. It was dis-covered at Ibadan University in 1951 (Elgood 1958,1964) and subsequent records, mainly during the 1960s, come from Ilaro, 110 km south-west of Ibadan (Button 1964,1967b), Iperu, 60 km south-south-west of Ibadan (Elgood 1975), Ife, 70 km east of Ibadan (Farmer 1979), Olokemeji, 40 km west of Ibadan (Elgood 1975) and Gambari Forest, 25 km south of Ibadan (Elgood 1975). It is possible that the species occupies all suitable areas between the Dahomey Gap and the Niger River, a total area of 60,000 km^2 (Elgood 1975) but this has not been confirmed.

Population No estimates of numbers have been made. The species has been noted as locally not uncommon around Ibadan and the Gambari Forest, 25 km south of Ibadan (Elgood 1958,1964,1975). At Ilaro it has been described as occasional (Button 1964,1967b) and at Ife it is a resident in very small numbers (Farmer 1979). Numbers appear to have declined drastically in recent years and in 1977 it was "difficult enough to find any forest, let alone birds" at Gambari (R. E. Sharland *per* J. H. Elgood pers. comm. 1983). Its appearance in gardens around Ibadan has long since ceased (J. H. Elgood *in litt.* 1983, J. A. Mackenzie *in litt.* 1984). However, several birds were seen in forest patches not far from Ibadan in 1976-1977 and in 1980 (M. Dyer pers. comm. 1983, M. E. Gartshore pers. comm. 1983).

Ecology Although sometimes seen in farmland and gardens (Elgood 1958,1964), the species is best described as a bird of forest edges and secondary growth (Elgood 1975,1982). It is usually seen in pairs, though sometimes solitarily or in groups of up to five birds, often associating with the Red-headed Malimbe *Malimbus rubricollis* (Elgood 1958,1964). Most observations have been of birds 5-15 m up in trees, especially oil palms (Elgood 1958). The breeding of the species has been summarised (Elgood 1964,1975) and birds have been seen chasing a Lesser Honeyguide *Indicator minor* from the vicinity of a nest (Button 1967a). The breeding season is not very restricted and nesting has been recorded in February, May, June, July, September, October and December (Elgood 1982).

Threats Although this species appears to have been tolerant of distur-bance to its forest environment, adapting to gardens and nearby farmland (Elgood 1958,1964), its recent apparent decline suggests that there is a limit to the degree of forest clearance that it can withstand (J. H. Elgood *in litt.* 1983). Forest clearance is so intense in south-western Nigeria (M. Dyer pers. comm. 1983, M. E. Gartshore pers. comm. 1983) that the survival prospects of the Ibadan Malimbe must now be very poor.

Conservation Measures Taken None is known.

Conservation Measures Proposed A new survey is urgently needed to determine the status of this species and to pinpoint localities where reserves might be established for its conservation.

Remarks The possibility of the Ibadan Malimbe being a hybrid between the Red-headed Malimbe and the Red-vented Malimbe *Malimbus scutatus* is not considered a plausible hypothesis (Elgood 1958, Moreau 1958). It is more likely to form a superspecies with the Red-bellied Malimbe *M. erythrogaster* which ranges widely though the equatorial forest belt of Africa from east of the Niger River to western Uganda (Elgood 1975, Hall and Moreau 1970).

References

Button, J. A. (1964) Synopsis of the status of birds at Ilaro. *Bull. Nigerian Orn. Soc.* 1(1): 5-6.

Button, J. A. (1967a) The birds of Ilaro. Part I. *Bull. Nigerian Orn. Soc.* 4(13/14): 17-27.

Button, J. A. (1967b) The birds of Ilaro. Part IIB. *Bull. Nigerian Orn. Soc.* 4(16): 10-19.

Elgood, J. H. (1958) A new species of *Malimbus*. *Ibis* 100: 621-624.

Elgood, J. H. (1964) A new species of *Malimbus*. *Bull. Nigerian Orn. Soc.* 1(3): 7-9.

Elgood, J. H. (1975) *Malimbus ibadanensis*: a fresh statement of biology and status. *Bull. Brit. Orn. Club* 95: 78-80.

Elgood, J. H. (1982) *The birds of Nigeria*. London: B.O.U. Checklist no. 4.

Farmer, R. (1979) Checklist of the birds of the Ile-Ife area, Nigeria. *Malimbus* 1: 56-64.

Hall, B. P. and Moreau, R. E. (1970) *An atlas of speciation in African passerine birds*. London: Trustees of the British Museum (Natural History).

Moreau, R. E. (1958) The *Malimbus* spp. as an evolutionary problem. *Rev. Zool. Bot. Afr.* 57: 243-255.

GOLA MALIMBE   INDETERMINATE
Malimbus ballmanni Wolters, 1974

Order PASSERIFORMES   Family PLOCEIDAE
                                                  Subfamily PLOCEINAE

Summary This recently described weaver is known only from Sierra Leone, Liberia and Ivory Coast. Its numbers are unknown and although it might be more widely distributed, it is probably in severe danger from forest destruction.

Distribution The Gola Malimbe is confined to the rainforest zone west of the Dahomey Gap, West Africa. The type-specimen was collected in 1972 between the Cavally and Keibli Rivers, north-west of Tai in south-western Ivory Coast (Wolters 1974). There have also been sight records of the species in the Gola Forest in eastern Sierra Leone between 1971 and 1976, where despite extensive searches it appears to be restricted, for no obvious reason, to a single tiny area (Field 1979). Recently ten specimens have been collected in the northern part of Grand Gedeh County in eastern Liberia (W. Gatter *in litt.* 1983). It is possible that the species occurs elsewhere in Sierra Leone, Liberia and Ivory Coast and perhaps also in Ghana and Guinea; but it is unlikely to occur to the east of the Dahomey Gap (see Remarks).

Population Numbers are not known, although records indicate that it is highly localised. In the Gola Forest birds were seen on 15 occasions between December 1971 and June 1972, and subsequently through until 1976 (Field 1979). In the northern part of Grand Gedeh County in Liberia the species has been seen on over 50 occasions in recent years (W. Gatter *in litt.* 1983).

Ecology The type-specimen was collected in forest dominated by *Eremospatha* and *Diospyros manii* trees (Wolters 1974). All records of the species from the Gola Forest are from lowland rainforest along a logging track, where it was usually seen searching through thick tangles of liana-covered branches 6-15 m above ground, though it has been seen in the top of the canopy (Field 1979). There have been several records of the bird in mixed-species bird parties (Field 1979).

Threats Forest clearance and over-exploitation are very severe within the probable range of this species (Roth 1982, Verschuren 1982,1983, Halle 1983, G. D. Field pers. comm. 1983, W. Gatter *in litt.* 1983, A. Tye *in litt.* 1983). Although the Gola Malimbe has evidently tolerated the cutting of roads through the Gola Forest (Field 1979), it is doubtless unable to withstand the large-scale commercial logging which is now taking place (G. D. Field pers. comm. 1983, A. Tye *in litt.* 1983). The forests in which this species has been recorded in Liberia are all in the process of being cleared for farming (W. Gatter *in litt.* 1983). The Tai Forest is also suffering from illegal encroachment (Roth 1982, Halle 1983, J.-M. Thiollay *in litt.* 1983). The rate of forest destruction in Africa west of the Dahomey Gap is so severe that any bird species endemic to primary forest in this region must be considered gravely at risk (see Remarks under Rufous Fishing Owl *Scotopelia ussheri* for the species in question).

Conservation Measures Taken None is known.

Conservation Measures Proposed Further studies are needed in Ivory Coast, Sierra Leone and Liberia to determine the distribution of the Gola Malimbe. If it does not occur within some national parks it is likely to be seriously endangered and immediate conservation action will be necessary. Attempts to locate the species in the Sapo National Park and the Grebo National Forest, both in Liberia, have so far been unsuccessful (W. Gatter *in litt.* 1983). Details of the protected areas of rainforest in West Africa and of the ornithological importance of Tai and Gola Forests are given in Remarks under Rufous Fishing Owl. The Gola Malimbe is perhaps most likely to occur in the huge Tai National Park in south-western Ivory Coast, which is very near to (and possibly even includes) the type-locality (but see Threats).

Remarks The birds seen in the Gola Forest from 1971 to 1976 were recognised as a new species and the name *M. golensis* was suggested (Field 1979). It was subsequently noticed that "*M. golensis*" was identical with *M. ballmanni* (Prigogine 1981). The Gola Malimbe is apparently most closely related to Rachel's Malimbe *M. racheliae* (Wolters 1974, Field 1979), which occurs to the east of the Dahomey Gap and probably, therefore, replaces it in that part of West Africa.

References

Field, G. D. (1979) A new species of *Malimbus* sighted in Sierra Leone and a review of the genus. *Malimbus* 1: 2-13.
Halle, M. (1983) Timber pressure on last Ivory Coast forest. *WWF News* 22: 2.
Prigogine, A. (1981) A new species of *Malimbus* from Sierra Leone? *Malimbus* 3:55.
Roth, H. H. (1982) We all want trees – case history of the Tai National Park. 3rd World National Parks Congress, Bali, Indonesia. Unpublished.
Verschuren, J. (1982) Hope for Liberia. *Oryx* 16: 421-427.
Verschuren, J. (1983) Conservation of tropical rain forest in Liberia. Recommendations for wildlife conservation and national parks. Gland, Switzerland: IUCN/WWF.
Wolters, H. E. (1974) Aus der Vogelsammlung des Museums Koenig. *Bonn. zool. Beitr.* 25: 283-291.

MAURITIUS FODY   ENDANGERED
Foudia rubra (Gmelin, 1789)

Order PASSERIFORMES   Family PLOCEIDAE
                                                          Subfamily PLOCEINAE

Summary This upland forest-dwelling weaver, endemic to Mauritius, suffered catastrophically from clearance of its habitat in the 1970s and continues to suffer extremely heavy nest predation by introduced animals. Provision of food-plants (it is a nectar- and insect-feeder) and some habitat creation are needed, and introduction to Réunion is counselled.

Distribution The Mauritius Fody is confined to upland areas of south-west Mauritius, Indian Ocean. On the basis of present habitat preferences, this species should have been widespread in upland forests in Mauritius before the arrival of man (Cheke 1983, in press). In the 1890s it was found in gardens in Curepipe and its neighbourhood, but in 1902-1903 it disappeared from them and was thereafter only found in forest (Carié 1904). In 1973-1975, following the cutting of Les Mares in 1972-1973, the majority of remaining birds were to be found in pockets of native vegetation throughout the high plateau south-west of Curepipe and on the upper parts of its south-facing slopes, the chief areas being Plaine Champagne, Plaine Paul, Pétrin and the Montagne Savanne ridge, with a tiny outlying group on the isolated Piton du Fouge in the extreme south-west, the total area occupied by the species being, however, only c. 35 km² (Cheke 1974,1983, in press, Temple *et al.* 1974). The patchiness of its distribution within this area is attributed to very low breeding success (see Threats). In 1979 its distribution appeared to extend from forests at the base of Montagne Savanne at the extreme east of its range to the dwarf forest around Black River Viewpoint in the west, including the dwarf forest on Plaine Champagne around Alexandra Falls and above Bel Ombre (Jones 1980); this definition of range indicates no change from the period 1973-1975 (A. S. Cheke pers. comm. 1984).

Population Already at the start of the century this species's increasing rarity was being lamented (Carié 1904) and it was thought "fast disappearing" and "a rare bird even in the south-west of the island" (Meinertzhagen 1912), and although in the 1950s birds were considered to be "making a surprisingly successful stand" against habitat change (Rountree 1951) and "not uncommon" in the right environment (Newton 1959), they were still acknowledged to be decreasing (Rountree 1951) and very local (Newton 1959). Statements concerning the plight of the species and the numbers present in the early 1970s (in Cheke 1974, Temple 1974a,b, Temple *et al.* 1974) are, in the light of recent full analysis of data, now known to have been unduly pessimistic (Cheke in press). A total of 121 territories was found in the 1974-1975 breeding season, with a further three in 1973-1974 that were not checked in 1974-1975: given suitable habitat not censused and allowing for varying density, the total breeding population in the latter season was estimated at around 250 pairs, although high density in some areas was thought to have been caused by forest clearance displacing birds from Les Mares, so that the carrying capacity of habitat in 1974-1975 was probably only 150-170 pairs, "normal" population density being 6-7(-12) pairs per km² (Cheke 1983). In 1979 the species was thought very rare, with a population of 20-40 pairs (Jones 1980), but the observer now regards this as an underestimate (Cheke in press). At Mount Cocotte on 16 May 1984, during the last half-hour before sunset, about 60 birds flew past, singly, in pairs or loose groups, coming from the north-west and heading for the south-facing slopes of the mountain (C. G. Jones *in litt.* 1984).

Ecology The preferred habitat of this species has been given as areas of native scrub vegetation with a few scattered taller trees, also low native scrub and, to some extent, native forest, birds venturing only rarely outside native vegetation (Temple *et al.* 1974; also Temple 1974a), although an earlier characterisation of habitat referred to forest and bush generally above 450 m, with birds utilising taller trees, woodlands of exotics such as Japanese red cedar *Cryptomeria japonica* and eucalyptus as well as the remnants of old endemic forest, but even thick scrub composed of guava *Psidium cattleianum* and privet *Ligustrum robustum* var. *walkeri* (Newton 1959). Subsequent analysis has shown that climatic constraints appear to determine distribution and therefore habitat usage: the population is mostly above 450 m (but descends to 300 m on the southern scarp at Bel Ombre and Combo) and is almost entirely contained within the zone where the mean January temperature is below 23°C and annual rainfall is above 2,800 mm, birds occurring in all types of native forest – most of which is low, open and bushy – within these limitations (Cheke 1983, in press; also Cheke 1975a,1980); this correlation explains the species's rarity in or absence from otherwise suitable habitat, since high humidity is associated with a good growth of epiphytes and the rapid rotting of dead wood, both of which are necessary for its food supply (Cheke 1983, in press). Food is insects, nectar and small fruit, foraged from near ground level to the tops of tall trees (Newton 1959, Temple *et al.* 1974, Cheke 1983, in press). Insects and their larvae are taken by probing or stripping dead wood and searching bark and epiphytes in the manner of a nuthatch (Sittidae), though also directly from leaves and flowers and even out of spiders' webs (Newton 1959, Cheke 1983, in press); plants searched in this manner are always native, e.g. *Sideroxylon, Labourdonnaisia glauca, Mimusops petiolaris, Calophyllum tacama- haca* and *Syzygium glomeratum* (Cheke 1983, in press), and in the heath zone *Philippia abietina* (Procter and Salm 1974). Nectar is taken from native *Eugenia*, fandamane *Aphloia theiformis* and introduced swamp mahogany *Eucalyptus robusta* and bottlebrush *Callistemon citrinus*, berries from native *Eugenia* species and introduced *Ardisia crenata* and *Ossaea marginata* (Cheke 1983, in press). Breeding extends from October to the end of February (Newton 1959), as early as September and/or as late as March in some years (Cheke 1983, in press). Males are then highly territorial, territories 4-8 ha in area (Cheke 1983, in press); a report of territories being 8-20 ha in size (Cheke 1980) was derived from incomplete analysis of data (Cheke 1983, in press). In one report, the nest is located very near the ground and rarely more than 2 m up (Temple *et al.* 1974) but this seems to refer to the Mauritius Olive White-eye *Zosterops chloronothus* (A. S. Cheke pers. comm. 1984); other accounts give nest height as 1.5-5 m (Hartlaub 1877), 1-16 m (Newton 1959) and 2-9 m (Cheke 1983, in press), in dense thicket or the thick foliage of canopy (Newton 1959, Cheke 1983, in press). Clutch-size is two or (perhaps more usually) three (Hartlaub 1877, Newton 1959, Temple *et al.* 1974, Staub 1976, Cheke 1983, in press). Breeding success is evidently extremely low: of five nests for which the outcome was known, 1973-1975, none was successful, and in each of the two seasons in this period only one observation of free-flying young was made (Cheke 1983, in press). Birds tend to remain in pairs throughout the year and are not gregarious (Newton 1959), although some join bird parties composed chiefly of Mascarene Grey White-eyes *Z. borbonicus* outside the breeding season, and even when breeding may join them as they pass through the territory (Gill 1971, Cheke 1983). Although very tame (Meinertzhagen 1912), birds are silent and easily overlooked except in the breeding season (Newton 1959).

Threats A general account of the problems facing the endemic forest-dependent birds of Mauritius is given in Threats under Mauritius Kestrel *Falco punctatus*. Two major factors have brought the Mauritius Fody to its present situation: habitat destruction and nest predation. The (World Bank financed) clearance in 1971-1974 of half (c. 2,800 ha) of the upland *Sideroxylon-Helichrysum* dwarf forest at Les Mares on Plaine Champagne resulted in the loss of probably 200 pairs, thus more than halving the population (Jones 1980, Cheke 1983). Extremely low breeding success is attributed to nest predation: of the five nests that failed, 1973-1975 (see Ecology), four were destroyed by predators and one by a cyclone; introduced crab-eating macaques *Macaca fascicularis* were implicated in two instances, monkeys or black rats *Rattus rattus* in the other two (Cheke 1983, in press). These two mammals are probably the most serious predators (Newton 1959, Cheke 1983, in press), but the introduced mongoose *Herpestes edwardsi* possibly also destroys very low nests (Temple *et al.* 1974), although it is probably not much to blame (Cheke in press). That this species was regarded as well below the carrying capacity of the habitat in 1973-1975 as a result of this predation of nests, and despite the displacement of large numbers of birds during that period owing to the habitat destruction referred to above (Cheke 1983, in press), is an indication of the very serious nature of this problem. The introduced Madagascar Fody *Foudia madagascariensis* does not appear to compete directly with the Mauritius Fody, but has possibly displaced it from exotic or marginal habitat over much of the island (Newton 1959, Cheke 1983, in press).

Conservation Measures Taken This species has long been protected by law (Meinertzhagen 1912) and in 1974 its remaining native forest habitat received almost complete protection when the Macabé/Bel Ombre Nature Reserve was created through the linking of existing reserves at Petrin, Macabé and Bel Ombre by the addition of Les Mares and Plaine Champagne, forming a large block covering 3,594 ha (Owadally 1976; see map in Procter and Salm 1974). An attempt to introduce the species to the neighbouring French island of Réunion (see Conservation Measures Proposed) in 1975 was hampered by regulations, a postal strike, Cyclone Gervaise and the availability of personnel (Cheke 1975b,1980, Temple 1975,1976): on 12 February 1975, three birds (two males, one female) were released in the Forêt de Bébour on Réunion, having been captured on Mauritius the previous month in areas at risk of clearance (Cheke 1975a,b,1980,1983, in press), a brief, unsuccessful attempt at relocating the birds (or their offspring) being made in October 1978 (Cheke 1979, in press). No further introduction of birds was possible (Cheke 1980). Three birds (two males, one female) were also released at Montagne Lagrave in central Mauritius but were not seen subsequently (Cheke 1983, in press).

Conservation Measures Proposed In 1974 the declaration of the species's strongholds as reserves, the protection of all existing islands of native or largely native vegetation on the high plateau, and the control or elimination of monkeys there was considered the "ideal solution" (Cheke 1974), essential (Temple 1974a) and urgent (Temple *et al.* 1974). The creation of habitat by a careful admixture of evergreen trees, on a commercial basis (see Conservation Measures Proposed under Mauritius Cuckoo-shrike *Coracina typica*) might prove beneficial to this species (Cheke 1978; also Jones and Owadally 1982). The introduction and establishment of two species of nectar-producing shrubs on the high plateau (see Conservation Measures Proposed under Mauritius Olive White-eye) should also benefit the Mauritius Fody (Cheke 1978). Captive breeding has been discounted as an option (Cheke 1974), at least until success has been achieved with the Rodrigues Fody *Foudia flavicans* (Jones 1980; see relevant account). Introduction of the species to Réunion has been attempted (see Conservation Measures Taken), and is urged on the basis that monkeys are absent from the island and that there are extensive tracts of wet montane forest ("bois de couleurs") very similar to that (formerly) at Les Mares, with a high degree of species overlap in the composition of the vegetation; there would be no risk to cultivations and plantations, no risk from poaching, no competition with (or other consequences for) the endemic birds of the island, and no great danger to the birds from the Réunion Harrier *Circus maillardi* (Cheke 1974,1975). This measure has been argued as biogeographically valid (Temple 1981) and given tentative support (C. G. Jones and A. W. Owadally *in litt.* 1982; also Barré and Barau 1982, Moutou 1983). However, several considerations arise: (a) in the first place, whether or not translocation is to be attempted, the species needs to be re-censused as a matter of extreme urgency; (b) confirmation is required that the climatic features now considered to determine its distribution in Mauritius (see Ecology) are similar at the preferred release-site on Réunion, the Forêt de Bébour, or at one of the alternatives (Forêt du Grand Matarum, Bras Sec: Cheke 1975a); (c) at least five pairs (Cheke 1975a) and preferably ten or more should be used (ideally at the start of the breeding season: Temple 1976); (d) released birds should be fully monitored and preferably radio-tracked; (e) a short-term campaign is desirable to eliminate monkeys from the particular area of Mauritius from which birds are caught, so that breeding success over one or two seasons could to some extent compensate for the birds lost to Réunion. Further consideration should also be given to the introduction of birds to Montagne Lagrave in central Mauritius. Work to safeguard this species will now proceed within the framework of the Mauritius Wildlife Research and Conservation Programme (see Conservation Measures Taken under Mauritius Kestrel).

Remarks It is a sad reflection on the impact of Red Data Books to read that, in May 1970, a year or more before clearance began at Les Mares, an entry on this species was published by Vincent (1966-1971) "in a 'last ditch' attempt to emphasize the need for immediate action" to save it. This attempt has yet to begin.

References

Barré, N. and Barau, A. (1982) *Oiseaux de la Réunion*. St.-Denis [Réunion]: Imprimerie Arts Graphiques Modernes.

Carié, P. (1904) Observations sur quelques oiseaux de l'île Maurice. *Ornis* 12: 121-128.

Cheke, A. S. (1974) British Ornithologists' Union Mascarene Islands Expedition: interim report on the Mauritian Fody *Foudia rubra*. Unpublished.

Cheke, A. S. (1975a) Proposition pour introduire à la Réunion des oiseaux rares de l'île Maurice. *Info-Nature* no. 12: 25-29.

Cheke, A. S. (1975b) British Ornithologists' Union Mascarene Islands Expedition: official report on the introduction of the Mauritius Fody *Foudia rubra* to Réunion. Unpublished.

Cheke, A. S. (1978) Recommendations for the conservation of Mascarene vertebrates. Conservation memorandum no. 3 (arising out of the B.O.U. Mascarene Islands Expedition). Unpublished.

Cheke, A. S. (1979) The Rodrigues Fody *Foudia flavicans*. A brief history of its decline, and a report on the 1978 expedition. *Dodo* 15 [1978]: 12-19.

Cheke, A. S. (1980) Urgency and inertia in the conservation of endangered island species, illustrated by Rodrigues. *Proc. IV Pan-Afr. orn. Congr.*: 355-359.

Cheke, A. S. (1983) Status and ecology of the Mauritius Fody *Foudia rubra*, an endangered species. *Natn. Geog. Soc. Res. Reports* 15: 43-56.

Cheke, A. S. (in press) The surviving native land-birds of Mauritius. In A. W. Diamond, ed. *Studies of Mascarene island birds*. Cambridge: Cambridge University Press.

Gill, F. B. (1971) Ecology and evolution of the sympatric Mascarene white-eyes, *Zosterops borbonica* and *Zosterops olivacea*. *Auk* 88: 35-60.

Hartlaub, G. (1877) *Die Vögel Madagascars und der benachbarten Inselgruppen*. Halle.

Jones, C. G. (1980) The conservation of the endemic birds and bats of Mauritius and Rodriguez (a progress report and proposal for further activities). Unpublished.

Jones, C. G. and Owadally, A. W. (1982) Conservation priorities for Mauritius and Rodrigues. Report submitted to ICBP, July. Unpublished.

Meinertzhagen, R. (1912) On the birds of Mauritius. *Ibis* (9)6: 82-108.

Moutou, F. (1983) Propositions pour la réintroduction à la Réunion d'espèces aujourd'hui disparues. *Info-Nature* no. 20: 49-50.

Newton, R. (1959) Notes on the two species of *Foudia* in Mauritius. *Ibis* 101: 240-243.

Owadally, A. W. (1976) *Annual report of the Forestry Service for the year 1974*. Port Louis, Mauritius: L. Carl Achille, Government Printer.

Procter, J. and Salm, R. (1974) Conservation in Mauritius 1974. IUCN/WWF consultancy report for Government of Mauritius. Unpublished.

Rountree, F. G. R. (1951) Some aspects of bird-life in Mauritius. *Proc. Roy. Soc. Arts Sci. Mauritius* 1(2): 83-96.

Staub, F. (1976) *Birds of the Mascarenes and Saint Brandon*. Port Louis, Mauritius: Organisation Normale des Enterprises.

Temple, S. A. (1974a) Appendix 6. The native fauna of Mauritius: 1, the land birds. In J. Procter and R. Salm, Conservation in Mauritius 1974. IUCN/WWF consultancy report for Government of Mauritius. Unpublished.

Temple, S. A. (1974b) Wildlife in Mauritius today. *Oryx* 12: 584-590.

Temple, S. A. (1975) A report on the conservation program in Mauritius, 15 October. Unpublished.

Temple, S. A. (1976) Conservation of endemic birds and other wildlife on Mauritius. A progress report and proposal for future activities. Unpublished.

Temple, S. A. (1981) Applied island biogeography and the conservation of endangered island birds in the Indian Ocean. *Biol. Conserv.* 20: 147-161.

Temple, S. A., Staub, J. J. F. and Antoine, R. (1974) Some background information and recommendations on the preservation of the native flora and fauna of Mauritius. Unpublished report to the Government of Mauritius.

Vincent, J. (1966-1971) *Red data book, 2: Aves*. Morges, Switzerland: IUCN.

SEYCHELLES FODY   RARE
Foudia sechellarum E. Newton, 1867

Order PASSERIFORMES   Family PLOCEIDAE
                                              Subfamily PLOCEINAE

Summary This species is now confined to three islands – Cousin, Cousine and Frégate – in the Seychelles with a combined surface area of less than 3 km^2. It is abundant on Cousin and fairly widespread on the other two. Its survival may depend on the continuing absence of rats from these islands, but competition from an introduced congener may yet constitute a threat.

Distribution The Seychelles Fody (locally Toc-toc) occurs on the small islands of Cousin (27 ha), Cousine (c. 50 ha) and Frégate (210 ha), in the Seychelles archipelago. In the last century it was found on Marianne (Newton 1867, Oustalet 1878, Ridgway 1896), Frégate (Oustalet 1878), Cousine (Oustalet 1878), Cousin (Ridgway 1896) and reportedly La Digue (Newton 1867), though it was not seen there in 1871 (Pike 1872): this hearsay evidence of past occurrence on La Digue was recently considered acceptable, as was unpublished hearsay of former populations on Aride (Diamond and Feare 1980). Two specimens in BMNH, labelled from Praslin and dated 1907 (Moreau 1960, Crook 1961), may have come from Cousin (Gaymer *et al.* 1969). Since 1940, breeding populations have been confined to Frégate, Cousin and Cousine (Vesey-Fitzgerald 1940, Crook 1960, 1961, Gaymer *et al.* 1969). A single bird has been recorded on Bird Island (Diamond and Feare 1980), and an introduction to D'Arros in the Amirantes has been attempted (Gaymer *et al.* 1969, Penny 1974).

Population An estimated 50-100 were seen on Marianne in 1867, when the species was reportedly "not plentiful" on La Digue (Newton 1867). In the 1930s it was considered abundant on Frégate, Cousin and Cousine (Vesey-Fitzgerald 1940). In 1959, the populations were estimated at 250-300 on Frégate, 105 on Cousin, and 80 on Cousine, with somewhat lower numbers for the introduced Madagascar Fody *Foudia madagascariensis* (Crook 1960). Despite apparent two-fold (and more) increases in the numbers of the latter species, population estimates in 1964-1965 were 250-350 on Frégate, 400-600 on Cousin, and 100-150 on Cousine (Gaymer *et al.* 1969). In 1975 it was guessed that numbers on Cousin had reached about 1,000 birds, with only 30-40 pairs of Madagascar Fodies (Diamond 1975); the birds were again guessed to number about 1,000 in 1980-1981 (Bathe and Bathe 1982), with c. 20 pairs of Madagascar Fodies in early 1982 (Phillips 1982a).

Ecology Many of the Seychelles Fody's characteristics indicate that it was originally a forest species, but its present refuges do not coincide with relict patches of endemic forest (Crook 1961). As a generalist feeder, its habitat constraints appear to be minimal: in one study on Cousin, 28% of feeding observations were in *Casuarina equisetifolia*, 20% in *Pisonia grandis*, 12% in *Morinda citrifola*, 8% in *Cocos nucifera*, 6% in *Ficus reflexa* and 4% (probably more) in the herb *Achyranthes aspera* (Bathe and Bathe 1982), while in another, *Casuarina* and

Morinda were the most important plants for feeding, with *Pisonia*, *Cocos* and *Carica papaya* fairly extensively used (Lloyd 1973). Birds exploit food-sources at any height and range widely to visit them (but see below concerning territories), the diet being highly catholic: insects and other invertebrates caught on leaves, in cracks in bark, among flowers and by fly-catching, seeds of *Casuarina*, nectar from *Morinda*, *Kalanchoe pinnata*, *Musa sapienta* and possibly *Cocos*, fruit whenever available (especially in the dry south-east monsoon when, on Cousin, they are an important source of moisture, birds gathering in the island's few *Carica* trees and squabbling over their yield), young skinks and geckos, gecko eggs, fish scavenged beneath seabird colonies, fallen and unattended eggs of seabirds, notably Fairy Tern *Gygis alba* and Black Noddy *Anous tenuirostris* (birds following parties of visitors to Cousin, systematically searching for nests of disturbed seabirds), domestic scraps (Lloyd 1973; also Bathe and Bathe 1982). Of 94 invertebrates extracted from vomitus of 23 birds, only 16% were active jumping or flying species: larvae were commonly found, also the fierce ant *Odontomachus troglodytes* (other ants were apparently largely avoided), eggs of (probably) the shield bug *Bathycoelia*, and beetles (Bathe and Bathe 1982); certain birds specialise in taking (e.g) grubs and paralysed geometrid larvae from cells of potter wasps, termites by breaking open their earthen trails, and ant pupae in nests (Bathe and Bathe 1982; also Lloyd 1973). On Frégate, feeding observations were 72% on insects, 25% on seeds (notably the vetch *Crotolaria anagroides*), and 3% on rotting fruit, 45% of all such observations concerning insect-gleaning on the undersides of palm leaves (Crook 1961); on Cousin, 51% were on insects, 38% on fruit and seeds, and 11% on nectar (Bathe and Bathe 1982). When feeding on insects in foliage, birds are less agile than the Seychelles Warbler *Acrocephalus sechellensis* (see relevant account), taking fewer flying insects (apart from termite alates), instead using the bill to pull open rolled-up leaves, break off pieces of bark and dead wood, open up flowers and the pinnae of palm fronds, and catching the animals thus exposed (Lloyd 1973; also Crook 1961, Bathe and Bathe 1982). The young are fed on insects (Crook 1960). During the day there is a decline in the use of *Morinda* and an increase in that of *Musa*, presumably owing to diurnal changes in their nectar supply, with an increase in feeding on *Casuarina* seeds in the afternoon and before dusk and a peak of insect-feeding in *Pisonia* from 09.00 to 12.00 hrs (Lloyd 1973); the proportion of insect food rises while nectar declines through the day (Bathe and Bathe 1982). Slight peaks in feeding activity, February/April and October/November, corresponded with increased food availability in, respectively, *Casuarina* and *Pisonia*, but feeding activity showed no correlation with nesting, which appears to extend throughout the year (Bathe and Bathe 1982), though possibly with greater intensity in the rainy season (Crook 1961). Nesting on Frégate is solitary (successive nests are built close together, this possibly explaining an earlier report of breeding in colonies), most nests being placed in bushy, "twiggy" trees, mainly oranges and limes, clutch-size generally two (Crook 1961; also Moreau 1960). On Cousin birds are reported to be non-territorial at least for much of the year, this allowing a less restricted choice of food-plants (Bathe and Bathe 1982); on fledging, the young bird moves away from the nest-site, often a considerable distance, and usually with the female parent (which continues to feed it), the male often remaining near the nest for at least a while (Phillips 1982a,b). However, those on Frégate hold territories (normally not contiguous) of 30-50 m radius and may remain in or near them throughout the period of reproductive inactivity, probably not moving much about the island and maintaining the pair-bond for several years and perhaps for life (Crook 1961); but although they keep in pairs or small family parties, they gather occasionally, e.g. to drink, to exploit localised food sources, and to roost (Crook 1961). Although birds are very confiding on Cousin they become extremely shy in the vicinity of the nest, and although they frequently attempt to breed success apppears low (N. J. Phillips and V. E. Wood *in litt.* 1984).

Threats The extinction of this species on certain islands has been attributed to the combined effect of rapid felling of the endemic vegetation and the appearance there of rats *Rattus*, mice *Mus* and cats, these animals being responsible for its absence from Félicité where much endemic vegetation remains (Crook 1961). Given the survival of the species on islands with heavily modified vegetation, one of which (Frégate) holds (or at least held) both cats and mice (Crook 1961), rats clearly emerge as the major and perhaps only cause of local extinction (see also Remarks). Competition from Madagascar Fodies was thought possibly responsible for its very restricted distribution (Vesey-Fitzgerald 1940, Moreau 1960), but an investigation found no evidence of this (e.g. Madagascar Fodies are largely granivorous, Seychelles Fodies largely insectivorous: details under Ecology) and instead placed the blame on the introduction of rodents and cats (Crook 1961). However, since the Madagascar Fody becomes insectivorous when breeding it may be premature to assume that effects of competition will be negligible in the long term (Gaymer *et al.* 1969). Moreover, as considered possible, the Madagascar Fody appears to be extending its breeding season from the September/March period (Crook 1960): in August 1976 birds were seen on Praslin (feeding on insects and nectar) that had apparently bred a month earlier (Evans 1977). Finally, the Madagascar Fody is known to be capable of imitative foraging (e.g. Greig-Smith 1978) and on Frégate, where it has been established much longer than Cousin or Cousine, it has learnt its congener's major feeding method of gleaning insects from the undersides of coconut leaves (Diamond 1973). Several members of the endemic herpetofauna are suspected nest-predators (Crook 1961). It would be surprising if the introduced Indian Mynah *Acridotheres tristis* were not a serious nest-predator on Frégate. On Cousin, the ultimate domination of the vegetation by *Pisonia* as currently planned and the permitted die-off of *Casuarina* as proposed (see Threats and Conservation Measures Proposed under Seychelles Warbler) seem unlikely to be negative influences on the Seychelles Fody population since *Morinda* continues to grow in mature residual *Pisonia* stands (N. J. Phillips *in litt.* 1984).

Conservation Measures Taken Cousin Island, where the Seychelles Fody is now most plentiful, has been managed by ICBP since 1968 as a nature reserve, and in 1975 was created a Strict Nature Reserve by the Seychelles Government (Diamond 1975). Cats are now heavily reduced and perhaps wholly eradicated from Frégate (see Conservation Measures Taken under Seychelles Magpie-robin *Copsychus sechellarum*) and also Cousine (H. V. Bathe *in litt.* 1984). In 1965 five birds were taken to D'Arros in the Amirantes in an attempt at introduction

(Gaymer *et al.* 1969); birds were claimed still to be present in 1968 (Penny 1974) but none was seen in 1976 (Stoddart and Coe 1979).

Conservation Measures Proposed Probably the single most important requisite is to maintain Cousin, Cousine and Frégate free of rats (see Remarks). Introduction to other suitable islands was recommended in 1960 in order to avoid disasters caused by introduced predators, fires, extensive vegetation changes, etc. (Crook 1960): despite the unexplained extinction of the species on Aride, this island seems a major candidate for such an experiment. Removal of bushy-topped trees (used for nesting) should not be allowed to become extensive (Loustau-Lalanne 1962). On Frégate, the suggested elimination of Indian Mynahs (see Conservation Measures Proposed under Seychelles Magpie-robin) would seem likely to benefit the fodies (see Threats). On Cousin and elsewhere, the planting of certain seed- and fruit-producing trees, such as the relatively highly utilised *Acalypha indica* (Bathe and Bathe 1982), might serve to stabilise or increase food-supply, and some *Casuarina* planted inland would probably be useful in offsetting the loss of coastal *Casuarina* under current policy (see Threats).

Remarks It has recently emerged that fodies (probably the Red-headed Forest Fody *Foudia eminentissima*) may have been present on Astove, Cosmoledo and Assumption in 1878, and their early extinction there is considered attributable to rats (Diamond 1981, Prys-Jones *et al.* 1981), which are known to inflict severe damage on breeding Aldabra Fodies *F. e. aldabrana* (Frith 1976).

References

Bathe, H. and Bathe, G. (1982) Feeding studies of three endemic landbirds, *Acrocephalus (= Bebrornis) sechellensis* (Seychelles Brush Warbler), *Foudia sechellarum* (Seychelles Fody), and *Nectarinia dussumieri* (Seychelles Sunbird), on Cousin Island, Seychelles, with implications for their conservation through vegetation management. Unpublished.

Crook, J. H. (1960) The present status of certain rare land birds of the Seychelles Islands. Seychelles Government Bulletin.

Crook, J. H. (1961) The fodies of the Seychelles Islands. *Ibis* 103a: 517-548.

Diamond, A. W. (1973) Report on a visit to Frigate Island, L'Ilot and St.Marie, 17-20 November 1973. Cousin Island Research Station, Techn. Rep. 4. ICBP, unpublished.

Diamond, A. W. (1975) Cousin Island Nature Reserve management plan 1975-1979. ICBP (London), unpublished.

Diamond, A. W. and Feare, C. J. (1980) Past and present biogeography of central Seychelles birds. *Proc. IV Pan-Afr. orn. Congr.*: 89-98.

Diamond, E. P. (1981) An early report of the flora and fauna of the Aldabra group. *Atoll Res. Bull.* no. 255: 1-10.

Evans, P. G. H., ed. (1977) Aberdeen University Expedition to Praslin, Seychelles, 1976: preliminary report. Unpublished.

Frith, C. B. (1976) A twelve-month study of the Aldabran Fody *Foudia eminentissima aldabrana*. *Ibis* 118: 155-178.

Gaymer, R., Blackman, R. A. A., Dawson, P. G., Penny, M. and Penny, C. M. (1969) The endemic birds of Seychelles. *Ibis* 111: 157-176.

Greig-Smith, P. W. (1978) Imitative foraging in mixed-species flocks of Seychelles birds. *Ibis* 120: 233-235.

Lloyd, D. E. B. (1973) Habitat utilisation by land birds of Cousin Island, and the Seychelles (incomplete). Cousin Island Research Station, Techn. Rep. 5. ICBP, unpublished.

Loustau-Lalanne, P. (1962) Land birds of the granitic islands of the Seychelles. *Seychelles Soc. Occ. Publ.* 1.

Moreau, R. E. (1960) The Ploceine weavers of the Indian Ocean islands. *J. Orn.* 101: 29-49.

Newton, E. (1867) On the land-birds of the Seychelles archipelago. *Ibis* (2)3: 335-360.

Oustalet, M. E. (1878) Etude sur la faune ornithologique des Iles Seychelles. *Bull. Soc. Philomath. Paris* (7)2: 161-206.

Penny, M. (1974) *The birds of Seychelles and the outlying islands.* London: Collins.

Phillips, J. (1982a) Forty-fifth report of the Scientific Administrator, 1st January – 31st March 1982, Cousin Island, Seychelles. ICBP British Section, unpublished.

Phillips, J. (1982b) Forty-sixth report of the Scientific Administrator, 1st April – 30th June 1982, Cousin Island, Seychelles. ICBP British Section, unpublished.

Pike, N. (1872) A visit to the Seychelles Islands. *Trans. Roy. Soc. Arts Sci. Mauritius* N.S. 6: 83-143.

Prys-Jones, R. P., Prys-Jones, M. S. and Lawley, J. C. (1981) The birds of Assumption Island, Indian Ocean: past and future. *Atoll Res. Bull.* no. 248.

Ridgway, R. (1896) On birds collected by Doctor W. L. Abbott in the Seychelles, Amirantes, Gloriosa, Assumption, Aldabra, and adjacent islands, with notes on habits, etc., by the collector. *Proc. U. S. Natn. Mus.* 18 [1895]: 509-546.

Stoddart, D. R. and Coe, M. J. (1979) Geography and ecology of D'Arros Island. *Atoll Res. Bull.* no. 223: 3-17.

Vesey-Fitzgerald, D. (1940) The birds of the Seychelles. I. The endemic birds. *Ibis* (14)4: 480-489.

RODRIGUES FODY   ENDANGERED
Foudia flavicans A. Newton, 1865

Order PASSERIFORMES   Family PLOCEIDAE
                                                      Subfamily PLOCEINAE

Summary Competition from the introduced Madagascar Fody *F. mada-gascariensis*, combined with loss of mature forest, and the impact of cyclones, has rendered this insectivorous weaver, endemic to the island of Rodrigues in the Indian Ocean, in danger of extinction for as long as it takes either to establish a healthy (i.e. entirely self-sustaining) captive stock or to introduce it successfully to another island. Recent evidence that black rats *Rattus rattus* are now on Rodrigues appears to make the situation highly critical.

Distribution The Rodrigues Fody is confined to a small area on the northern slopes of the island of Rodrigues (part of Mauritius) in the Indian Ocean. In 1864 birds were found west of Port Mathurin in the north of the island, and in the far south-west (Newton 1865), and it seems very probable – although it was not explicitly stated (*contra* Vinson 1964, Cheke 1974,1979a) – that the species was then widespread. By 1930 it had retreated to wooded areas on higher ground, being especially noted at Les Choux on the slopes of Mont Malartic (Vinson 1964) and this situation, with birds throughout the *Syzygium* (i.e. *Eugenia*) thickets covering the spine of the island from Grant Montagne in the east to Mont Malartic in the west, continued until the late 1950s or early 1960s (Cheke in press). Following felling of forests at various localities including Les Choux, post-1965 records have been almost exclusively from Solitude, Cascade Pigeon and Sygangue, these all being (in) adjacent north-facing valleys above Port Mathurin on the central-north slopes of the island (Cheke 1974). In 1974 a comprehensive survey of Rodrigues, with every area describable as wooded being visited, resulted in the plotting of 36 "sites" for the species, 27 at Solitude (all in an area of 16 ha), seven in Cascade Pigeon and two in Sygangue, birds also moving in December to Roseaux, Vangar and above Gros Mangue, these sites all being close to Solitude (Cheke 1974, in press). In early 1982 the main distribution was still at Solitude and Cascade Pigeon, with some birds also at Sygangue, Roseaux and Vangar, with one further to the south at Mont Lubin (Jones 1983); in April 1983 the species was found in all these localities and at St.Gabriel (see Population). A pair on Ile aux Crabes in July 1970 was probably blown there by a cyclone, there being no records before or since (Cheke in press; also Staub 1973, Cheke 1974).

Population Birds were "exceedingly numerous" in 1864 (Newton 1865), "very abundant" a decade later (Slater c. 1875), "still relatively common" in 1930 but evidently in a "steady decline" at the start of the 1960s (Vinson 1964); a "substantial population" was, however, encountered in Cascade Pigeon in 1964 (Gill 1967). It is believed the species was reduced to as few as five or six pairs after Cyclone Monica in 1968 and, after a minor recovery, to seven or eight pairs after Cyclone Fabienne in 1972 (Gill 1967, Cheke 1979a, in press). In early 1974 the population was still only 20-30 pairs plus a number of unattached males, though in

July juveniles were counted in 12 territories (Cheke 1974). There were 50-60 pairs in 1976 (Cheke 1980) and roughly 100 pairs in September 1978, when four pairs and 16 unpaired birds (eight males, eight females) were taken for captive breeding (Cheke 1979a,1980, in press) and five birds were released in another part of the island (see Conservation Measures Taken). In April 1979, following Cyclone Celine II, there were 42 pairs and seven unpaired males, all of these being at Solitude except five pairs at Cascade Pigeon and three at La Source (Mungroo 1979), these results being rounded up to 60 pairs (Cheke 1979a, Jones 1980), since many birds were believed missed (Y. Mungroo *per* C. G. Jones *in litt.* 1984). In October/November 1981 72 territories were found, with active pairs in 55, only males being located with certainty in the other 17 (Carroll 1981; also Carroll 1982, Jones 1983) – the population was then also reported as 200 birds (Jones 1982a; see Remarks) – and, following the close passage of Cyclone Damia, in February/March 1982 these had reduced to an estimated 60 pairs: 111 birds were counted (148 estimated), 60 (80 estimated) at Solitude, 37 (54 estimated) at Cascade Pigeon, nine at Roseaux/Vangar, four at Sygangue and one at Mont Lubin (Jones 1983). A survey in early April 1983 yielded the following results: 90-91 birds were counted (110-112 estimated), 44 (55 estimated) at Solitude, 27-28 (35 estimated) at Cascade Pigeon, nine (10-12 estimated) at Roseaux/Vangar, six at Sygangue, two at Mont Lubin and two at St.Gabriel (C. G. Jones *in litt.* 1984). This reduction in numbers may partly be explained by almost no breeding (or at least breeding success) in the months prior to the survey, and to the suspected under-counting of females (C. G. Jones *in litt.* 1984).

Ecology The species inhabits tall (up to 20 m high) mixed evergreen forest (though tolerating a high proportion of deciduous tecoma *Tabebuia pallida*), important trees being *Swietenia mahogani, Araucaria cunninghami, Vitex cuneata, Mangifera indica, Elaeodendron orientale, Terminalia catappa, T. arjuna, Cinnamomum camphora, Pterocarpus indicus, Aleurites moluccana* and *Syzygium jambos* (Cheke 1978b; for further details and review see Cheke in press). It is impossible to judge whether clearings or forest edges are important (all birds of necessity have access to them) but the variety of trees may be crucial; moreover, the extremely limited dispersal of young birds indicates that natal location helps determine habitat "choice" (Cheke in press). The concentration of birds at Solitude in 1974 was inexplicable in terms of vegetation but was possibly related to lack of disturbance, while the species's confinement to three north-facing valleys may have been the result of cyclones (Cheke 1974). In 1864 the species was apparently found fairly near the coast in hilly grassland with scattered trees and in an area of flat rock with "some stunted growth" (Newton 1865), and its retreat from such areas is considered the result of competition (see Threats). Birds forage by gleaning on flowers, leaves and twigs, sometimes probing bark, in the manner of a large tit (Paridae); food is arthropods, chiefly insects (stick insects, black ants, coccids, planthoppers, leaf-rollers) and spiders; also nectar of jamrose *Syzygium jambos* and tecoma *Tabebuia pallida* (Gill 1967, Staub 1973, Cheke 1974, in press) and, when available, the seeds of *Casuarina equisetifolia* (C. G. Jones *in litt.* 1984). Breeding seems opportunistic and not clearly or regularly seasonal, presumably related to the inconsistency of the weather (for details see Cheke in press).

Araucaria is evidently favoured for nesting in, if present in the territory; otherwise *Syzygium, Swietenia, Ravenala, Psidium, Mangifera* and *Eucalyptus* are generally used (Cheke in press). Clutch-size is three (Cheke in press), sometimes two (C. G. Jones *in litt.* 1984). Sometimes all three young are reared, though one or two seem more usual, and two broods per year may be normal (Cheke 1974); there may, however, be a high post-fledging mortality (Cheke in press). Young birds are very reluctant to disperse from the breeding area (Cheke 1980). Territories are tightly packed and very small, c. 0.2 ha on average (Cheke in press; this revises sizes given in Cheke 1980). Males are highly site-faithful, and apparently longer-lived than females: of 11 males ringed in 1974, seven were still alive in 1978, and of the five that were then re-trapped, all were still in the territories they had been holding in 1974; of six females ringed in 1974, only one was still alive in 1978 and had divorced her 1974 mate and moved to a territory c. 130 m away (Cheke 1979a). In April 1983 the population was strongly skewed towards males and, although this might in part have been more apparent than real (females being less conspicuous), a homosexual pairing of male birds was observed (C. G. Jones *in litt.* 1984). Birds generally remain in pairs throughout the year (Staub 1973); they are tame, noisy and conspicuous (Newton 1865, Cheke in press), and spend most of their time in trees (Cheke in press).

Threats The decline of this species was first attributed to the clearance of wooded regions and probably the introduction of the Madagascar Fody *Foudia madagascariensis* (Vinson 1964), and from subsequent research and analysis it appears that it is these two factors in combination that are responsible: the presence of the Rodrigues Fody in lowland scrublands in 1864 (see Ecology) indicates its adaptation to habitat other than woodland, but it would seem that only in woodland with mixed tree species over 9-12 m high does it have a competitive edge over the (now far more numerous and widespread) introduced species, which though normally a granivore has adapted itself to gleaning insects and even drinking nectar from tecoma and jamrose (Cheke 1974; also Moreau 1960, Gill 1967, Cheke in press). The cutting in the early 1960s of forest at Les Choux, St.Gabriel, Mont Lubin and La Source, i.e. within a wide area in which the native species was then present (Cheke 1974), would therefore have contributed to the Madagascar Fody's advantage. The resulting concentration of Rodrigues Fodies has rendered them susceptible to several serious threats, particularly from cyclones: the presence of 75% of the 1974 population in just 16 ha exposed the species then (and probably, without management, permanently) to annihilation by a single localised gust (Cheke 1980; for evidence of the effect of cylones on numbers in recent decades, see Population); even a near miss by Cyclone Damia in 1982 appeared to wipe out all nests, eggs and young (Jones 1983). The forest at Solitude having been the only one free from disturbance, it was assumed that disturbance, caused by habitations in woodland and illegal woodcutting, is a deleterious factor (Cheke 1974), illegal woodcutting having increased sharply on the island between 1974 and 1978 (Cheke 1979a) and being widespread, 1982-1984 (C. G. Jones and W. Strahm *in litt.* 1984); moreover, in 1983 Solitude itself was found to be daily disturbed by woodcutters, and the only nest then found was destroyed by children (C. G. Jones *in litt.* 1984). Human persecution (notably children destroying nests and killing birds with catapults) was reported in 1975 and may be a persistent and therefore intolerable factor (Cheke 1980, in press). The use of nests by the introduced House Sparrow *Passer domesticus*, first noted in 1979 and observed again in 1983 (Mungroo 1979, C. G. Jones *in litt.* 1984), is a further cause for disquiet (see Conservation Measures Proposed). The colonisation of Rodrigues by the black rat *Rattus rattus*, a notorious nest predator of arboreal birds, has been warned against (Cheke 1979b), but the species has recently been recorded from the island (C. G. Jones *per* A. S. Cheke pers. comm. 1984). The possibility of pet crab-eating macaques *Macaca fascicularis* being brought to the island and escaping is a real threat (A. S. Cheke pers. comm. 1984).

Conservation Measures Taken Legal protection for this bird, called for (in Staub 1973, Cheke 1974,1978a), has recently been given (C. G. Jones *in litt.* 1984). Natural dispersal being so poor, in September 1978 five birds (two males, three females) were released at a new site, Jamblong, in apparently suitable habitat (Cheke 1979a) but were not seen subsequently (Mungroo 1979, Cheke in press). At the same time, in an important initiative to take advantage of relatively high numbers before the next cyclone, 24 birds were taken for captive breeding (see Population), 12 birds being left in the government aviaries at Black River, Mauritius, 12 others being transported to JWPT (Cheke 1979a, Hartley 1979, Steele 1979). In 1982 only two pairs survived at Black River and were transferred to JWPT, where first breeding occurred, with two young raised, in 1983 (Darby 1983a,b, Jones 1983). In the course of 1984 these two young died, but the five adult males and four adult females in captivity hatched 15 young, of which 10 were still alive in September (K. Taynton pers. comm. 1984).

Conservation Measures Proposed The declaration and fencing off of Cascade Pigeon as a protected area was considered urgent over a decade ago (Staub 1973). Planting of mixed evergreen forest for areas requiring permanent cover and to extend the species's habitat (and that of the threatened Rodrigues Flying Fox *Pteropus rodricensis*) has been urged (Cheke 1974,1978a), and a detailed and comprehensive set of suggestions and management proposals in respect of this and other factors (e.g. disturbance) ultimately bearing on the species's conservation, but giving due consideration to the needs of local people, has been put forward (Cheke 1978b). Several areas that have been planted up with tecoma would, if provided with some variety (e.g. *Araucaria*, *Vitex*, *Pterocarpus*), make more suitable future habitat (Cheke 1974). The formal protection and active conservation of the important relic of native forest at Cascade St.Louis, the rich sheltered vegetation in Anse Quitor, and the upland forest at Grande Montagne would result in habitats that could be restocked with the Rodrigues Fody and Rodrigues Warbler *Acrocephalus rodericanus* (see relevant account) (Cheke 1974,1978b). Attempts to restock certain other localities (e.g. Cascade Ollier, Camp du Roi) with the former species requires consideration (Cheke 1974,1978b). Introduction of birds to suitable habitat in lowland Mauritius (e.g. Bras d'Eau plantations) has been repeatedly put forward as a measure that could have no repercussions on the threatened endemic (upland-dwelling) Mauritius Fody *Foudia rubra* (Cheke 1974,1975,1978a,b,1979a,1980; see relevant account), but concern for the latter has weighed against this proposal (Cheke 1980, Jones and Owadally 1982). An alternative suggestion of introducing birds to the small coralline islands of Agalega (a dependency of Mauritius, c. 1,000 km to the north) has met with approval, despite the more complex problems of logistics, management and monitoring, and the fact that only a small amount of suitable habitat exists there (Cheke 1978a,1979a,1980, Jones and Owadally 1982). Four considerations in respect of this are (a) that the adaptability of the Madagascar Fody is such that there can be no long-term guarantee that it will not eventually outcompete the native form in the habitat where the latter at present holds sway, so introduction to another island is a vital step whatever habitat conservation may take place, (b) that there are Madagascar Fodies on Agalega already (A. S. Cheke pers. comm. 1984), (c) that if the introduction of Mauritius Fodies to Réunion proceeds (see Conservation Measures Proposed under that species) and is manifestly successful, the introduction of Rodrigues Fodies to Mauritius can be considered far less of a risk, and (d) that, with the present predictable build-up of numbers on Rodrigues in the absence of a direct hit by a cyclone, action to make best use of the birds now available becomes more urgent by the month (for other considerations apropos introductions, see Conservation Measures Proposed under Mauritius Fody). Despite the work already undertaken on this species, considerably more valuable data could be gathered by a longer-term study using marked birds; such work could be combined with a now much-needed study to determine whether House Sparrows actually usurp nests from breeding birds or merely occupy disused nests (Cheke in press; see Threats) and with an educational campaign to prevent any more persecution by children (see Threats). Work to safeguard this species will now proceed within the framework of the Mauritius Wildlife Research and Conservation Programme (see Conservation Measures Taken under Mauritius Kestrel *Falco punctatus*).

Remarks The report of 60 pairs in May 1979 after Cyclone Celine II (Cheke 1979a, Jones 1980) appears to have been in error. The report of 200 pairs in late 1981 (Jones 1982b) is in error for 200 birds.

References

Carroll, J. B. (1981) The wild status and behaviour of the Rodrigues fruit bat *Pteropus rodricensis*. A report of the 1981 field study. *Dodo* 18: 20-29.

Carroll, J. B. (1982) Rodrigues. *On the Edge (Wildlife Preservation Trust Jersey Newsletter)* no. 43.

Cheke, A. S. (1974) British Ornithologists' Union Mascarene Islands Expedition: Report on Rodrigues. Unpublished.

Cheke, A. S. (1975) Proposition pour introduire à la Réunion des oiseaux rares de l'île Maurice. *Info-Nature* no. 12: 25-29.

Cheke, A. S. (1978a) Recommendations for the conservation of Mascarene vertebrates. Conservation memorandum no. 3 (arising out of the B.O.U. Mascarene Islands Expedition). Unpublished.

Cheke, A. S. (1978b) Habitat management for conservation in Rodrigues (Indian Ocean). Conservation memorandum no. 4 (arising out of the B.O.U. Mascarene Islands Expedition). Unpublished.

Cheke, A. S. (1979a) The Rodrigues Fody *Foudia flavicans*. A brief history of its decline, and a report on the 1978 expedition. *Dodo* 15 [1978]: 12-19.

Cheke, A. S. (1979b) The threat to the endemic birds of Rodrigues (Indian Ocean) from the possible introduction of ship rats *Rattus rattus* from vessels coming alongside the proposed new wharf at Port Mathurin. Conservation memorandum no. 5 (arising out of the British Ornithologists' Union Mascarene Islands Expedition). Unpublished.

Cheke, A. S. (1980) Urgency and inertia in the conservation of endangered island species, illustrated by Rodrigues. *Proc. IV Pan-Afr. orn. Congr.*: 355-359.

Cheke, A. S. (in press) Observations on the surviving endemic birds of Rodrigues. In A. W. Diamond, ed. *Studies of Mascarene island birds*. Cambridge: Cambridge University Press.

Darby, P. (1983a) Watching the fody. *On the Edge (Wildlife Preservation Trust Jersey Newsletter)* no. 45.

Darby, P. (1983b) A first for the fodies. *On the Edge (Wildlife Preservation Trust Jersey Newsletter)* no. 46.

Gill, F. B. (1967) Birds of Rodriguez Island (Indian Ocean). *Ibis* 109: 383-390.

Hartley, J. (1979) Fodies from Rodrigues. *Wildlife Preservation Trust Jersey Newsletter* no. 34.

Jones, C. G. (1980) The conservation of the endemic birds and bats of Mauritius and Rodriguez (a progress report and proposal for further activities). Unpublished.

Jones, C. G. (1982a) The conservation of the endemic birds and bats of Mauritius and Rodrigues. (Annual report 1981, WWF Project 1082.) Unpublished.

Jones, C. G. (1982b) Struggle for survival on tropical islands. *WWF Monthly Report* February: 37-42.

Jones, C. G. (1983) The conservation of the endemic birds and bats of Mauritius and Rodrigues. Annual Report, 1982. Unpublished.

Jones, C. G. and Owadally, A. W. (1982) Conservation priorities for Mauritius and Rodrigues. Report submitted to ICBP, July. Unpublished.

Moreau, R. E. (1960) The Ploceine weavers of the Indian Ocean islands. *J. Orn.* 101: 29-49.

Mungroo, Y. (1979) Report of post Cyclone Celine II survey of the endemic passeriformes, and bats and sea birds of Rodrigues. Unpublished.

Newton, E. (1865) Notes of a visit to the island of Rodriguez. *Ibis* (2)1: 146-154.

Slater, H. H. (c. 1875) Notes on the birds of Rodrigues. Manuscript in the Alfred Newton Library, Department of Zoology, University of Cambridge.

Staub, F. (1973) Birds of Rodriguez Island. *Proc. Roy. Soc. Arts Sci. Mauritius* 4(1): 17-59.

Steele, F. N. (1979) Conservation of birds on Mauritius, final report for 1978. Unpublished.

Vinson, J. (1964) Quelques remarques sur l'île Rodrigue et sur sa faune terrestre. *Proc. Roy. Soc. Arts Sci. Mauritius* 2(3): 263-277.

GRAND COMORO DRONGO   RARE
Dicrurus fuscipennis (Milne Edwards and Oustalet, 1887)

Order PASSERIFORMES   Family DICRURIDAE

Summary This is a rare and locally distributed insectivorous bird of forest clearings, confined to a certain altitude band on Mount Karthala, Grand Comoro, in the Comoro Islands; the habitat is somewhat vulnerable, and deserves to be fully protected.

Distribution The Grand Comoro Drongo is restricted to Mount Karthala on Grand Comoro, in the Comoro Islands. In 1958 and 1965 it was found only at Nioumbadjou (Benson 1960, Forbes-Watson 1969) but in 1981 it was found there and also at Malakoff (M. Louette *in litt.* 1981), and in 1983 at Kourani and Boboni (M. Louette *in litt.* 1984). Its distribution is therefore highly localised: birds are apparently restricted to the 500-900 m altitudinal zone around Mount Karthala (M. Louette *in litt.* 1984).

Population Numbers are unknown, but certainly low: birds were described as "not at all common" in 1958 (Benson 1960) and "very rare" in 1981 (M. Louette *in litt.* 1981).

Ecology The requirements of this species are very little known, but probably largely as in other drongos of the region. Apart from one record from a cacao plantation, all sightings in 1958 were from forest clearings at c. 500 m (Benson 1960); in 1983 it was again noted to be confined to forest clearings (M. Louette *in litt.* 1984). Birds collected in August that year contained grasshoppers, cockroaches, a mantid and fruit, but were not in breeding condition (Benson 1960); nesting was, however, noted in birds observed in October 1965 (Forbes-Watson 1969).

Threats The restricted range of this species within a notoriously vulnerable habitat (forest on a relatively small island) must be a permanent cause of concern and vigilance for its welfare. At present no human interference is known and the habitat is unaffected (M. Louette *in litt.* 1981), although there is some cutting of the lower forest for local use (R. Potvliege pers. comm. 1983). A hiking track now under construction to the crater rim on Mount Karthala will, however, bring many more people to higher elevations and carry the risk of being upgraded as a road, which might then increase the chances of disturbance and destruction of habitat (M. Louette *in litt.* 1984).

Conservation Measures Taken None is known.

Conservation Measures Proposed Protected area status, with a concomitant educational programme, for a representative section of the forest and heathland on Mount Karthala would enhance the prospects for survival of this species, the Grand Comoro Scops Owl *Otus pauliani*, the Grand Comoro

Flycatcher *Humblotia flavirostris* and the Mount Karthala White-eye *Zosterops mouroniensis* (see relevant accounts).

References

Benson, C. W. (1960) The birds of the Comoro Islands: results of the British Ornithologists' Union Centenary Expedition 1958. *Ibis* 103b: 5-106.

Forbes-Watson, A. D. (1969) Notes on birds observed in the Comoros on behalf of the Smithsonian Institution. *Atoll Res. Bull.* no. 128.

MAYOTTE DRONGO   RARE
Dicrurus waldeni Schlegel, 1866

Order PASSERIFORMES   Family DICRURIDAE

Summary This is a sparse and locally distributed insectivorous bird, confined to forest on the French island of Mayotte, in the Comoro Islands; conservation planning on the island should take full account of its needs.

Distribution The Mayotte Drongo is restricted to the French possession of Mayotte, in the otherwise independent Comoro Islands. When first discovered, it was only located in the forests behind Joungoni Bay in the south-west (Schlegel and Pollen 1868), but in 1958 it was found "towards the west coast" and at La Convalescence, in the north (Benson 1960), in 1965 above Passamainte in the east (Forbes-Watson 1969), in 1970 only on the north coast (Salvan 1972), and in 1983 at three localities (in one day) in the east above Passamainte and Mamoutzou at 200-300 m (M. Louette *in litt.* 1984). Its distribution is therefore fairly widespread but seemingly rather localised.

Population When first discovered, it was considered to be low in numbers (Schlegel and Pollen 1868), and in 1958 it was found "sparingly" (Benson 1960).

Ecology Although accounts indicate that the Mayotte Drongo is confined to primary evergreen forest (Schlegel and Pollen 1868, Benson 1960), there is a record of a pair holding a territory in an ylang-ylang *Cananga odorata* plantation (Salvan 1972). Beetles (including waterbeetles), Diptera, Homoptera, spiders, a myriapod and a wasp have been found in stomachs (Benson 1960; also Schlegel and Pollen 1868). Breeding occurs in October/November; clutch-size is three (Benson 1960; also Forbes-Watson 1969). Birds at this season are in pairs, but groups of three and four were reported for April to July, these presumably being families (Schlegel and Pollen 1868, Benson 1960); nevertheless song and display (by males towards females) are described from this latter period (see Schlegel and Pollen 1868).

Threats The restricted range of this species within a notoriously vulnerable habitat (forest on a relatively small island) must be a permanent cause of concern and vigilance for its welfare. The overall condition of forests on Mayotte is not known; however, there is still fairly extensive secondary forest in the part of the island where birds were seen in 1983 (M. Louette *in litt.* 1984).

Conservation Measures Taken None is known.

Conservation Measures Proposed Any analysis of conservation needs in Mayotte and resulting action should take full account of this endemic species. A study of its status, distribution and ecology would be a welcome first contribution to plans for its conservation.

References

Benson, C. W. (1960) The birds of the Comoro Islands: results of the British Ornithologists' Union Centenary Expedition 1958. *Ibis* 103b: 5-106.

Forbes-Watson, A. D. (1969) Notes on birds observed in the Comoros on behalf of the Smithsonian Institution. *Atoll Res. Bull.* no. 128.

Salvan, J. (1972) Quelques observations aux Comores. *Alauda* 60: 18-22.

Schlegel, H. and Pollen, F. P. L. (1868) *Recherches sur la faune de Madagascar et de ses dépendances, d'après des découvertes de François P. L. Pollen et D. C. van Dam*. 2me partie. Mammifères et oiseaux. Leyde.

ETHIOPIAN BUSH-CROW   RARE

Zavattariornis stresemanni Moltoni, 1938

Order PASSERIFORMES   Family CORVIDAE

Summary The factors restricting this species, remarkable both for its habits and for its uncertain affinities, to its small range in thorn-bush savanna in southern Ethiopia are unknown and, although it is common, without an understanding of these factors or a measure of protection for its habitat, it must always be considered at some risk.

Distribution The Ethiopian Bush-crow is restricted to an area of something less than 6,000 km^2 around (mainly east of) Yavello (Yabelo) and Mega, Sidamo province, southern Ethiopia. The species is apparently most abundant in the country immediately around Yavello (the type-locality) itself (Benson 1942,1946) but it has been reported from up to 15 km to the north (C. Erard pers. comm. 1983) and north-north-east (J. S. Ash *in litt.* 1983), 60 km to the east (C. Erard pers. comm. 1983), i.e. near Arero (Benson 1946), 70 km to the south (C. Erard pers. comm. 1983), i.e. towards Mega (Benson 1946), and 10 km to the west (C. Erard pers. comm. 1983), though previously reported as entirely absent west of Yavello (Benson 1946). There is also a record from 15 km east of Mega (Benson 1946) and another from 25 km south-east of Mega (J. S. Ash *in litt.* 1984). Two birds, confidently identified as of this species, were seen in acacia near Bahir Dar at the southern end of Lake Tana (i.e. some 700 km north of Yavello) on 13 February 1984 (N. A. Tucker pers. comm. 1984).

Population Birds are evidently very common at least at Yavello (Benson 1942,1946); and elsewhere they are considered fairly common and widespread (J. S. Ash *in litt.* 1983).

Ecology The species inhabits park-like thorn-bush and short-grass savanna (Benson 1942,1946, Urban and Brown 1971). It is reported to eat insects (Goodwin 1976) and has been observed on the ground in a mixed species flock feeding on dead termites (J. S. Ash *in litt.* 1983); when feeding, it commonly consorts with the Superb Starling *Spreo superbus* and White-crowned Starling *S. albicapillis* (J. S. Ash *in litt.* 1983; also C. Erard pers. comm. 1983), and outside the breeding season it is gregarious, in flocks of "half a dozen" (Benson 1942) or 10-30 (C. Erard pers. comm. 1983). It breeds in February/March (not colonially), the normal site being the top of an acacia (c. 6 m high); the nest is an untidy spherical structure of thorn twigs, entrance in the top; clutch-size is up to six (Benson 1942). Breeding has also been noted in May/June, so birds may be double brooded or have an extended breeding season (J. S. Ash *in litt.* 1984). It is normal for three birds to attend the nest but egg-patterns suggest only one female lays (Benson 1942). The factors restricting this species to its small range are unknown, there being nothing unique or distinctive about its habitat (Benson 1946); to the south of Yavello the country becomes more open, and to the north higher, which may limit distribution in these directions (Hall and Moreau 1962); see Remarks. The species has been recorded in most months of the year, so is presumably resident; but it obviously wanders since in areas near Yavello where birds were breeding commonly in June there were none in November and few in December (J. S. Ash *in litt.* 1984). A Tawny Eagle *Aquila rapax* has been observed opening up the top of a nest (J. S. Ash *in litt.* 1984).

Threats No part of the very limited range of this species is known to be protected. Programmes to improve the efficiency of land-utilisation, called "range management schemes", were being implemented in Ethiopia in the 1970s, and in some cases these involved removal of 50% of trees to improve grazing: one large scheme (whose nature and impact was not determined) was known to have included part of the Bush-crow's range, and any such scheme in the heart of its range may affect the species (J. S. Ash *in litt.* 1983). The main threat, however, is probably from removal of trees for charcoal and firewood, now greatly facilitated by a surfaced road through its range, especially as the Rift Valley acacias to the north are already disappearing for these needs so that pressure will always be mounting on vegetation further to the south (J. S. Ash *in litt.* 1983).

Conservation Measures Taken None is known.

Conservation Measures Proposed A study of this species is needed to determine its ecological requirements, status and exact distribution, and to prepare sound recommendations for its permanent conservation. Such work could be doubled with similar studies of the White-tailed Swallow *Hirundo megaensis* (see relevant account) and could form a central component of a general programme of conservation-oriented research on the threatened birds of southern Ethiopia (the others being Prince Ruspoli's Turaco *Tauraco ruspolii*, Sidamo Lark *Heteromirafra sidamoensis* and Degodi Lark *Mirafra degodiensis*: see relevant accounts). The anomalous record of the species from near Lake Tana requires following up.

Remarks This and the Congo Peacock *Afropavo congensis* (see relevant account) may be judged to represent the two most remarkable ornithological discoveries made in Africa this century. The Ethiopian Bush-crow is an extraordinary anomaly, and has generated considerable debate about its affinities (or lack of them) to the crows (Corvidae) and starlings (Sturnidae) (Benson 1942,1946, Lowe 1949, Ripley 1955, Goodwin 1976), and bafflement over its restricted distribution (see Ecology above). With the additional evidence that it may be a cooperative breeder (see Ecology), this species poses important questions in the (related) realms of behaviour, ecology, evolution and taxonomy, and its scientific interest can hardly therefore be overstated. Apropos its distribution, it is possible that the same factors are at play as those restricting the range of the White-tailed Swallow and that these are related to altitude, although it is clear that the habitats of the two species are somewhat different (which may explain the slight difference in their ranges; see Remarks under White-tailed Swallow).

References

Benson, C. W. (1942) A new species and ten new races from southern Abyssinia. *Bull. Brit. Orn. Club* 63: 8-19.

Benson, C. W. (1946) Notes on the birds of southern Abyssinia. *Ibis* 88: 444-461.

Goodwin, D. (1976) *Crows of the world*. London: British Museum (Natural History).

Hall, B. P. and Moreau, R. E. (1962) A study of the rare birds of Africa. *Bull. Brit. Mus. (Nat. Hist.) Zool.* 8: 313-378.

Lowe, P. R. (1949) On the position of the genus *Zavattariornis*. *Ibis* 91: 102-104.

Ripley, S. D. (1955) Anatomical notes on *Zavattariornis*. *Ibis* 97: 142-145.

Urban, E. K. and Brown, L. H. (1971) *A checklist of the birds of Ethiopia*. Addis Adaba: Haile Sellassie I University Press.

Appendices

List of threatened bird species in Africa and related islands arranged by country

In compiling this list by reference to the main text, discretion has been used in determining the weight to be given to particular records: vagrancy ("accidental") records have been excluded where they are known to be such, as have casual ("incidental") records (e.g. of Jackass Penguin *Spheniscus demersus* off Gabon and Congo), dubious records (e.g. of Monteiro's Bush-shrike *Malaconotus monteiri* in Kenya), and records for countries where the species concerned is likely or reported no longer to occur (e.g. Wattled Crane *Bugeranus carunculatus* in Lesotho, Yellow-throated Olive Greenbul *Criniger olivaceus* in Senegal). This reduction is aimed at clarifying for the conservationist which the countries are that individual species truly depend on. The number in brackets after a species's name indicates the total number of countries on which it may be said to depend: those with no number depend solely on the country under which they are listed. Threatened bird species whose distribution lies chiefly outside the limits defined in the Introduction are not included in this breakdown, so that this list is not entirely complete, especially for North Africa (a candidate list of such species is given in Appendix D). Islands that are not independent nations are listed alphabetically but treated under the country responsible for them.

Algeria

Northern Bald Ibis *Geronticus eremita* (6)
Algerian Nuthatch *Sitta ledanti*

Amsterdam Island: see France

Angola

Jackass Penguin *Spheniscus demersus* (3)
Swierstra's Francolin *Francolinus swierstrai*
Wattled Crane *Bugeranus carunculatus* (11)
Damara Tern *Sterna balaenarum* (3)
Fernando Po Swift *Apus sladeniae* (4)
Gabela Helmet-shrike *Prionops gabela*
Monteiro's Bush-shrike *Malaconotus monteiri*
Gabela Akalat *Sheppardia gabela*
White-headed Robin-chat *Cossypha heinrichi* (2)
Pulitzer's Longbill *Macrosphenus pulitzeri*
Black-chinned Weaver *Ploceus nigrimentum* (2)
Loango Slender-billed Weaver *Ploceus subpersonatus* (3)

Ascension Island: see Great Britain

Botswana

Slaty Egret *Egretta vinaceigula* (3)
Cape Vulture *Gyps coprotheres* (7)
Wattled Crane *Bugeranus carunculatus* (11)

Burundi

Grauer's Swamp Warbler *Bradypterus graueri* (4)
Papyrus Yellow Warbler *Chloropeta gracilirostris* (6)
Kungwe Apalis *Apalis argentea* (4)

Cameroon

Mount Cameroon Francolin *Francolinus camerunensis*
Bannerman's Turaco *Tauraco bannermani*
Fernando Po Swift *Apus sladeniae* (4)
Yellow-footed Honeyguide *Melignomon eisentrauti* (2)
Green-breasted Bush-shrike *Malaconotus gladiator* (2)
Mount Kupe Bush-shrike *Malaconotus kupeensis*
White-throated Mountain Babbler *Lioptilus gilberti* (2)
Grey-necked Picathartes *Picathartes oreas* (2)
Dja River Warbler *Bradypterus grandis* (2)
River Prinia *Prinia "fluviatilis"* (3)
Banded Wattle-eye *Platysteira laticincta*
Bannerman's Weaver *Ploceus bannermani* (2)
Bates's Weaver *Ploceus batesi*

Canary Islands: see Spain

Cape Verde

Gon-gon *Pterodroma feae* (2)
Raso Lark *Alauda razae*

Central African Republic

Shoebill *Balaeniceps rex* (8)

Chad

River Prinia *Prinia "fluviatilis"* (3)

Comoros (excluding Mayotte)

Madagascar Heron *Ardea humbloti* (2)
Grand Comoro Scops Owl *Otus pauliani*
Grand Comoro Flycatcher *Humblotia flavirostris*
Mount Karthala White-eye *Zosterops mouroniensis*
Grand Comoro Drongo *Dicrurus fuscipennis*

Congo

Black-chinned Weaver *Ploceus nigrimentum* (2)

Djibouti

Djibouti Francolin *Francolinus ochropectus*

Equatorial Guinea (including Fernando Po [Bioko])

Fernando Po Swift *Apus sladeniae* (4)
Fernando Po Speirops *Speirops brunneus*

Ethiopia

Shoebill *Balaeniceps rex* (8)
Northern Bald Ibis *Geronticus eremita* (6)
Wattled Crane *Bugeranus carunculatus* (11)
White-winged Flufftail *Sarothrura ayresi* (4)
Prince Ruspoli's Turaco *Tauraco ruspolii*
Degodi Lark *Mirafra degodiensis*
Sidamo Long-clawed Lark *Heteromirafra sidamoensis*
White-tailed Swallow *Hirundo megaensis*
Yellow-throated Serin *Serinus flavigula*
Ankober Serin *Serinus ankoberensis*
Ethiopian Bush-crow *Zavattariornis stresemanni*

Fernando Po: see Equatorial Guinea

France (Amsterdam Island)

Amsterdam Albatross *Diomedea amsterdamensis*

France (Mayotte)

Mayotte Drongo *Dicrurus waldeni*

France (Réunion)

Mascarene Black Petrel *Pterodroma aterrima*
Réunion Cuckoo-shrike *Coracina newtoni*

Gabon

Grey-necked Picathartes *Picathartes oreas* (2)
Dja River Warbler *Bradypterus grandis* (2)
Loango Slender-billed Weaver *Ploceus subpersonatus* (3)

Ghana

White-breasted Guineafowl *Agelastes meleagrides* (4)
Rufous Fishing Owl *Scotopelia ussheri* (5)
Western Wattled Cuckoo-shrike *Campephaga lobata* (4)
Yellow-throated Olive Greenbul *Criniger olivaceus* (5)
White-necked Picathartes *Picathartes gymnocephalus* (6)

Gough Island: see Great Britain (Tristan da Cunha group)

Great Britain (Ascension Island)

Ascension Frigatebird *Fregata aquila*

Great Britain (St.Helena)

St.Helena Plover *Charadrius sanctaehelenae*

Great Britain (Tristan da Cunha group)

Inaccessible Rail *Atlantisia rogersi*
Gough Moorhen *Gallinula comeri*
Gough Bunting *Rowettia goughensis*
Tristan Bunting *Nesospiza acunhae*
Grosbeak Bunting *Nesospiza wilkinsi*

Guinea

Rufous Fishing Owl *Scotopelia ussheri* (5)
Yellow-throated Olive Greenbul *Criniger olivaceus* (5)
White-necked Picathartes *Picathartes gymnocephalus* (6)

Ivory Coast

White-breasted Guineafowl *Agelastes meleagrides* (4)
Rufous Fishing Owl *Scotopelia ussheri* (5)

694

Ivory Coast *(cont'd)*

Western Wattled Cuckoo-shrike *Campephaga lobata* (4)
Yellow-throated Olive Greenbul *Criniger olivaceus* (5)
White-necked Picathartes *Picathartes gymnocephalus* (6)
Nimba Flycatcher *Melaenornis annamarulae* (2)
Gola Malimbe *Malimbus ballmanni* (3)

Kenya

Sokoke Scops Owl *Otus ireneae*
Sokoke Pipit *Anthus sokokensis* (2)
East Coast Akalat *Sheppardia gunningi* (4)
Spotted Ground-thrush *Turdus fischeri* (6)
Taita Thrush *Turdus helleri*
Hinde's Pied Babbler *Turdoides hindei*
Papyrus Yellow Warbler *Chloropeta gracilirostris* (6)
Tana River Cisticola *Cisticola restricta*
Turner's Eremomela *Eremomela turneri* (3)
Chapin's Flycatcher *Muscicapa lendu* (3)
Amani Sunbird *Anthreptes pallidigaster* (2)
Clarke's Weaver *Ploceus golandi*

Lesotho

Southern Bald Ibis *Geronticus calvus* (3)
Cape Vulture *Gyps coprotheres* (7)
South African Long-clawed Lark *Heteromirafra ruddi* (2)

Liberia

White-breasted Guineafowl *Agelastes meleagrides* (4)
Rufous Fishing Owl *Scotopelia ussheri* (5)
Yellow-footed Honeyguide *Melignomon eisentrauti* (2)
Western Wattled Cuckoo-shrike *Campephaga lobata* (4)
Yellow-throated Olive Greenbul *Criniger olivaceus* (5)
White-necked Picathartes *Picathartes gymnocephalus* (6)
Nimba Flycatcher *Melaenornis annamarulae* (2)
Gola Malimbe *Malimbus ballmanni* (3)

Madagascar

Madagascar Little Grebe *Tachybaptus pelzelnii*
Alaotra Grebe *Tachybaptus rufolavatus*
Madagascar Heron *Ardea humbloti* (2)
Madagascar Teal *Anas bernieri*
Madagascar Pochard *Aythya innotata*

Madagascar *(cont'd)*

Madagascar Fish Eagle *Haliaeetus vociferoides*
Madagascar Serpent Eagle *Eutriorchis astur*
White-breasted Mesite *Mesitornis variegata*
Brown Mesite *Mesitornis unicolor*
Subdesert Mesite *Monias benschi*
Slender-billed Flufftail *Sarothrura watersi*
Sakalava Rail *Amaurornis olivieri*
Madagascar Plover *Charadrius thoracicus*
Snail-eating Coua *Coua delalandei*
Madagascar Red Owl *Tyto soumagnei*
Short-legged Ground-roller *Brachypteracias leptosomus*
Scaly Ground-roller *Brachypteracias squamiger*
Rufous-headed Ground-roller *Atelornis crossleyi*
Long-tailed Ground-roller *Uratelornis chimaera*
Yellow-bellied Sunbird-asity *Neodrepanis hypoxantha*
Appert's Greenbul *Phyllastrephus apperti*
Dusky Greenbul *Phyllastrephus tenebrosus*
Grey-crowned Greenbul *Phyllastrephus cinereiceps*
Van Dam's Vanga *Xenopirostris damii*
Pollen's Vanga *Xenopirostris polleni*
Benson's Rockthrush *Monticola bensoni*
Madagascar Yellowbrow *Crossleyia xanthophrys*
Red-twiled Newtonia *Newtonia fanovanae*

Madeira: see Portugal

Malawi

Wattled Crane *Bugeranus carunculatus* (11)
East Coast Akalat *Sheppardia gunningi* (4)
Thyolo Alethe *Alethe choloensis* (2)
Spotted Ground-thrush *Turdus fischeri* (6)

Mauritania

Northern Bald Ibis *Geronticus eremita* (6)

Mauritius (and Rodrigues)

Mauritius Kestrel *Falco punctatus*
Pink Pigeon *Nesoenas mayeri*
Mauritius Parakeet *Psittacula eques*
Mauritius Cuckoo-shrike *Coracina typica*
Mauritius Black Bulbul *Hypsipetes olivaceus*
Rodrigues Warbler *Acrocephalus rodericanus*

Mauritius (and Rodrigues) *(cont'd)*

Mauritius Olive White-eye *Zosterops chloronothus*
Mauritius Fody *Foudia rubra*
Rodrigues Fody *Foudia flavicans*

Mayotte: see France

Morocco

Northern Bald Ibis *Geronticus eremita* (6)

Mozambique

Cape Vulture *Gyps coprotheres* (7)
Wattled Crane *Bugeranus carunculatus* (11)
Swynnerton's Forest Robin *Swynnertonia swynnertoni* (3)
East Coast Akalat *Sheppardia gunningi* (4)
Dappled Mountain Robin *Modulatrix orostruthus* (2)
Thyolo Alethe *Alethe choloensis* (2)
Long-billed Apalis *Apalis moreaui* (2)

Namibia

Jackass Penguin *Spheniscus demersus* (3)
Slaty Egret *Egretta vinaceigula* (3)
Cape Vulture *Gyps coprotheres* (7)
Wattled Crane *Bugeranus carunculatus* (11)
Damara Tern *Sterna balaenarum* (3)

Niger

River Prinia *Prinia "fluviatilis"* (3)

Nigeria

Fernando Po Swift *Apus sladeniae* (4)
Green-breasted Bush-shrike *Malaconotus gladiator* (2)
White-throated Mountain Babbler *Lioptilus gilberti* (2)
Anambra Waxbill *Estrilda poliopareia*
Bannerman's Weaver *Ploceus bannermani* (2)
Ibadan Malimbe *Malimbus ibadanensis*

Portugal (Madeira)

Gon-gon *Pterodroma feae* (2)
Freira *Pterodroma madeira*

Portugal (Madeira) *(cont'd)*

Madeira Laurel Pigeon *Columba trocaz*

Réunion: see France

Rodrigues: see Mauritius

Rwanda

Shoebill *Balaeniceps rex* (8)
Albertine Owlet *Glaucidium albertinum* (2)
Grauer's Swamp Warbler *Bradypterus graueri* (4)
Papyrus Yellow Warbler *Chloropeta gracilirostris* (6)
Kungwe Apalis *Apalis argentea* (4)

St.Helena: see Great Britain

São Tomé e Príncipe

Dwarf Olive Ibis *Bostrychia bocagei*
Maroon Pigeon *Columba thomensis*
São Tomé Scops Owl *Otus hartlaubi*
São Tomé Fiscal Shrike *Lanius newtoni*
São Tomé Short-tail *Amaurocichla bocagii*
São Tomé White-eye *Zosterops ficedulinus*
São Tomé Grosbeak *Neospiza concolor*

Seychelles

Seychelles Kestrel *Falco araea*
Seychelles Scops Owl *Otus insularis*
Seychelles Swiftlet *Collocalia elaphra*
Seychelles Magpie-robin *Copsychus sechellarum*
Seychelles Warbler *Acrocephalus sechellensis*
Aldabra Warbler *Nesillas aldabranus*
Seychelles Black Paradise Flycatcher *Terpsiphone corvina*
Seychelles White-eye *Zosterops modestus*
Seychelles Fody *Foudia sechellarum*

Sierra Leone

White-breasted Guineafowl *Agelastes meleagrides* (4)
Rufous Fishing Owl *Scotopelia ussheri* (5)
Western Wattled Cuckoo-shrike *Campephaga lobata* (4)
Yellow-throated Olive Greenbul *Criniger olivaceus* (5)

Sierra Leone *(cont'd)*

White-necked Picathartes *Picathartes gymnocephalus* (6)
Gola Malimbe *Malimbus ballmanni* (3)

Somalia

Somali Pigeon *Columba oliviae*
Ash's Lark *Mirafra ashi*
Somali Long-clawed Lark *Heteromirafra archeri*
Warsangli Linnet *Acanthis johannis*

South Africa

Jackass Penguin *Spheniscus demersus* (3)
Southern Bald Ibis *Geronticus calvus* (3)
Cape Vulture *Gyps coprotheres* (7)
Wattled Crane *Bugeranus carunculatus* (11)
White-winged Flufftail *Sarothrura ayresi* (4)
Damara Tern *Sterna balaenarum* (3)
South African Long-clawed Lark *Heteromirafra ruddi* (2)
Botha's Lark *Spizocorys fringillaris*
Spotted Ground-thrush *Turdus fischeri* (6)

Spain (Canary Islands)

Canarian Black Oystercatcher *Haematopus meadewaldoi*
Dark-tailed Laurel Pigeon *Columba bollii*
White-tailed Laurel Pigeon *Columba junoniae*
Fuerteventura Stonechat *Saxicola dacotiae*
Blue Chaffinch *Fringilla teydea*

Sudan

Shoebill *Balaeniceps rex* (8)
Northern Bald Ibis *Geronticus eremita* (6)
Spotted Ground-thrush *Turdus fischeri* (6)

Swaziland

Southern Bald Ibis *Geronticus calvus* (3)
Cape Vulture *Gyps coprotheres* (7)

Tanzania

Shoebill *Balaeniceps rex* (8)
Wattled Crane *Bugeranus carunculatus* (11)
Usambara Eagle Owl *Bubo vosseleri*

Tanzania *(cont'd)*

Sokoke Pipit *Anthus sokokensis* (2)
Uluguru Bush-shrike *Malaconotus alius*
Swynnerton's Forest Robin *Swynnertonia swynnertoni* (3)
East Coast Akalat *Sheppardia gunningi* (4)
Dappled Mountain Robin *Modulatrix orostruthus* (2)
Usambara Ground Robin *Dryocichloides montanus*
Iringa Ground Robin *Dryocichloides lowei*
Spotted Ground-thrush *Turdus fischeri* (6)
Karamoja Apalis *Apalis karamojae* (2)
Kungwe Apalis *Apalis argentea* (4)
Long-billed Apalis *Apalis moreaui* (2)
Mrs Moreau's Warbler *Bathmocercus winifredae*
Amani Sunbird *Anthreptes pallidigaster* (2)
Banded Green Sunbird *Anthreptes rubritorques*
Rufous-winged Sunbird *Nectarinia rufipennis*
Tanzanian Mountain Weaver *Ploceus nicolli*

Togo

White-necked Picathartes *Picathartes gymnocephalus* (6)

Tristan da Cunha Group: see Great Britain

Uganda

Shoebill *Balaeniceps rex* (8)
Nahan's Francolin *Francolinus nahani* (2)
African Green Broadbill *Pseudocalyptomena graueri* (2)
Forest Ground-thrush *Turdus oberlaenderi* (2)
Kibale Ground-thrush *Turdus kibalensis*
Grauer's Swamp Warbler *Bradypterus graueri* (4)
Papyrus Yellow Warbler *Chloropeta gracilirostris* (6)
Karamoja Apalis *Apalis karamojae* (2)
Turner's Eremomela *Eremomela turneri* (3)
Chapin's Flycatcher *Muscicapa lendu* (3)

"Western Sahara"

Northern Bald Ibis *Geronticus eremita* (6)

Zaire

Shoebill *Balaeniceps rex* (8)
Nahan's Francolin *Francolinus nahani* (2)
Congo Peacock *Afropavo congensis*

Zaire *(cont'd)*

Wattled Crane *Bugeranus carunculatus* (11)
Itombwe Owl *Phodilus prigoginei*
Albertine Owlet *Glaucidium albertinum* (2)
Schouteden's Swift *Schoutedenapus schoutedeni*
African Green Broadbill *Pseudocalyptomena graueri* (2)
Prigogine's Greenbul *Chlorocichla prigoginei*
White-headed Robin-chat *Cossypha heinrichi* (2)
Forest Ground-thrush *Turdus oberlaenderi* (2)
Spotted Ground-thrush *Turdus fischeri* (6)
Grauer's Swamp Warbler *Bradypterus graueri* (4)
Papyrus Yellow Warbler *Chloropeta gracilirostris* (6)
Kungwe Apalis *Apalis argentea* (4)
Kabobo Apalis *Apalis kaboboensis*
Turner's Eremomela *Eremomela turneri* (3)
Chapin's Flycatcher *Muscicapa lendu* (3)
Marungu Sunbird *Nectarinia prigoginei*
Rockefeller's Sunbird *Nectarinia rockefelleri*
Black-lored Waxbill *Estrilda nigriloris*
Loango Slender-billed Weaver *Ploceus subpersonatus* (3)
Lake Lufira Weaver *Ploceus ruweti*
Golden-naped Weaver *Ploceus aureonucha*
Yellow-legged Weaver *Ploceus flavipes*

Zambia

Slaty Egret *Egretta vinaceigula* (3)
Shoebill *Balaeniceps rex* (8)
Wattled Crane *Bugeranus carunculatus* (11)
White-winged Flufftail *Sarothrura ayresi* (4)
Black-cheeked Lovebird *Agapornis nigrigenis* (2)
White-chested Tinkerbird *Pogoniulus makawai*
Papyrus Yellow Warbler *Chloropeta gracilirostris* (6)

Zimbabwe

Cape Vulture *Gyps coprotheres* (7)
Wattled Crane *Bugeranus carunculatus* (11)
White-winged Flufftail *Sarothrura ayresi* (4)
Black-cheeked Lovebird *Agapornis nigrigenis* (2)
Swynnerton's Forest Robin *Swynnertonia swynnertoni* (3)

List of threatened bird species in Africa and related islands arranged by category of threat

Since this list begins with two species treated as Extinct, it is perhaps worth noting that a world list of bird species and subspecies known or believed to have become extinct since 1600 is given in Preamble 8 of King (1978-1979), although this includes one species, the São Tomé Grosbeak *Neospiza concolor*, here treated as Indeterminate. We offer no such list for the region currently under review, partly because it would very shortly be superseded by information to be published concerning the Mascarenes (see Diamond in press). Aside from the Mascarenes, in any case, it would appear that the region has fared relatively well in terms of species survival (or perhaps just moderately badly in their documentation), and from an essentially casual acquaintance with sources we can identify the following victims (at species level) of human influence: *Aepyornis maximus* on Madagascar (King 1978-1979), *Atlantisia elpenor* on Ascension Island (Olson 1973), *Atlantisia podarces* and *Porzana astrictocarpus* on St.Helena (Olson 1973), *Gallinula nesiotis* on Tristan da Cunha (Beintema 1972) and, possibly, a rail and a duck from Amsterdam Island (Jouventin and Roux 1984). Species not seen in the wild for over 50 years, which by CITES criteria qualify as "extinct" (see Introduction under "Red Data Book categories of threat"), are Dwarf Olive Ibis *Bostrychia bocagei*, Madagascar Serpent Eagle *Eutriorchis astur* (if unconfirmed reports are discounted), São Tomé Fiscal Shrike *Lanius newtoni*, São Tomé Short-tail *Amaurocichla bocagii*, Red-tailed Newtonia *Newtonia fanovanae*, Yellow-throated Serin *Serinus flavigula*, São Tomé Grosbeak and Golden-naped Weaver *Ploceus aureonucha*. It is possible that the Slender-billed Flufftail *Sarothrura watersi* should be added to this list.

Extinct

Canarian Black Oystercatcher *Haematopus meadewaldoi*
Snail-eating Coua *Coua delalandei*

Endangered

Alaotra Grebe *Tachybaptus rufolavatus*
Amsterdam Albatross *Diomedea amsterdamensis*
Mascarene Black Petrel *Pterodroma aterrima*
Freira *Pterodroma madeira*
Northern Bald Ibis *Geronticus eremita*
Madagascar Pochard *Aythya innotata*
Madagascar Fish Eagle *Haliaeetus vociferoides*
Madagascar Serpent Eagle *Eutriorchis astur*
Mauritius Kestrel *Falco punctatus*

Endangered *(cont'd)*

Djibouti Francolin *Francolinus ochropectus*
White-breasted Guineafowl *Agelastes meleagrides*
Pink Pigeon *Nesoenas mayeri*
Mauritius Parakeet *Psittacula eques*
Bannerman's Turaco *Tauraco bannermani*
Sokoke Scops Owl *Otus ireneae*
Raso Lark *Alauda razae*
Thyolo Alethe *Alethe choloensis*
Seychelles Magpie-robin *Copsychus sechellarum*
Taita Thrush *Turdus helleri*
Rodrigues Warbler *Acrocephalus rodericanus*
Aldabra Warbler *Nesillas aldabranus*
Banded Wattle-eye *Platysteira laticincta*
Marungu Sunbird *Nectarinia prigoginei*
Seychelles White-eye *Zosterops modestus*
Clarke's Weaver *Ploceus golandi*
Ibadan Malimbe *Malimbus ibadanensis*
Mauritius Fody *Foudia rubra*
Rodrigues Fody *Foudia flavicans*

Vulnerable

Madagascar Teal *Anas bernieri*
Maroon Pigeon *Columba thomensis*
Sokoke Pipit *Anthus sokokensis*
Mauritius Cuckoo-shrike *Coracina typica*
Réunion Cuckoo-shrike *Coracina newtoni*
Western Wattled Cuckoo-shrike *Campephaga lobata*
Prigogine's Greenbul *Chlorocichla prigoginei*
Yellow-throated Olive Greenbul *Criniger olivaceus*
Mauritius Black Bulbul *Hypsipetes olivaceus*
Hinde's Pied Babbler *Turdoides hindei*
White-necked Picathartes *Picathartes gymnocephalus*
Grauer's Swamp Warbler *Bradypterus graueri*
Mauritius Olive White-eye *Zosterops chloronothus*
Bannerman's Weaver *Ploceus bannermani*
Yellow-legged Weaver *Ploceus flavipes*

Indeterminate

Slaty Egret *Egretta vinaceigula*
Dwarf Olive Ibis *Bostrychia bocagei*
Swierstra's Francolin *Francolinus swierstrai*
White-winged Flufftail *Sarothrura ayresi*
Slender-billed Flufftail *Sarothrura watersi*

Indeterminate *(cont'd)*

Madagascar Red Owl *Tyto soumagnei*
Itombwe Owl *Phodilus prigoginei*
Schouteden's Swift *Schoutedenapus schoutedeni*
White-chested Tinkerbird *Pogoniulus makawai*
Yellow-bellied Sunbird-asity *Neodrepanis hypoxantha*
South African Long-clawed Lark *Heteromirafra ruddi*
Somali Long-clawed Lark *Heteromirafra archeri*
Sidamo Long-clawed Lark *Heteromirafra sidamoensis*
Botha's Lark *Spizocorys fringillaris*
Gabela Helmet-shrike *Prionops gabela*
Monteiro's Bush-shrike *Malaconotus monteiri*
Mount Kupe Bush-shrike *Malaconotus kupeensis*
São Tomé Fiscal Shrike *Lanius newtoni*
Gabela Akalat *Sheppardia gabela*
White-headed Robin-chat *Cossypha heinrichi*
Kibale Ground-thrush *Turdus kibalensis*
Madagascar Yellowbrow *Crossleyia xanthophrys*
Pulitzer's Longbill *Macrosphenus pulitzeri*
São Tomé Short-tail *Amaurocichla bocagii*
Nimba Flycatcher *Melaenornis annamarulae*
Red-tailed Newtonia *Newtonia fanovanae*
São Tomé White-eye *Zosterops ficedulinus*
Yellow-throated Serin *Serinus flavigula*
São Tomé Grosbeak *Neospiza concolor*
Golden-naped Weaver *Ploceus aureonucha*
Gola Malimbe *Malimbus ballmanni*

Rare

Gon-gon *Pterodroma feae*
Ascension Frigatebird *Fregata aquila*
Southern Bald Ibis *Geronticus calvus*
Cape Vulture *Gyps coprotheres*
Mount Cameroon Francolin *Francolinus camerunensis*
Nahan's Francolin *Francolinus nahani*
White-breasted Mesite *Mesitornis variegata*
Subdesert Mesite *Monias benschi*
Inaccessible Rail *Atlantisia rogersi*
Gough Moorhen *Gallinula comeri*
Madagascar Plover *Charadrius thoracicus*
St.Helena Plover *Charadrius sanctaehelenae*
Damara Tern *Sterna balaenarum*
Somali Pigeon *Columba oliviae*
Madeira Laurel Pigeon *Columba trocaz*
Dark-tailed Laurel Pigeon *Columba bollii*

Rare *(cont'd)*

White-tailed Laurel Pigeon *Columba junoniae*
Black-cheeked Lovebird *Agapornis nigrigenis*
Prince Ruspoli's Turaco *Tauraco ruspolii*
Grand Comoro Scops Owl *Otus pauliani*
Seychelles Scops Owl *Otus insularis*
São Tomé Scops Owl *Otus hartlaubi*
Usambara Eagle Owl *Bubo vosseleri*
Rufous Fishing Owl *Scotopelia ussheri*
Albertine Owlet *Glaucidium albertinum*
Seychelles Swiftlet *Collocalia elaphra*
Short-legged Ground-roller *Brachypteracias leptosomus*
Scaly Ground-roller *Brachypteracias squamiger*
Rufous-headed Ground-roller *Atelornis crossleyi*
Long-tailed Ground-roller *Uratelornis chimaera*
African Green Broadbill *Pseudocalyptomena graueri*
White-tailed Swallow *Hirundo megaensis*
Appert's Greenbul *Phyllastrephus apperti*
Dusky Greenbul *Phyllastrephus tenebrosus*
Grey-crowned Greenbul *Phyllastrephus cinereiceps*
Green-breasted Bush-shrike *Malaconotus gladiator*
Uluguru Bush-shrike *Malaconotus alius*
Van Dam's Vanga *Xenopirostris damii*
Pollen's Vanga *Xenopirostris polleni*
Swynnerton's Forest Robin *Swynnertonia swynnertoni*
East Coast Akalat *Sheppardia gunningi*
Dappled Mountain Robin *Modulatrix orostruthus*
Usambara Ground Robin *Dryocichloides montanus*
Iringa Ground Robin *Dryocichloides lowei*
Fuerteventura Stonechat *Saxicola dacotiae*
Forest Ground-thrush *Turdus oberlaenderi*
Spotted Ground-thrush *Turdus fischeri*
White-throated Mountain Babbler *Lioptilus gilberti*
Grey-necked Picathartes *Picathartes oreas*
Seychelles Warbler *Acrocephalus sechellensis*
Papyrus Yellow Warbler *Chloropeta gracilirostris*
Kungwe Apalis *Apalis argentea*
Kabobo Apalis *Apalis kaboboensis*
Long-billed Apalis *Apalis moreaui*
Mrs Moreau's Warbler *Bathmocercus winifredae*
Turner's Eremomela *Eremomela turneri*
Chapin's Flycatcher *Muscicapa lendu*
Grand Comoro Flycatcher *Humblotia flavirostris*
Seychelles Black Paradise Flycatcher *Terpsiphone corvina*
Algerian Nuthatch *Sitta ledanti*
Amani Sunbird *Anthreptes pallidigaster*

Rare *(cont'd)*

Banded Green Sunbird *Anthreptes rubritorques*
Rufous-winged Sunbird *Nectarinia rufipennis*
Rockefeller's Sunbird *Nectarinia rockefelleri*
Mount Karthala White-eye *Zosterops mouroniensis*
Fernando Po Speirops *Speirops brunneus*
Gough Bunting *Rowettia goughensis*
Tristan Bunting *Nesospiza acunhae*
Grosbeak Bunting *Nesospiza wilkinsi*
Blue Chaffinch *Fringilla teydea*
Ankober Serin *Serinus ankoberensis*
Warsangli Linnet *Acanthis johannis*
Bates's Weaver *Ploceus batesi*
Tanzanian Mountain Weaver *Ploceus nicolli*
Seychelles Fody *Foudia sechellarum*
Grand Comoro Drongo *Dicrurus fuscipennis*
Mayotte Drongo *Dicrurus waldeni*
Ethiopian Bush-crow *Zavattariornis stresemanni*

Insufficiently Known

Madagascar Little Grebe *Tachybaptus pelzelnii*
Madagascar Heron *Ardea humbloti*
Brown Mesite *Mesitornis unicolor*
Sakalava Rail *Amaurornis olivieri*
Fernando Po Swift *Apus sladeniae*
Yellow-footed Honeyguide *Melignomon eisentrauti*
Ash's Lark *Mirafra ashi*
Degodi Lark *Mirafra degodiensis*
Benson's Rockthrush *Monticola bensoni*
Dja River Warbler *Bradypterus grandis*
Tana River Cisticola *Cisticola restricta*
River Prinia *Prinia "fluviatilis"*
Karamoja Apalis *Apalis karamojae*
Anambra Waxbill *Estrilda poliopareia*
Black-lored Waxbill *Estrilda nigriloris*
Black-chinned Weaver *Ploceus nigrimentum*
Loango Slender-billed Weaver *Ploceus subpersonatus*
Lake Lufira Weaver *Ploceus ruweti*

Out of Danger

Seychelles Kestrel *Falco araea*

Of Special Concern

Jackass Penguin *Spheniscus demersus*
Shoebill *Balaeniceps rex*
Congo Peacock *Afropavo congensis*
Wattled Crane *Bugeranus carunculatus*

References

Beintema, A. J. (1972) The history of the Island Hen (*Gallinula nesiotis*), the
    extinct flightless gallinule of Tristan da Cunha. *Bull. Brit. Orn. Club* 92: 106-113.
Diamond, A. W. ed. (in press) *Studies in Mascarene island birds*. Cambridge:
    Cambridge University Press.
Jouventin, P. and Roux, J.-P. (1984) L'Albatross d'Amsterdam va-t-il disparaître à
    peine découvert? *La Recherche* 15: 250-252.
King, W. B. (1978-1979) *Red data book, 2: Aves*. 2nd edition. Morges,
    Switzerland: IUCN.
Olson, S. L. (1973) Evolution of the rails of the South Atlantic islands. *Smithsonian
    Contrib. Zool.* 152.

A list of near-threatened bird species in Africa and related islands

Red Data Books tend perhaps to render the distinction between "threatened" species and the "safe" remainder too sharp and certain. It is obvious, however, that in reality there is a very broad area where certainty is impossible, and where evaluation of candidacy proceeds from a reasonably informed (but still too subjective) sense of probability. The following list and notes concern 93 species that have been on the "fringe" of full treatment in this book and which, at other authors' hands, might well have been so treated; in particular, many of them could easily have qualified for the Insufficiently Known category. In a few cases, previously unpublished information is given as a means of forestalling doubt on the judgement we have exercised in excluding a species from the main text; but in general the provision of this list is a reflection of our own concern to indicate what further species are in need of some attention, although in almost all cases the main or at least first requirement is simply monitoring.

Barau's Petrel *Pterodroma baraui* is known from the Mascarene islands, with its principal breeding stations almost certainly in inaccessible cliffs in the higher parts of Réunion (France) (see Jouanin and Gill 1967, Brooke 1978, Jouanin in press). A nest has been found on Rodrigues (Cheke 1974) and a bird has been seen flying inland at Tamarin Falls, Mauritius (Jouanin in press). It is unlikely to be at risk, but gadfly-petrels *Pterodroma* are notoriously vulnerable birds and this species deserves further investigation (which on Réunion could largely double with any work done in attempting to track down the Mascarene Black Petrel *P. aterrima*: see relevant account in the main text).

Crowned Cormorant *Phalacrocorax coronatus* is restricted to the coast of South Africa and Namibia between Walvis Bay and Bredasdorp, where at least 2,665 pairs were counted between 1977 and 1981 in 39 colonies (Crawford *et al.* 1982, *contra* older data in Brown *et al.* 1982). The species appears to be under no immediate threat, but recommendations for its conservation have been made (see Crawford *et al.* 1982).

Bank Cormorant *Phalacrocorax neglectus* is restricted to the coast of South Africa and Namibia between Hollamsbird Island and Quoin Rock (Cooper 1981). In 1980 the population was estimated at 18,000 birds in 44 colonies, with 71% of the population occurring on Ichaboe and Mercury Islands on the Namibian coast (Cooper 1981, *contra* older data in Brown *et al.* 1982). The species is not considered to be facing any serious threat (Cooper 1981).

Madagascar Pond-heron *Ardeola idae* apparently breeds throughout much of Madagascar (Delacour 1932, Milon *et al.* 1973) and winters in a wide area of

Central and East Africa (Brown *et al.* 1982), including Somalia (Ash 1983), but there was a massive post-war decline in the only well known breeding area – c. 1,500 birds in 1945 (Milon 1949), c. 50 in 1970 (Salvan 1970,1972b) – that was scarcely compensated by the species's colonisation of Aldabra atoll (Seychelles) (Benson and Penny 1971). Birds are, however, still in good numbers on Madagascar (O. Langrand *in litt.* 1984), though sample monitoring of breeding and wintering populations is desirable. That the species breeds on Réunion (France) (Moutou 1984) is wholly in error (A. S. Cheke pers. comm. 1984).

Madagascar Crested Ibis *Lophotibis cristata* was treated (under a heading with both subspecies) as Vulnerable in King (1978-1979) and, despite statements that its forest habitat is disappearing and it is hunted for food by natives (Benson *et al.* 1976-1977, O. Langrand per G. Archibald *in litt.* 1983, D. A. Turner pers. comm. 1983), it is now apparent that the western subspecies *urschi* is still widespread and common (D. A. Turner pers. comm. 1983; also Appert 1966) while the nominate eastern *cristata* shows a degree of adaptability, being recorded from secondary forest (e.g. Salvan 1972a) and, at Maroantsetra, nesting in large trees shading vanilla plantations (O. Langrand *per* G. Archibald *in litt.* 1983).

Madagascar Cuckoo-falcon *Aviceda madagascariensis* is widely distributed in a variety of habitats in Madagascar, but is generally considered "uncommon", except for one report ("not uncommon") from Ivohibe in the south-east (Rand 1936, Milon *et al.* 1973, Thiollay and Meyburg 1981). Its crepuscular activity (Milon *et al.* 1973) may partly be responsible for the paucity of records.

Southern Banded Snake Eagle *Circaetus fasciolatus* occurs in coastal forests from Somalia south to South Africa (Snow 1978). Although habitat is declining it is very widespread and in no immediate danger.

Réunion Harrier *Circus maillardi* is confined to Réunion (France), the Comoros and Madagascar: it has recovered in numbers on Réunion since receiving protection in 1966 and may now number 130-200 pairs (Cheke in press b), on the Comoros it was fairly common in 1975 (A. S. Cheke pers. comm. 1984), while in Madagascar the species is inexplicably uncommon although suitable habitat is abundant (Langrand and Meyburg in press). The taxonomy of this form is considered by Cheke (in press b), whom we follow.

Black Harrier *Circus maurus* is largely restricted to South Africa with some outlying records in Namibia and Botswana (van der Merwe 1981). It is generally rare but is common in some areas and possibly increasing (van der Merwe 1981). The population is probably between a few hundred and 1,000 pairs and it appears to be under no immediate threat (van der Merwe 1981).

Henst's Goshawk *Accipiter henstii* is widely distributed in a variety of habitats in Madagascar, but is generally considered "uncommon", and in the 1970s was "certainly in decline" (Milon *et al.* 1973; also Delacour 1932, Rand 1936, Thiollay and Meyburg 1981).

Madagascar Sparrowhawk *Accipiter madagascariensis* is largely confined to areas in Madagascar below 1,000 m; it is apparently extremely rare in the east and uncommon in the west, though somewhat commoner in the subdesert region of the south-west (Lavauden 1932, Rand 1936, Milon *et al.* 1973). Its distribution appears complementary to that of the Madagascar Goshawk *A. francesiae* (Thiollay and Meyburg 1981).

Banded Kestrel *Falco zoniventris* is widely distributed in a variety of habitats in Madagascar, but is generally considered "rare"; it may be commonest in the north-east and south-west (Rand 1936, Milon *et al.* 1973, Benson *et al.* 1976-1977, Thiollay and Meyburg 1981). As it is noted to perch "quietly for long periods" (Rand 1936) it may be greatly overlooked, as experience with the Seychelles Kestrel *F. araea* has shown (see relevant account in the main text).

Taita Falcon *Falco fasciinucha* is scarce but widespread in eastern and central Africa, and unlikely to be at risk (see Snow 1978, Britton 1980, Irwin 1981, and Dowsett 1983).

Harwood's Francolin *Francolinus harwoodi*, of the Ethiopian highlands, has recently been shown to range more extensively than was previously known, and there is "no reason to believe that it is at any particular hazard" (Ash 1978).

Finsch's Francolin *Francolinus finschi* has a fairly restricted distribution in Angola, Congo and Zaire (Snow 1978). Being a bird of woodland savanna (Traylor 1963) and *Brachystegia* woodland, bare mountain slopes and grassland (Snow 1978) it is unlikely to be in any serious danger (A. A. da R. Pinto *in litt.* 1983).

Grey-striped Francolin *Francolinus griseostriatus* is restricted to the escarpment zone of western Angola, occurring in two populations (probably racially distinct) separated by 400 km, in Cuanza Sul and southern Benguela Provinces; it lives in secondary and gallery forest, and penetrates thickets and weed-covered areas in the north of its range, and in general it is relatively common (Pinto in press, A. A. da R. Pinto *in litt.* 1983; also Heinrich 1958, Hall 1961, Traylor 1963 and Pinto 1970).

Nubian Bustard *Neotis nuba* is a very poorly known species of the sahelian subdesert zone, the majority of records being between 13° and 17°N (see map in Snow 1978), extending from the Red Sea coast in Sudan (Butler 1905, Cave and Macdonald 1955) east through Chad (Friedmann 1962, Simon 1965, Salvan 1968, Newby 1979) to Niger (Vaurie 1961, Fairon 1975), with an apparently vagrant pair, northern Nigeria, May 1959 (Elgood 1982). In the 1970s the species was found to be present in Mali, from Azaouak near the Niger border right across the country, being described as "common in the Sahel and the Sahara as far as 20°N in the cold season" (Lamarche 1980), and it was also discovered in Mauritania north of Tidjikja, Tichit and Nouakchott and at the coast near the Banc d'Arguin (Gee 1974, Dick 1975, Lamarche 1980, J. P. Gee *in litt.* 1984, P. J. Knight pers. comm. 1984). Uncommon to fairly common throughout its range, the species was considered particularly threatened by hunting in Niger a decade ago (Fairon 1975) and the prolonged sahelian drought combined with the effects of overgrazing is expected to have had a substantial impact on its populations (Cramp and Simmons 1980). Hunting of bustards by Arab dignitaries is now believed to be widespread in the sahelian subdesert zone (P. D. Goriup pers. comm. 1984) and this species, being roughly equivalent in size and ecology to the much prized and persecuted Houbara *Chlamydotis undulata* of the northern fringes of the Sahara, is likely to be suffering seriously as a consequence. Although its massive range must at present be assumed to keep it from becoming threatened, the true status of this bird requires evaluation.

Little Brown Bustard *Eupodotis humilis* is known from Somalia and Ethiopia, in the former "common south to 7°N, but scarcer beyond to 4°N" (Ash and Miskell 1983; also Ash 1977). The effect of recent drought and war in this region on the species is unknown, but they are unlikely to have been beneficial and closer investigation of the situation is required.

African Black Oystercatcher *Haematopus moquini* is endemic to southern Africa, along coasts from southern Namibia to Transkei, the total population being estimated at about 4,800 birds in the early 1980s (Hockey 1983). Wide distribution of breeding sites and protection at some of them (further protection is recommended) indicates that this species, though low in numbers, is currently safe (Hockey 1983).

White-naped Pigeon *Columba albinucha* is restricted to a few areas of transition forest in eastern Zaire (Prigogine 1965), western Uganda (Britton 1980) and the Rumpi Hills in western Cameroon (Eisentraut 1973). It is localised and little known.

White-winged Dove *Streptopelia reichenowi* is much commoner than originally thought in southern Ethiopia and southern Somalia (Ash *et al.* 1974, Brown 1977, Ash and Miskell 1983). It also extends into northern Kenya (Britton 1980).

Verreaux's Coua *Coua verreauxi* has a highly restricted distribution in south-west Madagascar, between the Fiherenana and the Menarandra Rivers (Milon 1952). Various reports indicate that it is fairly common within this area (e.g. Rand 1936, Milon 1952, Milon *et al.* 1973, D. A. Turner *in litt.* 1983) and it occurs within the Lac Tsimanampetsotsa Nature Reserve (R.N.I. no. 10) (see Andriamampianina 1981). A recent account indicates that it is apparently "confined to an area of thick coastal scrub on coral rag" (D. A. Turner *in litt.* 1983).

Mascarene Swiftlet *Collocalia francica*, endemic to Mauritius and Réunion (considered specifically distinct from the Seychelles Swiftlet *C. elaphra*: see relevant account in main text), has always been reckoned common and widespread in both islands (e.g. Oustalet 1897, Meinertzhagen 1912, Milon 1951a, Rountree *et al.* 1952, Temple *et al.* 1974, Jones 1980, Jones and Owadally 1982,

Cheke in press a,b). In the mid-1970s there were several thousand birds on Mauritius (Cheke in press a) and around 1980 there were c. 5,000 on Réunion (Barré 1983). Nevertheless, there is strong evidence of a serious decline in the species in the past century, for reasons not entirely obvious (Cheke in press a,b). Vandalism of nests is a known cause of breeding failure on both islands (Jadin and Billiet 1979, Cheke in press a,b), and although many nest-caves at least on Réunion are considered inaccessible (Barré and Barau 1982) all those on Mauritius are easily reached (A. S. Cheke pers. comm. 1984). A simple programme of declaring certain vulnerable caves nature reserves and of barring public access by lockable metal grilles is urgently required on Mauritius (Cheke 1978) and highly desirable on Réunion (Barré and Barau 1982). A project on both islands aimed at identifying as many nest-caves (which are traditional) as possible and providing quantifiable data on abundance for long-term monitoring of population trends should form a component of future ornithological work in the Mascarenes.

Pitta-like Ground-roller *Atelornis pittoides* was treated as Rare in King (1978-1979), but is nonetheless much the most widespread of Madagascar's ground-rollers, ranging from Montagne d'Ambre in the far north (where around 1930 it was common) to the Chaînes Anosyennes in the far south (Delacour 1932, Milon *et al.* 1973). Apart from the localities mentioned in King (1978-1979) it is also known from Mangabe (north of Antananarivo) (Kaudern 1922), Antananarivo, in a garden (perhaps on migration: see below) (Wills 1893), the Périnet-Analamazaotra Special Reserve, where it breeds (Benson *et al.* 1976-1977, Turner in press; also Roch and Newton 1862, Newton 1863, Webb 1954), eastern Imerina forests (now felled) (Oberholser 1900) but also secondary forest at Ambatoloana in the eastern Imerina region (Salvan 1972a), Tsarafidy (= Ankafana) forest (Deans Cowan 1882, Fisher 1981; see Griveaud 1961), Iampasika and Vondrozo (Delacour 1932), breeding being recorded in 1984 in the Vondrozo region (O. Langrand pers. comm. 1984), and in view of it being "common" or "not rare" at several localities (see Milon *et al.* 1973) it is no longer to be regarded as at risk. However, it appears to be migratory (Turner in press) so that its conservation needs cannot yet be determined with confidence.

Red-faced Barbet *Lybius rubrifacies* is restricted to Rwanda, north-western Tanzania and south-western Uganda (Snow 1978). It can withstand cultivation (Britton 1980) but it has recently declined in Rwanda because of excessive habitat clearance although it survives in the Akagera National Park (J.-P. Vande weghe pers. comm. 1983).

Chaplin's Barbet *Lybius chaplini* occurs in a few hundred square kilometres in western Zambia, being sparsely distributed although it occurs in Kafue and Blue Lagoon National Parks; it is probably not under serious threat since the fig trees on which it depends are not usually disturbed by the human population (treated in Collar 1982).

Pygmy Honeyguide *Indicator pumilio* is known from five montane areas along the Albertine Rift: Itombwe Forest and the mountains west of Lakes Kivu and Edward (Zaire), Nyungwe Forest (Rwanda) and Impenetrable Forest (Uganda) (Prigogine in press). Birds from Kakamega in western Kenya have been judged aberrant Least Honeyguides *I. exilis pachyrhynchus* (Prigogine 1978) but their identity as Pygmy Honeyguides is strongly reaffirmed (A. D. Forbes-Watson pers. comm. 1984). The species is apparently mainly a montane forest species, long confused with *I. exilis* (Chapin 1958,1962). In the Itombwe Mountains it has a narrow altitudinal range between 1,850-2,220 m (Prigogine 1980a) and in Impenetrable Forest it is found between 1,500-2,400 m (Keith and Twomey 1968). Although the species is probably not in any immediate danger, the few records suggest that it is uncommon.

Stierling's Woodpecker *Dendropicos stierlingi* is common in two areas of southern Malawi, with the remainder of the population in the v̈ry poorly explored parts of southern Tanzania and northern Mozambique (treated in Collar 1982).

Williams's Bush Lark *Mirafra williamsi* is a very uncommon though probably not threatened species, endemic to arid and semi-arid grass plains on black lava soil in northern Kenya (Britton 1980). There are two apparently isolated populations: at Marsabit and the Dida Galgalla Desert, and between Isiolo and Garba Tula (Britton 1980).

Friedmann's Bush Lark *Mirafra pulpa* is a very uncommon though probably not threatened species whose taxonomic history is given by Lack (1977). It is a bird of bushy grasslands, known from one locality in southern Ethiopia and from Archer's Post, Voi and Ngulia in eastern Kenya (Hall and Moreau 1970, Lack 1977, Britton 1980).

Short-clawed Lark *Mirafra chuana* occurs locally below 500 m in northern Cape Province (east of 22°N), north-western Orange Free State, south-western and western Transvaal north-east to Bandolierkop (South Africa), also in south-eastern Botswana (Brooke in press). It inhabits *Acacia* and *Tarchonanthus* savanna where grass does not exceed 30 cm in height (Brooke in press). Its habitat is being cleared in places but otherwise there is no evidence of a decrease: several pairs breed in Pietersburg Municipal Nature Reserve, where it is a breeding visitor, but in general it does not wander far (Brooke in press).

Red Lark *Mirafra burra* is endemic to red sand (semi-desert) country of north-west Cape Province, east to near Prieska (South Africa). All records are south of the Orange River except one from Kleinkaras, southern Namibia, which might have involved a misidentification (Clancey 1980). The species is highly nomadic depending on localised rainfalls (Lawson 1961, Winterbottom 1963, Brooke in press). In some areas it is quite common (Winterbottom 1963,1968). There is no evidence of a decrease (Brooke in press). The taxonomic history of this species is highly confused (see Lawson 1961, Clancey 1967,1980).

Sclater's Lark *Spizocorys sclateri* is endemic to the heart of the south-western arid region of Africa, with the nominate form in northern Cape Province

(South Africa) and Namibia north to Great Namaqualand, *S. s. capensis* occurring in Cape Province south of the nominate form: the species inhabits semi-desert within accessible distance of drinking water, is often gregarious and breeds opportunistically when it rains (Winterbottom 1961, Hockey and Sinclair 1981, Brooke in press). It is sometimes fairly common (Winterbottom 1961) and there is no evidence of a decrease (Brooke in press) but it remains very little known.

Obbia Lark *Calandrella obbiensis* is a species endemic to Somalia, previously known from a single specimen from Obbia in 1903, two from Mogadishu in 1954 and two from Uarsciek in 1962, but now known to be abundant along a very narrow coastal belt for 570 km from Obbia in the north to just south of Mogadishu, eastern Somalia, and although the total area occupied may be only 1,200 km^2 the species is apparently at no risk (Ash 1981, Ash and Miskell 1983; also Collar and Violani in press).

Blue Swallow *Hirundo atrocaerulea* has a restricted breeding distribution that includes South Africa (Natal and eastern Transvaal), Zimbabwe (eastern highlands), Malawi and south-western Tanzania, also the Zambian part of the Nyika Plateau; birds from the southern part of this range winter north to Uganda (Grant and Mackworth-Praed 1942, Benson and Pitman 1966, Snell 1979, Brooke in press). It is a species of upland grasslands, breeding along streams in potholes and old burrows of antbears *Orycteropus*, and has declined towards extinction in South Africa and Zimbabwe (Snell 1979, Irwin 1981, Brooke in press) although there has been no evidence of a decline in the numbers wintering in Uganda (M. Carswell *in litt.* 1984). In Malawi, a very large population is considered to occur on the 1,000 km^2 grasslands of the Nyika Plateau, and the species is not uncommon on the Viphya Plateau, very scarce on the Misukus, and extinct on the Zomba Plateau following heavy plantation (R. J. Dowsett *in litt.* 1983). Although it is reportedly threatened in south-western Tanzania (Brooke in press), there is in fact a great amount of suitable habitat on the Kitulo Plateau and elsewhere (R. J. Dowsett *in litt.* 1983) where the species is known to be common (A. J. Beakbane pers. comm. 1984, E. M. Boswell pers. comm. 1984); this part of Tanzania may in fact prove to be the species's stronghold.

Cameroon Mountain Roughwing *Psalidoprocne fuliginosa* was thought to be restricted to Mount Cameroon (Cameroon) and the island of Fernando Poo (Equatorial Guinea), where it is common and under no immediate threat (Basilio 1963, Serle 1965, SNS). It has also been reported from montane areas in Cameroon away from Mount Cameroon itself (Elgood 1976) and from the Obudu Plateau in Nigeria (Elgood 1965,1976, M. E. Gartshore *in litt.* 1984), but such records of this species, easily confused with other hirundines, probably require the support of specimen material.

Cameroon Mountain Greenbul *Andropadus montanus* is restricted to montane forest in western Cameroon and eastern Nigeria, but a somewhat anomalous record from Togo (see Hall and Moreau 1970) was based on a specimen now lost whose identification is regarded as highly suspect (A. Brosset *per* L. G.

714

Grimes *in litt.* 1983). It occurs on Mount Cameroon, the Rumpi Hills, Mount Kupe, Mount Nlonako, Mount Manengouba, the Bamenda Highlands and the Obudu Plateau (Serle 1950,1954,1965, Eisentraut 1973, SNS). It is very rare through most of its range but common on Mount Manengouba and the Bamenda Highlands, where, however, the forest is being rapidly cleared (SNS).

Grey-headed Greenbul *Phyllastrephus poliocephalus* is restricted to submontane forest in western Cameroon and eastern Nigeria. It occurs on Mount Cameroon, the Rumpi Hills, Mount Kupe, Mount Nlonako, the southern slopes of the Bamenda Highlands at Foto, and the Obudu Plateau (Serle 1950,1954,1965, Eisentraut 1973, SNS). It has a fairly narrow altitudinal range in which some forest clearance is taking place, but it is not seriously threatened at present (SNS).

Sassi's Olive Greenbul *Phyllastrephus lorenzi* is a rare bird, of lowland in middle altitude forest, restricted to eastern Zaire and the Bwamba Forest in western Uganda, where one was collected in 1967 (Britton 1980), though this latter locality has since been largely felled (K. D. Bishop pers. comm. 1983). In eastern Zaire it occurs in the Semliki and Ituri Forests, forests west of Lake Edward, forests west of Lake Kivu, and the foothills of the Itombwe Mountains (Prigogine in press).

Grey-crested Helmet-shrike *Prionops poliolopha* is an uncommon species endemic to woodlands in Kenya and northern Tanzania, having possibly decreased although the evidence is very inconclusive (see Lewis 1981,1982).

Turati's Boubou *Laniarius turatii* has a restricted distribution in Sierra Leone, Guinea and Guinea-Bissau (see Hall and Moreau 1970), being common in the first two in a variety of non-forest habitats (A. Tye *in litt.* 1982, G. D. Field pers. comm. 1983).

Mfumbiri Bush-shrike *Laniarius mufumbiri* is a papyrus endemic, found in pure and mixed papyrus and never outside. It is a bird of the middle strata, occasionally using upper and lower levels to acquire its food from emergent vegetation (Vande weghe 1981). It has been recorded from eastern Zaire, Uganda, western Kenya at Yala Swamp and Kisumu (Hall and Moreau 1970, Britton 1978) and Rwanda and Burundi (Vande weghe 1981).

Bernier's Vanga *Oriolia bernieri*, although treated as Indeterminate in King (1978-1979), is nevertheless widely distributed in rainforests in Madagascar (Delacour 1932, Milon *et al.* 1973). Its habit of keeping to high trees (Delacour 1932) may be responsible for the paucity of records. In the northern part of its range, pairs of birds show an association with flocks of Helmetbirds *Euryceros prevosti* and have regularly been seen, and on this evidence the species is considered no longer under threat (D. A. Turner pers. comm. 1983).

Herero Chat *Namibornis herero* is a rare species of arid *Acacia* scrub in Namibia and Angola (Jensen and Jensen 1971, C. J. Stutterheim *in litt.* 1981). It has a very restricted distribution but appears not to be threatened (C. J. Stutterheim *in litt.* 1981).

Angola Cave-chat *Xenocopsychus ansorgei* is locally common in the escarpment of Angola and also on some mountain peaks (Traylor 1963, Hall and Moreau 1970). It lives amongst rocky cliffs and caves and is, therefore, unlikely to be threatened (A. A. da R. Pinto *in litt.* 1983).

Kivu Ground-thrush *Turdus tanganjicae* is a rare and little known thrush of highland forest ground-stratum (Britton 1980). It is known from only a few localities around the Albertine Rift in eastern Zaire, Rwanda and south-western Uganda (details in Prigogine 1977).

São Tomé Thrush *Turdus olivaceofuscus* is common in the wooded parts of São Tomé up to 1,600 m, and occurs in well shaded plantations; but the subspecies *xanthorhynchus* on Príncipe, never common, might now be extinct, for reasons unknown (de Naurois 1983,1984a).

Rufous-winged Illadopsis *Trichastoma rufescens* is endemic to the forests west of the Dahomey Gap. It is the commonest *Trichastoma* in the Sierra Leone forests and can withstand considerable habitat damage (G. D. Field pers. comm. 1983). Eighteen specimens were collected at Mount Nimba, Liberia, in 1966-1969 (Colston and Curry-Lindahl in press), it is recorded from Lamto in Ivory Coast (Brunel and Thiollay 1969) and there are old records from Ghana (Bates 1930a). J.-M. Thiollay (pers. comm. 1983) does not consider it rare in Ivory Coast; it is presumably overlooked and in no serious danger.

Wedge-tailed Jery *Hartertula flavoviridis* is a generally uncommon bird of the eastern rainforests of Madagascar, with its stronghold in the Sihanaka forest (see Conservation Measures Proposed under Madagascar Serpent Eagle *Eutriorchis astur* in the main text) and other records from Vondrozo (in the south), Périnet-Analamazaotra Special Reserve, Bejofo-Bealanana (at roughly 14°30'S 48°45'E) and Tsaratanana Nature Reserve (R.N.I. no. 4) (Rand 1936, Albignac 1970, Milon *et al.* 1973, Benson *et al.* 1976-1977). The species appears in little danger but deserves monitoring.

Red-collared Flycatcher-babbler *Lioptilus rufocinctus* is only known from Nyungwe Forest in Rwanda and Itombwe Forest and Mount Kabobo in eastern Zaire (Prigogine in press). It is a species of montane forest above 1,500 m (Prigogine 1980a) and it is probably not immediately threatened (A. Prigogine *in litt.* 1983).

Chapin's Flycatcher-babbler *Lioptilus chapini* is only known from Itombwe Forest and the forests west of Lakes Mobutu (Albert), Edward and Kivu, at altitudes between 1,000 and 1,650 m (Prigogine 1980a) and it is probably not immediately threatened (A. Prigogine *in litt.* 1983).

White-winged Warbler *Bradypterus carpalis* is largely restricted to papyrus swamps in eastern Zaire, Rwanda, Burundi, Uganda and Kenya (Chapin 1953, Britton 1978,1980, Vande weghe 1981). It faces the threat of swamp drainage and papyrus exploitation.

Bamboo Warbler *Bradypterus alfredi* is a widely distributed but curiously uncommon and rare bird. Two subspecies are currently recognised. The nominate form is known from early records from north-eastern Zaire and south-western Uganda (all summarised in Chapin 1953). The subspecies *kungwensis* was discovered on Mahale Mountain, western Tanzania, in 1941 (Moreau 1942); other birds referable to this race have been found in Upemba National Park in southern Zaire (Prigogine 1980b) and in the Mwinilunga District of north-western Zambia (see Benson and Irwin 1964,1965). More recent records of birds collected in three localities in southern and western Ethiopia (Ash 1977) and Sudan (van den Elzen and König 1983) might be referable to a new race. Very little is known of this species, though it has been found in long grass, forest and bamboo. The reasons for its rarity are obscure, though it is unlikely to be in any great danger.

Mrs Benson's Warbler *Nesillas mariae* occurs on Moheli and Grand Comoro (Comoro Islands), and is known from five specimens (Benson 1960). On Moheli it was found to be common in 1975 (Cheke 1980), and again in 1983, though only occurring above 200 m (M. Louette *in litt.* 1984); on Grand Comoro it was discovered on the lower slopes of Mount Karthala in 1974 (A. D. Forbes-Watson pers. comm. 1984).

Socotra Cisticola *Cisticola haesitata* is confined to Socotra (Yemen Democratic Republic) where it is unaccountably uncommon (see Ripley and Bond 1966). That it is distinct at species level from the Fan-tailed Warbler *C. juncidis* is borne out by the different structure of their respective nests (A. D. Forbes-Watson pers. comm. 1984).

White-eyed Prinia *Prinia leontica* occurs locally in north-eastern Sierra Leone, Guinea, Liberia and Ivory Coast, in thickets bordering streams, wooded highlands, and in mountain gallery forests (apparently being commonest in mountain ravines), though rarely at mountain bases (Bates 1930b, Bannerman 1939, Walker 1939, Brunel and Thiollay 1969, Colston and Curry-Lindahl in press, G. D. Field pers. comm. 1983). On Mount Nimba it occurs on the upper forest edge, where the fragmentation of the forest as a result of mining activities has probably increased the amount of suitable habitat (A. D. Forbes-Watson pers. comm. 1984).

Forest Prinia *Prinia robertsi* is restricted to the highlands of eastern Zimbabwe and adjacent Mozambique where it is common (Irwin 1981); it does not, however, occur on Mount Gorongosa in Mozambique (Irwin 1979).

White-winged Apalis *Apalis chariessa* is known only from the lower Tana River in coastal Kenya, the Uluguru Mountains and the Mwanihana and Chita forests in the Uzungwa Mountains in eastern Tanzania, Mount Chiperone in Mozambique, and 11 small forests in southern Malawi (Benson 1950, Britton 1980, Stuart and Jensen 1981, R. J. Dowsett *in litt.* 1983, F. P. Jensen pers. comm. 1984). There has been only one record this century from the Tana River, in 1961 (Britton 1980), where it might now be extinct. The type-locality, Mitole, on the Tana River, had been cleared of forest by the mid-1960s (A. D. Forbes-Watson pers. comm. 1984). The total population in Malawi is only about 100 pairs and it is under severe threat from forest clearance, including on Chiradzulu (or Lisau) where the largest population occurs (R. J. Dowsett *in litt.* 1983). The Tanzanian populations are in much more extensive forests which are under less immediate threat.

Rudd's Apalis *Apalis ruddi* occurs in southern Mozambique and KwaZulu (South Africa) in thickets and forest edges where it is apparently not common (Clancey 1971), although a new subspecies has recently been discovered in southern Malawi (Hanmer 1979).

Chirinda Apalis *Apalis chirindensis* is restricted to but common in the highland forests of eastern Zimbabwe (Irwin 1981) and neighbouring Mozambique including Mount Gorongosa (Clancey 1971).

Pearson's Warbler *Apalis melanura* is known from only a few localities in Angola and Zaire. The type was collected "somewhere in northern Angola" (see Chapin 1953) and it was subsequently found to be reasonably common in an area of dry woodlands 50 km south-west of Cacolo at 1,400 m, especially around grassy clearings (Ripley and Heinrich 1960). In Zaire it is known from Ndola District near Kipushi and the upper Lufupa valley where it is apparently not uncommon in woodland on the upper Lufupa River (Chapin 1953). It occurs in areas where little fieldwork has taken place and is no doubt much commoner than it appears. There is considerable taxonomic confusion about this species, referred to in some older publications as *Cisticola pearsoni*.

Brown Emu-tail *Dromaeocercus brunneus* is known principally from the central-eastern rainforests of Madagascar, in a circle whose diameter is between Antananarivo and Tamatave: localities include three now destroyed (D. A. Turner pers. comm. 1983) – "near Antananarivo" (Sharpe 1877), east Imerina forests (Oberholser 1900), and Fanovana (Delacour 1932, Rand 1936) – but birds occur fairly commonly in the Périnet-Analamazaotra Special Reserve (Milon *et al.* 1973) and are locally abundant in Sihanaka forest (its stronghold) – see Conservation Measures Proposed under Madagascar Serpent Eagle *Eutriorchis astur* in the main text – and in Fierenana forest, and the species even occurs in partially exploited forest at Nangarana (Delacour 1932, Rand 1936, Malcolm 1970, Milon *et al.* 1973). It was common last century in Tsarafidy (= Ankafana) forest (Deans Cowan 1882; see Griveaud 1961). It was found in the Tsaratanana Nature Reserve (R.N.I. no. 4) in 1966 (Albignac 1970), in 1984 near Vondrozo (O. Langrand pers. comm. 1984).

Black-headed Stream Warbler *Bathmocercus cerviniventris* is a bird of streams in primary and secondary forest west of the Dahomey Gap where it is not common (Walker 1939). Early records come from Ghana (Bannerman 1939) and there is an Ivory Coast specimen collected in 1960 (Louette 1976). Eight specimens were collected on Mount Nimba, Liberia, in 1968 (Colston and Curry-Lindahl in press). In Sierra Leone it was collected at Sandaru (Bannerman 1931-1932) and at Sefadu and in the Nimmini Mountains (Walker 1939). It is fairly common in eastern Sierra Leone in gallery and streamside vegetation, both montane and lowland (G. D. Field pers. comm. 1983). In 1959 a specimen was collected from Guinea at Seredon (Berlioz and Roche 1960).

Somali Short-billed Crombec *Sylvietta philippae* is known from Somalia and Ethiopia, and has recently been found sufficiently widespread to be considered at no risk (Ash 1982, Ash and Miskell 1983).

Rand's Warbler *Randia pseudozosterops* is endemic to the eastern rainforests of Madagascar; it was originally considered to be very rare (e.g. Delacour 1932) but is now known to be commoner and fairly widespread (Salvan 1970, D. A. Turner pers. comm. 1983).

Ward's Flycatcher *Pseudobias wardi* is a generally uncommon bird of the eastern rainforests of Madagascar; though found the length of the humid east, it has only been recorded from nine localities: from near Fort Dauphin (specimen in MNHN: NJC), this record extending the known range 250 km to the south of the southern limit given in published literature, Ivohibé, Fanovana (Delacour 1932), Périnet (Benson *et al.* 1976-1977), Sihanaka forest, Maroantsetra, Andapa (Delacour 1932) and Tsaratanana Nature Reserve (R.N.I. no. 4) (Milon 1951b). It is observed most often in large, dense, humid, evergreen forests and frequents what is variously noted as tree-tops and bushes (Sibree 1891, Rand 1936, Milon *et al.* 1973).

Margaret's Batis *Batis margaritae* occurs in Angola only in forest on the upper slopes of Mount Môco and the Manje Mountains (Traylor 1963, A. A. da R. Pinto *in litt.* 1983) and in north-western Zambia and Katanga in southern Zaire (Chapin 1953). It is not uncommon in parts of Zambia (Bowen 1979).

Woodward's Batis *Batis fratrum* occurs in forest in South Africa (coastal KwaZulu), southern Mozambique, southern Malawi and south-eastern Zimbabwe, where it is common in several places (Collar 1982, J. Burlison *in litt.* 1983).

Gabon Batis *Batis minima* is only known from Gabon and was formerly believed to be very rare, but recent fieldwork has shown it to be common and tolerant of forest disturbance (A. Brosset pers. comm. 1983, C. Erard pers. comm. 1983).

White-fronted Wattle-eye *Platysteira albifrons* is found in gallery forests and coffee plantations along the Angolan coast and escarpment from Luanda to Benguela (Traylor 1963, Hall and Moreau 1970, A. A. da R. Pinto *in litt.* 1983) but is little known.

São Tomé Paradise Flycatcher *Terpsiphone atrochalybea* is endemic to São Tomé where it is common but appears to have suffered from pesticide spraying (de Naurois 1983,1984b).

Bedford's Paradise Flycatcher *Tersiphone bedfordi* is endemic to eastern Zaire, occurring in transition forest between 980 m and 1,500 m, exceptionally in mountain forest up to 1,800 m (Prigogine 1976,1980c, in press). In the southern part of its range it hybridises with the Red-bellied Paradise Flycatcher *T. rufiventer* but introgression is very limited (Prigogine 1976,1980c).

Plain-backed Sunbird *Anthreptes reichenowi* occurs in southern Mozambique in forest and *Brachystegia* woodland, extending to south-eastern Zimbabwe (Clancey 1971). It also occurs in the forests of the Kenya coast south to the Usambara foothills in north-eastern Tanzania (Britton 1980). It is common in places (SNS).

Uluguru Violet-backed Sunbird *Anthreptes neglectus* is known by a very few records from the Kenya coast and otherwise from several forest sites in eastern Tanzania and northern Mozambique (Hall and Moreau 1970, Britton 1980) but it is probably in no immediate danger (SNS).

Giant Sunbird *Dreptes thomensis*, the largest representative of its family outside the aberrant Oriental genus *Arachnothera* (Amadon 1953), is restricted to forest in the centre and west of São Tomé, where it is reasonably common, feeding along branches, probing in bark, and at banana blossoms (Correia 1928-1929, Snow 1950, R. de Naurois pers. comm. 1983).

Ursula's Mouse-coloured Sunbird *Nectarinia ursulae* is known from submontane forest in western Cameroon on Mount Cameroon, the Rumpi Hills, Mount Nlonako and the southern slopes of the Bamenda Highlands at Foto (Serle 1950,1954,1965, Eisentraut 1963, SNS). It has a narrow altitudinal range in which some forest clearance is taking place, but it is not seriously threatened at present (SNS).

Moreau's Sunbird *Nectarinia moreaui* is restricted to forest at Nguru, Ukaguru, Uvidunda and on the eastern escarpment of the Uzungwa Mountains, all in Tanzania, where it is very common (Stuart and van der Willigen 1980).

Neergaard's Sunbird *Nectarinia neergaardi* occurs along the coast of southern Mozambique in woodland and dry forest, where it is not very common (Clancey 1971), and also in South Africa as far as St.Lucia and KwaZulu (McLachlan and Liversidge 1978).

Loveridge's Sunbird *Nectarinia loveridgei* is restricted to the Uluguru Mountains, Tanzania, where it is abundant (SNS). It can also tolerate some forest clearance (Williams 1951).

Pagulu White-eye *Zosterops griseovirescens* is confined to the small (17 km²) island of Pagalu (Equatorial Guinea), 1°25'S 5°37'E, in the Gulf of Guinea where, however, it is universally reported as abundant and occurring wherever bush- or tree-cover exists (Bocage 1893, Bannerman 1915, Basilio 1957, Fry 1961), on which evidence it seems unlikely to be at risk.

Gurney's Sugarbird *Promerops gurneyi* breeds in *Protea* veld from the Amatole Mountains, eastern Cape Province, discontinuously northwards to the highlands along the Zimbabwe/Mozambique border (Clancey 1980, Brooke in press). It has probably declined with the destruction, either by burning or afforestation, of *Protea* but it is adequately conserved in several protected areas in South Africa (Brooke in press).

Papyrus Canary *Serinus koliensis* is largely restricted to papyrus swamps, avoiding lowland areas with rainfall of less than 1,000 mm, in eastern Zaire, Rwanda, Burundi, Uganda and Kenya (Chapin 1953, Britton 1978,1980, Vande weghe 1981). It faces the threat of swamp drainage and papyrus exploitation.

Salvadori's Serin *Serinus xantholaema* is known from central Harar, northern Bale and central Sidamo provinces, Ethiopia (Erard 1974) and, though rare, is probably spread widely enough to be at no risk.

Lemon-breasted Canary *Serinus citrinipectus* is mainly known from southern Mozambique where it is generally fairly uncommon but can be locally abundant (Clancey 1971). It is also known from southern Malawi (Benson and Benson 1977, Hanmer *et al.* 1983), Zimbabwe (Irwin 1981) and parts of South Africa (McLachlan and Liversidge 1978).

Protea Serin *Serinus leucopterus* is endemic to South Africa and confined to the mountains of the south-western Cape Province from the northern Cedarberg southwards and east in the southern mountains to the Groot Winterberge (Clancey 1980). It is restricted to mature *Protea* fynbos, and feeds extensively on *Protea* seeds (Milewski 1978).

Drakensberg Siskin *Serinus symonsi* is restricted to but plentiful at high altitudes on the Drakensberg massif in Lesotho and South Africa, frequenting plateau grasslands, boulder-strewn hillsides and gullies with low scrub (Clancey 1964,1980, Cyrus and Robson 1980).

Shelley's Crimson-wing *Cryptospiza shelleyi* is known from many of the mountain ranges along the Albertine Rift: in eastern Zaire, in the Itombwe Mountains and mountains west of Lake Kivu; in Rwanda, in the Virunga Volcanoes, Nyungwe Forest, Gishwati Forest and Makwa Forest; in Burundi, in Bururi Forest and elsewhere; in Uganda, Mount Rwenzori and Impenetrable Forest (Britton 1980, J.-P. Vande weghe pers. comm. 1983, Prigogine in press). It is generally rare throughout its range though common in a few small and threatened forest patches (Gishwati, Makwa, Bururi) in Rwanda and Burundi (J.-P. Vande weghe pers. comm. 1983). There is some evidence of a decline in the Virunga Volcanoes (J. R. Wilson *in litt.* 1983), perhaps owing to forest clearance. In general, however, a considerable area of montane forest, suitable for this species, survives, and it seems unlikely to be in any immediate danger.

Pink-throated Twinspot *Hypargos margaritatus* occurs in southern Mozambique in scrub and bush, locally common in places (Clancey 1971). It extends to St.Lucia, KwaZulu and parts of Transvaal (Clancey 1980, Edmonds 1984).

Neumann's Waxbill *Estrilda thomensis* is very locally distributed in Angola from Dondo south to Benguela, Huila and Moçâmedes provinces, occurring in the south in dry mopane and acacia woodland (A. A. da R. Pinto *in litt.* 1983). Its occurrence on São Tomé is questioned (Hall and Moreau 1970).

Fox's Weaver *Ploceus spekeoides* was first collected in 1913 but described as a full species only in 1947 (Grant and Mackworth-Praed 1947). Twelve specimens were collected in June/July 1948 (all in BMNH: SNS): the collector reported many nests of the species at Aketa, Usulu, Nariam and Katakwi in Teso District, Uganda (Pitman 1948). The species is fairly common in north-eastern Teso District during the rains (Mann 1976). In the dry season the birds apparently leave their breeding areas but it is not known where they go to, possibly Karamoja or southern Sudan (Pitman 1948). The species breeds in swamps in a limited part of Uganda, though it probably occurs more widely around Lake Kyoga than has so far been proved (Turner 1977). It is common where it occurs (Pitman 1948, Mann 1976).

Copper-tailed Glossy Starling *Lamprotornis cupreocauda* is restricted to forests west of the Dahomey Gap. It is very common in the eastern forests of Sierra Leone (G. D. Field pers. comm. 1983). In Liberia 14 specimens were collected at Mount Nimba in 1967-1970, where it prefers secondary swamp forests (Colston and Curry-Lindahl in press). It is probably widespread in forest-edge habitat in Liberia (A. D. Forbes-Watson pers. comm. 1984). In Ivory Coast it is localised in the semi-deciduous forest zone at 6-7°N (Brunel and Thiollay 1969). Recent Ghana records come from Bia National Park where it has been seen singly and in small groups (Taylor and Macdonald 1978).

Abbott's Starling *Cinnyricinclus femoralis* is known from a few mountain forests in Kenya and northern Tanzania including Arusha National Park, Kilimanjaro National Park and Mount Kenya National Park (Britton 1980). Forest destruction on Mount Kenya has been reported (P. L. Britton pers. comm. 1982, A. W. Diamond pers. comm. 1982) and is now also known to be occurring extensively in prime habitat for the species on Mount Kilimanjaro (including inside the national park) (H. Grossmann pers. comm. 1984). Given that its occurrence in Arusha National Park may be only periodical (Beesley 1972, H. Grossmann pers. comm. 1984), studies are urgently needed to clarify the conservation status of this species.

Aldabra Drongo *Dicrurus aldabranus* is restricted to Aldabra atoll (Seychelles) where it is frequent in dense scrub, *Casuarina* and mangrove, preferentially using the latter two for breeding; based on territory sizes (2.25 ha in *Casuarina* woodland, 4.5 ha in mixed scrub) and habitat distribution, the population is considered to number roughly 1,500 birds and, although the influence of rats *Rattus* on the species is unknown, no conservation measures are currently felt to be needed (O. E. Prys-Jones and R. P. Prys-Jones *in litt.* 1983).

References

Albignac, R. (1970) Mammifères et oiseaux du Massif du Tsaratanana. *Mém. ORSTOM* 37: 223-229.

Andriamampianina, J. (1981) Les réserves naturelles et la protection de la nature à Madagascar. Pp. 105-111 in P. Oberlé, ed. *Madagascar, un sanctuaire de la nature*. Paris: Lechevalier.

Appert, O. (1966) Beitrag zur Biologie und zur Kenntnis der Verbreitung des Madagaskar-Mähnenibisses, *Lophotibis cristata* (Boddaert). *J. Orn.* 107: 315-322.

Ash, J. S. (1977) Four species of birds new to Ethiopia and other notes. *Bull. Brit. Orn. Club* 97: 4-9.

Ash, J. S. (1978) The undescribed female of Harwood's Francolin *Francolinus harwoodi* and other observations on the species. *Bull. Brit. Orn. Club* 98: 50-55.

Ash, J. S. (1981) Field description of the Obbia Lark *Calandrella obbiensis*, its breeding and distribution. *Bull. Brit. Orn. Club* 107: 379-383.

Ash, J. S. (1982) The Somali Short-billed Crombec *Sylvietta philippae* in Somalia and Ethiopia. *Bull. Brit. Orn. Club* 102: 89-92.

Ash, J. S. (1983) Over fifty additions of birds to the Somalia list including two hybrids, together with notes from Ethiopia and Kenya. *Scopus* 7: 54-79.

Ash, J. S., Erard, C. and Prévost, J. (1974) Statut et distribution de *Streptopelia reichenowi* en Ethiopie. *Oiseau et R.F.O.* 44: 340-345.

Ash, J. S. and Miskell, J. E. (1983) *Birds of Somalia: their habitat, status and distribution. Scopus* Spec. Suppl. 1. Nairobi: Ornithological Sub-Committee, EANHS.

Bannerman, D. A. (1915) Report on the birds collected by the late Mr Boyd Alexander (Rifle Brigade) during his last expedition to Africa. Part III. The birds of Annobon Island. *Ibis* (10)3: 227-234.

Bannerman, D. A. (1931-1932) Account of the birds collected (i) by Mr G. L. Bates on behalf of the British Museum in Sierra Leone and French Guinea; (ii) by Lt.-Col. G. J. Houghton, R.A.M.C., in Sierra Leone, recently acquired by the British Museum. *Ibis* (13)1: 661-697; (13)2: 1-33, 217-261.

Bannerman, D. A. (1939) *The birds of tropical West Africa*, 5. London: Crown Agents for the Colonies.

Barré, N. (1983) Distribution et abondance des oiseaux terrestres de l'île de la Réunion (Ocean Indien). *Rev. Ecol. (Terre et Vie)* 37: 37-85.

Barré, N. and Barau, A. (1982) *Oiseaux de la Réunion*. St.-Denis [Réunion]: Imprimerie Arts Graphiques Modernes.

Basilio, R. P. A. (1957) *Caza y pesca en Annobon*. Madrid: Instituto de Estudios Africanos.

Basilio, A. (1963) *Aves de la Isla de Fernando Poo*. Madrid: Editorial Coculsa.

Bates, G. L. (1930a) *Handbook of the birds of West Africa*. London: John Bale, Sons and Danielsson.

Bates, G. L. (1930b) [New birds from West Africa.] *Bull. Brit. Orn. Club* 51: 47-54.

Beesley, J. S. S. (1972) Birds of the Arusha National Park, Tanzania. *J. E. Afr. Nat. Hist. Soc. and Natn. Mus.* 132: 1-32.

Benson, C. W. (1950) A collection from Chiperoni Mountain, Portuguese East Africa. *Bull. Brit. Orn. Club* 70: 51.

Benson, C. W. (1960) The birds of the Comoro Islands: results of the British Ornithologists' Union Centenary Expedition 1958. *Ibis* 103b: 5-106.

Benson, C. W. and Benson, F. M. (1977) *The birds of Malawi*. Limbe, Malawi: Montfort Press.

Benson, C. W. and Irwin, M. P. S. (1964) Some additions and corrections to *A checklist of the birds of Northern Rhodesia*. Number 5. *Occ. Pap. Natn. Mus. S. Rhod.* 27B: 106-127.

Benson, C. W. and Irwin, M. P. S. (1965) Some birds from the North-western Province, Zambia. *Arnoldia Rhod.* 1(29): 1-11.

Benson, C. W. and Pitman, C.,R. S. (1966) Further breeding records from Zambia (formerly Northern Rhodesia) (No. 5). *Bull. Brit. Orn. Club* 86: 21-33.

Benson, C. W. and Penny, M. J. (1971) The land birds of Aldabra. *Phil. Trans. Roy. Soc. Lond.* B 260: 417-527.

Benson, C. W., Colebrook-Robjent, J. F. R. and Williams, A (1976-1977) Contribution à l'ornithologie de Madagascar. *Oiseau et R.F.O.* 46: 103-134, 209-242, 367-386; 47: 41-64, 167-191.

Berlioz, J. and Roche, J. (1960) Etude d'une collection d'oiseaux de Guinée. *Bull. Mus. Natn. Hist. Nat.* (2)32: 272-283.

Bocage, J. V. B. (1893) Note sur deux oiseaux nouveaux de l'île Anno-Bom. *J. Sci. Math. Phys. Nat. Lisboa* (2)9: 17-18.

Bowen, P. St.J. (1979) Some notes on Margaret's Batis *Batis margaritae* in Zambia. *Bull. Zambian Orn. Soc.* 11(2): 1-10.

Britton, P. L. (1978) Seasonality, density and diversity of birds of a papyrus swamp in western Kenya. *Ibis* 120: 450-466.

Britton, P. L. ed. (1980) *Birds of East Africa: their habitat, status and distribution*. Nairobi: EANHS.

Brooke, M. de L. (1978) Inland observations of Barau's Petrel *Pterodroma baraui* on Réunion. *Bull. Brit. Orn. Club* 98: 90-95.

Brooke, R. K. (in press) *The rare and vulnerable birds of South Africa*.

Brown, L. H. (1977) The White-winged Dove *Streptopelia reichenowi* in S. E. Ethiopia, comparisons with other species, and a field key for identification. *Scopus* 1: 107-109.

Brown, L. H., Urban, E. K. and Newman, K. (1982) *The birds of Africa*, 1. London: Academic Press.

Brunel, J. and Thiollay, J.-M. (1969) Liste préliminaire des oiseaux de Côte d'Ivoire. *Alauda* 37: 230-254, 315-337.

Butler, A. L. (1905) A contribution to the ornithology of the Egyptian Soudan. *Ibis* (8)5: 301-401.

Cave, F. O. and Macdonald, J. D. (1955) *Birds of the Sudan: their identification and distribution*. Edinburgh and London: Oliver and Boyd.

Chapin, J. P. (1953) The birds of the Belgian Congo. Part 3. *Bull. Amer. Mus. Nat. Hist.* 75A.

Chapin, J. P. (1958) A new honey-guide from the Kivu District, Belgian Congo. *Bull. Brit. Orn. Club* 78: 46-48.

Chapin, J. P. (1962) Sibling species of small African honeyguides. *Ibis* 104: 40-44.

Cheke, A. S. (1974) British Ornithologists' Union Mascarene Islands Expedition: Report on Rodrigues. Unpublished.

Cheke, A. S. (1978) Recommendations for the conservation of Mascarene vertebrates. Conservation memorandum no. 3 (arising out of the B.O.U. Mascarene Islands Expedition). Unpublished.

Cheke, A. S. (1980) [Review of King (1978-1979).] *Ibis* 122: 545.

Cheke, A. S. (in press a) The surviving native land-birds of Mauritius. In A. W. Diamond, ed. *Studies of Mascarene island birds*. Cambridge: Cambridge University Press.

Cheke, A. S. (in press b) The ecology of the surviving native land-birds of Réunion. In A. W. Diamond, ed. *Studies of Mascarene island birds*. Cambridge: Cambridge University Press.

Clancey, P. A. (1964) *The birds of Natal and Zululand*. Edinburgh and London: Oliver and Boyd.

Clancey, P. A. (1967) Comments on *Ammomanes burra* Bangs. *Bull. Brit. Orn. Club* 87: 13-14.

Clancey, P. A. (1971) *A handlist of the birds of southern Moçambique*. Lourenço Marques: Instituto de Investigação Científica de Moçambique.

Clancey, P. A. ed. (1980) *S.A.O.S. checklist of southern African birds*. [Pretoria:] Southern African Ornithological Society.

Collar, N. J. (1982) Extracts from the red data book for the birds of Africa and associated islands. Cambridge: ICBP, unpublished.

Collar, N. J. and Violani, C. G. (in press) Specimens of the Obbia Lark *Calandrella obbiensis* and White-winged Flufftail *Sarothrura ayresi* in Milan Museum. *Bull. Brit. Orn. Club*.

Colston, P. R. and Curry-Lindahl, K. (in press) The birds of the Mount Nimba region in Liberia. *Bull. Brit. Mus. (Nat. Hist.) Zool.*

Cooper, J. (1981) Biology of the Bank Cormorant, part 1: distribution, population size, movements and conservation. *Ostrich* 52: 208-215.

Correia, J. G. (1928-1929) Unpublished typescript concerning his São Tomé expedition, held in AMNH.

Cramp, S. and Simmons, K. E. L. eds. (1980) *The birds of the western Palearctic*, 2. Oxford: Oxford University Press.

Crawford, R. J. M., Shelton, P. A., Brooke, R. K. and Cooper, J. (1982) Taxonomy, distribution, population size and conservation of the Crowned Cormorant *Phalacrocorax coronatus*. *Gerfaut* 73: 3-20.

Cyrus, D. and Robson, N. (1980) *Bird atlas of Natal*. Pietermaritzburg: University of Natal Press.

Deans Cowan, W. (1882) Notes on the natural history of Madagascar. *Proc. Roy. Phys. Soc. Edinburgh* 7: 133-150.

Delacour, J. (1932) Les oiseaux de la Mission Franco-Anglo-Américaine à Madagascar. *Oiseau et R.F.O.* 2: 1-96.

Dick, W. J. A. ed. (1975) Oxford and Cambridge Mauritanian Expedition 1973 report. Unpublished.

Dowsett, R. J. (1983) Breeding and other observations of the Taita Falcon *Falco fasciinucha*. *Ibis* 125: 362-366.

Edmonds, E. (1984) Pinkthroated Twinspots in Transvaal. *Bokmakierie* 36: 47-48.

Eisentraut, M. (1963) *Die Wirbeltiere des Kamerungebirges*. Hamburg and Berlin: Paul Parey.

Eisentraut, M. (1973) Die Wirbeltierfauna von Fernando Poo und Westkamerun. *Bonn. zool. Monog.* 3.

Elgood, J. H. (1965) The birds of the Obudu Plateau, Eastern Region of Nigeria. *Nigerian Field* 30: 60-69.

Elgood, J. H. (1976) Montane birds of Nigeria. *Bull. Nigerian Orn. Soc.* 12: 31-34.

Elgood, J. H. (1982) *The birds of Nigeria*. London: B.O.U. Check-list no. 4.

van den Elzen, R. and König, C. (1983) Vögel des (Süd-)Sudan: taxonomische und tiergeographische Bemerkungen. *Bonn. zool. Beitr.* 34: 149-196.

Erard, C. (1974) Taxonomie des serins à gorge jaune d'Ethiopie. *Oiseau et R.F.O.* 44: 308-323.

Fairon, J. (1975) Contribution à l'ornithologie de l'Air (Niger). *Gerfaut* 65: 107-134.

Fisher, C. T. (1981) Specimens of extinct, endangered or rare birds in the Merseyside County Museums, Liverpool. *Bull. Brit. Orn. Club* 101: 276-285.

Friedmann, H. (1962) The Machris expedition to Tschad, Africa. Birds. *Los Angeles County Mus. Contrib. Sci.* 59.

Fry, C. H. (1961) Notes on the birds of Annobon and other islands in the Gulf of Guinea. *Ibis* 103a: 267-276.

Gee, J. P. (1974) Ornithological observations in Mauritania, 1971-1974. Unpublished.

Grant, C. H. B. and Mackworth-Praed, C. W. (1942) A new race of Blue Swallow from Tanganyika Territory. *Bull. Brit. Orn. Club* 62: 43-45.

Grant, C. H. B. and Mackworth-Praed, C. W. (1947) A new species of weaver from Uganda. *Bull. Brit. Orn. Club* 68: 7-8.

Griveaud, P. (1961) Un interesant vestige forestier malgache. *Bull. Acad. Malgache* 39: 9-10.

Hall, B. P. (1961) The faunistic importance of the scarp of Angola. *Ibis* 102: 420-442.

Hall, B. P. and Moreau, R. E. (1970) *An atlas of speciation in African passerine birds*. London: Trustees of the British Museum (Natural History).

Hanmer, D. B. (1979) An undescribed subspecies of Rudd's Apalis *Apalis ruddi* from southern Malawi. *Bull. Brit. Orn. Club* 99: 27-28.

Hanmer, D. B., Stephens, W. and Evans, D. (1983) Notes on the Lemon-breasted Canary *Serinus citrinipectus*. *Nyala* 9: 60.

Heinrich, G. H. (1958) Zur Verbreitung und Lebensweise der Vögel von Angola. Part 2. *J. Orn.* 99: 322-362.

Hockey, P. A. R. (1983) The distribution, population size, movements and conservation status of the African Black Oystercatcher *Haematopus moquini*. *Biol. Conserv.* 25: 233-262.

Hockey, P. A. R. and Sinclair, J. C. (1981) The nest and systematic position of Sclater's Lark. *Ostrich* 52: 256-257.

Irwin, M. P. S. (1979) The Zimbabwe-Rhodesian and Moçambique highland avian endemics: their evolution and origins. *Honeyguide* no. 99: 5-11.

Irwin, M. P. S. (1981) *The birds of Zimbabwe*. Salisbury, Zimbabwe: Quest Publishing.

Jadin, B. and Billiet, F. (1979) Observations ornithologiques à la Réunion. *Gerfaut* 69: 339-352.

Jensen, R. A. C. and Jensen, M. K. (1971) First breeding records of the Herero Chat *Namibornis herero*, and taxonomic implications. Proc. III Pan-Afr. orn. Congr. *Ostrich* suppl. 8: 105-116.

Jones, C. G. (1980) The conservation of the endemic birds and bats of Mauritius and Rodriguez (a progress report and proposal for further activities). Unpublished.

Jones, C. G. and Owadally, A. W. (1982) Conservation priorities for Mauritius and Rodrigues. Report submitted to ICBP, July. Unpublished.

Jouanin, C. and Gill, F. B. (1967) Recherche du Pétrel de Barau, *Pterodroma baraui*. *Oiseau et R.F.O.* 37: 1-19.

Jouanin, C. (in press) Notes on the nesting of Procellariiformes in Réunion. In A. W. Diamond, ed. *Studies of Mascarene island birds*. Cambridge: Cambridge University Press.

Kaudern, W. (1922) Sauropsiden aus Madagaskar. *Zool. Jahrb.* 45: 395-457.

Keith, S. and Twomey, A. (1968) New distributional records of some East African birds. *Ibis* 110: 537-548.

King, W. B. (1978-1979) *Red data book, 2: Aves*. 2nd edition. Morges, Switzerland: IUCN.

Lack, P. C. (1977) The status of Friedmann's Bush-lark *Mirafra pulpa*. *Scopus* 1: 34-39.

Lamarche, B. (1980) Liste commentée des oiseaux du Mali. 1ère partie: Non-passereaux. *Malimbus* 2: 121-158.

Langrand, O. and Meyburg, B.-U. (in press) Birds of prey and owls in Madagascar: their distribution, status and conservation. Second symposium on African predatory birds, 22-26 August 1983.

Lavauden, L. (1932) Etude d'une petite collection d'oiseaux de Madagascar. *Bull. Mus. Natn. Hist. Nat.* (2)4: 629-640.

Lawson, W. J. (1961) The races of the Karoo Lark *Certhilauda albescens* (Lafresnaye). *Ostrich* 32: 64-74.

Lewis, A. D. (1981) The past and present status and distribution of the Grey-crested Helmet-shrike *Prionops poliolopha*. *Scopus* 5: 66-70.

Lewis, A. D. (1982) Further records of the Grey-crested Helmet Shrike. *Scopus* 6: 47-48.

Louette. M. (1976) Notes on the genus *Bathmocercus* Reichenow. Part 1. The different plumages of *B. cerviniventris* and its relationship to *B. rufus*. *Rev. Zool. Afr.* 90: 1021-1027.

McLachlan, G. R. and Liversidge, R. (1978) *Roberts birds of South Africa*. 4th edition. Cape Town: Trustees of the John Voelcker Bird Book Fund.

Malcolm, N. S. (1970) Birds of some forest and degraded forest habitats in Madagascar. Conférence internationale sur l'utilisation rationelle et la conservation de la nature, Tananarive, 7-11 October 1970. Typescript.

Mann, C. F. (1976) The birds of Teso District, Uganda. *J. E. Afr. Nat. Hist. Soc. and Natn. Mus.* 156: 1-16.

Meinertzhagen, R. (1912) On the birds of Mauritius. *Ibis* (9)6: 82-108.

van der Merwe, F. (1981) Review of the status and biology of the Black Harrier. *Ostrich* 52: 193-207.

Milewski, A. V. (1978) Diet of *Serinus* species in the southwestern Cape, with special reference to the Protea Seedeater. *Ostrich* 49: 174-184.

Milon, P. (1949) Tableaux d'identification des échassiers blancs et des échassiers noirs observés aux abords de Tananarive. *Naturaliste Malgache* 1(2): 93-100.

Milon, P. (1951a) Notes sur l'avifaune actuelle de l'île de la Réunion. *Terre et Vie* 98: 129-178.

Milon, P. (1951b) Etude d'une petite collection d'oiseaux du Tsaratanana. *Naturaliste Malgache* 3(2): 167-183.

Milon, P. (1952) Notes sur le genre *Coua*. *Oiseau et R.F.O.* 22: 75-90.

Milon, P., Petter, J.-J. and Randrianasolo, G. (1973) *Faune de Madagascar, 35. Oiseaux*. Tananarive and Paris: ORSTOM and CNRS.

Moreau, R. E. (1942) New races of Slaty Flycatcher, Bracken-warbler and Grey-headed Negro-finch from Tanganyika Territory. *Bull. Brit. Orn. Club* 62: 41-43.

Moutou, F. (1984) Wildlife on Réunion. *Oryx* 18: 160-162.

de Naurois, R. (1983) Les oiseaux reproducteurs des îles de São Tomé et Príncipe: liste systématique commentée et indications zoogéographiques. *Bonn. zool. Beitr.* 34: 129-148.

de Naurois, R. (1984a) Les *Turdus* des îles de São Tomé et Príncipe: *T. o. olivaceofuscus* (Hartlaub) et *T. olivaceofuscus xanthorhynchus* Salvadori (Aves Turdinae). *Rev. Zool. Afr.* 98: 403-423.

de Naurois, R. (1984b) La moucherolle endémique de l'île de São Tomé, *Terpsiphone atrochalybeia* (Thomson, 1842). *Alauda* 52: 31-44.

Newby, J. E. (1979) The birds of the Ouadi Rime – Ouadi Achim Faunal Reserve: a contribution to the study of the Chadian avifauna. *Malimbus* 1: 90-109.

Newton, E. (1863) Notes of a second visit to Madagascar. *Ibis* 5: 333-350.

Oberholser, H. C. (1900) Catalogue of a collection of birds from Madagascar. *Proc. U. S. Natn. Mus.* 22: 235-248.

Oustalet, E. (1897) Notice sur la faune ornithologique ancienne et moderne des îles Mascareignes et en particulier de l'île Maurice d'après des documents inédits. *Ann. Sci. Nat. Zool.* (8)3: 1-128.

Pitman, C. R. S. (1948) *in litt.* to C. H. B. Grant (letter held in BMNH).

Pinto, A. A. da R. (1970) Um catálogo das aves do distrito da Huíla (Angola). *Mem. Trab. Inst. Invest. Cient. Angola* no. 6.

Pinto, A. A. da R. (in press) *Ornitologia de Angola.* Lisbon.

Prigogine, A. (1965) Le pigeon à nuque blanche pour la première fois dans un jardin zoologique. *Zoo Antwerp* 30(3): 94-95.

Prigogine, A. (1976) Relations entre les gobe-mouches de paradis, *Terpsiphone rufiventer ignea* et *Terpsiphone bedfordi* et statut de ce dernier. *Gerfaut* 66: 171-205.

Prigogine, A. (1977) The Orange Ground-thrush *Turdus tanganjicae* (Sassi) a valid species. *Bull. Brit. Orn. Club* 97: 10-15.

Prigogine, A. (1978) Note sur les petits indicateurs de la Forêt de Kakamega. *Gerfaut* 68: 87-89.

Prigogine, A. (1980a). Etude de quelques contacts secondaires au Zaire oriental. *Gerfaut* 70: 305-384.

Prigogine, A. (1980b) *Bradypterus alfredi kungwensis* au Zaire. *Gerfaut* 70: 279-280.

Prigogine, A. (1980c) Hybridization between the paradise flycatchers, *Terpsiphone rufiventer* and *Terpsiphone bedfordi. Proc. IV Pan-Afr. orn. Congr.*: 17-21.

Prigogine, A. (in press) The conservation of the avifauna of the forests of the Albertine Rift. *Proceedings of the ICBP Tropical Forest Bird Symposium, 1982.*

Rand, A. L. (1936) The distribution and habits of Madagascar birds. *Bull. Amer. Mus. Nat. Hist.* 72: 143-499.

Ripley, S. D. and Bond, G. M. (1966) The birds of Socotra and Abd-el-Kuri. *Smithsonian Misc. Coll.* 151 no. 7.

Ripley, S. D. and Heinrich, G. H. (1960) Additions to the avifauna of northern Angola. I. *Postilla* 47.

Roch, S. and Newton, E. (1862) Notes on birds observed in Madagascar. Part I. *Ibis* 4: 265-275.

Rountree, F. G. R., Guérin, R., Pelte, S. and Vinson, J. (1952) Catalogue of the birds of Mauritius. *Mauritius Inst. Bull.* 3(3): 155-217.

Salvan, J. (1968) Contribution à l'étude des oiseaux du Tchad. *Oiseau et R.F.O.* 38: 53-85.

Salvan, J. (1970) Remarques sur l'évolution de l'avifaune malgache depuis 1945. *Alauda* 38: 191-203.

Salvan, J. (1972a) Essai d'évaluation des densités d'oiseaux dans quelques biotopes malgaches. *Alauda* 40: 163-170.

Salvan, J. (1972b) Statut, recensement, reproduction des oiseaux dulçaquicoles aux environs de Tananarive. *Oiseau et R.F.O.* 42: 35-51.

Serle, W. (1950) A contribution to the ornithology of the British Cameroons. *Ibis* 92: 343-376, 602-638.

Serle, W. (1954) A second contribution to the ornithology of the British Cameroons. *Ibis* 96: 47-80.

Serle, W. (1965) A third contribution to the ornithology of the British Cameroons. *Ibis* 107: 60-94, 230-246.

Sharpe, R. B. (1877) On new species of warblers in the collection of the British Museum. *Proc. Zool. Soc. Lond.*: 22-24.

Sibree, J. (1891) On the birds of Madagascar, and their connection with native folk-lore, proverbs, and superstitions. Part II. *Ibis* (6)3: 416-443.

Simon, P. (1965) Synthèse de l'avifaune du massif montagneux du Tibesti et distribution géographique de ces espèces en Afrique du nord et environs. *Gerfaut* 55: 26-71.

Snell, M. L. (1969) The vulnerable Blue Swallow. *Bokmakierie* 31: 74-78.

Snow, D. W. (1950) The birds of São Tomé and Príncipe in the Gulf of Guinea. *Ibis* 92: 579-595.

Snow, D. W. ed. (1978) *An atlas of speciation in African non-passerine birds.* London: Trustees of the British Museum (Natural History).

Stuart, S. N. and Jensen, F. P. (1981) Further range extensions and other notable records of forest birds from Tanzania. *Scopus* 5: 106-115.

Stuart, S. N. and van der Willigen, T. A. (1980) Is Moreau's Sunbird *Nectarinia moreaui* a hybrid species? *Scopus* 4: 56-58.

Temple, S. A., Staub, J. J. F. and Antoine, R. (1974) Some background information and recommendations on the preservation of the native flora and fauna of Mauritius. Unpublished report to the Government of Mauritius.

Taylor, I. R. and Macdonald, M. A. (1978) The birds of Bia National Park, Ghana. *Bull. Nigerian Orn. Soc.* 14: 36-41.

Thiollay, J.-M. and Meyburg, B.-U. (1981) Remarques sur l'organisation d'un peuplement insulaire de rapaces: Madagascar. *Alauda* 49: 216-226.

Traylor, M. A. (1963) Check-list of Angolan birds. *Publ. cult. Co. Diam. Angola, Lisboa* no. 61.

Turner, D. A. (1977) Status and distribution of the East African endemic species. *Scopus* 1: 2-11, 56.

Turner, D. A. (in press) The ground rollers of Madagascar. *Proc. V Pan-Afr. orn. Congr.*

Vande weghe, J.-P. (1981) L'avifaune des papyraies au Rwanda et au Burundi. *Gerfaut* 71: 489-536.

Vaurie, C. (1961) A new subspecies of the Nubian Bustard. *Bull. Brit. Orn. Club* 81: 26-27.

Walker, G. R. (1939) Notes on the birds of Sierra Leone. *Ibis* (14)3: 401-450.

Webb, C. S. (1954) *A wanderer in the wind.* London: Hutchinson.

Williams, J. G. (1951) Notes of *Scepomycter winifredae* and *Cinnyris loveridgei*. *Ibis* 93: 469-470.

Wills, J. (1893) Notes on some Malagasy birds rarely seen in the interior. *Antananarivo Annual* 5 (no.17): 119-120.

Winterbottom, J. M. (1961) On the edge of drought. *Bokmakierie* 13: 7-8.

Winterbottom, J. M. (1963) Notes from Namaqualand and Bushmanland. *Ostrich* 34: 156-159.

Winterbottom, J. M. (1968) A checklist of the land and freshwater birds of the western Cape Province. *Ann. S. Afr. Mus.* 53: 1-276.

Threatened bird species recorded in Africa and related islands to be treated elsewhere

The species listed below are those with a current or very recent distribution in Africa or related islands, but whose main area of distribution lies beyond the limits set for this volume in the Introduction. They are candidates for treatment as threatened in the proposed Europe and Asia volume of the *ICBP/IUCN Red Data Book* or else as Species of Special Concern in that or another volume. The countries or regions where they occur or occurred within the limits set for the present volume are very briefly indicated. A new species of cliff swallow, found in the Red Sea in 1984, is probably of Afrotropical origin (Fry and Smith in press), but may of necessity be included in the Europe and Asia volume of this work.

Herald Petrel *Pterodroma arminjoniana*: Mauritius (Round Island)
Socotra Cormorant *Phalacrocorax nigrogularis*: Somalia, Ethiopia, South
  Yemen (Socotra)
Pygmy Cormorant *Phalacrocorax pygmeus*: Algeria
Dalmatian Pelican *Pelecanus crispus*: Egypt
White Stork *Ciconia ciconia*: Africa widespread
Marbled Teal *Marmaronetta angustirostris*: North Africa
White-headed Duck *Oxyura leucocephala*: North Africa
Red Kite *Milvus milvus*: North Africa
White-tailed Sea Eagle *Haliaeetus albicilla*: Tunisia
Bearded Vulture (Lammergeier) *Gypaetus barbatus*: North-west and north-east
  Africa, South Africa
Black Vulture *Aegypius monachus*: North Africa
Spanish Imperial Eagle *Aquila adalberti*: Morocco
Peregrine Falcon *Falco peregrinus*: Africa widespread
Demoiselle Crane *Anthropoides virgo*: Morocco, north-central Africa
Corncrake *Crex crex*: East to southern Africa
Little Bustard *Tetrax tetrax*: North Africa
Great Bustard *Otis tarda*: Morocco
Houbara Bustard *Chlamydotis undulata*: North Africa
Sociable Plover *Chettusia gregaria*: North-east Africa
Slender-billed Curlew *Numenius tenuirostris*: North Africa
White-eyed Gull *Larus leucophthalmus*: Red Sea coast
Audouin's Gull *Larus audouinii*: North African coast
Roseate Tern *Sterna dougallii*: Atlantic and Indian Oceans, African coasts
Red-necked Nightjar *Caprimulgus ruficollis*: Morocco, Algeria, Tunisia

Reference

Fry, C. H. and Smith, D. A. (in press) A new swallow from the Red Sea. *Ibis*

Some incipient species at risk or requiring monitoring in Africa

Although it has been policy to exclude subspecies from this study (see Introduction), there are several instances in Africa of forms of bird which are so distinct that it is a matter of opinion as to where the species divisions should be placed: we refer to these birds as incipient species, following the terminology of Hall and Moreau (1962,1970). Treated briefly below are sixteen such incipient species which are threatened or at least deserving of closer study and monitoring. Data on these forms were gathered opportunistically in the course of preparing the main text of this book, and no attempt has been made to provide a comprehensive survey of threatened incipient species.

Etchécopar's Barred Owlet *Glaucidium (capense) etchecopari* and the **Chestnut Barred Owlet** *G. (c.) castaneum* are distinctive forms of the Barred Owlet *G. capense*. The race *etchecopari* was discovered at Lamto in Ivory Coast in 1962 with two other specimens from the same locality being collected in 1967 and 1976 (Erard and Roux 1983; specimens all in MNHN: SNS). Three birds were taken at Mount Nimba, Liberia, in 1967 (Colston and Curry-Lindahl in press). It was believed to be uncommon in Liberia (Forbes-Watson undated), but it has been found to be quite common in central and southern Ivory Coast, including the Tai National Park, in primary and secondary and even gallery forests (J.-M. Thiollay *in litt.* 1983). Nevertheless, this subspecies appears to have a very restricted distribution and the rapid forest clearance which is taking place in this part of West Africa is likely to be detrimental to its survival. Whether in fact it should be considered as merely a race of *capense* is doubtful, its voice being rather different (A. D. Forbes-Watson pers. comm. 1984). *G. (c.) castaneum* has been thought of as a distinct species, but this is due to confusion with the threatened Albertine Owlet *G. albertinum* (see relevant account in the main text). Only two specimens of *castaneum* are known. The type, described in 1893, came from Andundi, on the west bank of the Semliki River, eastern Zaire (Reichenow 1893, Chapin 1939). In 1968 a bird was collected at 700 m at Ntandi, Bwamba Forest, western Uganda, on the east bank of the Semliki River (Friedmann and Williams 1971). The other subspecies of *G. capensis* are less closely associated with forest, and occur widely in eastern and southern Africa. *G. (c.) etchecopari* is particularly isolated from other races of the species.

Thyolo Green Barbet *Stactolaema (olivacea) belcheri*, **Ngoye Green Barbet** *S. (o.) woodwardi* and **Rondo Green Barbet** *S. (o.) hylophona* are distinctive forms of the Green Barbet *S. olivacea*; *belcheri* is a very distinct form, known only from forest on Thyolo Mountain in southern Malawi and on Namuli Mountain in northern Mozambique (Benson and Benson 1977, R. J. Dowsett *in litt.* 1983), while *woodwardi* and *hylophona* are closely related to each other but highly distinct from the rest of *S. olivacea. S. (o.) woodwardi* is known only from Ngoye (Umgoye) Forest, Natal, South Africa, where a population of 1,000 individuals is estimated (Brooke in press); *S. (o.) hylophona* is only known from Nchingidi on the Rondo Plateau, south-eastern Tanzania, where a few birds were collected in the 1930s (Clancey 1979b), but there has been no subsequent exploration. A move to place *woodwardi* and *hylophona* in a different species (with its own genus, *Cryptolybia*) (see Clancey 1979a,b) is perhaps premature, since *woodwardi* answers and reacts to playback calls of nominate birds (from coastal Kenya) (R. J. Dowsett *in litt.* 1982; see also "The problem of subspecies" in the Introduction). All three forms, *belcheri, woodwardi,* and *hylophona,* are likely to be at risk from forest clearance.

Angola White-headed Barbet *Lybius (leucocephalus) leucogaster* is a very isolated and distinctive offshoot of the White-headed Barbet *L. leucocephalus,* restricted to a relatively small area of south-western Angola where it is, however, fairly common (Pinto 1962,1970, Brooke 1970; A. A. da R. Pinto *in litt.* 1983).

Braun's Bush-shrike *Laniarius (luhderi) brauni* and the **Amboim Bush-shrike** *Laniarius (luhderi) amboimensis* are two highly distinct and very rare Angolan forms of Luhder's Bush-shrike *L. luhderi, brauni* confined to the secondary and gallery rainforest region in Cuanza Norte (Traylor 1963), *amboimensis* only known from evergreen forest in a restricted area around Gabela on the escarpment of Cuanza Sul, with the most recent records dating from 1960 (Pinto 1962).

Somali Olive Thrush *Turdus (abyssinicus) ludoviciae* is a very dark form of the Northern Olive Thrush *T. abyssinicus,* a widespread montane forest bird: *ludoviciae* is restricted to forest in northern Somalia, where it is "locally very common" (Ash and Miskell 1983).

Bamenda Apalis *Apalis (sharpii) bamendae* is known from middle altitudes around Bamenda and Dschang in western Cameroon and from Tello in the Adamawa Plateau in the centre of the country (Serle 1950, Louette 1981). It is very rarely recorded and appears to favour riverine thickets rather than forest (SNS). Its taxonomic position is very unclear and it may be closer to the Chestnut-throated Apalis *A. porphyrolaema* of eastern Africa than to Sharpe's Apalis *A. sharpii* (Chappuis 1979).

Taita Apalis *Apalis (thoracica) fascigularis* and **Namuli Apalis** *A. (t.) lynesi* are two very well marked and restricted subspecies of the Bar-throated Apalis *A. thoracica,* a widespread montane forest bird, *fascigularis* restricted to the tiny area of forest remaining on the Taita Hills in south-east Kenya (Britton 1980), *lynesi* only known from Namuli Mountain in northern Mozambique (Vincent 1935).

Kulal White-eye *Zosterops (poliogaster) kulalensis,* **Taita White-eye** *Z. (p.) silvanus* and **South Pare White-eye** *Z. (p.) winifredae* are all highly distinct grey-bellied forms of the Montane White-eye *Z. poliogaster,* confined to very small patches of forest on Mount Kulal and the Taita Hills (Kenya) and the South Pare Mountains (Tanzania) respectively (Britton 1980).

Thick-billed Seed-eater *Serinus (burtoni) melanochrous* is known from Tandala to Uwenda in the Southern Highlands of Tanzania according to Britton (1980) but also occurs some 200 km north-east in the Uzungwa Mountains at Mufindi and Dabaga and 70 km to the west at Mount Rungwe (Stuart and Jensen 1981). It is a forest bird but in no immediate danger (though probably not common).

References

Ash, J. S. and Miskell, J. E. (1983) *Birds of Somalia: their habitat, status and distribution. Scopus* Spec. Suppl. 1. Nairobi: Ornithological Sub-Committee, EANHS.

Benson, C. W. and Benson, F. M. (1977) *The birds of Malawi.* Limbe, Malawi: Montfort Press.

Britton, P. L. ed. (1980) *Birds of East Africa: their habitat, status and distribution.* Nairobi: EANHS.

Brooke, R. K. (1970) The White-headed Barbet in Angola. *Bull. Brit. Orn. Club* 90: 161-162.

Brooke, R. K. (in press) *The rare and vulnerable birds of South Africa.*

Chapin, J. P. (1939) The birds of the Belgian Congo. Part 2. *Bull. Amer. Mus. Nat. Hist.* 75.

Chappuis, C. (1979) Illustration sonore de problèmes bioacoustiques posés par les oiseaux de la zone éthiopienne. *Alauda* 47: 195-212.

Clancey, P. A. (1979a) Miscellaneous taxonomic notes on African birds 53. *Durban Mus. Novit.* 12: 1-17.

Clancey, P. A. (1979b) Miscellaneous taxonomic notes on African birds 55. *Durban Mus. Novit.* 12: 47-61.

Colston, P. R. and Curry-Lindahl, K. (in press) The Birds of the Mount Nimba region in Liberia. *Bull. Brit. Mus. (Nat. Hist.) Zool.*

Erard, C. and Roux, F. (1983) La Chevêchette du Cap *Glaucidium capense* dans l'ouest africain. Description d'une race géographique nouvelle. *Oiseau et R.F.O.* 53: 97-104.

Forbes-Watson, A. D. (undated) Checklist of the birds of Liberia. Non-passeriformes. Unpublished.

Friedmann, H. and Williams, J. G. (1971) The birds of the lowlands of Bwamba, Toro Province, Uganda. *Los Angeles County Mus. Contrib. Sci.* 211.

Hall, B. P. and Moreau, R. E. (1962) A study of the rare birds of Africa. *Bull. Brit. Mus. (Nat. Hist.) Zool.* 8: 313-378.

Hall, B. P. and Moreau, R. E. (1970) *An atlas of speciation in African passerine birds.* London: Trustees of the British Museum (Natural History).

Louette, M. (1981) *The birds of Cameroon. An annotated check-list.* Brussels: Verhandeling Wetenschappen, Jaargang 43, no. 163.

Pinto, A. A. da R. (1962) As observações de maior destaque das expedições ornitológicas do Instituto de Investigação Científica de Angola. *Bol. Inst. Invest. Cient. Angola* 1: 21-38.

Pinto, A. A. da R. (1970) Um catálogo das aves do distrito da Huila (Angola). *Mem. Trab. Inst. Invest. Cient. Angola* no. 6.

Reichenow, A. (1893) Diagnosen neuer Vogelarten aus Central-Afrika. *Orn. Monatsber.* 1: 60-62.

Serle, W. (1950) A contribution to the ornithology of the British Cameroons. Part II. *Ibis* 92: 602-638.

Stuart, S. N. and Jensen, F. P. (1981) Further range extensions and other notable records of forest birds from Tanzania. *Scopus* 5: 106-115.

Traylor, M. A. (1963) Check-list of Angolan birds. *Publ. cult. Co. Diam. Angola, Lisboa* no. 61.

Vincent, J. (1935) The birds of northern Portuguese East Africa. Comprising a list of, and observations on, the collections made during the British Museum Expedition of 1931-32. – Part VIII. *Ibis* (13)5: 485-529.

Notes on the subspecies from Africa and related islands treated in King (1978-1979)

As part compensation for the exclusion of subspecies from consideration in this volume (see Introduction), we provide here brief notes concerning the subspecies from the region under review that were treated as threatened (status category is given after the scientific name) in King (1978-1979).

Madeira Soft-plumaged Petrel *Pterodroma mollis madeira* (Rare) is now considered a full species and treated in the main text under Freira *P. madeira*.

Aldabra Sacred Ibis *Threskiornis aethiopica abbotti* (Rare) was treated in Collar (1982), where it was reported that positive overall management policy on Aldabra (Seychelles) was likely to be responsible for good breeding success in recent years, with numbers "reaching support level".

Anjouan Sparrowhawk *Accipiter francesii pusillus* (Endangered) is confined to 9,000 ha of forest on Anjouan, Comoro Islands, but there is no new information on its status.

Aldabra Kestrel *Falco newtoni aldabranus* (Rare) was treated in Collar (1982), where it was reported that the population on Aldabra (Seychelles), estimated at 100, might be at carrying capacity for the habitat and was at no ostensible risk, although its racial distinctness was put in question.

Cape Verde Peregrine Falcon *Falco peregrinus madens* (Rare) has a tiny but apparently stable population of six pairs or so in the Cape Verde Islands, but there is no new information on its status.

Aldabra White-throated Rail *Dryolimnas cuvieri sandvicensis* (Rare) was treated in Collar (1982), where it was reported that intensive (but as yet still largely unpublished) studies (by C. R. Huxley) of this flightless bird on Aldabra (Seychelles) in the 1970s had shown a total population of around 8,000 individuals and that the threat believed posed by feral cats was unlikely to be serious. This judgement appeared to be borne out by studies on numbers and distribution in 1983 (C. Hambler *in litt.* 1983). Hope that this or a closely allied form might still survive on South Island, Cosmoledo (near Aldabra), has been proved misplaced (Mortimer 1984).

Canarian Black Oystercatcher *Haematopus moquini meadewaldoi* (Endangered) is now considered a full species and treated in the main text under *H. meadewaldoi*.

Azores Woodpigeon *Columba palumbus azorica* (Rare), although reportedly much diminished in numbers in the Azores archipelago, has been found in fact to be still fairly common in places (Brien *et al.* 1982, G. Le Grand pers. comm. 1982).

Seychelles Turtle Dove *Streptopelia picturata rostrata* (Endangered) is being genetically swamped in its native Seychelles by its congener, the introduced Madagascar Turtle Dove *S. p. picturata*; the form was treated in Collar (1982), where it was suggested that captive breeding could possibly save it from complete disappearance.

Moheli Green Pigeon *Treron australis griveaudi* (Rare) was considered possibly confined to 3,000 ha of forest on Moheli, Comoro Islands, where it was under pressure from hunting, but in 1975 it was still "common" (Cheke 1980).

Seychelles Black Parrot *Coracopsis nigra barklyi* (Endangered) was treated in Collar (1982), where it was reported to number about 90 birds in 1976: great local interest exists in conserving this bird on its native Praslin (Seychelles) and it has recently been the subject of an ICBP project by R. E. Merritt.

Zanzibar Red-crested Lourie (Zanzibar Fischer's Turaco) *Tauraco fischeri zanzibaricus* (Rare) is (or was thought to be) restricted to the Jozani Forest on Zanzibar, Tanzania, from which there have been no recent reports except the sighting of a "turaco" to the north of Jozani in a drier forest area near Mapopwe (W. A. Rodgers *in litt.* 1983). No other species of turaco is known to occur on Zanzibar (Pakenham 1979).

Madagascar Thick-billed Cuckoo *Pachycoccyx audeberti audeberti* (Indeterminate) has not been seen since the account in King (1978-1979), to which three minor corrections may be made: (a) the statement that "the most recent reports date from the 1930s" refers to reports from natives gathered by Lavauden (1932,1937), who was in Madagascar approximately 1928-1931, so that his reports almost certainly stem from the 1920s at the latest; (b) the suggestion that the cuckoo's disappearance "may be connected with a diminution of the species which it is believed to parasitise, the Vanga *Leptopterus chaberti*" appears to be a mistaken translation of Benson *et al.* (1976), as no such diminution is anywhere reported; (c) the two other subspecies recognised in the most authoritative recent study (Benson and Irwin 1972,1973) are *P. a. validus* and *P. a. brazzae* (*canescens* being synonymous with *validus*). This species as a whole is very uncommon, and is treated in Brooke (in press); see also the account in Rowan (1983).

Nduk Eagle Owl *Bubo poensis vosseleri* (Rare) is now considered a full species and is treated in the main text under Usambara Eagle Owl *B. vosseleri*.

Anjouan Scops Owl *Otus rutilus capnodes* (Endangered) is presumably confined to 9,000 ha of forest on Anjouan, Comoro Islands, but there is no new information on its status.

Ngoye Green Barbet *Stactolaema olivacea woodwardi* (Rare) is considered an incipient species in Appendix E; see also Brooke (in press) where it is treated under the name *Cryptolybia woodwardi.*

Tristan Starchy *Nesocichla eremita eremita* (Rare) survives in low numbers on Tristan da Cunha, but there is no new information on its status (the presence of this population on the main island in the Tristan group was responsible for the decision not to treat the species in the main body of this book: if nominate *eremita* becomes extinct, the species must automatically be considered threatened on the same basis as are the Tristan Bunting *Nesospiza acunhae* and Grosbeak Bunting *N. wilkinsi* – see relevant accounts in the main text – all three then being confined to Nightingale and Inaccessible Islands).

Mauritius Paradise Flycatcher *Terpsiphone bourbonnensis desolata* (Rare) was reported in the 1970s still to be numbered "in the thousands" (King 1978-1979) but analysis of data then gathered shows this to have been over-optimistic, a maximum number of pairs for Mauritius in 1974 being 250 (Cheke in press).

Mauritius White-eye *Zosterops olivacea chloronothos* (*sic*) (Vulnerable) is now considered a full species and is treated in the main text under Mauritius Olive White-eye *Z. chloronothus.*

São Miguel Bullfinch *Pyrrhula pyrrhula murina* (Endangered) is now known to have a range of about 4 km^2 in one valley on São Miguel in the Azores, where perhaps some 30-40 pairs survive; strong efforts with ICBP involvement are now being made to ensure the long-term conservation of this bird and its habitat (G. Le Grand *in litt.* 1982; also Brien *et al.* 1982, Le Grand 1983).

Usambara Weaver *Ploceus olivaceiceps nicolli* (Rare) is now considered a full species and is treated in the main text under Tanzanian Mountain Weaver *P. nicolli.*

References

Benson, C. W. and Irwin, M. P. S. (1972) The Thick-billed Cuckoo *Pachycoccyx audeberti* (Schlegel) (Aves: Cuculidae). *Arnoldia (Rhod.)* 5(33).

Benson, C. W. and Irwin, M. P. S. (1973) *Pachycoccyx audeberti*: some addenda. *Bull. Brit. Orn. Club* 93: 160-161.

Benson, C. W., Colebrook-Robjent, J. F. R. and Williams, A. J. (1976) Contribution à l'ornithologie de Madagascar. *Oiseau et R.F.O.* 46: 209-242.

Brien, Y., Bessec, A. and Lesouef, J.-Y. (1982) Observations du Bouvreuil et du Pigeon ramier des Açores. *Oiseau et R.F.O.* 52: 87-89.

Brooke, R. K. (in press) *The rare and vulnerable birds of South Africa.*

Cheke, A. S. (1980) [Review of King (1978-1979).] *Ibis* 122: 545.

Cheke, A. S. (in press) The surviving native land-birds of Mauritius. In A. W. Diamond, ed. *Studies in Mascarene island birds.* Cambridge: Cambridge University Press.

Collar, N. J. (1982) Extracts from the red data book for the birds of Africa and associated islands. Cambridge: ICBP, unpublished.

King, W. B. (1978-1979) *Red data book, 2: Aves*. 2nd edition. Morges, Switzerland: IUCN.

Lavauden, L. (1932) Etude d'une petite collection d'oiseaux de Madagascar. *Bull. Mus. Natn. Hist. Nat.* (2)4: 629-640.

Lavauden, L. (1937) Supplément. A. Milne Edwards and A. Grandidier, *Histoire physique, naturelle et politique de Madagascar, 12. Oiseaux*. Paris: Société d'Editions Géographiques, Maritimes et Coloniales.

Le Grand, G. (1983) Der wiederentdeckte Azorengimpel. *Wir und die Vögel* no. 1: 37-38.

Mortimer, J. A. (1984) Rediscovery of the Turtle Dove *Streptopelia picturata* on Cosmoledo Atoll in the Seychelles. *Ibis* 126: 81-82.

Pakenham, R. H. W. (1979) *The birds of Zanzibar and Pemba*. London: B.O.U. Checklist no. 2.

Rowan, M. K. (1983) *The doves, parrots, louries and cuckoos of southern Africa*. Beckenham: Croom Helm.

A list of candidate bird species for treatment as threatened in Africa and related islands

This list comprises all those species which were seriously considered for treatment in the main text or in Appendix C of this study. Notwithstanding that we elected against discussing them further, all of them can, we think, lay some claim to the attention of the conservationist. The opinion has been expressed to us from several quarters that any species confined to a single island must be thought of as at some risk: although we are inclined to agree, we also feel that, as in the case of subspecies (see the Introduction), practical considerations militate against treating "single island endemics" even in an appendix, but we list all such species here except those for Madagascar and, obviously, those treated elsewhere in the book (a world list of single island endemic species has been prepared by ICBP – see Bishop in prep.). We are by no means certain that the following is as complete a list as it should have been, nor of course are we entirely sure that we have correctly judged the selection of those species treated in Appendix C from this original list: we welcome comment and suggestions. Two taxa that might at one stage have been considered for treatment are invalid, these being *Apus toulsoni* (see Brooke 1971) and *Anthreptes pujoli* (see Erard 1979), while a third, *Andropadus hallae*, is doubtful (see Devillers 1980), and three further taxa known from single specimens are currently too problematic to warrant more than a mention here, these being *Hirundo andrewi* (see Williams 1966, Hall and Moreau 1970, Dowsett 1972), *Anthus latistriatus* (see Prigogine 1981) and *Sylvia ticehursti* (see Mayer [*sic*] and Meinertzhagen 1951).

Cape Gannet *Sula capensis*
Tiger Bittern *Tigriornis leucolopha*
White-backed Night-heron *Nycticorax leuconotus*
Saddle-billed Stork *Ephippiorhynchus senegalensis*
Olive Ibis *Bostrychia olivacea*
Spotted-breasted Ibis *Bostrychia rara*
Meller's Duck *Anas melleri*
Congo Serpent Eagle *Dryotriorchis spectabilis*
Long-tailed Hawk *Urotriorchis macrourus*
Ayres's Hawk-eagle *Hieraaetus ayresii*
Cassin's Hawk-eagle *Spizaetus africanus*
Grey-breasted Francolin *Francolinus rufopictus*
Jackson's Francolin *Francolinus jacksoni*
Handsome Francolin *Francolinus nobilis*
Ahanta Francolin *Francolinus ahantensis*
Hartlaub's Francolin *Francolinus hartlaubi*
Ring-necked Francolin *Francolinus streptophorus*
Schlegel's Francolin *Francolinus schlegeli*

Madagascar Partridge *Margaroperdix madagarensis*
Black Guineafowl *Agelastes niger*
Madagascar Wood-rail *Canirallus kioloides*
Long-toed Flufftail *Sarothrura lugens*
Black Crowned Crane *Balearica pavonina*
Blue Bustard *Eupodotis caerulescens*
Spot-breasted Plover *Vanellus melanocephalus*
Brown-chested Plover *Vanellus superciliosus*
Chestnut-banded Sandplover *Charadrius pallidus*
Madagascar Snipe *Gallinago macrodactyla*
African Black Skimmer *Rynchops flavirostris*
Cameroon Olive Pigeon *Columba sjostedti*
Comoros Olive Pigeon *Columba polleni*
Gulf of Guinea Bronze-naped Pigeon *Columba malherbii*
Pink-bellied Turtle Dove *Streptopelia hypopyrrha*
Pemba Green Pigeon *Treron pembae*
São Tomé Green Pigeon *Treron sanctaethomae*
Comoros Blue Pigeon *Alectroenas sganzini*
Seychelles Blue Pigeon *Alectroenas pulcherrima*
Niam-Niam Parrot *Poicephalus crassus*
Yellow-fronted Parrot *Poicephalus flavifrons*
Black-collared Lovebird *Agapornis swinderniana*
Angola Red-crested Turaco *Tauraco erythrolophus*
Rwenzori Turaco *Tauraco johnstoni*
Fischer's Turaco *Tauraco fischeri*
Thick-billed Cuckoo *Pachycoccyx audeberti*
Sandy Scops Owl *Otus icterorhynchus*
Pemba Scops Owl *Otus pembaensis*
Maned Owl *Jubula lettii*
Shelley's Eagle Owl *Bubo shelleyi*
Akun Eagle Owl *Bubo leucostictus*
Vermiculated Fishing Owl *Scotopelia bouvieri*
Red-chested Owlet *Glaucidium tephronotum*
Sjostedt's Barred Owlet *Glaucidium sjostedti*
Madagascar Long-eared Owl *Asio madagascariensis*
Brown Nightjar *Caprimulgus binotatus*
Star-spotted Nightjar *Caprimulgus stellatus*
Madagascar Collared Nightjar *Caprimulgus enarratus*
Bates's Nightjar *Caprimulgus batesi*
Madagascar Spinetail *Zoonavena grandidieri*
São Tomé Spinetail *Zoonavena thomensis*
Black Spinetail *Telecanthura melanopygia*
Cape Verde Swift *Apus alexandri*
Forbes-Watson's Swift *Apus berliozi*
Bates's Swift *Apus batesi*
Red-backed Mousebird *Colius castanotus*
Bare-cheeked Trogon *Apaloderma aequatoriale*

Rosy Bee-eater *Merops malimbicus*
Monteiro's Hornbill *Tockus monteiri*
Brown-cheeked Hornbill *Bycanistes (cylindricus) cylindricus*
Yellow-casqued Hornbill *Ceratogymna elata*
Green Tinkerbird *Pogoniulus simplex*
Zenker's Honeyguide *Melignomon zenkeri*
Kilimanjaro Honeyguide *Indicator narokensis*
Lyre-tailed Honeyguide *Melichneutes robustus*
Little Green Woodpecker *Campethera maculosa*
Tullberg's Woodpecker *Campethera tullbergi*
Golden-backed Woodpecker *Dendropicos abyssinicus*
Grey-headed Broadbill *Smithornis sharpei*
Schlegel's Asity *Philepitta schlegeli*
Somali Long-billed Lark *Mirafra somalica*
Gray's Lark *Ammomanes grayi*
Lesser Hoopoe Lark *Alaemon hamertoni*
Masked Lark *Calandrella personata*
African River Martin *Pseudochelidon eurystomina*
Congo Sand-martin *Riparia congica*
Madagascar Swallow *Phedina borbonica*
Dusky Swallow *Hirundo fuliginosa*
Black-and-rufous Swallow *Hirundo nigrorufa*
Sharpe's Longclaw *Macronyx sharpei*
Grimwood's Longclaw *Macronyx grimwoodi*
Malindi Pipit *Anthus melindae*
Grauer's Cuckoo-shrike *Coracina graueri*
Eastern Wattled Cuckoo-shrike *Campephaga oriolina*
Sjöstedt's Bulbul *Baeopogon clamans*
Joyful Greenbul *Chlorocichla laetissima*
Cameroon Olive Greenbul *Phyllastrephus poensis*
Tiny Greenbul *Phyllastrephus debilis*
Yellow-crested Helmet-shrike *Prionops alberti*
Chestnut-fronted Helmet-shrike *Prionops scopifrons*
Yellow-breasted Boubou *Laniarius atroflavus*
Black Boubou *Laniarius fuelleborni*
Mountain Sooty Boubou *Laniarius poensis*
Lagden's Bush-shrike *Malaconotus lagdeni*
Helmetbird *Euryceros prevostii*
Coral-billed Nuthatch-vanga *Hypositta corallirostris*
Northern Bearded Scrub-robin *Cercotrichas leucosticta*
Brown Scrub-robin *Cercotrichas signata*
Sharpe's Akalat *Sheppardia sharpei*
White-bellied Robin-chat *Cossypha (Sheppardia) roberti*
Cameroon Mountain Robin-chat *Cossypha isabellae*
Chorister Robin-chat *Cossypha dichroa*
Spot-throat *Modulatrix stictigula*
Olive-flanked Ground Robin *Dryocichloides anomalus*

Archer's Ground Robin *Dryocichloides archeri*
Red-throated Alethe *Alethe poliophrys*
White-chested Alethe *Alethe fuelleborni*
Sombre Rock Chat *Cercomela dubia*
Réunion Stonechat *Saxicola tectes*
Rüppell's Chat *Myrmecocichla melaena*
Subdesert Rockthrush *Monticola imerina*
Black-eared Ground-thrush *Turdus camaronensis*
Grey Ground-thrush *Turdus princei*
Comoros Thrush *Turdus bewsheri*
Puvel's Illadopsis *Trichastoma puveli*
Grey-chested Illadopsis *Trichastoma poliothorax*
Scaly Babbler *Turdoides squamulatus*
Príncipe Thrush-babbler *Horizorhinus dohrni*
Crossley's Babbler *Mystacornis crossleyi*
Victorin's Warbler *Bradypterus victorini*
Knysna Scrub Warbler *Bradypterus sylvaticus*
Grey Emu-tail *Amphilais (Dromaeocercus) seebohmi*
Uganda Woodland Warbler *Phylloscopus budongoensis*
Red-faced Woodland Warbler *Phylloscopus laetus*
Black-capped Woodland Warbler *Phylloscopus herberti*
Aberdare Cisticola *Cisticola aberdare*
Boran Cisticola *Cisticola bodessa*
Churring Cisticola *Cisticola njombe*
Carruthers's Cisticola *Cisticola carruthersi*
São Tomé Prinia *Prinia molleri*
Sharpe's Apalis *Apalis sharpii*
Collared Apalis *Apalis ruwenzori*
Socotra Warbler *Incana incana*
Green Longtail *Urolais epichlora*
White-tailed Warbler *Camaroptera (Poliolais) lopesi*
African Tailorbird *Orthotomus metopias*
Neumann's Bush Warbler *Hemitesia neumanni*
Banded Graueria *Graueria vittata*
Kretschmer's Longbill *Macrosphenus kretschmeri*
Kemp's Longbill *Macrosphenus kempi*
Olivaceous Flycatcher *Muscicapa olivascens*
Tessmann's Flycatcher *Muscicapa tessmanni*
Ussher's Flycatcher *Muscicapa ussheri*
Yellow-eyed Black Flycatcher *Melaenornis ardesiaca*
Violet-backed Hyliota *Hyliota violacea*
Rwenzori Batis *Batis diops*
Ituri Batis *Batis ituriensis*
Fernando Po Batis *Batis poensis*
Red-cheeked Wattle-eye *Platysteira blissetti*
White-spotted Wattle-eye *Platysteira tonsa*
Little Yellow Flycatcher *Erythrocercus holochlorus*

White-bellied Crested Flycatcher *Trochocercus albiventris*
Mascarene Paradise Flycatcher *Terpsiphone bourbonnensis*
Stripe-breasted Tit *Parus fasciiventer*
White-backed Black Tit *Parus leuconotus*
Cape Sugarbird *Promerops caffer*
Socotra Sunbird *Nectarinia balfouri*
Príncipe Sunbird *Nectarinia hartlaubi*
São Tomé Sunbird *Nectarinia newtonii*
Cameroon Blue-headed Sunbird *Nectarinia oritis*
Rwenzori Blue-headed Sunbird *Nectarinia alinae*
Anjouan Sunbird *Nectarinia comorensis*
Regal Sunbird *Nectarinia regia*
Bocage's Copper Sunbird *Nectarinia bocagii*
Purple-breasted Sunbird *Nectarinia purpureiventris*
Congo River Sunbird *Nectarinia congensis*
Mayotte Sunbird *Zosterops mayottensis*
Pemba White-eye *Zosterops vaughani*
Réunion Olive White-eye *Zosterops olivaceus*
Príncipe Speirops *Speirops leucophaeus*
Black-capped Speirops *Speirops lugubris*
Socotra Bunting *Emberiza socotrana*
Príncipe Canary *Serinus rufobrunneus*
Golden-winged Grosbeak *Rhynchostruthus socotranus*
Little Olive-back *Nesocharis shelleyi*
White-collared Olive-back *Nesocharis ansorgei*
Dusky Crimson-wing *Cryptospiza jacksoni*
Crimson Seed-cracker *Pyrenestes sanguineus*
Lesser Seed-cracker *Pyrenestes minor*
Dusky Twinspot *Euschistospiza cinereovinacea*
Senegal Black-faced Firefinch *Lagonosticta (larvata) vinacea*
Strange Weaver *Ploceus alienus*
Taveta Golden Weaver *Ploceus castaneiceps*
Príncipe Weaver *Ploceus princeps*
Giant Weaver *Ploceus grandis*
Yellow Capped Weaver *Ploceus dorsomaculatus*
São Tomé Weaver *Ploceus sanctaethomae*
Rufous-tailed Weaver *Histurgops ruficauda*
Rachel's Malimbe *Malimbus racheliae*
Golden-backed Bishop *Euplectes aureus*
Marsh Widowbird *Euplectes (hartlaubi) psammocromius*
Jackson's Widowbird *Euplectes jacksoni*
Kenrick's Starling *Poeoptera kenricki*
Socotra Starling *Onychognathus frater*
Emerald Starling *Lamprotornis iris*
Príncipe Glossy Starling *Lamprotornis (Coccycolius) ornatus*
Green-headed Oriole *Oriolus chlorocephalus*
São Tomé Oriole *Oriolus crassirostris*

References

Bishop, K. D. (in prep.) *The ICBP list of single island endemic birds*. Cambridge: ICBP Techn. Publ. no. 7.

Brooke, R. K. (1971) Geographical variation in the swifts *Apus horus* and *Apus caffer* (Aves: Apodidae). *Durban Mus. Novit.* 9(4): 29-38.

Devillers, P. (1980) Projet de nomenclature française des oiseaux du monde. *Gerfaut* 70: 121-146.

Dowsett, R. J. (1972) Geographical variation in *Pseudhirundo griseopyga*. *Bull. Brit. Orn. Club* 92: 97-100.

Erard, C. (1979) What in reality is *Anthreptes pujoli* Berlioz? *Bull. Brit. Orn. Club* 99: 142-143.

Hall, B. P. and Moreau, R. E. (1970) *An atlas of speciation in African passerine birds*. London: Trustees of the British Museum (Natural History).

Mayer [sic], E. and Meinertzhagen, R. (1951) What is *Sylvia ticehursti* Meinertzhagen. *Bull. Brit. Orn. Club* 71: 47-48.

Prigogine, A. (1981) The status of *Anthus latistriatus* and the description of a new subspecies of *Anthus cinnamomeus* from Itombwe. *Gerfaut* 71: 537-573.

Williams, J. G. (1966) A new species of swallow from Kenya. *Bull. Brit. Orn. Club* 86: 40.

Index

This index is for species accounts in the main text and for Appendices C, D and E, i.e. it excludes species mentioned in the Introduction, in other species accounts than their own, or in appendices A, B, F (subspecies) and G.